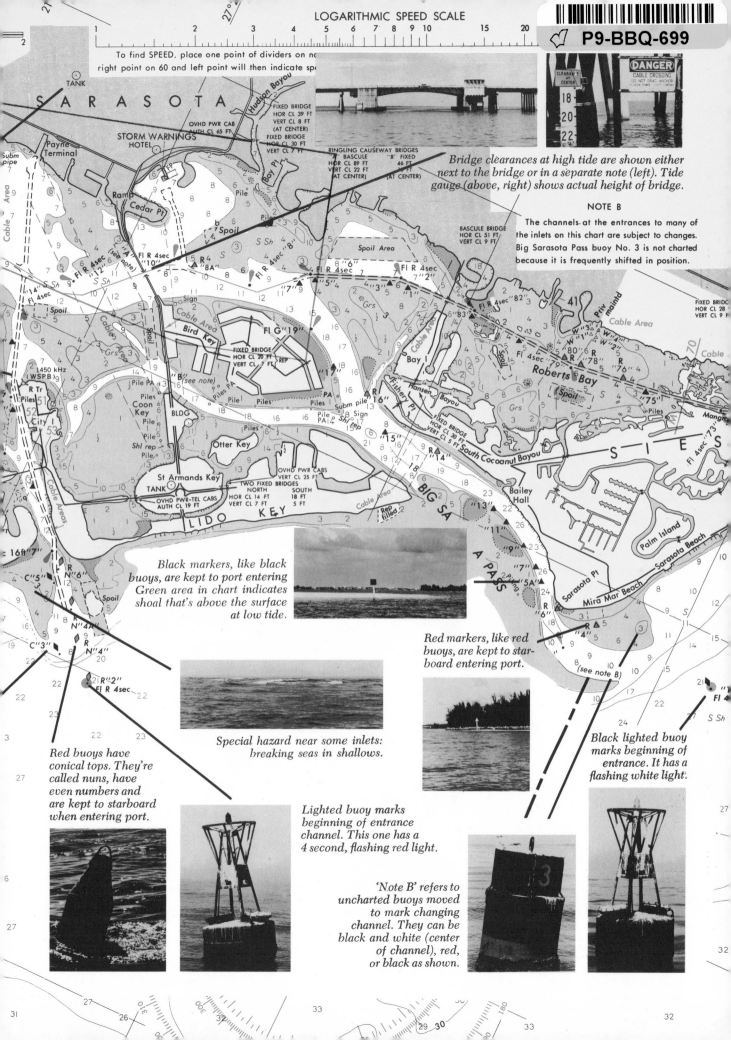

LOGARITHMIC SPEED SCALE

To find SPEED, place one point of dividers on n[...]
right point on 60 and left point will then indicate sp[...]

DANGER
CABLE CROSSING

Bridge clearances at high tide are shown either next to the bridge or in a separate note (left). Tide gauge (above, right) shows actual height of bridge.

NOTE B

The channels at the entrances to many of the inlets on this chart are subject to changes. Big Sarasota Pass buoy No. 3 is not charted because it is frequently shifted in position.

Black markers, like black buoys, are kept to port entering. Green area in chart indicates shoal that's above the surface at low tide.

Red markers, like red buoys, are kept to starboard entering port.

Special hazard near some inlets: breaking seas in shallows.

Black lighted buoy marks beginning of entrance. It has a flashing white light.

Red buoys have conical tops. They're called nuns, have even numbers and are kept to starboard when entering port.

Lighted buoy marks beginning of entrance channel. This one has a 4 second, flashing red light.

'Note B' refers to uncharted buoys moved to mark changing channel. They can be black and white (center of channel), red, or black as shown.

PILOTING,

SEAMANSHIP AND
SMALL BOAT HANDLING

CHAPMAN

PILOTING,
SEAMANSHIP AND
SMALL BOAT HANDLING

CHAPMAN

 51st EDITION

CHARLES F. CHAPMAN

With Revisions By ELBERT S. MALONEY,
WILLIAM KOELBEL, JOHN WILDE,
and GARDNER EMMONS

About the Author

CHARLES FREDERIC CHAPMAN completed more than 56 years of distinguished service to Motor Boating magazine and the boating public before he retired in January, 1969. For 48 of those years he was both editor and publisher of Motor Boating and a Vice President of Hearst Magazines, the parent organization.

Born in Norwich, Conn., in 1881, Chap was graduated from Norwich Academy in 1900, and went on to earn a degree in Mechanical Engineering at Cornell University where he majored in mechanical and marine engineering, and naval architecture.

Always active in boat racing, Chap served as Chairman of the American Power Boat Association's Racing Commission, sanctioning body for all motor boat races, and as the Association's Secretary—a post he held for 25 years. He was the first to be elected to the Honor Squadron of APBA.

Chap was also a leader in organization of the U. S. Power Squadrons in 1914, and holds USPS Certificate #A 1. He conducted the first national tests for USPS members, designed the USPS ensign, and served as Treasurer, Chairman of the Committee on Rules, and as Vice-Commander before his two terms as Chief Commander in 1946-47. Most recently he has been Chairman of the Flag and Etiquette Committee, and a Member of the Governing Board.

And in 1955, the Ole Evinrude Boating Foundation, in recognition of "long contributions to recreational boating," awarded Chap a silver bowl with a citation which read:

"No other man deserves so much from so many of us in the World of Boating."

MOTOR BOATING & SAILING BOOK DIVISION

Business Manager—JOHN R. WHITING

Editor—THOMAS R. BOTTOMLEY

Layout & Production — MERRILL A. LAUCK

Type Composition — BORO TYPOGRAPHERS, Inc.

Printed in the United States of America by
R. R. DONNELLEY & SONS COMPANY, Willard, Ohio

CONTENTS

COMPLETE INDEX
ON PAGE 623

Chapter		Page
1	NAUTICAL TERMS	1
2	BOATING LAWS AND REGULATIONS	29
3	EQUIPMENT FOR BOATS	51
4	RULES OF THE ROAD: LIGHTS AND DAY SHAPES	64b
5	RULES OF THE ROAD: RIGHT OF WAY	67
6	ANCHORING	89
7	THE SKIPPER	116
8	BOAT HANDLING	120
9	SEAMANSHIP	158
10	SAFETY AFLOAT	190
11	MARLINESPIKE SEAMANSHIP	215
12	WEATHER AND THE YACHTSMAN	232
13	THE MARINER'S COMPASS #1	267
14	THE MARINER'S COMPASS #2	287
15	AIDS TO NAVIGATION #1	300
16	AIDS TO NAVIGATION #2	317
17	GOVERNMENT PUBLICATIONS	327
18	THE NAUTICAL CHART	337
19	PILOTING: DEAD RECKONING	373
20	PILOTING: TIDES AND CURRENTS	392
21	PILOTING: POSITION DETERMINATION	417
22	FLAG ETIQUETTE	458
23	YACHTING CUSTOMS AND ETIQUETTE	473
24	BOATING CLOTHING AND UNIFORMS	479
25	ELECTRONIC EQUIPMENT AND ITS USE	486
26	SIGNALING	517
27	INLAND BOATING	529
28	OUTBOARD BOATING	549
29	BOAT TRAILERING	571
30	BOAT MANAGEMENT	587
31	USPS	593
32	USCG	597
	WHERE TO OBTAIN CHARTS AND CRUISING INFORMATION	608
	APPENDIXES	601
	INDEX	623

Preface to the 51st Edition

IN THE FEBRUARY 1922 issue of *Motor Boating,* there appeared an advertisement reading as follows: "Ready February 15, 1922, the *Greatest Motor Boating Book Ever Published;* PILOTING, SEAMANSHIP AND SMALL BOAT HANDLING by Charles F. Chapman—*Motor Boating's* Correspondence Course, Complete in Book Form—Profusely Illustrated, Questions and Problems on all Phases of Boating, etc., etc.

"Price $2.00."

Besides being more than 50 years since the advertisement was published, it is now more than 60 years since the author of this "Greatest Motor Boating Book Ever Published," joined the editorial staff of *Motor Boating* (now *Motor Boating & Sailing*), then a magazine selling for 10 cents a copy, one dollar per year, and with a circulation of but a few thousand copies a month.

The forecasting of 1922 was excellent. Not only was *Piloting, Seamanship and Small Boat Handling,* "Chapman's," as it is affectionately called by most boatmen, the greatest book of its kind, it has remained just that during its entire existence. It has maintained its position as the leading book in its field; nothing has ever approached it in its scope, its comprehension and its authority. Edition by edition, it constantly has been improved, up-dated and expanded to reflect the latest in boating trends and legislative requirements. Probably two million copies have been printed and sold to meet the demands of the boatmen.

During some of the war years, several editions per year were necessary to meet the demands of young men, wishing to join the Army, Navy, Coast Guard, and other branches of the service.

In one of the earliest editions, this was published—"While no claim is made that navigators or even good boatmen can be made by printed instructions alone, yet we feel certain that anyone who will faithfully study the following pages will learn to get a great deal more enjoyment out of his boating."

This must have been good advice, as along with edition after edition, recreational craft, both power and sail, increased from the few thousand which were underway at that time to the millions which are sailing our waterways at present.

It was just a few years before the first edition of the book that the United States Power Squadrons were formed. Their members became busy from the outset, instructing boatmen in the proper handling of their boats as a means to prevent the licensing of motor craft, which was then a very great threat.

It was this idea, "Instructing the Boatmen," which originally led to the publication of this book. This theme has been carried through all editions, from the first to the present.

To successfully carry out the idea, it has been necessary and desirable to completely revise, in many cases, each new edition as it was published. The boating field and sport, changing and growing as it has during the past two decades, has required a broadening of the subjects covered in the book. The size of the publication has increased from the original 100 pages to almost 700.

Originally planned as a text and instruction book for use by those preparing themselves for membership in the USPS, and later the Coast Guard Auxiliary, it has received acceptance by all yachtsmen to be classed as their "marine Bible."

Perhaps with the changing times, when many boatmen take their craft home with them every night, after a cruise, and "moor" the boat in the garage alongside of the towing automobile, the compass, chart, lead line, etc. may not be as important to safe navigation as they once were, yet we have always urged that a knowledge of these and allied subjects greatly aids in the safety and enjoyment of all pleasure boating. The book will continue to feature such subjects in an interesting, non-technical and instructive manner.

Acknowledgement must be made to the host of yachtsmen, government agencies and others who have contributed suggestions and assistance to the author in the original preparation of the book, as well as in his effort to keep the contents of the book up to date, revised, and to properly cover the subject of boating from all angles. In the early days it was officers and members of the Power Squadrons who acted as examiners for the original correspondence course—awarding a "Pilot Certificate" to all who "passed" the course.

My assistant, William Koelbel of Motor Boating, was the Master Mariner who kept the ship on an even keel, his knowledge of all phases of boating being reflected on most of the pages of all editions as they came off the press. He wrote the chapter on anchoring, with able assistance from Robert Ogg of Danforth.

A few years ago, early boating had so changed and grown that a complete revision became necessary. The result: the New Chapman's, which you know today—with much added material ever since the New Chapman's was first started.

To effect these important revisions, the most authoritative boating talent in the world did the job. Under the guidance of Skipper Koelbel, such authorities as Jack Wilde took over such important chapters as the Compass and Compass Errors, and Gardner Emmons wrote the chapter on Weather. Special recognition must be given the outstanding work of Elbert S. Maloney, who since 1966 has prepared chapters on Marine Electronics, Seamanship, Government Publications, Aids to Navigation, Charts and Piloting (four chapters), Signalling, Safety, Customs and Etiquette, and Clothing and Uniforms. For the 1971 edition, he supplied new chapters on Nautical Terminology, Government Regulations, Equipment Requirements, Rules of the Road, Boat Management, the U. S. Power Squadrons, and the U. S. Coast Guard and its Auxiliary.

For the 50th Anniversary edition, he prepared new chapters on Inland Boating, Outboard Seamanship, and Boat Trailering, plus a revised chapter on Government Regulations to include provisions of the Federal Boat Safety Act of 1971. For this edition, he has up-dated the chapter on Anchoring, again with the assistance of Robert Ogg of Danforth. This work of Mr. Maloney has greatly increased the scope, authoritativeness and value of the publication. Now under the leadership of Tom Bottomley, Editor of Motor Boating & Sailing Books, the prestige of the book continues to grow.

So, now in conclusion, the author, who recently celebrated his 94th birthday and has spent much of his active boating life in the preparation and distribution of this remarkable book, a really enjoyable avocation and occupation, can dedicate this 51st Edition to those who assisted in its preparation and to the millions who have found enjoyment and help from previous editions.

Could the author live over again those glorious 60 boating years, without change, he would be happy. Perhaps a better Piloting, Seamanship and Small Boat Handling would result.

Charles F. Chapman

Charles F. Chapman
Bylandorsea
Lat. 41°21'56" North
Long. 72°23'22" West

Foreword

You stand watching the compass, listening for a buoy, keeping your boat moving slowly through the fog. Or, you watch someone come into your harbor and pick up his mooring during a rainy squall. You talk to a Coast Guard chief about boat handling. You watch the smooth handling of a cruiser backing into a slip at a marina, with the U.S. Power Squadron ensign as a sign.

All of these things mean "expert boat handling," and that is a high skill. Yet, how do you pin it all down to one book? One book . . . all these persons learned how to handle a boat by reading a book?

If you could have watched the midshipmen aboard a frigate nearly two hundred years ago—were they studying books, learning to navigate with pieces of paper? The truth is, they were. At the same time they were working with their hands.

Of all the practical skills in the world, requiring a hand that feels the bubbling water as it vibrates the tiller, ears that are sensitive to gongs, bells, horns, and the dampness in the wind, some strength of fingers to make an eye-splice—of all the practical skills there are, boating needs books perhaps the most.

Half a century ago this book first saw the light—as pickups from magazine articles, as a sort of scrapbook, as the beginning of a course in boat operation. It has grown, changed, been revised, been re-edited and rewritten. In the same way that the skills of the sailor grow by experience, the pages of "Piloting, Seamanship and Small Boat Handling" have grown from the experiences of the readers, the practical lore of the countless teachers who have used the book as a text, and the expertise of the various writers and contributing editors who have been a part of it.

Perhaps fifteen million persons owe some part of their boating knowledge to "the blue book," as Chapman's is often called. It is impossible to estimate how many boats have had a copy aboard. It is even impossible to say precisely "the blue book is fifty years old," for a small volume, with a slightly different title, first came out fifty-five years ago in a green binding. So let us say "half a century ago."

Yet in certain ways, it truly goes back to the days of sailing ships and midshipmen. In some of the early volumes, for example, can be found a memo of advice to deck officers of Cunard liners, and they *had* to have experience under sail. Some of the maxims of the sea and of weather are five centuries old.

So—when you stand with a copy of Chapman's in your hand, a part of this book is as old as the wind that ruffles its pages or the knots and hitches you teach your son.

—John R. Whiting
Motor Boating & Sailing

SEE PAGE 639 FOR USPS AND USCGAux REFERENCES FOR COURSE INSTRUCTION

CHAPTER 1

Photo by Peter Smyth

FIG. 101 Both of the above watercraft are "boats"—the term encompasses a wide variety of sizes. They are also both "vessels" in the language of the law.

NAUTICAL TERMS

The Language of Boats and Boating—it's different from that of the land and landsmen, having developed over centuries of use by men who go down to the sea in ships, yet flavored by terms invented in our generation. When you speak of the "stern" of a boat you are using a word that goes back centuries through several languages; yet when you say that in the stern is an "inboard-outboard" engine, you are using a perfectly correct term that has been in existence only a relatively few years.

No, a boatman doesn't have to be excessively "salty" in his speech, nor should he be, but there are strong reasons for knowing and using the right terms for objects and activities and the like around boats. It shows a degree of interest and knowledge, a desire to call things by their right names. In times of emergency, many seconds of valuable time may be saved when correct, precise terms are used for needed tools or actions. In correspondence and other written material, the right word often shortens long explanations and eliminates doubt or confusion.

So learn and use the proper nautical terms for the parts of your boat, her equipment, and activities aboard her—to

do so will mark you as one who is truly interested in his boating and who cares enough to learn about it. But above all, form the habit of *thinking directly* in nautical terms, not in "shore" terms with subsequent mental translation—use the proper words consistently and you will soon find them coming naturally.

BASIC BOATING TERMS

The terms to be discussed in this chapter are not all-inclusive for the field of boating. No two "experts" would agree on what constituted a "complete" list, and any such list would far exceed the available space. What follows is intended as a basic nautical vocabulary, to prepare you for the various boating topics presented in detail in succeeding chapters. Many terms will be repeated and covered more fully later in the book, and more specialized words and phrases will be introduced at that time. Terms in this chapter will be described in simple, brief remarks rather than comprehensively defined as in dictionaries. Glossaries are available for those who need or desire exhaustive definitions.

FIG. 102 A motorsailer combines features of the motorboat and powered sailboat. This design includes many of the advantages of each type and is excellent for certain applications, but also suffers from the deficiencies of any compromise.

General Terms

What is a *boat*? The term has no really precise definition. It is a water-borne vehicle smaller than a *ship*, which is usually thought of as being used for ocean travel. Indeed, one definition of a boat is a small craft carried aboard a ship, such as a lifeboat. Many consider a boat as a craft not over 65 feet in length—this being the maximum length of vessels subject to certain federal boating laws. The term *small craft* is often used interchangeably with boat.

Vessel is a broad term for water-borne vehicles and is used *without* reference to size, particularly in laws and regulations relating to all water traffic. A *yacht* is a vessel used for recreation and pleasure, as opposed to work or business. Usually it is not used for boats under approximately 40 feet in length, but there are no established limits in this respect. The term is also applied to government craft used by officials and dignitaries, such as a presidential yacht or a state governor's yacht.

Although more and more people are coming to refer to boats with the neuter pronoun "it," the traditional "she" remains fully correct in speaking or writing about any size of vessel.

Categories of boats

Boats may be subdivided into *powerboats (motorboats)*, *sailboats*, and *rowboats* as determined by their basic means of propulsion. Remember, however, that sailboats may have *auxiliary engines* in which case they are often called *auxiliaries;* they are considered legally to be motorboats when propelled either by engine alone or by the engine and the sails. A *motor sailer* is a subcategory in which sails can still be used but their area has been reduced and the engine power has been increased. Like most compromises, motor sailers are somewhat less efficient under sail than sailboats and slower under power than motorboats—they

do, however, have desirable features taken from both major categories. There are no precise rules to differentiate between auxiliary-powered sailboats and motor sailers. Some pure motorboats used offshore will have a *steadying sail;* this is not for propulsion but rather for an easier ride in rough seas. See fig. 913.

The term "cruiser" indicates a type of boat with at least minimum accommodations and facilities for overnight trips. The type of propulsion may be added so as to form the terms *outboard cruiser* and *inboard cruiser*. The term is also applied to many sailboats to distinguish them from others designed primarily for racing. Other types of boats include *runabouts* for day fishing or recreational outings on the water and *utility boats* for general service applications.

A *dinghy* is a small open boat carried on or towed by a larger boat or yacht; it may be propelled by oars, sails, or a low-power outboard motor. The slangy contraction, "dink" is often used. *Prams* are small craft with square bows which serve as dinghies and are frequently used for youth program instruction and competitions. *Tenders* include dinghies and larger boats employed to carry persons and supplies to and from large yachts or ships.

Houseboats include both cruising yachts whose superstructure is larger and more designed for living aboard, and many smaller vessels that appear to have evolved from land trailers and mobile homes. Houseboats offer more living space than cruisers, but generally at some sacrifice of seaworthiness and rough water cruising ability.

Hydrofoil boats have structures called *foils* extending below the normal hull that are scientifically designed to give lift, like the wings of an airplane, when moving through the water at high speeds. These submerged foils

FIG. 103 The very large cruising houseboats have largely disappeared from today's boating scene, but they have been more than replaced by the modern high-speed design in the 30 to 50 foot size. These are excellent for all but the most exposed boating waters.

FIG. 104 Hydrofoil craft "fly" on subsurface structures contoured much like the wings of an airplane. The foils may be of the "surface piercing" type, as above, or of the "fully submerged" style.

around and facing the stern, one is looking *aft*.

The bow is the *fore* part of a boat; the stern is the *after* part. When one point on a boat is aft of another it is said to be *abaft* it; when nearer the bow, it is *forward* of the other. When an object lies on a line or in a plane parallel to the centerline of the vessel it is referred to as lying *fore-and-aft,* as distinguished from *athwartships,* which means right angles to the centerline.

The term *amidships* has a double meaning. In one sense, it refers to an object or area midway between the boat's sides. On the other hand, it can relate to something midway between the bow and the stern. *Inboard* and *outboard,* as directional terms, draw a distinction between objects near or toward amidships and those away from the centerline or beyond the sides.

To express the idea of upward or overhead, one says *aloft. Below* means the opposite direction. Note, though, that *abovedeck* means on deck, and not actually above it as does "aloft." We should not say that a person is in or on a boat—rather he is *aboard,* or *on board.*

Terms Relating to the Boat

The basic part of a boat is its *hull,* usually consisting of a major central structural member, the *keel,* with *frames* (also called *ribs*) set into it at right angles; this skeleton is covered with a skin—*planks* in the case of a planked wooden boat; *plates* for a metal boat—to make a watertight vessel that provides buoyancy to float the weight of the craft and its load. Boats may be of the *open* type or the hull may be covered over with a *deck;* some boats are partially open, partially decked. As boats get above the smallest sizes, they may have a *superstructure* above the main deck level, variously referred to as a *deckhouse* or *cabin* (cabins also extend below the level of the deck). Small, relatively open boats may have only a *shelter cabin,* or *cuddy,* forward.

The hulls of boats made of metal—usually aluminum or steel—or of fiberglass-reinforced plastics, will differ in some respects from wooden boats, but the basic components of keel, frames, and covering normally will be retained in at least modified form.

Terms denoting shape

Sheer is the term used to designate the curve or sweep of the deck of a vessel as viewed from the side. The side

permit the boat to "fly" just above the water surface with little drag and at much increased cruising speeds.

Boatmen and yachtsmen

The owner-operators of recreational small craft can be referred to as *yachtsmen* or *boatmen,* the usage often depending on the size of the craft involved, but again without any clear line of demarkation in boat length. The term *boater* is often heard, but it is generally less acceptable than the two just mentioned—perhaps because a "boater" is also an old-fashioned straw hat with a flat top and a broad brim! The term "rag men" and "stink potter" are applied in many areas to the skippers of sailboats and motorboats respectively—sometimes good-naturedly, and sometimes not. A *Corinthian* is any non-professional in the field of boating.

Directions Aboard a Boat

The front end of a boat is of course its *bow;* the other end is its *stern. Port* and *starboard* (pronounced starb'd) are lateral terms—port designating the left side and starboard the right when on the vessel and facing the bow, or, to express it differently, when facing *forward.* Turning

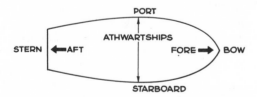

FIG. 105 The basic directions on a boat. Port and Starboard may be kept straight in one's mind by remembering that port is the shorter word and that "left" is shorter than "right."

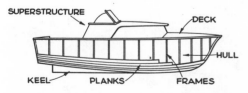

FIG. 106 The basic hull structural parts of a boat are its keel and frames. Planks close in the sides and bottom on the above type craft and the deck closes over the top. Other types of construction may not employ planking.

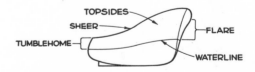

FIG. 107 Flare is the outward curvature of the sides near the bow. It is characteristic of modern designs, providing more usable forward deck area and making for a "drier" boat by turning aside spray. Tumblehome is the inward curving of topsides near the stern.

FIG. 108 Different bottom designs are used for various types of boats. A flat-bottom craft is inexpensive to build; a vee-bottom is used on fast craft. The "cathedral" hull is used on many small craft for speed and stability.

3

skin of a boat between the waterline and deck is called the *topsides*. If these are drawn in toward the centerline away from a perpendicular as they go upward, as they often do near the stern of a boat, they are said to *tumble home*. Forward, they are more likely to incline outward to make the bow more buoyant and to keep the deck drier by throwing spray aside; this is *flare*.

The bottom of a boat may be one of three basic shapes—*flat, round,* or *vee*—or it may be a combination of two shapes, one forward gradually changing to the other toward the stern. There are also more complex modern shapes such as *cathedral-hull, deep-vee, multi-step,* and others.

A *displacement* hull is one that achieves its buoyancy or flotation capability by displacing a volume of water equal in weight to the hull and its load, whether under way or at rest. A *planing hull,* on the other hand, is one that achieves the major part of its load-carrying ability by the dynamic action of its underside with the surface of the water over which it is rapidly traveling; at rest, a planing

FIG. 109 A planing hull at high speeds rides more "on" the water than "in" it. Hydrodynamic forces support the craft rather than displacement. Friction is reduced and higher speeds are achieved with the same horsepower.

hull reverts to displacement buoyancy. A *semi-planing* (or *semi-displacement) hull* is one that gets a portion of its weight-carrying capability from dynamic action, but which does not travel at a fast enough speed for full planing action. It is often a hull that is round-bottomed forward gradually flattening out toward the stern to provide a planing surface.

Two main types of *multi-hull* craft are the *catamaran* with two hulls of equal size held apart by rigid structural members, and the *trimaran* with a principal central hull flanked on either side by smaller outboard hulls.

Bows and sterns

The *stem* is the near-vertical major structural member at a vessel's bow. A stem is common to all boats with the conventional type of bow, whereas the square-nosed *pram* or *punt* type has a bow resembling its square stern. The stem of a boat is *plumb* if it is perpendicular to the waterline or *raked* if inclined at an angle for better appearance. The term *overhang* describes the projection of the upper part of the bow or stern beyond a perpendicular from the waterline. *Eye bolts* or *ring bolts* are frequently fitted through the stems of small boats for towing or for pulling aboard trailers.

Flat planking across the stern is called the *transom*. If, however, the stern is pointed, resembling a conventional bow, there is no transom and the boat is called a *double-ender*. The *quarter* of a boat is the after portion of her sides particularly the furthermost aft portion where the sides meet the transom.

Terms relating to the keel

The keel is the major longitudinal member of a hull. When another timber is fastened along the top of the keel to strengthen it, or as a necessary part of the construction, this is the *keelson,* sometimes *apron*. On some boats an extra piece is fastened externally to the bottom of the keel to protect it. This is termed a *false keel* or *worm shoe*. A metal fitting extending back from the under side of the keel to provide additional protection for the boat is called a *skeg*.

The *rudder* of a craft is the flat surface at or near the stern that is pivoted about a vertical or near-vertical axis so as to turn to either side and thus change the direction of movement of the vessel through the water. The upward extension of the rudder through which force is applied to turn the rudder is the *rudderpost* (or *rudderstock*). A *stuffing* box keeps the hull watertight where the rudderpost enters. A stuffing box is also used where a propellor shaft goes through the hull; see page 12 and fig. 133.

Planking terms

Each continuous line of planking along the hull from bow to stern is called a *strake*. The lowest strake, next to the keel, is termed the *garboard strake*. The *gunwale* (pro-

FIG. 110 Left, multihull sailing craft have become very popular. The catamaran, above, is seen in all sizes from small day sailers to large ocean racers. Trimarans are generally found in sizes from 30 feet upward.

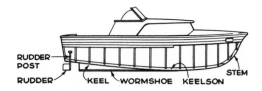

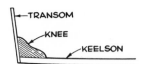

FIG. 113 Reinforcing pieces are often used where two structural members meet. This "transom knee" strengthens the stern and adds rigidity to the craft.

FIG. 111 The stem of a boat is the major structural member at the bow of a planked design or the reinforced area of a fiberglass hull where the forward ends of the sides come together.

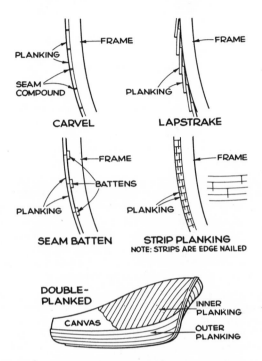

FIG. 112 Despite the increase in popularity of fiberglass and other modern boat construction materials, many craft are still made of wood using one of the traditional planking methods.

nounced gun'l) is the upper part of the *sheer strake*, the top plank of the topsides. It less-than-full-length planks are used in any one strake, the ends of each are *butted* and joined on *butt blocks* on the inside of the hull.

When the topsides are carried substantially above the level of the deck, they are called *bulwarks*, and at the top of the bulwarks is the *rail*. More common than bulwarks are *toe rails*, narrow strips placed on top of the gunwale to finish it off and provide some safety for personnel on deck. *Lifelines* are used on larger craft at the edges of the side decks to aid in preventing people from falling overboard. These lines usually consist of wire, often plastic-covered, supported above the deck on *stanchions*. If made of solid material—wood or metal—they are called *liferails*. Boats may also have waist-high *bow rails* of solid tubing for the same safety purpose. A *pulpit* is an extension, usually a heavy plank with rails extending up from it, beyond the bow of a sport-fishing boat used for spearing or harpooning large game fish. Bow rail installations on sailboats are also often called pulpits, whether they extend forward of the stem or not.

The planking of a boat is termed *carvel*—and the boat is said to be *carvel-built*—if the edges of the planks meet flush, resulting in a smooth surface. The *seams*, joints between adjacent strakes, are usually *caulked* to make the hull watertight. *Batten-seam* construction uses strips of wood, *battens*, on the inside of the hull behind each seam. These are fastened to the planks on either side of the seam with nails or screws and eliminate the need for caulking.

Strip planking, a variant of carvel, uses a greater number of "planks" which are much smaller, being roughly square in cross-section. Each of these is *edge-nailed* (and often glued as well) to the strip below it in addition to being fastened to the frames. This type of hull is quite strong but relatively more costly. Construction is *clinker*, or *lapstrake*, if each successive strake away from the gunwale laps over the one below it as the clapboards of a house are sometimes lapped. The overlapping edges are often fastened with rivets.

Some hulls are *double-planked*, in which case there is commonly an inner *skin*, or layer, of planking laid diagonally to the keel and an outer skin laid fore and aft, with waterproof glue, or fabric and glue, between the layers. In other boats, the two skins are both run *diagonally* at an angle of 45° from the keel to the gunwale, planks of the two layers being at right angles to each other. Due to the strength of double-planked hulls, some frames may be omitted.

Floors and ceilings

These are two terms that have different meanings afloat than ashore. *Floors*, nautically speaking, are not laid as in a house to be walked upon. In a boat they are important transverse structural members, tying together the keel and the lower ends of the frames. *Ceiling* is not overhead, as ashore; it is light planking or plywood sheeting on the inside of the frames.

Reinforcing pieces

Various kinds of *knees* are used throughout the hull to connect members joined at an angle to each other. These may be of metal, but often a natural growth of wood is selected in which the grain runs in the desired direction for maximum strength.

Deck openings

Hatches (sometimes *hatchways*) are openings in the deck of a vessel to provide access below. *Companion ladders* or steps lead downward from the deck; these are also termed *companionways*.

Cockpits are open wells in the deck of a boat outside of deckhouses and cabins. *Coamings* are vertical pieces around the edges of cockpit, hatches, etc., to prevent water on deck from running below.

Scuppers are holes permitting water to drain overboard from decks and cockpits. A cockpit is said to be *self-bailing* when it has scuppers to drain it.

Interior terms

Vertical partitions, corresponding to walls in a house, are called *bulkheads*. *Watertight bulkheads* are solid or are equipped with doors that can be secured so tightly as to be leak-proof. The interior areas divided off by bulkheads are termed *compartments*—such as an engine compartment —or *cabins*—such as the main cabin, aft cabin, etc. Some areas are named by their use; the "kitchen" aboard a boat is its *galley*. The toilet area is the *head* (the same name is also given to the toilet itself).

Overhead is the nautical term for what would be the ceiling of a room in a house; the nautical use of the term ceiling has been explained above.

The *forepeak* of a boat is the compartment furthest forward in the bow, usually used for the storage of line and/or chain, sometimes for sails. The *forecastle* (pronounced fo'c's'l), if any small craft can be said to have one, is the cabin furthest forward. The term is generally used today to mean the crew's quarters forward.

Cabin styles

A *trunk cabin* is one that extends above the main deck level, but less than the full width of the boat so that walkways—side decks—are left on either side; such a boat is re-

TRUNK CABIN   RAISED DECK CABIN

FIG. 114 The cabins of some motorboats and sailing craft are of the "raised deck" type extending the full width of the hull. Other boats have "trunk cabins" with a smaller superstructure set above the level of the deck.

ferred to as a *trunk cabin cruiser*. Conversely, a *raised deck* cruiser is one in which the cabin is formed by extending the topsides above the normal deck level—it extends for the full width of the hull, thus eliminating side decks. A *sedan cruiser* has the main cabin on the same level as an aft cockpit and opening out into it. A *sport fisherman* is a motorboat, usually fast, with special equipment for offshore trolling for large game fish.

The *bridge* of a vessel is the location from which it is steered and its speed controlled. On small craft, the term *control station* is perhaps more appropriate; *helm* is often used aboard sailboats. Many modern motorboats have a *flying bridge,* an added set of controls above the level of the normal control station for better visibility and more fresh air. Flying bridges are usually open, but may have a removable cloth top for shade.

Portholes and portlights

On a boat, a *port* (or *porthole)* is an opening in the hull to admit light and air. The glass used in it to keep the hull weathertight is termed a *portlight* if it can be opened, a *deadlight* if it cannot.

The dimensions of a vessel

The length of a boat is often given in two forms. *Overall length* (l.o.a.) is measured from the fore part of the stem to the after part of the stern. The *waterline* of a boat is the

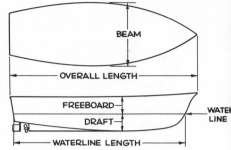

FIG. 115 The principal external dimensions of a boat are shown above. Don't confuse "draft" with "depth" — an internal measurement used in connection with the documentation of vessels.

plane where the surface of the water touches the hull when she is loaded normally; *length on the waterline* (l.w.l.) is measured along this plane. The greatest width of a vessel is her *beam;* boats of greater than normal beam are described as *beamy*. A vessel's *draft* is the depth of water required to float her. Draft should not be confused with the term *depth,* which is used in connection with larger vessels and documented boats and is measured inside the hull from the underside of the deck to the top of the keel.

The height of a boat's topsides from the waterline to the deck is called her *freeboard. Headroom* is the vertical distance between the deck and the cabin or canopy top, or other overhead structure.

Other terms aboard a boat

The lower interior areas of the hull of a vessel are called her *bilge* (or *bilges)*. It is here that water that leaks in, or is blown aboard as spray, collects as *bilge water,* to be later pumped overboard by a *bilge pump.*

When something is put away in its proper place on a vessel, it is *stowed*. The opposite of stowing, to *break out,* is to take a needed article from its locker or other secure place. To *unship* an item of equipment is to remove it from its normal working location or position.

Berths and *bunks* are seagoing names for beds aboard a boat. Closets are termed *lockers,* and a *hanging locker* is one tall enough for full-length garments. Chests and boxes may also be called lockers. A *rope* or *chain locker* is often found in the bow of a boat for stowing the anchor line or chain. *Lazarettes* are compartments in the stern of a vessel used for general storage.

Helm is a term relating to the steering mechanism of a craft. An individual is *at the helm* when he is the controls of the boat; he is then the *helmsman.*

Terms Used in Boating Activities

In addition to the numerous terms for the boat itself, there are many others to be learned in connection with boating in general and the use of craft of all sizes. The list of these is virtually endless, and those that follow are only the more basic and often-used ones.

Docks, piers, and harbors

There is a difference between a strict definition and popular usage for the term "dock." Most properly speaking, a *dock* is the *water* area in which a boat lies when she is *made fast* to shore installations (and "made fast" is the proper term rather than "tied up"). A *drydock* is one that can be shut off from the surrounding water and pumped out in order to make repairs on the vessel's bottom. *To dock* a vessel is to bring her to the shore installation and make her fast.

FIG. 116(a) A wharf is a facility along and parallel to a shore to which vessels may be made fast for loading, fueling, etc.

FIG. 116(b) Right, piers extend outward from the shoreline and craft may be made fast alongside the main structure or in slips separated by catwalks.

FIG. 117(a) Marine railways are widely used for hauling out craft of all sizes. A cradle is pulled down into water deep enough for the boat to be floated onto it. She is then blocked in place and the cradle is slowly pulled up rails until it is clear of the water.

FIG. 117(b) Craft up to 60 feet or more in length are now being taken out of the water by travelling lifts that straddle a wet slip. Broad slings are lowered, passed under the hull, and then raised. When the boat is high enough, the lift moves back on shore under tow or its own power.

In boating, however, the term "dock" is usually applied to structures bordering the water area in which boats lie. A *wharf* is properly a structure generally parallel to the shore, while a *pier* projects out from the shoreline. *Piles* are substantial stakes driven into the bottom to which craft may be made fast; a *dolphin* is a group of piles driven close together and bound with wire cables into a single structure. (The name dolphin is also given to the species of sea mammal often called porpoises, and quite separately to a species of ocean game fish.) Piles are often used to form *slips* out from a pier or wharf in which boats can be *berthed*; short *catwalks* (or *finger piers*) may extend out between the slips for easier access to the boats. A boat is made fast *to* a pile, *in* a slip, and *alongside* a pier or wharf.

A *harbor* is an anchorage which affords reasonably good protection for a vessel, with shelter from wind and sea. Strictly speaking, it applies to the water area only. *Port* is a more comprehensive term, including not only the harbor but, collectively, all the facilities for freight, passengers, and services as well, such as wharves, piers, warehouses, etc. A *yacht basin* or *marina* is a protected facility primarily for recreational small craft.

Jetties are dikes or embankments connected to the shore; when these are used to protect a harbor, and have no connection to the land, they are generally referred to as *breakwaters*. *Groins* are jetty-like dikes built out at roughly a 90° angle from the shore to prevent erosion of the beach.

Boats are *hauled out* of the water on inclined planes at the water's edge called *ways* (also *marine ways* or *marine railways*). The framework which supports a boat as she is hauled out is termed a *cradle*. Small and medium sized boats are also lifted bodily out of the water and set on shore for storage or work with *slings,* which are lowered, passed under the hull, and raised by *cranes* or *traveling lifts.*

Ropes and lines

Generally speaking, the word *rope* is used but little aboard a boat; the correct general term is *line*. "Rope" may be bought ashore at the store, but when it comes aboard and is put to use it becomes "line." *Marlinespike seamanship* is the term applied to that portion of the art related to the use of line and the making of *knots, bends, hitches,* and *splices.* Chapter 11 is devoted to this important subject.

Lines used to make a boat fast to a shore structure are usually called docking lines. *Bow lines* and *stern lines* lead forward and aft from these respective parts of the craft. *Spring lines* lead from the bow aft or from the stern forward to prevent the boat from moving ahead or astern. See fig. 841.

A *painter* is a line at the bow of a small boat, such as a dinghy, for towing or making fast. The line by which a boat is made fast to a mooring buoy is called a *pennant* (sometimes *pendant*).

Heave is a nautical term for throw or pull. One *heaves in* on a line when he pulls in the slack and *takes a strain* on it. When a line is let out, one *pays it out*; to lessen the strain on a line or let it out slightly or slowly, one *eases* it. A line is *snubbed* when its outward run is checked; it is *cast off* when it is let go. (A boat is cast off when all lines have been taken off the pier or other object to which it has been made fast.)

The *bitter end* of a line is the extreme end, the end made fast when all line has been paid out. The middle part of a line not including either end is the *bight*, particularly when formed into a loop. If a strain is put on a line heavy enough to break it, it *parts*.

Heaving lines are light lines, usually with a knot or weight at one end which makes it easier to throw them far and accurately. The knot that encloses a weight at the end of a heaving line is called a *monkey's fist*. *Belay* has two meanings—a line is belayed when it is made fast without knotting to a *cleat* or *belaying pin; belay* as a command signifies "stop" or "cease."

Ends of lines are *whipped* or *seized* when twine or thread is wrapped around them to prevent strands from untwisting or *unlaying*. Ragged ends of lines are said to be *fagged*. *Hawsers* are very heavy lines, in common use on tugboats and larger vessels but rarely found on boats.

Tackle is a broad, general term applied to equipment and *gear* used aboard a boat. It has a specific use, however, to mean a combination of line and *blocks* (pulleys)

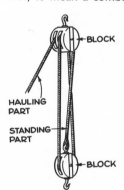

FIG. 118 A set of blocks and some line can be used to increase lifting or pulling power. The set shown here has a theoretical "mechanical advantage" of 3 — actually less due to friction in the blocks.

used to increase a pulling or hoisting force. The wheels or rollers of the blocks are the *sheaves* (pronounced shivs). When a line is passed through a block or hole it is *reeved*; to *render* is to ensure that the line will pass freely through the block or hole.

Lines have *standing parts* and *hauling parts*. The standing part is the fixed part, the one which is made fast; the hauling part is the one that is taken in or let out as the tackle is used. Lines are *foul* when tangled, *clear* when in order to run freely.

Anchors and moorings

An *anchor* is a specially shaped metal device designed to dig efficiently into the bottom under a body of water and hold a vessel in place despite winds and currents.

FIG. 119 There are many types of anchors used on boats. The old-fashioned, or yachtsman's type, left, and the modern patent (Danforth), right, are only two; many others are illustrated in Chapter 6.

Ground tackle is a general term embracing anchors, lines, and other gear used in anchoring. On boats, the anchor line may be referred to as a *rode*. A *mooring* is a semi-permanent anchorage installation, consisting of a heavy anchor (usually of the *mushroom* type), chain, a mooring buoy, and pennant of nylon or manila. See fig. 652.

The anchor carried on a boat for most normal uses is its *working anchor*. A heavier model carried for emergencies is termed a *storm anchor*, and a smaller, lighter anchor for brief daytime stops when the craft will not be left unattended is popularly called a *lunch hook*.

Anchors come in many styles—*kedge, stockless, grapnel,* and modern *light-weight* types such as the *Danforth, Northill,* and *plow*. More on this subject will be found in Chapter 6.

The term *kedge* is also applied to an anchor of any type that is used for getting a boat off when it has run aground. The kedge is carried out by a dinghy or other means and set so that a pull on the line will help get the boat off or at least keep it from being driven harder aground; this process is called *kedging*.

When a boat is anchored, the ratio of the length of line

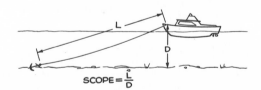

SCOPE = $\frac{L}{D}$

FIG. 120 A boat must always be anchored with adequate "scope." This is the ratio of the length of the anchor line in use to the distance from the bow chocks to the bottom of the water (not just the depth of the water!). See also fig. 631.

in use to the distance to the bottom of the water as measured from the deck is termed *scope*. An *anchorage* is an area specifically designated by governmental authorities in which vessels may anchor; special regulations may prevail in these areas.

Motions of a boat

A vessel *grounds* when she touches bottom, and if stuck there she is *aground*. When a boat moves through the water, she is said to be *underway* (or *under weigh*). According to government laws and regulations, a vessel is underway at any time that she is not aground, at anchor, or made fast to the shore. The direction in which she is moving may be made more specific by stating that she makes *headway* (moving forward), *sternway* (backwards), or *leeway* (to one side or the other, as when pushed by a beam wind). A boat is said to be *underway with no way on* when she is free of the bottom or shore but is making no motion through the water *(adrift)*. A vessel has *steerageway* if she is making enough speed through the water for her rudder to be effective. A vessel's anchor is said to be *aweigh* when it has broken out of the bottom and has been lifted clear.

FIG. 121 Nearly all boats leave an area of disturbed water—wake—behind them as they move forward through the water. Each skipper must be careful that the waves caused by this motion do not disturb or damage others.

The disturbed water that a boat leaves astern as a result of her motion is her *wake*. *Wash* is the flow of water that results from the action of her propeller or propellers. Both of these effects are commonly lumped together as "wake."

Sidewise rotational motion in rough water is called *roll;* vertical motion as the bow rises and falls is termed *pitching*. A craft *yaws* when she runs off her course to either side as she might if she didn't steer properly. If she yaws too widely and is thrown broadside into the *trough* of the sea (between the crests and parallel to them), she *broaches to,* a dangerous situation that should be carefully avoided. In very rough seas a small boat can be thrown end-over-end; this is *pitchpoling*.

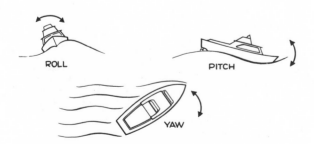

ROLL PITCH YAW

FIG. 122 The three basic motions of a boat are roll, pitch, and yaw. At sea, these are often combined with uncomfortable results!

A boat may *capsize* without *foundering*—in the first instance she turns over, in the latter she fills with water and sinks. If a boat fills with water from over the side, she *swamps*. Before his vessel is reduced to such straits, the wise skipper *heaves to,* reducing headway and generally lying with the bow slightly off from meeting the waves head on. He may put out a *sea anchor (drogue)* that will hold the bow at the most favorable angle; a sea anchor does not go to the bottom, it merely serves as a drag.

Trim

Trim relates to the way a boat floats in the water. When she floats properly as designed, she is on an *even keel;* but if she inclines to port or starboard, she *lists. Heel* conveys the same idea as list, a sideward inclination from the vertical. If a vessel is too heavily loaded forward, she *trims by the head;* if her draft is excessive aft, she *trims by the stern*.

Directions from the boat

Dead ahead refers to any point which the vessel is approaching directly on a straight course. *Dead astern* is, of course, the opposite direction. To convey the idea of opposite, or at right angles, we say *abreast*. An object that is at right angles (90°) to the centerline (keel) of a craft is *abeam,* or *broad on the beam*. If the boat passes near to it, it is said to be *close aboard*. (Vessels are *abreast* of one another when they are side-by-side.)

If we look ahead from abeam to a direction that is midway between abeam and dead ahead, this is *broad on the bow,* port or starboard as the case may be. Going in the other direction, an object seen midway between abeam and dead astern is *broad on the (port or starboard) quarter*.

To express the direction of another vessel or object relative to our boat, we say that it *bears* so-and-so, using the phraseology above. For intermediate directions through a circle centered on the observer's boat, the *point* system can be used, with 32 points making a complete circle. Each direction in the point system is named. A ship or other object seen from your craft might be said to bear *two points abaft the port beam, one point on the starboard bow, etc.* See fig. 123. Half-points and quarter-points exist

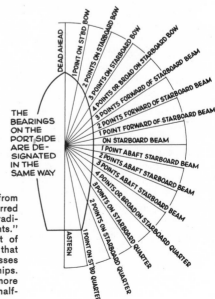

THE BEARINGS ON THE PORT SIDE ARE DESIGNATED IN THE SAME WAY

DEAD AHEAD
1 POINT ON ST'B'D BOW
2 POINTS ON STARBOARD BOW
3 POINTS ON STARBOARD BOW
4 POINTS OR BROAD ON STARBOARD BOW
3 POINTS FORWARD OF STARBOARD BEAM
2 POINTS FORWARD OF STARBOARD BEAM
1 POINT FORWARD OF STARBOARD BEAM
ON STARBOARD BEAM
1 POINT ABAFT STARBOARD BEAM
2 POINTS ABAFT STARBOARD BEAM
3 POINTS ABAFT STARBOARD BEAM
4 POINTS OR BROAD ABAFT STARBOARD BEAM
3 POINTS ON STARBOARD QUARTER
2 POINTS ON STARBOARD QUARTER
1 POINT ON STARBOARD QUARTER
1 POINT ON ST'B'D QUARTER
ASTERN

FIG. 123 Directions from on board are still referred to at times in the traditional system of "points." This is the same unit of angular measurement that was used with compasses in the days of sailing ships. See Chapter 13 for more on points, including half- and quarter-points.

but are rarely used. The direction of a remote object is its *bearing*.

Windward (pronounced wind'ard) means toward the direction from which the wind is blowing. A boat goes to windward, but in speaking of the side of a vessel and the parts on that side on which the wind is blowing, it is better to refer to the *weather* side.

Opposite to windward is *leeward* (pronounced *loo*ard), the direction away from the wind, toward which it is blowing. The *lee* side of a boat is the side away from the wind, and a boat makes *leeway* when blown sideways off her course. Don't confuse, however, the lee side of a boat with the *lee shore* of a land mass—this is the side *onto which* the wind is blowing, the dangerous shore; it is a confusing term, but one that has been used for many years.

Terms Relating to Equipment

Chocks are deck fittings, usually of metal, with inward curving arms through which lines such as mooring or anchor lines are passed so as to lead them in the proper

FIG. 125 For protection against rough piers or other boats, a skipper will often need to hang fenders (don't call them "bumpers") over the side. Modern ones are made of rubber or plastic. Where necessary, fenders may be hung horizontally, or two of them may be used vertically behind a fenderboard; see fig. 855.

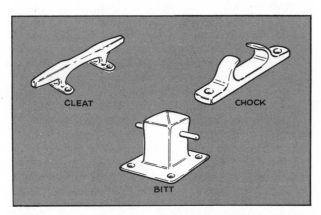

FIG. 124 Cleats, bits, and chocks are found on both motorboats and sailboats. Their shape and size may vary with the craft that they are on, but all are basic forms of deck hardware.

direction both on board and off the boat; they should be smooth so as to prevent excess wearing of the line. *Cleats* are fittings of metal or wood with outward curving arms or horns on which lines can be made fast *(belayed)*.

While cleats are generally satisfactory for most purposes on a boat, wooden or metal *bitts* are often preferred where heavy strains are to be taken. These are stout vertical posts, either single or double. They may take the form of a fitting bolted securely (never screwed) to the deck, but more often, as in the case of a wooden *samson post,* passing through the deck and *stepped* at the keel or otherwise strongly fastened. Sometimes a round metal pin is fitted horizontally through the head of a post or bitt to aid in belaying the line; this is a *norman pin.*

Fenders are relatively soft objects of rubber or plastic (older models were canvas cases filled with cork) used between boats and piles, pier sides, seawalls, etc. to protect the topsides from scarring and to cushion any shock of the craft striking the fixed object. Fenders, sometimes referred to in a landlubberly fashion as "bumpers," are also used between boats when they are tied, or *rafted,* together. *Fender boards* are short lengths of stout planking, often with cushion material or metal rubbing strips on one side.

They may be used with two fenders hung vertically, or occasionally by themselves, to provide a wider bearing surface against a single pile.

Life preservers provide additional buoyancy to keep a person afloat when he is in the water. They take the form of cushions, belts, vests, jackets, and ring buoys. Life preservers must be of a Coast Guard-approved type to meet the legal requirement as set forth in Chapter 2.

A *boathook* is a short shaft of wood or metal with a fitting at one end shaped to aid in extending one's effective reach from the side of a boat, such as when putting a line over a pile or picking up an object dropped overboard. It can also be used for pushing or fending off.

A *boarding ladder* is a set of steps temporarily fitted over the side of a boat to assist persons coming aboard from a low pier or float. A *swimming ladder* is much the same except that it extends down into the water. A *swimming platform* is a narrow wooden shelf attached to a boat's transom just above the waterline.

Grab rails are hand-hold fittings mounted on cabin tops or sides for personal safety when moving around the boat, both on deck and below. Whenever these or other fittings such as cleats and chocks are installed, *bedding compound* should be smeared on the surface of the fitting that will be in contact with the hull, deck, etc., to seal out moisture.

Magnetic *compasses* are mounted near the control station in boxes or other protective casings known as *binna-*

FIG. 126 A boarding ladder can either be hung over the gunwales of a small boat or fitted into brackets on the topsides of a larger craft to make easier boarding from a low float or dinghy. A longer ladder reaching down into the water is used for swimming.

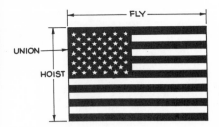

FIG. 127 The principal parts and dimensions of a flag are shown at left. For boat flags the usual ratio between the fly and the hoist is 3:2. This may vary in the case of some pennants.

cles. Compasses are swung in *gimbals,* pivoted rings that permit the compass *bowl* and *card* to remain relatively level regardless of the boat's motion. To enable the helmsman to steer a compass course, a *lubber's line* is marked on the inside of the compass bowl to indicate direction of the vessel's bow. Much more on compasses will be found in Chapters 13 and 14.

A *lead* (pronounced led) *line* is a length of light rope with a weight (the lead) at one end and markers at accurately measured intervals from that end. It is used for determining the depth of water alongside a vessel. A *depth sounder* is an electronic device for determining depths; often such devices are referred to as "fathometers"—this is incorrect as that term is the trademark of one particular manufacturer of electronic depth sounders. Boats used frequently in shallow waters may be equipped with a long slender *sounding pole* with depth in feet and fractions marked off from its lower end.

A *barometer* is often carried aboard a boat; it measures and indicates (in some cases, records) atmospheric pressure. Knowledge of the amount and direction of change in atmospheric pressure is useful in predicting changes in the weather.

Binoculars are hand-held optical devices that aid in detecting and identifying distant objects. Separate sets of lenses and prisms enable the user to see with both eyes at the same time.

A *winch* is a mechanical device, either hand or power operated, for exerting an increased pull on a line or chain, such as an anchor line.

Flags

Strictly speaking, a vessel's *colors* are the flag or flags that she flies to indicate her nationality, but the term is often expanded to include all flags flown. An *ensign* is a flag to denote the nationality of a vessel or her owner, or on a boat to denote the membership of her owner in an organization (other than a yacht club).

The *hoist* of a flag is its inner vertical side; also its vertical dimension. The *fly* is its length from the hoist out to the free end. The *union* is the upper portion near the hoist —in the U.S. national flag, the blue area with the white stars. The *union jack* is a flag consisting solely of the union of the national flag.

A *burgee* is a triangular, rectangular, or swallow-tailed flag usually denoting yacht club or similar unit membership. A *pennant* is a flag, most often triangular in shape, used for general designating or decorative purposes. See Chapter 22 for additional information on flags and how they should be flown.

Terms of Distance and Speed

On salt water, distances are measured in *nautical miles,* a unit about 1/7th longer than the land or *statute* mile with

which we all are more familiar. The international nautical mile is slightly more than 6076 feet; the statute mile used on shore and fresh water bodies is 5280 feet.

Where nautical miles are used for distance, the unit of speed is the *knot,* one nautical mile per hour. Note carefully that the "per hour" is included in the definition—to say "knots per hour" is incorrect. *Miles per hour* is the correct term for most inland fresh water bodies, as it is on shore. A *speed curve* is a plot of speed through the water versus engine speed in revolutions per minute (RPM), ex-

In boating, depths are usually measured in feet, but offshore the unit *fathom* may be used—it is six feet.

Increasingly, metric units are coming into use—*meters* and *kilometers* (1000 meters) for distance; *meters* and *decimeters* (1/10 of a meter) for depths and heights.

FIG. 128 Patent logs indicate distance traveled through the water by the turning of a rotor at the end of a line trailed astern. Other designs use a small impeller mounted on a strut a few inches below the hull; speed and distance are indicated mechanically or electrically.

Miscellaneous Terms

When any part of the vessel's gear or equipment breaks or gives way, it *carries away;* an object goes *by the board* when it goes *overboard.* If a boat is *stove* (planking broken in from outside), the craft *springs a leak* or *makes water.* When water is dipped out of a small boat the process is called *bailing.*

The term *clear* has many meanings. Before leaving for a foreign port, a ship must clear through Customs authorities. She clears the land when she leaves it, clears a shoal when she passes it by safely. The bilges are cleared of water when they are pumped out. Tangled *(foul)* lines are cleared by straightening them out and getting them ready for use.

A boat *stands by* when she remains with another craft to give her assistance if necessary. When used as an order, stand by means to be prepared to carry out an instruction. *Aye,* or *aye aye,* is a properly nautical (if somewhat military) way of acknowledging an order or instruction, indicating that it has been heard and understood, and will be obeyed.

Entries are made in a *log* (book) to record all events occurring aboard; more on this in Chapter 30. A *patent log* is a device to record distance traveled. One *raises* a light or landmark when it first becomes visible; he makes a *landfall* when the shore is first sighted on coming in from sea. *Passage* is generally construed to mean a run from one port to another; *voyage* includes both the outward and homeward passages. *Watches* are periods of duty, usually four hours long, aboard a vessel; *dog watches* are shorter, two-hour periods between 4:00 and 8:00 pm (1600 and

2000 in the 24-hour system of time, see page 376). A period of duty at the helm is a *trick*.

Tides and currents

The word *tide* is almost certainly one of the most misused of nautical terms, so much so that its misapplication has come to be widely accepted even though incorrect. Properly speaking, it means only the rise and fall, the vertical movement, of bodies of water as a result of the interacting gravitational pulls of the moon and sun. Commonly, but wrongly, "tide" is also used to refer to the inflow and outflow of water as a result of changes in tidal level. *Current* is the proper term for a horizontal flow of water, *tidal current* for flows resulting from tidal influences. It is proper to say a two-knot current, but not a two-knot tide.

The incoming tidal current running toward the shore, or upstream in a river, is the *flood*; the retreating, or downstream, current is the *ebb*. The *range* of the tide (difference between the height of *high water* and *low water* (or *high tide* and *low tide)* is not always the same as the days go by. *Spring tides* occur when the moon is new or full and have a greater range than those at other times. *Neap* tides are those occurring at quarter moons; and these have a less than average range.

Water movements and conditions

Various terms are used to describe specific water movements or conditions of the surface. A broad term, *waves*, is frequently used for disturbed conditions on a body of water; these actually represent vertical movement of water particles regardless of their apparent forward motion. *Sea* is a general term often used to describe waves and water action on the surface, but properly it should be applied only to waves produced by wind. *Rips* are short, steep waves caused by the meeting of currents. The confused water action found at places where tidal currents meet is also called a *chop*, but this term is more often applied to

FIG. 129 The horizontal motion of water is current, not tide, although they are termed tidal currents if they result from tidal influences. Such currents "flood" (flow in from sea) and "ebb" (flow out). Tides, vertical changes in water level, do not "come in" and "go out"; they "rise" and "fall."

FIG. 130 Waves result from local wind action on the water surface. Large deep-water swells may come from great distances away; they crest over and become breakers as they move into shallower water near shore.

U.S. Coast Guard Photo

small, closely spaced waves resulting from wind action on inland bodies of water.

Swells (ground swells) are long heavy undulations of the surface resulting from distubances some distance away on oceans and sea. *Surf* is produced when waves leave deep water forming *breakers* on the shore as they *crest* and curl over. A *following sea* is one that comes up from astern, running in the same direction as the boat is going. A *head sea* is just the opposite; one where the progress of the waves is against that of the craft which must meet them head on. *Beam seas* come from either side. *Cross or confused seas* are irregular ones with components from two or more directions.

Powerboat Terms

A number of basic boating terms are applicable specifically to boats equipped with some form of engine, whether *inboard* (mounted within the hull) or *outboard* (mounted on the transom and detachable).

Propulsion

Thrust for the movement of the boat through the water is achieved by the rotation of a *propeller* (or *screw*) which draws in water from ahead and pushes it out astern. Boats with two engines and propellers are referred to as *twin-screw* craft. An often-used slang term for a propeller is *wheel*. A very few boats achieve their thrust from the reaction of a *water jet*.

A more recent development is the *inboard-outboard* (or *I-O*, or *stern-drive*, or *outdrive*). Here the motor is of the inboard type mounted within the hull at the stern with an external driving unit closely resembling the *lower unit* of an outboard motor, even to the extent of being capable of being tilted up. Power is applied to the propeller through two right-angle sets of gears resulting in another name sometimes used, *Z-drive*.

Engine mountings

An inboard engine is mounted on *engine beds*, stout structural members running fore-and-aft across the floor timbers. On single-screw boats, the *deadwood* is a heavy fore-and-aft timber that lies above the keel and may extend beyond it. (On sailboats the deadwood may be beneath the keel timbers of the hull.) *Shaft logs* are timbers through which the *propeller shaft* passes; a *stuffing box* prevents water from entering at this point. The *propeller post*, if one is used, stands vertically behind the deadwood and is joined to it and to the keel. On many boats, the propeller shaft is supported externally under the hull by one or more *struts*.

In some designs of boats, the engine is turned about so that the shaft leads forward to a gear box which reverses its direction to come out under the hull in a normal manner; this *V-drive* permits a compact engine-in-the-stern arrangement.

Reverse and reduction gears

Reverse gears change the direction of rotation of the propeller to give a thrust in the opposite direction for stopping the craft or giving it sternway. *Reduction gears* are often combined with the reversing function so that the propeller, turning at a slower rate than the engine, will have increased efficiency.

12

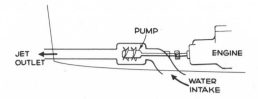

FIG. 131 Some small craft are "jet propelled." The engine drives a multistage pump and the reaction from the high-speed stream of water coming out of the stern provides the forward propulsion. Such systems are excellent for very shallow water but are less efficient overall than conventional drives.

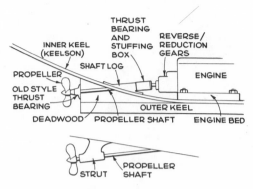

FIG. 133 On displacement-type hulls of heavy construction, the propeller shaft normally runs through a "deadwood" above the keel. On higher-speed hulls, struts extend downward from the bottom of the craft to support the exposed shaft. Long shafts on larger craft may have two or more struts.

FIG. 132 Inboard-outboard drives combine the advantages of using conventional inboard engines with the flexibility of outside drive units much like an outboard motor. Steering is accomplished without rudders by pivoting the drive units; these can also be tilted up for service.

The gears of outdrive and V-drive units include the reversing capability and a reduction ratio if required.

Engine accessories

A complete engine normally includes a *fuel pump* to feed fuel under pressure (to the *carburetor* if gasoline is used), an *oil pump* to supply lubricating oil where needed within the engine, and one or more *water pumps* for circulating cooling water. An engine is *raw water cooled* if water for cooling is drawn in through a hull fitting, circulated in the engine, and then discharged overboard. A *closed cooling system* uses a separate quantity of fresh water to circulate solely within the engine; heat picked up by this water is transferred to raw cooling water in a *heat exchanger,* or is dissipated to the water in which the boat is floating by means of a *keel cooler.*

Engine instruments usually include gauges for indicating oil pressure, cooling water temperature, and battery charging or discharging (ammeter). Speedometers and odometers (distance traveled indicators) are not normally used on powerboats although they do exist; instead a *tachometer* indicates the speed of the engine in revolutions per minute (RPM) and may indicate the total revolutions or operating hours as a guide for the performance of routine maintenance. Gasoline engines are fitted with *flame arresters,* screen-like metal fittings over the air intakes of carburetors so that any flame from a backfire will not come out dangerously into the *engine compartment.*

On many small outboard motors a *shear pin* is part of the propeller assembly. This small pin of relatively soft metal breaks apart—shears—when the propeller strikes a hard underwater object, thus saving the motor from more serious damage; the pin is easily replaced.

Sailboat Terms

Although some powerboat terms will also be applicable to many sailboats (especially those with auxiliary engines), "ragmen" really have a language of their own. All boatmen, including powerboat skippers, should have a working knowledge of the basic terminology of sailing and sailboats.

Basic sailboat components

The principal components of a sailboat are its *hull, spars,* and *sails.* The hull is essentially as decribed before in this chapter with certain modifications and additions resulting from the use of the wind as a means of propulsion. A portion of the wind forced on the sails drives the boat forward, but another portion tends to make it move sideways. To counteract this, the exterior keel is much enlarged in area, or the craft is fitted with a *centerboard,* a relatively thin plate that can be put down vertically through the keel for greater lateral area, but which can be raised when it is desired to lessen the boat's draft. To permit this raising and lowering action, the centerboard is normally pivoted on a pin near the lower forward corner.

To maintain the watertight integrity of the hull, the centerboard is housed in a *centerboard trunk* which extends internally to above the waterline. On some very small sailboats, a *daggerboard* is forced down vertically in lieu of a pivoted centerboard.

Ballast

The sideward thrust of the wind, besides making leeway, also causes a sailboat to heel to leeward. To lessen such heeling and to increase stability, many larger sailing craft carry *ballast,* additional weight either *external* in the form of a heavy mass (usually lead), on the bottom of the keel, or *internal* ballast within the hull. In smaller sailboats, the crew shifts its weight about within the craft (or just over the side) as a form of readily movable internal ballast.

Spars

The term *spars* is used broadly to cover masts, booms, gaffs, etc. *Masts* are, of course, the principal vertical spars from which sails are *set.* They are *stepped* when put in position and are *raked* if the mast is inclined aft at an angle rather than being exactly vertical.

Nautical Terms / CHAPTER 1

The horizontal spar along the lower edge of a fore-and-aft sail is a *boom*. A four-sided fore-and-aft sail has an additional spar along its upper edge; this is a *gaff*.

Rigging

All of the various lines about a vessel that secure the sails, masts, and other spars are collectively referred to as *rigging*. Lines or wires bracing the mast and certain other fixed spars comprise the *standing* rigging; those used for hoisting and adjusting the sails make up the *running rigging*.

The standing rigging—usually wire—from the mast to the sides of the boat are called *shrouds*. Those commonly used to support the mast in a fore-and-aft plane are *stays*—*forestays* run to the bow and *backstays,* if used, support the mast from aft.

The slack is usually taken out of a stay or shrouds by the use of a *turnbuckle,* a metal sleeve threaded right-handed in one end and left-handed in the other so that when turned in one direction eyebolts in both ends are drawn in so as to shorten the fitting; turning the sleeve in the other direction increases its overall length and provides slack.

Sails

Canvas is a general term for a boat's sails, although most modern sails are made of lighter synthetic materials. Sails *draw* when they fill with wind and provide power to drive the craft through the water. One *makes sail* when the sails are hoisted; he *shortens* sail when the area of sails in use is reduced. A sail is *reefed* by partly lowering it and securing it so that it continues to draw, but with reduced area and power. The sail is *dowsed* (or *doused*) when it is lowered quickly, *furled* when it is folded and

FIG. 136 Square-rigged vessels no longer sail in great numbers as they did before the days of steam, but some are still seen as training ships or cruise vessels. There are many types of rigs for these ships.

rolled and then secured to a boom or yard. One *looses sail* when *unfurling* it.

Most recreational sailing craft are now fitted with tri-angular-shaped sails and are said to be *Marconi rigged* (or *jib-headed*). If a four-sided sail with gaff is used, the boat is described as *gaff-rigged.*

A *suit of sails* is a complete set for any particular boat.

Sailing rigs

Rig is the general term applied to the arrangement of a vessel's masts and sails. The principal sail of a boat is its *mainsail*. If the boat has only this one sail, it is a *catboat,* and may be either Marconi- or gaff-rigged.

A sail forward of the mast, or ahead of the most forward mast if there are more than one, is a *headsail;* a single headsail is usually termed a *jib*. A boat having a single mast, with a mainsail and a jib, is a *sloop*. On some sloops additional headsails are set from a *bowsprit,* a spar projecting forward over the craft's bow. A sloop without a bowsprit,

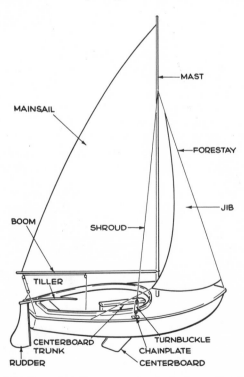

FIG. 134 The principal components of a basic small sailboat are identified above. Every boatman, even those only active with motorboats, should be familiar with these terms.

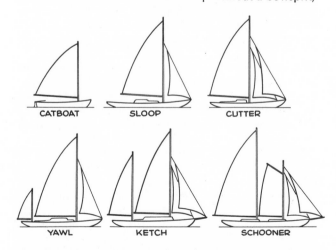

FIG. 135 The various rigs of modern sailing craft are shown above. Careful attention is sometimes necessary to differentiate between sloops and cutters; yawls and ketches are more easily distinguished from one another.

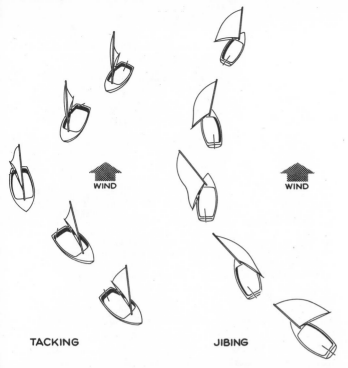

WIND

WIND

TACKING   JIBING

FIG. 137 A sailboat normally changes direction by bringing her bow through the wind—this is "tacking." If the wind passes astern, she "jibes," a maneuver that can be dangerous if not carefully controlled.

FIG. 138   (a) A sailing craft pointing as close to △ the wind as possible is "beating."

(b) As the wind moves more aft, she is "reaching." ▽

(c) With the wind astern or nearly so, she is "running." ▷

on which the jib is set from a stay to the stem, is sometimes called a *knockabout,* but this term has fallen into relative disuse.

A modern *cutter* is a variation of the sloop rig in which the mast is stepped further aft, resulting in a larger area for headsails. A cutter normally sets two headsails, a *forestaysail* and a jib ahead of it.

Yawls have two masts, the after one of which is much smaller and is stepped abaft the rudder post. A *ketch* likewise has two masts with the after one smaller, but here the difference in height is not so marked and the after mast is stepped forward of the rudder post. The taller mast is the *mainmast;* the shorter after mast of both rigs is the *mizzenmast,* and the sail is the *mizzen* (may be either jib-headed or with a gaff).

Schooners are *fore-and-aft rigged* (as distinguished from square-rigged) and have two or more masts. Unlike yawls and ketches, the after mast of a two-masted schooner is taller than the forward one (in rare designs, the two masts may be the same height). Thus the after mast becomes the mainmast and the other the *foremast.* Additional names are used if there are more than two masts.

Square-rigged vessels

Vessels on which the principal sails are set generally athwartships are referred to as *square-rigged.* These four-sided sails are hung from horizontal spars known as *yards.* Headsails are carried as on other rigs, forward of the foremost mast. Staysails may be used, and the aftermost mast of square-rigged vessels normally carry a fore-and-aft sail.

Sailing terms

As sailboats cannot sail directly into the wind, the wind is almost always coming over one side or the other. If the wind is coming over the starboard side, the boat is said to be on a *starboard tack;* the *port tack* is, of course, just the opposite. A boat *tacks* when she *comes up* (heads) into the wind and changes the side over which it blows. In tacking, a boat *goes (comes) about.* Changing tacks with the wind passing astern rather than ahead of the boat is called *jibing* (pronounced with a long *i* as in ice), or *wearing*

ship; jibes (also spelled gibes or gybes) sometimes occur accidentally when sailing downwind (the wind nearly dead astern) and can be dangerous.

After the sails have been *hoisted* by their *halyards,* they are trimmed with their *sheets (jibsheets, mainsheets,* etc.), lines used to control their lateral position and movement. To *harden* is to haul in and tighten up on the sheet attached to a jib, mainsail, etc. Sheets are *eased* when they are let out. Headsails normally have two sheets so that they can be trimmed on either tack; other sails have only one sheet.

Although a detailed discussion of sailing techniques is beyond the scope of this chapter, all boatmen should know that a sailboat is *close hauled (full and by)* when she is sailing with the wind as far ahead as possible, about 45° off the bow in most boats (this is also termed sailing *on the wind,* to *windward,* or *beating*). As the boat is steered further away from the wind, it *bears off* and is *reaching,* with *close* reaching, *beam* reaching, and *broad* reaching occurring successively as the wind moves aft. With the wind astern, the sailboat is *running* (or sailing *downwind, off the wind, free,* or *scudding*).

Miscellaneous Basic Terms

There are many other basic boating terms that do not fit neatly into one of the above categories. Among these are words and phrases relating to the operation of the vessel, navigation, etc.

Navigation and piloting

Navigation is the art and science of safely directing the movements of a vessel from one point to another. The basic boatman is primarily interested in one of its subdivisions, *piloting,* which is navigation using visible references, the depth of the water, etc. Other forms of navigation include *celestial,* taking *sights* by *sextant* on the sun, moon, planets, and stars, used for long offshore passages; and *electronic,* which may be used in varying degrees by inshore and offshore boatmen.

Courses

A *course* is the direction of movement prescribed for a vessel from one place to another. A *true course* is one taken from the chart with reference to true (geographic) north—it is the angle between the boat's keel and the geographic meridian when she is on course. The *magnetic course* is the angle between her keel and the magnetic meridan passing through that position; it is almost always different from the true course. A *compass course* is the course indicated by the vessel's compass—it is the angle between the vessel's keel and the direction indicated by the north point on the compass card when she is on course. The *heading* is the direction a vessel's bow points at any given time.

Bearings

A *bearing* is the direction of a terrestial object from the observer and may be stated in terms of true, magnetic, or compass values. A *relative bearing* is the direction of a terrestial object from the observer measured from the vessel's heading clockwise from 000° to 360°.

Variation and deviation

Variation is the angular difference between true north and the direction of magnetic north at a given point on

FIG. 139 Navigation includes all methods of safely directing the movements of a vessel from one point to another. The techniques range from simple buoy-to-buoy coastal piloting to celestial navigation on the high seas using a mariner's sextant.

earth. It is the direction indicated by a magnetic compass that is unaffected by local influences. Variation is "easterly" if the north mark of a compass card points to the east of true north, "westerly" if the opposite.

Deviation is the error in a magnetic compass caused by local magnetic influences on the boat. It is easterly or westerly as the compass points east or west of magnetic north. *Compass error* is the algebraic sum of variation and deviation.

Plotting and charting

In navigation, one *plots* various data on a *chart* (never map), takes *bearings* to determine his *position (fix),* and takes a *departure* to establish an exact point from which to commence his *dead reckoning* (a plot of courses steered and distances travelled through the water). *To chart,* a verb, is to record information, usually additional information, on an existing chart of the area.

Much more on the above terms will be found in Chapters 13, 14, 17, 19, and 21.

Aids to navigation

Various governmental authorities establish and maintain *aids to navigation,* artificial objects to supplement natural landmarks. These may be used to indicate both safe and unsafe waters; the boatman must know the meanings and use of each.

Buoys are floating aids to navigation of characteristic shapes and colors. They may be lighted or unlighted; they may or may not have audible signals such as bells, gongs,

FIG. 140 Relative bearings are measured as angles from dead ahead clockwise around the starboard side, past the stern, and back up the port side to the bow. Directions are always described in three-digit groups using zeros as necessary, i.e., 050°, not 50°

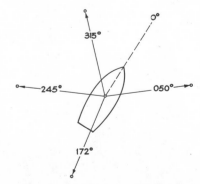

RELATIVE BEARINGS

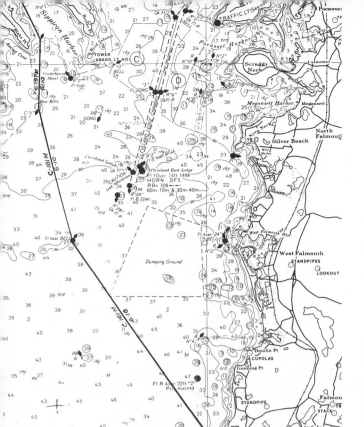

Other terms

Lubberly is used to describe the doing of any task aboard a boat or ship in an ignorant or sloppy manner.

In nautical terminology, *hard* means fully or completely as in turning a steering wheel *hard aport* (fully to the left) or *hard over* (in either direction).

A *beach* is the land immediately in from the water's edge. In tidal regions, it includes the area between the high- and low-water lines. To go *to the beach* is a nautical expression meaning to go ashore, even if not to an actual beach.

A *bar* is a build-up, usually of sand, that reduces the depth of water; it may or may not be partially exposed above the surface of the water and it usually has an elongated shape. Bars frequently form across the openings *(mouths)* of rivers, creeks, harbors, etc. Larger, broader areas of shallow water are often termed *flats*.

Advanced Boating Terminology

Once a boatman has mastered the basic "language" of this field of interest, he is ready to go further into the subject, learning terms perhaps not necessary to everyday operation of his boat, but rather words and phrases that will expand and broaden his knowledge. The terms discussed here will by no means exhaust the possibilities, but they will add to the skipper's understanding of his craft and its use.

These additional terms occur in many areas of boating; they are, however, perhaps most noticeable in those relating to boat construction and sailing—these fields of interest have extensive vocabularies all their own.

Additional Boat Construction Terms

Vessels, including boats, are normally designed by a *naval architect.* In so doing, he prepares detailed *plans* and *specifications,* including the *lines* (shape) of her hull. *Clean* is a term applied, not to a boat's condition, but rather to her lines. If the lines are *fine,* so that she slips easily through the water, the lines are said to be clean.

A *marine surveyor* is a highly qualified expert who makes detailed inspections—the *survey*—of boats and ships to determine the condition of their hull, equipment, machinery, etc.

Hull shape terms

In addition to being used for the lower interior portions of a vessel, the term *bilge* is also applied to the area of the hull of a round-bottom craft where the bottom gradually becomes the topsides; a somewhat longer but perhaps more descriptive term for this is *turn of the bilge.* If the boat is flat or vee-bottomed, the bottom and the topsides meet at a well-defined angle rather than a gradual curve—this is the *chine* of the boat. The smaller the angle of intersection of these planes, the *harder* the chine. *Soft* chine craft have a lesser angle; this term is sometimes applied to round-bottom boats, but this is not correct. Some modern boats are designed with *multiple chines (longitudinal steps)* for a softer ride at high speeds in rough water.

Larger round-bottom vessels may be built with *bilge keels,* secondary keels at the turn of the bilge to reduce their tendence to roll in beam seas.

FIG. 141 A skipper makes a plot on his chart to record his position at various times and his craft's movements, past and projected, through the water. This is important should an emergency arise as he must be able to quickly and accurately determine his location.

whistles, etc.

Daybeacons (not "markers") are fixed aids normally consisting of a distinctive sign, the *daymark,* mounted on a pile or group of piles driven into the bottom. Daymarks will have a characteristic shape and color or colors.

Lights (not "flashers") are aids consisting of a light source mounted on a fixed object (as distinguished from lighted buoys). Each light will have a characteristic color and on-off pattern; most light structures will also have a daymark for daytime identification. The term "light" covers all such aids from the relatively weak minor light on a single pile to the largest seacoast lighthouses.

Detailed information on aids to navigation will be found in Chapters 15 and 16.

FIG. 142 Aids to navigation are among a boatman's best friends. Unlighted buoys and daybeacons are the most numerous types of aids; these and many others are described and discussed in Chapters 15 and 16.

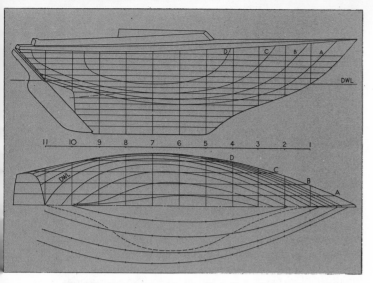

FIG. 143 The shape of a vessel's hull, particularly the underwater portions, is shown by her "lines" in several views. These are the basic determinations of a naval architect when he designs a boat.

The significance of the term *deadrise* can be appreciated by visualizing a transverse section across a hull. If the bottom were flat, extending horizontally from the keel, there would be no deadrise. In a round- or vee-bottom boat, where the bottom rises at an angle to a horizontal line outward from the keel, the amount of such rise is the deadrise, expressed in inches per foot or as an angle.

With normal sheer, the bow of a boat, as viewed from the side, rises and the stern is at least level with amidships. *Reverse sheer*, however, has the deck sloping downward at the bow, or stern, or both.

Flam is that part of the flare of the topsides just below the deck. If it curves outward sharply, it will both increase deck width and reduce the amount of bow spray that blows aboard. The *cutwater* is, naturally enough, the forward edge of the stem, particularly near the waterline. *Stem bands* of metal are frequently fitted over the stem for protection from debris in the water, ice, pier edges, etc. The *forefoot* of a boat is where the stem joins the keel.

If the boat has an *overhanging* stern, this part of the hull is the *counter*. Her lines aft to her stern are her *run*; lines forward to the stem are her *entrance* (or *entry*). The descriptions "fine" and "clean" are often applied to the entrance and run. The term *bluff* is applied to bows that are broader and blunter than normal.

FIG. 144 Some modern high-speed deep-vee hulls are designed with multiple chines or longitudinal steps for better rough-water performance. The skipper shown above, though, is driving his boat too hard for existing conditions, despite its special design!

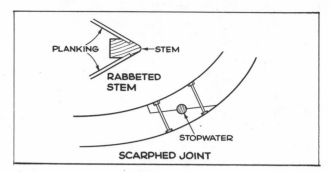

FIG. 145 Much expert carpentry work goes into a planked wooden boat to provide a strong, watertight hull.

Planking details

On a planked wooden hull, the sheer (or uppermost) strake is sometimes thicker than other lines of planking. When a second plank, next below the sheer strake, is also thicker than the others it is called a *binding strake*. *Bilge strakes* are those fitted at the turn of the bilge and these, too, may be heavier than others in the topsides.

A heavier strake in the topsides extending beyond the exposed face of the planking is termed a *rubbing strake* and is intended to protect the topsides from the roughness of piles, pier faces, etc. A strip of wood for the same purpose added externally to the planking is generally called a *rubrail* or *guard*. Both of these may be faced with metal strips for their own better protection.

Many hulls are fitted with a *spray rail* external to the planking just above the waterline. Such a rail usually extends about halfway aft from the stem and deflects downward any spray from the bow wave.

Frame members such as the keel and stem are *rabbeted* to receive the ends and edges of the planks. This *rabbet* is merely a longitudinal recess cut into the wood in the proper size to take the plank. Plank ends at the stem and stern are the *hood ends*.

The term *fastening* is applied to the screws or specially-designed nails which hold the planks to the frames. It may also be applied to screws, bolts, and similar items used to hold down equipment, cleats, chocks, etc. *Through fastenings* are bolts that go all the way through the hull or other base timbers and are secured with a washer and nut on the inside; a *backing block* is generally advisable to spread the stress for additional strength.

Waterways are gutters along the edge of a boat's deck to aid in draining off water through the *scuppers*. (This same term is also applied to water areas suitable for navigation, particularly improved channels in rivers, lakes, etc.)

Wedges are sometimes placed on the underside of a boat's hull at the transom to provide additional "lift" to the stern, preventing *squat* and so improving running trim. Wedges provide a fixed action; more sophisticated electrical-mechanical-hydraulic devices can be built-in or installed to provide adjustable amounts of wedge action.

Bulwarks and taffrails

When the topsides are carried above the level of the deck, this portion is called *bulwarks* and the top of the bulwarks is the *rail*. The *taffrail* is the rail at the stern, farthest aft. A *taffrail log* is a type of patent log that is

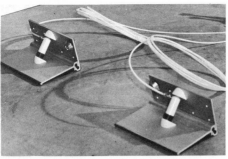

FIG. 146 Adjustable electro-mechanical or hydraulic "trim tabs" are a modern replacement for the wedges often added at the stern of a boat to reduce "squat." These can markedly change the riding angle of many hulls, increasing both speed and fuel economy.

mounted on the taffrail for measuring speed and distance traveled according to the rotation of a spinner at the end of a length of line towed astern.

Interior details

For strengthening the hull, there are *bosom* knees, and *carling* knees, *dagger* knees and *hanging* knees, *lodging* knees, *panting* knees, *thwart* knees, and many others. The name of each is derived from its location in the boat. They are strength members used wherever two structural members meet at an angle and reinforcing is required. For example, *quarter* knees are used at each side of the transom.

A *breasthook* is a triangular reinforcing member, usually of wood but sometimes of metal, placed horizontally behind the stem of a boat to strengthen her bow.

On a boat whose stern extends beyond the end of her keel, the *horn timber* is the backbone structural member to which the after frames are fastened. One-piece timbers running the full length of the keel are often not available. In such cases, shorter pieces are bevelled and bolted together in a joint called a *scarph* (scarf); similar joints may be used elsewhere, such as in the stem. A *stopwater* is a dowel (round rod or pin) of soft wood driven into a hole drilled through the joint line of a scarph; it swells when wet and prevents water from entering.

Sister frames are additional frames added at a later date next to original frames that may have cracked or split. Such a frame is not fastened to the broken frame but to the planking.

Limber holes are passages cut into the lower edges of floors and frames next to the keel to allow bilge water to flow to the lowest point of the hull from whence it can be pumped out. These limber holes must be kept clean so that drainage to the lowest point can occur; on some larger vessels a *limber chain* is run through these holes so

that it can be pulled back and forth a short distance to clean them out.

Some boats are severely damaged by "dry rot," a fungus attack on wooden areas. The name is incorrect, as moisture is essential for the growth and spread of the fungus. The wood is greatly weakened by the action of the fungus. Prevention of standing water in corners and pockets, and adequate ventilation, are the best defenses against dry rot; chemical treatments can be used to attack existing rot infestations.

A *collision bulkhead* is sometimes found in larger craft; it is a solid one near the bow intended to preserve flotation in case of a bow-on accident.

Stringers, beams, and carlines

Stringers are longitudinal members fastened inside the hull for additional structural strength. If they run along the turn of the bilge (the turn of the hull below the waterline) they are termed *bilge stringers*. Stringers fastened inside the gunwale are referred to as *clamps*.

Deck beams are the athwartships members that support the deck. Their outer ends usually rest on the clamps, although a horizontal *shelf* may be used above the clamp in which case the beams rest upon this on either side.

A *carline* (also spelled *carlin* or *carling*) is a short timber running fore-and-aft between deck beams. These will be found, for example, at the port and starboard sides of any opening in the deck.

Open boats often have a *finishing piece* which runs along the gunwale, lying on the top of the *clamp* or *inwale* and covering the top edge of the planking and the heads of the frames. This is *capping*. In many boats, however, capping is omitted so that there is nothing to catch dirt and water when the boat is heeled over on its side to be emptied, instead of being bailed out. Such a boat would be said to have *open gunwales*.

Deck terms

The sheer plank has been defined as the topmost strake of the topsides, where the sides join the deck. The *plank sheer,* on the other hand, means the outermost plank of the deck. Sometimes called a *covering board,* it covers the tops of frames and the upper edge of the sheer strake on a decked boat, just as capping does in an open boat. Covering boards are usually wider than any of the other deck planks. The center plank of a deck is the *king plank*. If a deck is arched to aid in the draining off of water, it is said to be *cambered*. Similarly, camber occurs on the tops of cabins, deckhouses, etc.

The deck over the forward part of a vessel, or the forward part of the total deck area, is termed a *foredeck*. Similarly, the *afterdeck* is located in the after part of the vessel. The deck of a cockpit or interior cabin is often called a *sole*.

Other construction terms

Composite construction is the use of two or more materials in the hull of a vessel. Often this consists of wood planking over iron or steel frames.

Sea cocks are valves installed just inside *through-hull fittings* and ahead of the piping or hose running from the fittings. They are important safety devices. See fig. 1010.

The *boot top* is that portion of the exterior hull at the

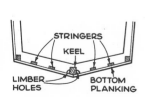
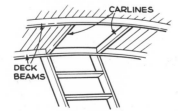

FIG. 147 Limber holes are notches cut into frames or floor timbers where they join the keel so that bilge water can run to the lowest point to be pumped out. These must be periodically checked to make sure that they are free of any obstructions.

waterline. It is usually finished with special paint—*boot-topping*—of a color to contrast with the *anti-fouling paint* of the bottom and the paint of the topsides.

Areas that are varnished to a high gloss are termed *brightwork*. (In naval usage, this term may be applied to polished brass.) A *tack rag* is a slightly sticky cloth that is wiped over surfaces that are to be varnished just before the brush is applied in order to remove all dust and grit.

When the rudder of a boat is exactly centered, one spoke of the steering wheel should be vertical; this is the *king spoke* and is usually marked with special carving or wrapping so that it can be recognized by feel alone.

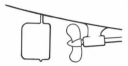

FIG. 148 A balanced rudder has a portion of its blade surface—much less than half—forward of the axis of rotation. This design considerably reduces the force required to turn the rudder against the pressure of the passing flow of water.

A boat's rudder is said to be *balanced* when a portion of its blade area extends forward of the axis of rotation. Such a rudder is easier to turn than one that is not so designed.

Many motorboats will have a small *signal mast* from which flags can be flown—see Chapter 22. These flags are hoisted on signal halyards. When partially hoisted they are said to be *at the dip;* when fully hoisted, they are termed *two-blocked.*

Sailboat and Sailing Terms

An *offshore* wind blows from the land; an *onshore* wind, towards it. A *weather shore* is one from which wind is blowing toward a vessel. A *lee shore* is a good one to *give a wide berth* (keep well clear of). Many use this term in the opposite, erroneous, sense, thinking that there is protection under the lee shore. But since this is the shore on the lee side of the vessel, it is the one onto which the wind is blowing, and thus it is a dangerous one. When a sailboat is caught on a lee shore and has to work her way clear, she is *clawing* off. To be *under the lee* of an island is to be on the sheltered side, the safe side in stormy weather.

Wind *veers* when it shifts by changing its direction clockwise as would be seen looking down from above the earth. It *backs* when it shifts in a counter-clockwise direc-

tion, such as going from southerly to more easterly.

On a sailboat, wind changing from abeam to further forward *hauls;* moving from abeam aft toward the stern, it *veers.*

Measurement and classes

One-design class sailboats are virtually identical craft built and equipped to the same set of plans for racing. *Measurement-rule* boats are not identical, but the total effect of design variations theoretically cancel out differences in performance so that they can compete without handicaps. Other racing sailboats are individually *measured* and *rated* to determine the *time allowance* (handicap) to be used in any given competition.

Details of sails

The forward edge of a triangular (Marconi or Bermudan) sail is its *luff;* its after edge is its *leech* (also spelled leach); and the lower edge is the *foot.* The foot is normally attached to a boom, but if it is not, or is attached only at the ends, the sail is said to be *loose-footed.*

The upper corner of such a sail is the *head;* the lower forward corner, as where the boom and the mast meet, is the *tack;* and the after lower corner, at the outer end of the boom if there is one, is the *clew.* The same terms apply to the sides and corners of all triangular fore-and-aft sails.

For four-sided (gaff-rig) sails, the term "head" is applied to the upper edge, with the upper forward corner, where the gaff and the mast meet, being the *throat;* the upper after corner, at the outer, higher end of the gaff, is the *peak.*

A *bolt rope* is often sewed into the edges of a sail to strengthen it. *Tabling* is the reinforced part of a sail to which the bolt rope is sewed. The leech of a fore-and-aft sail is usually cut with an outward curve called the *roach* of the sail. To support the roach and preserve its shape by flattening the leach, *battens* (thin flat strips of wood or plastic) are inserted in *batten pockets* in the sail along its after edge. This flattening results in a more efficient sail. A few designs use *full battens* extending across the sail from luff to leech.

Most sails are *bent* (attached or fastened) to the mast by the use of *slides* attached to the luff which ride on or in a track attached to the mast. A similar arrangement holds

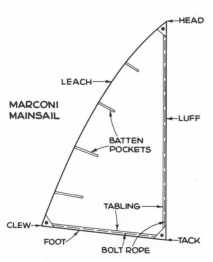

FIG. 149 The marconi style of sail is by far the most popular design for sailboats today. The major parts are labeled in the above sketch. Such sails may be made of cotton canvas or of dacron and other synthetic materials.

FIG. 150 Gaff-rig sails are still seen but not so often as formerly. They are usually found on larger or older sailing craft. Note that the term "head" here applies to a side of the sail rather than to a corner as on the marconi rig.

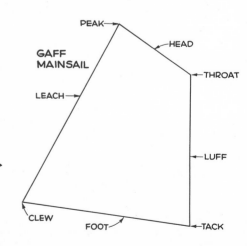

Fig. 151(a). This ketch is flying a mizzen staysail between her masts in addition to mainsail, spinnaker, and fore staysail.

Fig. 151(b). Right: A spinnaker is a foresail of very light material that is full in shape, nearly spherical. It is set in light or moderate breezes that come from well astern; usually in lieu of a regular jib.

FIG. 152 The masts of some sailing craft are mounted in "tabernacles" located above the deck. These permit the mast to be easily lowered rather than unstepped for inland cruising or shipment.

the foot of the sail to the boom. Headsails are fastened to the *jibstay* (or to the *forestay*) with *snaps*.

On some small sailboats the sail is held to the mast by sliding the bolt rope of the luff up an internal groove in the mast. If gaff-rigged, *hoops* encircling the mast are used to hold the luff in place with respect to the mast.

Jibs are headsails set forward of the foremost mast, but they often *overlap* and extend aft of this mast. Large overlapping jibs are called *Genoas*, in slang terms, "gennies," and *reaching jibs* or *reachers*. In coming about, care must be taken that the clew of an overlapping jib gets around the mast without fouling so that the new tack can be assumed smoothly. Smaller, non-overlapping jibs lack the "power" of larger jibs, but these can be self-trimming when tacking; to make them so, a light spar, called a *club*, not a boom, may be attached to the foot of such a jib.

Spinnakers are large, three-sided sails of very light material set from booms called *spinnaker poles* on the opposite side of the main or fore boom when running before a *fair wind*.

Staysails are triangular jib-like sails set from the stays which support the masts, including the stays between the masts of yawls, ketches, and other multi-masted sailing craft.

Plain sails are the ordinary working sails, not including the lighter jibs and staysails. *Storm canvas*, on the other hand, includes jibs, staysails, and *trysails* of extra heavy material for use in strong winds.

Masts and booms

The foot of a mast, its lower end, is called the *heel*; it fits into a *step* in the keel. Masts are often secured in place where they pass through the deck or cabin top with *mast wedges* which bear against the *mast partners* (or *mast bench)*, the heavier framing around the opening, the *mast hole*, through which the mast passes. In some sailing craft, the mast ends in a *tabernacle*, a pair of side-by-side vertical

timbers, or equivalent metal fitting, on the deck or cabin top, this fitting often has a pin so that the mast is in effect hinged and can easily be lowered for passing under bridges, trailering, etc.

The topmost end of a mast is the *masthead*, often capped with a *truck*, a flat circular piece of wood. Hence the expression "from truck to keel" as including everything in a ship from top to bottom. At the masthead there will normally be a *masthead fitting*, a metal fixture for the attachment of shrouds and stays; it may also include one or more sheaves for halyards.

A *jury mast* is any spar rigged temporarily as a mast in the event that the mast itself has carried away. If such an accident occurs, the vessel is said to have been *dismasted*. A *jury rig* is any device or arrangement fashioned from available materials in an emergency as a substitute for regular gear that has broken.

The *jaws* of a gaff are the extensions of the forward end that partially encircle the mast.

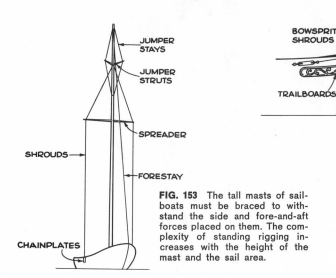

FIG. 153 The tall masts of sailboats must be braced to withstand the side and fore-and-aft forces placed on them. The complexity of standing rigging increases with the height of the mast and the sail area.

FIG. 154 Larger sailboats usually have a bowsprit to extend further forward the lower end of the forestay. The bowsprit in turn needs its stays and shrouds for bracing. Trailboards are merely decorative.

FIG. 155 (a) Sail area must be reduced by "reefing" when the wind blows too hard for safety. The sail is lowered slightly and the reef points are tied around the foot of the sail, never around the boom. Many larger sails have two or more rows of reef points.

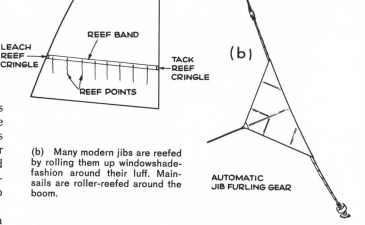

(b) Many modern jibs are reefed by rolling them up windowshade-fashion around their luff. Mainsails are roller-reefed around the boom.

Standing and running rigging

Horizontal spars fitted on a mast to spread the shrouds for more effective bracing are called *spreaders*. *Tangs* are metal plates attached to a mast where standing rigging is to be made fast; they distribute the strain over a wider area of the mast. The lower ends of shrouds are attached to *chainplates,* metal fittings in the form of straps that extend downward on the topsides across several strakes to distribute the load.

Jumper stays are short stays on the forward side of a mast that come down from the masthead and back into the upper part of the mast rather than extending down to the deck. The *jumper strut* holds these stays out from the mast so that bracing action is achieved.

A *topping lift* is a portion of the running rigging used to support or hoist the outer end of a boom. A *peak halyard* is used on a gaff-rigged sailboat to hoist the peak end of the gaff and the head of the sail. A separate *throat halyard* is used to hoist the throat end of the gaff.

A *clew outhaul* is a short length of line attached to the clew of the sail which is led outward to the end of the boom, around the sheave, and back to a cleat or small winch; it is used to stretch the foot of the sail.

A *boom vang* (or *boom jack*) is a line or tackle used to hold a boom down in a more effective position when reaching or running before the wind.

Lazy jacks are light lines run down from the masthead to the boom on either side of a sail. Their purpose is to contain the sail when it is lowered, keeping it from spilling onto the deck or over the side, and thus making it easier to furl.

Pin rails and fife rails

Belaying pins are short bars or pins, usually of wood, about which the lines of a sailboat's running rigging may be made fast. The same line is always *belayed* to the same pin for quick and easy identification at night or in an emergency. Belaying pins are mounted in *pin rails*, racks at a boat's side, usually at the shrouds, and in *fife rails* around the lower part of a mast at a handy height above deck level.

Cleats are more often used for securing sheets and halyards of modern sailing boats, but pin rails and fife rails will be found on larger and more tradition-minded vessels.

Bowsprits and boomkins

While a mast is stayed in a vertical position, bowsprits are *guyed* horizontally (or at a slight angle) by *bowsprit shrouds* at the sides and in a vertical plane by a *bobstay*— often chain—from below. A short, downward spreader to the bobstay is a *dolphin-striker.*

A bowsprit projects forward from the stem, and on quite large sailing vessels a *jib-boom* may be rigged out beyond the bowsprit. A jib-boom is thus a fixed spar and not like the other "booms" (remember, too, a spar along the foot of a jib is not a boom either, but a "club").

Short spars sometimes project aft from the stern, particularly on yawls, where the mizzen boom overhangs the stern considerably; these are *boomkins.*

Trailboards are added pieces of wood on either side of the bow of a sailboat, often elaborately carved and painted or gilded. They sometimes lead forward to a *figurehead.*

Reefing

To permit reefing a sail when the wind increases beyond a safe strength, there are usually strips of additional material, *reef bands,* sewed to the sail parallel to the foot. Short lengths of line, *reef points,* are attached at intervals along these bands; these are tied around the foot of the sail— never around the boom—to reduce the sail area.

A *reef cringle* is an eye in the leech or luff of a fore-and-aft sail in line with the reef points. *Reef earings (or pendants)* are short pieces of line spliced into the cringles to permit the latter to be secured to the boom when the sail is reefed.

Many modern sailing rigs use *roller reefing* in which the *gooseneck* fitting where the boom attaches to the mast is designed with a swivel to permit the boom to be rotated and thus roll up the foot of the sail like a window shade as the halyard is slacked off. In a few smaller rigs, the mainsail is reefed by winding it around the mast.

Jibs are sometimes roller furled around the stay upon which they are set; a single jib can have its effective area varied so widely that it will eliminate the need for carrying and setting various sizes of jibs for many different wind conditions.

Construction details

A metal rod called a *horse* (or *deck horse* or *boom horse*) is sometimes bolted to the deck and on it the ring of a *sheet block* can travel from side to side as the boom swings over on a change of tack. This is the *traveller*. A more modern rig uses a section of metal track instead of a horse; the sheet block is attached to a *slide* or *car* that rides the track. On small boats, a wire bridle often takes the place of the metal rod type of horse or track. Often, but inaccurately, the deck fitting or wire bridle is itself called the "traveller."

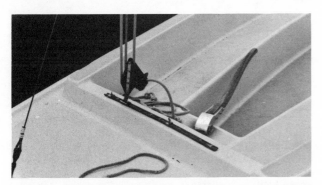

FIG. 156 Many sailboats are fitted with a traveller across the deck near the stern. With this device, the trim of the mainsail on each tack can be more closely controlled. Stops may be used to limit the movement to either side of the lower block on the mainsheet.

A *tiller* is a horizontal arm extending forward from the top of the rudder or rudderstock and which is moved from side to side for steering. It is much used on sailboats as it is said to provide a better "feel" of the boat's performance than a wheel, and is also cheaper.

On small sailing craft, the rudder is often detachable from the transom or stern post. Ordinarily, the rudder is fitted with downward pointing hooks or pins, called *pintles,* which fit into metal eyes, *gudgeons,* on the hull of the boat.

A *fin. keel* is one in the form of a relatively thin plate extending below the hull to give a sailboat greater *lateral resistance;* it may have a concentrated weight of metal on its lower edge for increased stability effectiveness, this is a *bulb keel.*

A *boom crutch* is an upright strut temporarily put in place to support a boom when the sails have been lowered.

Small, shallow-draft sailboats, such as sailing canoes, are sometimes equipped with *leeboards* in lieu of a center-board or daggerboard. These are a pair of flat surfaces extended over each side of the boat, normally pivoted at the top for easy lowering and raising. Only the leeward board is lowered when underway. They are also used on certain types of foreign sailing craft of considerable size.

Sailing terms

A sailboat *carries weather helm* if she has a tendency to *head up* into the wind and the tiller must be kept to windward to hold her on course. Lee helm is the opposite with a tendency to *fall off* the wind and a need to hold the tiller to leeward. A boat with *balanced helm* shows neither of these tendencies.

Generally speaking, it is well for a sailboat to carry a small amount of weather helm. Then if the tiller is accidentally let go, the boat will *round up* into the wind, a relatively safe action, instead of falling off into what might become a dangerous jibe. Too much weather helm, however, is undesirable as the constant rudder angle creates drag and slows the boat down. The angle of rake of the mast and the trim of the boat, determined by the distribution of the weight of the crew and ballast, have much to do with what helm and how much of it the boat will carry.

A *stiff* vessel returns quickly to her normal upright position from a rolled or heeled position. If she rolls in a seaway without quick action or sudden movements, her roll is *easy.* When a boat's center of gravity is too high and stability is low, she is *tender; crank* conveys the same idea.

A skipper *fetches* a given objective if he is sailing a course to windward and reaches the mark without tacking. When working to windward, each *leg* or tack may be called a *board,* and, depending upon the length of each leg, there may be *long boards* and *short boards.*

If a sailboat attempts to come about and the bow does not fall off on the other tack, she is *caught in* (or *misses*) *stays,* or is said to be *in irons.* A sailboat is *pinched* when she is steered so close to the wind that the sails shiver. A vessel is said to *luff* when she is brought up into the wind so as to spill some of it out of the sails, thus relieving the pressure and *easing* her.

Sailing before the wind, sails are sometimes set on opposite sides of the boat; this is called *wing and wing.* A light

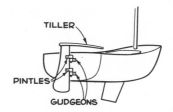

FIG. 157 Daysailers often have easily detachable rudders. Pintles on the rudder fit into brackets — "gudgeons" — on the transom. The boat may be more easily beached or trailered with the rudder removed.

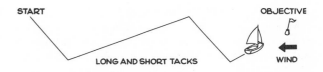

FIG. 158 When a sailboat's objective is more nearly upwind than the craft can sail, a series of tacks, or boards, must be used. These will be a combination of long and short legs if the objective is not directly upwind.

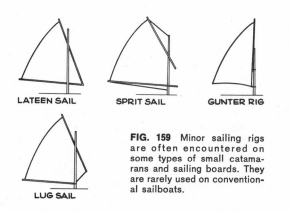

LATEEN SAIL   SPRIT SAIL   GUNTER RIG

LUG SAIL

FIG. 159 Minor sailing rigs are often encountered on some types of small catamarans and sailing boards. They are rarely used on conventional sailboats.

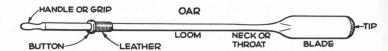

HANDLE OR GRIP   OAR   TIP
BUTTON   LEATHER   LOOM   NECK OR THROAT   BLADE

FIG. 160 Engines do fail and gas tanks do run dry! Every boatman should know at least the fundamentals of oars and rowing. Small outboards should be equipped with oars or paddles as determined by their design.

FIG. 161 Canoes are light, easily propelled craft for protected inland waters. Paddles are sometimes double-ended for convenience in solo operation.

whisker pole may be used to wing out the jib so that it will draw more effectively.

One boat *blankets* another when, being just to windward, she takes the wind out of the other's sails. She *outfoots* another craft by sailing faster, *outpoints* her by sailing closer to the wind.

Minor sailing rigs

A *lateen* rig consists of a single mast and a triangular sail whose forward edge is sharply raked aft at an angle of roughly 45°. This edge is attached to a light spar, or yard, which in turn is attached to the mast, the near mid-point of the yard to the near top of the mast. A boom is used which extends forward of the mast to the lower end of the yard. This rig is widely used for small catamarans and, in modified form, for *sailboards,* small sailing craft whose hulls resemble surfboards.

A *sprit* rig is used on some dinghies and other small craft. In this type of rig the upper aft corner (peak) of the four-sided fore-and-aft sail is held aloft by a light spar known as a *sprit* inserted in an eye in the sail called a grommet. The *sprit* at its lower end is supported by a *snorter* or *becket* consisting of a light line about the mast with an eye in the lower end to take the sprit. Although the sail is four-sided, no gaff at the head or boom at the foot is required, although a boom is sometimes used with its forward end held in a becket as the sprit above it.

Lug rigs are of various types and their use is also confined to small craft. The *standing lug* has a yard which crosses the mast obliquely while the tack of the four-sided sail (forward lower corner) is made fast to the mast. In a *dipping lug* the tack is made fast to the stem, ahead of the mast, so that the yard must be *dipped* around the mast when tacking.

A *gunter* (or *sliding gunter*) rig uses a triangular sail whose luff is attached to a spar which is hoisted much like a gaff except that it is hoisted to a fully vertical position where it becomes an extension of the short mast. A jib may also be used.

Rowboats and Rowing

Although this book is primarily for the skippers of motorboats and sailing craft, the well-informed boatman knows the essential facts about boats propelled by muscle-power. Dinghies are often rowed, and light motorboats are at times rowed or paddled to safety when the engine fails. The technique of paddling and rowing is an art unto itself and is best learned by practice under proper instruction, but the terms involved can be made familiar here.

Rowboats and oars

Rowboat is the term generally applied to a light craft propelled by one or more persons using *oars*. These are long slender wooden shafts shaped into a round *handle* (or *grip*) at one end and a flat *blade* at the other; between these ends the shaft of the oar is termed the *loom*.

The transverse seats in rowing craft are called *thwarts*. The ends of thwarts land on *risers* (or *risings*) which are fore-and-aft pieces or stringers fastened to the inside of the frames. To support the thwart, a vertical piece is often fitted amidships, called a *thwart stanchion*. Stretchers (also called *foot boards,* although this creates confusion with an alternate term for bottom boards) are sometimes fitted athwartships against which the *oarsman* can brace his feet.

The terms *rowlock* and *oarlock* are synonymous. These are the fittings in the gunwale which hold the oars when rowing. There are many styles of rowlocks; some open, others closed; some mounted permanently, others removable; some attached to the oars. In place of rowlocks, wooden *thole pins* are sometimes driven into holes or sockets.

Where the loom of the oar bears against the rowlock, it is often protected from excess wear by a *leather* (which may be of leather or rubber). On the side of the leather toward the handle, there may be a *button,* a ring around the oar to keep it from slipping outward through the rowlock. Where the loom becomes the blade is the *neck* (or *throat*) of the oar. The *tip* of the blade, its outer end, may be metal sheathed for protection from wear, but this is not common on oars used with light rowboats.

A man who is *sculling* would stand in the stern and propel the boat by working a single oar back and forth, using either one or two hands.

Canoes and paddles

Canoe is the term applied to very lightly built open craft of narrow beam and shallow draft that are *paddled* rather than rowed; they are normally double-ended. A *paddle* is much like an oar except that it is shorter. The various parts of a paddle are named the same as for an oar. The grip is shaped differently as the paddle is used vertically rather than horizontally; the blade will normally be somewhat wider for its length in comparison with an oar.

Some paddles are *double-ended* (double-bladed) so that they may be more conveniently dipped alternately on either side of the canoe, an advantage when one person is propelling the boat rather than two.

Documentation and Tonnage

Large ships and many commercial vessels are *documented* by the United States government (and foreign vessels by their governments). This procedure can also be used for medium and large size recreational craft. Such documentation is in lieu of *registration (numbering)* with state authorities. Before documentation can be considered, however, a discussion of "tonnage" is in order. The procedures and effects of documentation are covered in Chapter 2.

Admeasurement and tonnage

The *tonnage* of ships and boats is determined in several different ways; it may be a measurement of either (1) weight, or (2) size without regard to weight. Persons unfamiliar with the term as it is used in connection with vessels are likely, in error, to think only of the common ton which is a measure of weight—either 2000 pounds in a short ton or 2240 pounds in a long ton. This is a part, but only a part, of the situation when ships are considered.

The determination of the "tonnage" of a vessel is called *measurement* or *admeasurement,* the latter term being found mainly in legal documents. (This measurement should not be confused with the measurement of racing sailboats for rating purposes, a quite different process.)

Gross and net tonnage

The documentation law repeatedly refers to vessels of a certain tonnage, as for example when it states that a yacht of 5 net tons or over may be documented. *Net tons* are derived from gross tonnage which is a measurement of volume rather than weight.

FIG. 162 Large vessels are measured in various kinds of tonnage —gross and net, displacement and register. See text for differences and how each is measured.

Gross tonnage is the total enclosed space or internal capacity of a vessel, calculated in terms of "tons" of 100 cubic feet each. This was agreed upon many years ago as the average space or volume required by a ton (by weight) of general merchandise. Gross tonnage includes all spaces below the upper deck as well as permanently closed-in spaces on that deck.

Net (or *registered*) tonnage is a measurement of the earning power of a vessel when carrying cargo. Thus to arrive at a net tonnage figure it is necessary to deduct from the gross the volume of such spaces as would have no earning capacity or room for cargo. For example, on a ship there would be deducted the volume of the fuel compartments, engine room, crew's quarters, bridge, etc. In the case of recreational boats and yachts, deductions would mainly be for engine compartments and control stations. Many charges against vessels, such as canal tolls, harbor dues, etc., are based on net tonnage.

Displacement and deadweight tonnage

Although not closely related to documentation or boats, a yachtsman should have some knowledge of several other forms of "tonnage" used in connection with ships.

Displacement tonnage is the actual weight, in tons of 2240 pounds, which a vessel displaces when floating at any given draft, such as "light" or "loaded." The displacement is calculated by figuring the volume of the vessel under the water in cubic feet and dividing by 35, as 35 cubic feet of sea water weighs one long ton.

Deadweight tonnage is the carrying capacity of a vessel figured by weight in terms of tons of 2240 pounds. If her displacement were calculated when the vessel was "light" (with fuel and supplies but no cargo) and again when she was loaded (with the same fuel and supplies aboard), the difference would express the deadweight tonnage.

Miscellaneous Terms

The meaning of the word *lay* depends on its usage. One *lays aft* when he goes to the stern of the vessel. The lines of a boat are *laid down* before she is built. A boat is *laid up* when she is decommissioned for the winter in northern climates. A sailboat *lays her course* when she can make her objective without tacking. When an oarsman stops rowing, he *lays on his oars.* Referring to rope, *lay* is the direction of the twist (right or left hand) and its tightness (hard or soft).

When a vessel is hauled out of the water she is *shored up* with supports to hold her upright. If she is not supported properly, so that she is held amidships while the bow and stern settle, the boat will assume a shape that is described as *hogged.* Contrarywise, if the amidships portion of the keel is not adequately supported and droops, she is said to be *sagged.*

A vessel is said to *hail* from her home port; one *hails* another vessel at sea to get her attention, *speaks* to her when communicating with her.

The direction in which a current flows is its *set* and its velocity is its *drift.* (The amount of leeway that a vessel makes is also its drift.) *Slack* is the period of time between flood and ebb currents when there is no flow in either direction. *Stand* is the period when there is no rise or fall in the tidal level; slack and stand usually do not occur simultaneously at any given place.

FIG. 163 The lines of any craft should be protected from chafing and wear wherever they come in contact with abrasive surfaces, other lines, etc. Modern devices such as shown above may be slipped over the line, or in an emergency the line may be wrapped with old rags.

FIG. 164 A shackle permits the attachment of a line or chain to an anchor or any sort of ring. The pin of the shackle should be secured with safety wire to prevent its accidental loosening. The thimble in the eye splice prevents excessive wear on the line at a point of high stress.

A line *chafes* when it rubs on a rough surface and wears excessively. To prevent this, *chafing gear* is used; the line may be encased with plastic or rubber tubing. *Baggy-wrinkle* consists of short lengths of old line matted together and placed on shrouds, spreaders, etc. to protect sails from chafing and wearing.

A *shackle,* or *clevis,* is a roughly U-shaped metal fitting with a pin that can be inserted through a hole in one arm of the U and screwed or pinned in the other arm to close the link. Some special-purpose shackles close with a hinged *snap* or have a *swivel* built in. A *thimble* is a round or heart-shaped metal fitting with a deep outer groove around which line or wire can be eye-spliced. It protects the line from wearing on a shackle where it is joined to a chain, fastened to a deck fitting, etc.

A *fid* is a smooth, tapered pin, usually of wood, used to open up the strands of a rope for splicing.

A *waterlight* is an electric light, often automatically operated, that is attached to a life ring with a short length of line. It is intended for use in man-overboard accidents at night.

The term "charter" has usage both as a verb and a noun. *To charter* a craft is to lease her from the owner for a temporary period of time. She may be chartered on a *bare boat* basis, without crew, or as a *time charter* with crew. The contract covering the use of the boat is termed the *charter.*

Ships and large vessels may have compartments below deck used solely for carrying cargo, these are *holds.* The hatch giving access through the deck to such a hold is covered over with canvas and *battened down* with wooden strips around the edges (*battens*) to secure it against storms and water across the deck. The same term is used for the general securing of a boat against adverse weather conditions.

Another vessel is said to be seen *hull down* when she is at such a distance that her superstructure and/or masts are visible but the hull is not seen due to the curvature of the earth.

Flotsam is material floating on the surface of the water after a vessel has broken up and sunk. Larger pieces may be dangerous to the hull or shaft and propeller of small craft. *Jetsam* consists of items of equipment or cargo that have been deliberately *jettisoned* (thrown overboard) to lighten a vessel endangered by heavy seas.

A *bollard* is a heavy single or double post set into the edge of a wharf or pier to which the lines of a ship may be made fast.

FIG. 165 Ocean cruising, and particularly ocean racing, sailboats usually are fitted with a horseshoe type of life preserver mounted aft near the helmsman's position so that it can be quickly thrown to a man overboard. For nighttime use, an automatic waterlight is attached to the life preserver.

FIG. 166 Bollards are massive metal fittings placed along wharves and piers to which the heavy lines of large vessels are made fast.

Cavitation occurs when a high-speed propeller loses its "bite" on the water, creating a partial vacuum, loss of thrust, and excessive shaft speed; continued cavitation can result in blade wear. On outboard motors where the propeller is relatively near the surface of the water and aft of the transom, there may be a *cavitation plate* mounted above the propeller to deflect downward the water discharge from the blades—a more correct term might be "anti-cavitation plate" but this is not used.

If the galley stove is of the type that requires its own vent above deck, the pipe for this is sometimes referred to as a *Charlie Noble.*

A boat is *ship-shape* when everything is in good order;

FIG. 167 The anchors for large yachts and ships become too heavy to be hoisted on deck. They are drawn up into hawse pipes with power-operated winches.

well-found when it is well equipped. *Bristol*-fashion is a term used to describe an especially well-cared-for vessel. One *swabs* (or *swabs down*) the deck when he washes it down with a mop, called a *swab* in nautical language.

A task aboard a boat—such as lowering the dinghy—is done *handsomely* when it is done slowly and carefully. To do something *smartly* is to do it in a quick and lively manner.

The term *gangway* is applied both to the area of a ship's side where people *come aboard (board)* and *disembark,* and to the temporary ramp or platform used between the vessel and the wharf or pier. In the latter case, the terms *gangplank* and *brow* are also used.

A *windlass* is a particular form of winch with its *drum* on which the line is wrapped turning on a horizontal axis. If the drum's axis is vertical, the device may be called a *capstan.*

When an anchor line or chain is brought through the topsides rather than over the rail, it enters through a *hawse hole* and runs upward through a *hawse pipe.* An *anchor chock* is a fitting for holding an anchor securely on a deck.

Small boats, such as dinghies and runabouts, are hoisted aboard larger craft by *davits,* mechanical arms extending over the side or stern, or which can be swung over the side, plus the necessary lines and blocks.

When subjected to heavy strains in working her way through high seas, a vessel is said to *labor.* If she takes the large waves easily, she is said to be *sea kindly.* A boat that takes head seas heavily and comes down hard on successive waves is said to *pound;* this is more likely to occur with a hard-chined hull. If she takes little spray aboard when running into a choppy sea, she is termed *dry.*

To *flemish down* a line is to secure it on deck in a tight, flat coil roughly resembling a mat. When a line is laid down in loose, looping figure-eights it is said to be *faked* (or *flaked*) down; each loop is a *fake,* see pages 229–230.

To *put* is to take action, as to *put about, put into port,* etc.

A boat is said to be *off-soundings* when she is so far out from the shore *(offshore)* that depths *(soundings)* cannot be conveniently measured nor are used in navigation; this is commonly taken as the 100-fathom line. Contrary-wise, a boat is *on-soundings* when she is within this line.

Admiralty law is the body of law pertaining to ships and to navigation and commerce on the seas.

Pollution Control Systems

Boatmen on almost all waters have been faced with a rising tide of water pollution control laws. State and local regulations have varied widely as to the restrictions imposed and the type of device, if any, that will be accepted. Standards have been set by the Environmental Protection Agency and regulations have been issued by the Coast Guard covering the certification and use of *marine sanitation devices.* Various types of MSDs are described below.

The *macerator-chlorinator* device takes the discharge of a marine toilet, grinds up all solids to very fine particles, and treats the resultant waste with a disinfectant to reduce the bacteria to a safe count. This chemical is usually a chlorine compound which may be introduced either as a liquid (such as the household bleach, sodium hypochlorite, bought as "Clorox" or the equivalent), or in tablet form. The mixture of waste and treatment chemical is retained in a small tank until the next time the "head" is used, at which time it is pumped overboard and a fresh batch is taken in from the toilet. These units may be added to an existing toilet, or may be installed as a complete, self-contained device.

Holding tanks are simply what their name says, additional tanks installed on a boat to take the waste fluids

FIG. 168 Dinghies and small speedboats may be hoisted to the upper decks of large yachts with hand or power operated davits. On smaller yachts, dinghies are often carried on stern davits.

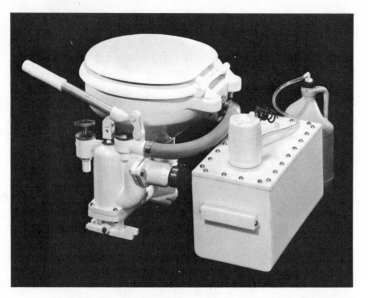

FIG. 169 Marine sanitation devices are coming into widespread use aboard all types of boats large enough to have one or more installed toilets. A number of different designs are available, but not all are acceptable on specific bodies of water.

and solids from the toilet and retain them temporarily. Some models provide the option of overboard discharge—for use when in waters where this is permitted—as well as pumping-out to a shore facility, but many states withhold approval of a system that would allow overboard discharge. Tanks are available in various sizes such as 10 and 20 gallons which will permit a few days' use of the head (with restraint!) before pump-out is necessary. A chemical is usually added to the tank for partial disinfecting action and to deodorize the contents. A vent over the side is required.

Self-contained toilets are closely related to holding tanks. These devices are "charged" with a few gallons of water and special chemicals. The internal mechanism recirculates this treated water plus the wastes that are added each time the head is used. The toilet can be used a number of times over a period of several days before pump-out is required. This is the type of facility used on modern airliners.

Incinerators dry liquid wastes pumped into them from marine toilets and reduce the resultant solids to ash. This final product is of low volume and need be removed only at infrequent intervals, roughly monthly. Heat is obtained from either bottled LP gas or electricity.

But Don't Overdo It!

There is literally no end to the list of boating terms that could be included here, but practical limitations of space must prevail. What has been covered in this chapter will serve as a framework for the remainder of the book. As the boatman gains experience in this form of recreation, his vocabulary will broaden proportionately and naturally.

It is to be hoped, however, that his enthusiasm for boating will not cause him to toss indiscriminate Avasts, Ahoys, and Belays into every conceivable nook and corner of his conversation. The natural, proper use of correct terms is much to be desired; strained efforts to effect a salty lingo are conspicuously inappropriate.

CHAPTER 2

BOATING LAWS and REGULATIONS

FIG. 201   All boating, commercial and recreational, is subject to certain laws
and regulations for the safety of the craft involved and all on board.
Federal rules are often supplemented by state and local requirements and restrictions.

Although boating is certainly not an inherently unsafe form of recreation, there are dangers and hazards for ignorant and careless individuals. To protect such persons, and "innocent bystanders," too, there has arisen a body of federal, state, and local laws and regulations. The basic intent of such restrictions is the safety of persons and property; to a much lesser degree do such factors enter as registration and taxation.

Boating laws and regulations can be roughly divided into two major categories. The first subdivision includes those that relate to the craft and its equipment; the second group covers the operator of the boat and his use of it. Formerly, the first category was greatly predominant, but in recent years regulations regarding boat operation have expanded rapidly.

Comparison of boating and motor vehicle laws

A quick comparison may be made between recreational boating and the field of ownership and operation of automobiles, an activity so much a part of our everyday lives. Here the trend has been rather in the reverse direction. Some years ago motor vehicle laws focused almost entirely on operational matters such as driving and parking, with a minimum of attention to details of equipment. In more recent times we have seen a considerable push toward legislated standards for safety equipment and design features. The obvious comparisons can be drawn in such areas as the requirements for headlights and turn signals on cars with the need for navigation lights on boats; and the necessity for both types of vehicles to observe rules as to relative right-of-way in congested areas. The principal point of difference at the present time is the lack of any requirement for an operator license or permit for the noncommercial skipper; the duration of this difference is a matter of some doubt. Some states are now requiring operator licenses on wholly inland bodies of water, but as yet there is no overall federal requirement.

In both boating and automobile operation the goals are essentially the same—the prevention of accidents insofar as possible, and the minimization of death and injury in those that regrettably do occur. Restrictive laws and regulations are irksome to all of us, but they should be known, understood, and accepted as proper guidance for our self-protection and the protection of others' lives and property.

Registration and numbering

A third category of boating laws and regulations includes those relating to registration and assignment of identification numbers to craft. This may perhaps be considered a minor category as compared with rules for safety

Boating Laws & Regulations / CHAPTER 2

FIG. 202 Water traffic must be subject to "Rules of the Road" which prescribe relative right-of-way between boats encountering each other. They are especially important in congested waters.

as they can be navigated continuously from the sea, often a considerable distance for such great waterways as the Mississippi, Missouri, Ohio, and Tennessee Rivers.

A second type of body of water subject to federal jurisdiction is any that overlaps or separates two or more states, even though not connected with the ocean. Inland rivers and lakes often fall into this category which is based on the fact that one can travel by water from one state to another; this is "interstate commerce" and subject to regulation by the U.S. Congress. A typical example is Lake Mead that borders both Nevada and Arizona. A third qualification places waters under federal jurisdiction if they can be used for travel to or from a foreign nation.

equipment and boat operation, but still these must be known and obeyed.

Again a close comparison can be drawn with motor vehicles, although in the case of boats it is probable that regulation is rather more related to taxation and revenue-raising than it is to identification—not many watercraft get "tickets" for overtime parking. The regulations relating to numbering must be followed by boatmen even though they have little to do with his safety or that of others.

FEDERAL VS. STATE JURISDICTION

This book will concentrate on federal laws and regulations relating to boating rather than state and local ordinances, rules, etc., due to the obviously wider applicability of the former. State and municipal regulations will be touched upon later in this chapter, but only in broad terms because of the wide variations between different jurisdictions. Each conscientious boatman must individually familiarize himself with the local requirements and restrictions for the waters that he uses.

Limits of federal jurisdiction

"Navigable waters of the United States"—where federal law prevails—are defined in broad terms by law and are specifically delineated by Coast Guard regulations. These include waters off the beaches along the coast and all bodies of water open to the sea or connected to the open sea by navigable rivers and channels. Typical of this category are all harbors and bays as well as major rivers as far

FIG. 204 The construction of dams, and locks for the passage of vessels around them, have extended far inland the limits of navigable waters subject to Federal jurisdiction. These limits are set forth in official publications.

The construction of a dam does not change the navigable status of a river. In fact, the building of a dam and lock system may serve to extend the river's navigability. The Coast Guard makes determinations of the bodies of water that do or do not fall under federal jurisdiction; such rulings are subject to challenge in Federal courts. The determinations will be found in Part 2 of Title 33, Code of Federal Regulations; changes are published in the daily Federal Register.

An understanding of federal jurisdiction over navigable waters is essential for all boatmen, especially those far from the coasts of our nation. Federal jurisdiction means the

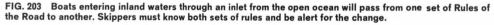

FIG. 203 Boats entering inland waters through an inlet from the open ocean will pass from one set of Rules of the Road to another. Skippers must know both sets of rules and be alert for the change.

applicability of federal laws and regulations, aids to navigation by the Coast Guard, and charting by the Coast & Geodetic Survey or Army Corps of Engineers. It does *not* deprive state and local authorities of their rights to regulate certain aspects of the use of the waters that are *not in conflict* with an applicable federal law or regulation; local rules might relate to speed limits, restrictions on water skiing, etc. Many state boating laws also require safety equipment on boats in excess of that called for by Acts of Congress and Coast Guard Regulations.

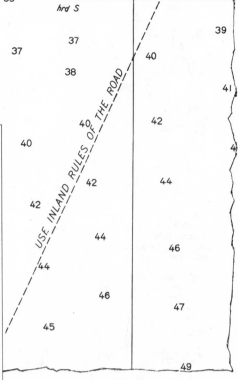

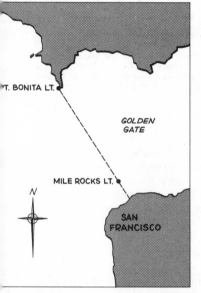 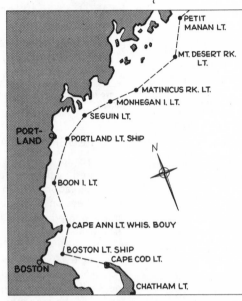

FIG. 205   At the entrances to major rivers, harbors, bays, etc., and along some, but not all, stretches of shoreline, there have been established boundaries to mark the transition from International to Inland Rules of the Road. These boundaries are defined in terms of geographic features and aids to navigation.

FIG. 206   The boundaries between the International and the Inland Rules of the Road are marked on coastal charts by a broken magenta line appropriately labeled.

"INLAND" WATERS DEFINED

Within the areas subject to the jurisdiction of the federal government there is a sub-category known as "inland waters." By an Act of Congress of 1895, with subsequent amendments, authority was established for the prescribing of boundary lines dividing the "high seas" from rivers, bays, sounds, harbors, etc. These boundaries are of primary importance in connection with the Rules of the Road as will be discussed in Chapters 4 and 5.

Federal waters inshore of these boundary lines are subject to the Inland Rules of the Road and the Inland Pilot Rules, except for certain interior areas where other laws and regulations known as the Great Lakes Rules and the Western Rivers Rules are in effect. Offshore of the boundary lines, the International Rules of the Road are effective. It should be noted that the International Rules have been adopted by the United States and legally govern all vessels in applicable U.S. waters within the limit of national sovereignty, as well as to U.S. vessels anywhere on the high seas. The United States applies the term "territorial sea" out to three miles and "contiguous zone" for waters from three to twelve miles offshore.

Delineation of boundary lines

The International-Inland boundary lines are drawn at all major entrances to harbors, rivers, bays, etc., roughly paral-lel with the general trend of the shoreline. The lines are established with respect to aids to navigation—lighthouses, lightships, buoys—for ease of identification; see fig. 205. Boatmen in waters where such boundaries exist should be familiar with them. Boundary lines are printed in various government publications—such as the Rules of the Road, International-Inland, CG-169; see fig. 1708—and are printed on applicable charts, fig. 206. As a result of their being defined in terms of such objects as buoys, boundary lines between the Inland and International Rules are subject to change as these aids to navigation may be relocated or changed. Such modifications to the boundaries are published in the daily Federal Register available at many libraries.

Formal boundary lines are established only at major harbor and other entrances, or where there are a series of offshore islands such as along the Maine coast and the Florida Keys; this procedure is not applied to the islands off the southern California coast. At other buoyed entrances from seaward for which official boundary lines have not been established, the waters inshore of a line approximately parallel with the general trend of the shore, drawn through the outermost buoy or other aid to navigation, are considered "inland" waters. Along relatively open straight stretches of the coast, the International Rules are applicable right up to the shore except for minor coves and other indentations.

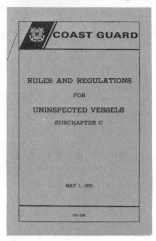

FIG. 209 Boats are divided into "classes" by the regulations of the Motorboat Act of 1940. Shown above is a Class 1 craft. Smaller boats, those under 16 feet in length, are Class A; those of 26 feet or more in length are in Classes 2 and 3, with 40 feet being the dividing line.

FIG. 207 Coast Guard Publication CG-258 contains the full text of regulations that were issued to implement the Motorboat Act of 1940, now repealed for recreational small craft. These rules do, however, remain in effect until specifically superceded by regulations implementing the Federal Boat Safety Act of 1971.

FIG. 208 This small and convenient USCG pamphlet summarizes in simple language the basic federal requirements for recreational craft. It is available without charge from most Coast Guard offices.

Federal Laws and Regulations

Recreational boating—and commercial boating and shipping, too—is subject to "laws" and "regulations." The former consist of Acts of Congress and provide basic policies and rules upon which more specific and detailed regulations may be promulgated. Regulations have the advantage of greater flexibility, being more easily created, modified, or revoked than laws which are subject to the full legislative process for any changes.

Coast Guard regulations

Most federal boating regulations are issued by the United States Coast Guard under authority given by Congress to the "Secretary of the Department in which the Coast Guard is operating." This rather cumbersome wording is necessary as federal laws make possible the transfer of this armed service from its normal peacetime Department (now Transportation, but formerly Treasury until 1967) to its wartime Department (Navy). The authority given by Congress to the Departmental Secretary is, in most instances, routinely delegated to the Commandant of the Coast Guard.

Coast Guard regulations cover a wide variety of matters including boat equipment and operation, lights for special-purpose vessels, aids to navigation, inland water boundary lines as mentioned above, and many other topics.

Other regulatory agencies

Boatmen on some waters will also be affected by regulations issued by other federal agencies such as the Corps of Engineers, U.S. Army; and the National Park Service. The operation of radio and radar transmitters on boats on all waters is subject to the rules and regulations of the Federal Communications Commission as explained in Chapter 25.

FEDERAL BOAT SAFETY ACT OF 1971

Recreational boating in the United States is now largely governed by the *Federal Boat Safety Act of 1971 (FBSA/71)* and regulations drawn from its authority. This law came into effect on 10 August 1971 but has not yet been fully implemented. Extracts from this act will be found on pages 611–614.

The 1971 Act differs in many respects from the 1940 and 1958 laws which formerly controlled boating. The FBSA/71 is quite broad in its terms, leaving the details to be spelled out in regulations. This is decidedly advantageous to the government, the boating industry, and boatmen; regulations are far more easily modified when required by changing conditions than are laws which require action by the Congress. No longer will such matters as whistles and bells, fire extinguishers and life saving devices be a part of relatively rigid laws; Coast Guard regulations will contain all such requirements.*

Scope

The Federal Boat Safety Act of 1971 is much broader than the previous boating laws. It provides authority to the "Secretary," as defined above, to establish minimum safety standards for boats and "associated equipment," provides for the numbering of all undocumented vessels equipped with propulsion machinery, directs that a Boating Safety Advisory Council be established, and authorizes financial assistance to the States for boating safety programs. The new law essentially repeals the 1958 Federal Boating Act and so amends the Motorboat Act of 1940 as to virtually exclude recreational boats and smaller passenger-carrying craft. (The 1940 Act remains on the books, applicable to commercial craft such as fishing vessels and diesel towboats.)

Definition of terms

The FBSA/71 contains a number of definitions that must be clearly understood, as they directly affect its applicability.

The word "vessel" includes every description of watercraft, other than a seaplane on the water, used or capable of being used as a means of transportation on the water.

The term "boat" is limited to the following categories of vessels—

*As of September, 1974, a few regulations had been issued and more were in the proposal stage; boatmen should be alert for new rules and requirements.

(1) Those manufactured or used primarily for non-commercial use.

(2) Those leased, rented, or chartered to another for the latter's noncommercial use.

(3) Those engaged in the carrying of six or fewer passengers for hire.

The distinction between "vessels" and "boats" is necessary because certain aspects of the bill (notably those sections dealing with safety standards and equipment) pertain *only* to the category called "boats." Other sections (those dealing with numbering) pertain to a broader category, all undocumented vessels equipped with propulsion machinery. Still other provisions of the Act (the prohibition of negligent operation) pertain to *all* vessels. Note that there is *no upper size limit* in the definition of "boat" as used in the FBSA/71.

Despite its general aim toward the regulation of noncommercial boats and boating, craft carrying six or less passengers for hire are included as these are not covered by existing laws regulating vessels carrying a greater number of passengers for hire. Livery and charter boats are included in the FBSA/71 as their operation is closely akin to noncommercial recreational use even though they are a part of a commercial enterprise.

The term "associated equipment" means—

(1) Any system, part, or component of a boat as originally manufactured, or any similar part, or component manufactured or sold for replacement, repair, or improvement of such system, part, or component.

(2) Any accessory or equipment for, or appurtenance to a boat.

(3) Any marine safety article, accessory, or equipment intended for use by a person on a boat.

The term "associated equipment" does *not* include radio equipment.

The word "State" means a State of the United States, the Commonwealth of Puerto Rico, the Virgin Islands, Guam, American Samoa, and the District of Columbia.

Applicability

The FBSA/71 applies to vessels and associated equipment used, or to be used, or carried on vessels on waters subject to the jurisdiction of the United States. This Act *also* applies to every vessel owned in a "State" and *used*

FIG. 210 Federal law does not require the registration and numbering of sailboats with no mechanical power, but some states do make this requirement. All boats, including such sailboats, are subject to Coast Guard requirements for equipment such as personal flotation devices.

FIG. 211 Boating accidents must be reported if they involve more than specified levels of damage or personal injury. This is true whether one or more craft are concerned. In many areas, reports are made to state authorities rather than the Coast Guard.

on the high seas, the waters beyond the territorial jurisdiction of the United States.

Certain limited categories of vessels are excluded from coverage by the FBSA/71; these include foreign vessels, military or public vessels of the United States (except for recreational-type craft which are included), vessels owned by a State or political subdivision thereof and used primarily for governmental purposes, and ships' lifeboats.

Regulations

Although the Motorboat Act of 1940 (MBA/40) is no longer applicable to the "boats" of the 1971 Act, the Coast Guard regulations which implemented the MBA/40 are retained and remain in effect until replaced.

Classes of boats

For the purpose of applying graduated requirements for equipment as the size of the craft increases, the regulations of the MBA/40 divide all motorboats into four "classes" based on length. This is "overall length" as measured in a straight line parallel to the keel from the foremost part of the vessel to the aftermost part, excluding sheer and excluding bowsprits, boomkins, rudders aft of the transom, outboard motor brackets, etc.

Class A—less than 16 feet in length

Class 1—16 feet and over, but less than 26 feet in length

Class 2—26 feet and over, but less than 40 feet in length

Class 3—40 feet and over, but not more than 65 feet

(Note: The new regulations will not have a upper limit on length of boats.)

Required Equipment

The regulations of the MBA/40, applicable until superceded by new rules, contain many provisions for required equipment, including fire extinguishers, whistles, bells, and other items. It is specifically stated in the FBSA/71 that

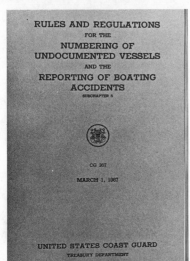

FIG. 212 The regulations issued under the 1958 Boating Act covering the registration and numbering of boats and the reporting of boating accidents were published in Coast Guard pamphlet CG-267. These remain in effect until superceded by new rules under the 1971 law which requires numbers for all motorboats regardless of horsepower.

FIG. 213 In addition to their frequent rescue missions, Coast Guard patrol craft have enforcement powers for the Federal Boat Safety Act and other federal laws and regulations. They are always clearly marked, fly the Coast Guard Ensign, and are manned by uniformed personnel.

regulations will be issued covering items not now required on board, such as ground tackle and navigation equipment. The new requirements will not become effective without considerable study and wide publicity. Because of the importance of equipment, this topic is covered separately in Chapter 3.

The MBA/40 regulations also prescribe navigation lights for boats, but as these are also included in the Rules of the Road, they are considered separately in Chapter 4.

Registration and Numbering

Although the Federal Boat Safety Act of 1971 repeals the Federal Boating Act of 1958 (FBA/58), it continues the numbering provisions of that law with one major and several minor changes. States were allowed until August 1974 to bring their boat registration systems into conformity with the 1971 Act, but many acted sooner.

The FBSA/71 provides for a system of boat registration and numbering that is uniform throughout the "States" although the actual process of issuing certificates and number assignments may be done individually by the States. As of late 1971, all but four had elected to perform this function within their jurisdiction; in the states of Alaska, New Hampshire, Washington, and in the District of Columbia, boats are registered by the Coast Guard.

The FBSA/71 establishes broad standards for the numbering of vessels and provides for the issuance of more detailed and specific regulations by the "Secretary." The individual States prepare their boat registration laws and regulations in accordance with Federal standards and then submit them to the Secretary for approval The Act provides for the withdrawal of approval if the State does not administer its system in accordance with the Federal requirements.

Vessels subject to numbering

The 1971 Act requires the registration and numbering of all vessels used on waters subject to Federal jurisdiction, or on the high seas if owned in the U.S., which are equipped with propulsion machinery *regardless of horsepower*. Exempted are foreign boats temporarily in U.S. waters, documented vessels, ships' lifeboats, and governmental vessels other than recreational-type craft.

A state numbering system *may* require the numbering of other craft (sailboats, rowboats, etc.) unless prohibited by Federal regulations.

Special provisions are made for tenders (dinghies) carried aboard for other than lifesaving purposes.

"State of principal use"

It is important to note that the FBSA makes it mandatory for the owner of a boat subject to the Act to secure a number "in the State in which the vessel is principally used." This has been interpreted literally—where the boat is most often used on the water, not the state of residence of the owner nor the state in which the boat might set on land on a trailer for a far greater proportion of the time. The term "used" is taken as meaning the time that the vessel is "on" the navigable waters of the United States whether in motion, at anchor, or moored.

Certificate of number

The identification number issued for a vessel is shown on a *Certificate of Number*. This Certificate must be on board whenever the vessel is in use (with exceptions for small rental boats). The FBSA/71 specifies that the certificate of number must be of "pocket size." Each person using a boat must present its Certificate for inspection at the request of any law enforcement officer.

The Federal law states that a certificate may not be valid for more than three years; many states are issuing registrations for shorter periods. All certificates, may, of course, be renewed at or prior to their expiration date.

Numbering systems

The specific details of the numbering of boats are now covered by regulations originally issued under the FBA/58 and still in effect. These will be replaced in due time, but no significant differences are anticipated.

The number pattern is divided into two parts. The first part consists of a two-letter symbol identifying the state of principal use. This is followed by a second part consisting of a combination of numerals and letters for individual identification. The list of state designators appears on page 620.

The individual vessel's identification consists of not more than four arabic numerals and two capital letters, *or* not more than three such numerals and three such letters. The letters "I," "O," and "Q" might be mistaken for the numerals one and zero, and therefore they are not used as part of individual boat identification suffixes.

Numbers for dinghies

If used with a numbered vessel, a dinghy equipped with a motor of less than 10 horsepower need not be individually registered and numbered *if* "used as a tender for direct transportation between that vessel and the shore and for no other purpose." It must display the number of the parent boat followed by the suffix "1" separated from the last letter by a space or hyphen as used in the basic number; for example, DC-4567-ED-1 or DC 4567 EF 1.

A dinghy used with a vessel not having a number, such as a documented boat, must be registered and have its own number as for any other craft if it is propelled by a motor of *any* horsepower.

Size and style of numbers

The regulations require that boat numbers provide good legibility and contain certain specifications as to their style and size. The letters and numerals must be plain (no border or trim), vertical block characters not less than three inches in height. They must *not* be of slanting or script style; see Fig. 218. The numbers and letters should all be of one color.

Contrast

Numbers must provide good contrast with their background—black on white or white on black best meets this requirement.

A backing or mounting plate may be used. If so, it must be of sufficient size to provide good contrast, and thus good legibility, for the numbers without regard to the hull.

Display of numbers

The identification number must be painted on, or attached to, either side of the forward half of the vessel, and no other number may be displayed there. (This does not apply to serial numbers on small validation stickers that some states and the Coast Guard issues as a visual indication of payment of current fees.) In most cases, the numbers are quite near the bow, but since they have only to be displayed on the "forward half" of the boat, it is frequently desirable, in the case of boats with considerable flare to their bows, to place the numbers well aft from the stem so that they will be on a more nearly vertical surface and so will be more easily seen and read.

Numbers are placed on a boat so as to read normally from left to right on both sides of the bow. They may be on the hull or on a permanent superstructure. The group of digits appearing between the two sets of letters in the total number *must be separated* from those letters by hyphens or spaces. The hyphen or blank space must be equal to the width of any letter other than "I" or any numeral other than "1"; see Fig. 217.

Identification numbers must be maintained properly to ensure legibility at all times.

Names or insignia may be displayed on the bow of a boat, but only in such a manner that they will not detract from the legibility of the registration numbers. Only one set of numbers may be displayed at any time. If transferred to a new state, the old numbers must be removed.

FIG. 214 A boat must be registered in, and receive its numbers from, "the state of principal use" even though this is not the owner's state of residence nor where the boat is stored on a trailer and out of the water for more days than it is used in the water.

FIG. 215 The assignment of identification numbers issued by the Coast Guard is made on a "Certificate of Number" which must be on board whenever the craft is in use. State numbering authorities issue a generally similar registration card.

Applications for numbers

The addresses of State and other authorities to whom application for a Certificate of Number must be made are listed on page 640.

The same numbers are assigned by a regular renewal Certificate. Upon transfer of ownership, if the boat continues in the same state of principal use, the old numbers stay on the craft and are assigned to the new owner.

Numbers may not be transferred from one boat to another, except for special dealers' and manufacturers' numbers issued for demonstrating, transporting, or testing boats.

Fees

Under the FBSA/71, States may set their own fees to be charged for registration and numbering of boats. The fees vary widely from state to state—and in some jurisdictions, these merely cover the cost of administering the numbering program; in others, they are used as sources of revenue for the state.

The 1971 law specifically provides that a State may require proof of payment of State and local taxes before issuing a Certificate of Number. Withholding of certification on any other grounds is *not* authorized, except that a title or proof of ownership may be required.

Reciprocity

When a vessel is numbered in the State of principal use, it will be considered as in compliance with the numbering system of any State in which it is *temporarily* used. There is no specific time limit stated if such use is truly "temporary." This is of considerable advantage to boatmen who may cruise or trailer their craft to other state waters for vacation periods.

When a vessel is taken to a *new* "State of principal use," that state must recognize the validity of the number issued by the authority for a period of at least 60 days before requiring new registration.

Notification of changes

If a boat is destroyed or abandoned, or it is sold, or it is used for more than 60 days in a state other than the one where its Certificate of Number was issued, or it is documented, a report must be made to the issuing office within 15 days. The Certificate is invalid and must be surrendered. The numbers (and validation stickers, if any) must be removed from the craft. A report must also be made if the boat is stolen or recovered.

A change of address of the owner must be reported to the issuing office within 15 days. If the state of principal use is changed, application must be made for a number in the new state within 60 days. A change of motor only is not required to be reported.

Operators' "Safety Certificates"

The Federal Boat Safety Act of 1971 continues the provision in the 1958 law that gives States optional authority to require the operator of a vessel that comes within the scope of the numbering provisions of the Act to "hold a valid safety certificate issued under terms and conditions set by the issuing authority."

No Coast Guard regulations have been issued for this purpose, and little use of the authority has been made by the States except in the case of young persons.

Termination of Unsafe Use

The Federal Boat Safety Act of 1971 includes a provision that is entirely new to the general concept of boating laws and regulations If a Coast Guard boarding officer observes a boat being used without sufficient lifesaving or fire fighting devices, or in an overloaded or otherwise unsafe condition as defined in regulations (lack of proper navigation lights when required, fuel system leakage or fuel in the bilges or elsewhere outside of tanks, ventilation of engine and fuel tank areas, or flame arrestors, that do not meet requirements), and which in his judgement such use creates an especially hazardous condition, he may direct the operator to take whatever immediate and reasonable steps would be necessary for the safety of those aboard the vessel. This may include directing the operator to return to mooring and remain there until the situation creating the hazard is corrected or ended. Failure to comply with an order to terminate unsafe use of a vessel could result in the arrest of the operator.

MI 2345 AB

OR

MI-2345-AB

CORRECT

MI2345AB

INCORRECT

FIG. 217 Undoubtedly the most widespread violation of boating regulations is the faulty application of numbers. There must be either a space or a hyphen (dash) before and after the block of numerals to set them off from the letters that precede and follow them. In some areas, as much as a majority of boats will be seen with the letters and numerals run together.

ME 456 R

AND

ME 456 R

INCORRECT

ME 456 R

CORRECT

FIG. 218 The regulations that govern the shape of boat's numbers specify "block letters in good proportion." This phrase has been officially interpreted to mean vertical characters of plain style — script, slanting, or other "fancy" style characters are not acceptable.

Negligent Operation

The FBSA/71 clearly states that "no person may use any vessel in a negligent manner so as to endanger the life, limb, or property of any person." Foreign vessels, governmental vessels, and other craft normally excluded from coverage under this Act are *not* exempted from the prohibition against negligent operations.

The endangerment of "any person" is so phrased as to *include* the operator of the vessel, no other person need be involved.

Boating Accidents

Sometimes, despite the best of care, boating accidents of one kind or another do occur. This may involve only a single craft, or two or more vessels may be concerned. In any case, there are obligations imposed on the skippers at the scene and afterwards.

Duties in case of accident

In case of collision, accident, or other casualty involving a vessel subject to the FBSA/71 (including such exempted vessels as foreign or governmental craft), it is the duty of the operator, to the extent that he can do so without serious danger to his vessel or those on board, to render such assistance as may be necessary and practicable to other persons affected by the incident in order to save them from danger as a result thereof. The operator must also give his name and address, and the identification of his vessel, to any person injured and to the owner of any property damaged.

The duties described above for the operator of a vessel are applicable whether or not the incident was the result of apparent negligence. They are also in addition to any other duties provided by law.

"Good Samaritan" provision

Any person who complies with the duties described above, or any other person who gratuitously and in good faith renders assistance at the scene of an accident or other boating casualty without the objection of any person being assisted, is protected by a provision of the FBSA/71.

FIG. 218 A common misconception is that the numbers must be on the "bow" of a boat. The legal requirement is that they must be on the "forward half of the vessel" and actually they should be sufficiently aft from the stem to ensure ease of readability despite any pronounced flare of the forward hull.

FIG. 219 When a boat is taken from one state to another, Federal law requires that the new state of use grant at least 90 days recognition to the existing registration and numbers. This is of great value to skippers who may trailer their craft to distant vacation areas.

He cannot be held liable for any civil damages as a result of the rendering of assistance or for any act or omission in providing or arranging salvage, towage, medical treatment, or other assistance where the assisting person acts as an ordinary, reasonably prudent man would have done under the same or similar circumstances.

Accident Reporting

In case of collision, accident, or other casualty involving a vessel subject to the Boat Safety Act of 1971, the operator of the craft must make a report under certain circumstances. A report is required if the incident results in death, unconsciousness, need for medical treatment, or disability for over 24 hours; or property damage of more than $100; or if a person disappears from a vessel.

If the accident causes a person's death or disappearance, an immediate report must be made by quickest means available. If death occurs within 24 hours, or unconsciousness, medical treatment, or disability is involved, a report must be made within 48 hours; otherwise, within five days.

Most state boating laws require that reports of boating accidents be made to a designated state office or official If, however, there is no state provision for reporting such incidents, a report must be made to the Coast Guard Officer in Charge, Marine Inspection, nearest to the place where the accident occurred.

The Coast Guard regulations on boating accident reporting (see pages 618-619) list the information that must be furnished. The Boating Accident Report — CG-3865 — may be used in reports to the Coast Guard. States normally use this form or one of their own patterned after it. See fig. 222.

Accident Statistics

The 1971 Federal Boat Safety Act provides that as a part of an approved state registering and numbering system there shall be a casualty reporting plan in accordance with regulations issued by the Secretary. The recording, compilation, and forwarding of accident statistics is, for the time being, covered by regulations from the 1958 Act.

National statistics

The Coast Guard, in turn, is charged with the responsibility of combining state reports with its own to form national statistics as to the number of registered boats by classes; accidents by type, cause, surrounding circumstances, etc.; and other related data. Reports are compiled on the basis of calendar years.

Privacy of information

Information as to the identity and ownership of vessels numbered under the Act will be made available to Federal and local officials as needed in any enforcement or assistance program.

In general, files relating to the numbering of boats are considered "public records," and information from them may be released to anyone, subject only to reasonable restrictions necessary to carry on the work of the records office.

On the other hand, individual "Boating Accident Reports" or extracts therefrom are *not* releasable. These are intended to furnish information necessary for the Coast Guard to make findings as to the cause of accidents and recommendations for their prevention, and to compile appropriate statistics. Their privacy permits the filing of full and accurate reports without the possibility of their contents being used against the individual in civil suits.

Enforcement Authority

Federal boating regulations in general are enforced by the Coast Guard. USCG boarding vessels are identified by the Coast Guard ensign (see pages P, T) and uniformed personnel. A vessel underway upon being hailed by a Coast Guard vessel or patrol boat is required to stop immediately and lay to, or maneuver in such a way as to permit the boarding officer to come aboard.

Many state and local governmental units have navigation regulations backed up with patrol boats. Skippers should be alert for posted signs or regulatory buoys indicating speed limits, "no wake," etc., and should stop immediately upon being hailed by an official craft.

Many law-enforcement vessels—Coast Guard and state or local—are now equipped with a characteristic blue revolving light like those seen on police cars in many areas; see page 64(n) and Fig. 430.

Boat and Equipment Standards

Another area of "new law" with respect to boating is that of safety standards for boats and associated equipment. Prior to the FBSA/71, all responsibility for meeting equipment regulations fell upon the operator of the craft; a manufacturer could make and sell a boat which, for example, did not have "legal" navigation lights. He had no federal requirements to meet on such matters as flotation, stability, capacity plates, etc. He had no responsibility to notify purchasers if later information revealed a safety defect. *All this is changed by the 1971 Act.*

The Federal Boat Safety Act of 1971 authorized minimum safety standards for "boats" and "associated equipment." Each standard must be reasonable, must meet the need for boating safety, and must be stated, insofar as

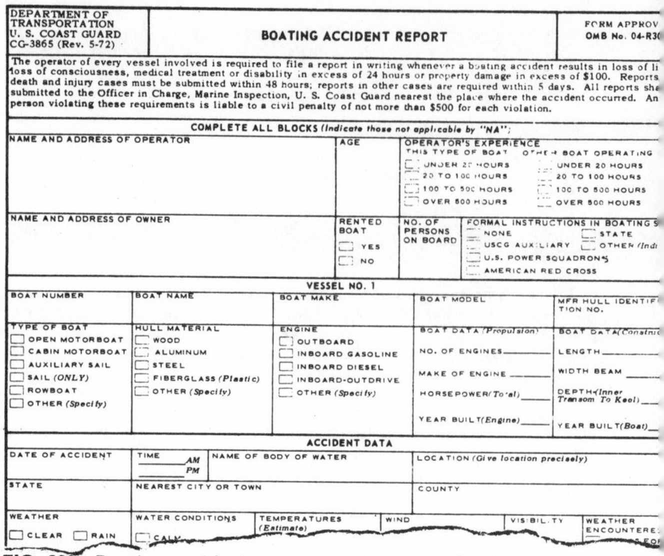
DEPARTMENT OF TRANSPORTATION
U. S. COAST GUARD
CG-3865 (Rev. 5-72)

BOATING ACCIDENT REPORT

FORM APPROV
OMB No. 04-R3(

The operator of every vessel involved is required to file a report in writing whenever a boating accident results in loss of li
loss of consciousness, medical treatment or disability in excess of 24 hours or property damage in excess of $100. Reports
death and injury cases must be submitted within 48 hours; reports in other cases are required within 5 days. All reports sha
submitted to the Officer in Charge, Marine Inspection, U. S. Coast Guard nearest the place where the accident occurred. An
person violating these requirements is liable to a civil penalty of not more than $500 for each violation.

COMPLETE ALL BLOCKS (*Indicate those not applicable by "NA"*)

NAME AND ADDRESS OF OPERATOR
AGE
OPERATOR'S EXPERIENCE
THIS TYPE OF BOAT: UNDER 20 HOURS; 20 TO 100 HOURS; 100 TO 500 HOURS; OVER 500 HOURS
OTHER BOAT OPERATING: UNDER 20 HOURS; 20 TO 100 HOURS; 100 TO 500 HOURS; OVER 500 HOURS

NAME AND ADDRESS OF OWNER
RENTED BOAT: YES; NO
NO. OF PERSONS ON BOARD
FORMAL INSTRUCTIONS IN BOATING S: NONE; USCG AUXILIARY; U.S. POWER SQUADRONS; AMERICAN RED CROSS; STATE; OTHER (*Indi*

VESSEL NO. 1

BOAT NUMBER
BOAT NAME
BOAT MAKE
BOAT MODEL
MFR HULL IDENTIF TION NO.

TYPE OF BOAT: OPEN MOTORBOAT; CABIN MOTORBOAT; AUXILIARY SAIL; SAIL (*ONLY*); ROWBOAT; OTHER (*Specify*)
HULL MATERIAL: WOOD; ALUMINUM; STEEL; FIBERGLASS (*Plastic*); OTHER (*Specify*)
ENGINE: OUTBOARD; INBOARD GASOLINE; INBOARD DIESEL; INBOARD-OUTDRIVE; OTHER (*Specify*)
BOAT DATA (*Propulsion*): NO. OF ENGINES ____; MAKE OF ENGINE ____; HORSEPOWER (*Total*) ____; YEAR BUILT (*Engine*) ____
BOAT DATA (*Constru*: LENGTH ____; WIDTH BEAM ____; DEPTH (*Inner Transom To Keel*) ____; YEAR BUILT (*Boat*) ____

ACCIDENT DATA

DATE OF ACCIDENT
TIME ____ AM ____ PM
NAME OF BODY OF WATER
LOCATION (*Give location precisely*)
STATE
NEAREST CITY OR TOWN
COUNTY
WEATHER: CLEAR; RAIN
WATER CONDITIONS: CALM
TEMPERATURES (*Estimate*)
WIND
VISIBILITY
WEATHER ENCOUNTERE

FIG. 222 Boating accident reports must contain all information required by regulations. The use of an official form will aid in ensuring completeness. States will either use the Coast Guard form shown above or one much like it.

practicable, in terms of performance. Under the 1971 Act's provisions, it will be the duty of the manufacturer to deliver to purchasers boats and associated equipment meeting all safety standards.

The FBSA/71 allows the Secretary to permit or require the use of seals, labels, plates, insignia, or other devices that indicate compliance with Federal safety regulations and standards. Severe penalties are provided for the misuse of such labels.

Penalties

The Federal Boat Safety Act of 1971 provides for both civil and criminal penalties for various violations of its provisions. It allows for variable penalties to meet situations of different degrees of seriousness, and provides for a flexible system of assessment and collection.

Civil penalties

A basic civil penalty of not more than $500 may be assessed for *any* violation of the FBSA/71 or any regulation issued thereunder. If the violation involves a vessel, that vessel may be liable and may be proceeded against in the Federal courts. The basic penalty may be assessed by administrative action; no trial in court is required, but procedures are established for appeals.

Criminal penalties

Any person who uses a vessel in a "grossly" negligent manner so as to endanger the life, limb, or property of any person (including himself) may be subjected to a criminal penalty of a fine of not more than $1,000 or imprisonment for not more than one year, or both. ("Simple" negligence comes under the civil penalty noted above.)

Boating Safety Advisory Council

The FBSA/71 establishes the *Boating Safety Advisory Council* of 21 members, each of whom it is expected will have special knowledge and experience in boating safety. Membership of the Council will consist equally of representatives from State and local governments, boat and associated equipment manufacturers, and boating organizations and the general public. All boating safety standards and other major safety matters will be referred to the Council prior to being issued.

State Boating Safety Programs

The Federal Boat Safety Act of 1971 contains extensive provisions for State participation in boating safety programs. These State programs will include registration and numbering systems, boating safety educational programs, and patrol and other enforcement activities.

Authorization is contained in the Act for the appropriation of Federal funds to partially support such State programs. Federal participation will initially be 75% of the total cost, gradually reducing to 33⅓%. The sum of $7½ million is authorized for each of five fiscal years, but the actual FY 72 and FY 73 appropriations were only $4.5 million each. The FY 74 appropriation was just under $3½ million, but larger sums are hoped for in the future.

RULES OF THE ROAD

The "Rules of the Road" are sets of statutory requirements enacted by Congress to promote safety of navigation. The rules consist of requirements for navigation lights and day shapes, steering and sailing rules, sound signals for both good and restricted visibility situations, rules for conduct in restricted visibility, and distress signals.

There are different sets of Rules for various bodies and areas of waters.

International Rules

The International Regulations for the Prevention of Collisions at Sea—generally referred to as the International Rules of the Road—have been adopted at international conferences and amended at various times. They have been made effective for U.S. waters and U.S. vessels by Act of Congress.

The International Rules are effective outside the boundary lines described on page 31. Boatmen who go offshore along the coast must be familiar with their provisions.

Rules for U.S. waters

There are currently three sets of Rules of the Road for U.S. inland waters. The "Inland Rules" are applicable inside of the boundary lines mentioned above, *except* where the "Great Lakes Rules" or the "Western Rules" are in effect.

The **Great Lakes Rules** are applicable on the Great Lakes and their connecting and tributary waters as far east as Montreal for all U.S. vessels, and for all vessels, including foreign ones, while within the portions of these waters that are under U.S. jurisdiction. This phraseology is required by the fact that a considerable portion of the Great Lakes and St. Lawrence River are Canadian waters.

The **Western Rivers Rules** are applicable on the Mississippi River from its source to the Huey P. Long Bridge (at New Orleans) and all of the tributaries emptying into the Mississippi, and their tributaries. These Rules are also in effect on that part of the Atchafalaya River above its junction with the Plaquemine-Morgan alternate waterway, and on the Red River of the North.

It should be noted carefully that the "Western Rivers" Rules do *not* apply to rivers on the West Coast of the United States—such rivers as the Sacramento or the Columbia; the Inland Rules are in effect for all rivers emptying into the Pacific Ocean.

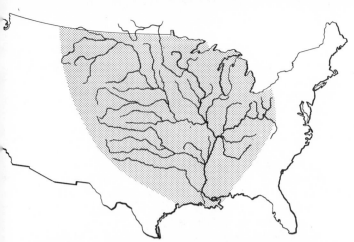

FIG. 223 The Western Rivers Rules of the Road apply to specific inland waters of the United States. They are not applicable to rivers on the West Coast, such as the Sacramento and Columbia, that empty into the Pacific Ocean.

Provisions of the Rules

The four sets of Rules of the Road are of such importance and contain such extensive information that two chapters in this book are devoted to them and their implementing regulations.

Matters relating to navigation lights and day shapes are covered in Chapter 4 for all sets of Rules. Chapter 5 covers other topics of the Rules such as the steering and sailing rules, whistle signals, etc.

Official publications

The Coast Guard publishes three pamphlets covering the Rules of the Road. CG-169 includes both the International Rules and the Inland Rules; see fig. 1708. CG-172 contains the Great Lakes Rules, and CG-184 covers the Western Rivers Rules.

Copies of these publications are not required to be on board motorboats, but they are desirable documents to have at hand. They are available, without charge, from Coast Guard District offices or from Headquarters in Washington, see page 608.

Additional regulations

Each of the three sets of U.S. Rules of the Road contains authority for the issuance of additional rules and regulations by the Secretary of the Department in which the Coast Guard is operating. These are termed "Pilot Rules" and are covered later in this chapter.

Penalties against persons

The Inland, Great Lakes, and Western Rivers Rules contain essentially the same language as to penalties for their violation, or violation of regulations issued under the authority of the Rules. There are minor differences in wording but the maximum penalties are the same.

A licensed or unlicensed master, mate, pilot, or engineer of any vessel subject to the Rules who is in violation is liable to a penalty not to exceed $500. In addition, the Inland and Western Rivers Rules specify that such person shall also be liable for all damages sustained by any passenger in his person or baggage as a result of such violation. (It is provided that these penalties against the individual do not relieve the vessel, its owner, or corporation from any liability as a result of the violation.)

Penalties against vessels

Penalties may also be assessed against any *vessel* subject to the Rules that may be navigated in violation of them. The penalty is fixed at $500, and the Inland and Western Rivers Rules provide that one-half of this sum may be paid to "the informer." Under all sets of these Rules the vessel may be seized and proceeded against in the Federal courts for the collection of the penalty.

Penalty for failure to give aid

As noted before, the master or person in charge of a vessel in collision has duties to the other vessel and her crew and passengers (see page 36). A specific penalty is provided for failure, without reasonable cause, to meet these responsibilities. Such a person may be found guilty of a misdemeanor and subjected to a fine of $1000, or imprisonment for not more than two years, or both. The vessel may be proceeded against in Federal court with the penalty assessed being divided equally between the informer and the United States.

International Rules

The statutory enactment of the International Rules of the Road as U.S. law does not prescribe any specific penalties for violation of the Rules. Individuals and vessels, would, of course, be liable for civil suits for damages as a result of violations of these Rules.

OTHER FEDERAL REGULATIONS

It is not feasible to attempt to include in this chapter a complete set of federal boating regulations—and probably no two authorities would agree as to what constituted a "complete" set—but major items of regulatory matter will be discussed or referenced. If needed, additional information can be obtained from Coast Guard offices.

Regulations to implement the Federal Boat Safety Act of 1971 are being issued slowly following careful study in each area to be controlled. In the meanwhile, recreational boats remain subject to regulations issued under the Motorboat Act of 1940 where these are not in conflict with the provisions of the 1971 Act.

PILOT RULES

The implementing regulations issued under the authority of each of the three sets of U.S. Rules of the Road are termed **"Pilot Rules."** (There are no parallel regulations for the International Rules of the Road.) There are thus three sets of Pilot Rules varying in considerable detail for the different waters for which each are effective.

Most of the contents of the Pilot Rules have to do with the same topics as the basic Rules of the Road: navigation lights, steering and sailing rules, whistle signals, etc. These regulatory provisions are covered with the basic Rules in Chapters 4 and 5.

Duplication of the Rules of the Road

As a result of certain old administrative requirements, each of the sets of Pilot Rules contain a number of provisions that are directly duplicatory of some provisions of the applicable Rules of the Road. This duplication has no

FIG. 224 The Rules of the Road, and related information, for the various areas of United States waters are published in a series of small Coast Guard pamphlets which may be obtained without charge from major USCG offices. They make excellent reference reading for any skipper.

significance and can be ignored. Other provisions of the Pilot Rules—the majority of them—are, of course, not duplicatory and must be understood.

Use of searchlights

The Inland Pilot Rules and those for the Great Lakes contain a specific regulation prohibiting the flashing of a searchlight or other blinding light onto the bridge or into

FIG. 225 All sets of Pilot Rules contain specific prohibitions against the use of a searchlight in such a way as to flash its rays onto the bridge or into the pilothouse of any vessel underway.

the pilothouse of another vessel while underway. Violation may lead to the suspension or revocation of the offending person's license or certificate.

Penalties

The penalties for violation of the Pilot Rules are the same as for offenses against the basic Rules of the Road; see page 39.

BILGE VENTILATION REGULATIONS

Of particular interest to the owners of motorboats using *gasoline* as a fuel are the Coast Guard regulations relating to the ventilation of engine and fuel tank compartments. The regulations are discussed and illustrated on pages 604-607.

REGATTAS AND MARINE PARADES

The Coast Guard has established a set of regulations covering the holding of regattas and marine parades. In some areas, the authority to regulate such events has been passed on to State authorities, but under the same general requirements and procedures.

The term "regattas and marine parades" includes all organized water events of limited duration conducted on a prearranged schedule; this covers races of all types.

An application must be submitted to the Commander of the Coast Guard District in which the event is to be held no less than 30 days prior to the start of the proposed event; late applications are normally rejected. The application must contain a number of items of information as specified

in Coast Guard regulations; see CG-169, 172, or 184.

Approved events will often result in the promulgation of "special local regulations" governing the conduct of the event, spectator craft restrictions, patrolling plans, etc. These are usually issued with Local Notices to Mariners and carry specific penalties for violations.

PARK REGULATIONS

The use of boats on many natural lakes and man-made reservoirs are subject to regulations issued by the National Park Service of the Department of the Interior. Other such bodies of water are controlled by state or local authorities. These rules and restrictions will vary from one body of water to another and each area must be individually checked to ensure that laws are not inadvertently violated.

State Boating Laws and Regulations

Federal laws and regulations now preempt State controls in the area of boat and equipment safety standards, but the Federal Boat Safety Act of 1971 does allow States to impose requirements for safety equipment beyond Federal rules if needed to meet uniquely hazardous local circumstances. The Act does *not* preempt State or local laws and regulations directed at safe boat operation. In addition, there are usually laws and regulations relating to boat trailers and their use.

The old saying that "Ignorance of the law is no excuse" is quite applicable to skippers of recreational boats. Each should know the requirements and restrictions of his state, and should take steps as appropriate to expand his knowledge if he plans to cruise in other states. He should particularly be alert to varying state laws about boat trailering on highways.

Information on applicable state laws and regulations may be obtained from each state, usually from the same office that handles registration and numbering; see page 504. The Outboard Boating Club of America publishes four regional handbooks that are thorough compilations of laws and regulations relating to boats of all sizes, trailers, boating activities, and taxation. These are up-dated when necessary by supplements. These may be ordered from OBC at 333 N. Michigan Avenue, Chicago, Ill. 60601.

TEMPORARY SUSPENSION OF FEDERAL PREEMPTION

Immediately following the enactment of the Federal Boat Safety Act of 1971, the Secretary of Transportation exercised his authority under Section 9 of the Act which allows him to grant exemptions to its provisions. He granted a blanket exemption to all States and political subdivisions thereof from Section 10 which sets forth the Federal preemption over State and local regulations in the area of boat and equipment safety standards and requirements.

This action was taken to avoid a temporary "vacuum" of regulation. The new Federal boat safety program will be implemented by regulations to be issued under the authority of the Act, rather than by specific provisions of the basic law. Time will be required to prepare, coordinate, and publish these regulations, and for them to become effective. To avoid the cancellation of State and local laws and regulations before rules come in, the exemption was granted, allowing them to temporarily continue in effect in the interim.

FIG. 227 State boating laws and regulations vary widely. The Outboard Boating Club has prepared sectional compilations of these requirements and restrictions, with supplements published as required by changes.

Miscellaneous Regulatory Matters

Boatmen will have need of knowledge of other regulatory matters in varying degrees as determined by the size of their craft, their cruising area, etc. Skippers should be alert to changes in these factors which may require additional knowledge in matters previously of no interest to them.

DOCUMENTATION

Not all boats are numbered—many are "documented." This is a process whereby official papers on the craft are issued by the Coast Guard in much the same manner as for large ships. (Formerly this was done by the Bureau of Customs of the Treasury Department, but the function was transferred to the Coast Guard in 1966.) The *numbering*

requirements of the 1971 Federal Boat Safety Act do not apply to documented vessels; other provisions of this Act, however, do apply to "boats" as defined therein.

Documentation of a craft used solely for non-commercial recreational purposes is *optional,* and certain requirements must be met. The vessel must be owned by a citizen of the United States (or a corporation 51% or more owned by U.S. citizens) and it must be of a specified minimum size, 5 net tons as explained below. The captain of a documented vessel, if other than the owner, must be a U.S. citizen.

Tonnage

Before a vessel can be documented it must be *measured* for its tonnage. ("Admeasured" is the more formal term, but it means the same and is gradually being dropped in favor of the simpler language.) The details of gross and net tonnage are explained on page 25.

Types of Documents

The documents that are issued to vessels are of five forms—register, enrollment and license, license, yacht enrollment and license, and yacht license. Only the latter two are of interest to the owners of noncommercial craft, but all should be generally understood.

Yacht documents

A **yacht enrollment and license** may be issued to a vessel used *exclusively for pleasure* of 20 net tons or more. A **yacht license** may be issued to such a vessel of 5 net tons or over but less than 20 net tons.

Other types of documents

An **enrollment and license** may be issued to a vessel of 20 net tons or more and, if the vessel meets certain qualifications, may authorize it to engage in the coasting trade, the mackerel fishery, the cod fishery, the whale fishery, or

---

A TRUE COPY OF THE LATEST CONSOLIDATED CERTIFICATE OF ENROLLMENT AND YACHT LICENSE

The United States of America OFFICIAL NO.

Measured at

Rebuilt at

Remeasured at Horsepower

CONSOLIDATED CERTIFICATE OF ENROLLMENT AND YACHT LICENSE†
LICENSE OF YACHT UNDER TWENTY TONS:

In conformity to Title L, "Regulation of Vessels in Domestic Commerce," and Chapter Two, Title XLVII, "Regulation of Commerce and Navigation," of the Revised Statutes of the United States, and to "An act to amend Sections 4214 and 4218 of the Revised Statutes Relating to Yachts," approved August 20, 1912

having taken and subscribed the oath required by law, and having sworn that

citizen of the United States and the sole owner of the vessel called the of and that the said vessel was built in the year 1 at of as appears by and having certified that the said vessel is a ; that she has deck mast, a stem, and a stern; that her register length is feet, her register breadth feet, her register depth feet, her height feet; that she measures as follows:

To have and to hold the said vessel and appurtenances thereunto belonging unto the said buyer(s) executors, administrators, successors, and assigns, to the sole and only proper use, benefit, and behoof of the said buyer(s) executors, administrators, successors, and assigns forever; And the said seller(s) ha promised, covenanted, and agreed, and by these presents do promise, covenant, and agree, for executors, administrators, successors, and assigns, to and with said buyer(s) executors, administrators, successors, and assigns, to warrant and defend the said vessel and all other before-mentioned appurtenances against all and every person whomsoever

FIG. 228 Craft over a specified minimum size may be "documented" in much the same way as are large ships. This action, in lieu of state or Coast Guard registration and numbering, has both advantages and disadvantages.

	TONS	100ths
Capacity under tonnage deck		
Capacity between decks above tonnage deck		
Capacity of enclosures on the upper deck, viz: Forecastle ; bridge ; poop ; break		

the coasting trade and mackerel fishery. A vessel authorized to engage in the "mackerel fishery" may be used in the taking of fish of any description.

If a vessel is to be used for towing, dredging, freight or passenger carrying, or a combination of any of these functions, its document must so state.

Special enrollments and licenses are issued on the frontiers, authorizing vessels to engage in the foreign and coasting trades. Vessels of 5 net tons or more may be granted an enrollment and license for navigating the waters of the northern, northeastern, or northwestern frontiers.

A **license** may be issued to a vessel of 5 net tons or over but of less than 20 net tons and, if the vessel meets certain qualifications, may authorize the vessel to engage in any one of the employments for which an enrollment and license may be issued as discussed above.

A vessel under a **register** which is not limited by a prohibitive endorsement on its face may engage in any trade, including the foreign trade, the coastwise trade, and the American fisheries. Registered vessels, however, may be required upon arrival in a port of the United States to pay certain pilotage fees and other charges from which other documented vessels are generally exempted.

Temporary and permanent documents

Marine documents are also described as "permanent"—issued to vessels at their home ports, or "temporary"—granted to vessels at ports other than their home port.

Advantages of Yacht Documentation

Important privileges extended by documentation of vessels as yachts include (1) legal authority to fly the yacht

FIG. 229 Much useful information on documentation requirements and procedures can be obtained from this free Coast Guard pamphlet. A copy should be obtained and studied before any decision is made regarding the possible documentation of a boat.

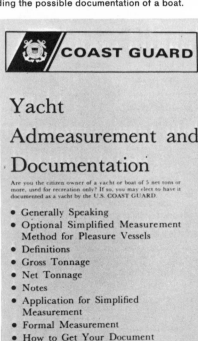

ensign, which authority is not formally granted to other boats; and (2) the privilege of recording bills of sale, mortgages, and other instruments of title for the vessel with federal officials at her home port, giving constructive legal notice to all persons of the effect of such instruments and permitting the attainment of a preferred status for mortgages so recorded. This gives additional security to the purchaser or mortgagee and facilitates financing and transfer of title for such vessels.

The former advantages of documented yachts over registered (numbered) non-commercial motorboats when returning to the U.S. from a foreign port have now been eliminated in the general simplification of procedures that has occurred in recent years; see pages 48-49.

Obtaining Documentation

A procedure has been established under which the owner of a boat used *exclusively for pleasure* may file an "Application for Simplified Admeasurement" with the Officer in Charge, Marine Inspection in his local Coast Guard District.

In brief, the simplified measurement method uses the numerical product of three dimensions—the overall length (L), overall breadth (B), and depth (D)—note that this is "depth," an internal dimension, and not the boat's "draft." The **gross tonnage** of a vessel designed for sailing is assumed to be $1/2$(LBD/100); for vessels not designed for sailing it is calculated to be 2/3(LBD/100).

The gross tonnage of a catamaran or a trimaran is determined by adding the gross tonnages of each hull as calculated above.

Where the volume of the deckhouse is disproportionate to the volume of the hull—as in some designs of houseboats—the volume of the deckhouse, calculated by appropriate geometric formulas and expressed in tons of 100 cubic feet each, is added to the gross tonnage of the hull as calculated with L, B, and D.

The **net tonnage** of a sailing vessel is recorded as 9/10 of the gross tonnage; for a non-sailing vessel, the multiplying factor is 8/10. If there is no propelling machinery in the hull, the net tonnage will be the same as the gross tonnage.

Application for simplified admeasurement is by letter; there is no standard form of application unless one has been prepared by the local Officer in Charge, Marine Inspection. The owner may take his own length, breadth, and depth measurements and complete the transaction by mail, quickly and without cost.

Considerable information on documentation can be obtained from the Coast Guard pamphlet "Yacht Admeasurement and Documentation"—CG-177, available without charge from Coast Guard offices.

Formal measurement

The owner of a boat may elect to have formal measurement rather than use the simplified method; this is *required* if the vessel is to be used *commercially*.

If an owner is contemplating formal admeasurement, it is suggested that he first make an estimate of the tonnage by using the simplified method. If the resulting net tonnage is less than 5 tons, it is not likely that the vessel will be 5 net tons or more when formally measured.

An application for formal measurement should be prepared in writing and submitted to the Officer in Charge,

FIG. 230 A documented vessel, including a boat, must have its "official number" and "net tonnage" deeply carved or permanently marked on her "main beam." Special provisions have been made for fiberglass boats.

Marine Inspection, for the area in which the vessel is located. The information that must be submitted is listed in CG-177.

Under formal measurement procedures, a definite date and place should be agreed upon between the measuring officer and the owner, or his agent, so that the vessel may be physically measured and examined by the measuring officer.

Application for document

The measuring officer who calculates the tonnages by the simplified method, or who visits the vessel for formal measurement, will provide the necessary forms which must be filled out to receive the document. Further assistance may be obtained by writing, calling, or visiting the nearest Documentation Office, U.S. Coast Guard.

Establishing title

A vessel may be documented only in the name of the holder of legal title. It is necessary therefore for the owner

FIG. 231 A craft documented for pleasure only—no commercial use—must have her name and hailing port marked "on some conspicuous place on the hull." This is normally done on the stern, but such is not mandatory. Detailed specifications must be met regarding the lettering.

to present adequate title papers with his application.

If the vessel was built for the present owner and has never been owned by anyone else, that person should have the builder furnish a "Builder's Certificate" on Form 1261 to establish title.

If there were previous owners, the proper documents are the Builder's Certificate and bills of sale in recordable form from each of the previous owners, preferably on Form 1346, available without charge from the Documentation Office. If these steps are impracticable, consult the Officer in Charge, Marine Inspection, for alternative procedures.

Fees

No charge is made for the documentation of a yacht or for renewing a yacht license. There is no charge for measuring and certifying the tonnages of a vessel, except that if the physical presence of a measuring officer is required outside certain local limits, a charge is made to cover his salary, travel, and subsistence expenses. If a vessel is to be measured on a Saturday or Sunday, substantial charges for overtime may be involved; it is suggested that a convenient weekday be proposed in the application to avoid such charges.

A small charge is made for recording each bill of sale or other recordable title instrument; the average cost of recording a bill of sale is approximately $2.

Markings of a Documented Boat

The owner or master of a vessel to be documented must file a certification with the Coast Guard Documentation Officer that the boat is properly *marked*. He must arrange for an official inspection of the marking if this is requested by the Coast Guard.

Official number and net tonnage

Every documented vessel, as a prerequisite to documentation, must have its official number and net tonnage carved or permanently marked on the *main beam* of the vessel.

The main beam is the beam at the forward end of the largest hatch on the weather deck and is usually located forward of amidships. If the vessel has no hatch on the weather deck, the main beam is any structural member integral to the hull.

The *official number* must be preceded by the abbreviation "NO." and the net tonnage must be preceded by the word "NET"; see fig. 230.

In a wooden vessel, the legend must be carved or cut on the main beam in arabic or block type letters three inches high, or as high as the width of the main beam will permit. In a vessel built of metal, the legend must be outlined by punch marks and painted over with oil paint using a color that contrasts with the background.

On fiberglass boats, the legend can be carved into a plastic sheet or plate in much the same manner as a wooden beam, and this plate then fastened with epoxy to the hull, usually in the bow. The plate will normally be six inches high by as long as required to carry the prescribed information.

Name and hailing port

All documented yachts are required to have their name and hailing port marked on *some conspicuous place* on their hull; this is usually done on the stern. The letters must be Roman type and not less than four inches in height. They may be painted, gilded, cut, or cast letters, and must be in a color that provides adequate contrast with the background surface.

The hailing port may be the port where the vessel is permanently documented, or the place in the same district where the vessel was built or where one or more of the owners reside.

Documented commercial vessels must have the name and hailing port marked in full on the stern, plus the name in full marked on both bows.

Special provisions are made for vessels with square bows and for double-enders.

Block letters required

For documented vessels, whether used for pleasure only or commercially, *the use of script or italic lettering is not acceptable.* It is *not* permissible to place the name or hailing port, on a board and attach the board to the hull, or to use cut or carved letters joined in one continuous piece. (For boats that are numbered rather than documented, there is no requirement that a name be shown nor specifications as to how one may or must be displayed.)

Use of Documented Boats

If a vessel is given a document as a yacht, that paper will authorize its use for *pleasure only.* A yacht document does *not* permit the transporting of merchandise or the carrying of passengers for hire, such as the taking out of fishing parties for a fee charged directly or indirectly. Any violation of this limitation may result in the imposition of severe penalties against the craft and its owner. See also section below on "Commercial Operation."

The documentation of a vessel as a yacht *does not exempt* it from any applicable State or Federal taxes. Further, the fact that a boat is federally documented will not excuse the owner from complying with safety and equipment regulations of the state or states in which it is operated.

Vessels that are documented are not required nor permitted to have a number issued under the 1971 Federal Boat Safety Act.

Renewal of Documents

A yacht license or enrollment and license must be renewed each year; this is probably the only disadvantage to documentation. The owner will ordinarily be notified by mail and will be sent the required renewal form and instructions several weeks in advance of the expiration date. Failure to receive this notice, however, will not affect the requirement for renewal.

For vessels under simplified measurement

At the discretion of the Officer in Charge, Marine Inspection, concerned, a document issued under the simplified measurement procedures *may* not be renewed, or another document issued, until the Coast Guard has verified the overall dimensions given in the application for such measurement.

Any correction of the stated overall dimensions of a vessel as a result of the above verification is deemed to be a change in the description of the vessel and the outstanding document will no longer be in force.

FIG. 232 A craft documented for any commercial use must be marked with her name and hailing port on the stern, and additionally must have her name on both sides of the vessel's bow. The style, size, and colors of the lettering are specified by regulation.

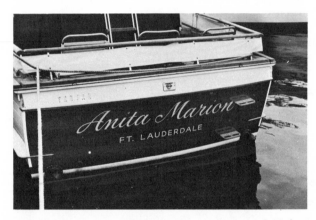

FIG. 233 The name in script-style letters on the stern of this boat is legal as she is numbered rather than documented. Such style of lettering is not acceptable on any documented boat or ship.

COMMERCIAL OPERATION

The Federal Government does not require that the owner of a motorboat or yacht of any size whatever have any knowledge of his boat or navigation or the handling of his vessel. Neither does the Government require that a *motorboat* or motor yacht under 300 gross tons not engaged in trade or carrying passengers for hire should have on board a licensed officer.

No licensed officers are required on *motor vessels documented as yachts* except on those of 200 gross tons and over when navigating the high seas.

Carrying Passengers For Hire

Persons wishing to operate a motorboat carrying passengers for hire must have a license. There are two categories of licensing as determined by the number of persons carried—six passengers and less, or more than six. Neither of these should be confused with the licenses required to be held by pilots and engineers on vessels of more than 15 gross tons or 65 feet length engaged in trade. Motorboats under 65 feet in length carrying freight for hire are not required to have licensed pilots and engineers.

Definition of "passenger"

Of particular interest to boatmen who use their craft exclusively for recreation is the definition of a "passenger" in the Federal Boat Safety Act of 1971. A person on board a vessel is *not* considered by law to be a passenger if he is in any of the following categories: (1) the owner or his representative; (2) the operator; (3) bona fide members of the crew who have contributed no consideration for their carriage and who are paid for their services; or (4) any guest on board a vessel which is being used exclusively for pleasure purposes who has not contributed any consideration, directly or indirectly, for his carriage.

The last exception noted above is the most troublesome. It is emphasized that to avoid being in a "passenger" status—which would subject the craft and its skipper to special requirements—the guest must not contribute *any* consideration, directly or indirectly, for his passage.

When is a boat carrying passengers for hire?

It is of considerable importance that a skipper have some understanding of circumstances that might be considered by the authorities as "carrying passengers for hire." Some situations are obvious—such as taking persons on a fishing trip for a specified amount of money for each individual or for the group as a whole—but other cases are more borderline and must be examined carefully.

It has been held that when the owner is a businessman who takes associates or customers aboard for the purpose of creating good-will or negotiating business matters not related to the trip this *does not* put the vessel and operator in the category of carrying passengers for hire.

On the other hand, the Coast Guard has ruled that the following situations *do* constitute instances of carrying passengers for hire.

1. When the boat owner invites guests aboard and one or more of them brings a gift of food or drink to be used on the trip.

2. Where the cruise guest takes the skipper ashore for dinner and entertainment.

3. Where during a cruise one of the guests aboard offers to buy a tankful of fuel or some like event.

4. If there is a prearranged plan or agreement in advance that the guests are to pay their proportionate share, or any specific amount, of the cruise expenses. The operator of the craft would have to be properly licensed and the vessel would have to be equipped in accordance with the requirements for those carrying passengers for hire.

If the participants in an expense-sharing cruise are members of a *bona-fide "joint venture,"* they are then all considered under the law to be "owners" and not "passengers" and thus no licensed operator would be required. It is essential, however, that this joint venture be legally sufficient and in writing. *Each person* must have *all* the incidents of ownership—the right to full possession, control, and navigation of the craft. A mere "share-the-expenses" agreement is not sufficient to establish a joint venture; rights of ownership and liability in case of accident and suit are necessary.

If a boat is chartered with the crew furnished by the owner, it has been held that the craft is then carrying passengers for hire and must be in charge of a licensed operator.

Licenses for Six or Less Passengers

Vessels equipped with propulsion machinery of any type, while carrying *not more than six* passengers for hire, must be "in the charge of" a person licensed for such service in accordance with regulations issued under the authority of the Federal Boat Safety Act of 1971.

Application for licenses

Licenses are issued by Officers in Charge, Marine Inspection, U.S. Coast Guard. These officers are located in many ports; check a nearby Coast Guard unit for the nearest Marine Inspection Office.

An applicant must submit a sworn application to one of these officers who will examine him concerning his character and fitness to hold such a license. The Officer in Charge, or his representative, investigates the proofs submitted concerning the applicant's character and ability, and determines whether his "capacity, knowledge, experience, character, and habits of life" qualify him for licensing as a Motorboat Operator.

The applicant must submit documentary evidence of at least one year's experience in operating motorboats.

FIG. 234 A craft carrying passengers for hire must be operated by a person possessing a valid Coast Guard license for the number of passengers on board and the waters navigated.

FIG. 235 The circumstances which distinguish between a "guest" on board and a "passenger for hire" are quite complex, but have been established with reasonable clarity. All boat operators should study the situation with some care to avoid law violations.

Examination

An oral examination is given which is based on subjects which any person operating a motorboat carrying passengers should know before being entrusted with its operation and navigation.

Questions deal generally with regulations governing motorboats, Rules of the Road and Pilot Rules for local waters, fire protection, lifesaving equipment, safe operation of gasoline engines, methods of operating and navigating boats carrying passengers for hire, and elementary first-aid.

As the Rules of the Road and Pilot Rules differ in various parts of the country, the holder of a license has the duty to familiarize himself with the prevalent rules if he should shift his operations to other waters.

Licenses to operate motorboats carrying passengers for hire are not issued to persons under 18 years of age. The applicant must be able to read and write.

Physical fitness required

Applicants must be physically fit or a license will not be granted. Normally, they must be examined by a U.S. Public Health Service surgeon or a reputable physician. Bad hearing or eye-sight, color blindness, use of narcotics, insanity, or presence of certain diseases are grounds for rejection of the applicant.

License issuance and renewal

Licenses are issued and signed by Officers in Charge, Marine Inspection; see fig. 236. Every license or certificate

FIG. 236 A "Motorboat Operator License" is one issued by the Coast Guard for carrying **six or less** passengers for hire. There are no restrictions on the size of the craft nor on the waters navigated.

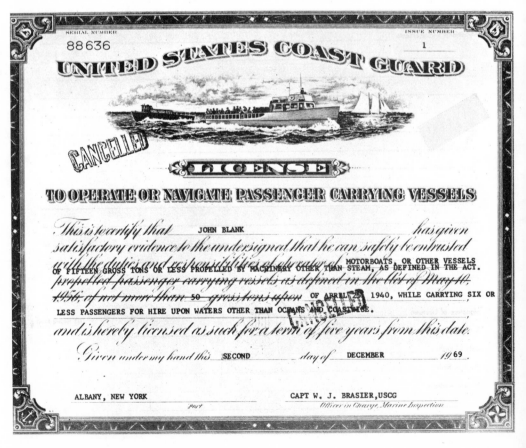

FIG. 237 To legally carry more than six passengers for hire, a skipper must have either an "Operator" or an "Ocean Operator" license. These are issued in terms of the gross tonnage of vessels that may be operated and with specific limitations as to the waters on which it is valid.

of lost license, see below) must be signed by the person to whom it is issued, who also places his thumbprint on the back. It is valid for five years, after which it can be renewed. There is no charge.

To renew the license, the individual must present it to an Officer in Charge, Marine Inspection, together with a certificate of color vision, within one year after its expiration date. If more than a year has elapsed since the license expired, the person must take another examination. In most situations, a brief test on the Rules of the Road will be a part of the renewal process. Except under extraordinary circumstances, renewal cannot be made more than 90 days before the expiration date.

Lost licenses

In the case of loss of license, except where it has been revoked or suspended, a certificate can be obtained from an Officer in Charge, Marine Inspection, on presentation of satisfactory evidence of the loss. This certificate is then as valid as the license for the unexpired term.

Suspension or revocation

If any operator is found guilty of incompetence, misbehavior, negligence, endangering life, or willfully violating any safety law or regulation, his license may be suspended or revoked. If revoked or suspended, the license must be surrendered to the official before whom the hearing was held. If an appeal is made, the license must still be surrendered but a certificate will be issued covering the period during which the appeal is pending.

Licenses for More Than Six Passengers

Rules and regulations for small passenger vessels are prescribed in an Act of 10 May 1956, frequently called the "Ray Act." Under this Act, a "passenger-carrying vessel" means any vessel which carries *more than six passengers* and which falls into one of the below categories.

1. Propelled in whole or in part by steam or by any form of mechanical or electrical power and is of 15 gross tons or less.

2. Propelled in whole or in part by steam or any form of mechanical or electrical power and is of more than 15 but less than 100 gross tons and is not more than 65 feet in length.

3. Propelled by sail and is of 700 gross tons or less.

A few exceptions are made, including: foreign vessels, vessels operating on non-navigable waters of the U.S., vessels laid up and out of commission, public vessels, and lifeboats.

Operator licenses

A person holding only a license under the 1971 Boat Act, as described above, is not authorized to operate passenger-carrying vessels under the Ray Act. A separate license issued under the terms of this Act is required and its scope varies according to the waters navigated. For offshore waters, an "Ocean Operator's License" is issued. Within the coastline and on the Great Lakes, it is an "Operator's License"; see fig. 237. In both cases, specific geographic limits are normally prescribed. Licenses are issued for a specified maximum gross tonnage, in multiples of 10, and are valid for five years.

Application is made to the nearest Officer in Charge, Marine Inspection. Physical fitness must be established and a written examination must be passed. Proof of appropriate experience is required.

Vessel Inspection

Vessels subject to the Ray Act must be inspected by an Officer in Charge, Marine Inspection, from whom applications for inspection may be obtained. These are among the vessels generally referred to in Coast Guard regulations and publications as "inspected vessels"; ordinary motorboats are categorized as "uninspected vessels."

Certificates of inspection are valid for three years. They describe the area in which the vessel may be operated, the maximum number of passengers that can be carried, the minimum crew required, minimum lifesaving and firefighting equipment to be carried, etc.

FIG. 238 A boat returning to the United States from foreign waters must report to the proper authorities at the first port touched. In some areas, a single Federal agency has been assigned to handle all forms and reports for all authorities concerned.

INTERNATIONAL VOYAGES

When an American boat crosses the national boundaries of the United States to visit a foreign port, or a foreign yacht visits an American port, certain customs, immigration, and other regulations must be obeyed. As a result of various provisions and exemptions applying to yachts, not engaged in trade, the procedure has been so simplified that there is nothing in these legal requirements to deter a recreational craft from enjoying a cruise outside the limits of U.S. waters. Severe penalties, however, are provided for failure to observe the applicable regulations.

Clearing and Entering

The terms "clearing" and "entering" are commonly used in connection with a vessel's voyage between ports of two nations. **Clearing** involves the obtaining of permission to sail by presenting the ship's papers to a customs official. **Entering** relates to arrival, when the owner or master "enters" his vessel by having his ship's papers accepted by customs authorities. Thus a U.S. vessel might be required to clear from an American port and enter on arrival at a foreign port. Then for the return passage, the vessel would clear from the foreign port and enter upon reaching an American harbor.

If desired, *bills of health* may be secured free of charge before leaving for a foreign port. This is not compulsory, but may make entry into the foreign port quicker and easier.

Report on arrival

There are four separate legal aspects to entering this country from a foreign nation, each involving its own government agency and officials. These are (1) **Customs,** relating to the bringing in of dutiable merchandise; (2) **Immigration,** relating to the eligibility for entry of persons; (3) **Public Health Service,** for the prevention of importation of human diseases; and (4) **Animal and Plant Quarantine,** for the prevention of entry of contaminated plants, fruits, and vegetables, or infected animals.

On arrival at a foreign port, the owner or captain of a yacht (any size) should report to the authorities mentioned above, or to such of them as exist for this port. The "Q" flag (plain yellow) should be flown where it can be easily seen—starboard spreader, radio antenna, fishing outrigger, etc.—to indicate that the vessel desires to be boarded by customs and other government authorities. When reporting, the crew and guests must remain aboard the boat until permission has been granted to land. Any additional or local regulations to be complied with, including details in connection with clearing from that port, will be supplied by the authorities.

Every vessel, whether documented or not, arriving in the United States from a foreign port or place must come into a *port of entry* and, within 24 hours, must report to the customhouse at that port. The crew and guests must remain aboard (one person may get off for the sole purpose of telephoning or otherwise notifying the authorities of the vessel's arrival), and no baggage or merchandise should be removed until the customs, immigration, and other officials have given their approval.

FIG. 239 Cruising with pets may introduce new problems into international voyages. Be sure to check the laws and regulations of all countries to be visited before departing from the United States. Investigate, too, any problems that may arise on your return to the U.S. from foreign shores with animals aboard.

All boats, regardless of size, must report to the immigration authorities on return to a United States port. Any alien passengers aboard must be reported and a heavy penalty may be imposed for failure to detain passengers and crew if ordered to do so by the authorities. A report giving names, nationalities, and other information concerning any paid crew aboard must be made on a crew manifest.

In many U.S. ports a "one-stop" service has been established whereby for the simple situations of a noncommercial craft from nearby foreign waters a single government official from one of the agencies will represent all of the authorities and bring all necessary forms to be filled in by the skipper.

Exemptions for non-commercial craft

Neither a licensed yacht nor an undocumented American pleasure vessel (not engaged in trade nor in any way violating the customs or navigation laws of the U.S.) is required to clear upon departure from the United States for a foreign port or place. Similarly a licensed yacht of any size or an undocumented American pleasure vessel (not engaged in trade nor in any way violating the customs or navigation laws of the U.S., and not having visited any other vessel "hovering" off the coast) is exempted from *formal* entry. These craft, however, *must* make a report to the proper authorities to cover such matters as the importation of items purchased while outside the United States.

At the Canadian border

U.S. yachts going into Canada may secure *cruising permits* with the right of free entry and clearance from 1 May to 1 October. These are issued without charge by the Canadian customs authorities at the Canadian port where the yacht first reports and must be surrenderd when leaving the country. Provided that the boat does not leave Canadian waters, she is then free to visit other Canadian ports until the permit is surrendered, though reports must be made at any port called where a custom officer is located.

Canadian boatmen with craft of less than 5 tons can enter the border waters of the United States for a day's outing without applying for admission at a U.S. port of entry. The Canadian Border Landing Card doesn't require advance application and is good for repeated 24-hour visits throughout the navigation season. It is good only for border waters; if the Canadian boatman wants to go farther into the U.S., he must apply at a port of entry and submit to inspection.

Arrival from coastwise cruises

There is a little-known law on the books that requires foreign vessels and documented vessels of the United States (but not numbered boats) navigating the "high seas" on coastwise cruises to give 24 hour's notice of their time of arrival to the Captain of the Port at their next intended port of call.

Bodies of water like Long Island Sound and Chesapeake Bay are excluded from the Act's definition of "high seas" but waters of the open sea below the low-water mark—as, for example, offshore along the Florida coast—are included.

This is basically a safety and security measure to control the entrance of commercial vessels into U.S. ports. For a time, the law was occasionally invoked against documented yachts, but now, however, these are specifically exempted in an amendment which excludes, among several types of vessels, "United States yachts, arriving at a U.S. port or place from a port or place outside the United States, or destined from one port or place in the United States to another port or place in the U.S."

Miscellaneous Provisions

Foreign yachts meeting certain requirements may receive from customs authorities in the United States a *cruising license* granting them special treatment while in United States waters.

Yacht "commission"

A documented yacht, belonging to a regularly organized and incorporated yacht club, may be issued a *commission* to sail for pleasure on a foreign voyage. Application for this document may be made to any Collector of Customs in the United States. The commission serves mainly as an identification of the vessel and her owner. It must be surrendered upon return from the foreign country.

Additional information

A boatman who *leaves* this country with foreign-made articles—such as cameras made in Japan or Germany—will find their reintroduction into the United States facilitated if these are registered with the U.S. Customs officials

prior to departure. Take such articles to a customs office at a port, airport, etc., and get a Form 4457 filled out and signed. Show this upon reporting in on your return and there will be no question of duty on such articles.

For further detailed information with regard to customs requirements, the boat owner should consult the nearest customs office. Likewise, for information regarding immigration, public health, etc., he should contact any convenient office of the applicable government agency. Information on the legal aspects of visiting a specific foreign country can best be obtained from that nation's consular offices in various major cities of the U.S. or its embassy in Washington, D.C.

FIG. 240 There are legal restrictions on the sale of American vessels to foreigners. Some blanket exceptions have been made for smaller numbered, but **not** documented, boats. An owner should carefully check the laws and regulations before completing such a transaction.

SALE OF CRAFT TO FOREIGNERS

A quite complex set of laws and regulations govern the sale of either documented or undocumented vessels to aliens. Some provisions are applicable at all times; others are in effect only in times of war or National Emergency (this latter condition exists *now* and has since 16 December 1950). The Maritime Administration of the Department of Commerce is the federal agency charged with the enforcement of these rules.

The war or National Emergency provisions extend to vessels of *any* size, including pleasure craft, motorboats, and yachts. Certain blanket approvals of transfer of title have been made for smaller *undocumented* craft, but these contain exceptions, and in any case do not apply to documented boats. A Maritime Administration pamphlet "Transfer and Sale of U.S. Ships to Aliens" is available without charge and contains the applicable laws and regulations. The general complexity of sales to foreigners, however, makes advisable the obtaining of expert advice before any such transactions are completed.

Federal Water Pollution Law

The basic law covering water pollution is the "Federal Water Pollution Control Act" as amended and extended by the "Water Quality Improvement Act of 1970" which was in turn amended in 1972. These cover far more than discharges from vessels, but they form the basis for all implementing standards and regulations.*

BASIC PROVISIONS

The newly-added section relates to all watercraft, large and small, commercial and recreational. The law does, however, permit enforcing authorities to distinguish among classes, types, and sizes of vessels (a boat is a vessel), as well as between new and existing vessels. There are pro-

*See also Page 622 for further regulations relating to water pollution control.

visions for waivers for groups of vessels, and for individual cases, where warranted, but it has been officially stated that very few waivers may be expected and only on the strongest justification for each situation.

Performance standards

The general approach of this federal legislation is the establishment of "standards of performance" for marine sanitation devices. These include all equipment on a vessel to "receive, retain, treat, or discharge sewage, and any process to treat such sewage." The term "sewage" is defined to mean human body wastes and the waste from toilets and other receptacles intended to receive or retain human body wastes."

(continued)

The law states that performance standards must be consistent with maritime safety standards and marine laws and regulations. It specifically notes that in the development of standards consideration must be given to "the economic costs involved" and "the available limits of technology."

Standards were developed by the Environmental Protection Administration (EPA) after consultation with the Coast Guard and other agencies; public hearings were held on the initial proposals. On 20 June 1972, intial performance standards were promulgated. These specified "no discharge"; thus requiring use of holding tanks and shore pumpout facilities. Such severe rules were adopted because of the inability of current models of flow-through devices to meet the high performance levels desired.

There was, however, an "escape clause" added to encourage the installation *now* of flow-through devices which, while the current models are not as effective as desired, are better than no treatment at all. The installation of current generation flow-through devices (provided they are certified by the Coast Guard as meeting a specified standard which is not too severe) will be accepted on *existing* boats if installed on or before the promulgation of Coast Guard regulations, or within three years thereafter. Such devices may be used for their full lifetime if maintained in an operable condition. Vessels installing such devices after the above three-year period, but before the effective date of the act (see below) for no discharges, may use them for three years following the effective date if they are kept operable.

Effective date

The Act does not require immediate compliance by boats. Its provisions will be enforced for *new* vessels *two* years, and for *existing* vessels *five years*, after the promulgation of initial EPA standards and initial USCG regulations; this "countdown" started on 30 January 1975.

There are advantages, however, for early action. The 1972 amendments provide that if a vessel is equipped with an approved marine sanitation device (MSD) and it is operated properly, the standards and regulations will then be *immediately effective for that vessel.* This status has certain advantages; see section below on "Preemption."

Previously installed equipment

All no-discharge devices installed prior to 30 January 1975 are considered "certified" and may continue in use.

If a craft had a flow-through MSD installed, there are provisions for its certification after similar units have been tested and found satisfactory.

Application of the Law

The Secretary of the department in which the Coast Guard is operating will establish testing procedures for marine sanitation devices. If these meet applicable performance standards, they will be "certified." Once these procedures are established, manufacturers must not import, sell, or deliver such units unless each is substantially the same as a device that has been certified.

Use and sale of vessels

After the *effective* date of the standards and regulations —*not the date of promulgation,* but two to five years later—

the Act states that it shall be unlawful for any vessel subject to these standards and regulations to operate on the navigable waters of the United States if such vessel is not equipped with an operable marine sanitation device of a certified design. The law does *not* apply to craft *without* an *installed* toilet.

The Act also states that after this effective date it will be unlawful to manufacture or distribute for sale, or sell or offer for sale, any vessel subject to the standards and regulations unless it has a marine sanitation device of certified type.

Enforcement

The regulations relating to Section 13 will be enforced by the Coast Guard and may be enforced by other federal agencies and state officers by agreement with the Secretary of the department in which the Coast Guard is operating.

The law specifically authorizes Coast Guard and other enforcement personnel to board and inspect any vessel upon the navigable waters of the United States to check compliance with the provisions of this section.

Penalties

The penalty for operation of a boat without an operable marine sanitation device of "certified" type is a civil penalty of not more than $2,000 for each violation. Note that this is an administrative type of penalty and one that does not require trial and conviction in court. No penalty will be assessed until the alleged violator has been given an opportunity for a hearing.

The penalty rises to $5,000 per violation for manufacturers and dealers in such devices and vessels.

PREEMPTION

A most important aspect of this federal anti-pollution law is "preemption." The Act provides that after the *effective* date of the initial standards and regulations "no state or political subdivision thereof shall adopt or enforce any statute or regulation with respect to the design, manufacture, installation, or use of any marine sanitation device on any vessel subject to the provisions of this Section."

As noted above, compliance by a vessel with the initial Federal standards and regulations before the mandatory date make these requirements *immediately effective* for that vessel, and thus give it the protection of Federal preemption. Craft not equipped to Federal rules must continue subject to State and local anti-pollution laws.

The 1972 amendments added a provision that, after the effective date of the initial standards and regulations, a State may completely prohibit all sewage discharges, whether treated or not, but that such prohibition will not become effective until the EPA has determined that *adequate pumpout and treatment* facilities exist; this determination must be made within 90 days after a State's request. The prohibition may apply to all or any part of a State's waters.

There is a further clause that allows EPA to prohibit the discharge of any sewage, treated or not, if a State can establish that such action is necessary to preserve water quality. This is expected to be applied only to special situations such as small lakes.

As anyone who has had the experience knows, buying a new boat is only the beginning. Then comes the purchase of equipment and accessories! The selection and installation of these items can be an interesting and educational part of a boatman's pursuit of his chosen field of interest.

CHAPTER 3
EQUIPMENT FOR BOATS

FIG. 301 Many items of equipment are required for any boat. Some are needed to meet legal requirements, others for safety in basic operations, and still others for the general comfort and convenience of the crew and guests.

Categories of equipment

Equipment for a boat can be conveniently divided into three categories for separate consideration. These major groupings are—

1. **Equipment required by law—federal, state, or local.** This list is rather surprisingly limited. It has little flexibility; items are strictly specified and usually must be of an "approved" type.

2. **Additional equipment for safety and basic operations.** This list is less limited and greater flexibility is possible in the selection of individual items.

3. **Equipment for convenience and comfort.** Here the skipper can turn loose his imagination and be limited only by his financial resources.

Factors affecting selection

In all of the above categories, the items and quantities will vary with the size of the craft involved and the use that is made of her. The legally required items will be determined in most cases by the "class" of the boat as set by regulations issued under the Act of 1940; see page 615. The equipment in the other categories will be governed by size generally, the waters boated upon, and the type of boating activities, together with other factors such as the amount of electrical power available on board, cost, etc.

Legally Required Equipment

The Federal Boat Safety Act of 1971 (FBSA/71) is the basic source of authority for the requirement for various items of equipment aboard boats. The specific details are to be spelled out in regulations rather than appearing in the Act itself. The types of vessels subject to this Act are listed in Chapter 2, page 33.

Federal equipment regulations

Pending the issuance of regulations under the 1971 Act, the requirements of the regulations stemming from the Motorboat Act of 1940 remain in effect for such boats. These are a part of the Code of Federal Regulations, Title 46, Parts 24, 25, and 26. They also appear in a small pamphlet "Rules and Regulations for Undocumented Vessels" —Publication CG-258, see page 609. The new FBSA/71 regulations for recreational craft will appear in Title 33 of the Code of Federal Regulations.

Craft to be considered

It should be noted that the FBSA/71 will regulate the equipment of all "boats" *including sailboats without mechanical propulsion.* This is true even though the regulations temporarily retained from the MBA/40 are in terms of "motorboats."

RULES AND REGULATIONS

FOR

UNINSPECTED VESSELS

SUBCHAPTER C

(Title 46, CFR Parts 24, 25, and 26)

CG-258

MARCH 1, 1967

UNITED STATES COAST GUARD
TREASURY DEPARTMENT

U.S. GOVERNMENT PRINTING OFFICE
WASHINGTON : 1967

◄

FIG. 302 The federal regulations regarding equipment on the various classes of boats will be found in a free Coast Guard pamphlet CG-258, "Rules and Regulations for Uninspected Vessels."

▶

FIG. 303 The Federal Boat Safety Act of 1971 has no upper limit for the length of "boats" subject to its provisions. This is a change from the 1940 Act which considered craft 65 feet or less in length as "motorboats" and those of greater lengths as "motor vessels."

The 1940 Act and its regulations will remain effective for commercial vessels such as fishing boats and diesel tugboats which are not subject to the 1971 law.

State Equipment Requirements

Although the Federal Boat Safety Act of 1971 provides for federal preemption over state controls regarding requirements for equipment on boats (and certain other aspects of boating safety), a blanket exemption has been granted which allows all State and local regulations in effect when the FBSA/71 became law to remain in force for the time being. When Federal requirements have been expanded beyond the regulations of the MBA/40, this exemption will be lifted and Federal rules will prevail.

The FBSA/71 allows States and political subdivisions thereof to have requirements for additional equipment beyond Federal requirements if needed to meet "uniquely hazardous conditions or circumstances" in a State or local area. The Federal government retains a veto over such additional State or local requirements.

Required Equipment as a Minimum

Skippers should regard the legal requirements as a minimum. If a particular boat is required to have two fire ex-

FIG. 304 The Federal Boat Safety Act of 1971 contains the authority of the issuance of regulations covering required equipment aboard craft propelled by machinery, sails, or a combination of both, if they are "boats" as defined in that Act.

tinguishers, for example, its owner should carefully consider if this number will give adequate protection for *his* craft. Two may satisfy the authorities, but a third might be desirable, even necessary, to ensure that one is available at each location on board where it might be needed in a hurry. Two bilge vents may satisfy the regulations, but four would certainly give greater safety. Think "safety," not just compliance with the minimum in order to be "legal"!

Non-approved items as excess

Some boatmen carry items of equipment no longer approved—older, superseded types, or items never approved, as "excess" equipment in addition to the legal minimum, or more, of approved items. This is not prohibited by regulations, but such action may give a false sense of protection and security. The danger of reaching for one of these sub-standard items in an emergency, rather than the proper item, must be recognized and positively guarded against. Some obsolete items of safety equipment, such as certain types of vaporizing-liquid fire extinguishers, see below, are actually hazardous on a boat and should not be on board even as "excess" equipment.

LIFESAVING EQUIPMENT

USCG regulations issued in 1973 under the authority of the Federal Boat Safety Act of 1971 require that *all* recreational boats subject to their jurisdiction, regardless of means of propulsion—motor, sails, or otherwise—must have on board an approved *personal flotation device (PFD)* for each person on board. (There are a few quite minor excep-

FIG. 305 The skipper of any craft must also know state and local laws that relate to his boating. These may differ in some details from Coast Guard regulations. Florida's Motorboat Law, for example, does not stop at 65 feet in length, and "FL" numbers may be seen on vessels quite large enough to be termed "ships."

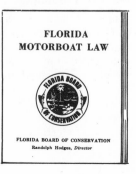

FLORIDA
MOTORBOAT LAW

FLORIDA BOARD OF CONSERVATION
Randolph Hodges, *Director*

tions such as racing shells, rowing sculls, and racing kayaks; foreign boats temporarily in U.S. waters are also exempted.) "Persons on board" includes those in tow, such as water-skiers. The PFDs must be in serviceable condition and so stowed or located as to be readily available in an emergency.

More stringent requirements are placed on craft carrying passengers for hire (any number) than are applied to recreational boats.

TYPES OF PERSONAL FLOTATION DEVICES

Each approved personal flotation device manufactured under the regulations of 1973 must be marked with a PFD "Type" designation to indicate to the user the performance level that the device is intended to provide. There are five PFD Type designations.

A *Type I PFD* is designed to turn an unconscious person from a face downward position in the water to a vertical or slightly backward position, and to have more than 20 pounds of buoyancy. A Type I PFD is, however, somewhat less "wearable" than other types of devices.

A *Type II PFD* is designed to turn an unconscious person in the same manner as a Type I, and to have at least 15½ pounds of buoyancy. A Type II device is more comfortable for wearing than a Type I PFD.

A *Type III PFD* is designed to keep a conscious person in a vertical or slightly backward position and to have at least 15½ pounds of buoyancy. Note that the Type III PFD has the same buoyancy as the Type II, but no turning requirement nor protection for a person who becomes unconscious while in the water. These factors make it possible to design a comfortable and wearable device for activities where it is especially desirable to wear a PFD because of the likelihood that the wearer will enter the water.

A *Type IV PFD* is designed to be thrown to a person in the water and to be grasped rather than worn; it must have at least 16½ pounds of buoyancy.

A *Type V PFD* is any approved device designed for a specific and restricted use.

APPROVED PERSONAL FLOTATION DEVICES

Coast Guard regulations recognize a number of different styles of personal flotation devices and contain specifica-

FIG. 306   This Class 3 boat carries several buoyant cushions for use as lifesaving equipment in the dinghy. Such cushions, however, are not acceptable toward meeting the requirements for life preservers on a craft of this size.

tions that must be met or exceeded if each is to be approved. Each device must be marked with its approval number and all other information, such as limitations on its use, required by the specifications.

Life preservers—Type I PFDs consist of life preservers of various styles; see figs. 308 and 311. The flotation material of the jacket type will be pads of kapok or fibrous glass material; these are inserted in a cloth cover fitted with the necessary straps and ties. Kapok or fibrous glass *must* be encased in sealed plastic film covers; older life preservers without plastic inner containers are no longer acceptable. Old style cork and balsa wood life preservers manufactured as approved items before 1 July 1965 may still be accepted as initial or replacement equipment if they are in good and serviceable condition.

Life preservers of the "bib" type may be of cloth containing unicellular plastic foam sections of specified shape, or they may be of uncovered plastic foam material with a vinyl dip coating. The bib type must have a slit all the way down the front and have adjustable body straps.

Life preservers come in two sizes—*adult,* for persons 90 pounds or more in weight, and *child,* for individuals weighing less than 90 pounds—and are so marked in large letters.

Approved life preservers will also be marked with the type, manufacturer's name and address, and USCG approval number, plus a date and place of individual inspection together with the inspector's initials. All USCG-approved life preservers are now required to be international orange in color.

Life preservers are distinguishable from other lifesaving gear by the words "Approved for Use on All Vessels and Motorboats" which appear near the other markings. (Life preservers manufactured before 1 July 1966 may not have this marking.)

Buoyant vests—Type II PFDs include *buoyant vests* which come in many styles and colors. They use the same flotation materials as life preservers and have the same requirement for plastic inner cases, but vests are smaller and

FIG. 307   The Type III personal flotation device being worn by this skier is an approved model and may be counted toward the required number of PFDs, one for each person including the skier. Ski belts are not approved PFDs and cannot be counted.

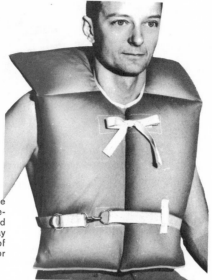

FIG. 308 The most desirable type of lifesaving equipment for a boat is the "life preserver." It is produced in two styles, one of which is the "jacket" type shown above. Such devices are individually inspected at the factory by a representative of the Coast Guard.

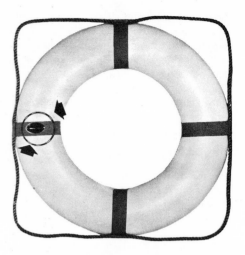

FIG. 310 Ring buoys are classed as Type IV personal flotation devices under the 1973 regulations. Standard sizes of 20, 24, and 30 inch diameters will bear a USCG inspector's markings. The smaller 18½-inch rings are approved as "special purpose" devices and are marked accordingly. These are all acceptable as "throwable" PFDs.

Fig. 309 Buoyant vests are smaller and less expensive devices than life preservers, and provide less buoyancy. They may be of any color. Inflatable vests of any type are **not** acceptable for boats of any class or use.

provide less buoyancy, hence somewhat less safety for a person in the water. Their design must be such as to float the wearer in the same safe position as required for life preservers.

Buoyant vests are made in three sizes—one for adults and two for children, medium and small; weight ranges for children's sizes are marked on each vest. Each PFD must be of the proper size for its intended user.

Buoyant vests are marked with the model number, manufacturer's name and address, approval number, and other information. These water safety items are approved by lot and are *not* individually inspected and marked.

Special purpose devices—Personal flotation devices in this category may be either Type II or Type III if they are designed to be worn; they are Type IV if designed to be thrown.

The design of *special purpose water safety buoyant devices* is examined and approved by recognized laboratories, such as the Yacht Safety Bureau, see page 193, and this approval is accepted by the Coast Guard. These devices are labeled with information as to the use for which intended, the size or weight category of the user, instructions as necessary for use and maintenance, and an approval number. Devices to be grasped rather than worn will also be marked "Warning: Do not Wear on Back."

Buoyant cushions—The most widely used style of Type IV PFD is the *buoyant cushion.* Although adequate buoyancy is provided, actually more than by a buoyant vest, the design of cushions does *not* provide safety for an exhausted or unconscious person.

This device consists of kapok, fibrous glass material, or unicellular plastic foam in a cover of fabric or coated cloth fitted with grab straps. Kapok or fibrous glass material pads must be encased in sealed plastic film covers.

Buoyant cushions are approved in various shapes and sizes, and may be of any color. Approval is indicated on a label on one side carrying generally the same information as for buoyant vests. Cushions are approved by lot number and are not individually inspected. All cushions manufactured since 1961 will carry the warning, "Do not wear on back."

Life rings—Another style of Type IV personal flotation device is the *life ring buoy* which may be of cork, balsa wood, or unicellular plastic foam. The ring is surrounded by a light grabline fastened at four points and used to obtain a better grasp of it; see fig. 310.

Standard sizes are 20, 24, and 30 inches in diameter. Life rings of 18½-inch diameter have been approved under the "special purpose water safety buoyant device" category and are authorized for use on boats of any size that are not carrying passengers for hire.

Balsa wood or cork life ring buoys will be covered with cloth after the core material has been coated with a waterproof glue. These will be marked as Type IV personal flotation devices and with other data general similar to life preservers. They may be either orange or white in color.

Rings of plastic foam with special surface treatment will carry a small metal plate with approval information including the inspector's initials. Ring buoys of this style may be either international orange or white in color.

Some skippers paint the name of the craft on their ring buoys; this is not prohibited by the regulations.

Work vests—Buoyant *work vests* are classed as Type V personal flotation devices. These are items of safety equipment for crew members and workmen when employed over or near water under favorable conditions and properly supervised. Such PFDs are not normally approved for use on recreational boats, but may be so authorized in limited specific circumstances; when so authorized, they may be carried in lieu of other type devices.

PFD REQUIREMENTS BY BOAT SIZES

Recreational boats *less than 16 feet in length* (and canoes and kayaks of any length) must have on board at least one approved personal flotation device of Type I, II, III, or IV for each person on board.

Recreational boats *16 feet or more in length* (except canoes and kayaks) must have on board at least one approved personal flotation device of Type I, II, or III for each

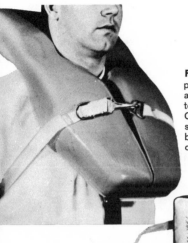

FIG. 311 The "bib" style of life preserver of approved design is acceptable on all classes of motorboats used for any purpose. Certain older models without the slit down the front may no longer be counted toward the legal requirements.

FIG. 312 Buoyant cushions have been the most widely used personal flotation devices on smaller boats. It is expected, however, that these will be eliminated as primary lifesaving equipment, but will be allowed on larger craft as a "throwable" item in addition to the required "wearable" devices.

person on board. Note that *buoyant cushions are no longer acceptable* as the basic type of PFD for craft of this size.

Recreational boats *16 feet or more in length* must comply with the above paragraph and *in addition* must have on board at least one Type IV "throwable" PFD.

Size of PFD

Where the style of PFD that is carried comes in sizes, such as adult and children's life preservers, and the three sizes of buoyant vests, the PFD used to meet the requirements of the regulations must be of an "appropriate" size for the person for whom it is intended.

Stowage of PFDs

The regulations are very specific about the stowage of personal flotation devices. Any required Type I, II, or III PFD must be "readily accessible." Any Type IV PFD that is required to be on board must be "immediately available." These rules are strictly enforced.

The PFDs must also be "in serviceable condition."

Equivalents

Personal flotation devices manufactured before the 1973 regulations will not be marked as to PFD Type. The equivalents in older terminology which are acceptable to the regulations are as follows:

Type I—Life preserver
Type II—Buoyant vest or wearable special purpose water safety buoyant device.
Type III—Wearable special purpose water safety buoyant device.
Type IV—Buoyant cushion, life ring buoy, or throwable special purpose water safety buoyant device.

Exceptions

A person in a canoe or kayak that is enclosed by a deck and spray skirt is exempted from the PFD requirement provided that he is wearing a vest-type lifesaving device that meets certain specifications in the regulations.

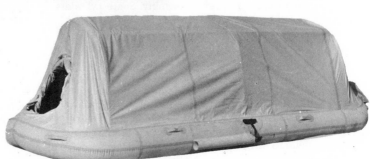

FIG. 314 This buoyant cushion is not in "good and serviceable condition" as required by Coast Guard regulations. It will not be counted toward the legal minimum requirements. Items such as this generally cannot be repaired and must be replaced.

FIG. 313 Special purpose water safety buoyant devices are produced in a wide variety of designs, including sport vests, water skiing vests, hunters' jackets, and others. Check carefully for a USCG approval number before purchasing any such device for use on a boat.

FIG. 315 In northern areas, survival times "over the side" are severely reduced by the cold temperatures of the water. Life rafts, preferably with a canopy, furnish protection that life preservers cannot provide from the elements.

FIG. 316 Hand-portable fire extinguishers using a dry powdered chemical as the extinguishing agent are widely used on boats. Such units must have a pressure indicator to show their readiness for use. (Certain exceptions permit the continued use of some older models without pressure gauges.)   Peter Smyth Photo

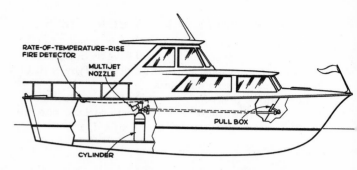

FIG. 317 Larger craft powered by inboard engines, particularly those using gasoline as a fuel, are often fitted with a built-in CO-2 fire extinguishing system. This is actuated automatically by temperature-rise detectors or it may be operated manually.

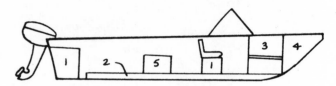

FIG. 318 Small outboard craft (not carrying passengers for hire) may or may not be required to have a fire extinguisher. Any one or more of the above construction features, see text for identification, will require one B-I fire extinguisher on board.

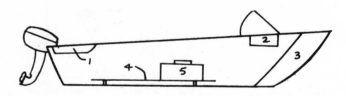

FIG. 319 The construction features identified above, see text for explanation of numbers, do **not**, in themselves, require that a fire extinguisher be carried—but one is still desirable for safety.

Cold weather areas

Boatmen who use colder northern waters should consider the purchase of a life raft to supplement other life-saving gear and increase the chances of survival offshore. A raft with a canopy provides the best protection.

FIRE EXTINGUISHERS

All hand-portable fire extinguishers and semiportable and fixed fire extinguishing systems must be of a type that has been approved by the Coast Guard. Such approvals are published in the pamphlet "Equipment Lists"—CG-190—with changes in the daily Federal Register.

All fire extinguishers and extinguishing systems approved for use on boats will have a metallic nameplate attached with information as to the manufacturer, type, and capacity. For those manufactured between 1962 and 1965, the nameplate must contain the wording "Marine Type USCG Type _____ Size _____"; those made since 1965 must have the above label plus "Approval No. 162.068/_____." (See below for information on "type" and "size").

Kinds of extinguishers

Fire extinguishers for boats are described in terms of their contents, the actual extinguishing agent.

Dry Chemical—This type of extinguisher is widely used because of its convenience and relative low cost. These have an advantage over other types in that they may be quickly "recharged" by screwing another cylinder onto the discharge nozzle and valve assembly. Spare cylinders may be carried on board for increased safety.

The cylinder contains a dry chemical in powdered form together with a propellant gas under pressure. Coast Guard regulations now require that such extinguishers be equipped with a gauge or indicator to show that normal gas pressure exists within the extinguisher. (Some older models do not have indicators and must be checked by very careful weighing. Such extinguishers must have been manufactured before 1 June 1965 to be acceptable, but may continue to be carried if they are in good and serviceable condition.)

Carbon dioxide—Some boats carry portable carbon dioxide (CO_2) extinguishers; such units are advantageous as they are the only type to leave no messy residue to clean up after use, and they cannot cause harm to the interior of engines as other types may do. This type may be used where a fixed system is installed in an engine compartment. Such a system may be operated either manually or automatically by heat-sensitive detectors.

Carbon dioxide extinguishers consist of a cylinder containing this gas under high pressure, a valve, and a properly designed discharge nozzle at the end of a short hose. The state of charge of a CO_2 extinguisher can only be checked by weighing the cylinder and comparing this figure with the one stamped on or near the valve. See page 210 for further details on the maintenance of CO_2 extinguishers.

Vapor systems—Other chemical vapors with a fire extinguishing action are available. Halon 1301 is a colorless, odorless gas that stops fire instantly by chemical action. It is heavier than air and sinks to lower parts of the bilge. Humans can tolerate a 7% concentration, more than enough to fight fire, for several minutes. It is used in built-in systems actuated manually or automatically; additional tanks can be carried to restore protection after use.

Foam—Fire extinguishers using chemical foam are legally acceptable on boats, but this type is rarely used as they leave a residue that is difficult to clean up after use and may require a partial engine disassembly.

Foam extinguishers are not pressurized before use and do not require tests for leakage. Such units contain water and must be protected from freezing. Foam extinguishers should be discharged and recharged annually.

Non-acceptable types—Vaporizing-liquid extinguishers, such as those containing carbontetrachloride and chlorobromomethane, are effective in fighting fires but produce highly toxic gases. They are *not* approved for use on motorboats and should NOT be carried as excess equipment because of their danger to the health or even life of a user in a confined space.

Classification of extinguishers

Fires are classified in three categories, A, B, and C, according to the general type of material being burned; see page 178. Fire extinguishers are similarly classified as to "type" and in addition are placed in size groups, I (the smallest) through V.*

The primary fire hazard on boats results from flammable liquids and so type "B" extinguishers are specified. (Some "B" extinguishers have adequate or limited effectiveness on other classes of fires; some should *not* be used on other types of fires, such as foam extinguishers on class "C" electrical fires.) Only the two smaller sizes, I and II, are hand portable, size III is a semi-portable fire extinguishing system, and sizes IV and V are too large for consideration here.

The type and size classifications for various extinguishing agents are shown in Table 3-1, page 64(a).

Requirements on Boats

Fire extinguisher requirements are prescribed in terms of the four "classes" of boats as established in the regulations which implemented the Motorboat Act of 1940.

Class A and 1 boats must have at least one type B-I hand portable fire extinguisher, except that boats of these classes propelled by outboard motors, not carrying passengers for hire *and* of such open construction that there can be no entrapment of explosive or flammable gases or vapors, need not carry an extinguisher.

A fire extinguisher is required on outboard boats under 26 feet in length if *one or more* of the following conditions exist, see fig. 318.

    1. Closed compartment under thwarts or seats in which portable fuel tanks may be stored.

    2. Double bottoms *not* sealed to the hull, or which are not *completely* filled with flotation material.

    3. Closed living spaces.

    4. Closed storage compartments in which combustible or flammable materials are stowed.

    5. Permanently installed fuel tanks. (To avoid being considered as "permanently installed," tanks must not be physically attached in such a manner that they cannot be lifted out with reasonable ease for filling off the boat; the size of the tank in gallons is *not* a specific criteria for determining whether it is a "portable" or a "permanently installed" tank.)

The following conditions do *not,* of themselves, require that fire extinguishers be carried, see fig. 319.

    1. Bait wells.

    2. Glove compartments.

    3. Buoyant flotation material.

    4. Open slatted flooring.

    5. Ice chests.

Class 2 boats must carry at least *two B-I* approved hand portable fire extinguishers, *or* at least *one B-II* unit.

Class 3 craft must carry at least *three B-I* approved hand extinguishers, *or* at least *one B-II* unit *plus* one B-I unit.

Boats with fixed extinguisher systems in the engine compartment may have the above minimum requirement for their size reduced by one B-I unit. The fixed system must meet Coast Guard specifications.

Exemptions—Motorboats propelled by outboard motors, while engaged in a previously arranged and announced race (and such boats designed solely for racing, while engaged in operations incidental to preparing for racing) are exempted by Coast Guard regulations from any requirements to carry fire extinguishers.

Keeping Safe

Don't merely purchase and mount fire extinguishers, and then forget all about them. All types require some maintenance and checking; see page 210 for guidance in keeping up the level of fire protection you gain when first installing new extinguishers.

All members of your regular "crew," and to a lesser extent any guests that may be aboard, should know both the location and operation of all fire extinguishers.

BACKFIRE FLAME CONTROL

Every inboard gasoline engine installed in a motorboat must be equipped with an acceptable means of backfire flame control (with certain quite limited exceptions to be discussed below). Such a device is commonly called a

FIG. 320 With certain quite minor and technical exceptions, a gasoline engine used on a boat must be equipped with a "flame arrestor." This metal grid over the air intake to the carburetor prevents the exit of backfire flames into the engine compartment.

"flame arrestor" and must meet specific Coast Guard specifications to be approved. Accepted models will be listed by manufacturer's number in equipment lists or will have an approval number marked on the grid housing.

In use, flame arrestors must be secured to the air intake of the carburetor with an air-tight connection, have clean elements, and have no separation of the grids that would permit flames to pass through.

Exceptions

There are four categories of engine installations that are not required to have an approved flame arrestor, but these will actually include very few craft. The exempted situations are (1) Engines installed prior to 25 April 1940. (2) Installations made prior to 19 November 1952 which meet

*These USCG classifications B-I, B-II, etc., are not to be confused with Underwriters Laboratories classification 1-B, 2-B, 10-B, etc., which may also appear on extinguishers. The UL classification provides a better guide to extinguisher capacity, but they have not been written into USCG regulations as yet.

the lesser requirements then in effect and which are still in a good and serviceable condition. (3) Engines of a design inherently free from any backfire flames; each design must be tested and specifically approved by the Coast Guard. (4) Installations such that any backfire flames would be vented outside the vessel in such a manner as to not be dangerous to the craft; no formal inspection and specific approval is required.

VENTILATION REQUIREMENTS

All motorboats, except open boats, which use fuel having a flashpoint of 110°F. or less—gasoline but not diesel—must have at least two ventilation ducts for every engine and fuel tank compartment. These ducts must be fitted with cowls or the equivalent for the efficient removal of explosive or flammable vapors. (Power exhaust blowers are desirable but are not legally required.)

Additional information on bilge ventilation will be found on pages 604 to 607.

OTHER REQUIRED EQUIPMENT

Additional items of equipment required by Coast Guard regulations to be on board a boat include whistles and bells. As with other equipment, the requirements are graduated with the size of the craft when used on inland waters.

Whistle

Motorboats operating on waters governed by the Inland, Great Lakes, and Western Rivers Rules of the Road must be equipped with an "efficient" whistle or other sound producing mechanical device (horn) as follows:

Class A — None required.
Class 1 — Mouth, hand, or power operated; capable of producing a blast audible at a distance of at least one-half mile.*
Class 2 — Hand or power operated; capable of producing a blast audible at a distance of at least one mile.*
Class 3 — Power operated; capable of producing a blast audible at a distance of at least one mile.*
*All blasts to be of at least two seconds duration.

The term "efficient" is nowhere defined in the laws or regulations. It has generally been held by enforcement authorities and the courts that the device must be suitable for the boat or vessel on which it is used—a horn (or bell) suitable for a small motorboat would not be suitable, and

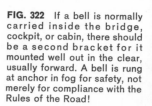

FIG. 322 If a bell is normally carried inside the bridge, cockpit, or cabin, there should be a second bracket for it mounted well out in the clear, usually forward. A bell is rung at anchor in fog for safety, not merely for compliance with the Rules of the Road!

thus not "efficient," for a large yacht, a ship, or a noisy tugboat.

Bell

Motorboats operated on waters subject to the above Rules of the Road must carry an "efficient" fog bell if they are 26 or more feet in length (boats of Classes 2 and 3).

Exceptions

Motorboats engaged in a race which has been previously arranged or announced, or engaged in operations incidental to preparing for such a race, need not carry a whistle or a bell.

May be needed although not required

Despite their not being required by USCG regulations to carry a whistle or bell, smaller boats of Class A or 1 are *not exempt* from sounding the whistle and fog signals required by the Rules of the Road; see Chapter 5.

Requirements of the International Rules

Watercraft of any size operated on waters governed by the International Rules of the Road, see page 38, must be provided with the whistle, bell, and fog horn required by those Rules. No range of audibility is specified, only that the device be "efficient."

FIG. 321 All motorboats 16 feet or more in length must be equipped with a "whistle" or horn. The type of device—mouth, hand, or power operated—and its audibility range varies with the size classification of the boat. All must be capable of producing blasts of at least two seconds duration. Shown here are a mouth-operated whistle, a freon-operated horn, and an electric horn.

FIG. 323 Navigation lights are part of the equipment requirements from the implementing regulations of the Motorboat Act. These are covered in Chapter 4 together with the lights for all types of vessels.

FIG. 324 Some boats use liquified petroleum (LP) gas for cooking, and possibly for heating. Such installations are acceptable on recreational craft (strict safety precautions in installation and use must be observed), but these are prohibited on boats carrying passengers for hire.

NAVIGATION LIGHTS AND DAY SHAPES

The requirements for navigation lights for "boats" are currently contained in regulations from the 1940 Motorboat Act. Essentially the same requirements, however, also appear in the Inland and other U.S. Rules of the Road, and so lights for boats are considered in Chapter 4 together with the navigation lights and day shapes of larger vessels.

Motorboats are permitted to carry the lights prescribed for them by the International Rules of the Road while operating in inland waters, but *not* vice versa. The International lights for small craft will also be found in Chapter 4.

EQUIPMENT FOR COMMERCIAL OPERATION

Boats used for carrying six or fewer passengers for hire, or for commercial fishing, are subject to different requirements for lifesaving equipment than recreational craft. These "commercial uninspected vessels" are subject to the Motorboat Act of 1940 and Coast Guard regulations issued under the authority of that Act. Also covered by these regulations are sailing and non-self-propelled vessels carrying six or fewer passengers for hire.

All non-recreational craft less than 40 feet in length, *not* carrying passengers for hire, such as commercial fishing boats, must have on board at least one life preserver, buoyant vest, or special purpose water safety buoyant device of a suitable size for each person on board. "Suitable size"

means that sufficient children's lifesaving devices (medium or small, as appropriate) must be carried in addition to adult sizes.

All vessels carrying passengers for hire (six or fewer), and all other vessels subject to the MBA/40 which are over 40 feet in length, must have at least one life preserver of a suitable size for each person on board.

Each vessel 26 or more feet in length must also carry at least one life ring buoy in addition to the life preservers or other wearable lifesaving devices required.

All lifesaving equipment must be in serviceable condition; wearable devices must be readily accessible and devices to be thrown must be immediately available.

Use of LP gas fuel

Vessels carrying passengers for hire are prohibited from using liquidified petroleum gases and certain other flammable liquids for cooking, heating, or lighting purposes.

More than six passengers

Motorboats carrying more than six passengers for hire are subject to a separate Act and set of Coast Guard regulations. These craft must be "inspected" and the certificate resulting from such action will specify minimum equipment such as lifesaving gear and fire extinguishers; see page 47.

FIG. 325 A sailboat without installed mechanical power and no detachable motor mounted will be subject to the regulations of the Federal Boat Safety Act of 1971 when issued. Federal regulations preempt State and local requirements for safety equipment unless specific exemptions have been granted for waters subject to unique hazards.

FIG. 326 Every skipper must understand that merely meeting Coast Guard requirements for equipment will not ensure the safety of his boat. Additional items are needed on board, some of which may be required by state laws.

FIG. 327 The Courtesy Motorboat Examination program of the Coast Guard Auxiliary lists equipment requirements over and above the legal minimums. These requirements are an excellent guide to all boat owners in equipping their craft for full safety.

FIG. 329 It is desirable on all but the smallest boats to carry two or more anchors. These may be of different types, or of the same type but of different sizes, to meet varying situations.

FIG. 328 Distress flares for night use **and** smoke signals for day use should be aboard all craft to aid in obtaining assistance in an emergency. Other devices, such as signalling mirrors and orange flags, are also available and should be considered.

FIG. 330 Small electric bilge pumps are found on most boats, but these should be backed-up with a hand-operated pump for emergency use. Larger craft may also be fitted with a high-capacity pump belt-driven from a main engine.

EQUIPMENT FOR SAILBOATS

Sailboats, including those without any form of mechanical propulsion, are "boats" as defined in the Federal Boat Safety Act of 1971. These craft will be subject to the equipment requirements of that Act when implementing regulations are issued. In the meanwhile, they must carry lights, fog horns, and bells to meet the requirements of the applicable Rules of the Road. They may also be liable for compliance with any local or State requirements for lifesaving or other equipment until these are preempted by the new Federal regulations.

SUMMARY

The federal equipment requirements for non-commercial motorboats are summarized, by class of boat, in Table 3-2, page 64(a). To these must be added any applicable state requirements.

FIG. 331 Coast Guard regulations do not require any lengths of line aboard a boat for use in docking, anchoring, etc., but these are essential for the operation of any craft. The number and length will vary with the size and use of the boat. Some state laws require an anchor and line of appropriate size and length.

Additional Equipment for Safety

In view of the many Federal regulations for mandatory safety equipment on boats, any newcomer to this activity might be excused for thinking that he would be fully set to go if he ordered his new craft with "all equipment required by regulations." Actually, such is far from the real situation if one considers only the existing federal requirements. The problem may be ameliorated somewhat if state requirements are added in, but their lack of uniformity clouds the picture.

No quarrel can be made with the statutory and regulatory federal requirements; the sole problem is that they stop too soon. Even the smallest rowboat requires at least one length of line with which to make fast to a pier, or mooring, or anchor; and a 40-footer will need some six to eight dock and anchor lines—yet none are required by Coast Guard regulations. Only the most foolhardy and ignorant venture far from shore without some sort of distress signalling equipment—but again none are required by federal law or regulation.

These are but two of the more obvious examples of *additional equipment required for safe operations*—with the emphasis on both operations and safety. This section will consider the above items and others, but can establish no firm, fixed list for all skippers. Each boat owner must carefully examine his own needs and equip his craft accordingly.

Possible liability

Another factor that cannot be ignored in considering what equipment is truly needed is the possibility of liability in case of an accident. It is a mistake to think that the boating equipment specified by the government is the only equipment that you are *legally* bound to have aboard. The boatman must consider as well the far-reaching rules of negligence, as developed over the years in court cases. Technically, negligence is the unintentional breach of a legal duty to exercise a reasonable standard of care, thereby causing damage to someone. More simply stated, it is the failure to conduct oneself as a *reasonable* man would have under the circumstances. If, for example, our reasonable man would have carried charts, you may be liable to an injured party for an accident arising out of not having them available. If he would have had an anchor, compass, flares, lines, tools and spare parts, etc., you may be held liable for not having them when needed. It is no defense to argue that no regulations require you to carry them on board.

Sources of information

The U.S. Coast Guard Auxiliary has a program of voluntary Courtesy Motorboat Examination; see pages 191-192 and 599-600. The requirements and recommendations of this program make an excellent list of items and actions so desirable as almost to be termed "essential."

ITEMS REQUIRED FOR USCGAUX DECAL

For a boat to receive the Auxiliary's Courtesy Motorboat Examination (CME) decal, it must, of course, first meet all of the legal requirements of the Coast Guard regulations derived from the 1971 Boat Safety Act. Also, some of the legal requirements are "beefed up" and made more stringent; additional items and conditions are imposed.

Personal flotation devices

An approved personal flotation device of the appropriate type is required for *each berth* on the boat; this may be more than the legal requirement of one PFD for each person on board at the time of a check. In addition, a boat with no bunks, or with only one, must still have a minimum of two lifesaving devices aboard.

Fire extinguishers

The Auxiliary standards for fire extinguishers on smaller boats are likewise more demanding than the law or regulations. Although a boat under 26 feet in length that is of "open construction," or one which has a built-in fire extinguisher system, need not carry an additional hand portable extinguisher to meet the legal minimum, it must have one for award of a CME decal.

Additional fire extinguishers—The prudent skipper considers whether he will be adequately safe with only the minimum required number of fire extinguishers. An im-

FIG. 332 Despite the convenience and widespread use of modern electronic depth sounders, an old-fashioned hand-held lead line is often handy to have aboard, such as for checking depths all around the sides of a craft that has gone aground.

portant safety factor is the ready availability of an extinguisher close at hand when a fire emergency suddenly bursts forth. An extinguisher should be considered for *each* of the following locations: (1) the helm, where there is always someone when underway; (2) the engine compartment; (3) the galley; and (4) adjacent to the skipper's bunk, for quick reach at night. On smaller craft, the legally required minimum, or even the USCG Aux requirements, may not be enough to provide one at all desirable locations.

Navigation lights

The law does not require that a boat operated only in the daylight have navigation lights, but these must be fitted and in good working order to meet the Auxiliary's standards.

Distress signals

At least one distress flare must be on a boat for it to pass the CME check, and preferably there should be several. Other emergency signalling equipment that is desirable includes smoke signals (better for day use than flares), dye marker (to aid aerial searches), a signalling mirror, and an orange flag or the new "Canadian" signal described on page 87 and fig. 552.

Anchor and line

An anchor of suitable type and weight together with line of appropriate size and length is required for the CME decal. This is a valuable safety item should the engine fail and the craft be in danger of drifting or being blown into hazardous waters.

Smaller craft requirements

All Class A boats must have an oar or paddle, a manual pump or bailer, and a whistle meeting the legal requirements for Class 1 boats.

Installation standards

In addition to requiring the above items of equipment, the CG Aux program has established standards for the installation of fuel systems, electrical systems, and galley stoves. Information on gasoline fuel systems and electrical systems will be found in pages 196-201.

FIG. 333 As determined by their normal use and area of operations, all craft should carry an emergency supply of drinking water, and possibly some emergency food supplies. These should be checked periodically and replaced if they show signs of deterioration.

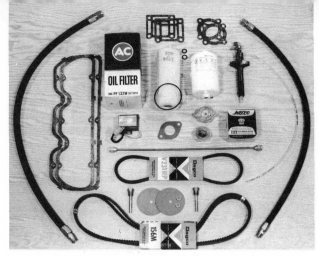

FIG. 334 The set of tools and spare parts carried on board must be individually tailored to the craft, her equipment, her use, and the capabilities of her crew. An item for all boats is a spare bulb of each type used in the navigation lights.

The Auxiliary requires that a galley stove be of a marine type and be installed so as to present no hazard to the craft and its occupants. Any common fuel is acceptable except gasoline and derivatives or distillates of naphtha and benzene. LP gas stoves or heaters which use an integral fuel container or one which fastens directly to the appliance are not acceptable for award of the decal.

Equipment Recommended by the USCGAux

The CME checklist also contains a number of items recommended for the proper operation of a craft or for its safety, items beyond those required for award of the decal. The actual selections of items from this list will vary with the size and use of the particular boat involved.

This list of generally recommended items includes many that are required for "Facilities" and "Operational Facilities," the boats of members of the Auxiliary that have been brought to higher standards for use in their programs of search and rescue, regatta patrolling, etc.

Anchors

The carrying of a second anchor is recommended in addition to the one required to pass the CME check. This additional anchor may be a lighter one for non-emergency daytime use. Chapter 6 of this book in general, and page 99 in particular, provide guidance as to the selection of the proper size of anchor in several varying styles.

It is recommended that a length of chain be used between the anchor and the nylon line. Shackles used on either end of this chain should have their pins secured with safety wire.

Bilge pumps

One or more mechanical or electrical bilge pumps are recommended for all boats, and these should, of course, always be in good working order. Motorboats more than 26 feet in length should have at least two means of pumping bilges; and their bilges must be clean and free of any oil or grease; wood chips or any other debris that could clog pumps and limber holes must be removed.

Lines

Every boat should have mooring (dock) lines suitable in length and size to that particular craft. These should be of

FIG. 335 Windshield wipers, manually or electrically operated, are essential for the good vision of the helmsman despite rain or spray. When spray, especially that from salt water, is intermittent, fresh water washers on the windshield help in keeping it clean.

several different lengths for convenience in use. No generalization can be made as to the lengths, but the diameter should roughly correspond to that of storm or working anchor rodes.

A heaving line of light construction is desirable if the craft is large enough to require the use of heavy mooring lines. The use of polypropylene line, or other material that is brightly colored and will float, is recommended for this purpose.

Life rings

A ring life buoy with a length of light line attached is recommended for rendering assistance to swimmers or accident victims in the water. This can also be used to float a heavier line across to a stranded boat. If of an approved type, this ring buoy may count as the required "throwable" PFD for boats of Classes 2 and 3. A water light (a device which automatically lights up in contact with the water) enhances the use of a ring buoy at night.

Operational equipment

Recommended operational equipment includes fenders in appropriate sizes and numbers for the craft involved. Not only will these be used in normal berthing, they are also necessary if two craft must make fast to each other while underway or at anchor. A boathook will be found very useful for fending off, placing lines over piles, picking up pennants of mooring buoys, recovering articles dropped over the side, and many other uses.

A searchlight—installed on larger craft, hand-held on smaller boats—serves both as a routine aid in night piloting and as an emergency signalling device. A multicell flashlight or electric lantern can serve these functions, but not so well as a searchlight.

Navigation publications and charts should be carried aboard boats in accordance with their use; see Chapters 17 and 18 for further details. Compasses are discussed in detail in Chapters 13 and 14; here we need merely to note that one is desirable on almost any boat for emergency if not regular use. Piloting and plotting instruments are covered in Chapter 19.

A hand-held lead line is a useful back-up to the more complicated electronic depth sounder; one is particularly handy when one must probe around a stranded boat in search of deeper water.

An emergency supply of drinking water—and perhaps food, too—should be carried on all craft. It may never be used, but when needed it can literally be a "lifesaver." Supplies of this nature should be periodically freshened or replaced to ensure acceptable quality when needed. Distilled water should be carried for periodic replenishment of any storage batteries on board; this can, of course, serve as an emergency source of drinking water.

A first aid kit is an essential item of safety equipment; see pages 211-214. The kit should be accompanied with a manual or separate book of instructions.

The list of tools and spare parts to be carried aboard must be developed by each skipper individually for his craft. The items will be governed by the type of boat, its normal use, and the capabilities of the crew to use them. An item required on USCGAux Facilities is one or more spare bulbs for the navigation lights. Items for all craft include simple tools, plugs, cloth, screws, nails, wire, tape, and other objects for the execution of emergency repairs at sea. Mechanical and electrical spares will be highly individualized by the particular boat and skipper.

Further Operational and Safety Items

A sea anchor or drogue, see pages 165-166, is an essential item of safety equipment for boats operating in many areas, but one is not legally required. As noted above, life rafts, preferably with a canopy, are much needed safety items in many waters.

Electric windshield wipers are excellent items of equipment when running into rainy or rough weather; safety is

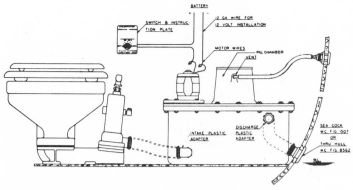

FIG. 337 The conscientious skipper does his part in keeping our waters clean. Pollution control equipment of several basic types is rapidly becoming standard equipment on new boats. The variations in state and local laws do, however, confuse the situation at present.

often much improved by their availability and use. The installation of washers that squirt fresh water on windshields will help greatly when spray, particularly of salt water, is intermittently received over the bow.

Many electronic items that will add to operational safety are described in Chapter 25. These include radiotelephones, electronic depth sounders, radio direction finders (RDFs), and fuel vapor detectors for engine rooms and bilges of gasoline-powered craft. Alarm systems are available to alert the skipper of dangerous conditions of engine overheating, low oil pressure, or high water in the bilge. Electric bilge exhaust blowers will add to the safety of the required ventilation systems for all engine and fuel tank compartments. All of these are in the "desirable," or even "necessary," category. Less vital items are discussed in the next major subdivision of this chapter.

Pollution control equipment is rapidly moving from the operationally desirable to the necessary category. All skippers should be looking forward to their needs and problems in this area.

Cleaning gear may not be "glamorous," but it is certainly operational. Specific lists will vary from boat to boat, but all may be expected to contain a swab (mop), bucket, sponges, chamois, metal polish and rags, and similar items.

Sailboats

Sailboats without mechanical power, either installed or detachable, are now required to have personal flotation devices for each person on board; the type of PFD varies with the size of the craft. They are not checked as a part of the Courtesy Motorboat Examination program. Such craft over 16 feet in length are, however, eligible to become Auxiliary Facilities and must meet certain prescribed standards. These requirements can serve as a guide to all owners of sailing craft as to desirable safety equipment above the legal requirements.

Sailing Facilities under 26 feet in length are required to have one B-I hand fire extinguisher and larger craft must have on board two such units. These sailboats must meet the CME standard of one approved lifesaving device on board for each berth, with a minimum of two such devices. Further, such craft must meet all standards for motorboats other than those relating to propulsion machinery, fuel systems, and ventilation of related compartments. This would leave in the requirements such items as an anchor with line, distress flare, galley stove installation and general electrical system—all matters appropriate to the safe operation of any sailboat.

FIG. 336 Electric-motor-driven blowers for bilge vents are not required by regulations but are actually essential for safety, especially when starting up engines with no wind across the deck to provide natural ventilation.

FIG. 338 An automatic steering mechanism — often called an "autopilot" — offers much convenience on long open-water passages. Provided that a proper lookout is maintained, use of such a device increases safety through the elimination of fatigue.

FIG. 340 An anchor windlass on the foredeck can supply mechanical power for breaking the anchor out of the bottom and raising it to the surface. These are most useful if the anchor is drawn up into a hawsehole rather than being lifted onto the deck.

Equipment for Convenience and Comfort

Many, but certainly not all, of the items of *equipment for convenience and comfort* fall into the electronic or electrical categories. These items are covered more fully in Chapter 25 and include navigational aids such as automatic radio direction finders, radar, and sophisticated positioning equipment including loran, decca, and others. Speedometers and logs will provide speed and distance information that will assist in piloting. An automatic steering mechanism—the so-called "autopilot"—adds greatly to the convenience of cruising. Loudhailers and intercom systems increase the convenience of operating or living aboard larger boats. Twin engine craft will benefit from engine synchronization indicators, and even more from equipment that will automatically do the function of matching engine speeds.

Electrical equipment items include pressure fresh water systems, water heaters, electrical refrigeration, showers with drain pumps, plus heating and/or air conditioning equipment.

All of these demand increased electrical power from the boat's system, either AC or DC. Auxiliary generating plants will permit the use of "shore-type" heavy-drain equipment when underway or at anchor. Inverters are very useful items to permit the operation of moderate-drain AC equipment without the noise of running a gasoline or diesel engine driven generator. Marine converters will supply the needed DC power without operation of the main engine if AC power is available; these will keep the boat's storage batteries at full charge when in port.

Outside the electrical-electronic field, equipment items for convenience and comfort are numerous and varied. Many skippers will want to have a boarding/swimming ladder for ease in going over the side and returning. A platform across the stern of larger boats is a great convenience for swimming or using a dinghy. The dinghy itself, perhaps with sails or a small outboard motor, may well be classed as an item of convenience equipment.

Fresh water making equipment—stills to convert salt water to potable water—will often add immeasurably to a boat's cruising endurance. Stabilizers are now available for medium and larger motor yachts to eliminate much of the rolling from offshore cruising.

An anchor windlass on the foredeck will remove a major part of the physical labor involved in "getting the hook up" —it may even put this chore back into the category of duties of the "first mate."

Weather instruments — barometer, thermometer, and anemometer, and perhaps a hygrometer for measuring the relative humidity—will add to the interest of boating. With study and practice, they can add to the safety, too, of a craft and its crew. A recording barograph will provide interesting permanent records of atmospheric, and thus weather, changes.

The spare parts inventory of a boat can be expanded beyond the limits of necessity into the area of convenience. Carrying spare propellors, and even shafts, can often greatly reduce delays at a strange port away from home if these major components should become damaged. These may be beyond the capability of the crew to install, but their ready availability can often reduce repair times from days to hours.

Diving gear, either of the simple mask and snorkle style or the more complex SCUBA type, can make boating in many areas more interesting and can at times be of real value in making underwater inspections and repairs. "Wet suits" may be required for colder water areas.

Boating Insurance

Insurance coverage is not something ordinarily thought of as boating "equipment," but to a prudent skipper it is as much a part of the outfitting of his craft as the compass or anchor.

Various coverages of marine insurance include those against loss of or damage to the boat itself, its hull, machinery, sails, and equipment; protection against liability for damages to the persons or property of others; and medical payments to cover the care and treatment of the owner or guests resulting from accidents on board. Other coverages can include boat trailers and the land transportation of the craft itself.

It is beyond the scope of this book to go into details of marine insurance, but the boat owner is reminded that an insurance policy can be one of his most valuable items of "equipment." Consult a reputable insurance agent for specific information on coverages applicable to your craft and her use—better yet, talk with two or three agents for proposals on coverages and quotations of rates.

FIG. 339 A platform across the stern of a motorboat is a convenience item in connection with either swimming or the use of a dinghy. Some installations are fixed in place; others fold up against the transom when not in use.

TABLE 3-1

Hand Portable types	Foam (minimum gallons)	Carbon Dioxide (minimum pounds)	Dry Chemical (minimum pounds)	Freon (minimum pounds)
B–I	1¼	4	2	2½
B–II	2½	15	10	(none)

TABLE 3-2

Minimum Required Equipment

EQUIPMENT	CLASS A (Less than 16 feet)	CLASS 1 (16 feet to less than 26 feet)	CLASS 2 (26 feet to less than 40 feet)	CLASS 3 (40 feet to not more than 65 feet)
BACK-FIRE FLAME ARRESTER	One approved device on each carburetor of all gasoline engines installed after April 25, 1940, except outboard motors.			
VENTILATION	At least two ventilator ducts fitted with cowls or their equivalent for the purpose of properly and efficiently ventilating the bilges of every engine and fuel-tank compartment of boats constructed or decked over after April 25, 1940, using gasoline or other fuel of a flashpoint less than 110°F.			
BELL	None.*	None.*	One, which when struck, produces a clear, bell-like tone of full round characteristics.	
PERSONAL FLOTATION DEVICES	One Type I, II, III, or IV for each person.	One Type I, II, or III for each person on board or being towed on water skiis, etc., plus one Type IV available to be thrown.		
WHISTLE	None.*	One hand, mouth, or power operated, audible at least ½ mile.	One hand or power operated, audible at least 1 mile.	One power operated, audible at least 1 mile.
FIRE EXTINGUISHER— PORTABLE — When NO fixed fire extinguishing system is installed in machinery space(s).	At least One B–I type approved hand portable fire extinguisher. (Not required on outboard motorboat less than 26 feet in length and not carrying passengers for hire if the construction of such motorboats will not permit the entrapment of explosive or flammable gases or vapors.)		At least Two B–I type approved hand portable fire extinguishers; OR At least One B–II type approved hand portable fire extinguisher.	At least Three B–I type approved hand portable fire extinguishers; OR At least One B–I type Plus One B–II type approved hand portable fire extinguisher.
When fixed fire extinguishing system is installed in machinery space(s).	None.	None.	At least One B–I type approved hand portable fire extinguisher.	At least Two B–I type approved hand portable fire extinguishers; OR At least One B–II type approved hand portable fire extinguisher.
	Note: Dry Chemical and Carbon Dioxide (CO_2) are the most widely used types, in that order. The others, while acceptable, are seldom seen on boats.			
	Fire extinguishers manufactured after 1 January 1965 will be marked, "Marine Type USCG Type ―― Size ―― Approval No. 162.028/EX . . ."**			

*NOTE.—Not required by the Motorboat Act of 1940; however, the "Rules of the Road" require these vessels to sound proper signals.

**NOTE.—Toxic vaporizing-liquid type fire extinguishers, such as those containing carbon tetrachloride or chlorobromomethane, are not accepted as required approved extinguishers on uninspected vessels (private pleasure craft).

CHAPTER 4

RULES OF THE ROAD

Lights and Day Shapes

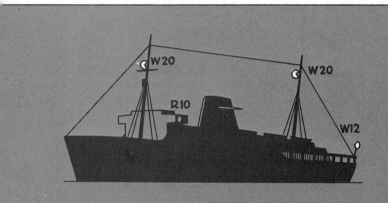

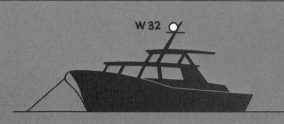

FIG. 401 The navigation lights shown by a vessel at night identify her as a water craft and give some indication of her type, size, and relative heading. (left) Lights are also used at night to indicate the status of a vessel. The single white light shown above signifies to another vessel that the boat is at anchor. This is often called a "riding light" to distinguish it from a "running light."

Nautical Rules of the Road are somewhat broader than their land counterparts. On the water, such sets of rules include not only the expected "keep to the right" and the "vessel to your right has the right-of-way" provisions, but they also cover many other matters related to safety of operations, principally through the avoidance of collisions.

Although requirements for navigation lights are included in regulations for "boats" as defined in the Federal Boat Safety Act of 1971, the various Rules of the Road prescribe lights for *all* vessels and thus those for boats will be considered together with lights for larger ships.

WHY NAVIGATION LIGHTS AND DAY SHAPES

On a vessel, *navigation lights* are lights shown of specified color (white, red, green, amber, blue), arc and range of visibility, and location as required by law and regulations. Their basic purpose is the prevention of collision by providing identificaton of a vessel and some information regarding her activities. Lights will indicate the relative heading of one vessel as seen from another, and may give some clue as to her size, special characteristics, and/or current operations. Most important is the information as to her relative orientation with respect to your vessel; a fact that must be known to determine who has the right-of-way.

Navigation lights are sometimes referred to as *running lights* (those shown under way) and *riding lights* (those shown while at anchor or moored), but this terminology is unofficial and does not appear in the Rules of the Road.

Day shapes are objects of specified shape, size, color, and placement on a vessel as required by law and regulations. They serve some of the same purposes by day that navigation lights do by night. In normal visibility situations, the relative aspect and motions of two vessels can be determined by observation and no day shapes are required. They are, however, used to indicate special situations, such as being anchored or engaged in fishing, and some conditions not detectable by eye, such as a sailboat with her sails up but engine also in use—as will be noted in Chapter 5, such a craft is regarded as a power-driven vessel and is not entitled to any of the right-of-way privileges of sailing craft merely because her sails are up.

SEQUENCE OF CONSIDERATION

As noted in Chapter 2, there are *three separate sets* of Rules of the Road currently in effect on U.S. waters, the Inland, Great Lakes, and Western Rivers Rules. For the sake of simplicity, these sets of Rules will be collectively referred to in this book as the "U.S. Rules," although this is not an official designation. Further, the boatman is faced with the applicability of the International Rules of the Road along the seacoasts outside of the boundary lines specified in page 31.

Because of their applicability to a greater number of

boatmen, the Inland Rules will be the primary consideration of this chapter. The Great Lakes and Western Rivers Rules will be discussed in terms of their differences with the basic provisions of the Inland Rules. This will in turn be followed by an explanation of the provisions of the International Rules of the Road regarding navigation lights and day shapes; this will be of particular interest to boatmen whose activities take them offshore along the coasts. The chapter is concluded with a review of the status of pending legislation that would extensively change the requirements for navigation lights and day shapes on the inland waters of the United States.

Regulations issued by state or local authorities on the topics of this chapter are too detailed and varying for consideration. Each skipper should check for those that will affect his boating.

The various sets of Rules of the Road also cover matters other than navigation lights and day shapes—such as right-of-way, whistle signals, fog signals, distress signals, etc.; these are the topics of Chapter 5.

Numbered "Rules"

All of the sets of Rules of the Road, except the Inland Rules, consist of various sections which are numbered as Rule 1, Rule 2, etc. (The Inland Rules consist of a series of numbered "Articles" which are essentially the same as "Rules.") This chapter will deal only with those Rules relating to navigation lights and day shapes.

While there is some parallelism in the contents and numbering of Rules and Articles in the various sets, this, unfortunately, is not complete and cannot be relied upon when going from one set to another. There is some hope for greater uniformity in the future, though, see page 66 or 88 for pending changes in the U.S. Rules.

Indication of references

Numbers and letters shown in brackets are references to the applicable Article or Rule.

DEFINITION OF TERMS

The verbatim U.S. Rules make considerable use of the term "steam vessel," but specifically state that the term includes any vessel propelled by machinery; this would, of course, include motorboats and auxiliary-engine driven sailboats. For the sake of clarity, in this chapter and Chapter 5, the phrase "power-driven vessel" will be used; this is the same, more inclusive phraseology that is used in the International Rules.

Sailing vessel—Every vessel which is under sail and is *not* being propelled by machinery is a *sailing vessel* for the purposes of the Rules of the Road.

Power-driven *(steam)* vessel—A vessel propelled by machinery, *whether or not she is also under sail,* is a *power-driven (steam) vessel.*

Underway—A vessel is *underway* when she is not at anchor, made fast to the shore, or aground.

Visible—Where the Rules require a navigation light to be visible for a stated distance, this visibility is understood to be on a "dark night with a clear atmosphere."

Arcs of visibility—"points"

With the exception of the International Rules, the arc of visibility of navigation lights is specified in terms of "points"—in the International Rules, both points and degrees are used. These "points" are the same units of angular measurement as used for compasses and bearings —see page 9 and pages 260 to 271. One point is equal to 11¼°. See Fig. 123.

Lights are generally 10-point (112½°), 12-point (135°), 20-point (225°), or 32-point (360° or all around the horizon). Lights *should not,* of course, show through any wider arc than that prescribed by the Rules. It must, however, be recognized that in most practical cases, especially on quite small craft, the arcs will not exactly conform to the requirements and combination red-and-green bow lights in particular may show over somewhat wider arcs than 10 points for each color.

The Inland Rules

The **Inland Rules of the Road** are applicable to all U.S. waters inside boundary lines established to limit the application of the International Rules of the Road—see page 31—*except* for waters specifically excluded and placed under the Great Lakes and Western Rivers Rules.

The Inland Rules consist of introductory material and 31 "Articles" numbered 1 through 32, less #4, containing the actual requirements, restrictions, etc. Not all Articles are applicable to the topics of this chapter; certain ones are covered in Chapter 5. With changes over the years, some sub-sections have been deleted without re-numbering the Rules as a whole; for example, there is no Article

FIG. 402 During the day, when lights would be ineffective, "day shapes" are used to indicate the special status of vessels. Other information provided at night by lights—type, size, and relative heading—can be determined in daylight by direct observation.

FIG. 403 The U.S. Inland Rules of the Road are written in terms of requirements for "steam vessels," but this is defined as including all vessels propelled by machinery of any type.

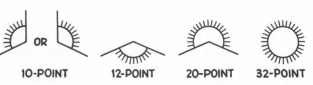

FIG. 404 The arc of visibility of navigation lights are specified in the Inland Rules in terms of "points." Each of these units of angular measurement equals 11¼°. A complete circle consists of 32 points.

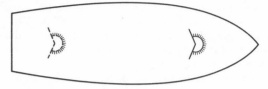

FIG. 405 Under the Inland Rules, all power-driven vessels carry a white forward light in the forepart of the vessel. This is a 20-point light, visible on ships for at least five miles and on motorboats for at least two miles. A sea-going vessel may also carry a similar light aft and higher.

15(b) although there is a 15(a), (c), etc., and there is now no Article 4 in the Inland Rules.

NAVIGATION LIGHTS

Navigation lights will be discussed for various categories and sizes of vessels in the sub-sections below; they are also summarized in Tables 4-3 and 4-4 in this chapter.

When lights are shown

Vessels are required to show the proper navigation lights from *sunset to sunrise* in all weathers, good and bad. During these times, no other lights which might be mistaken for navigation lights may be displayed. [Article 1]

Although not specifically provided for in the Inland Rules, nor prohibited by them, the prudent skipper does not hesitate to turn on his navigation lights during the day between sunrise and sunset under conditions of reduced visibility.

Lights for Power-driven Vessels Underway

Lights for power-driven vessels underway will be first considered from the viewpoint of "vessels," all waterborne vehicles other than sailing vessels and seaplanes on the water. Special provisions for "motorboats" will be considered separately.

Forward lights

A power-driven vessel, when underway, must carry in the forward part of the vessel (on or in front of the foremast if there is one), a white light showing over an unbroken arc of 20 points, from dead ahead to 2 points abaft the beam on either side. This white forward light must be visible at a distance of at least five miles. [Article 2(a)]

A *sea-going* power-driven vessel—one which goes into waters subject to the International Rules—*may,* while in waters of the Inland Rules, carry a second white light similar to the one described above. These two lights must be placed in line over the keel so that the after light will be at least 15 feet higher than the forward light, and their horizontal spacing must be greater than their difference in height above the hull. [2(e)]

Power-driven vessels, *except* sea-going vessels and ferryboats, *must* carry a central range of two white lights with the after light at least 15 feet higher than the forward

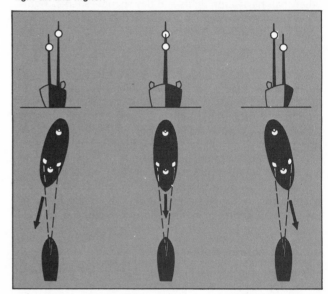

FIG. 406 The two white lights forming a central range on a vessel are an excellent indicator of her relative heading as seen from another vessel. These lights will normally be seen well before the colored side lights.

light. The forward light must meet the 20-point arc of visibility requirements of the light of Article 2(a); the after range light must be a 32-point light showing all around the horizon. This Article, 2(f), does not include a requirement as to the distance to which the after light must be seen.

Value of range lights. Range lights are a valuable aid in determining the relative heading of another vessel when she is first sighted at night. These white lights are both brighter and higher than the side lights, and consequently they normally will be seen well before the colored light or lights can be detected and read for their meaning.

The relative location of the two range lights will be the key. Should they be seen one directly over the other, the other vessel is headed *directly toward* the observer and danger of collision exists. Should the lower forward range light be seen to the right or left of the higher light, the other vessel is on an oblique course and the angle can be roughly gauged by the horizontal separation between the lights. See fig. 406.

FIG. 407 Any vessel or craft not showing a white light visible from astern must, under the Inland Rules, carry a separate white 12-point light visible for two miles or more. This light must be at the stern and should be on the same level as the sidelights.

If the lower light is to the left of the upper one, the red port light of the other vessel should be visible or become visible later. This has particular significance as it means that the other vessel is in the observer's "danger zone" and has the right-of-way; see page 72.

Any change in the horizontal separation of the other vessel's range lights, together with any change in the relative bearing of the other ship or craft will provide information as to the degree of danger of collision that exists. The relative speeds of the two vessels and any change of distance separating them, as each of these can be roughly judged at night, must be taken into consideration.

Stern light

A vessel, when underway, *if not carrying one or more lights visible from aft,* such as the after range light of Article 2(f), must carry at her stern a white light showing over an arc of 12 points, six points on either side of dead astern, and visible for at least two miles. This stern light is to be mounted on the same level as the side lights, or as nearly so as practicable. [10(a)]

Side lights

Power-driven vessels, when underway, will show a green light on the starboard (right) side and a red light on the port (left) side. These lights must show through an unbroken arc of 10 points from dead ahead to two points abaft the respective beam. Note that the sum of the arcs of the side lights is the same as the arc of the white forward light. The red and green lights must be visible for at least two miles. [2(b) and (c)]

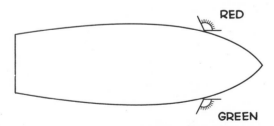

FIG. 408 In addition to white navigation lights, vessels show colored "sidelights"—red to port (left) and green to starboard (right). These lights show through an arc of 10 points each, from dead ahead to two points abaft the respective beam.

These side lights are required to be fitted with *inboard screens* projecting a minimum of three feet forward of the light. These screens are installed so as to prevent the side lights from being seen across the vessel's bow. [2(d)] On boats, the hull is frequently used to screen the side lights from being seen across the bow.

FIG. 409 Sailing vessels, with no mechanical propulsion being used, show the colored sidelights but not the white forward light. Since no other light would show aft, they also carry the 12-point white stern light (on small craft in bad weather, a white lantern or flashlight to be shown when needed).

Lights for Sailing Vessels Underway

A sailing vessel underway—and remember that if any propelling machinery is in use, she is not a "sailing vessel" —will carry the same side lights of power-driven vessels. They will *not,* however, carry any white forward light or lights, and their stern light will be *12 points.* [5, 10]

Lights for Small Craft

The requirements for lights on vessels subject to the 1971 Boat Safety Act are generally similar to the above, but with modifications as might be expected for smaller craft.

Boats of Classes A and 1

Motorboats of Classes A and 1, those under 26 feet in length, see page 33, carry one white light which must be visible all around the horizon to a distance of not less than two miles. It is to be located aft and is normally on the centerline, but if necessary because of the construction of the boat, it may be located off the centerline. This

FIG. 410 Boat less than 26 feet in length meet the requirements of Coast Guard regulations stemming from the Motorboat Act by showing a white 32-point light located aft and as near the centerline as practicable. They also show a combination red-green light forward over 10-point arcs to either side.

permissive variation takes into account the small craft with an outboard motor mounted on the center of the transom; there, the light would be mounted to either side of the motor well or bracket.

Boats of this size must also carry a combined red and green light in the fore part of the craft with each light covering its normal 10-point sector to a distance of at least one mile.

Boats of Classes 2 and 3

Boats of from 26 to 65 feet length, Classes 2 and 3, must under the requirements of current Coast Guard regulations, carry a white 20-point forward light as near the stem as possible, a white 32-point light aft, and separate 10-point red and green side lights. The stern light must be on the centerline and higher than the forward white light. The white lights are required to be visible for two miles and the colored lights for one mile. Inboard screens or other shielding (hull or superstructure) must be used to prevent side lights from being seen on the wrong side across the bow. [Section 3, MBA]

Sailboats

"Motorboats when propelled by sail alone" are sailboats insofar as the Inland Rules are concerned. Those of Classes A and 1 show only the combination red and green light, *not* the all-around white light aft. Such craft of Classes 2 and 3 show only the screened separate side lights and *neither* of the white lights. There is conflict between the Inland Rules which require a stern light and USCG regulations which require only the availability of a lantern or flashlight. In the interest of safety, a motorboat of any class under sail alone should carry the 12-point stern light of Article 10 for otherwise she would have no light regularly visible from astern.

FIG. 411 Under regulations of the Motorboat Act, still in effect, powered craft of 26 feet and more in length carry separate sidelights and a 20-point white forward light in addition to the all-around light aft. The white lights must be visible for at least two miles, and the colored lights to a distance of not less than one mile.

"Bad weather"

The Inland Rules permit certain variations "if it is not possible on account of bad weather or other sufficient cause" for normal stern and side lights to be mounted in accordance with the requirements of the Rules.

When the regular stern light of Article 10(a) cannot be mounted, the operator of the vessel must have a lantern or flashlight readily available in order to show a white light in time to prevent a collision with an overtaking vessel. [10(b)]

If bad weather prevents vessels of less than 10 gross tons from showing the prescribed colored side lights, such lights may instead be kept close at hand, lighted, and ready for use upon the approach of another vessel. When

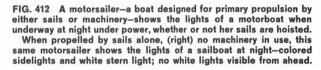

FIG. 412 A motorsailer—a boat designed for primary propulsion by either sails or machinery—shows the lights of a motorboat when underway at night under power, whether or not her sails are hoisted.

When propelled by sails alone, (right) no machinery in use, this same motorsailer shows the lights of a sailboat at night—colored sidelights and white stern light; no white lights visible from ahead.

Rosenfeld Photo

FIG. 413 Quite small craft, propelled by oars or sails, need not carry regular navigation lights, but instead must have a lantern or flashlight showing a white light and this must be exhibited in sufficient time to prevent collision.

FIG. 414 A boat on inland waters has the option of displaying either the lights called for by regulations stemming from the Motorboat Act of 1940 or those in the International Rules.

this occurs, the red and green lights must be shown on the appropriate sides and over the normal arcs of visibility soon enough to prevent an accident. Care must be taken that the red and green lights are not accidentally reversed, and to help prevent this, the outsides of the lanterns must be painted with the color of the light. The requirement for adequate inboard screens remains in effect. [6]

Miscellaneous small craft

Rowing boats, whether propelled by oars or sails, do not carry any regular navigation lights, but instead must have a white light to be shown in ample time to prevent collision with another craft. [7]

Rafts or other watercraft not specifically provided for in the Rules, operated by hand power, horse power, or the current of the river, will carry one or more white lights as prescribed by the Commandant of the Coast Guard. [9(d)] These lights are spelled out in detail in the Pilot Rules.

Option for International Rules

Boats subject to the Federal Boat Safety Act of 1971 (and so to the regulations of the Motorboat Act of 1940) *may* carry lights complying with the requirements of the International Rules of the Road for their size *in lieu of* the lights specified by those regulations even when in "inland waters." See pages 64(t) to 64(u) for the applicable provisions of the International Rules.

This option is of value to the owners of boats that may be operated outside the Inland Rules boundary lines at night as it eliminates any need for making a change in lights when going from one body of water to the other. The navigation lights of the International Rules are permitted on inland waters, *but not vice versa*. A boat lighted for the Inland Rules may be in violation when proceeding seaward of the boundary lines.

Candlepower requirements

Although the statutory requirements remain in terms of being seen for so-many miles on a clear, dark night, the Coast Guard has, by regulation, established a more scientific criteria for the power of lights. Data have been worked up translating miles range to candlepower *immediately outside the light;* see Table 4-1, page 66. These values must not be confused with the candlepower rating of the bulb used, an entirely different matter.

These light intensity standards are applicable as of 1

FIG. 415 Navigation lights of the Fresnel lens type are generally considered "old-fashioned" and seldom appear on new boats. They are, however, considerably more efficient than the plain lens type and permit the use of smaller bulbs.

July 1974. New navigation lights installed and replacement of existing lights made on and after that date must meet the external intensity standards of Table 4-1.

Misuse of navigation lights

Boats are often seen underway at night showing *both* running lights and the anchor light. This presents a confusing picture to another boat approaching from astern of the first craft—two white lights such as would be seen from ahead of a larger motorboat under the Inland Rules. This illegal situation is usual caused by carelessness on the part of the skipper—he turned on one too many switches! Check your lights each time after you have turned them on.

Another problem is the smaller Class A and 1 boat at anchor showing her combination red and green light as well as her all-around white light aft. Here the illegal situation is caused by the manufacturer who installed only one switch for all navigation light, making it impossible for the boat to show only the white light as an anchor light without simultaneously showing the red and green side lights. The solution is for the skipper to install a second switch so that the colored and white lights may be controled independently.

Maintenance of navigation lights

Many boats are used only in the daytime, but the wise skipper checks his navigation lights once a month whether used or not. In this way, he can be sure that they are ready when needed. He also carries one or more spare bulbs and fuses, each of the proper type and size.

text continued on page 64(j)

LIGHTS FOR VARIOUS TYPES OF VESSELS—INLAND RULES
TABLE 4-3

Note: Vessels lighted according to the International Rules are not required to change their lights when navigating waters subject to other Rules of the Road.

		Bow (Foremast or Forward)	Side	Range	Remarks or Additional Lights
1	MOTOR BOATS Class A—under 16' Class 1—16' to less than 26'	None	Combination red and green each color showing 10 pts.*	White 32 pt.[1] Visible 2 mi.	[1]Placed higher than combination *Visible 1 mi.
2	Class 2— 26' to less than 40'	White—20 pts. Visible 2 mi.	Red—10 pt. Green—10 pt. Screened so as not to show across bow. Visible 1 mi.	White—32 pt. Visible 2 mi. Placed higher than bow light.	
3	Class 3— 40' to 65'				
4	Motorboats and auxiliaries, when they are driven by *sail only,* show the colored lights appropriate to their class, and fixed white 12 pt. stern light showing aft, visible 2 miles, carried as nearly as possible at the level of the side lights. Motorboats and auxiliaries, under *motor and sail,* are lighted as motorboats of their respective classes. In bad weather, small boats may, if necessary, show an electric torch or lighted lantern to overtaking vessels. Small sailing vessels under way in bad weather, if they cannot keep their side lights fixed, may keep side lights at hand ready to show in time to avert collision. Note:—Under Coast Guard regulations, motorboats of any class, may, optionally, carry lights prescribed by International Rules while operating on other than the high seas; on the high seas they must carry such lights.				
5	Sailing vessel or vessel in tow (except barges, canal boats, scows, etc.	None	Red—10 pt. Green—10 pt.	None	*12 pt. white showing aft, visible 2 mi., at level of side lights (See comments in item above regarding bad weather)
6	Steam or motor vessels over 65' in length (except those vessels falling in classifications noted below)	White 20 pt. Vis. 5 mi.	Red—10 pt. Green—10 pt. Vis. 2 mi. 36 in. screen	White 32 pt.[2]	[2]At least 15 feet higher than foremast light (On *sea-going* vessel, horizontal spacing must be at least as great as vertical separation)
7	Double-ended[3] ferry boat	White 32 pt.[4] Vis. 2 mi.	Red—10 pt. Green—10 pt. Vis. 2 mi. Three-foot screens	White—32 pt.[4]	[3]If not of double-ended type, carries same lights as inland steamer [4]On both ends at same height. Special light amidships may designate line
8	Steam pilot vessel on station[5] on pilotage duty and underway[6]	None	Red—10 pt. Green—10 pt. Three-foot screens[6]	None	White 32 pt. at masthead 8' above red 32 pt., each vis. 2 mi. Shows flares at intervals of not more than 15 min. [5]If not on station, carries same lights as other steam vessels [6]On station at anchor, side lights are extinguished
9	Fishing vessel underway engaged in commercial fishing[7]	None	None	None	Red 32 pt. 6' to 12' above white 32 pt. not more than 10' apart horizontally. White vis. 3 mi. red 2 mi. [7]If underway, but not fishing carries usual lights of her class except vessel under 10 gross tons may show combination red and green lantern to other vessels, in lieu of fixed side lights
10	Inland[10] tug without tow[8]	White 20 pt. Vis. 2 mi. if not over 56'; vis. 5 mi. over 65'	Red—10 pt. Green—10 pt. Three-foot screens	White 32 pt.[9]	[8]Lighted same as ordinary inland steam vessel [9]At least 15' higher than foremast light [10]For lights of ocean-going tug on inland waters, see International Rules, Table 4-5
11	Inland tug with tow alongside or pushed ahead	Two white 20 pt. vertically arranged, at least 3' apart *or* lights mentioned in fourth column. Vis. same as item 10, above	Red—10 pt. Green—10 pt. If side light is obstructed by vessel towed, light is transferred to outside of tow.	Two white 32 pt. vertically arranged, at least 3' apart *or* foremast lights mentioned in second column	With 20-pt. towing lights forward, may carry 32-pt. white range light aft. May carry small white light aft for tow to steer by, not visible forward of beam. With 32-pt. towing light aft, may carry 20-pt white light forward. When pushing tow ahead and using 20 pt. white towing lights forward, carries two amber 12 pt. lights aft vertically arranged
12	Inland[10] tug with tow astern	Three white 20 pt. vertically arranged, at least 3' apart *or* lights mentioned in fourth column. Vis. same as item 10, above	Red—10 pt. Green—10 pt.	Three white 32 pt. vertically arranged, at least 3' apart *or* foremast lights mentioned in second column	
13	Rowboat (under oars or sail)	None	None	None	White light shown on approach of another vessel
14	Vessels working on a wreck	White 32 pt. (each outside vessel) at least 6' above decks	None	White 32 pt. stern light (each outside vessel) at least 6' above decks	Two red 32 pt. in verticle line, 3' to 6' apart, at least 15' above decks

11 and 24

1

2

6

5

7

9

13

LIGHTS FOR VARIOUS TYPES OF VESSELS—INLAND RULES
TABLE 4-3 (Continued)

		Bow (Foremast or Forward)	Side	Range	Remarks or Additional Lights
15	Dredge (held in position by moorings or spuds)	None	None	None	White 32 pt. each corner at least 6' above deck Two red 32 pt. in verticle line 3' to 6' apart, at least 15' above deck Scows moored alongside show white 32 pt. on each outboard corner, at least 6' above deck
16	Dredge (self-propelling suction type, underway, with suction on bottom)	White 20 pt. Vis. 2 mi. if not over 65'; vis. 5 mi. over 65'	Red—10 pt. Green—10 pt.	White 32 pt.	Two red 20 pt. under the white 20 pt. foremast light, 3' to 6' apart Upper red light 4' to 6' below white light At stern two red 4 pt. showing aft, in verticle line 4' to 6' apart
17	Vessel towing wreck	Carries lights same as described for inland tug with tow astern (see No. 12) except that in lieu of the regular 3 white towing lights she shows 4 lights vertically arranged, 3' to 6' apart, upper and lower white, two middle lights red, 20-point if carried on the foremast, 32-point if carried aft			
18	Naval and other U.S.	12	12		[12]Both the Inland and International Rules provide, in Article 13, that these rules shall not interfere with special rules made by the Government of any nation with respect to additional station and signal lights for two or more ships of war or for vessels sailing under convoy, or with exhibition of recognition signals adopted by ship owners, properly authorized by their respective Governments
19	At anchor—vessel under 150' in length	One white 32 pt. forward, vis. 2 mi. where best seen	None	None	In specially designated anchorage areas, vessels under 65' need no anchor light.
20	at anchor—vessel 150' in length or over	One white 32 pt. forward at least 20' above hull. Vis. 2 mi.	None	None	One white 32 pt. aft. at least 15' lower than forward light. Vis. 2 mi.

LIGHTS FOR BARGES, CANAL BOATS AND SCOWS IN TOW ON INLAND WATERS
TABLE 4-4

		Bow	Side	Stern	Remarks or Additional Lights
	Except Great Lakes, east to Montreal—Red River of the North—Mississippi River and tributaries above Huey P. Long Bridge—that part of the Atchafalaya River above its junction with the Plaquemine-Morgan City alternate waterway—Gulf Intracoastal Waterway and certain connecting waters, from the Rio Grande to Cape Sable—Hudson River (Troy to Sandy Hook)—East River and Long Island Sound—Narragansett Bay—Lake Champlain—and other tributaries.				
21	One barge or canal boat towed astern of tug	None	Green—10 pt. Red—10 pt. Vis. 2 mi.	Two white 32 pt. athwartship horizontal. At least 5' apart and at least 4' above deckhouse	None
22	More than one barge or canal boat towed astern in tandem	None	Green—10 pt. Red—10 pt. Vis. 2 mi.	[13]One white—12 pt. Vis. 2 mi.	[13]Except last vessel of tow which carries instead two 32 pt. white athwartship horizontal at least 5' apart and at least 4' above deckhouse
23	More than one barge or canal boat towed astern abreast (one tier)[14]	None	Green—10 pt. Red—10 pt. Vis. 2 mi. (carried at outer sides of bows of outside boats)	[14]One white—32 pt. on each outside boat	[14]If more than one tier, white stern lights are placed on outside boats of last tier only
24	Barges, canal boats or scows towed alongside of tug	None	Colored side lights carried on outer side of outside barge if side lights of towing vessel are obstructed by barge	None	None
25	Scows towed singly or tandem	White 32 pt.[15] Vis. 5 mi.	None	White 32 pt.[15] Vis. 5 mi.	[15]Lights to be carried at least 8' above surface of water.
26	Scows massed in tiers, two or more abreast, astern	White 32 pt. on outer side of all outside scows. Vis. 5 mi.[15]	None	White 32 pt. on outer side of outside scows last tier only. Vis. 5 mi.[15]	[15]Lights to be carried at least 8' above surface of water.

NOTE:—When barges, canal boats or scows are *pushed ahead* of the tug, head boat carries red 10-pt. and green 10-pt. side lights on outer bows, or if more than one abreast, they are shown from outer bow of outside boats.

12 and 22

11 and 24

19

20

12 and 23

12 and 25

10 PT. LT.

12 PT. LT.

20 PT. LT.

32 PT. LT.

C

LIGHTS FOR VARIOUS TYPES OF VESSELS—INTERNATIONAL RULES
TABLE 4-5

		Bow (Foremast or Forward)	Side	Range	Remarks or Additional Lights
27	Power-driven vessels less than 65 feet in length[17] NOTE—Small power-driven boats may carry white light forward at height less than 9 feet but it must be carried not less than 3 feet above the side lights or combination red and green light.	White—20 pt. at least 9' above gunwale. Vis. 3 mi.	Red—10 pt. Green—10 pt. Vis. 1 mi. or combination red and green, each color showing 10 pts. At least 3' below foremast light	None	12-pt. white showing aft. [17]Instead of the lights called for here these vessels may optionally carry those lights intended for larger power-driven vessels (see item 31)
28	Vessels under oars or sails under 40 feet	None	Combination red and green, each color showing 10 pts. shown to approaching vessels	None	12-pt. white showing aft.
29	Rowboats, under oars or sails	None	None	None	Show electric torch or lighted lantern to prevent collision
30	Sailing vessel or vessel in tow	None	Red—10 pt. Green—10 pt. Vis. 2 mi. 36 in. screens	None	12 pt. white light showing aft. Vis. 2 mi. Sailboats may optionally carry on top of foremast two 20 pt. lights, upper red, lower green, visible 2 mi., sufficiently separated for distinction
31	Power-driven vessels generally (ocean liners, sea-going yachts, etc.)	White 20 pt. 20' to 40' above hull. Vis. 5 mi. Both (see "range") 20-pt. white lights must be in line with, and over, the keel	Red—10 pt. Green—10 pt. Vis. 2 mi. Three-foot inboard screens	White 20 pt. at least 15' higher than foremast light vis. 5 mi. Optional on vessels under 150 feet. Horizontal distance between white lights at least 3 times the vertical distance	White 12 pt. showing astern. Vis. 2 miles. Carried at, or near, level of side lights
32	Pilot vessels (power-driven	On station, under way, carry white 32-pt. masthead light not less than 20 ft. above the hull, and 8 feet below it a red 32-pt. light, both vis. 3 mi.	Normal red and green side lights only when underway	Normal stern light when underway	Show flare or intermittent 32-pt. white light at intervals of not more than 10 minutes. Normal anchor lights if at anchor
33	Vessels engaged in trolling	[18]	[18]	[18]	[18]Show only lights appropriate for power-driven or sailing vessel
34	Vessels engaged in fishing but not trolling or trawling	None[19]	When making way through the water same side lights as under items 27, 28, or 31 above	Two vertical 32-pt. lights, upper red, lower white, 4' to 12' apart. Boats under 40' may show the white 3' under red and not less than 9' above gunwale; larger craft must show it at height above side lights of at least twice distance between vertical lights[19]	12-pt. white stern light. If outlying gear extends more than 500', another 32-pt. white light 6' to 20' away from vertical lights toward outlying gear and neither higher than white light nor lower than side lights [19]When not actually engaged in fishing, show normal lights of vessel their size
35	Vessels engaged in trawling	None[19]	Same as item 34	Same as item 34 except that upper of two vertical lights is green[19]	Same as item 34
36	Vessels at anchor	32-pt. white light at or near bow, vis. 2 mi. On ships 150 feet or more, at least 20' above hull, vis. 3 mi.	None	None	At or near stern of vessels 150' or more, a 32-pt. white light at least 15' lower than forward one and vis. for 3 mi. After light is optional for vessels under 150' in length
37	Vessel aground	Same as in item 36	None	None	Same as in item 36 plus two red vertical 32 pt., at least 6' apart. Vis. 2 mi.
38	Vessel not under control	None	None, unless under way with way on, when side and stern lights are carried	None	Two red 32 pt. in vertical line at least 6' apart. Vis. 2 mi.
39	Cable-laying vessel	Three 32-pt in vertical line at least 6' apart. Upper and lower red; middle white. Vis. 2 mi.	None, unless under way with way on, when side and stern lights are carried	None	Same rules apply to vessels laying or picking up a navigation mark, or engaged in surveying or underwater operations
40	Power-driven vessel with one vessel in tow, or more, if tow is 600' or less in length from stern of tug	Two white 20 pt. in verticle line not less than 6' apart. Lower light must be not less than 14' above the hull.	Red—10 pt. Green—10 pt. Vis. 2 mi. three-foot screens	White 20 pt. (optional if tug is less than 150' in length)	Must show either the fixed white 12-pt. stern light, or small white light aft for tow to steer by, not visible forward of beam
41	Power-driven vessel with tow over 66' in length	Three white 20 pt. in vertical line at least 6' apart. Lower light may be not less than 14' above hull	Red—10 pt. Green—10 pt. Vis. 2 mi. three-foot screens	White 20 pt. (optional if tug is less than 150' in length)	Must show either the fixed white 12-pt. stern light, or small white light aft for tow to steer by, not visible forward of beam

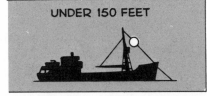

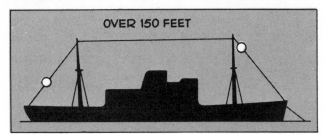

FIG. 416a The Inland Rules require a single white all-around light in the forward part of vessels at anchor that are under 150 feet in length. This light need not be shown on craft 65 or less feet in length if in a designated "special anchorage area."

FIG. 416b Larger vessels—150 feet or more in length—must show a second white light aft in addition to the basic anchor light shown forward. The forward light must be at least 20 feet above the hull with the after light at least 15 feet lower.

continued from page 64(g)

Lights for Vessels at Anchor

Under the Inland Rules, vessels less than 150 feet in length at anchor display a single white light in the forward part of the vessel where it can best be seen all around the horizon. This light must be visible for at least two miles. [11(a)]

If the anchored vessel is 150 feet or more in length, she must show a white 32-point light in the forward part of the vessel at least 20 feet above the hull, *and* a second white all-around light at or near the stern at least 15 feet lower than the forward light. Both of these lights must be visible for a distance of not less than two miles. [11(b)]

Special anchorage areas

There are, however, locations on the inland waters designated as "special anchorage areas" where anchor lights need not be shown by vessels 65 feet or less in length. In these special areas, barges and similar craft 150 feet and more in length may display only the one anchor light of Article 11(a) rather than the two required by 11(b) of the Inland Rules. If two or more barges or similar craft are tied together and anchored as a unit in such areas, the anchor light need be shown only by the vessel having its anchor down. [11(c)]

These special anchorage areas are frequently found off yacht clubs and similar facilities. For the boatman, they offer the possibility of legally leaving his craft unattended at a mooring for extended times without having an anchor light burning continuously or turning one on each sunset.

Lights for Towing

Vessels which are either towing another or are being towed have, because of this condition, much less maneuverability than vessels proceeding singly. To indicate this situation at night, special navigation lights are prescribed for vessels towing or being towed.

Towing alongside or pushing ahead

A power-driven vessel when towing another alongside

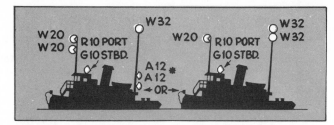

FIG. 417 A tug towing a barge alongside or pushing one ahead in waters of the Inland Rules displays special towing lights which indicate her status. See text for permissive, but not mandatory, range lights. *The two amber stern lights are used only when pushing ahead, not for towing alongside, and only when the towing lights are carried forward.

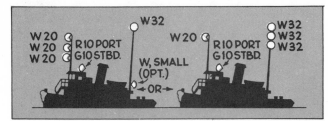

FIG. 418 A different set of towing lights is prescribed for a tug towing a barge or string of barges astern on a hawser. Boatmen should know all towing lights so as to recognize the situation when underway at night.

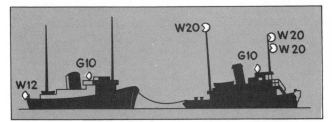

FIG. 419 A towed vessel—not a barge—shows lights prescribed by the Inland Rules of the Road. Lights for towed barges are regulated by the Inland Pilot Rules and vary for different bodies of water.

or pushing another ahead carries, in addition to her normal side lights, *two* white lights, one over the other and not less than three feet apart. These lights must be shown, but may be carried at *either* the position of the white forward light of Article 2(a) *or* the after range light of Article 2(f). In each case, they have the same arc of visibility and distance seen requirements as the 2(a) or 2(f) lights and one of the towing lights replaces such light so that there are only two lights at that location. [3(a)]

Towing astern

If the towed vessel is astern of the towing vessel, regardless of distance, there will be *three* white lights vertically as described above for either variation, with the third light three feet above or below the others. (Note that in this case the "not less than" phraseology is not used and the separation is specific.) [3(a)]

Range lights when towing

The Inland Rules are simply not clear as to the whole picture of white lights carried by towing vessels. If Article 3 is read as the sole requirement for white lights, it would then result that a towing vessel *would not* show a central range of lights. If, on the other hand, Article 3 is read in conjunction with Article 2, then range lights *would* be shown.

It has generally been held that the showing of range

Red 32 Points

White 32 Points

FIG. 420 Fishing vessels—those trawling, dredging, or fishing with any sort of drag nets or lines—show special red-over-white all-around lights at night to indicate their occupation and limited maneuverability. When not fishing, they show normal navigation lights.

ably in different geographic areas. The prudent skipper knows well those of his home waters, and he checks the applicable regulations before venturing into new areas.

Lights for Fishing Vessels

All vessels when trawling, dredging, or fishing with any kind of drag nets or lines must show from some part of the vessel where they can best be seen a red light above a white light with a vertical separation of not less than 6 nor more than 12 feet. If these lights are separated horizontally, this distance must not be more than 10 feet. These are 32-point all-around lights, the white must be visible for at least three miles and the red light for not less than two miles. [9(c)] The phrase "Red over white, inland fishing at night" will aid in remembering this combination of special lights, but note it is for Inland waters only.

Fishing vessels of 10 gross tons or more, when underway and *not* fishing, will carry the same lights as other vessels underway. [9(b)] Such vessels under 10 gross tons *may* substitute for fixed side lights a portable lantern with red and green glasses to be shown upon the approach of another craft. [9(a)]

Lights for Pilot Vessels

Pilot vessels, when on station and engaged in pilotage duty, do not show normal lights for vessels of their size, but rather they display a white all-around light at the masthead and will also show a "flare-up" light at intervals of 15 minutes or less. On the near approach of or to other vessels, the pilot vessel must have her side lights ready and flash or show them at short intervals to indicate the direction in which she is headed.

A pilot vessel of such smaller size as needing to go alongside another vessel to put the pilot aboard may "show" the required white light rather than having it fixed at the masthead, and may show a portable lantern with red and green glasses in lieu of the regular side lights.

A power-driven pilot vessel engaged in pilotage duty and on station, but *not* at anchor, displays the all-around and flare-up white lights of such a vessel as described above, and in addition will show normal side lights plus a red light mounted eight feet below the white light and visible out to two miles or more all around the horizon. If anchored, she omits the colored side lights but shows the others. This combination of lights has led to the memory-aiding phrase—"White over red, pilot ahead," which is suitable for both Inland and International waters.

A pilot vessel when not engaged in pilotage duty on her station will carry the usual lights of a vessel of her size and type. [8]

lights by towing vessels is *permissible, but not mandatory.* In view of the safety value of range lights—they usually provide another vessel with relative heading information before the colored side lights can be seen—it would appear the wiser procedure to show a white 32-point light higher aft if the two or three "towing" lights are carried as 20-point lights forward *or* show a single 20-point white light forward if the towing lights are 32-point lights located aft. In both cases, a range is established and no confusion is likely to result, despite the vagueness of the rules.

Amber lights

If the white towing lights are carried in the forward location in lieu of the light of Article 2(a), a vessel pushing another ahead *must* carry at or near her stern *two amber* 12-point lights vertically one above the other and spaced not less than three feet apart. Each of these lights must show six points to either side of dead astern for a distance of not less than two miles. [3(b)]

Such a vessel *may* carry the after range light of Article 2(f), but if she does, then the amber lights must be shown in a vertical line with and at least three feet lower than this after range light.

Steering light

A vessel towing one or more other vessels astern and carrying the three white towing lights in the forward location *may* carry, in lieu of the normal stern light of Article 10, a small white light abaft the funnel for the towed vessel to steer by, but this "steering light" must not show forward of the beam. [3(b)] This Rule assumes that the tug is *not* carrying the optional and recommended 32-point after range light—such light, if carried eliminates the need for either the regular stern light or a steering light.

Lights for towed vessels

Any vessel being towed by a power-driven vessel, except a barge, scow, etc., will carry her normal side lights but will *not* show the white forward or range lights of Article 2. She will, however, display the Article 10(a) white stern light. [5]

Lights for towed barges

Navigation lights for barges, scows, and the like are covered by regulations in the Pilot Rules. Lights for such towed craft are, in many cases, quite complex.

These rules for lights on towed craft may vary consider-

FIG. 421 A motorsailer underway with sails up and engine not in use may hoist a day shape of one black ball to indicate that she is then a "sailing vessel" and entitled to the right-of-way privileges of such a craft over a power-driven vessel.

FIG. 422 A ship anchored or moored in a channel or fairway is required by the Pilot Rules for Inland Waters to hoist a day shape of one black ball not less than two feet in diameter. This is not required for craft 65 feet or less in length.

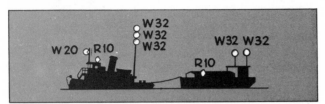

FIG. 423a A barge towed astern is lighted in accordance with one of several sets of requirements as determined by the waters being traversed. See the various applicable sections of the Inland Pilot Rules.

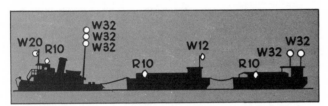

FIG. 423b A group of barges towed astern is fitted with navigation lights as prescribed by the section of the Inland Pilot Rules applicable to the waters traveled. Any one of several sections may be applicable.

FIG. 424a A barge being pushed ahead will carry sidelights on each outside corner of the bow; these must be fitted with suitable inboard screens. If there are several barges being pushed as a unit, the sidelights will be on the outside bow of the outside leading barges of the group. In some waters, an additional quick flashing amber light is required at the forward center point of the barge or barges.

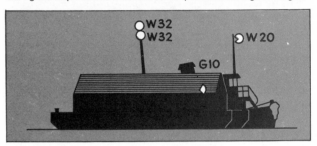

FIG. 424b If the height of the tow alongside is such as to obscure the tug's sidelight, then such colored light must be shown from the barge. On some waters, a scow towed alongside must have white lights at each outer corner.

Special Purpose Lights

Article 12 of the Inland Rules authorizes any vessel to additionally show a "flare-up" light, or make any detonating signal that cannot be mistaken for a distress signal, if this is necessary in order to attract attention.

Naval lights and recognition signals

The Inland Rules contain a section that allows the use of additional special lights on vessels sailing in convoy. It also allows the use of recognition signals adopted by shipowners and authorized by the government if such have been duly registered and published. [13]

DAY SHAPES OF THE INLAND RULES

The Inland Rules prescribe only one day shape; many others, however, will be found in the Pilot Rules for Inland Waters to be discussed later in this chapter.

Power-driven vessel under sail only

Article 14 provides that a power-driven vessel proceeding under sail only—meaning a power-driven type of vessel not then using her machinery—"but having her funnel up" *may* carry in the daytime, where it can best be seen, one black ball or shape two feet in diameter. This rather archaic language can be interpreted in more modern terms as meaning a vessel which gives the outward appearance of being power-driven but at the moment is not so propelled. The carrying of this optional day signal is advantageous to such a vessel as it identifies her as a sailing vessel under the Rules and aids her in claiming her proper right-of-way over power-driven vessels.

EXEMPTIONS FOR GOVERNMENT VESSELS

Any requirements regarding lights—their number, placement, or arc of visibility—shall not apply to those displayed on vessels of the Navy or Coast Guard if the Secretary of the Department concerned certifies that this is not possible due to the special construction of these vessels—for example, submarines and aircraft carriers. In such cases, however, their lights must comply as closely as the Secretary finds to be feasible.

Details of the non-complying lights for each vessel or class of vessel are published in Notices to Mariners and other official documents.

PILOT RULES FOR INLAND WATERS

The **Pilot Rules for Inland Waters** are issued under authority contained in the preamble to the Inland Rules and are applicable to the same waters.

These Pilot Rules for Inland Waters are a part of the Code of Federal Regulations, Title 33, Part 80. For boatmen however, they are more conveniently found in Coast Guard publication CG-169, pages 43-66.

Lights and day shapes prescribed by the Inland Pilot

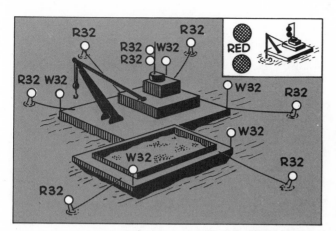

FIG. 425 At night, a moored dredge shows two red lights arranged vertically to indicate her status, plus a white light at each corner to mark her outer limits. Anchor marker buoys are fitted with a red light, and scows alongside show a white light at each outside corner. All lights are 32-point and must be visible for two miles.

Rules will be considered concurrently where both are applicable for a type of vessel or situation. In most instances, the reason for such lights and day shapes is to provide for early recognition of the limited maneuverability of the particular vessel displaying them.

Numbers in brackets are references to the applicable sections of the Pilot Rules.

Day shape for vessels anchored or moored

Vessels *over 65 feet in length,* when anchored or moored in a channel or fairway, must display during the day a black ball not less than two feet in diameter. This is shown in the fore part of the vessel where it can best be seen by other vessels. [80.25]

Lights for barges and related craft

The navigation lights for barges and similar towed craft are relatively complicated, and are made all the more so by the fact that the requirements differ on various bodies of water.

On much of the waters subject to the Inland Pilot Rules, side lights are carried on barges towed astern or on the outer sides of the outer barges if two or more are abreast. A barge towed astern, or the last barge if a string is towed astern, carries *two* white all-around stern lights not less than five feet apart *horizontally,* and not less than four feet above the deckhouse. Barges in a string, other than the last one, carry a normal single 12-point white stern light. If more than one abreast, each barge carries a single white light at its stern. Normal arcs of visibility are prescribed for side lights and a two-mile range of visibility is required for both white and colored lights.

Barges and similar craft towed alongside are fitted with an outboard side light if their height is sufficient to obscure the corresponding side light of the towing vessel. Barges, scows, etc., pushed ahead are lighted with side lights on the outboard bows of the leading barge, or on the outboard bows of the outboard leading barges if there are two or more abreast. [80.16]

Somewhat different sets of requirements prevail on inland waters along the Gulf Coast, on the Hudson River and Lake Champlain, and on Long Island Sound and cer-

tain adjacent waters. These modified requirements will be found in the Pilot Rules for Inland Waters and should be studied by boatmen whose activities will bring them into these areas. [80.16a and 80.17]

The Pilot Rules recognize that barges and related craft being towed by power-driven vessels may pass from waters where one set of lights is used into an area where the requirements are different. Such transients are not obliged to change their lights from those specified at the place where the trip begins or ends. If, however, such barges are used for local purposes in other than their home waters, then their lights must be changed to comply with local rules. [80.16b]

Under an "Interpretative Ruling" of the Inland Pilot Rules, a barge which travels on waters subject to the International Rules *and* on those of the Inland Rules may, for the duration of such a voyage, display the navigation lights and shapes required by international Rule 5; see pages 64(v), 65. [86.05-10]

Moored dredges

By day, dredges which are held in place by moorings or spuds (pile-like metal tubes that are forced into the bottom under the water) are identified by two red balls not less than two feet in diameter carried in line vertically between three and six feet apart. These must not be less than 15 feet above the deckhouse and where they can best be seen from all directions.

At night, such dredges show a white light at each corner of the deck plus two vertically spaced red lights where they can best be seen from all directions. These red lights must be not less than three feet nor more than six feet apart and must be at least 15 feet above the deck. [80.20]

The two paragraphs immediately above well illustrate the complexity of the rules and regulations relating to navigation lights, and the care that must be taken to read and study them carefully. Note that the red lights shown at night must be a minimum of 15 feet above the "deck," but that the day shapes must be displayed the same distance above the "deckhouse." These are two quite different levels aboard a dredge. The use of two different reference points adds considerably to the complexity of the requirements of a single section of the Inland Pilot Rules.

Where scows are made fast alongside a dredge, a white light must be shown from each outboard corner of them not less than six feet above the deck.

Pipelines attached to dredges, and either floating or supported by trestles, must display a line of *amber* lights between 8 and 12 feet above the water approximately equally spaced horizontally and sufficient in number to mark the length and course of the pipeline. The interval between lights where the pipeline crosses navigable channels must not be more than 30 feet. The shore or discharge end of the line is marked by two red lights in a vertical line three feet apart with the lower one at least eight feet above the water. If the pipeline is to be opened at night for the passage of vessels, a similar vertical pair of red lights will mark each side of the opening. [80.23]

These white and red lights must each be visible for a distance of at least two miles.

Vessels working on submarine construction

Vessels which are moored or anchored and are engaged in laying cables or pipes, dike construction, excavation, or

FIG. 426   A pipeline extending from a dredge must be properly lighted at night to prevent its being a hazard to the safe navigation of vessels. The pipeline must be lighted along its length and have special lights at the discharge end or any point of opening for the passage of vessels.

similar submarine construction work will display by day two balls not less than two feet in diameter. These balls will be hoisted one over the other with three to six feet separation. The upper one will be painted with alternate black and white vertical stripes; the lower one will be solid red. They must be shown not less than 15 feet above the deck and where they can best be seen from all directions.

Note the use of height above "deck" here as distinguished from height above "deckhouse" for dayshapes in the preceding subsection.

This type of working vessel will display at night three red lights in a vertical line with three to six foot separations and the lowest light not less than 15 feet above the deck. These lights are to be located where they can best be seen from any direction to a distance of not less than two miles.

If there is a "stringout" of such vessels, the three red lights are carried on the channelward end of the series. If the stringout crosses a navigable channel and will be opened at night for the passage of vessels, two sets of such red lights will be displayed, one at either side of the opening, in lieu of a single display at the channelward end of the stringout. The series of vessels must also be marked by a row of amber lights not less than four feet above the deck (above the deckhouse if there is one) in a position where they can best be seen from all directions at a distance of two miles or more. The spacing between such amber lights must not exceed 50 feet. [80.22]

Day shapes for fishing vessels

The Inland Pilot Rules require that all vessels or boats fishing with nets, lines, or trawls, when underway in the daytime, display a basket where it can best be seen as an indication of their activity to an approaching vessel. If such fishing vessels or boats have their gear out while at anchor, they must, on the approach of other vessels, show the same signal in the direction from their anchor back toward the nets or gear. [80.32a]

Coast Guard vessels at aids to navigation

A vessel of the Coast Guard while handling or servicing an aid to navigation during the daytime will display two orange and white vertically striped balls not less than two feet in diameter. These will be hoisted in a vertical line

FIG. 427   Vessels that have restricted maneuverability because they are working on submarine cables or pipelines, or other forms of sub-surface construction work, must show special lights or day shapes as appropriate to indicate their status.

FIG. 428   The Inland Pilot Rules require that day shapes be shown by fishing vessels much the same as special lights are required at night by the Inland Rules of the Road. Such craft hoist a basket as their distinctive day signal.

separated not less than three nor more than six feet.

By night, Coast Guard vessels engaged in such work will show two red lights arranged and separated as above, from a location on board where they can best be seen. [80.33a]

Distinctive light for law-enforcement craft

The Pilot Rules for Inland Waters authorize a distinctive light for law-enforcement vessels which may be shown by day or night whenever such vessel is engaged in direct law enforcement and identification of its status is desirable or where necessary for safety reasons. This light is in addition to normal navigation lights.

This light is authorized for law-enforcement vessels of the United States, or its political subdivisions, including municipalities, having administrative control over navigable waters as authorized by a controlling Federal or

FIG. 429 Coast Guard buoy tenders and other vessels working at aids to navigation show a special day signal of two orange-and-white vertically-striped balls. The night signal is two red lights, one over the other.

FIG. 430 (Below) A distinctive light is authorized for law-enforcement craft and may be used by day or night in addition to normal navigation lights. It is a blue revolving beam of low intensity mounted on the forward part of the craft.

when the pilot is in total darkness except for the lowest possible of illumination for the compass or other essential instruments; this illumination should be dim red in color.

Other special lights and day shapes

The Pilot Rules for Inland Waters also contain provisions for lights and day shapes for other special vessels and situations which are less likely to be encountered by the average boatman. These are listed below with the applicable section number from the Code of Federal Regulations, Title 33, Part 80; they are also included in publication CG-169.

> Ferryboats—80.15
> Dredges underway and engaged in dredging
>   operations—80.21
> Vessels made fast alongside a wreck or
>   moored over a wreck—80.19
> Vessels engaged in hydrographic surveying—
>   80.33
> Vessels towing a submerged or partially sub-
>   merged object not carrying lights—80.18
> Rafts and other miscellaneous craft—80.32

These sections of the Inland Pilot Rules may be consulted for information on these lights as required by the individual boatman's circumstances.

State governmental agency.

The distinctive light is a *blue* revolving horizontal beam of low intensity light. It may actually rotate, or may appear to do so because of a revolving reflector behind a steady light which results in a pulsating or periodic peak intensity effect.

The blue light will be located at any effective point on the forward exterior of the craft. A shield or other device, fixed or movable, to restrict the arc of visibility of this light may be used if desired. [80.45]

Warning signal for dangerous cargo

A vessel made fast to a dock, when loading or unloading dangerous cargo such as explosives or flammable liquids or gasses, must display a red flag by day—this is usually the "B" flag of the International Code of Signals—or a red light at night. There are no specifications in the Pilot Rules as to the height or placement of this red flag or light although it may be assumed that each should be visible from all directions.

A vessel engaged in such operations while at anchor must fly a similar flag in the daytime, but there is no requirement, or authorization, for a red light at night. [80.38]

No unauthorized lights

The Pilot Rules contain a prohibition against the display of *any* light not required by law which would in any way interfere with the prescribed lights. [80.36]

At night, good practice dictates that no lights other than the legally required navigation lights be shown anywhere on the decks of a vessel. Not only are extraneous lights disconcerting to the pilots of other vessels, but the direct or reflected rays of lights on his own craft will interfere with the night vision of the skipper. Vision at night is best

FIG. 431 When necessary to pass under a bridge, a vessel may lower any navigation light or day shape. After passing under the bridge, the light or shape must be promptly restored to its required height or position.

Modifications while passing under bridges

Any vessel, when passing under a bridge, may lower any light or day shape if required to do so by the available vertical clearance. When clear of the bridge, such lowered lights or day shapes must be immediately raised to the positions or heights required by law or regulations. [80.40]

PENALTIES

The penalties for violation of the Inland Rules or Pilot Rules for Inland Waters are described in Chapter 2; see page 59.

For certain specified violations, the penalty is prescribed as the possible suspension or revocation of a master's or pilot's license.

Great Lakes Rules

The **Great Lakes Rules of the Road** are derived from an Act of Congress of 8 February 1895 with subsequent amendments. From this Act, authority is granted to the Secretary of the Department in which the Coast Guard is operating, and on to the Commandant of the Coast Guard, for the issuance of regulations which become the **Pilot Rules for the Great Lakes;** these will be covered later in this chapter.

These Rules apply on waters that may be generally described as the Great Lakes and their tributaries and connecting waterways—exact limits are set forth in Chapter 2.

The format of the Great Lakes Rules is generally the same as for the Inland Rules except that the term for major subdivisions is "Rule" rather than "Article." Also, as noted before in this chapter, there is little parallelism in the numbering of rules relating to the same general subject matter although in some places identical, or nearly

FIG. 433 On the Great Lakes a sailing vessel regularly shows only her red and green sidelights at night, but will, on the approach of a power-driven vessel, show a "lighted torch" in that direction.

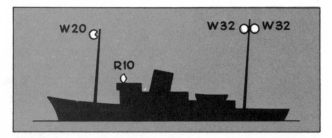

FIG. 432 The Great Lakes Rules of the Road allow a double after range light. The horizontal separation of the two lights must not be greater than 30 inches, and one or the other, or both, of the lights must be visible from all directions.

identical, language is used.

The Great Lakes Rules will be considered here in terms of their differences from the Inland Rules discussed in detail above. Identical requirements, even though appearing in differently numbered rules, will *not* be repeated.

Lights for Power-driven Vessels Underway

The white navigation lights required by the Great Lakes Rules (GLR) are generally the same as those of the Inland Rules (IR). The GLR do, however, require that the forward white light be at a greater height above the water than the colored side lights. [3(a)]

Range lights

On the Great Lakes, a power-driven vessel *over 100 feet in length* must carry a central range of white lights. The after light is visible all around the horizon to a distance of three miles; it must be at least 15 feet higher and 50 feet further aft than the forward light (which must be visible for five miles. [3(e)]

In lieu of such a single second light aft, there may be carried *two* white lights placed not more than 30 inches apart horizontally and arranged so that one or the other, or both, will be visible from all directions. (The logical placement of such lights would be on either side of a mast or stack.) [3(e)]

Vessels *100 feet or less in length* must carry a bright white all-around light aft higher than the forward light, but with no specified difference in height or horizontal separation, and with no specified minimum distance of visibility. [3(f)]

Lights for Towing

A Great Lakes power-driven vessel having a tow other than a raft must carry the basic forward 20-point white light plus a second white light of the same characteristics not less than six feet above or below the basic light. The towing vessel must also carry a small bright light abaft the funnel or aftermast for the towed craft to steer by; this "steering light" must not be visible forward of the beam. The towing vessel carries the usual side lights, but does *not* show the after range light of Rule 3(e) or 3(f). [4]

Towing a raft

The lights of Rule 4 above do not apply if the tow is a raft. In this case, there are two white *all-around* lights arranged *horizontally* athwartships not less than eight feet apart. Each light must be visible for at least five miles. These lights are to be mounted in the fore part of the ship (on or in front of the foremast if there is one) at a height above the hull of at least 20 feet, except that if the beam of the vessel exceeds 20 feet, then the height must equal the beam up to a maximum height of 40 feet. Such a vessel carries normal side lights and the steering light aft. [5]

Towed vessel

A vessel in tow carries normal side lights and must also show a small bright light aft, but such light must not be visible forward of the beam. Rule 6 does not, however, define or specify any details of "small" or "bright." Neither does the Rule state a color for this light, but it is set as white in the Pilot Rules for "canal boats" being towed.

Lights for Other Vessels

A sailing vessel underway carries *only* the usual red and green side lights. She will, however, upon the approach of any power-driven vessel show a "lighted torch" in the direction of approach of the other vessel. [6 and 12]

Open boats

On the Great Lakes, "open boats" are not required to carry the side lights specified for vessels; but if they do not, then they must carry a lantern with a green glass on one side and a red glass on the other which shall be exhibited in sufficient time to prevent collision.

Open boats, when at anchor or stationary in the water, must show a bright white light. They may also use a flare-up light if this is considered expedient. [11]

Miscellaneous craft

Tugs under 100 feet in length in harbor service, fishing boats, canal boats, rafts, and other miscellaneous craft are lighted in accordance with regulations issued by the Commandant of the Coast Guard. [7 and 10]

Anchor Lights

The Great Lakes Rules require that the anchor light of a vessel under 150 feet in length be at a height not exceeding 20 feet above the hull and be visible for one mile. (The Inland Rules do not specify a height and require two miles range.) [9]

For larger vessels, those 150 feet and more in length,

the anchor lights of the GLR are *very* different from those of the IR. For such ships, there must be *two pairs* of lights plus additional lights along the deck. In the fore part of the ship, there will be two white lights at the same height of not less than 20 feet nor more than 40 feet above the hull. These lights must be not less than 10 feet apart on an athwartships line, and arranged so that one or the other, or both, is visible all around the horizon to a distance of at least one mile. At or near the stern, there must be another pair of white lights similarly arranged but not less than 15 feet lower than the forward pair. In addition to these four anchor lights, there shall be at least one white light shown for every 100 feet along the deck measured from the forward pair of lights; these lights must be at least two feet above the deck and insofar as intervening structures permit, they should be visible from any angle of approach. No range of visibility is specified for these deck lights. [9]

Lights for Special Situations

The Great Lakes Rules prescribe lights for vessels of *over 65 feet length* in two special situations. There are no similar lights in the Inland Rules.

Vessels not under command

A vessel "not under command"—a better phrase might be "not under control"—is one such as might have suffered a breakdown of propulsion machinery or a steering failure. At night, such a vessel must show two red lights one over the other in lieu of the basic white forward light of Rule 3(a). These are 32-point lights separated by at least three feet vertically, shown where they can best be seen and visible for not less than two miles.

Such a vessel will show her usual colored side lights if she is making way through the water, but will not show side lights if no way is being made. [30(b)]

Vessels aground

A vessel of over 65 feet in length, when aground at night, will show the two red "not under command" lights of the above paragraph *plus* the appropriate white anchor lights of the GLR for a vessel of her size. No other navigation lights will be shown. [30(c)]

Inland Rules Lights Not Used

The Great Lakes Rules do *not* contain any provisions for lights comparable to the distinctive lights for pushing ahead or towing alongside as distinguished from towing

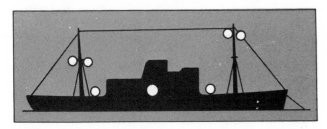

FIG. 434 The Great Lakes anchor lights for vessels 150 feet or more in length are quite complex. A pair of white lights is shown forward with another pair aft and lower. In addition, white lights must be shown at 100-foot intervals along both sides.

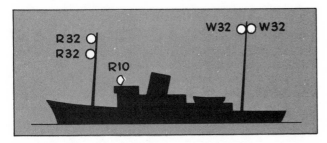

FIG. 435 A vessel is "not under command" when it is underway but incapable of maneuvering, such as might result from a steering system failure or breakdown in propulsion machinery. Such a ship shows two red lights at night in lieu of the white forward lights. Sidelights are shown only if she is making way through the water.

FIG. 436 By day, a vessel not under command indicates her situation by hoisting two black ball shapes similar to the one used when at anchor. A vessel aground hoists three such shapes. Craft 65 feet or less in length need not show these day shapes of the Great Lakes Rules.

astern; amber lights for towing vessels; special lights for fishing or pilot vessels; 12-point stern lights; and signal lights to attract attention.

Day Shapes

The Great Lakes Rules prescribe day shapes for three situations, all for vessels *over 65 feet in length*. An additional day shape appears in the Pilot Rules for the Great Lakes.

FIG. 437a On waters subject to the Great Lakes Pilot Rules, small harbor tugs of under 100 net tons show sidelights plus a 20-point white "headlight" (usually located on top of the pilothouse). An additional white forward light is shown when actually towing.

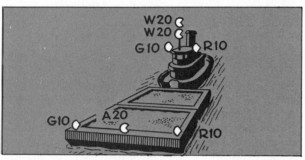

FIG. 437b Barges ("canal boats") pushed ahead on the Great Lakes carry the usual colored sidelights with inboard screens on the leading outer bows, and may show a 20-point amber light visible for three miles on the centerline forward on the barges.

Vessels anchored

When at anchor between sunrise and sunset, one black ball not less than two feet in diameter must be displayed in the forward part of the vessel where it can best be seen. The GLR omit the "or moored" language of the Inland Pilot Rules and do *not* limit the application of this requirement to vessels anchored "in a fairway or channel." [30(a)]

Vessels not under command

When not under command during the day, a vessel hoists two black balls in a line vertically similar to the anchor ball described above; the separation between the shapes must be three feet or more. [30(b)]

Vessels aground

The day signal for vessels *over 65 feet in length* when aground is three "anchor" balls hoisted vertically and separated by not less than three feet. [30(c)]

PILOT RULES FOR THE GREAT LAKES

As in the case of the Inland Rules, the Great Lakes Rules authorize the issuance of Coast Guard regulations which are known as the *Pilot Rules for the Great Lakes.* These are a part of the Code of Federal Regulations, Title 33, Part 90, but are most conveniently found in Coast Guard publication CG-172.

Small harbor tugs

Tugs under 100 net tons used primarily for harbor towing carry the normal side lights and a white 20-point forward light ("headlight") on the top of the pilothouse (at the foremast head if there is one).

When towing, other than towing a raft, such a tug will show an additional white light of the same characteristics as the headlight not less than three feet above or below the headlight.

When towing a raft, the two headlights will be all-around lights carried on a horizontal line not less than four feet apart.

All of these headlights must be visible to a distance of at least three miles. [90.16]

Canal boats (barges)

The term "canal boat" as used in certain sections of the Great Lakes Pilot Rules also includes barges, scows, and "other craft of nondescript type not otherwise provided for by statute or regulations."

Canal boats (barges) towed astern of a tug must show a green light on the starboard side, a red light on the port side, and a "small bright white light" aft. The colored lights show through the usual 10-point arcs and must be screened from showing across the bow; they must be visible for two miles. The white light aft must not show forward of the beam; no visibility range is specified.

When two or more barges are towed in tandem abreast, the appropriate colored light is shown from the outboard side of the outer barges and a white light is shown from both of the outer barges aft. If there is more than one tier, the outside barge in each *tier* shows side lights.

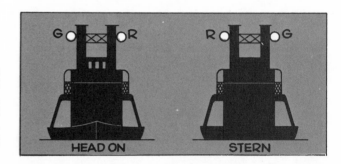

FIG. 438 On the waters governed by the Western Rivers Rules, a "river-type" power-driven vessel—one with two stacks in line athwartships—may carry red and green lights that show forward, abeam, and aft on their respective sides. These are in lieu of normal 10-point sidelights.

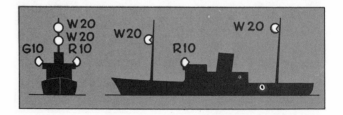

FIG. 439 The after range light is mandatory in the International Rules of the Road for vessels 150 feet or more in length, and it is optional for smaller vessels. Note that it is a 20-point light, not 32-point as in Inland Article 2(f). The required 12-point white stern light is not visible in these views.

Barges towed alongside a tug carry a red or green light on the outboard side of the barge or barges.

When a tow of one or more barges is being pushed ahead of a tug, the red and green side lights are placed so that they mark the outermost projections and a 20-point *amber* light *may* be shown from the extreme forward end of the tow. The colored lights must be visible for two miles and the amber light for three miles.

Other lights

The Pilot Rules for the Great Lakes also prescribe lights for miscellaneous craft and situations as follows—numbers refer to sections of Title 33 of the Code of Federal Regulations; these will also be found in CG-172.

Ferryboats—90.18

Craft propelled by handpower, horsepower or by current—90.20

Rafts—90.21

Boats navigated only on the River St. Lawrence—90.17

Applicability of Certain Inland Pilot Rules

The Great Lakes Pilot Rules prescribe the same lights and day shapes for Coast Guard vessels working at aids to navigation as the Inland Pilot Rules, and the same lights and warning flags for vessels handling dangerous cargo. They authorize the same distinctive blue light for law-enforcement craft, and they contain the same prohibition on the carrying of unauthorized lights that would interfere with seeing and understanding the required lights.

PENALTIES

The penalties for individuals and vessels violating the Great Lakes Rules of the Road or the Pilot Rules for the Great Lakes are discussed on page 39 . They are close to, but not exactly the same as those provided for the Inland Rules.

Western River Rules

The **Western Rivers Rules of the Road** consist of numbered "Rules" like the Great Lakes Rules, but again the numbering is not parallel in most cases although often the provisions are essentially the same.

An unusual provision of the WRR, not found in any of the other sets of Rules, pertains to special lights for "river steamers"—vessels with two stacks on a line athwartships, typical of the old-time stern-wheelers. Such vessels *may* carry, *in lieu of* normal side and range lights, a red light on the outboard side of the port stack and a green light similarly on the starboard stack. These lights show *forward, aft, and abeam* on their respective sides. [6] Barges towed alongside or pushed ahead now show a quick-flashing *amber* light all the way forward on the centerline.

Because of their lesser applicability to boatmen as compared with other sets of U.S. Rules of the Road, the Western Rivers Rules and their associated Pilot Rules will not be considered in detail in this chapter. The skipper concerned with these waters—principally the Mississippi River and its tributaries, see page 38, for exact limits—should obtain a copy of Coast Guard pamphlet CG-184 and study it carefully.

International Rules of the Road

Careful study of the U.S. Inland Rules of the Road provides an excellent basis for an understanding of the "International Regulations for the Prevention of Collisions at Sea"—the full and formal name for what is generally referred to as the **International Rules of the Road.**

These regulations—created by international conferences and made applicable to U.S. waters and U.S. vessels by Act of Congress and Presidential proclamation—consist of a series of numbered "Rules" plus an "Annex." Certain of these Rules relate to lights and day shapes, and will be discussed in this chapter. Other Rules and the Annex are covered in Chapter 5.

The consideration of the International Rules in this chapter will be focused on their differences and variations from the basic U.S. Inland Rules. Where no difference is pointed out, the provisions of a Rule of the International Rules of the Road (IntRR) are the same as those of the Inland Rules (IR) although not necessarily the Article with the corresponding number.

Applicability

The International Rules, as established under U.S. authority, are applicable to two situations:

1. To *all* vessels in waters within United States sovereignty outside the prescribed boundary lines at entrances to bays, rivers, harbors, etc.; see page 31.

2. To all U.S. vessels *on the high seas* not subject to another nation's geographic jurisdiction.

Additional definitions

International Rule 1(c) formally defines a number of terms used in the Rules in addition to those in the Inland Rules. (The IR definitions, page 64(c), are applicable except that the IntRR uses "power-driven vessel" instead of "steam vessel" for the same meaning.)

Vessel—The word "vessel" includes every description of watercraft, other than a seaplane on the water, used or capable of being used as a means of transportation on water. This definition obviously includes a boat of any size or means of propulsion.

Seaplane—The word "seaplane" includes a flying boat and any other aircraft designed to maneuver on the water.

Height above deck — The term "height above deck" means height above the uppermost continuous deck.

Length and breadth—The length and breadth of a vessel shall be her length overall and her largest breadth. (Length and span of a seaplane are also defined in the IntRR.)

Fishing — The term "engaged in fishing" means fishing with nets, lines, or trawls, but does *not* include fishing with trolling lines.

NAVIGATION LIGHTS

In general, the requirements of the International Rules regarding navigation lights are for brighter lights placed at greater heights or with greater separation. These factors stem from the larger size of vessels normally affected by the IntRR and the need for detection and comprehension at greater distances.

The IntRR specifically authorize the showing of navigation lights between sunrise and sunset in conditions of restricted visibility and in all other circumstances where they are deemed necessary. This is, of course, in addition to the requirement that they must be shown from sunset to sunrise. [1(b)]

Lights for Power-driven Vessels Underway

As before, lights for vessels in general will be considered first, followed by exceptions and variations for small craft.

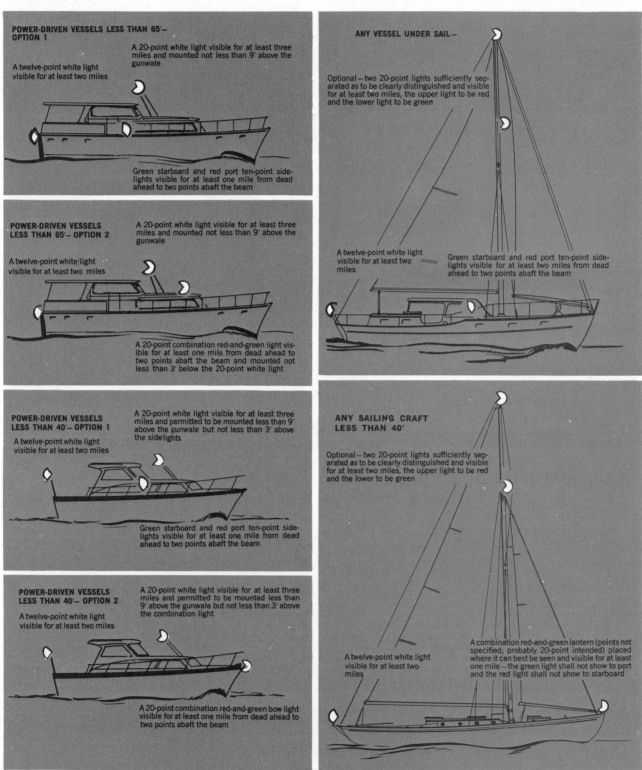

POWER-DRIVEN VESSELS LESS THAN 65'— OPTION 1

A 20-point white light visible for at least three miles and mounted not less than 9' above the gunwale

A twelve-point white light visible for at least two miles

Green starboard and red port ten-point sidelights visible for at least one mile from dead ahead to two points abaft the beam

POWER-DRIVEN VESSELS LESS THAN 65'— OPTION 2

A 20-point white light visible for at least three miles and mounted not less than 9' above the gunwale

A twelve-point white light visible for at least two miles

A 20-point combination red-and-green light visible for at least one mile from dead ahead to two points abaft the beam and mounted not less than 3' below the 20-point white light

POWER-DRIVEN VESSELS LESS THAN 40'— OPTION 1

A 20-point white light visible for at least three miles and permitted to be mounted less than 9' above the gunwale but not less than 3' above the sidelights

A twelve-point white light visible for at least two miles

Green starboard and red port ten-point sidelights visible for at least one mile from dead ahead to two points abaft the beam

POWER-DRIVEN VESSELS LESS THAN 40'— OPTION 2

A 20-point white light visible for at least three miles and permitted to be mounted less than 9' above the gunwale but not less than 3' above the combination light

A twelve-point white light visible for at least two miles

A 20-point combination red-and-green bow light visible for at least one mile from dead ahead to two points abaft the beam

ANY VESSEL UNDER SAIL—

Optional—two 20-point lights sufficiently separated as to be clearly distinguished and visible for at least two miles, the upper light to be red and the lower light to be green

A twelve-point white light visible for at least two miles

Green starboard and red port ten-point sidelights visible for at least two miles from dead ahead to two points abaft the beam

ANY SAILING CRAFT LESS THAN 40'

Optional—two 20-point lights sufficiently separated as to be clearly distinguished and visible for at least two miles, the upper light to be red and the lower to be green

A combination red-and-green lantern (points not specified; probably 20-point intended) placed where it can best be seen and visible for at least one mile—the green light shall not show to port and the red light shall not show to starboard

A twelve-point white light visible for at least two miles

FIG. 440 Rule 7 of the International Rules of the Road provides for lesser light requirements for craft less than 65 feet in length. Two options are available for power-driven boats and two size groups are established. These lights must be shown by craft on offshore waters beyond established boundary lines. They are acceptable on inland waters in lieu of the lights of the various U.S. Rules of the Road and USCG regulations.

Forward lights

The International Rules require a central range of two white lights (except on small craft). The basic forward 20-point white light must have the same characteristics as for the Inland Rules. [2(a)(i)]

The after light of the two must be higher by at least 15 feet with both lights in line over the keel. The IntRR require that the horizontal distance between these two white lights be at least three times their vertical separation. The lower of the lights, the forward one, must be at least 20 feet above the hull; if, however, the breadth of the vessel is greater than 20 feet, then it must be above the hull by a distance equal to that breadth, but need not be more than 40 feet above for wider vessels. In all instances these white forward lights must be so placed as to be above and clear of all other lights and obstructing superstructures. [2(a)(iii)]

It should be noted that the International Rules do *not* allow the alternative of a 32-point after range light as in the Inland Rules, but rather require a 20-point after light for vessels 150 or more feet in length, and permit one for smaller vessels. A separate 12-point stern light is required; see below.

Stern light

International Rule 10(a) does *not* contain the Inland Rules requirement that the stern light be carried as nearly as practicable on the same level as the side lights. The IntRR are silent as to the height of the 12-point white stern light visible for at least two miles.

Side lights

The requirements for and specifications of side lights and inboard screens under the International Rules are the same as for the Inland Rules with one exception. Rule 6(a) allowing side lights to be kept ready rather than fixed in position in bad weather does *not* contain the Article 6 size limitation to "vessels of less than ten gross tons," and so would be applicable to all size vessels.

Lights for Sailing Vessels Underway

International Rule 5(a) spells out the requirement for sailing vessels underway to carry the normal stern light of Rule 10, which requirement exists in the Inland Rules but is not so explicitly stated.

Additional optional light

International Rule 5(b) has no counterpart in the Inland Rules. It describes *optional* additional forward lights for sailboats to be carried at the top of the foremast. These are a red upper light and a green lower light sufficiently separated so as to be clearly distinguished. They are 20-point lights and must be visible for at least two miles.

Basic Lights for Small Craft

Power-driven vessels of less than 65 feet in length, vessels under oars or sails under 40 feet in length, and rowing boats may carry *either* the forward and side lights specified in the basic rules for "vessels," *or* alternatively may follow the special provisions of Rule 7 which allow for several options.

Power-driven craft under 65 feet

Power-driven vessels of less than 65 feet length may carry in the forepart of the craft where it can best be seen a 20-point, 3-mile, white light not less than 9 feet above the gunwale. They must also show normal red and green side lights visible for one mile *or* a combination red-and-green light carried not less than three feet below the white forward light. [7(a)] (The regular stern light requirement of Rule 10(a) must also be met.)

Power-driven craft under 40 feet

If the power-driven craft is less than 40 feet in length, she may carry the white forward light at a height of less than nine feet above the gunwale, but such light must be not less than three feet above the separate side lights or the combination red-and-green light. [7(c)]

Sailing craft under 40 feet

Vessels of less than 40 feet in length, under sails or oars, may carry, in lieu of fixed side lights, a lantern showing a green light on one side and a red light on the other, of such intensity as to be visible for at least one mile and so fixed that the colors show only on the proper sides. Where this light is not fixed in place, it must be kept ready for immediate use and exhibited in sufficient time to prevent collision. [7(d)]

Smaller craft

Small rowing boats, whether under oars or sail, are required only to have an electric torch (flashlight) or a lighted lantern showing a white light which will be exhibited in time to prevent a collision. [7(f)]

The term "small" is not precisely defined in the Rule, but it apparently would apply to dinghies and the like.

In "a small vessel"—again not precisely defined as to size—if it is not possible to carry a fixed stern light by reason of bad weather or other sufficient cause, then an electric torch or lighted lantern may be kept at hand and shown to an overtaking vessel in sufficient time to prevent a collision. [10(b)]

Lights for Vessels at Anchor

International Rules of the Road require the same anchor lights as the Inland Rules with two exceptions: (1) for vessels *under* 150 feet in length, the second, or after, light is *permitted,* although not required as it is for larger ships (this option is not available under the IR); (2) for vessels 150 feet or more in length, the required visibility range is increased from two to three miles. Further, International Rule 11 does not contain any provisions for "special anchorage areas" where the requirements for lights and shapes are lessened.

FIG. 441 Vessels 150 feet or more in length at anchor in waters subject to the International Rules must show two anchor lights at night similar to the Inland Rules. Here, however, the second light may also be shown by smaller vessels.

Lights for Towing

The requirements of the International Rules for lights on towing vessels are quite different from the corresponding Inland Rules provisions, being rather briefer and simpler.

Basically, International Rule 3 does *not* provide lights to distinguish between towing astern and towing alongside or pushing ahead as does Inland Article 3. Rather, the differences in IntRR lights serve to distinguish between tows that are more or less than a certain overall length behind the towing vessel. The IntRR require two towing lights for tows measuring 600 feet or less from the stern of the towing vessel to the stern of the last vessel towed. Three lights are prescribed for tows exceeding 600 feet.

Light characteristics

These towing lights are white, show through an arc of 20 points to a distance of five miles, and one of them replaces the basic forward light of Rule 2(a)(i). The vertical separation between the lights must be at least six feet, and if there are three lights the two separations must be the same; the lowest light must be at a height of not less than 14 feet above the hull. [3(a)]

The towing vessel must also show her normal side lights and *either* the usual stern light or a small white light abaft the funnel for the towed vessel to steer by, but such light, if used, must not show forward of the beam. [3(b)] The after 20-point range light is *not* carried.

Lights for towed vessels

Vessels being towed carry the side lights of Rule 2, but not the forward white lights of that Rule. They also show the normal stern light of Rule 10, except that vessels other than the last one in a string of two or more may substitute a small "steering light" for the stern light. [5(a)]

A vessel being pushed ahead—a rather uncommon procedure on the more open waters of the International Rules—will carry red and green lights at her forward end that meet the usual requirements of Rule 2 for arc of visibility, range, and side screens. A group of vessels being pushed ahead will be lighted as if they were a single large vessel. [5(c)]

Small craft

Power-driven craft less than 65 feet in length, when towing or pushing ahead another vessel, will carry two white lights in a vertical line one over the other and not less than four feet apart. These are 20-point lights visible to a distance of at least three miles. One of these two lights replaces the basic white forward light of Rule 7(a); in a vessel with a single mast, these lights may be carried on the mast. Such craft will show their usual separate side lights or combined red-and-green light, plus a stern light or a steering light. [7(b)]

Vessels less than 65 feet in length, when towed or pushed ahead, may carry either the separate side lights or the combined red-and-green light for craft of their size. If, however, a group of small craft being pushed exceeds 65 feet in length, these provisions of Rule 7(e) do not apply and the regular lights of Rule 5(c) must be exhibited.

If such craft are being towed astern, they also carry the usual stern light of Rule 10(a), except that if more than

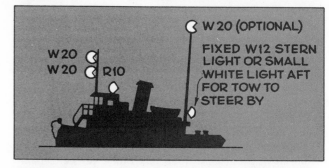

FIG. 442a The towing lights of the International Rules distinguish between tows longer than 600 feet and those of shorter overall length from the stern of the towing vessel. Towing alongside or pushing ahead is seldom done on these waters.

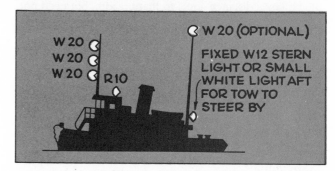

FIG. 442b Tows longer than 600 feet are identified by the three white towing lights of the tug. The after 20-point light shown above is optional rather than required as this tug is less than 150 feet in length.

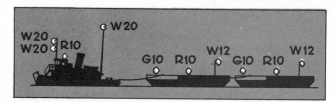

FIG. 443 Vessels towed on waters of the International Rules will carry normal side lights but not white forward (range) lights. At their stern, they will show the usual 12-point stern light except that all but the last vessel in a string of several may substitute a small white "steering" light.

one are being towed, all but the last one may substitute a steering light.

Lights for Special Purpose Vessels

Specific lights or combinations of lights are prescribed for various categories of vessels so that they may be more easily and quickly identified as such at night.

Power-driven pilot vessels

Under the International Rules the white masthead light of a power-driven pilot vessel underway and engaged in her duties must be at least 20 feet above the hull and visible for three miles or more (no height or range for this light is specified in the Inland Rules). An all-around red light visible to the same distance is carried eight feet below the white light. If, however, the pilot vessel is less than 65 feet in length, she may show the white masthead light at a lower height but not less than nine feet above the gunwale with the red light four feet lower. As in the Inland Rules, a "flare-up" light or lights must be shown, but the maximum interval is specified as 10 minutes rather than 15. The IntRR permit the use of an intermittent white all-around light in lieu of the flare-up lights. [8(a)]

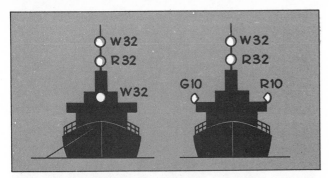

FIG. 444 A power-driven pilot vessel shows white over red all-around lights, and when underway, normal side and stern lights. Flare-up lights are shown at intervals of not more than 10 minutes. When not underway, stern and side lights are extinguished and an anchor light, below red light on illustration at left, is shown if appropriate.

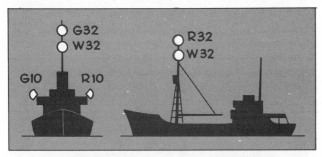

FIG. 445 The fishing lights of the International Rules are of two types. Vessels trawling show a green-over-white combination; vessels other than trawlers show red over white lights. When making way through the water, side lights are shown. When gear extends more than 500 feet into the seaway, a white light must be shown to that side.

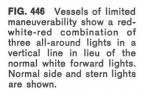

FIG. 446 Vessels of limited maneuverability show a red-white-red combination of three all-around lights in a vertical line in lieu of the normal white forward lights. Normal side and stern lights are shown.

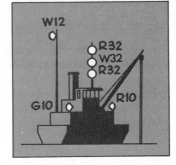

Such vessels also carry the normal side and stern lights for their size.

Sailing pilot vessels

Sailing pilot vessels are specifically provided for in the International Rules. Such a vessel shows a white all-around three-mile light at the masthead (no minimum height above the hull specified) plus normal side and stern lights. She does *not* show the red light beneath the white masthead light as provided for power-driven pilot vessels, but she does show the flare-up lights (the substitution of an intermittent white light for the flare-up lights is not mentioned for sailing pilot vessels). [8(b)]

Pilot vessels generally

All pilot vessels engaged in pilotage duties but not underway will carry the white-over-red (power-driven) or white only (sail) all-around lights and show flare-up lights as appropriate; if at anchor, they will also exhibit the normal anchor lights. [8(c)] They will not show colored side lights in these situations.

Pilot vessels *not* engaged in pilotage duty show only the usual lights for craft of their size. [8(d)]

Fishing vessels

International Rule 9 regarding lights for fishing vessels · is rather different from Inland Article 9. Separate sets of lights are provided for trawling and for other forms of fishing.

Trawling—Vessels engaged in trawling—the dragging of a dredge net or other apparatus through the water—must carry two lights in a vertical line with not less than 4 nor more than 12 feet separation between them and the lower light must be above the level of the side lights a distance not less than twice the amount of separation. The upper light is to be green and the lower will be white; both are 32-point lights.

Such vessels *may* also carry a white 20-point light, but if so, it must be carried lower than and abaft the all-around green and white lights. [9(c)]

Fishing other than trawling—Vessels engaged in fishing other than in trawling, carry a pair of lights as above except that the upper light is red rather than green. If such a vessel is less than 40 feet in length, the upper red light may be carried at any height not less than nine feet above the gunwale with the white light not less than three feet below it. [9(d)]

If such vessels have outlying gear extending more than 500 feet into the seaway, they must carry an additional all-around white light at a horizontal distance of from 6 to 20 feet away from the vertical lights in the direction of the outlying gear. This additional white light must not be higher than the white lower light of the vertical pair, nor lower than the side lights. [9(f)]

All fishing vessels—All lights referred to above must be visible for at least two miles. [9(b)]

Fishing vessels, when making way through the water, must also show the appropriate side lights or combined red-and-green light, plus the usual stern light. When *not* making way through the water, they will show neither the side lights nor the stern light. [9(e)]

In addition to the lights of this section, a vessel engaged in fishing of any sort may, if necessary to attract the attention of an approaching vessel, show a flare-up light or direct the beam of her searchlight in the direction of a danger threatening the other vessel. [9(g)]

Fishing vessels may use working lights on deck, but their skippers must take into account that especially bright or insufficiently screened working lights may impair the visibility and distinctive appearance of the mandatory lights of the Rules.

Fishing vessels when not engaged in fishing will show the normal lights for similar vessels of their size. [9(a)]

Lights for vessels not under command

A vessel not under command will show, *in lieu of* the normal white forward (or range) lights, two red lights, in a vertical line one above the other and separated not less than six feet. These are 32-point lights that must be visible for at least two miles. [4(a)]

Vessels less than 65 feet in length, when not under command at night, are *not* required to show these two red lights. [7(g)]

Lights for vessels aground

A vessel aground at night will show the same lights as for one of her size anchored, see page 64(u), plus the two lights of Rule 4(a) above for a vessel not under command and unable to get out of the way.

Vessels less than 65 feet in length are not required to show the two red lights when aground at night. [7(g)]

Lights for vessels with limited maneuverability

A vessel engaged in laying or picking up a submarine cable or navigation mark, or a vessel engaged in surveying or underwater operations, or a vessel engaged in replenishment at sea, or in the launching and recovery of aircraft, when from the nature of her activities she is unable to get out of the way of approaching vessels, will show, *in lieu of* the forward white lights, three lights in a vertical line, red—white—red. The spacing of these lights must be equal and not less than six feet. All lights are 32-point and must be visible for at least two miles. [4(c)]

A vessel engaged in minesweeping operations will carry at the fore truck a green light and at the end of the fore yard on the side or sides on which danger exists another green light or lights. These lights are carried *in addition to* the normal white forward lights. Such green lights are 32-point and must be visible for at least two miles. [4(d)] The showing of these lights indicates that it is dangerous for other vessels to approach closer than 1000 yards astern or 500 yards on the side on which danger is indicated.

General—The vessels referred to in this and the preceding subsection, when making way through the water, will show normal side and stern lights, but when not making way through the water, they will not show either. [4(e)]

The lights described in Rules 4(a), 4(c), and 4(d) above are to be understood by other vessels as signals that the vessels showing them is not under command and therefore cannot get out of the way. They are *not* to be taken as signals of vessels in distress and requiring assistance. [4(f) and (g)]

General Provisions

Rule 13(a) generally follows the provisions of Article 13 of the Inland Rules regarding the operation of special rules by governmental authority. The IntRR adds the category of "fishing vessels fishing as a fleet" to those for which special lights may be authorized.

Naval vessels

International Rule 13(b) provides the authority for variation of the regulations regarding lights where required by the special construction characteristics of naval or military vessels.

Signals to attract attention

International Rule 12 closely parallels Inland Article 12 in allowing the use of a flare-up light (or detonating or other efficient sound signal) if needed in order to attract attention. The IntRR wording is slightly different, but the effect is the same.

Lights for Seaplanes

The International Rules include requirements for navigation lights on seaplanes while on the water. The Inland

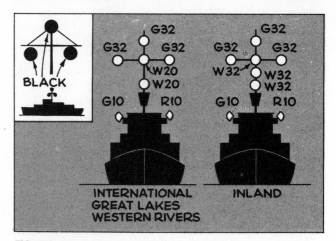

FIG. 447 Naval minesweepers show special lights and day shapes to indicate the hazardous nature of their operations. Ships and boats should keep well clear of all vessels displaying green lights at night and black balls by day at the fore truck and end or ends of the fore yardarms.

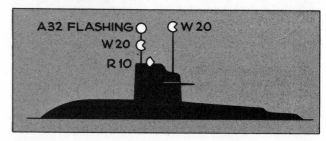

FIG. 448 Submarines show normal navigation lights but with vertical and horizontal placement and separations modified as made necessary by their special design. A special amber quick flashing (rotating) light serves to distinguish submarines from other craft.

Rules do not touch on this subject, leaving it to the regulations of the Federal Aviation Agency.

Because of their rather limited applicability and interest to boatmen, portions of rules relating to such lights have been omitted. If needed, full details can be found in the International Rules in CG-169.

Submarine Special Lights

The normal navigation lights of submarines have been found to be easily mistaken for those of small craft whereas actually submarines are large, deep-draft vessels with limited maneuverability when they are on the surface. In accordance with International Rule 13(a) and Inland Article 13, the display of a special distinctive light by U.S. naval submarines in international and inland waters of the U.S. has been authorized. This light is in addition to all other lights prescribed by law or regulation.

The distinctive light for submarines is an amber rotating light producing 90 flashes per minute all around the horizon to a distance of at least three miles. The light will be located not less than two feet nor more than six feet above the masthead navigation light.

DAY SHAPES OF THE INTERNATIONAL RULES

In the interests of collision prevention and greater overall safety on the water, the International Rules prescribe a number of day shapes for certain situations and categories of vessels.

Vessels at anchor

International Rule 11(c) requires that "every vessel" at anchor between sunrise and sunset must carry, in the forepart of the vessel where it can best be seen, one black ball not less than two feet in diameter.

This requirement is modified, however, by Rule 7(g) which allows a smaller "anchor ball" on vessels less than 65 feet in length.

Vessels under sail and power

A vessel proceeding under sail, when *also* being propelled by machinery in the daytime, *must* carry forward where it can best be seen, a black conical shape, point downwards. The base of this shape must be not less than two feet in diameter. There is *no exception* for smaller craft. [14]

International Rule 14 should not be confused with Inland Article 14 for they cover different situations regarding a vessel which is power-driven in appearance but which has sails up. The Inland Article prescribes an optional signal that will assist a vessel with sail propulsion only in getting the right of way to which she is entitled. On the other hand, International Rule 14 sets a mandatory signal to indicate. that the vessel, although having sails set, has mechanical propulsion also and this is *not* entitled to the right-of-way privileges of a sailing craft. For this reason, the day shapes of the two rules are different.

Vessels towing and being towed

Between sunrise and sunset, a power-driven vessel having to tow astern the length of which exceeds 600 feet must carry where it can best be seen a black diamond shape at least two feet in diameter. [3(c)]

In such cases, the vessel being towed must carry a similar shape where it can best be seen. [5(d)]

Vessels engaged in fishing

Vessels engaged in fishing by day must indicate their occupation by displaying where it can best be seen a black shape consisting of two cones point to point one over the other, each cone being not less than two feet in diameter.

If the vessel is less than 65 feet in length, a basket *may* be substituted for the two-cone shape.

If their outlying gear extends more than 500 feet into the seaway, vessels engaged in fishing must additionally show one conical shape, point up, in the direction of the outlying gear. [9(h)]

FIG. 450 By day, a vessel aground in waters of the International Rules hoists three black balls not less than two feet in diameter. A vessel "not under command" displays two such shapes. Neither of these requirements are applicable to craft less than 65 feet in length.

FIG. 449 International Rule 14 requires a vessel proceeding under sail and power to show a special day shape; there is no corresponding light for night use. This identifies her to other vessels as a power-driven craft not entitled to the right-of-way of a sailboat despite her sails being up.

Photo by Gary Miller

Vessels aground

A vessel aground by day must hoist three black balls, each not less than two feet in diameter, in a vertical line with not less than six feet separation. [11(e)] This signal is *not* required of vessels less than 65 feet in length. [7(g)]

Vessels not under command

A vessel not under command, see page 64(w), must hoist by day two black balls, each not less than two feet in diameter, in a vertical line with not less than six feet separation. [4(a)] This signal is *not* required of craft less than 65 feet in length. [7(g)]

Vessels with limited maneuverability

A vessel engaged in laying or picking up a submarine cable or navigation mark, and certain similarly restricting tasks, see page 64(x), displays by day three shapes in a vertical line not less than six feet apart. The upper and lower shapes must be globular and red in color, the middle one must be diamond in shape and white in color; all must be not less than two feet in diameter, except that they may be smaller if the vessel is of less than 65 feet in length. [4(c) and 7(g)] Such vessels if at anchor also hoist the usual anchor ball day shape.

A vessel engaged in minesweeping by day displays black balls in locations where green lights would be shown at night, page 64(x). [4(d)]

The shapes prescribed in the preceding two paragraphs are to be understood by other vessels that the vessel displaying them is not under command and therefore cannot get out of the way. They are *not* to be taken as signals of vessels in distress and requiring assistance. [4(f) and (g)]

Day Shapes for Small Craft

As noted in the various sections above, International Rule 7(g) relaxes the requirements for day shapes for craft less than 65 feet in length. In summary, such craft need not show the day shapes generally required for vessels aground or not under command, and may display smaller shapes for vessels at anchor or involved in activities restricting their ability to get out of the way of other vessels, such as laying or picking up submarine cables or navigation marks, etc.

Size limitations

It might be noted that the Inland Rules (and the regulations from the Motorboat Act of 1940) refer to craft "not more than 65 feet in length," whereas the International Rules use the phraseology "less than 65 feet in length." Where this leaves the owner of a vessel measuring exactly 65'—0" is not quite certain!

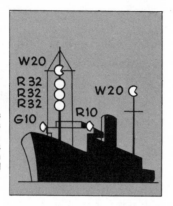

FIG. 451 Deep-draft vessels operating in narrow channels may carry a special day shape. Small craft may not demand a normal right-of-way over such larger vessels with limited maneuverability.

Additional Signals for Deep-draft Ships In Narrow Channels

Although not strictly a part of the International Rules of the Road, an agreement has been reached by maritime nations regarding an additional signal—lights or day shape —that *may* be carried by deep-draft ships when operating in narrow channels. In view of the provisions of Rules 20 and 25 (see Chapter 5, pages 73 and 75) that small craft may not demand a normal right-of-way over such larger vessels with limited maneuverability, these lights and day shapes should be known by all boatmen.

It is officially *recommended*, but not required, that deep-draft ships operating in narrow channels carry at night, in addition to all normal navigation lights, three red lights in a vertical line one over the other so that the upper and lower lights are the same distance and not less than six feet above and below the middle light. Such lights must be carried where they can best be seen and must be visible all around the horizon to a distance of at least two miles. By day, such a vessel *may* carry, where it can best be seen, a black cylinder not less than two feet in diameter and 3½ feet in height.

PENALTIES

As noted in Chapter 2, the International Rules prescribe no specific penalties for violation of their provisions, including, of course, the requirements for various navigation lights and day shapes.

Distance of visibility, in nautical miles	Candlepower
1	1.0
2	5.5
3	17.6
5	100.0

TABLE 4-1 To translate the visibility requirements of navigation lights from the rather inexact terms of "seen for so-many miles on a clear dark night" into more precise terms, the Coast Guard has established a set of intensity standards for the brightness of each type of light. These are in terms of candlepower measured outside the lens and must not be confused with candlepower ratings of the bulbs used. See text for effective date of these standards which will supplement, but not replace, the basic requirements of the Rules of the Road and Coast Guard regulations.

The differences between the U.S. Inland, Great Lakes, and Western Rivers Rules of the Road have long been recognized. Legislation was introduced in the 90th Congress (1968) to replace these three sets of Rules with a single set to be known as the "U.S. Nautical Rules." Prompt Congressional action was not forthcoming, and finally after several years the proposals were shelved completely pending the adoption of new international rules.

An international conference in 1972 adopted a new set of Rules of the Road which now must be ratified by the requisite number of maritime nations. The "International Regulations for the Prevention of Collisions at Sea, 1972" will not become effective before mid-1976, and it could be later if some nations are slow to take the necessary ratifying and implementing actions. The new International Rules are very different in format, and in some cases in substance, from the present IntRR.

The 1972 International Rules have been sent to Congress for enactment into U.S. law, with subsequent Coast Guard regulations. Following this adoption, action will be resumed to establish a single set of U.S. inland rules which will be consistent with the new IntRR. An effective date for this action cannot be forecast, but it probably would be one year after enactment.

CHAPTER 5

RULES OF THE ROAD

Right-of-Way
Whistle Signals
Fog Signals
Distress Signals

MOST OF US have had the experience, when walking down a street, of meeting another pedestrian, giving way to the right and having him turn to our right, then turning to the left and having him dodge to the same side, and finally bumping into him. To pedestrians on a sidewalk, such actions and subsequent collision are merely comical; between vessels on the water, it is very serious. Yet the skippers of ships and boats are human and might do the very same thing if there were not rules to guide them.

In the case of pedestrians on sidewalks, and even cars and trucks on highways, it is a fairly simple matter to keep clear of approaching danger. Both individuals and vehicles follow well-defined paths or lanes, and by keeping to their right, the danger of collision is nearly eliminated.

On the water, however, it is often a far different matter. Except in a limited number of areas, there are no narrow paths or channels to follow. Boats generally have a wide and open expanse of water on which to navigate, with their courses constantly crossing the tracks of other craft and vessels that may be in the vicinity. Thus the caution that must be observed on the water, even though the total traffic is much less than on land, is just as important as on sidewalks, streets, and highways.

RULES AND REGULATIONS

With the objective of preventing collisions, very carefully considered rules have been laid down so that the duty of the skipper of any vessel at the time of an encounter with another vessel is quite definitely prescribed. These rules are of three general classes. First, there are the International Rules of the Road, adopted at conventions of maritime nations and subsequently enacted into United States law. Secondly, there are the three sets of U.S. Rules —Inland, Great Lakes, and Western Rivers—enacted by Congress as laws of this country. These rules will be referred to *collectively* in this book as the "U.S. Rules," but this is *not* an official designation. On the third level are regulations issued by the various departments and agencies of the federal government. Most of these are promulgated by "the Secretary of the Department in which the Coast Guard is operating" (see page 32) or by the Commandant of the Coast Guard under authority delegated by the Secretary; these are termed "Pilot Rules." State and local authorities may also issue regulations covering the topics of this chapter, but these are too varying to be considered in this book. In general, these conform to the Coast Guard rules and go further with certain minor de-

tails. Skippers should inform themselves of such regulations for the waters that they use.

Numbered "Rules"

The International Rules and two of the three sets of U.S. Rules—Great Lakes and Western Rivers—contain various sections which are designated as numbered "Rules." These concern the relative right-of-way between two vessels encountering each other, whistle signals, fog signals, distress signals, the general conduct of vessels in reduced visibility situations, etc. The provisions of the U.S. Inland Rules are in numbered "Articles," but these are in effect rules and are often so referred to in everyday speech.

These "rules of the nautical road" for both inland and offshore waters also prescribe navigation lights to be carried at night and certain shapes to be displayed by vessels during daylight; these are covered in Chapter 4.

"Privileged" and "Burdened" Vessels

In any consideration of the right-of-way aspects of a set of rules, two terms that almost invariably will enter the discussion are "burdened" and "privileged" with respect to the status of the vessels involved.

The "privileged" vessel is the one that has the right-of-way, the right to proceed unhindered by the other.

FIG. 501 Many boating areas are relatively open expanses of water without specific channels. Craft may approach from one or more directions, often several at the same time. Knowledge of the right-of-way rules and whistle signals is important to every skipper.

The "burdened" vessel is the one that does **not** have the right-of-way, the one that must take any necessary action to keep out of the way of the privileged vessel.

Sequence of Consideration

As in the preceding chapter, the rules will first be considered in terms of the provisions of the U.S. Inland Rules (IR) as these cover the activities of a greater percentage of recreational boatmen than any of the others. Then the Great Lakes Rules (GLR) and the Western Rivers Rules (WRR) will be relatively briefly reviewed in terms of their differences and variations from the Inland Rules. This will in turn be followed by an explanation of the International Rules of the Road (IntRR) covering the topics of this chapter, again primarily in terms of how the IntRR differ from the IR. Because of their importance, distress signals will be discussed in a separate section at the end of this chapter.

Indication of references

Numbers and letters shown in brackets are references to the applicable Article or Rule, or portion thereof; or to the Section or Paragraph of the Pilot Rules.

U.S. Inland Rules

The **Inland Rules** consist of introductory material and 31 numbered "Articles" containing the actual requirements, restrictions, etc. Not all of the Articles are applicable to the topics of this chapter; certain ones are covered in Chapter 4 as noted above.

With changes over the years, some subsections have been deleted without a renumbering of the Rules as a whole. Article 18 has subsections designated as "Rules I, III, V, VIII, and IX," but not the intervening numbers. There is no Article 4 in the Inland Rules.

AREA OF APPLICABILITY

The Inland Rules apply to all federal navigable waters of the United States (see page 31) inside of boundary lines established at the mouths of rivers, bays, harbors, etc., to

limit the applicability of the International Rules, *except* for waters specifically excluded and placed under the Great Lakes or Western Rivers Rules. These boundary lines are described in Coast Guard publications and are printed on charts; see fig. 206.

As noted in Chapter 2, the boundaries between waters of the International Rules and those of the Inland Rules should not be confused with territorial limits of national authority. The *IntRR* apply outside these boundary lines over wide expanses of ocean waters that are *within* the three-mile limit of U.S. sovereignty.

Where not applicable

There are portions of the "inland waters" of the United States where the Inland Rules do not apply. One such area may be broadly defined as the Great Lakes and their tributaries and connecting waterways. The other waters consist of the Mississippi River above New Orleans, its tributaries and their tributaries, and certain other specified rivers. Information on the specific limits of the Great Lakes and Western Rivers Rules will be found in Chapter 2, page 38.

DEFINITION OF TERMS

The definitions of the Inland Rules that were discussed in Chapter 4, page 64(c), are also equally applicable in this chapter. Additional definitions are as follows:

Prolonged blast—A *prolonged blast* in the whistle signals is formally defined to mean a blast of from four to six seconds duration.

Short blast—The Inland Rules make frequent use of the term "short and distinct blast," or merely "short blast," but no definition or specification is provided in the Rules. It should be noted, however, that the regulations known as the Pilot Rules for Inland Waters specify that "a short blast means a blast of about one second duration."

Long blast—The Inland Rules and related Pilot Rules require a signal for each of two situations which is termed "one long blast." Nowhere, however, does either of these sets of rules define a "long" blast. By general acceptance, this has come to mean a blast of approximately 8 to 10 seconds in duration, sufficient to distinguish it from a "pro-

FIG. 502 Coast Guard pamphlet CG-169 shows the International and Inland Rules of the Road in parallel column format with material covering the same situation side-by-side. International "Rules" and Inland "Articles" are numbered, but not always the same for similar situations.

POWER-DRIVEN VESSELS MEETING END ON	*(e) A vessel which has the wind aft shall keep out of the way of the other vessel.* RULES AND WHISTLE SIGNALS FOR VESSELS MEETING, NEARING BENDS, LEAVING BERTHS AND OVERTAKING
RULE 18 (a) When two power-driven vessels are meeting end on, or nearly end on, so as to involve risk of collision, each shall alter her course to starboard, so that each may pass on the port side of the other. This Rule only applies to cases where vessels are meeting end on, or nearly end on, in such a manner as to involve risk of collision, and does not apply to two vessels which must, if both keep on their respective course, pass clear of each other. The only cases to which it does apply are when each of two vessels is end on, or nearly end on, to the other; in other words, to cases in which, by day, each vessel sees the masts of the other in a line, or nearly in a	ART. 18. RULE I. *When steam vessels are approaching each other head and head, that is, end on, or nearly so, it shall be the duty of each to pass on the port side of other; and either vessel shall give, as a signal of her intention, one short and distinct blast of her whistle, which the other vessel shall answer promptly by a similar blast of her whistle, and thereupon such vessels shall pass on the port side of each other. But if the courses of such vessels are so far on the starboard of each other as not to be considered as meeting head and head, either vessel shall immediately give two short and distinct blasts of her whistle, which the other vessel shall answer*

FIG. 503 The Inland Rules of the Road are not applicable on all "inland" waters. Specific areas are subject to the Great Lakes Rules or the Western Rivers Rules. Boundaries for all sets of rules are given in free Coast Guard publications.

longed" blast but not so long as to be unreasonable or objectionable. (This duration is supported by the Great Lakes Rules which describe the signal for a similar situation as being a blast of "at least 8 second's duration.") Remember—"long" is longer than "prolonged" insofar as the Inland Rules are concerned.

"Steam" vessels

As in Chapter 4, the more modern and more inclusive term "power-driven vessel" will be used rather than the verbatim phraseology of the Inland Rules, "steam vessel"— the meaning is the same.

STEERING AND SAILING RULES

The basic purpose of any set of rules of the nautical road is the prevention of collisions. A major subdivision known as the "Steering and Sailing Rules" is particularly aimed at that goal.

Technically, the right-of-way rules do not come into effect in a situation between two vessels until the possibility of a collision exists—they are not applicable otherwise. Privilege and burden are *not* necessarily established when vessels first sight each other, as many seem to feel, but rather at the point where a "risk of collision" develops.

If, however, a collision does result, the rules must have been applicable—a "risk of collision" obviously existed before the event itself occurred. Although not a "rule," a basic principle of collision prevention is that, where the depth of the water permits, two vessels should not get so close to each other that risk of a collision need materially

FIG. 504 Believe it or not— this is a "steam vessel" insofar as the Inland Rules of the Road are concerned! The rather dated term is applicable to all power-driven craft. She is also a "boat" under the Federal Boat Safety Act of 1971 and must be registered and carry numbers as she is "mechanically propelled."

arise. A collision between two vessels is almost an impossibility provided that *each* skipper *fully and properly* obeys the applicable rules of the nautical road.

Early and decisive action necessary

In interpreting and applying the rules of the road, any action that is taken should be positive and in ample time. For example, a change of course to clear another vessel should be of sufficient magnitude that the action will be noticed and understood by the other skipper. Your judgment—your "seaman's eye"—may tell you that only a slight change will be sufficient, but such might well go undetected, leaving the other skipper in doubt as to your assessment and reaction to the situation. Make your actions both timely and boldly!

Determining risk of collision

An excellent method of determining whether your craft is on a collision course with another is to watch the relative bearing of the other vessel. If this bearing does not change appreciably, either forward or astern, a risk of collision exists, the rules of the road apply, and appropriate action should be taken. More on this subject will be found on pages 449 and 450.

Boatmen are cautioned, however, against presuming the absence of any risk when there is an appreciable change in bearing. The courts have held (112 F. 161) that such a presumption might, under some circumstances, be unwarranted. Each situation must be considered on its own merits.

Whistle Signals

One- and two-blast whistle signals to be used between power-driven vessels encountering each other on the water will be discussed with the consideration of the relative right-of-way and necessary actions to be taken by the vessels. Under the Inland Rules, these signals are to be used *only* when the vessels are within sight of each other and the position and course of the other can be determined in daytime by an actual sighting of the vessel, or at night by seeing her navigation lights. These signals must never be used in fog, mist, falling snow, or heavy rain storms when the vessels are not visible to each other; only fog signals may be used at such a time. [Article 18, Rule IX] The Pilot Rules for Inland Waters require an exchange of such signals at all times when the vessels, visible to each other, will pass within one-half mile or less. [Section 80.3]

Danger signal

If in any situation where two power-driven vessels are approaching each other, either one fails to understand the course or intentions of the other, the vessel so in doubt should sound the **danger signal**—four or more short blasts rapidly following one another. [18-III]

This is also used by a skipper as a signal that he considers the actions of the other vessel as dangerous to *either* vessel—such as a *negative* reply to a proposal to pass in a certain manner. *The giving of such a danger signal does not relieve a vessel of her obligations or responsibilities under any rule.*

Whistle signals by boats

Although the Pilot Rules specify that whistle signals "shall be given on an efficient whistle or siren sounded by

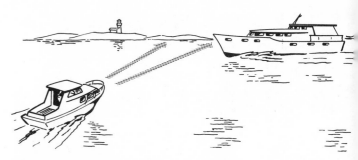

FIG. 506 When you are possibly on a collision course with another vessel, keep a close check on her relative bearing. To be safe, there should be a distinct change in either direction; this will indicate that she will pass either ahead or astern of you. A constant or slowly changing bearing indicates probably danger.

FIG. 505 All changes of course in the presence of a ship or another boat should be so pronounced and definite that they will be noticed and properly evaluated by the other skipper. Slight changes may be technically enough, but may fail to make intentions clear.

FIG. 507 Whistle signals are prescribed for various encounters between vessels under the Inland Rules of the Road. These are used only when the vessels are within sight of each other and the position and course can be determined.

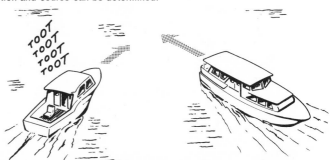

FIG. 508 In a confused situation—here caused by a boat backing into a dangerous encounter—it is important that the Inland Rules "danger signal" of four or more blasts be sounded promptly by a skipper uncertain of the other's intentions.

steam or by some substitute for steam," it is recognized that this cannot be accomplished literally on all small craft. Coast Guard regulations require that all motorboats be equipped with "an efficient whistle or other sound producing mechanical device" with certain minor exceptions. Thus a boat will normally make its "whistle signals" by sounding its horn. These regulations prescribe graduated requirements for horns on various classes of motorboats; see Chapter 3, page 58.

The Rules require an "efficient" whistle or horn without in any way defining or describing this term (which is similarly used in connection with fog horns and bells). In general, enforcement authorities and courts have held that the item must be suitable to the size and nature of the vessel on which it is used. For example, a whistle or bell that would be suitable—"efficient"—on a motorboat would not so qualify on a large ship or a noisy tugboat.

Rules for Power-driven Vessels

The rules of the road recognize *three* types of encounters between two approaching vessels—*meeting, crossing,* and *overtaking.* These may be collectively referred to as "passing situations"; see fig. 510. The rules governing the relative right-of-way, whistle signals to be given, and actions to be taken with regard to course and speed changes are given below for power-driven vessels. Remember that a boat being propelled by both machinery and sails is treated as a power-driven vessel.

Meeting situation

When two power-driven vessels are approaching one another head on, or nearly head on, this is a *meeting situation.* In this situation, it is the duty of each to pass on the port side of the other. [Article 18, Rule 1] *Neither vessel has the right of way over the other* and both must alter course to starboard if necessary to provide sufficient clearance for safe passage. This is exactly the same, it will be noted, as for two cars meeting on a narrow road.

For the rule of the meeting situation to be applicable, *both* of two requirements must be met. First, the vessels

must be meeting in such a manner as to involve risk of collision. Secondly, each must be end on, or nearly end on, to the other. Although the Rules do not set specific limits for the meeting situation, court interpretations and decisions over the years have established one point (11¼°) on either side of the bow as the practical boundaries within which vessels will be considered as meeting each other.

FIG. 509 A small hand-held horn powered by compressed gas in a cylinder meets the Rules of the Road requirements for an "efficient whistle" for small and medium size craft. Its audibility range should be checked against the requirements of current Coast Guard regulations. Range may be reduced in very cold weather.

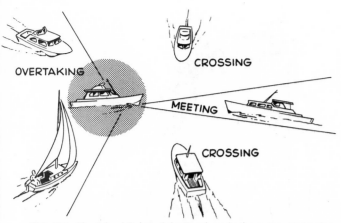

FIG. 510 The Inland Rules of the Road—and others, too—recognize three types of "passing" situations—meeting, crossing, and overtaking. Specific procedures are established to govern the actions and signals of both vessels in such encounters.

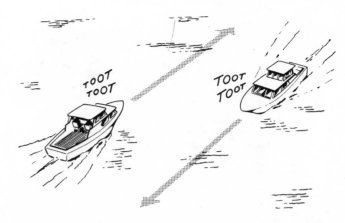

FIG. 512 Only if their courses are sufficiently well clear of each other's will a starboard-to-starboard meeting situation be legal without a change of course. The signal is two blasts, answered with the same; either vessel may signal first.

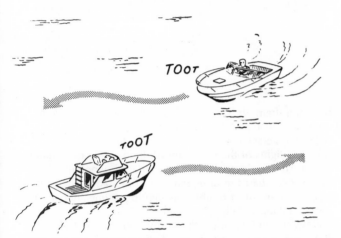

FIG. 511 In a nearly head-on meeting situation, both vessels must give way to starboard and sound one blast; neither has the right-of-way. If their projected courses are such that they will pass clear of each other, port-to-port, then neither must change course, but either signals one blast and the other answers similarly.

Rule I of Article 18 does *not* apply to two vessels which will, if both keep on their respective courses without change of heading or speed, pass clear of each other. It also does *not* apply to situations by day in which a vessel sees another ahead crossing her own course; nor by night to cases where the red light of one vessel is opposed to the red light of the other, or where the green light of one vessel is opposed to the green light of the other. It does *not* apply to situations where a red light without a green light, or a green light without a red light, is seen ahead; nor to where both the red and green lights of another vessel are seen anywhere but ahead.

Article 18, Rule I also recognizes the meeting situation in which the courses of the two vessels are in opposite directions but are so far to starboard of each other as to not be considered meeting "head to head." In such circumstances, each vessel may continue on to pass on the starboard side of the other after exchanging the proper whistle signals as described below.

Signals—This rule also requires that in a normal meeting situation *either* vessel must give, as a signal of her intention to pass port-to-port, one short and distinct blast of her whistle. This signal must be answered by the other vessel with a similar one-blast signal, *or* with the danger signal if she considers such passing dangerous or is in doubt as to the situation. There is no rule as to which vessel should signal first—both craft are on an equal basis and either can make the first signal to the other.

If it is the second situation with vessels well clear to starboard of each other, the whistle signal to be given and answered is two short and distinct blasts.

Note that a vessel must **never** answer a one-blast signal with two blasts, or a two-blast signal with one blast. This is known as "cross signals" and is strictly prohibited. [Pilot Rules, Section 80.2]

When in a meeting situation one vessel sounds the danger signal, *both* vessels must *immediately* reduce their forward speed to bare steerageway. Neither vessel should attempt to proceed or pass until agreement is reached through the exchange of the same whistle signal, either one blast or two.

Crossing situations

When two vessels are *not* meeting head on, or nearly so, *and* each has the other forward of a direction two points (22½°) abaft the beam, there exists a *crossing situation*.

When two power-driven vessels are crossing, so as to involve risk of collision, the vessel that has the other on her own starboard side must keep out of the way of the other. [19] See fig. 514.

This rule leads to the definition of a craft's "danger zone." This is the arc from nearly ahead to two points abaft the starboard beam; fig. 515. If you see another vessel within this danger zone, she has the right-of-way in a crossing situation—she is the privileged vessel, yours is the burdened vessel.

The Pilot Rules require that the vessel that has the other in her danger zone must keep out of the way of the other by directing her course to starboard so as to not cross ahead but rather to cross the other vessel's stern. She must slacken her speed, or stop or reverse, if necessary. The privileged vessel, on the other hand, must hold her course and speed. [80.7]

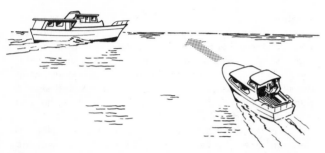

FIG. 513 It is strictly forbidden to answer a one blast signal with two blasts—or a two-blast signal with one. If a signal cannot be properly and safely answered with the same, the skipper must sound the danger signal, and take immediate action to stop or reduce his speed to mere steerageway.

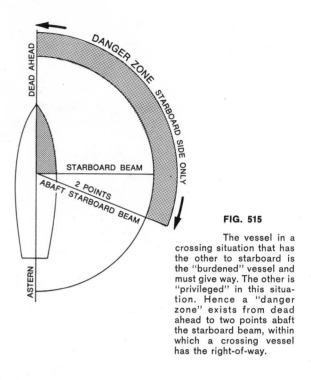

FIG. 515

The vessel in a crossing situation that has the other to starboard is the "burdened" vessel and must give way. The other is "privileged" in this situation. Hence a "danger zone" exists from dead ahead to two points abaft the starboard beam, within which a crossing vessel has the right-of-way.

FIG. 514 Vessels are "crossing" if they are not meeting head on, or nearly so, and each has the other on a relative bearing forward of two points abaft either beam, port or starboard. The Rules of the Road determine relative right-of-way if there is risk of collision.

Signals—Whistle signals are *not required* by the Inland Rules in a crossing situation, but the Pilot Rules *permit* the privileged vessel to sound a one-short-blast signal as an indication that she will hold her course and speed. [80.03(a)(3)] Although not specifically covered in the Pilot Rules, it would be normal for the burdened vessel to acknowledge with the same signal.

If from any cause the situation is such that either vessel cannot take the prescribed action or comply with the other vessel's signals, this condition must be made apparent to the other vessel at once by sounding the danger signal of four or more short, rapid blasts. When this happens, both vessels must immediately be stopped, and backed if necessary, until signals for passing with safety have been made and understood.

Note that this rule is applicable only if there is risk of collision. If the situation is such that the vessels will pass free and clear of each other, there is *no* privileged or burdened vessel, and whistle signals are not appropriate. In case of doubt, however, the safer procedure is to assume that the rules *do* apply and exchange signals to be sure that the intentions of each are known to each other.

Overtaking situation

If one vessel is coming up on another, she being astern of a direction two points abaft the beam of the other vessel and making greater speed so as to close the distance between them, the first vessel is said to be *overtaking* the latter vessel; fig. 517. At night, this situation would exist when the vessel astern could not see either of the navigation side lights of the vessel ahead. By day, the overtaking vessel cannot always know with certainty whether she is forward or abaft the direction two points abaft the other vessel's beam—if in doubt, she should assume that she is an overtaking vessel. [24]

Notwithstanding *any* other provision in the Rules of Road, *every* vessel overtaking another must keep out of the way of the overtaken vessel. The overtaking vessel is burdened; the overtaken vessel is privileged. [24]

The Rules are very specific that once a vessel is in an overtaking status, she remains as such for the remainder of the encounter—no subsequent alteration of the bearing between the two vessels will serve to make the overtaking vessel a crossing vessel within the meaning of the rules, or relieve her of her duty of keeping clear of the overtaken vessel until she is finally past and clear. In other words, should the overtaking vessel come upon the starboard side of the overtaken vessel, and so into the latter's normal danger zone, she does *not* by this movement become the privileged vessel with the right-of-way over the overtaken craft. [24]

Signals—If the overtaking vessel desires to pass on the port side of the vessel ahead—as would be normal if the slower vessel were keeping to the right of a channel, see fig. 519a, she must sound a two-short-blast signal. If the privileged vessel agrees with such a passing, she should immediately sound the same signal of two blasts. The faster vessel then directs her course to port and passes as proposed and agreed.

Should the vessel astern desire to pass on the other's starboard side—not normal, but legal, see fig. 519b, she sounds a one-short-blast signal which is returned in kind by the privileged vessel if she consents.

If in either of the above situations, the vessel ahead

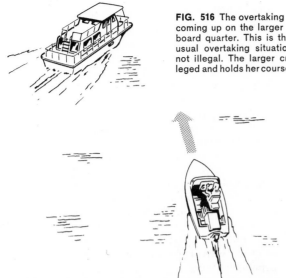

FIG. 516 The overtaking boat is here coming up on the larger craft's starboard quarter. This is the less-than-usual overtaking situation, but it is not illegal. The larger craft is privileged and holds her course and speed.

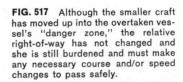

FIG. 517 Although the smaller craft has moved up into the overtaken vessel's "danger zone," the relative right-of-way has not changed and she is still burdened and must make any necessary course and/or speed changes to pass safely.

does *not* consider that the passing can take place safely as proposed by the burdened vessel, she must *immediately* sound the danger signal of four or more short, rapid blasts. (The danger signal would likewise be applicable if the overtaking craft attempted an unsafe passing without first giving a whistle signal of her intentions.)

An overtaking vessel that receives a danger signal in reply to her stated intention to pass should immediately cease all actions related to passing and reduce speed so as to not close further on the overtaken vessel; fig. 518c. No attempt should be made to pass until the proper signals have been given and answered. [18-VIII] Although not provided for in the Rules, it is reasonable for a privileged vessel to give the danger signal, pause, and then give the other passing signal to the burdened vessel—in effect saying, "The side that you proposed is unsafe, but the other is ok." This initiation of the proposal and agreement for passing by the privileged vessel is not normal, but often it is logical considering that the leading vessel has better observation of the conditions ahead.

As in the meeting situation, "cross signals"—answering one blast with two, or two blasts with one—are *prohibited*. Answer a signal **only** with the same signal as given by the other vessel, or with the danger signal.

Although the slower vessel ahead is privileged, she must in no case attempt to cross the bow or crowd upon the course of the passing vessel. [18-VIII]

Meeting in restricted waters

Every power-driven vessel when proceeding along the course of a narrow channel shall, when it is safe and practicable, keep to the side of the fairway or midchannel that lies on the starboard side of such vessel. [25] This is merely the same general provision as used on streets and highways—keep to the right of center. Although the Rules are silent as to which side an overtaking vessel should pass the slower craft, it is a logical extension of the above rule that the faster craft moves to the left with a two-blast signal and passes as two automobiles might do on a road.

In narrow channels, a power-driven vessel of less than 65 feet length must not hamper the safe passage of a vessel which can navigate only inside that channel. The size or nature of this latter vessel is not relevant if she meets the requirement of having to stay within the channel. [25]

Rounding bends in a channel

A special "alarm" or "bend" signal is provided in the Rules for a situation in which a power-driven vessel approaches a bend in a channel where another vessel approaching from the opposite direction on the other side of the bend cannot be seen for a distance of a half-mile because of the height of the banks or other cause. In this case, when within a half-mile of the bend, a vessel must sound one "long" blast (generally taken as 8 to 10 second's duration) of her whistle. This signal will be answered with a similar long blast by any vessel within hearing around the bend. If such an answer is received, normal whistle signals must be exchanged *when* the vessels come within sight of one another. If no reply to her alarm signal is heard, the vessel may consider the channel ahead to be clear and govern herself accordingly. [18-V, and 80.5(a) and 86.10-1] Normal good judgment, however, dictates special alertness and moderate speed at blind bends.

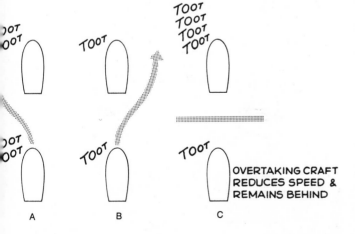

FIG. 518 **a, b, c** The overtaking craft signals first as indicated by the numbers above. The overtaken (privileged) vessel replies with the same signal (and the passing occurs normally) or with the danger signal (and the overtaking craft must not attempt to pass until the proper signals have later been exchanged).

Rules of the Road / CHAPTER 5

FIG. 519 Vessels, including boats, approaching a bend in a river, where a craft approaching from the other direction could not be seen at a distance of a half-mile, must sound a special signal of one "long" blast. This is generally considered to mean one of 8 to 10 seconds duration.

In a winding channel, a vessel may *first* sight the other at an oblique angle rather than "head on, or nearly head on". Nevertheless, the situation is to be regarded as a *meeting* situation as such will be the case when the actual passing occurs. Each should keep to her own right side of the channel and neither has the right-of-way over the other.

Leaving a berth

Whenever a power-driven vessel is moved from a berth or dock, she shall give a signal of one long blast (approximately 8 to 10 second's duration) on her whistle. Immediately *after* clearing the berth so as to be fully in sight, she is then governed by the applicable steering and sailing rules. [18-V and 80.5(b)]

Note that although it is not explicitly so stated in the Rules of the Road or the Pilot Rules, it may be inferred that a craft just emerging from a slip or berth does *not* have the right-of-way over another vessel passing in the channel or nearby open water even though she is in the other's danger zone. Her privileged status in a crossing situation is *not* established until she is "fully in sight."

FIG. 520 A boat leaving its slip in a marina, or exiting from between parallel piers, should sound a long blast of 8 to 10 seconds duration. She does not have right-of-way until out in the clear.

Ferry boats

Although there are no express provisions in the Inland Rules of the Road and related Pilot Rules that give any special privileges to ferry boats, the courts have repeatedly ruled that ferries are entitled to a reasonable degree of freedom of entrance to and exit from their slips. The same is true in regard to other craft using slips and piers. Boats should avoid passing unnecessarily close to piers, wharves, etc., where they may be caught unawares by the unanticipated movements of other craft.

Sailing Vessels

The provisions of Inland Article 17 are applicable only to situations involving two sailing vessels—*neither* may be under power or a combination of sail and power.

When two sailing vessels are approaching one another, so as to involve risk of collision, one of them must keep out of the way of the other in accordance with the following conditions.

(a) A vessel that is running free must keep out of the way of a vessel that is closehauled.

(b) A vessel that is closehauled on the port tack must keep out of the way of a vessel that is closehauled on the starboard tack.

(c) When both vessels are running free with the wind on different sides, the vessel that has the wind on the port side must keep out of the way of the other.

(d) When both are running free with the wind on the same side, the vessel that is to windward must keep out of the way of the vessel that is to leeward.

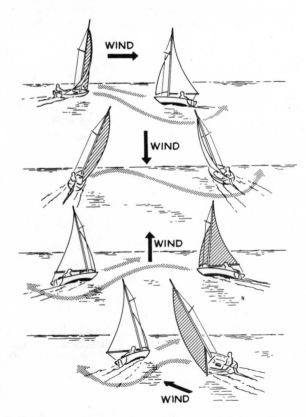

FIG. 521 The Inland Rules contain right-of-way statements for five situations between two sailing vessels. These rules are not the same as those of the International Rules and the differences must be kept in mind. Burdened sailboats are shown with shaded sails.

74

FIG. 522 a In any encounter between a sailing vessel and a power-driven vessel, the former has the right-of-way unless she should be overtaking the other. Whistle signals are not sounded by a motorboat in such a situation as the sailboat is not equipped to reply.

FIG. 522 b The right-of-way of a sailboat over a power-driven vessel does **not** prevail if the latter cannot safely navigate outside the limits of the channel she is using.

(e) A vessel that has the wind aft must keep out of the way of the other vessel.

It should be noted that the right-of-way rules between two sailing vessels under the Inland Rules currently *differ* in wording and effect from the International Rules and from the right-of-way rules commonly used in yacht racing. This difference is expected to disappear when the pending action on new U.S. rules takes effect; see page

Signals—Sound signals are *not* used in passing situations between two sailing vessels.

Encounters Between Sailing and Power Vessels

In general, a sailing vessel has the right-of-way over a vessel propelled by machinery or by sail and machinery concurrently. The power-driven vessel must keep out of the way of the sailing vessel. [20] There are, however, some exceptions and they should be thoroughly understood.

Should a sailing vessel overtake a power-driven vessel —not likely, but possible—the overtaking situation rule prevails and the sailing vessel is the burdened one regardless of the means of propulsion.

Likewise, a sailing vessel is not the privileged vessel in an encounter with certain vessels engaged in fishing.

Further limitation

The normal privileged status of a sailing vessel over a power-driven vessel does *not* give her the right in a narrow

channel to hamper the latter vessel if such can navigate safely only within the limits of the channel. [20]

No whistle signals

Power-driven vessels do *not* give whistle signals when encountering sailing vessels as the latter are not equipped to reply, and an unanswered signal would create a situation of doubt.

FIG. 523 Fishing vessels are accorded certain special privileges over other vessels when they are engaged in their work. These privileges are not, however, unlimited; see Inland Article 26. Yachts should stay well clear of fishing craft at work.

Right-of-Way of Fishing Vessels

Inland Article 26 accords special right-of-way status, within limitations, to vessels engaged in fishing.

Sailing vessels underway must keep out of the way of sailing vessels or boats fishing with nets, lines, or trawls. Although not explicitly stated in the Inland Rules (as it is in the IntRR), power-driven vessels likewise should also keep clear of fishing vessels.

This rule does *not* give any vessel or boat engaged in fishing the right of obstructing a fairway used by vessels other than fishing vessels or boats.

General Right-of-Way Rules

There are a number of Inland Rules of the Road that relate generally to all vessels regardless of their means of propulsion.

Privileged vessel's duty

Where the Rules of the Road require that one vessel is to keep out of the way, the other—the privileged vessel—*must* maintain her course and speed. [21]

Although the matter is not very clearly covered in the Inland Rules, it should be obvious that if such action by the privileged vessel brings her into a situation where collision cannot be avoided by the actions of the burdened vessel, then she, too, must take such measures as will best avert an accident. When such a situation becomes apparent (and this is usually a very difficult decision), the privileged vessel is to take whatever action she deems necessary to avoid or minimize disaster. The courts have consistently held that *any* action (except *no* action) is proper in such circumstances.

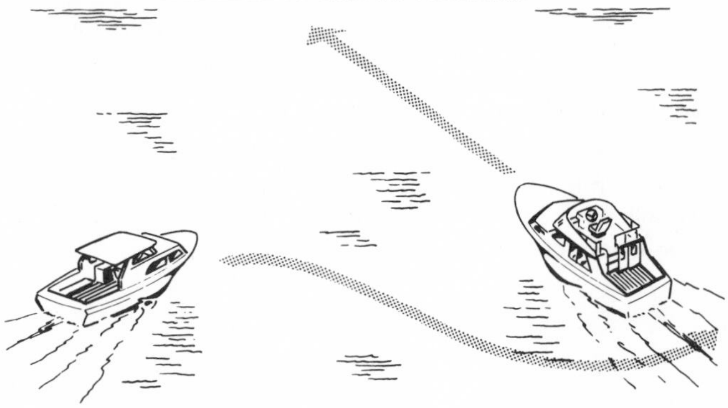

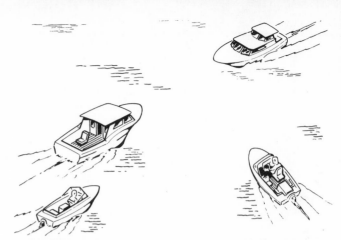

FIG. 524 In any encounter between two vessels where one has the right-of-way over the other, both have responsibilities. Not only must the burdened vessel give way; the privileged vessel has the duty of maintaining her course and speed.

FIG. 525 The "General Prudential Rule" requires that due regard be given to any special circumstances that may render a departure from the Rules necessary to avoid immediate danger. A typical example occurs when more than two craft are involved in an encounter and strict compliance cannot be had for all pairs of vessels.

Burdened vessel's duty

Every vessel that is directed by the Rules of the Road to keep out of the way of another is a burdened vessel and must, if the circumstances of the situation permit, avoid crossing ahead of the other—the privileged vessel. [22]

Every power-driven vessel that is burdened must, on approaching the privileged vessel, slacken her speed if necessary, or stop or reverse. [23]

GENERAL PRUDENTIAL RULE

Article 27 is often termed the "general prudential rule" and is of great importance because of its wide applicability.

In obeying and construing the Rules of the Road, due regard must be given to all dangers of navigation and collision, and to any special circumstance that may render a *departure* from the Rules necessary to avoid immediate danger.

Interpretation of "immediate danger"

Courts have placed considerable emphasis on the words "immediate danger" of Article 27 in rendering their decisions. The basic principle is that the Rules must *not* be abandoned whenever perceptible risk of collision exists, but *only* when *imperatively* required by special circumstances in order to avoid such danger.

SOUND SIGNALS FOR VESSELS WITHIN SIGHT

In the Inland Rules, sound signals, given on the horn in the case of most motorboats, are used for the purpose of indicating the intention of the skipper of a craft, his agreement to a proposed action, or to warn others of a situation considered dangerous.

Although sailing vessels *never* give whistle signals, if such a craft is equipped with an auxiliary engine, then she must have a horn for use when under sail and power or power alone.

Passing signals

Whistle signals for power-driven vessels encountering one another have been discussed above in connection with the passing situations, pages 69 to 74.

The danger signal of four or more short, rapid blasts was discussed on page 69.

Backing signal

The Inland Rules contain provision for a "backing signal." When vessels are within sight of one another, a power-driven vessel underway whose engines are going at full speed astern must indicate this fact by sounding three short blasts on her whistle. [28]

FIG. 526 The Inland Rules call for a three-blast signal when a vessel's engines are going at "full speed astern." In normal practice, it is used whenever engines are in reverse or the vessel is beginning to make sternway.

Note that the Rules *require* this signal only when the engines are going at *full speed* astern—in actual practice, a three-blast signal is sounded by vessels whose engines are going astern at any speed, or who are making sternway, in the presence of other vessels. Note also that this signal may be made to sailing vessels as it does not require a reply.

"Alarm" or "bend" signal

As noted on prior pages of this chapter, the Rules provide for an "alarm signal" of one long blast (generally taken as from 8 to 10 seconds duration, although no length is officially specified), for vessels approaching a blind bend in a channel. This same signal is used by a vessel about to be moved from a berth or slip.

Caution in use of whistle signals

Whistle signals should be used with caution in conditions of heavy traffic on the water. Such a circumstance might exist when three or more vessels were in the vicinity

FIG. 527 Signals for the opening of a drawbridge vary somewhat with different geographic areas, but the one most often used is three blasts. This is also used for canal locks on many waterways. There are also signals of reply from the bridge or lock. See appropriate Coast Pilot or equivalent publication for details.

and there existed a combination of meeting, crossing, and/or overtaking situations, there being no way to direct a whistle signal to one vessel exclusively. In such cases, the omission of whistle signals might well be a safer course of action than indiscriminate "tooting."

Signals for drawbridges and canal locks

The whistle signals for opening drawbridges are not a part of the Rules of the Road, but should be known by boatmen. Such signals vary somewhat with different localities; a three-short-blast signal is common in many areas. The bridge tender will sometimes reply with a three-blast signal if he is going to open without delay, or with four blasts (two blasts in some areas) if not able to open immediately.

A skipper should always consult the applicable volume of the Coast Pilot, or corresponding publication for other waters, for the specific signals for bridges, and for canal locks which usually follow similar procedures.

No whistle salutes

Yachts and boats should never exchange salutes or greetings by means of whistle blasts. Commercial craft sometimes do this, but it is not authorized by the Rules. By Coast Guard regulation, the "unnecessary sounding of the whistle is prohibited within any harbor limits of the United States."

SOUND SIGNALS IN REDUCED VISIBILITY

Article 15 of the Inland Rules prescribes sound signals to be given by different types of vessels in various circumstances when visibility conditions are reduced from "normal." These are often termed "fog signals," but they are equaly applicable in cases of mist, falling snow, heavy rainstorms, or any other condition similarly restricting visibility. They are equally applicable by day or night.

Courts have held that fog signals should be sounded when visibility is reduced to the distance at which side lights are required to be seen, one mile in the case of waters subject to the Inland Rules.

These sound signals serve two purposes. Basically, they alert other vessels to the presence in the vicinity of the vessel sounding the signal and a rough indication of her position. Secondly, they may provide an indication of her

activities (which tack a sailboat is on) or limitations on her maneuverability (towing, at anchor, etc.).

Equipment

The Inland Rules require that a power-driven vessel be provided with an efficient whistle or siren sounded by steam or by some substitute for steam, so placed that the sound will not be intercepted by any obstruction.

Article 15 also requires that such vessels be equipped with an efficient fog horn and with an efficient bell. Sailing vessels of 20 or more gross tons must have an efficient fog horn and bell.

FIG. 528 Coast Guard motorboat regulations do not require a bell on craft under 26 feet in length. The Rules of the Road, however, make no exception for such boats from the requirement for sounding a bell when certain conditions prevail.

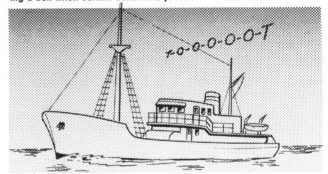

FIG. 529 On waters governed by the Inland Rules of the Road, a power-driven vessel underway in reduced visibility sounds one prolonged blast—four to six seconds duration—at intervals of not more than one minute.

Although the Inland Rules state "all vessels" and contain no clear exception for small craft, the implementing regulations of the Motorboat Act of 1940 (retained in effect by the 1971 Federal Boat Safety Act) prescribe lesser requirements for vessels 65 feet or less in length; see page 58. This, however, does not excuse them from compliance with the requirement for giving the specified signals should they become involved in a reduced visibility situation where they are applicable. For example, a 24-foot Class 1 motorboat is not required by USCG regulations to be equipped with a bell—yet if this "power-driven vessel" were to be anchored in a fog, she is not excused from the need for ringing a bell. Boats must be equipped for situations in which they may find themselves even though this require items on board over and above the minimum requirements of laws and regulations.

How sounded

All signals prescribed by Article 15 for vessels underway

in reduced visibility shall be given—

    By power-driven vessels, on the whistle;

    By sailing vessels, on the fog horn.

It is interesting to note that although the Inland Rules require a power-driven vessel to be equipped with a whistle or siren *and* a fog horn, the same Article states that fog signals are to be made on the whistle or siren—no mention whatever is made of any use of the fog horn for such vessels!

Motorboats sound their fog signals on their whistle or horn.

Power-driven Vessels Underway

On waters subject to the Inland Rules, a power-driven vessel underway in conditions of reduced visibility, day or night, sounds one prolonged (four to six seconds) blast of her whistle at intervals of not more than *one* minute. [15(a)] It has been held by court rulings that a vessel approaching an area of reduced visibility, such as a well-defined fog bank, should start her signals before she herself actually enters the area.

Sailing Vessels Underway

A sailing vessel, when underway in restricted visibility of any kind, is required by Article 15(c) to sound the following signals at intervals of not more than one minute (the length of the blasts is not stated as prolonged or any other specific duration)—

    When on a starboard tack, one blast;

    When on a port tack, two blasts;

    When with the wind abaft the beam, three blasts.

Vessels Towing and Being Towed

A power-driven vessel, when towing another in fog, gives a special signal *in lieu of* the usual one prolonged blast to indicate her more limited maneuverability. She sounds one prolonged blast followed by two short blasts; the same one-minute maximum interval is observed. [15(e)]

A towed vessel *may* give this signal, but no other.

Other vessels of limited maneuverability, such as fishing vessels with their nets out have no special signal in the waters of the Inland Rules and can only indicate whether they are underway or at anchor. If concern arises over the apparent too-close approach of another vessel, the danger signal may be sounded, see below.

Miscellaneous Vessels

All rafts and other types of craft not otherwise provided for in Article 15, navigating by hand power, horse power, or by the current of the river, when in conditions of reduced visibility must sound one blast (duration not specified) on a fog horn, or an equivalent signal, at intervals of not more than one minute. [15(f)]

Vessels at Anchor

A vessel at anchor in fog or other condition reducing normal visibility, whether by day or night, must ring a bell rapidly for about five seconds at intervals of not more than one minute.

The same signal is used by vessels made fast to a mooring buoy. Vessels made fast to a pier or wharf do not sound fog signals unless they project out into a channel or fairway and so constitute a hazard to others.

This requirement for ringing a bell is waived for vessels

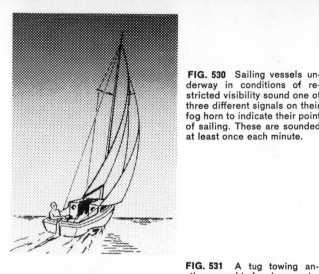

FIG. 530 Sailing vessels underway in conditions of restricted visibility sound one of three different signals on their fog horn to indicate their point of sailing. These are sounded at least once each minute.

FIG. 531 A tug towing another vessel in fog, heavy rain, snow, etc., sounds a special signal of one prolonged blast followed by two short blasts. The towed vessel **may** give this same signal, but no other.

FIG. 532 A vessel at anchor in fog or other conditions reducing visibility must ring her bell rapidly for about five seconds at intervals of not more than one minute. A craft of 65 feet or less length anchored or moored in a "special anchorage area" is not required to sound this signal.

FIG. 533 The Inland Rules have no specific signal for vessels aground in conditions of reduced visibility, but it is logical for them to sound the danger signal of four or more blasts rather than ringing the bell. This will warn other vessels not only of her presence, but also of the hazard.

FIG. 534 A boat underway in reduced visibility must not only sound the proper fog signals but also must go no faster than a "moderate" speed. This is not defined in the Rules of the Road but numerous court interpretations exist.

not more than 65 feet in length, and barges, scows, and similar craft, if located in a "special anchorage area" as discussed in Chapter 4, page 64(j). [15(d)]

Fog Signals in General

Although not specifically covered in Article 15 of the Inland Rules, several aspects of fog signals have arisen from court interpretations and rulings, and from general experience.

Danger signal

It is reasonable for a vessel to sound the danger signal of four or more short blasts in rapid succession if the skipper considers that another vessel is approaching with risk of collision; this can be done underway or at anchor. Other "steering signals" are *not* given in reduced visibility situations until each vessel has actually sighted the other.

Vessel aground

A vessel *aground* should sound the *danger signal* as a warning to other vessels that the shoal water may be dangerous to them, information that the normal signal of an anchored vessel would not convey.

Not too often!

The Inland Rules prescribe an interval of "not more than one minute" between the successive soundings of fog signals. This is a rather brief time and should not be further reduced by skippers concerned over the risk of collision. The interval between signals—used for listening for other vessels' blasts—is equally as valuable for safety as the actual blowing of one's own whistle or horn. The timing, if not done by automatic means, should be measured to reasonable accuracy by a second hand on a clock or watch.

CONDUCT IN RESTRICTED VISIBILITY

In addition to providing for sound signals, the Inland Rules set forth restrictions on the navigation of vessels when visibility is reduced for any reason. The basic rule for the operation of vessels in fog, mist, falling snow, heavy rainstorms, or other conditions similarly restricting visibility is quite brief and logical. It is required that all vessels in such conditions go at a "moderate" speed having careful regard for the existing circumstances. [16]

It is, of course, impossible to define "moderate" in terms of knots or miles per hour—this is a judgment that must be left for each situation to the individual skipper concerned, who must be prepared to defend it should he be in a collision. A general interpretation is that a vessel should be going no faster than a speed which would permit her to be brought to a complete stop in *one-half* of the range of existing visibility—the theory being that thus both of two vessels on a collision course could stop short of each other if action were initiated as soon as one became visible to the other.

It should be carefully noted that courts have held that the only "moderate" speed in some dense fog situations was *zero,* meaning that the vessel should not have gotten underway, or should have stopped and anchored or laid to.

On hearing another vessel

A power-driven vessel hearing—apparently forward of her beam—the fog signal of another vessel the position of

FIG. 535 A good listening as well as visual lookout is essential in reduced visibility situations. On power-driven boats, this normally means sending a man to the bow, farther away from the noise of the craft's own engines.   Kodachrome by Bill Koelbel

which has not been ascertained, must, so far as the circumstances of the case permit, stop her engines and then navigate with caution until danger of collision is over. [16] The phrase "so far as the circumstances of the case permit" allow for situations where power must be kept on for safe control, such as in swift currents, but should not be abused to the extent of continuing ahead.

Radar is an aid in determining position of other vessels in conditions of limited visibility, but it is not a justification for immoderate speed. The possession of information obtained from radar does not relieve any vessel of the obligation of conforming strictly with the Rules and in particular with the obligations of Article 15, Sound Signals in Restricted Visibility, and Article 16, Conduct in Restricted Visibility.

THE RULE OF GOOD SEAMANSHIP

Article 29 is the broad, summing-up "rule of good seamanship." It provides that nothing in the Rules shall exonerate any vessel, or the owner, master, or crew thereof, from the consequences of any neglect to carry lights or signals, or any neglect to keep a proper lookout, or the neglect of any precaution which may be required by the ordinary practice of seamen, or by the special circumstances of the case.

Lookouts

The need for a proper lookout is often taken rather too lightly by the skippers of boats and yachts, and this is a *serious* mistake. Under normal circumstances, the helmsman will satisfy the need, but he must be qualified, alert, and have no other responsibilities. The use of an automatic steering mechanism (so-called "autopilot"), see page 512, is *no* justification for the absence of a human helmsman at the controls observing *all around* the horizon and ready to immediately take over if needed. The use of radar at night or in fog is *no* justification for the absence of an additional person as a lookout, stationed outside the bridge, usually forward, where he can *hear* as well as see. The noise level at the control station of most motorboats renders the helmsman totally ineffective as a listening watch.

Supplementary Signals

Every vessel may, if necessary in order to attract attention, in addition to the lights which she is by the Rules required to carry, show a flare-up light or use any detonating signal that cannot be mistaken for a distress signal. [12]

PILOT RULES FOR INLAND WATERS

As noted in Chapters 2 and 4, the statutory Inland Rules of the Road provide authority for the issuance of regulations which are known as **Pilot Rules.** This material sometimes repeats what is in the basic Rules of the Road, but also additionally expands and implements them.

Many of the provisions of the Inland Pilot Rules covering topics of this chapter have been discussed above in connection with the applicable basic Article.

REGULATIONS [1]

TITLE 33—NAVIGATION AND NAVIGABLE WATERS

Chapter I—Coast Guard, Department of the Treasury

Subchapter D—Navigation Requirements for Certain Inland Waters

PART 80—PILOT RULES FOR INLAND WATERS

General

Sec.
80.01 General instructions.
80.02 Definition of steam vessel and vessel underway; risk of collision.

Signals

80.03 Signals.
80.1 Danger signal.
80.2 Cross signals.
80.3 Vessels passing each other.

Situations

80.4 Vessels approaching each other head and head, end on.
80.5 Vessels nearing bend or curve in channel; moving from docks.
80.6 Vessels running in same direction; overtaking vessel.
80.7 Vessels approaching each other at right angles or obliquely.
80.8 Meeting of steam and sailing vessels; right-of-way.
80.9 Avoidance of crossing ahead.
80.10 Keeping to right in narrow channels.
80.11 Departure from rules.
80.12 Fog signals.
80.13 Speed in fog; pamphlet containing Pilot Rules; diagrams.

Lights for certain classes of vessels

80.14 Lights; time for.

Sec.
80.16a Lights for barges, canalboats, scows, and other nondescript vessels on certain inland waters on the Gulf Coast and the Gulf Intracoastal Waterway.
80.16b Lights for barges, canalboats, scows, and other nondescript vessels temporarily operating on waters requiring different lights.
80.17 Lights for barges and canalboats in tow of steam vessels on the Hudson River and adjacent waters and Lake Champlain.

Lights and day signals for vessels, dredges of all types, and vessels working on wrecks and obstructions, etc.

80.18 Signals to be displayed by a towing vessel when towing a submerged or partly submerged object upon a hawser when no signals can be displayed upon the object which is towed.
80.19 Steam vessels, derrick boats, lighters, or other types of vessels made fast alongside a wreck, or moored over a wreck which is on the bottom or partly submerged, or which may be drifting.
80.20 Dredges held in stationary position by mooring ...

FIG. 536 Pilot Rules are Coast Guard regulations that implement and supplement the statutory Rules of the Road. They exist for all sets of U.S. Rules, but there are none for the International Rules.

Passing Coast Guard vessels

Paragraph 80.33(b) requires that all vessels passing a Coast Guard vessel servicing an aid to navigation must reduce speed sufficiently to ensure the safety of both vessels. If passing within 200 feet of the Coast Guard vessel—which will be displaying two orange-and-white vertically-striped balls by day or two red lights by night in a vertical line—the other vessel's speed must not exceed five miles per hour.

Unnecessary whistling prohibited

Section 80.35 of the Pilot Rules prohibits any unnecessary sounding of the whistle "within any harbor limits of the United States." Any licensed officer who authorizes or permits a violation of this regulation may face hearings which could result in the suspension or revocation of his license.

Distress signal

The Inland Pilot Rules, Section 80.37, authorize a daytime distress signal which is covered with the other distress signals on pages 87 to 88.

Copy required on board

Paragraph 80.13(b) requires that all vessels and craft *over 65 feet* in length must, where practicable, carry on board a copy of the current edition of CG-169 and have it available for ready reference.

Motorboats subject to the 1940 Act are specifically exempted, but this does not excuse a boat operator from knowing its contents. The conscientious skipper keeps a copy of this Coast Guard pamphlet on board whether required or not; it is a handy publication to have and occasionally review.

PENALTIES

The penalties for violation of the Inland Rules or Pilot Rules for Inland Waters are described in Chapter 2; see page 39.

For certain specified violations, the penalty is prescribed as the possible suspension or revocation of a master's or pilot's license.

Great Lakes Rules

The **Great Lakes Rules of the Road** are derived from an act of Congress of 8 February 1895 with subsequent amendments. These Rules apply on waters than can be broadly described as the Great Lakes, their tributaries, and connecting waterways. Exact limits are set forth in Chapter 2 on page 38.

The format of the Great Lakes Rules is generally the same as for the Inland Rules discussed above, except that the term for each major provision is "Rule" rather than "Article." Also as noted before in this chapter, there is little parallelism in the numbering of rules relating to the same general subject matter although in some places identical, or nearly identical, language is used.

The Great Lakes Rules will be considered here in terms of their differences from the Inland Rules discussed in detail above. Identical requirements, even though appearing in differently numbered rules, will not be repeated.

STEERING AND SAILING RULES

The Steering and Sailing Rules for the Great Lakes are roughly the same as those of the Inland Rules. Rule 16 relating to right-of-way of sailing vessels is identical with Article 17 except that subsection (e) of that Article, which states that a vessel with the wind aft must keep out of the way of the other vessel, is omitted.

Power-driven Vessels

The right-of-way and maneuvering rules for the meeting, crossing, and overtaking situations are generally similar to the provisions of the Inland Rules as discussed above, but they contain nothing on the whistle signals to be given; these are contained in separate Rules, see below.

The Great Lakes Rules of the Road do *not* specifically recognize the alternative situation of Inland Article 18, Rule I, where meeting vessels are sufficiently to starboard of each other so as to make a port-to-port passing un-necessary, but this is contained in the Pilot Rules. [90.5]

Likewise, the situation of a vessel approaching a blind bend or curve in a channel is covered (in a manner generally similar to the Inland Rules) by the Great Lakes Pilot Rules rather than the basic Rules of the Road. The duration of the long blast here is specified as "at least 8 seconds." [90.6]

The requirement for a similar long blast on the whistle by a vessel leaving a dock also appears in the Great Lakes Pilot Rules [90.7] rather than in the basic Rules of the Road.

Whistle Signals

Great Lakes Rule 23 prescribes whistle signals for course changes authorized or required by any of the other Rules. These signals are given **in all weathers** whether or not the vessels are within sight of each other; note carefully the difference from the Inland Rules.

One blast means "I am directing my course to star-board."

Two blasts mean, "I am directing my course to port."

Every power-driven vessel receiving a signal as above from another vessel must promptly respond with the same signal or the danger signal as described below.

This Rule specifically states, however, that the giving or answering of any whistle signal does not change the responsibilities and obligations of the vessels involved.

On the Great Lakes, there is **no** three-blast "backing" signal—actually this signal is used in reduced visibility situations as the basic underway vessel signal, see below.

Danger signal

The danger signal on the Great Lakes is described in Rule 26 as consisting of "several short and rapid blasts," but the Pilot Rules are more specific in requiring "not less than **five** blasts. If the vessels have approached within one-half mile of each other at the time of sounding the danger signal, *both* must be immediately slowed to bare steerage-way, and if necessary, stopped and reversed, until the proper signals have been given and answered or the vessels have passed. [90.2]

Crossed signals prohibited

The Great Lakes Pilot Rules also specifically forbid "cross signals"—answering one blast with two, or vice versa. If a pilot considers it injudicious to reply with the

FIG. 537 The danger signal for waters subject to the Great Lakes Pilot Rules consists of **five** or more short and rapid blasts of the whistle or horn. It is used to indicate dissent to another vessel's signalled intentions as well as for danger.

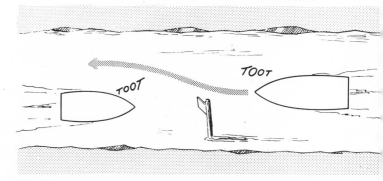

FIG. 538 The Great Lakes Rules of the Road give the right-of-way to vessels traveling with a current over those making their way up-stream. This is based on the relative controllability of the craft involved; it is a courteous action on waters of the Inland Rules although not legally required.

same signal sounded by the other vessel, he must sound the danger signal in lieu of a "cross" signal. [90.3]

Restricted Waters

In all channels less than 500 feet in width, no power-driven vessel shall overtake and pass another going in the same direction unless the privileged vessel consents to being passed. This restriction does not apply to passing a disabled vessel. [Rule 25]

When two power-driven vessels going in opposite directions meet in such a channel, both vessels must slow down to a "moderate" speed as determined by the circumstances. [25]

In all "narrow" channels (no width specified) a power-driven vessel less than 65 feet in length must not hamper the safe passage of a vessel (no size specified) that can navigate only inside the channel. [25] A similar restriction applies to sailboats. [19]

Rivers and channels with currents

In all narrow channels where there is current, and on five specified rivers, a power-driven vessel going *with* the current ("descending") has the right-of-way when meeting another such vessel proceeding against the current ("ascending"), and she must initiate the exchange of whistle signals before the separation of the vessels is reduced to a half-mile. [24]

FOG SIGNALS

The Great Lakes Rules' requirements for fog signals for power-driven vessels differ *considerably* from the provisions of the Inland Rules. A skipper going from waters governed by one set of rules to those of the other set should carefully prepare himself with knowledge of the new signals.

The fog signals for sailing vessels under the two sets of rules are in effect identical. The only difference is that the GLR specify that the wind must be forward of the beam for the one- and two-blast signals, whereas the IR merely imply such a condition. The GLR also specify that the sailing vessel is "not in tow." [14(d)]

Equipment

On the Great Lakes, a power-driven vessel must be provided with an efficient whistle sounded by steam or by some substitute for steam *and* this whistle must be placed forward of the funnel not less than eight feet from the deck. It must be of such character as to be heard "in ordinary weather" at a distance of at least two miles. The vessel must also be equipped with an efficient bell. (There is no mention of fog horn as required by the Inland Rules.) [14]

For craft subject to its provisions, however, the implementing regulations of the Motorboat Act of 1940 prescribe lesser requirements than the preceding paragraph, see page 58.

A sailing vessel must be equipped with an efficient fog horn and an efficient bell. [14]

When required

Fog signals are sounded on the Great Lakes either by day or night whenever there is "thick weather" resulting from fog, mist, falling snow, heavy rainstorms, or other cause.

Power-driven Vessels Underway

A power-driven vessel, other than one with a raft in tow, must sound *three distinct* blasts of her whistle at intervals of not more than one minute; the duration of the blasts is not specified. [14(a)] (Note carefully the difference between the basic fog signal of the GLR and the IR.)

Vessels Towing and Towed

A power-driven vessel towing other than a raft sounds the basic three-blast signal.

A power-driven vessel with a raft in tow will sound a unique fog signal at the same interval—a screeching or "Modoc" whistle for from three to five seconds.

A vessel *being towed* by another *must* sound a bell signal of four strokes in two groups of two strokes each. This is to be sounded at intervals of one minute. [14(b)] Note that here the interval is specific, rather than maximum— the usual "not more than one minute" of other sections of Great Lakes Rule 15 is not used; note also that the fog signal of a towed vessel is mandatory on these waters, rather than optional as in the Inland Rules. The GLR require that the bell be "good and efficient and properly placed."

Vessels Anchored or Aground

A vessel at anchor or one aground in or near a channel or fairway must sound *two separate signals*. At intervals of not more than *two* minutes, she must ring her bell rapidly for from three to five seconds. *Additionally,* at intervals of not more than *three* minutes, she must sound on her whistle or horn a signal of one short, two long, and one short blasts in quick succession. [14(e)] (This requirement might possibly have been made more complicated, but just how is not readily apparent!)

Special Provisions

Vessels of less than 10 tons registered tonnage, *not* power-driven, need not give the above fog signals, but if they do not, then they must make some other efficient sound signal at intervals of not more than *one* minute. [14(f)]

Fishing boats, produce boats, rafts, and other watercraft navigated by hand power or by the current of the river, or anchored or moored in or near a channel or fair-

FIG. 539 The Great Lakes fog signal—sounded in any kind of "thick weather"—is three distinct blasts of the whistle at intervals of not more than one minute. Note carefully the difference between this signal and the corresponding one of the Inland Rules.

way and not in any port, and not covered by any of the preceding rules, will sound a fog horn or equivalent signal at intervals of not less than *one* minute. [14(g)]

CONDUCT IN RESTRICTED VISIBILITY

The Great Lakes Rules differ slightly from the Inland Rules in the action to be taken by a vessel in conditions of reduced visibility, called "thick weather" on these waters.

Rule 15, in addition to requiring moderate speed as in the Inland Rules, also requires a power-driven vessel, hearing another, apparently not more than four points from dead ahead, to at once reduce speed to bare steerageway and navigate with caution until the vessels have passed each other. This zone of 45° on either side of the bow contrasts with the zone of 90° to either side specified by Inland Article 16.

RULE OF PRECAUTIONS

The Great Lakes "Rule of Precautions," Rule 28, is the same as the Rule of Good Seamanship of the Inland Rules; see page 79.

Supplementary signals

There are no provisions in the GLR comparable to Inland Article 12 which authorizes a flare-up light or detonating signal if necessary to attract attention.

PILOT RULES FOR THE GREAT LAKES

The regulations authorized by the Act of Congress which established the Great Lakes Rules of the Road are known as the **Pilot Rules for the Great Lakes.** These will be found in Title 33 of the Code of Federal Regulations, Chapter I, Subchapter E, Part 90. They are more readily available to boatmen in the free Coast Guard pamphlet CG-172 which also contains Part 92 of this CFR title, "Anchorage and Navigation Regulations; St. Mary's River, Michigan."

Fig. 540. If in or near a channel or fairway, a vessel anchored or aground in fog on the Great Lakes must sound two separate signals —one at two-minute intervals and the other at three-minute intervals. See text for the characteristics of each signal.

Portions of the Pilot Rules are duplicatory of the provisions of the basic Great Lakes Rules and will not be repeated here. Other portions of the Pilot Rules have been discussed above in connection with the specific requirements of the Rules of the Road.

Boundaries with the Western Rivers Rules

Two demarcation lines are established to separate waters subject to the Great Lakes Rules from those of the Western Rivers Rules.

These are the Thomas J. O'Brien Lock and Controlling Works on the Calumet River and the Ashland Avenue Bridge over the Chicago River. [90.03]

Posting of Pilot Rules

Paragraph 90.15(b) requires that vessels must keep the Pilot Rules posted in *two* conspicuous places, one of which shall be the pilothouse. (This requirement for the posting of a copy of the "Pilot Rules" rather than the "Great Lakes Rules of the Road" is one reason that some of the GLR provisions are repeated in the Pilot Rules.) The posting can consist of a placard containing the Pilot Rules or a copy of the CG-172 pamphlet secured in plain sight.

Motorboats, as defined in the Motorboat Act of 1940, are exempted from the requirement above for posting copies of the Pilot Rules or for carrying them on board. This exemption from the legal requirement, however, should not serve to keep a boat skipper in these waters from having a copy of the latest edition of CG-172 on board—he is still responsible for knowing its contents.

Other provisions

Many provisions of the Pilot Rules for the Great Lakes are similar to those for the Inland Waters, such as rules prohibiting any unnecessary sounding of a vessel's whistle. Other provisions are unique to the Great Lakes Pilot Rules, such as the inclusion of a set of signals between the master or pilot and the engineer for controlling the direction and speed of the vessel's engine. [90.15(a)]. These Pilot Rules also contain many more distress signals than the single one listed in the Inland Pilot Rules. [90.15(a)] See pages 87 to 88.

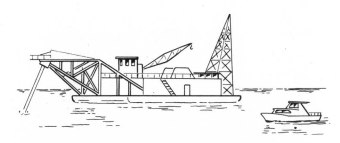

FIG. 541 The Great Lakes Pilot Rules now require that craft passing within 200 feet of "floating plant"—moored dredges and the like—must reduce their speed to not more than five miles per hour.

Recent additions to Pilot Rules

The Great Lakes Pilot Rules were amended in 1974 to add provisions formerly covered in Navigation Regulations of the Army Corps of Engineers. These regulations have now been revoked, but they will still appear in CG-172 until a new edition of that pamphlet can be prepared.

These newly added Pilot Rules relate to navigation and whistle signals of vessels passing "floating plant"—dredges, pile drivers, and the like—working in navigable channels. The provisions do not conflict with nor contradict the Rules of the Road, but do add some specifics such as a speed limit of five miles per hour when passing within 200 feet of floating plant and the stopping of propulsion machinery when passing over the lines of a plant. [90.31]

The locations of anchors used to hold a floating plant in position must be marked with barrels or other suitable buoys. [90.33] Light-draft vessels must keep outside of such markers wherever possible. [90.32], and all vessels must avoid running over these buoys, or any buoys, stakes, and marks placed for the guidance of floating plant operations. [90.36]

With the new additions, the Great Lakes Pilot Rules now cover the required lights for vessels towing a submerged object or working alongside a wreck and for dredges.

Western Rivers Rules

The **Western Rivers Rules of the Road** consist of numbered "Rules" like the Great Lakes Rules, but again the numbering is, in most cases, not parallel between the two sets of rules although the provisions are essentially the same.

Major differences include a different "bend" signal, several important variations in fog signals, and the requirement that a privileged vessel hold only her course (rather than course and speed). The **Pilot Rules for Western Rivers** contain a section covering the right-of-way between two vessels meeting at the junction of two rivers.

The Western Rivers Pilot Rules provide right-of-way to a vessel "descending" a river, running down with the current. The "ascending"—upbound—vessel must yield to the

other craft when both are about to enter a narrow channel, when they meet in such a channel (the descending vessel must pass at a slow speed), and when they meet at a bridge span or draw. This is a logical procedure as the skipper of an upbound craft has greater and easier control.

Because of their lesser applicability to the majority of boatmen, in comparison with the Inland and Great Lakes Rules, the Western Rivers Rules of the Road and their associated Pilot Rules will not be considered in detail in this chapter. The skipper concerned with these waters—principally the Mississippi River and its tributaries, but also including two other rivers—see page 38 for exact limits—should obtain a copy of Coast Guard pamphlet CG-184 and study it carefully.

International Rules of the Road

An individual who has carefully studied the provisions of the U.S. Inland Rules will have few problems when faced with the "International Regulations for the Prevention of Collisions at Sea"—the full and formal name for what is generally referred to as the **International Rules of the Road.**

These regulations—created by international conferences and made applicable to U.S. waters and vessels by Act of Congress and Presidential proclamation—consist of a series of "Rules" numbered from 1 to 31 without omission of any numbers, plus an "Annex." Those Rules relating to the topics of this chapter, and the Annex, will be discussed below primarily in terms of their differences and variations from the U.S. Inland Rules. Where no difference is pointed out, the provisions of a Rule of the International Rules of the Road (IntRR) are the same as those of the Inland Rules (IR), although not necessarily of the Article with the corresponding number.

Rules of the IntRR dealing with navigation lights and day shapes are discussed in Chapter 4.

Applicability

The International Rules of the Road, as established under U.S. authority, are applicable to two situations:

1. To **all** vessels in waters of the United States sovereignty outside the prescribed boundary lines at entrance to bays, rivers harbors, etc.; see page 31.

2. To *all* U.S. vessels. *on the high seas* not subject to another nation's geographical jurisdiction.

DEFINITION OF TERMS

International Rule 1(c) includes definitions of two terms related to the topics of this chapter which were not formally defined in the U.S. Inland Rules.

Many of the Chapter 4 basic definitions of the Inland Rules [page 64(c)] and the International Rules [page 64(s)] are also applicable to this chapter.

Additional definitions

In sight—Vessels are deemed to be within sight of one another when one can be visually observed from the other.

Whistle—the word "whistle" means any appliance capable of producing the prescribed short and prolonged blasts. (These blasts are also specifically defined in Rule 1(c) in the same terms as in the Inland Rules of the Road or Pilot Rules.)

STEERING AND SAILING RULES

The "Preliminiary Statement" to the Steering and Sailing Rules of the International Rules includes a directive that is not a part of the Inland Rules, but which is an excellent one that should be known and heeded on all waters.

"In construing and obeying these Rules, any action taken should be positive, in ample time, and with due regard to the observance of good seamanship."

The Preliminary Statement also contains a caution regarding the limitations of seaplanes in the act of landing or taking off, or operating under adverse weather conditions. This, too, is applicable to all waters by reason of logic if not law.

International Rules 17 through 24 relating to right-of-

FIG. 542 The International Rules of the Road not only affect all vessels in U.S. off-shore waters, but they also apply to all U.S. vessels anywhere on the high seas—the ocean waters not subject to the jurisdiction of any nation.

way between vessels are specifically limited to vessels "in sight of one another." This limitation does not appear in the Inland Rules, except indirectly in Article 18.

Passing Situations

International Rules 18, 19, and 24 direct the same actions for power-driven vessels in meeting, crossing, and overtaking situations as the Inland Rules, but **without** the whistle signals of intent and agreement as to the side to be passed on.

Sailing vessels

International Rule 17 covering the right-of-way between two sailing vessels encountering each other is phrased quite differently from the provisions of the Inland Rules.

When each has the wind on a different side, the vessel which has the wind on the port side must keep out of the way of the other.

When both have the wind on the same side, the vessel which is to windward must keep out of the way of the vessel that is to leeward.

For the purpose of Rule 17, the windward side is considered to be the side opposite to that on which the mainsail is carried (or in the case of a square-rigged vessel, the side opposite to that on which the largest fore-and-aft sail is carried).

Sound Signals for Vessels Within Sight

The one- and two-blast sound signals of good visibility situations in the International Rules are indications of *taking action to alter course* rather than the U.S. Rules signals of intent and agreement. The International Rules signals are frequently termed "rudder signals"; they do not involve a reply and the IntRR do not speak of an "exchange" of whistle signals.

FIG. 543 The whistle signals of the International Rules of the Road indicate changes of course (rudder signals) rather than intentions to pass under certain conditions. In this well-clear, port-to-port meeting, no signals would be exchanged.

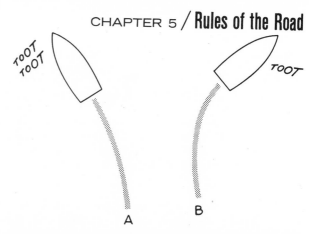

Rule 28 of the IntRR states that one short blast means "I am altering my course to starboard" and two short blasts mean "I am altering my course to port." The three-short-blast signal has the meaning "My engines are going astern"—the same generally as the Inland Rules, but without including the words "full speed."

Signal of doubt (Danger signal)

Whenever a power-driven vessel that is required to hold her course and speed in a situation with another is in sight of that other vessel and is in doubt as to whether sufficient action is being taken to avoid a collision, she *may* indicate such *doubt* by sounding *at least five* short and rapid blasts on her whistle. The giving of this signal does not relieve a vessel of her obligations under the Rule of Good Seamanship, the General Prudential Rule, or any other of the rules of the road, including her duty to sound other whistle signals as indicative of her intentions to alter course. [28(b)]

Note that the International Rule signal is *limited* to a *privileged* vessel, and thus to those situations wherein there is relative right-of-way—crossing and overtaking. Its use is optional, as contrasted with some situations under the Inland Rules where the danger signal must be sounded.

Whistle light

Any International whistle signal *may* be further indicated by a visual signal consisting of a white light visible all around the horizon to a distance of at least five miles. This light, if used, must be so installed that it operates simultaneously and in conjunction with the sound signal mechanism; it must light and remain lighted for the same period as the sound signal. [28(c)]

This is essentially the same visual signal as required by the Western Rivers Pilot Rules for many types of vessels, except for color and required distance of visibility.

FIG. 545 a, b Under the International Rules a power-driven vessel starting a change of course within sight of another vessel must sound a whistle signal. This is not returned by the other vessel, and thus there is no "exchange" of signals.

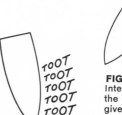

FIG. 546 In waters subject to the International Rules of the Road, the danger signal may only be given by a privileged vessel in doubt as to whether the action being taken by the burdened vessel is sufficient to avert collision.

FIG. 547 Any whistle signal authorized by the International Rules may be visually indicated by a light synchronized with the sound-producing apparatus. This is to be an all-around white light visible to at least five miles.

Sound Signals in Reduced Visibility

The principal difference here between the requirements of the IntRR and those of the IR is that power-driven vessels need sound their fog signal only at intervals of *two* minutes or less, rather than one minute. [15(c)(i)]

An additional signal is prescribed for power-driven vessels underway but stopped and making no way through the water—as might be the case in fog so dense as to make any speed at all greater than "moderate," often in water too deep to anchor. This is a two-prolonged-blast signal with about one second's spacing between blasts; it is repeated at the normal interval of not more than two minutes. [15(c)(ii)]

Sailing vessels

The International Rules prescribe the same fog signal for sailing vessels as do the Inland Rules, including the *one* minute interval.

Vessels of limited maneuverability

In situations of reduced visibility, a vessel towing another, or a vessel engaged in laying or picking up a submarine cable or navigation mark, or a vessel underway

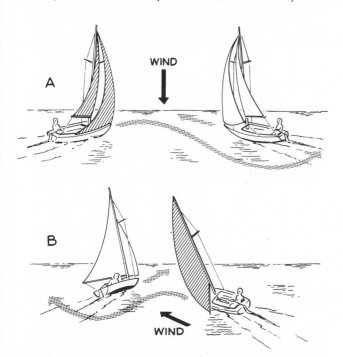

FIG. 544 a, b International Rules 17 covers the relative right-of-way between two sailboats encountering each other an off-shore waters. The language of this Rule varies considerably from Inland Article 17. Burdened sailboats are shown with shaded sails.

that is not under command or is unable to maneuver as required by the rules of the road, *must* sound a special signal *in lieu of* the normal fog signals of power-driven and sailing vessels. This consists of three blasts in succession—one prolonged, and two short—sounded at intervals of not more than *one* minute. [15(c)(v)] For vessels engaged in towing, this is the same signal as prescribed in the Inland Rules; the other classes of vessels covered by this rule are not mentioned in the Inland fog signals.

Vessels being towed

If manned, a vessel being towed (or the last vessel if several are being towed in a string) must sound a fog signal of four blasts—one prolonged and three short blasts—at intervals of not more than *one* minute. When practicable, this signal should be sounded immediately after the signal of the towing vessel. [15(c)(vi)] This signal differs from that of the Inland Rules and is mandatory rather than optional.

Vessels at anchor

The IntRR prescribe the usual fog signal for a vessel at anchor, the ringing of a bell for about five seconds at intervals of not more than one minute, and provide an *additional* signal for vessels over 350 feet in length. In such vessels, the regular bell must be rung in the fore part of the ship *and* in the after part at the same interval there must be sounded for about five seconds a gong or other instrument the tone and sounding of which cannot be confused with that of the bell.

Further, *any* vessel at anchor in waters of the International Rules, regardless of size, *may* sound a three-blast signal—one short, one prolonged, one short—to give warning of her position and status to an approaching vessel that might collide with her. [15(c)(iv)]

Vessels aground

A vessel which is aground in International Rules' waters in reduced visibility must give the normal bell signal of a vessel at anchor (and the gong signal if required by her size), and *additionally* sound three separate and distinct strokes of the bell *before and after* the rapid ringing of the bell. [15(c)(vii)] There is no parallel signal in the Inland Rules; as noted above, such vessels there should sound the danger signal on their whistle in lieu of ringing a bell.

Fishing vessels

A vessel "engaged in fishing" [see definition on page 64(s)] *when underway or at anchor* must sound the signal described above for vessels of limited maneuverability—one prolonged blast followed by two short ones. A vessel fishing with trolling lines and underway sounds only the normal signal of a sailing vessel underway or a power-driven vessel underway or underway with no way on. [15(c)(viii)]

Exceptions

A vessel of less than 40 feet in length or a rowing boat is not obliged to give the signals of the above subsections of Rule 15(c), but if she does not, she must make some other efficient sound signal at intervals of not more than *one* minute. [15(c)(ix)]

A major difference between the IntRR and the IR for

FIG. 548 In waters of the International Rules, the one prolonged blast—four to six seconds—signal for vessels making way through the water when visibility is reduced need be sounded only once every two minutes. If the vessel is "underway with no way on," the signal is two prolonged blasts.

FIG. 549 A vessel towed astern in waters of the International Rules (the last vessel if more than one is being towed in tandem) must, if manned, sound a signal of one prolonged blast followed by three short blasts; this should be sounded immediately following the tug's fog signal.

FIG. 550 The International Rules prescribe the same fog bell signal for smaller vessels as in the Inland Rules, but require an additional—gong—signal for vessels over 350 feet in length. Further, **any** vessel at anchor in these waters **may** sound a one short—one prolonged—one short whistle signal also.

sound signals in conditions of reduced visibility is that there are no exceptions in the International Rules for "special anchorage areas." This is logical as the usually open waters of these Rules are less likely to provide safe anchorages for small craft and barges.

A further, but minor, difference is that International Rule 15(a) requires that power-driven and sailing vessels over 40 feet in length must have an efficient fog horn "to be sounded by mechanical means"; this language does not appear in the Inland Rules.

Pilot vessels

When engaged in her duties, a power-driven pilot vessel *may* sound an "identity" signal of four short blasts. This would be in addition to the normal signals of a vessel underway, underway with no way on, or at anchor.

CONDUCT IN RESTRICTED VISIBILITY

Subsections (a) and (b) of International Rule 16 regarding speed and conduct in fog or other situations of reduced visibility are essentially the same as Inland Article 16, but the IntRR contains a subsection (c) with an *additional requirement.*

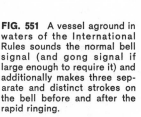

FIG. 551 A vessel aground in waters of the International Rules sounds the normal bell signal (and gong signal if large enough to require it) and additionally makes three separate and distinct strokes on the bell before and after the rapid ringing.

A power-driven vessel which detects the presence of another vessel forward of her beam before hearing her fog signal or sighting her visually—this would normally mean detection by radar—*may* take early and substantial action to avoid a close-quarters situation, but if this cannot be avoided, she *must,* insofar as the circumstances of the situation permit, stop her engines in proper time to avoid collision and then navigate with caution until danger of collision is over.

The "may take early and substantial action" in the above paragraph is the way that the International Rule is formally worded—for all practical purposes, however, considering the Rule of Good Seamanship, it ought to be "should take early action," or even "must."

GENERAL RIGHT-OF-WAY RULES

With respect to the "duty" of the privileged vessel, In-

ternational Rule 21 contains the same language as Inland Article 21 regarding her requirement to keep her course and speed, but the IntRR go on to state that when, for any cause, the privileged vessel finds herself so close that collision cannot be avoided by the actions of the burdened vessel alone, she, too, must take such action as will best aid in the prevention of a collision. This is only logical, but does not so clearly appear in the Inland Rules.

Burdened vessel's duty

International Rule 22 contains the same requirement as Inland Article 22 for the burdened vessel to keep out of the way and avoid crossing ahead, but also specifically states that she must, so far as possible, take positive early action to comply with her obligation.

Rule 23 regarding the slackening of speed, or stopping or reversing, is identical with Article 23.

RADAR ANNEX

The International Rules contain an "Annex" which has no counterpart in the Inland Rules. This annex is entitled "Recommendations on the Use of Radar Information as an Aid to Avoiding Collisions at Sea."

Skippers of boats equipped with radar should be thoroughly familiar with the contents of this Annex—it is mandatory on waters subject to the International Rules, and it makes good sense on all waters.

Distress Signals

Because of their great importance, the accepted forms of distress signals have been written into the various Rules of the Road or related Pilot Rules.

Some signals are the same, or nearly so, in all sets of Rules; others appear in only one or two sets. Table 5-1 lists the various *officially recognized* signals for each set of Rules of the Road or Pilot Rules, but in a true emergency a skipper can use *any* means within his capabilities to summon help.

Additional distress signals

The Coast Guard also recognizes two additional distress signals that are particularly well-suited to the needs of small craft. One is an excellent signal, developed in Canada, that any boat owner can make (it is also available for purchase in many stores). This signal consists simply of a 45" x 72" rectangular piece of fluorescent orange-red cloth on which are marked a black 18" square and a black 18" circle separated by an 18" space, symmetrically arranged with a 9" space at each end. It is based on the International Rule signal of "a square flag having above or below it a ball . . . " This piece of cloth could be displayed vertically to other vessels or horizontally across the boat cabin top as a signal to aircraft.

Also recognized is a simple orange-red flag of any size, waved from side to side.

Use of inverted ensign

Most American boatmen would recognize the flying of an *inverted* U.S. national or yacht ensign as a signal of

distress. It should be carefully noted, however, that such a signal has **no** official sanction. This stems from the fact that the national flags of many maritime nations have no "top" or "bottom" and would appear exactly the same if turned upside down!

Radio alarm signals

The radiotelephone is, of course, a major means of announcing a distress situation and requesting help; see pages 496 to 498. Vessels in distress may use the radiotelephone alarm signal to secure attention to distress calls and messages. This consists of two different tones transmitted alternately and rapidly for from 30 seconds to one minute. It is very distinctive and effective.

There is also a radiotelegraph alarm signal, but this is of little interest to boatmen.

Submarine distress signals

Distress signals used by submarines of the U.S. Navy are not included in the U.S. or International Rules, but these should be known by the skippers of all craft plying offshore waters.

U.S. submarines are equipped with signal ejectors which may be used to launch identification signals, including emergency signals. Two general types of signals are used: smoke floats, and flares or stars. The smoke floats, which burn on the surface, produce a dense colored smoke for a period of 15 to 45 seconds. The flares or stars are propelled to a height of 300 to 400 feet from which they descend by small parachute, burning for about 25 seconds.

The color of the smoke or flare/star has the following meaning:

Green or black—Used for training exercises only to indicate that a torpedo has been fired or the firing of a torpedo has been simulated.

Yellow—Indicates that the submarine is about to come to periscope depth from below periscope depth. Surface ships and craft should clear the area; do *not* stop propellers.

Red—Indicates an emergency condition within the submarine, and that it will surface immediately, if possible. Surface ships and craft should clear the area and stand by to give assistance after the submarine has surfaced. In case of repeated red signals, or if the submarine fails to surface within a reasonable time, she may be assumed to be disabled. Mariners should determine the location, buoy it, look for the submarine's marker buoy, and advise U.S. Naval or Coast Guard authorities immediately.

The differences between the U.S. Inland, Great Lakes, and Western Rivers Rules of the Road have long been recognized. Legislation was introduced in the 90th Congress (1968) to replace these three sets of Rules with a single set to be known as the "U.S. Nautical Rules." No Congressional action was taken, however, and the proposals were subsequently shelved pending the adoption of new international rules.

An international conference in 1972 adopted a new set of Rules of the Road which now must be ratified by the requisite number of maritime nations. The "International Regulations for the Prevention of Collisions at Sea, 1972" will not become effective before mid-1976, or later. The new International Rules are very different in form, and in some cases, in substance, from the old IntRR.

The 1972 International Rules have been sent to Congress for enactment into U.S. law, with subsequent Coast Guard regulations. Following this adoption, action will resume to establish a single set of U.S. inland rules which will be consistent with the new IntRR. An effective date for such new inland rules cannot be forecast, but it probably would be one year after enactment. This chapter will be revised before the effective date of any new Rules.

Know the Rules

It cannot be emphasized too strongly that (1) a skipper of any boat must know the rules of the road relating to his craft and waters; and (2) it is too late to start learning them when he gets into a tight situation! Rules must be studied carefully and thoroughly, and they should be periodically reviewed as a refresher.

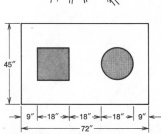

FIG. 552 The various Rules of the Road and Pilot Rules each list a set of distress signals; no two sets are the same, however. The square flag and round shape, and the code flags "NC" are from the International Rules but do not appear in the Inland Rules of the Road or Pilot Rules.

Table 5–1   DISTRESS SIGNALS

Distress Signal	Rules of the Road or Pilot Rules			
	Inland	Great Lakes	Western Rivers	Inter-national
Continuous sounding with any fog-signal apparatus	D/N	D/N	D/N	X
Firing of a gun or other explosive signal	D/N	D/N(2)	D/N(2)	X(2)
Flames on the vessel (as from a burning tar or oil barrel, etc.)	N	N	N	X
A signal consisting of a square flag having either above or below it a ball or some object resembling a ball		D	D	X
Slowly and repeatedly raising and lowering arms outstretched to each side	D	D	D	X
Rockets or shells, throwing stars of any color or description, fired one at a time at short intervals		N	D/N	X
The International Code signal of distress indicated by NC			D	X
The signal SOS sent in the Morse Code (. . . — — — . . .) sent by any means				X
The spoken word "Mayday" by radiotelephone				X
A rocket parachute flare or a hand flare showing a red light				X
A smoke signal giving off a volume of orange colored smoke				X

The above signals can be used singly or in any combination.

Notes 1—D = Day use; N = Night use;
D/N = Day or night use;
X—IntRR do not specify in terms of day or night use.
2—fired at intervals of about one minute

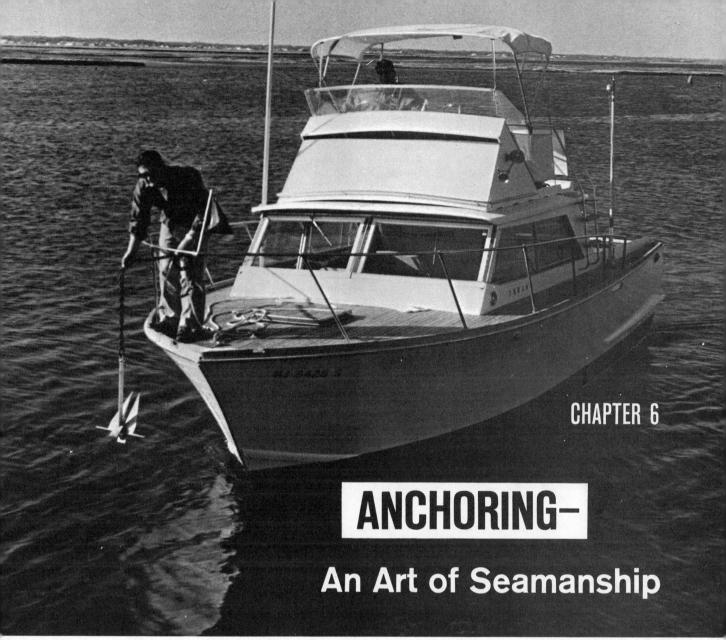

CHAPTER 6

ANCHORING—

An Art of Seamanship

Of all the skills involved in seamanship, the art of anchoring is one the boatman must master if he is to cruise with an easy mind. Perhaps he is just getting by with inadequate gear, despite bad practices acquired in home waters. Sooner or later, carelessness and ignorance will lead to difficulty—probably inconvenience, possibly danger.

The essence of successful anchoring is to "stay put," without dragging, whenever the anchor is let go. Corollary to this is the need to respect the rights of nearby boats which could be fouled or damaged by your dragging.

Though the art may not be learned from the printed page alone, this chapter should help the tyro to get off to a good start, the seasoned boatman to round out and update his technique.

In quiet anchorages, in familiar surroundings, *ground tackle* (the gear we use) and the methods used are seldom put to test. Cruising into strange waters, find inadequate shelter in an exposed anchorage during a hard blow, and the elements will surely take the measure of both tackle and technique. The ultimate test, of course, would come in deep water on a lee shore with nothing between you and breakers on the beach except dependable gear. Ask yourself *now,* in a situation like that, would I hold . . . or hope?

The problem, then, breaks down into two principal parts—(1) the equipment we should carry, and (2) knowledge of how to use it. It is in this sequence that we treat the subject here, however anxious the reader may be to plunge headlong into the "how" aspect before he is quite familiar with the "what."

Anchoring / CHAPTER 6

Conditions vary

In approaching the subject, it is imperative to have a sense of perspective, impossible to achieve if one is so wedded to the lore of one locality (no matter how good or effective) as to be blinded to practices proved in other areas. Lay down universal rules based on experience solely with one type of anchor in one kind of bottom, and the gale that would test your "rules" would be but a breeze compared to the storm of controversy you might raise in other knowledgeable quarters.

When we realize that the gear we see aboard that visiting boat from a distant port may have been dictated by proved and practical experience foreign to our own, we will have gone a long way toward broadening that perspective we need ... and, who knows, perhaps improving our own anchoring skill as well.

Some of the variables

The man who has cruised in many areas, over many years, knows he can list nine or ten important variables. To cite a few: the size and type of boat; whether she is of light or heavy draft; the size and design of anchor; the nature of the bottom in which the anchor is bedded; the protection afforded by the anchorage; and the amount of sea running.

To say that any one kind of ground tackle would be ideal under all conceivable conditions for all boats of a given length is to discount the combined knowledge of the saltiest boatmen in waters all up and down our coastline. To rule out completely the value of certain specialized equipment is to overlook the fact that many a seasoned skipper has his own well-founded preferences ... or prejudices.

FIG. 601 A century ago, wooden stock anchors were still in use. This one snagged the net of a dragger in the late 1940's, off Chatham, Cape Cod, offshore of Pollock Rip Lightship. It's likely that it was lost by a four- or five-masted coastal cargo schooner.
(From Kodachrome by Wm. H. Koelbel)

Evolution of the modern anchor

It is beyond the scope of this chapter to delve deeply into the history of anchors, interesting though that may be. Touching on it briefly, however, we get an insight into the evolution from ancient to modern design, and what lies behind the quest for an anchor that will *bury*, not drag. At this point it will be helpful to refer to the sketches, fig. 602, and labeled diagram, fig. 604, which, later, will clarify the meaning of terms used to describe the anchor's parts.

Going back to primitive times, the earliest "anchor" of which we have record was a simple stone used with a crude rope. Though it may have served under ideal conditions to prevent the drift of an ancient watercraft, dragging at times was inevitable, when sheer weight was unable to hold against the pull of wind and current.

Obviously what was needed was a device to engage the bottom, giving rise to the addition of simple wooden (and later, iron) hooks, forerunner of the arms and flukes found in later developments. To this day, survivors of this early anchor concept may be found Down East in Nova Scotia, where fishermen still fashion by hand their "killicks" of wood, stone and manila. Colloquially, we drop a "hook" when we lower an anchor.

Modifications of the hooking type of anchor evolved and, roughly 4,000 years ago, the Chinese added a stock at the crown end of the shank, perpendicular to the plane of the hooking arms, to put them in position to get a bite in the bottom. Junks still use this type today. In an ancient Greek design (about 750 B.C.) the stock had moved to the ring end of the shank.

In due course, in an effort to increase holding power, broad triangular flukes were added to the arms, giving rise to the old-fashioned kedge, fig. 603, often with a wooden stock, fig. 601, at the ring end of the shank, as used on naval vessels well into the 19th century. In 1821 the first of a series of stockless (patent) Navy anchors was invented Elimination of the stock permitted the shank to be drawn up into the hawsepipe of a vessel, flukes lying flat against the topsides.

Toward the middle of the 19th century, the mushroom anchor appeared, its design restricting its principal value to use in permanent moorings. Though their holding power is low, very small craft often use them for brief stops in light weather.

The principle of placing the stock at the crown end was brought to a relatively high state of development in the Northill design (now marketed as the Danforth Utility), where short, broad, thin flukes provided better penetration and a folding stock improved stowage characteristics.

In 1933, a radical innovation in design was introduced in England—the plow, a stockless type in which conventional flukes were replaced by a casting resembling a plow, pivoted at its point of attachment to the shank.

Supplanting mass and weight with scientific design, R. S. Danforth in 1939 developed what has been referred to by the U.S. Navy as the *lightweight-type* anchor in which broad pivoted flukes, stabilized by a stock, not only penetrate the bottom but bury completely until firm holding ground is reached. It is this feature, primarily, which distinguishes the *burying* anchor from a type that is prone to drag.

So much for history.

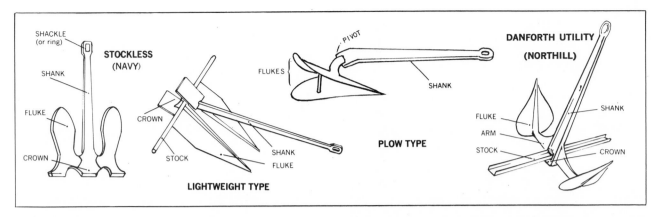

Ground Tackle

Some terms and definitions

To prevent possibility of confusion in the use of terms, refer again to the labeled illustration of the parts of an anchor, fig. 604, and the more general definitions in Table 6-1. A popular version of the kedge was chosen to illustrate the parts, because it is a type frequently visualized as a conventional anchor. Subsequently we shall see how the proportioning and placement of parts have varied with the introduction of later designs. Many otherwise well-informed boatmen have often spoken of the shank and stock as though the terms were interchangeable. In fact, however, most anchors (with few exceptions) have shanks, but some are stockless.

To illustrate graphically the basic fundamentals in anchoring, one authority sketches, in fig. 605, what has been referred to as *the anchoring system*. Though *scope* has been defined in Table 6-1 as the ratio between the length of the anchor line and the distance from the bow chocks to the bottom, there are other important factors, such as the range of any tidal rise and fall. This will be dealt with more fully later, as scope is one of the most important of all factors in determining holding power.

Finally, to forestall argument as to the validity of the term *rode*, it should be noted that the word has, on rare occasions, been challenged. Without going to its defense here, we can say that our best boating authorities have long accepted its usage in nautical jargon, and it is unlikely that it will ever be lost to the language.

TYPES OF ANCHORS IN USE

Lightweight type (LWT)

Scan a marine hardware catalog and, without experience, you may be confused by the diversity of designs offered today. What you should be buying, essentially, is holding power; sheer weight is no index of that. On the contrary, scientific design is the key to efficiency and a lightweight type, *if properly manufactured,* unquestionably stands at the top of the list today on a holding power-to-weight basis.

The lightweight type was originated just prior to World War II by R. S. Danforth. Its efficiency in war service was so high that it made possible the retraction of amphibious craft in assaults on enemy-held beachheads. After the war, models were developed specifically for recreational and small commercial craft and these are widely used. Such an anchor is excellent in mud and sand, and, with caution, can be used on rocky bottoms; however, it often does not hold well in grassy bottoms.

In this type of anchor, flukes are long and sharp, designed so that heavy strains bury the anchor completely. Tests have proved that it tends to work down through soft bottoms to firmer holding ground below, burying part of

---

TABLE 6-1. SOME BASIC DEFINITIONS

Anchor—A device designed to engage the bottom of a waterway and through its resistance to drag maintain a vessel within a given radius.

Anchor Chocks—Fittings on the deck of a vessel used to stow an anchor when it is not in use.

Anchor Rode—The line connecting an anchor with a vessel.

Bow Chocks—Fittings, usually on the rail of a vessel near its stem, having jaws that serve as fairleads for anchor rodes and other lines.

Ground Tackle—A general term for the anchor, anchor rodes, fittings, etc., used for securing a vessel at anchor.

Hawsepipe—A cylindrical or elliptical pipe or casting in a vessel's hull through which the anchor rode runs.

Horizontal Load—The horizontal force placed on an anchoring device by the vessel to which it is connected.

Mooring Bitt—A post or cleat through or on the deck of a vessel used to secure an anchor rode or other line to the vessel.

Scope—The ratio of the length of the anchor rode to the vertical distance from the bow chocks to the bottom (depth plus height of bow chocks above water).

Vertical Load—The lifting force placed on the bow of a vessel by its anchor rode.

Definitions (except scope) are from a code of standards and recommended practices adopted by the American Boat & Yacht Council.

the rode as well, fig. 609(b).

In place of a stock through the head, the lightweight type has a round rod at the crown end to prevent the anchor from rolling or rotating. This placement of the stock does not interfere with its being drawn into the hawse-pipes of larger craft for stowage. (Many skippers place protective rubber tips over the stock ends; others merely plug the ends of the rod, which is hollow, to prevent mud and sand from entering and so being brought on deck.)

A key element in the high performance of Danforth Anchors is the design of the crown. The two flat, inward-sloping surfaces force the thin, sharp flukes to dig into the bottom and penetrate deeply. The surfaces of the crown are placed away from the plane of the flukes in order to help reduce clogging with mud, grass, or bottom debris that might possibly interfere with the penetration of the anchor and its holding power.

For recreational and commercial small craft, Standard Danforth anchors are made in approximate weights from 2-1/2 to 180 pounds, the Hi-Tensile model in sizes from 5 to 90 pounds. For comparable weights, Hi-Tensile models provide roughly 20% to 30% more holding power.

A number of other manufacturers produce anchors of the light-weight, burying type. The development of suitable alloys has made possible anchors of this style in aluminum (Viking) with considerable savings in dead weight.

In selecting an anchor, remember that all manufacturers have their own concepts of design, and "look-alikes" do not necessarily hold alike; data on holding power under similar conditions should be carefully compared.

The plow

The plow anchor is unique in design, resembling none of the other types. It was invented in England by Professor G. I. Taylor of Cambridge University; he called it the CQR (secure). It found wide acceptance because of its demonstrated efficiency in a variety of bottoms. Opinions vary as to its effectiveness in heavy weed, which is not surprising in that certain weed growths resist penetration by any anchor. The Plowright, fig. 608, is a model since developed and manufactured in the United States.

When a plow is lowered, the anchor first lies on its side on the bottom. See fig. 609(a). Then when a pull is put on the rode, it rights itself, driving the point of the plow in, and finally burying the plow completely. The Plowright is claimed to hold up to 300 times its weight, depending naturally on the kind of bottom. CQR suggested catalog weights vary from 10 pounds for a 20-footer to 75 pounds for 75—125-footers.

Because of the pivoting feature of the shank, the tendency of the plow is to remain buried when the angle of pull is changed by wind or current. There is no projecting fluke to foul the rode and it breaks out easily when the pull is vertical, in position to bring the anchor up on deck.

Kedges

In discussing kedges it is important to make a sharp distinction between the more massive ancient types and later versions which have been designed for yacht use. In glossaries, "kedge anchors" as a rule are light anchors (of any design) carried out from a vessel aground to free her by winching in on the rode. Here, however, we refer to the kedge as an anchor with the more conventional type of

FIG. 604 Wilcox Crittenden's Yachtsman anchor, with parts labeled. The stock can be folded to lie along the shank.

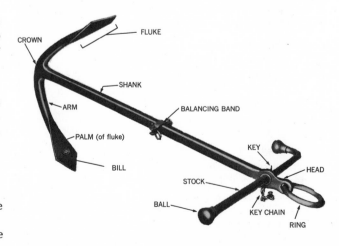

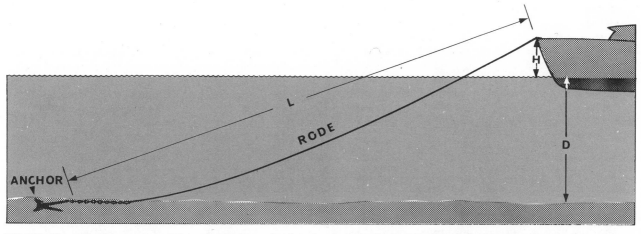

FIG. 605 The anchoring system includes not only the anchor but also the rode, the length of which is referred to in terms of "scope" (the ratio of L to D + H). It is important that the depth, D, be considered as that at high tide for it is at this time that the scope will be least.

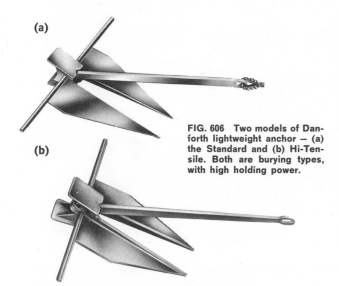

FIG. 606 Two models of Danforth lightweight anchor — (a) the Standard and (b) Hi-Tensile. Both are burying types, with high holding power.

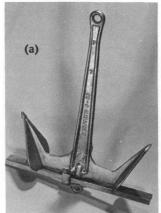 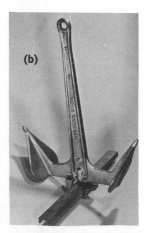

FIG. 607 The Danforth Utility anchor, a modification of the Northill design, is shown (a) with the stock folded and (b) with the stock set up in position for use.

arms, flukes and stocks as distinguished from newer light-weight types.

The earliest kedges, aside from their mass, were characterized by roughly triangular flukes and relatively dull bills. See fig. 610. The shoulders on the flukes, being nearly square with the arm, invited fouling of the rode as a vessel swung at her anchorage with shifts in wind and current. The dull bills made it difficult to bite in hard bottoms. Other kedges, like sand and trawl anchors, designed for use primarily on hard bottoms, had very small flukes and sharp bills. Both of these types left much to be desired for general yacht use, though often right for special purposes.

Yachtsman and Herreshoff anchors

Types of anchor which evolved from earlier kedges include the Yachtsman, fig. 604, and Herreshoff, fig. 611(b), designs. Though varying in details of construction, the principle used in both was a redistribution of the weight, a different proportioning of the length of stock to the chord measured from bill to bill, and a drastic change in the shape and size of fluke relative to the arm.

A major distinguishing feature of these modified kedges is the diamond-shaped fluke, embodied in the design to reduce risk of fouling, on the theory that the rode would slip off an exposed fluke where no squared shoulder was presented. At the same time, sharpening of the bill permitted better penetration in hard bottoms.

Neither of these kedges is claimed to be a "burying" type, as the shank lies on the bottom and one fluke remains exposed. On the other hand, its "hook" design recommends it, probably above all other types, on rocky bottoms where one fluke can find a crevice, and retrieval, with proper precautions, is not too difficult. (More about this later.)

Northill-type anchors

The concept of light weight was first brought to kedge-type anchors with the introduction of the Northill design. Originally made in stainless steel, the current model, called the Danforth Utility, is made of malleable iron, hot-dip galvanized for resistance to corrosion.

The Northill design is unique, resembling the kedge only to the extent that it is a "hooking" type. Here, however, the stock has been placed at the other end of the shank, square with the arms, but moveable to fold along the shank or across the arms for better stowage.

Patterned after a principle utilized on wooden anchors in Malaysia through thousands of years, the Northill stock adds to the anchor's holding power when the fluke is buried. Arms are at right angles to the shank, and the broad reinforced flukes with sharp bills are set at a carefully computed angle to assure a quick bite. See fig. 613. Narrow fluke arms allow the anchor to penetrate well.

The Northill has demonstrated its efficiency in sand and mud, and has performed well even in heavy kelp and on rocky bottoms.

Other types

All the anchors discussed thus far have been of the so-called *stock-type*, though the stock, as we have seen, may be placed at either the ring or crown end of the shank. Although some stock anchors are made with a fast stock, for pleasure boat use they are more likely to have a loose stock which can be folded for better stowage. Frequently, a key is required to pin the stock of a kedge in its open position when set up ready for use, the key in turn being lashed in its slot to hold it in place.

Some anchors, however, are *stockless*. Frequently these are cataloged as Navy-type anchors. Inexperienced boatmen, seeing them on large vessels, sometimes jump to the conclusion that they are consequently the best for all vessels, including boats. Nothing could be further from the truth. Ships use them because stockless anchors can be hauled up with power into hawsepipes. On pleasure boats, the ratio of weight to holding power is so great that, if it is heavy enough to hold, it is a back-breaker; if weight is held within reason, holding power is far below the limits of safety. The Sea-Claw is an improved version of the Navy anchor, with a different proportioning of its parts, and round stock at the crown. See fig. 614.

Grapnels, though used more extensively by some commercial fishermen than many boatmen realize, are not recommended for general anchoring service aboard pleasure boats. These are also stockless models with, as a rule, five curved sharp-billed claw-like prongs symmetrically arranged around the crown end of the shank. Eyes may be cast in both ends of the shank—at the head in lieu of a ring for attachment of a rode (if used as an anchor) and at the crown end for a buoyed trip line. By dragging a small grapnel back and forth, a boatman may *grapple* for a piece of equipment lost on the bottom. See fig. 615.

When we speak of *folding anchors,* we think not so much in terms of a Yachtsman's kedge with movable stock as a highly specialized design in which, at some sacrifice of holding power, all parts fold against the shank into the smallest possible space for most convenient stowage. In one stockless type, the Norwegian SAV (imported by Canor Plarex) there are two pairs of flukes at right angles to each

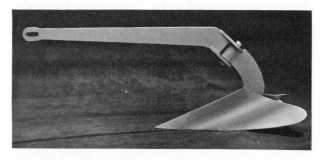

FIG. 608 Woolsey's Plowright anchor has plow-shaped flukes, causing the anchor to bury deep. The shank is pivoted.

FIG. 609 How burying anchors work when an anchoring strain is put on the rode. In (a) below, a plow lands on the bottom on its side (1) gets a quick bite (2) and rights itself (3), digging deep. In (b) a lightweight anchor lands with flukes flat (1), penetrating (2) as the strain comes on the rode, and (3) burying in the holding position.

FIG. 610 Early kedges used aboard yachts had dull bills and shoulders on flukes that often fouled the rode when the boat swung in a complete circle at an anchorage.

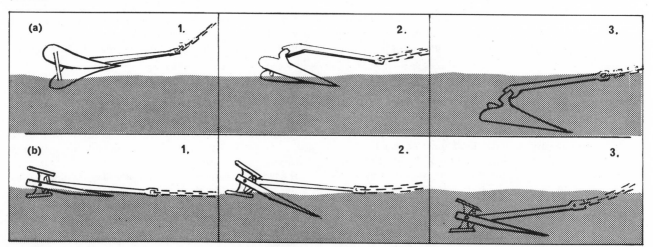

(a) 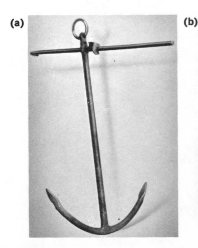 (b)

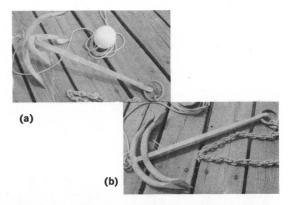

(a)

(b)

FIG. 612 (a) This four-prong grapnel anchor is excellent for use in grassy bottoms. or in coral or rocks; a buoyed trip line is usually fastened to the eye in the crown. (b) The shank is square as is the hole in the moveable arm. By sliding this arm up to the other end of the stock, which is smaller and rounded, the moveable arm can be rotated 90° so that when it slides back down it nests inside the fixed arm and the anchor stows flat.

FIG. 611 (a) Flukes of this sand anchor are relatively small, the bills sharp, to penetrate hard bottoms. In soft bottoms holding power is low. (b) The Herreshoff version of the kedge. Note difference in fluke area.

other, almost in the manner of a grapnel. In rocky bottoms, they hook readily and may be rigged to pull out easily, crown first. See fig. 646.

Discussion of *mushroom* anchors, fig. 652, will be reserved till later as, properly, their principal use is in conjunction with permanent moorings, at anchorages. Modified versions of the mushroom are manufactured for small craft like canoes and rowboats, but their efficiency as "anchors" is at the lowest end of the scale.

All the anchors under discussion in this chapter are devices designed to keep a boat from drifting, by engagement with the bottom. *Sea anchors* do not fall in this category. These are intended to float at or just below the surface, serving merely as a drag to hold a boat's bow (or stern) up toward the seas to prevent her from lying in the trough. Sea anchors are rarely used aboard pleasure boats, and then only in the heaviest weather offshore, where there is room to drift to leeward. See chapter 9, Seamanship (pages 165-166) for a discussion of sea anchors and their use. *Drogues*, like the highly effective Fenger-type, are devices made up with planks, chain, weights and rode, to serve the purpose of a conventional sea anchor which, in some cases, they are reported to have bettered in efficiency.

THE RODE

All of the gear, taken collectively, that lies between a boat and her anchor is called the *rode*—whether it be synthetic fiber (like nylon), vegetable fiber (like manila), chain, wire, or a combination of fiber and chain. When his rode is nylon or manila, a knowledgeable boatman will not refer to his anchor "rope," as rope in a coil becomes "line" when cut for specific uses. Thus, with fiber rodes, it is quite appropriate to refer to the "anchor line."

Nylon

Since the introduction of synthetics, a quiet revolution has been taking place in the choice of material for anchor rodes. Good quality manila was once the accepted type of line. Synthetics, however, have brought new properties that make them even better adapted to the boatman's use.

FIG. 613 Pitch of the flukes of a Northill-type anchor causes it to penetrate and dig in quickly. Here the anchor is turning to its ultimate horizontal position. Such an anchor can also be used to "hook" a hold on rocks.

Because other synthetics, such as dacron, polypropylene, polyethylene, etc., have little elasticity, they are not recommended for anchoring and towing. Nylon, on the other hand, has high elasticity and is the outstanding choice today.

Any differential in cost between nylon and manila is more than made up by differences in strength and longer life, both on the side of nylon. (See Table 11-1, breaking strengths, page 216.) Several times the strength of manila, nylon can be used in smaller diameters, light and easy to handle. See fig. 616. Though it can be damaged by rust from iron fittings or rusty chain, it is highly resistant to the rot, decay and mildew that attack vegetable fibers.

For anchoring purposes, nylon's greatest asset is its elasticity, stretching a third or more under load. Its working elasticity of 15 to 25% is several times greater than that of manila. When a boat surges at anchor in steep seas, there is a heavy shock load on fittings and ground tackle unless provision is made to absorb it gradually. Nylon's elasticity does exactly that.

Some boatmen unwittingly lose part or most of the advantage inherent in nylon by buying too strong a line. Within the limits of safe working loads, the smaller the diameter the better the elasticity for given conditions. A

95

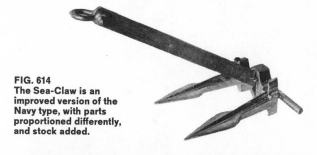

FIG. 614
The Sea-Claw is an improved version of the Navy type, with parts proportioned differently, and stock added.

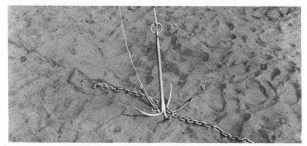

FIG. 615 A grapnel, shown here as it might be used in grappling to recover a mooring chain.

FIG. 616 Nylon (a) and manila (b). Nylon's great elasticity makes it popular for anchor rodes. A 3/8-inch diameter nylon line (breaking strength 3650 lbs.) will replace 9/16-inch manila (3450 lbs.).
(Gordon S. Smith photo)

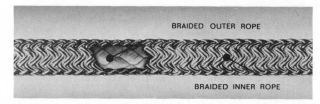

BRAIDED OUTER ROPE

BRAIDED INNER ROPE

FIG. 617 Because of its construction, braided synthetic line has no tendency to twist. Braided nylon, for anchor rodes, retains high elasticity; braided polyester, with little stretch, is better for sheets and halyards.

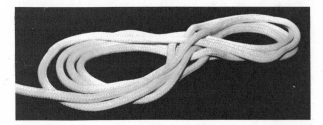

FIG. 617 (a) Braided line coils best when faked (or flaked) down in a figure 8.

FIG. 618 On this large yacht, *wildcats* in the winch engage the links of the all-chain rodes. Chain, leading down to the anchors through hawsepipes, is shown here *stoppered*, held by split-hook *devil's claws.*

practical limit is reached when small diameters (though rated high enough for breaking strength) are not convenient to handle. Some of the most experienced boatmen use nylon as light as 3/8-inch diameter on the working anchors of their 30- to 40-foot cruisers.

Braided synthetic line

Most of the nylon currently in use today for anchor rodes is the type that is laid up by twisting three strands, in the same manner as manila. Synthetics, however, may also be laid up by braiding. For anchoring, mooring and towing, a braided outer cover of nylon surrounds a braided inner synthetic core. See fig. 617. The result is a line of exceptional stability with no inherent tendency to twist because of the nature of its lay. Consequently, it can be fed down into rope lockers without fear of kinking.

When braided nylon is handled on deck, it is advisable to fake it down in figure-8 pattern, rather than the conventional clockwise coil used with twisted fibers to prevent kinking. Because of the relatively smoother surface of braid, with more fibers exposed, chafe is less of a problem than it is with the twisted three-strand lay. Braided nylon retains a high degree of elasticity (14% at working loads, as against 25% for twisted nylon).

For sheets and halyards, where it is preferable to eliminate the stretch, an outer cover of polyester is used. Double-braided nylon is becoming increasingly popular for mooring pennants.

Double-braided synthetic rope is a quality product, its smooth, soft handling characteristics recommending it highly as a "yacht" line. Obviously it requires a special splicing technique; step-by-step instructions will be found in figs. 1108a through 1108h.

Manila

Most of the arguments that could once have been advanced for the selection of manila have quite generally been settled with the increasing trend toward nylon. It is a fact that manila is still in common use on many lighter anchors and in some areas it survives among boatmen of

FIG. 619 Manila line, badly chafed on a rough coral bottom. A fathom of chain, shackled between the anchor and fiber rode, would have prevented this.

FIG. 620 A thimble, shackle, and eye splice are commonly used to secure fiber rodes to the anchor ring or to a shackle in a short length of chain between the line and the anchor.

the old school who are not yet ready to give up the line they've grown up with. They find it easy to handle, light in weight (for required strength), comparatively inexpensive, and capable of enough stretch to absorb some shock load. Above all, it holds knots and splices better than the more slippery synthetics. Even at that, the experience of some of the hardest working commercial craft, like the charter fishermen who anchor day in and day out in open water in all weathers, is hard to deny. They've turned to nylon.

Chain

Nylon in diameters up to 1 inch is used on boats up to 50 or 60 feet in length—even larger, under normal conditions. Any fiber line, however, more than $1^1/_2$ inches in diameter, is hard to handle, so chain is often chosen for larger craft. BBB chain is recommended (its size designated by the diameter of material in the links). To handle it, the boat should be equipped with a winch having a *wildcat* to fit the chain. See fig. 618.

From this it should not be inferred that chain is not also in use on smaller craft. On boats that cruise extensively and have occasion to anchor on sharp rock or coral, chain is often preferred—in cases, regarded as indispensable, as it stands chafing where fiber won't. Some boatmen with wide cruising experience have used one or more fathoms of chain shackled between the anchor and fiber line. Others prefer chain throughout.

In the larger diameters, the weight of chain tends to produce a sag in the rode which cushions shock loads due to surging. Once the sag is out, it is quite generally agreed that the shock on both boat and anchor is greater than with nylon or even manila. Too much emphasis should not be placed on the cushioning effect of a chain's sag, in small sizes. One test made in a moderate wind with generous scope of 10-to-1 revealed not a single link of chain resting on the bottom. On the other hand, in larger sizes, exhaustive tests on a 104-footer with $1/_2$-inch and $5/_8$-inch chain showed the weight of chain to be beneficial, reducing the maximum load on the anchor to as little as 5% of that recorded in a similar test with wire rope. Wire cable has

been used on some larger craft; though strong, it has no elasticity.

Nylon-and-chain

Today the concensus appears to be that for most average conditions, the ideal rode consists of a combination of nylon and short length (a fathom, more or less) of chain between the nylon and anchor. The only exception to this is in the very softest bottoms where one authority claims that the lightweight anchor bites best without chain.

The effect of chain in a combination rode is to lower the angle of pull, because chain tends to lie on the bottom. Of equal, perhaps greater, significance is the fact that modern lightweight anchors often bury completely, taking part of the rode with them. Chain stands the chafe, fig. 619, and sand has less chance to penetrate strands of the fiber line higher up. Sand doesn't stick to the chain, and mud is easily washed off. Without chain, nylon gets very dirty in mud.

Chain used in this manner may vary roughly from $1/_4$-inch diameter for 20-footers up to $7/_{16}$-inch for 50-footers. It should be galvanized, of course, to protect against rust. Neoprene-coated chain is an added refinement, as it will not mar the boat.

SECURING THE RODE

Eyesplice, thimble, and shackle

Various methods are used in securing the rode to the anchor ring. With fiber line, the preferred practice is to work an eye splice around a thimble and use a galvanized shackle to join the thimble and ring. See fig. 620. Using manila, the common galvanized wire-rope thimble is satisfactory; with nylon more care must be taken to keep the thimble in the eye. A tight, snug splice will help and seizings around the line and the legs of the thimble, near the V, will keep the thimble in the eye splice when the line comes under loads that stretch the eye. A better thimble, fig. 621, is available in bronze alloy or plastic for use with synthetic rope. This is designed to hold and protect the line.

FIG. 621 Improved types of Newco thimble in plastic or bronze alloy for use with synthetic rope prevent line from jumping out of the thimble when an eye splice stretches under load.

TABLE 6-2 ANCHOR WEIGHT* (pounds)			
BOAT LENGTH (Maximum)	Lunch hook	Working anchor	Storm anchor
20'	**4** (10)	**5** (20)	**12** (40)
30'	**5** (15)	**12** (30)	**18** (60)
40'	**12** (20)	**18** (40)	**28** (80)

*Bold-face figures based on modern lightweight burial-type anchors of efficient design. Figures in parentheses show how weights would be increased, using a formula of ½, 1 lb. and 2 lbs. per foot for certain kedges.

With this kind of rig, it is a good idea to put a bit of silicone spray, Lubriplate or graphite grease on threads of the shackle pin. This will keep the threads from seizing. Wire the pin to prevent its working out accidentally. For convenience, and to prevent loss of the pin, many prefer to bend a piece of marline to the eye of the pin, so that it can be lashed to a link of the chain. Watch for corrosion if different metals are used in thimbles, shackles and rings. Also beware of rust stains on nylon; cut out and resplice on new thimbles if the line is rust-stained.

With a thimble and shackle, a ready means is provided of backing up your line with a length of chain, if desired, shackling the chain in turn to the anchor ring. Shackles should be large enough so as not to bind the fiber against the ring and cause chafing.

When an anchor has an eye cast into the head of the shank, but no ring, it is generally convenient to use a shackle in the eye, even if the rode is to be bent to the anchor without an intermediate length of chain.

Anchor bends and bowlines

Some boatmen would rather bend their line directly to the ring using an anchor bend, fig. 622, seizing the free end to the rode. In the Chesapeake, and elsewhere, they use a bowline with an extra round turn around the ring, fig. 623, pointing out that this makes it easy to turn the line end-for-end occasionally or to remove the line from the anchor for easy handling when stowing.

Turning a line end-for-end greatly extends its useful life, as the lower end which has chafed on the bottom becomes the inboard end. Shackles and eye splices may be used at both ends of the rode, or may be added as necessary when the rode is turned.

Another convenient rig on small craft is merely to work a big eye splice in the end of the line, pass it through the ring, over the anchor while the stock (on stock types) is folded along the shank and then tighten the eye by hauling it up on itself at the ring.

Even where the regular working anchor is kept made-up with a combination of line and chain, it is well to know how to bend a line directly to the anchor. Often this is the handiest way to drop a light "lunch hook" for a brief stop, or to make up a second anchor when a bridle or stern anchor is needed.

Shackles, fig. 624, must be used to secure chain cables to the anchor, stout swivels, fig. 625, being an added re-

FIG. 622 Some boatmen prefer to make the rode fast to the anchor ring with an anchor bend. For added security, the free end may be seized to the rode. Line illustrated is braided nylon.

finement on combination rodes. As swivels are a weak point, they must be large. On an all-chain rode, they are a *must*. Swivels, however, should *not* be used with twisted soft-laid synthetic lines; a hockle, fig. 626, may be the result. Double-braided synthetic lines will not hockle, even though subjected to very heavy strains.

At the bitter end

To guard against loss in case the anchor goes by the board accidentally, the bitter (inboard) end of an anchor cable should preferably be made fast to some part of the boat. Sometimes this is accomplished by leading the line below, perhaps through a deck pipe, and securing to a Samson post or other strong timber. On sailboats, it may be secured to a mast. On small boats where the entire length of rode is carried on deck, it is usually feasible to have an eye splice in the bitter end to fit the post. Run this down close to the deck and use a clove hitch above the eye splice to adjust the scope.

HOW MANY—AND HOW HEAVY?

The number of anchors to be carried aboard will be conditioned upon several things—the size of boat, whether she is used only in sheltered waters or cruises extensively offshore and, to some extent, the type of anchor.

Though some small boats, like runabouts and utilities, are occasionally found with only a single anchor, this can by no stretch of the imagination be considered adequate. Even discounting the possibility of fouling one anchor so badly that it cannot be retrieved, there are many occasions when it is desirable to lie to two. Again, one anchor heavy enough for extreme conditions could be a nuisance in ordinary weather.

Many boats carry two anchors, proportioning the weight in the ratio of about 40 percent in one, 60 percent in the other. For cruising boats, three are undoubtedly better. This allows for two to be carried on deck—a light *lunch hook* for brief stops while some one is aboard, and a *working anchor* for ordinary service, including anchorages at night in harbor. The third might well be a big spare *storm anchor,* carried below, selected with an eye to its holding no matter what else lets go, even under extreme conditions of wind and weather. Break this out when you find it necessary to anchor overnight in an exposed anchorage, and you will sleep better. On long cruises, some experienced yachtsmen carry four.

Anchor size and holding power

Down through the years there have been repeated attempts to reduce anchor weights to a simple formula or table based on boat length or tonnage. Recommendations varied widely, up to as high as 3 or 4 pounds per foot for the heavy spare on cruising boats, assuming this would be a kedge type.

With the introduction of new anchors of lightweight design, it becomes obvious that the older figures no longer apply. Recognizing further that inefficient copies of a well

FIG. 623 The anchor bowline, an alternate method of bending the rode to the anchor ring. Note the extra round turn around the ring.

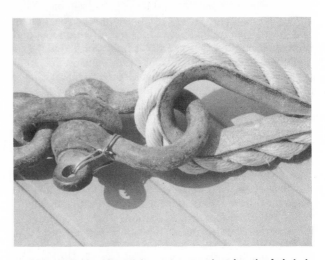

FIG. 624 This shackle, used to connect a short length of chain in a nylon-chain rode, should be secured in place with a short piece of non-corroding wire through the eye in the pin and around the side of the shackle.

TABLE 6-3   SUGGESTED RODE AND ANCHOR SIZES*

For Storm Anchor (Winds up to 60 knots)

L.O.A.	BEAM SAIL	BEAM POWER	RODE NYLON	RODE CHAIN	ANCHOR NORTHILL	ANCHOR STANDARD	ANCHOR HI-TENSILE
10′	4′	4′	100′-¼″	3′-³⁄₁₆″	12 lb. (6-R)	8-S	5-H
15′	5′	5′	125′-¼″	3′-³⁄₁₆″	12 lb. (6-R)	8-S	5-H
20′	6′	7′	150′-⅜″	4′-¼″	27 lb. (12-R)	13-S	12-H
25′	6′	8′	200′-⅜″	4′-¼″	27 lb. (12-R)	22-S	12-H
30′	7′	10′	250′-⁷⁄₁₆″	5′-⁵⁄₁₆″	46 lb. (20-R)	22-S	20-H
35′	8′	12′	300′-½″	6′-⅜″	46 lb. (20-R)	40-S	35-H
40′	10′	14′	400′-⅝″	8′-⁷⁄₁₆″	80 lb. (30-R)	65-S	60-H
50′	12′	16′	500′-⅝″	8′-⁷⁄₁₆″	105 lb. (50-R)	130-S	60-H
60′	14′	19′	500′-¾″	8′-½″	105 lb. (50-R)	180-S	90-H

For Working Anchor (Winds up to 30 knots)

L.O.A.	BEAM SAIL	BEAM POWER	RODE NYLON	RODE CHAIN	ANCHOR NORTHILL	ANCHOR STANDARD	ANCHOR HI-TENSILE
10′	4′	4′	80′-¼″	3′-³⁄₁₆″	6 lb. (3-R)	4-S	5-H
15′	5′	5′	100′-¼″	3′-³⁄₁₆″	6 lb. (3-R)	8-S	5-H
20′	6′	7′	120′-¼″	3′-³⁄₁₆″	12 lb. (6-R)	8-S	5-H
25′	6′	8′	150′-⅜″	3′-³⁄₁₆″	12 lb. (6-R)	8-S	5-H
30′	7′	10′	180′-⅜″	4′-¼″	27 lb. (12-R)	13-S	12-H
35′	8′	12′	200′-⅜″	4′-¼″	27 lb. (12-R)	22-S	12-H
40′	10′	14′	250′-⁷⁄₁₆″	5′-⁵⁄₁₆″	46 lb. (20-R)	22-S	20-H
50′	12′	16′	300′-½″	6′-⅜″	46 lb. (20-R)	40-S	35-H
60′	14′	19′	300′-½″	6′-⅜″	80 lb. (30-R)	65-S	35-H

For Lunch Hook

L.O.A.	BEAM SAIL	BEAM POWER	RODE NYLON	RODE CHAIN	ANCHOR NORTHILL	ANCHOR STANDARD	ANCHOR HI-TENSILE
10′	4′	4′	70′-¼″	3′-³⁄₁₆″	6 lb. (3-R)	2½-S	5-H
15′	5′	5′	80′-¼″	3′-³⁄₁₆″	6 lb. (3-R)	2½-S	5-H
20′	6′	7′	90′-¼″	3′-³⁄₁₆″	6 lb. (3-R)	2½-S	5-H
25′	6′	8′	100′-¼″	3′-³⁄₁₆″	6 lb. (3-R)	4-S	5-H
30′	7′	10′	125′-¼″	3′-³⁄₁₆″	6 lb. (3-R)	4-S	5-H
35′	8′	12′	150′-¼″	3′-³⁄₁₆″	12 lb. (6-R)	4-S	5-H
40′	10′	14′	175′-⅜″	4′-¼″	12 lb. (6-R)	8-S	5-H
50′	12′	16′	200′-⅜″	4′-¼″	12 lb. (6-R)	8-S	12-H
60′	14′	19′	200′-⅜″	4′-¼″	27 lb. (12-R)	13-S	12-H

*Suggested sizes assume fair holding ground, scope of at least 7-to-1 and moderate shelter from heavy seas.

PLOW ANCHORS—Woolsey, manufacturer of the Plowright anchor, makes the following recommendations for winds up to 30 knots: for *working anchors*, 10′-21′, 6 lbs.—22′-32′, 12 lbs.—32′-36′, 18 lbs.—36′-39′, 22 lbs.—39′-44′, 35 lbs. For *lunch hooks*, they advise stepping down one size. For *storm anchors*, up one size.

KEDGES—Holding powers vary widely with the type. Best to consult manufacturer for individual recommendations.

FIG. 625 Swivels are required on all-chain rodes to prevent snarls.

designed anchor may vary tremendously in holding power, it is equally evident that a hard-and-fast table of anchor weights could easily be an over-simplification. With this caution, Table 6-2 is offered, merely as a point of departure, to be modified as necessary in individual cases. This same caution applies to Table 6-3, giving suggested rode and anchor sizes for boats from 10 to 60 feet in length.

Horizontal loads as criteria for anchor sizes

In a recent project to establish an advisory code of safety standards for all kinds of small craft up to 65 feet in length, the equipment division of the American Boat and Yacht Council took a different tack in recommending practices and standards for ground tackle. They have set up a Table (6-4) specifying, for boats of 10 to 60 feet in length, typical minimum *horizontal loads* (in pounds) which an anchor should be able to hold, assuming freedom to swing and moderate shelter from seas proportionate to hull size. This, too, is broken down into three sizes of anchor—lunch hooks, working anchors, and storm anchors. Armed with these figures, you can consult the recommendations of the manufacturer of the particular anchor you prefer.

TABLE 6-4   TYPICAL HORIZONTAL LOADS (pounds)

Length over all	Lunch hook	Working anchor	Storm anchor
10'	40	160	320
15'	60	250	500
20'	90	360	720
25'	125	490	980
30'	175	700	1,400
35'	225	900	1,800
40'	300	1,200	2,400
50'	400	1,600	3,200
60'	500	2,000	4,000

STOWAGE

The boatman's seamanship is often measurable by the amount of common sense and foresight he displays in every-day boating practice. It shows up, for example, in the attention he gives to stowage of his ground tackle. Exactly how he goes about it depends to some extent on the kind of boating he does, the size of his boat, and the way it is equipped. In any case, unless his deck is uncluttered, with gear ready for immediate use, yet secured so that it cannot shift, he will never rate high as a seaman.

Ordinarily a cruising boat will carry one, sometimes two, anchors on deck, made up ready for use. On some small boats, where it is not feasible to leave anchors on deck at all times, or in cases where lines are stowed below at the home anchorage, one anchor and line at least should be prepared and made ready before getting under way from the dock or mooring. Engines have been known to fail and, when they do, it's likely to be at an embarrassing moment, with wind or current setting you down on a shoal or reef. Then it's too late to think about breaking out gear that should have been ready at hand.

An anchor lying loose on deck is a potential hazard. If the boat happens to roll deep in a seaway or be caught by the heavy wash of a passing boat, it may slide across the deck, leaving in its wake scars on woodwork and damage

to equipment, conceivably going over the side, and taking line with it, at the risk of fouling a propeller. To forestall this, every anchor on deck should be stowed in chocks. See fig. 627. These are available at marine supply stores to fit standard anchors. Lashings hold them down to prevent their jumping out of the chocks. Hardwood blocks, prop-

FIG. 627 Anchors stowed on deck should be lashed down in chocks.

FIG. 628 A short "pulpit" on this motor sailer provides for the housing of a plow anchor.

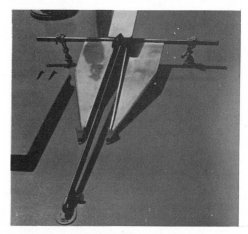

FIG. 626 To avoid a hockle, swivels should not be used with twisted soft-laid synthetic lines.

FIG. 629 Hawsepipes are commonly seen on large vessels, and may also be used on some yachts. The planking is protected by a circular pad.

erly notched, have often been used in lieu of metal chock fittings. Rubber caps should be fitted over the round stock ends of lightweight type anchors.

As an alternate to chocking on deck, anchors carried aboard auxiliaries may be lashed to shrouds, off the deck, where there is no risk of their getting underfoot, and less risk of their fouling running rigging. In one Dutch yacht, a foreign-built lightweight type anchor is carried in hooks provided in the bow rail. Some cruisers and motor sailers equipped with bowsprits or pulpits have a roller at the outboard end so that a plow can be carried in this outboard position as a regular working anchor. See fig. 628. There are devices that combine the anchor with a kind of well fixture to be let in flush with the deck. In considering such equipment, be sure the anchor weight and design are such as to meet the boat's requirements as to holding power. On some yachts provision is made to haul the anchor into a hawsepipe fitted into the topsides forward. See fig. 629.

Stowing the storm anchor

As the big spare storm anchor is used only on rare occasions, it is customary to carry it in some convenient location below. Frequently this will be a lazarette or in stowage space below a cockpit deck, accessible through a hatch. Chocks here should be arranged to carry the weight on floors or frames, never on the planking. If the big anchor gets adrift, it could easily loosen a bottom plank and start a leak.

The big risk in stowing a spare anchor away in some out-of-the-way corner is the possibility that other gear may be allowed to accumulate over and around it. Guard against that. Its sole value may some day depend upon your being able to get that big hook over quickly, bent to a long and strong spare rode that must be equally accessible.

Lunch hooks are small and seldom needed in a hurry, so there's justification for stowing them in some convenient

locker. Keep them away from the compass, however, as they can be a potent cause of deviation. That goes for all anchors and any ferrous metal that might inadvertently be left too close to the compass.

Rope and chain lockers

Though small craft frequently carry their lines coiled on a forward deck or in an open cockpit, many cruising boats are built with rope lockers in the forepeak. Nylon dries quickly and can be fed down into lockers almost as soon as it comes aboard. Manila, on the other hand, must be thoroughly dried on deck before stowing below. Gratings are sometimes provided as an aid to drying lines on deck before stowage. Lockers must be well ventilated and arranged to assure good air circulation at all times. See fig. 630. Dark, wet lockers are an invitation to dry rot. A hatch over the rope locker will permit exposure to sun and air.

The rode should always be ready to run without fouling. Line is often passed below through a deck pipe, slotted so that it can be capped even when the line is in use. Slots must face aft to prevent water on deck from finding its way below. Caps are usually connected with a length of chain, preferably of brass, as galvanized chains may rust out too quickly. Some cast mooring bitts are also made with an opening on the after face, through which line can be passed below.

Chain won't soak up moisture like manila and is easy to stow in lockers. Where weight of chain in the bow of a small offshore cruising boat is objectionable, this can be overcome by splitting a long cable into two or three shorter lengths, stowed where convenient and shackled together as necessary. The chain portion of a combination nylon-and-chain rode is ordinarily shackled in place for regular use, but small-diameter nylon, if left on deck, should preferably be shaded from the sun to protect surface fibers from damage by ultraviolet rays.

SCOPE

Later, in a discussion of anchoring techniques, we will go into the matter of holding power but at this point it seems appropriate to cover, in advance, the subject of *scope*. See fig. 631. Once an anchor of suitable design and size has

FIG. 630 Lightweight anchors chocked on deck, their round stock-ends fitted with rubber tips. A grating provides ventilation to the forepeak. Inboard ends of the nylon dock lines are *flemished* in spiral mats.

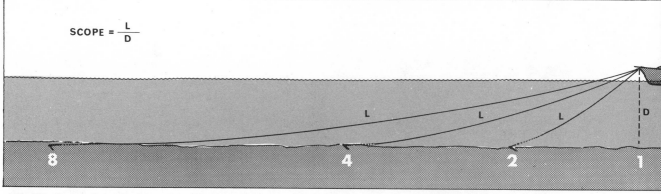

$$\text{SCOPE} = \frac{L}{D}$$

FIG. 631 Scope, the ratio of L to D in the sketch above, is critically important in safe anchoring. At (1) length of rode just equals depth of water plus height of bow above water. At (2) rode length is twice distance D, but still much too short. At (4) note how the greater scope has decreased the angle between the rode and the bottom. At (8) the scope is 8:1 and the short length of chain at the anchor lies flat on the bottom for a horizontal pull.

been chosen to provide adequate holding power, scope is the factor that will determine whether you will, in fact, hold or drag. Too short a scope can destroy the efficiency of the best anchor.

Although definitions may be found that would refer to scope as "the length of cable from hawsepipe to anchor," and others that roughly call it the ratio between length of rode paid out (between boat and anchor) and depth of water, two important factors are frequently overlooked: the height of bow chocks above water and the range of tide.

Let's assume we anchor in 10 feet of water with 60 feet of rode paid out. Theoretically, one might suppose this is a reasonable scope of 6:1. Our bow chock, however, is 5 feet above the surface. Immediately the ratio is cut to 4:1 (60:15). Six hours later the tide has risen another 5 feet. So now we have an actual scope of 3:1 (60:20), exactly half of the original theoretical ratio.

What is a proper scope? Under favorable conditions, 5:1 might be considered a *minimum*; under average conditions, 7 or 8:1 is regarded as satisfactory. Government tests have indicated that proper scope ratios will range between 5:1 and 10:1, the latter for heavy weather. Even in a very hard blow, in an exposed anchorage, the chances are that you will never need a scope of more than 15:1 with an anchor of suitable holding power. Boatmen who carry more than one kind of anchor have found that effective scope required under a given set of conditions may vary with the type.

In our hypothetical example above, the length of rode paid out should have been 140 (7:1) to 160 (8:1) feet; 100 feet (5:1) might be regarded as a minimum.

To provide maximum efficiency, all anchors require a low angle of pull—preferably less than 8 degrees from the horizontal. With short scope, holding power is reduced because the angle of pull is too high, tending to break the anchor out. As the pull is brought down more nearly parallel with the bottom, flukes dig in deeper with heavier strains on the line. Surging, as a boat pitches in a sea, throws a great load on the anchor, particularly on short scope. With long scope, the angle of pull is not only better, but the elasticity of a long nylon line cushions the shock loads materially.

FIG. 632 A plastic marker used to indicate the scope of anchor line paid (or veered) out.

Marking a rode for scope

Granting that we know how much scope is required, how do we know when we have paid out enough? Estimates are risky. Plastic cable markers, fig. 632, may be bought in sets to mark various lengths such as 25, 50, 75, 100, 125, 150, and 200 feet, or generally similar lengths. These are attached by inserting them under a strand of the line. In daylight, when the figures can be read, such markers are fine. In the dark, however, the traditional markers of strips of leather, bits of cotton or flannel cloth, and pieces of marline with knots have the advantage of being able to be "read" by feel.

For all practical purposes, five or six marks at intervals of 20 feet (say 60-140 feet) should be adequate. One practical method would be to paint wide and narrow bands of a red vinyl liquid called Whip-End Dip at significant points, calling wide bands 50 feet, narrow ones 10. On chain rodes, as a measure of scope, some boatmen have painted links white at intervals.

One method that has proved successful on a 150-foot line with an additional 8 feet of chain is to whip the line at 50 and 100 feet from the chain with red sail twine. This gives an exact measure of 58 and 108 feet; other lengths can easily be estimated with sufficient accuracy.

Anchoring Techniques

HOW TO ANCHOR

Thus far we have discussed only equipment, or ground tackle. Let's consider now the technique—the art of anchoring. As a matter of fact, good equipment is more than half the battle; anyone can easily learn to use his gear correctly.

If, on the other hand, your anchors are of doubtful holding power, and your lines too short, then you can never escape the uneasy feeling associated with wondering whether, some day, you'll find yourself dragging on a lee shore. No part of your boat's equipment is more important, so don't stint here.

Before you can think about *how* to anchor, you must decide *where* you'll anchor, and here, as in all other phases of seamanship, a little foresight pays off handsomely.

Selecting an anchorage

There will be times, of course, when you will stop briefly in open water, coming to anchor for lunch, a swim, to fish, or perhaps to watch a regatta—but, in the main, the real problem of finding an anchorage comes down to choice of some spot where there's good holding bottom, protection from the wind, and water of suitable depth. Such an anchorage is the kind you'd look for in which to spend the night, free from anxiety about the weather.

Use the chart

The chart is the best guide in selecting such a spot. Sometimes you will be able to find a harbor protected on all sides, regardless of wind shifts. If not, the next best choice would be a cove, offering protection at least from the direction of the wind, or the quarter from which it is expected. As a last resort, anchorage may be found under a windward bank or shore—that is, where the wind blows from the bank toward the boat. In this case, watch for wind shifts, which could leave you in a dangerous berth on a lee shore.

Anchorages are sometimes designated on charts by means of an anchor symbol. Areas delineated on the chart by solid magenta lines, marked perhaps by white buoys, are often shown as special anchorage areas, where lights are not required on vessels less than 65 feet in length. See fig. 633. Never anchor in cable areas or channels, both indicated by broken parallel lines.

Shallow depths are preferred for an anchorage, because a given amount of scope will then provide better holding and reduce the diameter of the circle through which the boat will swing. Consideration, however, must be given to the range of tide, so that a falling level does not leave you aground, impaled perhaps on the exposed fluke of your own anchor, or bottled up behind a shoal with not enough water to get out at low tide.

Characteristics of the bottom

Character of the bottom is of prime importance. While the type and design of anchor fluke has a direct bearing on its ability to penetrate, as already noted, it may be stated broadly that mixtures of mud and clay, or sandy mud, make excellent holding bottom for most anchors; firm sand is

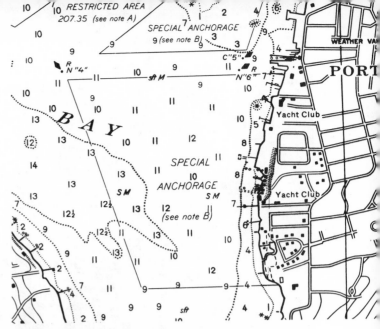

FIG. 633 In special anchorage areas shown on the chart, lights are not required on boats less than 65 feet in length.

Bottom characteristics:				
Cl. clay	M. mud	Oys oyster	stk. sticky	gn. green
Co. coral	Rk. rock	hrd. hard	bk. black	gy. gray
G. gravel	S. sand	rky. rocky	br. brown	wh. white
Grs. grass	Sh. shells	sft. soft	bu. blue	yl. yellow

FIG. 634 Abbreviations of some bottom characteristics as shown on charts.

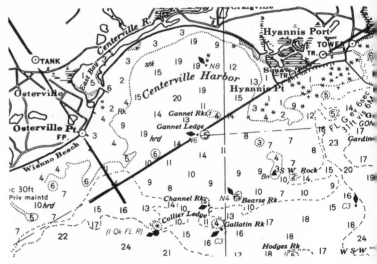

FIG. 635 How ranges may be used to select an anchorage by lining up visible charted objects. At the intersection of one range through the tank and flagpole, and another through two towers, the boat has 14 feet of water (at low tide) in hard bottom, clear of rocks, with room to swing outside of shoal water.

good *if* your anchor will bite deep into it; loose sand is bad. Soft mud should be avoided if possible; rocks prevent an anchor from getting a bite except when a fluke is lodged in a crevice; grassy bottoms, while they provide good holding for the anchor that can get through to firm bottom, often prevent a fluke from taking hold.

Sometimes bottoms which ordinarily provide reasonably good holding will be covered with a thick cabbage-like

FIG. 636 In this crowded anchorage, there's risk that the swinging circles of boats may overlap.

growth that positively destroys the holding power of any anchor. Even if you happen to carry one of the fisherman's sand-anchor types, with its thin spidery arm and small flukes, expect it to pick up half a bushel of this growth. All you can do is clean it off and try elsewhere.

Characteristics of the bottom are always shown on charts. By making a few casts with the hand lead, a check can be had on the depth, and if the lead is armed with a bit of hard grease or tallow, samples of the bottom will be brought up as a further check. Abbreviations for some bottom characteristics are shown in fig. 634.

Approaching the anchorage

Having selected a suitable spot, try to run in *slowly* on some range ashore, selected from marks identified on the chart, crossing ranges, fig. 635, or referring your position to visible buoys and landmarks to aid you in locating the spot. Later these aids will also be helpful in determining whether you are holding or dragging, especially if the marks are visible at night and it comes on to blow after dark.

If there are rocks, shoals, reefs or other boats to consider, give them all as wide a berth as possible, keeping in mind a possible swing of 360 degrees about the anchor with wind shifts or current changes.

Remember, too, that large yachts nearby may swing to a much longer scope than you allow—and, conversely, that you may swing much further than a smaller boat nearby lying on short scope. See fig. 636. Such conditions bring about an overlapping of the swinging circles.

The risk of fouling a neighboring craft is aggravated when, in a current, the deep-draft vessel holds her position while a light-draft boat swings to a shift of wind not strong enough to influence the other. Keel sailboats may lie one way in a light current, power boats another.

The boat that has already established her location in an anchorage has a prior claim to the spot and can't be expected to move if you later find yourself in an embarrassing position. Consequently, allow room enough so that you

can pay out more scope if necessary in case of a blow, without being forced to change your anchorage, perhaps at night.

The way other boats lie, together with the set of nearby buoys, will help to determine how you should round up to the chosen spot. Estimate the relative effects of wind and current on your own boat and come up, *slowly*, against the stronger of these forces—in other words, heading as you expect to lie after dropping back on the anchor. Running through the anchorage, take care that your way is reduced to a point where your wake cannot disturb other boats.

FIG. 637 With its stock set up, this anchor can be let go quickly by casting off the lashing. Chain leads outboard through a hawsepipe up to the ring. Davit tackle can be hooked into the ring of the balancing band on the shank. On the port side of the winch a gipsy is provided for use with fiber rode.

Letting the anchor go

These preliminaries disposed of, you are ready to let the anchor go. Unless you are forced to work single-handed, one man should be stationed on the forward deck. Enough line should be hauled out of the locker and coiled down so as to run freely without kinking or fouling. If previously detached, the line must be shackled to the ring, stock set up (if of the stock type) and keyed. See fig. 637. Many an anchor has been lost for failure to attach the rode properly. Rodes, too, have gone with the anchor when not secured at the bitter end. Lightweight anchors are always ready for use and do not have to be set up, but always check to see that the shackle is properly fastened.

Despite the fact that in certain localities some experienced boatmen have adopted the practice of letting go while the boat has headway, depending on way to snub the anchor and give it a bite, the small-craft skipper would do well to make it a standing rule to *never* let go the anchor while his boat has any forward way on.

In a motorboat, or auxiliary under power, the bow should be brought *slowly* up to the spot where the anchor is to lie, and headway checked with the reverse gear if necessary. Then, just as the boat begins to gather sternway slowly in reverse, the anchor is lowered easily over the side till it hits bottom, crown first.

Never stand in the coils of line on deck and don't attempt to "heave" the anchor by casting it as far as possible from the side of the boat. Occasionally, with judgment, a light anchor in a small boat can be carefully thrown a short distance—taking care that it lands in its holding position—but the best all-around rule is to *lower* it as described. That way, the possibility of fouling is minimized.

Setting the anchor

An anchor must be *set* properly if it is to yield its full holding power. The best techniques for setting an anchor will vary from type to type; only general guidelines can be given here, and a skipper should experiment to determine the best procedures for his boat, his anchors, and his cruising waters.

With the anchor on the bottom and the boat backing down slowly, line should be paid out (sometimes spoken of as veering) as the boat takes it, preferably with a turn of line around the bitt. When the predetermined scope has been paid out, the line is quickly snubbed and the anchor will probably get a quick bite into the bottom. A light-weight, burial type, such as a Danforth, is frequently set with a scope as short as 2 or 3, especially in a soft bottom. Anchors such as a kedge or grapnel seem to set better with a scope of 5 to 8.

Sometimes the anchor may become shod with a clod of mud or botton grass adhering to the flukes; in these cases, it is best to lift it, wash it off, and try again.

After the anchor is set, rode can be paid out or taken in to the proper length for the anchorage being used and the prevailing and expected weather conditions. Scope must be adequate for holding, but in a crowded anchorage consideration must be given to other craft.

When you must work single-handed, you can get your ground tackle ready to let go, long before you arrive at the anchorage, bring the boat up to the chosen spot, and then lower the anchor as the boat settles back with wind and current, paying out line as she takes it.

Regardless of the type of anchor, after full scope has been paid out, a back-down load in excess of any anticipated loads should be applied. This is particularly important if the boat is to be left unattended.

Making fast

After the anchor has gotten a good bite, with proper scope paid out, the line can be made fast and the motor shut off.

On boats equipped with a forward bitt (sampson post), an excellent way to secure the anchor line is to make two or three full turns around the bitt and finish off with a half-hitch around each end of the pin through the bitt; see fig. 638. The bitt takes the load and the pin secures the line; this is more easily taken off the bitt than a clove hitch or any other hitch.

Where a stout cleat is used to make fast, take a full turn around the base, one turn over each horn crossing diagonally over the center of the cleat, and finish with a half-hitch around one horn; see fig. 1103h. Clove hitches should not be used on cleats as they may jam.

The fundamental idea in making fast is to secure in such a manner that the line can neither slip nor jam. If the strain comes on top of a series of turns on a cleat, fig. 1103(i), then it will be practically impossible to free if you want to change the scope, without first taking the strain off it by using power.

If it becomes necessary to shorten scope, clear the bitt

FIG. 638 Although a clove hitch can be used, a better way to make a line fast to a bitt or mooring post is to take two turns around it (to bear the load) and then finish with a half-hitch around each end of the pin (to secure the line). This is easily unfastened or slacked even under considerable strain.

first of old turns or hitches. Don't throw new ones over the old.

A trick worth using when the sea is so rough that it is difficult to go forward on deck—especially if you are single-handed—is to set up the anchor in the aft cockpit, lead the line forward on deck through a closed chock, and back aft to the cockpit. If there are stanchions for life lines, the lead of the rode from chock to anchor must obviously be outside any such obstructions. When you're ready to let go it can be dropped on the weather side from the cockpit, and the line secured on a bitt or cleat aft.

Anchoring without power

When anchoring under sail you don't have the same maneuverability that power supplies and, of course, there is no positive way to dig your anchor in. Here it is best to approach your anchorage with wind abeam so that you can spill most of the wind out of your sails, thereby slowing the boat down. If necessary trim your sail in to gain more headway as needed. Approach the anchorage with all sails down except the mainsail and with enough headway to keep the boat under control. Just before you are ready to let the anchor go, you should have steerageway, but no more. Let your sheet run and, with tiller hard-alee, shoot your bow directly into the wind and drop the mainsail. As your boat loses headway her bow will fall off and the boat will begin to drift to leeward; now lower your anchor.

Pay out scope as the boat drifts back and, occasionally, give a few jerks on the line. This usually helps to set the anchor. Hand-test the line by pulling it. You will be holding when the boat is drawn toward the anchor. Then pay out the usual scope of 7 or 8:1.

Hand signals

Anchoring, like docking, is one of the situations where it's a great help to have another hand aboard. The problem is communication between the anchor man on deck and the skipper at the wheel. With engine and exhaust noise, it's usually difficult for the skipper to hear, even though the man on deck can. Wind often aggravates the problem. If the skipper is handling the boat from a flying bridge, he can usually hear better and, from his higher position, can see the trend of the anchor line.

In any case, it helps to have a pre-arranged set of hand signals. There is no need for standardization on this, as long as the helmsman clearly understands the crew's instructions. Keep the signals as simple as possible. Motion of the hands, calling for the helmsman to come ahead a little, or back down, can take the most obvious form. Pointing ahead or aft accomplishes the same purpose. A simple vertical wave of the hand may be used to signal "stop."

WHEN THE ANCHOR DRAGS

Let's assume now that you have anchored with a scope of 8:1, have inspected the rode, and taken bearings, if possible, as a check on your position. Though the wind has picked up, you turn in, only to be awakened at midnight by the boat's roll. Before you reach the deck you know what has happened—the anchor's dragging and the bow no longer heads up into the wind.

This calls for instant action—not panic. A quick check on bearings confirms what the roll indicated. You're dragging, with the wind abeam. Sizing the situation up swiftly, you note that danger is not imminent; there is still plenty of room to leeward and no boats down-wind to be fouled. Otherwise you would have to get under way, immediately.

The first step in trying to get the anchor to hold is to pay out more scope. Don't just throw over several more fathoms of line; pay it out, with an occasional sharp pull to try to give it a new bite. If you're dragging badly and can't handle the rode with your hands, take a turn around the bitt and snub the line from time to time. If this doesn't work, start the engine and hold the bow up into the wind

FIG. 639 Two schools of thought on the use of sentinels (kellets). In (a) below, the traditional use of a weight (about 25 pounds) or light anchor sent down the rode by means of a shackle over the rode, with light line to control the scope between sentinel and boat. In (b) below, a buoy rather than a weight has been proposed as a superior method, utilizing the principle commonly found in permanent mooring systems.

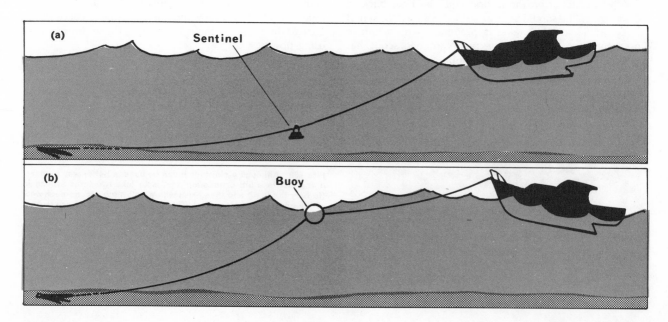

with just enough power to take the strain off the rode. This gives the anchor a chance to lie on the bottom and perhaps get a new bite as you ease the throttle and let the boat drift back slowly. If you haven't held when the scope is 10:1, get the anchor back aboard and try again with your larger storm anchor.

Sentinel—or buoy?

Suppose, now, that we have no spare storm anchor to fall back on. Can anything be done to increase our holding power? Here we enter an area of controversy with weight of experience on two opposing sides. We'll present both views.

For generations, seasoned cruising boatmen have known of the device known as a *sentinel*, or kellet. See fig. 639(a). Many have reported using it successfully; few have challenged its effectiveness. In principle, the sentinel is nothing more than a weight sent more than half-way down the rode to lower the angle of pull on the anchor and put a sag in the rode that must be straightened out before a load is thrown on the anchor. Working only with what came readily to hand in such a case, boatmen have shackled or snapped their light anchor to the main anchor rode, and sent it down the main rode with a line attached to the ring of the lunch hook, to be stopped at a suitable distance. A pig of ballast or other weight would do as well, provided it could be readily attached.

The other school of thought claims that when this principle is used with short scope in order to limit swinging room, it has proved inadvisable and dangerous, on the theory that, under storm conditions, a resonant condition

FIG. 640 A plastic foam buoy. Note how the strain is transmitted by solid rod through the buoy.

may be encountered which could quickly snap the line. Their alternative would be to use a buoy, fig. 639(b) rather than a weight, claiming that, properly used, the buoy can carry most of the vertical load in an anchoring or mooring system, limiting the basic load on the boat to the horizontal force required to maintain the boat's position. The argument is advanced that the buoy permits the boat's bow to ride up easily over wave crests, rather than being pulled down into them, with excessive loads on both rode and anchor.

What to watch

From these opposing views, certain conclusions may be drawn. To be most effective, a buoy, if used, should preferably be of the type found in a permanent mooring system, fig. 640, where its efficiency is undoubted. Its connection into the system should be as positive as it would be in a

mooring buoy, all strain being carried directly by the rode —in short, no "weak link" here! Provision should be made for carrying it as part of the "emergency" equipment, rather than trusting to a makeshift device improvised under stress of weather.

On the other side of the picture, if the sentinel is to be used, it should be done *with ample scope,* and every precaution taken to avoid a chafing condition on the main rode.

In support of advocates of the sentinel, we cite the scientific test made under controlled conditions aboard a 104-footer in which a *30-pound* weight, suspended from $5/8$-inch wire cable used as the main rode, cut the maximum anchor load practically in half. Obviously, wire rope is less suited to the average pleasure boat than it was to this test boat, it has no stretch and stands chafe of the sentinel's shackle, but figures on reduction of the load are irrefutable.

An alternate system

We offer a compromise. Carry a boat-length of substantial chain and a 25-pound pig of lead with a ring bolt cast in it. Stow them away somewhere in lieu of ballast. When the chips are down, with breakers to leeward, shackle the chain to your biggest and best anchor, and the chain in turn to your best and longest nylon rode, with the ring of the pig lead shackled in where chain and nylon join. It cannot be anything but an improvement over the same long scope of nylon without benefit of the extra scope of chain and added weight. This would seem to eliminate the twin problems of chafe (at the sentinel) and any tendency to hold the boat's bow down in the surge of pitching seas.

GETTING UNDER WAY

When you are ready to *weigh anchor* and get under way, run up to the anchor slowly under power, so that the line can be taken in easily without hauling the boat up to it. Ordinarily the anchor will break out readily when the line stands vertically.

As the line comes in, it can be whipped up and down to free it of any grass or weed it may have picked up. This clears the line before it comes on deck. If the anchor is not too heavy, mud can be washed off by swinging it back and forth near the surface as it leaves the water. With care, the line can be snubbed around a bitt and the anchor allowed to wash off as the boat gathers way, preferably astern. Two things must be watched: don't allow the flukes to hit the topsides, and be careful that water flowing past the anchor doesn't get too good a hold and take it out of your hands.

Manila, if used, must be coiled loosely on deck and allowed to dry thoroughly before stowing below. When the anchor is on deck, the stock (if there is one) can be folded and the anchor lashed down securely in its chocks.

On larger craft, equipped with a davit, the anchor is brought up with the winch to a point where a light tackle can be hooked into a ring in the balancing band on the anchor's shank. With the anchor suspended over the side, mud can be washed off with a hose.

In all this anchor handling, try to avoid letting the anchor hit the hull at any time as planking is soft and will get badly gouged and dented. Fiberglass finishes and metal hulls can also be marred. Guests often are eager to "help" by getting the anchor up, but unless they have had some experience, it's better to handle this part of the job your-

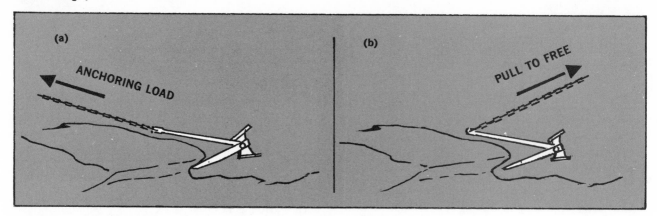

FIG. 641 In rocky bottoms when an anchor fouls, the first attempt to clear it should be made by reversing the original angle of pull (a), with moderate scope, so as to draw it out as shown in (b).

self. Handle and stow lines carefully. If a bight or end of line slips over the side it is almost certain to run back under the bottom and get hopelessly fouled in the propeller.

In a boat under sail alone, have your mainsail up before you break the anchor loose. The same procedure is used as stated above but there is no motor to help. However, it is possible to use your sails to assist.

Clearing a fouled anchor

If an anchor refuses to break out when you haul vertically on the line, snub it around the bitt and go ahead with the engine a few feet. If it doesn't respond to this treatment, it's an indication that the anchor may have fouled under some obstruction. To clear it, try making fast to the bitt and running slowly in a wide circle on a taut line. Changing the angle of pull may free it, or a turn of line may foul an exposed fluke (if it's a kedge) and draw it out.

Sometimes a length of chain can be run down the anchor line, rigged so that another boat can use her power to haul in a direction opposite to that in which the anchor line tends, thus changing the angle of pull 180 degrees. With kedges, if one fluke is exposed, a chain handled between two dinghies can occasionally be worked down the rode to catch the upper arm and draw the anchor out, crown first.

If the anchor is not fouled in something immovable, it may be broken out by making the line fast at low water and allowing a rising tide to exert a steady strain. Or, if there is a considerable ground swell, the line may be snubbed when the bow pitches low in a trough. There's some risk of parting the line this way, in case the fluke is fouled worse than you think.

In rocky bottoms, the first thing to try is reversing the direction of pull, opposite to that in which the anchor was originally set, using a moderate amount of scope. See fig. 641.

There is a type of anchor in which the ring is free to slide the full length of the shank. Properly rigged, it is claimed to be virtually snag-proof. More about this later.

If you have been anchored for a day or two in a brisk wind, the anchor may be dug in deep. Don't wait till you're ready to sail; 20 minutes before departure shorten the scope—*but keep a sharp watch.* Motion of the boat will tend to break the anchor out and save a lot of work.

HOLDING POWER

Before getting into some of the special techniques of anchor use, some understanding of holding power is in order. We have already seen how important anchor design and scope are in determining relative holding power, assuming of course that we are comparing anchors of equal weight. To understand just how critical design can be, remember that a change of as little as 1 degree in fluke angle may cause as much as a 50 percent reduction in efficiency. Lacking equipment to make individual scientific tests, one can readily appreciate how essential it is to rely on the reputability of the manufacturer.

Some factors involved

Tests have shown that the normal strain on an anchor due to wind and current in average weather is comparatively small. Current is a relatively small factor as compared with the pressure exerted by wind on exposed surfaces. Surge when a boat pitches in a seaway may throw a tremendous strain on the boat and all her ground tackle. Weight of the boat is also significant.

In calculating holding power required under average conditions, manufacturers have taken into account all of these factors, including such boat dimensions as length, beam, hull depth, draft, displacement, and height of superstructure. One has tabulated it as a percentage of gross

TABLE 6-5   HORIZONTAL HOLDING POWER DANFORTH ANCHORS (pounds)

Hi-Tensile	Soft Mud	Hard Sand	Standard	Soft Mud	Hard Sand
5-H	400	2,700	2½-S	140	800
12-H	900	6,000	4-S	230	1,600
18-H	1,250	8,750	8-S	480	3,200
28-H	1,600	11,000	13-S	720	4,900
60-H	2,400	17,000	22-S	1,200	8,000
90-H	2,900	20,000	40-S	1,500	10,000
200-H	5,000	35,000	65-S	2,300	15,000
500-H	7,500	50,000	85-S	2,700	19,000
3000-H	21,000	140,000	130-S	3,100	21,000

weight—for centerboard sailboats 5%; small motorboats 6%; larger cruisers 7%; keel-type sailboats 10%. As wind pressure varies as the square of the velocity, the same manufacturer has suggested another formula for extreme conditions where a boat is anchored in a gale. For sailboats, the formula says that pull (in pounds) = $AV^2/186$, for motorboats $AV^2/220$. (V is wind velocity in miles per hour, A a factor derived by multiplying height, from waterline to deckhouse top, by overall beam.) An added safety factor of one-third should be allowed.

Varies with bottom

In preparing tables of holding power for specific anchor sizes, the manufacturer must give proper consideration to the kind of bottom in which his tests are run. Table 6-5 illustrates how wide the discrepancy can be between results in soft mud and hard sand. The figures also bring into sharp focus the variation in holding power between different models of equal weight offered by the same manufacturer.

One test the boatman can make

A simple test that any boatman can make has been suggested by the owner of a 40-foot auxiliary sloop. He found that a well-powered boat can use her engine to throw a load on an anchor greater than she will normally register when riding to that anchor.

The pull of an engine can be approximated by multiplying the horsepower by 20, a value that works out about right for a fairly heavy-duty propeller. With a high-speed propeller of small diameter, the pull is reduced somewhat.

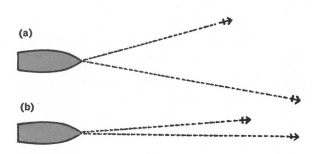

(a)

(b)

FIG. 642 Using two anchors out ahead, it is better to have the rodes form an angle as at (a), instead of in line as at (b).

FIG. 643 Anchoring in a narrow waterway with reversing tidal current, two anchors should be used, but they must be set properly. Two anchors, both from the bow and set as shown in the sketch, are better than one from the bow and one from the stern. Adequate scope should be used, but the lines must be pulled tight against each other with the boat's bow on the line between them.

The anchor to be tested is let go astern and scope of 7 or 8:1 paid out before making fast. Then the engine is speeded up till the anchor drags. Sufficient speed is maintained to drag the anchor at one or two knots, meanwhile noting the engine rpm. Testing other anchors the same way provides a basis for comparison in the varying rates of rpm required to move each.

Actual test readings of the load can be made by using spring scales in the line, rigged if necessary to permit a small scale to register heavy loads. If a lever-operated winch is available, the scale can be attached at the end of the lever. The scale's reading is then multiplied by the ratio of the radius of the lever arm to the radius of the drum on which the chain or rope is carried.

The originator of this idea determined that his 40-footer, powered with a 52 hp engine driving a 20-by-12 propeller through 2:1 reduction, under full power pulled about 1,000 pounds. Under normal conditions of anchoring, he found that the boat would rarely surge to a value higher than 400 pounds, especially if generous scope were paid out.

When making a comparison of holding powers it is interesting to note that holding power is proportional to the area of buried fluke multiplied by the distance it is buried in the bottom. Consequently, for given areas of fluke, the design which permits deepest penetration is the most effective.

USING TWO ANCHORS

Two anchors are sometimes laid for increased holding power in a blow. If your working anchor drags, you can run out your spare storm anchor, without picking up the working anchor. The important thing to remember is to lay them out at an angle, not in line, to reduce the risk of having one that drags cut a trough in the bottom for the other to follow. See fig. 642.

To stop yawing

Deep-draft sailboats lie well head to the wind but motorboats often "tack" back and forth at anchor. Skiffs, with high freeboard and little draft forward, are among the worst offenders in this respect.

You can stop this yawing by laying two anchors, lines leading out from either bow, making an angle of about 45 degrees between them. To do this, get one anchor down first and have a man tend the line carefully as you maneuver the bow off to one side before letting the other go. Then you can settle back on both lines, adjusting scope as

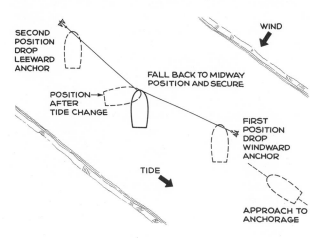

necessary. *Fouling the wheel in slack line under the boat in maneuvers like this is disastrous.*

With good handling, it is possible to get two anchors down single-handed. The easiest way is to settle back on one anchor, making fast when the proper scope has been paid out. Then go ahead easily with the propeller, rudder over enough to hold the line out taut so you can keep an eye on it at all times. When the line stands out abeam, stop your headway, go forward and let the other anchor go, then drop back and adjust the lines to equal scope.

If a dinghy is available, the second anchor can be carried out in it, lines being adjusted as required after both anchors are set.

To guard against wind or current shifts

It is sometimes necessary to anchor where tidal currents reverse or wide wind shifts are likely. Here it is wise to set two anchors as security against an anchor breaking out and failing to set itself again.

The anchors are set 180° apart with the bow of the boat at the midpoint between them; see fig. 643. With both lines drawn up tight, the bow remains over essentially the same spot and swinging is limited to the boat's length.

When setting a second anchor for use as described above, set the up-wind anchor in the conventional way and then back down till double the normal scope is out. After the down-wind anchor is set, adjust the scope at the bow chocks until both are equal. Going ahead, with a rode tending aft, use great care not to foul the propeller.

If the two-anchor technique is used in a crowded anchorage to limit swinging radius, remember that other nearby boats may lie to one anchor only, so risk of having the swinging circles overlap is increased.

Stern anchors

In some anchorages, boats lie to anchors bow and stern. The easiest way to get these down is to let the bow anchor go first, and then drop back with wind or current on an extra long scope (15-18 times the depth), drop the stern anchor, and then adjust the scope on both as necessary, taking in line forward. In tidal waters make allowance for increasing depth as the tide rises. The value of this arrangement is pretty well restricted to areas where permanent moorings are set explicitly for this purpose, as in narrow streams, or on occasions where there is no risk of getting a strong wind or current abeam. Under such conditions, the strain on ground tackle could be tremendous.

Sometimes a stern anchor will be useful if you seek shelter under a windward bank. The stern anchor can be let go aft, carefully estimating the distance off as it is dropped, and scope paid out as the boat is run up toward the bank or beach. A second anchor can then be bedded securely in the bank, or a line taken to a dock or tree ashore.

The stern anchor will keep the stern off and prevent the boat from ranging ahead. But, again, *watch that stern line, while the propeller is turning!*

At piers and wharves

A berth on the weather side of a dock is a bad one, as considerable damage can be done to a boat pounding heavily against piles, even with fenders out. Anchors can help to ease the situation in a case where such a berth is unavoidable. Keeping well up to windward, angling into

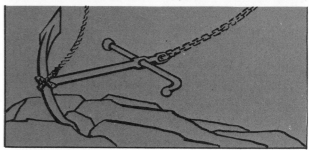

FIG. 644 When a boat swings with wind or current about an anchor, fouling a line around an exposed arm, holding power is destroyed.

FIG. 645 A buoyed trip line to the crown will permit an anchor fouled in rocky bottom to be hauled up fluke first.

the wind as much as is practicable, have a man let one anchor go on a long scope off the quarter (the port quarter, if you'll lie starboard side to the pier). As he pays out scope, run ahead and get another off the port bow, judging positions of both so you can drop down to leeward toward the pier on equal scope, with lines tending off at a 45-degree angle. Properly executed, this maneuver will prevent you from hitting the pier, and the lines you then carry ashore will be needed only to prevent the boat from moving ahead or astern.

RAFTING

At rendezvous several boats frequently lie to a single anchor. As many as ten boats have been observed rafted together, too many for safety even in a quiet cove. After one boat is anchored, the second pulls alongside with plenty of fenders out on both. Stay six to ten feet away from the anchored boat and heave bow and stern lines. If this can't be done, run up to the anchored boat's bow at an angle of about 45° and pass a bow line first, then your stern line. Make sure you have no headway when lines are passed. As soon as the bow line is aboard the anchored boat, stop your engine so that there will be no chance of going ahead, breaking the anchor out.

Allow your boat to drift astern until transoms align. Then let the bow swing off and pull the sterns in close so it will be easier to step from one boat to another. To keep the transoms in line and fenders in position a spring line

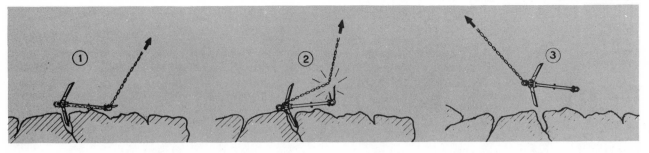

FIG. 646 Scowing an anchor. The rode to this Norwegian SAV folding anchor is attached to the crown and led back along the shank, to be lashed at the ring. When it fails to release at (1), an upward strain (2) parts the lashing and the anchor is drawn out as shown at (3).

must be run from the stern of the second boat forward to the anchored boat.

If a third boat ties up, the anchored boat should be in the middle; if more tie up always alternate them, port and starboard of the anchored boat. Each succeeding boat should use the same technique, always with a spring from the stern of the outboard boat forward to the one next inboard. Keels of all boats in the group should be nearly parallel. Naturally boats should raft only when there is little wind and a relatively smooth surface. When four or more are tied together, it is a good precaution for the outboard boats to carry anchors out at a 45° angle. When it's time to turn in for the night, every boat should have its own separate anchorage.

OTHER TECHNIQUES

On rocky bottoms

Earlier we spoke of certain steps that could be taken to clear a fouled anchor. Hazardous at best, rocky bottoms should preferably be avoided, regardless of the type of anchor used. Before leaving a boat unattended, a load should be applied to the anchor, after setting, well in excess of any expected load.

If you normally anchor in rocky bottoms or suspect that the bottom is foul in the area where you must anchor, it is better to forestall trouble. One time-tested device is the *buoyed trip line*. See fig. 645. Make a light line fast to the crown (in some anchors an eye is provided). This trip line should be long enough to reach the surface (with allowance for a rising tide) where it is buoyed with any convenient float—a block of wood, ring buoy or plastic disposable bottle. If the anchor doesn't *trip* readily at the first pull on the rode, haul in the trip line and the anchor will be withdrawn, crown first.

An alternate scheme is to *scow* the anchor, fig. 646, by bending the rode to the crown, leading it back along the shank, and stopping it to the ring with a light lashing of marline. With sufficient scope, the strain is on the crown and not on the lashing. When hove up short, the strain is on the lashing. When this parts, the anchor comes up crown first.

There are anchors (the Sure-Ring, fig. 647, is typical) that have a slotted shank in which the ring can travel freely from end to end. If the anchor should snag, the theory is that when the boat is brought back over the anchor, the sliding ring can slip down the shank so the anchor will be drawn out backwards. The Sure-Ring has an added refinement—a unique ring design that permits the rode to be

bent to an eye in the shank for overnight or unattended anchoring. A general similar design is the Benson "Snag Proof" anchor; here, too, the ring can slide up to the crown end if the anchor must be backed out.

Kedging off a bar

The term *kedging* is often, and properly, applied to the use of a light anchor (not necessarily kedge-type) carried out to deep water in a dinghy to haul a stranded boat off a shoal. If you ever have to resort to this, coil the line down carefully in the dinghy, so that it pays out freely from the stern as you row. The dink might well become unmanageable in a wind or strong current if an attempt is made to pay the line out from the deck of the stranded boat.

Anchoring at night

Anchoring at night, you must display a white 32-point light, visible at least 2 miles, rigged forward where it can be best seen. Vessels over 150 feet in length show a white light forward at least 20 feet above the hull, and another aft at least 15 feet lower than the forward light. Vessels over 65 feet at anchor display a black ball as a day mark.

FIG. 647 In the Danforth Sure-Ring anchor, a ring slides in a slot down the shank so the anchor can be drawn out backwards if it snags. For overnight use, the line can be shackled through the eye in the shank.

In certain specially designated anchorage areas, fig. 633, no lights need be displayed at night on vessels less than 65 feet in length.

When anchoring overnight, if you have no ranges to check your position (or if those you have are unlighted) you can rig a *drift lead* (the lead line will do). Lower it to the bottom, leave some slack for swinging, and make fast. If it comes taut, you've dragged. Don't forget to pick it up before getting under way.

FIG. 648 Salisbury plastic Chafe-Gard protects mooring lines from abrasion at the bobstay of this auxiliary.

FIG. 649 Chafe-Gard is lashed by thongs to the rode to hold it in place to protect against chafe at the chock.

FIG. 650 The drum of an electric windlass and, behind it, a substantial well-rounded wooden Samson post. The horizontal Norman pin keeps line from slipping off the top. At lower left, a deck pipe through which the rode is passed below.

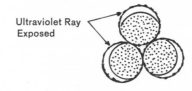

Ultraviolet Ray Exposed

FIG. 651 Small-diameter nylon line must be protected from damage by exposure to ultraviolet rays of the sun.

SOME CAUTIONS

Guard against chafe

Every possible precaution must be taken to avoid chafe on fiber lines. Wherever the line comes in contact with chocks or rails and rubs back and forth under continuous strain, outer fibers may be worn to such an extent as to seriously weaken the line. Mooring pennants, fig. 648, are particularly susceptible to this.

When lying at anchor, you can *freshen the nip* by paying out a little more scope from time to time, or parcel the line at the point of chafe with strips of canvas wrapped around it. Modern chafing gear is available in the form of plastic or rubber sleeves, fig. 649, which can be snapped over the line, centered in a chock and seized with thongs to prevent shifting. Chafing gear also comes in the form of a white waterproof tape, to be applied around the line at bitts, chocks and other points of contact.

The increasing use of relatively light anchor rodes of small diameter (frequently $3/8$ inch) points up the necessity of preventing chafe. The chafe that a $3/4$-inch line could tolerate might render a $3/8$-inch line unsafe.

Chocks, bitts, cleats and other fittings

Chafe is aggravated wherever a fitting has a rough surface to accelerate abrasion of the fiber. Even small nicks and scratches in a chock can damage a line by cutting fibers progressively, one at a time. Serious weakening of a line develops when it is forced to pass around any fitting with relatively sharp corners, such as a square bitt with only a minimum chamfering of the edges, especially when the bitts are too small for the job they have to do. Theoretically the ideal bitt is round, of generous diameter. The best chocks are those of special design with the largest possible radius at the arc where the line passes over it.

Mooring bitts especially must be fastened securely. The best bitt is the old-fashioned wooden bitt, fig. 650, long enough to have its heel fastened deep in the boat's frame. If a cast fitting must be used on deck, it should be through-bolted, the deck below reinforced with husky partners. Bitts have been torn completely off the decks of boats anchored in open water with chain rode.

All fittings playing a part in the use, handling or stowage of ground tackle should be designed and installed not with

an eye to just getting by in fair weather, but proof against failure in the worst blow the vessel will ever encounter.

Damage from ultraviolet rays

The outer layers of all types of rope are subject to some degree of damage from ultraviolet rays of the sun. See figure 651. With nylon line of relatively large diameter (upwards of $3/4$ inch) damage from this cause is probably negligible. As the diameter decreases, the problem becomes proportionately more serious. In $3/8$-inch nylon it is an important factor to be reckoned with. Every possible precaution should be taken to shield such lines from unnecessary exposure to direct sunlight. Often the rode can be fed down into a locker. If it must be carried on deck, it pays to shade it.

CARE AND INSPECTION

Anchors and chain

Galvanized anchors are usually coated by the hot-dip process which leaves a tough protective finish, normally requiring no care except ordinary washing off of mud that may be picked up in use. Occasionally, they are freshened up in appearance by a coat of aluminum paint.

On soft bottoms chain may come up fouled with mud

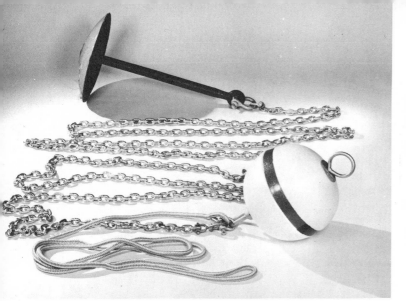

FIG. 653 This mushroom anchor has a heavy bulb cast into the shank at the shackle end.

FIG. 652 A small permanent mooring system consisting of mushroom anchor, chain, buoy and pennant, with necessary swivels, shackles, thimble and eye splices. Rigged as shown, no strain is carried by the buoy.

because its weight has caused it to lie on the bottom, where even a light strain would keep all but a few feet of fiber line from touching bottom. Obviously, the chain needs thorough cleaning and on some larger yachts a hose is carried on deck for the purpose.

Fiber Lines

Fiber lines should be kept free from sand and grit; manila must be dried before stowing. A low-pressure hose can be used to wash off grit or you can slosh the line overboard, tied in a loose coil. Throwing a strain on a kinked fiber or wire line can be fatal. To a lesser degree, short bends are injurious.

Good practice dictates the need for one long spare rode in good condition. Too often this is an "old but new" unused manila line, which has rotted in its locker. This might fail in the emergency for which it is broken out.

Lengths of line in regular use may be turned end-for-end periodically, as most of the chafe and wear come on the anchor end. If one size is used for all lines, a new spare anchor line could be put aboard each spring, the former spare put into regular use, and the oldest anchor line made into dock lines, cutting out any chafed sections.

Nylon should be unreeled from the coil like wire, not up through the coil like manila. Neither should it be towed like manila when new to take out the kinks. When splicing, tape and fuse the ends with a hot knife or flame. Strands should be kept twisted, and an extra tuck taken, the ends to be left a little longer, when trimming, until the splice is well set under strain. Use synthetic rope thimbles or splice thimbles in tightly to prevent them from dropping out when the nylon stretches. On deep-sea tugs the "legs" of thimbles are seized to the line. All whipping and seizings should be made tightly so they cannot slip.

Periodic inspection

Periodic inspection of all lines, particularly anchor lines, pays big dividends. Look for and appraise the effect of abrasion, cuts, rust on nylon, broken or frayed yarns, variations in strand size or shape, burns, rot and/or acid stains, and fiber "life." Rotten manila fibers have little or

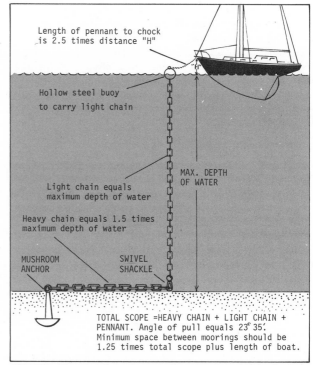

Length of pennant to chock is 2.5 times distance "H"

Hollow steel buoy to carry light chain

MAX. DEPTH OF WATER

Light chain equals maximum depth of water

Heavy chain equals 1.5 times maximum depth of water

MUSHROOM ANCHOR

SWIVEL SHACKLE

TOTAL SCOPE = HEAVY CHAIN + LIGHT CHAIN + PENNANT. Angle of pull equals 23° 35'. Minimum space between moorings should be 1.25 times total scope plus length of boat.

FIG. 654 Diagram of mooring practice recommended by the Lake Michigan Yachting Association and approved by the U.S. Coast Guard. A weight added at the shackle between lengths of heavy and light chain would increase holding power.

no strength when broken individually. Nylon line may fuzz on the surface although the yarns are not broken. This seems to act as a cushion, reducing further outside abrasion.

Consider the remaining cross-sectional area as compared to new rope. Untwist and examine the inside of strands. They should be clean and bright as in new rope. If powder or broken fibers appear, the line has been overloaded or subject to excessive bending. Nylon may be fused or melted, either inside or out, from overloads.

Most old-timers in yachting know cordage. If you are in doubt, replace your line or get an expert's opinion. For a more detailed discussion of marlinespike seamanship, see Chapter 11.

Permanent Moorings

Permanent moorings, as distinguished from ordinary ground tackle in daily use, consist of the gear used when boats are to be left unattended for long periods, at yacht club anchorages, for example. See fig. 652. The traditional system has often consisted of a mushroom anchor, chain from the anchor to a buoy and a pennant of stainless steel or nylon from the buoy to a light pick-up float at the pennant's end.

Mushroom anchors, especially the type with a heavy bulb cast in the shank, fig. 653, have been able through suction to develop great holding power under ideal conditions if they are allowed time enough to bury deep in bottoms that will permit such burying. Unfortunately ideal bottom conditions are not always present.

Complicating the problem is the fact that anchorages are becoming increasingly crowded so that adequate scope cannot be allowed each boat because of overlapping swinging circles. Add to this the threat of abnormally high hurricane tides, reducing scope to a ratio allowing no safety factor and you have the explanation for devastation wrought by several hurricanes along the Atlantic Coast, beginning in 1938.

Systems used by typical yacht clubs

The problem faced by the Manhasset Bay Yacht Club at Port Washington, N. Y., is typical of that existing in numerous anchorages. Here about 200 boats are moored in a limited space. If it were possible to permit each boat to use a length of chain equal to 5 to 7 times the depth of water (maximum 30 feet), safety would be assured, but this would require a swinging radius of several hundred feet for each boat, which is not possible. After exhaustive study, they prepared a set of recommended standards, given in Table 6-6.

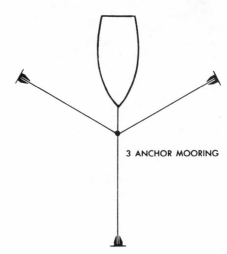

3 ANCHOR MOORING

FIG. 655 A modern permanent mooring system scientifically designed as a vast improvement over single-mushroom systems. Three lightweight anchors are bridled 120 degrees apart. From the intersection a relatively short rode limits swing.

A similar system was adopted by the Lake Michigan Yachting Association, their standards approved by the U.S. Coast Guard. See figure 654.

Guest moorings are often available at yacht clubs. The launch man will know which of those not in use for the night will be heavy enough to hold your boat. As a rule, it's easier and safer to pick up such a mooring. In some places, a charge may be made.

A multiple anchor system

One hurricane that ravaged the North Atlantic Coast swept through an anchorage in the New York area and tore almost every boat from her moorings. Only two survived. What these two had in common was an "unconventional" mooring system—multiple (3) anchors bridled to a common center, with chain and pennant leading from that point to the boat. The principle is diagrammed in fig. 655.

TABLE 6-6-   **SUGGESTIONS FOR PERMANENT YACHT MOORINGS**
For Wind Velocities Up to 75 M.P.H.

Boat Length Overall	Mushroom Anchor (Min. Wt.)	Heavy Chain Length	Heavy Chain Diameter	Light Chain Length	Light Chain Diameter	Pennant Length (Minim.)	Pennant Diameter Manila	Pennant Diameter Nylon	Pennant Diameter Stainless Steel	Total Scope (Chocks to Mushroom)
—FOR MOTOR BOATS—										
25	225	30	7/8	20	3/8	20	1	7/8	9/32	70
35	300	35	1	20	7/16	20	1-1/4	1	11/32	75
45	400	40	1	20	1/2	20	1-1/2	1-1/4	3/8	80
55	500	50	1	20	9/16	20	2	1-1/2	7/16	90
—FOR RACING TYPE SAILBOATS—										
25	125	30	5/8	20	5/16	20	1	7/8	9/32	70
35	200	30	3/4	20	3/8	20	1-1/4	1	11/32	70
45	325	35	1	20	7/16	20	1-1/2	1-1/4	3/8	75
55	450	45	1	20	9/16	20	2	1-1/2	7/16	85
—FOR CRUISING TYPE SAILBOATS—										
25	175	30	3/4	20	5/16	20	1	7/8	9/32	70
35	250	30	1	20	3/8	20	1-1/4	1	11/32	70
45	400	40	1	20	7/16	20	1-1/2	1-1/4	3/8	80
55	550	55	1	20	9/16	20	2	1-1/2	7/16	95

NOTE:—Heavy chain to be shackled to mushroom anchor, light chain shackled to end of heavy chain.
With stainless steel pennants, use special bow chocks and mooring bitts to eliminate sharp bends.

LENGTH O.A.	BEAM		PENNANT NYLON	*RODE (COMBINATION)		RODE CHAIN⊕ ONLY	ANCHOR		DANFORTH	
	SAIL	POWER		NYLON	CHAIN		†MUSHROOM	NORTHILL	STANDARD	HI-TENSILE
10′	4′	4′	4′-³⁄₈″	³⁄₈″	5′-¼″	¼″	250 lb.	12 lb. (6-R)	8-S	5-H
15′	5′	5′	6′-³⁄₈″	³⁄₈″	6′-⁵⁄₁₆″	⁵⁄₁₆″	400 lb.	27 lb. (12-R)	13-S	12-S
20′	6′	7′	8′-³⁄₈″	³⁄₈″	6′-⁵⁄₁₆″	⁵⁄₁₆″	550 lb.	27 lb. (12-R)	22-S	12-H
25′	6′	8′	10′-⁷⁄₈″	⁷⁄₁₆″	8′-³⁄₈″	³⁄₈″	750 lb.	46 lb. (20-R)	40-S	20-H
30′	7′	10′	12′-⁷⁄₁₆″	⁷⁄₁₆″	8′-³⁄₈″	³⁄₈″	1050 lb.	80 lb. (30-R)	65-S	35-H
35′	8′	12′	14′-½″	½″	10′-⁷⁄₁₆″	⁷⁄₁₆″	1350 lb.	105 lb. (50-R)	85-S	60-H
40′	10′	14′	16′-½″	½″	10′-⁷⁄₁₆″	⁷⁄₁₆″	1800 lb.	105 lb. (50-R)	130-S	60-H
50′	12′	16′	18′-³⁄₄″	³⁄₄″	12′-½″	½″	2400 lb.	—	180-S	90-H
60′	14′	19′	20′-1″	1″	14′-⁵⁄₈″	⁵⁄₈″	3000 lb.	—	300-S	90-H

TABLE 6-7   SUGGESTED ANCHOR SYSTEMS FOR PERMANENT MOORINGS — (Winds up to 75 knots)

NOTE: *Total scope with combination rode to be a minimum of 7:1. ⊕Scope with chain only to be a minimum of 5:1. Buoy with each system to have lifting power (in pounds) of 1½ times the submerged weight of total rode. †Suggestions offered (by Danforth) in table above may sound excessive to those accustomed to lighter tackle. Experience, however, under storm conditions has proved the wisdom of providing for loads of unexpected severity. Sizes suggested assume fair holding ground, scopes as recommended, and moderate shelter from heavy seas.

A casual inspection of figure 655 reveals the obvious advantages of the system. Regardless of how the wind shifts, the boat swings through a small circle, despite the advantage of a relatively long total scope from boat to anchor. The short rode up from the three-way bridle minimizes any "tacking" tendency. Always there will be one or two anchors to windward, the strain tending in the same direction. Using modern lightweight anchors instead of mushrooms, the greater the load the deeper they bury. Mushrooms often need a relatively long period to bed in securely, but lightweight anchors will dig in almost immediately. Using a safety factor of 1.5, each anchor in the 3-anchor system should have a holding power equal to the design holding power of the moorings.

A scientific 3-anchor system of this kind overcomes all of the weaknesses inherent in poor systems using inadequate scope and concrete blocks, railroad car wheels and old engines, all categorized as "dragging" types of "anchor."

Mooring buoys

To comply with new uniform state waterway regulations (applicable on waters under state control), mooring buoys should be white with a horizontal blue band. Buoys used in any mooring system should be of a type that transmits strain directly through chain or rod. See fig. 640. Buoys perform a useful function in removing much of the vertical load, the pennant is under a more nearly horizontal load, and the boat's bow is freer to lift to heavy seas.

Pennants of stainless steel have often been preferred because failures frequently were traceable to chafing of fiber pennants. When fiber is used for the pennant, it should be carefully protected with chafing gear, especially if there is a bobstay against which it can saw. See figure 648.

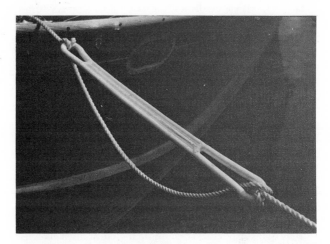

FIG. 656 The Rubbermaid snubber, bent into a mooring line with clove hitches as shown, leaving a loop of slack, absorbs heavy shock loads on line and fittings. Tensile strength is 2000 pounds.

Annual inspection necessary

Because ordinary moorings often depend for holding power on a period of time to silt in, annual inspection of chain, links, shackles and pins should be made early in the season—never disturbed just about the time storm warnings are issued. On the other hand, it is also wise to give the pennant from buoy to boat a double-check in midseason, just before the August-September months when hurricanes most often strike.

Table 6-7 includes figures suggested for Danforth and Northill anchors when used in place of mushroom anchors in a permanent mooring system.

CHAPTER 7

THE SKIPPER

His Duties and Responsibilities

The yachtsman is properly interested in the pleasure and comradeship that he obtains with his boat; the rigorous routine of a battleship has little, if any, place on the bridge of a 40-foot cruiser. However, we amateurs can learn from Navy practices. As many of these practices have as their sole purpose insurance of the safety of the ship and her personnel, it is especially appropriate for us to know something of them and apply to our own cruising those that will contribute to our own safety. *The first responsibility of a skipper is the safety of his ship and his people.*

LEADERSHIP AND DISCIPLINE

Suppose we think first about leadership and discipline. These are subjects that are rarely considered by the yachtsman but in them we find much that can be of value in that sudden emergency for which all of us who cruise must always be prepared.

Discipline; shades of a hickory stick. But, discipline is not subservience, discipline is self-control. It means prompt and cheerful obedience to necessary laws and regulations, laws and regulations designed for the sole purpose of our safety. It also means a square deal to our shipmates; the skipper who expects discipline of his crew must likewise discipline himself. A well-disciplined boat is a secure and safe boat.

Discipline does not mean a long string of commands with a crew constantly scurrying about the deck. Gold braid is not necessary to discipline. Discipline does not mean that all the joy is gone out of the job. There can be discipline on board the smallest yacht without there being any apparent show of it. Real discipline is a function of leadership and leadership can be exercised in dungarees on board a 20-foot sailboat; it is a characteristic that all of us should cultivate and practice.

Leadership is based on three things: (1) each man must know himself, his abilities and his limitations; (2) he must know his job, know it so well that he doesn't have to think about the details of doing it; (3) he must know his men and his boat and what he can reasonably expect of them in an emergency.

Authority and obligations

From the lowest third class Petty Officer to the Admiral of the Fleet, every man of the Navy charged with authority has two functions to perform: (1) his function as a military leader; (2) his function as a specialist in some technical phase of his profession. It is relatively easy for any of us to become technically skilled in shaping a course, making

FIG. 701   The primary responsibility of every skipper is the safety of his boat and crew.

a mooring, even swabbing a deck. All of these have to do with our technical ability and are equally applicable in the Navy and in amateur cruising.

But there usually comes a time, and it is always an emergency when seconds count, when there are too many jobs for even the most skillful of us to handle them all. This is the time when our capacity for leadership will bring us to port or put us aground. In one way, leadership on a motor cruiser is even more important than it is on an aircraft carrier; our friends on board may not be skilled in the operation of a boat. We have to make up for their lack of technical ability.

Let's look at it another way. There is an old saying that you get more out of a job when you have to work at it; the average guest on board should more quickly feel at home and should have pleasanter memories of his cruise if he has some of the boat's work to perform, if he must coordinate his efforts with those of his shipmates. As skippers, we all welcome the guest who is eager to turn to and do his share.

Assignment of tasks

A good skipper will privately catalog in his own mind the abilities of his guests and think ahead to the tasks that he will request them to do should an emergency arise. See fig. 702. He may and should go one step further; without making it obvious, he should see to it that all on board are given various jobs to do not only so that he can find the best spot for each but also so that they are able to do more than one thing. *Our first obligation is the safety of our boat and her people.*

One good U. S. Power Squadron skipper makes it a practice to have "informal formal" watches, which amount to Navy watch, quarter, and station bills. From the stories told of cruises in his schooner, everyone on board has a bang-up good time, as well as a safe cruise. This man is a real leader and he doesn't hesitate to work at it.

Let's not try to define leadership; there have been as many definitions of this word as there have been writers. Any intelligent man thoroughly understands the meaning and significance of the term. Taking honesty and integrity for granted, it is the first characteristic that a man should develop. Out of leadership comes confidence, pride, emulation on the part of our associates; out of it will come the pleasant cruise that all of us want.

FORESIGHT

Next to leadership comes forehandedness or foresightedness. A first class skipper doesn't wait for an emergency to arise; he has long before formulated several solutions to any emergency with which he may be faced. Commander Frost, one of the foremost destroyer captains in the Navy, put it something like this: "The most expert captain is the first to admit how often he has been fooled by some trick of wind or current. Dangerous situations develop with startling suddenness so even when things look easiest, watch out. Have an answer to every threat and a trick to take you out of every danger." An officer must always look ahead, a minute, an hour or a day as the circumstances of his situation dictate. And, whether we like it or not, a yacht skipper is an officer, good or bad.

VIGILANCE

Next in importance to forehandedness is vigilance. In no position more than that of the skipper is "eternal vigilance the price of safety." He must see intelligently all that comes within his vision, outside and inside the ship. And his vigilance must extend beyond this to the faculty of foreseeing situations as well as seeing them. The rule of the airlines that a pilot must be able to get into alternate fields as well as the airport of his destination holds meaning for the boat skipper too.

COMMON SENSE

One more check point; it is common sense. The successful skipper has a sense of proportion and of the fitness of things; let us adjust ourselves to our situation. For example, it is obviously ridiculous to dress in white flannels and blue coat when kedging off, although we might do so when the ladies are on board of a quiet Sunday afternoon. Yet we all probably can recall cases where, through a failure to exercise common sense, we did things as silly as that suggested above. The old adage "use your head" applies equally well on shipboard.

One more quotation from Commander Frost. He has defined the art of handling a ship: "Systematic application of knowledge and skill, acquired by study, observation and experience, in effecting the safe, smart, effective and economical operation of your ship." Think it over.

COURTESY

There is a courtesy extended by large ships that is worthy of attention: dipping the ensign when passing a ship of the Navy. Pleasure craft frequently do not do this but it is a mark of respect that is highly desirable for all to show. As your bridge draws abeam the bridge of the Naval vessel, dip the ensign and immediately hoist it two-blocks. All persons on board except the helmsman should face the warship and stand at attention. Any in uniform should salute.

DUTIES AND RESPONSIBILITIES

We come now to the duties and responsibilities of a skipper, of those activities with which you must be familiar while on the bridge.

Approximately in the order of their importance, the responsibilities of the skipper or of the man having the watch are as follows:

• Safe navigation of his boat.

• Safe and efficient handling of the boat in company with or in the presence of other boats. See fig. 703.

• Safety of personnel and materiél on board.

• Rendering assistance to all in danger or distress.

• Smart handling and smart appearance of the boat.

• Comfort and contentment on board.

• A good log.

These are some of the instructions that the U. S. Navy gives to watch officers, men who are charged with the

FIG. 702   The good skipper will catalog in his mind the abilities of guests and crew, assigning tasks accordingly.

responsibility for the ship. They form a pattern that all of us, whatever the size of our craft, can follow with benefit. They presuppose that a man know himself, his job, his crew, and his ship. Let's see what they mean in terms of actual practice.

Check of equipment

Before a boat can be gotten under way, it is important that a check-up be made to determine if she is ready to sail. Not alone should the equipment required by law be on board and in proper condition for use but all navigational and other equipment should be at hand. See fig. 704. Water and gasoline tanks should be sounded, the ground tackle inspected, stores checked, and all those other little odd jobs that can be done at the mooring, but not at sea in an emergency, completed. These things sound elementary and worthy of little consideration but all of us can recall results that might have been different had the proper attention been given in advance to such minor details.

The Navy provides each ship with a check list that the officer must use before he takes charge or gets the ship under way. The yachtsman could profitably make up his own check list and either actually or mentally go over it as he steps from the dock to the deck. The whole subject of safety is so important that every yachtsman should consider himself disqualified until he so thoroughly knows the requirements that he executes them as second nature.

Physical condition of the skipper

Another point in the safe navigation of a ship has to do with the physical condition of the skipper. The constant vigil which is necessary requires the complete possession of all faculties as well as a sense of physical well-being. No man should expose his boat or his people to danger, except in an extreme emergency, unless he is in good physical and mental condition.

Avoidance of risk

The good skipper will not permit any of his personnel to take needless risks. If a dangerous job that may result in a man's being swept overboard has to be done, he will insist that that man wear a life jacket. This may not be customary in yachting circles but that omission does not justify contempt for danger. In this connection, the state of the weather should be carefully observed and every effort made before getting under way to ascertain what the weather will be for the period of the cruise. A little foresight in this regard may save a ship or a life.

In conclusion, for those of us who wish to cruise tomorrow as well as today, let us think first of the things that spell safety; then the fun will take care of itself.

IMPORTANT THINGS TO DO

Here is a short check list of things to do:

• Frequently check and plot the boat's position when in sight of land or aids to navigation; be certain of the identification of the objects used to fix position.

• Take soundings and heed their warning.

• Note the effect on the boat of wind and current, especially in close waters or when maneuvering with other boats.

• Do not follow other boats blindly; steer a safe course and do not assume that the other fellow is on a safe course.

• When in doubt as to position, slow down promptly; do not wait until the last minute.

• Remember that the other fellow may not see us and always be alert immediately to take such steps as will prevent a collision.

FIG. 703 One of the major responsibilities of a skipper is the safe and efficient handling of his boat in the presence of other craft.

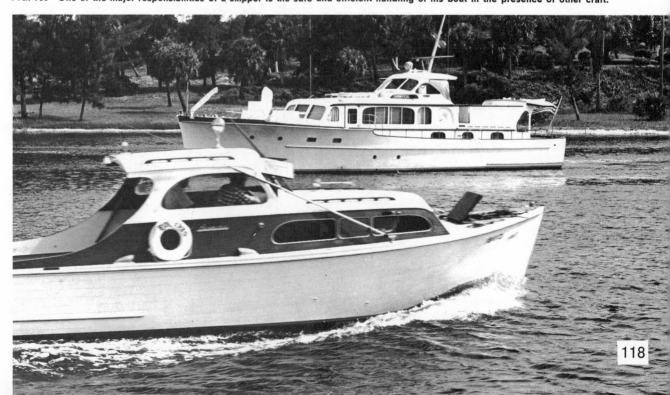

Maintenance of a lookout

A small cruiser cannot readily utilize the lookout routine of the large vessel but the implication of vigilance and caution of that routine should be acknowledged. We should make it a matter of pride that we, as skippers, will observe any danger before any other person on board sights it; this is definitely our responsibility.

Regarding Refuse   The admonition (see item below) against throwing refuse overboard is more than a matter of etiquette alone—it is based on law. Complaints received by both the Coast Guard and Army Engineers concerning refuse in coastal waters have fostered an official appeal by both agencies to the public. While asking each citizen to do his part voluntarily the appeal pointed out that "throwing, discharging, or depositing either from or out of any floating craft or from the shore refuse matter of any kind into any navigable waters of the U.S. or into any tributary of any navigable waters from which the same shall float or be carried into such navigable water is a violation of federal law (33 USC 407)." And for any who might take the warning lightly the appeal adds that such violation is punishable by a fine not exceeding $2500, not less than $500 or by imprisonment for not more than one year nor less than 30 days, or by both fine and imprisonment.

Official U.S. Coast Guard photo.

FIG. 704   The skipper must take full responsibility for seeing that all essential equipment, including that required by law, is aboard (and in proper condition for use) before casting off.

YACHT_____

Glad To Have You On Board

The Skipper and Mate welcome you on board. We look forward to your company during our cruise and ask

Please

DO make yourself at home. The mate will show you your locker. There is no lock on the refrigerator and the berths are said to be comfortable. Decks are usually swabbed down at 0900.

DO be informal. Old clothes are fit companions for swabbing decks, weighing anchor, and securing from chow.

DO ask us all the questions you wish—while we are not handling the boat. If you have a yen for rope-work or other ship's business, let us know. Too, you may find a helpful magazine or book on board.

DO locate your life-belt and learn how to use it. We will show you how to toss a life-ring, if you do not know. Not looking for trouble, but we want to be ready for it.

DO the same for the fire extinguishers. In case of fire, the Skipper will tell you what to do—and not to do.

DO report any danger or unusual occurrence to the Skipper at once: what it is, where it is, what it is doing.

DO go swimming at every opportunity. Swim upstream, keeping an eye on your shipmates and on the boat.

DO fish too, if you wish. But watch out for fouling the propeller and mooring lines, watch out for that fish-hook.

DO conserve fresh water. Use all that you need but remember, the supply is limited.

DO likewise conserve electricity. Lights out on the bridge when under way at night.

DO learn to work the "head." The Skipper or Mate will gladly show you.

DO stand clear of dock lines and anchor rode, of all boat controls.

DO remember that sound carries far over the water especially late at night.

Please

DO NOT smoke or strike a match or cigarette lighter or touch off the galley stove while fueling or starting the engines.

DO NOT take chances on deck, especially if the sea kicks up. Remember, rubber-soled shoes often slip on a wet deck.

DO NOT fall overboard or cause another to do so, while under way or at anchor.

DO NOT use any equipment with which you are not familiar. See the Skipper or Mate.

DO NOT jump from deck to dock without watching your footing. Landing on a rope-end usually results in a sprained ankle.

DO NOT jump into the dinghy; it isn't built to "take it."

DO NOT let go the dinghy painter until you are ready to clear.

DO NOT jump over the side while wearing a life-belt; your chin may be the worse for wear.

DO NOT throw refuse overboard without instructions from the Mate. Puncture cans at both ends; fill bottles with sea water and jettison only in deep water.

DO NOT use the "head" for cigarettes, matches, chewing gum or bulky articles; plumbers are scarce afloat.

DO NOT wear hard-soled or high-heeled shoes on deck; a good varnish job is too hard to come by.

DO NOT use the Skipper's binoculars or chart without permission; he may need them in a hurry.

DO NOT intrude on the privacy of others.

Morning colors at 0800—Evening colors at sunset—Recognition Signal—COOPERATION

_____Mate   _____SKIPPER

CHAPTER 8
BOAT HANDLING

Without a doubt some of the finest exhibitions of skill in the art of handling motor boats are often given by men who may never have read a printed page on the subject of seamanship. Their facility at the helm of a motor boat is their sheepskin from the sea's school of experience — in which the curriculum, admittedly, may be tough.

Witness, for example, the consummate skill some commercial fisherman might display in maneuvering his skiff into a tight berth under adverse weather conditions, finally to bring her up against the wharf in a landing that wouldn't crack an egg. Such proficiency, developed over long years of meeting every conceivable kind of situation, eventually manifests itself almost as an instinct, prompting the boatman to react right whether he has time to think the problem out in advance or not.

Sometimes the old-timer's methods might appear, to a novice, to verge on carelessness, but that's probably be-cause the old salt in a practical way understands exactly what the minimum requirements are for the safety of his craft and therefore doesn't waste any time on non-essentials. Consequently if he uses three lines where the text book says six, don't jump to the conclusion that he wouldn't know how to use more if they were needed.

So, in approaching a study of the principles of boat handling, it's helpful to keep in mind that the goal is not so much to be able to repeat verbatim definitions or the prescribed answers to a set of questions for the sake of passing a quiz as it is to understand the "why" of some of the curious capers your boat may cut when you're out there handling her. If she stubbornly refuses to make a turn under a given set of conditions, or persistently backs one way when you want her to go the other, you will be less likely to make the same mistake twice when you understand the reasons behind her behavior.

The Basic Principles

The paragraphs above lead up to a very fundamental thought. Learn all you possibly can about the principles according to which average boats respond under normal conditions; supplement this with all the experience you can get aboard your own boat and other types as well, and then learn to act so that controlling elements aid you rather than oppose you.

In consideration of boat handling, there are three primary types of powerboats — single-screw, inboard, twin-screw inboard, and outboard (including inboard-outboard propulsion). The first two of these use a rudder or rudders in combination with a constant direction of thrust from the propeller or propellers; the latter type uses directed thrust without a rudder. The handling characteristics of each type is different from the others, but as the single-screw, single rudder inboard is the basic type, it will be given first consideration. An understanding of its principles is necessary to a study of the other types.

Although you may develop boat handling skills for your own present craft without knowing the "whys" (through the "school of hard knocks"—and that's no pun!), an understanding of the basic principles is very desirable when you change to your next, and probably larger, boat, or when at the helm of a strange craft.

No two boats will behave in identical manner in every situation, so great is their individuality. Just how a boat performs depends on many things—among them the design; the form and shape of the hull's underbody; the construction; the shape, position and area of the rudder; the trim; speed; the weight; load; strength and direction of wind and current; and the nature of the sea, if any.

EFFECT OF WIND AND CURRENT

Wind and current are particularly important factors in analyzing a boat's behavior as they may cause her to respond precisely opposite to what you would expect without these factors to reckon with. As a case in point, many motor boats have a tendency to back into the wind despite anything that can be done with the helm.

Given two boats of roughly the same size, one of which (A) has considerable draft forward but little aft, and another (B), with relatively greater draft aft but more superstructure forward—you will find radical differences in their handling qualities. What governs is the relative area presented above water to the wind as compared with the areas exposed to the water, both fore and aft.

The former (A), with wind abeam, might hold her course reasonably well when the bow of the latter (B) would persistently pay off, requiring considerable rudder angle to hold her up. On the other hand, with wind and sea aft, B might go along about her business with little attention to the helm while A insisted on "rooting" at the bow and yawing off her course despite the best efforts of the helmsman.

As a general rule, the boat with low freeboard and superstructure but relatively deep draft tending toward the sailboat type, fig. 801, will be less affected by wind and more by current than the light draft motor boat, fig. 802, with high freeboard and deckhouses. The latter floats relatively high in the water and has little below the waterline to hold her against wind pressures acting on areas exposed above water to drive her to leeward.

In the type of motorboat where the greatest draft and least freeboard are aft, the greatest exposure to windage is presented by the relatively higher bow and cabin forward. Obviously her bow will be affected by wind pressures more than the stern. With wind abeam, the tendency would be for her bow to be driven to leeward more than the stern. To offset that, she would need a certain amount of rudder angle to hold her on her course and compensate for leeway.

For the same reason if she is drifting in a smooth sea with engine stopped, wind pressure on her bow will make the bow pay off so that the wind finally is brought abaft the beam. The action might also be compared to that of a sailboat in which a flattened jib, but no other canvas, is set.

But, just as an illustration to show how boat behavior may vary, suppose it is raining and cockpit curtains are buttoned down on that same cruiser. Here a new factor is introduced and the windage aft is increased to such an extent that it may more than offset the effect of the windage forward. Under such conditions she might be very hard to handle in close quarters because of the great amount of total windage compared to her draft.

Although flying bridges, fig. 803, on modern cruisers tend to add to the windage, they have an undeniable ad-

FIG. 803 A modern cruiser being brought up to a finger pier. The flying bridge and twin screws are a great advantage in handling, from the standpoint of visibility and control. Crew tends bow line.

vantage in better visibility when maneuvering, and running at night or in strange waters.

Some boats require humoring under certain conditions. For example, because of a combination of excessive superstructure forward and little draft at the bow, it may be practically impossible to turn a boat in close quarters by the conventional technique.

HELMSMAN MUST DEVELOP JUDGMENT

From these and many other variations in boat behavior it begins to be evident that the boatman must develop judgment, based on understanding of the individual boat he is handling and the forces acting upon her. Combina-

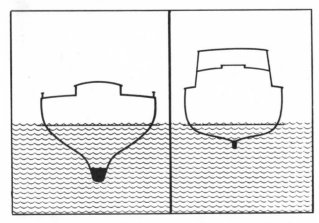

FIG. 801 Section of a deep-draft sailboat with relatively low freeboard, as compared with a typical motorboat.

FIG. 802 In this motorboat the draft is small compared to the height of superstructure exposed to windage.

Boat Handling / CHAPTER 8

FIG. 804 Approaching a bridge. At this point the helmsman waits for the span to open. When about to enter the opened span, he will square away parallel with the center line.

tions of conditions are infinite, so he must be able to appraise the situation and act promptly, with decision.

A good helmsman will be prudent and try to foresee possibilities, having a solution in mind for the problem before it presents itself. On that basis, it's likely that he'll never meet an "emergency." To cite a simple example, if you're running down a narrow channel with a strong wind abeam, and you have a choice as to which side to take, the windward side is the better bet. If the engine should stop, you'll probably then have a chance to get an anchor down before going aground on the leeward side.

By the same token, you wouldn't skirt the windward side of a shoal too closely. To leeward, in case of engine failure, you would drift clear, but to windward you'd be driven down on the shoal. A strong current might have the same effect, and would have to be taken into account.

As another example of how the helmsman should try always to be prepared for possibilities, suppose you are approaching a bridge, fig. 804, having a narrow draw opening with a strong wind or current setting you down rapidly on it. If you were to approach the opening at an angle,

and power or steering gear failed, you'd be in a jam. On the other hand, if you are prepared and straighten out your course while still some distance off so you will be shooting down the center of the opening in alignment with it, the chances of doing any damage are practically nil because her straight course will tend to carry her through in the clear in any case.

In developing your boat sense, draw from as many sources as possible. Observe the way experienced yachtsmen, fishermen and Coast Guardsmen handle their boats, making due allowance for differences in your own boat when you try similar maneuvers.

TERMINOLOGY OF BOAT HANDLING

Before getting too deep into discussion of actual problems of maneuvering it is necessary in advance to get some of the correct terminology fixed in mind.

The *port* side of a boat is the *left* side facing forward; the *starboard* is the *right* side. This is easy to visualize while the boat has headway but when the boat is reversing the operator may face aft and get all mixed up when the terms right, left, starboard and port are used.

Therefore, bear in mind that the port side is the port side *no matter which way the boat is going*. When we speak of the boat's going to port it means that her bow turns to port when she has headway and her stern to port when she has sternway. Figure 805 makes this clear. At A the boat has headway and her bow is turning to port. At B she is going astern and her stern is going to port.

The old terms of port helm and starboard helm have now given way to new terms which prevent misunderstanding. In Figure 805 the boat has *left rudder* in both cases and with headway, as at A, her bow goes to port. *Right rudder,* which is not illustrated, is just the opposite. The rudder is then on the starboard side of the boat's centerline and her bow goes to starboard when the boat has headway.

A *balanced rudder,* fig. 806, is one in which the area of the blade surface is distributed so that part of it lies ahead of the rudder stock. An unbalanced rudder would have the stock attached at the edge of the blade.

While the proportion of this balanced area may be only

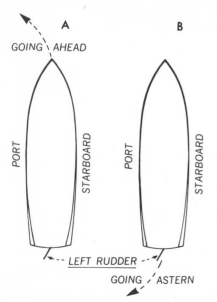

FIG. 805 With left rudder in a boat going ahead (A) the stern is thrown to starboard, bow to port. Going astern, left rudder throws stern to port.

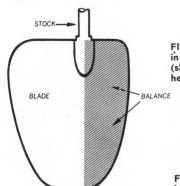

STOCK

BLADE — BALANCE

FIG. 806 A balanced rudder, in which part of the blade area (shaded section) projects ahead of the rudder stock.

FIG. 807 Left-hand and right-hand propellers. This is how they turn when you stand astern of them, looking forward at the aft side of the blades.

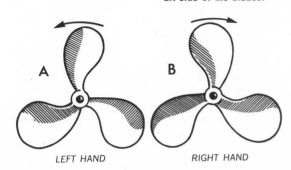

LEFT HAND   RIGHT HAND

20 per cent of the total rudder area, it exerts considerable effect in taking strain off the steering gear and making steering easier, though it may slow the boat on a turn more than the unbalanced type.

RIGHT- AND LEFT-HAND PROPELLERS

Propellers are right-handed or left-handed, depending on the direction of their rotation. It is vital that the difference be understood because this has a great bearing on how a boat maneuvers, especially when reversing. To determine the hand, stand outside the boat, astern of the propeller, and look forward at the driving face of the blades, fig. 807. *If the top of the propeller turns clockwise when driving the boat ahead, it is right-handed; if counter-clockwise, left-handed. A is left-handed; B, right-handed.*

Most propellers on marine engines in single-screw installations are right-handed although some are left-handed. In any maneuvering problems which follow, the assumption is that the propeller on a single-screw boat under dis-

FIG. 808 Direction of rotation is marked on this marine engine flywheel housing. This is a left-hand engine, as shown by the counterclockwise direction of the arrow. It takes a right-hand propeller.

FIG. 810 Boats under sail only have no propeller discharge current to increase the rudder's effect in steering. Their maneuverability is limited, and there are many tight places into which a motor boat could be worked where the sailboat (without power) could not.

FIG. 812 Regardless of differences in size or the number of blades, the same basic principles of propeller action apply and should be understood by all skippers.

twin-screw cruiser is likely to have twin rudders, one behind each propeller, thus keeping their blades at all times more directly in the propeller's discharge current. Exactly what the effect of each part of the screw current on the boat's behavior will be depends upon what part of the boat it is acting upon.

There is also a *wake current*. This is a body of water carried along by a vessel with her as she moves through the water due to friction on her hull. This has its maximum effect near the surface, is practically of no consequence at the keel.

Unequal blade thrust

Finally, there is another factor of some moment that needs to be understood in analyzing a boat's reaction to propeller rotation. While this has been sometimes referred to as sidewise blade pressure, it is more properly an unequal thrust exerted by the ascending and descending blades of the propeller, fig. 813.

Here we are looking at the starboard side of a propeller shaft, inclined, as most shafts are, at a considerable angle to the water's surface and to the flow of water past the propeller blades. The actual pitch of the blades as manufactured, of course, is the same, but the water flows diagonally across the plane in which the blades revolve.

Figure 813 shows clearly how the effect of this is to increase the pitch of the descending starboard blade as compared with the ascending port blade, when considered relative to the direction of water flow past the propeller.

The importance of this factor is reduced as the shaft angle is decreased, and naval architects, taking cognizance of this, sometimes take pains to have the engine installed as low as possible to keep the propeller shaft nearly parallel to the water's surface and the flow of water past the blades. This naturally contributes to propeller efficiency, and is a worth-while factor to be considered wherever consistent with other requirements of the design. Limitations in some designs, however, make it necessary for the engine and shaft to be installed at a considerable angle.

Effect of unequal blade thrust

The relatively greater pitch of the blade on the starboard side has the effect of creating a stronger thrust on this side with the result that the bow of the boat tends to turn to port. Putting it another way, insofar as this single factor is concerned, there is a natural tendency for the stern of a single-screw boat with right-hand propeller to go to starboard when the propeller is going ahead, and for the stern to go to port when it is reversing.

FIG. 813 With rudder amidships, bow of boat with right-hand propeller may swing to port. Angularity of the propeller shaft has the effect of increasing the pitch of the descending blade relative to that of the ascending blade, so greater thrust is exerted on starboard side.

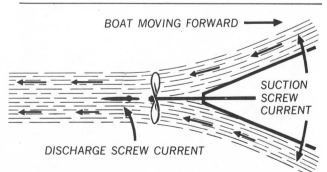

FIG. 811 The screw current which drives a boat through the water. Here the boat has headway. Suction current is shown leading into the propeller, the discharge current driven out astern.

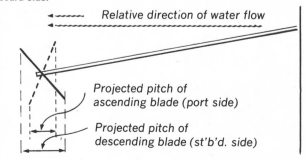

Again, when such a boat has headway, the bow apparently wants to turn to port if the rudder is held amidships, so a certain amount of right rudder may be necessary to maintain a straight course. To correct it, a small trimming tab may be attached to the after edge of the rudder and bent to an angle that provides the proper correction.

The effect is a great variable, so small in some cases as to be negligible; quite pronounced in others.

HOW THE RUDDER ACTS

The conventional arrangement for steering on most inboard boats a vertical rudder blade at the stern pivoted in hangers or on its own stock so that movement of the steering wheel or tiller throws it to port or starboard.

Steering gears on motor boats are almost invariably rigged today so that they turn with the rudder, that is, turning the top of the wheel to port throws the rudder to port. Consequently, with the usual rig, the boat having headway, putting the wheel over to port gives her left rudder which kicks the stern to starboard so that the bow, in effect, moves to port. Conversely, turning the wheel to starboard gives her right rudder, throwing the stern to port so that the boat turns to starboard.

Sailboat rudder action

In a sailboat, or auxiliary, fig. 810, when the engine is not driving a propeller, when the boat has headway water flows past the hull and if the rudder is moved to one side of the keel a resistance on that side is created together with a current at an angle to the keel. The combined effect is to throw the stern to port with right rudder, to starboard with left rudder.

But note that *any control from the rudder is dependent on the boat's motion through the water.* Even if she is drifting, with motion relative to the bottom, but none so far as the surrounding water is concerned, her rudder has no effect. Only when the water flows past the rudder and strikes it at an angle does the boat respond. The faster she is moving, the stronger the rudder effect. It makes no difference how her headway has been produced—she may even be in tow—there is control as long as there is motion relative to the water.

FIG. 815 With an outboard motor, the basic principles do not apply. Directed thrust from the pivoting lower unit is used for steering; there is no rudder.

Propeller current's action on rudder

In a motor boat the situation is different from that encountered in a sailboat. Here the rudder blade is almost invariably directly in the discharge current of the propeller which is pumping a strong stream of water astern. Moving the rudder to one side of the keel deflects the stream to that side. The reaction which pushes the stern in the opposite direction is much stronger than it would be in the absence of that powerful jet.

At very slow propeller speeds the boat's headway may not be sufficient to give good control over the boat if other forces are acting upon her at the time. For example, with a strong wind on the port beam, even with rudder hard over to port, it may not be possible to make a turn into the wind until the propeller is speeded up enough to exert a more powerful thrust against the offset rudder blade.

Here is a fundamental principle to remember in handling motor boats. In close quarters a motor boat can often be turned in a couple of boat lengths by judicious use of the power. If, for example, the rudder is set hard to starboard (that is, right rudder) while the boat has no headway and the throttle is suddenly opened, the stern can be kicked around to port before the boat has a chance to gather headway. The exact technique of turning in limited space will be described in detail further along.

FIG. 814 On inland waterways, boats may get into shoal water. This reduces the speed and also affects their handling qualities, response to the rudder being sluggish.

FIG. 816 The inboard-outboard, like the inboard boat, has an inboard engine. Unlike the inboard, it has an outboard drive unit which pivots like the outboard. This boat has twin engines.

TURNING CIRCLES

When the boat has headway and the rudder is put over to make a turn (to starboard, let us say), the stern is first kicked to port and the boat then tends to slide off obliquely, "crab-wise." Due to its momentum through the water it will carry some distance along the original course before settling into a turn, in which the bow describes a smaller circle than the stern, fig. 818. The pivoting point about which she turns may be between one-fourth and one-third of the boat's length from the bow, varying with different boats and changing for any given boat with the trim.

The distance a vessel moves in the direction of her original course, after the helm has been put over, is called the *advance*.

While there is always a loss of speed in making a turn, the size of a boat's turning circle will vary but little with changes in speed, assuming a given rudder angle. Whether she makes it at slow speed or at wide open throttle, the actual diameter of the turn is about the same.

There is, however, a great difference in the size of turning circles for single-screw inboards as compared with outboards or inboard-outboards because, as has been noted, the shaft and propeller of the inboard are fixed on the center line and cannot be rotated. This is dramatically illustrated in fig. 818. The twin-screw inboard, on the other hand, provides excellent maneuverability, as will be seen later.

Stops are invariably put on a rudder to limit its maximum angle. Beyond that point an increase of rudder angle would result, not in a smaller turning circle, but a larger one. That's why Naval vessels usually have a maximum rudder angle of 35 degrees.

When the boat has sternway (reversing) the rudder normally would be turned to port (left rudder) to turn the stern of the boat to port, while right rudder should normally tend to turn the stern to starboard in backing. However, the subject cannot be dismissed as easily as that and we shall see later how, under certain circumstances, the effect of the reversing propeller may more than offset the steering effect of the rudder.

Just as the speed of a boat is cut down in shallow water fig. 814, so the depth has an effect on a boat's steering. Even though the keel may not actually be touching the bottom, it will be noticed that the boat's response to rudder action in shallow water is almost always sluggish.

KEEP STERN FREE TO MANEUVER

As soon as the boatman understands the underlying difference between the steering of a boat and a car, he will always be conscious of the need to keep the stern free to maneuver in close quarters. Furthermore, when he lies alongside a dock, a float or another boat, and wants to pull away, he will never, automobile-fashion, throw the wheel over until the stern is clear.

To set the rudder to starboard, for example, while lying port side to a dock and then attempt to pull away by going ahead, fig. 817, would only throw the port quarter against the dock piles and pin it there, to slam successively into one pile after the other as the boat moves ahead, with the likelihood of doing damage.

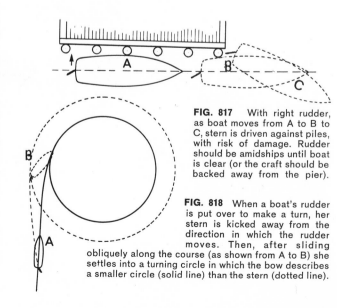

FIG. 817 With right rudder, as boat moves from A to B to C, stern is driven against piles, with risk of damage. Rudder should be amidships until boat is clear (or the craft should be backed away from the pier).

FIG. 818 When a boat's rudder is put over to make a turn, her stern is kicked away from the direction in which the rudder moves. Then, after sliding obliquely along the course (as shown from A to B) she settles into a turning circle in which the bow describes a smaller circle (solid line) than the stern (dotted line).

FIG. 819 A dramatic comparison of the turning circles of two boats at high speed. At "B" (left) the outdrive unit permits a tight turn in less than two boat lengths. At "A" (right) the inboard's propeller is fixed, and she responds only to rudder angle for steering.

HOW INDIVIDUAL BOATS DIFFER

We have seen how the helmsman has many things to consider when handling boats, due partly to individual characteristics which cause them to respond differently under identical conditions of wind, weather and current.

We have dealt too with the effect which draft and freeboard have on a boat's behavior, showing how high freeboard creates windage which acts to drive a boat to leeward whereas deep draft gives her a grip on the water with which to oppose that tendency.

The general principle is easily observed in the case of a deep keel sailboat, where deep draft acts to hold her on her course, and minimum freeboard is designed into her to reduce the windage factor.

Not only the draft, but the trim, has a bearing on a boat's handling qualities. Later we will see how the effect of rudder action in steering is to cause a boat to pivot about a point near the bow. But if she trims by the stern, that is, deeper than normal aft, the tendency is for that pivoting point to move aft.

The tendency to stray off course

Different boats require varying degrees of rudder angle to compensate for any tendency to fall off from a straight course. Depending on differences in construction, arrangement of rudder blade, and the hand of the propeller, the bow may tend to fall off to port or starboard. These are all factors that the helmsman should understand before attempting maneuvers with a boat.

Using a concrete example to make the significance of the last point more clear, a certain group of boats of almost identical design were found to have a strong tendency to pull off course to port. In some of these, the condition was corrected by the simple expedient of lowering the rudder blade, without changing its size or shape but merely by lengthening the stock an inch or two.

Before correcting that condition, these boats would make a quick and easy turn to port but would be obstinate in turning to starboard. As a matter of fact, unless steering controls were rigged with worm and gear to hold the wheel against pressure on the rudder, the boat would immediately swing into a short circle to port the instant the wheel was left unattended. While this is an exaggerated condition, far from normal, it does illustrate the handling characteristics the helmsman must pay attention to, especially in an unfamiliar boat.

Then again, the state of the sea will have an effect on a boat's performance. A heavy, deep draft boat or one which is heavily loaded will carry her way through the water longer than a light one when the propeller is disengaged by throwing the reverse gear lever into neutral. This is likely to be even more marked in a seaway, the light displacement boat losing her way against the sea much sooner than a heavier craft would.

Response of Boat to Propeller and Rudder

Let us consider now a number of typical situations to see how the average inboard motor boat will respond to propeller and rudder action (*assuming a single-screw boat with right-hand propeller*).

NO WAY ON, PROPELLOR NOT TURNING

When a boat is "dead in the water"—making no way forward or sternward through the water, although she may be drifting with respect to the bottom—and her propeller is not in gear, turning the rudder has no more effect than turning a car's front wheels while it is parked. There must be a flow of water past the rudder for it to be effective, from either the boat's motion through the water or the propeller's discharge current, or both.

NO WAY ON, PROPELLER TURNING AHEAD

Picture her first without any way on, engine idling and rudder amidships. Being dead in the water there is no wake current to act on the propeller blades. Now the clutch is engaged and the propeller starts to turn ahead.

Until she gathers headway, the unequal blade thrust (refer back to fig. 813) tends to throw her stern to starboard. As she gets headway, wake current enters the picture, increasing pressure against the upper blades (remember wake current is strongest at the surface, has little effect at the bottom of the keel) and this tends to offset the effect of unequal blade thrust.

What happens under identical conditions, except that the rudder is hard over at the time the propeller is engaged? In this case the propeller's discharge current strikes the rudder and exerts its normal effect of kicking the stern to port with right rudder, or stern to starboard with left rudder. With right rudder the kick to port would be much stronger than the effect of unequal blade thrust.

WITH HEADWAY, PROPELLER GOING AHEAD

After the boat has gathered normal headway, with rudder amidships, the average boat tends to hold her course in a straight line fairly well. From a purely theoretical standpoint, the unequal blade thrust, with a right-hand wheel, should tend to move the stern to starboard, and bow to port. On most boats, however, the effect is quite slight. Only in a comparatively few cases will unequal blade thrust have a pronounced effect on steering, and in these it can be corrected by a small rudder tab.

Now, the boat having headway, assume the rudder is put to starboard. The water flowing past the hull hits the rudder on its starboard side, forcing the stern to port. The propeller's discharge current intensifies this effect by acting on the same side and the boat's bow turns to starboard, the same side on which the rudder is set. With rudder to port the action would naturally be just the opposite.

WITH HEADWAY, PROPELLER REVERSING

A boat has no brakes as does a car, so she depends on reversing the propeller to bring her to a stop. Assuming that the boat has headway, rudder amidships, and the propeller is reversed, the effect is to throw the stern to port as the boat loses headway. The rudder has no steering effect in this case, and unequal blade thrust of the pro-

peller (which, remember, is reversing) tends to throw the stern to port. At the same time the propeller blades on the starboard side are throwing their discharge current in a powerful column forward against the starboard side of the keel and bottom of the boat, with nothing on the port side to offset this pressure. The stern, of necessity, is thrown to port.

This principle explains why a boatman will bring his boat up to a landing port side to the dock, if he has a choice. The stern then is thrown in toward the dock by the reversing propeller instead of away from it.

With rudder to port

Going back now to the case where the boat has headway and the propeller is reversed—this time with rudder over to port, let us say. Here the situation is more complicated. As before, we have the unequal blade thrust and propeller discharge current both driving the stern to port.

In addition there are two opposing factors. If the boat has much way on (ahead) her left rudder tends to throw the stern to starboard. However, her propeller suction current is being drawn in from astern in such a manner that it strikes the back of the rudder blade, tending to drive the stern to port.

Which combination of factors will be strongest depends on the amount of headway that the boat is carrying. If she has been running at some speed, the steering effect of left rudder will probably be the dominant factor and her stern would be thrown to starboard at first. As this steering effect weakens with reduced headway, the propeller slowing her down, then the effect of the suction current is added to help the tendency of the stern to port until eventually, with all headway killed, even the steering tendency to starboard is lost and all factors combine to throw the stern to port.

NO WAY ON, PROPELLER REVERSING

Now if the boat is lying dead in the water with no headway, rudder amidships, and the propeller is reversed, we again have that strong tendency of the stern to port as the

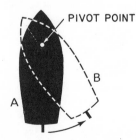

FORWARD - RIGHT HAND WHEEL RUDDER DEAD AHEAD

PIVOT POINT

Boat lying dead in water. When controls are set for forward motion, the first movement is a kick to starboard. The amount of side kick will depend on the boat and the amount of throttle given.

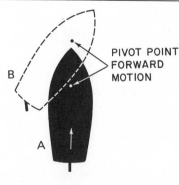

PIVOT POINT FORWARD MOTION

With forward motion when the helm is put over, the boat pivots around a point about ⅓ aft of the stem.
Note that the stern swings through twice as wide an arc as the bow.

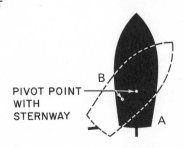

When backing down:

PIVOT POINT WITH STERNWAY

Pivot point is about ⅓ forward of stern, so bow describes twice as wide an arc as the stern.

FIG. 820 In the above series of sketches, the solid figure "A" represents the position of the boat before the action starts, and the broken outline "B" indicates its postion afterwards.

discharge current strikes the starboard side of the hull. You see, in each of the. cases where the discharge current of the reversing propeller is a factor, the strong current on the starboard side is directed generally toward the boat's bow but upward and inward in a spiral movement. The descending blade on the port side, on the other hand, tends to throw its stream downward at such an angle that its force is largely spent below the keel. Therefore, the two forces are never of equal effect.

Until the boat gathers sternway from her backing propeller it would not matter if the rudder were over to port or starboard. The discharge current against the starboard side is still the strong controlling factor and the stern is thrown to port. (Come back to this later when we discuss the matter of turning in a limited space.)

WITH STERNWAY, PROPELLER REVERSING

Now visualize the boat gathering sternway as the propeller continues to reverse. Here arises one of the seemingly mystifying conditions that baffle many a helmsman during his first trick at the wheel. The novice assumes that if he wants to back in a straight line his rudder must be amidships, just as it must be when he goes ahead on a straight course. Under certain conditions his boat may even respond to *right* rudder as he reverses by going to *port,* which is exactly what he doesn't expect, and if he is learning by trial-and-error he comes to the conclusion that it depends on the boat's fancy, while rudder position has nothing to do with control.

Let's analyze the situation, however, to see if he's right and whether there is anything that can be done about it. Fortunately, there is.

Backing with left rudder

At the outset we can rule out any effect of wake current as that force now is spent at the bow. Considering first the most obvious case, let's assume we have left rudder. Here there are four factors all working together to throw the stern to port. Unequal blade thrust is pushing the stern to port; the discharge current of the propeller is adding its powerful effect; and now we add the steering effect of the rudder acting on the aft side of the rudder blade, against which the suction current of the propeller is also working.

Remember this condition well for it is the answer to why *practically every single-screw vessel with right-hand propeller naturally backs to port* easily when she may be obstinate about going to starboard when reversing, fig. 821.

Backing with rudder amidships

Now, while backing to port, let's bring the rudder amidships and see what happens. Here we have eliminated the effects of suction current and steering from the rudder, leaving unequal blade thrust and the discharge current to continue forcing the stern to port.

Backing with right rudder

Assuming further that we have not yet gathered much sternway, let's put the rudder to starboard and see if we can't possibly make the boat back to starboard as you might expect she should with right rudder. The forces of unequal blade thrust and discharge current still tend to drive her stern to port, but the suction current of the pro-

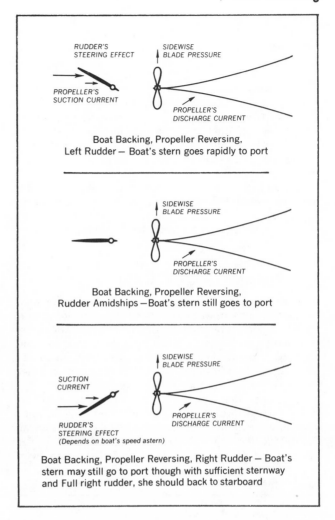

FIG. 821 **Three different situations where a boat is backing, her propeller reversing, with rudder set in various positions. Some boats back to port no matter how the rudder is set, but usually with right rudder and good sternway, they can be turned to starboard, though the turn to port is much better.**

peller wants to offset this. The effect of the discharge current is stronger than the suction so the tendency is still to port. Now, with sternway, the steering effect of right rudder is to starboard, but as yet we haven't way enough to make this offset the stronger factors.

STEERING WHILE BACKING

Just about the time we are about to give it up on the assumption that she can't be made to back to starboard, we try opening the throttle to gain more sternway. This finally has the desired effect and with full right rudder we find that the steering effect at considerable backing speed is enough (probably) to turn her stern to starboard against all the opposing forces. How well she will back to starboard—in fact, whether she will or not—depends on the design.

All of this means that if the boat will back to starboard with full right rudder, she may also be made to go in a straight line—but not with rudder amidships. There's no use trying. She will need a certain amount of right rudder depending both on her design and the speed. Some boats, while their backing to port is always much better than to starboard, can be controlled with a reasonable degree of precision by one who understands the particular boat he is handling.

In cases, boats may even be steered backwards out of crooked slips or channels—not, however, without a lot of backing and filling if there is much wind to complicate the situation. Generally the trick is to keep the boat under control, making the turns no greater than necessary so as to prevent the boat from swinging too much as a result of momentum and making it correspondingly difficult to get her straightened out again.

In maneuvers of this kind it is best to set the rudder first and then get added maneuvering power by speeding up the propeller in the desired direction, instead of trying to swing the rudder after the propeller is turning fast either ahead or astern.

WITH STERNWAY, PROPELLER TURNING AHEAD

There is one other situation to be considered, where we wish to kill our sternway by engaging the propeller to turn ahead. Regardless of rudder position, unequal blade thrust with the propeller going ahead now tends to throw the stern to starboard while the suction current is of no consequence. Unequal blade thrust may or may not be offset by the steering effect and the discharge current.

With rudder amidships, there is no steering effect and the discharge current does not enter our calculations. Therefore the stern will go to starboard. Now if you throw the rudder to port the discharge current of the propeller hits the rudder and drives the stern to starboard—even though the normal steering effect of left rudder would be to send the stern to port, with sternway. The powerful dis-

charge current from the propeller going ahead is the determining factor.

If the rudder is put to starboard, the steering effect works with the unequal blade thrust tending to move the stern to starboard but the discharge current strikes the starboard side of the rudder and acts to kick the stern to port. Application of enough power so that the force of the discharge current outweighs the other factors will result in the stern's going to port.

PROPELLER ACTION GOVERNS

From this analysis it will be seen that in a single-screw inboard boat one must constantly keep in mind what the propeller is doing in order to know how to use the rudder to best advantage. What the propeller is doing is even more important than whether the boat at the time may have headway or sternway.

To cite an example to make this clear, let's suppose you are backing in a direction that brings your port quarter up toward a dock. The tendency if you were to try to steer away from it would be to use right rudder. But the efficacy of that would be doubtful, because of the boat's inclination to back to port.

Therefore, we plan to kick the stern away by going ahead with the propeller so we set the rudder to port (left rudder, *toward* the dock), throw the reverse gear lever into the forward position and go ahead strong with the engine. The discharge current checks the sternway and, striking the rudder, throws the stern to starboard, clear of the dock.

It takes a lot of experience with any given boat to learn all her whims and traits—to know her strong points and use them wisely to overcome the weak ones. But boats, like individuals, do respond to understanding treatment.

Applying the Principles _____

Proficiency in motor boat handling is a matter of 10 percent principles, 90 percent application of these principles in practice. Therefore, the sooner we get afloat and start experimenting, the better. We've absorbed enough of the theory to have a broad idea of what to expect in practice; the next step is to get at the helm of a boat and actually learn by doing.

POINTS TO REMEMBER

Here are a few basic ideas to keep in mind, summarized from what has gone before.
• Remember that *the boat is always under better control with headway* than when she has sternway, because of the effect of the propeller's discharge current on the rudder when steering.
• Until the boat has gathered headway the stern has a tendency to swing (to starboard, with right-hand propeller) even with rudder amidships, as the propeller starts to turn ahead. *With good headway, rudder angle is the principal factor affecting control.*

• *Backing, there is a strong tendency to go to port* regardless of rudder angle, except (ordinarily) with full right rudder and considerable sternway. To back in a straight line you need a certain amount of right rudder varying, probably, with the speed.

• *With no way on there is no rudder control,* yet the stern can be kicked rapidly to port or starboard by putting the rudder over and applying plenty of power before the boat has a chance to gather way.
• *With left-hand propeller, the boat's reaction will be contrary to that outlined for the right-hand propeller.*

THE FIRST TIME OUT

The first step in applying these principles will be to take the boat out in open water—preferably on a day when there is little wind and no current. These factors should be ruled out at first and studied separately later, after the boat's normal reactions are fully understood.

With unlimited room to maneuver and no traffic to worry about, try putting the boat through all the maneuvers already discussed. Practice with every combination of

FIG. 822 In channels like this, speed must be held down to avoid damage to other craft and discomfort to their passengers. A boat is liable for damage caused by her wake.

better and quicker with the propeller engaged.

Before casting off, check the oil pressure and see that the cooling water is circulating. Whether your engine is "raw-water cooled" or "fresh-water cooled" with a heat exchanger, there should be a visible flow of water overboard, usually through the exhaust line. Until this water flows, it is unsafe to get underway.

If the water doesn't circulate, investigate at once as overheating can cause much damage, especially in a raw-water cooled engine if the cold water is suddenly picked up and pumped into the hot cylinder block. Cracking of the block could result.

Never race the motor as it idles, especially when cold. If the propeller is the right size and the throttle stop properly set, the motor should be able to take the propeller when the clutch is engaged at idling speeds. Boats don't require transmissions with a change of speeds as in cars, because the propeller slip automatically takes care of picking up the load gradually as the clutch is engaged.

After the clutch is in, the throttle (which almost invariably is hand-operated) can be opened gradually. Roughly speaking, normal cruising should be done at about two-thirds or three-quarters throttle. The extra few hundred revolutions available at wide open throttle seldom yield an increase in speed proportionate to the extra power required and the corresponding increase in fuel consumption. In congested waterways speed should be moderate, taking care that no damage is done by the wake, fig. 822.

One caution to observe when first learning to maneuver the boat is to avoid operating at too high a speed. Later, after you have become more familiar with the boat and its response to wheel and throttle, you will be able to use more power in certain situations—to accomplish a quick turn, for example—without getting into a jam.

CHECKING HEADWAY

Before attempting the maneuver of picking up a mooring you will want to experiment with the technique of checking the boat's headway while she is out in open water. Having no brakes, you must reverse the propeller to bring the boat to a stop. Caution must be exercised, *and docks or other craft must be approached at a very slow speed.* Unexpected failure of the clutch and reverse gears, or an unintentional killing of the engine, can result in embarrassing situations, if not actual damage, as you are unable to check your boat's forward motion.

Your experiments will show how effective the propeller is in killing the boat's headway. Generally speaking the larger diameter propellers, acting on a large volume of water, will exert the greatest effect. Small propellers, poorly matched to heavy hulls, may churn up much water before they are able to overcome the boat's momentum.

Many fast boats can be stopped in an incredibly short distance. When their throttles are closed, the boat changes her trim suddenly and headway is quickly lost, even before the propellers are reversed.

Whenever it is necessary to go from forward into reverse or vice versa, close the throttle to slow the engine down while going through neutral. If you make a practice of shifting the reverse gear from full ahead to full astern, look out for trouble. This is hard on the gear even if it doesn't fail—which it might do just when you're counting on it most.

conditions—with headway, sternway, and no way on; with right-rudder, left rudder and rudder amidships; with propeller turning in the direction of the boat's way, and also those cases where the propeller is turning opposite to the direction of the boat's way.

In each of these maneuvers note whether the rudder or propeller has the greater effect; note, too, how changing the speed alters the boat's response. Put the rudder hard over each way and see what happens when considerable power is applied before the boat has any way on.

Practice turns to determine the size of the boat's turning circle and the space required to bring the boat to a full stop with varying amounts of way, up to full speed.

GAINING EXPERIENCE

Later, when these fundamentals are mastered, go out again and observe how wind and current and sea alter the situation. Note how she tends to back into the wind until good steerageway is reached. How, if she is lying in the trough in a seaway, she tends to stay there with rudder amidships, because wave action is stronger than her natural tendency in smooth water to back to port.

Watch too how her stern starts to settle, and the bow comes up, when you get into shoal water. If there's just enough water to permit her to run without grounding, a wave will pile up on her quarter, steepest on the shallower side, as the natural formation of the wake is disturbed.

You should, of course, pick your maneuvering grounds from the chart to avoid danger of grounding, but if you see the first wave of your wake stretching away on the quarter in a sharp inverted V, tending to break at the top, beware of shoal water on that side.

GETTING UNDER WAY

Whenever you are about to get under way, assuming that you are starting a cold motor, don't spend too much time at the dock or mooring "warming up." There are a few things to check before getting under way and by the time these have been taken care of you will be ready to cast off and let the warming up of the motor be accomplished under load, at about half speed. Long periods of idling are bad for the clutch and the motor will warm up

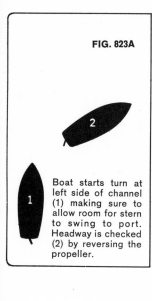

FIG. 823A

Boat starts turn at left side of channel (1) making sure to allow room for stern to swing to port. Headway is checked (2) by reversing the propeller.

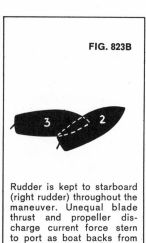

FIG. 823B

Rudder is kept to starboard (right rudder) throughout the maneuver. Unequal blade thrust and propeller discharge current force stern to port as boat backs from (2) to (3), propeller reversing.

FIG. 823C

Going ahead again, sternway is checked at (3) and propeller turning ahead kicks stern to port as shown at (4) before the boat has had a chance to gather headway.

FIG. 823D

Reversing once more, headway is checked at (4) and boat backs to (5). If necessary, alternate going ahead and backing can be repeated. Space available for the turn governs this. Turning in two boat lengths is easy.

FIG. 8

At (5) boat is in a position to go ahead with right rudder, bringing it amidships at (6), where she ready to proceed, having versed her course 180° from her original position at (

TURNING IN CLOSE QUARTERS

Turning a boat in a waterway not much wider than the boat's length often seems a bugbear to the novice but, once he has mastered the technique, it's no more difficult than turning a car on a narrow road.

Take a look at fig. 823. The situation sketched might apply in many cases. Perhaps you've run to the head of a dead-end canal and must turn around. Or possibly the waterway is a narrow channel, flanked by shoals. In the former case you must allow room so the swinging stern doesn't hit the canal bulkhead; in the latter, a similar allowance must be made to avoid throwing the stern up on shoal water.

Referring to fig. 823A, we start at (1), on the left side of the channel, running at slow speed. Putting the rudder hard over to starboard, the boat swings toward position (2), her headway being checked by reversing. *Always* execute this maneuver (if the propeller is right-handed) by going ahead to starboard, backing to port, to take advantage of the boat's natural tendency, as explained before.

Now (see 823B) *leave the wheel hard over to starboard* (right rudder). Normally you would expect to use left rudder in backing from (2) to (3), but this is unnecessary as the boat has no chance to gather sternway. As the reversing propeller stops the boat at (2), open the throttle for an instant and the stern will be kicked around to port to position (3).

Any attempt to shift from right rudder while going ahead to left rudder while going astern only results in extra gymnastics at the wheel at a time when you want your hands free for the throttle and reverse gear lever.

Throttling while we engage the clutch to go ahead, the sternway is checked at (3). Opening the throttle again, just for an instant, keeps the stern swinging to port toward position (4)—see fig. 823C. Now the operation described in 823B is repeated, backing from position (4) to (5) as shown in 823D.

If this happens to be a bulkheaded slip you are maneuvering in, allow plenty of room so that the port quarter is not thrown against the head of the slip as you go ahead

again at (5)—see 823E. The stern will continue to swing to port as the boat straightens away toward (6). At this point the rudder can be brought amidships, the boat having executed a 180-degree turn.

Backing around a turn

Fig. 824 illustrates the successive steps required to work out another practical problem in boat handling. Suppose (see 824A) you are in a narrow slip or canal at position (1) and want to back around a sharp turn, to starboard.

Reversing with full right rudder, you will not be able to turn short enough to steer around the 90-degree angle. Most likely you will back to a position about as indicated at (2), gaining a little to starboard. Now (see 824B) by going ahead with left rudder the stern is kicked over to starboard, placing the boat at (3).

Reversing once more, with full right rudder, the boat backs to (4), necessitating our going ahead once more with left rudder. This puts the boat at (5) (824D) in a position to back down on the new course.

Note that if she is expected to back down in a straight line from (5) she will need right rudder, though not necessarily hard over.

Backing to port from a slip

Fig. 825 illustrates a variation of the maneuver just described. Suppose the boat is lying in a slip, at A, and wishes to back out into the channel, space being limited. Fig. 824 showed how it would be necessary to work her around if the turn were to starboard. In fig. 825 her problem would be exactly the same if she had to back around in the direction of C.

However, if there is a choice, and she can back out to port, the probability is that with left rudder she will work around from A to B without any special maneuvering. To do it, her initial position in the slip must be about as shown at A with some clearance on her port side, but considerably more on the starboard side.

Clearance on the port side is needed because in reversing her stern immediately starts to move to port. More clearance on the starboard side is necessary because the

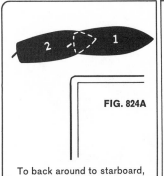

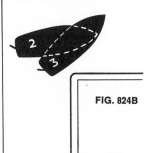

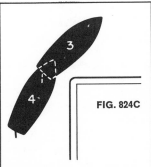

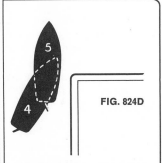

FIG. 824A

To back around to starboard, where space is limited, as in a slip, boat starts at (1) with right rudder, and backs to (2). She cannot turn short to starboard.

FIG. 824B

At (2) rudder is shifted to port and, with full left rudder, stern is kicked around to starboard by going ahead strong for a few revolutions of the propeller.

FIG. 824C

From position (3) boat can be backed down to (4) by reversing with full right rudder. Boat may back nearly in a straight line or gain a little to starboard.

FIG. 824D

At (4) wheel is swung hard over again, to give left rudder, while propeller, turning ahead, moves boat to (5). Backing down from (5) she will need right rudder to hold a straight course.

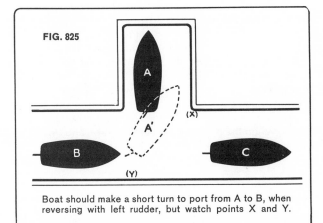

FIG. 825

Boat should make a short turn to port from A to B, when reversing with left rudder, but watch points X and Y.

bow will swing over toward point (x) as she backs.

In fact, points (x) and (y) are the ones to watch in executing this maneuver. If the boat shouldn't turn as short as expected, and doesn't swing directly from A to B, but takes a position as shown by the dotted lines at A', the starboard bow is in danger of touching at (x) and the starboard quarter at (y). This could be corrected at A' by going ahead with the propeller a few revolutions, using right rudder, to kick the stern over to port. This must be done carefully as there is no latitude here for much headway.

Having straightened her up, you could then back with left rudder to B and finally square away with rudder amidships to proceed toward C.

LEAVING A MOORING

Many yacht clubs have anchorages for members' boats, using mushroom anchors or heavy concrete blocks and mooring buoys to which the boat is secured by a pennant or mooring line over the forward bitt. Boats at moorings are reached from shore by dinghy or the club launch.

Getting away from the mooring when you are about to start a cruise is among the simplest of maneuvers, yet there is a right and a wrong way to go about it. The principal hazard in doing it wrong is the possibility of getting either the mooring line or dinghy painter fouled in the propeller. Handling of the boat is dictated by whatever is necessary

to accomplish this with a minimum of fuss.

If a dinghy was used to reach the boat, shorten up its painter so that the reversing propeller cannot pull any slack down into it, to be hopelessly fouled around the shaft and wheel. See that any boarding ladders, fenders or boat booms are aboard and send a man forward to let the mooring line go. The pennant usually has a small block of wood or metal buoy to float the end, making it easy to pick up again on return to the mooring.

In a river or stream where there is a current, the boat will lie head to that current (unless the wind is stronger). But in a bay on a calm day there may be neither wind nor current to move the boat even when the mooring line is let go. To go ahead under such conditions would almost certainly result in fouling the propeller.

To avoid this, back away a few boat lengths, far enough so you can keep the buoy in sight and allow sufficient room to clear it when you go ahead, with particular regard for any swinging of the stern. Whether you back away straight or turn as you reverse depends largely on the position of neighboring boats in the anchorage.

Until you are clear of the anchorage, run well throttled so as not to create a nuisance with your wake. Then, as you open up to cruising speed, the dinghy can be dropped back near the crest of the second wave astern. If she is astern of that crest, she will tow too hard, running "uphill" with bow too high. Shorten the painter from this point until the pull on it lessens as she flattens out to a better trim, but don't have her run "down-hill" either, if there is any tendency for her to yaw off the course. Exactly how you trim the dinghy by the length of the painter will depend largely on boat speed and sea conditions, fig. 826.

When there is wind or current

When your mooring is in a stream or if a tidal current flows past it, the boat will be set back when the mooring line has been let go. This usually simplifies the problem of getting away; reversing may not be necessary.

In a wind (assuming the current is not stronger) the boat will be lying head to the wind. As she drops back from the mooring, whether or not the reverse gear is used, the bow will pay off to one side and shape the boat up to get away without additional maneuvering.

All boats with considerable freeboard have a strong tendency to "tack" back and forth as they lie at anchor in a wind, and the same is true to an extent at permanent moorings unless the gear is so heavy as to retard this action.

If the bow is "tacking" this way and you want to shape the boat up to leave the buoy on one side or the other, wait till the boat reaches the limit of her swing in the right direction and then let the pennant go. The bow will pay off rapidly as she catches the wind on that side.

Sometimes, if the boat isn't too big or the wind too strong, you can help to cast the bow in the right direction by holding the pennant to one side so that the wind will catch that side and cause her to pay off toward the other.

PICKING UP A MOORING

Returning to the anchorage when the cruise is finished, approach your mooring at slow speed, noting carefully how other boats are lying at their buoys. They are heading into the wind or current (whichever is stronger) and your course in approaching the buoy should be roughly parallel to the way they align up-wind or against the current. Shorten the dinghy painter as necessary.

Now slip the clutch into neutral when you estimate that you have just way enough to carry you up to the buoy. A man should be stationed on the bow with a boathook to pick up the pennant float when it comes within reach. If you see that you are about to overshoot the mark, reverse enough to check the headway as the bow comes up to the buoy. If you fall short, a few extra kicks ahead with the propeller should suffice.

FIG. 826 Length of the dinghy painter will determine how well she tows.

Don't expect the man forward to do the work that the engine should accomplish in holding the boat in position until the signal is given that the pennant eye has been secured on the bitt. Watch especially that the boat doesn't tend to drop astern while the man forward tries to hang on with the boathook. Also try to avoid having the buoy chafe unnecessarily against the hull.

When running through an anchorage keep an eye peeled for other moorings so as not to foul or cut them. If yours is the only mooring in the anchorage, you will have to gauge the effect of wind and current on your own boat as best you can so as to approach up-wind or against the current or directly against any combination of these factors. Don't try to execute this maneuver with wind abeam or astern. When the pennant is secure forward, and only then, the motor can be stopped.

Landing at a Dock

The knowledge you have already acquired in turning a boat where space for maneuvering is limited will stand you in good stead when you tackle the next problem of bringing her in neatly to a dock or float.

The factors involved here are, in part, the same as in coming to a mooring, with certain modifications. For example, when you pick up a mooring you have wind and

FIG. 827 This boat, properly, is being maneuvered near her berth at slow speed.

current to consider, generally determining the angle of your approach. Wind and current must also be reckoned with at docks, but there are many occasions when the angle of approach to a dock is not a matter of choice.

With no wind or current to complicate the situation, landing, with a right-handed propeller, can be accomplished most effectively by bringing the boat in port side to the dock. Our previous analysis of propeller action when reversing makes the reason for this clear.

Keep boat under control

Don't come in with a grand flourish at high speed but throttle down gradually to keep the boat under control, fig. 827. When you see that you have way enough to reach the dock, slip the clutch into neutral and use the reverse gear as and when necessary to check headway as the boat goes into her berth.

If your speed has been properly estimated you will be several boat lengths from the dock when the clutch is thrown into neutral. Coming in at too high a speed you will be forced to go into neutral a long way from the dock (losing maneuverability with the propeller disengaged) or face the alternative of trusting the reverse gear to check excessive headway.

This is a good time to exercise judgment, keeping the way necessary for good maneuverability, yet using no more

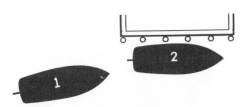

FIG. 828 When landing port side to a dock, approach at an angle of 10 to 20 degrees as shown. Discharge current of the reversing propeller (if R.H.) will set the stern to port, as at (2), even though rudder is amidships.

than required. If you have been running at any speed, it is desirable to hold off briefly and let your own stern wave catch up with and pass your boat. It is embarrassing to "cuss" about being rocked by a wake just as you are coming alongside—and then find out that it was your own wake that upset your smooth approach and docking.

As the reversing propeller throws its discharge current against the starboard side aft, the stern is carried to port. For this reason it is customary to approach, not exactly parallel with the dock, but at a slight angle—say 10 to 20 degrees. Then as she comes up to the dock her stern will be brought alongside, fig. 828, with the boat parallel to the dock, properly berthed.

In docking, lines should be kept ready to run fore and aft and fenders placed if necessary to keep the boat from chafing against unprotected piles.

WIND OR CURRENT PARALLEL TO DOCK

When a berth happens to be on the shore of a river or bank of a tidal stream so that the current flows parallel to it, it is best to govern the direction of approach by the current flow, even though this puts the starboard side toward the dock. Heading into the current will enable you to keep the propeller turning over slowly—right up to the moment of reaching the dock, if the current is strong enough.

The same is true if wind is the force you are opposing. If your course puts the wind over the stern you will have to make a wide swing, starting far enough from the dock to permit you to round up to leeward of it, coming in against the wind. To miscalculate here by not allowing room enough for the turn would be embarrassing, as you head for the bank with wind or current sweeping you downstream. Hence the importance of preliminary practice in open water, noting the size of turning circles under various conditions, before attempting the actual docking maneuvers.

In starting a turn like this, even at some distance from the dock, it will be necessary to throttle down long before the dock comes abeam. Otherwise the wash the boat throws may carry along and leave you wallowing in your own wake just when you're trying to come alongside.

In coming up against wind or current, you use that force to check your headway, instead of the reverse. Therefore, allowance usually need not be made for the effect of a reversing propeller.

LANDINGS DOWN-WIND OR WITH CURRENT

Avoid, if you can, the landing in which wind or current is setting you down towards the dock in the direction of

your course. In cases of this kind you are dependent on your reverse gear and even though they are practically 100 percent dependable an error in judgment or minor motor ailment would put you on the spot.

However, you will meet such situations, where space does not permit a turn before docking. For example, suppose you are coming in to a canal lock with a strong wind astern. Hold the speed down to a minimum consistent with adequate control and by all means take the port side of the lock, unless there is no choice.

Plan to get a line out from the stern or port quarter as soon as headway is checked. If necessary, the boat would lie well enough temporarily to this line alone, whereas to get a bow line fast first and then miss making the stern line fast would be to risk being turned end-for-end by the wind. This has happened repeatedly to inexperienced boatmen on their first cruise through canals, to the embarrassment of other boats already berthed along the lock walls.

Handling the lines

If you have a couple of hands aboard, assign one to the bow and one to the stern to handle lines, with instructions not to make fast until headway is checked. The seriousness of checking the boat's way by means of a snubbed bow line instead of reversing the propeller is only too obvious. If single-handed, you will have to work smartly, with a stern line fast to the after bitt coiled ready to carry ashore, and a bow line, preferably run in advance along the deck back to the cockpit. Such lines of course would have to be led outboard of all stanchions, to be clear when taken ashore.

The problem is no different if you are making your landing with a following current. In either case, be ready with the reverse on the approach, using it as strongly as necessary to hold the boat against its momentum and the push of wind or current. The propeller ordinarily should be turning over slowly in reverse for the last boat length or two of headway, the throttle being opened gradually and as needed to kill all headway at the right instant.

WHEN BOATS LIE AHEAD AND ASTERN

Let's vary the problem by assuming that boats are already lying at a wharf, leaving you little more than a boat length to squeeze into your berth. The technique is decidedly not the one you are accustomed to in parking a car at a curb.

Referring to fig. 829, boats A and B are already in their berths astern and ahead, respectively, of the berth we, in

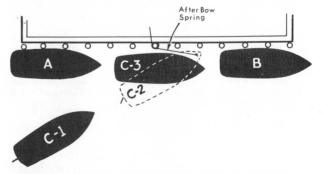

FIG. 829 Landing at a dock between boats (A) and (B), C approaches at an angle. At (C-2), a spring line is run aft to dock from forward bitt. Going ahead with propeller and right rudder, boat swings into berth at (C-3).

boat C, want to slip into. The position of boat A necessitates our going in at a greater angle than if the dock were clear, and there is no room to go either ahead or astern once we have nosed up to position C-2.

Consequently a man is stationed forward to take a line (in this case technically called an after bow spring) leading aft from the forward bitt to a pile or bollard on the dock. He takes a turn around the pile and holds fast while we go ahead with the propeller, setting the rudder to starboard. The spring prevents the boat from going ahead and the stern is thrown in toward the dock until she assumes her final position against the dock, as at C-3.

As the boat swings in, the spring must be slacked off a little and often a fender or two will be necessary at the point of contact.

USING WIND OR CURRENT

In a case such as that covered by fig. 829, with conditions the same except for a wind from the south (assume boats A and B are headed east) we could have used the wind to advantage in bringing the boat in.

Under such conditions the boat could be brought up parallel to her final position at C-3, allowing the wind to set her in to her berth at the dock. The bow, probably, would come in faster than the stern, but this would not matter.

During this maneuver, the engine would be idling and, if there were any tendency for the boat to go ahead or astern, it could be offset by a turn or two of the propeller as needed, to maintain her position midway between A and B.

Balancing current against propeller action

A variation of this problem is sketched in fig. 830, where a current is flowing east. Here the boat is brought up to a position C-1 parallel to her berth at C-2. The propeller will have to be turning over very slowly in reverse (perhaps at the engine's idling speed) to hold her at C-1 against the current.

Now if the rudder is turned slightly to port the boat will tend to move bodily in toward the wharf, but the stern is likely to come in first. An after quarter spring should be

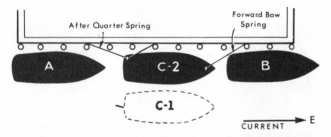

FIG. 830 The boat can be worked into her berth, using the current, by setting the rudder to port and using just enough power to offset drift of the current. In this case, propeller must be reversed to hold her against the current.

run first, to hold the boat against the current as the propeller stops turning.

Only enough rudder and power should be used to work the boat slowly sidewise. Too much power will put her out of control and too much rudder may cause her stern to go to port too fast, permitting the current to act on the boat's starboard side.

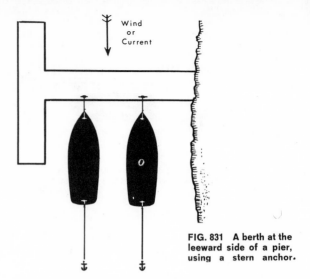

FIG. 831 A berth at the leeward side of a pier, using a stern anchor.

Under identical conditions, except for a current setting west instead of east, the propeller would be allowed to turn slowly ahead, just enough to hold the boat against the current. Then, with rudder slightly to port, the boat would edge off sidewise to port, the bow coming in slightly ahead of the stern. The forward bow spring would be the first of the mooring lines to make fast in this case.

LANDING ON THE LEEWARD SIDE

Sometimes you will run into situations where a pier juts out into the water, with wind blowing at right angles to it, giving you a choice of sides on which to land. If there is much wind and sea, the windward side can be uncomfortable as the boat will pound against the piles.

The rougher it is, the more important it becomes to take the leeward side. The wind will then hold her clear, at the length of her mooring lines. If there is much wind you will have to work smartly when bringing the boat up to such a berth and it will help to have men ready at both bow and stern to run the mooring lines.

Bow line first

The bow line of course must be run first and made fast. The stern line may present more of a problem since the boat has had to approach at an angle to allow for the wind's tendency to blow the bow off. The stern line can be heaved ashore by the man aft to the other on the dock, after the latter has made his bow line fast. The bow line, if necessary, can be used as a spring to bring the stern in by going ahead with rudder to starboard, on the principle sketched in fig. 829.

This maneuver, single-handed, would be difficult. It could be accomplished by getting a bow line off to use as a spring, working the stern up to the dock with the power, and lashing the wheel (unless you have a worm-and-gear steerer) to keep the rudder to starboard while you get a stern line fast.

Often it is a question of just how smartly the boatman works as to how much maneuvering he must go through. If he knows his boat and his crew know their job, he probably will get his lines ashore fast enough so that the spring line may not be needed to get the stern in.

STERN ANCHOR TO LEEWARD

Fig. 831 illustrates a method by which boats often line up at a pier beam to beam. Each has a secure berth on the leeward side of the pier and a maximum number of

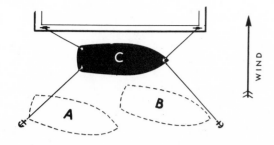

FIG. 832 Laying anchors to windward from the bow and quarter to keep a boat from pounding on the windward side of a pier or wharf.

boats are accommodated for a given amount of dock space. The principal objection is the difficulty of stepping ashore from the bow.

The arrangement shown makes a snug berth even in a hard blow but a shift of wind might necessitate a shift of berth if the wind came abeam, throwing a heavy strain on the stern line and anchor.

The principle of getting into a berth like this is obvious from the sketch. Simply run up against the wind or current, propeller turning over just fast enough to give steerageway, and have a man let the anchor go over the stern, paying out line until the bow is close enough to get a line on the dock. The stern line is available as a check though the helmsman should make it his business to bring the bow up as required without over-shooting his mark and hitting the dock.

After passengers have been discharged the bow line can be slacked and the stern anchor line shortened, though this means that one person must be aboard. If all are to go ashore, adjust the stern line so that it just checks the boat from touching the dock. Then if there is room, carry the bow line off at an angle to another pile. This increases the clearance at the bow, and the wind or current acting on one side will help to hold her clear.

The sketch is not to scale. Often the scope of the anchor line astern will need to be much greater than that indicated to provide holding power in a given depth. Seven times the depth of water is a rough-and-ready rule to determine the scope of anchor lines though this is qualified by dozens of factors.

USING ANCHORS TO WINDWARD

If you see that a berth on the windward side of a dock is inevitable and there is reason to believe that the hull will suffer even with fenders strategically placed, plan in advance to get anchors out to windward. This trick is not used nearly as often as it should be, especially if the boat is to occupy such a berth for a considerable time.

You will need a man on the bow and another on the stern to handle anchor lines, though in a pinch the helmsman can handle the stern line if he takes every precaution to keep slack lines from fouling the propeller. Referring to fig. 832, the stern anchor is let go from the quarter when the boat is at A, moving slowly ahead, to be checked at B, when the man forward lets his anchor go. If someone is tending the line aft, the helmsman can back a little as necessary to place the boat as the wind carries her down to her berth at C.

Tend lines carefully

On the other hand, if the helmsman must leave his wheel and tend the stern line, then the boat can be jockeyed into position merely by adjusting the length of the various lines. This probably will necessitate hauling in some of the stern line while the bow line is slacked away. Throughout, the lines should be carefully tended. Dock lines can be run from the port bow and quarter.

Note that at A and B the boat is not parallel to the dock, but has been headed up somewhat into the wind. As she drifts in, after the engine is put in neutral at B, the bow will come in faster than the stern.

This plan should be used with a full understanding of the great strain the anchor lines are carrying with the wind hitting the boat abeam, especially if there is some sea running as well. The stronger the wind and the rougher the sea, the longer the scope required if the anchors are to hold without dragging.

If you plan to land on the windward side of the dock without using anchors to hold her off, make due allowance for leeway on the approach and keep the bow somewhat up to windward if possible, checking headway while abreast of the berth you will occupy. Then have fenders handy as she drifts in.

WHEN CURRENT SETS TOWARD DOCK

Let's suppose now a situation in which the boat must find a berth off a pier in such a position that the current will be flowing from the boat toward the pier, fig. 833.

In this hypothetical case it may be assumed that the outside of the dock, which ordinarily would be the natural choice for landing, must be kept clear for ferries, perhaps, or other boats, while the lower side of the dock is also restricted for some reason. The only remaining berth is above it, at A in the illustration.

This situation should be sized up to determine exactly where the anchor is to be let go, with certainty that you will have sufficient scope. If your anchor drags here, you will be in a bad spot as the current will set the boat down on the dock. Therefore make sure that the anchor really gets a bite.

The spot where the anchor is to be let go may be approached from any direction as long as the boat is rounded up into the current. The procedure, if we wish to land bow to the dock with a stern anchor out, has already been outlined in fig. 831. This, however, is not feasible above the dock because of the difficulty of backing away into the current when leaving.

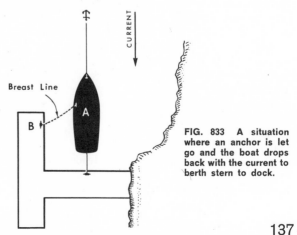

FIG. 833 A situation where an anchor is let go and the boat drops back with the current to berth stern to dock.

Tending scope of anchor line

After the anchor has been let go, the boat can be dropped back toward her berth at A, simply by paying out more scope on the anchor line. The current will do the work though the engine could be used to help control the

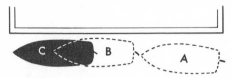

FIG. 834 Making a landing with starboard side of the boat toward the dock. Approaching slowly at (A), nearly parallel with the dock, rudder is shifted to full left at (B), swinging stern to starboard. At this point, give the boat a kick ahead with the propeller (if necessary) to swing the stern. Then reverse to check headway.

FIG. 835 A bow line run well forward restrains this yacht from moving astern and against another boat. It also provides adequate length for vertical changes with the rise and fall of the tide.

boat's position if wind tended to throw her out of line.

Just before the stern reaches the dock, a stern line can be made fast to a pile, after which the boat's position can be adjusted by the lines as desired. If the anchor is holding securely (and the berth should be left if it isn't) the stern can be brought close enough to the dock for passengers to step comfortably ashore.

The boat should not be left unattended in this position as she may safely be if berthed as in fig. 831. In fig. 833, where a convenient wing of the dock is available alongside the boat, a breast line could be run as shown. Then, before leaving the boat, the anchor line could be shortened to give ample clearance at the stern. Slacking the stern line would permit stepping ashore at B, after which the stern line could be adjusted from the dock.

The breast line is left slack but is available to haul the boat back in to B when boarding again after slacking the stern line. If the breast line is made fast too far aft it would be difficult to haul the stern in because of the "tacking" action of the boat in the current. Made fast forward of amidships, the boat will come in readily.

LANDING STARBOARD SIDE TO DOCK

Though a dock on the port side is preferable, as already explained, a good landing at a dock on the starboard side can be made, if care is exercised.

Referring to fig. 834, the boat is approaching the dock at (A), nearly parallel to it, engine idling or turning over just enough to insure control.

Just before it is necessary to reverse to check the headway, the rudder is shifted to full left (at B) to swing the stern in toward the dock. If she does not respond, give the propeller a kick ahead while the rudder is full left. This definitely kicks the stern in and, as she swings, the reverse can be used to kill the headway.

Dock Lines and Their Use

Lines play an important part in the handling of vessels at a dock. Obviously, the larger the craft the more lines are likely to be called into play. It would be absurd for the motor boatmen to burden his 30-footer with a spider-web of breasts, springs and other lines that would be appropriate only on a large vessel.

TERMINOLOGY

Nevertheless, it is well to be familiar with correct terms and the functions of lines that may be used. They may come in handy some time—though not necessarily all at once.

Motor boatmen often speak loosely of bow and stern lines—and little else—depending on whether the line is made fast forward or aft and regardless of the direction in which it leads or the purpose it serves. To be strictly correct, according to nautical terminology, there is *only one bow line*. This is made fast to the forward bitt and run along the dock as far as practicable to prevent the boat from moving astern.

Conversely, a *stern line,* properly, leads from the after bitt to a distant pile or bollard on the dock astern of the boat, to check her from going ahead. The special virtue of

such lines as applied to small boats is the fact that, with but little slack, they may allow for considerable rise and fall of the tide.

Breast lines, on the other hand, lead athwartships nearly at right angles to the vessel and to the dock, to keep her from moving sidewise away from her berth. Large craft may use bow, waist or quarter breasts, depending on whether they are made fast forward, amidships or aft.

Naturally breasts on large vessels are more important than on small craft. If a vessel has a 100-foot beam, her bow is 50 feet from the dock and the bow breast must be somewhat longer than that. On a small boat with 10-foot beam, the bow is only 5 feet from the dock, and other lines may serve to keep her from moving away from the dock.

Smaller recreational boats will frequently have only one bitt or cleat forward and one or two aft to which dock lines may be made fast. Additional cleats along the sides, properly through bolted, are desirable to provide flexibility in using dock lines.

As we shall see later, a small boat might be adequately moored with springs alone, using no breasts. Sometimes boatmen attempt to make fast to a dock with bow and stern breasts only and get into trouble because slack must

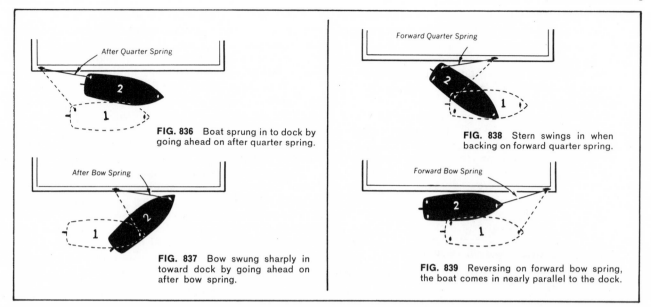

FIG. 836 Boat sprung in to dock by going ahead on after quarter spring.

FIG. 837 Bow swung sharply in toward dock by going ahead on after bow spring.

FIG. 838 Stern swings in when backing on forward quarter spring.

FIG. 839 Reversing on forward bow spring, the boat comes in nearly parallel to the dock.

be left in the line to allow for tide. If adjusted right for low water, they may be entirely too slack at high water and the boat gets a chance to catch in some stringer or projection of the dock when her bow or stern swings in.

SPRING LINES

Springs are especially useful lines in preventing undesired movement ahead or astern in a berth. They are also useful in keeping a craft in position where it is made fast to a fixed structure and there is a significant rise and fall of tide. There may be four spring lines—the *forward bow spring*, the *after bow spring*, the *forward quarter spring*, and the *after quarter spring*; see fig. 841.

Bow springs are made fast to the vessel at or near the bow, quarter springs at or near the stern. Forward springs lead forward from the vessel to the pier or wharf, and thus check any movement sternward. After springs lead aft from the vessel and check any movement ahead.

Remember that the terms *forward* and *after* relate to the *direction* in which the spring line runs from the vessel, and not to where it is made fast on board, this being indicated by the terms *bow* and *quarter*.

Going Ahead on a Spring

We have already seen, fig. 829, how, by means of an after bow spring, the stern can be brought in to a dock by going ahead with the rudder set away from the dock; it is more easily done with line made fast farther aft. This technique is especially useful when a boat must be gotten in to a dock against a stiff offshore wind.

Now if the boat lay parallel to the dock but some distance off, she could be breasted in bodily by hauling in on bow and stern breasts, but with the wind off the dock and a sizable craft this might require much effort.

Again with an after bow spring, but with the rudder set amidships, let's see what would happen; fig. 837. This will cause the bow to be swung abruptly in toward the dock, as the bitt describes an arc of a circle, the length of the spring its radius. With left rudder, the bow turns in even faster as the stern is thrown to starboard further away from the dock.

Ahead on a quarter spring

If it were possible to secure an after spring at the boat's center of gravity, she could be sprung in bodily to the dock and her parallel alignment (or any other position) could be held by means of the rudder as the propeller goes ahead, because the stern would be free to swing as the discharge current acts on the rudder.

Actually this is more theoretical than practical on many boats as we will normally have only the bow and stern (or quarter) cleats to make any spring lines fast to, while the center of gravity may be nearly amidships. Now if we rig an after quarter spring, and go ahead with rudder amidships, the combination of forces is such that the boat will be sprung in nearly parallel to the dock. Her stern will come in till the quarter touches the dock, while the bow may stand off somewhat, fig. 836.

If the rudder were put to port at position (1) in fig. 836, in the expectation that the bow would thus be thrown to port, it would be seen that the effect is negligible, as the stern is prevented from being kicked to starboard by the taut spring. Putting the rudder to starboard would throw the stern in to port fast, however.

Reversing on a Spring

The action is just the opposite if we reverse on a spring. Turning to fig. 838, note how the stern is swung sharply in toward the dock by the action of the forward quarter spring when reversing. Compare this action with that illustrated in fig. 837, picturing the boat turned end for end.

Now note what happens, as in fig. 839, when backing on a forward bow spring. The turning effect of the spring on the boat is not important here, and she springs in nearly parallel to the dock in an action which might be compared with that in fig. 836—once again considering the boat turned end for end.

Allow for Tidal Range

Boatmen located on fresh water streams and lakes have no tidal problem confronting them when securing to a dock with mooring lines, but failure to take this action into account in tidal waters can part lines, and even sink the boat.

Springs provide an effective method of leaving a boat free to rise and fall, while preventing her from going ahead or astern or twisting in such a way as to get caught on dock projections.

The longer a mooring line can be, the more of a rise and fall of tide it can take care of with a minimum of slack,

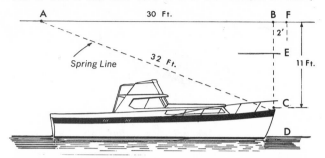

FIG. 840 How long spring lines act with great changes in tidal level. If water level drops 11' from E to D, a 32-foot spring line (A to B) would cause the boat to move astern to the position shown; cleat C would be at F at the higher level. Principle is a right triangle ($32^2 = 30^2 + 11^2$ approximately). Advantage of long spring lines is obvious.

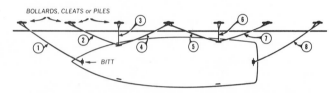

FIG. 841 Shown above are most of the possible docking lines for a vessel with the identification of each. These are (1) bow line, (2) forward bow spring, (3) forward (bow) breast, (4) after bow spring, (5) forward quarter spring, (6) after (quarter) breast, (7) after quarter spring, (8) stern line. Don't try to use them all on a small boat! Aboard ships, mooring lines are numbered from the bow aft, depending on where they are secured aboard the vessel.

FIG. 842 Spring lines (3) and (4) are often crossed to gain a greater length for them, especially where significant rise and fall of tide occurs. The stern line (2) is often run to the off-shore quarter cleat.

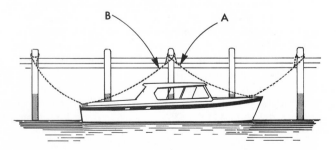

FIG. 843 Where two spring lines must be placed on the same pile or cleat. Note that eye splice of after bow spring (A) is run up through eye (B) of forward quarter spring. Either can be cleared without removing the other.

fig. 840. Yet every line must be allowed slack enough so that all do not come taut together at either extreme stage of the tide.

Manila lines are left slack, too, to allow for shrinkage when wet or, if "made up" wet, must be checked when dry for excessive stretch. When nylon is used, generally the lines are "made up" taut, as they don't change much with the weather and will stretch to take up changes in wind strength. This point must be carefully observed in narrow slips or close quarters. Better tight than so loose the boat will move too far.

As a general rule, where space permits, a bow line should be run well ahead of the boat to the dock, and a stern line well aft. If these two lines are run off at an angle of about 45 degrees to the centerline of the boat, they will often prove sufficient for small pleasure boats, breasts being entirely unnecessary and the springs (one or two) resorted to only if the necessary slack of bow and stern lines allows the boat to move about too much at her berth.

MOORING A BOAT

Eight mooring lines that might be used to make fast a ship or boat are illustrated in fig. 841. They are *not* all used at the same time! What might be considered a typical satisfactory arrangement of mooring lines for a boat or yacht—20 to 65 feet—is illustrated in fig. 842. The two spring lines are shown crossed and running to separate dock cleats or piles. This provides longer spring which can be drawn up rather snugly and yet allow for a rise and fall of tide. If only one pile or cleat is available, position the craft so that this point is opposite amidships and run both springs to it; see fig. 843.

The bow and stern lines should make roughly a 45° angle with the dock face. The stern line is most easily run to the near-shore quarter cleat, but a better tie-up is made if it is run to the off-shore quarter cleat, as shown by the dotted line in fig. 842.

Breast lines here would be superfluous and should be omitted. An exception might be a slack line to the near-shore quarter cleat used solely for pulling the boat in against an offshore wind for easier and safer boarding.

If lines are doubled

If two lines are used anywhere with the idea of getting double the strength of one, they must be of equal length when strain is put upon them. Otherwise one carries the load first and parts, and then the other follows suit.

Two lines on one bollard

Frequently, mooring lines may have an eye splice of suitable size in the end which goes ashore, to be dropped over the pile or bollard. Fig. 843 shows both the after bow spring and the forward quarter spring secured to a single bollard about amidships. If these are dropped one over the other, the upper one must first be cleared in order to get the lower one free.

Inasmuch as one or the other of these springs may be needed to get clear of the dock, depending on wind and current conditions at the time, it is well to rig these so that either can be freed without disturbing the other.

Assuming that the eye splice of the forward quarter spring has been placed on the pile first, take the splice of the after bow spring and run it up from below through the eye of the quarter spring and then drop it down over the pile, fig. 843.

This way either line can be cleared without disturbing the other, though it may be necessary to use a little power to ease the strain on one if its eye happens to nip the other line between itself and the pile.

If a boat has much freeboard, the tide is high, and dock piles are relatively short, so that a mooring line leads down at a fairly sharp angle from deck to dock, there may be some risk of its slipping up over the top of the pile. An extra round turn of the eye splice taken over the pile will prevent this, fig. 844.

Dock or Mooring Lines

On recreational boats, mooring lines are generally of nylon, either the usual twisted rope or the newer type with a braided core and a braided cover. The size of the line will vary with the size of the craft. Typically, a 30- to 40-footer will use lines of ⅝" nylon, with larger yachts going to ¾" lines, and smaller boats to ½" or even ⅜" nylon for under-20-footers. Manila lines are rather infrequently used these days—1" manila would not be as strong as ⅝" nylon, yet it would be 2½ times heavier and correspondingly harder to handle. Nylon also has desirable properties of stretch, longer life, and softness in one's hands.

Heaving lines and monkey's fists

Part of the essence of good seamanship lies in knowing when a certain method of procedure is applicable to the size of vessel one is handling. Use of big ship technique on small motor boats is amusing to a seasoned boatman. Application of motor boat principles aboard a big vessel may be distressing to a ship captain.

An excellent example of this is in the technique used to get the mooring lines from the ship or boat to the dock. The lines of a big vessel are heavy hawsers, hard to handle, and impossible to heave. Therefore they make use of heaving lines, which are light lines weighted at the end by a "monkey's fist" (an intricate woven knot which encloses the weight). This heaving line is bent to the hawser near the eye splice—not in the loop where it might be jammed when a strain is thrown on the hawser—and the line is sent from ship to dock, dock to ship, or ship to ship as soon as possible as a messenger, fig. 845.

FIG. 844 An extra round turn in the eye splice of a mooring line should be taken around a pile if the lead is high from dock to deck. This prevents it from slipping up.

Small craft practices

On boats, heaving lines are more of a technique to be learned and then filed away in your memory for possible emergency use. Normally your crew can simply step ashore with the necessary lines or hand them to someone there.

Even if necessary to heave your regular mooring lines on a small boat, they will carry some distance if properly coiled, half held loosely in the left hand and the remaining half heaved by the right, fig. 846, all uncoiling naturally in the air, without fouling up into a knot and falling short. If necessary, a weight can be added at times to carry a line but this is seldom used.

If, in passing a line for towing purposes, for example, you had to send a heavier line a long distance, then break out the heaving line principle and use it to good advantage.

HOLDING WITH ONE SPRING

While we are talking of springs there is another trick worth remembering that deserves to be used more often, fig. 847.

In the illustration we assume that you have run up along the leeward side of a dock, to remain there for a short time while you pick up guests or perhaps put some one ashore. Instead of getting lines out to make fast fore and aft as you would for a longer stop, or expect the crew to hold the boat against the wind's pressure, try using one line as an after bow spring, as illustrated.

After coming alongside, rig the line and go ahead easily till it takes a strain; then go ahead, with left rudder, with power enough to hold the stern up against the dock. This is a maneuver that you can accomplish single-handed with-

FIG. 845 A monkey's fist carries this light heaving line to a lightship from a Coast Guard cutter. The end will be bent to a heavier line or hawser.

FIG. 846 Mooring lines on pleasure boats are usually light enough to heave, if held properly coiled.

out too much difficulty, by having your spring fast to the forward bitt as you come in, with the end ready to pass ashore for someone on the dock to drop over a pile.

Doubling the spring

Single-handed, you might prefer to use the spring double, with the bight of line around the pile and both ends of the line fast to your bitt. Then, when your guests are all aboard, you can slip the engine into neutral, cast off one end and haul the spring back aboard without leaving the deck. This would be helpful if the wind were of some force, the bollard well back from the dock edge, and no one ashore to assist. This way there would be no risk of the boat's being blown off as you step ashore to cast off the line.

In any case, when the line has been cast off forward, the wind will cause the boat to drift clear of the dock, the

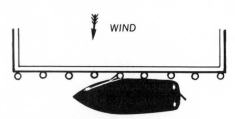

FIG. 847 Making a brief stop on the leeward side of a dock, boat can be held in postion by going ahead on an after bow spring with rudder hard over (in this case, to port).

bow ordinarily paying off faster than the stern. Whether you go ahead or reverse to get under way will be dependent on the proximity of other docks and boats, etc., and whether your course is to be up- or down-stream. The same maneuver would be applicable if current were setting in the direction that the wind is blowing in the illustration.

Getting Clear of a Dock

As a matter of strict terminology, you should never refer to a "dock" when you actually mean "pier" or "wharf." A pier projects out from the shoreline. A wharf is a structure generally parallel to and not far from the shore. Technically, a dock is the adjacent water area, but in boating it is customarily applied to the structure itself.

When the master of a ship takes her out of a berth, he calls it "undocking," a term applicable to all vessels but which may seem inappropriate to some for small boats. For a 20-footer, "undocking" may sound affected.

WIND OR CURRENT AHEAD

Probably the first situation to consider is with the wind or current parallel to the face of the dock to which the boat is made fast and in the opposite direction than that in which she is headed. This is the result of making a landing against the current, the easiest and "basic" technique of coming alongside.

A safe way of getting clear of the dock is to go ahead on an after bow spring with the rudder turned in toward the dock. The natural propeller action plus rudder action will swing the stern clear of the dock. The boat can then be backed down a short distance and will have sufficient clearance to go ahead and away, but don't try to cut away too sharply lest your stern come back in and your port quarter strike the dock face.

Another technique for the same situation is shown in fig. 848. If all lines were cast off, the boat might drift back along the dock, or if she went ahead, the helmsman would have to exercise care that the boat was kept exactly parallel in order to pull away without damage.

Again, it is more seamanlike to use a spring (unless the boat is so small that a person stepping aboard at the bow can merely push her bow out enough). This time we need a forward quarter spring on the port side. It is likely that this is already in use as one of the dock mooring lines, so all other lines can be cast off.

If the bow does not swing out at once with the effect of wind or current, backing easily on the spring will pull the stern in toward the dock, probably necessitating use of a fender on the port quarter to protect the hull.

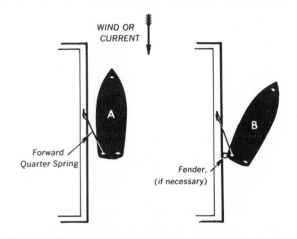

WIND OR CURRENT

Forward Quarter Spring

Fender, (if necessary)

FIG. 848 When wind or current is ahead, backing on a forward quarter spring turns the stern in and bow out, shaping the boat up to get clear by going ahead.

In maneuvers where the bow swings in toward the dock, the fender is not always important if the bow has a good metal rub strip and the topsides are well flared. On the other hand, in cases like the one under discussion, the stern comes in against the dock and a fender is usually in order, especially if the topsides tumble home. Good stout metal-shod rubrails are a fine thing on any boat that has occasion to maneuver much around docks.

In fig. 848, when the bow has swung out as sketched at (B), the boat has been shaped up to pull directly away by casting off the spring and going ahead with rudder amidships.

FROM A WINDWARD BERTH

When either wind or current tends to set the boat off the dock as shown in fig. 847 there is little difficulty in getting clear when you are ready to get under way. In fig. 849, however, we have assumed a situation in which the wind (or current) tends to hold the boat in her berth against the windward side of the dock. This is a bad berth if there is wind enough to raise much of a sea.

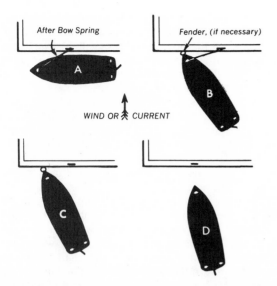

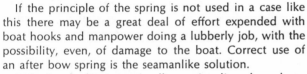

FIG. 849 How an after bow spring is used to leave the windward side of a dock. Boat goes ahead on the spring with rudder set toward dock, then backs away into the wind.

FIG. 850 Rigging an after bow spring.

If the principle of the spring is not used in a case like this there may be a great deal of effort expended with boat hooks and manpower doing a lubberly job, with the possibility, even, of damage to the boat. Correct use of an after bow spring is the seamanlike solution.

Referring to fig. 849 (A), all mooring lines have been cast off except the after bow spring. If the boat has been lying to bow and stern lines only, the stern line can be cast off and the bow line transferred to a position on the dock as shown in fig. 850 to convert it into a spring.

Going ahead easily on the spring with right rudder tends to nose the bow in and throw the stern up into the wind away from the dock. If it does not respond with the rudder hard over, open the throttle to provide the kick necessary to work the stern around against wind pressure. Depending on the nature of the dock and type of boat, you may need a fender or two at the critical spots between dock and boat.

Ease the spring

At (B), fig. 849, it is evident that the continued turning of the stern would throw a great strain on the spring. Therefore, it is generally necessary to ease the spring, yet keep the stem from slipping along the dock. One of the best ways to accomplish this is to have the spring made fast on the bitt by means of several round turns and a half hitch. With the half hitch cast off, the turns can be allowed to slip a little to ease the spring as necessary.

Here, again, remember the stretch of nylon with the possible reversal of direction when power is removed. In addition, if sufficient load is placed on a nylon line wound around a cleat or bitt the first turn or two may seize and grab the cleat so the line cannot be eased or slipped if there is a strain or load on the line. It may "jump" loose when turns are removed, causing a rapid and sudden change in control of the vessel by the line.

At (C), the boat has turned far enough so that the stem is not likely to slip, though the boat could be allowed to turn further till her stern was squarely into the wind. At

this point the spring and fender can be gotten aboard and the boat backed away with rudder amidships.

When single-handed

This is another of those maneuvers that can be accomplished single-handed with little effort if done in a seamanlike manner. If single-handed, the rudder must be set amidships when the stern has worked up into the wind, giving the helmsman a chance to go forward and cast off the spring. Furthermore, it will not be easy for him to go forward and ease his spring, but this can sometimes be done by momentarily going into neutral, which allows the spring to pull the stem toward the bollard. This, however, may not be expedient with much wind, requiring the help of a man forward to handle it properly.

When the boat lies with head to the dock and rudder amidships, there may be a natural tendency for her to work her stern around to starboard, because of the effect of unequal blade thrust (with a right-handed wheel). This usually is of little consequence as it takes but a moment to get forward and cast off.

With a worm-and-gear type steerer, which holds its position against pressure on the rudder, or any other type of control that will maintain rudder angle without a hand on the wheel, it can be set in a case like this for just enough right rudder to compensate for the effect of unequal blade thrust.

WITH WIND OR CURRENT ASTERN

The procedure just outlined can be used in getting away from a dock if the wind or current comes from astern.

Instead of merely casting off all lines and going ahead in such a situation, it is better to get the maneuverable stern out away from the dock, shaping the boat up to go astern first, before going ahead on the course. Let us look again at fig. 849, but now assuming that the wind is east or that the current sets westward (top of diagram being north) the after bow spring allows her stern to go out into the stream, to be kicked out if necessary by power, going ahead with right rudder. Often in such a case the stern swings out without aid from the power.

When the boat has swung anywhere from 45 to 90 degrees, depending on circumstances of the particular case, the spring is cast off and the boat reverses far enough to clear the dock nicely when you go ahead with left rudder.

BACKING AROUND

Elsewhere we have discussed the technique of backing a boat out of her slip, turning either to port or starboard, preparatory to getting under way. A variation of this is illustrated in fig. 851, where the boat is pictured lying in a slip at right angles to the outer side of a dock.

The problem may be to back her around so as to have her lying along the outside of the dock, or the principle might be used as a method of backing clear of the slip, preliminary to getting under way, especially if there is little room for maneuvering. The idea in this case is to use a forward quarter spring.

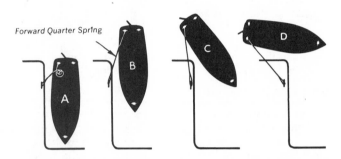

Forward Quarter Spring

FIG. 851 Use of a forward quarter spring when backing a boat out around the end of a dock. When spring is taut, boat reverses with full right rudder.

At (A) in the illustration, the boat is shown lying starboard side to the dock. The first step is to make the spring ready from a point near the corner of the dock to the after bitt, either amidships if there is only one, or the bitt on the starboard quarter, if there are two.

With the spring ready, but left slack and tended, the bow line is cast off, or slacked away and tended by a man on the dock and the boat is backed easily with full right rudder. At (B), a strain is taken on the spring to prevent her from backing further and this causes her to pivot as the stern is pulled around to starboard, as at (C). As she continues to back toward (D), the boat assumes a position parallel to the outer face of the dock.

At (D), the spring can be cast off the bollard and carried further up the dock to be made fast elsewhere as a stern line, if the boat is to remain in this new berth. The bow line in turn can be used to control the bow and prevent the boat's swinging too far; then made fast as necessary, perhaps to the bollard formerly used to secure the spring.

This method is especially useful when there is a breeze off the dock that would tend to blow her away if maneuvering without lines. No manpower is required and it can be accomplished leisurely in a seamanlike manner.

Getting under way

In the event that the maneuver is used preparatory to getting under way, the bow line is not required. When the

boat has pivoted far enough, with starboard quarter near the corner of the dock, the engine can be idled while the spring is cast off the bollard and brought aboard. Getting under way from such a position, the rudder must be set amidships till the quarter clears the dock, then full left rudder turns her bow out into the stream.

Spring lines used this way should have a loop of convenient size in the end, formed either by an eye splice or a bowline so as to slip quickly and easily off the pile, bollard, or cleat, yet stand the strain of holding the boat against application of power, without slipping. The eye splice is best; the bowline is quickly turned into the end of a line having no splice.

In this or any other maneuver involving the application of engine power against the spring, it is obvious that strain must be taken up slowly, easily. A sudden surge of power puts a shock load on deck fittings that they were never designed to carry—may even tear cleats right out by the roots, so to speak. If the fastenings hold, the line may part —perhaps with a dangerous snap, as the parted ends lash out.

Once the strain has been taken up easily, proper deck fittings and good line of adequate size will stand the application of plenty of power, in those cases where the power is really needed. Bear this principle in mind when you are preparing to tow or in passing a line to a stranded boat with a view toward hauling her off.

TURNING AT A DOCK

Turning a boat at a dock—called *winding ship* in the case of a large vessel—is easy if wind or current is used as an aid, or if the engine is used in the absence of these factors.

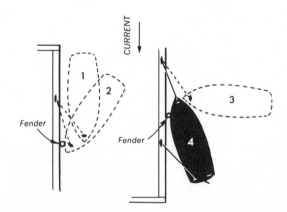

FIG. 852 Turning a boat at a dock, using the current and springs.

Fig. 852 illustrates a boat lying, at position (1), with her stern toward the current and the problem is to turn her to head into the current. The first step is to let all lines go except the after bow spring.

Normally the effect of the current will then be sufficient to throw her bow in toward the dock and her stern out into the stream toward the position sketched at (2). If any factor, such as a beam wind, tends to keep her stern pinned against the dock, the stern can be kicked out by going ahead easily with right rudder. A fender should be kept handy as a protection to the starboard bow.

Some steps should be taken to prevent the bow from catching on the dock as she swings, thus exerting a great leverage on the spring. A small boat may roll the fender a little and the boat can be eased off by hand, but in larger craft it is customary to reverse the engine just enough to keep the bow clear, as shown at (3).

As she swings in with the current, the fender should be made ready near the port bow as shown at (4). At this point she may tend to lie in this position, depending on just how much strain there is on the bow spring. If she does not come alongside readily, perhaps helping her by going ahead a little with right rudder, a forward quarter spring can be rigged. Then, by taking a strain on the quarter spring, and easing the bow spring, she will set in to her new berth.

Larger vessels executing this maneuver would get a forward bow spring out on the port bow when the ship reaches position (3), rigging it not from the extreme bow but a point further aft. Going ahead easily with right rudder on this spring alone (the first one having been cast off), the ship could be kept under control and eased in nicely.

In turning a boat this way it is always easier and better to make the turn with the bow to the dock rather than the stern. The procedure would be the same as outlined in a case where wind is blowing in the direction in which the current sets in the illustration.

Turning with power

Considering a problem similar to that sketched in fig. 852, except that we assume there is neither wind nor current to assist in turning, the power of the engine can be used to swing her.

Going ahead on an after bow spring with right rudder (starboard side being toward the dock as in the figure) would throw the stern out away from the dock, a fender being used as in the previous illustration to protect the bow. In this case the stem is allowed to nose up against the dock, using another fender if necessary to cushion it.

As the boat swings toward a position at right angles to the dock, the spring will have to be eased. With the bow against the dock, engine going ahead slowly, and rudder amidships, the boat can be held in this position while the bow spring is cast off from the dock and re-rigged as an after bow spring on the port side. With right rudder again, the stern will continue to swing all the way around, fenders being shifted once more to protect the port bow.

[CAUTION: If nylon springs and lines are used, remember that they stretch and can store energy enough to snap the boat back when power is removed. If nylon is stretched to the breaking point, it can snap back with lethal effect.]

This principle has many applications and will be found useful in dozens of situations when the theory is understood. In a berth only inches wider than the overall length of the boat, without room to go ahead and astern, she can be turned end for end with no line-hauling or manual effort of any kind.

If there happens to be wind or current holding her against the dock, the first half of this maneuver may be used to get the stern out into the stream, preliminary to backing away when ready to get clear of the dock.

MAKE USE OF FENDERS

We have noted from time to time in the foregoing illustrations the necessity of protecting the hull with fenders in maneuvering around rough dock piles, or in lying alongside other craft, fig. 853. Articles on equipment have repeatedly pointed out the desirability of carrying plenty of good fenders, but often the equipment actually provided falls far short of being adequate.

The standard types of yacht fenders are satisfactory if large enough and provided in sufficient number. When a boat lies at a dock with no motion, except the rise and fall of tide and the flow of current, even the lightest of guardrails may be alright. But you can't count on these ideal conditions to prevail at all times.

The combination of topsides that are heavily flared forward, tumble home aft, high superstructure that reaches out practically to the deck edge, and comparatively light guard moldings, possibly of wood not even metal-shod with half-oval, all make for potential damage when the boat starts to roll and pound against piles, either as a result of the swell created by passing craft or wave action from the wind or a ground swell.

The ordinary fenders (not "bumpers") for pleasure boats are of several types of construction—canvas covers filled with ground cork for small craft; woven manila or cotton covers, also cork-filled; and all manila rope, braided so that no central core or filler is required. Newer types, fig. 854, include those of synthetic or rubber construction containing air or minute gas-filled cells; others have canvas covers enclosing sponge rubber, shredded rubber or cork and rubber. Kapok is also used as a filling.

FIG. 853 Rafted boats properly protected by substantial fenders.

FIG. 854 Light-weight pneumatic fenders which can be inflated to various pressures for the service required. Lines may be run through them lengthwise to hang them horizontally.

The smallest of these fenders sometimes have a grommet, eye or rope ring at one end only, to take the pennant by which it is suspended from fender hooks on the boat. Better practice is to have an eye at each end so that the fender can be rigged horizontally as well as vertically, sometimes by hanging it over the pile, instead of from the boat where it moves as the boat moves. Some modern fenders have a longitudinal hole through which a line can be run, especially convenient when the fender is used horizontally.

Half a dozen substantial fenders are not too many to carry and if the boat is equipped with few, or no, hooks, go over it with a critical eye to see that stout fender hooks are placed where needed.

Maneuvering at Slips in Tight Quarters

Many marinas and yacht clubs provide "slips" in which boats are berthed at right angles to a pier or wharf and made fast to piles as shown in figs. 827 and 856. Normally, a short secondary pier, or "catwalk," extends out between each slip or pair of slips.

A BERTH BETWEEN PILES

Figure 856 illustrates a problem where a boat must be backed into such a berth in a basin. Complicating the situation is a bulkhead along the east (leeward) and south sides, which prevents approach from any direction except west, down-wind.

If the space between piles and the south bulkhead is sufficient to allow the boat to make a turn, going ahead with right rudder, as in 2-3-4-5, she may round up this way, until, as in (5), she has headed partly into the wind.

If space, turning power, or wind prevent her from getting around any further than the position sketched at (4), her position is awkward as the wind will tend to blow her bow down to leeward faster than the stern so that her angle of approach will not conform with the path sketched

Fenderboards

If fender's are hung vertically from the boat's side, they give protection in cases where there is a vertical dock face to bear against as the craft moves fore and aft. If there are vertical piles to lie against, vertical fenders cannot be expected to stay in place. Movement of boat fore and aft shifts them between the piles and their protection is eliminated. Hanging a fender horizontally by both ends sometimes is satisfactory against piles; this is most effective when the fender is attached to the pile, but don't go off and forget it!

The solution to protecting the hull in many situations has been found in the use of *fenderboards*. These are short

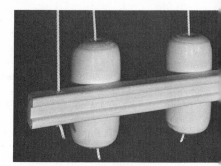

FIG. 855 A side board or plank used in conjunction with ordinary fenders proves invaluable in cases where adequate protection to the hull cannot be provided by fenders alone. The rubber cushion-board illustrated is encased in a thick cover of tough white Nordel rubber with two rubber cushions to absorb the shock of impact.

lengths (approximately 4 to 6 feet) or heavy boards (2" by 6") is a common size faced on one side with metal rub strips or rubber cushions. Holes are drilled and lines attached so that the board may be hung horizontally behind two fenders with the wider face vertical, see fig. 855.

Fenderboards are excellent for providing the necessary cushioning between two or more craft "rafted" together as in fig. 853. One boat should put over the usual two fenders behind a fenderboard; the other puts over only its own two fenders. A second fenderboard should not be used as one board could tangle with the other as the "nest" of boats was rocked by waves, wash from other craft, etc.

at 6-7-8. In that case, she would have to work out another technique.

Assuming that she can round up under power to position (5) with right rudder, she has been placed so that she

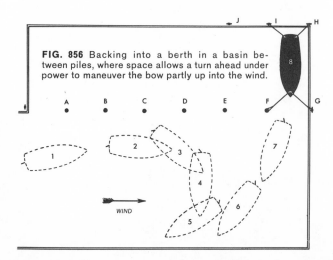

FIG. 856 Backing into a berth in a basin between piles, where space allows a turn ahead under power to maneuver the bow partly up into the wind.

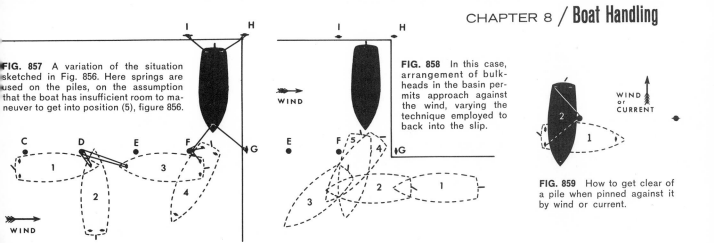

FIG. 857 A variation of the situation sketched in Fig. 856. Here springs are used on the piles, on the assumption that the boat has insufficient room to maneuver to get into position (5), figure 856.

FIG. 858 In this case, arrangement of bulkheads in the basin permits approach against the wind, varying the technique employed to back into the slip.

FIG. 859 How to get clear of a pile when pinned against it by wind or current.

can back along the line 6-7-8 without shifting her rudder. Remembering that the stern normally tends to port, and that with full right rudder she might back practically in a straight line, it can be seen how her position at (5) allows for the wind to blow the bow down to leeward.

At (7) her bow should still be somewhat up into the wind, and her starboard quarter close to the pile (F). Having her head up into the wind more than is shown at (7) is alright as a kick ahead with left rudder will straighten her out to exactly the right angle. If that kick throws her stern too close to the pile (F), idling a moment allows the wind to carry her down into position.

As she passes pile (F), a line should be passed to it—or picked up if one is attached to the pile—and made fast forward when a man at the stern has been able to get another line on cleat (I). Lines to cleats (G) and (H) can be run at leisure.

Before the line to (G) is fast, backing easily draws the stern close enough for a man to step ashore from the stern. Adjusting and securing the line at (G) after all are ashore prevents the boat from going too far astern.

Using springs to the piles

With a good breeze, it might be impossible to get the bow around as shown at (5). In that case there is an alternative, using springs. You might approach close to the line of piles A B C D with the intent of bringing her up alongside piles (C) and (D), heading east, as at position (1), fig. 857. Now run an after bow spring, doubled, from the bitt around pile (D) and back to the bitt. Going ahead easily with left rudder will cause the stern to swing around to the south as at (2). Engine idling, she will swing completely around and if the spring is slacked a little she will lie starboard side against piles (E) and (F), as at (3). It may be necessary to back a little between positions (2) and (3).

Next rig a forward quarter spring on the starboard side to pile (F) and cast off the bow line to (D). The reason why this was doubled is now evident, as you can get the line back aboard by casting off the second hitch.

Reversing on the quarter spring throws her bow to the south and her stern in toward her berth as at (4). This spring can be carried forward by a crewman walking along the starboard side to the bow, where it becomes the forward bow spring to (F) when secured to the forward bitt.

Approaching up-wind

In fig. 856 and 857, if this were not a closed basin, so

that approach could be made against the wind, heading west, it would be comparatively easy to swing up into a position approximately as shown at (7) in fig. 856, heading perhaps more closely into the wind—say a 45-degree angle from the line of piles—with starboard quarter close to pile (F). This would have been accomplished by turning with left rudder as the berth came abeam.

Fig. 858 illustrates such a case. At (2) left rudder, while the boat is still moving ahead, throws the stern in toward the slip and pile (F) as at (3). Backing with right rudder brings her down to position (4), the bow sagging off to leeward somewhat, while the rudder is set to port and the propeller given a strong kick ahead. This throws the stern up to windward as at (5), shaping the boat up to back in with right rudder.

Between positions (4) and (6) it may be necessary to go ahead and back several times but in any case the combination of the engine kicking the stern to windward while the wind blows the bow to leeward can be used effectively to work her in neatly.

Another alternative, at (3), would be to pass a line around the pile (F) and hold on while the wind blew the bow to leeward just enough to shape the boat up, as at (5), to back in. A little reversing between positions (3) and (5) might be indicated. At (5), of course, the line from the starboard quarter is cast off and carried forward to become the forward bow spring on the starboard side, secured to pile (F) for mooring.

Getting clear of a pile

In maneuvering around piles, there is a possibility that you may be caught in a position where the wind or current, or both, will act to pin the boat against the pile and hold her there so that she cannot maneuver.

The solution to this is to rig a forward spring from the pile to a bit aft, preferably on the shore side of the boat away from the pile, as shown in fig. 859. Then, by reversing with left rudder, the boat can be wound around the pile and her bow brought into the wind or against the current as in position (2), properly shaped up to draw clear by going ahead with power as the spring is cast off.

In getting clear from this point, it may be necessary to use a little left rudder to keep the stern clear of the pile, but not enough to throw her stern so far over that the starboard quarter is in danger of hitting the other pile.

As a matter of fact, at position (2) the wind may catch the bow on the port side, easing the boat away from the pile, so that you will be in a position to pull directly away with rudder amidships—always alert, however, to throw the stern one way or the other if needed by proper use of the rudder.

MAKING A TIGHT TURN

There are situations in which a burst of engine power for a short period may help the boat to turn within the limits of a channel or restricted waterway where she couldn't turn at low engine speeds.

Consider the following case in point. In fig. 860, we have a boat bound south in a narrow canal or stream with a strong northerly wind, her dock being on the west side. The south end of the illustration may represent the dead end of a canal or the stream may continue further. This is irrelevant except that if the stream widens further on it would be wise to go on down-stream and take advantage of the greater width for turning, then come back upstream against the wind to dock.

Preferably, if there is room, the helmsman should wait till he is beyond the dock before he starts his turn as this would allow more room for straightening out at the dock. Referring to the illustration, he has slowed down, the boat is under control and he gauges his distance from the east bank so that there is just sufficient room for the stern to swing to port with right rudder at (B) without hitting the bank.

From experience in this maneuver he knows that in the absence of wind he can round up nicely through track A-B-C-D-E-F with full right rudder at low speed. Now if he tries the same thing at low engine speed with the northerly wind, instead of moving from (C) to (D), the wind catches him abeam and tends to hold the bow down to leeward as at (D').

Using power at slow speed

At (D') he would be in a bad way, forced to reverse to avoid hitting the west bank and fortunate if he could back out quickly enough to prevent his bow from being driven down by the wind on the south bank, if this is a dead end.

Therefore at (B), if the boat is moving slowly, a sudden

FIG. 861 A boatman's skill is often quickly revealed by the way he handles his lines.

burst of power at the propeller acting on the full right rudder will bring her around quickly. At (D) the helmsman must be ready to close his throttle in order to prevent the boat from gathering so much way that landing at the dock is difficult.

This is not a maneuver to be guessed at, but if you have occasion to make the same one repeatedly in bringing her in to her usual berth, you will soon get to know whether the strength of the wind will allow you to use these tactics or whether you must resort to some other procedure such as landing down-wind and allowing her to turn at the dock on a spring.

PLAN MANEUVERS IN ADVANCE

In previous pages we have outlined most of the basic ideas or principles by means of which the average single-screw motor boat can be handled when maneuvering around docks and moorings. Obviously the number of possible situations, considering the differences in boats, and the strength, direction, and effect of wind and current is almost infinite. Usually, however, the application of one of the principles we have mentioned, modified perhaps to suit conditions, will permit a seamanlike handling of the problem.

Understanding these principles as a background, you will be less likely to work in opposition to the forces of the elements and will use the control you have over the boat with propeller, rudder, and lines to best advantage. The seamanlike solution usually requires the least manpower and is accomplished with a minimum of confusion, fuss, shouting of orders, and other unnecessary hindrances to an orderly accomplishment of the task.

Even though you know the principles you are to use in executing a maneuver, you will find that it pays to think out in advance the steps you will take, and their succession. With a plan of action clearly worked out, you can take each step slowly and easily, and have time to keep the boat under perfect control. This does not conflict in

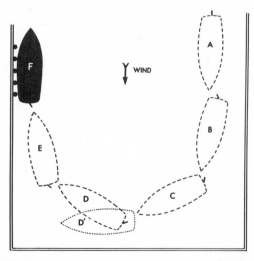

FIG. 860 Turning downwind in close quarters with wind astern. As boat approaches slowly at (B), a sudden short burst of power will turn her, when she may not be able to get around at slow speed.

any way with the truth that there will be occasions that call for bold, swift, and decisive action. Rather, under such circumstances, the need for calm ordered judgment is accentuated.

The lubberly handling of a situation may eventually achieve the end that is sought, but often at the expense of strained lines, fittings, and equipment, not to mention the nerves, muscles, and temper of both skipper and crew.

Common sense in executing the plan

If your planned line of action requires amendment or even complete abandonment because of unforeseen conditions, don't hesitate to act accordingly. If, for example, your plan for a clean approach to a dock has been upset by a freak current you couldn't calculate, back off and square away for another attempt. That in itself is good seamanship and good judgment regardless of how others may judge your apparent "miss" on the first try.

Common sense, if you act with deliberation, will enable you to work out a solution for any combination of conditions. Sometimes, understanding the idiosyncrasies of your own boat, you may put it through evolutions never mentioned in the books but if it achieves your end better than conventional practice, it's still good seamanship.

When you are at the helm and you have men on deck handling lines, fig. 861, issue the necessary orders to each so that all action is coordinated and under your control, instead of having two or three acting independently to cross purposes. This is especially imperative when your crew is not familiar with boats or your method of handling one.

ORDERS TO THE CREW

On larger vessels here are some of the orders used in connection with the handling of lines at a dock. You can be the judge as to whether you consider them appropriate on your own boat, having due regard for its size and the number of men in the crew. Use these orders *only* if *all* persons concerned with them thoroughly understand what actions you want them to take.

When docking, the order *"Stand by to dock"* puts the crew in readiness, each standing by his respective line, seeing that it is properly coiled ready to heave. If no men are available on the dock to receive lines, others aboard stand ready to step ashore to receive the lines.

At the command *"Heave——(bow line, stern line, or whatever line is named)"* deck men heave the line named to the dock.

"Take in slack on——" requires deckmen to take a turn on the cleat or bitt and pull in slack.

"Take a strain on——" means that deckmen are to pull lines named up tight, taking an extra turn if necessary on the cleat or bitt, but allowing it to slip.

"Ease off on——" means that the line should be allowed to slip off more freely.

"Hold (or snub)——" means to check the line temporarily.

"Secure lines" means to make fast permanently, adjusting to proper length and rigging chafing gear if necessary.

In each case the blanks above imply that a line or lines will be named to complete the order.

On leaving a dock, the order *"Stand by the lines"* prepares men on the dock to stand by bollards ready to cast off lines and men on deck to take them in. *"Cast off the lines"* directs the dock men to clear all lines from the cleats or bollards ashore and toss them to the deck men, keeping them out of the water if possible. This may be modified to *"Cast off the —— line"* if the skipper wishes to clear only certain dock lines at that time, or wants them cast off one by one in a certain sequence.

Easy does it

As previously explained, the procedure is so simplified on a small boat that docking may involve only the stepping ashore of one man each at bow and stern with their respective lines, others to be passed as and if required after these are secured.

One mistake that crewmen often make in helping to handle lines on a small boat is that, in their eagerness to assist, they insist on snubbing them immediately when as a matter of fact the skipper wants them merely to be tended and left slack so that his boat is free to be maneuvered further with the power. A case in point is where the boat is coming in to a landing at a dock and the bow man snubs his line instead of allowing the boat to ease up and draw alongside as the skipper intended.

One caution that cannot be emphasized too strongly is that, in handling lines, whether they are mooring lines, anchor lines, or any other kind, they must not be allowed to get over the side in such a way that they will be sucked down into the propeller and wrapped around the shaft and wheel.

RESUME OF FACTORS AFFECTING CONTROL OF SINGLE-SCREW BOAT

To sum up all the effects which the skipper of a single-screw (R. H.) boat must have in mind as he maneuvers his craft, the following will provide a condensed summary.

I—ENGINE
  (1) *Going ahead*—No effect (or slight tendency of bow to port).
  (2) *Going astern*—Stern goes to port, bow to starboard.

II—RUDDER
  (1) *With headway*
    (a) Left rudder turns stern to starboard, bow to port.
    (b) Right rudder turns stern to port, bow to starboard.
  (2) *With sternway*
    (a) Left rudder turns stern rapidly to port, bow to starboard.
    (b) Right rudder usually turns stern to starboard, bow to port, if sternway is sufficient. With little sternway, boat may back in a straight line, or stern may even go to port.

III—CURRENT
  (1) Sets boat bodily in direction of its flow.
  (2) Other factors interacting (boat held, for example, by waist breast), current normally acts with greater effect on the stern because of deeper draft here.

IV—WIND
  (1) Usually affects bow more than stern, throwing it to leeward.
  (2) Engine backing, boat backs into wind.

V—TWO OR MORE FACTORS COMBINED
  (1) Helmsman must determine relative effects of each on basis of his experience with the boat.

149

Handling Twin-Screw Boats

Practically everything that has been said thus far in this chapter has been related to a single-screw inboard boat. Although this permits a better study of the basic factors of boat handling, attention must now be given to twin-screw craft. These are increasingly popular, partly because of their superior maneuverability. In the twin-screw boat, the propellers are usually arranged so that the tops of the blades turn outward, so that the starboard wheel is right-hand, the port wheel is left-hand. The effect of this is to give a maximum of maneuverability.

Going ahead with the starboard wheel for a turn to port, the offset of the propeller from the center line is adding its effect by throwing the stern to starboard. Similarly, offset of the port wheel going ahead helps the steering effect when the port propeller is turning ahead for a turn to starboard.

When reversing, the starboard wheel throws its discharge current against the starboard side of the hull to help the turn of the stern to port. Likewise, the port pro-

FIG. 863 Twin-screws give control independent of rudder position. Helmsman here is backing on his port engine, throwing his stern to starboard. Photo, courtesy of Vermont Development Department.

FIG. 862 For maximum maneuverability, twin rudders are placed behind propellers of twin-screw boats, in the discharge currents.

peller reversing throws its stream against the port side of the hull to help the swing of the stern to starboard.

The important factors in turning and steering are thus combined by the outward-turning wheels. The steering effect is exerted in the same direction as the turning moment caused by the off-center location of the propellers.

Twin rudders for twin screws

Almost all twin-screw craft have two rudders, one directly behind each propeller in the discharge current, fig. 862. This provides much greater effectiveness than would a single center rudder not behind either propeller.

BASIC TURNING MANEUVERS

It can be readily seen that having two propellers, one each on the port and starboard sides at some distance from the centerline, gives a skipper the means of throwing one side or the other ahead or astern, independent of rudder control. In fact, much of a boat's maneuvering at low speed is done without touching the steering wheel as the two throttles are the key to the boat's control.

One propeller going ahead or backing

The stern of a boat may be put to one side or the other by going ahead or backing on one propeller only without turning the other. Some headway or sternway in these cases accompanies the turn.

Referring to (A), fig. 864, a kick on the port propeller throws the stern to port, bow to starboard, as in a single-screw boat with right rudder. If there are twin rudders, right rudder helps this kick. A kick ahead with the starboard wheel throws the stern to starboard, bow to port, as shown at (B). Reversing the port wheel only, pulls the stern around to starboard and vice versa. See sketches (C) and (D).

When reversing with one propeller, the other being stopped, unequal blade thrust, discharge screw current and the offset of the working propeller from the center line all combine to throw the stern in a direction away from the reversing propeller.

Response to rudder while backing

A twin-screw vessel starting from a position dead in the water, with both propellers backing at the same speed, is at a great advantage over the single-screw vessel as she can

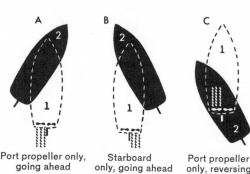

Port propeller only, going ahead   Starboard only, going ahead   Port propeller only, reversing   Starboard only, reversing

FIG. 864 What happens in a twin-screw boat when one propeller is thrown ahead or astern.

be made to take any desired course by steering with her rudders whereas the single-screw vessel, it will be remembered, is obstinate about backing her stern to starboard. In the twin-screw vessel opposite rotation of the propellers means that the forces which normally throw the single-screw vessel off course are balanced out.

In addition to use of the rudders, the twin-screw vessel offers the possibility of using her throttles to speed up one motor or the other as an aid to steering while maintaining her sternway or she can even stop one propeller or go ahead on it for maximum control in reverse, fig. 865.

While the twin-screw vessel backs as readily to starboard as to port, she is still subject to the effect of wind, waves, and current though the helmsman is in a better position to exercise control over them as we have seen in the case of leeway, offset by different engine speeds instead of holding the rudder offset from the midships line.

Steering with the Throttles

In maintaining a straight course with a twin-screw vessel, the speed of the motors can be adjusted so that the leeward engine compensates for the effect of leeway. That is, the leeward engine can be turned a little faster to hold the bow up into the wind.

If she happens to sustain some damage to her steering gear, whether it be the rudder(s) or any part of the gear inboard, she can still make port by steering with the throttles. One motor can be allowed to turn at a constant speed—the starboard one, let us say. Then opening the throttle of the port motor will speed up the port propeller and cause a turn to starboard. Closing the throttle of the port motor slows down the port propeller and allows the starboard wheel to push ahead, causing a turn to port. And we have also shown that she is at no great disadvan-

FIG. 865 Maneuvering his twin-screw boat, the helmsman can leave his rudders amidships, may even set his throttles, and handle the boat with a touch of one or both of his reverse gear controls.

tage when she finally maneuvers into her berth after getting into port as the throttle and reverse gears are adequate for complete control here too.

A disadvantage of this technique is that you must run the engine out of synchronism, with the accompanying audible "beat" sound which may be annoying.

Turning in a Boat's Length

With practice, a twin-screw boat can easily be made to turn in a circle the diameter of which is only a little greater than her length, fig. 868. The turn to port is accomplished as readily as a turn to starboard, since such effects as un-

A Typical Docking Maneuver with a Twin-screw Cruiser

1 FIG. 866-a In this case, the slip is on the starboard side of a canal. The helmsman turns to port to place his boat in position to back into the berth.

2 FIG. 866-b Here he goes ahead easily with the starboard engine, his port engine backing. He turns without making headway and watches clearance at the stern.

equal blade thrust on two propellers rotating in opposite directions offset each other.

Turning bow to starboard, the rudder can be set amidships, while the port engine goes ahead and the starboard engine reverses, fig. 868. The engines will probably be turning at nearly, not exactly, the same speed. The boat drives forward more easily than it goes astern and the pro-

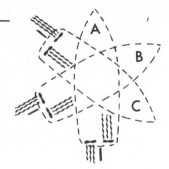

FIG. 868 Turning twin-screw boat, bow to starboard, stern to port, in her own length. Rudder amidships, port propeller going ahead, starboard propeller reversing (probably at somewhat higher r.p.m. than port propeller). Changing r.p.m. can give her headway or sternway as she turns.

peller at a given r.p.m. has more propelling power ahead than astern. Therefore the r.p.m. on the reversing starboard wheel may be somewhat higher than that on the port propeller, to prevent her from making some headway as she pivots.

By setting the throttle for the reversing starboard engine this can be left alone and the port throttle is adjusted till the size of the turning circle is established. A rate of r.p.m. can be found where she is actually turning in her own length. If the port engine is then speeded up a little, the circle is larger and she makes some headway. If the port

engine is slowed down, the circle is also larger but she makes some sternway as the reversing starboard wheel pulls her around, stern to port.

DOCKING A TWIN-SCREW BOAT

Landing at a dock, a twin-screw vessel will approach at slow speed at an angle of 10 to 20 degrees, as is the case with a single-screw boat. When she has just way enough to carry her in nicely, the rudder is swung over to the side away from the dock to bring the stern in as the engines are thrown into neutral. To check headway as she comes up parallel to the dock, the outboard engine is reversed.

Landing either port or starboard side to the dock is accomplished with equal ease because of the starboard propeller turning counter-clockwise as it reverses in a port-side landing, or the port propeller turning clockwise in reverse on a landing starboard side to the dock.

USING SPRINGS WITH TWIN SCREWS

When a twin-screw vessel is lying at a dock and a spring is used to throw the bow or stern out as an aid to getting clear, one engine may be used. For example, with an after bow spring, going ahead on the outside engine only, throws the stern out away from the dock. Or propellers can be turned in opposite directions.

Sometimes a twin-screw vessel is gotten clear of a dock by rigging a forward bow spring and reversing the propeller on the dock side to throw the propeller discharge current on that side forward between the boat and dock as a "cushion." Naturally this is most effective if the dock under water is solidly bulkheaded rather than built on open piling. The discharge current from the inside wheel forces the boat away from the dock and the line is then

A Typical Docking Maneuver . . . (continued)

3 **FIG. 866-c** Now the transom is centered at the entrance to the slip and the boat is making neither headway nor sternway. Crewman stands ready in the cockpit.

4 **FIG. 867-d** With his boat aligned as carefully as wind and current permit, the helmsman starts to back easily. With rudders amidships, he tends the throttles.

cast off. Further reversing on the propeller nearest the dock while the other propeller turns ahead, as necessary, shapes the boat up to get the stern clear. The speed of the two motors will vary with conditions of wind and current and the rudder is left amidships till the boat is clear and ready to pull away.

OTHER TWIN-SCREW MANEUVERS

If one propeller is stopped while the boat has headway, the bow necessarily turns in the direction of the propeller that is dead. Consequently, if one engine of a twin-screw power plant fails, and the boat is brought in on the other, a certain amount of rudder angle on the side of the operating propeller is necessary in order to maintain a straight course, or some kind of drag must be towed on the side of the working propeller.

A basic principle in the maneuvering of a twin-screw vessel is to use the rudder primarily in relation to the direction of the vessel's movement through the water (that is, whether she had headway or sternway). Elsewhere, it will be recalled, the principle as given for the single-screw vessel was that the rudder should be considered in relation to the direction in which the propeller happens to be turning, regardless of whether the vessel has headway or sternway.

When a twin-screw vessel has headway, both propellers turning ahead, and a quick turn to starboard is desired, the starboard engine is reversed with right rudder. The fact that the vessel has headway in this instance means that the right rudder adds its steering effect to shorten the turn.

With sternway, both propellers reversing, if a quick turn to port is wanted, the port engine is thrown ahead, with left rudder. Again, due to the vessel's sternway, the rudder's effect is added to that of the propellers in causing a short turn to port.

If a twin-screw vessel has considerable headway and her engines are reversed with rudder hard over, the stern will normally swing away from the rudder (to port with right rudder and vice versa) until the headway is overcome by the reversing engines. After she has gathered sternway, her stern tends to work toward the side on which her rudder is set. Then the vessel's stern in the illustration just cited would eventually move to starboard with right rudder, after her headway had changed to sternway.

HANDLING A LARGE YACHT

As a rule, most of our average sized pleasure boats are handled by their owners; the larger yachts are frequently in charge of professional skippers. It's of interest, nevertheless, to note an instruction technique regarded as applicable to craft in the 100-foot category when leaving and returning to a berth alongside other vessels.

In fig. 869 this vessel is the middle one of three tied abreast lying port side to a dock headed toward the beach. Let's call the boats A, B, and C. Our boat is B, the middle one; A is at the dock; C is the outside boat.

The engines are warmed up preliminary to getting under way and when they are ready lines are cleared as follows: First, C's bow breast is cast off from B's bow and run to A, forward of B's stem, with some slack to allow B to maneuver a little.

C now casts off all lines except the bow breast which has been transferred to A and gets a heaving line ready for use after B has pulled out.

B then casts off all lines securing her to A except an after bow spring which is slacked a little to allow B, going

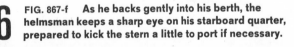
FIG. 867-f   As he backs gently into his berth, the helmsman keeps a sharp eye on his starboard quarter, prepared to kick the stern a little to port if necessary.

5 FIG. 867-e   With barely enough clearance on both sides, the helmsman is alert to keep his alignment parallel with the dock, the boat centered as closely as possible.

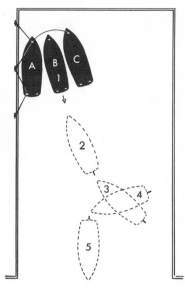

FIG. 869 Large twin-screw vessel leaving berth between two others in a slip. At (1) stern has been sprung out by going ahead on bow spring to (A), starboard engine going ahead, port engine reversing. At (2) spring having been cast off, she has backed clear with both engines reversing. At (3) sternway is checked and stern kicked around to (4) by going ahead on the starboard engine. At (5) she is straightened out and, after headway is gained, responds to her rudder which has been left amidships during the maneuver.

ahead, to get the bulge of her bow past that of A's bow and thus permit B to pivot better.

B now goes ahead 1/3 on the outside (starboard) engine and back 1/3 on the inside (port) engine. Two men are standing by with fenders. As B moves slowly ahead a few feet, the spring line takes the strain and the stern works out, to starboard.

Backing clear

C is being swung along with B but no lines secure the two vessels and there is nothing to prevent B from drawing clear as she backs both engines 1/3 after having swung her stern far enough around to starboard.

With B clear, C heaves to A the line she has already pre-

pared. At this point she can either run a stern breast to A and heave in on it or else rig an after bow spring to draw alongside A by using power. In the latter case, she will go ahead on the inside (port) engine and reverse the outside (starboard) engine. If the bow breast to A tends to check the swing of C's bow, it must be slacked. Back alongside A, C rigs all mooring lines to A as she was formerly secured to B.

B, in the meantime, has backed out into the slip and backs the port engine 2/3 while the starboard engine continues to back at 1/3. The effect of this will be to give her better clearance from the dock and swing her while backing.

Checking sternway and turning

The boat draws well clear of the dock under this maneuver but presently gathers too much sternway so that the starboard engine is thrown ahead 2/3 which checks the sternway and causes her to turn more rapidly, throwing the bow around to port.

When finally straightened out in the slip, both engines are run at 1/3 ahead to gather steerage-way. Then both are stopped (idled in neutral in the case of a boat with reverse gears) while steering with the rudder and a long blast is blown on the whistle as a warning prior to leaving the slip.

Moving out of the slip, the current catches the port bow and tends to set the vessel back toward the dock so she is given a short kick ahead on the starboard engine to offset it. Clear of the dock, she goes ahead 2/3 on both engines.

Returning to her berth

The same craft is now ready to return to her berth alongside another vessel. Keeping well out in the stream till the

---

A Typical Docking Maneuver . . . (continued)

7 **FIG. 867-g Settled in her berth, the crewman makes fast with docklines, giving attention first to the spring that will prevent the boat's ranging too far astern.**

8 **FIG. 867-h As the boat eases astern, the helmsman keeps his eye on the transom, using his controls to turn his propellers ahead just enough to check the sternway.**

Leek Pacemaker photographs by Rosenfeld

FIG. 870 In tight quarters, the twin-screw boat can turn in her own length. Here she backs on the port engine. Under perfect control, she could be made to complete a 180° turn, with starboard engine going ahead. With starboard engine idling, her reversing port engine would probably bring her up to the bulkhead, stern toward the transom of the docked cruiser. (Photo courtesy Palm Beach Isles Sales Corp.)

slip is almost abeam, she turns and passes into the slip about midway between the piers, favoring one side a little to allow for current. No abrupt changes of course will be needed.

Engines are stopped (or, with reverse gears, idling in neutral) passing the pier heads while the vessel is steered to a point just ahead of the other vessel's pilot house. The angle of approach to the other vessel should be small. If it appears that the angle is too wide the helm should be used decisively to place her in position in plenty of time to straighten out.

With reduced speed, the helmsman handles the wheel smartly, using considerably more helm to achieve a given response than he would need if the vessel had good headway. What he does is to get the bow to swing, then shifts the rudder smartly for a moment, then shifts back to the midships position.

Engines are kept stopped (or idling, as the case may be) as she comes in at a moderate angle, her bow about six feet from that of the other vessel. A bow spring is passed, slack taken up and secured. Now the outside (starboard in this case) engine is backed 1/3 while the inside (port) engine goes ahead 1/3. This is just a momentary kick to be repeated if necessary.

The effect of the reversing outside engine is to kill the headway and swing the stern to port toward the other vessel, assisted by the kick ahead on the inside engine. The last of the headway, acting on the spring, also contributes to the same effect. No heaving lines have been used during this maneuver and, under ideal conditions, only the outside engine will be called on for a short kick astern while the inside engine may not be needed at all.

Outboard and I-O Handling

Boat handling with outboard motors or inboard-outboard (I-O) drives is quite different from the procedures and techniques discussed earlier in this chapter for inboard craft. The skipper who makes a too quick and brash change from inboards to outboards may find himself severely embarrassed. This is true whether he had a single- or a twin-screw inboard boat, and whether he has one or two outboard motors or outdrives. (Boats propelled by outboard motors and I-O drives have essentially the same handling characteristics; for the balance of this chapter, the two types will be considered together with the terms used interchangably.)

Major Differences

In a way, boat handling with outboard drives is easier than it is with inboard propulsion, but different, too! There are two differences, each of major importance. First, the direction of propeller discharge current of an inboard boat is always parallel to the craft's keel, although it may be forward or reverse; thrust is parallel to the direction that the boat is *headed*, regardless of the direction that it may momentarily be *traveling*. With a single-screw inboard craft, the thrust line is coincident with the boat's centerline (although angled down somewhat); with a twin-screw inboard, the thrust line of each engine is not coincident with the centerline, but each is parallel to it. On the other hand, with outboard propelled boats the situation is radically different. The thrust line of the propulsion is easily changed from dead ahead or astern to either side. On quite small motors not having reverse gears, thrust can be pointed in any direction through a full 360° circle; on other motors, those with reverse gears, the angle of thrust is limited to perhaps 40° either side of the centerline. It should be noted that the pivot point around which the thrust is rotated is *outside* the boat, just aft of the transom (this ignores

FIG. 871 Boats propelled by outboard motors and those with inboard-outboard drives handle in generally the same manner. Both of these types, however, with their directed thrust and lack of rudders maneuver quite differently than inboard craft.

155

FIG. 872 Smaller outboard motors frequently have no reverse gears, but pivot in a full circle so that their propeller thrust may be "aimed" in any direction.

a very few specialized boats with interior motor wells). This external turning point of the thrust will combine with the natural turning point of the hull to result in a pivot point for a craft that is highly·individualized and must be learned from experience.

No rudder

The second major point of difference between inboard and outboard boats is the *absence of a rudder* on the latter. A rudder is unnecessary for the normal steering of outdrive craft as the change of direction of thrust very efficiently changes the heading of the boat, and consequently its direction of travel. When, however, the outdrive propeller is giving little or no thrust, as when the motor is idling or is stopped, the absence of rudder blade area deprives the skipper of control that he would have with an inboard boat from the flow of water past the rudder as the boat "coasts" along. The lower unit of the outboard does in a small measure act as a rudder, but it is a very inefficient and ineffective one. This lack of positive steering action without engine power is something that must be kept in mind; it is not a major problem, but it can't be overlooked or forgotten.

Torque effect

The propeller shaft of an outboard motor or outdrive is horizontal, and thus this form of propulsion is free of the side-turning tendencies which result from unequal blade pressures as described earlier in this chapter for inboard boats with inclined propeller shafts. Large outboard motors and I-O units do, however, tend to have a *torque effect* from their high rotational power. To correct for this, many such underwater units have a small tab or adjustable exhaust nozzle which can be offset from center to correct for torque effect. Properly adjusted, even the largest motors can be run at high speeds with little or no tendency of the boat to pull to one side.

BASIC PRINCIPLES

The thrust of an outboard motor is parallel to the fore-and-aft axis of the powerhead, but remember that the steering handle is on the opposite side of the pivot point

from the propeller—the handle must be moved to the side that is *opposite* to the direction in which you wish the craft to head. When you are going ahead, the motor handle must go to the left if you wish to turn to the right, and vice versa. (If the boat is equipped with a remote steering wheel, the connecting cables or other mechanism will turn the motor so as to make the boat go in the direction that the wheel is turned.) Just as with inboards, the new heading will be attained by having the stern initially swing out in the other direction; watch out for this action when maneuvering in close quarters.

When backing down, the reversed outdrive propeller can be thought of as moving itself through the water, pulling the hull after it. The craft will both build up sternway and at the same time head off in a new direction as the motor is turned to either side. Again, the motor's steering handle is moved to the opposite side to that in which it is desired that the stern go.

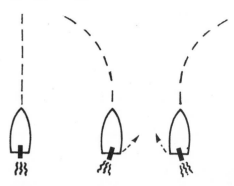

FIG. 873 When an outboard motor is centered, its thrust drives the boat straight ahead. When the motor is turned to one side, the thrust is to the opposite side and the stern swings in that direction, turning the craft onto a new course.

FUNDAMENTAL MANEUVERS

The essential maneuvers of outboard handling are the same as for inboard craft, and relate to getting away from alongside a pier or wharf ("undocking") and coming back in to such a position. The basic aspects of outboard boat handling while underway in open waters are covered in Chapter 28.

Leaving a Pier

In many instances it is possible to get away from the face of a pier in a small, light outboard boat by merely pushing off, waiting a moment until space opens up between the hull and the pierface, and then going ahead slowly with a very gentle outward turn. Care must be taken not to turn so sharply that the quarter of the boat strikes the pierface or piles, but with reasonable caution this maneuver can be executed without problems.

Backing out

If the wind or current is tending to pin the craft against the pier, it is wiser to back out. The outboard motor, or I-O drive unit, is turned *away* from the pier, power in reverse is applied slowly, and the propeller draws the boat smoothly and safely away. (This is a good way to leave a pier in any circumstaances and is often taken as the sign of a prudent skipper.) Care must be exercised to get far

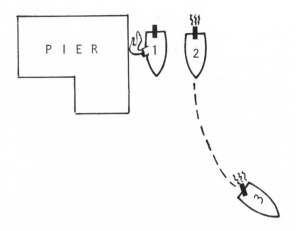

FIG. 874 Light outboard craft can be gotten clear of a pier by simply pushing off parallel and then going ahead under power with a slow gentle curve away from the pier. Don't attempt to turn away too sharply lest the stern of the boat come in and strike the pier.

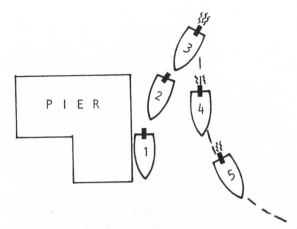

FIG. 875 A better way for clearing from a pier or wharf is backing out; this will be necessary with larger and heavier outboard and I-O craft. Be sure to back clear far enough that you can go ahead without bumping into the pier.

enough out from the pier so that when forward thrust is applied the boat does not come right back in to the pier and strike it—it is better to err on the safe side and back out farther than necessary than to back out too little and have to repeat the whole procedure.

Docking

Bringing an outboard safely in to a pier or wharf is relatively easy with the directed thrust of this type of propulsion, but as with all kinds of vessels, any favorable influences of wind or current should be used to help you.

Against the wind or current

If there is wind and/or current, or a net effect of the two if they both exist but oppose each other, it is advisable to head into this opposing force as this allows the most positive control of the boat. Approach the pier in a gradual turn, bring the boat up parallel with the face of the pier, and stop with a touch of reverse power. If the stern of the boat is not quite in to the pier, the motor should be turned in toward the pier when reversed so as to complete the docking process. A bow line can be gotten across as

the boat comes parallel with the pier, but under favorable conditions it is often possible not to use any lines until the boat is snug against the pier; this is helpful if the skipper is alone in his craft.

Other conditions of wind and current

If the wind or current is off the pier, the approach should be made at a relatively steep angle to the pier which will be nearly into the wind or current. Then with a sharp, but smooth, turn just as the pier is reached, the boat is brought around parallel to the face of the pier. Lines must be gotten across quickly so as to prevent the boat from being blown away. Reverse is used to check headway and to bring the stern in as required.

If there is no wind or current acting on the craft, the skipper has his choice of approach methods, but usually the best technique is to approach at a moderate angle, 30° to 60°, to the pier, checking forward motion with reverse power and pulling the stern in at the same time.

In all of these maneuvers, it is essential that the pier be approached at a slow speed with the boat fully under control. Any reverse, or forward, power should be applied positively but smoothly to avoid any risk of stalling the motor. Reverse power must be applied gently if the anti-tilt latch has not been locked; otherwise, the lower unit

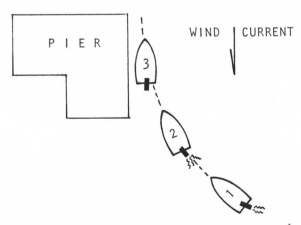

FIG. 876 If possible, approach a pier with your boat headed into the wind or current as this gives you the best control. If the elements oppose each other, head into the stronger of the two, the one having the greater effect on your boat.

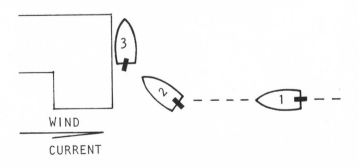

FIG. 877 When the wind (or current) is off the pier, approach at a steep angle to the pierface; this will make the wind nearly dead ahead to your movement through the water. When very close, turn and come in parallel; check your headway with a touch of reverse with the motor turned in toward the pier.

will pull itself up and out of the water, and the motor will race without effect.

FIG. 878 If twin outboard motors or I-O drive units are used, the propellers should turn in opposite directions, the starboard propeller being right-hand and the port left-hand. This will provide a balance of torque and the greatest ability in maneuvering.

TWIN-SCREW OUTBOARDS

Boats with twin outboard motors or I-O drives are generally handled in the same manner as single installations. Because of the principle of steering by directed thrust, there is not the difference in handling characteristics between single and twin outboards that exists between single- and twin-screw inboard craft.

With larger outboard and I-O craft, the horsepower of the motors is frequently considerable. Although there is not the problem of unequal blade thrust, there is considerable torque. It is highly desirable that the propellers rotate in opposite directions for balance of torque. Without opposite rotation, the skipper may find himself constantly fighting a tendency of the boat to turn off to one side, usually port. Adjustable tabs on each motor will help, but opposite rotation will give the best balance and is the preferred installation.

TO SUM UP...

- Try to visualize just what conditions will be at the dock before you get there.
- Use fenders generously and pad your slip or dock well.
- Keep your engine in good shape and your control cables taut.
- Keep your mooring lines healthy and use chafing gear whenever possible.
- Favor a bight of line around a pile as the last line to let go (as it is an easy matter, when casting off, to let go the end on the vessel.
- Watch lines to see that they don't foul your propeller.
- Remember that a boat will pivot about a point about 1/3 of her length aft from the bow and will not "follow the front wheels" as does a car. When the bow goes to starboard the stern will also swing out to port so that, when turning, a boat cuts a considerably wider path than its beam. It goes around a turn "crab-fashion."

Try the maneuvers (in easy weather first) and see how they treat you. I believe you'll find them kind to your boat, safe under most conditions, and easy to learn and use.

Every good boatman aspires to be known, ultimately, as a good seaman. Perhaps it would be difficult to make a nice distinction between the two. Their skills merge, and overlap. Yet, one may handle his boat effectively in ordinary maneuvers in day-to-day sailing, but lack the inborn instinct of a "good seaman" when faced by a critical situation at sea. The subtle qualities of a seaman can be conveyed neither by word of mouth nor by printed page alone. Instruction can, however, go a long way toward teaching principles based on experience, which the seasoned skipper applies in practice. It is on this premise that the Seamanship chapter which follows has been prepared. Its text is completely new, generous use has been made of illustrations, and both are combined in the new format to which all revised material in recent editions conforms. Its subject matter has been keyed closely to requirements of instruction courses given by the United States Power Squadrons. Studied in conjunction with related chapters which form an integral part of the subject, we believe it constitutes the best and most practical seamanship text ever presented.

SEAMANSHIP

Photograph by Pacific Studio

CHAPTER 9 SEAMANSHIP

The term "seamanship" is a broad one. It encompasses many topics and probably would be defined differently by various persons qualified in the subject. In its broadest scope, *seamanship* for the recreational craft skipper may be considered to cover such areas as knowledge of his craft, its construction and maintenance, its handling under favorable and adverse weather conditions, and the actions to be taken in emergencies. It also covers such subjects as nautical terms and language, and the use of lines, knots, and splices.

Several topics that fall under the general heading of "seamanship" are of such major importance that they are presented as separate chapters. Typical of these are boat handling, anchoring, and marlinespike seamanship. Other subject areas, highly specialized, are also covered separately—seamanship in breaking inlets and outboard seamanship. This chapter will include topics that are not considered elsewhere and thus complete the coverage of this broad but most essential subject area, seamanship.

THE CREW

Recreational boating is usually a family affair—indeed, one of its most pleasing aspects is that essentially the whole family can share in the activities.

One aspect of boating that should not be overlooked is the *training* of the crew. No boat of any appreciable size should depart its slip or mooring for an afternoon's run or a cruise measured in days without an adequately trained crew, especially an alternate for the skipper. The first mate, usually the skipper's wife, should be fully competent to take the helm under all normal conditions of wind and

FIG. 901 In a family crew, the "First Mate"—the Skipper's wife—should be qualified to take the helm and make simple maneuvers, such as coming alongside a pier or anchoring. (Gordon Manning photo)

waves, and hopefully to do so under adverse weather conditions. The mate should be capable of bringing the boat alongside a pier or of anchoring it. A sudden incapacitating illness (heart attack, stroke, etc.) or accident such as a broken arm or leg or blow on the head, may thrust heavy responsibilities upon the mate completely without warning. If that person has been trained ahead of time, the emergency will be significantly less drastic and much more easily handled.

Training the crew

A training program need not be either onerous or unpleasant. It should be planned and carried out on a formal basis so that the skipper can be *sure* that everyone knows what he has to know. The secret to a successful family crew training program is to make it *fun,* and not let it take the pleasure out of pleasure boating. This is not an impossible task; it is not even a difficult one.

With just a little imagination a man-overboard drill can be made into a game without losing one bit of its effectiveness. With patience and adequate opportunities for practice, the mate and older children can be developed into skillful helmsmen. Every member of the crew should know where the fire extinguishers are located *and should have had actual experience in using them*. It is well worth the small price of recharging one or two extinguishers to have had the experience of having put out a fire with one. (By the way, skipper, have *you* ever actually put out a fire with an extinguisher of the type now on your boat?) This practice should not, of course, be carried out on the boat, but it is easily done ashore.

The mate, at least, and preferably several others of the crew, should know how to place the radio set in operation,

how to change channels, which channel is to be used for emergencies, and what to say. All persons aboard, crew or guests, should know where the life preservers are stowed *and how they should properly be worn.*

Instruction plus practice

A proper training program consists of two parts—instruction and practice. The skipper first learns for himself what should be done and how, and then passes this information on to his crew. For routine matters such as boat handling, ample opportunity should be given each crew member to acquire proficiency—it may be quicker and easier on the nerves for the skipper always to bring the boat alongside a pier, but he must have the patience to let others learn how by doing. For emergency procedures, there should be both planned and snap, unannounced drills.

All aboard, *including the skipper,* can be trained to do the right thing instinctively, quickly and unquestioningly should a real emergency ever occur. Not only can they be trained, they must be—this is part of "seamanship" for the crew.

Boat Handling Under Adverse Conditions

Perhaps the greatest test of a skipper's seamanship abilities comes in his handling of his boat under adverse conditions of wind and waves.

The size of his craft will have little bearing on its seaworthiness. This is fixed more by design and construction. The average power cruiser or sailboat is fully seaworthy enough for all of the conditions that she is likely to encounter in the use for which she is intended. Note carefully that qualifying phrase—"for which she is intended." Don't venture into water areas or weather conditions beyond those for which your boat was obviously designed. It is only good common sense that a craft designed for lake and river use should not be expected to be suitable in all weather offshore.

FIG. 902 Boating is usually a family affair and all members of the "crew" should be given informal training in their duties. Guests should be given a few of the essential "do's" and "don'ts" soon after coming aboard.

FIG. 903 "Rough" seas is a relative term. This ocean-racing sailboat can weather almost any condition of wind and waves if her skipper and crew are good seamen. (Rosenfeld photo)

It is a fact, however, that just what a boat will do is governed to a great extent by the skill of the man at the helm. Thus a good seaman will bring a poor craft through a blow that a novice might not be able to weather in a larger, more seaworthy craft.

"Rough" weather

Rough weather is purely a relative term and what seems a terrible storm to the fair-weather man may be nothing more than a good breeze to the man who has known the sea in all its tantrums.

On large, shallow bodies of water, such as Long Island's Great South Bay, Delaware Bay and River, or Lake Erie, even a moderate wind will cause a steep, uncomfortable sea with crumbling crests because the depth of water is not great enough to permit waves to assume their natural form. Offshore, or in a deeper inland body of water, the same wind force might result in a moderate sea, but the slow, rolling swells would be no menace to a small craft.

Use good judgment—don't panic

Sane small craft skippers don't ask for trouble afloat. Nobody wants to grip the spokes of a wheel when seas are breaking green over the bow or coming over the transom— at least nobody in his right mind. Unfortunately, however, at some time during your cruising career, you may be caught by an unexpected line squall, or obliged to thread your way through an inlet while breakers crash on the bar. *If you apply the fundamentals of good rough weather seamanship, you'll moor at your home berth and have a whopping good yarn to tell.* The casualties stem from those who panic—from boatmen who lose their heads when the going gets rough.

Know your boat

Boat handling under adverse conditions is a quite flexible and individual matter, since no two boats are exactly alike in the same sea conditions. When the going begins to get heavy, each different hull design reacts differently— and even individual boats of the same class will behave differently because of such factors as the way they are loaded and trimmed.

Each skipper must learn his own boat to determine the precise application of general principles to be covered in the following sections. Reading this book and taking courses are important first steps, but they won't be enough when the chips are down. You can pick up the basics of good seamanship by absorbing factual data and principles, but you'll have to pick up the remainder—the elusive quality that makes the "real" skipper—by applying your book and classroom learning on the spot when the wind blows.

Preparations for rough weather

In anticipation of high winds and rough seas, there are certain precautions and preparations that a prudent skipper takes. No single list will fit all boats or all weather conditions, but among the actions that should be considered are these:

1. Secure all hatches; close all ports and windows.
2. Pump the bilges dry and repeat this action as often as required. ("Free" water in bilges adversely affects the

FIG. 904 Each skipper must learn the individual traits of his own boat—how she handles under good and adverse conditions, and what weather she can safely take. Study seamanship, but learn by doing. (Loyd Sandgren photo)

craft's stability.)

3. Secure all loose gear; put away small items and lash down the larger ones.
4. Break out life preservers and have all on board wear them if the situation worsens; don't wait too long.
5. Break out emergency gear that might be needed, such as hand pumps or bailers, sea anchor, etc.
6. Get a good check of your position if possible and update the plot on your chart.
7. Prepare plans for altering course to a protected harbor or sheltered waters if necessary.
8. Reassure your crew and guests; instruct them in what to do and not to do; give them something to do if possible to take their minds off the situation.

HEAD SEAS

Little difficulty should be experienced by the average well-designed power cruiser when running generally into head seas. Spray will be thrown, and in some hull designs there may be a tendency to pound against the waves. If the seas get too steep-sided, or if pounding is encountered, it will be necessary to slow down. This will give the bow a chance to rise in meeting each wave rather than being driven hard into it.

Match speed to sea conditions

Should the conditions get really bad, and there be any danger of "starting" leaks in the planking or tearing loose heavy objects in the bilge, slow down until you're making bare headway, holding your bow at an angle of about forty-five degrees to the swells. The more headway is reduced in meeting heavy seas, the less will be the strain on the hull.

Avoid propeller "racing"

You must reduce speed to avoid damage to either the hull or powerplant for your propeller will "race" as the seas lift the screw clear of the water. It sounds dangerous—and it may be. First, there's a rapidly increasing crescendo of sound as the engine winds up. Then an excessive vibration as the screw bites the water again. Don't panic—simply slow down and change your course till these effects are minimized. Keep headway so that you can maneuver her readily.

Adjust trim

It is possible to swamp your boat if you drive her ahead too fast or if she is poorly trimmed. In a head sea, a vessel with too much weight forward will plunge rather than rise. Under the same conditions, too much weight aft will cause her to fall off. You must give the bow time to rise as she meets the swells instead of driving straight into them. The ideal speed will vary with different boats and power plants —experiment with your craft and discover her best riding speed before you have to utilize the knowledge under storm conditions.

Change the weight aboard if necessary. On outboards, you can shift your tanks and other heavy gear. In any boat, you can direct your passengers and crew to remain where you place them. Under dire emergency situations, you can tow a pail or other form of sea anchor behind you, helping to steer a straight course, slowing your speed forward while enabling you to keep the throttle open wide enough to maneuver. Be careful, however, that you don't foul the line in your propeller.

Meet each wave as it comes

You will be able to make reasonable progress by carefully nursing the wheel—spotting the steep-sided combers coming in and varying your course, slowing or even stopping momentarily for the really big ones. If the man at the wheel is able to see clearly so he can act before dangerous conditions develop, you should be able to weather moderate gales with little discomfort. *Make sure the most experienced seaman aboard acts as helmsman!*

FIG. 905   Close-hauled, with lee rail awash, this yawl is being driven hard. Wind pressure on sails keeps her from rolling as a motor boat would in a beam sea.   (Rosenfeld photo)

IN THE TROUGH

If the course to be made good is such that it will require you to run broadside to the swells, bouncing from crest to trough and back up again, you will be rolling heavily, perhaps dangerously. It would probably be wise to resort to what might be called a series of "tacks" much like a sailboat.

Tacking across the troughs

Change course and take the wind and waves at roughly a 45° angle, first broad on your bow and then broad on your quarter. This results in a zig-zag course that makes good the desired objective, while the boat is in the trough for only brief intervals while turning. With the wind broad on the bow, the behavior should be satisfactory; on the quarter, the motion will be less comfortable but at least it it will be better than running in the trough. Make each tack as long as possible for the waters that you are in so as to minimize the number of times that you must pass through the trough when changing tacks.

If you want to turn sharply, allow your powerboat to lose headway for a few seconds, throw the wheel hard over, then suddenly apply power. She will wheel quickly as a powerful stream of water strikes the rudder, kicking you to port or starboard, *without making any considerable headway.* You won't be broadside for more than a minimum length of time. This is the same technique as used in docking in close quarters with adverse current or wind conditions; it is particularly effective with single-screw powerboats.

RUNNING BEFORE THE SEA

Your course may be such that the swells are coming from directly behind you. Running directly before the sea is well enough if the stern of your craft can be kept reasonably up to the seas without being thrown around off course. This is known as *yawing.* But when the seas get too heavy, the boat tends to rush down a slope from crest to trough, and, stern high, the propeller comes out of the water and races. The rudder, also partly out of water, loses its grip, and the sea may take charge of the stern. At this stage, the boat may yaw so badly as to *broach,* to be thrown broadside into the trough out of effective control. This must be avoided through every possible action. Unfortunately, modern cruiser design emphasizes beam at the stern so as to provide a large, comfortable cockpit or afterdeck—this added width at the transom increases the tendency to yaw and possibly broach.

Reducing yawing

Slowing down so as to let the swells pass under the boat usually will reduce the tendency to yaw, or at least will reduce the extent of yawing and so lessen the chances of broaching. While seldom necessary, consideration can be given to towing a heavy line or small sea anchor astern to help check the boat's speed and keep her running straight.

FIG. 906 Sharp lines at the stern of this double-ender make for easier handling in a following sea. Motorboats with wide transoms are much more difficult to keep from yawing as heavy seas pass under the stern. (Rosenfeld photo)

Obviously the line must be carefully handled and not allowed to foul the propeller. Do not tow soft-laid nylon lines which may unlay—even though seized—and cause hockles (strand kinks).

Cutting down the engine speed will reduce the strain imposed on the motor by alternate laboring with stern deep down before an overtaking sea and racing as the head goes down and the propeller comes out at the crest.

Pitchpoling

The ordinary swell off shore is seldom troublesome on this point of running, but the steep wind sea of the lakes and shallow bays makes steering difficult and reduced speed imperative. Excessive speed down a steep slope may cause a boat to *pitchpole,* that is, drive her head under in the trough, tripping the bow, while the succeeding crest catches the stern and throws her end over end. When the going is bad enough to result in risk of this, it helps to keep the stern down and the bow light and buoyant, by shifting weight if necessary.

Shifting any considerable amount of weight aft will reduce a boat's tendency to yaw but too much might cause her to be "pooped" by a following sea breaking into the cockpit. *Do everything in moderation rather than in excess.* Find out if she acts more stable, adjusting her trim bit by bit rather than doing it all at once. Too much speed forward with the incorrect weight distribution might cause a small boat to pitchpole.

Tacking before the seas

Previously, a form of tacking was suggested for avoiding the necessity of running dead into heavy seas or with them directly abeam. This same technique of alternately heading to either side of the base course can also be used when it is desired to avoid large swells directly astern.

Try a zig-zag track so that the swells are off your quarter, minimizing their effects—experiment with slightly different headings to determine the angle at which the waves will have the least tendency to cause your boat to yaw off course. Be careful at all times to keep your craft under control and prevent an unexpected broach.

RUNNING AN INLET

When offshore swells run into shallower water along the beach, they build up a steeper ground swell because of resistance created by the bottom. Natural inlets on sandy beaches, unprotected by breakwaters, usually build up a bar across the mouth. When the ground swell reaches the bar, its form changes rapidly, and a short steep-sided wave is produced which may break where the water is shallowest.

This fact should be taken into consideration when approaching from offshore. A few miles off, the sea may be relatively smooth while the inlet from seaward may not look as bad as it actually is. The breakers may extend clear across the mouth, even in a buoyed channel.

The shoals shift so fast with the moving sand that it is not always feasible to keep buoys in the best water. Local boatmen often leave the buoyed channel and are guided by appearance of the sea, picking the best depth by the smoothest surface and absence of breakers. A stranger is handicapped in such a situation because he may not have knowledge of uncharted obstructions and so may not care to risk leaving the buoyed channel. In a case of this kind,

FIG. 907 Boats that must cross a bar with breaking waves must avoid "pitchpoling"—being thrown end over end if caught driving hard down the face of a steep sea, burying the bow. This double-ended fisherman just misses being caught on the forward face of a breaker. This is no place for pleasure boats.

he should have a local pilot if possible. Otherwise it will sometimes be well to anchor off, if necessary, until you can follow a local boat in.

If it becomes necessary to pick a way through without local help, there are several suggestions which may help to make things more comfortable. Don't run directly in but wait outside the bar until you have had a chance to watch the action of waves as they pile up at the most critical spot in the channel, which will be the shallowest. Usually they will come along in groups of three, sometimes more, but always three at least. The last sea will be bigger than the rest and by careful observation it can be picked out of the successive groups.

When you are ready to enter, stand off until a big one has broken or spent its force on the bar and then run through behind it. Watch the water both ahead *and behind* your craft; control your speed carefully and match it to that of the waves. Ebb tide builds up a worse sea on the bars than the flood, due to the rush of water out against and under the incoming ground swell. If the sea looks too bad on the ebb, it may be better to keep off a few hours until the flood has had a chance to begin.

This section has concentrated on entering inlets rather than departing through them. This latter action is less hazardous as the boat is on the safe side of the dangerous area and usually has the option of staying there. If the skipper does decide to go out, dangerous areas are more easily spotted from the inside, and a boat heading into surf is more easily controlled than one running with the swells. On the other hand, the skipper of a boat outside an inlet may have little option as to whether or not he can remain in the open sea indefinitely; he may have to enter and can only attempt to do it in the safest possible manner.

HEAVING TO

When conditions get so bad offshore that a boat cannot make headway and begins to take too much punishment, it is time to *heave to,* a maneuver that varies in its execution with the type of craft under consideration. Motor boats, both single and twin screw, will usually be most comfortable if brought around head to the seas, or a few points off, using just enough power to make bare steerageway without trying to make any considerable progress through the water. In fact, the boat is likely to be making some sternway or leeway even though kept nearly bow on to the waves.

Sailing craft, when heaving to, will shorten sail, carrying just enough canvas, principally aft, to keep the vessel's head to the sea or nearly so where she can ride comfortably without making progress ahead.

The object always is to lay the craft in such a position that she will take the seas most comfortably, in a manner that is easiest on both the hull and the crew. For some vessels, this may mean allowing her to drift naturally, perhaps with the seas on the quarter, but this is not normal for small craft. For short periods, when the fuel supply permits, the average motorboat will be most comfortable when the propeller is allowed to turn over slowly, giving steerageway enough to keep her head in the desired relationship to the swells as determined by the period of the waves and the natural motion of the boat.

THE SEA ANCHOR

In extreme cases, a *sea anchor* is occasionally used. Normally, this will consist of a canvas cone-shaped bag having an iron hoop to keep it open at the mouth. To this hoop, a bridle and a heavy line is attached which is paid out from the bow and made fast to the forward bitt. A trip line is

165

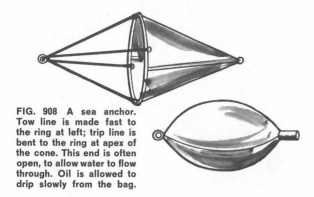

FIG. 908 A sea anchor. Tow line is made fast to the ring at left; trip line is bent to the ring at apex of the cone. This end is often open, to allow water to flow through. Oil is allowed to drip slowly from the bag.

attached to a ring at the end of the cone. This is used to spill the bag and make it easier to haul the anchor back aboard. In use, the theory of the anchor is not to go to the bottom and hold, but merely to present a drag or resistance which will keep the boat's head up within a few points of the wind as she drifts off to leeward. A sea anchor, sometimes called a *drogue,* will usually float a short distance beneath the water's surface.

There are also available on the market, sea anchors made up of a series of plastic floats of a more modern design. These fold compactly for storage and are said to be more effective in holding a boat's head to the sea.

Whatever style of sea anchor is carried on your boat, make sure that it is of sufficient size to be effective. A small one may be easier to stow, but there's no point to having it if it won't do the job.

Improvised sea anchors

In the absence of a regular sea anchor, any form of drag rigged from spars, planks and canvas or other material at hand that will float just below the surface and effectively keep the boat from lying in the trough, would be worth trying. If it could be launched successfully and swamped, with a stout line securely attached, a dinghy could be tried in lieu of the sea anchor, but such procedure is easier to talk about than to accomplish when conditions are bad enough to justify the attempt.

Use of oil with sea anchors

Sea anchors are sometimes equipped with an *oil can* which permits oil to ooze out slowly and form a slick on the surface, thus preventing seas from breaking. The oil might be distributed from a bag punctured with a few holes and stuffed with oakum or waste saturated with oil. (See also the following section on the use of oil.)

Make sure this equipment—sea anchors, trip lines, oil bag lines, lead lines, etc.—is in good condition and not rotten from long disuse or old age. Cotton and manila emergency equipment should be discarded in favor of synthetics.

Sea anchors and lee shores

Sea anchors can be used only if there is sufficient sea room as there is naturally a steady drift to leeward. When a vessel is driven down onto a lee shore and is forced to use her regular ground tackle to ride out a gale, it is imperative that a constant watch be maintained to guard against dragging. Engines may have to be used to ease the strain during the worst of the blow, and a long scope will give the anchor its best chance to hold. (Don't confuse

"lee shore"—a shore onto which the wind is blowing, a dangerous shore—with being "in the lee" of an island or point of land which is being on the sheltered side.

THE USE OF OIL ON ROUGH WATER

Many years of experience at sea have established the value of using oil for the purpose of modifying the effect of breaking seas. Oil is easily dispensed and quickly dispersed; the effect of even small amounts is significant.

The following summary of information on the use of oil on rough waters can guide the small craft skipper should he ever be in a situation requiring its use.

1. On free waves, *i.e.,* waves in deep water, the effect is greatest.

2. In a surf, or waves breaking on a bar, where a mass of liquid is in actual motion in shallow water, the effect of the oil is uncertain, as nothing can prevent the larger waves from breaking under such circumstances, but even here it is of some value.

3. The heaviest and thickest oils are most effectual. Kerosene is of little use; crude petroleum is serviceable when nothing else is obtainable; but all animal and vegetable oils, and waste oil from the engines, will have a useful effect.

4. A small quantity of oil suffices, if applied in such a manner as to spread to windward.

5. In cold water, the oil, being thickened by the lower temperature and not being able to spread freely, will have its effect much reduced. This will vary with the type of oil used.

6. For a boat at sea, the best method of application appears to be to hang over the side, in such a manner as to be in the water, small canvas bags, capable of holding from 1 to 2 gallons of oil, the bags being pricked with a sail needle to facilitate leakage of the oil.

The position of these bags should vary with the circumstances. Running before the wind, they should be hung on either bow and allowed to tow in the water.

With the wind on the quarter, the effect seems to be

FIG. 909 The skipper of this sailboat is a good seaman. Note lifelines around the decks for safety. Note, too, the absence of any clutter of lines or gear on deck.

less than in any other position, as the oil goes astern while the waves come up on the quarter.

Lying-to, the weather bow, and another position farther aft, seem the best places from which to hang the bags, using sufficient line to permit them to draw to windward while the vessel drifts.

7. Crossing a bar with a flood tide, to pour oil overboard and allow it to float in ahead of the boat, which would follow with a bag towing astern, would appear to be the best plan. As noted before, however, under these circumstances, the effectiveness of oil can not always be depended upon.

On a bar, with the tidal current ebbing, it is probably useless to try to use oil for the purpose of entering.

8. For approaching a stranded boat, it is recommended that oil be poured overboard to windward of her before going alongside or close. The effect in this case will greatly depend upon the set of any current and depth of water.

9. For a boat riding in rough water from a sea anchor, it is recommended that the oil bag be fastened to an endless line rove through a block on the sea anchor. By this means, the oil can be diffused well ahead of the boat and the bag can be readily hauled on board for refilling whenever necessary.

10. The general principle involved is to get the oil slick to spread to windward if possible and around the boat in such a way that she stays in the slick. If the oil goes off to leeward or astern, it is of no use.

SEAMANSHIP IN "THICK" WEATHER

Another form of "adverse condition" that will require special skills in seamanship is "thick" weather—conditions of reduced visibility. The cause for this lessoned range of vision may be fog, heavy rain or snow, haze, etc. Of all these, fog is probably the most often encountered and most severe. The general rules and procedures to be considered here are, however, applicable whatever the situation.

Avoiding collisions

Seamanship in fog is primarily a matter of safety, avoiding collisions. Piloting and position determination, the legal requirements for sounding fog signals, and the meterological aspects of fog are all covered elsewhere in this book. Here we will consider only the aspects of boat handling and safety.

The primary needs of safety in fog or other conditions of reduced visibility are to *see and be seen—to hear and be heard*. The wise skipper takes every possible action to see or otherwise detect other craft and hazards, and simultaneously takes all steps to ensure that the presence of his boat will be most surely and easily detected by others.

Reduce speed

The detection by sight or sound must be made early enough to allow proper corrective action. All of the Rules of the Road—International, Inland, and others—require a reduction in speed for all vessels in circumstances of low visibility. Specifically, the Rules require that all vessels "go at a moderate speed, having careful regard to the existing circumstances and conditions." Admiralty court decisions over the years have generally established "moderate speed" as that at which the vessel can come to a complete stop in one-half the existing range of visibility. This, obvi-

ously, is subject to varying interpretation rather than precise definition, but it should always be conservatively considered from the viewpoint of safety.

The preferred situation is to be able to stop short in time, rather than having to resort to violent evasive maneuvers to dodge the hazard. The Rules also require that a power-driven vessel hearing the fog signal of another vessel forward of the beam, and not knowing the position of the other vessel, shall insofar as circumstances permit, stop her engines and then navigate with caution until the danger of collision is past.

Lookouts

Equally important with a reduction in speed is the posting of *lookouts*. This, too, is a requirement of the Rules of the Road, but it is also simple common sense. Many, if not most, modern motor and sail boats are designed in a manner such that the helmsman is *not* so located as to be an effective lookout, and thus one or two additional persons are required for this function in thick weather.

Look . . . and listen

Despite the "look" in "lookout," such a person is as much for *listening* as he is for seeing. A person assigned as a lookout should have this duty as his sole responsibility while on watch. A skipper should certainly post a lookout as far forward as possible when in fog, and, if his helmsman is at inside controls, another lookout for the aft sector is desirable. Lookouts should be relieved as often as nec-

FIG. 910 The primary needs of safety in fog are to see and be seen—to hear and be heard. (Bob Ruskauff photo)

essary to ensure their alertness. If the crew is small, an exchange of bow and stern duties will provide some change in position and relief from monotony. If there are enough persons on board a larger craft, a double lookout forward is not wasted manpower. Care should be taken that they do not distract each other from their duties.

A bow lookout should keep alert for other vessels, sound signals from aids to navigation, and hazards in general. In the latter category are rocks and piles, breakers, and buoys—in thick weather, aids to navigation without audible signals can indeed become hazards. A lookout aft should be primarily alert for overtaking vessels, but he may also hear fog signals missed by the man on the bow.

The transmission of sound in fog is uncertain and tricky. It may seem to come from directions other than that toward the true source, and it may not be heard at all at ranges which would be expected as normal. See the discussion of fog signals in Chapter 16.

Stop your engine

When underway in fog in a powerboat, consideration should be given to slowing the engines to idle, or shutting them off entirely, at intervals in order to aid in hearing the fog signals of other vessels and aids to navigation. This is not a legal requirement of the Rules of the Road, but it is an excellent, practical action to take.

During these periods, silence should be maintained on the boat so that even the faintest signal will be heard. These periods of listening should be at least one minute in length in inland waters and two minutes on the high seas to conform with the legally required maximum intervals between the sounding of fog signals. Don't forget to continue to sound your own signal during the listening period —you may get an answer from close-by!

When proceeding in fog at a moderate speed, any time your lookout indicates that he has heard something, immediately cut your engines to idle, or stop them altogether, in order that the lookout may have the most favorable conditions for verifying and identifying what he believes he has heard.

Radar and radar reflectors

Radar comes into its greatest value in thick weather conditions. If you are so equipped, be sure to turn it on and use it; but not at the expense of posting a proper lookout.

Even if you do not have a radar set, you should have a passive radar reflector (see page 509); then is the time to open it and hoist it as high as possible.

Cruising with other boats

If you are cruising with other boats and fog closes in, you may be able to take advantage of a procedure used by wartime convoys. Tie onto the end of a long, light line some object that will float and make a wake as it moves through the water. A life ring, or a glass or plastic bottle with a built-in handle, will do quite well. This object is towed astern with the boats traveling in column, one object behind each craft except the last.

When the object is kept in sight by the bow lookout on the next boat in column, he knows just where the boat ahead of him is located even though he cannot see her and perhaps cannot even hear her fog signal.

Anchoring and laying-to

If the weather, depth of water, and other conditions are favorable, consideration should be given to anchoring rather than proceeding through conditions of low visibility; but do not anchor in a heavily-traveled channel or traffic lane.

If you cannot anchor, then perhaps laying-to—underway with no way on—may be safer than proceeding at even a much reduced speed. Added quiet will provide increased safety.

Remember that different fog signals are required when you are underway, with or without way on, and when you are at anchor. By all means, sound the proper fog signal and keep your lookouts posted to *look* and *listen* for other craft and hazards.

Helmsmanship

One of the characteristics of a good seaman is the ability to steer well. This is called *helmsmanship*. Here is another quality that cannot be learned entirely from the book, or in a classroom, but there are basic principles that can and should be studied. Knowledge of these, coupled with experience, can make a skipper a better man at the helm than one who has not taken the time and trouble to develop his ability.

Boat's individuality

When considering the general principles of helmsmanship, it must always be borne in mind that these are truly "general" principles. Boats are nearly as individualistic as people, and nowhere is this more noticeable than in their steering characteristics.

Deep-draft and shallow-draft vessels will handle differently. Boats that steer by changing their thrust direction— outboards and inboard-outboards—will respond entirely different than boats steered by rudders. Heavy, displacement hulls will react to helm changes quite unlike light, planing hulls.

FIG. 911 Handling characteristics of various boats are nearly as different as personalities of people. Not all boats will turn as sharply as this fast runabout. A good helmsman knows well the response to the helm of his own craft.

The secret of good helmsmanship is to "know the boat." If you are the skipper of your own craft, this will come relatively quickly as you gain experience with her. If you are invited to take the wheel or tiller of a friend's boat, take it easy at first with helm changes, and make a deliberate effort to get the "feel" of the craft's response.

Steering by compass

At sea and in many larger inland bodies of water, steering is often done by compass. The helmsman must keep the lubberline of the compass (also referred to as the lubber's line; see Chapter 13) on that mark of the card that indicates the course to be steered. If the course to be steered is 100 degrees, and the lubberline is at 95 degrees, the helmsman must *swing the boat's head,* with right rudder, 5 degrees to the right, so that the lubberline is brought around to 100. **Remember, the card stands still while the lubberline swings around it.** Any attempt to bring the desired course on the card up to the lubberline will produce exactly the *wrong* result.

FIG. 912 **Steering by compass is a skill that must be acquired by practice. The compass card remains in essentially the same position with relation to the earth and the boat is moved about it.**

As a vessel swings with a change in course, there is a tendency for the inexperienced helmsman to allow her to swing too far, due to the momentum of the turn and the lag between turning of the wheel and the craft's response to rudder action. That's why it is necessary to "meet her" so that the vessel comes up to, and steadies on, the new course without over-swinging. This often requires, partic-

ularly in larger and heavier cruisers, that the helmsman return the rudder to the neutral, amidships position noticeably before the craft reaches the intended new heading. It may even be necessary to use a slight amount of opposite rudder to check the boat's swinging motion.

A crooked course, yawing from side to side, brands the inexperienced helmsman. A straight course is the goal to shoot at; this can be achieved, after the boat has steadied, by only slight movements of the wheel. It calls for anticipation of the vessel's swing and correction with a little rudder instead of letting her get well off the course before the rudder is applied. A zig-zag course is an inefficient course. The mileage is longer and any offset of the rudder from the center-line tends to retard the craft's progress.

A good helmsman will not only use small amounts of rudder, but he will also turn the wheel slowly and deliberately. The actual manner of steering is again a characteristic of each individual boat and can only be learned by experience with that particular craft.

In piloting small craft, it is often better to pick out a distant landmark, if there is one, or a star at night, to steer by. This helps to maintain a straight course as the compass is smaller and less steady than aboard a larger vessel. The helmsman can then drop his eye periodically to the compass to check his course. Avoid steering on a particular cloud formation as these move with the wind and change shape. In some situations, a boat may be steered for a short time with reference to reflections on the water from the sun or moon, but always remember that these are moving rather than fixed reference points.

EFFECT OF WIND AND SEA

A beam wind will have considerable effect on the steering as the bow, with its relatively greater proportion of freeboard to draft, tends to be driven off more than the stern, and the rudder angle must be sufficient to compensate for this. In a heavy sea, the direction from which the seas are coming will have an effect on the steering. A head sea will be less troublesome than a following sea.

Driving into a head sea, a boat will probably be slowed down to prevent unnecessary pounding, and the swing of the bow will have to be corrected with *slight* rudder changes. In a following sea, the tendency for the stern to be thrown around by overtaking waves (yawing) must be anticipated and checked as much as possible. When the stern is tossed high before an overtaking sea, if it tends to be thrown to starboard, the helmsman must meet her by applying right rudder; a considerable amount of rudder may be required.

Broaching should be avoided at all costs. Ordinarily, if the seas are not too bad, it is possible in handling a small boat to watch astern for the big seas that might cause the boat to yaw excessively. Then by speeding up the engine, with rudder set against the direction of the yaw, the corrective effect of the rudder will be enough to straighten her out and keep the stern up to the sea. As the wave passes the bow, the throttle can be closed again to its previous setting and the rudder brought back to amidships.

SHALLOW WATER

Small craft in heavy following seas such as are built up on inlet bars and in big shallow bodies of water sometimes tend to broach despite anything that can be done by the

FIG. 913 A small steadying sail may be used to advantage to damp the rolling action of a motor cruiser in a beam sea. (F. Raymond Photo)

helmsman. Rudder hard over one way, the boat may run in the opposite direction. When conditions are as serious as that, a drag astern, consisting of a small sea anchor or length of heavy line has been recommended as an aid in keeping the stern up to the sea. The great risk in speeding up too much when the boat has acquired considerable momentum down the descending side of a wave is that of pitchpoling. If she is allowed to trip by running the bow under in the trough between steep seas, the next sea astern may throw her end over end.

Shallow water, besides tending to create a more bothersome steep-sided sea when the wind blows hard, also has a decided effect on the speed and steering of a vessel. A suction is created, the stern settles, and speed is decreased because of the change in the vessel's trim. Propeller and rudder action are both sluggish, so that response to the wheel is not as good as it will be in deep water.

In a small motor boat with exhaust at the stern near the waterline, warning of shallow water is often had before actual grounding, as the exhaust starts to bury under water and a difference in its sound is detected. This happens without any change in the throttle setting.

BEAM SEAS

All craft have what is known as a "natural" period of oscillation, or rolling period, which is the time required by a vessel to roll from one side to the other. If this period happens to coincide with the period of the waves in which she is running, as in a beam sea, the synchronism should be broken by a change of course (and speed, if necessary), to avoid excessive rolling. It is seldom necessary, in such a case, to meet the seas squarely bow-on.

Slight changes of course often damp the rolling enough to make the vessel comfortable. If the craft is disabled, with power not available, then the only way to prevent heavy rolling is to get out a sea anchor or drogue to hold the bow up to the sea, used perhaps in conjunction with storm oil if the waves are breaking.

Occasions may arise, as in preparing to heave to, when a vessel that has been running before a following sea must be brought around head to sea. This calls for skill and judgment and a knowledge of the steering qualities of the particular craft involved. By watching carefully the procession of waves as they pass, taking into consideration their height and the distance between them and space required for the turn, it will usually be possible to avoid having her caught broadside to a dangerous swell.

Invariably a boat is under better control when her engine is going ahead rather than in reverse. The propeller, in the first instance, is throwing a stream of water past the rudder blade. In general, if left to her own devices, with engines stopped, the bow of the average boat will fall off until the wind comes somewhat abaft the beam, because of the relative height of bow and superstructure forward as compared with that aft where the draft is normally greater.

Stranding, Assisting, and Towing

It is an unwritten law of the sea that one should never pass an opportunity to render assistance to any vessel in need of aid. Of course this is one of the primary functions of the Coast Guard, but there are plenty of occasions when a little timely help on the part of a fellow boatman may save hours of labor later after the tide has fallen or wind and sea have had a chance to make up.

As often as not, assistance is likely to take the form of a tow line passed to another skipper to get him out of a position of temporary embarrassment or perhaps to get him to a Coast Guard station or back to port in case of failure of any of his gear.

Or perhaps the situation will be the other way around. If you do a normal amount of boating, and poke your bow into a number of strange places, the chances are that some day *you* may go aground. It is equally possible that some day a balky motor may force you to ask a tow from a passing boat, or you may be on the passing boat from which a tow is requested.

In either case, you should know what to do, and why. Let us consider the problem and possible solutions from each of two points of view—being in need of help yourself, and being the boat that assists another.

STRANDING

Simple stranding, running aground, is more often an inconvenience than a danger and, with a little "know how" and some fast work, the period of stranding may be but a matter of minutes.

If it should happen in that before-mentioned strange harbor, the very fact that it is strange presupposes that you have been feeling your way along and so, probably, have just touched bottom lightly, in which case you should be off again with a minimum of difficulty, *provided* that your immediate actions do not tend to put you aground more firmly.

Right and wrong actions

One's first instinctive act on going aground is to throw one's engines into reverse and gun them to the limit in an effort to pull off; this may be the one thing that you should *not* do.

If in tidal waters, the first thing to consider is, of course, the stage of the tide.

If the tide is rising, and the sea quiet enough so that the hull is not pounding, time is working for you, and whatever you do to assist yourself and the boat will be much more effective after a little time has passed. If, on the other hand, you grounded on a falling tide, you will have to work quickly and do exactly the right things or you will be fast for several hours or more.

About the only thing you know offhand is the shape of the hull, its point of greatest draft, and consequently the part most apt to be touching, but bottom contours may be such that this premise will not be true. If, however, the hull shows any tendency to swing, due to the action of wind or waves, the point about which it pivots is most apt to be the part grounded.

Cautions in getting off

The type of bottom requires immediate consideration. If it is sandy, and you reverse hard, you will be apt to wash a quantity of sand from astern and throw it directly under the keel, with the obvious result of bedding the boat more firmly to the bottom. Always exercise discretion in reversing while aground due to the risk of pumping sand or mud into the engine. If the bottom is rocky and you insist on trying to reverse off, you may drag the hull and do more damage than with the original grounding. Also, if grounded forward, the well known tendency of

the stern to swing to port, when reversing with a single-screw boat having a right-hand wheel, may swing the hull broadside onto exposed pinnacles or to a greater contact with a soft bottom.

How to use a kedge

The one *right* thing to do immediately after grounding is to take out an anchor and set it firmly; this is called a *kedge;* the act of using it is *kedging.*

Unless the boat has really been driven on, the service anchor should be heavy enough. Put the anchor *and* the line in the dinghy, make the bitter end fast to the stern bitts or to something solid and row out as far as possible, letting the line run from the stern of the dinghy as it uncoils. Taken out this way, the oarsman's task will be much easier than if he tries to drag the line from the large boat through the water.

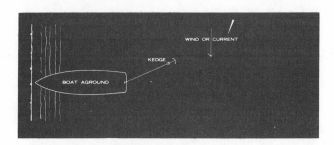

FIG. 914 **The most important thing to do after going aground is to get out a** *kedge*—**an anchor to keep you from being driven further aground and possibly a means of pulling yourself free as waves or the wake from another boat lifts your craft.**

If you do not carry a dinghy, it is often possible to swim out with an anchor provided that the sea and weather conditions do not make it hazardous to go into the water. Life preservers or buoyant cushions—one or two of either —can be used to support the anchor out to where you wish to set it. Be sure to wear a life jacket or buoyant vest yourself so as to save your energy for the work to be done.

If there is *no* other way to get a kedge anchor out, you may consider throwing it out as far as possible. Although this is, of course, contrary to the basic principle that an anchor is never thrown over the side, the importance of getting a kedge set is sufficient to warrant the use of this technique under the circumstances. It may be necessary to pull in the anchor and throw again one or more times to get it set firmly.

When setting out the kedge, consider again the sideways turning effect of a reversing single screw and, unless the boat has twin screws, set the kedge at a compensating angle from the stern. If the propeller is right hand, as those of most boats are, set the anchor slightly to starboard of the stern. This will give two desirable effects. When pulling together with kedge line and reverse the boat will have practically a straight pull on it, and when used alternately, first pulling on the line and then giving a short surge with the reverse, the action may give a sort of wiggling action to the stern and the keel, which will be a real help in starting the boat moving.

Getting added pulling power

If you can find a couple of double-sheave blocks (pulleys) and a length of suitable line on board, make up a handy-billy or fall and fasten it to the kedge line. Then you can really pull! Such a handy-billy should be a part of the boat's regular equipment, anyhow.

Whatever else you may do, during the entire period of grounding, persist in keeping that kedge-line as taut as the combined strength of those on board can make it. You may be agreeably surprised by having the boat yield suddenly to that continued pull, especially if a passing boat throws a wake to help lift the keel off the bottom.

Two kedges set out at an acute angle from either side of the stern and pulled upon alternately may give that desired stern wiggle that will help you work clear.

Working off

If the bottom is sandy, that same pull, with the propeller going *ahead* may result in washing some sand *away* from under the keel, with the desired result. If the kedge line is kept taut, you may try it with a clear mind. At least you will not do any harm.

Move your crew and passengers quickly from side to side to roll the boat and make the keel work in the bottom. If you have spars, swing the booms outboard and put men on them to heave the boat down, thus raising the keel line. Shift ballast or heavy objects from over the portion grounded to lighten that section and if you can, remove some internal weight by loading it into the dinghy or by taking it ashore if that is possible.

When to stay aground

All of the above is predicated on the assumption that the boat is grounded, but not holed or strained open. If either of these last has happened, you may be far better off where she lies than you would be if she were in deep water again. If she is badly stove, you may want to take an anchor ashore, to hold her on or pull her further up until temporary repairs can be made. Perhaps, as the tide falls, the damaged portion may be exposed far enough to allow some outside patching; always presupposing that you have something aboard to patch with! A piece of canvas, cushions, bedding, these are all illustrative of items that can be used in an emergency as temporary hull patches.

What to do while waiting

While waiting for the tide to rise, or for the Coast Guard to come, you do not need to sit idle. Take soundings all around the position where the boat lies aground. It is possible that a swing of the stern to starboard or port may do more for you than any amount of straight backward pulling; soundings will reveal any additional depth that may exist to either side to help you out.

If there is another boat present, she may be able to help you even if she is not suitable for pulling. Have the other skipper run his craft back and forth at a speed that will make as much wake as possible. The rise and fall of his wash may lift your boat just enough to permit you to back clear.

Even though the hull is unharmed, and you are left with a falling tide to sit it out for a few hours, you may as well be philosophical and get over the side and make good use of those hours. Undoubtedly you would prefer to do it under happier circumstances, but this may be your chance to get a good check on the condition of the bottom, or do any one of a number of little jobs that you could not do otherwise, short of a haulout.

FIG. 915   If you go aground on a falling tide, you may find yourself "high and dry." If so, try to brace the boat so that she will stay upright; she will refloat easier if you do. While you are out of water, make an inspection of the bottom. (Photo by Charles True)

If she is going to be left high and dry, keep an eye on her layover condition. If there is anything to get a line to, even another kedge, you can make her lie over on whichever side you choose, as she loses buoyancy. If she is deep and narrow she may need some assistance in standing up again, particularly if she lies over in soft mud. Both the suction of the mud and her own deadweight will work against her in that case.

ASSISTING

If, rather than being stranded, you are in a position to render assistance to another skipper who has been so unlucky as to go aground, it is just as important that you know what to do, and what not to do, in the circumstances.

It is of *primary* importance to see that the assisting boat does not join the other craft in its trouble! Consider the probable draft of the stranded vessel in comparison with the draft of your boat. Consider also the size and weight of the boat that is aground in comparison with the power of your engines—don't tackle an impossible job; there are other ways of rendering assistance.

Getting a line over

It may seem easiest to bring a line in to a stranded boat by coming in under engine power, bow on, passing the line and then backing out again, but the maneuver should not be attempted unless one is sure that there will be water enough under the assisting boat, and also, unless the boat backs well, without too much stern crabbing due to the action of the reversed screw. Wind and current direction will greatly affect the success of this maneuver. If all conditions are adverse and tend to swing the boat broadside to the shallows as she backs, it will be best to try to pass the line in some other manner.

Perhaps the assisting boat may back in, with wind or current compensating for the reversed screw, thus keeping her straight and leaving the bow headed out with consequent better maneuverability. In any case, after the line is once passed and made fast, the assisting boat should do the actual pulling with engines going ahead, to get full power into the pull.

If conditions are such that a close approach is unwise, it will be far better for the second boat to drop anchor, or even two anchors, well off the stranded boat and then send the line over in a dinghy, or else buoy the line and attempt to float it in to the grounded boat.

Making the pull

If wind or current or both are broadside to the direction of the pull, the assisting boat would best stay anchored even while pulling. Otherwise, as soon as she takes the strain (particularly if the line is fast to her stern) she will have lost her own maneuverability, and will gradually make leeway, which could eventually put her aground broadside.

If the pulling must be done with the assisting boat under way, the line should be made fast well forward of the stern so that while hauling, she can angle into the wind and current and still hold her own position.

Tremendous strains can be set up, particularly on the stranded boat, by this sort of action, even to the point of carrying away whatever the tow-line is made fast to. Ordi-

nary recreational craft are *not* designed as tug boats! It is probable that the cleats or bits available for making the line fast are not strong enough for such pulling, and even more likely that they are not located advantageously for such work.

It is far better to run a bridle around the whole hull and pull against this bridle rather than to risk starting some part of the stern by such straining. The assisting boat should also be bridled if there is any doubt of her ability to withstand such concentrated strains.

When operating in limited areas, the stranded craft should have a kedge out for control when she comes off. She should also have another anchor ready to be put over the side if necessary; this may be required to keep her from going back aground if she is without power.

Through all of this maneuvering, it is imperative to see that all lines are kept clear so as not to foul the propeller and that no sudden surge is put on a slack line.

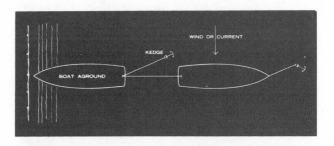

FIG. 917 Most small craft must make the pull with the line made fast near the stern. This restricts maneuverability and, for safe control, a bow anchor should be put out. Slack of the anchor line should be taken up as the stranded boat comes free to prevent the pulling boat from being carried around into shoal water.

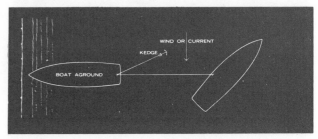

FIG. 918 To aid in maneuverability if a bow anchor cannot be set, the tow line may be made fast to a cleat forward of the stern on the up-wind or up-current side. This cleat *must* be capable of taking heavy strain.

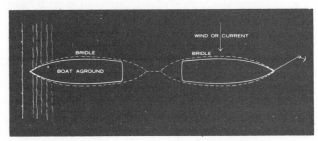

FIG. 919 Tremendous strains are set up when trying to free a stranded boat. Most bitts and cleats on recreational small craft cannot take such a load. It is safer to put a bridle around the superstructure of both boats. Pad pressure points to protect against chafing and scarring.

FIG. 916 If a line is to be sent to another boat, you can heave a light line which can then be used to pull the heavier towing line across. A weighted end on the light line will make it easier to throw —this can be a "monkey's fist," as shown.

TOWING

Somewhere in the course of your boating experience you are likely to run up against a situation where you wish to take another vessel in tow. In good weather with no sea running, the problem is comparatively easy, involving little more than the maneuvering of your boat into position in line with, and ahead of, the other boat and the passing of a tow line.

FIG. 920 It is generally desirable to pass a line from the assisting boat to the one being aided. If the weather is rougher than as shown here, or for any reason the other boat cannot be approached, the rescuing boat can float a line over, using a life ring or buoyant cushion.

Generally speaking, it is best for the towing boat to pass her tow-line to the other craft. It may be desirable to emulate large-ship practice and first send over a light line, using that to haul over the actual towing line. Plastic water ski tow lines that float are excellent for use as this initial ("messenger") line to the other boat.

When approaching a boat, dead in the water, with the intention of passing a line, if there is any kind of sea running, do not be dramatic and try to run in too close. Just buoy a long line with several life preservers, tow it astern and take a turn about the stern of the disabled one, but don't foul their propeller in so doing. The occupants will be able to pick it up with a boathook from the cockpit with far less fuss than by any heave-and-catch method.

The forward bitts are usually rugged and so the towed one may make the line fast at that point; then, with someone at the wheel to assist by steering, there is little more

to do than to have an anchor ready to drop if, for any reason, the tow-line parts or is cast loose.

Handling the towing boat

The tow boat, however, requires some real handling!

The worst possible place to make the tow-line fast is to the stern of the lead boat, because the pull of the tow prevents the stern from swinging properly in response to rudder action and thus interferes with the boat's maneuvering ability. The tow-line should be made fast as far forward as practicable, as in tug and tow boat practice. If no suitable place is provided, it is best to make a bridle from the forward bitts, running around the superstructure to a point in the forward part of the cockpit. Such a bridle will have to be wrapped with chafing gear wherever it bears on the superstructure or any corners, and even then, some chafing of the finish is almost bound to occur.

Towing lines

Manila makes a good tow line; nylon is even better because of the spring in it. The "poly" ropes have an added advantage in their floatability. Size and strength must be considered, whatever the choice.

Anything that tends to produce a spring to ease heavy shocks when towing in heavy weather is helpful. It is on this principle that long heavy tow lines are used for easy towing. The sag in the tow line is desirable and can be increased if necessary by bending an anchor to the middle of the line. This will relieve excessive strains on the towing hawser. In rough weather a long tow line should be used, even if the tow is light.

Cautions in towing

The tow-line should be made fast so that it can be cast loose if necessary or, failing that, have a knife or hatchet ready to cut it. This line is a potential danger to anyone near if it should break and come whipping forward. Nylon, when it breaks or lets go, acts like a huge rubber band and there have been some bad accidents. In one case a cleat pulled loose from the deck and came through the air like a projectile. Never stand near or in line with a highly strained line and keep a wary eye out at all times.

If for any reason you have to approach a burning vessel, be sure to approach it in such a manner that the flames are blowing away from you. If there are reasons it must be towed (for instance, to prevent it from endangering other boats or property) your light anchor with its length of chain thrown into the cockpit or through a window could act as a good grappling hook.

Never at any time in the process of towing have people on deck to fend off with hands or feet as even the smallest boats coming together under these condition can cause broken bones or severed fingers. Also never allow anybody to be caught between two large vessels where they will be exposed to this danger. The risk here could be the loss of a whole limb.

Never allow anyone to hold a towing line while towing another vessel regardless of size. Badly torn tendons and muscles could make them cripples for life, or they could be dragged overboard.

Starting the tow

Start off easy! Don't try to dig up the whole ocean with

your screw, and merely end up with a lot of cavitation and vibration without getting anywhere in particular. A steady pull at a reasonable speed will get you there just as fast and with far less strain on boats, lines, and crews.

Towing principles

When towing, boats should be kept "in step," as it were, by adjusting the length of tow line so that the lead boat and her tow are both on the crest or in the trough of seas at the same time. Under certain conditions, with a confused sea, this may be largely a theoretical consideration, but the general principle is to prevent, if possible, a situation where the tow is shouldering up against the back of one sea, presenting a maximum of resistance, while the towing boat is trying to run down the forward slope of another sea. Then when this condition is reversed, the tow alternately runs ahead and surges back on the tow line with a heavy strain. If there is any degree of uniformity to the waves, the strain on the hawser will be minimized by adjusting it to the proper length.

As the tow gets into protected, quiet waters, shorten up on the line to allow better handling in close quarters. Swing as wide as possible around buoys, channel turns, etc., so that the tow will have room to follow.

A small boat in tow should preferably be trimmed a little by the stern because trimming by the head causes her to yaw. In a seaway this condition is aggravated and it becomes increasingly important to keep the bow relatively light.

In smooth water motor boats may at times borrow an idea from tugs which often, in harbor or sheltered waters, take their tow alongside for better maneuverability. If the tow is a big one the tug will make fast on the other craft's quarter.

It is easy for a larger boat to tow a smaller vessel too fast, causing it to yaw and capsize. Always tow at a moderate speed and make full allowance for adverse conditions of wind and waves.

FIG. 922 A boatman should always be ready to render assistance. In some cases, the best that can be done is to call for assistance and stand by. The Coast Guard 40-footer shown is well equipped to pull a stranded boat free and take her in tow; her crew, too, is better trained and more experienced. (U.S. Coast Guard photo)

When not to tow

Towing can be a dangerous undertaking, as well as an expensive one, if not properly done. If you are not equipped to do a proper towing job, stand by the disabled vessel. It may, however, be feasible to put a line across and assist by holding the other craft's bow into the sea at a comfortable angle while waiting for a more suitable towing vessel.

Call the Coast Guard or other salvage agency and turn the job over to them when they arrive. Don't try to be a hero, as you are more than likely not experienced or trained for this type of work. No boat is worth a life.

Emergency Procedures

The average boatman is a relatively typical person in that he tends to believe that emergencies and accidents happen to "the other guy," and not to him. The seasoned skipper—the good seaman—reasons otherwise. It is not likely to happen to him, but it *could,* and so he prepares himself just in case it does. He also prepares his crew, and, to a lesser extent, the guests aboard his boat.

The best seaman is the one who is prepared for any emergency, before the need arises to meet it.

Value of planning

An emergency is, by definition, not a planned event, but actions to cope with foreseeable ones can be preplanned and rehearsed. Any emergency will be much less severe and much more easily countered if there is a routine to be executed almost instantly when needed.

It must be recognized, of course, that the actual circumstances will surely vary somewhat from those used for planning and practice, but nevertheless a basic approach and assignment of duties will be of immense help in coping with the unexpected. There is nothing more valu-

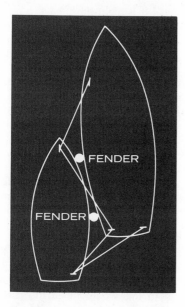

FIG. 921 How springs are used when a boat takes a larger vessel in tow alongside. Fenders are rigged at points of contact, springs made up with no slack. When the towing boat puts her rudder to port or starboard for a turn, both boats respond as a unit.

able than fast and correct action when something goes wrong.

Need for drills and practice

The best plans are of little value if they have not been tried out and evaluated to the best extent practicable short of having a full occurrence of the emergency.

When the plans have been tried out and modified as needed, the next step is to have periodic drills. This should not be done so much as to become boring or irksome, but there are reasonable minimums that should be met. Every boating family should run through its emergency procedures at the beginning of each boating season, and once again on a staggered schedule later in the season. As mentioned earlier in this chapter, every effort should be made to make the drills enjoyable without reducing their business-like nature.

Guests aboard

Crew training extends, of course, to preparation for emergencies. But do not overlook any guests whom you may have aboard; on most boats, they are at least "temporary crew." You may not be able to train them in drills, but as a minimum they should be shown the location of life preservers and instructed, if necessary, in their use. Do this in a casual, relaxed manner so that they are informed but not alarmed.

If the guests are going to be aboard for an extended cruise, their indoctrination can be correspondingly extended to such items as the location and operation of fire extinguishers, bilge pumps, etc. Use your good judgment as to how far this should be carried with various individuals.

Types of emergencies

The preceding major section of this chapter dealt with what is probably the most common of boating accidents, running aground. Here we will consider emergencies that are more serious, but fortunately much less likely to happen—man overboard, fire, sudden leaking, and abandoning ship.

MAN OVERBOARD

At the cry "Man Overboard" fast—immediate—action is of the utmost importance; every second counts, particularly at night, in heavy weather, or in cold water. The actions of the helmsman and other crew members should be automatic and without many shouted orders.

It is helpful to the following action if the cry of "Man Overboard" is supplemented by an indication of which side he went over—Port or Starboard, or even Left or Right. This focuses attention of those who did not see the accident and guides their actions.

Immediate actions

It is customary for the person at the helm to cut the throttle immediately, put the engines in neutral, and swing the stern to the side away from the person in the water. In actual practice, this is of questionable value—a 30-foot boat doing 12 knots moves one boat length in 1½ seconds. Thus even if the person fell off the bow, the stern would be past him before effective action at the controls could be taken. If the victim should fall overboard from

the cockpit, you will be well beyond him almost instantly —don't waste time with throttles or gear shifts, go on immediately with the next steps of the rescue.

Post a lookout

It is imperative that the person in the water be kept in sight at all times, or at least the spot where he was last seen. Heave over some buoyant object *at once*. Preferably, this will be a standard life ring or a buoyant cushion, but throw something over *immediately*. This will serve to mark the spot and perhaps provide assistance to the person overboard. Designate a specific crewman to do *nothing*

FIG. 923 The "Sav-a-Life" plastic ball can be thrown farther and more accurately than a standard life ring or cushion. When it hits the water, it automatically opens and inflates into a buoyant ring that will support a person in the water. Although not an accepted substitute for legally-required life preservers, it can be helpful in man-overboard emergencies.

but watch the person or his last known location. If more than one crew member is available, assign two to this as their *sole* duty. If it is night-time, have a member of the crew man the searchlight and keep it on the person in the water while the boat maneuvers to pick him up.

Throw over a life preserver

Throw overboard a life ring or buoyant cushion even though the person in the water is known to be a strong swimmer. Throw as closely as possible to the person without directly hitting him. He may have had the breath knocked out of him when he hit the water, he may be burdened with clothing and shoes, he may even panic despite his swimming ability—for all these reasons, he should have added buoyancy as soon as possible. A water-activated light attached to a life ring is the most effective nighttime device for man-overboard emergencies.

No "heroes"

Don't let a would-be "hero" jump over the side immediately to rescue the victim—then you would only have two persons rather than one to fish out of the water. The only exception to this would be in the case of a small child or an elderly or handicapped adult. If this must be done, be sure that the rescuer takes with him a life ring or cushion; never let a person enter the water without some added buoyancy.

Maneuvering to return

Whether you turn to port or starboard had best be decided by experiment in advance. Ordinarily a boat with a right-handed propeller turns quickest to port, but practical experience shows that some boats behave otherwise. By this maneuver you should be able to get back to the scene, with boat under perfect control, in less than a minute. You might find that reversing and backing will be more effective for your boat, but the odds are against it. At any rate make a few tests. Throw a paper or cardboard box overboard and experiment in recovering it until you know precisely what to do if the need should ever arise.

If your craft is a sailboat, the maneuvers necessary to return to the location of the accident and recover the victim will vary widely with your point of sailing at the time and the direction of the wind. In some situations, the boat should come about; in others, jibing will result in faster action. If a spinnaker is in use, it will probably have to be gotten down immediately before the boat can maneuver. For sailboats, man overboard drills are far more important than for power craft, and should be executed under a wide variety of situations.

Use additional markers

In some circumstances, particularly at night, it may be desirable to throw overboard additional small objects that will float while the boat maneuvers so as to ensure that the path back to the victim can be retraced. A single marker may be lost to sight; multiple objects increase the probability of returning to the proper location.

Maneuvering for the pick-up

Circumstances will dictate best procedure as to how to approach the man in the water. Although the boat can best be kept under control by approaching from leeward, maneuvering into a position to windward of him will provide a lee as the boat drifts toward him.

The particular maneuver that you use in approaching the victim depends upon common sense and good judgment based on existing conditions such as the sea condition, the temperature of the water, physical condition and ability of the man in the water, boat maneuverability, and the availability of other assistance.

A good procedure is to stop the boat a short distance from the victim in the water, throwing him a light line (such as a skiing tow line of material that floats), and pulling him over to the boat. This will be considerably less hazardous than trying to maneuver the boat right up to him.

Getting the victim on board

While the boat is being maneuvered back to the victim in the water, make all preparations for getting him back on board. Have a member of the crew, who is physically capable, prepare to go into the water, *if necessary*. He should remove any excess clothing and shoes and *always* put on a life jacket. He will need the added buoyancy in order to save his strength to aid the victim. The rescuer should also have a light safety line; it may be useful in transferring it to the accident victim.

Assisting the unlucky victim back into the boat is a highly individualized matter determined by the craft, the person, and the prevailing sea conditions. The availability

of a transom boarding platform if the boat is so equipped will be most helpful. A swimming ladder can usually be quickly rigged if one is carried aboard. Lines with a loop in one end tied with a bowline may be hung over the side for handholds or footholds in climbing back aboard.

Obviously, the propeller should be stopped whenever there is a person in the water near the stern of the boat.

Call for help if needed

If the victim is not immediately rescued, get on the radio with the urgent communications signal "Pan" to summon assistance from the Coast Guard, marine police, and nearby boats. (Do *not* use "Mayday" as your vessel is not in distress.) Continue the search until released by competent authority.

Importance of drills

Man overboard drills are most important. It is not necessary for an individual to go over the side, any floating object about the size of a human head can be used as the "victim." For such drills, one crew member should be told to stand aside and take no part in the "rescue"-just as if it were he who was in the water. And don't forget that for some drills this non-participant should be the skipper—some day it just might be he who was the "man overboard" and his rescue had to be effected by the rest of the crew without his guidance.

Always hold a "critique" after each drill. Discuss what was done right and what was done wrong, how the procedures could be done better. Learn from your mistakes, and don't repeat them.

FIG. 924 On every boat, large or small, it is wise occasionally to conduct a "man-overboard" drill. The exact techniques may vary with conditions, but the essence of the idea is: be prepared.

FIRE EMERGENCIES

Fire on a boat can be a serious experience. A person's surroundings are burning, and he is faced with nowhere to go except into the water. In a sense, he is trapped.

Keep in mind that most fires are preventable. A skipper who keeps his boat in shipshape condition, which includes clean bilges and proper stowage of fuel and gear, will probably never be faced with the emergency condition of fighting a fire. This requires constant attention; whenever a condition is observed that might contribute to a fire, it should be corrected at once.

Despite the skipper's best efforts, fires are a possibility and do occur. Every boatman should be foresighted in this regard. Shipshape conditions include the proper stowage and maintenance of firefighting gear. Having this equipment handy and in good working condition is the first step in combating fire.

Explosions and fires

Fires may start with either a "bang"—an explosion—or on a much smaller scale. Should your craft have a gasoline explosion, there usually is little that you can do except grab a life preserver, if possible, and go over the side.

When clear of danger, check about and account for all those who were aboard. Render such assistance as you can to those who may be in the water without a buoyant device and those who may have been burned or injured in the blast. Keep all individuals in the water together in a group for their morale and to aid rescue operations.

Fires and extinguishment

Fires require four elements for their existence—fuel, oxygen (air), heat, and uninhibited chemical chain reactions; remove or interrupt any of these and the fire will go out. Many fires are fought by smothering (shutting off the flow of air) or by cooling them below the temperature that will support combustion. Others are extinguished by interrupting the chain reactions of the combustion process —this is the action of dry-chemical extinguishers so widely used on small boats.

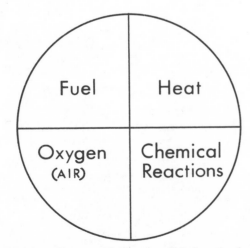

FIG. 925 Shown above are the four essential elements of a fire. If any one is removed or interrupted, the fire will go out. Different types of extinguishers attack different elements—water cools, CO_2 smothers (cuts off the air), and dry-chemicals or chemical vapors disrupt the chain reactions of the combustion process. Fires may also be fought by shutting off the flow of liquid or gaseous fuel.

FIG. 926 Risk of explosion or fire is greatest when the engines are being started or are running. The helmsman should have an extinguisher within easy reach.

Classes of fires

Fires are classified into three categories:

Class A—fires in ordinary combustible materials such as wood, paper, cloth, etc., where the "quenching-cooling" effect of quantities of water or solutions containing large percentages of water is most effective in reducing the temperature of the burning material below the ignition temperature, and is, therefore, of first importance.

Class B—fires in flammable petroleum products or other flammable liquids, greases, etc., where the "blanketing-smothering" effect of oxygen-excluding media is most effective.

Class C—fires involving electrical equipment where the electrical conductivity of the extinguishing media is of first importance.

Fire extinguishers

Fire extinguishers are classified on the same "A", "B", "C" system as are fires. Some types of extinguishers, however, have a suitability greater than their basic classification. Extinguishers required by law on boats are in the "B" category, but a carbon-dioxide or dry-chemical extinguisher will also have value in fighting an electrical ("C") fire. On the other hand, a foam-type "B" extinguisher is effective on ordinary Class "A" fires but is *not* safe on Class "C" electrical fires. Boatmen should remember that for typical Class "A" fires in wood, paper, or bedding, the popular dry-chemical extinguishers are *not* as suitable as an ordinary bucket of water.

Fire extinguishers should be distributed around the boat in relation to potential hazards. One should also be near the boat's control station where it can be grabbed quickly by the helmsman. Another should be mounted near the skipper's bunk so that he can roll out at night with it in his hand. Other locations include the galley (but remember that water is best on a stove alcohol fire!) and any other compartment at some distance from the location of other extinguishers. Fire extinguishers should be mounted where they are clearly visible to all on board as they move about the boat.

Fighting fires

Burning items such as wood, mattresses, and rags are best extinguished by the cooling effect of an agent such as water. For this reason a bailer or bucket can be a most valuable piece of equipment. You will have an unlimited supply of water available on all sides. Throwing burning materials over the side should not be overlooked.

If a fire occurs in a relatively confined space, the closing of hatches, doors, vents, and ports will tend to keep oxygen from fanning the flames. The hatch or door should not be reopened until fire-fighting equipment is ready for use. In addition, should the fire be in a machinery space, shut off the fuel supply and activate the fixed fire-extinguishing system, if your boat is so equipped.

It is *very important* to note that small fire extinguishers typically found on boats have a discharge time of *only 8 to 20 seconds*. They must be used effectively from the very first instant of discharge.

Maneuvering the boat

Now let us consider vessel maneuvers that will assist in extinguishing fires. When underway, wind caused by the boat's motion fans the flames; stopping or reducing speed helps to reduce the wind effect. Also it would make sense to keep the fire downwind—that is, if the fire is aft, head the bow of the boat into the wind; if the fire is forward, put the stern of the boat into the wind. Such action helps to reduce any tendency of the fire to spread to other parts of the boat, and may reduce the hazard of smoke enveloping persons on board.

Stow some life preservers well forward in case of fire aft or the necessity of abandoning ship over the bow.

Summary of actions

The following suggested steps are listed and may be performed, not necessarily in the order shown:
1. If possible, apply the extinguishing agent by:
   a. Using a fire extinguisher,
   b. Discharging fixed smothering system, or
   c. Applying water to wood or materials of this type.
2. If practical, burning materials should be jettisoned (thrown over the side).
3. Reduce the air supply by:
   a. Maneuvering the vessel to reduce the effect of wind, and
   b. Closing hatches, ports, vents, doors, etc. if the fire is in an area where this action will be effective.
4. Make preparation for abandoning ship, which include:
   a. Putting on lifesaving devices, and
   b. Signaling for assistance by radio or any other means available.

LEAKS AND DAMAGE CONTROL

A boat floats properly only so long as the water is kept outside. A small boat with sufficient built-in flotation ability may stay afloat when filled with water, but it will be rather uncomfortable for the crew and passengers. A skipper who is a good seaman prepares a plan of action to be put into effect should his craft suddenly start taking on water as a result of a collision, striking a submerged object, failure of a through-hull fitting, etc.

Planning ahead

The circumstances of suddenly taking on water are so varied as to permit only the most generalized advance planning. Drills are usually not possible for this type of emergency, but a checklist of probably desirable actions can be prepared.

Standard procedures

It should be, to use a military term, SOP (Standard Operating Procedure) to immediately switch on *all* bilge pumps if there is any suspicion of hull damage that might result in taking on water. There are no legal requirements for pumps, as there are for life preservers, fire extinguishers, etc., and many small craft are equipped to handle only a very small inflow of water. The risk of harm to the pumps by running them dry is far less than that of having water in the bilge get a head start on you because of a delay in starting pumping. Remember to turn off the pumps as soon as you are sure that they are not needed.

Actions of the crew

Members of the crew should be assigned immediately to man the manual bilge pump if you have one (and you certainly should have one!). Another crewman should be told to start at once to inspect for leaks; pull up floor boards and check the bilges, don't wait for the water to rise above the cabin sole.

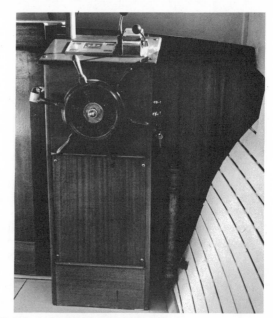

FIG. 927 In addition to electrical bilge pumps, a boat should be equipped with at least one manually-operated pump. This can be used even if rising water in the bilge shorts out the boat's batteries.

If it is determined that the boat is taking on water, it is probably advisable for the skipper to turn over the helm to a qualified member of the crew so that he can go below and personally take charge of the damage control actions.

In most situations, the boat should be slowed or brought to a stop to minimize the inflow of water, but it is possible that a hole in the hull could be in such a location that it would be held above the waterline by maintaining speed.

Emergency pumping

It is sometimes possible in grave emergencies, where the regular electric and manual bilge pumps cannot keep up with the inflow of water, to use the water pumps of the main engines. Shut off an engine, close the seacock on the raw water intake, break the connection between the seacock and the hose, and move the latter into the now rising bilge water; restart the engine. Engine raw water pumps have quite a capacity and may make the difference between sinking and staying afloat.

Two precautions must be observed. First, there must be enough water already in the bilge and flowing in to meet the engine's needs for cooling. Secondly, caution must be exercised to keep bilge dirt and trash from being sucked into the engine's intake. To lose power if the engine overheats might be disastrous. These two precautions will usually require that the intake hose be watched and tended at all times by a crew member assigned to that specific duty.

Operating USCG droppable pumps

Coast Guard aircraft are equipped with pumps that can be dropped in floating containers to boats that need them. The following operating instructions are applicable:

1. Make sure suction hose is tight—connect discharge hose.
2. Fill gas tank.
3. Pull stop switch away from spark plug.
4. Close carburetor choke—turn lever in direction of arrow.
5. Open throttle at base of engine.
6. Attach starting cord and spin engine.
7. After engine starts, open choke.
8. Normally, pumps are self-priming—if difficulty arises, prime.
9. When finished, flush out pump with fresh water.

Emergency repairs

Almost anything can be stuffed into a hole in the hull to help stop the inflow of water—cushions, pillows, bedding, spare sails—all of these will have some beneficial effect.

Material used to stop a leak will be more effective if it can be applied from the outside where water pressure will aid in holding it in place. This will, of course, require that the boat be stopped while the temporary patch or plug is positioned and secured. If a hole must be plugged from the inside, the pillow, bedding etc., can sometimes be held in place by nailing a batten or bed slat across it. If no better solution can be found, a member of the crew can be assigned to hold the plug in place. In any event, station a crewman or passenger to watch the patched hole and give immediate alarm if the patch or plug fails to hold.

ASSISTANCE

In any form of emergency, it is well to alert possible sources of assistance without delay. Use your radio with an urgent ("Pan") call to advise the Coast Guard and other craft of your problem. Don't put out a "Mayday" distress call unless you are in obvious danger of sinking, have an uncontrollable fire on board, etc. Don't panic and make a distress call under conditions that do not warrant such action, but also don't fail to alert others to your possible need for assistance soon.

FIG. 928 A radio is probably the primary means of summoning assistance. Do not put out a "Mayday" call unless you are in distress. If you need help, but are not in danger, use the urgent signal "Pan" on 2182 kHz or 165.8 MHz.

Summoning assistance

A boat's radio is probably the primary means of obtaining assistance, although it is far from being the only method. Use 2182 kHz and follow the procedures of Chapter 25.

Other distress signals are listed on pages 87 and 88.

Any signal that will attract attention and bring help is a satisfactory distress signal. However, if your signal is a known or recognized distress signal, your chances of obtaining assistance are enhanced.

Don't overlook the possible use of a small signal mirror equipped with sighting hole and cross-line target. The reflected mirror signals can be seen as flashes of light for many miles and may be just the device that could attract the attention of aircraft.

There are several recently recognized distress signals for small boats on waters of the United States. A simple orange-red flag may be waved from side to side. Even better is a 72-inch by 45-inch fluorescent orange-red panel cloth bearing an 18-inch black square and an 18-inch black circle, 18-inches apart on the major axis of the flag. This could be tied across a hatch or cabin top as a signal to aircraft. A signal may also be made by slowly and repeatedly raising and lowering arms outstretched to each side. This is a distinctive signal, not likely to be mistaken for a greeting. To be as effective as possible, this signal should be given from the highest vantage point on the boat with consideration given to color contrasts.

Helicopter rescue

In more and more instances, Coast Guard assistance is being provided by helicopters rather than patrol craft. This new technique requires new knowledge on the part of the boat skipper and is most effective with advance preparations.

Prior to arrival of helicopter

1. Provide continuous radio guard on 2182 kc/s or specified frequency if possible.
2. Select and clear most suitable hoist area. This must include securing of loose gear, awnings and antenna wires. Trice up running rigging and booms.
3. If hoist is at night, light pick-up areas as well as possible. Be sure you do not shine any lights on the helicopter and blind the pilot. If there are obstructions in the vicinity, put a light on them so the pilot will be aware of their positions.
4. Advise location of pick-up area before the helicopter arrives so that he may adjust for and make his approach as required.
5. Remember that there will be a high noise level under the helicopter, so conversation between the deck crew will be almost impossible. Arrange a set of hand signals between those who will be assisting.

Rescue by hoist

1. Change course so as to permit the craft to ride as easily as possible with the wind on the bow, preferably on the port bow.
2. Reduce speed if necessary to ease the boat's motion, but maintain steerageway.
3. If you do not have radio contact with the helicopter, signal a "Come on" when you are in all respects ready for the hoist; use a flashlight at night.
4. Allow basket or stretcher to touch down on the deck prior to handling to avoid static shock.
5. If a trail line is dropped by the helicopter, guide the basket or stretcher to the deck with the line; line will not cause shock.
6. Place person in basket sitting with hands clear of sides, or strap person in the stretcher. Place a life

FIG. 929 The Coast Guard is making increased use of helicopters for rescue and assistance work. The gas-turbine powered HH-52A shown can land on the water if necessary. Note the hoisting winch above the door. Skippers should know how to cooperate with helicopter crews. (U.S. Coast Guard photo)

jacket on the person if possible. Signal the helicopter hoist operator when ready for hoist. Person in basket or stretcher nods his head if he is able. Deck personnel give "thumbs up."
7. If necessary to take litter away from hoist point, unhook hoist cable and keep free for helicopter to haul in. *Do not secure cable to vessel or attempt to move stretcher without unhooking.*
8. When person is strapped in stretcher, signal helicopter to lower cable, hook up, and signal hoist operator when ready to hoist. Steady stretcher from swinging or turning.
9. If a trail line is attached to basket or stretcher, use to steady. Keep feet clear of line.

ABANDONING SHIP

Many boats involved in casualties have continued to float indefinitely. If it becomes necessary to abandon your boat due to fire, danger of sinking, or other emergency, don't leave the area. Generally a damaged boat can be sighted more readily than a person, and it may help to keep you afloat.

Keep in mind that distance over water is deceptive. Usually the estimated distance is much shorter than the actual distance. Keep your head and restrain your initial impulse to swim ashore. Calmly weigh the facts of the situation such as: injuries to passengers, the proximity of shore, and your swimming abilities, before deciding upon your course of action.

Before abandoning your craft, put on your life preserver and give distress signals. Don't foolishly waste signaling devices where small likelihood of assistance exists. Wait until you sight someone or something. If your vessel is equipped with a radio telephone, a distress message should be sent.

Maintenance

The condition of a boatman's craft can be an indication of his overall seamanship knowledge and abilities. Using a boat is only part of its ownership—maintenance, keeping her shipshape and Bristol Fashion, is the other part.

For most recreational boat owner-skippers, his craft represents a considerable investment of family funds. She must be properly and continuously maintained to keep up the value of this investment. The secret of getting the fullest measure of pleasure from your boat is to make the necessary maintenance effort enjoyable, even fun, and not a grudging chore. The key to this happy situation is proper planning and a low but continuous level of effort.

Don't let your boat get run down; it will not only look worse, but will require more total maintenance than if it had been properly cared for. Deferred maintenance is always more of a burden and more expensive. Maintain the value of your boat—and your pride in her—by continuous attention to maintenance, perhaps peaking in the spring of each year, but not neglected at any time.

USE AND CARE OF EQUIPMENT

A planned maintenance program can start with the use and care of the boat and its equipment. Let us first consider equipment and supplies. To have one's craft in true ship-shape condition means a place for everything and every-

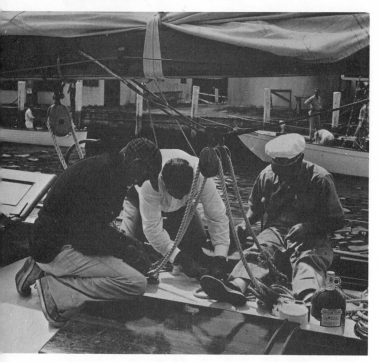

FIG. 930 The key to proper and adequate maintenance, without its becoming a burdensome chore, is a low but continuous level of effort. Do small jobs when they need it—don't put them off. Have a regular schedule for preventive maintenance. (Peter Stackpole photo)

thing in its place; and, too, everything in good working condition.

Lines and sails

There is nothing that we depend upon so much as lines. We use them to anchor, to tie up, and in fact almost everything we do depends upon their use. For our safety, these must be kept in good condition. We must be sure that lines are dry before stowing; if not, they will rot if they are of manila. And, we must be sure that they are stowed in a well-ventilated compartment, for if it is not, we might just as well have not dried them. While synthetic cordage and sail cloth are not subject to rot, mildew can form from deposited spores of fungus unless these items are clean and dry when stowed. The unseamanlike practice of stowing wet ropes and sails below decks will inevitably result in a damp condition, which is uncomfortable.

The same reasoning goes for cotton sails, foul weather gear, and any other materials of the same sort.

Clean, dry, and well-ventilated compartments not only save lines, sails, etc. but contribute to safety of the hull itself. If these compartments, as well as all other parts of the boat, are not well ventilated, dry rot may set in, and this may involve extensive repairs and a big bill. Nothing could be sadder than the boat that at a distance looks fine with a new coat of paint, but which underneath is a rotting shell.

Stowage of supplies

Every item of equipment should be well marked and kept in its specific place. Any article with labels should have the contents painted on the bottle or can proper; it is a good idea even to remove any paper labels, as they may come off in any dampness and cause problems. Some skippers use adhesive tape on the articles and print the contents on the tape; others merely place a letter on each different item (A means potatoes, B means beans, C means sunburn ointment) and keep a key list on board. The only trouble with the latter method is if you lose the key list you're in trouble.

The new felt-tip marking pens are excellent for labeling cans and other containers. Experiment with different ones until you find the most moisture-resistant type.

Use a checklist

If all equipment is clearly marked and always in its proper place it eases the skipper's mind, to say nothing of adding to his safety. Not only is he sure of having everything, but he doesn't worry for the first day trying to remember what he has forgotten. In order to carry this thought out successfully, it is necessary and good seamanship to have and use a sailing checklist. A sailing checklist is a list of all items that a competent skipper will provide for the boat, her equipment, supplies, stores, and condition prior to shoving off from the mooring. If this list is kept aboard, and if the skipper checks off each item before he shoves off, there will never be any need to worry about being without the necessary equipment.

THE HULL

The hull is, to say the least, a very important part of a boat. No matter how good your superstructure is, if your hull is rotten you just have no boat. In order to preserve a wooden hull, we must keep it well painted. Every year the old coat of paint should be sanded down before new is applied, and every so often, depending on how thick the

FIG. 931 Prepare a checklist to be sure all necessary supplies and equipment are on board before setting out on a cruise. Use it every time, modifying and updating from experience.

old coats of paint are, all paint should be removed, the hull sanded, and seams and scars filled before a new coat of paint is applied.

Selection of paint

The number of different types of paint has expanded remarkably in recent years. While there is nothing wrong with "old fashioned" marine paint as used for many years, the modern skipper should give consideration to some of the new paints with exotic names such as polyutherane, epoxy, acrylic, etc. If you don't feel qualified to make a selection, ask the professionals at your boatyard and talk to other skippers about their experiences with various hull finishes.

Painting techniques

No matter which paint you select, proper surface preparation and application of the paint are *absolutely essential* if the desired results are to be obtained. Follow the manufacturer's directions explicitly from start to finish. Select the proper weather conditions for your work—wait until the morning dew has evaporated, and stop well before sundown.

"Between wind and water," that part of the vessel at or near the waterline, is the most difficult part of the hull to keep protected. This is because it is always getting wet and drying off and also that the water causes a lot of friction at this location. A special quick-drying paint called boot-topping is used here, the principal ingredients of which are varnish and dryer.

Fiberglass hulls

The above comments have been directed to the owners of boats with wooden hulls. If yours is of fiberglass, you will have less maintenance, but some will still be required. Don't neglect the care of your hull just because it requires less attention.

A fiberglass hull should be cleaned as required to keep it free of dirt and oily scum; more cleaning will be needed near the waterline than higher on the topsides. Try to get the job done using only a detergent without an abrasive powder that can dull a high-gloss finish. If you must use a scouring powder to remove marks and greasy streaks, use a mild one and use it with caution.

Liquid cleaner wax is excellent for fiberglass hulls, particularly for mid-season continuing maintenance. Once a year, usually at spring fitting-out, do a more thorough two-step job with a paste cleaner followed by a paste wax. This is also the time to patch up any hair-line cracks that have appeared in the gel (surface) coat of the fiberglass.

After a few years of use, a fiberglass hull may require painting to restore it to top appearance. Many paints are available for this purpose, most of which are two-part products to be mixed just prior to application. Advances in chemical and plastics technology are now resulting in one-part paints for fiberglass surfaces that are easier to use and will give satisfactory results. The problem is to get proper adhesion to the fiberglass plus a high-gloss finish. As with painting a wooden hull, the best procedure is to ask a professional and talk with people who have used various products to get their opinions. Again, too, it is most important that the manufacturer's instructions for surface preparation and paint application be adhered to exactly.

FIG. 932 Two secrets to success in painting are proper preparation of the surface and application of the paint in strict conformity with manufacturer's instructions.

BOTTOM MAINTENANCE

Special attention must be given to the maintenance of the bottom of the boat; this is a most important item as it is usually available for inspection only once or twice a year.

Except for small boats that are taken out of the water after each period of use, the bottom must be kept covered with anti-fouling paint. This type of paint, usually with a copper base, has properties that tend to keep worms out of the bottom as well as to discourage marine growth that attaches itself to the bottom.

Coming into wider use are bottom paints employing other metals and chemicals toxic to marine life. With these, bottom paints are now available in a wide range of colors.

FIG. 933 In most locations, antifouling paint must be applied to a boat's underwater surfaces to protect against worms and marine growth. Bottom finishes are available in many colors as well as the old familiar "copper" paint. (Wm. H. Koelbel photo)

Launching wet or dry

There are two theories about applying bottom paint. Some say that the boat should be put into the water as soon as the paint has been applied, that is, while it is still fairly wet, while others state that the paint should be dry before launching. Follow the manufacturer's directions on the can for the best results.

BRIGHTWORK

Brightwork, natural wood surfaces finished with varnish or similar products, requires special care. Horizontal areas of brightwork should be wiped clear of morning dew each day to prolong their life. All brightwork will require a good sanding at least yearly followed by a fresh coat of varnish. Those parts of the brightwork that receive a lot of wear or spray will need to be given more than one coat each season. Unless varnished areas are kept well covered, moisture will get into the wood and the result will be that

FIG. 934 Varnished surfaces, called "brightwork," require more care than painted or natural wood or fiberglass areas, but to many boat owners their added beauty is worth the effort. Often, care of brightwork can be turned over to the "first mate." (Rosenfeld photo)

it will turn dark, in extreme cases, black.

Wooding down

To keep brightwork looking well is a lot of work, but the beauty of it can make it worthwhile. No matter how much care is taken, it will turn just a little darker each year. Many modern varnishes and synthetic equivalents now include a "filter" to screen out ultraviolet rays of the sun that are most damaging to brightwork. The additive slows down the aging process. Even with this added protection, however, it will be necessary every few years to remove all of the varnish with varnish remover, sand the bare wood, and start with a fresh coat. From four to six separate coats will generally be required.

Reduction of brightwork

In recent years more and more boats have appeared with almost no brightwork at all. The cabins and spars are painted and in fact the only parts left natural may be the handrails, toerails, and trim around hatches.

This move toward little or no brightwork has even invaded interiors. A few years ago this would have been looked upon as sacrilege. No matter how much oldtimers view this trend with alarm, it does have this advantage—it does not reduce the protective qualities which are the main reasons for keeping surfaces covered, and it does make less work. In many cases, natural, unfinished teak is being substituted for mahogany that must be kept varnished.

DECK CARE

Canvas decks present a special problem. They must be kept covered with a good deck paint for protection, but the less paint you put on the better. If you get too much paint on the decks, not only will it crack but they will become smooth. This is not good especially on a small boat, as a smooth deck makes for precarious footing in wet weather. This has been overcome on some boats by sprinkling fine sand on the decks while the paint is still wet. Also, some paint manufacturers are putting out a special paint with a non-skid surface.

Fiberglass decks

Decks of fiberglass require little care other than rinsing off dirt and salt spray. On most boats, anti-slip protection is built in by the manufacturer. In some cases, however, additional non-skid strips or specially painted areas will be required for safety. If it becomes necessary to paint a fiberglass deck, don't fail to provide for continued anti-skid protection where needed.

Teak decks

Decks on large power and sail craft are often made of unfinished teak. Such decks are attractive, quite non-skid, and require little maintenance. They may be allowed to assume a natural, weathered appearance, or they can be periodically bleached to a lighter color, as the individual skipper prefers.

Teak decks should be washed down to keep them free of dirt that might get ground in when walked upon. Salt sea water is excellent for washing down teak decks. A periodic scrubbing with a special teak cleaner is not a difficult chore and will improve overall appearance, but it should not be done too often.

FIG. 935 Teak is an excellent material for decks. The wood can be left unfinished or given a light treatment with special preservatives. It weathers well and provides a non-skid surface. (Rosenfeld photo)

Decks of teak wood are subject to staining from oily liquids or solids—particularly from some types of food such as bits of potato chips or mayonnaise drippings from sandwiches—but special paste or spray cleaners will efficiently remove these spots.

PAINTING METAL SURFACES

If any metal is to be painted, be sure to use a priming coat of anti-corrosive paint against the metal first. Popular types of such paint include the familiar red lead, zinc chromate, and aluminum. Paints for this purpose will be so labeled on the container; don't use a paint for anti-corrosion protection unless it is so designated.

If your boat has a metal bottom it is specially important that anti-corrosive paint be used before the anti-fouling paint. Ingredients of most bottom paint are oxides of mercury and copper, and if these come in contact with steel, corrosion will result. The anti-fouling paints offer no protection to the hull against sea-water corrosion, but the anti-corrosion paints have no anti-fouling properties, so both must be used.

Painting aluminum

Boats having aluminum hulls may be painted for protection against corrosive attack although this is not generally required with modern alloys properly selected. Underwater anti-fouling paint will be needed for aluminum bottoms under the same conditions as for wood or fiberglass boats.

Aluminum will hold paint very well *provided* that the metal surface has been properly prepared and a suitable primer has been used. Greater care must be taken with this metal than with others commonly used. The aluminum must be *absolutely clean,* free of all oil, scale, dirt, etc., even free of fingerprints. Sand-blasting or wire brushing will be needed to etch the surface slightly in order to make the paint adhere. Zinc chromate is a suitable primer; two

coats should be used to insulate the aluminum hull from any lead-pigmented paint or copper-bearing bottom coating so as to prevent galvanic action between the dissimilar metals.

When patching up the paint job on any area of an aluminum hull, always be sure to prepare the metal surface thoroughly and use a primer coat next to the aluminum.

GENERAL RULES FOR PAINTING

There are a few simple rules for painting. If observed, they will make such work simpler and more satisfactory. These are:

1. Never paint over a wet, dirty, or greasy surface.
2. Never paint during wet weather.
3. Never paint before cleaning and sanding.
4. Do not continuously apply new over old coats.
5. Never apply paint heavily.
6. Paint with reasonable frequency.
7. Use surfacing putty (trowel or brushing cement) to fill nicks and gouges after the prime coat of paint, unless manufacturer's instructions indicate otherwise.
8. Never use a blow torch immediately after applying paint remover.
9. Never scrape or sand near fresh paint.

Sequence for painting

There is a generally preferred order for painting the various parts of a boat as follows:

1. All interiors, including bilge (if painted) and engines.
2. Spars.
3. All deck gear, cockpits, ventilators, hatches, etc.
4. Cabin exterior and decks.
5. Hull topsides.
6. Bottom.
7. Boot-topping.

FIG. 935(a) For boatmen, a power sander can be a real energy-saver. These come in many styles, both as a separate tool as above, and as an attachment for an electric drill.

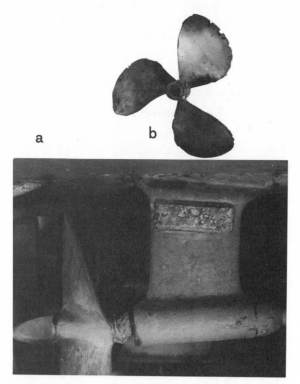

a   b

FIG. 936 Whenever your boat is hauled, inspect underwater areas. Zinc blocks and collars, as shown in (a), are used to control galvanic corrosion and must be regularly checked and replaced when needed. Failure to do this may have the results pictured in (b).

INSPECTION NECESSARY

Besides keeping all appropriate surfaces well covered with paint or varnish, there are many other parts that must be inspected regularly. For example, on some boats you must be constantly on the lookout for galvanic corrosion. This chemical reaction is caused when different metals such as brass or bronze and iron come together or in close proximity to each other in salt or impure water. This is often noticeable on boats between an iron rudder and a bronze propeller. Cases have been known where the rudder is just eaten up. This can be checked by placing a zinc plate nearby so that the zinc, in contact with the part to be protected, will be affected instead of the iron. However, if this is done, care must be taken to watch the zinc plate and replace it whenever necessary. Systems may be installed in which a reverse flow of current is used to equalize and offset any destructive current.

Make regular checks

Regular checks of shaft logs, stuffing boxes, bearings, underwater fittings, and the propeller are essential. Your steering system and cables should be gone over often. If your steering system goes wrong in a tight place, you will not only damage your own vessel but may also injure some person or another boat.

Keep your boat clean

All equipment as well as the hull itself must be kept clean at all times. This also includes the bilges. Dirty bilges can result in stopped-up inlets to bilge pumps, and this is sure to happen just when the pump is most needed. There is nothing that gets dirty easier than a boat. Not only is it uncomfortable to try to live on, but it is injurious to the hull and the equipment. Regular cleaning makes for little work to keep your boat spick-and-span; if you let it go, it is a hard job to clean up.

Inspection checklist

Earlier in this section, a sailing checklist was described that all good skippers use before each run. In order to assist the skipper in preventing breakdowns, every boat should have an *inspection checklist* on board and in use. An inspection checklist is a list of all items that the skipper will regularly inspect, and the scheduled periods for such inspections, with a place for the skipper to write in the date of each inspection in order to keep his boat well found.

ENGINE CARE

In a motor boat the engine is the only means of propulsion, and in an auxiliary it is the means of getting in and out of tight places. Therefore, the engine is something that should be in the best of shape at all times and should always start at once. All of us are not good mechanics, but all of us should be able to (1) obtain, read, and follow the manufacturer's instruction book; (2) know enough not to fool with something we are not sure of; and (3) get instruction on simple trouble diagnosis and emergency repairs—U.S.P.S. members can and should take the Engine Maintenance Course.

Routine care

There are, however, a number of things that any skipper can do not only to keep his engine running well for whenever it is needed, but also to keep down the cost of repair bills. All should be done at intervals and in the manner prescribed by the maker's operating manual.

FIG. 937 Regular cleaning makes for little work to keep a boat spick-and-span.

(Rosenfeld photo)

FIG. 938 The average powerboat skipper is not expected to be a mechanic, but he must have an idea of how to maintain his engines. The manufacturer's instruction book should be aboard and its preventive maintenance procedures carried out. (Charles Anderson photo)

Typical routine maintenance items include:
1. Frequently check oil level; change oil regularly.
2. Check cooling system, including intake, regularly.
3. Keep batteries filled and fully charged.
4. Oil starter, generator, and distributor regularly.
5. Keep grease cups filled; turn down and clean regularly.
6. Keep engines clean, especially all filters.
7. Keep fuel lines tight; check for vibration.
8. Check all electric wiring periodically.
9. Do not race a cold motor.
10. Cool down engine before stopping it.
11. Engage clutch only at moderate speeds.
12. Carry spare parts and know how to install them.
13. Carry proper tools.

CARE OF SAILS

Modern sailboats use nearly all synthetic sailcloth—dacron and nylon. These materials have greatly improved characteristics over canvas, but they do require proper use and maintenance.

Care in use

Protect sails from chafing—use wooden or rubber protectors over turnbuckles and at the tips of spreaders. Don't let sails slat needlessly; it wears the stitching and tears batten pockets. Use properly fitted battens and remove them when the sail is furled.

Care in stowage

The greatest enemy of synthetic sailcloth is the sun. Excessive sunlight ultimately causes the material to break down and lose its strength. If sails are left on, they should be furled *and covered*. Water and moisture will not harm dacron and nylon and so such sails can be stored damp if necessary. It is, however, advisable to dry them if you can in order to avoid mildew and the general carrying of mois-

ture below decks.

Wash sails once or twice a season with pure water and soap—no detergents; and never use a washing machine. Hose off, spread to dry, and inspect before folding. Try to keep them as free from salt as possible.

When storing for the winter, wash, clean, and dry. In folding, lay out on the floor, fold lengthwise accordion fashion. When you have a 2- to 3-foot-square bundle, fold head to foot, tie up and store safely or hang to protect from vermin.

Sail maintenance

Although any major repairs should be left to a professional sailmaker, every sailor should be familiar with four basic emergency repairs: the round stitch, the herringbone stitch, the patch, and sail repair tape.

Round Stitch. The round or overhand stitch is used particularly for light sails and in repairing minor tears of from one to four inches. Gather the two sides of the rip, starting about an inch above it. Secure the thread *not* by knotting, but by passing it under the first few stitches; then

FIG. 939 Sails of modern craft are almost entirely synthetic—dacron, nylon, and others. While more resistant to damage from misuse, they still require proper care and maintenance for good service and long life. (Rosenfeld photo)

FIG. 940 When sails are furled on the boom, they should be protected by a cover. Sunshine, more than use, rain, or salt spray, is the greatest enemy of synthetic sails. (Schwarm, Sheldon photo)

sew over it and continue round and round, ending about an inch below the tear. Finish your job in the same turn-under way.

Herringbone Stitch. This is used for more serious repairs. Before placing the two sides of the rip together, fold under a narrow margin on each and "iron" it like a pair of pants by gently scraping the edge of the sailcloth with your knife. Then make alternate long and short stitches to avoid an even line, starting about a quarter-inch from the end of the tear, and finish a quarter-inch below it. Tuck the end of the twine under the final few stitches as in the round job, and cut it. This is a stitch that is best learned from someone who knows how.

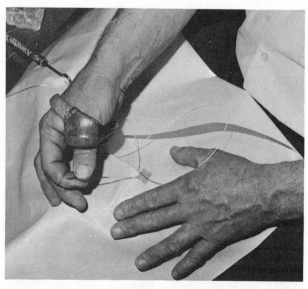

FIG. 941 A sailboat skipper should be able to make minor repairs, but all major maintenance and alteration work should be referred to a professional sailmaker. The herringbone stitch, above, is used for tears too extensive to permit use of the simpler round stitch. Start ¼-inch from the tear and finish below it. (Frank Rohr photo)

Patch. Cut your patch, if possible, from the same weight and type of material as the damaged sail. Allow about one and one-half inches of margin on either side of the tear and turn the patch under a half-inch all the way round, "ironing" folds with knife treatment to keep them manageable, especially with heavier weight cloths. Try to get the weave of the patching cloth to run identically with the sail being repaired. Measuring the approximate area and marking the patch material with pencil before cutting will help.

Miter corners of the patch and, pinning it to sail with extra needles, use the round or overhand stitch to sew your patch to the sail. Pound it into submission with a knife handle; turn the whole lot over; miter the corners of the torn sail itself; sew it to the back of the patch, and hoist away.

Tape. Spinnaker and white rigging tape can be pressed into service swiftly and efficiently to help you finish—even win—a race, or perhaps withstand the wind in some cruising crisis till you reach port.

In making the repair, separate the sticky part from its guard which comes as part of the roll; then, as you unroll the ready tape, press with your fingers on both sides of the rip or seam. It should hold till you can get to it with needle and thread, or bring it ashore to the sailmaker.

Sail repair kit

Various sailmakers can supply emergency repair kits suitable for the sails used on your boat. These include sewing twine, needles, beeswax, a sewing palm, and other useful items, including a booklet of instructions on the care and repair of sails.

WINTER LAY-UP

Perhaps the greatest damage is done to a boat during the long winter months when she is laid up. In the north boats are usually pulled out during the winter, while in the south they are usually left in the water. Of course these call for slightly different techniques.

Storage on land

In general, these are the things to do when laying up for the winter hauled out on shore:

1. Thoroughly clean the bottom, decks, cockpit, bilge, all compartments, and lockers.
2. Apply a coat of good anti-fouling paint to the bottom, and sand down and prime all other marred surfaces.
3. Drain the fuel system, tanks, lines, pumps, and carburetor.
4. Drain and flush out all water systems and tanks; drain the toilets.
5. Winterize the engine in accordance with the manufacturer's instruction manual. This will normally include draining and flushing the cooling system; draining and refilling the crankcase; applying oil to inside of each cylinder through the sparkplug holes; and other preservative actions. Thoroughly clean the exterior of the engine; sand and touch up with paint any scarred areas to prevent rusting.
6. Remove the batteries from the boat; store in an area not subject to freezing temperatures and place on a "trickle" charge.
7. Place a light coating of grease over all chromeplated

8. Leave all floorboards up, doors ajar, ports and sky-lights open, hatches partly open, drawers and lockers open.

9. Carefully fit a well-made winter cover, provided with ventilation ports, if boat is to be stored outdoors.

Storage afloat

When making plans for your boat's winter lay-up, don't fail to give consideration to "wet storage." New ice-protection techniques are coming into wider usage, and more owners are leaving their craft in the water for the winter months—it has many advantages.

The cost is often less, but the real gains are in the better storage conditions for the boat. Water temperatures do not fluctuate so widely or rapidly as do those of the air, and so there is less "sweating" inside the hull. Properly protected with antifreeze, the engine can be periodically started and run, which is better for it than standing idle for several months.

Another advantage of wet storage is that there is less danger of the hull's warping or becoming distorted. A boat's structure is designed to be uniformly supported by water; resting on a few blocks, or even in its own special cradle, is distinctly "unnatural" for it. If protected against ice, covered, in-water storage is the best way for your boat to sit out the winter months until the next boating season.

FIG. 943 More and more boats are being kept in the water over the winter season even where ice normally is a problem. Air pumped through pipes on the bottom brings warmer water to the surface and prevents formation of ice near the hull. (Chicago Sun-Times photo)

FIG. 944 An electric drill is a virtually indispensable tool in boat maintenance. Many models feature variable speed operation and some can be reversed in rotation.

Winterizing procedures afloat

The actions to be taken for a winter lay-up afloat will, of course, be somewhat different from those in the list above for when the boat is to be hauled out. The engine should be winterized, but the details, as in connection with the cooling system, will vary. Gas tanks may be filled, to reduce condensation, rather than being drained. Excess gear should be removed from the boat, and all lockers, drawers, etc., should be left open to promote ventilation.

Getting a head start on fitting out

Some annual maintenance chores may be suitable for accomplishment in the fall at the time of laying-up. Any that can be done at this time will reduce the effort required the following spring and so expedite your next boating season.

KEEP YOUR BOAT WELL MAINTAINED

Once a boat is "Shipshape and Bristol Fashion" it doesn't take much work to keep her so. It is only when she is allowed to run down that the work is heavy.

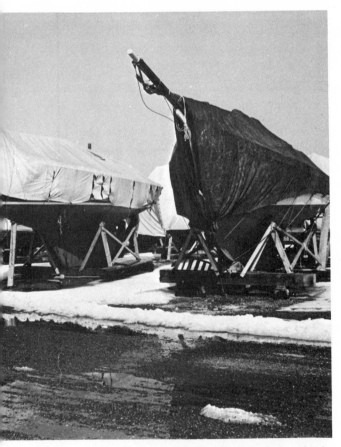

FIG. 942 In northern waters, boats are normally hauled out for dry storage during the winter. Proper blocking and shoring are necessary so that the hull is adequately supported and will not distort in shape. Canvas cover should provide protection and ventilation.

189

CHAPTER 10

SAFETY AFLOAT

No one should ever be deterred from enjoying the wholesome pleasures of boating by hazards that *might* be encountered; neither should he take safety for granted. No one—skipper, first mate, crew, nor guests—need fear the water and recreational boating if it is approached in a sensible manner.

While not allowing it to detract from the enjoyment of boating, the wise skipper practices safety at *all* times while afloat and studies it frequently ashore. He recognizes its importance, and safety is always in the back of his mind, never forgotten nor ignored. He views safety not as an arbitrary set of rules, but rather as the practical application of knowledge, as commonsense requirements and practices that should be thoroughly understood and followed. If "hazards" of any nature are recognized and respected, they largely cease to be hazards.

It is an established fact that most boating accidents and difficulties arise from ignorance, and could have been avoided. A man does not knowingly put his life, and the lives of others, and the safety of valuable property in jeopardy, but he may do so through lack of knowledge. Serious study and thought toward safety can significantly reduce the problems encountered while on the water.

Photograph by Schwarm and Sheldon, Inc.

Safety afloat is a broad topic encompassing essentially all aspects of boating. It is involved in the construction of boats, their equipment, operation, and maintenance. Safety matters are touched on in other chapters of this book in their relationship to government regulations, Rules of the Road, boat handling, seamanship, and other major topics. Here, safety afloat will be the *principal* consideration, with appropriate cross-references to other sections.

SAFETY ORGANIZATIONS

There are a number of public and private organizations devoted to the promotion of safety in boating. Several of these approach safety as an educational matter; others are concerned with the material and operational aspects of boats and boating. Each plays an important part in enhancing the safety of small craft, their crews and passengers.

Educational organizations

The **United States Power Squadrons** is a volunteer organization of more than 87,000 members organized into over 425 local Squadrons. These units, located throughout the United States and in some overseas areas, offer educational programs of basic boating safety and piloting to the public, and more advanced courses to their membership.

It is a nonprofit, self-sustaining, private membership organization dedicated to the teaching of better and safer boating. Despite the word "Power" in its name, the USPS today includes many sailboat skippers in its ranks. The boats of members can usually be identified by the USPS Ensign with its blue and white vertical stripes; see color page R.

More than 70,000 boatmen and members of their families receive free instruction in the USPS Boating Course every year. Information on local classes is published often in *Motor Boating & Sailing* magazine or an inquiry can be addressed to USPS Headquarters, P.O. Box 345, Montvale, N.J. 07645.

Additional information on the USPS will be found in Chapter 31.

In Canada, the Canadian Power Squadrons are organized in a manner generally similar to the USPS, with modifications to fit that country's laws and customs. Power Squadron ideals and programs are spreading also to other nations and parallel organizations may be seen developing throughout the world in future years.

The **United States Coast Guard Auxiliary** is a voluntary civilian organization of owners of boats, private airplanes, and amateur radio stations; it is a non-military group although administered by the U.S. Coast Guard. Its mission is to promote safety in the operation of small craft through education, boat examinations, and operational activities.

Although uniformed and organized along military lines, and closely affiliated with the regular Coast Guard, the Auxiliary is strictly civilian in nature; it has no law enforcement powers. See color pages T and U for illustrations of USCG Aux flags and uniform insignia.

The Auxiliary carries on a program of free public instruction and members take specialty courses to increase their knowledge and abilities.

Courtesy Motorboat Examinations are a well-known program of the Coast Guard Auxiliary. Specially trained members conduct annual checks on boats, but only at the request of an owner. Boats that meet a strict set of require-

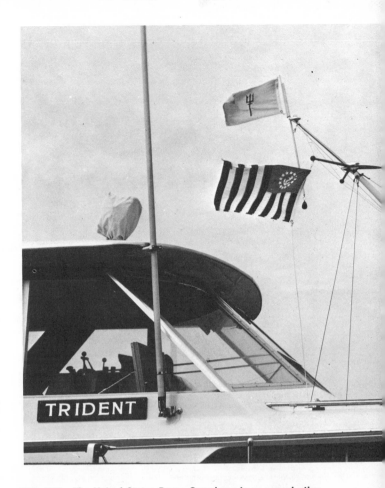

FIG. 1001 The United States Power Squadrons is an organization of volunteers dedicated to making boating safer through education. Craft skippered by USPS members are usually identified by the distinctive flag, with blue and white vertical stripes, shown here at the starboard yardarm. The flag at the masthead identifies the owner as an officer of the USPS; in this case, the blue trident on a white field signifies Rear Commander.

ments are awarded a distinguishing decal, fig. 1002. No report is made to the authorities of craft that fail to qualify; the owner is urged to remedy the defect and request reexamination.

Operationally, the Auxiliary promotes safety afloat by assisting the Coast Guard in patrolling marine regattas and racing events. In many areas, the Auxiliary also participates in search and rescue for craft that are disabled, in distress, or have been reported overdue.

Information on public classes of the Auxiliary or membership in the organization may be obtained from the Flotilla in your vicinity or by writing to the appropriate Coast Guard District Headquarters; see fig. 1502, page 301.

More information on the USCG Aux will be found in Chapter 32.

The **American National Red Cross** offers programs of water safety education through its more than 3,000 local chapters in all areas of the country. The swimming and water safety skills taught by the Red Cross range from beginning through advanced swimmer, survival swimming, and life saving. (Many schools, YMCAs, and other organizations also teach these subjects by Red Cross methods and to its standards.) The small craft safety instructional programs include courses in canoeing, rowboating, outboard boating, and sailing.

Red Cross first aid training is also available to the public

FIG. 1002 The Coast Guard Auxiliary makes Courtesy Motorboat
Examinations, but only at the request of the craft's owner. Boats
meeting all legal requirements
and certain additional safety
standards of the Auxiliary are
awarded the "Seal of Safety"
sticker for the current year.
(Official Coast Guard photograph)

FIG. 1003 Local chapters of the American National Red Cross
teach swimming, lifesaving, and other water safety subjects to persons of all ages. Every boatman should set a personal goal of being a competent swimmer and having enough lifesaving knowledge
to help others in trouble in the water.

through local chapters. A wise skipper would do well to
learn the proper action to be taken in cases of bleeding,
fractures, stoppage of breathing, shock, burns, and other
common emergencies.

Textbooks used in Red Cross training programs may be
purchased from larger bookstores or through local chapters; all of these are valuable reference publications. Texts
which are available include *Swimming and Water Safety,
Lifesaving and Water Safety, First Aid, Basic Canoeing,
Canoeing, Basic Rowing, Basic Outboarding,* and *Basic
Sailing.* All are priced at less than $2.

The Red Cross publishes a variety of safety pamphlets
and posters, and produces a number of informational and
instructional films; these are made available to interested
groups free of charge. Full information on classes, publications, films, and other safety activities can be obtained
from local chapters.

Equipment organizations

In addition to the national volunteer organizations
working toward greater safety afloat through education,
there are nonprofit groups within and related to the boating industry that promote safety through higher standards
for equipment, including its installation and use.

The **American Boat & Yacht Council, Inc.** is a nonprofit,
public service organization founded for the purpose of
"improving and promoting the design, construction,
equipage, and maintenance of small craft with reference to
their safety." Membership in the Council is open to anyone
interested in furtherance of its objectives. Regular Members may serve in administrative offices and on administra-

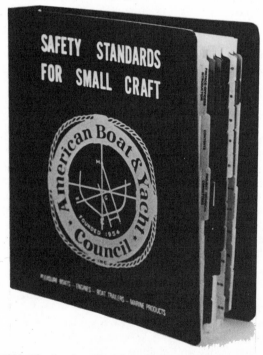

FIG. 1004 The American Boat & Yacht Council, Inc. is a non-profit,
public service organization founded to increase safety in the design,
construction, equipment, and maintenance of small craft. It periodically publishes a compilation of its "Safety Standards"—worthwhile
reading for all skippers.

tive committees, but only Technical Members (highly qualified individuals) may serve on the Council's Technical Board and technical committees.

The American Boat & Yacht Council publishes "Safety Standards." These recommended specifications and practices are intended as good guidance toward making small craft as free from dangerous defect or deficiency as practicable in the interest of minimizing loss of life, injury, and loss of property. Standards are stated largely in terms of desired performance and are not intended to preclude attainment of the desired safety level by other means.

Safety Standards are prepared by Project Technical Committees formed as broadly based groups of recognized authorities with the objective of obtaining a maximum of agreement and acceptance. All technical reports and safety standards are advisory only; the Council has no powers of enforcement.

The AB&YC does not "approve" boats, equipment, materials, or services. Compliance with appropriate standards may be indicated by listings of nationally recognized testing laboratories whose findings may be used as a guide to approval. All standards are reviewed at intervals of three years, or more frequently if necessary because of comments received or advances in technology.

The American Boat & Yacht Council publishes its "Adopted" and "Proposed" standards as they complete a careful review and approval process. The standards are sent out as supplements to the complete compilation published in loose-leaf form. Included are standards for such diverse matters as "good visibility from the helm position," "life saving equipment," "engine exhaust systems," "electrical grounding of DC systems," "lightning protection," "sewerage treatment systems," and "distress signals." The full set of recommended practices is published as "Safety Standards for Small Craft," available for $35 from the Council at 15 East 26th Street, New York, N.Y. 10010. The serious skipper can well devote some spare time to reading this volume; it is a good book to have on hand for reference.

The **Yacht Safety Bureau, Inc.,** for many years a non-profit public service organization under joint sponsorship of the National Association of Engine and Boat Manufacturers and major marine insurance underwriters, has now become the Marine Division of Underwriters Laboratories. This will not change the organization's primary purpose of inspection, testing, and safety evaluation of products intended for use on, in, or in conjunction with small boats, including hulls and entire boats.

Simply stated, the Bureau's objective is to see that marine equipment is available to the boating public that has been measured for safety of operation when used as intended. This objective is based on the logic that safety begins with safe products and continues with how they are used.

The Yacht Safety Bureau does not solicit work. Manufacturers voluntarily submit products for evaluation. Extensive laboratory facilities are maintained in New Jersey; field testing is frequently accomplished at other sites.

The word "approved" is frequently misused in connection with YSB product certification. The Bureau does not approve or disapprove anything. What it does is operate a product listing and labeling service.

Satisfactory completion of safety evaluation results in an item's being "listed" by the Yacht Safety Bureau. Listing of a product, with its related privilege of use of the Bureau's label, means that production samples of it have been evaluated and found acceptable under the Bureau's requirements. Listing is an expression of the Bureau's good faith opinion, based on tests, that the item meets minimum applicable safety standards. It is not a warranty of quality or performance, nor are listed products of the same class necessarily equivalent in quality, performance, or merit.

The Bureau's labels include the words "LISTED PRODUCT" in a copyrighted design, fig. 1005. These symbols may be seen in advertisements and on tags, stickers, etc., on products. This label will gradually be replaced with the well-known UL label widely used on electrical items.

The presence of the YSB or UL label on any device means that a production sample has been successfully evaluated to related safety requirements, and nothing else. The label may, however, be the basis on which "authorities having jurisdiction" grant approval. Such authorities include individuals making judgments for their own purposes, industry people making judgments for components or original equipment installations, marine surveyors for insurance purposes, and administrators of regulations making judgments required by law.

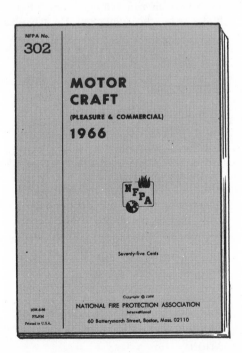

FIG. 1006 **Fire Protection Standards for Motor Craft, No. 302, is a small yet valuable safety bulletin issued by the National Fire Protection Association. A copy should be studied by every boat owner and carried aboard as a useful reference document. See text for how a copy may be obtained.**

FIG. 1005 **Boating products that have passed a safety evaluation are "listed" by the Yacht Safety Bureau. The YSB seal can be used in advertising the items and may be found on it in the form of a sticker, tag, etc. Periodic re-testing ensures the continued safety of all listed products.**

Only products commercially available are eligible for listing. New products may be submitted in their model stage for evaluation, but no final listing action is taken until production units are submitted. Continuity of a Bureau listing is provided for by means of its periodic re-inspection service. This is directed only toward confirming that originally tested qualities of listed and labeled products are maintained so long as the listing continues.

The **National Fire Protection Association** is an organization whose activities extend far beyond boating and marine interests to include all aspects of the science and methods of fire protection. NFPA issues codes, standards, and recommended practices for minimizing losses of life and property by fire.

NFPA does not approve, inspect, or certify any installations, procedures, equipment, or materials, nor does it approve or evaluate testing laboratories. It does prepare, by coordinated action of committees of experts, codes and standards for the guidance of all persons in the matter of fire protection. Frequently, NFPA codes and standards are written into law or regulations by various governmental units.

Of interest to boatmen is NFPA Fire Protection Standard No. 302 for Motor Craft (Pleasure and Commercial).

Originally issued in 1925, it has been amended and revised many times. The small booklet, available for 75c from NFPA, 60 Batterymarch Street, Boston, Mass. 02110, is a useful guide to any skipper.

Construction for Safety

In one respect, safety afloat may be considered to start with the design and construction of the craft itself. The average skipper is not likely to build his own boat, but he should be able to recognize proper design features and sound construction characteristics. He should be at least broadly familiar with safe and unsafe aspects of boat construction—the points that should be checked in determining whether or not a particular craft, new or used, should be bought. There is little the average yachtsman can do directly to influence the design and construction of boats, but he can, through knowledge and careful inspection, avoid those that fail to measure up to desirable standards.

A boatman contemplating purchase of a used boat should seriously consider use of the services of a qualified marine surveyor. He is an expert in determining the condition of the hull, engine, and equipment. He may well discover hidden defects that the would-be buyer overlooked in his enthusiasm. An impartial survey is sound protection for a purchaser; the modest cost involved will be well-justified. Such a survey is often required to obtain insurance, particularly on older boats.

HULL CONSTRUCTION

Modern boats, built by reputable manufacturers, are basically seaworthy because they are honestly constructed to proven designs. This points out the proper course in the selection of a good, sound boat. There is no necessity of trying some freak of questionable worth. If you have no experience in selecting a boat, it is easy enough to avail

FIG. 1008 Anti-slip protection on deck walkways and at boarding areas is a *must* for safety. This can be obtained from the natural qualities of the deck, ingredients added to the deck paint, or by applying special strips of material having a no-slip surface and an adhesive backing.

yourself of the advice and guidance of others who are better qualified; be sure to talk to several persons to avoid personal biases.

Construction materials

For seaworthiness and safety, suitable materials for boatbuilding and highgrade construction are equally essential. Use of fire-retardant materials wherever practicable is suggested. Boats may be built equally well of wood, fiberglass, steel, or aluminum. Combinations of materials may also be used, such as a fiberglass superstructure on a wooden hull.

ABC BOAT CO.
ANY STREET, YOUR TOWN

THIS BOAT COMPLIES WITH U. S. COAST GUARD SAFETY STANDARDS IN EFFECT ON THE DATE OF CERTIFICATION

MODEL T–205
ABC456781272
1973 MODEL

FIG. 1007 The Federal Boat Safety Act of 1971 provides for the promulgation of safety standards by Coast Guard regulations. It is required that manufacturers attach a "certification plate" to each craft produced. The plate may appear as above, or the certification statement may be combined into the required "capacity plate," see fig. 1023.

FIG. 1009 Lifelines are important on all boats, but are an absolute must on offshore cruising and racing sailboats. The lines must have adequate strength and the stanchions must be securely through-bolted. Note how lines merge into metal pulpit rails at bow and stern.
(Photograph by Romaine-Skelton)

It should be noted, too, that boats can also be built poorly in any of these materials. Many arguments can be made for and against each hull material, but basically the decision is one for the individual owner, considering the use of the boat, cost factors, maintenance, and not least, his personal preferences.

Water-tight bulkheads (or as tight as practicable) are recommended to isolate bilges of fuel and machinery spaces from those of living quarters. Where feasible, two means of exit should be provided from compartments where persons may congregate or sleep. Thus, in a small craft having only one cabin and cockpit, a forward hatch is a desirable feature.

Safety on deck

A Class 1 or larger boat may have side decks on which individuals move forward to the bow and back. It is essential that four safety features be present. First, these decks must be wide enough for secure footing. People will attempt to pass forward from the cockpit, around the cabin, and to the forward deck. There must be adequate space for their feet to be placed fully on deck, even though the space may be measured in inches and they have to make their way forward sideways. Secondly, if the deck is of a material that is slippery when wet (and most are), anti-slip protection must be provided at critical points. This may consist of a built-in roughness in fiberglass decks, added material to deck paint, or special anti-slip strips attached to the deck with their own adhesive backing. Any place that a person can or has slipped, even once, is a potential area for anti-slip protection.

Thirdly, there must be adequate hand-holds, places to grab and hold on. These must be sufficient in number and so spaced that no one need be beyond a secure grasp of the boat at any time in moving forward and aft, or when coming aboard or leaving the boat. The old saying "one hand for the boat and one for yourself" is an excellent one —even in calm waters; hold on at all times to something strong enough to bear your weight.

Lifelines, also referred to as liferails, are the fourth item of deck security for personnel. No boat large enough for lifelines should be without them. They are often carried forward to join low metal rails (pulpits) at the bow and stern to completely enclose the deck.

Owners of offshore cruising sailboats would be wise to meet the requirements set by the North American Yacht Racing Union: Fixed bow and stern pulpits (unless lifelines are arranged to adequately substitute for a stern pulpit); pulpits and stanchions through-bolted or welded to the deck; taut, double life lines with wire upper line secured to pulpits and stanchions; pulpits and upper life line not less than 24" above deck at any point; and stanchions spaced not more than 7' apart except in the way of shrouds when the lifelines are permanently attached to the shrouds. The lifelines need not be affixed to the bow pulpit if they terminate at, or pass through, 24" high stanchions set inside of and overlapping the bow pulpit. These requirements are compatible with those of the American Boat & Yacht Council for lifelines and rails on both power and sail boats. There are also nine other AB&YC safety standards relating to hulls of small craft, all of which will make interesting reading to those seriously concerned with safety afloat.

Superstructure and stability

The mistaken notion that a boat can carry weight anywhere as long as she appears to trim right in the water must be corrected. Addition of more superstructure, such as a flying bridge, is particularly bad, as is the shifting of heavy weights such as motors, ballast, tanks, machinery, etc. Where stability is concerned, no shifts of major weights or changes in design should be considered without the advice of a qualified naval architect. Amateur boat-builders sometimes ruin boats and reduce their safety factors by deviating from architect's plans in which the proportioning of weights has been given the most painstaking attention.

Through-hull fittings

Fittings which pass through the hull near or below the water line should have sea-cocks installed internally close to the planking to permit positive closing. It is desirable that solid, seagoing metal pipe extend from the sea-cock to a level above the water line, from which point flexible hoses may be run to the pump or other accessory. Where hose is placed over pipe nipples for connections, hose clamps should be used.

There are now available through-hull fittings and sea-cocks that have been safety evaluated by the Yacht Safety Bureau and "listed" by that organization. AB&YC Safety Standard A-2 furnishes additional information on these.

FIG. 1010 Seacocks are important items of safety equipment on boats of all sizes. Every through-hull fitting should have one for cutting off the entry of water in case of hose leakage or for working on equipment. Seacocks should be tested for easy shut-off action at least twice each year; adjust or replace without delay any seacock stuck in the open position.

Engines and Fuel Systems

Probably the first thought that comes to mind in connection with safety afloat is that of preventing fire and explosion. Fire is usually traceable to the engine room or galley where improper equipment, faulty installation, or careless operation is the direct cause. All of these are under the owner's control.

ENGINE INSTALLATION

Engines should be suited to the hulls they power. Extremes of underpowering and overpowering are both bad. Original installations and subsequent changes require the advice of a naval architect or one thoroughly familiar with this phase of boat design.

Conversions of automobile engines for marine duty by amateur mechanics are invariably a source of trouble because of basic differences between the two types. Lubrication and cooling are the chief problems. Selection of an accepted type of marine engine or a commercially-produced conversion is advisable.

Pans, preferably made of copper, are recommended for installation under the engine to catch any oil and grease drippings and prevent these from getting into the bilge. Accumulations should be removed promptly for fire safety.

FUEL SYSTEMS

The primary aspect of fuel system safety is the prevention of fires and explosion. Not to be forgotten, however, are the reliability aspects of the system that will ensure a continuous flow of clean fuel to the engine.

The discussion that follows will be principally concerned with boats using gasoline engines; exceptions and special requirements relating to diesel fuel systems will be covered separately.

Fire prevention

It is of primary importance that the entire fuel system be liquid- and vapor-tight with respect to the hull interior. Gasoline fumes, mixed with air, form an explosive combination. These fumes, several times heavier than air, settle to the bottom of the bilge. A concentration of gasoline in air as low as 1¼% can be exploded by a slight spark with tremendous effect—a half-teacup of gasoline can create

enough explosive vapor to totally destroy a large motorboat.

The obvious answer for safety is *prevention*—make it impossible for gasoline, either in liquid or gaseous form, to get into the bilge in the first place. Then keep the bilge clean and ventilate the engine compartment thoroughly, and there will be nothing that can be ignited.

Leakage of liquid gasoline into the bilge can be prevented by proper installation, using strongly built gasoline tanks, copper tubing for fuel lines, leakproof connections, tight fittings, and lengths of flexible metallic fuel hose to take care of vibration. Gasoline vapors created when the tanks are filled must be prevented from finding their way down through open hatches and companionways. Finally, avoidable sparks and flames should not be permitted in the engine room.

Carburetors

Carburetors must be equipped with flame arresters for protection against backfire; see fig. 1011. If not of the downdraft type, they should also have a pan covered with a fine mesh screen attached under the carburetor to collect any drip. Leakage will be sucked back into the engine if a copper tube is run from the bottom of the pan to the intake manifold. Flame arresters should be kept clean both for safety and best engine operation.

Air intakes to the engine compartment should be directed so that any backfires will not tend to blow into the bilges.

Fuel tanks

Fuel tanks should be permanently installed in such a manner as to be secure against moving about in a seaway. The use of portable tanks below decks is not good practice.

Fuel tanks must be constructed of a metal that is compatible with both the fuel and a normal marine environment. Copper, copper alloys of certain specific compositions, hot-dipped galvanized sheet steel, and terneplate steel are all used for gasoline tanks. In each case, construction, installation, and inspections should be in accordance with standards of the American Boat & Yacht Council. The AB&YC also provides specifications for fiberglass reinforced plastic tanks, but notes that "Compliance with these requirements does not necessarily guarantee acceptance by the authority having jurisdiction."

Gasoline tanks must not be integral with the hull. The shape of the tank should be such that there are no exterior pockets that would trap moisture after the tank is in its installed position. Tank bottoms must not have sumps or pockets in which water could accumulate.

Internal stiffeners and baffle plates will normally be used to provide necessary rigidity and resistance to surging of liquid in the tanks. Baffles must meet certain specified design criteria to prevent formation of liquid pockets in the bottom of tanks and vapor pockets in the tops.

There should be no drains or outlets for drawing off fuel from the tank, nor outlets or fittings of any type in the bottom, sides, or ends of tanks. Fuel lines to the engine should enter the tank at its top and internally extend nearly, but not quite all the way, to the bottom.

Fuel filler pipes and vents

One of the most essential requirements in the proper installation of a fuel system is that there be a completely tight connection between the gasoline tank and the filling plate on deck. The fuel fill must be located so any spillage will go overboard, not inside the hull, and tight pipe connections between deck plate and tank will prevent leakage or spillage below. Fill pipes, at least 1½" inside diameter, should run down inside the tank nearly to the bottom to lessen the production of vapors.

A suitable vent pipe for each tank should lead *outside the hull*; vents should *never* terminate in closed spaces such as the engine compartment or under the deck. Minimum inside diameter of vent pipes should be 9/16". Where a vent terminates on the hull, the outlet should be fitted with a removable flame screen to protect against flash-backs from outside sources of ignition. In boats that normally heel, such as auxiliary sailboats, it may be necessary to have dual vents with the port tank vent led to the starboard side and vice versa.

Non-metallic hose may be used as a coupling between

sections of metallic piping. The hose must be reinforced or of sufficient thickness to prevent collapse. A grounding jumper wire must be installed across the non-conducting section so as to provide a complete electrical path from the deck fitting to the fuel tank, which in turn is grounded.

A fuel level indicator, if used, should be of an approved type. If the fuel supply for an auxiliary electric plant is not drawn from the main tank, the separate tank should be installed with fillers and vents similar to those of the main tank.

Fuel lines

Fuel lines should be of seamless copper tubing, run so as to be in sight as much as possible for ease of inspection, protected from possible damage, and secured against vibration by soft non-ferrous metal clips with rounded edges. A short length of flexible tubing with suitable fittings should be used between that part of the fuel line that is secured to the hull and that part which is secured to the engine itself; this will prevent leakage or breakage as a result of vibration.

Reinforced non-metallic hose in the fuel line should be limited to the short flexible section described above, but may be used for the full distance from the tank shutoff valve to the engine if the line is fully visible and accessible for its entire length. Wherever used, non-metallic hose must be dated by the manufacturer and not be used for a period longer than that recommended by the maker.

Tube fittings should be of non-ferrous drawn or forged metal of the flared type, and tubing should be properly flared by tools designed for the purpose, preferably annealing the tube end before flaring.

A shut-off valve should be installed in the fuel line directly at the tank connection. Arrangements should be provided for ready access and operation of this valve from outside the compartment in which tanks are located, preferably from above deck. Where engine and fuel tank are separated by a distance exceeding 12 feet, an approved-type manual stop-valve should be installed at the engine end of the fuel line to stop fuel flow when servicing accessories.

Valves should be of non-ferrous metal with ground seats installed to close against the flow. Types which depend on packing to prevent leakage at the stem should not be used. For fuel, gas, and oil lines a type of diaphragm packless valve is available which is pressure-tight in any position. A YSB-listed electric fuel valve shuts off the flow of gasoline whenever the ignition switch is turned off; it can also be independently turned off in an emergency.

Fuel pumps and filters

Electric fuel pumps, where used, should be located at the engine end of fuel lines. They must be so connected as to operate only when the ignition switch is on and the engine is turning over.

A filter should be installed in the fuel line inside the engine compartment, properly supported so that its weight is not carried by the tubing. Closure of the filter must be so designed that its opening for cleaning will minimize fuel spillage. It should also be designed so that the unit can be disassembled and reassembled in dim light without undue opportunity for crossing threads, displacing gaskets

FIG. 1011 Carburetors on marine engines (other than outboards) must be equipped with a flame arrester. Out of sight beneath the updraft carburetor shown above is a drip pan for further safety. Downdraft carburetors do not need such a pan.

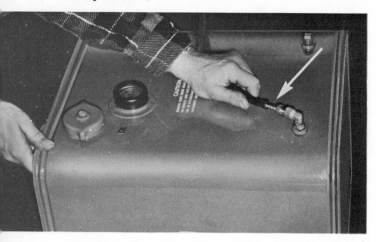

FIG. 1012 Portable gasoline tanks used with outboard motors may have a quick-disconnect fitting on the fuel line. This fitting must be designed so as to minimize leakage of gasoline when it is detached.

or seals, or assembly of parts in an improper order, resulting in seepage of fuel after reassembly. Fuel filter bowls should be highly resistant to shattering due to mechanical impact and resistant to failure from thermal shock.

Fuel systems for outboards

Fuel tanks and systems permanently installed in the hull of outboard-powered boats should be designed, constructed, and installed in accordance with the above principles. No pressurized tanks should be built into or permanently attached to hulls. A quick-disconnect coupling may be used between motor and fuel line but, when disconnected, it must automatically shut off fuel flow from the tank. Arrangements should be provided so that the operation of making and breaking the connection can be accomplished with a minimum of spillage.

Extreme caution must be exercised in the use of plastic containers for storing gasoline. These can accumulate a static electricity charge that is not drained off by grounding connections. A static electricity-generated spark could ignite vapors in the container.

Plastic containers, if used, should meet fire retardance and compatibility with fuel requirements of the AB&YC. Such containers will carry the approval of a national listing agency or a major city fire department. Do not use any other plastic container for gasoline or other flammable liquid. Any portable fuel container must be stowed on the boat in a well-ventilated place, protected from both physical damage and exposure to direct sunlight. Any leakage or vapors must drain overboard.

Every possible precaution must be taken to ensure that not even a single drop of gasoline can find its way into the bilge. Bilge ventilation is most important. It is a strict legal requirement and it is a vital safety measure; see pages 607 to 610.

Fuel systems of diesel-powered boats

Fuel systems of diesel-powered boats will generally conform to safety standards for gasoline-fueled craft, with a few exceptions as required or permitted by the nature of the fuel and characteristics of diesel engines.

Tanks for diesel fuel may be made of iron or steel as well as nickel-copper. Tanks may be painted if not galvanized externally; iron tanks must not be galvanized internally. Diesel tanks may have a sump or pocket in the bottom for collection of water but, if so, must have a positive means for removal of any accumulations from above deck. Tanks for diesel fuel may be integral with the hull.

Fuel lines for diesel oil may be of iron or steel pipe or tubing in addition to the metals approved for gasoline. A return line to carry excess fuel from the engine back to the tank will be needed.

Additional information

Many additional technical details on gasoline and diesel fuel systems for boats will be found in AB&YC Safety Standard P-2.

Underwriters Laboratories Marine Division has evaluated and accepted for listing a number of tanks, filters, valves, and related equipment by various manufacturers.

EXHAUST SYSTEMS

Exhaust lines and pipes should be installed so that they cannot scorch or ignite woodwork. Where necessary, gratings can be used to prevent gear from touching the line. Exhaust systems must be gas-tight, constructed and installed so that they can be inspected and repaired readily along their entire length. Any leaks must be rectified at once to prevent escape of exhaust gases into various compartments. *Carbon monoxide is a deadly gas.*

A "wet" exhaust system requires a continuous flow of cooling water (from the heat exchanger or the engine block) discharged through the exhaust line, entering as near the manifold as practicable. Exhaust systems of the "dry" type (no cooling water) operate at considerably higher temperatures and their use is relatively rare except on larger yachts.

An exhaust system should be run with a minimum number of bends. Where turns are necessary, long-sweep elbows or 45° ells are recommended. The exhaust system must not result in back pressure at the exhaust manifold greater than that specified by the engine manufacturer. A $1/8$" pipe tap, located not more than 6" from the exhaust-manifold outlet, should be provided for measuring back pressure.

The exhaust system should be designed to prevent undue stress on the exhaust manifold, particularly where an engine is shock-mounted. All supports, hangers, brackets, and other fittings in contact with the exhaust should be noncombustible and so constructed that high temperatures will not be transmitted to wood or other combustible materials to which fittings are secured.

The exhaust piping or tubing should have a continuous downward pitch of at least $1/2$" per foot when measured with the vessel at rest. It must be so designed and installed as to eliminate any possibility of having cooling water or sea water return to the engine manifold through the exhaust system.

Exhaust systems for sailboat engines

Exhaust systems for auxiliary sailing craft should be carefully designed to prevent sea or cooling water from running back into the engines because such engines are usually installed close to or below the water line. A riser must

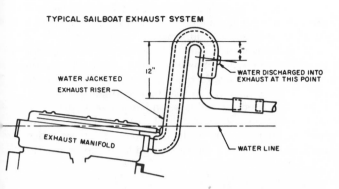

TYPICAL SAILBOAT EXHAUST SYSTEM

WATER JACKETED
EXHAUST RISER

WATER DISCHARGED INTO
EXHAUST AT THIS POINT

EXHAUST MANIFOLD

WATER LINE

FIG. 1013 The AB&YC Safety Standard for small-craft exhaust systems has special provisions for auxiliary-powered sailboats. Unusual precautions must be taken in such installations as the engine is often below the waterline and a normally-sloping exhaust line cannot be installed.

reach sufficiently high above the water line to allow a steep drop-off of at least 12"; the rest of the piping or tubing should have a downward pitch to the outlet of at least 1/2" per foot. The high point of the line should form a gooseneck, with cooling water injected aft of this point; see fig. 1015. The vertical dry section must be either adequately insulated and provided with a metallic bellows flexible section or water-jacketed. As an alternate arrangement, a water-trap silencer is recommended.

Flexible exhaust lines

Steam hose or other non-metallic material may be used for exhaust lines where greater flexibility is desired. Every flexible line of this type must be secured with adequate clamps of corrosion-resistant metal at each end. Hose used for this purpose must have a wall thickness and rigidity sufficient to prevent panting (internal separation of plies) or collapse. Full-length nonmetallic exhaust tubing may be used in wet exhaust systems providing it is water-cooled throughout its length and is not subjected to temperatures above 280° F. Tubing used for engine exhaust service should be specifically constructed for that purpose and so labeled by the manufacturer. Tubing should be installed in a manner that will not stress or crimp the inner or outer plies, or permit any local impingement of exhaust gases or cooling water.

Additional information

The AB&YC Safety Standard P-1 provides much additional information on "wet" and "dry" exhaust installations. It should be studied by persons building or rebuilding any boat equipped with an inboard engine.

ELECTRICAL SYSTEMS

The entire electrical installation should comply rigidly with the best and most modern safety practices. Requirements of marine installations are more exacting than other applications where salt- and moisture-laden atmospheres are not prevalent. Wiring and other electrical equipment should be installed correctly in the beginning and kept safe by frequent inspection.

Information on electrical systems will also be found in chapter 25 on pages 487 and 488.

The sources of electrical power for engine starting, lights, pumps, electronic gear, and other electrical accessories are usually lead-acid storage batteries kept charged by a generator or alternator integral with the main engine. Larger craft equipped with electrical cooking and air-conditioning will have a separate engine-driven generator producing AC electrical power similar to shore current. The discussion in this section will be directed to the more-common 12- and 32-volt DC electrical systems found on all boats, even though also equipped with AC power.

All direct-current electrical systems should be of the two-wire type with feed and return wires parallel throughout the system. Conductors should be twisted together where their magnetic field would affect compasses or automatic pilots. Where one side of a DC system is grounded, connections between that side and ground should be used only to maintain that side at ground potential and should not normally carry current.

Wiring diagrams

All boats should be provided with a complete wiring diagram of the electrical system as originally installed. It is recommended that the diagram be enclosed in a suitable plastic envelope and secured to an accessible panel door, preferably near the main switchboard. Diagrams should include an indication of the identification provided for each conductor.

Additions to and/or changes in electrical circuits should be drawn in on the wiring diagram without delay so that it is correct at all times.

Batteries

Storage batteries should be so located that gas generated during charging will be quickly dissipated by natural or mechanical ventilation. They should be located as high as practicable, where they are not exposed to excessive heat, extreme cold, spray, or other conditions which could impair performance or accelerate deterioration. Caution should be taken to avoid locating batteries in areas subject to accumulation of gasoline fumes and also in proximity to any electrical or electronic devices. Engine starting batteries should be located as close to the engine as practicable.

Batteries must be secure against shifting. Care also should be taken to secure a battery against vertical motion which would allow it to pound against the surface on which it is resting while cruising in rough water. Batteries should be chocked on all sides and supported at the bottom by non-absorbent insulating supports of a material that will not be affected by contact with electrolyte. These supports should allow air circulation all around. Where the hull or compartment material in the immediate vicinity of the battery is aluminum, steel, or other material readily attacked by the acid, a tray of lead, fiberglass, or other suitable material resistant to the deteriorating action of electrolyte should be provided.

Batteries should be arranged to permit ready access for inspection, testing, watering, and cleaning. A minimum of 10" clear space above the filling openings should be available.

A non-conductive, ventilated cover or other suitable means should be provided to prevent accidental shorting

FIG. 1014 Storage batteries should have a cover to protect terminals from being shorted by an accidentally dropped tool or other metal object. Such covers must be ventilated to prevent accumulation of gases during charging.

of the battery's terminals; fig. 1014.

An emergency switch capable of carrying the maximum current of the system (including starter circuits) should be provided in each ungrounded conductor as close to the battery terminal connection as practicable. This switch should be readily accessible; a switch with a remote operating handle that can be opened or closed from the bridge or other location outside the compartment containing the batteries is highly desirable.

Generators and motors

Generators, alternators, and electric motors intended for use in machinery spaces or other areas which might contain flammable or explosive vapors must be designed and constructed so as to prevent such devices from becoming a source of ignition of these vapors. These units must be of a type approved for marine service.

Generators, alternators, and electric motors must be located in accessible, adequately ventilated areas as high above the bilge as possible. They must not be located in low or pocketed positions.

Ground connections from battery to starter should be made as close to the starter as possible. It is recommended that all other ground connections to the engine be made at this same point. By making all ground connections at one point, damaging stray-current flow through the metal of the engine will be minimized.

Distribution panels and switches

Switchboards and distribution panels should be located in accessible, adequately ventilated locations, preferably outside of engine and fuel-tank compartments. They should be protected from rain and spray; where necessary, panels should be provided with a drip shield to prevent wetting of terminals or electrical components from overhead dripping.

Totally enclosed switchboards and distribution panels of the dead-front type are recommended. Metal enclosures are desirable, but wood may be used if all terminal strips,

fuse blocks, switches, etc., are mounted on non-absorbent, non-combustible, high-dielectric insulating material. It is recommended that the interior of enclosures be lined with asbestos sheet or other fire-resistant material.

All switches should have suitable electrical ratings for the particular circuits on which they are used; distribution panels should have several spare switches to take care of additional equipment that may be added later.

Switches used in fuel-tank and machinery spaces, or other hazardous locations, must be designed so as to prevent ignition of flammable or explosive vapors. Such switches must be of a type approved for marine use.

Wiring

Conductors used for general wiring throughout the boat should be approved for marine use to indicate adequate mechanical strength, moisture resistance, dielectric strength, insulation, and current-carrying capacity for the intended marine service.

The table of wire gauges on page 488, fig. 2504, is for an allowable voltage drop of 3% on a 12-volt system. For lighting and other non-critical purposes, the wire size shown there may be reduced to the gauges shown in fig. 1015 (wire gauge number varies *inversely* with conductor size). The "length" for these tables is the distance from the source to the load, one way, measured along the route followed by the wires; this is much greater than the direct distance—don't estimate; measure.

Current in Amps.	Length of Wire, in feet					
	10	15	20	30	40	50
5	14	14	14	14	14	12
10	14	14	14	12	10	10
15	14	14	12	10	8	8
20	12	12	10	8	8	6
25	10	10	10	8	6	6

FIG. 1015 Table above, extracted from AB&YC Safety Standard E-9, 1970, specifies the wire gauge to be used versus conductor length for a voltage drop of not more than 10% in a 12-volt system. This drop is satisfactory for all but the most critical electronic equipment. For such critical applications, see Fig. 2504 which provides for a drop not exceeding 3%

All wiring must be routed as high above the bilge as possible with consideration given to protection of wire and connections from physical damage. Wiring should be secured throughout its length, at intervals not exceeding 14 inches, in a manner that will not crush or cut insulation around the conductor. Non-metallic clamps are excellent; if metallic clamps are used, they must be lined with a suitable insulating material. All non-metallic material must be resistant to the effects of oil, gasoline, and water.

Unless absolutely necessary, wire splices should not be made in any circuit vital to the operation of the boat nor in the navigation light circuit. Splices, where made, should be taped to relieve all strain from the joint. If solder is used, it should be a low-temperature resin-core radio solder. Acid-core solder must *not* be used.

Terminal connections

Terminal connections should be designed and installed so as to insure a good mechanical and electrical joint without damage to conductors. Metals used for terminal studs, nuts, and washers should be corrosion-resistant and galvanically compatible with the wire and terminal lug.

Terminals should be of solderless type, preferably with ring-type ends. Solderless terminals should be attached with crimping tools specified by the manufacturer of the terminal. The holes in ring-type terminals should be of a size that will properly fit the terminal stud. Formed and soldered wire terminal connections should not be used. It is recommended that terminal lugs include a means of clamping the wire insulation for mechanical support. A short length of insulated sleeving over the wire at each terminal connection is desirable.

No more than four conductors should be secured to any one terminal stud. Where additional connections are necessary, two or more terminal studs should be used and connected together with copper jumpers or straps.

Wires terminating at switchboards, in junction boxes or fixtures, etc., should be arranged to provide a surplus length of wire sufficient to relieve all tension, allow for repairs, and permit multiple wires to be fanned at terminal studs, etc.

Electrical shock hazards

Voltage is only one factor in determining whether a shock will be fatal or only startling. Many people have received shocks from spark-plugs, where the voltage is 10,000 or more, with no more harm than a few bruised knuckles. The actual factors that determine the extent of harm are: (1) the amount of current that flows through the body, the amperage; (2) the path of the current through the body; and (3) the length of time that the current flows.

The effects of different levels of current are not exact and will vary with the individual victim and the path of current through his body. Unfortunately, there is no way of predicting in advance how much current will flow in any given situation—play safe, work only on de-energized circuits.

Additional information

Further guidance and recommendations for DC electrical systems for boats will be found in Safety Standards E-1, E-3, E-5, E-6, E-9, and E-10 issued by the American Boat & Yacht Council.

AC electrical systems

More and more boats are being wired for 115-volt AC electrical systems so that larger, home-type appliances and equipment may be used afloat. Power may be obtained from dockside connections only or from such sources plus an engine-driven generator for use while under way. From a safety viewpoint, it is important to recognize the increased hazards from this higher-voltage wiring and devices.

All component parts of a 115-volt AC system must be designed, constructed, and installed so as to perform with safety under environmental conditions of continuous exposure to vibration, mechanical shock, corrosive salt atmosphere, and high humidity. The system must provide maximum protection against electrical shock for persons on the boat, in the water in contact with the boat, or in contact with the boat and a grounded object on shore.

Appliances and fixed AC electrical equipment used on boats must be designed so that current-carrying parts of the device are effectively insulated from all exposed metal parts by a dielectric material suitable for use in damp and/or wet locations as determined by location of the item and its intended use.

Further technical specifications for AC electrical systems on boats will be found in AB&YC Safety Standard E-8. Portions of standards E-3, E-5, and E-6 are also applicable.

LIGHTNING PROTECTION

One seldom hears of a boat, power or sail, being struck by lightning, yet cases have been reported. A skipper can add to both his physical safety and his peace of mind by obtaining some basic information and taking a few precautionary actions.

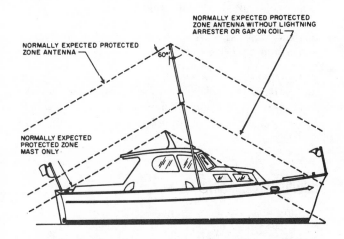

FIG. 1016 Under *certain* **conditions, a grounded radio antenna can provide a "cone of protection" from lightning strikes for a boat and its occupants. See text for details.**   (from A.B. & Y.C. Safety Standards)

Protective principles

A grounded conductor, or lightning protective mast, will generally divert to itself direct lightning strokes which might otherwise fall within a cone-shaped space, the apex of which is the top of the conductor or mast and the base a circle at the water's surface having a radius approximately twice the conductor's height. Probability of protection is considered to be 99.0% within this 60° angle as shown in fig. 1016. Probability of protection can be increased to 99.9% if mast height is raised so that the cone apex angle is reduced to 45°.

To provide an adequately grounded conductor or protective mast, the entire circuit from the masthead to the ground (water) connection should have a conductivity equivalent to a #8 gauge wire. The path to ground followed by the conductor should be essentially straight, with no sharp bends.

If there are metal objects of considerable size within a few feet of the grounding conductor, there will be a strong tendency for sparks or side flashes to jump from the grounding conductor to the metal object at the nearest point. To prevent such possibly damaging flashes, an interconnecting conductor should be provided at all likely places.

Large metallic objects within the hull or superstructure of a boat should be interconnected with the lightning protective system to prevent a dangerous rise of voltage due to a lightning flash.

Protective measures

For power boats, a radio antenna may serve as a lightning or protective mast provided it is equipped with a transmitting-type lightning arrester or means for grounding during electrical storms, and that the antenna height is sufficient to provide an adequate cone of protection for the length of the craft. Antennas with loading coils are considered to end at a point immediately *below the coil* unless the coil has a suitable gap for bypassing lightning current. This protection can be obtained *only* with an antenna of metal rod or tubing. Fiberglass whip antennas with a spirally-wound wire conductor—the type almost universally used—will *not* provide lightning protection.

Sailboats with metallic standing rigging will be adequately protected provided that all rigging is bonded together and connected to ground. A wooden mast must have a heavy metal conductor running down the mast from a short, sharp-pointed "lightning rod" at the masthead; this conductor is tied into the grounding system.

Metal objects situated wholly on a boat's exterior should be connected to the grounding conductor at their upper or nearest end. Metal objects within the boat may be connected to the lightning protective system directly or through the bonding system for underwater metal parts.

Metal objects that project through cabin tops, decks, etc., should be bonded to the nearest lightning conductor at the point where the object emerges from the boat and again at its lowest extreme end within the boat. Spotlights and other objects projecting through cabin tops should be solidly grounded regardless of the cone of protection.

A ground connection for lightning protection may consist of any metal surface, normally submerged, which has an area of at least one square foot. Propellers and metallic rudder surfaces may be used for this purpose; the radio ground plate is more than adequate. A steel hull itself constitutes a good ground connection to the water.

Protection for personnel

As the basic purpose of lightning protection is safety of personnel, the following precautions should be taken by the crew and guests.

Individuals should remain inside a closed boat as much as practicable during an electrical storm.

Persons should avoid making contact with any items connected to a lightning protective conductor, and especially in such a way as to bridge between two parts of the grounding system. For example, it is undesirable to touch either the reverse lever or spotlight control, particularly in contact with both at the same time.

No one should be in the water during a lightning storm.

Equipment for Safety

Some items of safety equipment are required by laws and Coast Guard regulations. These are generally written, however, in such broad language that additional knowledge and guidance are required for the greatest degree of safety afloat.

Additional items of equipment above legal minimums are required to receive the approval decal of the Coast Guard Auxiliary Courtesy Motorboat Examination.

Still further pieces of equipment are desirable for safety or convenience, or both. Many of these are discussed in Chapter 3 and other chapters. This chapter will supplement rather than duplicate equipment considerations covered elsewhere in the book.

LIFESAVING EQUIPMENT

As noted in Chapter 3, each boat must, by law, have a lifesaving device for each person aboard; few specific details are stated. A wise skipper has, in addition to his regular buoyant devices, several jackets of smaller size to protect children. On boats under 40 feet in length, life "jackets" are not required, but a buoyant cushion is not fully safe for a small child who might lose his grasp on the straps.

Although non-commercial boats under 40 feet may carry buoyant cushions, buoyant vests, or special-purpose buoyant devices (ski vests, racing vests, flotation jackets, etc.), the skipper who is really safety-conscious will carry an adequate number of *life jackets,* the canvas jackets with flotation material (usually kapok) sealed in plastic pouches; fig. **1017. These are clearly marked with the words "Approved for use on all vessels and motorboats." Such jackets** provide ample buoyancy and, most importantly, float the wearer in the position that will best hold his face clear of the water so that he can breathe adequately even though he may be semi-conscious or unconscious. Jackets of this type (or life rings) are required on Class 3 boats; they are actually of even greater importance on·smaller craft as statistics show that over 97% of all accidents involve boats of the smaller classes. Jackets may be bulkier and harder to stow than vests, and they don't make sitting easier as do cushions (even though these should not be sat upon), but when needed to keep you afloat until help comes, nothing else does the job half so well!

PUMPS AND BAILERS

Oddly enough, there are no federal legal requirements for a boat (if used exclusively for pleasure) to be equipped with a device of any type for removing water that leaks in or comes aboard as spray. Essentially all boats are, of course, equipped with some form of pump or bailer, but too many skippers place their *full* dependence on electrical bilge pumps, and perhaps on only one of those. Once water rises in the bilge to a level sufficient to short out the battery, there is no way to combat the further rise of water. (Incidentally, on most boats the batteries are placed low in the bilge—excellent for stability, but not for safety if the craft starts taking on water.)

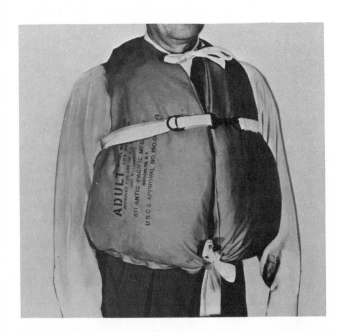

FIG. 1017 Life jackets of the type shown provide a greater measure of safety than other lifesaving devices that may be acceptable on small craft. Properly worn, they will not only provide buoyancy but will float an individual in the best position for breathing. As these are strapped to the person, he cannot lose his grasp as he could with a buoyant cushion. Two children's sizes are also available.
(Courtesy Atlantic-Pacific Mfg. Corp.)

Only the smallest boats should depend on a hand bailer or bucket. Other boats should be equipped with a hand-operated pump of generous capacity. Such an item can be either a fixed installation or a portable pump stowed where it can be quickly and easily reached when needed.

DISTRESS SIGNALING EQUIPMENT

A boat's radiotelephone is probably the most often used means of summoning assistance in an emergency. Use of the radio for this purpose is covered on pages 496-498. See also pages 87 and 88.

Without special equipment a distress signal can be made to other craft in sight by standing where one is clearly visible and slowly raising and lowering one's arms. Another visual distress signal is a fluorescent red-orange rectangular panel displayed where most visible to boats and/or aircraft. This item of safety equipment is described more fully on page 87.

Signal flares may be projected several hundred feet into the air by a special type of pistol, or to a lesser height from a pocket "tear gas" gun that resembles an old-fashioned fountain pen. The laws of several states regulate possession of these and similar explosive projectile devices; check carefully before putting one aboard, but if permissible, these are effective and desirable items of safety equipment.

There are also hand-held flares of the single- and double-ended types, the latter producing a bright flame at one end for night use and a dense smoke at the other end for day distress situations. Before using any flare, read all instructions carefully so as to avoid personal injury or aggravation of the emergency. Read carefully *before* any emergency arises, you won't have time then!

MISCELLANEOUS ITEMS OF SAFETY EQUIPMENT

There are many small items of equipment that serve to increase safety and convenience.

Every boat should be equipped with several **flashlights** and at least one battery-powered **electric lantern,** fig. 1019. If provided with an adjustable head, the beam can be directed where needed. Flashlights should be distributed so as to be quickly available in an emergency. One should be within reach of the skipper's bunk and the first mate's, too. There should also be a flashlight in the guest cabin, if any, and another on the bridge. The electric lantern should be kept in an accessible place. Batteries in all units should be checked at least monthly to be sure that they have sufficient power.

An installed searchlight of adequate intensity is desirable on medium-sized and large boats operated at night. It is useful both in routine navigation and docking, and in emergencies such as man-overboard situations or assisting another boat in distress. On smaller boats, the electric lantern can serve as a hand-held searchlight.

FIG. 1018 A night distress signal will be seen at much greater distances if projected to a height of several hundred feet. Flare pistols and related devices will do this, but in some states these items of boating safety equipment are subject to firearms laws and regulations.
(Courtesy Abercrombie & Fitch)

FIG. 1019 An electric lantern should be aboard every boat. If provided with adjustable head, it projects a stronger beam of light than most flashlights and has the added advantage of being able to be set down with the light directed where needed, thus making both hands available for working.

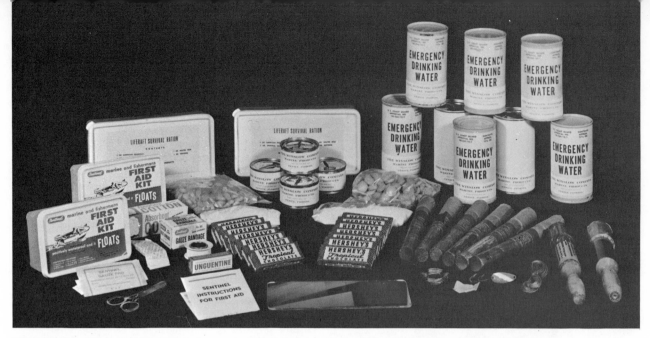

FIG. 1020 Every boat should have aboard some emergency drinking water and food. The quantity and type of these supplies will vary, of course, with the number of persons aboard and the cruising area. Prepared kits of long shelf-life food and water can be purchased, or the boat owner can assemble his own supplies. (Courtesy Winslow Company Marine Products)

Boats of medium or large size should have on board a small **hand axe** to be used in cutting lines in an emergency. The axe should be stowed on deck, where it might be needed in a hurry.

Tools and **spare parts** for the engine and major accessories can be considered parts of a boat's essential safety equipment. Personal experience and conversation with seasoned skippers will offer the best guidance to just what tools and parts should be carried aboard any particular craft. Insofar as practicable, tools should be of rust-proof metal; tools susceptible to rust or corrosion, and all spare parts, should be properly protected from adverse effects of a marine environment.

All but the smallest craft should be equipped with **emergency drinking water** and **food** supplies. The amount will vary with the number of persons normally on board. The type of food is not important—anything will do when you get hungry enough! Non-perishability over a long period is important, but it might be wise once each year to consume your emergency supplies (a shipwreck party?) *after* they have been replaced with a fresh stock. Such items can usually be purchased from marine supply stores or from Army-Navy surplus stores; food should be simple and compact, but sustaining and energy-producing.

First aid kits are essential safety items; they will be considered in more detail later in this chapter.

Navigation equipment, charts, and **ground tackle** are all items of safety equipment, but each is considered in detail elsewhere in this book, see index.

SAFETY ASPECTS OF OTHER EQUIPMENT

Several items generally found on boats are not "safety equipment" per se, but have definite aspects of safety about their design, installation, or operation that must be considered by boat owners.

Galley stoves

All boatmen seem to love to eat, especially when out on the water. Cabin boats will normally have a galley, the de-

gree of size and elaborateness varying with the design and use of the craft.

Galley stoves should be designed, manufactured, and approved for marine use. Types of fuel that are ordinarily used include alcohol, electricity, and liquified petroleum gas (LPG—normally propane or butane). Stoves fueled with kerosene, coal, wood, or canned heat (solidified alcohol) are only rarely seen now. Gasoline is *not* a safe stove fuel and should *never* be used on a boat.

Electricity is probably the safest source of heat for cooking, but an auxiliary generating plant is required to produce the large amounts of AC power required. Because of the inexpensive and simple nature of the equipment,

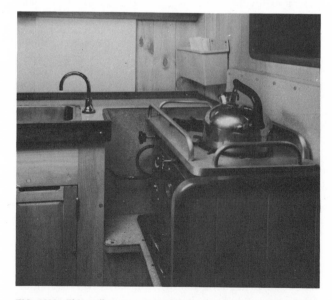

FIG. 1021 This galley stove installation shows the use of insulating board behind, beside, and below the stove to protect woodwork from unsafe high temperatures. The stove also has a drip pan beneath it, another safety feature.

alcohol stoves are widely used on boats despite their rather high fuel costs; with moderate and reasonable precautions, such installations can be quite safe. Plain water will extinguish alcohol fires.

LPG stoves are excellent for cooking, but can present a serious safety hazard unless installed and operated in accordance with strict rules—their use is prohibited on certain classes of commercial vessels.

Stoves should be permanently and securely fastened in place when in operation. Portable stoves are not recommended; if one must be used, it should be secured temporarily while in use. Adequate ventilation should be provided to prevent any excess rise in temperature of an area in which a stove is operated for extended periods of time (for the sake of safety as well as the cook's comfort!). All woodwork or other combustible material directly above or immediately surrounding a stove, including smoke stacks, must be effectively protected with non-combustible sheathing; see fig. 1021. A recommended means is the use of 1/8-inch asbestos board covered with sheet metal.

Fuel for alcohol and kerosene stoves may be supplied to the burners either by gravity or pressure systems provided fuel tanks cannot be filled while the burners are in operation except where the supply tank is remote from burners and the filling operation will not introduce a fire hazard. A removable or accessible liquid-tight metal drip pan at least 3/4" deep should be provided beneath all burners. Pressure tanks should have suitable gauges and/or relief valves.

Refrigeration

Ice is used on many boats as a means of keeping food fresh and for cooling beverages. It offers no safety hazards, but water from melting ice should be piped overboard rather than into the bilge. Fresh-water drip tends to promote dry rot. A collection sump, with pump, may be used if desired.

Mechanical refrigeration will normally be of the electric-motor-driven compressor type similar to units found in the home. Occasionally, a compressor will be belt-driven from a main engine, but this is rare.

Safety aspects of mechanical refrigeration include use of a non-toxic and non-flammable refrigerant, non-sparking motors, safety valves on high-pressure portions of the system, and general construction adequate to survive rigors of marine service.

Kerosene and bottled-gas refrigerators have a constant small open flame. This can produce an explosion hazard, and the use of such absorption-type units is presently excluded from the AB&YC Safety Standard A-6.

Heaters

Cabin heaters are sometimes used on boats in northern waters to extend the boating season or to ward off the chill of a sudden cold snap. Gasoline should never be used as a fuel and portable kerosene or alcohol heaters are not recommended. Built-in electrical heaters are safe; portable electrical heaters should be used only if secured in place while in operation.

Gas-burning heaters should be equipped with an automatic device to shut off the fuel supply if the flame is extinguished. Pilot lights should not be used. Coast Guard regulations prohibit use of LPG fuel for any purpose on certain commercial craft.

Many models of air-conditioning equipment used on boats are of the "reverse cycle" or "heat pump" type and can supply warmth rather than cooling when the former is needed. This is a thoroughly safe method of heating.

Safety in Operations

Safety should be a part of every aspect of the operation of small craft. Boat handling has been covered in Chapter 8. Safety in such operations as stranding and towing was considered in Chapter 9. Navigation and piloting—essential for safety—are discussed in Chapter 21 and other chapters. The aspects of operational safety afloat to be considered here are those that do not fall under other major headings.

FUELING PRECAUTIONS

Certain precautions must be carefully and completely observed *every* time a boat is fueled with gasoline. Step by step, these are:

Before fueling

1. Make sure that the boat is securely tied to the fueling pier. Fuel before darkness, if possible.

2. Stop engines, motors, fans, and other devices capable of producing a spark. Open the master switch if the electrical system has one. Put out all galley fires and open flames.

3. Close all ports, windows, doors, and hatches so that fumes cannot blow aboard and below.

4. Disembark all passengers and any crew members not needed for the fueling operation.

FIG. 1022 Fueling must be accomplished in a safe manner to reduce hazards of gasoline explosion and fire. Refer to the text for a 16-point checklist of actions before, during, and after fueling.

5. Prohibit all smoking on board and in the vicinity.

6. Have a filled fire extinguisher close at hand.

7. Measure the fuel in the tanks and do not order more than the tank will hold; allow for expansion.

While fueling

8. Keep nozzle or can spout in contact with the fill opening to guard against static sparks.

9. Do not spill gasoline.

10. Do not overfill. The practice of filling until fuel flows from the vents is highly dangerous.

11. For outboards, remove portable tanks from boat and fill on shore.

After fueling

12. Close fill openings.

13. Wipe up any spilled gasoline; dispose of wipe-up rags on shore.

14. Open all ports, windows, doors, and hatches; turn on bilge power exhaust blower. Ventilate boat this way *at least* five minutes—time it, don't guess.

15. Sniff low down in tank and engine compartments. *If any odor of gasoline is present, do not start engine;* continue ventilation actions until odor can no longer be detected.

16. Be prepared to cast off lines as soon as engine starts; get clear of pier quickly.

SAFETY IN LOADING

Overloading is probably the greatest cause of accidents in smaller boats and dinghies, and is even a significant factor in medium-size boats such as those of Class 2. Overloading is particularly hazardous as it is not so feared as are fires and explosions. Many a skipper, cautious in his handling of gasoline, will unknowingly load his craft far beyond safe limits. The number of seats in a boat is *not* an indication of the number of persons it can carry safely.

Determining capacity

"Loading" and "capacity" are terms primarily related to the weight of persons, fuel, gear, etc., that can be safely carried. The safe load of a boat in persons depends on many of its characteristics, such as the hull volume and dimensions; the material of which it is built, if it is an outboard hull, whether there is an effective engine well inboard of the transom notch where the engine is mounted; how heavy the engine is; and other factors.

BIA capacity plates. Many small boats manufactured before 31 October 1972 *may* carry a "capacity plate" in accordance with standards of the Boating Industry Association. These show the recommended maximum loading in terms of number of persons and in total weight (pounds) for gear, fuel, persons, and outboard motors.

USCG capacity plates. Boats under 20 feet in length—inboard, outboard, inboard-outboard, and unpowered, other than sailboats and certain special types—manufactured after 31 October 1972 *must* carry a capacity plate specified by Coast Guard regulations issued under the Federal Boat Safety Act of 1971. These capacities are computed from rather complex formulas. Plates on outboard craft show both maximum weight, in pounds, for persons (not the number of persons), and maximum total weight for motor, fuel, gear, *and persons.* Plates for inboard, inboard-out-

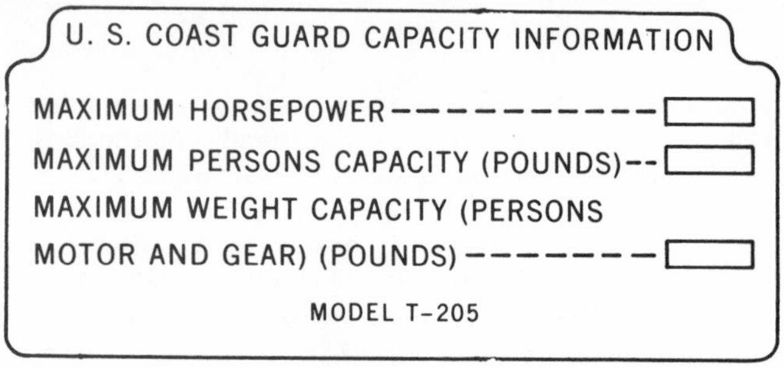

U. S. COAST GUARD CAPACITY INFORMATION

MAXIMUM HORSEPOWER — — — — — — — — ☐

MAXIMUM PERSONS CAPACITY (POUNDS)-- ☐

MAXIMUM WEIGHT CAPACITY (PERSONS

MOTOR AND GEAR) (POUNDS) — — — — — ☐

MODEL T-205

FIG. 1023 A Coast Guard required capacity plate for outboard boats. For inboards and I-Os, the horsepower limit is omitted, as is motor weight from the last line of the plate. Compliance with safety standards may be certified on this plate, or on a separate plate such as fig. 1007. Inclusion of model number or name is optional.

board, and unpowered craft show only the maximum weight for fuel, gear, and persons. A capacity plate must be displayed where it is clearly visible to the operator when he is getting the craft underway.

If there is no capacity plate on a boat, the skipper can make a rough determination for himself by applying the formulas for safe capacity in persons and weight-carrying capacity which are given on page 551.

Capacities from plates or self-determination are based on good weather conditions and should be reduced in rough waters. The presence of a capacity plate does not relieve the boatman of the responsibility for exercising sound judgment. This includes knowledge of probable future weather conditions as well as those prevailing at the start of a period of use of the boat.

Safe loading

It must always be remembered that people represent a "live" load (no pun intended); they move about and affect a boat quite differently than a "dead" or static load such as the engine or fuel tank. If the capacity of the boat is fully utilized, or the weather gets rough, distribute the load evenly, keep it low, and don't make abrupt changes in its distribution. Any shifting of human or other weights should be done only after stopping or slowing the boat so that the change can be made safely.

Horsepower capacity

A second aspect of the capacity of an outboard boat is the maximum horsepower motor that can be *safely* put on it. This is exceeded perhaps as often as the weight-carrying capacity. The safe maximum horsepower will also be included on both the older BIA and the newer USCG regulation capacity plates. If a boat does not have such a plate, the maximum horsepower can be determined from the tables and graphs on pages 554 and 555.

The maximum horsepower that is safe need not be used; most boats will give satisfactory, and more economical, service with motors of less horsepower. A larger engine does not always mean more speed. If the horsepower of the engine is doubled, it does not mean that boat speed will be doubled. It does mean, however, that because of the increased weight of the engine, fuel and accessories it will require, the number of persons that can be safely carried will be significantly reduced.

Boarding a boat

There is a safe way to step aboard a small boat—outboard or dinghy—and an unsafe way. In boarding from a pier, step into the boat as near to the center as possible, keeping body weight low. If you're boarding from a beach, come in over the bow. Keep lines tight or have someone steady the boat.

Never jump into a boat or step on the gunwale (edge of the hull). If you have a motor or other gear to take aboard, pile it on the pier so that you can easily reach it from the center of the boat. Better still, have someone hand it to you after you're aboard.

SAFETY IN THE WATER

Anyone who goes boating regularly should know how to care for himself in the water. Fortunately, most boatmen and their families do know "how to swim," but this is often limited to taking a few strokes in a calm, relatively warm pool, with safety and rest only a few feet away. More attention should be given to staying afloat under adverse conditions of water temperature, waves, etc. Seldom is it necessary, or even desirable, to "swim" any distance; the problem is that of remaining afloat until help arrives. The skipper and crew should all have instructions in "drownproofing."

Safety *in* the water can well start with swimming and/or lifesaving class at the local "Y" or community recreation center. Local chapters of the American Red Cross also give instruction in these subjects.

Lifesaving devices

A person in the water following a boating accident should, of course, have a life jacket or buoyant cushion. It is of extreme importance that these devices be worn or used properly. Buoyant cushions are far from the best flotation device, but are widely used because of their convenience and low cost. Buoyant cushions are *not* intended to be worn. The straps on a buoyant cushion are put there primarily for holding-on purposes and also to aid in throwing the device. Because they must be grasped, cushions are

not suitable for small children or injured persons, and are not desirable for non-swimmers. Cushions should never be worn on a person's back since this tends to force his face down in the water.

As mentioned earlier in this chapter, the lifesaving device providing the greatest safety is the canvas jacket with flotation material in sealed plastic pouches. But the real potential of this most important safety item will be realized *only* if several conditions are met. Life preservers should be stored in several locations about the boat so that fire or other disaster cannot cut you off from all of them, and they must be stowed so as to be easily and quickly accessible. Everyone on board, including guests who may be aboard for only a few hours, *must* know where the life preservers are stowed. The skipper and regular crew must have tried them on and must be able to get into them quickly even in the dark (practice wearing a blindfold). Most importantly, the skipper must not delay in ordering everyone into life preservers in advance of their need if the emergency is of the type that builds up rather than striking suddenly without warning. It is far better to put them on, as bulky and uncomfortable as they may be, when trouble first threatens than it is to wait until near-panic develops. At night, anyone on deck should routinely wear a life jacket; non-swimmers, young children, and persons physically handicapped should wear one at all times—a person with a cast on an arm or leg goes down like a rock without added buoyancy.

The wise skipper never carries non-approved, damaged, or condemned lifesaving devices as "extra"—someone might grab one of them in an emergency.

Swimming tips

Even with the best of lifesaving equipment aboard, a boatman may find himself in the water without the aid of a buoyant device. If the boat remains afloat or awash, *stay with it.* Search vessels and aircraft can spot a boat or its

FIG. 1024 Swimming is a fine sport and an excellent capability to have for anyone who goes boating. Every skipper and his crew should know how to stay afloat and swim moderate distances. Take lessons at your local "Y" or Red Cross if you do not have this most desirable ability.

wreckage far easier than an individual whose head only is above water.

A swimmer may find temporary relief from fatigue by floating or by varying his style of swimming. Cold or tired muscles are susceptible to cramps. A leg cramp can often be overcome by moving your knees up toward your chest so that you can massage the affected area. Save your breath as much as possible; call for help only when there is someone definitely close enough to hear you.

PRE-DEPARTURE SAFETY

A worthwhile degree of increased safety afloat can be achieved if certain actions are taken routinely before departing on a short cruise. If it is to be an extended cruise of days or weeks, most of these items should be repeated each day.

Final weather check

Few, if any, boats are of such size for the waters on which they are operated that no heed need be given to possible worsening of weather conditions before return to the home berth or reaching the next port. The wise skipper makes a final weather check just as close as possible to his departure time so as to have the latest weather report of current conditions and most up-to-date forecast. He learns the time of best weather broadcasts, radio and TV, in his home area (such broadcasts vary widely in their scope and suitability for boating); he knows the telephone numbers of agencies that he can call for last-minute information. When away from his home area, he finds on arrival at each overnight stop how he can get early. morning forecasts before his departure.

The Coastal Warning Facilities Charts published each year in early summer by the Weather Bureau (see pages 264 and 265) provide information on major radio and TV weather broadcasts as well as the location of day and night storm warning displays. The Weather Bureau also is steadily expanding the number of VHF-FM radio transmitters that broadcast continuous weather information on 162.55 Mc/s.

Pre-departure check list

Each skipper should prepare his own pre-departure checklist *and use it.* The following items are of general applicability; all may not be needed, and others certainly will have to be added for your own boating.

1. All safety equipment is aboard, accessible, and in good working condition, including one Coast Guard-approved life-saving device for each person embarked.

2. The bilge has been checked for fuel fumes and water. Ventilate or pump out as necessary.

3. Horn and all navigation lights operate satisfactorily.

4. All loose gear is stowed securely. Dock lines and fenders should be stowed immediately after getting under way.

5. All guests aboard have been properly instructed in safety and operational matters, both do's and don'ts.

6. Engine oil levels have been checked, both crankcase and reverse/reduction gears; water level has been checked in closed cooling systems. After starting engines, check overboard flow of cooling water.

7. Fuel tanks have been checked for quantity of gasoline or diesel fuel. Know your tank capacity and fuel consumption at various RPMs, thus knowing your cruising radius.

FIG. 1025 Although boating is generally a leisure-time activity, a skipper often leaves his pier or mooring in a hurry. A "pre-departure checklist" will ensure that no essential preparatory step has been left undone. This is especially important for safety when running single-handed and the skipper cannot leave the helm once underway.

FIG. 1026 A "Float Plan" is a handy means of leaving behind on shore essential information when you go out fishing or for a cruise. Should you become overdue and a search must be made, much valuable time may be saved. Be sure, however, to report in when you return so as to avoid needless concern and wasted action.

Make sure there is enough fuel aboard for your anticipated cruising, plus an adequate reserve if you must change your plans for weather or other reasons.

8. There is a second person on board capable of taking over from the skipper should he become disabled or excessively fatigued.

Float plan

Before departing on a cruise, the skipper should advise a responsible relative or friend as to where he intends to cruise and when he expects to make port again; make sure that this person has a good description of the boat. Keep him advised of any changes in your cruise plans. By doing these things, this person will be able to tell the Coast Guard where to search and what type of boat to look for if you are overdue. Be sure to advise this relative or friend when you return so as to prevent any false alarms about your safety.

An excellent means of accomplishing the foregoing is through use of "Float Plan" forms made available by the Marine Office of America, a leading insurer of boats. These forms, fig. 1026, provide a simple and convenient way of filing the necessary information. A pad of forms may be obtained by writing to 123 William Street, New York, N. Y. 10038, or from a local agent of the company.

SAFETY IN WATER SKIING

Water skiing has become an ever more popular sport and its spread brings with it new problems in safety afloat. The following guides should do much to reduce hazards.

1. Allow no one who is not qualified as a basic swimmer to engage in water skiing. A ski belt or vest is intended to keep a stunned or unconscious skier afloat.

2. Water ski *only* in safe areas, out of channels and away from other craft. Some bodies of water will have areas designated for this sport with skiing prohibited elsewhere.

3. Install a wide-angle rear-view mirror or take along a second person to act as lookout. This will permit watching the skier *and* the waters ahead. Some state laws require this mirror or a second person in the boat to assist the operator, or both; check before starting to ski.

4. Make sure that the skier is wearing a proper lifesaving device.

5. If the skier falls, approach him from the lee side; stop your motor before starting to take him aboard.

6. In taking the skier on board, be careful not to swamp the boat. For smaller craft, it is usually safer to take a person aboard at the stern.

Skiing signals

The following set of signals is recommended by the American Water Ski Association; see fig. 1027. Make sure that the skier, boat operator, and safety observer all know and understand the signals.

Faster—palm of one hand pointing upward.

Slower—palm pointing downward.

Speed O.K.—arm upraised with thumb and finger joined to form a circle.

Right Turn—arm outstretched pointing to the right.

Left Turn—arm outstretched pointing to the left.

Return to Drop-off Area—arm at 45° from body pointing down to water and swinging.

Cut Motor—finger drawn across throat.

Stop—hand up, palm forward—policeman style.

Skier O.K. After Fall—hands clenched together overhead.

Pick Me Up or **Fallen Skier, Watch Out**—one ski extended vertically out of water.

FASTER SLOWER

SPEED O.K. RIGHT TURN

LEFT TURN BACK TO DROP-OFF AREA

CUT MOTOR STOP

SKIER O.K. AFTER FALL PICK ME UP OR FALLEN SKIER — WATCH OUT

FIG. 1027 This simple set of hand signals will allow adequate communication from the skier to the operator or observer on the towing craft. They must all be thoroughly familiar with the full set of signals if maximum safety is to be achieved.
(from the USCG Recreational Boating Guide)

Maintenance for Safety

Safety afloat is achieved, as we have seen in this chapter, by good design, sound construction, proper equipment, and sensible operating practices. The remaining element is continued maintenance for safety. Continual attention is needed for some of the material aspects of safety; for others, periodic checks at weekly, monthly, or annual intervals is sufficient. The important thing is that these checks of safety equipment be made *regularly* when needed.

Keep your boat clean

Cleanliness aboard a boat is an important aspect of safety. Accumulations of dirt, sawdust, wood chips, and trash in the bilge will soak up oil and fuel drippings and become a fire hazard. Such accumulations may also stop up limber holes and clog bilge pumps. Keep your bilge absolutely free of dirt and trash; check frequently and clean out as often as needed.

LIFESAVING EQUIPMENT

Lifesaving equipment usually requires no maintenance, but such items should be carefully inspected at the beginning of each boating season and again near its mid-point. These devices are not permanent; they do slowly wear out. Check for cut or torn fabric, broken stitches, and other signs of deterioration. **Do not delay in replacing below-par lifesaving devices;** attempt repairs *only* where *full* effectiveness can be restored. In case of doubt, ask the Coast Guard.

FIRE EXTINGUISHERS

Portable fire extinguishers and installed systems should be checked at least annually; the best time is at the beginning of the year's activities afloat and again at mid-season if required.

Dry chemical extinguishers

Pressurized dry chemical extinguishers are widely used on boats. These will have a gauge that should be checked every six months for an indication of adequate pressure—needle in center or green area of scale. Do not, however, merely read the gauge; tap it lightly to make sure that it is not stuck at a safe indication. If it drops to a lower reading, take the extinguisher to a service shop for recharging. Even if the gauge reads O.K., take the unit out of its bracket and shake it a bit to loosen the dry chemical inside to keep it from settling and hardening. Any areas on the exterior of the cylinder showing rust should be cleaned and repainted.

CO2 extinguishers

Carbon dioxide extinguishers must be checked annually by weight. Any seals on the valve trigger must be unbroken. Portable units and built-in systems have a weight stamped at the valve. If the *total* weight is down by 10% or more of the *net* weight of the contents, the cylinder must be recharged. Weighing is normally the only check for CO_2 fire extinguishers, but it must be done accurately. Portable units can be checked by the skipper if he has suitable scales. Built-in systems are best checked by a professional serviceman with his special knowledge and equipment.

CO2 cylinders should also have verified the date on which the cylinder was last hydrostatically pressure-tested. This should be done every 12 years if the cylinder is not discharged. If the extinguisher is used, it must be pressure-tested if this has not been done within the preceding five years. If a used CO2 extinguisher is purchased, it should be discharged, hydrostatically tested, and recharged before it is installed aboard. Remember that the pressure confined in these cylinders is tremendous, and if the cylinder has been damaged (through rust or corrosion), it is just like having a time bomb aboard, not knowing when it is set to go off!

Carbon dioxide extinguishers should not be installed where bilge or rain water will collect and cause rust. Any exposed metal should be painted at each annual inspection If a cylinder becomes pitted from rust, have it hydrostatically tested for safety. Replace any damaged hoses or horns on this type of extinguisher.

Foam-type extinguishers

Foam-type fire extinguishers are acceptable on boats, but are seldom actually installed because they are messy in use and need annual recharging. If you do have one, it must be completely discharged and recharged each year. There is no other method of checking it.

Periodic discharges

It is a good policy to discharge a fire extinguisher periodically even though it is not needed for fighting a fire. An effective way of doing this would be to discharge one of the portable units each year on a regular rotation basis. This should be done in the presence of the whole crew and preferably in the form of a drill, putting out an actual small fire—off the boat, of course—in a metal pan or tub. Probably 99% or more of all persons who go boating have never discharged a fire extinguisher, let alone used one to put out an actual fire! There is no time to read the instructions carefully and practice after a real fire has started on the boat.

A word of warning with respect to CO2 extinguishers—*never* unscrew the hose from the cylinder and then discharge it openly. This would have the same effect as trying to hang onto a rocket. A strong, heavy man would have trouble in hanging onto the cylinder, and if it were to get loose, it could cause a great deal of trouble.

Make sure that when fire extinguishers are removed for testing or practice discharge they are serviced by a competent shop and reinstalled *as soon as possible*. Sitting empty in the basement or garage at home or in the trunk of your car, an extinguisher cannot protect your boat. It is also wise not to denude your boat of fire protection by removing all extinguishers at the same time for servicing; do a half or a third at a time.

Log entries

An entry should be made in the boat's log of all inspections, tests, and servicing of fire extinguishers. This will help keep these essential checks from being overlooked and may prove valuable in the event of insurance surveys or claims.

ENGINE AND FUEL SYSTEM

Frequent safety checks should be made of the engine and fuel system for cleanliness and leaks. Any drippings of oil or grease should be kept wiped up and stopped as soon as possible. Immediate action must be taken in the case of any gasoline leaks—do not use the boat and disconnect the leads from the battery (with all loads turned off so that no spark will jump) in order that the engine cannot be started.

Annually, the entire fuel system should be checked inch by inch, including fuel lines in areas not normally visible. Look for any evidence of weepage of fuel or external corrosion of the lines. If any suspicious joints or lengths of tubing are found, it would be well to call in a qualified mechanic without delay.

ELECTRICAL SYSTEMS

A thorough annual inspection should be made of a boat's electrical system, including all wiring in areas not normally visible. This should be done by a person qualified to evaluate what he finds—the skipper if he has the necessary knowledge and experience, or an outside expert if needed. A search should be made for any cut or chafed insulation, corrosion at connections, excessive sag or strain on conductors, and other visible signs of deterioration. A leakage test should be made by opening each circuit at the main distribution panel and measuring current flow when all loads are turned off. Ideally there should be no current flow; current of more than a few milliamperes indicates electrical "leakage" that should be traced down and corrected without delay.

Bonding systems

If all through-hull fittings, struts, shafts, etc., are electrically connected by an internal bonding system, this wiring should be checked annually. Especially careful checks should be made where connections are made to the fitting or other metal part; connections in the bilge are subject to corrosion and development of poor contacts with high electrical resistance.

The skipper can make a visual check of the bonding system, but an electrical expert with specialized equipment is needed for a thorough evaluation. Should any signs of corrosion at points of connection of bonding wires to through-hull fittings be noted, a complete electrical test is recommended.

With respect to possible electrolysis damage, a bonding system with one or more poor connections is worse than no system at all. Electrolysis can and does cause weakening of through-hull fittings, bolts on struts and rudder posts, etc., that could result in serious safety hazards.

HULL SAFETY MAINTENANCE

Boats that are kept in the water will be hauled out periodically for bottom cleaning and repainting. This occasion should not be overlooked as an opportunity for a *safety* inspection of hull and fittings below the waterline.

Hull planking should be carefully checked for physical damage from having struck floating or fixed objects, and for any general deterioration from age. In general, it is best to call upon the services of an expert if any suspicious areas are found.

Through-hull fittings

An inspection should be made each time the boat is hauled to see that through-hull fittings and their seacocks are in good condition. This check should include fastenings susceptible to damage from electrolytic action.

Underwater components

Underwater fittings should get an annual inspection. This includes such parts as shafts, propellers, rudders, struts, stuffing boxes, and metal skegs. Stuffing boxes should be repacked as often as necessary to keep them from leaking excessively, shafting checked for alignment and excessive wear at strut bearings, and propellers examined to see if they need truing up.

FOLLOW-UP OF INSPECTIONS

Nothing is gained if prompt and thorough follow-up actions are not taken on findings of periodic safety inspections. *Maintenance related to the safety of the craft and those aboard must not be delayed. Do not operate a boat that has a known safety defect.*

First Aid Afloat

No one who is not educated and properly qualified to practice medicine should attempt to act as a doctor. There are, however, many instances where availability of a first aid kit, some knowledge on the part of the boatman, and a ready reference book have materially eased pain or even saved the life of a sick or injured person on a boat. All skippers should prepare themselves and their craft to render emergency first aid, doing no more than is absolutely necessary while getting the victim to a doctor or hospital as rapidly as possible.

FIRST AID KITS

There are many published guides to the proper contents of a first aid kit. Probably each of these has merit, and the list that follows can, and should, be modified for the size of boat, the number of persons aboard, the length of an average cruise, the area to be cruised, and the hazards likely to be encountered.

The first aid kit must be accessible and each person aboard should be made aware of its location.

Basic first aid materials

There are certain basic first aid materials that should be carried aboard all classes of boats. Bandages should be ready for instant use—each dressing individually wrapped, a complete dressing in itself. Each should be sterilized and designed to provide protection against infection and contamination.

Antiseptic liquids are preferably packaged so that the solution stays at its original strength until used. This type of packaging is available as a swab that contains a sealed ampoule in a sleeve of multi-layered cardboard; when the ampoule is broken there is no chance for the user to be

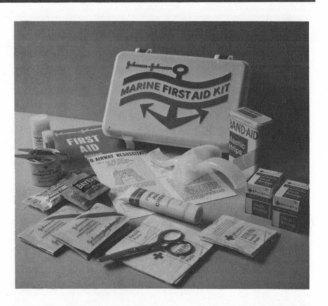

FIG. 1028   All boats should have on board adequate first aid equipment, supplies, and instructions. Kits may be either home-assembled or bought ready-made. See text for recommended items to be included. Skippers should also consider taking a standard first-aid course of instruction.

cut by glass. A close-packed cotton tip saturates instantly and then is applied to the wound area. There is no wastage, spillage, or deterioration.

Basic first aid materials should also contain burn treatment compounds to take care of sunburn or burns caused by other hazards. Scissors have multiple uses. Forceps, to remove splinters, should be blunt-end, to preclude possi-

Artificial Respiration

Every boatman should have a working knowledge of the principles of artificial respiration. When the need for it arises, there is no time to search for instructions nor to study each step while, at the same time, attempting to apply the treatment. A boatman who has familiarized himself in advance with one of the accepted methods is more likely to work with calm assurance, saving precious minutes that could mean the difference between success and failure.

Through the courtesy of The American National Red Cross, we reproduce below the simplified illustrated methods they advocate. In recent years the mouth-to-mouth method, illustrated in steps 1 to 5, has come into widespread use. Recognizing, however, that some rescuers cannot or will not apply this method, the Red Cross includes instructions for the older manual chest pressure—arm lift (Silvester) and back pressure—arm lift (Holger Nielsen) methods. Study carefully the additional instructions at the bottom of the page applicable to all methods.

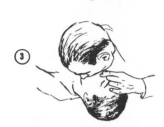
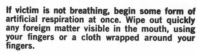

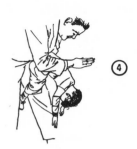

If victim is not breathing, begin some form of artificial respiration at once. Wipe out quickly any foreign matter visible in the mouth, using your fingers or a cloth wrapped around your fingers.

MOUTH-TO-MOUTH (MOUTH-TO-NOSE) METHOD

Tilt victim's head back. (Fig. 1). Pull or push the jaw into a jutting-out position. (Fig. 2).

If victim is a small child, place your mouth tightly over his mouth and nose and blow gently into his lungs about 20 times a minute. If victim is an adult (see Fig. 3), cover the mouth with your mouth, pinch his nostrils shut, and blow vigorously about 12 times a minute.

If unable to get air into lungs of victim, and if head and jaw positions are correct, suspect foreign matter in throat. To remove it, suspend a small child momentarily by the ankles or place child in position shown in Fig. 4, and slap sharply between shoulder blades.

If the victim is adult, place in position shown in Fig. 5, and use same procedure.

MANUAL METHODS OF ARTIFICIAL RESPIRATION

Rescuers who cannot, or will not, use mouth-to-mouth or mouth-to-nose technique should use a manual method.

THE CHEST PRESSURE-ARM LIFT (SILVESTER) METHOD

Place the victim in a face-up position and put something under his shoulders to raise them and allow the head to drop backward.

Kneel at the victim's head, grasp his wrists, cross them, and press them over the lower chest (Fig. 6). This should cause air to flow out.

Immediately release this pressure and pull the arms outward and upward over his head and backward as far as possible (Fig. 7). This should cause air to rush in.

Repeat this cycle about 12 times per minute, checking the mouth frequently for obstructions.

If a second rescuer is available, have him hold the victim's head so that the jaw is jutting out (Fig. 8). The helper should be alert to detect the presence of any stomach contents in the mouth and keep the mouth as clean as possible at all times.

THE BACK PRESSURE-ARM LIFT (HOLGER NIELSEN) METHOD

Place the victim face-down, bend his elbows and place his hands one upon the other, turn his head slightly to one side and extend it as far as possible, making sure that the chin is jutting out. Kneel at the head of the victim. Place your hands on the flat of the victim's back so that the palms lie just below an imaginary line running between the armpits (Fig. 9).

Rock forward until the arms are approximately vertical and allow the weight of the upper part of your body to exert steady, even pressure downward upon the hands (Fig. 10).

Immediately draw his arms upward and toward you, applying enough lift to feel resistance and tension at his shoulders (Fig. 11). Then lower the arms to the ground. Repeat this cycle about 12 times per minute, checking the mouth frequently for obstruction.

If a second rescuer is available, have him hold the victim's head so that the jaw continues to jut out (Fig. 12). The helper should be alert to detect any stomach contents in the mouth and keep the mouth as clean as possible at all times.

RELATED INFORMATION FOR ALL METHODS

If vomiting occurs, quickly turn the victim on his side, wipe out the mouth, and then reposition him.

When a victim is revived, keep him as quiet as possible until he is breathing regularly. Keep him from becoming chilled and otherwise treat him for shock. Continue artificial respiration until the victim begins to breathe for himself or a physician pronounces him dead or he appears to be dead beyond any doubt.

Because respiratory and other disturbances may develop as an aftermath, a doctor's care is necessary during the recovery period.

bility of doing further injury by probing, which is *not* a first aid measure.

Pre-packed first aid kits, available at most drug stores and marine supply stores, are generally acceptable, but their contents should be checked against recommendations that follow. Consideration should be given to separate purchase of any significant shortages; such items should be stored in or near the kit.

The container

The container for a first aid kit for a boat should not be made of a metal that could rust, nor of cardboard that could soak up moisture. A plastic box such as is often used to hold fishing tackle or tools is a good choice. It should close securely and be moisture-tight. It should *never* be locked, although it may be sealed with tape. Keep it on a high shelf out of the reach of small children. The kit may be lightly secured in place for safety in rough weather, but it must be portable and capable of being quickly unfastened and taken to the scene of an emergency.

Contents (instruments)

First aid kits should contain both simple instruments and consumable supplies. In the first category, the following are recommended:

Scissors—small and sharp; if there is room for two pairs, one should be of the blunt-end surgical type. Also a packet of single-edge razor blades.

Tweezers—small, pointed; tips must meet exactly to pick up small objects.

Safety pins—assorted sizes.

Thermometer—inexpensive oral-rectal type, in case.

Tourniquet—use only for *major* bleeding that cannot be controlled by compresses; follow instructions *exactly*.

Eye-washing cup—small, metal.

Cross Venti-breather—resuscitation device for drowned or asphyxiated person; aids in mouth-to-mouth resuscitation; follow directions on box.

Hot-water bottle and **ice bag**—these items, or a single unit that will serve both purposes, can do much to ease pain. Use with caution, following instructions in the first aid manual or medical advice book; improper use can aggravate conditions, sometimes seriously.

Contents (supplies)

The first aid kit should contain approximately the following types, sizes, and quantities of consumable supplies. Within reasonable limits, substitutions can be made to reflect local availabilities, personal preferences, etc.

Bandages—1", 2", and 4" sterile gauze squares, individually wrapped. Bandage rolls, 1" and 2". Band-aids (or equivalents) in assorted sizes, plus "butterfly closures." A minimum of one unit of each item, more on larger craft with greater number of persons aboard.

Triangular bandage—40" for use as sling or major compress.

Elastic bandage—3" width for sprains or splints.

Adhesive tape—Waterproof, 1" and 2" by 5 or 10 yards.

Absorbent cotton—standard size roll, for cleaning wounds, padding, etc.

Applicators—cotton-tipped individual swabs (Q-tips or equivalent) for applying antiseptics, removing foreign objects from cuts, eyes, ears.

Antiseptic liquid—Tincture of iodine of merthiolate; or zephiran chloride, aqueous solution, 1:1,000. Antiseptic may be in bottle, but preferably in form of individual crushable ampoule applicators. Also a 4 oz. or larger bottle of antiseptic (70% alcohol) solution, or Phisophex solution.

White petroleum jelly—small jar, or preferably tube; plain, not carbolated; for small burns, dressings. An antiseptic burn cream may be substituted. This may be supplemented by a tube or bottle of sunburn remedy and a package of sterile petroleum-jelly-saturated gauze squares.

Antiseptic ointment—1 oz. tube of Bacitracin or Polysporin, or as recommended by your physician (prescription required); for general cuts, abrasions, and infections of the skin.

Nupercainal ointment—1 oz. tube; for local anesthetic purposes—apply to raw surface before cleaning or if painful. Calamine lotion is good for relief from itching.

Pain killer—Aspirin or related compound for ordinary pain. Also Darvon Compound, Codeine, or Demerol tablets or capsules for more severe pain (prescription required).

Sleeping pills—Seconal or equivalent as prescribed by your physician; use with caution as directed. If sleeplessness is related to pain, also give aspirin or Darvon Compound.

Antibiotics—Use *only* if there will be a delay in reaching a doctor and infection appears serious. Use Achroymcin, Eryothromycin, or similar drug as prescribed by your doctor.

Ophthalmic (eye) ointment—small tube of butyn sulphate with metaphen. If necessary to flush out eye, use sterile solution of 1 teaspoon of salt in 1 pint of water; do *not* use sea water.

Antihistamine—Pyrabenzamine tablets or as prescribed by your physician; use for allergies and allergic reactions to stings and insect bites. Also an antihistamine ointment.

Ammonia inhalants—crushable ampoules; for relief of symptoms of faintness or dizziness.

Seasickness remedy—Dramamine, Marezine, Bonamine, or Bonine tablets; may also be obtained in suppository form. Prescription required for all except Bonine. These should be taken before embarking; usually not effective after vomiting starts.

Anti-acid preparation—liquid or tablet, or both, for heartburn and indigestion.

Laxative—one or two forms for variations in personal preferences; Milk of Magnesia is excellent. Also Fleets disposable enemas are desirable items to have an board.

Anti-diarrhea drug—3 oz. bottle of Paregoric (prescription required) or 8 oz. bottle of Kaopectate.

First aid manual

A compact first aid manual should be packed in the top of the first aid kit. A larger medical-adviser and first aid book may be carried in a book shelf, but there should always be a small booklet of instructions in or immediately adjacent to the container of instruments and supplies.

First aid manuals can be obtained from the American Red Cross and other safety agencies. Books relating specifically to medical problems afloat and their management can be obtained through book stores and at many marine supply stores.

Replenishment

A first aid kit missing some items does not provide a full measure of safety afloat. As supplies are used, they should be replenished promptly. Further, some drugs do not last indefinitely. They may lose their strength, become unstable and toxic, or evaporate to increased concentrations that could be harmful. Ask your physician about the safe shelf-life of drugs prescribed by him and other supplies carried in your first aid kit. Replace questionably-old supplies whether used or not.

If instruments, or the first aid manual, become lost or damaged, they, too, should be replaced at the earliest opportunity.

Medicine cabinet

Most cruisers have medicine cabinets in the head where additional first-aid supplies may be found. A word of caution should be sounded here—this cabinet should supplement rather than replace the first-aid kits as outlined above because its contents are not portable to the scene of the emergency. It should contain the items which normally are stocked in a medicine cabinet at home such as aspirin, upset stomach remedies, etc.

ADMINISTERING FIRST AID

It would be highly impractical to attempt the instruction of first aid in the few paragraphs that can be devoted to that topic in this book. It is the skipper's responsibility to his passengers and crew to acquaint himself with the proper first-aid procedures. This can be done through classes given by each Chapter of the American Red Cross in a standard first-aid course. It should be remembered that when you are aboard your boat and at sea, you are out of immediate touch with professional medical attention and thus advance preparedness is necessary.

Rule one. Always take first aid to the victim, not the victim to the first aid. You may well aggravate an injury by attempting to move an accident victim. You will add to a sick person's discomfort by requiring him to move about. Limit movement of the affected individual to that absolutely necessary to get him clear of a hazardous area.

Rule two. When giving first aid, take your time. Usually there is more damage done by the well-meaning amateur than was ever caused by the actual injury. Remember, there are only three instances when speed in giving first aid is required: (1) when the victim has stopped breathing; (2) when there is arterial bleeding; and (3) when the victim has been bitten by a poisonous snake. The measures required in these instances are taught in the standard Red Cross first aid course available locally; get a group of your fellow boatmen together and attend one soon.

It should be noted that we have eliminated splints from the first-aid kit. The average first-aider is not qualified to set a broken limb; it is much safer to place the limb in pillows or blankets, tying them securely around the fractured member so that no further damage will be done. And always remember that first-aid should stop at first aid . . . which is administering aid and comfort to avert further complications until professional medical attention can be obtained.

Radio advice

In many emergency situations, a call to the Coast Guard can bring medical advice for treatment of serious injuries or illnesses. Initial contact should be made on 2182 kc/s, but it is most desirable that the boat be capable of shifting to a Coast Guard working frequency such as 2670 kc/s. On VHF-FM, the initial contact should be on 156.8 Mc/s (Channel 16).

Basic Guides to Boating Safety

1. Carry proper equipment—know how to use it.
2. Maintain boat and equipment in top condition.
3. Know and obey the Rules of the Road afloat.
4. Operate with care, courtesy, and common sense.
5. Always keep your boat under complete control.
6. Watch posted speeds; slow down in anchorages.
7. Under no circumstances, overload your boat.
8. See that life-saving equipment is accessible.
9. Check local weather reports before departure.
10. Inspect hull, engine, and all gear frequently.
11. Keep bilges clean, electrical contacts tight.
12. Guard rigidly against any fuel system leakage.
13. Have fire extinguishers instantly available.
14. Take maximum precautions when taking on fuel.
15. Be sure to allow adequate scope when anchoring.
16. Request a USCG Auxiliary courtesy examination.
17. Enroll in a US Power Squadrons piloting class.

CHAPTER 11
MARLINESPIKE SEAMANSHIP

The Selection and Care of Rope—

Knots, Bends,

Hitches and Splices—

Blocks and Tackles—

The Bosun's Locker—

FIG. 1101 Running rigging on a windjammer. Sails are power on wind-ships; their rigging is as important as the engines of motorboats.

Cordage

Earlier editions of Piloting, Seamanship and Small Boat Handling, before the coming of many types of synthetic cordage, were much concerned with the prevention of rot, which is one of the two worst enemies of natural or vegetable fiber rope. The other is abuse. Abuse rather than proper use, today, is probably the cause of most cordage failure.

In Table 11-1 you will note the variation in weight and strength—size being equal—between ropes made of different fibers or fiber combinations. Manufacturers compare rope of different fibers, or different constructions of the same fiber, by calculating "breaking length." This means the length of rope that would break from its own weight if it were hung on a sky hook. For instance, the "breaking length" of nylon is approximately 100,000 vs. manila at approximately 32,000. The strength of the fiber, the unit weight of the fiber and the rope construction all enter into breaking strength and breaking length.

It would appear that ropes could be substituted on the

215

basis of strength alone. NOT SO!, except perhaps in some limited applications. A *working* line must have other attributes beyond strength alone. For instance, abrasion resistance; a small line presents less surface area over which to distribute the surface wear. Notice the proportion of cross section area the same size cut or nick makes in two lines of different diameters which might be of the same strength. (Fig. 1102)

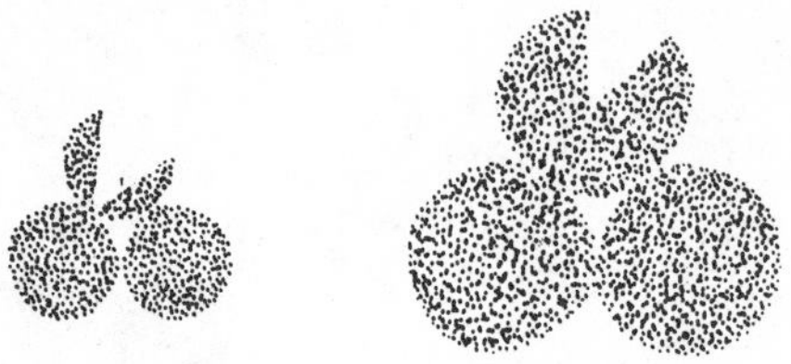

FIG. 1102 Relative effect on strength of cuts or nicks in rope of different diameter.

Perhaps as important in size selection, even for large hawsers for ships and tugs, is handling convenience. On a small sailboat a *Dacron 3/16" diameter sheet might be strong enough but it would not be easy to hold or grasp. Therefore, a 3/8" main sheet and 5/16" jib sheets are about the smallest that can be handled except in very light wind.

Another factor in the surface area is that twisted rope has "crowns" which reduce this area and abrade more rapidly; as contrasted to double braided rope which essentially is round and presents some 30% greater surface area to distribute the wear. Double braid also provides a visible safety check, because severe abraiding of the cover can be spotted while there is still more than 50% of the strength left in the line from the inner core.

SELECTION OF SIZE

Now, to select the size synthetic to substitute for manila or cotton lines, and referring to Table 11-1 of weights and strengths, the following method has worked out in practice:

There are two ways to approach selection. The first is a straight synthetic substitute for manila or cotton line. The other is to select a different type and fiber combination such as 2-in-1 double braid, depending on the use. For sheets and halyards, where low stretch is required, you can use Dacron, or a double braid that combines a polyester cover with a polypropylene core that has 25% less stretch than Dacron alone. For mooring, anchor, and tie-up lines, you can select nylon twisted, or double braided nylon for a better stretch and strength combination. For example, a 3/4" diameter, 2 1/4" (2.25") circ. manila rope (@ 16.3 lbs. per 100; 5400 lb. strength) could well be replaced by 9/16" dia. (1 3/4" circ.) or 5/8" dia. (2" circ.) twisted nylon or Dacron; or by a 7/16" dia. 2-in-1 double nylon braided line. Added strength and less weight and

FIBER CORDAGE – TYPICAL WEIGHTS AND MINIMUM BREAKING STRENGTHS (POUNDS)

NOMINAL SIZE (inches)		MANILA Fed. Spec. TR 605			NYLON (High Tenacity—H.T.)			DU PONT DACRON or H.T. POLYESTER			POLYOLEFINS (H.T.) (Polypropylene and/or Polyethylene)			DOUBLE NYLON BRAID			POLYESTER/POLYOLEFIN DOUBLE BRAID		
Dia.	Circ.	Net Wt. 100′	Ft. per lb.	Breaking Strength	Net Wt. 100′	Ft. per lb.	Breaking Strength	Net Wt. 100′	Ft. per lb.	Breaking Strength	Net Wt. 100′	Ft. per lb.	Breaking Strength	Net Wt. 100′	Ft. per lb.	Breaking Strength	Net Wt. 100′	Ft. per lb.	Breaking Strength
3/16	5/8	1.47	68	450	1	100	1,000	1.3	77	1,000	.73	137	750	NA	NA	NA	.75	133	900
1/4	3/4	1.96	51	600	1.5	66.6	1,700	2.1	47.5	1,700	1.24	80	1,250	1.66	60.3	2,100	1.7	60.2	1,700
5/16	1	2.84	35	1,000	2.5	40	2,650	3.3	30	2,550	1.88	53	1,850	2.78	36	3,500	2.6	38.4	2,600
3/8	1 1/8	4.02	25	1,350	3.6	28	3,650	4.7	21.3	3,500	2.9	34.5	2,600	3.33	30	4,200	3.5	28.5	3,500
7/16	1 1/4	5.15	19.4	1,750	5	20	5,100	6.3	15.9	4,800	3.9	25.5	3,400	5.0	20	6,000	5.1	20	5,100
1/2	1 1/2	7.35	13.6	2,650	6.6	15	6,650	8.2	12.2	6,100	4.9	20.4	4,150	6.67	14.9	7,500	6.8	15	6,800
9/16	1 3/4	10.2	9.8	3,450	8.4	11.9	8,500	10.2	9.8	7,700	6.2	16	4,900	8.33	12	9,500	NA	NA	NA
5/8	2	13.1	7.6	4,400	10.5	9.5	10,300	13.2	7.6	9,500	7.8	12.8	5,900	11.1	9	12,000	11	9	11,000
3/4	2 1/4	16.3	6.1	5,400	14.5	6.9	14,600	17.9	5.6	13,200	11.1	9	7,900	15.0	6.7	17,000	15	6.7	15,000
7/8	2 3/4	22	4.55	7,700	20	5	19,600	24.9	4	17,500	15.4	6.5	11,000	20.8	4.8	23,700	20	5	20,000
1	3	26.5	3.77	9,000	26	3.84	25,000	30.4	3.3	22,000	18.6	5.4	13,000	25.0	4	28,500	28	3.6	28,000
1 1/8	3 1/2	35.2	2.84	12,000	34	2.94	33,250	40.5	2.5	26,500	24.2	4.1	17,500	35.0	2.8	39,000	35	2.8	35,000
1 1/4	3 3/4	40.8	2.45	13,500	39	2.56	37,800	46.2	2.16	30,500	27.5	3.6	20,000	40.0	2.5	44,000	40	2.5	40,000
1 5/16	4	46.9	2.13	15,000	45	2.22	44,500	53.4	1.87	34,500	31.3	3.2	23,000	45.0	2.2	49,500	45	2.2	45,000
1 1/2	4 1/2	58.8	1.7	18,500	55	1.8	55,000	67	1.5	43,000	39.5	2.5	29,000	60.0	1.6	65,000	60	1.6	60,000

Table 11-1

NOTE:—The figures on synthetics, above, are an average of those available from four large cordage manufacturers. Those for the rope you buy should be availabe at your dealers. Check them carefully. Also check the rope. In general a soft, sleazy rope may be somewhat stronger and easier to splice but it will not wear as well and is more apt to hockle or unlay than a firm, well "locked-up" rope. Blended ropes, part polyolefins and part other fibers, may be found. Multifilament (fine filament) polypropylene looks like nylon—don't expect it to be as strong or do the job of nylon. (It floats, nylon doesn't.) Spun, or stapled, nylon and Dacron are not as strong as ropes made from continuous filaments but are less slippery and easier to grasp. Sometimes used for sheets on sailing craft.

*Du Pont registered trademark.

storage room, in addition to long life and other advantages, would be gained.

By similar method, use 80 to 85% factor to find the polyolefin size to use. (2" circ. ⅝" dia. indicated by previous example). The polys are not as strong and have lower melting points, thus are not as abrasion-resistant. They are, however, the lightest weight and they float which are advantages for "female hands" for tie-up lines and towing, such as dinghies and passing a tow line.

Table 11-3 gives the preferred ropes for different uses. Others may be used if care is taken in the selection, and the limitations are taken into account.

CARE AND PROTECTION OF ROPE

The anchor and mooring lines, standing and running rigging, and similar gear that constitute one of the most important parts of a yachtsman's equipment may be used with intelligent care—to which it will respond with years of useful service—or it may be abused by ignorance and neglect, ruining it in short order.

TEN RULES TO LENGTHEN ROPE LIFE

These ten commandments for the care of rope may not be all-inclusive, but it is safe to say that if they are observed a boatman may very well, in many cases, be able to double the useful life of his rope.

1. Look Out for Kinks

One sure way to destroy the value of a piece of line is to allow it to get a kink in it and then put it under strain. For example, you decide to play the Good Samaritan and break out your new spare line to haul a stranded boat off a bar. The new line is unruly and doesn't handle like the well-used anchor line, so there are a dozen kinks between your quarter bitt and his samson post when you ease the clutch in and open the throttle. In thirty seconds, you'll take more out of that line than you would in thirty weeks of normal service—if you don't shake those kinks out first.

What happens is this: The fibers are overstressed at the sharp bend, weakening fibers of the strands. Rapid wear follows and later the line may part at that spot, right at a critical time—through no fault of its own.

The time to start watching for kinks is in the very beginning when the rope is first taken from the coil or reel. There are right and wrong ways of doing this. The right way is to lay the coil on deck with the inside end down according to direction on the tag attached to the coil. Now reach down into the coil and pull this inner end up through the center, unwinding counter-clockwise. (See fig. 1120.) If it uncoils in the wrong direction, turn the coil over and pull the end out from the other side.

Synthetic rope should be shipped on reels and should be pulled or rolled off, disturbing the lay as little as possible. If it becomes unruly when coiling, try "faking down" in a figure 8. Do not "loop" off over the end of the reel—let it roll.

In natural fiber ropes kinks are most troublesome in wet weather; yachtsmen therefore have more to watch than those who use their rope ashore. Wet manila rope shrinks in length and swells in diameter and the lay shortens, making it more difficult to handle.

Knots have the same effect as a sharp kink. Some knots

Table 11-2

ROPE AND FIBER COMPARISON CHART				
	MANILA	NYLON	DACRON	POLY-OLEFINS
Relative Strength	1	4	3	2
Relative Weight	3	2	4	1
Elongation	1	4	2	3
Relative Resistance to Impact or Shock Loads	1	4	2	3
Mildew and Rot Resistance	Poor	Excellent	Excellent	Excellent
Acid Resistance	Poor	Fair	Fair	Excellent
Alkali Resistance	Poor	Excellent	Excellent	Excellent
Sunlight Resistance	Fair	Fair	Good	Fair
Organic Solvent Resistance	Good	Good	Good	Fair
Melting Point	380° (Burns)	410°F.	410°F.	about 300°F.
Floatability	Only when new	None	None	Indefinite
*Relative Abrasion Resistance (*Depends on many factors— whether wet or dry, etc.)	2	3	4	1
KEY TO RATINGS: 1 Lowest—4 Highest				

may take 40 to 50 per cent out of a rope's efficiency. (See table 11-4.) A good splice, on the other hand, will allow a rope to retain 85 to 95 per cent of its original strength. Therefore, if a splice is indicated, don't use a knot.

2. Keep Your Rope Clean

Simple cleanliness in taking care of rope pays big dividends. In the course of use it is bound to pick up mud and sand. When this occurs, the rope should be draped in loose loops over a rail and hosed down gently, with fresh water if available. Don't use a high pressure stream with the intent of doing a more thorough job, as this will only force dirt and grit deeper into the rope. After washing, allow it to dry and then rap or shake it thoroughly to get out any remaining particles of dirt. Grit cuts the fibers.

3. Stow Carefully

Natural fiber rope will rot so it must be dried and carefully stowed in a place with adequate ventilation. This applies to manila, sisal, cotton and, to a lesser extent, linen and flax. Many a yachtman has been embarrassed or worse because of rot. Dry lines on deck before stowing. Hang up light lines. Loosely coil heavier ones on gratings so air can circulate. Don't subject them to intense heat.

Synthetic rope *may* be stowed wet but introduces unpleasant dampness below. Iron rust from rusty chain and thimbles is not good for nylon.

Keep lines away from exhaust pipes and batteries.

4. Guard Against Chafe and Abrasion

Chafe and abrasion are among rope's worst enemies. Heavy coils are sometimes dragged along the ground instead of being carried on the shoulder. Dragging over a rough surface causes the outside fibers to be cut or rubbed off while grit works inside the strands and is equally destructive in cutting inside fibers.

Rope should never be allowed to rub on sharp edges, or one rope chafe against another. Surface wear is accelerated and fraying often starts as a result of it. If it is necessary to have a rope pass over a sharp edge like a rail on the deck edge or a badly designed chock, rig a canvas

RECOMMENDED ROPE FOR VARIOUS USES								
	Tie-Up or Mooring Lines	Anchor Ropes or Mooring Pennants	Sheets and Halyards	Flag Halyards	Seizing and Whipping	Bolt Rope Synthetic Sails	Towing	Water Skiing
MANILA	✓	✓	✓	✓			✓	
NYLON	✓	✓		✓			✓	
DACRON	✓		✓	✓		✓		
POLYOLEFIN	✓						✓	✓
BRAIDED DACRON			✓	✓				
BRAIDED NYLON	✓	✓		✓	✓		✓	
WIRE (Stainless)		Pennants	✓					
BRAIDED COTTON				✓	✓			
NYLON SEINE TWINE					✓			
LINEN or FLAX			✓	✓	✓			

pad to prevent excessive wear from damaging the fibers.

When riding to an anchor for considerable periods, it is always well to "freshen the nip" by paying out a little line to bring the chafe of chocks in another place.

Chafing gear of canvas will protect the line from this source of trouble; it is particularly desirable on mooring lines where chafing always comes in one spot. Some boatmen carry a split length of rubber hose which can be readily clapped on the line where required. Specially molded rubber and plastic chafing gear is available.

Another trick to lengthen the life of a line like an anchor line or halyard, where most of the wear comes on one end, is to turn the line end-for-end occasionally. Any rope ends that do not terminate in a splice should be whipped to prevent fraying.

When making fast at a dock, select smooth round piles of good diameter to make fast to, and shun square or rectangular timbers with sharp corners. If there is no alternative, pad the sharp edges.

5. Prevent Slipping

When using rope on the drums of winches or hoists it is bad practice to let the rope slip on the drum as it revolves. This not only increases wear on the rope, but the sudden jerks as the rope is snubbed, strain the fibers badly.

Similarly the rope should not be allowed to lie against the revolving drum of a hoist or winch. In addition to objectionable chafe, there is the element of heat from friction to be considered; this may be enough to burn or melt the fibers.

Synthetic ropes that are highly strained and/or repeatedly stretched while around a cleat or winch may melt and grab so they will not run or pay out smoothly.

6. Avoid Small Blocks

There are two sources of trouble when rope is expected to run over too small a block. On the one hand there is excessive internal friction. Wear from such friction is always present when rope runs over the sheaves of blocks and the smaller the sheave diameter, the greater the friction. On the other hand, there is the external wear as the rope chafes against the inside of sheave holes providing insufficient clearance. Faulty alignment of blocks which causes the rope to rub against the sides, or cheeks, of the

blocks is also bad. A combination of this internal friction and external chafe breaks down fibers much faster than would be expected in normal use.

One place where trouble of this kind shows up quickly if installation is faulty is in the use of small sheaves in the steering lines or cables. These get a great deal of hard usage and their life can be extended by the use of sheaves of generous diameter.

In tackles, when matching blocks to rope, use a block with a shell length of at least 3 inches for $3/8$-inch (diameter) rope; 4 inches for $1/2$; 5 inches for $5/8$; 6 inches for $3/4$; 8 inches for $7/8$; 9 inches for 1 inch; and 12 inches for $1^1/4$-inch rope. (See table 11-5.)

Care should be exercised to see that sheaves are never allowed to become rough or rusty. See to it that they are well lubricated to reduce friction and to prevent their seizing. A sheave frozen by rust or corrosion on its pin would work havoc on a piece of rope.

7. Don't Lubricate

For natural fiber, the manufacturer has already treated the rope with an oil or solution which preserves it and lubricates internal fibers. This may account for roughly 10 per cent of the rope's weight. Even some synthetics have special fiber treatments.

Users are cautioned not to attempt to improve upon the manufacturer's work by using additional lubricant of any kind upon it. The treatment given the rope originally when manufactured prolongs its life and retains its strength.

8. Beware of Chemicals

Both acids and alkalis attack vegetable fiber rope and some synthetics. See fiber comparison table 11-2. Consequently it should never be stowed any place where it might be brought into accidental contact with chemicals or even be subject to exposure to the fumes. In testing storage batteries with a hydrometer, for example, acid dropped on a rope will burn it badly. Even paint and drying oils, like linseed, should not be allowed to get in contact with it.

Alkalis and acids burn the fibers and kill the life of rope by rendering the fibers brittle. Wet rope is more susceptible to chemical fumes than if it were dry. Rust, too, is bad for rope. If a line must be used around chemicals, it is essential to check it frequently. Spots of discoloration are a danger sign showing when fibers have broken down.

In the case of double braided rope, excessive wear will show up on the cover (or outside braid) by a parting of the strands. The inner core is rarely, if ever, affected by abrasion and provides 50% strength retention as a safety factor.

9. Never Overload

Many tables have already been published giving suitable sizes of anchor and mooring lines for motor and sailing craft of all sizes. See Tables 6-2 and 6-3, pages 98-99.

Table 11-1 will serve as a guide in this respect. It shows the minimum breaking strain carried by standard brands of manila, and typical synthetic ropes. It should be understood these strengths are for new cordage.

The factor of safety to be allowed in determining the working load on a rope is commonly taken as 5. That is, if a rope must lift 500 pounds, a rope with tensile strength of 2,500 pounds should be selected. With synthetic ropes the same factor of 5 or sometimes 4 (2,000 lbs. in the example above) may be used. The condition of the rope must be considered when making a selection. If the load ever exceeds 75 per cent of the rope's breaking strength the chances are good that it will be permanently injured. In that case, it may fail unexpectedly, without warning.

10. Don't Use Frozen Rope

While this is a problem seldom encountered by the average yachtsman whose boat is normally laid up in freezing weather, it is still a matter of moment to those such as charter boat fishermen, etc., whose activities often run right through the winter. Manila rope that has been allowed to freeze after a wetting is readily broken and therefore cannot be trusted. Since synthetics absorb very little moisture this is not too much of a problem and is one of the reasons tow boats and fishermen are using synthetics. However, reasonable care should be exercised to prevent internal damage of the rope structure by internal ice formation and subsequent heavy loading while frozen. The only practical solution if this happens is to thaw it out and dry it thoroughly before putting it back into service in extreme weather.

HOW TO INSPECT YOUR ROPE

Careful periodic inspection should, in a practical way, enable you to renew lines long before they have deteriorated to a point where they might be considered unsafe, even though theoretically a scientific breaking test might be insisted upon for some services. Here are things to look out for:

In an external examination of the rope, watch out for abrasion, cuts and broken fibers, variations in size and shape of the strands, and uniformity of the lay. Excessive wear on the outside is revealed when fibers appear to be about half worn out and yarns 1/2 or 2/3 worn through. Then, depending on the rope size and percentage of good yarns remaining, it may be time to down-grade to lighter work loads or time to renew the rope. Acid stains, frayed strands and broken yarns should all be revealed in such an examination, which should include the entire length of the rope.

Now twist the strands so as to open the rope up, revealing the condition of interior fibers. Evidence of powdered or melted or fused fiber is a danger signal warning of excessive internal bending, tension and wear. Repeat this test in several places. If yarns (the twisted fibers inside) appear to be clean, bright and free from spots of discoloration or melting (harsh and brittle) the chances are that the rope is still in good condition—assuming the exterior is also OK.

Signs of damage due to overloading are also found in the interior yarns of the strands. A rope in which these inner yarns have been broken or partly broken or melted by excessive or repeat loading can never be trusted.

Natural fibers should have a certain luster, and evidences of dryness or brittleness should be viewed with suspicion. A good manila rope will have a certain feel that distinguishes it from another out of which the life has gone. The sound rope will have a certain pliability, stretch and flexibility that is never present in a limp, dead worn-out rope. A good rope will be free from splinters of fiber—just another earmark of quality in good rope. A rough and ready breaking test that the owner can apply is to unlay about a foot of one yarn and break it, or fibers taken from it, with the hands. If this single yarn breaks easily, or fibers have little strength, the rope undoubtedly has lost strength from old age or perhaps has rotted.

Again scientists may demand more scientific tests. When black or brown discoloration spots reveal the action of acid or chemical fumes, use this breakage test frequently.

Table 11-4

		% EFF.
	Normal rope	**100%**
KNOTS	Anchor or Fisherman's bend	76
	Timber hitch	70-65
	Round turn	70-65
	Two half-hitches	70-65
	Bowline	60
	Clove hitch	60
	Sheet bend or Weaver's knot	55
	Square or Reef knot	45
SPLICES	Eye splice (over thimble)	95-90
	Long splice	87
	Short splice	85

**HOW KNOTS AND SPLICES
REDUCE THE STRENGTH OF ROPE**

Based on a normal rope strength of 100% (without knots) the figures above show what percentage of strength is left in a straight rope after a knot has been tied in it. Under differing conditions of test and stress, results vary. Therefore the percentages of efficiency tabulated are necessarily approximate, but they do serve as a base for general calculations.

The real problem in advising the boatman as to the knots he should learn to tie and use is to select the few that are of real utility on the average cruiser and exclude the numerous knots which, although serving a special purpose excellently, are of little practical use to the average boatman.

The short list of knots described below and illustrated in the accompanying sketches will meet all ordinary situations. Better know these knots—practice until they can be tied with certainty in the dark or blindfolded—than to have a superficial knowledge of a greater number of knots, including many that are of little practical value.

A knot or splice is never as strong as the rope itself. See table 11-4. Splices are preferred for heavy loads. It may be of some interest to recall that the strength of a rope is derived largely from the friction that exists between the individual fibers, yarn and strands, of which the rope is made. The twisting of these fibers into yarn, then into strands, hawsers and finally cables is always carried out in such a manner as to increase the amount and effectiveness of the friction between the rope elements. In the tying of knots this principle of making use of friction is also applicable, for in this manner, much more can be accomplished by the use of a simple knot, so tied that the strain on the rope adds to the knot's holding power, than will ever develop from a conglomeration of hitches, many of which serve no useful purpose, and which, moreover, make it more practicable in the end to cut the rope than to untie the knots. From the examples which follow it will be evident that wherever possible the most effective use is made of friction between two or more portions of a knot in order to increase its holding power.

Knots, Bends and Hitches

FIG. 1103a   Overhand

The simple overhand knot is used to keep the end of a rope from unlaying. This knot jams and may become impossible to untie. A better knot for the purpose is shown below.

FIG. 1103b   Figure Eight

The figure eight knot. This does not jam.

FIG. 1103c   Square or Reef Knot

The square or reef knot is perhaps the most useful and common knot The rope manipulated by the right hand (this is the rope leading from the left side of the sketch and terminating in the arrow in A) is turned over the other rope in tying both the first and second half of the knot. Learn to always turn this rope over the other and the knot can be tied with certainty in the dark. If the rope manipulated by the right hand is first turned over and then under the other rope the treacherous granny knot will result.

Do not use the square knot to tie together lines of different sizes, as it will slip. The reef or square knot is used for tying light lines together (not for tying heavy hawsers), for tying awning stops, reef points, cord on packages, and in fact is put to such numerous uses by sailors that many landsmen call it the sailor's knot. The knot has one serious fault. It jams and is difficult to untie after being heavily stressed.

FIG. 1103d   Sheet or Becket Bend

The sheet or becket bend has been known to landsmen as the weaver's knot, and it is used for tying two lines together. It will not slip even if there is great difference in the sizes of the lines. To make the knot secure for connecting hawsers for towing, the free ends of the lines should be stopped down with twine in the manner illustrated in fig. 1103j, the reeving line bend.

FIG. 1103e   Bowline

The bowline is considered a knot second in usefulness only to the square knot. The bowline will not slip, does not pinch or kink the rope as much as some other knots, and does not jam and become difficult to untie. By tying a bowline with a small loop and passing the line through the loop the running bowline is obtained. This is an excellent form of running noose.

Bowlines are used wherever a secure loop or noose is needed in the end of a line, such as a line which is to be secured to a bollard in making a boat fast to a pier or wharf. They may also be used in securing lines to anchors where there is no time to make a splice. Hawsers are sometimes connected by two bowlines, the loop of one knot being passed through the loop of the other.

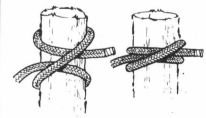

FIG. 1103f   Clove Hitch

The clove hitch is used for making a line fast temporarily to a pile or a bollard.

FIG. 1103g   Two Half Hitches

Two half hitches are used for making a line fast to a bollard, pile, timber, or stanchion. Note that the knot consists of a turn around the fixed object and a clove hitch around the standing part of the line.

FIG. 1103h   Correct Method of Making Fast to a Cleat

Correct method for making fast to a cleat is shown. The half hitch which completes the fastening is taken with the free part of the line. The line can then be freed without taking up slack in the standing part.

FIG. 1103i   Incorrect Method of Making Fast to a Cleat

Common incorrect method of making fast to a cleat is shown. The half hitch is taken with the standing part of the line and the line consequently can not be freed without taking up slack in the standing part. Accidents have been caused by the use of this type of fastening on lines which must be freed quickly.

**FIG. 1103j   Reeving Line Bend
Free ends must be
stopped down with twine**

The reeving line bend is so called because it is used to connect lines which must pass through a small opening, such as a hawsepipe.

FIG. 1103k   Fisherman's Bend

The fisherman's bend, also called the anchor bend, is handy for making fast to a buoy or spar or the ring of an anchor. In some localities it is preferred to the thimble and eye splice for attaching the anchor line to the ring. As is evident from the illustration, it is made by taking two round turns around the ring, then passing the end under both turns to form a half hitch around the standing part of the line. For further security, a second half hitch is taken around the standing part only, or in place of the last half hitch, the end may be stopped down or sized back to the line with twine.

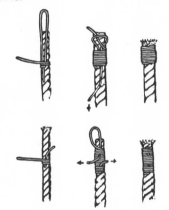

FIG. 1103l   Two Methods of Whipping a Rope End

All butt-ended ropes should of course be whipped to prevent raveling of the strands. Two common methods for doing this are illustrated above. While these figures are not strictly to scale this has been done purposely to avoid difficulty in following the several steps involved in either of the two methods.

FIG. 1103m   Sheepshank

The sheepshank is used to shorten a line. Lay the bight in three parts and take a half hitch around each doubled part.

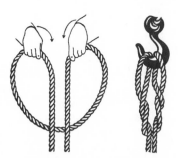

FIG. 1103n   Cat's Paw

The cat's paw is used to secure a line to a hook. Make a double loop by twisting two bights of the line as shown,

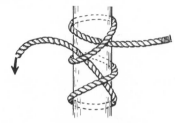

FIG. 1103o   Rolling Hitch

The rolling hitch is used to bend a line to a spar or rope. Close turns up tight and take the strain on the arrow-tipped end.

FIG. 1103p   Timber Hitch

The timber hitch is used to temporarily secure a line to a spar or timber, as in towing. The half hitch shown is sometimes omitted. If used, it should be taken first. In both hitches, strain should be kept on the line to make it hold.

FIG. 1103q   Blackwall Hitch

The Blackwall Hitch is easy to make and practical to use when *temporarily* securing a rope to a hook. It will carry a heavy load, *provided* the tension is constant.

The Art of Splicing

EYE SPLICE OR SIDE SPLICE

Start the splice by unlaying the strands, about six inches to a foot or more, or 6 to 10 turns of lay, depending on the size of rope you are splicing. Now whip the end of each strand to prevent its unlaying while being handled. If working with synthetic rope, it is sometimes helpful to use masking or friction tape wrapped around the unlaid strands every 4 to 6 inches to help hold the "turn" in the strand. The ends may be fused with a flame or whipped.

Next form a loop in the rope by laying the end back along the standing part. Hold the standing part away from you in the left hand, loop toward you. The stranded end can be worked with the right hand.

The size of loop is determined by the point X (fig. 1104) where the opened strands are first tucked under the standing part of the rope. If the splice is being made around a thimble, the rope is laid snugly in the thimble groove and point X will be at the tapered end of the thimble. The thimble may be temporarily taped or tied in place until the job is finished.

Now lay the three opened strands across the standing part as shown in fig. 1104 so that the center strand B lies over and directly along the standing part. Left-hand strand A leads off to the left; right-hand strand C to the right of the standing part.

Tucking of strand ends A, B and C under the strands of the standing part is the next step. Get this right and the rest is easy. See fig. 1105.

Start with the center strand B. Select the topmost strand (2) of the standing part near point X and tuck B under it. Haul it up snug but not so tight as to distort the natural lay of all strands. Note that the tuck is made from right to left, against the lay of the standing part.

Now take left-hand strand A and tuck under strand (1), which lies to the left of strand (2). Similarly take strand C and tuck under strand (3), which lies to the right of strand (2). Be sure to tuck from right to left in every case.

The greatest risk of starting wrong is in the first tuck of strand C. It should go under (3), from right to left. Of course, strands (1), (2), and (3) are arranged symmetrically around the rope.

It may help to visualize this by referring to fig. 1106, a cross-section through the rope at X, seen from below.

If the first tuck of each of strands A, B and C is correctly made, the splice at this point will look as shown in fig. 1107.

The splice is completed by making at least two additional tucks in manila rope or 4 full tucks in synthetic rope with each of strands A, B and C. As each added tuck is made be sure it passes over one strand of the standing part, then under the strand next above it, and so on, the tucked strand running against the lay of the strands of the standing part. This is clearly shown in fig. 1108, the completed splice. Note C, C¹ and C², the same strand as it appears after successive tucks.

Suggestions: The splice can be made neater by tapering. This is done by cutting out part of the yarns from the tucking strands, before the finishing tucks. In any case, the first

3 tucks in manila or 4 tucks in synthetics, are made with the full strands. (Synthetics are slippery and stretchy and thus require at least one extra tuck.) After that, some prefer to cut out one-third of the yarns, make a tuck, then cut out another third of the yarns, and make the last tuck. This produces an even taper. After the splice is finished, roll it on deck under foot to smooth it up. Then put a strain on it and finally cut off the projecting ends of the strands. Do not cut off the "tails" of synthetic rope too short. If possible seat the splice in use or whip down the ends before cutting. The loose fibers may be fused with a match or candle to finish off, but be careful not to melt the rope.

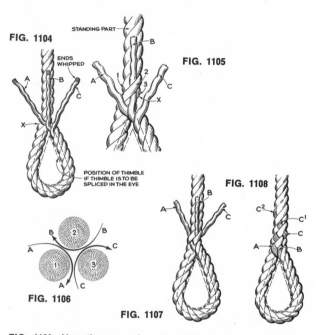

FIG. 1108 How the eye splice should look when completed. A thimble, if spliced in, would fit as shown by the dotted lines.

From the earliest days of rope, marlinspike seamanship had concerned itself with the splicing of 3-strand or twisted rope. With the increasing use of 2-in-1 double braided rope, however, a new method of splicing has

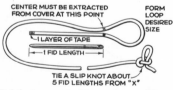

Fig. 1108a Tightly tape end with one layer of tape. Mark a big dot one fid length from end of line. From the dot, form a loop the size of the eye you want, and mark with an X as shown.

Fig. 1108b Bend line sharply at X, and spread strands apart firmly to make opening so center can be pried out. Mark one big line on center where it comes out (this is Mark #1), and use your fingers to pull all the center out of the cover from X to the end. Pull on paper tape inside center until it breaks back at slip knot; you need to get rid of it so you can splice. Put a single layer of tape on end of center.

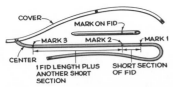

Fig. 1108c Pull out more of the center. From Mark #1 measure a distance equal to the short section of the fid, and mark two heavy lines (this is Mark #2). Mark three heavy lines at a distance of one fid length plus one short section of fid from Mark #2. This is Mark #3.

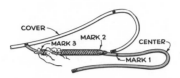

Fig. 1108d Insert fid into center at Mark #2, and slide it lengthwise through "tunnel" until point sticks out at Mark #3.

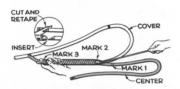

Fig. 1108e Cut across taped end of cover to form a point, and re-tape tightly with one layer of tape. Jam this point into open end of the fid. Jam pusher into fid behind the tape. Hold center gently at Mark #3, and push both fid and cover through the center until dot almost disappears at Mark #2.

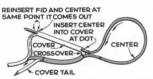

Fig. 1108f Note how center tail must travel through cover. It must go in close to dot, and come out through opening at X. On large eyes several passes may be necessary for fid to reach X. When this occurs simply reinsert fid at exact place it comes out and continue to X. To start, insert fid in cover at dot and slide it through tunnel to X. Form tapered point on center tail, jam it into open end of fid, and push fid and center through the cover. After fid comes out at X, pull all center tail through cover until tight, then pull cover tail tight.

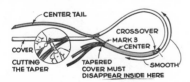

Fig. 1108g Unravel cover tail braid all the way to Mark #3, and cut off groups of strands at staggered intervals to form a tapered end. Hold crossover in one hand, and firmly smooth both sides of loop away from crossover. Do this until the tapered tail section completely disappears inside Mark #3.

Fig. 1108h Hold rope at slipknot, and gently begin to "milk" or slide the cover slack toward the loop. You'll see the center begin to disappear into the cover. Go back to the knot, and continue sliding cover more and more firmly until all center and the crossover are buried inside the cover.

come into being. The splicing of braided rope is best done by following an 8-step procedure that, in an over-simplified way, starts by extracting the core from inside the cover, then inserting the cover into the core in one direction, inserting the core back into the cover in the opposite direction, and then "milking" a slack section of cover over the core. A fid and pusher are used in the process. The holding power is related to the old Chinese finger trick, and the result is a sure and good looking splice. A thimble can be inserted during the splicing process. The 8 steps for a basic eye splice are shown in the sketches

HOW TO MAKE A SHORT SPLICE

A short splice is used where two ropes are to be permanently joined, provided they do not have to pass through the sheave hole, swallow or throat, of a block. The splice will be much stronger than any knot.

The short splice enlarges the rope's diameter at the splice, so in cases where the spliced rope must pass through a sheave hole, a long splice should be used.

To start the short splice, unlay the strands of both rope ends for a short distance as described for the eye splice. Whip the six strand ends, or fuse or tape them, to prevent unlaying. A seizing should also be made around each of the ropes to prevent strands from unlaying too far. These seizings can be cut as the splice is completed.

Next "marry" the ends so that the strands of each rope lie alternately between strands of the other as shown in fig. 1109. Now tie all three strands of one rope temporarily to the other. See fig. 1110. (Some omit this step; it is not absolutely essential.)

Working with the three free strands, remove temporary seizing from around other rope and splice them into the other rope by tucking strands exactly as described for the eye splice, working over and under successive strands from right to left against the lay of the rope. When first tucks have been made, snug down all three strands. Then tuck two or three more times on that side.

Next cut the temporary seizing of the other strands and the rope and repeat, splicing these three remaining strands into the opposite rope.

Just as in the eye splice, the short splice can be tapered as desired by cutting out yarns from the strands after the full tucks are made. Figure 1111 shows how the short splice would appear if not tapered, after finally trimming off the ends of strands. Never cut strand ends off too close. Otherwise when a heavy strain is put on the rope, the last tuck tends to work out, especially with synthetics.

Another method which some find easier, is to start as in fig. 1109 and tie pairs of strands from opposite ends in an overhand knot. See fig. 1112. This, in effect, makes the first tuck.

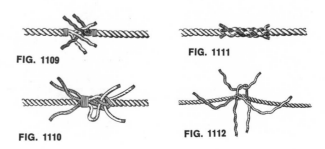

FIG. 1109

FIG. 1111

FIG. 1110

FIG. 1112

HOW TO MAKE A LONG SPLICE

The long splice (fig. 1113) is used where the spliced ropes are to reeve through blocks or sheaves. There are several methods of making this splice. Some splicers unlay both ends, marry as in the short splice and work from the center both ways. But by starting as in fig. 1113 you do not lose any of the lay of strands. For a long splice in a 3-inch circumference line allow not less than 6 feet, or about 2 feet for each inch of *circumference,* as the farther apart the three splices are staggered, the stronger will be the completed splice. In the illustration 2-inch circumference rope was used, but the illustration does not show proper spacing of tucks. After seizing or taping the ends of each strand, to start this splice, unlay one strand of one rope for about 6 feet and cut off, leaving about one foot as in Illustration 1, strand C. Then unlay one strand from other rope and lay in space formerly occupied by strand C, allowing a foot for splicing as in Illustration 1 at A.

When laying the first strand A (1), plan the spacing of splices so that B will be about central in the finished long splice. Next unlay a strand from right hand rope and a strand from left hand rope and lay the left hand strand in the respective space formerly filled by the strand from right hand rope as in Illustration 2. Continue strand C until all three strands are about equal distance as in Illustration 3.

Then with all pairs of strands (for example Illustration 4A) tie an overhand knot with all yarns flat and even. Next take spike and tuck strands over one and under one as in 4B, unlaying or untwisting strands sufficient to allow yarns to lay flat when tucked. The overhand knot at 4A and, after tucking as at 4B, should be as near as possible to an original strand in size and volume of fiber by reducing twist in the tucked strand. Make another full tuck with all strands.

You now have an overhand knot and two full tucks. Halve each strand and tuck as in 4C, again halve the re-maining yarns and tuck as in 4E. Roll tucks under foot and stretch before cutting off ends. Here, again, do not cut off too short. Much better a little fuzz or whiskers than tucks starting to pull out.

To make a long splice in fishing line, make the same as above, using a sail needle to tuck the strands. The small sail needle, used in fine work, takes the place of the larger fid.

SPLICING WIRE ROPE

In general, wire rope is spliced in a similar way except that tucks are made with the lay rather than against the lay. Splicing vises are used to hold the rope and metal tools and hammers are usually needed.

Splices of wire-to-fiber rope should be left to professional riggers. They can usually be found at sail lofts where wire halyards with rope tails can be made to specification. With the right tools and a lot of practice, you can work out a method yourself.

A FEW TIPS

Practice these knots and splices with a couple of short lengths of line and put them to practical use. Always keep lines dry and clean. Keep ends of lines neatly served or whipped with twine to prevent unlaying. Serving or whipping is preferable to the crown knots or splices sometimes used to prevent unlaying as these knots and splices prevent reeving the line through the openings of a block which would otherwise take the line nicely.

The knots, hitches, bends and splices just described are sufficient for all practical purposes aboard the average pleasure boat. To make them with facility in a seamanlike manner, have some experienced yachtsman, sailor or fisherman show you how he'd do it, especially the bowline, clove hitch and splice.

LONG SPLICE

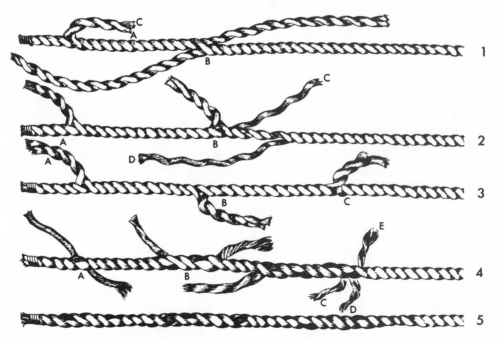

FIG. 1113   While the short splice is excellent for strength and neatness, as compared to a knot, there are times when the spliced line must reeve through a block. In such cases, the long splice should be used. Illustrated above are steps in the making of a long splice.

Blocks and Tackles

The use of blocks and tackle (pronounced tay-kle) or, to use a higher sounding name, mechanical appliances, on board a small cruising type boat is very limited. The competent seaman, however, should have a basic knowledge of them, as their use enables one man to do the work of many.

Blocks and tackle on small boats are almost entirely confined to sailboats where the hoisting of heavy sails, as well as setting them, requires some means for one or two men to match the strength of many. No matter how small the sailboat, the sheets usually run through one or more blocks, which means we have a mechanical appliance.

To see how this aids, go for a sail in a 20-foot boat, in a moderate breeze, and bend a line to the boom. While under way attempt to trim in the sail with your improvised sheet. It will come in but it will be a struggle, so try it with the regular system of blocks and tackle and you will see with what ease the sail comes in. About the most common use on a motorboat is in hoisting your dinghy.

A *block* consists of a frame of wood or metal inside of which is fitted one or more *sheaves* (pulleys—the word is pronounced shiv), and is designated according to the number of sheaves it contains, such as single, double, or triple. The size of the block to be used is, of course, de-termined by the size of the rope to be reeved. If a fiber rope is being used, the size of the block should be *about* three times the *circumference* of the rope and the sheave diameter about twice the circumference. Therefore, if 2-inch rope, $^5/_8$" diameter, is being used the block could be 6 inches (three times the circumference) and the sheave diameter 4 inches (twice the circumference). This is an approximation. See Table 11-5, block sizes and rope diameter, for recommended sizes.

Wire rope is also used but usually only as halyards on sailboats. Some larger sailing craft use wire sheets and guys. This should be stainless steel and sheaves should be as large as possible for long rope life. Make sure the rope cannot squeeze between the sheave and the cheeks of the block or a "panic party" may ensue.

The term *tackle* is used for an assemblage of *falls* (ropes) and *blocks*. When you pass ropes through the blocks, you *reeve* them and the part of the fall made fast to one of the blocks, or the weight, as the case may be, is known as the *standing part,* while the end upon which the force is to be applied is called the *hauling part.* To *overhaul the falls* is to separate the blocks; to *round in* is to bring them together; and *chock-a-block* or *two blocks* means they are tight together.

FIG. 1114 PARTS OF A BLOCK

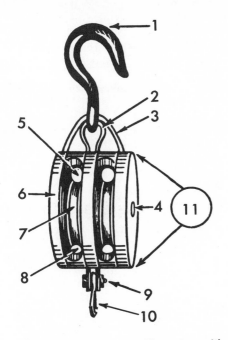

1. Hook
2. Inner Strap
3. Outer Strap
4. Pin
5. Swallows
6. Cheeks
7. Sheaves — either plain, roller, or self-lubricating
8. Breech
9. Becket
10. Thimble
11. Shell

DEFINITIONS:

Block
A frame of wood or metal within which are fitted sheaves or pulleys over which a rope runs. Blocks may be single, double, treble, etc. They are designated by the number of sheaves they contain. The lifting power is multiplied in ratio to the number of sheaves used.

Tackle
A combination of blocks, ropes and hooks for raising, lowering or moving heavy objects. A "tackle" increases lifting power but reduces lifting speed.

Fall Rope
That part of the tackle to which lifting power is applied.

Fall Block or Running Block
The block attached to the object to be moved.

Fled Block or Standing Block
Is fixed to a permanent support.

Standing End
The end of the fall fixed to the tackle.

Running End
The end opposite the standing end.

Return
Each part of the fall between the two blocks or between either end and the block.

Lifting Force
Is in ratio with the number of times the rope passes to and from the fall block.

To Overhaul
Is to separate the blocks.

To Round In
Is to bring the blocks closer together.

Two Blocks
Means the blocks of the fall are in contact.

Shell or Frame
Part which holds sheave or wheel.

(From Columbia Rope Co. rigger's booklet)

KINDS OF TACKLE

Tackles (fig. 1116) are named according to the number of sheaves in the blocks that are used (single, two-fold, three-fold purchases), according to the purpose for which the tackle is used (yard-tackles, stay-tackles, etc.), or from names handed down from the past (luff-tackles, watch-tackles, gun-tackles, Spanish-burtons, etc.). The tackles that may be found aboard cruising boats, and should be known are:

1. Single Whip—A single fixed block and fall—no increase in power. Gain only in height of lift or change in direction of pull.

2. Gun Tackle—Two single blocks. If lower block is movable, double force is gained. If upper block is movable, triple force is gained.

3. Luff Tackle—A double hook-block and single hook-block. Force gained three if single block is movable, four if double block is movable.

4. Two-Fold or Double Tackle—Two double sheave hook-blocks. Force gained four or five, depending upon application.

CALCULATING POWER OF A TACKLE

The force gained as given in all of these tackle combinations is theoretical only, as the friction of the blocks has been ignored. The method of calculating the actual force gained and compensating for this friction is to add

FIG. 1117 The size of rope should be matched to the block it reeves through. Chafe at blocks can cause serious damage. The second and fourth are swivel blocks.

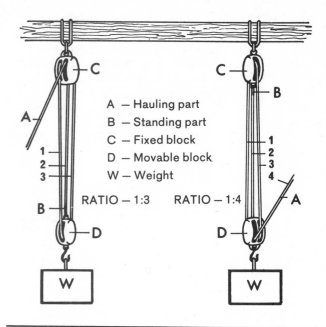

A — Hauling part
B — Standing part
C — Fixed block
D — Movable block
W — Weight

RATIO — 1:3   RATIO — 1:4

FIG. 1115 The number of falls leading to and from the movable block determines the ratio of force to weight necessary for lifting.

10% to the weight W, for each sheave in the tackle before dividing by the number of falls. Thus, in Illustration 4 (fig. 1116) if W is 1000 lbs.: 10% is 100 lbs.; 4 sheaves × 100 = 400 lbs.; total theoretical W then is 1000 plus 400 = 1400 lbs. With 4 falls the force needed on A to lift W would be 1400 ÷ 4 or 350 lbs. rather than an apparent 250 lbs., disregarding friction. This will vary with the type of bearings and pins and lubrication in the blocks and sheave diameter.

There are, of course, a number of other purchases, the heaviest commonly used aboard ship being a three-fold purchase, which consists of two triple blocks. It must be remembered the hauling part reeved through a triple block should be led through the center sheave. If not, the block will cant causing it to bind and, in extreme cases, to break the block. This is especially true with a three-fold purchase.

TO OBTAIN GREATEST EFFICIENCY

To get the greatest mechanical efficiency, the hauling part should lead from the block with the most sheaves, and if both blocks have the same number it is best for the hauling part to lead from the movable block. It is also best to have the block with the greatest number of sheaves the movable block, as the number of falls leading to and from the movable block determines the ratio of force-to-weight necessary for lifting.

In the illustration (fig. 1116) showing two arrangements of luff tackles, in one there are three falls leading from the movable block and ratio of force-to-weight would be 1:3. Now change the blocks—the single block fixed and the double block made movable with the weight attached and the hauling part leading from it. Notice that, counting the hauling part, there are four falls leading to or from the now movable block, and the ratio becomes 1:4, which is quite an increase.

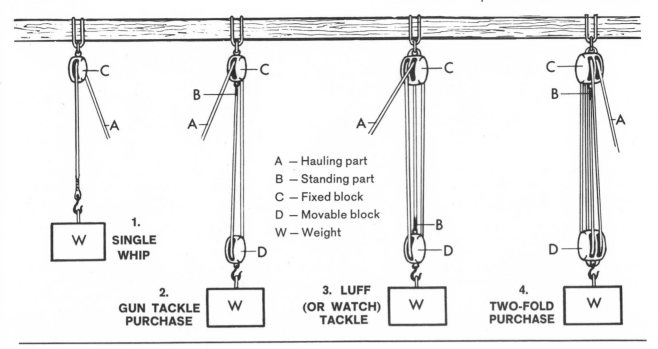

A — Hauling part
B — Standing part
C — Fixed block
D — Movable block
W — Weight

1.
SINGLE WHIP

2.
GUN TACKLE PURCHASE

3. LUFF (OR WATCH) TACKLE

4.
TWO-FOLD PURCHASE

FIG. 1116 Some of the common tackles that are found aboard cruising boats.

Table 11-5

BLOCK AND ROPE SIZES *			
Size of Block (Length of Shell)	Diameter of Rope	Size of Block (Length of Shell)	Diameter of Rope
3	⅜″	8	⅞″ — 1″
4	½″	10	1⅛″
5	9⁄16″–⅝″	12	1¼″
6	¾″	14	1⅜″–1½″
7	13⁄16″	16	1⅝″

*NOTE—Some heavy blocks can accommodate larger rope sizes but the use of smaller blocks for larger rope than recommended reduces rope life. Too small diameter sheaves cause extra strain on outer rope fibers and increase internal friction.

PROPORTIONING BLOCKS TO ROPE SIZE

In using blocks and tackle the utmost care must be taken in having the proper size blocks for the rope used. See Table 11-5. If the rope is too big it will jam and if too small it will slip out of the sheave and jam between the *cheeks* (sides of a block) and the sheave, which will cause untold damage. Also be careful that the proper size of rope and type of tackle is used in reference to the weight to be lifted. There are many tables to give you this. Also your blocks must be lubricated, clean, well painted or varnished (if wooden), and they must be so placed when in use that they will not be crushed or beaten against a spar or other gear.

The entire study of mechanical appliances is a lengthy and technical one, but also immensely interesting. There has been no effort to cover the subject, but only to give a few notes as an introduction. As said before, it allows one man to do many men's work, or it is a case of a "boy doing a man's job."

FIG. 1118 Main sheet tackle rigged with a double block (movable) on the boom, and single block (fixed, with becket) on deck. The extra single block (foreground) does not increase power but serves as a fairlead. Note eye splice around thimble.

THE BOSUN'S LOCKER

There is nothing that distinguishes a seaman from a lubber as much as his proficiency in marlinespike seamanship. There is nothing more pitiful than seeing someone make fast with a multitude of turns around a pile finished off with many fancy loops only to see a puff of wind cause the boat to tug and the entire conglomeration fall apart and the boat begin to drift. Again, it is impossible to keep a boat shipshape and Bristol fashion, if the ends of your lines have "cow's tails" (frayed or untidy ends of rope).

TERMINOLOGY

First let us all make sure that we understand certain terms. Marlinespike seamanship deals with rope and the methods of working it. *Rope* is cordage of all types and sizes: fiber, wire, small cordage. *Small stuff* is small cordage, usually made of tarred hemp, such as spun-yarn, seine twine, either cotton, linen or synthetic, marlin, ratline, houseline, roundline, frequently used as seizing for whipping, worming and serving line. *Line* is a general term applied on board ship to a piece of rope in use.

There are few ropes on shipboard. Here is a good question to ask boating friends or to send to a quiz program: "How many ropes are there aboard ship? Name them." There are but nine principal ropes on board ship. These are bell ropes, man ropes, top ropes, foot ropes, bolt ropes, back ropes, yard ropes, bucket ropes, and tiller ropes. There may be one or two more, of less importance. The main thing to remember is that you don't make fast with a rope, you use a line; you don't trim in a sail with a rope or a sheet-rope, but with a sheet.

KINDS OF FIBER ROPE

There are various types of fiber rope, mainly manila, nylon, polyesters such as Du Pont Dacron or the English Terrylene, and polyolefins such as polyethylene and polypropylene. In addition you may find linen or flax, cotton, sisal, ropes made of two or more fibers in many combinations, and other fibers. New ones seem to come out every year.

Because the *synthetics* have proved themselves, both as to ultimate cost and ease of handling, they are replacing much of the natural fiber rope. The exception seems to be where the rope is lost by accident or theft or rapidly worn out by abuse and where the higher cost, in most cases, of synthetics cannot be recovered by longer life.

Usually the rope is made from three strands but sometimes four-strand rope is made. A cable is made by twisting three ropes together. To keep rope from unlaying easily, each successive step is twisted in the opposite direction. This is done as follows: yarn—right-handed; strands—left-handed; rope—right-handed; and cable—left-handed. It is possible, however, to get left-handed rope and in this case the procedure is reversed. Left-laid genoa jib sheets and others that are winched hard run more freely (without kinks) when spun off the winch and released for tacking.

FIG. 1119 Anchor line neatly coiled, clockwise, on deck. Note the grating below it to aid in drying.

FIG. 1120 Taking line from a new coil, reach down inside and take inner fag end from bottom. Coil clockwise if rope is right-handed.

The newest kind of fiber rope is referred to as 2-in-1 double braid. This consists of an inner braided core of nylon or polypropylene and a braided cover of nylon or polyester. The double braid construction has gained wide acceptance for sheets because its fiber combinations provide very low stretch, and because it is non-rotational so it will always run free (not kink). The double braid also has greater bearing surface, so it holds better on winches and in the hand. It also retains flexibility, whether wet or dry, over extensive periods of use. These same characteristics also make the double braid construction useful for anchor lines where ease of storing, non-kinking, and high stretch/strength ratios are desirable.

HOW ROPE IS MEASURED AND SOLD

The size of rope is measured in different ways. Marine fiber rope is measured by its circumference, although most yachtsmen have always designated it by its diameter. On the other hand wire rope is designated by its diameter. Therefore, two-inch wire rope is much thicker than two-inch fiber rope (⅝ inch diameter).

The length of fiber and wire rope may be measured in feet or in fathoms. A fathom is 6 feet. Small stuff is sometimes designated by the number of *threads* it contains. The largest of small stuff is ratline stuff, which is usually 3-stranded, right-handed and may have 8 threads to the strand, in which case it would be 24-thread.

Cordage is sold by the foot or fathom or by the pound. Usually standard coils and reels are sold by the pound and cut lengths are sold by the foot or at a higher price per pound. Your dealer is entitled to increase the price for cuts because of the waste involved in fag ends and his investment and time.

Another method that is gaining in acceptance is "pre-packed" lines. Double-braided type rope comes as pre-spliced dock lines of specific lengths and diameters; and as pre-spliced anchor lines, ready to use.

POINTS TO REMEMBER

Vegetable fiber rope will shrink when wet, and because of this fact it is necessary to loosen all standing fiber rigging whenever wet. If this is not done the shrinking will cause an injurious strain on the rope.

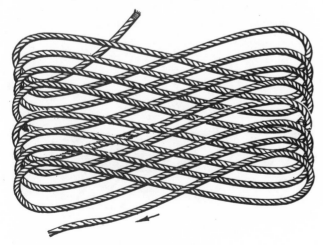

FIG. 1121   Line faked down ready to run out rapidly. Coils, in practice, would lie closer together.

FIG. 1122   Line is flemished down for neatness by laying it down in close concentric coils, one against the other, in the form of a flat mat, free end at the center. If left long in one spot it may discolor the deck. It does not dry as well as a loose coil. Sunlight may damage nylon and poly ropes.

Rope of natural fiber will deteriorate rapidly from continued dampness and therefore should always be dry before stowed. To dry, it is best to coil down loosely and place where the sun can get at the rope and the air can pass freely all about it. Of course, such rope should never be stowed in a locker that is not well ventilated and dry; for if not, there is not much use in drying the rope as it will rot in the locker.

One thing not generally understood about synthetic ropes is *cold flow*. Due to the nature of the fiber, a long sustained load may cause the fibers to stretch or elongate permanently with a consequent reduction in rope diameter and ultimate strength. Some synthetics are worse than others in this respect. Temperature affects the flow. In a surging load such as anchoring in moderate weather, the anchor line can recover. But in a hurricane or a long passage at sea the load might be continuous and cold flow could become a hazard.

USE AND CARE OF WIRE ROPE

Wire rope or strand is generally used on board cruising boats as standing rigging. On a number of sailboats, however, it is also used as running rigging. Steel is used almost exclusively in making wire rope. To preserve it from corrosion it is sometimes galvanized. Stainless steel is fine, but expensive. Some wire rope has a hemp core. This greatly increases flexibility and also acts as a cushion against sudden stress or heavy pull.

Great care must be taken of wire rope also. It should always be kept on a reel when not in use and must be reeled off and not slipped off over the ends of the reel. If kept in a coil it should be rolled off at all times. If a kink ever gets into a wire rope it is a disaster, as this practically ruins it. As with fiber rope, sharp bends will cause an excessive strain and greatly impair the efficiency.

It is important to note that whenever you see broken wires, "meat hooks" that surely cut up the hands, or when the diameter of the outside wires is worn to one-half the original diameter, it is time to condemn the rope as it is no longer safe.

COILING, FAKING AND FLEMISHING

When line is left on deck, or put in a locker, it should never be thrown down in a heap. Not only would this give a lubberly appearance, but if you needed to use the line, especially in a hurry, it might kink or tangle. For safety and good seamanship we always either coil, fake, or flemish down a line.

When it must be kept ready for emergency use, clear for running, a line is generally coiled down (figures 1119-1120) always with the lay (clockwise for right lay rope). To make a straight coil, a circular bight of the secured end is laid and successive bights are placed on top. When all the line has been used, the entire coil is capsized to leave it clear for running.

When the entire length of a line must be run out rapidly it is usually faked down (fig. 1121). To do this a short length of the free end is laid out in a straight line and then turned back to form a flat coil. Successive flat coils are then formed, laying the end of each coil on top of the preceding coils, rather like figure 8s.

When great neatness is desired a line is flemished down (fig. 1122). Successive circles of the line are wrapped about each other with the free end at the center. When it is finished it looks like a mat and with an old piece of line can be used as one.

A disadvantage of coiling down is that you must watch out for kinks. With a flemished-down line care must be taken to prevent coils from falling back and fouling the preceding coil. If a line is flemished down and left on deck

for some time it will mark the deck and remain wet on the under side. On small boats lines are usually either coiled down or flemished down.

KNOTS THE SEAMAN KNOWS

Before a person dares to take a boat out he should be able to make a bowline, two half hitches, clove hitch, square knot and sheet bend. (See figures 1103 c-g.) This is not all he should know, but they are the minimum. The following are those that every competent seaman should know:

A.—Knots in the end of a rope:

1. Overhand
2. Bowline
3. Running bowline
4. Bowline on a bight
5. French bowline
6. Sheepshank
7. Blackwall hitch
8. Figure 8
9. Cat's-paw

B.—Knots for bending two ropes, or two ends of the same rope, together:

1. Square or reef
2. Two bowlines
3. Single and double sheet or becket bend
4. Single and double carrick bend
5. Reeving line bend

C.—Knots for securing a line to ring or spar:

1. Fisherman's bend
2. Timber hitch
3. Timber and half hitch
4. Two half hitches
5. Round turn and two half hitches
6. Rolling hitch
7. Clove hitch
8. Studding sail tack bend
9. Studding sail halyard bend

D.—Knots worked in the end of a rope:

1. Wall knot
2. Wall and crown
3. Single Matthew Walker
4. Lanyard knot

Rope end dip. A new, effective way to treat rope ends is to dip them into a red vinyl liquid called Whip-End Dip. It seals all rope ends in seconds, setting into a tough, flexible permanent finish that eliminates whipping.

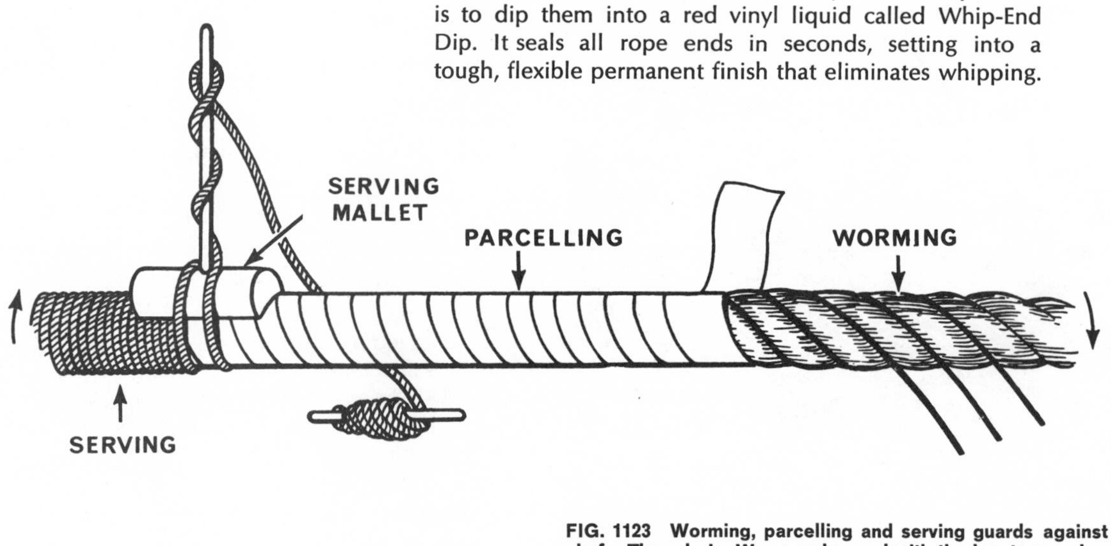

SERVING MALLET
PARCELLING
WORMING
SERVING

FIG. 1123 Worming, parcelling and serving guards against severe chafe. The rule is: Worm and parcel with the lay; turn and serve the other way.

OTHER ARTS OF THE SAILOR

Besides the general classes of knots and the splices shown earlier, there are other types of work that all seamen should be able to do.

Back Splice: To put an enlarged, finished end on a line.
Stopper on a rope: A length of rope secured at one end used in securing or checking a running line.
Strap on a rope: Turns taken around a standing part with the tackle hooked through the bights.
Mouse a hook: A method of closing the open part of a hook with small stuff to assist in preventing the object to which it is hooked from jumping out.
Grommet strap: A grommet or continuous loop of rope, used to attach a hook to a block permanently.
Seizing: The lashing together of two ends of rope by continuous turns of small stuff. Word sometimes used to mean whipping.

As said before there is nothing more unseamanlike than cow's tails on the end of a line. There are many ways to prevent this such as a back splice, wall knot, etc., but perhaps the best method is by whipping. See fig. 1103-l. Another method, sewed whipping, is preferred as it is easier to get taut and much harder to pull off. Plastic whips that are shrunk on with heat are available but good "fancy" work is preferred over substitutes like friction tape. The advantage of whipping over the other methods of eliminating cow's tails is that it does not increase the size of the rope. This can work as a disadvantage: for example, a sheet can run through all the blocks, making it necessary to re-reeve. Another type, such as a wall and crown, will not allow the end to run through a block.

HOW TO PREVENT CHAFE

There is nothing that wears rope so fast as chafing. In order to prevent this, it is necessary to rig *chafing gear*. When the chafe is of only temporary nature the rope can be protected by wrapping a piece of canvas around it. However, when the chafe will be more or less permanent

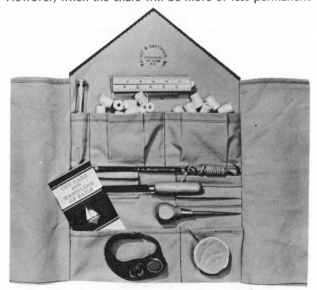

FIG. 1124 This sail repair kit, created by Ratsey & Lapthorn, contains a sailmaker's palm, bench hook, thread, seven needles, awl, knife, wax, rule, pencil and booklet on sail care and handling.

FIG. 1125 This ditty bag contains all the essentials for splicing and sail and canvas repair. Included are palm, assorted needles, marline, sail twine, and 6-inch heavy-duty steel spike.

or severe, the line should be wormed, parceled, and served or molded rubber gear, leather or rawhide, permanently attached.

Worming: consists of following the lay of the rope, between the strands, with small stuff, to keep the moisture out and for filling out the round of the rope.
Parceling: consists of wrapping the rope spirally with long overlapping strips of canvas, following the lay of the rope.
Serving: consists of wrapping small stuff over the parceling opposite to the lay of the rope to form a taut, protective cover. Should be hard-laid marline or seine twine for the best wear.

REPAIRS TO CANVAS

All seamen should be able to work with canvas and a needle. You should provide yourself with a sewing kit consisting of a small canvas kit bag, two or three short and long needles, some beeswax, and some small stuff. The long needle, usually triangular, straight, or curved, is generally used for sewing canvas, while the short needle, usually broad, straight or curved, is generally used for rope work.

There are four main types of stitches used in sewing canvas. Flat is used for seams in sails, tarpaulins, etc.; round is for making duffel bags; baseball, where a snug edge-to-edge fit in canvas is desired; and herringbone is for very stiff or painted canvas.

Have the right cordage for the job and take care of it well—then it will take care of you if you use it correctly.

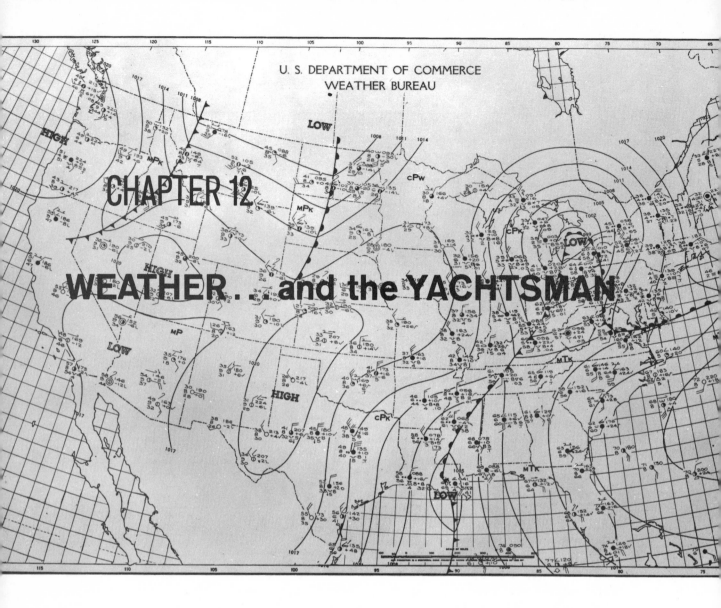

U. S. DEPARTMENT OF COMMERCE
WEATHER BUREAU

CHAPTER 12

WEATHER...and the YACHTSMAN

How to Read a Weather Map

THE WEATHER MAP provides a bird's-eye view of the weather over a large area. With its many figures, symbols and lines, the map at first appears to be puzzling. But with a little study of these markings and an understanding of their meaning, the map becomes a picture of the weather giving you a good idea of what's in store.

Some boatmen may receive the weekly compilations of daily weather maps mailed to subscribers by the National Weather Service, NOAA. Most skippers, however, depend upon newspaper maps for their information. These are drawn from Weather Service master weather charts. Four times each day, the Weather Service in Washington prepares and analyzes surface and upper air weather charts for the entire Northern Hemisphere.

On surface charts, weather data are plotted as received every six hours from more than 750 reporting stations in North America, more than 200 ships at sea, and 1500 stations in other countries. Each station reports the amount of sky covered by cloud, direction and speed of wind,

visibility distance in miles, present weather, weather during the last three hours, sea level barometric pressure, air temperature, kinds of low, middle and high clouds, dew-point temperature, character and amount of pressure change in the last three hours, and the character, duration and amount of rainfall in the last six hours. Many of these stations also furnish twelve-hour reports of pressure, temperature, moisture and wind conditions for several levels of upper air. Thus, the central weatherman with his daily surface and several upper air charts has a detailed picture of the weather occurring at the same time over the entire Northern Hemisphere. These charts are used in issuing the daily weather forecasts and warnings of approaching storms.

Over 150 *symbols* are used in entering data on weather maps. Although you may never need know what all the symbols mean, nor have occasion to plot them on a weather map, a knowledge of those most often used will help you to understand and interpret the daily maps appearing in newspapers. See fig. 1201.

THE STATION MODEL

Fig. 1202 shows the *"station model,"* a system weathermen the world over developed for entering data on weather maps. It presents a "model" or picture of the weather at a station, using symbols and numbers, which can be understood in any language. Not only the symbols and numbers but their positions around the station circle tell what each item means. Fig. 1202 represents a typical arrangement.

Study these for a few moments. By referring to fig. 1201 and reading the parenthetical explanations in fig. 1202, you can interpret the weather at this particular station.

For example, starting with the "station circle" itself (the black dot in the middle)—the fact that this circle is solid black indicates that the sky is completely covered with clouds here.

Let's go counterclockwise around the station circle to examine and understand what's shown. Take the wind first. The symbol indicates a pretty windy day, the wind being from the northwest at 21 to 25 mph. The wind arrows always "fly" with the wind.

Next is temperature in degrees Fahrenheit. As you can see, it was relatively cold, the thermometer registering only 31°.

Since we know the sky was completely overcast, the next two markings—Visibility and Present Weather—begin to give us a picture of conditions at the station. It was a nasty day with a stiff, cold wind blowing light snow all over the place.

PRECIPITATION SYMBOLS

A word about precipitation symbols is in order here. Fig. 1201 shows the symbols used to indicate different forms of precipitation—drizzle, rain, snow, etc. Increasing precipitation is indicated by more than one symbol being plotted, the range being from one to four identical symbols.

In fig. 1202 the use of the two stars (or asterisks) tells you that it is snowing continuously but lightly at this station. If there had been three stars the snow would have

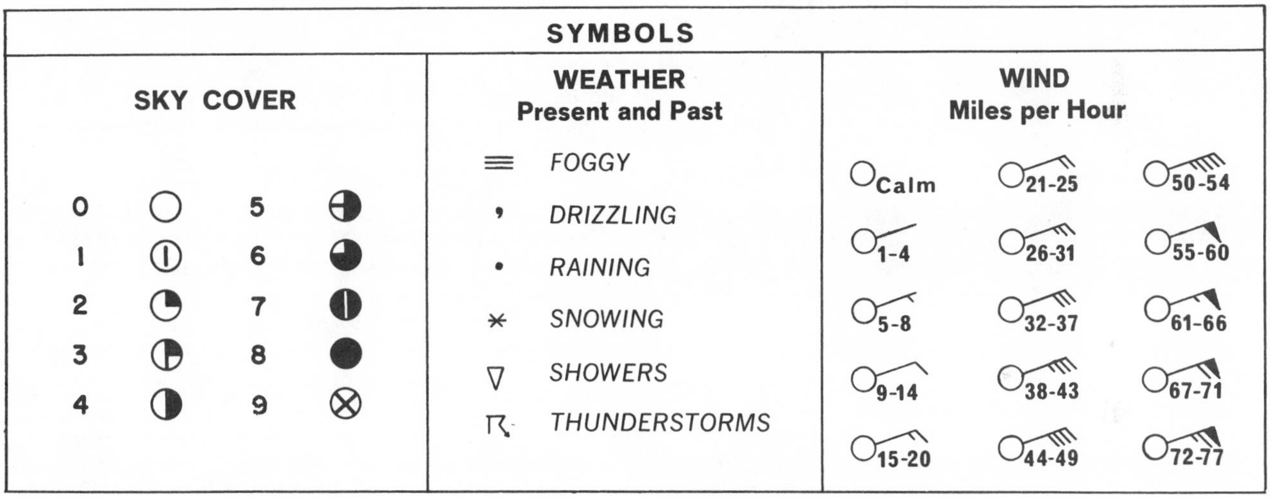

SYMBOLS		
SKY COVER	**WEATHER** Present and Past	**WIND** Miles per Hour

FIG. 1201

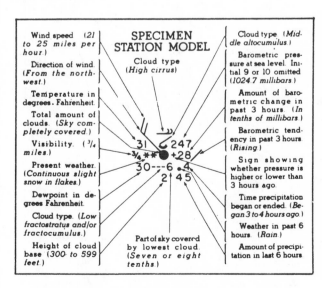

FIG. 1202   Illustrating how symbols in fig. 1201 are used by weathermen to show weather conditions at a station.

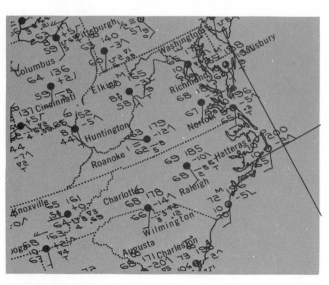

FIG. 1203 A section of the Atlantic coast from a National Weather Service Surface Chart with data for several stations.

been moderate to heavy. Now, if the *shower* symbol (a triangle) had been shown instead of the star it would have carried a star symbol above it to indicate that the showers were *snow* showers. If the showers were *rain* the shower symbol would have carried a dot (the rain symbol) above it.

Hail is indicated by a small triangle (inverted shower symbol) above the thunderstorm symbol. Fog is represented by three horizontal lines.

Other symbols around the station circle in fig. 1202 are interesting and important to weathermen and anyone wishing to use the information. They are worth studying but since most of them do not appear on the abbreviated maps appearing in newspapers we won't go into a detailed description here. Fig. 1202 does provide a brief explanation of each.

Fig. 1203 shows a small portion of a Weather Service surface chart with data plotted for several stations. By re-

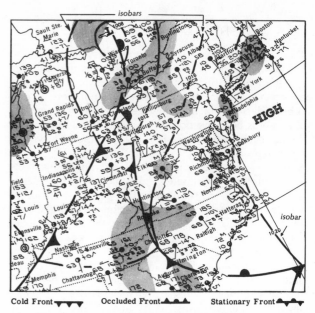

FIG. 1205 Section of a weather map with fronts, isobars, HIGHS, LOWS, and direction of fronts plotted on it.

ferring to figs. 1201 and 1202 you can tell what the weather conditions at any given station are. Let's take Raleigh, N. C. as a case in point:

You can see that the sky is completely overcast, the wind is south, at 9 to 14 mph, the temperature is 69°F., the dew point is 68°, the numeral 2 indicates the clouds were low, the letter T says that precipitation in the past 6 hours was very slight, T standing for "Trace," the barometer has fallen 1.0 millibar during the past 3 hours, there were thunderstorms at the station during the past 6 hours, and

Inches	Millibars	Inches	Millibars
28.44	963	29.77	1008
28.53	966	29.86	1011
28.62	969	29.94	1014
28.70	972	30.03	1017
28.79	975	30.12	1020
28.88	978	30.21	1023
28.97	981	30.30	1026
29.06	984	30.39	1029
29.15	987	30.48	1032
29.24	990	30.56	1035
29.32	993	30.65	1038
29.41	996	30.74	1041
29.50	999	30.83	1044
29.59	1002	30.92	1047
29.68	1005	31.01	1050

FIG. 1204 Conversion table for a weather map's millibars.

FIG. 1206 Typical abridged weather map commonly appearing in newspapers.

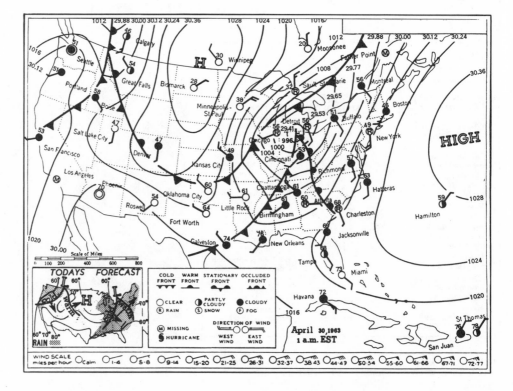

the pressure is 1018.5 millibars or 30.08 inches of mercury.

Fig. 1204 provides a conversion table for changing millibars to inches and vice versa.

ISOBARS AND FRONTS

When data from all stations are entered on the map, the weatherman draws black lines, called *isobars*. These are lines drawn through points having the same ("iso-" means equal) barometric pressure. For example, a 1020 millibar (30.12 inches) isobar is a line drawn through all points having a barometric pressure of 1020 millibars. Ad-

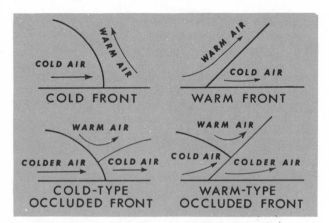

FIG. 1207 Diagrams indicate action of cold and warm fronts and show how their interaction forms occluded fronts.

ditional isobars are drawn for every four millibar intervals. The purpose of the isobars is to position the centers of low and high pressure — the familiar "LOWS" and "HIGHS" which govern our weather. The centers of high pressures are marked "H" or "High" and the low pressures are marked "L" or "Low." It is the movement of these HIGHS and LOWS which enables the weatherman to forecast weather, taking into consideration, of course, the various data supplied by the weather stations.

The heavier lines in fig. 1205 are drawn to indicate "*fronts*" — the boundaries between different air streams. Triangles and half circles are attached to these heavier lines pointing in the direction in which the fronts are mov-

ing. The triangle indicates a "*cold front*," the half circle a "*warm front*." (See also fig. 1207.)

A front which is not moving, one which is "*stationary*," is shown by attaching triangles on one side of the line and half circles on the opposite side. An "*occluded front*" is indicated by attaching both triangles and half circles to one side of the line. Fronts and their significance will be explained later.

WEATHER OFFICES

If you visit a Weather Service office you can see the latest surface and upper air weather maps. Maps prepared at the Weather Service Headquarters are sent to various stations over a picture (facsimile) transmission circuit. Maps prepared by local stations appear much the same as the Washington maps with a few exceptions. The cold fronts, for instance, will be drawn on the map in blue pencil, warm fronts in red, occluded fronts in purple, while the stationary front will be shown by a line of alternating red and blue dashes.

NEWSPAPER WEATHER MAP

Because of their reduced size, it is impossible to include on newspaper maps all of the data usually entered on a map prepared at a Weather Bureau office. To permit easier reading, only sky covered by cloud or other forms of present weather, wind direction and speed, and air temperature are plotted for each station. Barometric pressure at each station is omitted because it can be estimated for any place from the nearest isobar (remember—isobars represent lines of equal barometric pressure). Incidentally, on some weather maps, isobars may be drawn for 3 millibar intervals; for example, 996, 999, 1002, etc., rather than the 4 millibar intervals. Some maps show isobars marked at one end with the millibar pressure and at the other end in inches. Symbols used for entry of all this information, including those for types of fronts, are usually shown in the margin of newspaper maps. See fig. 1206.

Morning newspapers usually contain the weather map prepared from data collected the evening before, while afternoon editions publish the early morning chart. The time is noted on the newspaper chart.

Analysis of the Weather Map

We don't need to know how to draw the isobars and fronts on a weather map in order to be able to read one, but we can review to advantage the method used by the professional weatherman. First, the meteorologist enters on the chart the observations at all stations from which he has received reports. The entries, which include both instrumental and visual observations, are recorded partly in numerical and partly in symbolic form, as illustrated in fig. 1202. Second, he delineates any fronts that may exist, using preceding maps, in addition to present information, as a guide to their locations.

Let's take an actual case as analyzed by the late Dr. B. C. Haynes, Senior Meteorologist with the U.S. Weather Bureau, and published by the Bureau in its booklet "An-

alysis of a Series of Surface Weather Maps." Fig. 1208 is the finished map for 1930 EST Wednesday, 17 April, in the year the analysis was made. Given the observations at each station, how was analysis of the data accomplished?

LOCATING THE FRONTS

Consider first the location of the fronts. A *front* is the boundary between two contiguous bodies, or masses, of air which have come from different geographical regions and traveled along different routes (see fig. 1209) and which, therefore, have different physical properties. The *position of a front* is marked principally by the difference in the temperatures of the two air masses, the difference

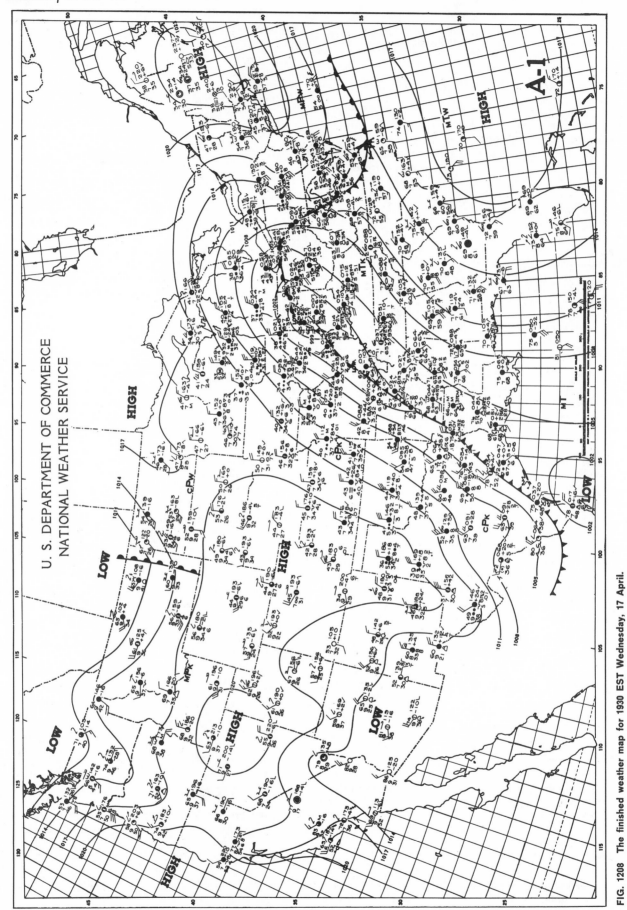

FIG. 1208 The finished weather map for 1930 EST Wednesday, 17 April.

in dew points (the temperature at which the air is saturated with moisture), differences in barometric pressure and pressure tendency, and differences in wind direction and velocity.

To make a start, we examine the plotted data and find that the lowest barometric pressure (998.0 millibars for this map) is at a station in western Indiana. Note that the general wind pattern over Kentucky, Tennessee and the southwestern states is from south to southwest. Over Illinois, Missouri, Kansas and the central plains states the general wind pattern is northwest to north. Different air masses must be over each of these regions and these air masses must be separated by a front. Beginning at our station in western Indiana we will draw this front.

To confirm our finding that a front exists, we look at the next station due west of our starting point; it is located in central Illinois. Here are the salient data at the two stations:

	Western Indiana	Central Illinois
Air temperature	65°	37°
Dew point	60°	36°
Pressure	998.0 mb	1,004.4 mb
Pressure tendency	−2.2 mb	+2.4 mb
Wind direction	SW	N

The differences are sharp; we are on the right track.

We continue southwestward across Illinois, southeastern Missouri, central Arkansas, the northwestern tip of Louisiana, eastern Texas, and into Mexico, all the time comparing the observations at different stations and placing the front between those showing critical contrasts.

Kinds of Fronts

We have drawn a front on our map, but what kind of front is it? To the west and northwest of this front, the observations show relatively colder air moving from the north or northwest; to the east and southeast they show relatively warmer air moving from the south. The colder air is moving toward the front. As it is colder and heavier, it pushes the warmer, lighter air eastward before it, at the same time driving under this warmer air and lifting it off the ground. Cold air is displacing warm; we have a *cold front.*

Are there any more fronts to be found? Starting again at our station in western Indiana, suppose we work eastward this time. Through southern Michigan and northern Ohio we again find differences in wind direction and velocity, in air temperature and dew point. These differences remain quite sharp all the way to western Pennsylvania. We have located another front, a *warm front* this time as the somewhat colder air north of our line is retreating to the northeast and warmer air south of the line is following and replacing the colder.

As we continue eastward from western Pennsylvania, the front becomes more obscure; the differences between the air masses become less pronounced. On the other hand, reports of rain, overcast skies and fog continue. The winds are lighter. We draw in a *stationary front* (neither air mass moving appreciably against the other), all the way across West Virginia, Virginia, and North Carolina to the sea.

Warm fronts and cold fronts are *active* weather factories; a stationary front is a *potential* weather factory. The latter may gradually dissipate or it may resolve itself into an active front.

Taking a final glance at the map, we notice another wind shift and temperature difference in eastern Montana. Applying the same technique, we locate another, a short, warm front in this region. We now have our frontal analysis complete.

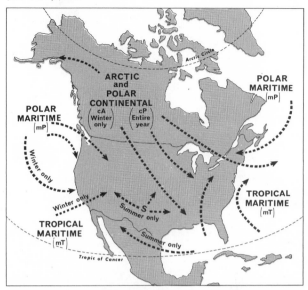

FIG. 1209 North American Air Masses. Source regions and directions of movement of air masses influencing North American weather are shown. Air remaining in contact with earth's surface gradually acquires properties characteristic of the surface beneath it. Then, as this air mass subsequently moves over the earth, its properties, and its conflicts with other air masses that it may encounter en route, cause changes in weather of the area invaded.
(Reproduced by courtesy of Aviation Training Division, U.S. Navy)

ANALYSIS OF PRESSURE INDICATIONS

The third step is to analyze our map for pressure indications; we need to know the pattern of the *isobars,* where high and low pressure centers exist, *the nature of the pressure field.* Because of the earth's rotation, the wind blows, not directly from high to low pressure, but nearly parallel to the isobars and only slightly across them toward low pressure. The more closely spaced the isobars, the stronger the winds in that area. The closely spaced isobars mean that a greater pressure difference exists, hence the winds are stronger, but the earth's rotation still makes them blow almost along the isobars. Observe the wind direction arrow at each station, then note the direction of adjacent isobars. Compare the velocity of the wind, as indicated by the number of feathers on the arrow, with the spacing of the isobars.

To get back to the map for 17 April, we have a low-pressure center in western Indiana. We find a high-pressure center in northeastern Nevada and another off the coast of Maine. There is a high over the central plains states, another over central Canada, and others off the South Atlantic and Pacific coasts. In addition to our western Indiana low, there are lows in the southwest, off the east coast of Texas, and over western Canada.

As we approach our long cold front, the isobars become more closely spaced; the pressure differences are greater and the winds are stronger. It is not too promising a time for a comfortable cruise along the east coast, the Gulf, Mississippi or Great Lakes.

FIG. 1210 Cumulonimbus cloud, indicative of very unstable air. Strong updrafts and severe turbulence are found in and around center of the cloud. Note heavy rain shower falling out of it.

FIG. 1211 A layer of stratus cloud, typical of moist, stable air. In this picture the stratus is very low; shreds of cloud trailing downward from base of the layer are visible against dark hillside.

LABELING THE AIR MASSES

The fourth step is to determine the *kinds of air masses* on either side of each front. A given air mass has its own individual properties; these properties tell us much about the kind of weather we can expect. Having located our fronts and completed the pressure analysis, we can label these air masses. Look at fig. 1208 again.

In the southeastern United States, the winds and pressure gradient indicate that a broad current of air is flowing from over the warm waters of the Gulf northward across the southeastern states. The high temperatures and high dew points in this area tell us that this air is warm and moist. As this is a late afternoon (1930 EST) map, the air has been further heated for many hours by re-radiation of the sun's heat by the earth, which means that the air probably is unstable. The thunderstorms and showers, cumulus and towering cumulonimbus clouds (see fig. 1210) reported at various stations confirm the diagnosis. We label this air with the symbol mTk, meaning that it is *unstable, tropical maritime air,* air that can result in foul weather.

Looking north of the front along the Atlantic Coast, we note that the winds and pressure gradient indicate an on-shore movement of air from over the Atlantic Ocean. Temperatures and dew points are fairly low; fog and low clouds (see fig. 1211) are shown at many stations. These are signs of *maritime, stable polar air* so we label it mPw, the w indicating that it is relatively warmer than the land over which it is moving and hence not given to heating from below. It will lose heat to the earth; more low clouds, fog and light rains are probable.

To the west of our main cold front, we observe northerly winds, low temperatures and low dew points. Many stations report stratocumulus clouds (see fig. 1212) and a few report cumulus clouds. The temperatures recorded tell us that this air mass is being warmed as it moves southward. Again we have unstable air. As it came, however, from the northward over Canada and not from over an ocean, it is

unstable, continental, polar air. We label it cPk.

Studying our map further, we find *stable continental polar air* over the Dakotas (cPw) and *unstable moist (maritime) polar air* (mPk) over the northwestern states.

ESTIMATING EXPECTED CHANGES

We can now make a rough estimate of the changes that will take place during the next 12 hours. The cold front extending from western Indiana to eastern Texas should move eastward in response to the push of the relatively cold northwesterly winds over Illinois, Missouri, Arkansas, Oklahoma and Texas. The warm front across northern Ohio and western Pennsylvania should advance across Lake Erie as the relatively cool air situated to the northeast of the warm front gives way to the moist tropical air flowing from the south. The low-pressure center over western Indiana should be displaced northeastward along the advancing warm front. We should expect this center to move toward the area where the largest negative pressure tendencies are observed, namely, southern Michigan.

A feature of the 1930 EST 17 April map which should not pass unnoticed is the small low-pressure center spotted in the Gulf of Mexico just southeast of the southern tip of Texas. This center appears to be unconnected with the cold front, and its future behavior is hard to judge.

Now let's look at the map for 0730 EST 18 April (fig. 1213). We find that the low-pressure center which was over western Indiana twelve hours earlier has moved in a general northeasterly direction and is situated somewhere between Lake Huron and Lake Ontario. The actual center may be spotted about 100 miles east of the station in eastern Michigan that reports a pressure of 1000.3 millibars, temperature 35°, dew point 35°, and a northwest wind. (Incidentally, twelve hours earlier this same station reported a due north wind, an indication that the cold air there was holding its ground against the advancing warm front. This fact explains why the low-pressure center

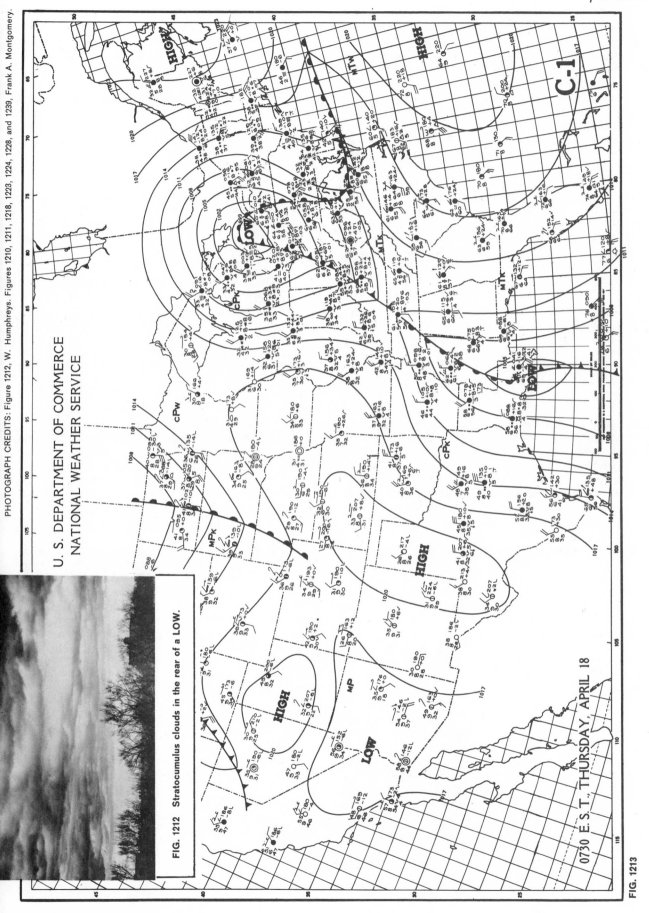

PHOTOGRAPH CREDITS: Figure 1212, W. Humphreys. Figures 1210, 1211, 1218, 1223, 1224, 1228, and 1239, Frank A. Montgomery.

U. S. DEPARTMENT OF COMMERCE
NATIONAL WEATHER SERVICE

C-1

FIG. 1212   Stratocumulus clouds in the rear of a LOW.

0730 E. S. T., THURSDAY, APRIL 18

FIG. 1213

239

moved in a slightly more easterly direction than we had expected from our consideration of the pressure tendencies reported at 1930 EST 17 April.)

From the point of lowest pressure north of Lake Erie we can start our diagnosis of the location of the cold front. The front quite clearly runs southwestward through Ohio and Kentucky, between the stations reporting northwest winds and the stations reporting southerly winds. To the east of the front, temperatures are quite uniformly in the low sixties and dew points in the upper fifties. To the west of it both temperatures and dew points decrease rapidly westward, being in the thirties at a distance of 200 miles from the wind-shift line.

In Tennessee the east-to-west contrasts of temperature and dew point become less sharp, but pronounced differences in wind direction still exist, with winds from the south over eastern Tennessee, Alabama and eastern Mississippi, in contrast to winds generally from the north over western Tennessee, northwestern Mississippi and central and western Louisiana.

If we look at the pressure reports from the region near the Gulf Coast we find a barometric reading at New Orleans of 1004.1 millibars (fig. 1213). This indicates the presence of another low-pressure center, which is almost certainly the same one that we noticed southeast of Texas twelve hours earlier. It has now made connections with the original cold front, and is affecting the movement of this front, as we shall now determine.

In drawing the 1008 millibar isobar northward from the Gulf Coast we find that it no longer can be traced with practically no change in direction all the way to western Pennsylvania, as it could on the preceding map (fig. 1208). It intersects the front in northeastern Mississippi and thence must make a sharp turn to the left, with the result that it returns to the Gulf via western Louisiana. It has become separated from the 1008 millibar isobar to the north, which crosses the front in southwestern Ohio and closes around the northern low-pressure center.

Changes in Wind Pattern

This splitting of the isobaric pattern means that changes in the wind pattern have taken place from Tennessee southward. In eastern Louisiana especially, it can be seen that the winds in the moist tropical air have backed to southeast, while on the other side of the front the winds in the cold air have, in general, veered to a straight northerly, or even north-northeasterly direction. Hence, the winds in the cold air have become more nearly parallel to the front. The result is that the eastward advance of the front has been abruptly stopped; the front has become stationary or is even beginning to reverse its course and to move slowly to the west. Therefore, from the point in Tennessee to just west of New Orleans the front may now be marked a warm front. Southwest of the low-pressure center near New Orleans we assume that the cold air is advancing eastward across the Gulf of Mexico and so we indicate there that the front is acting as a cold front.

RELOCATING THE WARM FRONT

Let us now see how to locate the warm front that extended eastward across northern Indiana, northern Ohio, and thence southeastward to the Middle Atlantic Coast at

1930 EST of 17 April (see fig. 1208). The determination of the position of this front has to be based largely on temperature differences and dew-point differences, since the contrast of wind directions on either side of it are nowhere near as marked as in the case of the cold front.

Beginning at the center of low pressure just east of Lake Huron (fig. 1213), the warm front runs southeastward and may be found in western New York lying between the station that reports a south-southwest wind, pressure 1001.0 millibars, temperature 60°, dew point 58°, and the station in central New York with a southeast wind, pressure 1006.1 millibars, temperature 52°, dew point 45°.

From this point the front extends southward through western Pennsylvania. We determine that it lies between the station in extreme southwestern Pennsylvania (Pittsburgh) which reports a south-southwest wind, temperature 61°, dew point 58°, and the station in central Pennsylvania reporting a southeast wind, continuous light rain, temperature 54°, dew point 47°. (The temperature-dew point combination of 61°/58° observed at Pittsburgh is characteristic, for that latitude, of the moist tropical air that has come from the Gulf of Mexico.)

Beyond this point the position of the front does not show up clearly, owing to the lack of reports from stations in Maryland and northeastern Virginia. We are on safe ground, however, if we draw it between stations reporting south to southwest winds and places where the winds range from northeast to southeast. On this basis we determine that the front intersects the coastline at about latitude 38°. From there we project it eastward out to sea.

We shall not take time to analyze the weather features over the western part of the United States at 0730 EST of 18 April, since little of interest is occurring there. And so we conclude our brief study of the weather map.

SUBSEQUENT DEVELOPMENTS— IN RETROSPECT

The reader, however, may be interested to hear what happened to the principal frontal system and its two associated low-pressure centers during the next four days. During the interval between 0730 EST of 18 April and 0730 EST of 19 April the northern low-pressure area continued its northeastward movement and reached a position just north of the St. Lawrence River. But, meanwhile it weakened considerably, its lowest pressure on 19 April being not less than about 1005 millibars. The northern part of the cold front which extended southwestward from it pushed across Pennsylvania, New York and New England, all the way to the Atlantic. Further south, however, the advance of cold air was slowed by the developing low-pressure center which we noted near New Orleans at 0730 EST of 18 April. During the next 24 hours this center moved north-northeastward to Tennessee, all the while strengthening; by 0730 EST of 19 April it had become more prominent than the northern center.

Subsequently it continued to intensify, as it changed course to a more easterly direction, and eventually it developed into a severe storm. At 0730 EST of 22 April it was located about 250 miles east of Nantucket; the pressure at its exact center had fallen to about 972 millibars (28.70''). It caused exceptionally strong northeast gales off the New England coast during 21 April.

CLOUDS—How they form—What they mean

Storm warning—the anvil-shaped cumulonimbus cloud associated with thunderstorms. The wind at high altitudes is stronger than lower down, so the top of the cloud is carried ahead of the main body and forms an anvil which points like a finger in the direction toward which the upper wind is blowing. (Photographed, on the Mississippi River, by J. D. Tennison, Jr.)

Out on the water you have a front row seat at one of the greatest shows on earth: the constantly changing and highly instructive spectacle presented by the clouds. The meteorological information that clouds convey can help you to estimate future weather developments and thereby make your boating safer and more enjoyable.

Everyone knows that clouds are composed of water In order to learn how to interpret them, one must first understand how water behaves in the atmosphere.

There is always a certain amount of water in gaseous form ("water vapor") present in the air, even on a perfectly clear day. However, there is a limit to the quantity of water vapor that can exist in a given volume of air.. When the amount of water vapor actually present in the air is equal to the limit, the air is said to be "saturated," because then no more water can evaporate into it from ocean, river, lake or other sources.

Saturated air can be thought of as air that contains its full quota of water vapor. This quota varies with the temperature of the air. The warmer the air, the more water vapor it can take up. Thus, if a volume of saturated air is heated, some additional water can be evaporated into it because the temperature of the air will be raised and, hence, the allowable proportion of water vapor will be increased.

Suppose, however, the air is cooled, rather than heated, as happens on a clear night. As its temperature is lowered its water-vapor quota is reduced. Eventually the air is cooled to a temperature for which the allowable propor-

tion of water vapor is equal to the actual amount in the air. This temperature is called the "dew point"; the air is now at saturation. If the air is cooled some more, its water-vapor content becomes excessive in relation to its temperature, and condensation results. This leads to the formation of liquid water particles, which form a cloud when the condensation process takes place in the air aloft, or fog when it takes place near the ground.

Air is cooled whenever it rises. As air ascends, the weight of the atmosphere above it decreases, and so the pressure upon the air diminishes. The decrease of pressure permits the air to expand and to cool. If the ascent and accompanying expansion is great enough to cool the air to a temperature below its dew point, clouds appear. (There are several other ways in which air may be cooled sufficiently to produce condensation, but they play a minor part in cloud formation.)

Clouds formed at heights greater than 4 miles, where the temperature is *always* below freezing, might be expected to consist solely of ice particles. However, at these altitudes clouds composed of liquid droplets also are found; such droplets are said to be "supercooled." Although unfrozen water clouds can exist at temperatures as low as −20°F, the introduction of a relatively small number of ice particles into a cloud composed of supercooled water droplets will, by means of a sort of chain reaction, transform it into an ice cloud, out of which snow will fall and produce a trail stretching downward from the underside of the cloud.

E

The Use of Cloud Observations in Weather Forecasting

It would be naive to believe that anyone can forecast weather 24 hours in advance solely from observations of clouds. Even if such a feat were possible it would provide no great advantage, since the universality of radio communication makes the official forecasts issued by the government weather service readily available to the boatman.

However, government forecasters, despite the enormous quantity of weather observations at their disposal, have difficulties. Greatest problem is probably that of timing; for example, estimating the time of arrival of a wind-shift line.

Here is where an understanding of the meaning of the clouds can be helpful. Clouds are the visible manifestations of physical processes that are taking place in the atmosphere. Some of these processes cause clouds to form and grow; others cause existing clouds to break up and disappear. The ability to interpret the clouds in terms of the physical processes that are going on aloft often will enable the boatman to decide for himself whether the latest official forecast is working out or not. In many cases he can amend the forecast and thereby still make use of it when the timing or some other feature has been miscalculated.

The formation and growth of a cloud or cloud system means that there is an upward component of motion of the air at the level of the cloud, because the cooling necessary to produce the cloud has resulted from expansion of the air. The general appearance of the growing cloud is determined by the stability of the air in which it forms. If the air is stable, then the upward motion responsible for the cloud is a "forced" one; characteristically it is uniformly smooth and gentle. Therefore, the clouds formed by the expansion and concomitant cooling of air that ascends in this fashion are layered, and they grow or thicken relatively slowly.

The pattern of cloud growth just described is illustrated by Photographs Nos. 5, 9, and 30, viewed in that order. The processes at work often produce long-lasting steady rain and, hence, this sequence of photographs typifies the evolution of the sky during the approach of a widespread rain area.

If the atmosphere is unstable, portions of it will rise spontaneously. The upward motion in this case is irregular and rapid; the clouds that form are of the cumulus type and are separated by clear spaces. The pattern of cloud growth in unstable air is illustrated by Photographs Nos. 15, 16 and 25, viewed in that order. This sequence is typical of pre-thunderstorm weather.

> This 4-page insert amplifies the discussion of cloud forms and their significance, which appears on pages 259 and 260.

CIRRUS—These are ice clouds in the form of tufts. Snow is falling out of tuft in upper left portion of photograph. Altitude—above 20,000 feet. The elements are isolated. 1

CIRRUS—This is a dense ice cloud. If viewed toward the sun it appears greyish. It appears to be the edge of an "anvil" cloud formed from Cumulonimbus. 2

ALTOSTRATUS — Thin, translucent water cloud sheet, often the forerunner of rain in most parts of the U.S. Small, dark clouds underneath are Cumulus. 7

ALTOSTRATUS — Translucent sheet cloud with fibrous characteristics. Difference in opacity produces a dark band (bottom). Dark clouds below are Cumulus. Alt —8,000 to 20,000 ft. 8

CUMULUS — Typical of fine weather. Appearance of sky indicates good weather continuing for 6 hours at least. Altitude—base of cloud 3,000 to 5,000 feet. 13

CUMULUS—These are less benign than those in Photograph No. 13. However, they do not have a threatening appearance. Altitude of cloud tops about 10,000 feet. 14

STRATOCUMULUS — Another example of an unbroken sheet of Stratocumulus. The elongation and alignment of the rolls suggest that strong wind is blowing. 19

STRATOCUMULUS and CUMULUS — Here is cloud-layer formed from decaying Cumulus. Fresh Cumulus are growing underneath. Altitude—base 5,000 to 8,000 feet. 20

CUMULONIMBUS—This is a "chaotic" sky with Cumulonimbus in the background and growing Cumulus in the foreground. Showers and thunderstorms are occurring nearby. 25

CUMULUS and CUMULONIMBUS — Cumulus are seen in lower portion. Cloud sheet above is part of a vast Cumulonimbus. Scene is typical of thunderstorm weather. 26

CLOUDS AND THE BAROMETER—There is very little correlation between individual cloud types and barometric indications. Most clouds shown here can occur in association with either a rising or falling barometer. However, if the sky is filled with Cumulus and the barometer is falling, look for the development of Cumulonimbus and showers. Thickening high-altitude ice clouds accompanying a falling barometer are particularly significant. This combination almost always indicates the approach of wet weather. But *isolated* Cirrus tufts or streaks occur without relation to the barometric trend.

CIRRUS — Ice clouds in the form of both tufts and hooks. The hooks are snow trails which are bent when they encounter changes in wind direction and velocity at lower altitudes. **3**

CIRROSTRATUS — This cloud covers the whole sky. Individual Cirrus tufts appear, but they merge with a sheet of ice filaments. Altitude—above 20,000 feet. **4**

CIRROSTRATUS — Ice cloud in the form of a veil. The halo is caused by refraction of sunlight through the ice crystals composing the veil. The halo is **not** a sure sign of rain. **5**

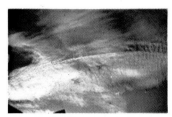

CIRROCUMULUS — Fairly typical in middle section. Cirrus streaks are visible at top. Altitude—above 20,000 feet. This cloud is often difficult to distinguish from Altocumulus. **6**

ALTOSTRATUS — This layer is sufficiently translucent to reveal the position of the sun. Dark patches in vicinity of sun probably are remains of Cumulus. **9**

ALTOCUMULUS — This sheet of lightly shaded white to dark grey elements displays the chief characteristics of Altocumulus. Altitude—8,000 to 20,000 feet. **10**

ALTOCUMULUS — This layer of Altocumulus has a wavy appearance. The billows are caused by irregularities in the wind at the altitude of the cloud. **11**

ALTOCUMULUS — This is clearly a water cloud, since it shows no signs of hair-like structure. The elements are ragged and apparently are evaporating. **12**

CUMULUS — The build-up in the left half of the picture appears to be sprouting rather rapidly. However, development of Cumulonimbus is not imminent. **15**

CUMULUS — The Cumulus in the right half of the picture has considerable vertical extent. The bulging upper part indicates strong ascending air currents. **16**

STRATOCUMULUS — Appearance indicates localized rising air currents. Stratocumulus is dark cloud in foreground. Cumulonimbus (white cloud). Altitude—base 3,000 to 5,000 feet. **17**

STRATOCUMULUS — This is a solid layer of Stratocumulus formed by the merging of numerous Cumulus clouds. Light showers may fall from it. Often accompanied by gusty winds. **18**

STRATOCUMULUS — Typifies Stratocumulus formed during the day and evaporating at sunset. Rising currents have stopped; a clear night can be expected. **21**

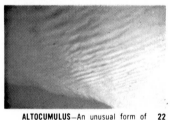

ALTOCUMULUS — An unusual form of Altocumulus. It might be identified as Cirrocumulus, but absence of streaks means it is a water rather than ice cloud. **22**

ALTOSTRATUS and CUMULUS — This combination and the general appearance of the sky suggest that the weather is beginning to improve following a rainstorm. **23**

CUMULUS and CIRRUS — The white clouds at top are Cirrus (note the streaks). Cumulus below suggest Cirrus have been derived from distant Cumulonimbus. **24**

CUMULONIMBUS — A rain shower can be seen falling from the darkest portion. This feature identifies the cloud as Cumulonimbus even though it is not a thunderstorm cloud. **27**

CUMULONIMBUS — Exhibiting hanging protuberances, called "mamma," caused by the descent of blobs of cloud-filled air. Associated with severe thunderstorms. **28**

CUMULONIMBUS — The heavy rain shower in the distance identifies the cloud as Cumulonimbus. The scene is common over warm ocean waters in summer. **29**

STRATUS — A featureless grey sheet whose base is within a few hundred feet of the ground. If rain falls from it, the cloud is called NIMBOSTRATUS. Note top of tower is obscured. **30**

STABLE vs. UNSTABLE AIR—These terms are best explained by first considering stability in a liquid. A light liquid can float on top of a heavier one without mixing, but a heavy liquid will not float on top of a lighter one. The first arrangement is stable, the second unstable. Heating of a kettle of water from below demonstrates the same fact. The water at the bottom of the kettle is heated and becomes lighter than the water above it. The warmed water rises from the bottom, its place being taken by colder water from above. This action occurs because water is unstable when cold water lies above warm. Because air is compressible, the condition for stability in the atmosphere is — *not* that the temperature shall increase with height, but that the temperature shall not decrease at a rate (*for unsaturated air*) greater than 5.4°F per 1,000 feet. If, due to heating at the earth's surface, the temperature decrease with height exceeds this rate, the air is unstable, or top-heavy, and tends to overturn.

G

BASIC CLOUD FORMS

Although 10 principal cloud types are defined in the International Cloud Classification (see pages 259-261), there are really only three basic cloud forms: (1) "streak" clouds, (2) "sheet" clouds and (3) "heap" clouds. The streak clouds are composed of tiny ice particles which often form trails, giving rise to the picturesque English name "mares' tails." ("Federwolke" is the German name for the same formation.)

HOW CLOUDS ARE NAMED

In the interest of conformity, however, the cloud designations chosen for international usage are derived from Latin words. Streak clouds are called *cirrus* (a hair or curl) A sheet-like cloud is called *stratus* (a spreading out) and a heap cloud *cumulus* (a heap). When appropriate, other Latin words are joined to these primary ones. Thus, for example, the Latin word *nimbus* (black rain cloud) is combined with *stratus* and with *cumulus* to give *nimbostratus* and *cumulonimbus,* meaning, respectively, "raining cloud sheet" and "raining heap cloud."

SHEET AND HEAP TYPES

Sheet clouds are produced mainly by a slow widespread ascent of stable air, less commonly by radiative cooling of air moving purely horizontally. Heap clouds, on the other hand, are formed in unstable air permeated with localized, strong updrafts created by spontaneous ascent of buoyant "bubbles" of air.

EFFECT OF WIND SHEAR

Numerous modifications of the basic cloud forms are observed. These may be caused by complex motions within the clouds or by the twisting effect of "vertical wind shear," that is, changes in the direction and velocity of the wind from one altitude to another. We have a demonstration of the latter in the not-uncommon sight of curving streaks of ice crystals which trail from a parent cirrus (see photograph No. 3).

IN MIDDLE LATITUDES

In middle latitudes, at elevations greater than about 10,000 feet, the wind velocity generally increases with height but the direction usually remains fairly constant right up to 30,000 feet at least. Tall cumulus clouds in this kind of environment will be bent by vertical wind shear, so that their tops lean forward. A striking example of this is provided in the photograph at top of page E. Here the cloud apparently has built up to the base of the stratosphere. At that altitude a temperature inversion has stopped its upward growth, and the stronger wind which exists there has spread the cloud top horizontally off to the right.

IN TRADE-WIND BELTS

In the tropical trade-wind belts, where easterly winds prevail in the lowest 10,000 feet of the atmosphere, cumulus clouds are sometimes seen to lean backwards. This happens because the easterly winds of the tropics ordinarily do not increase in velocity upward as do the westerlies of middle latitudes. It is not uncommon for the wind velocity to decrease with elevation, so that the vertical wind shear is directed from west toward east. If the top of a tall tropical cumulus cloud is seen to be bent sharply backward, perhaps pointing in an almost horizontal direction, it is probable that the cloud top has penetrated an upper layer where the wind is blowing from the west.

ROLLS OR BILLOWS

The roll formations, or billows, that often occur in a layer of middle-level clouds (see photograph No. 11) are usually caused by vertical wind shear. The upper part of the layer is moving faster than the lower part but is flowing in the same direction. The sliding of the upper part over the lower part sets up waves on the boundary between the two, with the result that the cloud deck is shaped into rolls which are oriented approximately at right angles to the direction of the air flow.

CLOUDS AND CLIMATE

The ten cloud types defined in pages 259-261 can be seen the world over. However, the frequency of each type varies considerably from one climate region to another. For example, *cumulus* is far more prevalent in the tropics than in the polar regions, whereas *stratus* occurs more often in middle and high latitudes than in the tropics. Moreover, the predominating cloud types in certain parts of the United States are quite different from those in others.

HEIGHT—RANGES

The table below gives the approximate height-ranges of the bases of the ten principal cloud types. In this table the overlapping of the upper limits of the middle-level water clouds (Ac and As) and the lower limits of the ice clouds is explained by latitudinal, seasonal, and day-to-day variations in temperature, which occur aloft as well as well as at the earth's surface.

APPROXIMATE HEIGHT-RANGES AT WHICH BASES OF VARIOUS CLOUDS ARE FOUND			
Cloud Type	In polar regions	In middle latitudes	In tropical regions
Ci, Cc, Cs	10,000-30,000 ft.	16,000-45,000 ft.	25,000-55,000 ft.
Ac, As	6,000-15,000 ft.	6,000-23,000 ft.	6,000-25,000 ft.
Ns, Sc, St, Cu, Cb	From near the ground to 8,000 feet		

Types of Storms

EXTRA-TROPICAL CYCLONES

The principal source of rain, winds and generally foul weather in the United States is the *extra-tropical cyclone.* There are other storms—the hurricane, the thunderstorm and the tornado—that are usually more destructive but it is a fact that the extra-tropical cyclone is the ultimate cause of most of our weather troubles. Fog is another enemy not to be taken lightly, as we shall see, but let's concentrate on storms right now. If we would take proper and timely precautions for them, we should know something of their characteristics.

A definition of an extra-tropical cyclone in the Northern Hemisphere is: a traveling system of winds rotating counterclockwise around a center of low barometric pressure and containing a warm front and a cold front.

How extra-tropical cyclones develop

We saw what one looked like on the daily weather map. Fig. 1214 is a diagram (plan view) of the birth, development and death of an extra-tropical cyclone. Our thanks are due Captain Charles G. Halpine, USN, for permission to reproduce this diagram from his book "A Pilot's Meteorology," published by D. van Nostrand Company.

In part (a) of fig. 1214, we have a warm air mass, typically moist tropical air, flowing northeastward and a cold air mass, typically polar continental, flowing southwestward. They are separated by a heavy line representing the boundary or front between them. The next stage is shown in part (b). The cold air from behind pushes under the warm air; the warm air rushes up over the cold air ahead of it. A cold front is born on the left, a warm front on the right. Where they are connected, the barometric pressure is lowered and the air starts circulating counterclockwise around this LOW. At the rear of the cold front, a high-pressure area

develops. At the same time, the whole system keeps moving in a general easterly direction. The crosshatched area represents rain. When warm, moist air is lifted, as it is when a cold air mass pushes under it or when it rushes up over cold air ahead, it cools by expansion. After its temperature has fallen to the dew point, excess water vapor condenses to form first clouds and then rain.

In parts (c) and (d) of fig. 1214, the storm matures, the low-pressure area intensifying more and more, the clouds and rain increasing and the winds becoming stronger. In part (e), the cold front begins to catch up with the warm front; an occluded front is formed. The storm is now at its height. It will do about one-half of its mischief while in occlusion. In part (f), it has begun to weaken; after a while, the weather should clear, as the high-pressure area reaches us.

Extra-tropical cyclones often occur in families of two, three or four storms. It takes about one day (24 hours) for this disturbance to reach maturity with three or possibly four days more required for complete dissipation. In winter, these storms occur on the average of twice a week in the USA; in summer they occur somewhat less frequently and are less severe. Their movement is eastward to north of east at a velocity in winter of about 700 miles per day and in summer of perhaps 500 miles per day. Finally, this storm usually covers a large area geographically; it can affect a given locality for two days or more.

Parts of the extra-tropical cyclone

The component parts of an extra-tropical cyclone are:
1. A warm front, with its two conflicting air masses and its weather.
2. A cold front, with its two conflicting air masses, one of which (the warmer) is situated between the cold front and the warm front.

FIG. 1214 Diagram of development of extra-tropical cyclone.
(Reproduced by courtesy of Captain C. G. Halpine, U.S.N., and D. van Nostrand Co., Inc.)

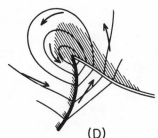

(A)

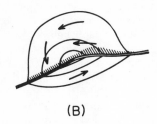

(B)

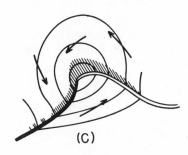

(C)

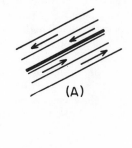

(D)

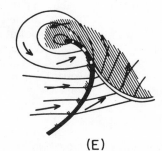

(E)

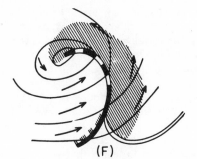

(F)

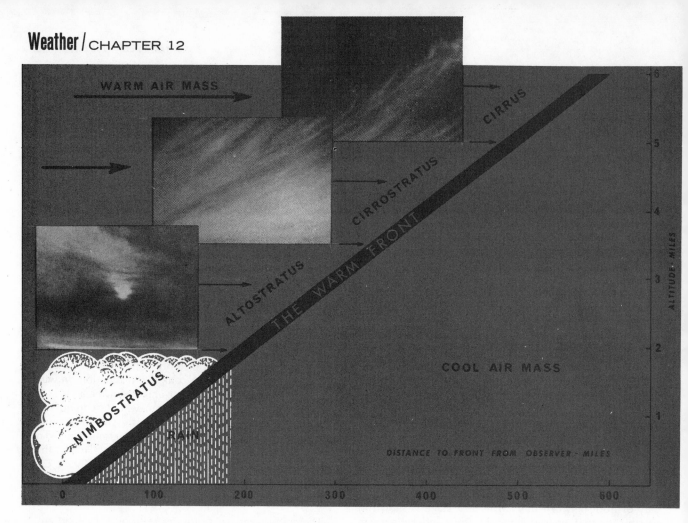

FIG. 1215

3. A center of low barometric pressure with its wind system, at the junction of the fronts.

4. A high pressure area behind the cold front.

A typical cruising experience

In early May a few years ago we were cruising down the Mississippi. We noticed on the weather map that there was an extra-tropical cyclone far to the WSW, its center moving NE along a path that would leave us SSE of it. The warm front, the warm sector between the fronts, and the cold front would pass over us if we continued our cruise. Being stubborn, we kept on but watched carefully for the approaching trouble.

The first day the weather was fine with gentle winds and light fluffy cumulus clouds. The next morning we observed cirrus (Ci) clouds (fig. 1215) to the westward and noted that the barometer was falling. As these slowly thickened, we knew that the warm front was perhaps 500 miles, about one day, away. As the day wore on, the barometer fell more rapidly, the wind blew increasingly strong from the southeast, and the clouds thickened to the cirrostratus (Cs) of fig. 1215. A halo appeared around the sun.

Altostratus (As) clouds (fig. 1215) next were seen approaching from westward. Knowing that these clouds precede a warm front by about 300 miles and that rain can be expected about 200 miles ahead of the front, it required no magician to tell us that we had better begin securing

ship and breaking out the oilskins. We observed that the spread between the air temperature and dew-point temperature was growing less and less; it looked as though we could also expect fog. We decided to anchor until the warm front had passed over.

Next came the low nimbostratus (Ns) clouds and the rain, the barometer continuing to fall and the temperature slowly to rise. The visibility grew worse and worse. The ship's bell began its clamor and we spent a not too comfortable night. By morning, however, the wind had veered to SSW, the clouds had begun to break, the barometer had stopped falling, the rain had ceased. Knowing that it might be 6 to 12 hours before the cold front struck us, we got under way, keeping our eyes peeled for altocumulus (Ac) clouds to the westward. The watch below was set to airing the cabins and our duffle as we ran through the warm sector.

About 1400 the lookout spotted the altocumulus clouds (fig. 1216); the cold front was perhaps 100 miles away. As the day was hot and quite humid, we thought that thunderstorms were probable and that they might be severe. We decided to anchor early, about 1500, and prepare for the worst. The barometer was again falling, the wind was SW and increasing. Nimbostratus (Ns) clouds with cumulonimbus (Cb) (fig. 1216) towering out of them appeared to the west. Rain set in and the wind rose sharply. We had a busy few hours—and were mighty glad that we had known enough to recognize and time the warning signs. By the

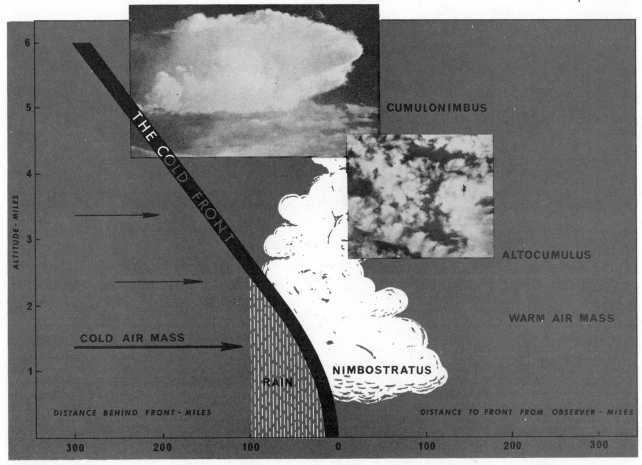

FIG. 1216

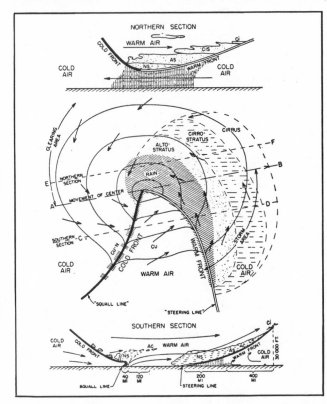

FIG. 1217 Cross-sections of extra-tropical cyclone. (Reproduced by courtesy of Captain C. G. Halpine, U.S.N., and D. van Nostrand Co., Inc.)

next morning the storm was over and we continued our cruise with a blue sky and fair winds.

Thus, we passed through an extra-tropical cyclone. Fig. 1217 is a picture of it, again with acknowledgement to Captain Halpine. The central portion is a plan view of the storm; the lower portion is a vertical cross-section along the line CD, our "course" through the storm. The cloud sequences and the rain are clearly shown (Cb symbol omitted). Had we passed north, instead of south, of the center, the upper diagram would represent the clouds and weather.

HURRICANES

Another type of cyclone which is of concern principally to those of us cruising the Gulf of Mexico and the southeast Atlantic coast is the *tropical cyclone,* which in its most violent (and best known) form is called a *hurricane.* Unlike the extra-tropical cyclone, it does not contain warm and cold fronts, and its occurrence (over waters adjacent to the United States) is restricted to summer and autumn.

The hurricane as a storm type is too well known among sailors to require any description here of the various premonitory signs, the violence of the wind and rain accompanying such a storm and the steps to be taken to minimize the dangers of encounter. These are fully detailed in standard nautical works, such as Bowditch's "American Practical Navigator."

243

FIG. 1218 Wall cloud around eye of a hurricane, as seen from an aircraft within the eye. Upper edge of wall cloud is at an altitude of nearly 40,000 feet. Note clear space in right foreground.

Over the years much statistical information on the frequency of hurricanes in various regions of the world has accumulated. In the Far East hurricanes (or *typhoons*, as they are called in the western Pacific) may occur in any month, although late summer and early autumn are the preferred seasons. In North American waters, however, the period from early December through May is hurricane-free. August, September and October are the months of greatest frequency; in these months hurricanes form over the tropical Atlantic, mostly between latitudes 8°N and 20°N. The infrequent hurricanes of June and November almost always originate in the southwestern part of the Caribbean Sea.

Development of a hurricane

The birthplace of a hurricane typically lies within a diffuse and fairly large area of relatively low pressure situated somewhere in the latitude belt just mentioned. The winds around the low-pressure area are not particularly strong, and, although cumulonimbus clouds and showers are more numerous than is usual in these latitudes, there is no clearly organized "weather system." This poorly-defined condition may persist for several days before hurricane development commences.

When development starts, however, it takes place suddenly. Within an interval of 12 hours or less the barometric pressure drops 15 millibars or more over a small, almost circular area. Winds of hurricane force spring up and form a ring around the area; the width of this ring is at first only 20 to 40 miles. The clouds and showers become well-organized and show a spiral structure. At this stage the growing cyclone acquires an eye. This is the inner area enclosed by the ring of hurricane-force winds, which, by the time the cyclone reaches maturity, has expanded to a width of 100 miles or more. Within the eye we find the lowest barometric reading.

Hurricane eyes average about 15 miles in diameter but may be as large as 25 miles. The wind velocities in the eye of a hurricane are seldom greater than 15 knots and often are less. Cloud conditions vary over a wide range. At times

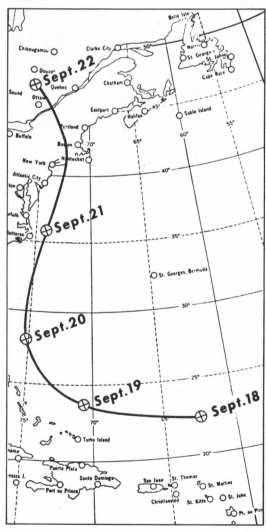

FIG. 1219 Path of the hurricane, showing positions of the center at 0700 EST, 18-22 September 1938.

there are only scattered clouds, but usually there is more than 50% cloud cover. Through the openings the sky is visible overhead and at a distance the dense towering clouds of the hurricane ring can be seen extending to great heights (fig. 1218). This feature has been given the name *wall cloud.*

Hurricane tracks

The usual track of an Atlantic hurricane describes a parabola around the semipermanent Azores-Bermuda high-pressure area. Thus, after forming, a hurricane will move westward on the southern side of the Azores-Bermuda HIGH, at the same time tending to work away from the equator. When the hurricane reaches the western side of this HIGH, it begins to follow a more northerly track, and its direction of advance changes progressively toward the right. Thus, the usual movement of Atlantic hurricanes at first is roughly westward, then northwestward, northward, and finally northeastward. The position where the westward movement changes to an eastward movement is known as the *point of recurvature.*

Occasionally when a hurricane is in a position near the

southeast Atlantic coast, the Azores-Bermuda HIGH happens to have an abnormal northward extension. In this type of situation the hurricane will fail to execute a complete recurvature in the vicinity of Cape Hatteras. It will skirt the western side of the HIGH and follow a path almost due north along the Atlantic coast, as occurred in the case of the famous New England hurricane of September 1938 (see figs. 1219 and 1220).

The rate of movement of tropical cyclones while they are still in low latitudes and heading westward is about 15 knots, which is considerably slower than the usual rate of travel of extra-tropical cyclones. After recurving they begin to move faster and usually attain a forward speed of at least 25 knots, sometimes 50 to 60 knots, as in the case of the September 1938 hurricane. A small proportion of hurricanes, however, do not recurve at all, and a few of these follow highly irregular tracks which may include a complete loop.

Hurricanes gradually decrease in intensity after they reach middle and high latitudes and move over colder water. Many lose their identity by absorption into the wind circulation around the larger extra-tropical cyclones of the North Atlantic.

THUNDERSTORMS

We stated at the beginning of this section that the extra-tropical cyclone was the ultimate cause of most of our foul weather. We said this advisedly, because in addition to the strong winds and generally wet weather which it generates, smaller-scale storms, such as *thunderstorms* and *tornadoes,* usually are created by the contrasting air masses and conflicting winds within the large-scale, overall air circulation of the extra-tropical cyclone. Thus, thunderstorms are commonly linked to the cold front of the cyclone. But if the air comprising the warm sector is sufficiently unstable, which is often the case in summer, thunderstorms together with general rain will occur during the approach of a warm front as the warm-sector air ascends over the cold air ahead. They also develop on their own in the middle of an air mass, unaided by frontal activity.

We know a thunderstorm as a storm of short duration, arising only in a cumulonimbus cloud, attended by thunder and lightning, and marked by abrupt fluctuations of temperature, pressure and wind. A *line squall,* now usually referred to in meteorological parlance as a *squall line,* is a lengthy row of thunderstorms stretching for 100 miles or more.

Incidentally, a *shower* (as opposed to gentle, steady rain) is a smaller brother, though the rainfall and wind in it may be of considerable intensity. It characteristically is the product of relatively large cumulus, or small cumulonimbus, clouds separated from one another by blue sky. It is not accompanied by thunder and lightning.

Features of the thunderstorm cloud

In all cases the prime danger signal is a cumulus cloud growing larger. Every thunderstorm cloud has four distinctive features, although we may not always be able to see all four as other clouds may intervene in our line of sight. Fig. 1221 shows these four features; the anvil top is better illustrated in fig. 1222. These three photographs of an anvil were taken from the same position over a period of one-half hour!

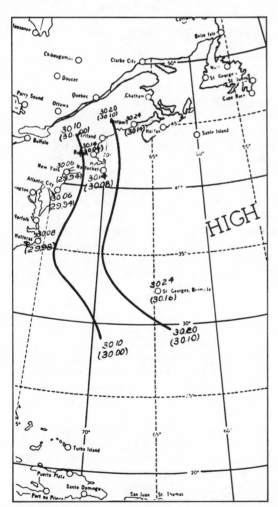

FIG. 1220 Constancy of anticyclonic flow, as shown by unchanged orientation of sea-level isobars from September 19 to September 20. Upper figure of each pair of numbers is barometric reading on September 19, lower figure that on September 20. Although a general fall of pressure took place during the interval, flow pattern remained the same.

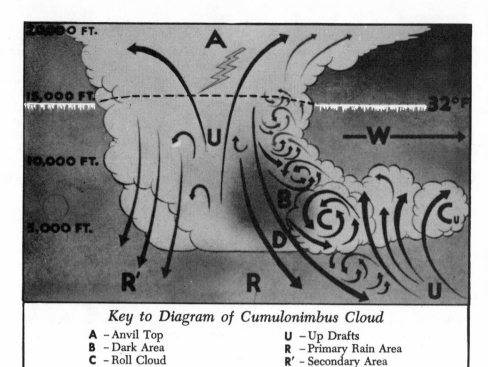

FIG. 1221 Diagram of thunderstorm cloud.
(Courtesy of Aviation Training Division, U.S. Navy)

Key to Diagram of Cumulonimbus Cloud

A – Anvil Top	**U** – Up Drafts
B – Dark Area	**R** – Primary Rain Area
C – Roll Cloud	**R′** – Secondary Area
C_u – Advance Cumulus Clouds	**W** – Wind Direction
D –Down Drafts	

Fig. 1221 is a drawing, by courtesy of the Navy Bureau of Aeronautics from their booklet "Thunderstorms" (Aerology Series Two), of a cumulonimbus cloud; it shows these four features diagrammatically. Starting at the top, we notice the layer of cirrus clouds, shaped like an anvil and consequently called "anvil top," leaning in the direction toward which the upper wind is blowing. This tells us the direction in which the storm is moving.

The next feature is the main body of the cloud; it is a large cumulus of great height with cauliflower sides. It must be of great height, as it must extend far above the freezing level if the cirrus anvil top is to form. Cirrus clouds are composed of ice crystals, not water droplets. The third feature is the roll cloud formed by violent air currents along the leading edge of the base of the cumulus cloud. The fourth and final feature is the dark area within the storm and extending from the base of the cloud to the earth; at the center this is rain, at the edges hail and rain.

Requirements for thunderstorm formation

There are three requirements for the formation of thunderstorms. One, there must be strong upward air currents such as are caused by a cold front burrowing under and lifting warm air or by heating of the air in contact with the surface of the earth on a summer day. Warm, humid air blowing up a mountain slope also can produce a thunderstorm. Two, the air parcels forming the storm must be buoyant relative to their neighbors outside the storm and willing, therefore, to keep on ascending higher and higher until they pass the freezing level. Third, the air must have a large concentration of water vapor. The most promising thunderstorm air is of tropical maritime origin; whenever it appears in our cruising area, especially when a cold front is approaching, we need to be suspicious.

Frequency of thunderstorms

Thunderstorms occur most frequently and with the greatest intensity in the summer over all parts of the USA. While they may strike at any hour, they prefer the late afternoon and early evening over inland and coastal waters. The surrounding land has been a good "stove" for many hours, heating the air to produce strong upward currents. Over the ocean, well away from shore, thunderstorms more commonly occur between midnight and sunrise. Finally, thunderstorms are most frequent and most violent in tropical latitudes; they are less common and less intense in the higher latitudes. The southeastern states experience as many as four thunderstorms per week in summer.

Ahead of a thunderstorm the wind may be either steady or variable, but as the *roll cloud* (fig. 1221) draws near, the wind weakens and becomes unsteady. As the roll cloud passes overhead, violent shifting winds, accompanied by strong downdrafts, may be expected. The wind velocity may reach 60 knots. Heavy rain and sometimes hail begins to fall just abaft the roll cloud. However, the weather quickly clears after the passage of the storm, which brings cooler temperatures and lower humidity.

If the cumulonimbus cloud is fully developed and towers to normal thunderstorm altitudes, 35,000 feet or more in summer, the storm will be violent. If the anvil top is low, say only 20,000 feet or so, as is usual in spring and autumn, the storm will be less severe. If the cumulonimbus cloud is not fully developed, particularly if it lacks the anvil top, and the roll cloud is missing, only a shower may be expected.

We can time the approach of a thunderstorm, once the cumulonimbus cloud is visible, by a series of bearings. If we wish, we can estimate its distance off by another

FIG. 1222 Growth of the anvil of thunderstorm cloud. Top photograph was taken at 1200, the middle at 1220, the lower at 1230 from same position as storm developed.
(Courtesy National Weather Service)

method. The thunder and lightning occur simultaneously at the point of lightning discharge, but we see the lightning discharge much sooner than we hear the thunder. Consequently, time this interval, in seconds. Multiply the number of seconds by 0.2; the result will be the approximate distance off in miles.

TORNADOES

When numerous thunderstorms are associated with a cold front, the storms are apt to be organized in a long, narrow band. The forward edge of this band is usually marked by a *squall line,* along which the cold downdrafts

from a series of thunderstorms meet the warm air (see fig. 1221). Here the wind direction changes suddenly in vicious gusts, and a sharp drop in temperature occurs. The importance of squall lines is that they often spawn a most destructive type of storm, the deadly *tornado.* We should keep firmly in mind the fact that tornadoes have wrecked boats on the Mississippi and elsewhere in the southern part of the USA.

Tornadoes formed at squall lines often occur in families and move with the wind that prevails in the warm sector ahead of the cold front. This wind direction is usually from the southwest. The warm air typically consists of two layers, a very moist one (source: Gulf of Mexico) near the

FIG. 1223 The terrifying "funnel" of a tornado is actually a cloud of water droplets mixed with dust and debris. Close to the ground, dust and debris are plentiful, because greatly reduced atmospheric pressure inside funnel (a lowering of pressure of the order of 50 millibars) causes air to whirl violently inward and upward.

FIG. 1224 Waterspout over St. Louis Bay, off Henderson Point, Mississippi. Note cloud of spray just above sea surface.

ground and a relatively dry layer above. The temperature decreases with altitude relatively rapidly in each layer. When this combination of air layers is lifted along a squall line or cold front, excessive instability develops and violent updrafts are created.

A tornado is essentially an air whirlpool of small horizontal extent which extends downward from a cumulonimbus cloud and has a funnel-like appearance (see fig. 1223). The average diameter of the visible funnel cloud is about 250 yards, but the destructive effects of the associated system of whirling winds may extend outward from the tornado center as much as $1/4$ mile on each side. The wind speed near the core can only be estimated, but it undoubtedly is as high as 200 knots. This means almost certain death for the occupants of a boat which might have the misfortune to be in the path of a tornado.

Fortunately, the tornado belt in the USA is in the interior section of the country, but still there are boating areas which can be affected. So, if you live in the Midwest or the southern tier of states, keep your radio tuned to your local station, if weather conditions look threatening. The U.S. Weather Bureau now has a highly refined and reliable system for forecasting the likelihood of tornadoes.

Waterspouts

The marine counterpart of the tornado is the *waterspout*. The conditions favoring the formation of waterspouts at sea are similar to those conducive to the formation of tornadoes over land. Waterspouts are much more frequent in the tropics than in middle latitudes. Although they are less violent than tornadoes, nevertheless they are a real danger to small craft.

A waterspout, like a tornado, forms under a cumulonimbus cloud. A funnel-shaped protuberance first appears at the base of the cumulonimbus and grows downward toward the sea. Beneath it the water becomes agitated and a cloud of spray forms. The funnel-shaped cloud descends until it merges with the spray; it then assumes the shape of a tube that stretches from the sea surface to the base of the cloud (see fig. 1224).

The diameter of a waterspout may vary from 20 feet to 200 feet or more. Its length from the sea to the base of the cloud is usually between 1000 feet and 2000 feet. It may last from 10 minutes to half an hour. Its upper part often travels at a different speed and in a different direction from its base, so that it becomes bent and stretched-out. Finally the tube breaks at a point about one-third of the way up to the cloud base, and the "spout" at the sea surface quickly subsides.

The existence of considerably reduced air pressure at the center of a waterspout can be inferred from visible variations of the water level. A mound of water, a foot or so high, sometimes appears at the core, because the atmospheric pressure on the water surrounding the spout is perhaps 30 to 40 millibars greater than that on the sea surface inside the funnel. This difference causes the rise of water at the center.

Like the tornado, the visible part of a waterspout is composed, on the whole, of tiny water droplets formed by the condensation of water vapor in the air. Considerable quantities of salt spray, however, picked up by the strong winds at the base of the spout, are sometimes carried far aloft. This has been verified by observations of the fall of salty rain following the passage of a waterspout.

FOG

How, Why, Where and When It Forms — Its Distribution in the United States

The essential part is not always to know things; it is to know how to reason about them. This truism applies to fog. The basic causes of fog are few in number and easy to understand. What we want is a working knowledge of these causes; then we can judge if and when fog is likely to upset our plans.

Fog is merely a cloud whose base rests upon the earth, be the latter land or water. It consists of water droplets, suspended in the air, each droplet so small that it cannot be distinguished individually, yet present in such tremendous numbers that objects close at hand are obscured.

If we are to have innumerable water droplets suspended in the air, there must be plenty of water vapor originally in that air. If droplets are to form from this vapor, the air must be cooled by some means so that the vapor will condense. If the droplets are to condense in the air next to the earth, the cooling must take place at the surface of the earth. If the fog is to have any depth, successively higher

layers of air must be cooled sufficiently to cause condensation in them. Fog forms from the ground up. Thus, the land or water must be colder than the air next to it; the lower layers of air progressively must be colder than the layers above them.

If water vapor is to condense out of the air, then the temperature of the air must be lowered to or below the *dew-point temperature,* that is, the temperature at which the air is saturated with water vapor and below which condensation of water vapor will occur.

Air is said to be *saturated* with water vapor when its water-vapor content would remain unchanged if it were placed above a level surface of pure water at its own temperature. The amount of water vapor which is required to saturate a given volume of air depends on the temperature of the air, and increases as the temperature increases. The higher the temperature the more water vapor can the air hold before it becomes saturated, and the lower the temperature the less water vapor can the air hold before it becomes saturated.

If a mass of air is originally in an unsaturated state, it can be saturated by cooling it down to a temperature at which its content of water vapor is the maximum containable amount, that is to say, to the dew-point temperature. Or we can saturate it by causing more water to evaporate into it, thereby raising the dew-point temperature to a value equal to the air temperature. In regard to the latter process, unsaturated air, as it passes over rivers and lakes, over the oceans or over wet ground, picks up water vapor and has its dew point raised. Also, rain falling from higher clouds will increase the amount of water vapor in unsaturated air near the earth.

JUDGING THE LIKELIHOOD OF FOG

In order to judge the likelihood of fog formation, we should periodically measure the air temperature and dew-point temperature and see if the spread (difference) between them is getting smaller and smaller. The Navy, in its Aviation Training booklet "Fog" (Aerology Series 3) has

provided us with a diagram of the change in spread; it is reproduced here as fig. 1225.

Fig. 1226 is a graph of a series of air and dew-point temperatures. By recording these temperatures and plotting their spread over a period of several hours, as is indicated by that part of the curve drawn as a solid line, we have a basis for forecasting the time at which we are likely to be fog-bound. The dot-dash portion of the curve represents actual data but it could just as easily have been drawn by extending the solid portion. If an error were made in this extrapolation, it would probably indicate that the fog would form at an earlier hour. This is on the safe side; we would be secure in our anchorage some time before the fifty-ninth minute of the eleventh hour!

Note that the curve is not a straight line. While the average decrease in spread is about one and one-half degrees (Fahrenheit) per hour, the decrease is at a much greater rate in the earlier hours. So long as we do not make unreasonable allowances for a slowing up in the rate of change of the spread, this also will help to keep us on the safe side.

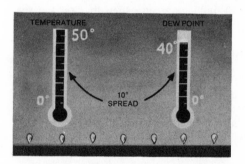

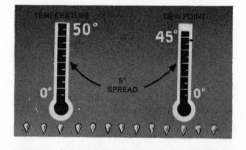

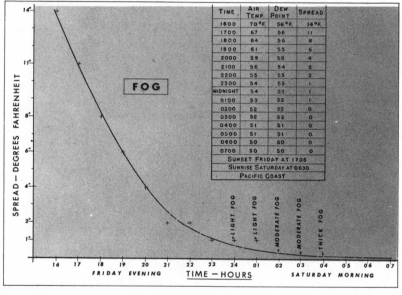

FIG. 1226 Graph of a series of air and dew-point temperatures.

TIME	AIR TEMP.	DEW POINT	SPREAD
1600	70°F.	56°F.	14°F.
1700	67	56	11
1800	64	56	8
1900	61	55	6
2000	59	55	4
2100	56	54	2
2200	55	53	2
2300	54	53	1
MIDNIGHT	54	53	1
0100	53	52	1
0200	52	52	0
0300	52	52	0
0400	51	51	0
0500	51	51	0
0600	50	50	0
0700	50	50	0
SUNSET FRIDAY AT 1705			
SUNRISE SATURDAY AT 0630			
PACIFIC COAST			

DETERMINING THE DEW POINT

How do we determine the dew point? By means of a simple-to-operate, inexpensive little gadget known as a *sling psychrometer* (fig. 1227). A sling psychrometer is merely two thermometers, mounted in a single holder with a handle that permits it to be whirled overhead. One thermometer, know as the *dry bulb,* has its bulb of mercury exposed directly to the air. This thermometer shows the actual temperature of the air. The other thermometer, known as the *wet bulb,* has its bulb covered with a piece of gauze. We soak this gauze in water so that the bulb is moistened. If the air is not saturated with water vapor, evaporation then takes place from the wet-bulb thermometer, and the wet bulb is cooled, since the process of evaporation requires the expenditure of heat. The reduced temperature shown by the wet-bulb thermometer, the so-

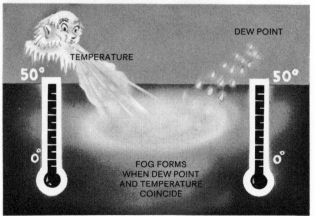

FIG. 1225 Why fog forms.
(Reproduced by courtesy of Aviation Training Division, U.S. Navy)

called "wet-bulb temperature," represents the lowest temperature to which the air can be cooled by evaporating water into it.

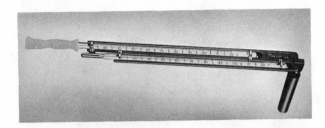

FIG. 1227   A pocket-type sling psychrometer, having two 5″ etched tubes, 20° to 120° in 1° divisions.
(Courtesy Taylor Instrument Companies)

When we whirl the psychrometer we create a draft around the instrument. The ventilation so produced increases the efficiency of the evaporation process and makes the wet-bulb reading more reliable than it would be if there were little or no air movement past the wet bulb. This is the reason why the psychrometer is designed for whirling.

From the wet-bulb temperature and dry-bulb temperature, the dew point may be determined by referring to a suitable table. As we are far more interested, however, in knowing the *spread, or difference, between the air temperature and dew point,* we will save ourselves some work by using another table (Table 12-1), its use being explained in the next two paragraphs.

If the air is already actually saturated with water vapor, then no water can evaporate from the gauze and both thermometers must show the same value. The dew point then has this same numerical value and so the spread between air temperature and dew point must be zero. But, as explained above, if the air is not already saturated with

water vapor, the wet-bulb thermometer will give a lower reading than the dry-bulb thermometer. We subtract the wet-bulb temperature from the dry-bulb temperature. With this difference and the dry-bulb (the air) temperature, we consult Table 12-1 and find directly the corresponding spread between the air temperature and the dew-point temperature. This is the figure we want.

If, in the late afternoon or early evening, the spread between the air temperature and dew point is less than approximately 6°F, and the air temperature is falling, fog or greatly restricted visibility will probably be experienced in a few hours. These critical values are emphasized by the heavy line above which they lie in Table 12-1. Incidentally, should we ever want to know the dew-point temperature itself, all we need do is to subtract the spread figure given in the table from the temperature shown by the dry-bulb thermometer. Thus, when the dry-bulb thermometer indicates an air temperature of 70°F and the difference between the dry-bulb and wet-bulb temperatures is 11°F, the spread is 19°F and the dew point is 51°F.

FOUR TYPES OF FOG

We can distinguish four types of fog: (a) *radiation fog,* formed in near-calm conditions by the cooling of the ground on a clear night as a result of radiation of heat from the ground to the clear sky; (b) *advection fog,* formed by the flow of warm air over cold sea or lake; (c) *steam fog,* or "sea smoke," formed when cold air blows over much warmer water; and (d) *precipitation fog,* formed when rain coming out of warm air aloft falls through a shallow layer of cold air at the earth's surface.

Radiation fog

There are four requirements for the formation of *radiation fog* (sometimes called "ground fog"). First, the air must be stable, that is, the air next to the earth must be colder than the air a short distance aloft. Second, the air must be relatively moist. Third, the sky must be clear, so that the earth readily can lose heat by radiation to outer space. This enables the ground to become colder than the overlying air, which subsequently is cooled below its dew point both by contact with the ground (conduction of heat) and by radiative loss of heat to the ground.

The fourth requirement is that the wind must be light to calm. If there is a dead calm, the lowest strata of air will not mix with the ones above, and fog will form only to a height of two to four feet. If there is a slight motion of the air (say a wind of three to five knots) and, hence, some turbulent mixing, the cooling is spread through a layer which may extend to a height of several hundred feet above the ground. With strong winds, the cooling effect is distributed through so deep a layer that the temperature nowhere falls to the dew point and fog does not form.

Radiation fog is most prevalent in the middle and high latitudes. It is local in character and occurs most frequently in valleys and lowlands, especially near lakes and rivers where we may be cruising. The cooled air drains into these terrain depressions; the lake or river aids the process of fog formation by contributing water vapor, which raises the dew point.

This type of fog, which may be patchy or uniformly dense, forms only at night. Shortly after sunrise, it will start

TABLE 12-1   AIR TEMPERATURE ── DEWPOINT SPREAD

(All figures are in degrees Fahrenheit at 30″ pressure)

Difference Dry-Bulb Minus Wet-Bulb	Air Temperature Shown By Dry-Bulb Thermometer												
	35	40	45	50	55	60	65	70	75	80	85	90	95
1	2	2	2	2	2	2	2	1	1	1	1	1	1
2	5	5	4	4	4	3	3	3	3	3	3	3	2
3	7	7	7	6	5	5	5	4	4	4	4	4	4
4	10	10	9	8	7	7	6	6	6	6	5	5	5
5	14	12	11	10	10	9	8	8	7	7	7	7	6
6	18	15	14	13	12	11	10	9	9	8	8	8	8
7	22	19	17	16	14	13	12	11	11	10	10	9	9
8	28	22	20	18	17	15	14	13	12	12	11	11	10
9	35	27	23	21	19	17	16	15	14	13	13	12	12
10	-	33	27	24	22	20	18	17	16	15	14	14	13
11	-	40	32	28	25	22	20	19	18	17	16	15	15
12	-	-	38	32	28	25	23	21	20	18	17	17	16
13	-	-	45	37	31	28	25	23	21	20	19	18	17
14	-	-	-	42	35	31	28	26	24	22	21	20	19
15	-	-	-	50	40	35	31	28	26	24	23	21	21

Opposite — Difference Dry-Bulb Minus Wet-Bulb and
Under   — Air Temperature Shown By Dry-Bulb Thermometer
Read   — Value of Spread: Air Temperature minus Dewpoint Temperature

Based on U.S. Weather Bureau Psychrometric Tables

FIG. 1228 Fog bank over Lake Huron. This is basically an advection-type fog which has formed over an area of relatively cold water. When the wind is very light and unsteady, as in this case, fog tends to concentrate in patches, even after it has drifted away from its source.

FIG. 1229 Sea smoke in Great Harbor, Woods Hole, Massachusetts, 0915 EST, 31 December 1962. Water temperature 31.6°F; air temperature (30 feet above sea level) +5°F. Wind NW 20 knots. Height of steaming approximately 15 feet. Rigging of vessel encountering this type of condition will become coated with rime ice. Note frosty deposit on beach grass in lower right corner of photograph.
(Courtesy of P. M. Saunders, Woods Hole Oceanographic Institution)

to evaporate ("burn off") over the land, the lower layers being the first to go. It is slow to clear over water, since the temperature of the water does not vary nearly as much from day to night as does the temperature of the land.

Advection fog

Radiation fog bothers us chiefly in the late summer and early autumn; *advection fog* can be an annoyance at any season. (Advection means transport by horizontal motion.) Winds carrying warm, moist air over a colder surface produce advection fog. The dew point of the air must be higher than the temperature of the surface over which the air is moving. Thus, the air can be cooled below its dew point by conduction and by radiation of heat to the colder surface. Other requirements for the formation of advection fog are as follows: (a) the air at a height of 100 feet or so must be warmer than the air just above the surface; (b) the temperature of the surface—be it land or water—must become progressively colder in the direction toward which the air is moving. Fig. 1230, again by courtesy of the U.S. Navy from its "Flying the Weather," illustrates the formation of advection fog along the coast and fig. 1231

its formation at sea. Advection fog may form day or night, winter or summer, over the sea.

Coastal Fog. For yachtsmen the most bothersome variety is *coastal fog* (fig. 1230). When steady winds blow landward and carry warm oceanic air across cold coastal water, the resulting fog may blanket a great length of coastline and, especially at night, may extend many miles inland up bays and rivers. For example, let's go to the Pacific coast, where the water close to the land is often colder than the water to westward. The prevailing winds in summer are onshore and the air, since it frequently has come from mid-Pacific, usually is nearly saturated with water vapor. Fig. 1230 illustrates the result; the same thing happens when southerly winds carry air across the Gulf Stream and thence northward across the colder Atlantic coastal waters. Advection fog also may form over the larger inland lakes whenever relatively warm and moist air is carried over their colder surfaces.

Advection fog is generally much harder to dissipate than is radiation fog. A wind shift or a marked increase in wind velocity usually is required. Sunshine has no effect on it over the water.

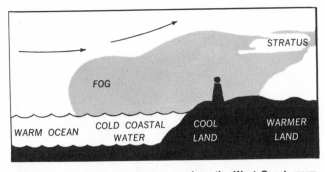

FIG. 1230 Coastal fogs are common along the West Coast—warm ocean, cool coastal water, frequent winds from the sea.
(Courtesy Aviation Training Division, U.S. Navy)

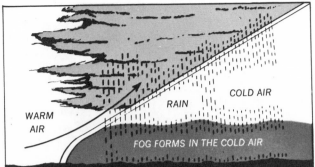

FIG. 1233 Formation of precipitation fog.

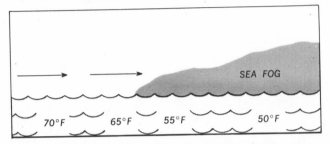

FIG. 1231 Most persistent sea fog is an advection fog that forms when air blows from warm sea to cold sea.

American coastal waters are concerned, this variety of steam fog occurs most frequently off the coasts of Maine and Nova Scotia, and in the Gulf of St. Lawrence, where it can be a serious navigational hazard. However, its occurrence is not restricted to the higher latitudes. Off the east coast of the United States it has been observed as far south as Florida and it occurs occasionally over the coastal waters of the Gulf of Mexico.

Steam fog

On the Mississippi and Ohio rivers, a special type of fog, known as *steam fog* is a particular hazard to late evening or early morning cruising in the autumn. When cold air passes over much warmer water, the lowest layer of air is rapidly supplied with heat and water vapor. Mixing of this lowest layer with unmodified cold air above can, under certain conditions, produce a supersaturated (i.e., foggy) mixture. Owing to the fact that the water is much warmer than the air, vertical air currents are created, and we observe the phenomenon of steaming. Hence, this type of fog is called "steam fog"; it forms in just the same way as steam over a hot bath.

Sea Smoke. When, in winter, very cold air (having a temperature less than about 10°F) blows off the land and across the adjacent coastal waters, steam fog may be widespread and very dense. It is then known as "sea smoke" (sometimes called "Arctic sea smoke"). As far as North

Precipitation fog

As mentioned earlier, we can distinguish a fourth type of fog, which we may call "*precipitation fog*," or "*rain fog*." When rain, after descending through a layer of warm air aloft, falls into a shallow layer of relatively cold air at the earth's surface, there will be evaporation from the warm raindrops into the colder air (see fig. 1233). Under certain conditions, this process will raise the water-vapor content of the cold air above the saturation point and fog will form. Its mode of formation is similar to that of the fog produced in the bathroom when one takes a hot shower.

It may be noted that both steam fog and rain fog are basically the result of evaporation from relatively warm water, a process which increases the dew point. These fogs can be placed in the single category of "warm-surface" fogs. Likewise, radiation fog and advection fog come under the single heading of "cold-surface" fogs.

FIG. 1232 Steam fog forming, then dissipating upwards, over pond near Mount Kisco, N.Y., 0700 EST, 12 October 1964. Air temperature approximately 25°F; water temperature not known, but probably 50°F or higher. Wind less than 1 knot.
(Photograph by Caroline S. Emmons)

253

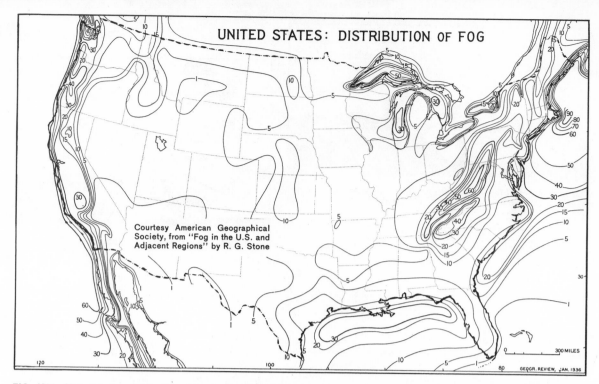

FIG. 1234 Map showing distribution of fog in the United States. Isopleths show mean annual number of days with "dense fog, i.e., fogs obscuring visibility to 1000 feet or less." In order to bring out more detail in the large portion of the country where fogginess is less than 20 days, an interval of 5 days was selected. For regions with more than 20 days of fog a 10-day interval is used.

DISTRIBUTION OF FOG IN THE UNITED STATES

Turning our attention now to the distribution of fog (all types included) in the United States, we find that the coastal sections most frequently beset by fog are (1) the area from the Strait of Juan de Fuca to Point Arguello (Calif.), on the Pacific Coast, and (2) the area from the Bay of Fundy to Montauk Point (N.Y.), on the Atlantic Coast. In these waters the average annual number of hours of fog occurrence exceeds 900, that is, more than 10% of the entire year. In the foggiest parts of these areas, namely, off the coast of Northern California and the coast of Maine, fog is present about 20% of the year.

As we go southward along both the Atlantic and Pacific Coasts the frequency of fog decreases, but it does so much more rapidly on the Atlantic Coast than on the Pacific. Hence, we find that the average annual fog frequency over the waters adjacent to Los Angeles and San Diego is about three times that in the same latitude along the Atlantic Coast.

SEASONAL FREQUENCIES

The *time of maximum occurrence* of fog off the Pacific Coast varies somewhat with the various localities and, of course, with the individual year. In general, however, over the stretch from Cape Flattery (Wash.) to Point Arguello the season of most frequent fog comprises the months of July, August, September and October, with more than 50% of the annual number of foggy days occurring during this period. However, along the lower coast of California, that is, from Los Angeles southward, the foggiest months are those from September through February, and the least foggy from May through July.

On the Atlantic side: Off the coast of New England the foggiest months are usually June, July and August, with a maximum of fog generally occurring during July, in which month fog normally is encountered from one-third to one-half of the time. Off the Middle Atlantic Coast, however, fog occurs mostly in the winter and spring months, with a distinct tendency toward minimum frequency in summer and autumn. Along the South Atlantic Coast (from Cape Hatteras to the tip of Florida) and in the Gulf of Mexico fog rarely creates a problem for the yachtsman. It is virtually non-existent during the summer, and even in the winter and early spring season (December through March), when it has maximum frequency, the number of days with fog hardly anywhere exceeds 20, on the average, during this four-month period.

The *fog regime of the Great Lakes* is essentially like that of the oceanic coastal waters in middle latitudes; the Great Lakes as a whole tend to have more fog in the warmer season. The explanation of this circumstance is to be found in the comparison of the lake temperatures with the air temperatures over the surrounding land. From March or April to the beginning of September the lakes are, on the average, colder than the air. Hence, whenever the dew-point temperature is sufficiently high, conditions are favorable for the formation of advection fog over the water.

The greatest fogginess occurs when and where the lakes are coldest in relation to the air blowing off the surrounding land. On Lake Superior, north-central Lake Michigan, and northwestern Lake Huron the *time* of maximum frequency is late May and June; elsewhere it is late April and May. As to the *location* of maximum fogginess, since the lake temperatures become colder from south to north and from the shores outward, the occurrence of fog increases northward and towards the central parts of each lake.

Observations Afloat—Weather signs

We have already discussed fog and how we can use a sling psychrometer to help us in forecasting its occurrence. There are a few other weather instruments which are practical on shipboard and which provide us with helpful information.

WIND OBSERVATIONS

Every sailor is familiar with the *wind direction indicators* that may be mounted at the masthead. Because a boat, at anchor or under way, can head in any direction all around the compass, a few mental calculations are necessary before we can use this indicator or an owner's flag or club burgee to determine the true direction of the wind. At anchor, the fly will give us the bearing of the wind relative to the boat's head; this must be converted to the true bearing of the wind itself. We can use our compass to obtain these values, provided we know its deviation on our heading and know the variation for our anchorage. Also, we need to remember that wind direction is always stated as the true direction *from* which, not toward which, the wind is blowing.

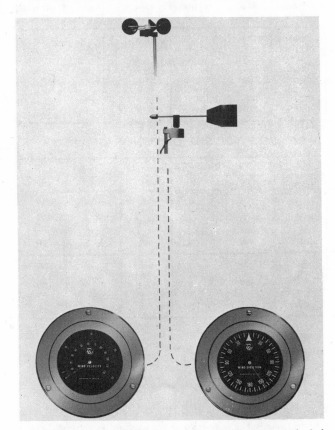

FIG. 1235 Danforth/White's anemometer with flush-mounted wind velocity indicator supplies accurate readings on two scales (0-25 and 0-120 knots). Two-wire conductor leads from indicator to masthead or spreader. Wind direction indicator is a matching unit.

The anemometer

For measuring *wind velocity* we need something else. This is an *anemometer;* the principal parts of the instrument are illustrated in fig. 1235. The anemometer is essentially a speedometer. It consists of a rotor with conical cups attached to the ends of spokes and is designed for mounting at the masthead, where the wind is caught by the cups, causing them to turn at a speed proportional to the speed of the wind. Indications of the rotor's speed are transmitted to an indicator which may be mounted in the cabin.

In the type of instrument illustrated in fig. 1235, the indicator is direct-reading, in two scales from 0 to 25 and 0 to 120 knots for velocity, gusts and variations. Battery drain (.09 amp.) is insignificant. A 60-foot wire cable is supplied to connect the rotor aloft with the illuminated indicator below. At anchor, the reading is the actual or true wind velocity at masthead height.

True and apparent wind

So far we have been considering the determination of the direction and speed of the wind while at anchor. Under way, the determination is more difficult, but the Oceanographic Office of the Navy has worked out the problem, so we may as well use their results. Table 12-2 is based on wind tables formerly published in Bowditch. Using our true course and speed, we can determine from this table the approximate *true* wind direction and velocity, provided we know the *apparent* direction and velocity. Our wind indicator or owner's flag will give us the apparent direction and our anemometer will give us the apparent velocity.

The Beaufort Scale

Another method is to estimate the strength of the wind in terms of the *Beaufort Scale* of Wind Force. Visually we can observe the sea condition and note the Beaufort number to which it corresponds (see Table 12-3). The range of wind velocity represented by each force number on the Beaufort scale is shown in the extreme left-hand column of Table 12-3.

Wind direction can be judged by observing the direction from which the smallest ripples are coming, since these ripples always run with the wind, responding instantly to changes in wind direction.

We don't need to determine wind direction and velocity with great precision, but reasonable estimates are helpful in preparing our own local forecasts. Estimating direction to two points is sufficient; within one Beaufort number is enough for velocity. By observing wind direction and velocity regularly and making a record of them we can obtain clues concerning potential weather developments as the wind shifts direction and changes its velocity.

TABLE 12-2

TRUE FORCE AND DIRECTION OF THE WIND FROM ITS APPARENT FORCE AND DIRECTION ON A BOAT UNDER WAY

APPARENT WIND VELOCITY (Knots)	SPEED OF BOAT							
	5 Knots		10 Knots		15 Knots		20 Knots	
	TRUE WIND		TRUE WIND		TRUE WIND		TRUE WIND	
	Points off Bow	Velocity Knots	Points off Bow	Velocity Knots	Points off Bow	Velocity Knots	Points off Bow	Velocity Knots
I. APPARENT WIND DIRECTION IS DEAD AHEAD								
Calm	D. As.	5 K.	D. As.	10 K.	D. As.	15 K.	D. As.	20 K.
4 K.	D. As.	1 K.	D. As.	6 K.	D. As.	11 K.	D. As.	16 K.
8 K.	D. As.	3 K.	D. As.	2 K.	D. As.	7 K.	D. As.	12 K.
12 K.	D. Ah.	7 K.	D. Ah.	2 K.	D. As.	3 K.	D. As.	8 K.
16 K.	D. Ah.	11 K.	D. Ah.	6 K.	D. Ah.	1 K.	D. As.	4 K.
22 K.	D. Ah.	17 K.	D. Ah.	12 K.	D. Ah.	7 K.	D. Ah.	2 K.
30 K.	D. Ah.	25 K.	D. Ah.	20 K.	D. Ah.	15 K.	D. Ah.	10 K.
42 K.	D. Ah.	37 K.	D. Ah.	32 K.	D. Ah.	27 K.	D. Ah.	22 K.
60 K.	D. Ah.	55 K.	D. Ah.	50 K.	D. Ah.	45 K.	D. Ah.	40 K.
II. APPARENT WIND DIRECTION IS 4 POINTS (BROAD) OFF THE BOW								
4 K.	11 pts.	4 K.	14 pts.	8 K.	15 pts.	12 K.	15 pts.	17 K.
8 K.	7 pts.	6 K.	11 pts.	7 K.	13 pts.	11 K.	14 pts.	15 K.
12 K.	6 pts.	9 K.	9 pts.	9 K.	11 pts.	11 K.	13 pts.	14 K.
16 K.	5 pts.	13 K.	7 pts.	11 K.	10 pts.	12 K.	11 pts.	14 K.
22 K.	5 pts.	19 K.	6 pts.	16 K.	8 pts.	15 K.	9 pts.	16 K.
30 K.	5 pts.	27 K.	6 pts.	24 K.	7 pts.	22 K.	8 pts.	21 K.
42 K.	4 pts.	39 K.	5 pts.	36 K.	6 pts.	33 K.	6 pts.	31 K.
60 K.	4 pts.	57 K.	5 pts.	53 K.	5 pts.	51 K.	6 pts.	48 K.
III. APPARENT WIND DIRECTION IS 8 POINTS OFF THE BOW (ABEAM)								
4 K.	13 pts.	6 K.	14 pts.	11 K.	15 pts.	16 K.	15 pts.	20 K.
8 K.	11 pts.	9 K.	13 pts.	13 K.	14 pts.	17 K.	14 pts.	22 K.
12 K.	10 pts.	13 K.	12 pts.	16 K.	13 pts.	19 K.	13 pts.	23 K.
16 K.	10 pts.	17 K.	11 pts.	19 K.	12 pts.	22 K.	13 pts.	26 K.
22 K.	9 pts.	23 K.	10 pts.	24 K.	11 pts.	27 K.	12 pts.	30 K.
30 K.	9 pts.	30 K.	10 pts.	32 K.	10 pts.	34 K.	11 pts.	36 K.
42 K.	9 pts.	42 K.	9 pts.	43 K.	10 pts.	45 K.	10 pts.	47 K.
60 K.	8 pts.	60 K.	9 pts.	61 K.	9 pts.	62 K.	10 pts.	63 K.
IV. APPARENT WIND DIRECTION IS 12 POINTS OFF THE BOW (BROAD ON THE QUARTER)								
4 K.	14 pts.	8 K.	15 pts.	13 K.	15 pts.	18 K.	15 pts.	23 K.
8 K.	14 pts.	12 K.	14 pts.	17 K.	15 pts.	21 K.	15 pts.	26 K.
12 K.	13 pts.	16 K.	14 pts.	20 K.	14 pts.	25 K.	15 pts.	30 K.
16 K.	13 pts.	20 K.	14 pts.	24 K.	14 pts.	29 K.	14 pts.	33 K.
22 K.	13 pts.	26 K.	13 pts.	30 K.	14 pts.	34 K.	14 pts.	39 K.
30 K.	13 pts.	34 K.	13 pts.	38 K.	13 pts.	42 K.	14 pts.	46 K.
42 K.	12 pts.	46 K.	13 pts.	50 K.	13 pts.	54 K.	13 pts.	58 K.
60 K.	12 pts.	64 K.	13 pts.	67 K.	13 pts.	71 K.	13 pts.	75 K.

CONVERSION OF POINTS OFF BOW TO TRUE DIRECTION OF WIND

POINTS OFF BOW	BOAT'S HEADING—TRUE							
	000°	045°	090°	135°	180°	225°	270°	315°
I. WHEN WIND DIRECTION OBTAINED FROM TABLE ABOVE IS OFF STARBOARD BOW								
Dead Ahead	N	NE	E	SE	S	SW	W	NW
4 points	NE	E	SE	S	SW	W	NW	N
8 points	E	SE	S	SW	W	NW	N	NE
12 points	SE	S	SW	W	NW	N	NE	E
Dead Astern	S	SW	W	NW	N	NE	E	SE
II. WHEN WIND DIRECTION OBTAINED FROM TABLE ABOVE IS OFF PORT BOW								
Dead Ahead	N	NE	E	SE	S	SW	W	NW
4 points	NW	N	NE	E	SE	S	SW	W
8 points	W	NW	N	NE	E	SE	S	SW
12 points	SW	W	NW	N	NE	E	SE	S
Dead Astern	S	SW	W	NW	N	NE	E	SE

TO USE THIS TABLE

Abreviations: D. As. = Dead Astern. D. Ah. = Dead Ahead. K. = Knots. pts. = Points off bow.

1. **With Wind Direction Indicator:** Determine Apparent Wind Direction off the Bow.
2. **With Anemometer:** Determine Apparent Wind Velocity, in Knots.
3. **Enter Upper Part of Table:** Use portion for nearest Apparent Wind Direction Opposite Apparent Wind Velocity and under nearest Speed of Boat, read Wind Direction in Points off Bow and True Wind Velocity in Knots. Note whether True Wind Direction is off Starboard or Port Bow.
4. **Enter Lower Part of Table:** Use portion for proper Bow: Starboard or Port. Opposite Points off Bow and under nearest Boat's True Heading, read True Wind Direction.
5. **Log:** Record True Wind Direction as obtained from Lower Part of Table and True Wind Velocity as obtained from Upper Part of Table in Boat's Weather Log.

TABLE 12-3

DETERMINATION OF WIND SPEED BY SEA CONDITION

Knots	Descriptive	Sea Conditions	Wind force (Beaufort)	Probable wave height (in ft.)
0-1	Calm	Sea smooth and mirror-like.	0	—
1-3	Light air	Scale-like ripples without foam crests.	1	¼
4-6	Light breeze	Small, short wavelets; crests have a glassy appearance and do not break.	2	½
7-10	Gentle breeze	Large wavelets; some crests begin to break; foam of glassy appearance. Occasional white foam crests.	3	2
11-16	Moderate breeze	Small waves, becoming longer; fairly frequent white foam crests.	4	4
17-21	Fresh breeze	Moderate waves, taking a more pronounced long form; many white foam crests; there may be some spray.	5	6
22-27	Strong breeze	Large waves begin to form; white foam crests are more extensive everywhere; there may be some spray.	6	10
28-33	Near gale	Sea heaps up and white foam from breaking waves begins to be blown in streaks along the direction of the wind; spindrift begins.	7	14
34-40	Gale	Moderately high waves of greater length; edges of crests break into spindrift; foam is blown in well-marked streaks along the direction of the wind.	8	18
41-47	Strong gale	High waves; dense streaks of foam along the direction of the wind; crests of waves begin to topple, tumble, and roll over; spray may reduce visibility.	9	23
48-55	Storm	Very high waves with long overhanging crests. The resulting foam in great patches is blown in dense white streaks along the direction of the wind. On the whole, the surface of the sea is white in appearance. The tumbling of the sea becomes heavy and shock-like. Visibility is reduced.	10	29
56-63	Violent Storm	Exceptionally high waves that may obscure small and medium-sized ships. The sea is completely covered with long white patches of foam lying along the direction of the wind. Everywhere the edges of the wave crests are blown into froth. Visibility reduced.	11	37
64-71	Hurricane	The air is filled with foam and spray. Sea completely white with driving spray; visibility very much reduced.	12	45

(Courtesy National Weather Service)

FIG. 1236   A modern aneroid barometer, graduated in both millibars (inner scale) and inches of mercury (outer scale). Pointer indicates reading at last setting.
(Courtesy Airguide Instrument Company)

THE BAROMETER

Another weather instrument with which we are all familiar is the *aneroid barometer*. The one illustrated (fig. 1236) has several interesting features.

First, there are two *pressure scales*. Not a few of us are accustomed to thinking of barometric pressure in terms of *inches of mercury*, so the outer scale is graduated in these units. Weather maps are now printed with the pressures shown in *millibars* and many radio weather reports specify this value. Consequently, the inner scale is graduated in millibars, and so we don't have to worry about conversions between units.

Second, it is a rugged instrument, a feature not to be despised on board a 40-footer. It has a high order of accuracy.

Third, it has the usual reference hand, so we can keep track of changes in pressure.

The words "Fair—Change—Rain," in themselves, when they appear on the face of an aneroid barometer, are meaningless. It is not the actual barometric pressure that is so important in forecasting; it is the *direction* and *rate of change of pressure*. The words may be misleading if this fact is not clearly understood.

How it is used

Now, a good barometer is a helpful instrument, *provided* a few things: provided we read it at regular intervals and keep a record of the readings; provided we remember that there is much more to weather than just barometric pressure.

An individual reading of the barometer tells us only the pressure being exerted by the atmosphere on the earth's surface at the particular point of observation. But, suppose we have logged the pressure readings at fairly regular intervals, as follows:

Time	Pressure	Change
0700	30.02 inches	—
0800	30.00	−0.02
0900	29.97	−0.03
1000	29.93	−0.04
1100	29.88	−0.05
1200	29.82	−0.06

The pressure is falling, at an increasing rate. Trouble is brewing. A fall of 0.02 inch per hour is a low rate of fall; consequently, this figure would not be particularly disturbing. But a fall of 0.05 inch per hour is a pretty high rate.

Next, there is a normal *daily change in pressure.* The pressure is usually at its maximum value about 1000 and 2200 each day, at its minimum value about 0400 and 1600. The variation between minimum and maximum may be as much as 0.05 inch change in these six-hour intervals (about 0.01 inch change per hour). Thus, when the pressure normally would increase about 0.03 inch (0700 to 1000) our pressure fell 0.09 inch.

Suppose, now, around 1200 we also observed that the wind was blowing from the NE with increasing force and that the barometer continued to fall at a high rate. A rocky lee shore close aboard would not be pleasant to contemplate as a severe northeast gale is on its way. On the other hand, given the same barometer reading of about 29.80, rising rapidly with the wind going to west, we could expect improving weather. Quite a difference.

Barometer rules

A few general rules are often helpful. First, *foul* weather is usually forecast by a *falling* barometer with winds from the *east* quadrants; *clearing* and *fair* weather is usually forecast by winds shifting to *west* quadrants with a *rising* barometer. Second, there are the rules formerly printed on every Weather Bureau daily surface weather map:

"When the wind sets in from points between south and southeast and the barometer falls steadily, a storm is approaching from the west or northwest, and its center will pass near or north of the observer within 12 to 24 hours, with the wind shifting to northwest by way of south and southwest.

"When the wind sets in from points between east and northeast and the barometer falls steadily, a storm is approaching from the south or southwest, and its center will pass near or to the south of the observer within 12 to 24 hours, with the wind shifting to northwest by way of north.

"The rapidity of the storm's approach and its intensity will be indicated by the rate and amount of fall in the barometer."

There are some other generally useful barometer rules.

With our sling psychrometer we can determine the air temperature, so: a falling barometer and a rising thermometer often forecast rain; barometer and thermometer rising together often forecast fine weather. A slowly rising barometer forecasts settled weather; a steady, slow fall of pressure unsettled or wet weather.

Barometric changes and wind velocity

We shall now give some rules relating barometric changes to changes in wind velocity. First, it is generally true that a *rapidly falling barometer* forecasts the development of strong winds. This is so because a falling barometer indicates the approach or development of a LOW, and the pressure gradient is usually steep in the neighborhood of a low-pressure center. On the other hand, a *rising barometer* is associated with the prospect of lighter winds to come. This is true because a rising barometer indicates the approach or development of a HIGH, and the pressure gradient is characteristically small in the neighborhood of a high-pressure center.

The barometer does not necessarily fall before or during a strong breeze. The wind often blows hard without any appreciable accompanying change in the barometer. This means that a steep pressure gradient exists (isobars close together, as seen on the weather map) but that the well-developed HIGH or LOW associated with the steep pressure gradient is practically stationary. In this case the wind may be expected to blow hard for some time; any slackening or change will take place gradually.

It not infrequently happens that the barometer falls quite rapidly, yet the wind remains comparatively light. If we remember the relation between wind velocity and pressure gradient, we conclude that the gradient must be comparatively small (isobars relatively far apart). The rapid fall of the barometer must be accounted for, then, in either one or both of two ways. Either a LOW with a weak pressure gradient on its forward side is approaching rapidly, or there is a rapid decrease of pressure taking place over the surrounding area, or both. In such a situation the pressure gradient at the rear of the LOW is often steep, and in that case strong winds will set in as soon as the barometer commences to rise. (It will rise rapidly under these circumstances.) The fact, however, that the barometer is now rising indicates that decreasing winds may soon be expected.

The barometer and wind shifts

Nearly all extra-tropical cyclones display an unsymmetrical distribution of pressure. The pressure gradients are seldom the same in the front and rear of an extra-tropical cyclone. During the approach of a LOW the barometer alone gives no clue as to how many points the wind will shift and what velocity it will have after the passage of the low-pressure system. This is particularly applicable to situations in which the wind blows from a southerly direction while the barometer is falling. The cessation of the fall of the barometer will coincide with a *veering* (gradual or sudden) shift of the wind to a more westerly direction. Unfortunately, an observer having no information other than that supplied by his barometer cannot foretell the exact features of the change.

In using barometric indications for local forecasting it is most important to remember that weather changes are

FIG. 1237 Forecast—Severe Storm. Squall line clouds mark an advancing cold front; storm will be severe, with sharp, violent shift in wind, rain and probably lightning and thunder. (Courtesy U.S. Weather Bureau)

influenced by the characteristics of the earth's surface in our locality. All rules should be checked against experience in our own cruising waters before we can place full confidence in their validity.

VISUAL WEATHER SIGNS

In addition to our instrumental weather observations there are certain *visual signs* that we can record. First, we should note the *visibility*. Haze, dust and smoke are nearly as important as fog. Many of the tiny particles which are suspended in the air and which reduce the visibility serve as nuclei on which water vapor can condense. Unless the water vapor in the air does condense, we can have no fog nor clouds. If haze thickens to a degree where it restricts the visibility to 3 miles, we have an indication that condensation has begun on the more active condensation nuclei and a warning that fog may soon develop.

Next, we should note the *clouds*. First, we ask ourselves: "What form (or forms) of cloud is (or are) present?" In order to answer this question we need to know the international system of cloud classification. This system resembles the method of classification used in the biological sciences. The different cloud types are given descriptive names which depend mainly upon appearance, but also sometimes upon the processes of formation as seen by an observer on the ground.

Cloud forms classified

Despite an almost infinite variety of shapes and forms, it is possible to define 10 basic types. The following definitions are taken from the 1956 edition of the International Cloud Atlas.

1. Cirrus (Ci)—Detached clouds in the form of white, delicate filaments, or white or mostly white patches or narrow bands. These clouds have a fibrous (hair-like) appearance, or a silky sheen, or both.

2. Cirrocumulus (Cc)—Thin, white patch, sheet or layer of cloud without shading, composed of very small elements in the form of grains, ripples, etc., merged or separate, and

H. T. Floreen

FIG. 1238 Cumulus clouds of fair weather, illustrating situation in which atmosphere is stable a short distance above bases of clouds which, therefore, cannot grow vertically. Appearance of sky indicates fine weather will continue for at least another 6 hours.

more or less regularly arranged; most of the elements have an apparent width of less than one degree.

3. Cirrostratus (Cs)—Transparent, whitish cloud veil of fibrous (hair-like) or smooth appearance, totally or partly covering the sky, and generally producing halo phenomena.

4. Altocumulus (Ac)—White or gray, or both white and gray, patch, sheet or layer of cloud, generally with shading, composed of laminae, rounded masses, rolls, etc., which are sometimes partly fibrous or diffuse, and which may or may not be merged; most of the regularly arranged small elements usually have an apparent width between one and five degrees.

5. Altostratus (As)—Grayish or bluish cloud sheet or layer of striated, fibrous or uniform appearance, totally or partly covering the sky, and having parts thin enough to reveal the sun at least vaguely, as through ground glass. Altostratus does not show halo phenomena.

6. Nimbostratus (Ns)—Gray cloud layer, often dark, the appearance of which is rendered diffuse by more or less continuously falling rain or snow, which in most cases reaches the ground. It is thick enough throughout to blot out the sun. Low, ragged clouds frequently occur below the layer, with which they may or may not merge.

7. Stratocumulus (Sc)—Gray or whitish, or both gray and whitish, patch, sheet or layer of cloud which almost always has dark parts, composed of tessellations, rounded masses, rolls, etc., which are non-fibrous (except for virga) and which may or may not be merged; most of the regularly arranged small elements have an apparent width of more than five degrees.

8. Stratus (St)—Generally gray cloud layer with a fairly uniform base, which may give drizzle, ice prisms or snow grains. When the sun is visible through the cloud, its outline is clearly discernible. Stratus does not produce halo phenomena except, possibly, at very low temperatures. Sometimes stratus appears in the form of ragged patches.

9. Cumulus (Cu)—Detached clouds, generally dense and with sharp outlines, developing vertically in the form of rising mounds, domes or towers, of which the bulging upper part often resembles a cauliflower. The sunlit parts of these clouds are mostly brilliant white; their bases are relatively dark and nearly horizontal. Sometimes cumulus is ragged.

10. Cumulonimbus (Cb)—Heavy and dense cloud, with a considerable vertical extent, in the form of a mountain or huge towers. At least part of its upper portion is usually smooth, or fibrous or striated, and nearly always flattened; this part often spreads out in the shape of an anvil or vast plume. Under the base of this cloud, which is often very dark, there are frequently low ragged clouds either merged

FIG. 1239 Semi-transparent altocumulus clouds. Clouds in this picture clearly show signs of evaporation; edges of individual elements are frayed and indistinct. This indicates continuing fair weather.

FIG. 1240 Altostratus clouds, together with some altocumulus, over Mt. Kisco, New York, 1655 EST, 11 February 1965. (Note aircraft condensation trail in lower left portion of photograph.) At this time a LOW was centered over southeastern Missouri, moving northeastward. Rain began to fall about 7 hours after picture was taken.
(Photograph by Caroline S. Emmons)

with it or not, and precipitation, sometimes in the form of virga (precipitation trails).

Significance of changing cloud forms

Having identified the cloud form (or forms) present in the sky, we should next note whether the clouds are *increasing* or *decreasing* in amount, and whether they are *lowering* or *lifting*. In general, thickening and lowering of a cloud layer, be it a layer of cirrostratus, altocumulus or altostratus, is a sign of approaching wet weather. On the other hand, when a layer of clouds shows signs of evaporation, that is, when holes or openings begin to appear in a layer of altostratus, or the elements of an altocumulus layer are frayed and indistinct at the edges, we have an indication of improving weather or, at least, delay of the development of foul weather.

Finally, we should note the *sequence of cloud forms* during the past few hours. Cirrus clouds are frequently the advance agents of an approaching extra-tropical cyclone, especially if they are followed by a layer of cirrostratus. In this case the problem is to forecast the track the low-pressure center will take to one side or the other, the nearness of approach of the center and the intensity of the low.

As the clouds thicken steadily from Ci to Cs and from Cs to As, we naturally expect further development to Ns with its rain or snow. There are usually contrary indications if such is not to be the case, or if the precipitation will arrive late, amount to little and end soon, or will come in two brief periods separated by several hours of mild, more or less sunny, weather.

If the northern horizon remains clear until a layer of altostratus clouds overspreads most of the sky, the low-pressure center will probably be passing to the south without bringing precipitation. If the northern horizon is slow in clouding up but becomes covered by the time the cloud sheet is principally As, there will probably be some precipitation but not much. If the cloud sheet, after increasing to As, breaks up into Ac and the sky above is seen to have lost most of its covering of Cs, the low-pressure area is either weakening or passing on to the north.

The approach of a squall line accompanied by thunderstorms may be detected an hour or more in advance by observing the thin white arch of the cirrus border to the anvil top of the approaching cumulonimbus cloud. The atmosphere ahead of a squall line is often so hazy that only this whitish arch will reveal the presence of a moderately distant Cb, for the shadowed air under the dense anvil will be invisible behind the sunlit hazy blue air near the observer. Thus this part of the sky will appear to be clear and will resemble the blue sky above the cirrus arch.

THE WEATHER LOG

Although the latest Weather Service forecasts are readily available to us via the medium of radio, it is often helpful to keep a record of our own observations of clouds and weather as they develop. This procedure will enable us to check the reliability of the latest prediction. Occasionally the professional forecaster misjudges the future rate of travel of the weather pattern, which may move faster or

TABLE 12-4A Boat Weather Log.

```
                    BOAT WEATHER LOG


  Yacht_____At/Passage_____to_____
  Day___Date_____Time Zone_____Skipper_____
  1. Latest Weather Map: Date___Time_____Summary of forecast and
     of principal regional weather features:_____
     _____
     _____
     _____
     _____

  2. Radio Weather Reports Received (state source and time):_____
     _____
     _____
     _____

  3. Local Weather Observations (see over for record)

  4. Remarks and Local Forecast for Next____Hours (state time fore-
     cast effective):_____
     _____
     _____
     _____
     _____
```

TABLE 12-4B Local Weather Observations.

```
                LOCAL WEATHER OBSERVATIONS


  Time -- ZT, Navy Style

  Latitude - degrees, minutes
  Longitude -    "         "
  Course - degrees psc
         -    "     true
  Speed - Knots

  Barometer - in. or mb.
            - tendency
  Clouds - form
         - moving from
         - amount
         - changing to
  Sea - condition
      - swells
      - moving from
  Temperatures - air, dry bulb
               - dewpoint
               - water
  Visibility
  Wind - direction, true
       - shifting to
       - velocity, true
       - force (Beaufort)
  Weather - present
```

more slowly than anticipated. (This is known as an error of timing.) Or there may occur a new, unforeseen development in the pattern.

Table 12-4 shows a form of *Weather Log* which is similar to that used in the Weather Course of the United States Power Squadrons. Table 12-4 A is the face sheet, Table 12-4 B the reverse side. The first weather items recorded are based on a perusal of the latest weather map (if available to us) and a summary of radio reports received. Then

we use the reverse side to jot down our local observations. Sufficient columns are available to permit the entry of these data six times during one 24-hour day, or at four-hour intervals. Entries may be made using the standard weather code symbols or any other way we choose, provided we use the same system consistently.

From these records we can estimate in what way and to what extent the actual weather during the next few hours is likely to differ from the official forecast.

FIG. 1241 Semi-transparent layer of altostratus clouds over Mt. Kisco, New York, 1445 EST, 14 February 1965, looking south-southwestward. Sun is dimly visible. Later in the afternoon, altostratus layer thickened and lowered. Light snow began to fall about 6 hours after picture was taken. (Photograph by Caroline S. Emmons)

FIG. 1241-A Squall line approaching Mt. Kisco, N.Y., late afternoon of 27 July 1965. View at left looking toward WNW, center and right toward NW. Time interval between pictures approximately three minutes. Thunderstorm overhead one hour later. (Photographs by Caroline S. Emmons.)

Appendix _____

The National Weather Service has an ascending series of alerting messages—advisories and warnings—for mariners, including boatmen. These are keyed to increasingly hazardous weather and sea conditions.

Each advisory or warning condition has both a day and a night signal. These are displayed at prominent locations ashore, such as Coast Guard stations and lighthouses, marinas, yacht clubs, etc.; at some but not all such locations, check locally to know where to watch for them. Some of the locations will display only the day signal, others both the day and night signals. Day signals only are flown from Coast Guard lightships while on station, in some areas the small craft advisory red pennant will be shown on local law enforcement patrol craft.

The Weather Service emphasizes that these visual storm warnings displayed along the coast are supplementary to —and not a replacement for—the written advisories and warnings given prompt and wide distribution by press, radio, and television. In most cases, important details of the forecasts and warnings in regard to the time, intensity, duration, and direction of storms cannot be given satisfactorily through visual signals alone.

Following is a detailed explanation of the signals:

Small Craft Advisory: One red pennant displayed by day and a red light above a white light at night to indicate winds up to 38 mph (33 knots) and/or sea conditions dangerous to small craft operations are forecast for the area.

Gale Warning: Two red pennants displayed by day and a white light above a red light at night to indicate winds ranging from 39 to 54 mph (34 to 47 knots) are forecast.

Storm Warning: A single square red flag with black center displayed by day and two red lights at night to indicate winds 48 knots (55 mph) and above (*no matter how high the velocity*) are forecast for the area. NOTE—If winds are associated with a tropical cyclone (hurricane) the *storm*

DISSEMINATION OF STORM WARNINGS AND ROUTINE WEATHER INFORMATION

warning display indicates forecast winds of 48 to 63 knots (55 to 73 mph). The *hurricane warning* is displayed only in connection with a tropical cyclone (hurricane).

Hurricane Warning: Two square red flags with black centers displayed by day and a white light between two red lights at night to indicate that winds 74 mph (64 knots) and above are forecast for the area.

The term *Small Craft Advisory* needs some explanation. In the first place, small craft, as defined by the Weather Service, consist of "small boats, yachts, tugs, barges with little freeboard, or any other low-powered craft." In the second place, a small-craft advisory does not distinguish between the expectation of a general, widespread, all-day blow of 25 knots or more and, for example, a forecast of the occurrence of isolated, late-afternoon thunder-squalls in which winds dangerous to small craft will be localized and of short duration. It is up to the individual skipper to deduce from his own observations, supplemented by any information he can obtain from radio broadcasts about the current over-all weather picture, to which type of situation the advisory applies and to plan his day's cruise accordingly.

Storm warnings and advisories issued by the National Weather Service are broadcast by designated United States Naval and Coast Guard radio stations. A large number of commercial radio stations also broadcast storm warnings, although at somewhat irregular intervals.

VHF-FM BROADcasts: At many places, the National Weather Service has *continuous* broadcasts of conditions and forecasts with emphasis on marine use. New tapes are prepared every few hours. The usual frequency is 162.55 MHz, but others, such as 164.00 MHz, may be used.

These can be received on regular VHF sets, on inexpensive transistor receivers, and on some newer AM-FM receivers and MF-band radiotelephones. The broadcasts are of excellent quality and are most useful to boatmen.

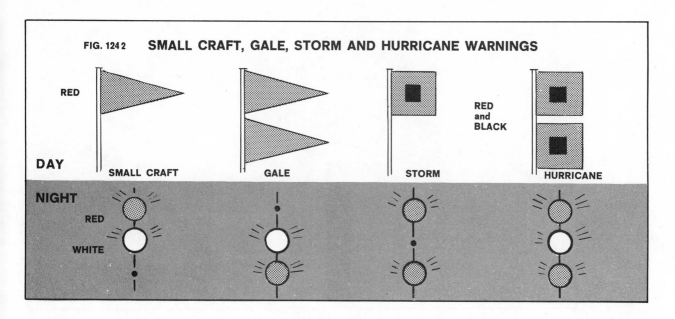

FIG. 124·2 **SMALL CRAFT, GALE, STORM AND HURRICANE WARNINGS**

RED

DAY — SMALL CRAFT — GALE — STORM — RED and BLACK — HURRICANE

NIGHT — RED — WHITE

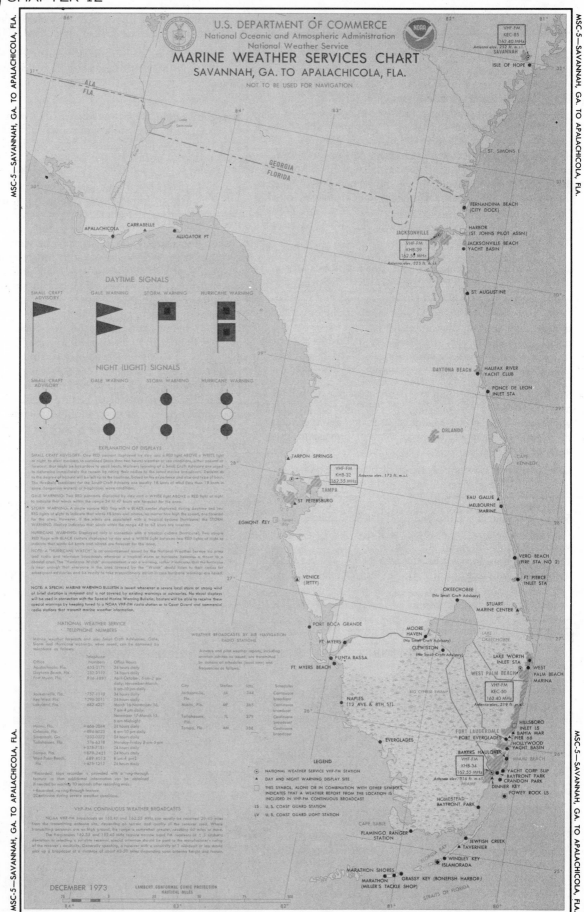

Fig. 1243 Marine Services Weather Chart. See text, page 265.

MARINE WEATHER SERVICES CHARTS

Coast Guard vessels now display storm warning signals. Headquarters of the Coast Guard are supplied with weather information by the Weather Service and Coast Guard vessels receive instructions to fly the proper signals when bad weather is approaching.

The shore stations where storm warning signals are displayed are prominently marked on the *Marine Weather Services Charts,* a series which is published annually by the Weather Service. These charts, of which fig. 2143 is an example, also contain detailed information concerning the times of weather broadcasts from commercial stations, the radio frequencies of marine broadcast stations, the specific type of storm warnings issued and the visual display signals (already described and illustrated in the text above) which are used in connection with the warnings. This series consists of fourteen charts, twelve of which cover the coastal waters of the United States and the Great Lakes. The remaining two charts are for (a) the Hawaiian Islands, and (b) Puerto Rico and the Virgin Islands. They can be purchased from the Superintendent of Documents, Government Printing Office, Washington, D. C. 20402.

Yachtsmen will find much interesting weather information on the various Pilot Charts of the North Atlantic and North Pacific Oceans issued by the Oceanographic Office of the Navy Department. The Pilot Charts show average monthly wind and weather conditions over the oceans and in addition contain a vast amount of supplemental data on subjects closely allied to weather.

WIND FORCE—AND ITS EFFECT ON THE SEA

Boatmen, like mariners at sea, frequently use the Beaufort Scale to log wind speed and the condition of the sea. Too often the description of sea conditions relies solely upon a verbal statement like "moderate waves, large waves, moderately high waves" (column 3, Table 12-3) which leaves the boatman pretty much "at sea" in trying to visualize exactly what these relative terms imply.

England's Meteorological Office has solved this problem by issuing a State of Sea card (M.O. 688A) with photographs to accompany each of the descriptions of thirteen wind forces of the Beaufort Scale. Thus the observer has a guide in estimating wind strength (*in knots*) when making weather reports or in logging sea conditions. Fetch, depth of water, swell, heavy rain, tide and the lag effect between the wind getting up and the sea increasing, may also affect the appearance of the sea. Range of wind speed and the mean wind speed are given for each force. By special permission, we are privileged to reproduce (figure 1244, page 248) seven of these photographs (Forces 1, 3, 5, 6, 8, 10, 12). Forces 0, 2, 4, 7, 9, and 11, though not illustrated, may be estimated in relation to those above and below them in the scale.

⟶

This table shows the velocity of sound at various air temperatures. Strictly speaking, the table is valid only for dry air, i.e., air containing no water vapor. However, the effect of water vapor on the speed of sound is quite small, so that the values in the table are entirely suitable for use in ordinary, rough calculations.

TABLE 12-5

WIND PRESSURE AT VARIOUS WIND VELOCITIES
(Air temperature 50°F, barometric pressure 1000 mbs.)

WIND VELOCITY (Knots)	WIND PRESSURE (Lbs. Per Square Foot)
0	0.0
5	0.1
10	0.3
15	0.8
20	1.3
25	2.1
30	3.1
35	4.2
40	5.5
45	6.9
50	8.5
55	10.3
60	12.3

This table gives the wind pressure exerted on the windward side of a flat surface oriented at right angles to the wind. The values in the table have been computed for air temperature equal to 50°F and barometric pressure equal to 1000 millibars. At greater barometric pressures and lower air temperature the wind pressure corresponding to a given wind velocity will be somewhat greater; at higher air temperatures and lower barometric pressures, somewhat less.

TABLE 12-6

VELOCITY OF SOUND IN DRY AIR

AIR TEMPERATURE	SOUND VELOCITY	
°F	Feet per second	Knots
100	1160	687
95	1155	684
90	1149	681
85	1144	678
80	1139	675
75	1133	671
70	1128	668
65	1123	665
60	1117	662
55	1112	659
50	1107	656
45	1101	653
40	1096	649
35	1090	646
30	1084	642
25	1079	639
20	1073	635
15	1067	632
10	1062	629
5	1057	626
0	1051	622
−5	1045	619
−10	1040	616
−15	1034	613
−20	1028	609
−25	1022	605
−30	1016	601
−35	1010	598
−40	1004	595

FORCE 1—Wind speed 1-3 kt.; mean 2 kt.

FORCE 3—Wind speed 7-10 kt.; mean 9 kt.

FORCE 5—Wind speed 17-21 kt.; mean 18 kt.

FORCE 6—Wind speed 22-27 kt.; mean 24 kt.

FORCE 8—Wind speed 34-40 kt.; mean 37 kt.

FORCE 10—Wind speed 48-55 kt.; mean 52 kt.

FIG. 1244 — HOW THE SEA LOOKS IN WINDS OF VARYING FORCE

Wind forces used in these illustrations are based on the Beaufort Scale. See column 3, table 12-3, for verbal description of the state of the sea for Forces 0-12.

(All photographs Crown Copyright, by R. R. Baxter, except Force 10, J. Hodkinson, and Force 12, G.P.O. Reproduced by permission of the Controller of Her Brittanic Majesty's Stationery Office.)

FORCE 12—Wind speed 64-71 kt.; mean 68 kt.

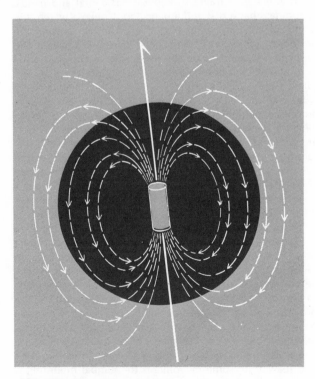

FIG. 1301 Typical spherical compass

*Planning a voyage,
or when under way,
the navigator or the
small boat pilot is always
concerned with direction
and distance.
Methods of determining
and recording distance
are thoroughly
covered elsewhere in
this book. This chapter
is about direction
and, more particularly,
about the most commonly
used direction
indicator afloat,
the mariner's compass.*

THE MARINER'S COMPASS

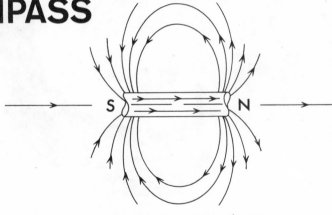

FIG. 1302 Lines of force, bar magnet

Why It Works

The operating principle is the behavior of a freely suspended bar magnet.

A permanent bar magnet has two poles, conventionally labeled north or south, in accordance with usage. The so-called force of the magnet is apparently concentrated at each of these poles. Actually it exists in the three-dimensional space, called the field, around the bar, roughly as shown in fig. 1302 and is presumed to consist of innumerable *lines of force,* a few of which are pictured. Another smaller magnet, brought into this field and free to move, will align itself along a line of force of the larger magnet.

The earth has only some of the properties of a large bar magnet. Fig. 1303. A bar magnet freely suspended in the

FIG. 1303 Lines of force, earth

earth's magnetic field will align itself along one of the earth's lines of force and thus establish a *direction*. As will appear later this direction will not necessarily be north or south, but at any particular point on the earth, for practical navigation, it may be considered relatively constant for periods of several years. It is true that the direction is always changing, has even a diurnal oscillation, but with occasional exceptions *(see the discussion of variation)* these movements are of an order far too miniscule to affect what is indicated by the best of mariner's compasses at any given location. The changes in the indicated direction when the compass is moved many miles to another place will be discussed in due course.

This fact, that a freely suspended bar magnet stably indicates a direction, is the secret of the operation of the mariner's compass. It should be remembered such an indicated direction is generally neither geographic north or south, nor the true direction of the magnetic pole. Nonetheless, it is relatively *constant at a place*. The navigator usually has at hand ready information and rapid means of converting what his compass shows to true directions. He knows that if the magnetic effects of his ship be

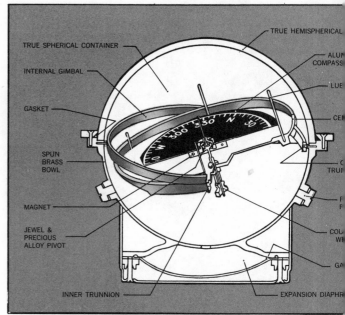

FIG. 1304   Compass with internal gimbal ring   Courtesy DANFORTH/WHI

neutralized *(see Chapter 14)* his compass is a magnetic direction finder; that its 'pointer' is aligned with one of the earth's lines of force. This line of force is called the *magnetic meridian* of the place; it will be referred to later.

Construction

Few wearers can describe or need to know the construction of a watch. Some know it contains a motor, an escapement and a gear train. All know it has a dial and hands. A compass has a dial and a hand too. Unlike a watch, the 'hand' of a typical mariner's compass *moves around the periphery of its 'dial.'* The 'hand' is a mark called the *lubber's line,* painted on the inside of the compass bowl or is a stile or a pointer fastened to its upper edge. The 'dial' is the compass card.

Several long thin permanent magnets, each enclosed in a non-magnetic tube, are affixed, parallel to each other, to a light non-magnetic wire frame. Like poles of the magnets are adjacent. In some modern instruments there is a different type of magnetic element. An annular disk, bearing suitable graduations, *the card,* is fastened to the frame above the magnets. Centrally placed under the frame is a bearing. Usually a float is attached to the frame to reduce wear on the pivot and bearing. This whole assembly serves as the dial. The user looks at its peripheral graduations.

The bowl, with its lubberline 'hand,' has a pivot atop a post in its center. See fig. 1306. The frame bearing rests on this pivot. A top of transparent material, either flat or hemispherical, is rigidly fastened with a liquid-proof seal to the top of the bowl. Through a pluggable aperture, the bowl is filled with a non-freezing liquid, formerly alcohol, but now usually a special oil. An expansion chamber is provided to allow for the effects of temperature changes. The sealed unit is mounted in gimbals so as to remain level in a seaway. In some instruments the gimbal mounting is inside the bowl. See fig. 1304.

FIG. 1305   Navy-type 7½" compass

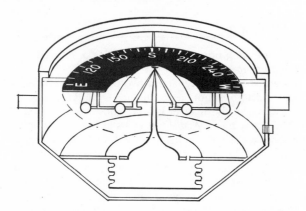

FIG. 1306   Cross section, typical compass

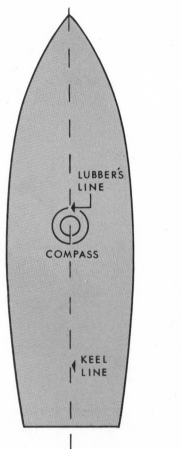
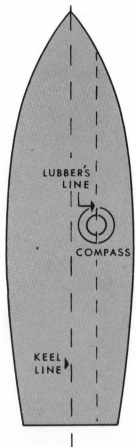

FIG. 1307 **Mounting parallel to keel**

Mounting

These are principles only. Most strongly is it suggested that pages 287-291 be read before using *any* tools.

The compass should be securely fastened aboard. A line through the lubber's line and the center of the card must be parallel to the keel. See fig. 1307. The instrument should be level, and so placed that it is within easy and unobstructed view of the helmsman. See fig. 1308. It must be lighted for night use with a minimum of illumination, preferably red. Magnetic material in its vicinity should be minimal. Wires near it, carrying direct current, should be twisted. Equipment generating strong magnetic fields should be as far away from it as is practical.

A box compass, fig. 1309, not permanently mounted, should have some permanent receptacle to receive it, so that upon each occasion of use it is correctly positioned.

Ships and larger yachts mount the compass in a stand called the binnacle, fig. 1404 though the term binnacle list does not indicate the need to shore up one side.

Photo by Dale Phillips

FIG. 1309 **Box Compass**

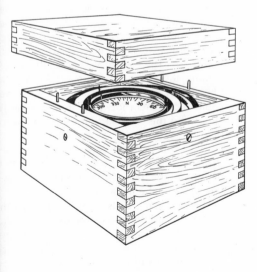

FIG. 1308 **Cruiser "bridge" or steering station showing compass mounted amidships and off centerline**

The Card

As previously stated the card serves as a dial; the lubber's line as a hand. A clock has a zero reference point. Time is told by observing the position of two or more hands relative to the twelfth or zero hour. Actually we observe an angle, but long ago each of us learned to ignore the angle, to read immediately what we see as time. The lubber's line indicates an angle, a direction relative to that of the north or zero point of the card, though most of us think not of the angle but of the direction. We think of east as a direction, paying no thought to the fact that it is one-quarter of a single clockwise rotation from north.

Modern compass cards are graduated in degrees, clockwise from north. Marks may be at each degree or for smaller craft at five-degree intervals. Numerals may be printed every ten degrees from 10° to 350°; every fifteen degrees from 15° to 345° or every thirty degrees from 30° to 330°, see figs. 1301, 1310 and 1311.

Still extant are older compasses with cards graduated only ninety degrees to the east and to the west from north and from south. In that system N 90°E means the same as S 90°E, i.e. East.

For many years the card bore only points. There are eight points to a quadrant; thus a point equals 11¼°. As the building of better hulls and the development of the fore and aft rig enabled vessels to hold course with greater accuracy, came need to use smaller units of arc. Each point was divided into fourths, giving rise to quarter-points, about 2¾°. There were various methods of naming these quarter-points. There was a time when no man was a salt unless he could recite them forwards and backwards all around the card starting from any given one. The age of steam brought the ability to hold a course regardless of all but the stronger winds and the need for a smaller division of the 'dial.' So the sexagesimal system came to the helmsman.

The cardinal points, North, East, South and West, and the intercardinals, Northeast, Southeast, Southwest and Northwest are still in common use as rough directions and as descriptions of wind direction. The combination points, as ENE, NNE and so on are but little used and as for the by-points, NxE, NExN, they and their like seem but to embellish (often erroneously) some TV or radio

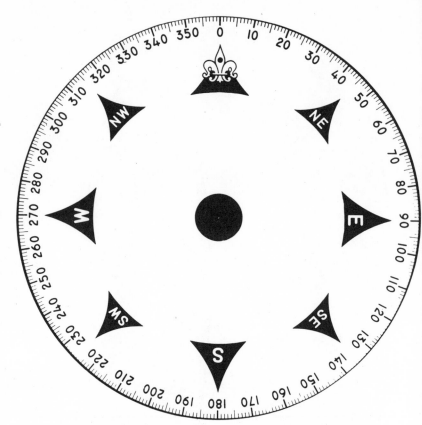

FIG. 1310   Compass Card—degrees, cardinals and intercardinals

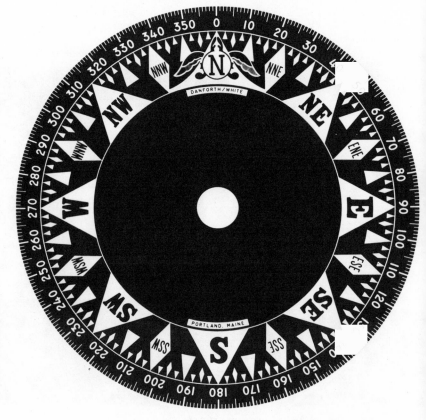

FIG. 1311   Compass Card—degrees, points and quarter points

drama. For those who do not wish to forget the past, and for those neophytes in sail who must learn points for ease in steering their wind-driven craft, there is included a table of comparisons of the various systems of nomenclature, fig. 1312.

Many modern compasses do label the cardinal and the intercardinal points, see fig. 1310, but the ensuing work here will be carried out in degrees.

CONVERSION TABLE—POINTS TO DEGREES

	Points	Angular measure ° ′ ″		Points	Angular measure ° ′ ″
NORTH TO EAST			**SOUTH TO WEST**		
North	0	0 00 00	South	16	180 00 00
N¼E	¼	2 48 45	S¼W	16¼	182 48 45
N½E	½	5 37 30	S½W	16½	185 37 30
N¾E	¾	8 26 15	S¾W	16¾	188 26 15
N by E	1	11 15 00	S by W	17	191 15 00
N by E¼E	1¼	14 03 45	S by W¼W	17¼	194 03 45
N by E½E	1½	16 52 30	S by W½W	17½	196 52 30
N by E¾E	1¾	19 41 15	S by W¾W	17¾	199 41 15
NNE	2	22 30 00	SSW	18	202 30 00
NNE¼E	2¼	25 18 45	SSW¼W	18¼	205 18 45
NNE½E	2½	28 07 30	SSW½W	18½	208 07 30
NNE¾E	2¾	30 56 15	SSW¾W	18¾	210 56 15
NE by N	3	33 45 00	SW by S	19	213 45 00
NE¾N	3¼	36 33 45	SW¾S	19¼	216 33 45
NE½N	3½	39 22 30	SW½S	19½	219 22 30
NE¼N	3¾	42 11 15	SW¼S	19¾	222 11 15
NE	4	45 00 00	SW	20	225 00 00
NE¼E	4¼	47 48 45	SW¼W	20¼	227 48 45
NE½E	4½	50 37 30	SW½W	20½	230 37 30
NE¾E	4¾	53 26 15	SW¾W	20¾	233 26 15
NE by E	5	56 15 00	SW by W	21	236 15 00
NE by E¼E	5¼	59 03 45	SW by W¼W	21¼	239 03 45
NE by E½E	5½	61 52 30	SW by W½W	21½	241 52 30
NE by E¾E	5¾	64 41 15	SW by W¾W	21¾	244 41 15
ENE	6	67 30 00	WSW	22	247 30 00
ENE¼E	6¼	70 18 45	WSW¼W	22¼	250 18 45
ENE½E	6½	73 07 30	WSW½W	22½	253 07 30
ENE¾E	6¾	75 56 15	WSW¾W	22¾	255 56 15
E by N	7	78 45 00	W by S	23	258 45 00
E¾N	7¼	81 33 45	W¾S	23¼	261 33 45
E½N	7½	84 22 30	W½S	23½	264 22 30
E¼N	7¾	87 11 15	W¼S	23¾	267 11 15
EAST TO SOUTH			**WEST TO NORTH**		
East	8	90 00 00	West	24	270 00 00
E¼S	8¼	92 48 45	W¼N	24¼	272 48 45
E½S	8½	95 37 30	W½N	24½	275 37 30
E¾S	8¾	98 26 15	W¾N	24¾	278 26 15
E by S	9	101 15 00	W by N	25	281 15 00
ESE¾E	9¼	104 03 45	WNW¾W	25¼	284 03 45
ESE½E	9½	106 52 30	WNW½W	25½	286 52 30
ESE¼E	9¾	109 41 15	WNW¼W	25¾	289 41 15
ESE	10	112 30 00	WNW	26	292 30 00
SE by E¾E	10¼	115 18 45	NW by W¾W	26¼	295 18 45
SE by E½E	10½	118 07 30	NW by W½W	26½	298 07 30
SE by E¼E	10¾	120 56 15	NW by W¼W	26¾	300 56 15
SE by E	11	123 45 00	NW by W	27	303 45 00
SE¾E	11¼	126 33 45	NW¾W	27¼	306 33 45
SE½E	11½	129 22 30	NW½W	27½	309 22 30
SE¼E	11¾	132 11 15	NW¼W	27¾	312 11 15
SE	12	135 00 00	NW	28	315 00 00
SE¼S	12¼	137 48 45	NW¼N	28¼	317 48 45
SE½S	12½	140 37 30	NW½N	28½	320 37 30
SE¾S	12¾	143 26 15	NW¾N	28¾	323 26 15
SE by S	13	146 15 00	NW by N	29	326 15 00
SSE¾E	13¼	149 03 45	NNW¾W	29¼	329 03 45
SSE½E	13½	151 52 30	NNW½W	29½	331 52 30
SSE¼E	13¾	154 41 15	NNW¼W	29¾	334 41 15
SSE	14	157 30 00	NNW	30	337 30 00
S by E¾E	14¼	160 18 45	N by W¾W	30¼	340 18 45
S by E½E	14½	163 07 30	N by W½W	30½	343 07 30
S by E¼E	14¾	165 56 15	N by W¼W	30¾	345 56 15
S by E	15	168 45 00	N by W	31	348 45 00
S¾E	15¼	171 33 45	N¾W	31¼	351 33 45
S½E	15½	174 22 30	N½W	31½	354 22 30
S¼E	15¾	177 11 15	N¼W	31¾	357 11 15
South	16	180 00 00	North	32	360 00 00

FIG. 1312

Conversion Table: points and degrees

(From BOWDITCH)

Variation

The point has been made that a freely suspended permanent magnet indicates a direction. That direction is, at any place, the vertical plane of the magnetic meridian. That the magnet may not be strictly horizontal and may dip slightly at one end is of no moment in the use of a mariner's compass.

In his normal day's work the navigator, or the small boat pilot, plotting his track on the chart, has need to know true directions, directions relative to the earth's geographic north. His courses and bearings are recorded with respect to the true north. His directional instrument, his mariner's compass, rarely indicates a direction as an angle referred to true north; always indicates an angle referred to the north point of the compass card, or compass north.

In a non-magnetic ship, one like the now non-existent CARNEGIE, a magnetic compass is subject only to the effect of the earth's magnetic field. In this unusual condition the north point of the compass card lies in the magnetic meridian. In general, the magnetic meridian does not coincide with the true meridian (which is the direction of the plane passing through the place and the geographic poles). There is an angle between them. This angle is termed variation. (V or Var)

The variation at any place is the angle there between the true meridian and the magnetic meridian. See fig. 1313. When that part of the magnetic meridian running towards the north magnetic pole lies to the east of the northern half of the true meridian, the variation is termed easterly. When it is to the west, the variation is westerly. Currently variation is expressed in degrees and minutes and labelled east or west, e.g. 7°30'W or 16°45'E. See fig. 1315. Its value may range from 0° to 180°.

Contrary to popular ideas the location of the magnetic poles is of little interest to the pilot or navigator. (Should he cruise in their vicinity he must perforce rely for directions on some instrument other than the magnetic compass.)

Variation is not the angle between the direction of the true and the magnetic poles. This supposition, a fictitious construct, useful in helping students to realize that true and magnetic north are usually in different directions, has been accepted by many as truth. Emphatically it is not so. It must be recognized as merely a learning aid, not a factual representation. The magnetic pole does not control the compass. The controlling force, as previously stated, is the earth's magnetic field. The compass magnet does not point to the magnetic pole.

Actually two antipodean points on the earth which are magnetic poles do not exist. There are north and south magnetic polar areas containing many magnetic poles, places where a dip needle would stand vertically. If this seems strange, give thought to pin-pointing the pole in the end of a bar magnet having a cross-sectional area of one square inch.

For scientific purposes rough approximate positions of theoretical north and south magnetic poles are computed from a large number of continuing observations made the

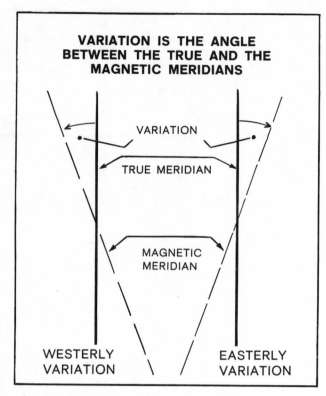

FIG. 1313 Defines Variation

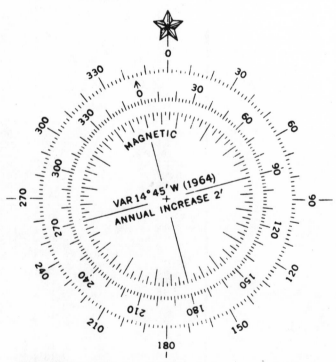

FIG. 1315 Typical chart rose, modern

world over through many years. In 1955 these adopted positions were respectively in latitude 74°N, longitude 101°W and latitude 68°S, longitude 144°E. In 1960 the adopted positions were in latitude 75°N, longitude 101°W and latitude 67°S, longitude 143°E.

Several facts become obvious. A magnetic compass in 79°N, 101°W would show north in a direction to the southward of the instrument! The magnetic poles are not stationary. They are not diametrically opposed as one conceives of the geographic poles. They are far from the geographic poles. A magnetic meridian is generally not a segment of a great circle passing through the magnetic poles, since but one great circle passes through any two surface points not at the end of a diameter. Not so obvious but nonetheless true is that, again generally, the magnetic meridian is not part of a great circle from the place to the adjacent magnetic pole.

Variation changes with location. Cognizance of this is part of the duty of every navigator or pilot. If he neglects it he will be in trouble, see fig. 1314. At any place the amount of the variation is relatively constant, though there is usually a small annual change. The navigator finds this data on the chart he is using. On all types of charts issued by the National Ocean Survey, including those of the Lake Survey, compass roses are printed suitably spaced for convenient use in plotting. See figs. 1315 and 1316. The rose has two concentric circular scales. The outer one is graduated in degrees and is oriented so that its zero point indicates true or geographic north. The inner one is graduated in degrees and points. Its zero point, identified by an arrow, shows the direction of the northern half of the magnetic meridian at that place. The angle at the center of the rose, between this arrow and the zero point of the outer, or true, rose, is the variation *at that place* for the year stated. This information is printed on the rose to the nearest 15', as "Var 14° 45'W (1964)," together with a further notation on the annual rate of change, to the nearest 1', and whether the variation increases or decreases as "ANNUAL INCREASE 2'," "ANNUAL DECREASE 10' or "NO ANNUAL CHANGE." See fig. 1315.

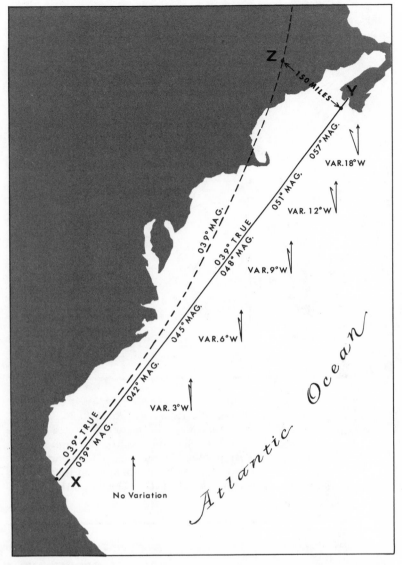

Fig. 1314.

The course from X to Y is 039° true. At X the variation is zero, so the magnetic course is also 039°. Because the variation changes with location, the magnetic course steered must be changed as the vessel enters regions having different variations. This must be done for each 1° change in the variation.

An airplane leaving X headed 039° magnetic for Y and held on this magnetic course would follow the curved track and ultimately be at Z, 150 miles from Y. To remain on the track XY, the magnetic course is altered in successive increments of 1°.

On smaller scale charts covering larger areas, variation is shown by labeled *isogonic lines*. Every point on such a line has the same variation. That line joining all the points having zero variation is called the agonic line.

The annual rate of change printed on chart roses permits the chart user to estimate the variation to be expected at some date subsequent to the publishing of the chart. Estimates based on information more than five years old should be used with caution. The annual rate of change is not due to the motion of the magnetic poles. It cannot be predicted accurately. The rate on the chart *is the best guess* of its trend, based upon prior observations of the gradual alterations in the earth's ever-changing magnetic field. Within the suggested time limit the prediction is adequate

for nautical use. It is well to know that there are recorded instances of sudden major changes and indeed reversals in the rate. Here then is another reason for not using old charts. Charts are cheap. Stranding is not.

LOCAL ATTRACTION

In some localities, fortunately few, over relatively small areas, the compass is subject to irregular magnetic disturbances in the earth's field. A striking example is found in Kingston Harbor, Ontario, Canada, where deflection of the compass may be as great as 45° in a distance of a mile and a half. This phenomenon is called local attraction. Charts of the area bear warnings to this effect.

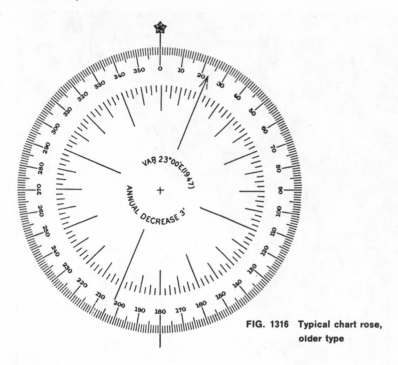

FIG. 1316   Typical chart rose, older type

Deviation

Usually the mariner's compass is subject to magnetic forces additional to those of the earth. Magnetic materials aboard the vessel cause the compass to deviate from its ideal position in the magnetic meridian. This angular swing or rotation on its pivot is called *deviation* (D or Dev) fig. 1317.

Deviation is the angle between the magnetic meridian and a line from the pivot through the north point of the compass card. Its amount can range from 0° to 180°, though large values are not to be tolerated. It is described east or west as the compass north lies to the east or west of the north branch of the magnetic meridian, fig. 1317.

It will be recalled that variation changes with geographic position. *Deviation changes with the ship's heading.* The causes will be explained subsequently. To cope with these changes a vessel carries a deviation table, a tabulation of the respective deviations, usually for every 15° of heading by the ship's compass. (See page 282.) For added convenience a table is made on the basis of magnetic headings (page 285), or the two combined in a direct reading table (page 285).

Reducing deviation to a minimum brought into existence professional compass adjusters. A yachtsman may avail himself of their expert services, but with common sense and an understanding of the causes, may *compensate* his compass himself. *(See Chapter 14.)* Note that a compass is not 'corrected'; its deviations are reduced; the process is called *compensating*. Rarely is a compensated compass entirely free of deviation on all headings. As will be seen, there will be residuals, quite possibly of small practical significance.

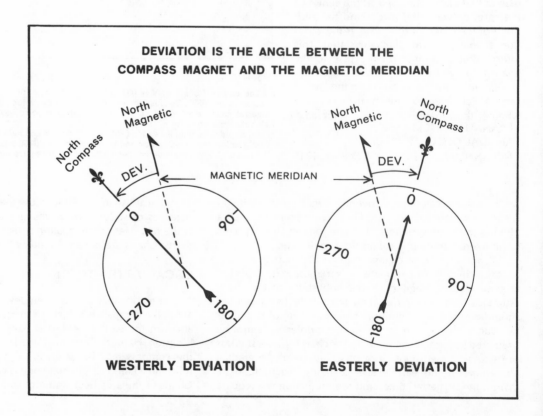

FIG. 1317
Deviation defined

DEVIATION IS THE ANGLE BETWEEN THE
COMPASS MAGNET AND THE MAGNETIC MERIDIAN

WESTERLY DEVIATION   **EASTERLY DEVIATION**

Compass Error _____

Because variation depends upon location and deviation upon the ship's heading, there are various possible combinations of the two, fig. 1318. The algebraic sum of the variation and the deviation is termed the *compass error, CE.* This is a semantic term. The compass is not in error. It is operating according to the forces that control its behavior. Compass error is merely another angle, that one between the direction of true north and the direction north as shown by the compass. Similarly to variation and deviation it is expressed in degrees and direction, i.e., 5°E or 7°W. The accomplished navigator uses this combined figure frequently in his work.

THE APPLICATION OF VARIATION AND DEVIATION

A course is merely an angle. It is the angle which the keel, or a line on a chart, makes with some other line of reference. Three lines of reference have been established: the direction of true north or the true meridian; the direction of the magnetic meridian; and the direction of the north point of the compass. Thus *there are three ways to name a course,* true, magnetic or compass. Always to be kept in mind, and sometimes this is difficult for the novice, is that no matter how the course be named among these three, *it applies to only one track, one direction*, fig. 1319.

The helmsman steers by compass. Bearings are observed by, or relative to, a compass. On the other hand, the navigator customarily plots and logs his courses, bearings and lines of position as true. Hence there is need for continual interconversion between the three systems of nomenclature.

Like learning to read, to tell time by a watch, to finger a musical instrument, facility in making these conversions comes with practice. At first one reasons out the steps. Later, reasoning is dropped as the process becomes one of habit.

Two of the many mnemonic aids available to help the student master conversion will be described. Both are applicable only when courses are stated in the conventional 0° to 360° system now in most common use. One is verbal, the other pictorial.

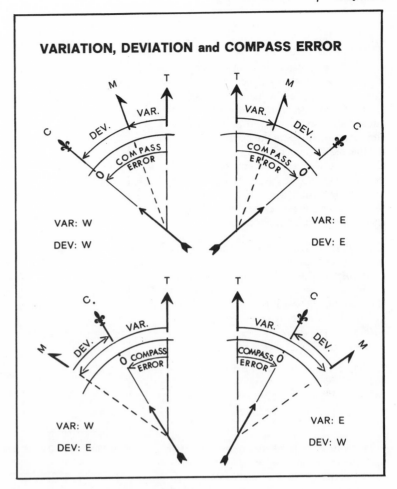

FIG. 1318   Variation, Deviation and Compass Error

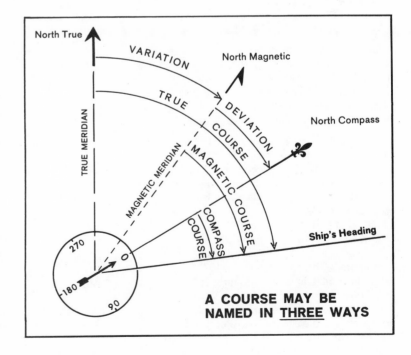

FIG. 1319   Three ways to name a Course

VERBAL AID

Assume the correct method of expressing a course as true, since no variable is involved. See fig. 1320. Assume the magnetic course to be less correct an expression because variation is involved and finally for a similar reason assume the compass course to be the least correct method of expression. Call the conversion of a course from compass to magnetic and from magnetic to true 'correcting.' Then the rule is: *"When correcting, add easterly errors"* which may be shortened to *"Correct add east."*

Example 1. The magnetic course is 061° and the variation is 11°E.
Required: The true course, TC.
The conversion is one of 'correcting' and the variation is easterly, so the basic rule, *"Correct add east"* is used.
061° + 11° = 072°
Answer: TC 072° See fig. 1321.

The rule is easily altered for application to the three other operations of conversion by remembering that *always two and only two* words are to be changed for any application.

Example 2. The magnetic course is 068° and the variation is 14°W.
Required: The true course, TC.
The conversion is 'correcting,' and the variation is westerly. The rule becomes: *"Correct subtract west."* Two words were changed in the basic rule.
068° − 14° = 054°
Answer: TC 054°. See fig. 1322.

Call the process of conversion from true to magnetic, or from magnetic to compass 'uncorrecting.' Now the two other forms of the rule are: *"Uncorrect east subtract"* and *"Uncorrect west add."* Two and only two words have been changed in each case.

Example 3. The true course is 088°. The variation is 18°W and the deviation 12°W.
Required: The compass course, CC.
Both conversions are 'uncorrecting' and both 'errors' are westerly. The rule is: *"Uncorrect west add."*
088° + 18° + 12° = 118°
Answer: CC 118°. See fig. 1323.

Example 4. The true course is 107°. The variation is 14°E and the deviation is 11°E.
Required: The compass course, CC.
Both conversions are 'uncorrecting' and both 'errors' are easterly. The rule: *"Uncorrect east subtract."*
107° − 14° − 11° = 082°
Answer: CC 082°. See fig. 1324.

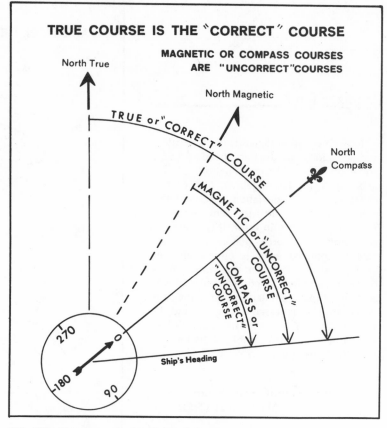

FIG. 1320   True Course is the "Correct" Course

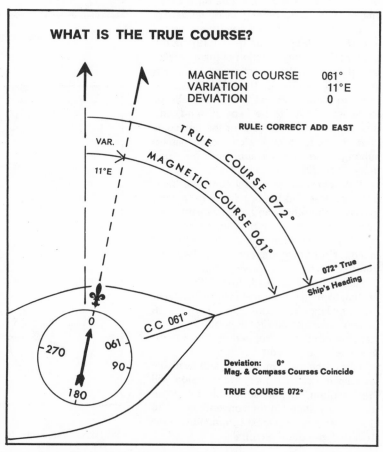

FIG. 1321   Problem What is the True Course Var E

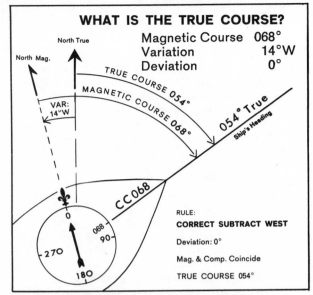

WHAT IS THE TRUE COURSE?

Magnetic Course 068°
Variation 14°W
Deviation 0°

RULE:
CORRECT SUBTRACT WEST

Deviation: 0°

Mag. & Comp. Coincide

TRUE COURSE 054°

FIG. 1322 Problem What is the True Course Var W

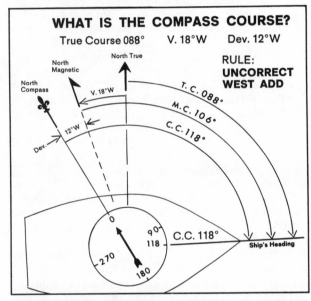

WHAT IS THE COMPASS COURSE?

True Course 088° V. 18°W Dev. 12°W

RULE:
UNCORRECT WEST ADD

FIG. 1323 Problem What is the Compass Course Var W, Dev W

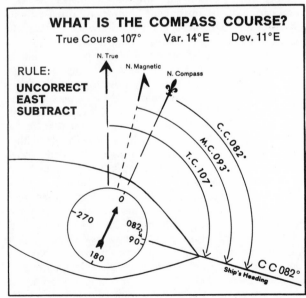

WHAT IS THE COMPASS COURSE?

True Course 107° Var. 14°E Dev. 11°E

RULE:
UNCORRECT EAST SUBTRACT

FIG. 1324 Problem What is the Compass Course Var E, Dev E

$$W- \quad \leftarrow \quad T V M D C \quad \rightarrow \quad -E$$

PICTORIAL SCHEMA

Vertically arrange the letters representing the three ways of naming a course, true, magnetic and compass, with the respective differences variation and deviation between them. Memorizing the reversal, Can Dead Men Vote Twice, may help to keep this arrangement in mind. On each side of the letters draw an arrow indicating the kind of conversion: on the left true to compass, on the right compass to true. Write in the appropriate arithmetic processes to be used with either easterly or westerly errors. The right side represents what has been called 'correcting' and the left side the reverse process, "uncorrecting." See fig. 1325. Memorize *DAW, DOWN ADD WEST* or WEST DOWN PLUS.

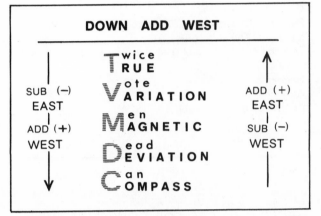

FIG. 1325 Verbal Aid, Down Add West etc

Example 5(a). From the chart the true course is 107° and the variation in the locality is 25°E.

Required: The magnetic course, MC.

The conversion is 'down' the picture. Use the left side. Easterly variation is to be subtracted.

107° − 25° = 082°

Answer: MC 082°. See below.

DOWN	T	107°
SUBTRACT	V	(−) 25°E
EAST	M	082°

Example 5(b). For this magnetic heading the deviation aboard this ship is 11°W.

Required: The compass course, CC.

The conversion is again 'down' the picture. Use the left side. Westerly deviation must be added.

082° + 11° = 093°

Answer: CC 093°. See below.

DOWN	M	082°
ADD	D	(+) 11°W
WEST	C	093°

Note that the so-called *compass error*, CE, the difference between true and compass, is 25°E − 11°W = 14°E. For any bearings taken over the ship's compass, while she is on the compass course 093°, applying the correction of 14°E yields the true bearing to be plotted on the chart.

277

Example 6(a). A ship is on compass course (CC) 193°. The deviation aboard this ship, for this compass heading is 11°E.

Required: The magnetic course, MC.

The conversion is 'up' the picture. Use the right side. Easterly deviation is to be added.

193° + 11° = 204°

Answer: MC 204°. See below.

ADD ↑	T	178°
EAST	V	(−) 26°W
SUBTRACT	M	204°
WEST	D	(+) 11°E
	C	193°

Example 6(b). The variation in the locality is 26°W.

Required: The true course, TC.

The conversion is 'up.' The westerly variation is subtractive.

204° − 26° = 178°

Answer: TC 178°

Note that CE is 26°W − 11°E = 15°W.

RULE CHANGES FOR COURSES NAMED IN POINTS

When courses are named in points and quarter points, the terms add and subtract should not be used. For this application the shortened rules become:

Correct easterly errors **clockwise**

Correct westerly errors **counter clockwise**

Uncorrect easterly errors **counter clockwise**

Uncorrect westerly errors **clockwise**

The serious student by this time has an understanding of the existence of variation and deviation and the means of making allowances for them in operating his craft. From what has been presented he should know that a chart will give him the variation and that if he has reliable deviation tables he can interconvert courses.

Before explaining why deviation changes with the ship's heading, how to determine the deviations and how to prepare deviation tables it seems well to present a little general information.

Always trust your compass. Failure to do this may be disastrous. The so-called errors of the compass, you have learned, are not errors. A compass does not usually exhibit erroneous behavior. It is subject to natural laws which

totally govern its operation. As will be shown, insofar as the small boatman is concerned, its errors are determinable; may be reduced and once determined make the compass an exceedingly accurate instrument. Unless abused or subjected to unusual extraneous magnetic effects caused by wrenches, knives, steel cans, radio or other equipment, it is far more reliable than a watch. For years it will faithfully indicate direction, if properly guarded. No watch is without some rate, which must be allowed for; not so a well treated compass.

No mention has been made of dry compasses. At one time mariner's compasses were dry. The needles were affixed to a card, and the assembly, extremely light in weight, supported on a pivot as in the wet compass. The installation of reciprocating engines in ships caused vibrations which affected the instruments' accuracy. The wet compass, literally damping these vibrations, came into general use.

Do not attempt to use the rules for conversion with a compass having a free needle supported above a card. In this type of compass the card and the magnet do not move as a unit. Such a compass has no lubber's line and is useful only for estimating directions from its center.

Detail on the gyro compass is outside the scope of this book. Interested readers are referred to texts such as: American Practical Navigator, Bowditch, published by the U.S. Oceanographic Office or to Dutton's Navigation and Piloting, The U.S. Naval Institute, publisher. The gyrocompass is a complex device designed to maintain a fixed direction in space. Contrary to the usual belief it is not without "errors." Aboard ship allowances have to be made for changes in geographic latitude and for rapid changes in the speed of the vessel. Its great advantages, of course, are the absence of the magnetic effects, variation and deviation. Gyro error is termed east or west and applied exactly as is deviation.

The sun compass is not a compass. It is an instrument for taking bearings of the sun. The observer looks, not at the sun, but at a shadow cast by a small pin in the center of a card. The card is graduated clockwise through 360° from a zero point at South. Thus the shadow marks the sun's true bearing. If the instrument be properly oriented with the vessel's heading, the shadow will show the vessel's true course. The difference between it and the ship's compass course is the compass error, CE. Applying the variation yields the deviation of the ship's own compass on that heading. Accuracy depends on knowledge of the sun's true bearing. Since latitude, date and time affect this and moreover since the rate of change of the sun's true bearing is inconstant, the method is not recommended to the uninitiate. Spherical compasses have been made with a shadow pin mounted centrally on the card directly above the pivot. The knowing navigator uses this device in checking deviation by azimuths of the sun.

A pelorus (see pages 378 and 379) is an instrument having sight vanes and a compass card, either of which may be clamped in a fixed position. Sometimes referred to as a dumb compass, it is used to take bearings when, because of obstructions, sighting across the compass is impossible. The pelorus is placed in a position suitable for observations, its zero point either on the ship's heading, or oriented to compass north depending on whether relative or compass bearings are desired.

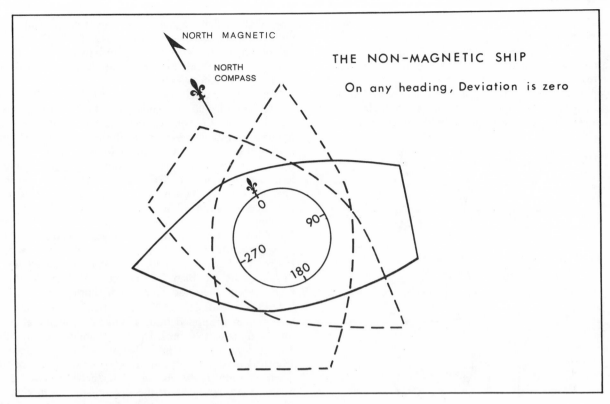

FIG. 1326   The Non-magnetic Ship

WHY DEVIATION DEPENDS ON THE SHIP'S HEADING

Aboard ship the mariner's compass is subject to two magnetic forces, that of the earth and that of the vessel. Were the vessel absolutely free of magnetism, there would be no deviation, regardless of her heading, fig. 1326. The earth's force depends upon geographic location. The compasses of all the ships in a harbor are subject to the same variation. The deviations aboard these ships will be unlike because of the magnetic characteristics of each hull. Further, if all these ships be put on identical magnetic courses, their corresponding compass courses will differ, except in the exceedingly remote circumstance that each compass be completely compensated.

Deviation, it was stated, *varies with the ship's heading,* because of the magnetic material aboard. A little investigation will demonstrate this. Refer again to fig. 1326, the non-magnetic ship. No heading of the vessel affects the compass card; its north point always lies in the magnetic meridian. The compass has no deviation. As the ship changes course, the lubber's line, turning with the ship's head, indicates on the "dial," the card, the magnetic course.

Now put aboard this ship, anchors, chain, rigging, pipe berths, steering gear, galley fittings, gas tanks, water tanks, stanchions, life lines, a host of similar magnetic material, not forgetting the all-important engine. The vessel has acquired a magnetic field of her own. To consider how this may affect the compass, assume the same field is created by fastening a large permanent magnet, slightly askew, in the vessel's stern. This artifact is exceedingly applicable; it simulates the magnetic condition aboard most wood or

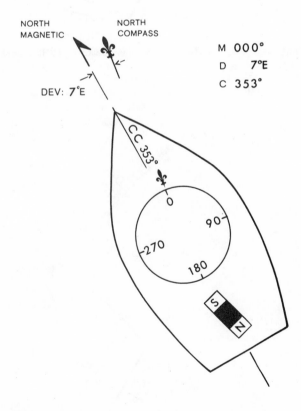

FIG. 1327   Heading North Magnetic aboard ANACHRONISM

plastic pleasure craft. Two forces, that of the earth and that of the stern magnet, now affect the compass magnets. The magnets behave as if they were subject to one force, the resultant of the two. When the two forces are aligned, the resultant force is in that same alignment; so are the compass magnets and there is no deviation. On all other headings the two forces are applied at an angle to each other and the resultant force will be in a direction different from that of the magnetic meridian. Consequently, on these other headings, north by compass (000° CC) will not be north magnetic, (000° M), but north by compass will be stable on any specific heading if no changes be made in the magnetic material aboard.

Consider a typical vessel, the yacht ANACHRONISM. Headed North (000°) magnetic, fig. 1327, the forces referred to cause the compass magnets and hence the card, to come to rest with compass north slightly to the right, or east, of the magnetic meridian. There is an easterly deviation. Its magnitude is of no moment in this instance. Important to realize is that whenever she is put on this heading, with no changes made in her magnetic materials, the same deviation will exist.

Swinging to the eastward the ship steadies on a course for which it has been found she has no deviation, fig. 1328. Now the earth's force, the force of the stern magnet and the resultant are all aligned. The compass magnets lie in the magnetic meridian. The direction compass north is identical with the direction magnetic north.

Next she heads East (090°) Magnetic, fig. 1329. Now the ship's force is applied from a direction roughly at right angles to the earth's force. This 90° coupling produces the largest deviations. The effect is just as if a small piece of iron had been brought near the left or west side of the compass north. The deviation will be large. In ANACHRONISM it is westerly. Had the polarity of the theoretical stern magnet been reversed, the deviation on this heading would likewise have been large, but in the opposite direction, to the east.

Coming now to head South (180°) Magnetic, fig. 1330, the stern magnet's force is approaching alignment with the earth's force, but in a direction diametrically opposite to that of the heading 000° Mag. shown in fig. 1327. The large westerly deviation so evident on the heading East mag-

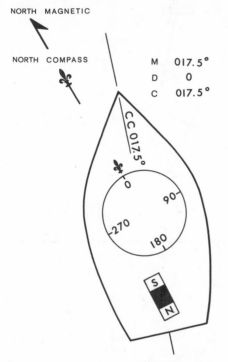

FIG. 1328 Heading with zero deviation aboard ANACHRONISM

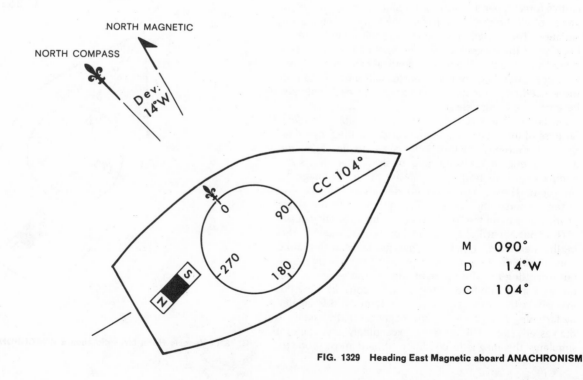

M	090°
D	14°W
C	104°

FIG. 1329 Heading East Magnetic aboard ANACHRONISM

netic is greatly reduced.

As the swing continues there will be a heading on which the two forces and their resultant will be again in line and the deviation zero. (In ANACHRONISM, as will appear later in this chapter, this occurs on the heading 187.5° Mag.)

Heading West (270°) Magnetic, fig. 1331, once more puts the two forces roughly at right angles, but the stern magnet's force is applied from the other side of the compass. The effect, now, is similar to that brought about by putting a small piece of iron close to the right or east side of the compass's north point. Again, as on the heading East, Magnetic, the deviation will be large, but now in the opposite direction, easterly.

Do not assume that on any other vessel these same deviations will exist. A ship's magnetic field does not necessarily lend itself to depiction as that of a single magnet. Indeed, changing the skew of the assumed magnet aboard ANACHRONISM a trifle would have altered the deviations.

To reiterate, were the ship non-magnetic, it would have no magnetic field, no deviation on any heading. Compensating a compass is an endeavor to so neutralize the magnetic field of the ship as to produce this non-magnetic environment for the mariner's compass. It is done by placing small magnets close to the compass in such positions as may be required. For this purpose many modern compasses have small magnets, adjustable as to position, built into their stands or binnacles. By their use and, if necessary, by adding other compensating magnets in the vicinity of the compass, the deviation on small boats is usually reducible to zero on most headings and leaving not more than three or four degrees in the others. Sailing craft, heeling out of the horizontal, frequently require heeling magnets to reduce their deviations. Iron and steel craft are subject to changes in deviation upon large changes in their geomagnetic latitude. This is outside the scope of this work.

It is not difficult for the small boat operator to ascertain and record the deviations for a number of headings. Such a record becomes a ready reference deviation table good until structural changes or other movements of magnetic material are made aboard.

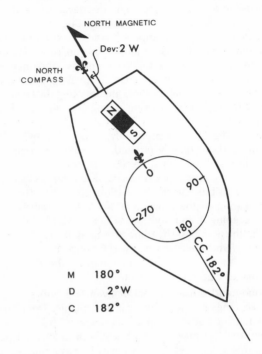

FIG. 1330 **Heading South Magnetic aboard ANACHRONISM**

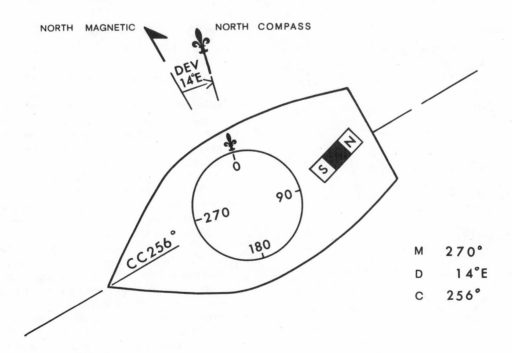

FIG. 1331 **Heading West Magnetic aboard ANACHRONISM**

Compass / CHAPTER 13

DETERMINING THE DEVIATIONS

Deviation is the angle between the compass card axis and the magnetic meridian, fig. 1317, page 274.

Aboard any craft the direction of compass north is sighted at a glance. Not so the direction of the magnetic meridian or, as it is loosely termed, magnetic north. So it is not possible to compare, visually, the deviation angle between these two reference directions. But the difference between an observed compass bearing, and its magnetic equivalent yields the same angle. The bearing is sighted over, or with reference to, the compass. The magnetic equivalent is taken from the chart. The navigator does this by observing celestial bodies, the piloting boatman by running ranges, or by crossing a range on different headings.

Two visible objects, preferably ashore or fixed to the bottom, both accurately charted, are selected. From the chart the magnetic range, i.e. the magnetic course, from the fore to the after mark is recorded. See fig. 1332. A and B are two visible objects; B is visible behind A. The magnetic bearing of the range is 075°. A vessel sails on the range, keeping A and B visibly in line. While held on this course, the compass heading is noted. It is 060°. The amount of the deviation is the difference between 075° and 060° or 15°. Reference to either of the conversion rules makes clear that its direction is East.

A buoy and a fixed object or even two buoys may be used if a range of fixed objects is unavailable. The charted position of a buoy is that of its anchor. Thus wind, or current, or both may move a buoy from its charted position. Large ships have been known to move buoys inadvertently by collision in thick weather. Steering a visible

course from buoy to buoy and noting the heading by compass, will, if the observation be made at the *start of the run,* give reasonably accurate results. (See fig. 1333.) Easiest perhaps is to swing the ship about its compass by sailing different headings across a range, recording the compass bearing of the range on each crossing.

Two prominent objects ashore are on a range bearing 087° from seaward. On a calm day the yacht ANACHRONISM sails across this range on compass headings successively 15° apart. Using sight vanes and an azimuth ring mounted on the compass (page 378) the compass bearing of the range is taken at each crossing. The results are recorded and tabulated. *(See below.)*

The navigator, noting the average compass bearing, 086.9°, was unusually close to the magnetic bearing of the range, decided the table was valid.

Ship's Head Compass	Range bears Compass	Range bears Magnetic	Deviation
000°	082°	087°	5°E
015°	086°	087°	1°E
030°	091°	087°	4°W
045°	096°	087°	9°W
060°	100°	087°	13°W
075°	104°	087°	17°W
090°	106°	087°	19°W
105°	106°	087°	19°W
120°	104°	087°	17°W
135°	101°	087°	14°W
150°	097°	087°	10°W
165°	093°	087°	6°W
180°	089°	087°	2°W
195°	085°	087°	2°E
210°	082°	087°	5°E
225°	079°	087°	8°E
240°	076°	087°	11°E
255°	073°	087°	14°E
270°	070°	087°	17°E
285°	069°	087°	18°E
300°	070°	087°	17°E
315°	072°	087°	15°E
330°	075°	087°	12°E
345°	078°	087°	9°E

The first and last columns in this tabulation now constitute a deviation table for ANACHRONISM'S compass provided *no changes are made in the magnetic environment of the compass.* Clearly indicated is the manner in which the deviation changes with the vessel's heading. To paraphrase Lecky, when on the heading 045° *magnetic* the ship's bow points in a direction quite different from where it does when she heads 045° by *compass.* The deviations in this table are applicable immediately to compass headings. It would not be difficult to interpolate visually for courses between the tabular values.

There is another problem. The navigator determines from the chart the magnetic course, wishes to know the compass course to steer. Use of this table for that purpose requires tedious, repetitive and time-consuming trial-and-error steps. To avoid these he makes a second table listing the deviations for *magnetic* headings. The second table is prepared without further observations by plotting a graph of the first. This nomogram or interconversion curve may be prepared in various forms. The simplest to plot and to use is still that of Admiral Sir Charles Napier, R.N., devised early in the nineteenth century, and bearing his name.

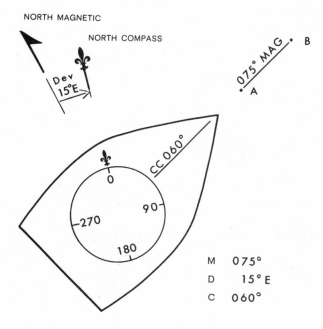

NORTH MAGNETIC

NORTH COMPASS

Dev 15°E

075° MAG. B

A

CC 060°

0

90

270

180

M 075°

D 15° E

C 060°

FIG. 1332 Determining the Deviation, sailing on a range

The Napier Diagram

The Napier Diagram is used to this day in most of the world's navies, including our own. One cannot now agree with Squire Lecky's statement that "it requires a man who has lived on the same street as a draughtsman to produce" it. Napier arranged his co-ordinates at angles of 60° instead of the usual 90° so that in place of a rectilinear grid, his is a series of equilateral triangles on a common base. This singularly simple device (see fig. 1334) makes the single scale, that of the base line, equally applicable to the inclined lines. The base line is laid off to represent 360°, with a dot every degree of its length. Every fifth dot is slightly heavier, for ease in identification. Every 15° along the base line is printed an angular value. Through these fifteen-degree stations are drawn the lines of the grid. Those sloping downward to the right are dotted every degree and like the base line, have the fifth dot accented. Those sloping downward to the left are solid.

Note that in the improved form of Napier diagram shown, the base line is not continuous but divided into two sections. To simplify its use for courses near the ends of these sections, this one, prepared by the United States

Power Squadrons, has 15° extensions at both ends of each section. When points were in vogue the base and dotted lines were spaced in quarter-points. Perhaps this, the difficulty of dividing 11¼° accurately into quarters, may have occasioned Lecky's caustic comment. Deviations for compass headings are plotted on the dotted lines, easterly deviations to the right of the base line, westerly ones to its left.

Consider now plotting a Napier curve of ANACHRONISM'S deviation table from the observations previously made. For the heading 000° CC the deviation is 5°E. On the dotted line passing through the point marked North or 000° on the base line, circle the fifth dot to the right. For the heading 015° CC the deviation is 1°E. Circle the first dot to the right on the dotted line passing through 015° on the base line. For 030° CC the deviation is 4°W. Circle the fourth dot *to the left* on the dotted line passing through 030° on the base line. Continue in this fashion, plotting each one of the deviations listed in the table. Stations 345°, 195°, 165° and 015° are plotted twice, once in each of their respective positions on the base line.

FIG. 1333 Chart Segment showing magnetic headings from buoy to buoy

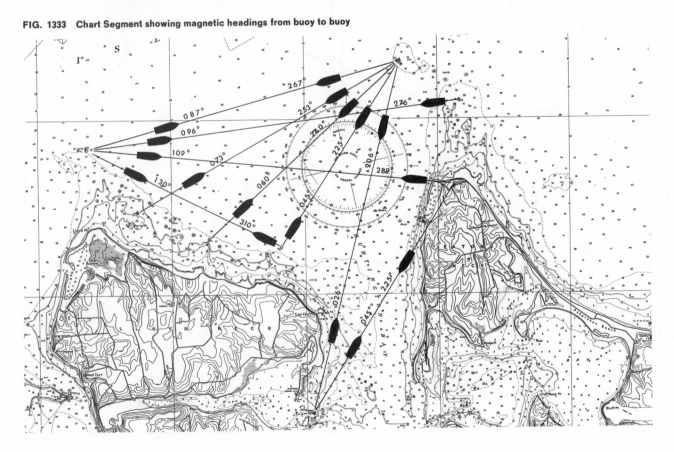

FIG. 1334 Napier Diagram

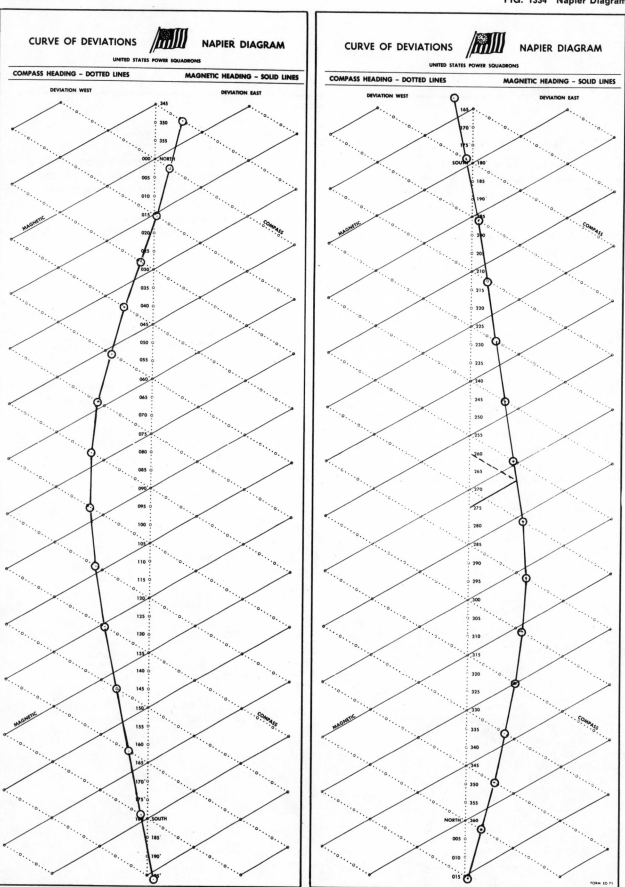

Now draw a fair curve through the plotted points. It may not pass exactly through every point because of observational or other errors, but if most of the points lie on the curve and those few which do not are within ½° of the curve, it will be sufficiently accurate. Should there be larger discrepancies the original observations or their subsequent computations are repeated. This is the conversion curve. All possible deviations of ANACHRONISM'S compass lie between this curve and the base line.

The length, from the base line to the curve, of any line of the diagram's grid, represents, to the baseline's scale, the magnitude of a deviation. Measured on the *dotted* lines are deviations for *compass* headings. Measured on the *solid* lines are deviations for *magnetic* headings. Where the curve is to the east (right) of the baseline, the deviations are east; where it is to the west (left), the deviations are west.

Making the second table, that of deviations for the magnetic headings, is now easy. The lengths of the respective solid lines are measured. Start with north. The curve is east of the baseline, hence this deviation will be east. See fig. 1334. Place one point of a pair of dividers on the center line at 000°. Adjust the dividers so that the other point is on the curve at its intersection with the solid line passing through 000°. Without changing the setting of the dividers' legs and keeping one leg on the base line, swing back to the base line. Record the number of degrees on the baseline between the divider points. It is 7° and the deviation for the heading 000° magnetic is 7°E.

Doing this for stations 15° apart produces the required second table for ANACHRONISM. It looks like this:

Ship's Head Magnetic	Deviation
000°	7°E
015°	1°E
030°	6°W
045°	12.5°W
060°	17°W
075°	19°W
090°	18°W
105°	17°W
120°	14°W
135°	11°W
150°	8°W
165°	5°W
180°	2°W
195°	2°E
210°	4°E
225°	6°E
240°	9°E
255°	11.5°E
270°	14°E
285°	16°E
300°	17.5°E
315°	17°E
330°	15°E
345°	11°E

Reverting to the Napier diagram, note that in swinging the dividers back to the base line it matters not, insofar as the amount of deviation is concerned, which way they are swung. If they be swung so that the two points on the baseline and the point on the curve form an equilateral triangle, the swung leg will indicate not only the deviation, but the corresponding compass course. Direct course conversion

is arrived at this way, or by drawing lines parallel to the grid lines. See fig. 1334 showing the inter-relationship between a magnetic course of 275° and a compass course of 260° aboard ANACHRONISM. This old jingle outlines procedure.

From compass, the magnetic course to gain,
Depart by dotted and return by plain.
But from magnetic, to gain the course allotted,
Depart by plain and then return by dotted.

From the Napier diagram a third table listing deviations in increments of 1°, applicable to either compass or magnetic headings, may be made. Appended is a portion of such a table, to the nearest integral degree, for ANACHRONISM. It has the advantage that no interpolations are required. For a known magnetic or a known compass course the deviation is immediately available.

Magnetic Heading	Deviation	Compass Heading
017°-018°	0°	017°-019°
019°-021°	1°W	020°-022°
022°	2°W	023°-025°
023°-025°	3°W	027°-028°
026°-027°	4°W	029°-031°
028°	5°W	032°-034°
029°-031°	6°W	035°-038°
032°-033°	7°W	039°-041°
034°-035°	8°W	042°-044°
036°-037°	9°W	045°-046°
038°-039°	10°W	047°-050°

For a compass with deviations as large as those of ANACHRONISM, such a table would be quite extensive, but nonetheless useful. For a compensated compass the table will be shorter because the deviations will be greatly reduced. *See: ANACHRONISM Compensated, Chapter 14.*

Instead of the three tables shown, some pilots prefer a circular deviation card, fig. 1335. The outer rose represents magnetic directions; the inner one directions by compass. Lines are drawn connecting corresponding values, as, for example, one between 275° on the outer rose and 260° on the inner. This really says that to make good 275° magnetic, ANACHRONISM must steer 260° by her compass or, conversely, that when she is steering 260° by compass she is making good 275° magnetic.

Some prefer a columnar arrangement. One column is headed: "For Magnetic"; the other: "Steer, Compass" and the corresponding values tabulated.

Using either of these two, conversion is performed by direct reading. No arithmetic is necessary and, with respect only to courses, not bearings, the user need know neither the amount nor the direction of the deviations.

Let the reader not infer that a Napier diagram or any similar conversion graph is to be used in daily piloting. That would be impractical. The diagram has but one function, to serve as a means of conversion in the preparation of those tables which the pilot chooses to use afloat.

See Chapter 14 for a further discussion of the compass

285

COMPASS DEVIATION CARD

MAGNETIC COURSE
FROM CHART
ON OUTER
ROSE

COURSE TO STEER
BY COMPASS
ON INNER
ROSE

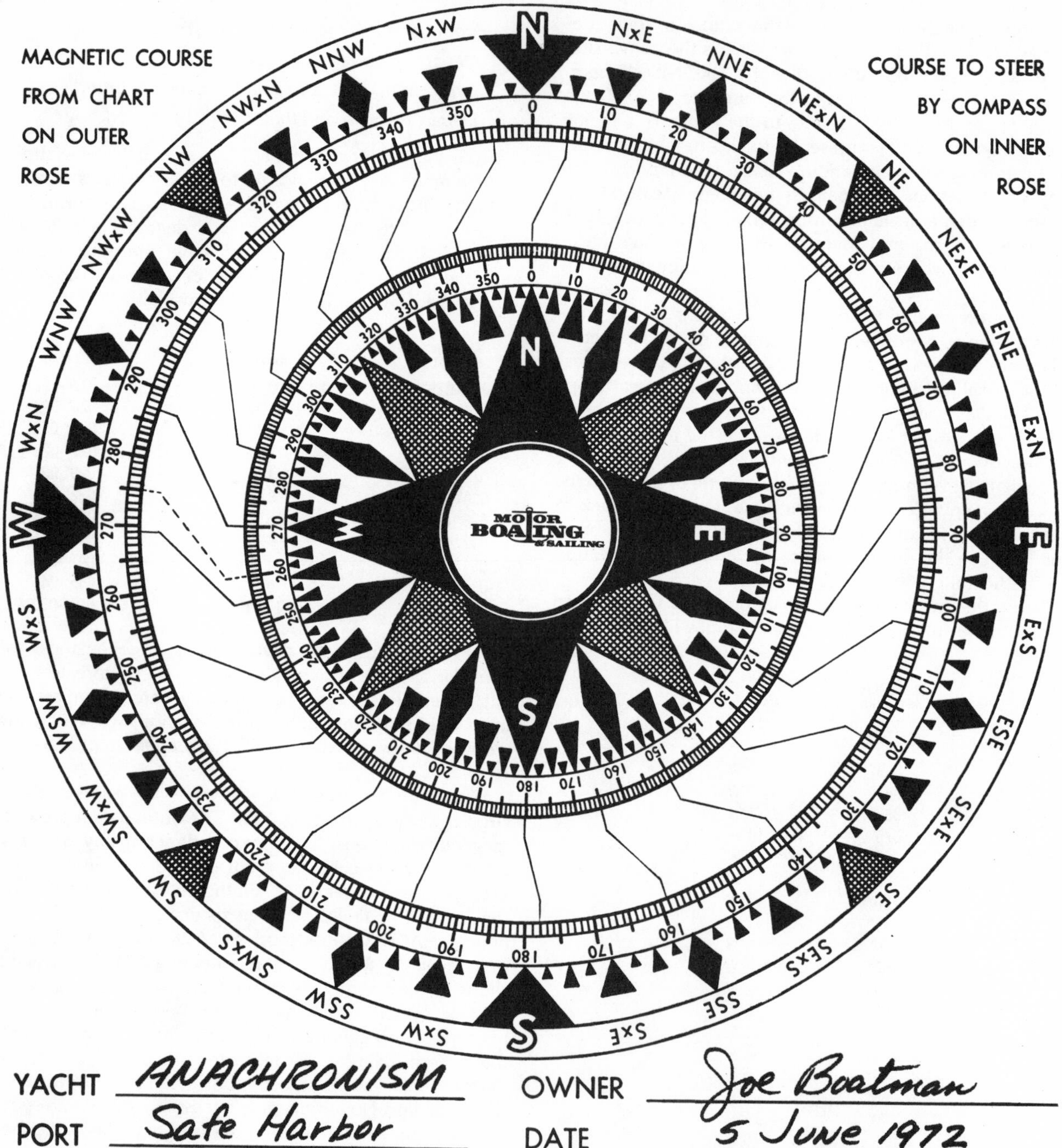

YACHT *ANACHRONISM*   OWNER *Joe Boatman*

PORT *Safe Harbor*   DATE *5 June 1972*

Read only MAGNETIC courses on the OUTER rose; only COMPASS courses on the inner one. For each compass heading (inner rose) apply the known deviation and draw a line from that degree or point to the corresponding magnetic heading (outer rose).

TO FIND THE COMPASS COURSE: Locate the magnetic course on the outer rose. Follow the lines to the inner rose and read the compass course.

TO CONVERT COMPASS COURSE TO MAGNETIC COURSE: Locate the compass course on the inner rose. Follow the lines to the outer one and read the magnetic course.

DO NOT CONVERT BEARINGS with this card. To do this find first the deviation for the boat's heading when the bearing was taken. Apply this deviation to the bearing.

FIG. 1335   Deviation Card

CHAPTER 14

THE MARINER'S COMPASS

**SELECTION,
INSTALLATION,
MAINTENANCE
and
COMPENSATION**

A VESSEL'S SAFETY may depend upon her compass. Cruising under conditions of poor visibility, the small craft pilot may have no other means of keeping to his desired track and, crossing a body of open water, no other means of making a good landfall. Running out the time on a given course in thick weather and neither seeing nor hearing the expected aid to navigation is not conducive to peace of mind. There is little comfort in a chain of soundings that does not match what the chart shows in the expected vicinity. Stranding because of unexpected contact with rock, shoal or any bottom is unnerving.

The preceding chapter gave some ways of ascertaining and using variation and deviation. Here will be discussed compensating, the reduction of deviations to a minimum, after some remarks on the choice of a compass and some further details as to its mounting aboard.

FIG. 1401 Inspecting the pivot action and instrumentally zeroing-in the compensators of a compass, prior to packaging for shipment.

Selecting a Compass

Almost any new compass looks fine in the store, or aboard in the quiet motion of the mooring or the marina slip. Its behavior under way, when the sea makes up and the little ship rolls, pitches and yaws, is of supreme importance. Will the card stick at some angle of heel? Will its apparent motion be jerky or smooth and easy? Are the card graduations legible and different headings easily distinguished? Is the instrument to be subject to large temperature changes? What if under its glass appears a bubble which may distract the helmsman? Answers depend on the quality of the compass.

No aviator will knowingly accept a cheap parachute, no sailor a bargain in life-jackets or fire extinguishers. No boatman should settle for a cheap compass. Select one adequate for your expected needs, erring on the side of luxury. Look at a number of them before buying. Pick them up, tilt and turn them, simulating motions to which they would be subject afloat. The card should have a smooth and stable reaction, come to rest without oscillations about the lubber's line. Reasonable tilting, comparable to the rolling and pitching of your boat, should not materially affect the reading. In fairness to the compass, if it has internal compensators, they must be zeroed-in (see below) before making these tests.

Pay particular attention to the card. Its graduation should be suited to the intended use. That a large craft may be held more easily on course than a small one is axiomatic. Hence the larger the ship, the greater is the number of divisions required on the card periphery. Owners of large ocean-going auxiliaries and cruisers seem to prefer cards which can be read to single degrees. Many of them also use quarter-point cards for long runs under sail.

Except under ideal conditions a small boat cannot long be held on a course with single-degree accuracy. The varying effects of wind, sea and indeed of trim brought about by the movement of a person aboard, swing her off the desired heading. Admittedly in the planning of a voyage, in the chart work, in the application of variation and deviation, accuracy to the nearest degree is essential. It gives the helmsman a goal. The experienced seaman knows little vessels cannot be steered so closely. Their track is an average, made up of headings at times on course, at times off to the right and to the left.

The novice, trying to steer 'too fine,' attempts to achieve the unachievable, to keep constantly on one heading. He cannot do so and, in the endeavor, repeatedly shifting his rudder, he overdoes it, makes steering needlessly laborious and is much less efficient than he would have been in a less effortful and more relaxed operation. Far from the smooth and easy performance of the skilled helmsman, his is that of the learner, most inept and suffering from a self-defeating concentration on precise control.

Steering is a bodily skill. The helmsman's brain, processing information received through his eyes, sends a signal to his muscular system to act in a certain way, to move the wheel or tiller. Lest the boat swing in a circle this muscular action must be stopped and a new one initiated to return the wheel to its previous position. Should the first action be too violent or too long continued, the vessel's head swings past the desired course, causing need for stronger action in the opposite direction in attempted rectification. There is little reason to believe the second action will be less violent than the first. Now the heading is off course in the opposite direction and the whole cycle must be repeated. The ship's head wanders from side to side about the course desired. (The modern science of control, of reducing in many operations this oscillating about a desired end, Norbert Wiener named cybernetics, using Plato's term for the steersman's art.)

Though most machines and electrical circuits respond much faster than man to specific orders, it cannot be denied that man does well when the orders allow him some latitude in performance. Consider attempting to steer 113° for a short 30-minute trick at the wheel using a small compass card. Close to the lubber's line are the graduations representing 111°, 112°, 113°, and 114° not in any way distinguishable from each other, except by position. More easily recognizable, because their marks are somewhat longer and perhaps heavier than the other four, are 110° and 115°. fig. 1402. Under any but the calmest conditions holding on 113° will not be possible. The effort of identifying 113° among the other close and cluttered marks will be difficult. Handling the wheel or tiller to keep the lubber's line on it for 30 minutes will be impossible.

To the best of his ability, the experienced small craft captain will hold the lubber's line midway between the more prominent graduations 110° and 115°, each clearly recognizable, and steer this course with the admonition "nothing to the left," gauging his handling to give her just

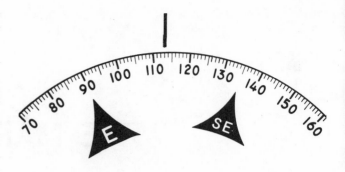

FIG. 1402 Segment of a card graduated in degrees, the lubber's line indicating a course of 113°. Compare fig. 1403.

FIG. 1403 Another card, graduated every 5°. Most helmsmen find this type of graduation easier to use.

"a little to the right." The orders to the operator of the boat's steering mechanism, a man, are not too specific and can be carried out with relative ease. The amount of error, the amount that the track sailed will wander from 113°, will be less than it would have been under rigorous endeavors to keep the lubber's line exactly on that course mark. Moreover the operation will be easier visually when there are no intermediate marks on the card between 110° and 115°. Thus a card graduated only every 5° is ideal for the small boatman's purpose. See fig. 1403.

CRITERIA FOR SELECTION

1. The card should remain level and not stick through reasonable angles of pitch and roll.

2. The card should move but slightly during any course change made by rotating the box or case through 90° or more. Some small motion due to the inertia of the fluid is permissible, but the card should be dead-beat, swinging but once to a steady position, not oscillating about the lubber's line.

3. The card should be easily read and graduated to your preference.

4. Provision should be made for lighting.

5. Hemispherically shaped, rather than a flat top plate.

6. Internally gimballed card and lubber's line.

7. Sturdy waterproof case.

8. Internal compensators, that is, built into the case.

9. Expansion bellows in the assembly to prevent bubbles in the liquid in lowered temperature.

10. For a larger boat a deck-mounted binnacle (fig. 1404), means for taking bearings and frequently for small steel boats soft iron compensators, those hollow iron balls you may have seen mounted on binnacles.

11. Do *not* consider a dry marching compass nor a dry tank compass. This is pure folly, inviting later disaster.

FIG. 1404 **Deck-mounted binnacle.**

Above all do not be niggardly. Buy an instrument made by a manufacturer of repute and pay his price. Hidden in the construction of a compass are things that make for accuracy and long life. Among them are: precise positioning of the magnetic element or the magnets under the card, so that its 000°-180° axis indicates exactly the direction of the magnetic meridian; the permanency of the markings on the card, of the expansion bellows, of the case seals; the life of the pivot bearing, its resistance to wear or to warping or distention from being, in the case of many little ships, tied up on one heading for five days every week. Here quality will pay off. In the long run the best is the least expensive.

ZEROING-IN

A modern compass having built-in compensators should be zeroed-in before being mounted aboard. If necessary such a compass already installed may be demounted and taken ashore for this purpose. Zeroing-in is nothing more than adjusting the compensators so that they have no effect on the compass. A compass subject only to the earth's field has no need of compensation; there are no deviations to remove. Therefore **before being installed, any deviation caused by improper positioning of the compensators themselves must be removed** and the unit go aboard just as an old-fashioned compass, ready for what magnetic changes may be wrought upon it by the ship's field. Setting the compensators by aligning screws with marks on the case or housing may not be sufficient for accurate navigation. Zeroing-in by trial-and-error is simple and effective, does not require any knowledge of the direction of magnetic North.

Do it in an area well away from any known magnetic influence: iron, steel girders, pipes, and ductwork concealed in walls, floors or ceilings; loud-speakers, radios, motors, refrigerators, freezers and so on. Don't work wearing a steel belt buckle, bracelet or watch band, nor a

yachtsman's cap containing a steel top grommet.

Using non-magnetic screws or tacks mount the compass temporarily on a small board having two parallel edges. Placing the lubber's line closely parallel to these edges is helpful but not essential. On a level flat board—be wary of a table or card table as it may have hidden steel screws or fittings—place a large book and the compass on its small board. Set the compass board with one of its parallel sides firmly against the edge of the book. Turn book and board as a unit until the compass reads North, fig. 1405. Hold the book steady. It serves as a fixed direction marker. Bring the opposite edge of the compass board snugly against the book. The lubber's line is now exactly reversed. If, now, the compass reads South, the N-S compensator is already zeroed-in and needs no adjustment.

If the reading is not South, half the difference must be removed. With a non-magnetic screw driver (a dime may do), slowly turn the N-S screw. Should the card move farther away from South, turn the screw in the opposite direction. With half the difference removed, realign the book and compass board, again as a unit, to the compass heading, South. Then without moving the book, reverse the compass.

If it does not now read North, halve the difference by turning the N-S adjusting screw. Again realign the book and compass on North, reverse the compass and if it does not read South, again halve the difference. Continue this process until the reversal is as nearly perfect as possible. When these adjustments are concluded, the direction of

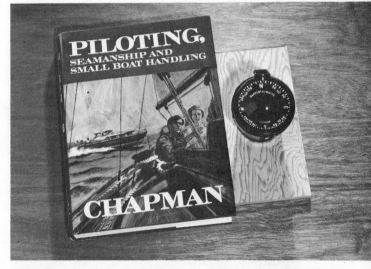

FIG. 1405 **Zeroing-in with book and board. Edges of small board should be parallel, and lubber's line of the compass should be parallel to these edges.**

the magnetic meridian (see Chapter 13) is that of the North-South axis of the compass card.

Next adjust the E-W compensators in the same way: line up on either an East or West heading, reverse and if the resultant heading is not exactly opposite, remove half the difference and continue working on East and West headings just as was done on North and South.

If exact reversals are not attainable move to a different

site; some magnetic influence may be at work.

If the adjusting screws are accessible and if the compass fits tightly in its packing box, zeroing-in can be done with the compass in its box instead of mounted on a board. If the compass, however, has to be removed from its box to adjust the screws, it is difficult to halve the differences and the chance of the compass not being exactly reversed is more probable.

Do not discard the temporary mounting board. It may be useful in testing the proposed permanent site aboard.

Installation

Intentionally Chapter 13 made only brief reference to the principles of mounting a compass. Now those should be amplified. There are definite steps to a good compass installation: inspect, test, mount, compensate and maintain.

Look critically at the proposed location. Clearly the compass should be directly in front of the helmsman, placed so that he may view it without bodily stress as he sits or stands in a posture of relaxed alertness. Give thought to his comfort in heavy weather and, in conditions of poor visibility, day or night. His position is fairly well determined by the wheel or tiller he handles. The compass is to be brought into what one might term his zone of comfort. Too far away, he bends forward to watch it. Too close, he rears backward for relief. Much of the time he may be not only the helmsman, but the forward and after lookout. So put the compass where he can bring his eyes back to it with a minimum of bodily movement. A distance of 22 to 30 inches from his eyes with the head tilted forward not more than 20° is about right, see fig. 1406.

Now inspect the site. It should be at least two feet away from engine indicators, bilge vapor detectors, other magnetic instruments and any steel or iron. Six or more feet is better than two, but there may have to be compromise on the small boat. When one or more of these magnetic influences is too close, either it or the compass must be moved. Vertical magnetic material is to be particularly avoided.

When, from this cursory inspection, the location seems satisfactory, test it. There may be magnets or magnetic influences concealed under the cabin top, forward of the cabin's after bulkhead, within the cockpit ceiling or in a wood-covered stanchion. You will test with the compass. If the compass has internal compensators, be sure, before testing, that they have been zeroed-in. If this has not been done, rotary motion of the case will make the card move, nullifying the test procedure.

Move the compass all around the area of the proposed site. Watch the card. One thing only will make it turn, a magnetic influence. Find it with the compass. If it cannot be moved away or replaced by non-magnetic material, test to determine whether it is merely magnetic, a random piece of iron or steel, or is magnetized. Successively bring the North and South poles of the compass near it. Both

FIG. 1406   Consider the helmsman's comfort when installing a compass.

FIG. 1407 Keep magnetic materials away from the compass. This light meter would cause deviation.

poles will be attracted if it is unmagnetized. If it attracts one pole and repels the other, it is magnetized. Demagnetization (see page 295), should be attempted.

Next hold or tape down the compass where you expect to mount it. Now the temporary mounting board used in zeroing-in will be helpful. Test everything that might affect the compass. Turn the wheel, switch on and off all the lights, radios, radio direction finder, radio telephone, depth finder and, if there is one, the shipboard intercom. Sound the electric 'whistle,' turn on the windshield wipers. Start the engine, work the throttle, move the gear shift. When there is an auxiliary generator, start it. In short, one at a time test everything that might cause deviation. When, on any one of these tests, the card moves, ideally the compass should be relocated or the cause demagnetized. Some of these things, windshield wipers, for example, you may

have to settle for, making a different deviation table to use when they are operating.

Be sure the site is firm. Vibration not only increases pivot wear, but may initiate that disconcerting phenomenon, a slowly spinning card!

Now prepare to mount the compass, following the principles given on page 269. The line through the lubber's line and the compass card pivot must be exactly parallel to the boat's keel to forestall an error constant on all courses. Establish the fore-and-aft line of the ship with stout cord or string. Carefully transfer this line to the compass site. If necessary shim the base so that a stile-type lubber's line affixed to the case and not gimballed, is vertical when the ship is on an even keel. Drill one hole, only. If, during compensation, the instrument has to be skewed slightly to counteract disalignment of the card or the fore-and-aft line, more than one hole will present problems.

Maintenance

Maintenance has two aspects. The first is the preservation of the magnetic environment of the compass. Except for occasional testing, no piece of iron or steel is to be brought or installed near it. An ashtray, a beverage can, camera, light meter, freon-powered horn, a portable radio, steel tools and a host of other common magnetic materials must be kept well away from the compass while it is in use. See fig. 1407. They will cause unknown deviations.

The second consists mainly of getting to know your compass. Watch how it appears to swing. Check that its readings are consistent on frequently sailed courses. Note if it appears to become sluggish and above all if it becomes erratic—these two warn you of alien magnetism or a damaged pivot bearing.

Test for a damaged pivot bearing or for undue pivot friction by deflecting the card a few degrees from the lubber's line with a piece of steel. There is need for repair

should the card not return to its former heading.

A bubble is removed by adding some liquid but the liquid must be that with which the compass is filled. No alcohol or water should be added to an oil-filled compass, no oil added to an alcohol-water-filled one lest the card, gaskets and internally painted marks be damaged.

Lightning and electric welding aboard may change the ship's own magnetic field. After exposure to either of these, test to see whether the deviations have changed.

On small welding jobs, placing the ground connection close to the weld limits the electric current flow and the resultant magnetic field to a small area, rendering large changes less likely.

Do read and follow the manufacturer's recommendations for winter storage. They may add years to the instrument's useful life.

PRINCIPLES OF COMPENSATION

It should be understood that what follows applies to compensation in the craft of the average pleasure boat owner. Though in these vessels deviations may be large initially *(see ANACHRONISM, Chapter 13)* and indeed the compass may even lock and swing with the ship after the ill-considered installation of some useful but strongly magnetic article, the causative factors are limited. With common sense, care in procedure and occasional ingenuity, the causes can be removed or their effects largely neutralized by the average boat owner if he will methodically follow the steps laid out in this chapter.

Usually absent in these craft are complications due to permanent hull magnetism acquired during building; the variable transient magnetism induced in vertical iron or steel members: the ship's sides, bulkheads, stanchions, masts; not forgetting those arising from a magnetic cargo. Solution of these and other problems should be left to an expert skilled and experienced in that field, a professional compass adjuster. The reader interested in the magnetic conditions aboard larger steel vessels is again referred to Dutton or Bowditch (page 278) or to still more technical treatises.

Compensating a compass is the process of reducing its deviations to a minimum. Deviation is caused by the magnetic field of the vessel. Compensation, then, is the elimination of the effects of this ship's magnetism on the compass. A small magnet very near the compass can negate the effect of more remote large magnetic masses.

In wooden or plastic power craft compensation is usually achieved by firmly fastening two small permanent bar or needle magnets, one parallel to the keel, the other athwartship, close to the compass. These two compensators need not be in the same horizontal plane, but there is one restriction upon their placement. Each must be centered on a line passing through the compass pivot. Thus the one parallel to the keel, called the fore-and-aft magnet, is placed to the right or left of the compass, with its center on a line running accurately athwartship through the compass pivot. The athwartship one is positioned forward or aft of the compass with its center on a truly fore-and-aft line through the pivot.

When, and only when, the compensators are placed that way, a unique condition exists which greatly simplifies the process of compensation. The athwartship compensator will not materially affect the compass on east or west magnetic headings, nor the fore-and-aft one on north or south headings.

A ship is headed east magnetic. An athwartship magnet, centered on a fore-and-aft line through the compass pivot and placed at A or B, fig. 1408, is approximately parallel to the compass's magnetic element. Irrespective of the direction of the compensator's poles, north to starboard or to port, it will exert no force bringing about any practical change in the deviation.

A compensator, centered on an athwartship line through the compass pivot, placed fore-and-aft at D or F, fig. 1409, is roughly at right angles to the compass magnet, exerts a strong torque or turning force upon it, and causes it to move, either increasing or decreasing the deviation.

Obviously similar conditions obtain on a heading of

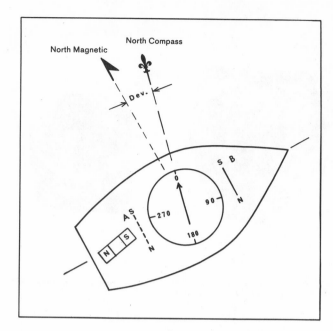

FIG. 1408   On E-W headings athwartship magnets have no effect.

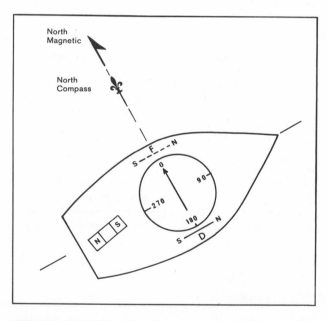

FIG. 1409   On E-W headings fore-and-aft magnets have maximum effect.

west magnetic. In the same way on north-south headings the effectivity of athwartship compensators and the nullity of those placed fore-and-aft could be demonstrated.

Of course both compensators come into use when sailing other than cardinal directions. The great value of the phenomena just explained is that they permit the pleasure craft operator to divide the causes of deviation into only two component parts and, without knowledge of their magnitude, remove each of them separately and uncomplicated by the other.

When the compensators have been fastened in what is found to be their most effective positions they could be replaced by one single horizontal magnet centered exactly under the pivot, at a specific distance from it and fixed at

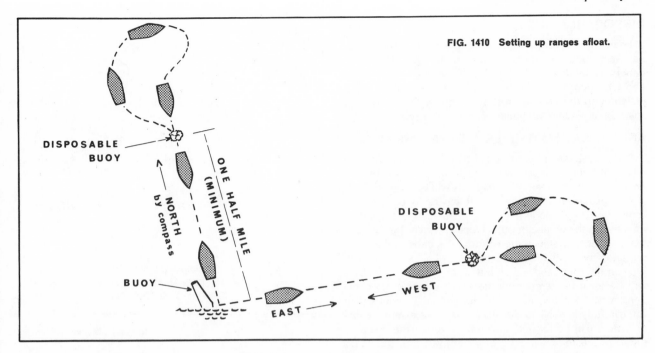

FIG. 1410 Setting up ranges afloat.

DISPOSABLE BUOY

ONE HALF MILE (MINIMUM)

NORTH by compass

DISPOSABLE BUOY

BUOY

EAST

WEST

some necessary angle to the ship's fore-and-aft line. This, the Admiralty method at one time used in the British Navy, is, to quote Lecky, "very elegant, . . . but somewhat more difficult than the ordinary one in vogue on merchant vessels." For "merchant vessels" read present-day pleasure craft and that understatement made twenty years before the twentieth century began still holds good.

Internal compensators, built in by the manufacturer, are so arranged that when the compass is installed they will be in the proper relative positions previously outlined. They are adjusted, as was shown in the discussion of zeroing-in, by means of a slotted bolt head, usually called a compensating screw. Casual inspection will show that one of the compensating screws is aligned with the lubber's line, the other at right angles to it. On some instruments the screws are marked N-S and E-W. Turning the screw varies the magnet's influence on the compass card from zero to maximum. Aboard many pleasure craft proper setting of these compensators will bring about compensation. When this does not suffice, because of powerful magnetic forces aboard, additional means, to be described later, will be necessary.

The astute reader will have perceived that compensation is analogous to zeroing-in. In zeroing-in, the book and board served to make certain that, at each reversal of the compass, its lubber's line turned exactly 180°. It was as if the compass had been aboard a ship, which, on each reversal, sailed an exactly reciprocal magnetic course.

Zeroing-in ashore began by using an unknown magnetic direction or course, identified only as North (000°) by compass. Zeroing-in was successful because this, or any other unknown magnetic heading, could be accurately reversed. Afloat, compensation may be started in the same way. Afloat, the nub of the problem is achieving accurate reversal, putting and holding the vessel on a course over the bottom, exactly the reciprocal of the original unknown magnetic heading. This, as will be shown, is not as difficult as one might surmise.

SAILING A RECIPROCAL COURSE

Between any two visible marks, or on a range, reversing the magnetic heading is obviously easy. In compensating there is need ultimately to sail at least the four cardinal magnetic directions North, South, East and West. Cardinal directions are seldom defined by aids to navigation or by landmarks in cruising waters. In a yacht anchorage or in waters adjacent to a marina, ranges may be built on these bearings and vessels easily steadied on them.

This then becomes a do-it-yourself project. *The skipper makes his own range.* Departing from a fixed mark (a buoy will do) he sails on a steady compass heading until ready to reverse course, then drops his own disposable buoy clear of the screw, creating the required range. Next he executes a buttonhook turn, lines up the disposable buoy and the original departure point, steadies on this range visually and, ignoring the compass, heads for the starting point, runs down the disposable buoy and continues back toward the mark originally left, fig. 1410. The turn is made as tightly as possible, keeping the buoy in sight, and is completed before the buoy has time to drift. The skipper, knowing the characteristics of his boat, will choose a right or a left turn.

This maneuver has accurately put the ship on a reciprocal course, providing that the buoy remained where it was dropped and that no wind or current sets the ship to either side of her heading on the outward or inward courses. Compensation will be inaccurate if she has moved crabwise over the bottom, going one way, but headed another; therefore the requisite courses are sailed where the current is negligible and when the wind or sea produces no leeway.

The skipper who has qualms about running the buoy down should take it very close alongside, touching it. On a range of 1/2 nautical mile, 1000 yds, when the buoy is 6¼ feet to one side of the vessel's center line the course error will be 8', less than 1/7 of 1°.

DISPOSABLE BUOYS

Excellent disposable buoys are plastic bleach bottles ballasted about one-quarter full of sand, fig. 1411. Newspapers wadded into a ball about the size of a basketball, tied with light string—no heavy stuff or wire, please—and weighted at the end of a four-foot cord with an old bolt, spark plug, washer or similar gear will also serve.

ADDITIONAL MATERIALS AND PREPARATIONS

For a compass without internal compensators or for one whose internal compensators are insufficient to remove deviation, two compensating magnets will be needed. Each is an encased permanent magnet having two holes for screw fastening. Modern units are small, but equally as effective as the original tubular types in which the magnets were either long steel wires or rods. The ends of the compensators will either be stamped N and S or be colored, blue on the south and red on the north end. Adhesive tape will be ideal for temporarily fastening the external compensators. Carefully mark their longitudinal centers. Lay out carefully in chalk in the areas where the external compensators will be located, two lines through the compass pivot, one fore-and-aft, the other athwartship, fig. 1412.

For the internally compensated compass a non-magnetic screw driver will be needed. A thin coin may do. The compass has been previously zeroed-in.

Every magnetic article of ship's gear should be stowed in its accustomed place, the windshield wiper blades be in their normal position of rest, no magnetic material near the compass, either obviously or hidden in the clothing of the helmsman or others. Realize that steel partial dentures, or the steel grommet of a yachting cap brought within a few inches of the compass may produce deviation. Someone may be working that close to the instrument during compensation. Keep external compensators far from the compass until they are to be installed.

COMPENSATION ON THE CARDINAL HEADINGS

With due regard for the conditions of wind, sea and current already mentioned steer 000° by compass from the

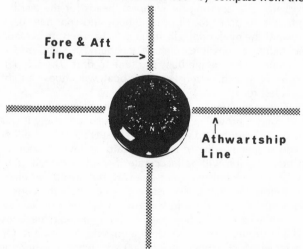

FIG. 1412 Chalk lines for positioning external compensators, laid out through the compass pivot.

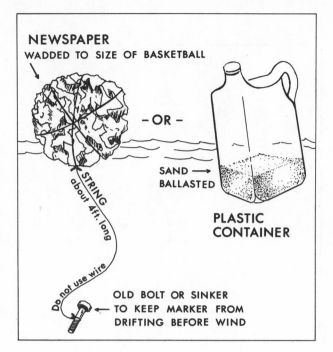

FIG. 1411 Disposable buoys.

chosen mark, holding rigorously to this course by the compass for half a mile or more. Next, have a crew member drop the disposable buoy over the stern, execute the turn and sail the reciprocal course, fig. 1410. This course, the reader will recall, is not sailed by compass, but by heading for the original departure point. The helmsman must hold this course visually. The compass heading is noted. If it is 180° there is no deviation on either the north or south compass headings. The athwartship internal compensator is not touched and no athwartship external compensator is necessary.

If the compass heading is not 180° compensation is required. Exactly as in the process of zeroing-in, half the difference between 180° and the observed compass course is to be removed. Halving the difference is based on the assumption that the deviation on reciprocal courses is equal and opposite. It may not be exactly so *(see again ANACHRONISM, Chapter 13)*, but it serves well as an approach.

Assume the compass heading is observed to be 200°. Then one half of the 20° difference, or 10°, is to be removed; adjustment is made until 190° is on the lubber's line while the helmsman continues to hold the course by steering for the buoy.

On an internally compensated compass turn the N-S adjusting screw. This controls the concealed athwartship magnet. If the compass course becomes more than 200°, turn the screw in the opposite direction. Move the screw slowly until the compass course is 190°.

For the externally compensated compass the correction will be made by *centering* a compensator athwartship on the chalked fore-and-aft line. If there is room, place a compensator forward of the compass in the position D, A or C, fig. 1413. Should the course become more than 200° the compensator is increasing the deviation and must be turned end-for-end. The card will move in the desired direction.

Should the card stop moving before 190° reaches the lubber's line, the compensator, in a position as at D, is too far from the compass. On the other hand, should the card swing past 190° the compensator is in the position as at C, too close to the compass. Move the compensator aft or forward as necessary until the course is 190°. Now tape the compensator firmly down; no screws yet. If there is no room for the compensator forward of the compass, place it in the vicinity shown as A'. *Do not place it off the center line as at E.*

In zeroing-in, the compass was next oriented so that 180° was on the lubber's line. This maneuver is not usable here before returning to the buoy because there is no means of laying out a reciprocal course. Return to the buoy, then run either south or north, repeat the procedure: outbound again on 000° (though the track will be 10° away from the original one), drop the disposable buoy, make the turn, head visually for the marker. If the observed course is not now 180° again remove only half the difference by turning the adjusting screw or moving the external compensator, as the case may be. Repeat if necessary until the N-S headings are error-free. Screw down the external magnet in its place, being careful not to move it. Do not touch

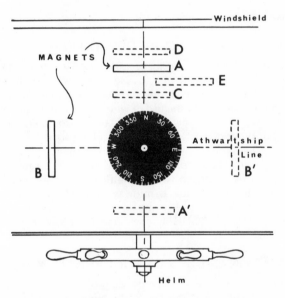

FIG. 1413 How compensating magnets are placed.

the internal compensator screw again. The smallest shift will nullify the careful work and re-introduce some deviation.

A similar method is pursued on east-west headings. Run from a buoy to the eastward on 090° or to the westward on 270°, drop the buoy, make the turn, head back visually for the departure point. Remove half the apparent error. On the internally compensated compass, adjust the E-W screw. With external compensation, place the compensator in a fore-and-aft position and *centered* on the athwartship chalk line, similar to B or B', fig. 1413, following the same techniques as on the north-south headings. When, after sufficient trials, the deviations are zero, *or as near to zero as is attainable*, screw down the external compensator with utmost care. Leave the internal compensator screw alone.

An alternate method of sailing reciprocal courses, credited to Darrach, uses a vertical shadow pin in the center of a horizontal graduated disc, preferably gimbal-mounted.

As the vessel heads north by the compass, the disc is rotated by hand so that the shadow falls on its zero point.

The ship comes about, steadies on a course such that the shadow falls on the opposite edge of the disc, exactly on the 180° mark. Now the course shown on the compass is noted. If it is 180° there is no deviation on N-S headings. If it is not, the procedure for compensation is undertaken, halving the difference and similarly on the E-W headings.

This appears to be simple. The vessel need not run far on any course. No departure mark nor disposable buoy is necessary. Neither wind nor current alters the result. But, reader, wait before you exclaim "this is for me." That shadow is not a fixed direction. The earth turns under the sun. While the ship holds a constant heading for a few minutes, that shadow moves. So time becomes a factor in the operation. Compensators must be adjusted or taped down before the shadow moves appreciably, taking the ship off the reciprocal heading. A navigator knows how to make the needed changes in his course by the shadow pin. The novice would best plan to use this method of course reversal only near the time of the summer solstice when the rate of change of the shadow movement is less than 1° in ten minutes of time, depending on the latitude.

COMPENSATION ON INTERCARDINAL HEADINGS

This is not for the amateur. However, in the average wooden, plastic or aluminum hull after cardinal compensation, the deviations on the intercardinals are usually small, not exceeding 4°.

Steel hulls may present problems whose solution may require installing soft iron spheres on the binnacle, use of Flinders bars and possibly heeling magnets. All this is for the professional, or for the exceptional amateur who, by study and practice in methods not discussed in this book, has achieved professional competence.

RESIDUALS ON INTERCARDINAL HEADINGS

The deviations remaining on the intercardinal headings may be determined by the methods discussed in Chapter 13 or estimated by making reciprocal runs on these headings. In the latter method half the difference between the outward course steered by compass and the observed inward course will be the deviation for the heading. Proper attention should be paid to the direction of the deviation, East or West.

FAILURE TO ACHIEVE COMPENSATION

When compensation cannot be achieved there is a strong magnetic field nearby. If care was used to remove or relocate the more obvious culprits in view of or hidden from the compass as earlier advised, look to the existence of a magnet nearby. Always suspect are tachometer cables and the steering mechanism. Test them with a thin piece of steel; a machinist's thickness gauge .001″ thick is ideal. Touch one end to the part being tested and gently pull it away. If the thin piece of steel tends to stick to the part, the latter is magnetized. Test thoroughly. Open the wheel housing and test all its metal parts. Finding a magnet, demagnetize it.

DEMAGNETIZATION

Robert C. Beard wrote: "When the offending part has been located, you can demagnetize it by borrowing from an electronics service shop either his color TV degaussing coil or his magnetic tape bulk erasing coil. Before doing any demagnetizing, *remove the compass from the boat* to prevent accidentally demagnetizing the compass needle.

"Connect the demagnetizing coil to the shore line. Holding it about one foot from the part to be demagnetized, turn it on and keep it on! Do not let it turn off for any reason, until this procedure is finished. Move the coil slowly toward the part until it is in contact with it. Then, still slowly, move it all over the part and around it. Finally, very slowly draw the coil away from the part for about five feet before turning it off. If your finger slipped and allowed the coil to turn off momentarily during the process, you will have to repeat the whole process to be sure of complete demagnetization."

Now test once more, with the thin piece of steel, the previously discovered permanent magnet or magnets. Inaccessibility may have precluded their complete demagnetization. Ideally, such parts should be disassembled, taken ashore, demagnetized and reassembled. Steel used in some linkages may be replaced by non-ferrous metals, aluminum or bronze.

Remount the compass, positioning the lubber's line with care and follow the procedure of compensation.

When the compass has been compensated preserve its magnetic environment as was suggested earlier in this chapter.

WORKING DEVIATION TABLE

Now that the compass has been non-professionally compensated a new deviation table must be made. That of ANACHRONISM is here reproduced.

ANACHRONISM COMPENSATED

Compass Heading	Deviation	Compass Heading	Deviation
000°	2.0°W	180°	2.0°E
015°	2.5°W	195°	2.5°E
030°	3.0°W	210°	3.0°E
045°	3.0°W	225°	3.0°E
060°	3.0°W	240°	3.0°E
075°	2.5°W	255°	2.5°E
090°	2.0°W	270°	2.0°E
105°	1.5°W	285°	1.5°E
120°	1.0°W	300°	1.0°E
135°	0°	315°	0°
150°	0.5°E	330°	1.0°W
165°	1.5°E	345°	1.5°W

From this the direct-reading table in the next column was prepared. Slight discrepancies, due to rounding, have no practical significance.

Either table makes quite evident those courses on which deviations are larger. In planning a voyage and in keeping track of position under way, using accurate deviation is essential. The knowing pilot, seeing at a glance where in ANACHRONISM the deviations are maximum, will be aware of those courses upon which compass bearings differ widely from their magnetic equivalents. Bearings taken on these headings must, before plotting, be converted by applying the deviation for the ship's heading. Bearings taken on headings in the vicinity of 135° and 315° may be plotted immediately as magnetic.

Magnetic	Deviation	Compass
133°-144°	0°	133°-145°
145°-153°	0.5°E	146°-153°
154°-163°	1.0°E	154°-162°
164°-176°	1.5°E	163°-174°
177°-187°	2.0°E	175°-185°
188°-211°	2.5°E	186°-208°
212°-251°	3.0°E	209°-248°
252°-264°	2.5°E	249°-262°
265°-279°	2.0°E	263°-277°
280°-294°	1.5°E	278°-292°
295°-303°	1.0°E	293°-302°
304°-310°	0.5°E	303°-309°
311°-319°	0°	310°-319°
320°-326°	0.5°W	320°-327°
327°-335°	1.0°W	328°-336°
336°-352°	1.5°W	337°-353°
353°-006°	2.0°W	354°-008°
007°-018°	2.5°W	009°-021°
019°-061°	3.0°W	022°-064°
062°-078°	2.5°W	065°-080°
079°-097°	2.0°W	081°-099°
098°-109°	1.5°W	100°-110°
110°-120°	1.0°W	111°-121°
121°-132°	0.5°W	122°-132°

TESTING FOR RANDOM DEVIATIONS

Random deviations are those existent only when some auxiliary equipment is put to use. They will not have normally been present during the compensation process, but may show up with the use of windshield wipers, radiotelephone, radio direction-finder, depth sounder, any lights or other electrical device used intermittently.

Testing is simple. Any single electro-magnetic influence that affects a fully compensated compass will cause a maximum deviation on two diametrically opposed headings. On the two headings midway between these there will be no deviation. A compass having residual deviations, as ANACHRONISM, may exhibit departure from this rule.

DEVIATION CAUSED BY WINDSHIELD WIPERS

Put the ship on a compass heading of 000° for a buoy or a landmark. Hold the course by steering, not by the compass, but visually for the mark. Repeatedly turn on the windshield wipers for five to ten seconds. Watch the compass closely. If the card swings even slightly, the wipers are affecting it. No motion of the card does not, at this point, support the conclusion that the wipers have no magnetic influence. By coincidence this might be the heading of zero deviation.

To continue the test, position the boat so that on a compass heading of 090° or 270° it may be steered visually for a buoy or landmark. Again turn on the wipers repeatedly for five- to ten-second periods. If the card is again motionless, the wipers cause no deviation.

When deviation does occur, the headings of maximum and zero deviations must be found. The opinion of experts is that rarely will these be cardinal points. The wise skipper is concerned with the maximum amount of deviation the wipers may cause. To find the maximum he looks first for a minimum, that heading on which the wiper-caused deviation is zero. Should this be hard to pinpoint he knows the maximum will be small and then hunts for it. He is dealing no longer with the whole 'magnetic mass' of the ship but with one small additional field either present or not present as the wipers are turned on or off.

The magnetic situation is as if, closely enough to affect the compass, a small magnet were sometimes placed in a definite position and orientation. When the wipers are off, the magnet is not there. When the wipers are on, the magnet is there—always in the same place and position, always exerting a deviation force on the compass, constant for any particular heading. Reason says eliminate the magnet. Practice says wipers are necessary; compensating for their magnetic effect is impractical and therefore allowance is to be made for their use. The allowance will be listed in a subsidiary deviation table to be used only when the wipers are running.

Slowly swing the boat, testing with the wipers for deviation on successive headings 15° apart. This is not too tedious. In any quadrant a point of either maximum or minimum deviation must occur. Hunt for a heading of no deviation, a null. Finding it, record the compass heading. If, as may well be, the precise null heading is not determinable, find and record the two headings on which the deviation is respectively 1°E and 1°W or 2°E and 2°W. Now determine arithmetically the mid-point between either of these pairs. Put the ship on a heading 90° from this mid-point. Now turn on the wipers and observe and record the deviation. It should be maximum. Further trial may be necessary to ascertain precisely the heading of maximum deviation.

When the maximum deviations are small, the values for the intermediate headings may be calculated by simple interpolation.

Example. Aboard EVOTZ the deviation is zero on the compass heading 060° and is maximum at 6°W on the compass heading 150°.

Required: The deviations for the intermediate headings at 15° intervals.

Answer. In 90° the deviation changes 6°. Therefore in 15° it will change $(\frac{15 \times 6}{90})°$ or 1° and the required deviations will be:

075° 1°W;   090° 2°W;   105° 3°W;   120° 4°W;   135° 5°W

As long as the wiper deviations are small, even though the headings of maximum and minimum are not exactly 90° apart (in the case of a not fully compensated compass), it is safe to estimate the intermediate values. A curve of deviations plotted on a Napier diagram would yield a table more accurate, but only in insignificant fractions of degrees.

A round of observations in ANACHRONISM produces these tables.

WIPERS OPERATING

Compass Heading	Deviation	Compass Heading	Deviation
000°	6°W	180°	6°E
015°	5.5°W	195°	5.5°E
030°	5°W	210°	5°E
045°	3°W	225°	4°E
060°	2°W	240°	2°E
075°	0.5°W	255°	0
090°	1°E	270°	2°W
105°	3°E	285°	3.5°W
120°	5°E	300°	5°W
135°	7°E	315°	6°W
150°	7°E	330°	6°W
165°	6°E	345°	6°W

Magnetic	Deviation	Compass
072°-085°	0°	073°-084°
086°-095°	1°E	085°-093°
096°-103°	2°E	094°-101°
104°-112°	3°E	102°-109°
113°-122°	4°E	110°-117°
123°-130°	5°E	118°-124°
131°-137°	6°E	125°-131°
138°-163°	7°E	132°-156°
164°-201°	6°E	157°-195°
202°-223°	5°E	196°-218°
224°-233°	4°E	219°-229°
234°-239°	3°E	230°-236°
240°-246°	2°E	237°-244°
247°-252°	1°E	245°-251°
253°-259°	0°	253°-260°
260°-266°	1°W	261°-267°
267°-274°	2°W	268°-276°
275°-282°	3°W	277°-285°
283°-292°	4°W	286°-296°
293°-303°	5°W	297°-308°
304°-010°	6°W	309°-015°
011°-028°	5°W	016°-033°
029°-040°	4°W	034°-043°
041°-053°	3°W	044°-055°
054°-062°	2°W	056°-064°
063°-071°	1°W	065°-072°

The existence of other random deviations which cannot be eliminated is unusual in small craft, but tests should be made for them. If present, knowledge of their existence first promotes safety, and second may impel the skipper to remove them.

Using alternate deviation tables is not difficult, particularly if they are made of different colored stock. With a little practice the skipper soon learns those headings on which wipers introduce important changes in deviation or, as in ANACHRONISM, those few headings where the change is slight. Turning on the wipers is an automatic order to recheck the compass course to be steered.

It is well to keep in mind the result of sailing off course. With a 10° error the ship will be set off course 1 mile for every 5.7 miles run. This may be serious when making a landfall in poor visibility. More hazardous are the risks of stranding when running a narrow channel through shallow water in fog or heavy rain. Note the following table.

Error in Course	Number of feet off course after sailing one nautical mile	Miles sailed to be one mile off course
1°	106	57.3
2°	212	28.6
3°	318	19.1
4°	424	14.3
5°	530	11.5
6°	635	9.6
7°	740	8.2
8°	846	7.2
9°	950	6.4
10°	1055	5.7

Properly installed, understood and used, the magnetic compass is the finest, least troublesome, inexpensive direction indicator obtainable by the small-craft sailor. Study and mastery of the principles and methods covered in these two chapters will be richly rewarding. A review of the highlights appears in the following two pages.

COMPASS BRIEFS

→ The heart of the compass is a magnetic element so mounted that on any heading of the ship, it lies in a constant direction in a horizontal plane. A card is rigidly attached to the magnetic element. To the helmsman the card may appear to move, but this is not so. The compass bowl, carrying the lubber's line, the 'hand,' moves around the card, the 'dial,' to mark the course. Except for movements caused by deviation, *the card is stationary*. The ship rotates about the card.

Card graduations are in degrees or points, or in various combinations of the two. Scales read from 000° at North clockwise through 360° or in points logically named by their positions relative to the cardinal or intercardinal points. There are eight points to a quadrant, thus a point is 11¼° and a quarter-point approximately 2¾°.

→ Buy the best compass you can afford or one a little better. A large card makes for easy steering. By virtue of its optical magnification, so does a spherical compass. Card graduations should suit your needs. Many craft sail on only short coastwise, lake or river voyages. On most of these, 'open' cards graduated every 5°, are adequate. Skippers of larger boats or of small ones making blue-water passages prefer graduations in single degrees and points. Many wind sailors still use quarter-points.

→ Before buying, test the compass by simulating the motions of rolling, pitching, yawing and deliberate course change. A good one behaves well under these conditions. It is also 'dead beat,' showing minimum over-swing as the vessel steadies on a new course.

→ Before taking it aboard, zero-in a compass having built-in compensators. Zeroing-in is done by adjusting the compensators so that they do not affect the compass. This is imperative if the unmounted compass is to be moved about its projected site testing for ship's magnetism or magnetic influences.

→ Mount the compass as far as possible from any known shipboard magnetic influences and yet where the helmsman may watch it without strain. There may have to be compromise here. Be sure that a line through the pivot and the lubber's line is parallel to the keel's fore-and-aft direction. See that the instrument is level at cruising speed and *particularly not canted* to port or starboard.

Once mounted, preserve the compass's magnetic environment, except for the adjustments made during compensation.

→ Keep the bowl filled with liquid. Should additions be made, check the tightness of the seals and top-off with nothing foreign to the original contents lest the card, bellows, seals and even the pivot and bearings be damaged. Watch the compass in operation. If it becomes sluggish, test for pivot friction. Should it oscillate in a seaway, look for and consider removing vertical iron aboard.

→ Magnetic meridians are lines of force of the earth's magnetic field. A compass, influenced by this field alone, aligns its N-S axis along a magnetic meridian. Such a compass *does not point to a magnetic pole* but does show accurately the direction of the magnetic meridian. Generally, the magnetic and the true meridians do not coincide. The angle between their similar parts is called variation. It is labelled East or West as the (magnetic) northerly part of the magnetic meridian lies to the east or the west of the true meridian. Variation ranges in amount from zero to 180°.

→ Variation exists where there is no compass. It is an attribute of the earth. Variation changes with geographical position. It is relatively constant in a locality. The small annual changes noted on charts are not persistent. The annual rate of change may itself change. The chart bears at best an educated guess, based on past observations. Therefore do not rely on computations projected from obsolete charts.

→ Magnetic materials aboard ship or alongside cause the compass magnet and card to swing out of the magnetic meridian. The resulting angle between the north-indicating branch of the magnetic meridian and the compass's N-S axis is called deviation. It, too, can range in amount from zero to 180° and, like variation, is termed East or West as the North point of the compass card deviates to the East or West of the magnetic meridian. Deviation exists only where there is a compass and some magnetic force additional to that of the earth. It is an attribute of the compass, not of the earth. Deviation changes with the ship's heading.

Though often so-called, variation and deviation are not errors of the compass, but are simply predictable magnetic effects to be reckoned with in course conversion.

→ A course may be named in three ways: true (TC), magnetic (MC) and compass (CC). A course (or a bearing) is a fixed direction. The scale zero, the line of reference for the angle, may be in one of three directions: the true meridian, the magnetic meridian or the direction of the north point of the compass. Hence courses have to be converted, that is, expressed with respect to the three different reference lines.

Converting courses expressed in degrees is simple.

True	Conversion from true through
Variation	magnetic to compass is in
Magnetic	the rule: *Down Add West* or
Deviation	*DAW*, which should be memorized.
Compass	The changes in the rule are obvious:

Down Subtract East, Up Subtract West, Up Add East.

→ When courses are expressed in points and quarter-points "add" and "subtract" can be confusing instructions. (Try adding ½ pt E to E ¾ N and you will be 1 point in error!) The direction in which the deviation or variation is to be applied is substituted. For 'add' use 'clockwise' and for 'subtract' use counterclockwise. Call conversion from compass to magnetic to true 'correcting' and the reverse conversion 'uncorrecting.' Then a basic rule emerges, Correct Easterly Errors Clockwise, shortenable to *Correct Easterly Clockwise, CEC*. With this in memory, remember further that in any change of this basic, *only two and always two* of the terms are changed. Thus there are UWC, UECC and CWCC. UWC is immediately recognizable as the DAW of the degree system.

→ Deviation changes with the heading because the ship

rotates about the compass card. Hence magnetic material aboard located in the compass's first quadrant while the vessel heads North, will be moved into the compass's fourth quadrant when she heads West. Similarly all the other magnetic material aboard shifts its position relative to the compass on this 90° course change. The compass card, subject to two influences, that of the earth and that of the moved field of the ship, may deviate from its original direction on CC north. Thus it should be seen that any change in heading may change the deviation.

→ Among the methods of determining deviation are running ranges or sailing across one range on different headings. Recording the deviations so observed yields a deviation table for compass headings. Plotting these on a Napier diagram and taking therefrom the deviations for magnetic headings gives a table of deviations on magnetic headings.

Thence for everyday use, deviation cards of various types, pictorial or tabular, are constructible, as the user desires.

→ A word of warning. *Never enter a deviation table with a bearing.* The deviation to be applied to a bearing is that of the ship's head at the time of bearing. For convenience in plotting bearings the proper deviation and the variation are algebraically combined to give one quantity, the so-called compass error (CE). CE = Var + Dev. When the two are in the same direction they are added, when opposite in direction the smaller is subtracted from the larger and the remainder takes the name of the larger.

→ Compensating, often called adjusting, a compass is the act of neutralizing, by small magnets near the compass, the effect on the compass of the ship's own magnetic field. Many compasses are equipped with two small magnets, whose position is adjustable, built into their cases. Adjust-

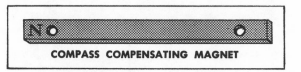

COMPASS COMPENSATING MAGNET

ment or compensation consists of positioning these compensators so that they negate the action of the ship's field. A compass not so equipped is compensated by fastening one or two small magnets near the compass. The proper position of these magnets is most important. Each must be centered on a line passing through the compass pivot. The athwartship magnet is centered on such a line running truly fore-and-aft; the fore-and-aft one on such a line running truly athwartship.

→ A table of deviations may be analyzed to ascertain approximately its components or coefficients and so determine, again approximately, the position of the compensators. This is usually unnecessary in small craft.

→ Compensation in small craft is not difficult. Run from a fixed mark on compass course North, establishing a range with a disposable buoy. Reverse course by sailing the range, ignoring the compass. Now observe the course the compass shows. The difference between 180° and the compass-indicated course is approximately twice the deviation. Remove half of this by adjusting the N-S internal compensator or temporarily taping down an athwartship

external compensator on the fore-and-aft line through the compass pivot. Repeat this operation on N-S and S-N headings until the deviations reach a minimum. Then do the same on the E-W compass headings, adjusting the E-W internal compensator or taping down, on the athwartship line through the pivot, a fore-and-aft external compensator. Permanently fasten the external compensators or leave the internal ones in the optimum positions found.

With a thin piece of steel (.001″) locate any strong magnetic influence which prevents reasonable compensation. Demagnetize it or remove it from the boat and recompensate. *Caution. Do not subject the compass to demagnetization.* Before turning on any demagnetizer unship the compass, take it ashore, well away from the influence of this powerful equipment.

Swing the ship for residuals and make a working deviation table or tables as desired.

Reasonable compensation is obtainable by this method. There may be residuals near the intercardinal points which merit some explanation here.

→ Broadly, deviations may be classified as observational, semicircular and quadrantal. The student need not be fearful of these names.

Observational deviation is that part of the total deviation due to errors in observation. It includes errors caused by lack of parallelism of the pivot-lubber's line axis and the keel. Observational deviation exists when a Napier diagram is symmetrical with respect not to its base line, but to a line parallel to the base line.

Semicircular deviation waxes and wanes, so to speak, in a semicircle. It increases from zero to maximum and decreases again to zero through a course change of 180°.

Quadrantal deviation does the same thing in one quarter of a circle. It increases from zero to maximum and decreases to zero through a course change of 90°.

A plotted curve of deviations includes all these elements. It follows, then, that when a Napier or other curve of deviations is unsymmetrical (i.e. of different shape on the opposite sides of its base line or a base line adjusted for observational error) quadrantal deviation exists. Fore-and-aft and athwartship compensators may not remove all the quadrantal deviations. Those remaining appear as residuals on the intercardinals. Generally, in wooden or plastic craft, they are not large enough to be troublesome.

Removing these residuals by hollow iron spheres, called quadrantal correctors, attached to the binnacle may not be within the competence of the amateur, is best left to the professional.

→ Windshield wipers in operation may cause significant deviations. Test for these. When existent, make a deviation table for use only when they are turned on. In reduced visibility, fog, rain or snow, comes greater need for trying to be sure that the course steered is the one desired to be made good.

→ Preserve the compass's magnetic environment. When it is altered by the installation of a new motor or other equipment, or by electric welding aboard, check the deviations.

→ Know your compass. Know its deviations. Above all, trust it. Not without good reason has it been dubbed the mariner's best friend.   *   *   *

CHAPTER 15

AIDS TO NAVIGATION

FIG. 1501 The skipper of a boat of any size is highly dependent on aids to navigation to warn him of unseen underwater hazards. He must be able to recognize such aids and know their significance.

Buoyage Systems

Although few mariners or boatmen may be aware of it, directing the movements of a vessel of any size in near-shore waters is closely akin to "flying blind" in an aircraft. It is not the few visible obstacles that are dangerous, but rather the more numerous shoals and rocks that lie unseen beneath the surface.

Natural landmarks may be used as reference points for navigation, but these are often few and far between, and may not be located to best advantage. It is to protect the mariner from these unseen dangers, and to allow him to safely direct his course, that government agencies and private individuals establish and maintain *aids to navigation*.

Figures 1502-1510, 1512, 1514, 1516 and 1517 reproduced from official U.S. COAST GUARD photographs.

The term *aid to navigation* may be applied to any man-made object prepared and located so as to indicate to a mariner the location of his vessel or the safe and proper course on which to proceed. The term includes buoys, day-beacons, lights, lighthouses, lightships, radiobeacons, fog signals, and loran, consolan, and other electronic systems. It covers unlighted objects, floating and non-floating; and visible, audible, and electronic signals and their supporting structures.

The term "aid to navigation" should always be stated thus, and not as "navigational aid". The latter term has been more broadly defined as also including "charts, instruments, devices, methods, etc., intended to assist in the navigation of a craft."

PURPOSE OF AIDS TO NAVIGATION

Aids to navigation are placed at various points along the coasts and navigable waterways as markers and guides to enable mariners to determine their position with respect to the shore and to hidden dangers. They assist mariners in making landfalls when approaching from the high seas, mark isolated dangers, make it possible for pilots to follow natural and improved channels, and provide a continuous chain of charted marks for coast piloting.

Establishment and maintenance of any aid must have economic justification. Aids established by the Federal government must, by law, be needed for the safety of a reasonable amount of water traffic, not just the occasional craft or the coming and going of a few local boats.

Within the bounds of actual necessity and reasonable cost, every aid to navigation is designed to be seen or heard over the greatest practicable area. As all aids serve the same broad purposes, such structural differences as those between an unlighted buoy or beacon, a minor light, or a major lighthouse with radiobeacon, are solely for the purpose of meeting requirements and conditions of the particular location at which the aid is established.

OPERATING AGENCIES

The United States Coast Guard, since 1967 a part of the Department of Transportation, is the agency responsible for maintenance of the system of aids to navigation on waters of the United States subject to Federal jurisdiction. Federal "navigable waters" are legally defined as coastal waters; rivers, bays, sounds, lakes, etc. navigable from the sea; and rivers, canals, and lakes *not* lying wholly within the boundaries of a single state. Such areas include the Atlantic, Gulf, and Pacific coasts of the continental United States, the Great Lakes, the Mississippi River and its tributaries, Puerto Rico, the Hawaiian Islands, and Alaskan waters. Aids to navigation may also be maintained by the Coast Guard at other places where required to serve the needs of our armed forces.

The senior officer of the Coast Guard is its Commandant, with headquarters in Washington, D.C. Functions of planning, procurement, establishment, operation, and maintenance of aids to navigation are carried on under his direction. Because of the wide geographic distribution of such aids on our coasts and inland waters, actual field work is executed by district organization.

There are 12 Coast Guard Districts. They maintain the system of aids to navigation and carry out other Coast Guard functions. The ten continental Districts are numbered from 1 to 13, omitting 4, 6, and 10; see fig. 1502. Hawaii is in the 14th Coast Guard District, Alaska in the 17th. Each District has its Commander, assisted by a suitable engineering and administrative force. Each District has the necessary supply and buoy depots, and specially designed and equipped vessels for the maintenance of aids to navigation. See fig. 1503.

"Private" aids to navigation

Aids to navigation may, with prior approval, be established in waters subject to Federal jurisdiction by agencies other than the Coast Guard. Information on procedures for obtaining such permission may be obtained from any Coast Guard District office. These aids must be patterned after Federal aids, and if a fixed structure is to be erected in navigable water, a permit must also be obtained from the Army Corps of Engineers.

All such aids to navigation—whether established by an individual, a corporation, a state or local government, or even a Federal agency other than the Coast Guard, such as the Navy—are termed "private" aids. These will have the same appearance as Coast Guard-maintained aids, but will be specially designated in the Light Lists.

State-maintained aids

On bodies of water wholly within the boundaries of a single state, and not navigable to the sea, the state government has the responsibility for the establishment and maintenance of aids to navigation.

Although each state retains authority over its waters, agreement has been reached on a uniform system of aids

FIG. 1502 Maintenance of aids to navigation is a district responsibility in the Coast Guard organization. There are ten districts covering the continental 48 states. District boundaries and headquarters are shown. Note that there are no districts numbered 4, 6, or 10.

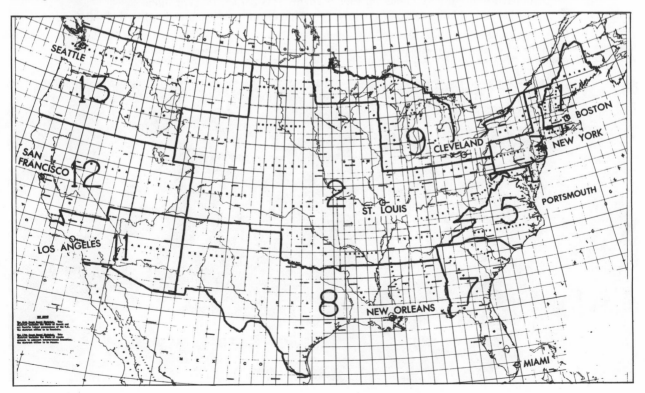

to navigation and regulatory markers. These will be described and discussed in detail later in this chapter.

PROTECTION BY LAW

Whether established by the Coast Guard or by another agency, all aids to navigation are protected by law. It is not only a violation of common sense, but also a criminal offense, to cause any damage or hindrance to the proper operation of any aid. Do not deface, alter, move, or destroy any aid to navigation. Never tie your boat to a buoy, daybeacon, or light structure. Avoid anchoring so close to a buoy that you obscure the aid from the sight of other passing craft.

If you should unintentionally or unavoidably collide with or damage an aid to navigation, this fact must be reported to the nearest Officer in Charge, Marine Inspection, U. S. Coast Guard in full detail and without delay.

For your own safety and that of others, cooperate with the Coast Guard and other agencies by promptly reporting any missing or malfunctioning aid. This will normally be done immediately after returning to port; if the safety of navigation is threatened seriously, the report should be made by radio without delay.

Types of Aids to Navigation

The term "aid to navigation" encompasses a wide range of fixed and floating objects from a single pile with a pointer or a small sixth-class buoy to manned lightships and lighthouses with an array of visible, audible, and electronic signals. Conspicuous shapes and objects on shore, such as mountain tops, radio antennas, smoke stacks, etc., may be charted and used to assist in piloting, but these are generally grouped under the term *landmark* and are excluded from the definition of an aid to navigation. This latter term is applied to objects that have been *primarily* established to assist in navigation. Also excluded are such informal aids as bush stakes placed in many side creeks by local watermen to mark minor natural channels or hazards. These do indeed help the skipper to pilot his boat safely, but they are not a part of the organized system of aids to navigation.

MAJOR TYPES

Buoys are floating objects moored or anchored to the bottom as aids to navigation; lightships fit this overall definition, but they are excluded as they form a separate category of aids. Buoys will have a distinctive shape and color as determined by their location and purpose. They may be equipped with visual, audible, and/or electronic signals.

Daybeacons are unlighted fixed structures established to aid navigation. They may be a single pile or a multiple-pile structure. Clusters of piles are called dolphins. Daybeacons are equipped with one or more signboards ("daymarks") of a distinctive shape and color as determined by the information that they indicate; see color pages I-K. (Pointers were used in some areas but are now being phased out.)

Lights are aids to navigation that have active visual signals. These are fixed aids (lighted floating aids are designated as lighted buoys or lightships). Lights are classified by the Coast Guard and other authorities as *primary seacoast lights, secondary lights,* or *minor lights,* as determined by their location, importance, and physical characteristics; the intensity of the light and its visible range will vary with the classification. The shape and color of the structure supporting the light source may be distinctive for purposes of identification, but will not convey information as, for example, in the case of buoys. The term *lighthouse* is often applied to primary seacoast lights and to some secondary lights.

Fog signals are audible signals transmitted to assist mariners during periods of low visibility, primarily fog. Occasionally they may be separate aids, as when located on the end of a jetty, but more often they will be part of a buoy, light, or larger aid to navigation.

Ranges are pairs of unlighted or lighted fixed aids so

FIG. 1503 The Coast Guard is the principal agency maintaining aids to navigation in U.S. waters. Specially designed and equipped vessels do this work. The USCGC Red Wood is the first of a class of 157-foot coastal buoy tenders.

FIG. 1504 "Large Navigation Buoys" are now used at some locations. The one shown, built of high-strength low alloy steel plate, is 40 feet in diameter with a 5,000 candlepower light 33 feet above the water. It replaces the old Scotland Lightship in the approaches to New York Harbor.

located that when observed in line the pilot is on the centerline of a channel. The individual structures may, in some cases, also serve as separate aids to navigation marking a turn in a channel.

Lightships are specially equipped vessels moored or anchored at specific locations to serve as aids to navigation. They are of distinctive shape and color, and will have lights and sound signals, and radiobeacons.

Radiobeacons are transmitters broadcasting a characteristic signal specifically to aid navigation at night, in fog, or at distances exceeding normal visibility. These, too, are usually at another aid, but may at times be located separately.

Electronic navigation systems are radio transmitters, usually in groups, which emit special signals that may be used for assistance in navigation when in fog or otherwise out of sight of land or offshore aids. Such systems include *Loran-A*, *Loran-C*, and *Omega* operated by the Coast Guard, aeronautical radiobeacons and "Omni" stations run by the Federal Aviation Agency, and other systems operated by various government or private interests. In general, only the USGC and FAA systems will be of use to boatmen.

Buoys

Buoys are floating objects, other than lightships, anchored or moored to the bottom at specific locations so as to serve as aids to navigation. They are shown on charts by special symbols and lettering that will indicate their shape, color, and visual and/or sound signals. They will vary widely in size from sixth-class buoys projecting only a few feet above the surface of the water to the new "super buoys" that are some 40 feet in diameter with a superstructure rising to 30 or more feet in height; see fig. 1504.

The buoyage system adopted for waters of the United States consists of several different types of buoys, each kind designed to serve under definite conditions. Broadly speaking, all buoys serve as daytime aids; those having lights are also available to aid navigation at night, and those having sound signals are especially useful in time of fog as well as at night.

The shape, color, and light characteristic, if any, will convey to a pilot information as to his location and the proper guidance of his vessel to remain in safe waters. The size of a buoy does *not* indicate such information and is usually determined by the importance of the waterway and size of vessels using it. The size of a buoy need not be taken into consideration by a skipper, except when estimating distances.

Buoys are normally anchored to the bottom using chain and heavy concrete sinkers weighing from one to five tons, fig. 1505. The length of chain will vary with the location, but will generally be two to three times the depth of water.

FIG. 1505 Buoys are anchored with cast concrete blocks called "sinkers." These range in weight from 500 pounds to more than six tons; a one-ton sinker is seen above. Normally, only a single sinker of appropriate size is used for any buoy.

BUOY CHARACTERISTICS

Buoys may be subdivided into types as lighted or unlighted, sound buoys, or combination buoys. This latter type is comprised of buoys that have both an audible and a visual signal.

The Coast Guard maintains about 21,000 unlighted and 3,700 lighted and combination buoys in waters under its jurisdiction. Many others are maintained by state and private agencies in non-federal waters.

Buoy shapes

Unlighted buoys may be further classified by their shape.

Can buoys are objects made up of steel plates so that the above-water appearance is cylindrical, like a can or drum floating with its axis vertical and flat end upward; see fig. 1506. Two lifting lugs may project slightly above the flat top of a can buoy, but these will not significantly alter its appearance.

Nun buoys are objects made up of steel plates so that the above-water appearance is that of a cylinder topped

303

(a)

(b)

FIG. 1506 Can buoys have a cylindrical shape with a flat top. An older-type, still used, is shown on the left. Newer can buoys have integral radar reflectors as shown in (b) above.

FIG. 1507 Nun buoys have a conical shape coming to a near-point at the upper end. This is a modern nun buoy with radar reflector plates in its upper section.

with a cone, pointed end up, fig. 1507. The cone may come to a point or the tip may be slightly rounded. Smaller nun buoys will have a single lifting ring at the top; larger buoys will have several lugs around the sides.

Unlighted buoys come in standardized sizes. These are designated in classes—first through sixth—and as standard or nonstandard. Knowledge of the various sizes is not important to the boatman, although it may be of general interest to note that the above-water visible portion of a nun buoy may vary from 2'-6" for a sixth-class standard to 14'-0" for a first-class tall. Can buoys are somewhat shorter, ranging from 1'-4" to 9'-9" above the waterline. The smaller buoys are, of course, lesser in diameter also, with a range of 1½ to 5 feet. Pilots should remember that a considerable portion of a buoy is under water, and that they are really much larger and heavier objects than they would appear to be from a casual observation.

The Coast Guard has now eliminated the use of *spar* buoys, but they may be found in some private or foreign systems of aids. These are usually large logs, trimmed, shaped, and appropriately painted; they are anchored from one end with a suitable length of chain.

Special shapes will sometimes be found in use as markers, but these are not regular aids to navigation. Spherical buoys are the most generally used of the special shape category.

Lighted, sound, and combination buoys are described by their visual and/or audible signals rather than by their shape.

Sound buoys

Buoys are often equipped with a characteristic sound signal to aid in their location during periods of reduced visibility, chiefly fog. Several different sound signals are available and are used to distinguish between different aids to navigation that may be within audible range of each other.

Bell buoys are steel floats surmounted by short skeleton towers in which a bell is mounted, fig. 1512. They serve

with considerable effectiveness both by day and night, and especially in fog; they are much used because of their moderate maintenance costs. Most bell buoys are operated by the motion of the sea—four tappers, loosely hung externally around the bell, are readily set in motion. When the buoy rolls as a result of waves, ground swells, or the wake of passing vessels, a single note is heard at irregular intervals. Some bell buoys are operated by electric batteries, their strokes sounding at regular intervals. These are particularly useful in sheltered waters where wave action is often insufficient to sound the signal.

Gong buoys are similar in construction to bell buoys, except that a set of gongs is substituted for the bell, fig. 1512. Gong buoys are used to give a distinctive character-

(a)

FIG. 1508 Buoys equipped with both a light and a sound signal are called combination buoys. Shown above in (a) is a lighted buoy with a whistle below the radar reflector. In (b) at the right, the lighted buoy has an electric horn fog signal.

AIDS TO NAVIGATION ON NAVIGABLE WATERS
except Western Rivers and Intracoastal Waterway

LATERAL SYSTEM AS SEEN ENTERING FROM SEAWARD

PORT SIDE
ODD NUMBERED AIDS
■ GREEN OR □ WHITE LIGHTS

FIXED
FLASHING
OCCULTING
QUICK FLASHING
EQ INT

9
LIGHTED BUOY   "9" Ra ref

7
CAN   "7" Ra ref

SB   SW
1   **3**

"1"▲   DAYMARKS   △ "3"
W

SG
3
△ "3"
G

MID CHANNEL
NO NUMBERS—MAY BE LETTERED
□ WHITE LIGHT ONLY

MORSE CODE

T   **N**   **B**
BW MoA "N" Ra ref

CAN   LIGHTED   NUN
BW C "T" Ra ref   BW N "B" Ra ref

A
MB   "A" BW   DAYMARK

JUNCTION
MARK JUNCTIONS AND OBSTRUCTIONS
NO NUMBERS—MAY BE LETTERED
INTERRUPTED QUICK FLASHING

□ WHITE OR ■ GREEN   □ WHITE OR ■ RED

M   **D**
"M" RB "D" Ra ref LIGHTED

N PREFERRED CHANNEL TO STARBOARD TOPMOST BAND BLACK
L PREFERRED CHANNEL TO PORT TOPMOST BAND RED

CAN   RB C "N" Ra ref   NUN   RB N "L" Ra ref

JB **L**   △ "L" RB   JR **J**   △ "J" RB

STARBOARD SIDE
EVEN NUMBERED AIDS
■ RED OR □ WHITE LIGHTS

FIXED
FLASHING
OCCULTING
QUICK FLASHING
EQ INT
GROUP FLASHING (2)

8
LIGHTED BUOY   R "8" Ra ref

6
NUN   R N "6" Ra ref

TR
4
DAYMARK   ▲ R "4"

BUOYS HAVING NO LATERAL SIGNIFICANCE—ALL WATERS

SHAPE HAS NO SIGNIFICANCE
NO NUMBERS—MAY BE LETTERED
MAY BE LIGHTED
ANY COLOR LIGHT EXCEPT
RED OR GREEN

WOr C Ra ref   SPECIAL PURPOSE

Y C Ra ref   QUARANTINE ANCHORAGE

FIXED
FLASHING
OCCULTING

N W C "N" Ra ref   ANCHORAGE

BW C Ra ref   FISH NET AREA

GW C Ra ref   DREDGING

UNLIGHTED

DANGER

EXCLUSION AREA

DAYMARKS HAVING NO LATERAL SIGNIFICANCE
MAY BE LETTERED

SUBMERGED DANGER JETTY   NW

M   NR

M   NB

Note: Square black (SB) and square white (SW) daymarks are being gradually phased out by replacement with square green (SG) daymarks with green reflective borders as shown above.

I

AIDS TO NAVIGATION ON THE INTRACOASTAL WATERWAY

AS SEEN ENTERING FROM NORTH AND EAST—PROCEEDING TO SOUTH AND WEST

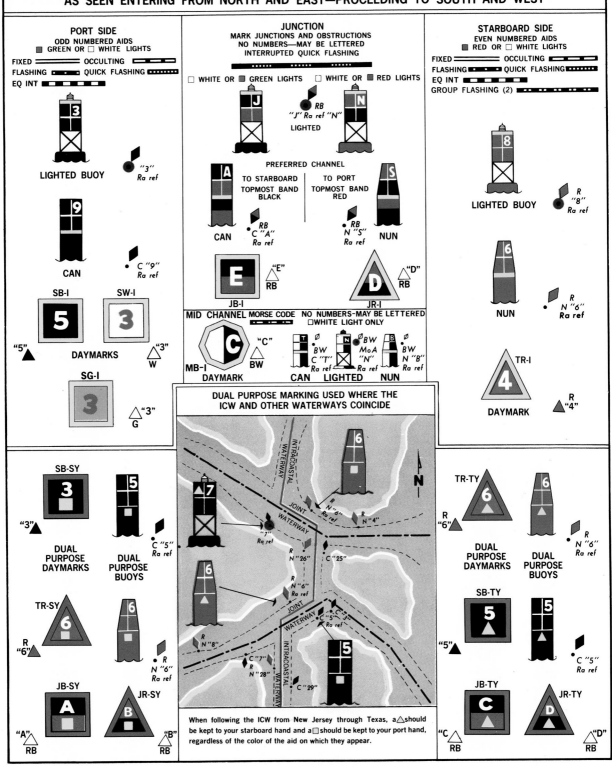

Note: The yellow-bordered ICW daymarks are being gradually phased out. Square daymarks will be green with green reflective border (SG); triangular daymarks will be red with red reflective border (TR). The ICW indication will be a yellow stripe immediately below the numeral or letter (not illustrated above).

AIDS TO NAVIGATION ON WESTERN RIVERS

AS SEEN ENTERING FROM SEAWARD

PORT SIDE	JUNCTION	STARBOARD SIDE

PORT SIDE

■ GREEN OR □ WHITE LIGHTS
FLASHING

LIGHTED BUOY

CAN

PASSING DAYMARK

SG   SW

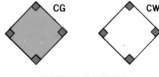

CROSSING DAYMARK

CG   CW

176.9

MILE BOARD

JUNCTION

MARK JUNCTIONS AND OBSTRUCTIONS
INTERRUPTED QUICK FLASHING

PREFERRED CHANNEL TO STARBOARD	PREFERRED CHANNEL TO PORT
TOPMOST BAND BLACK	TOPMOST BAND RED

□ WHITE OR   □ WHITE OR
■ GREEN LIGHTS   ■ RED LIGHTS

    LIGHTED

CAN   NUN

JB   JR

STARBOARD SIDE

■ RED OR □ WHITE LIGHTS
GROUP FLASHING (2)

LIGHTED BUOY

NUN

PASSING DAYMARK

TR

CROSSING DAYMARK

CR

123.5

MILE BOARD

RANGE DAYMARKS AS FOUND ON

	KWB	KWR	KRW	KRB	KBW	KBR	
NAVIGABLE WATERS EXCEPT ICW							MAY BE LETTERED

	KWB-I	KWR-I	KRW-I	KRB-I	KBW-I	KBR-I	
INTRACOASTAL WATERWAY							MAY BE LETTERED

K

UNIFORM STATE WATERWAY MARKING SYSTEM

AIDS TO NAVIGATION

PORT (left) SIDE

COLOR — *Black*
NUMBERS — *Odd*
LIGHTS — *Flashing green*
REFLECTORS — *Green*

THE LATERAL SYSTEM—In well-defined channels and narrow waterways, USWMS aids to navigation normally are solid-colored buoys. Though a can and a nun are illustrated here, SHAPES may vary. COLOR is the significant feature. When proceeding UPSTREAM or toward the head of navigation, BLACK BUOYS ← mark the *left* side of the channel and must be kept on the left (port) hand. RED BUOYS → mark the *right* side of the channel and must be kept on the right (starboard) side. This conforms with practice on other federal waterways. On waters having no well-defined inlet or outlet, arbitrary assumptions may be made. Inquire in the locality for further information and charts when available.

STARBOARD (right) SIDE

COLOR — *Red*
NUMBERS — *Even*
LIGHTS — *Flashing red*
REFLECTORS — *Red*

THE CARDINAL SYSTEM—Used where there is no well-defined channel or where an obstruction may be approached from more than one direction.

BLACK-TOPPED WHITE BUOY indicates boat should pass to NORTH or EAST of it. Reflector or light, if used, is white, the light quick-flashing.

RED-TOPPED WHITE BUOY indicates boat should pass to SOUTH or WEST of it. Reflector or light, if used, is white, the light quick-flashing.

RED-AND-WHITE VERTICALLY STRIPED BUOY indicates boat should not pass between buoy and nearest shore. Used when reef or obstruction requires boat to go *outside* buoy (away from shore). White stripes are twice the width of red stripes. Reflector or light, if used, is white, the light quick-flashing.

MOORING BUOY—White with horizontal blue band. If lighted, shows slow-flashing light unless it constitutes an obstruction at night, when light would be quick-flashing.

NOTE—The use of lights, reflectors, numbers and letters on USWMS aids is discretionary.

LIGHTS—On solid-colored (red or black) buoys, lights when used are flashing, occulting, or equal interval. For ordinary purposes, *slow-flashing* (not more than 30 per minute). *Quick-flashing* (not less than 60 per minute) used at turns, constrictions, or obstructions to indicate *caution*.

REFLECTORS—On lateral-type buoys, *red* reflectors or retro-reflective materials are used on solid-red buoys, *green* reflectors on solid-black buoys, *white* on all others including regulatory markers (except that *orange* may be used on orange portions of markers).

NUMBERS—*White* on red or black backgrounds. *Black* on white backgrounds. Numbers increase in an upstream direction.

LETTERS—When used on regulatory and white-and-red striped obstruction markers, letters are in alphabetical sequence in an upstream direction. (Letters I and O omitted.)

UNIFORM STATE REGULATORY MARKERS

Diamond shape warns of DANGER! Suggested wording for specific dangers: ROCK (illustrated), DAM, SNAG, DREDGE, WINGDAM, FERRY CABLE, MARINE CONSTRUCTION, etc.

Circle marks CONTROLLED AREA "as illustrated." Suggested wording to control or prohibit boating activities: 5 MPH (illustrated), NO FISHING, NO SKI, NO SWIM, NO SCUBA, NO PROP BOATS, SKI ONLY, FISHING ONLY, SKIN DIVERS ONLY, etc.

SWIM AREA

Diamond shape with cross means BOATS KEEP OUT! Explanatory reasons may be indicated outside the crossed diamond shape, for example SWIM AREA (illustrated), DAM, WATERFALL, RAPIDS, DOMESTIC WATER, etc.

Square or rectangle gives INFORMATION, names, activities. May give place names, distances, arrows indicating directions, availability of gas, oil, groceries, marine repairs, etc.

REGULATORY MARKERS are *white* with *international orange* geometric shapes. Buoys may be used as regulatory markers. Such buoys are *white* with two horizontal bands of *international orange*—one at the top, another just above the waterline. Geometric shapes, colored *international orange*,

are placed on the white body of the buoy between the orange bands. When square or rectangular *signs* are displayed on structures as regulatory markers, they are *white* with *international orange borders*. Diamond and circular shapes, when used, are centered on the signboard.

FIG. 1509 This is a late design of lighted buoy without sound signal. Note the straight sides of the tower-like superstructure; older designs had towers that first tapered in and then out near the top.

FIG. 1510 The Coast Guard is experimenting with an atomic power source for a buoy. This buoy is lighted from a strontium-90 thermo-electric system. It is hoped that the use of atomic power will increase the reliability of remote buoys and decrease the number of servicing visits required.

istic when there are several sound buoys in one vicinity. In these buoys, four gongs of different tones are mounted, with one tapper for each gong. As the sea rocks the buoy, the tappers strike against their respective gongs, sounding four different notes in an irregular sequence.

Whistle buoys provide yet another distinctive audible signal useful at night or in fog. The whistle is sounded by compressed air produced by the motion of the buoy in the sea. For this reason, such buoys are used principally in open and exposed locations where a ground swell normally exists, fig. 1508.

FIG. 1512 Shown here are models, all to the same scale, of four typical buoys. Note the range of sizes and large mass of the lighted buoys that is below the waterline. The smaller lighted buoy has a bell and the larger one four gongs; both have external "tappers" to strike and sound the fog signal. These are all of the so-called "1962" design, many of which are in use.

Horn buoys are rather infrequently used, but boatmen should be aware of their existence and know how to recognize them. They differ from whistle buoys in that they are electrically powered rather than depending upon the motions of the sea.

Lighted buoys

Buoys may be equipped with lights of various colors, intensities, and flashing characteristics (called "phase characteristics"). The color and characteristics of the light are used to convey information to the mariner. Intensity of the light will be determined by the distance at which the aid must be detected, influenced by such factors as background lighting, normal atmospheric clarity, etc.

Lighted buoys are constructed as metal floats with a short skeleton tower at the top of which the light is placed; see fig. 1509. The light is powered by electric batteries placed inside the lower body of the buoy below the waterline. Lighted buoys are designed to operate for many months without servicing.

Lighted buoys are now generally equipped with "daylight controls" that automatically turn the light on and off as darkness falls and lifts. Buoys equipped with such electric eye controls may be specially marked with a symbol in white paint consisting of a circular spot with a horizontal bar running through its center. This symbol was used for some years when the automatic daylight controls were being introduced, but are now being discontinued as conversion has essentially been completed.

Lights on buoys, as on other lighted aids, are either red, green, or white. The colors red and green have specific applications as will be discussed later in this chapter. White lights are prescribed for certain specific functions, and may also be substituted for red or green where a greater range of visibility is desired.

Color of buoys

Buoys used for navigation may be painted red, black, red-and-black, or black-and-white. Buoys for special purposes will use these colors and also yellow, green, orange, and blue. The specific meanings of the various colors will be discussed later in this chapter when buoyage systems are considered.

Optical reflectors

Many unlighted buoys are fitted with optical reflectors. These greatly facilitate the locating of the buoys at night when using a searchlight. Optical reflectors may be white, red, or green, and have the same significance as lights of these colors.

Reflective sheeting is used extensively by the Coast Guard for marking buoys. This flexible plastic film is easily attached to any reasonably smooth surface and has improved reflective characteristics over conventional glass reflectors. The reflective material may be in the form of square "patches" or as bands around the buoy.

Although primarily intended to make unlighted buoys more visible at night, reflective material is also placed on the numbers or letters of buoys to aid in their nighttime identification. Reflective numbers and/or letters will be found on both lighted and unlighted buoys of all types.

Radar reflectors

Many buoys are equipped with radar reflectors, vertical metal plates set at right angles to each other in such a manner as to greatly increase the echo returned to a radar receiver on a ship or boat. The plates are shaped and mounted so as to preserve the overall characteristic shape of an unlighted buoy or the general appearance of a lighted buoy. See fig. 1512.

LIGHT PHASE CHARACTERISTICS

The lights on lighted buoys will generally flash in one of several specific patterns. The flashing-light type of operation serves a number of useful purposes:

(1) It conserves the energy source within the buoy by having the light on only a small portion of the total time. Fixed lights, continuously lit with no variation of color or intensity, are not used on Coast Guard buoys, and only occasionally on buoys maintained by other agencies.

(2) Flashing assists in the detection of the lighted aid against a background of other lights.

(3) Flashing allows the signaling during hours of darkness of a limited amount of information, such as the need to exercise special caution at a certain point in a channel.

(4) The flashing characteristic of the light can be selected from a number of available patterns so as to be able to distinguish between several buoys of the same general function that may be within visible range of each other.

Lights are classed as *flashing* when the light comes on for a single brief flash at regular intervals; the period of light is always *less* than the period of darkness. Coast Guard-maintained buoys designated as of the flashing type will flash their light not more than 30 times per minute. This is the more-generally used characteristic for buoys. It is sometimes termed "slow flashing," but the official and correct description is simply "flashing."

Flashing (Fl)

Quick Flashing (Qk Fl)

Interrupted Quick Flashing (I Qk Fl)

Morse Code "A" (Mo A)

FIG. 1513 Buoys show various light phase characteristics which help in conveying information and assist in distinguishing between buoys of the same type located near each other.

Quick flashing lights will flash not less than 60 times each minute. These buoys are used for special situations where they will be more quickly spotted and where particular attention to piloting is required.

Interrupted quick flashing lights are characterized by a series of quick flashes separated by dark intervals of about five seconds' duration. This light characteristic, too, is used in special situations as will be described later.

Morse code "A" flashing lights have a cycle consisting of a short flash, a brief dark interval, a longer flash, and a longer dark interval. This is the "dot-dash" of the letter "A" in the International Morse Code; the characteristic was formerly known as "short-long flashing." The color of the light is always white.

The above light phase characteristics are shown diagramatically in fig. 1513. The *period* of a light is the time required for the completion of one full cycle of flash and dark interval, or flashes and dark intervals. A light de-

FIG. 1514 Buoys should be used with caution because of natural hazards to which they are exposed. A Coast Guardsman is seen here removing ice from a large lighted buoy; such ice may have interferred with the buoy's normal operation.

scribed as "Flashing 4 seconds" has a period of four seconds. One flash and one dark interval lasts just that long before the cycle is repeated.

Standardized flashing rates

As noted earlier, "flashing" lights may have various repetition rates for individual buoy identification, provided that there are not more than 30 flashes each minute. Over the years, the Coast Guard has used various characteristics involving different flash lengths and intervals. Buoys have been operated in the past that flashed at intervals of 2, 2½, 3, 4, 5, and 6 seconds; individual flashes have varied in length from 0.05 to 1.0 second. Standardization has now been introduced into the system of lighted buoys to reduce the number of different light phase characteristics.

Three standard characteristics will be used—flashing at intervals of 2.5, 4, and 6 seconds. These correspond to 24, 15, and 10 flashes per minute. These three light phase characteristics will provide sufficient differences for individual buoy identification and will provide economic battery service periods.

Another part of the Coast Guard's continuing effort to improve the reliability of its aids to navigation is the replacement of motorized mechanical flashers with solid-state (transistorized) electronic equipment having no moving parts. The use of precision moulded acrylic plastic lenses on buoys and minor lights has made possible substantial increases in the candlepower of such aids.

CAUTIONS IN USING BUOYS

A pilot should not rely on floating aids to navigation to always maintain their charted positions, or to constantly and unerringly display their specified characteristics. Obstacles to perfect performance are of such magnitude that complete reliability is manifestly impossible. The Coast Guard makes a continuous effort to keep aids working properly, but cannot be completely successful with all of the many thousands to be checked and maintained.

Buoys are heavily anchored, but they may shift in location, be carried away, capsized, or sunk as a result of violent storms or of having been struck by passing ships. A pilot must be prepared for the possible absence of a buoy he planned to use in his navigation, or its displacement off-station.

Buoys that have been placed to mark shifting shoals may not always be properly located in relation to the hazards they are meant to mark. This is particularly true during and immediately after heavy storms when shoals are liable to shift their positions relative to the buoys.

Lighted buoys may become extinguished, or their control apparatus become broken or deranged causing them to show improper light characteristics. Essentially all audible signals on buoys are operated by action of the sea, and may consequently be silent during periods of calm water. They may fail to sound, regardless of wave activity, due to mechanical defects in their sound-producing mechanism. Even if functioning properly, a sound buoy may not be heard at relatively close range due to erratic transmission of sound in air.

Buoys do not maintain their position directly over their anchors as they must be provided with some scope on their anchor chains; they swing in small circles around the anchor, which is the charted location. (See Chapter 18 for how buoys are charted.) For this reason, buoys are inferior

to fixed aids to navigation when precise bearings are desired.

Moored as they are, buoys have a tendency to yaw about under the influence of wind and current. This action is unpredictable, and a vessel attempting to pass close aboard risks collision with a yawing buoy. In extremely strong currents, buoys may even be pulled beneath the surface.

Buoys are sometimes removed to make way for dredging operations, or for other reasons. In northern waters, buoys may be discontinued for the winter, or smaller unlighted buoys substituted for lighted and combination buoys to prevent damage or loss from ice floes. The dates shown in the Light Lists for seasonal buoys, or seasonal changes in buoys, are only approximate and may vary slightly due to weather or other conditions.

Temporary or permanent changes in buoys may be made between editions of charts. A wise skipper keeps informed of existing conditions through reading Notices to Mariners or Local Notices to Mariners—see Chapter 17.

All buoys (especially those located in exposed positions) should, therefore, be regarded as warnings or guides, and not as infallible navigation marks. Whenever possible, a boat should be navigated by bearings or angles on fixed objects on shore (see Chapter 21), and by soundings, rather than by total reliance on buoys.

FIG. 1515 The simplest daybeacon is a single pile with one or two "daymarks" either square (green, black, or white) or triangular (red). Reflective borders of green or red, and reflective numbers of the same color, show up brilliantly in a searchlight. Other shapes are used for special purposes; see color pages I, J, and K.

Daybeacons

Daybeacons are unlighted structures established as an aid to navigation; they are "fixed" rather than "floating" aids. Daybeacons may be located either on shore or in waters up to perhaps 12 to 15 feet deep.

Daybeacons vary greatly in design and construction, depending upon their location and the distance at which they must be seen. A continuing effort is now being made by the Coast Guard to standardize daybeacon structures and markings for easier identification as aids to navigation.

FIG. 1516 Buoys must be periodically hauled out for servicing. A new buoy is placed on station, and the old one is taken in to a depot for scraping and repainting.

FIG. 1517 A minor light may consist of a single-pile structure with the light itself at the top and number identification on the daymark below. The light shown here is receiving periodic maintenance from a Coast Guard crew.

CHARACTERISTICS

The simplest daybeacon is a single pile with a number sign, called a "daymark," located at or near the top, fig. 1515. The pile may be wood, concrete, or metal.

A larger, more visible, and more sturdy daybeacon is the "three-pile dolphin" type. Here the single pile is replaced by three piles separated a few feet at their lower ends, but coming together at their tops where they are strongly held together with wire cables. Such structures are equipped with a daymark at the top, or more likely two daymarks facing in opposite directions. (Some dolphins may be made of five piles, four around one central pile.)

Daymarks and pointers

The daybeacon must be properly identified if it is to serve its purpose as an aid to navigation. Thus a daymark usually bears a number, occasionally a letter or letters.

Daymarks are normally either square or triangular in shape, corresponding to can and nun buoys; see page 304. Square daymarks will now be green with green reflective border (some older ones may be black or white). Triangular daymarks are red with red reflective border. The number or letters will be of the same color reflective material as the border. These reflective areas show up brilliantly at night in a boat's searchlight and aid in both the location and identification of the daybeacon. In some special applications, a daymark may be octagonal (eight-sided) or diamond-shaped carrying a brief warning or notice.

In some areas, pointers have been used in lieu of square or triangular daymarks. These are now being phased out, but some may remain for years to come.

THE USES OF DAYBEACONS

For obvious reasons, the use of daybeacons is restricted to relatively shallow waters. Within this limitation, however, a daybeacon is often more desirable than a buoy. From a navigator's point of view, it is a superior aid to navigation — firmly fixed in position, and more readily seen and identified. From the Coast Guard's viewpoint, a daybeacon is more desirable too—once established, it is in position and requires but little maintenance (buoys must be regularly hauled out for scraping and repainting, fig. 1516).

Daybeacons are used primarily for channel marking and serve in the same manner as buoys in the buoyage systems to be described later in this chapter.

Minor Lights

Just as daybeacons are sometimes substituted for unlighted buoys, so may lighted buoys be replaced with *minor lights*. These are fixed structures of the same overall physical features as daybeacons, but equipped with a light generally similar in characteristics to those found on buoys. Most minor lights are part of a series marking a channel, river or harbor; also included, however, are some isolated single lights if they are of the same general size and characteristics. The term "minor light" does not include the more important lights marking harbors, peninsulas, major shoals, etc.; these have lights of greater intensity and/or special characteristics — these are designated as "secondary" or "primary seacoast" lights and are discussed in detail in Chapter 16.

CHARACTERISTICS

Minor lights are placed on single piles, fig. 1517, on multiple-pile dolphins, fig. 1518, or on other structures in the water or on shore. Daymarks are placed on the structures for their identification, and reflective material is added for nighttime safety should the light be extin-

FIG. 1518 Structures for daybeacons or minor lights may also consist of three or more piles driven in a few feet apart and then bound together at their top. (Morris Rosenfeld photograph)

guished. In general, the description of daybeacons is applicable plus the addition of the light mechanism.

Light characteristics

A minor light will normally have the same color and flash with the same phase characteristics that a lighted buoy would have if the aid were of floating rather than fixed type. Intensity of the light will generally be of the same order as that of a lighted buoy, occasionally somewhat greater, but visibility may be increased by its greater height above water and its more stable platform.

Flashing characteristics of minor lights have been standardized with flashes at intervals of 2.5, 4 and 6 seconds. This is part of the same light modernization program as previously described for lighted buoys.

Sound signals

Minor lights may, in some locations, have an audible fog signal. These cannot, of course, be of a type operated by wave action, as in the case of bell and gong buoys. A bell, horn, or siren will be electrically operated on the structure, in some cases continuously for months during which fog may be expected.

Buoyage Systems

The primary function of buoys is to warn the mariner of some danger, obstruction, or change in the contours of the bottom, and to delineate channels leading to various points, so that he may avoid hazards and continue on his course safely. The greatest advantage is obtained from buoys used to mark specifically defined spots, for if a pilot knows his precise position at the moment and is properly equipped with charts, he can plot a safe course. Such features as shape, coloring, and signaling characteristics of buoys are but means to these ends of warning, guiding, and orienting the navigator.

Most maritime nations use either the *lateral system of buoyage* or the *cardinal system,* or both. In the lateral

system, the buoys indicate the direction to a danger relative to the course that should be followed. In the cardinal system, characteristics of buoys indicate location of the danger relative to the buoy itself. The term "cardinal" relates to cardinal points of the compass, see Chapter 13, page 270.

The Lateral System of Buoyage

In the United States, the lateral system of buoyage is uniformly used in all Federal-jurisdiction areas and on many other bodies of water where it can be applied. In this system, the shape, coloring, numbering, and light characteristics of buoys are determined by their position with respect to the navigable channel, natural or dredged, as such channels are entered and followed from seaward toward the head of navigation. The lateral system is described in detail in the subsequent sections covering each of the basic characteristics.

THE BASIC U. S. SYSTEM

The lateral system of buoyage employs a simple arrangement of shapes, colors, numbers, and light characteristics to indicate the side on which a buoy should be passed when proceeding in a given direction. The system is easily learned and should be known in detail by all boatmen.

As all channels do not lead from seaward, certain arbitrary assumptions must be made in order that the lateral system may be consistently applied. In coloring and numbering offshore buoys along the coasts, the following system has been adopted: proceeding in a southerly direction along the Atlantic Coast, in a northerly and westerly direction along the Gulf Coast, and in a northerly direction along the Pacific Coast will be considered the same as coming in from seaward. This can be remembered as proceeding around the coastline of the United States in a clockwise direction.

On the Great Lakes, offshore buoys are colored and

numbered as proceeding from the outlet end of each lake toward its upper end. This will be generally westerly and northward on the Lakes, except on Lake Michigan where it will be southward. Buoys marking channels into harbors are colored and numbered just as for channels leading into coastal ports from seaward.

On the Mississippi and Ohio Rivers and their tributaries, characteristics of aids to navigation are determined as proceeding from seaward toward the head of navigation, although local terminology describes "left bank" and "right bank" as proceeding with the flow of the river.

Coloring

All buoys are painted distinctive colors to indicate the side on which they should be passed, or their special purpose. In the lateral system, the significance of colors is as shown below.

TABLE 15-1	LATERAL SYSTEM IN U.S. AND CANADIAN WATERS					
Returning from sea*	Color	Number	Unlighted Buoy Shape	Lights or Lighted Buoys		Daymark Shape
				Light Color	Light Phase Characteristic	
Right side of channel	Red	Even	Nun	Red or White	Flashing or Quick Flashing	Triangular
Left side of channel	Black	Odd	Can	Green or White	Flashing or Quick Flashing	Square
Channel Junction or Obstruction	Red-and-black horizontally banded**	Not Numbered; May be Lettered	Nun or Can**	Red, Green or White**	Interrupted Quick Flashing	Triangular or Square**
Midchannel or Fairway	Black-and-white vertically striped	May be lettered	Nun or Can	White	Morse Code "A"	Octagonal

*or entering a harbor from a larger body of water, such as a lake.
**Preferred channel is indicated by color of uppermost band (shape of unlighted buoy), color of light, if any.

Black buoys mark the left (port) side of a channel when entering from seaward, or the location of a wreck or other obstruction that must be passed by keeping the buoy on the left hand.

Red buoys mark the right (starboard) side of a channel, or the location of a hazard to navigation that must be passed by keeping the buoy to starboard. It is from this color designation that the often-used phrase "Red — Right — Returning" is derived, meaning that *red* buoys should be kept on the *right* side of the boat when *returning* to harbor from the sea or other large body of water.

Red-and-black horizontally banded buoys mark junctions in a channel, or wrecks or obstructions that may be passed on *either* side. If the topmost band is black, the preferred channel will be followed by keeping the buoy on the left (port) hand. If the topmost band is red, the preferred channel is followed by keeping the buoy on the right (starboard) side of the vessel. (Note: When proceeding *toward* the sea, it may *not* be possible to pass such buoys safely on either side. This is particularly true in situations where you are following one channel downstream and another channel joins in from the side, see fig. 1519; always consult the chart for the area.)

Black-and-white vertically striped buoys mark the fairway or midchannel. They are also used to divide the "in" and "out" channels of a Traffic Separation Scheme.

It should be noted that when the areas of color run horizontally, they are "bands"; when they are arranged

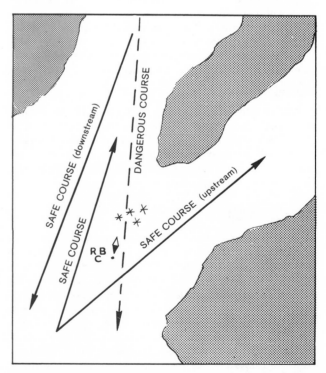

FIG. 1519 When proceeding upstream, a red-and-black horizontally-banded junction buoy may be safely passed on either side. This is not true, however, when going downstream, as examination of the above situation will quickly show.

vertically, they are "stripes." These terms are used in other color combinations in the case of special-purpose buoys.

Shapes of buoys

In the lateral system of buoyage, definite shape characteristics are given to the unlighted buoys to indicate which side of the channel they mark. The use of shapes is particularly valuable when a buoy is first sighted in line with the sun and only its silhouette rather than its color can be distinguished.

Can buoys, painted black, mark the left (port) side of the channel when returning from seaward, or the location of a wreck or shoal that must be passed by keeping the buoy on the left hand.

Nun buoys are used to mark the right (starboard) hand side of channels, or hazards that must be passed by keeping the buoy to starboard.

Channel junction and obstruction buoys may be of *either* can or nun shape. If the uppermost band is *black,* the buoy will be a *can;* if the uppermost band is *red,* it will be a *nun.*

Black-and-white vertically striped midchannel buoys may be either nuns or cans, and in this situation the shape has no significance.

No special significance is to be attached to the shape of spar buoys, bell buoys, gong buoys, whistle buoys, lighted buoys, or combination buoys. The purpose of these is indicated by their coloring, number or the characteristic of the light.

Numbering

Most buoys are given "numbers" that actually may be numbers, letters, or a combination of numbers and letters. These markings facilitate identification and location of buoys on charts.

In the lateral system, numbers serve as yet another indication of which side the buoy should be passed. The system is as follows:

Odd numbered buoys mark the left hand side of a channel leading in from seaward. In accordance with the rules stated above, these will be black buoys, cans if they are unlighted.

Even numbered buoys mark the right (starboard) side of a channel; these will be red (nun) buoys.

Numbers increase from seaward and are kept in approximate sequence on the two sides of a channel by omitting numbers as appropriate if buoys are not uniformly placed in pairs. Occasionally, several numbers will be omitted on longer stretches without buoys in order to allow for possible later additions.

Numbers followed by letters, such as 24A, 24B, 24C, etc., indicate buoys that have been added to a channel with the series not being immediately renumbered.

A buoy marking a wreck will often be designated with a number derived from the number of the buoy next downstream from it, preceded by the letters "WR". Thus, a buoy marking a wreck on the left-hand side of a channel between buoys 17 and 19 would be numbered "WR17A". A wreck buoy not related to a channel may be designated by one or two letters relating to the name of the wrecked vessel or a geographic location.

Letters, without numbers, are applied in some cases to black-and-white vertically striped buoys marking fairways, and to red-and-black horizontally banded buoys marking channel junctions or obstructions.

Numbers followed by letters may be used on some buoys marking offshore dangers. An example of this usage is the buoy marked "2TL" where the number has the usual sequential significance and the letters "TL" indicate the place as a shoal known as "Turner's Lump." This form of marking buoys is now more traditional than necessary.

Color of lights

For all buoys in the lateral system that have lights, the following system of colors is used.

Green lights on buoys are used only on those marking the left-hand side of a channel returning from seaward (black, odd-numbered buoys) or on red-and-black horizontally banded buoys that have the topmost band painted black.

Red lights on buoys are used only on those marking the right-hand side of a channel when entering from sea (red, even-numbered buoys) or on red-and-black horizontally banded buoys having a red topmost band.

White lights on buoys may be used on either side of channels in lieu of red or green. White lights are frequently employed where a greater visible range is desired, such as at a change in the direction of the channel. No special significance is derived from a white light, the purpose of the buoy being indicated by its color, number, or its light phase characteristic.

Light phase characteristics

Fixed lights (lights that do not flash) may be found on either red or black buoys, but are rare.

Flashing lights (flashing at a rate of not more than 30 flashes per minute) are placed only on black or red buoys, or on special purpose buoys.

Quick flashing lights (not less than 60 flashes each minute) are placed only on channel-edge-marking black and red buoys; these are used at points where it is desired to indicate that *special caution* in piloting is required, as at sharp turns or changes in the width of the waterway, or where used to mark wrecks or dangerous obstructions that must be passed only on one side.

Interrupted quick flashing lights are used only on buoys painted with red-and-black horizontal bands. These are the buoys at channel junctions and obstructions that can be passed on either side.

Morse code "A" flashing lights (short-long flashing) are placed only on black-and-white vertically striped buoys that mark a fairway or midchannel; these are passed close to, on either side. The lights are always white.

WRECK BUOYS

Buoys established by the Coast Guard to mark dangerous wrecks are generally placed on the seaward or channel side of the obstruction and as near to it as conditions permit. Wreck buoys are *not* placed directly over a wreck; they must be placed in position by a vessel and it is usually impossible for such vessel to maneuver directly over the hazard without incurring underwater damage to herself.

Caution must be exercised when navigating in the vicinity of buoys marking wrecks because, due to sea action, the wreck may shift in location between the time that the buoy is established and when it is later checked or serviced.

Buoyage Systems / CHAPTER 15

STATION BUOYS

Important buoys, usually large combination buoys, with both light and sound signals, are sometimes accompanied by *station buoys*. These are smaller, unlighted buoys, see fig. 1520, placed in the vicinity of the main buoy on the side away from marine traffic. They are colored and numbered the same as the main buoy. Station buoys are not charted; their existence is noted, however, in the Light Lists in the remarks column for the major aid to which they are related.

The purpose of the station buoy is to mark the location should the main buoy be sunk or carried away for any reason, such as being struck by a passing ship. The station buoy serves as a temporary substitute and aids in the replacement of the main buoy on the correct location.

DAYBEACONS AND MINOR LIGHTS

Although the lateral system of buoyage has been described in terms of unlighted and lighted buoys, the use of comparable daybeacons and minor lights is fully applicable.

Daybeacons with red triangular daymarks or red pointers may be substituted for nun buoys, and structures with black square daymarks or black pointers may replace can buoys where the water is shallow enough to make such installations practicable. Minor lights likewise may be used in place of lighted or combination buoys. It is not unusual to find a channel marked with a mixture of unlighted and lighted buoys, daybeacons, and minor lights.

Occasionally, daybeacons will be used to indicate a channel junction or obstruction. In such a case, the daymark will be red-and-black horizontally banded with the color of the uppermost band indicating the main or preferred channel. The shape of the daymark will be either square or triangular as determined by the color or the top band, similar to the use of a can or nun buoy for this purpose.

Daybeacons used to mark fairways or the middle of a channel will have an octagonal-shaped daymark, painted with the normal black-and-white vertical stripes.

A diamond-shaped daymark has *no* significance in the lateral system. A typical application might be to increase the daytime detectability of a minor light which is not a part of a channel or waterway series.

INTRACOASTAL WATERWAY AIDS

The Coast Guard maintains the system of aids to navigation along the Atlantic and Gulf Intracoastal Waterway (ICW). The coloring and numbering of buoys and daybeacons, and the color of lights on buoys and light structures, is in conformity with the lateral system of buoyage as described above. The system is applied by considering passage from north to south along the Atlantic coast, and from south to north and east to west along the Gulf coast, as corresponding to returning from sea in an entrance channel. Thus, red buoys and fixed aids are on the right side of the channel when proceeding from New Jersey toward Florida and then on to Texas; black aids are on the left hand side of the Waterway when proceeding in the same direction. This rule is applied in a uniform manner from one end of the Intracoastal Waterway to the other, regardless of widely varying compass headings on

FIG. 1520 Station buoys are occasionally used in conjunction with major combination buoys. These are placed near the main buoy on the side away from ship traffic. Such buoys are not separately charted, but they are mentioned in the Light Lists. The older tapered "wasp-waist" design of buoy superstructure is giving way to a newer straight-sided design.

many stretches, and the fact that rivers and other waterways marked by the seacoast system are occasionally followed.

The aids to navigation do differ in one respect, however, in that they carry on additional distinctive marking to identify the ICW route. This special marking is applied to the so-called "inside route" and to those portions of all connecting waterways that must be crossed or followed to make a continuous passage.

Distinctive ICW markings

All buoys, daybeacons, and light structures marking the Intracoastal Waterway have some portion of them painted *yellow*. This is the distinctive coloring adopted for the ICW. Buoys will be marked with a band of yellow at the top; daymarks and pointers have a band or border of yellow. For examples of these markings, see the color illustration on page J.

The numbering of Intracoastal Waterway aids follows the same basic rule as for entrance channels, with numbers increasing in the direction from New Jersey toward Florida and Texas. Aids are numbered in groups, usually not exceeding 99, beginning again with "1" or "2" at specified natural dividing points.

Lights on buoys follow the standard system of red or white lights on red buoys, and green or white lights on black buoys. The color of lights on fixed structures follows the same general system. Range lights, not being a part of the lateral system, may be any of the three standard colors.

Dual marking

In order that vessels may readily follow the Intracoastal Waterway where it coincides with another route such as an important river marked on the seacoast system, special *dual markings* are employed. These are applied to the buoys or other aids that mark the river channel for other traffic. Special marks consist of a yellow square or a yellow triangle painted on a conspicuous part of the dual-purpose aid. The yellow square, in outline similar to a can buoy, indicates that the aid on which it is placed should be kept on the left-hand side when following the ICW in the direction from New Jersey to Texas. The yellow triangle, in outline similar to a nun buoy, indicates that the aid should be kept on the right hand side when traveling in the same direction.

The yellow squares may appear on *either* a black can or a red nun of the river channel marks (or comparable daybeacons and light structures). Similarly, the yellow triangle dual markings may appear on any type of lateral aid. These similarly contradictory markings result from the fact that in some situations a southbound ICW route (red nuns on the right side) will be *up* a river channel from seaward (red nuns on the right side); and in other situations, the same ICW route will be down a river toward the sea where black cans will be on the skipper's right side. In both of these situations, however, the yellow triangle will be kept to the right. See page J.

Where the yellow squares and triangles are added to regular river or harbor aids to navigation, the ICW yellow band or border is omitted.

Where dual marking is employed, the boatman following the ICW disregards the shape and coloring of the aid on which the yellow square or triangle is placed and pilots his craft solely by the shape of the yellow markings. The numbers on the aids will be those of the river's lateral system, and in some instances where the southward ICW proceeds down a river, the numbers will be temporarily decreasing rather than increasing. See page J.

By this system of dual marking, the mariner approaching a body of water such as the Cape Fear River, and realizing that he must follow it for some distance before again entering a dredged land cut of the Intracoastal Waterway, knows that his course lies along such buoys or other aids as are specially marked in yellow. He determines the side of his craft on which these aids should be passed by the shape of the yellow marks, keeping always in mind the basic direction of his ICW travel.

Special Purpose Buoys

In addition to the lateral system of buoyage maintained by the Coast Guard in Federal-jurisdiction waters, several special-purpose buoy characteristics, having no lateral significance, are used to mark dredging areas, anchorages, quarantine areas, fish net areas, race courses, experiments or tests, etc.

The meaning of special-purpose buoys is indicated by their colors as follows:

White buoys mark *anchorage* areas.

Yellow buoys mark *quarantine anchorage* areas.

Note carefully the difference between an *anchorage* buoy and a *mooring* buoy — an anchorage buoy is an aid to navigation marking the boundary of an area in which vessels may be anchored in accordance with prescribed regulations; a mooring buoy is a strong, heavily anchored buoy to which vessels can be made fast in lieu of anchoring.

White buoys with green tops are used in connection with *dredging* and *survey* operations.

White-and-black horizontally banded buoys mark fish net areas. Particularly, but not exclusively, in the Chesapeake Bay area, such buoys are used to mark the boundaries of areas in which fish nets and traps may be placed; such areas and buoys are indicated on charts. (See fig. 1521.) These buoys may be cans or nuns, the shape has no significance; they carry identification numbers and letters.

White-and-international-orange buoys, with either horizontal bands or vertical stripes, are used for special purposes to which neither the lateral-system colors nor the other special-purpose colors are applicable. (See fig. 1522.)

Special-purpose buoys are illustrated in color at the bottom of page L

Yellow-and-black vertically striped buoys mark seaplane operating areas and have no marine significance other than to indicate the need for caution and a sharp lookout for aircraft.

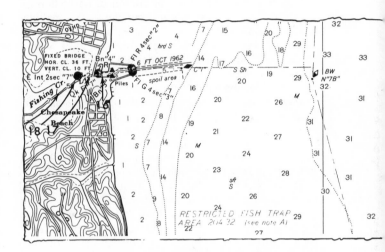

FIG. 1521 A black-and-white horizontally banded buoy is charted here at the intersection of lines (long and short dash) indicating outer limits of a fish trap area.

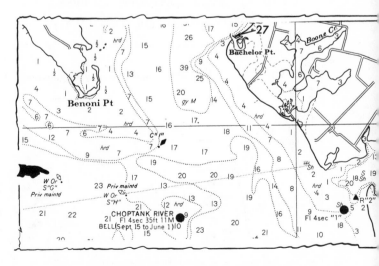

FIG. 1522 Positions of white-and-orange horizontally banded special purpose buoys near Choptank River Light are indicated on this chart. These are lettered for identification and it is indicated that they are privately maintained.

Special-purpose buoys may be lighted or unlighted, and some may have a fog signal. These buoys may be of any shape if unlighted—can, nun, or spherical.

SPECIAL—TYPE BUOYS

Special-type buoys may be encountered in all waters. Typical of these in inland waters are the buoys used in current surveys. The shape, size, color, lights (if any), markings, etc., vary too widely to be described here, but will be completely listed in the public notices that are always published before such buoys are placed in navigable waters.

Offshore boatmen may occasionally encounter large sea buoys used for gathering meteorological or oceanographic data, or those employed in naval defense operations.

Uniform State Buoyage System

Each state has authority over control of navigation on waters that lie wholly within its boundaries. This includes the responsibility for the establishment and maintenance of aids to navigation. Each state is free to mark its waters according to any system that it desires. Initially, the result of this freedom was a considerable variance in the ways that inland waters not subject to Federal jurisdiction were marked. More recently, however, although the states still retain their authority, they have agreed to adopt a single consistent system of markers. With trailer-borne craft traveling freely over the highways from state to state, the gain for boatmen from the uniform system is too obvious to discuss in detail. The rambling skipper no longer has to try to decipher the significance of what had been intended to serve him as an "aid to navigation."

By Act of Congress, the Uniform State Waterway Marking System (USWMS) may be extended to cover waters subject to Federal jurisdiction, but which have not been marked with aids by the Coast Guard. Agreements may be entered into between a Coast Guard District Commander and state officials for the designation of "state waters for private aids to navigation." In such waters, state or local governments may establish and maintain aids to navigation which comply with the standards of the USWMS.

MAJOR FEATURES OF THE USWMS

The Uniform State Waterway Marking System has been developed to provide a means to convey to the small craft operator, in particular, adequate guidance to indicate safe boating channels by indicating the presence of either natural or artificial obstructions or hazards. The USWMS also provides means for marking restricted or controlled areas and for providing directions. The system is suited for use in all water areas and designed to satisfy the needs of all types of small vessels. It supplements and is generally compatible with the lateral system of aids to navigation maintained by the Coast Guard.

The USWMS consists of two categories of aids to navigation:

(1) A system of regulatory markers to indicate to the pilot the existence of dangerous areas as well as those which are restricted or controlled, such as speed zones and areas set aside for a particular use, or to provide general information and directions.

(2) A system of aids to navigation to supplement the Federal lateral system of buoyage.

Regulatory markers

On Federal waters, the boatman can turn to his charts, Light Lists, Coast Pilots, and other publications for information on natural hazards, zoned areas, directions, distances, etc., to supplement the knowledge that he gets from buoys, daybeacons, and other aids. On state waters, he now has a uniform system of water signs or markers that, in themselves, convey their message without reference to any publication — an obvious advantage, especially for inexperienced boatmen.

Just as Intracoastal Waterway markers are distinguished by their special yellow borders or other yellow marks, state regulatory markers are identified by international-orange-and-white colors. On buoys, an orange band will be seen near the top and bottom; on the white area between these bands, a geometric shape, also in orange, will be noted. An open diamond shape indicates danger. A diamond with a cross inside indicates a prohibited area; vessels are excluded from the area marked by such buoys. A circle signifies zoning or control; vessels operating in such areas are subject to certain operating restrictions. A square or rectangular shape signals the conveying of information, the details of which are spelled out within the shape. (See fig. 1523 and color page L.)

Where the regulatory marker consists of a square or

FIG. 1523 Uniform state regulatory markers convey their meaning to the boatman without need for reference to charts or other publications.

DANGER! Warns of rocks, reefs, dams, snags, or other hazards.

BOATS KEEP OUT! Marks waterfalls, swim areas, rapids, and other restricted areas.

CAUTION! Type of control is indicated within the circle such as No ski, speed zone, No anchoring.

INFORMATION! Tells distances, locations, other official information.

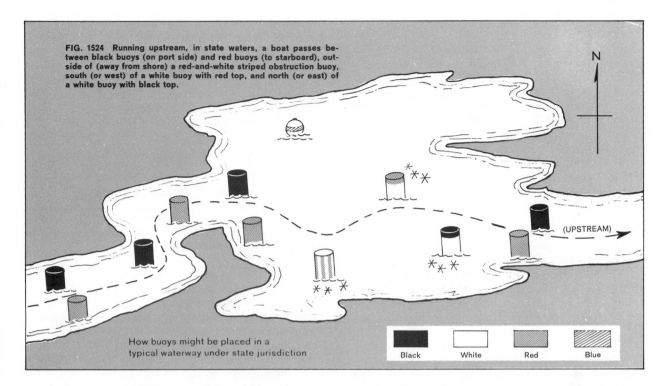

FIG. 1524 Running upstream, in state waters, a boat passes between black buoys (on port side) and red buoys (to starboard), outside of (away from shore) a red-and-white striped obstruction buoy, south (or west) of a white buoy with red top, and north (or east) of a white buoy with black top.

N

(UPSTREAM)

How buoys might be placed in a
typical waterway under state jurisdiction

| Black | White | Red | Blue |

rectangular shaped sign displayed from a structure, the sign is white with an international orange border. If a diamond or circular shape is associated with the meaning of the marker, it will be centered on the signboard.

The geometric shape displayed on a regulatory marker is intended to convey the basic idea of danger, or control, etc., so that the boatman can tell at a distance whether he should stay away or may safely approach for more information. To convey a specific meaning, spelled-out words or recognized abbreviations appear within the shape. The sole exception to this is the cross within the diamond shape that is used to absolutely prohibit boats from entering an area, because of danger to the boat, swimmers in a protected area, or for any other reason sufficient to warrant exclusion by law.

To minimize the risk of misinterpretation, initials, symbols, and silhouettes have not been used. In some cases, words may be needed outside the geometric shape to give the reason, authority, or some clarification of the specific meaning.

Aids to navigation

The second category of marker in the USWMS is the aid to navigation having lateral or cardinal meaning. In selecting types of buoys for use on waters not marked by the Coast Guard, the principal objective was to make the state system compatible with the Federal.

On a well-defined channel, including a river or other relatively narrow natural or improved waterway, an aid to navigation of the USWMS is normally a solid-colored buoy. A buoy that marks the left side of a channel viewed *looking upstream* or toward the head of navigation is colored *solid black*. A buoy that marks the *right* side, looking in the same direction, is colored *solid red*. (This, it will be noted, is the same as the Coast Guard lateral system.) On a well-defined channel, solid-colored buoys will be found

in pairs, one for each side of the channel that they mark, and opposite each other, leaving no doubt that the channel lies between the red and the black buoys, and that the skipper should pilot his boat between them.

On irregularly defined channels, solid-colored buoys may be used singly in staggered fashion on alternate sides provided that they are spaced at sufficiently close intervals to clearly inform the skipper that the channel lies between the buoys and that he should pass between them.

Where there is no well-defined channel, or when a body of water is obstructed by objects whose nature or location is such that the hazard might be approached from more than one direction, a *cardinal* system is used. The use of cardinal system aids to navigation is strictly limited to waters wholly subject to state jurisdiction or waters covered by a Coast Guard-state agreement. This restriction is necessary as the Coast Guard's lateral system makes no provision for markers of the cardinal system.

A white buoy with red top indicates that a boat must pass to the *south or west* of the buoy.

A white buoy with black top indicates that the safe water is to the *north or east* of the buoy.

A buoy with alternate red and white vertical stripes indicates that an obstruction extends from the nearest shore to the buoy, and that the boat must not pass between the buoy and that shore. The number of red and white stripes may vary, but the width of the white stripes will always be twice that of the red ones. See fig. 1524.

Characteristics of markers and aids

The size, shape, material, and construction of all markers, fixed or floating, is discretionary with the state authorities. They must, however, be such as to be observable under normal conditions of visibility at a distance such that the significance of the marker or aid will be recognizable before a craft stands into danger.

315

Numbers

State aids to navigation and regulatory markers may carry numbers, letters, or words. These must be placed in a manner so as to be clearly visible to approaching and passing boats, with characters in block style, well proportioned and as large as the available space permits. Numbers and letters on red or black backgrounds will be in white; on white backgrounds, they will be black. The use of numbers on buoys is optional, but if used will conform to the following system:

Odd numbers will be used on *solid black* buoys and on *black-topped* buoys.

Even numbers will be used on *solid red* buoys and on *red-topped* buoys.

All numbers will *increase* in an *upstream* direction or toward the head of navigation.

Letters only may be used to identify regulatory markers and red-and-white vertically striped obstruction buoys. If used, letters will follow an alphabetical sequence in the upstream direction; the letters "I" and "O" will not be used to prevent possible confusion with numbers.

Reflectors

The use of reflectors or reflective tape is discretionary with the local authorities maintaining the markers and aids. If used, red reflectors or reflective material will be used on solid red buoys, and green on solid black buoys.

All other buoys will have white reflectors or reflective material, as will regulatory markers, except that orange reflectors may be placed on the orange portions of such markers.

Lights

Lights may be used on USWMS regulatory markers and aids to navigation if desired by the state authorities. When used, lights on solid colored buoys will be regularly flashing, regularly occulting, or equal interval. (An "occulting" light is one that is on more than it is off.) For ordinary purposes, the rate of flashing will not be more than 30 times per minute.

When lights have a distinct cautionary significance, such as at sharp bends in a channel, the light may be quick flashing, not less than 60 flashes each minute.

When a light is placed on a cardinal system buoy or a red-and-white vertically striped buoy, it will always be quick flashing.

Red lights are used only on solid red buoys, green lights only on solid black buoys. White lights will be used on all other buoys and on regulatory markers.

Ownership markings

The use and placement of ownership identification is discretionary. If used, such markings must be worded and placed in such a manner that they will not detract from the meaning being conveyed as a regulatory marker or aid to navigation.

Mooring buoys

Mooring buoys in waters covered by the Uniform State Waterway Marking System will be white with a horizontal blue band around them midway between the waterline and the top of the buoy.

A lighted mooring buoy will normally show a slow flashing white light. If, however, its location is such that it is an obstruction to craft operating during hours of darkness, the light will be quick flashing white.

A mooring buoy may carry ownership identification provided that such markings do not detract from the meaning intended to be conveyed by the color scheme and identification letter, if assigned.

Illustration of the USWMS
The Uniform State Waterway Marking System is illustrated in color on page L.

Other Buoyage Systems

Buoyage on the "Western Rivers of the United States" (the Mississippi and its tributaries, and certain other designated rivers) conforms to the lateral system, but includes some additional shapes and daymarks not found in other areas. See the color illustration on page K.

On these rivers, unlighted buoys are not numbered, while the numbers on lighted buoys have no lateral significance, rather indicating the number of miles upstream from a designated reference point.

Additional details on the buoyage of the Western Rivers will be found in Chapter 28.

Foreign waters

Boatmen who carry their cruising into foreign waters should, prior to departure, fully acquaint themselves with the buoyage systems to be encountered. Significant differences from the U. S. lateral system may be found, and there will be variations between the systems used in different countries.

In Canadian waters, the lateral system of buoyage is essentially the same as in the United States. Minor differences in the physical appearance of buoys may be noted, but these should not be great enough to result in any confusion. Chart symbols, likewise, may be slightly different from those standardized for use on U. S. charts.

In British waters, however, quite a different situation exists. A lateral system of buoyage is employed, but the coloring, light characteristics, etc. are entirely at variance with the U. S. system. The "red-right-returning" rule becomes "black-right-returning." Buoys on the right side of entering channels are conical (nun), but they are painted black or black-and-white checkered; lights will flash in sequences of 1, 3, or 5. On the left side of such a channel, there are can buoys, as an American boatman might expect, but they are painted red or red-and-white checkered; lights will flash in sequences of 2, 4, or 6.

Junction (obstruction) buoys in British waters are spherical in shape and are horizontally banded, red-and-white or black-and-white, according to the general system for indication of the main or preferred channel as used in the United States. Midchannel buoys are of a distinctive shape — a shape other than can, nun, or spherical — and vertically striped in either black-and-white or red-and-white colors.

CHAPTER 16

AIDS TO NAVIGATION —
Lighthouses and Other Aids

The preceding chapter covered the many thousands of aids to navigation that mark rivers and channels for watercraft of all sizes. These constitute the majority in the system of aids in U.S. waters, but there are other, major aids to serve the mariner. These other aids and systems provide guidance to the navigator making a landfall after a sea voyage or piloting his vessel along a coast. Electronic systems serve to help the navigator fix his position when he is out of sight of land because of darkness, fog, or distance. Primary and secondary lights, lightships and offshore tower light stations, fog signals, and ranges and directional lights will be considered in this chapter to complete the topic of aids to navigation. Electronic navigation systems are covered in Chapter 25.

Primary Seacoast and Secondary Lights

Primary seacoast and *secondary lights* are so designated because of their greater importance as aids to navigation. In general, they differ from the minor lights considered in Chapter 15 by their physical size, intensity of light, and complexity of light characteristics. These lights are more individual in nature than minor lights and buoys; only broad, general statements can be made about them as a group.

Primary seacoast lights are maintained to warn the high-seas navigator of the proximity of land. They are the first aids to navigation to be seen when making a landfall (except where there may be an offshore lightship). A coast-wise pilot can use these lights to keep farther offshore at night than if he were using other visual aids. These are the most powerful and distinctive lights in the U.S. system of aids to navigation.

Primary seacoast lights may be located on the mainland or offshore on islands and shoals. When located offshore, they may mark a specific hazard or they may serve merely as a marker for ships approaching a major harbor.

Many primary seacoast lights are so classified from the importance of their location, the intensity of the light, and the prominence of the structure. Other aids will be classed as *secondary lights* because of their lesser qualities in one or more of these characteristics. The dividing line, however, is not clear cut, and lights that may seem to be more properly in one category may be classified in the other group in the Light Lists (see page 331). The difference in classification is of no real significance to boatmen and it can be ignored in practical piloting situations.

STRUCTURES

The physical structure of a primary seacoast light and many secondary lights is generally termed a *lighthouse,* although this is not an official designation used in the Light Lists. The principal purpose is to support a light source and

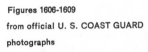

Figures 1606-1609
from official U. S. COAST GUARD
photographs

lens at a considerable height above water. The same structure may also house a fog signal, radiobeacon, equipment, and quarters for the operating personnel. In many instances, however, the auxiliary equipment and personnel are housed in separate buildings nearby; such a group of buildings is called a *light station.*

Lighthouses vary greatly in their outward appearance, determined in part by their location, whether in the water or on shore, the importance of the light, the kind of soil on which it is constructed, and the prevalence of violent storms; see fig. 1601.

Lighthouses also vary in appearance with the distance at which their lights must be seen. Where the need is for a relatively great range, a tall tower with a light of high candlepower is erected. Conversely, at points intermediate to the principal lights, where ship traffic is light, and where long range is not so necessary, a less expensive structure of more modest dimensions is constructed.

The terms, "secondary light" and "minor light," indicate in a general way a wide variety of lights, one class shading imperceptibly into the other. These lights may be displayed from towers resembling the most important seacoast lights, or from a relatively inexpensive structure. The essential features of a light structure where operating personnel are not in residence are: best possible location as determined by the physical characteristics of the site, sufficient height for the requirements of the light, a rugged support for the light itself, and proper shelter for the power source. Many

(Text continued on page 320)

MILE ROCKS LIGHT, at the entrance to San Francisco harbor, was built in 1906. In 1966, its tower superstructure was cut off to provide a landing platform for helicopters. No longer manned, operation is automatic. A horn fog signal is remotely controlled from Pt. Bonita Light.

During periods of low visibility, **CHARLESTON LIGHT** on south side of Sullivans Island (S.C.) shows a 28,000,000 candlepower flash visible 26 miles seaward. Built in 1962, this modern 140-foot elevator-equipped structure is one of the world's tallest lights. ▲

New and old lights at **CAPE HENRY,** Va., at the entrance to Chesapeake Bay. The old tower, no longer lighted, was the first built by the Federal Government.

On the lower coast of Maine, **CAPE NEDDICK LIGHT** is situated on a small rock islet called The Nubble, separated by a narrow channel from Cape Neddick, a headland which juts out a mile into the Atlantic.

AMERICAN LIGHTS –

▲ **PEMAQUID POINT LIGHT** (Maine) is a secondary light of 10,000 candlepower, visible 14 miles from a white pyramidal tower, 79 feet above water. Originally established in 1827, the rebuilt structure dates to 1857.

◄ **SPLIT ROCK LIGHT,** on a rocky cliff in Minnesota on Lake Superior, is one most frequently visited. Standing 178 feet above water, its 1,000,000 candlepower beam is visible 23 miles.

▲ **EASTERN POINT LIGHT** (Mass.) has guided Gloucestermen for more than a century. Its white brick tower, built in 1890, replaces one built in 1832.

▲ **PORTLAND HEAD LIGHT,** at Cape Elizabeth, Me., guards the entrance to Portland harbor with a 200,000 candlepower beam. The original station dates back to 1791.

◄ Isolated **CAPE SPENCER LIGHT,** 150 miles from a town, marks the northern entrance from the Pacific into the Inside Passage of southeastern Alaska. It is a primary light, fog signal and radiobeacon station.

► **FOWEY ROCKS LIGHT,** a skeleton iron structure, is typical of those used on the Florida Reefs at Carysfort Reef, Alligator Reef, Sombrero Key, American Shoal and Sand Key.

— Safeguards of Coastal Navigation

PHOTO CREDITS—Cape Henry, Sullivan's Island, Fowey Rocks, Dry Tortugas, Galveston, and Mile Rocks Official U.S. Coast Guard photos. Portland Head, Cape Neddick and Pemaquid from Kodachromes by Wm. H. Koelbel.

GALVESTON (Texas) **JETTY LIGHT** flashes white and red alternately from a height of 91 feet. Resident personnel attend it. Fog signal is a diaphone. There is a radiobeacon, with special RDF calibration service. ▼

◄ **DRY TORTUGAS LIGHT** on Loggerhead Key in the Gulf of Mexico was established in 1826, rebuilt in 1858. The conical black and white tower is 157 feet high, the light visible 19 miles.

forms of structures meet these requirements—small houses topped with a short skeleton tower, a cluster of piles supporting a battery box and light, and countless others.

Many lights originally tended by resident keepers are now operated automatically because of the availability of commercial electric power and reliable equipment. There are also a great many automatic lights on inexpensive structures, cared for by periodic visits of Coast Guard cutters or by attendants who are in charge of a group of such aids.

The recent introduction of much new automatic equipment means that the relative importance of lights can no longer be judged on the basis of whether or not they have resident personnel; a number of powerful lights in towers of great height are now operated without continuous attention.

Coloring of structures

Lighthouses and other light structures are marked with various colors for the purpose of making them readily distinguishable from the backgrounds against which they are seen, and to make possible the identification of individual lights among others that are in the same general area. Solid colors, bands of color, stripes, and various other patterns are used, fig. 1602.

LIGHT CHARACTERISTICS

Primary seacoast and secondary lights are assigned distinctive light characteristics so that one may be distinguished from another. These characteristics are achieved by using lights of different colors, and by having some that show continuously while others go on and off in regular patterns of great variety. Actually, in these days of modern electronic navigation there is much less need for special distinctive characteristics of major lights—those were necessary when a navigator making a landfall might have been in doubt as to whether he was approaching the coast of Maryland or Virginia, or even farther to the north or south.

The three standard colors used for the lights of major aids to navigation are white, red, and green.

Light phase characteristics

By varying the length of the intervals of light and darkness, a considerable number of individual *light phase characteristics* may be obtained.

The term "flashing" has already been defined in Chapter 15 as a light that is on less than it is off in a regular sequence of single flashes occurring less than 30 times each minute. Some primary seacoast and secondary lights will "flash" in accordance with such a definition although their characteristics will have no relation to the flashes of buoys and minor lights. In general, a flashing major light will have a longer period (time of one complete cycle of the characteristic) and may have a longer flash; for example, Cape Hatteras Light flashes once every 15 seconds with a 3-second flash. On the other hand, some of the newer aids are equipped with xenon-discharge-tube lights that give a very brilliant, but very brief, flash. The intensity of these lights can be varied for periods of good or bad visibility. A few major lights may be "fixed"—a continuous light without change of intensity or color.

Typically, however, the light phase characteristic of a primary seacoast or secondary light will be more complex. These are described below and are illustrated in fig. 1603.

MASONRY STRUCTURE   CYLINDRICAL TOWER SQUARE HOUSE ON CYLINDRICAL BASE   SKELET... IRON STRUCT...

TYPICAL LIGHT STRUCTURES

FIG. 1601. Primary seacoast and secondary lights are mounted on a wide variety of structures. The location of the light, whether on shore or rising from the water; the degree of exposure to violent storms; the need for great height; and many other factors determine the type of structure. Physical characteristics of the structures are described in the Light Lists.

Group flashing (Gp. Fl.)—the cycle of the light characteristic consists of two or more flashes separated by brief intervals and followed by a longer interval of darkness.

Alternating flashing (Alt. Fl.)—flashes of alternating color, usually white and red, or white and green.

Occulting (Occ.)—the light is on more than it is off. The interval of time that the light is *lighted* is greater than the time that it is *eclipsed*.

Equal interval (E. Int.)—the periods of light and darkness are equal; the light will be described in the Light List or on charts in terms of the period, the lighted and eclipsed portions each being just half of that time interval.

Group Occulting (Gp. Occ.)—intervals of light regularly broken by a series of two or more eclipses. This characteristic may have all eclipses of equal length or one may be greater than the others.

Fixed and Flashing (F. and Fl.)—a fixed light varied at regular intervals by a flash of greater intensity. The flash may be of the same color as the fixed light (usually white) or of another color. This characteristic may also appear as *fixed and group flashing (F. and Gp. Fl.)*.

Complex characteristics

The above light phase characteristics may be combined. Examples might include "Group flashing white, alternating flashing red" (Gp. Fl. W. Alt. Fl. R.)—Gay Head Light—with three white and one red flash in each 40-second period; or "Gp. Fl. W., (1 4 3)"—Minots Ledge Light where 1½-second flashes occur at 1½-second intervals in groups of one, four, and three separated by 5-second intervals and followed by a 15½-second longer interval to indicate the proper starting point of the 45-second period; or others of a generally similar nature.

Perhaps one of the most complex characteristics is that of Halfway Rock Light off the Maine Coast where the description is "Alternating fixed white, red, and flashing red" (Alt. F. W., R., and Fl. R.)—in a 90-second period, the light shows fixed white for 59 seconds, fixed red for 14 seconds, a high-intensity red flash for 3 seconds, and fixed red again for the final 14 seconds—this is certainly a distinctive enough characteristic to avoid any confusion.

BOSTON, MASS.

ST. AUGUSTINE, FLA.

CAPE HENRY, VA.

TYBEE, GA.

FIG. 1602. The physical structure supporting a primary seacoast light, usually referred to as a lighthouse, may be painted in a number of different patterns for better daytime identification. The colors are usually black and white. Details are given in the Light Lists.

COLORING OF TYPICAL LIGHTHOUSES

Sectors

Many lights will have *sectors,* portions of their all-around arc of visibility in which the normally white light is seen as red. These mark shoals or other hazards, or warn mariners of nearby land.

Lights so equipped show one color from most directions, but a different color or colors over definite arcs of the horizon as indicated on charts and in the Light Lists. A sector changes the color of a light when viewed from certain directions, but *not* the flashing or occulting characteristic. For example, a flashing white light having a red sector, when viewed from within the sector, will appear as flashing red, fig. 1604.

Sectors may be a few degrees in width, as when marking a shoal or rock, or of such width as to extend from the di-

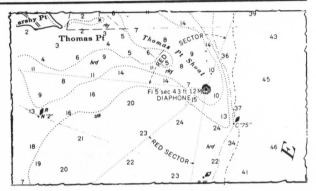

FIG. 1604. Many lights that are basically white in color have one or more **red sectors** to mark areas of shoal water or other hazards. The light will have the same phase characteristics in both the white and red sectors. Red sectors will be indicated on charts and described in the Light Lists.

rection of deep water to the shore. Bearings referring to sectors are expressed in degrees *as observed from a vessel toward the light.*

In the vast majority of situations, water areas covered by red sectors should be avoided, but in all cases the extent of the hazard should be determined from an examination of the chart for the vicinity. A few lights are basically red (for danger) with one or more white sectors marking the direction of safe passage through the hazards. A narrow white sector may also be used to mark a turning point in a channel.

Lights may also have sectors in which the light is *obscured* and cannot be seen. These will be shown graphically on charts and described in words and figures in the Light Lists, fig. 1605.

THE VISIBILITY OF LIGHTS

The theoretical visibility of a light in clear weather depends upon two factors, its intensity and its height above water. The intensity of the light fixes its *nominal range* which is defined in Coast Guard Light Lists as "the maximum distance at which the light may be seen in clear weather (meteor-

Illustration	Symbols and meaning		Phase description
	Lights which do not change color	**Lights which show color variations**	
	F. = Fixed . . .	Alt. = Alternating.	A continuous steady light.
	F. Fl. = Fixed and flashing	Alt. F. Fl. = Alternating fixed and flashing.	A fixed light varied at regular intervals by a flash of greater brilliance.
	F. Gp. Fl. Fixed and group flashing.	Alt. F. Gp. Fl. Alternating fixed and group flashing.	A fixed light varied at regular intervals by groups of 2 or more flashes of greater brilliance.
	Fl. = Flashing	Alt. Fl. = Alternating flashing.	Showing a single flash at regular intervals, the duration of light always being less than the duration of darkness.
	Gp. Fl. Group flashing.	Alt. Gp. Fl. Alternating group flashing.	Showing at regular intervals groups of 2 or more flashes.
	Gp. Fl. (1+2) = Composite group flashing.		Light flashes are combined in alternate groups of different numbers.
	E. Int. = Equal interval.		Light with all durations of light and darkness equal.
	Occ. = Occulting.	Alt. Occ. = Alternating occulting.	A light totally eclipsed at regular intervals, the duration of light always greater than the duration of darkness.
	Gp. Occ. Group Occulting.		A light with a group of 2 or more eclipses at regular intervals.
	Gp. Occ. (2+3) = Composite group occulting.		A light in which the occultations are combined in alternate groups of different numbers.

FIG. 1603. Primary seacoast and secondary lights flash with specific **light phase characteristics.** These permit rapid and positive identification at night. The time for a light to go through one full cycle of changes is called its **period.**

ological visibility of 10 nautical miles)." Height is, of course, important because of the curvature of the earth. It determines what is known as the *geographic range* which is not affected by the intensity (provided that the light is bright enough to be seen out to the full distance of the geographic range).

As a rule, the nominal range of major lights is greater than the geographic, and the distance from which such aids can be seen is limited only by the earth's curvature. Such lights are often termed "strong"; conversely, a light limited by its luminous range can be called a "weak light."

Often, the glare, or *loom,* of strong lights may be seen far beyond the stated geographic range. Occasionally, under rare atmospheric conditions, the light itself may be visible at unusual distances. On the other hand, and unfortunately more frequently, the range of visibility may be lessened by rain, fog, snow, haze, or smoke.

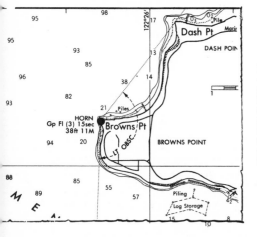

FIG. 1605. Some lights — particularly those on shore—will have sectors in which they cannot be seen at all. The light is said to be "obscured" in these sectors which are indicated on the chart and described in the Light Lists.

The Light Lists show the nominal range when such is 5 miles or more. Instructions are given for conversion of nominal range to *luminous* range, the maximum distance at which a light may be seen in *existing* visibility. Both nominal and luminous ranges take no account of elevation, observer's height of eye, or the curvature of the earth. For lights of complex characteristics, nominal ranges are given for each color and/or intensity.

The geographic range of lights is no longer given in the Light Lists, but may be calculated from information in the front pages of each Light List volume or from Table II, page 603. Boatmen should know their height of eye when at the controls of their craft and be aware of the greater range obtainable from a greater height above water.

Lights on inland waters, where their radius of usefulness is not great, are frequently "weak" lights of insufficient intensity to reach the full limit of their geographic range.

IDENTIFICATION OF LIGHTS

Charts can only briefly describe the characteristics of a primary seacoast or secondary light by means of abbreviations and a notation of the total period of the light cycle. It will often be necessary to consult the Light List for the details of the characteristic that may be needed for positive identification.

When a light is first observed, its color should be noted, and, by means of a watch or clock with a second hand, a check made of the time required for the light to go through its full cycle of changes. If color, period, and number of flashes per cycle agree with the information in the Light

List, correct identification has been accomplished. As a further check, however, the charts and Light List should be examined to see if any other light in the vicinity might have such similar characteristics that there could be a case of mistaken identity. If there is any doubt, a careful timing of the length of all flashes and dark intervals should be made and compared with the Light List entries; this will normally be conclusive.

CAUTIONS IN USING LIGHTS

Complex lights with several luminous ranges may appear differently at extreme distances where, for example, a white fixed (or flashing) light could be seen but a red flash of the same light was not yet within luminous range. Examination of a Light List will show that ordinarily the candlepower of a red or green light is only 1/4 or 1/5 that of a white light from the same aid. Caution must be exercised in light identification under such circumstances.

The effect of fog, rain, snow, haze, etc., on the visibility of lights is obvious. Colored lights are more quickly lost to sight than are white lights under weather conditions that tend to reduce visibility. On the other hand, refraction may cause a light to be seen at a greater distance than would normally be expected.

Caution must also be applied when using light sectors. The actual boundaries between the colors are not so sharp and distinct as indicated on the chart; the lights shade gradually from one color into the other. Allow an adequate margin for safety when piloting by colored light sectors.

The increasing use of brilliant shore lights for advertising, illuminating bridges, and other purposes may cause marine navigational lights, particularly those in densely populated areas, to be outshone and difficult to distinguish from the background lighting.

There is always the possibility of a light's being extinguished. In the case of unattended lights, this condition may not be immediately detected and corrected. If lights are not sighted within a reasonable time after prediction from the course and speed of the boat, a dangerous situation may exist requiring prompt action to ensure the safety of the craft and its crew.

Do not rely on any *one* light, except perhaps for making a landfall. Use several lights *together* as a system, checking each against the others.

At many lights, rip-rap mounds are maintained to protect the structures against ice damage and scouring action, fig. 1606. Skippers should not attempt to pass close to light structures rising out of the water in order to be sure of avoiding collision with uncharted, submerged portions of such rip-rap or with the structure itself.

Standby lights

Standby lights of reduced candlepower are displayed from many light stations when the main light is inoperative. These standby lights may or may not have the same characteristics as the main light. The existence of the standby light (if any) and its characteristics (if different) may be noted in the Light List.

Fog Signals

Any sound-producing instrument operated in time of fog from a definite point shown on a chart serves as a useful fog signal. To be effective as an aid to navigation, a pilot must be able to identify it and know from what location it is sounded.

The simpler fog signals used on buoys and at minor lights have been covered in Chapter 15. There it was noted that such signals operated by the action of the sea cannot be entirely depended upon and identification might be difficult. At all lighthouses and lightships equipped with fog signals, these devices are operated by mechanical or electrical means and are sounded on definite time schedules during periods of low visibility to provide the desirable feature of positive identification.

SIGNAL CHARACTERISTICS

Fog signal characteristics are described in terms of the length of a total cycle consisting of one or more *blasts* of specific length and one or more *silent intervals,* also of definite lengths. These times are shown in the Light Lists to aid in identification. (Normally, only type of fog signal, without further details, is indicated on charts.) Where counting the number of blasts and the total time for the signal to complete a cycle is not sufficient for identification, reference may be made to the details in the Light List.

Fog signal equipment

The various types of fog signals differ in tone, and this also aids in identification. The type of fog signal for each station is shown in the Light Lists and on charts.

Diaphones produce sound by means of a slotted reciprocating piston actuated by compressed air. Blasts may consist of two tones of different pitch, in which case the first part of the blast is higher pitch and the latter is lower. These alternate-pitch signals are termed "two-tone."

Diaphragm horns produce sound by means of a disc diaphragm vibrated by compressed air or electricity. Duplex or triplex horn units of different pitch are sometimes combined to produce a more musical signal.

Sirens produce sound by means of either a disc or cup-shaped rotor actuated by compressed air, steam, or electricity. These should not be confused with what might be called "police sirens"; these may produce a sound of constant pitch much like a diaphragm horn or a whistle.

Whistles produce sound by compressed air, emitted through a circumferential slot into a cylindrical bell chamber.

Bells are sounded by means of a hammer actuated by an electric solenoid.

Operation of signals

Fog signals at stations where a continuous watch is maintained (identified in the Light Lists by the words "Resident Personnel") are sounded whenever the visibility decreases below a limit set for that particular station; typically, this might be two to five miles. The audible fog signals at certain stations are synchronized with the radiobeacon signals of these stations for distance-finding; see page 506.

Fog signals at locations where no continuous watch is maintained may not always be sounded promptly when fog conditions occur, or may operate erratically due to mechanical difficulties.

Where fog signals are operated continuously on a seasonal basis or throughout the year, this information will be found in the Light Lists.

FIG. 1606. Light structures rising out of the water are often protected by piles of rocks known as "rip-rap." Skippers should keep well clear as obstructions below the surface may extend far out. This is the light shown in the chart extract of fig. 1604—note there how the rip-rap is indicated around the light.

CAUTIONS IN USING FOG SIGNALS

Fog signals depend upon the transmission of sound through air. As aids to navigation, they have certain inherent limitations that *must* be considered. Sound travels through air in a variable and unpredictable manner. It has been established as fact that:

(a) Fog signals can be heard at greatly varying distances, and the distance at which such an aid can be heard may at any given instant vary with the bearing of the signal, and may be different on different occasions.

(b) Under certain conditions of the atmosphere, when a fog signal has a combination of high and low tones, it is not unusual for one of them to be heard but not the other. In the case of sirens which produce a varying tone, portions of the blast may not be heard.

(c) There are occasionally areas close to the signal in which it will not be heard. This is particularly true when the fog signal is screened by intervening land masses or other obstructions, or when the signal is on a high cliff.

(d) The apparent loudness of a fog signal may be greater at a distance than in the immediate vicinity.

(e) A patch of fog may exist at a short distance from a manned station but not be seen from it. Thus the signal may not be placed in operation.

(f) Some fog signals require a start-up interval.

(g) A fog signal may not be detected when the vessel's engines are in operation, but may be heard when they are stopped, or from a quieter location on deck.

Based on the above established facts, a mariner must *not* assume:

(1) That he is out of ordinary hearing distance from a fog signal because he fails to hear it.

(2) That because he hears a fog signal faintly, he is at a greater distance from it.

(3) That he is near to it because he hears it loudly.

(4) That the fog signal is not sounding because he does not hear it, even when in close proximity.

(5) That the detection distance and sound intensity under any one set of conditions is an infallible guide for any future occasion.

In summary, fog signals are valuable as warnings, but the boatman should not place implicit reliance upon them in navigating his vessel. They should be considered solely as warning devices.

Standby fog signals

Standby fog signals are sounded at some of the more important stations when the main signal is inoperative.

Lighthouses and Other Aids / CHAPTER 16

The standby signals may be of a different type and characteristic than the main signal. If different, details are given in the Light Lists.

Lightships and Offshore Towers

Lightships are vessels of distinctive design and markings, equipped with lights, fog signals, and radiobeacons. They are anchored or moored at specific, charted locations to serve as aids to navigation; see fig. 1607.

Purpose

Lightships mark the entrances to important harbors, warn of dangerous shoals lying in much-frequented waters, and serve as departure marks for both ocean and coastwise traffic.

Lightships serve the same essential purposes as lighthouses. They take the form of vessels only because they are at locations where it is (or has been until recently) impracticable to build lighthouses. As will be noted later, modern construction technology has now made possible the replacement of all but a few of the traditional lightships with more efficient fixed structures.

LIGHTSHIPS

The hulls of lightships in U. S. waters are almost invariably painted red with the name of the station in large white letters on each side. All the signals—the light, fog signal, and radiobeacon—have distinctive characteristics so that the lightship may be identified under all conditions. As with lighthouses, details regarding these signals are shown briefly on charts and more completely in the Light Lists. A riding light on the forestay indicates the direction that the ship is heading, and since lightships ride to a single bow anchor, this also indicates the direction from which the current is flowing, whenever the current is stronger than the wind.

Modern U. S. lightships are self-propelled, capable of proceeding to and from their stations under their own power. All are diesel-powered and can use their main engines to either relieve the strain on their moorings during storms or work their way back to station if blown off by high winds and seas. Each lightship carries a crew of about 15 men.

FIG. 1607 Lightships are used to mark both offshore hazards and the entrance to major harbors. Nantucket Shoals have been marked since 1854. The lightship shown above is anchored in 192 feet of water; her 400,000 candlepower light is 67 feet above the water and can be seen for 14 miles geographic range and 23 miles luminous range. She is also equipped with a Diaphone two-tone fog signal synchronized with her radiobeacon signal.

Identification

A lightship underway to or from its station will fly the International Code flags "LO" which signify "I am not in my correct position," fig. 1608. She will not show or sound any of the signals of a lightship, but will display the lights prescribed by the International or Inland Rules for a vessel of her class.

When on station at night, a lightship shows only the aid to navigation and riding lights. By day, lightships will display the International Code signal of the station whenever a vessel is in the vicinity and there are any indications that her crew fails to recognize the station, or whenever a vessel asks for information. The International Code signal for each lightship station is stated in the Light Lists.

Relief lightships

Whenever the regular lightship must be withdrawn from her station for maintenance, she is temporarily replaced with a *relief lightship*. These are painted the same colors as regular lightships, but have the word "RELIEF" on each side in lieu of a station name.

Relief lightships will generally exhibit lights and sound signals having the regular characteristics of the station. They may differ in outward appearance from the regular lightship in minor details. Changes in lightships are announced in advance by Notices to Mariners.

Station buoys

Station buoys, also referred to as "watch buoys," are used to mark the position of lightship stations. These buoys are located from several hundred yards to as much as a mile from the station as shown on the chart; the distance and direction are given in the Light Lists. They are *not* separately charted.

Station buoys serve as a substitute if the lightship is forced to seek shelter in extreme weather, and they aid in later returning the lightship to its correct position. They are always of an unlighted type and are marked with "LS" and the initials of the lightship station.

Cautions in using lightships

A skipper should set his course so as to pass a lightship with sufficient clearance to avoid the possibility of collision from any cause. It should be borne in mind that most lightships are anchored by a very long scope of chain and as a result the radius of their swinging circle is considerable. The charted position is the location of the anchor.

It must also be remembered that during extremely heavy weather lightships may be carried off station despite the best efforts of their crews, and perhaps without their knowledge. A navigator should not, therefore, implicitly rely on the position of a lightship during and immediately after severe storms. A lightship known to be off station will secure her light, fog signal, and radiobeacon, and will fly the International Code signal "LO."

A craft steering toward a radiobeacon on a lightship, "homing" on it, should exercise particular care to avoid collision. Sole reliance should *never* be placed on sighting the lightship or hearing her fog signal in time to prevent hitting her. The risk of collision will be lessened by ensuring that the radio bearing does not remain constant.

Skippers must also use care in passing lightships so as

FIG. 1608. A lightship flies the International Code flags "LO" when she is not on her station. These are seen above flying from the foremast. The vessel shown here is used as a temporary substitute for other lightships when those must return to port for maintenance, hence the name "RELIEF" in white letters on the red hull rather than the name of a specific station.

FIG. 1609. The old and the new in offshore aids to navigation. Lightships have been used since 1820, but in 1961 the Coast Guard started their replacement along the Atlantic Coast with tower structures. The fixed towers offer many advantages over lightships and will be constructed wherever hydrographic conditions permit. Frying Pan Shoals Light off the coast of North Carolina stands in 46 feet of water.

to not collide with the station buoy, remembering that it is unlighted and may be at a considerable distance from the lightship. Particular caution must be exercised in fog and at night.

OFFSHORE LIGHT TOWERS

Along the Atlantic Coast, lightships are being gradually replaced with offshore light structures, fig. 1609. The first of these was placed in operation in 1961 and others will be added until only a few lightships remain. On the Pacific Coast, lightships will remain in use as the greater depths of water make tower construction impractical.

Characteristics

A typical tower deckhouse is 60 feet above the water, 80 feet square, and supported by steel legs in pilings driven nearly 300 feet into the ocean bottom. The deckhouse accommodates living quarters, radiobeacon, and communications and oceanographic equipment. The top serves as a landing platform that will take the largest helicopters flown by the Coast Guard. On one corner of the deckhouse is a 32-foot radio tower supporting the radiobeacon antenna and a 3½-million candlepower light. At an elevation of 130 feet above the water, it is visible for 18 miles. The construction details of other towers will vary slightly, but all are of the same general type.

Advantages

Fixed offshore light stations have five major advantages over lightships:

(1) Lower operating costs. The annual operating, personnel, and maintenance expenses of a tower light station are only about one-third of those of a lightship.

(2) Greater light range. Greater luminous range is made possible by more efficient optics, and greater geographic range results from the increased height of the light above the water—some 50 to 70 feet higher than one on a lightship.

(3) Better fog signal projection. By eliminating the swinging to which a lightship is subject, fog signals may be projected specifically in the most useful directions under all circumstances.

(4) More accurate guidance for ships. The location of a tower light is fixed; it does not swing about the charted position and cannot be blown off station in violent storms.

(5) Longer life. Towers are expected to last 75 years, as compared with the average 50-year lifespan of lightships.

Unmanned offshore aids

In addition to the manned offshore light stations, there are several unmanned light towers, such as the one at Brenton Reef, and an increasing number of "large navigational buoys" as replacements for lightships.

Ranges and Directional Lights

Ranges and directional lights serve to indicate the centerline of a channel and thus aid in the safe piloting of a vessel. Although they are frequently used in connection with channels and other restricted waterways, they are not a part of the lateral system of buoyage and so were not covered in Chapter 15.

RANGES

A *range* consists of two fixed aids to navigation so positioned with respect to each other that when seen in line they indicate that the observer's craft *may* be in safe waters, fig. 1610. The aids may be lighted or unlighted as determined by the importance of the range, and may take a wide variety of physical appearances.

The conditional phrase "may be in safe waters" is used in the definition above since observation of the two markers in line is *not* an absolute determination of safety. A range is "safe" only within specific limits of distance from the front marker; a vessel too close or too far away may be in a dangerous area. The aids that comprise the range do not in themselves indicate the usable portion of the range; reference *must* be made to a chart of the

325

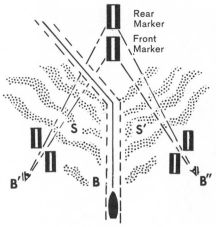

FIG. 1610. The principle of range markers. A boat B follows a safe mid-channel course between shoals S and S' by aligning the front marker directly below the rear marker. If the range opens and the rear marker shows to the **left** of the front marker, the boat is off course, displaced toward B'. If the rear marker shows to the **right** of the front marker, she is displaced toward B''. Ranges may be lighted or unlighted.

area and to other aids.

Ranges are described in the Light Lists by first giving the position of the front marker, usually in terms of geographic coordinates—latitude and longitude; and then stating the location of the rear marker in terms of direction and distance from the front marker. This direction, given in degrees and minutes, true, need not be used in ordinary navigation, but is useful in making checks of compass deviation. The rear daymark (and light, if used) is always higher than the one on the front aid.

Because of their fixed nature, and the accuracy with which a vessel can be positioned by using them, ranges are among the best aids to navigation. Preference should always be given to using a range when one is available; buoys should be referred to only in order to determine the beginning and end of the usable portion of the range.

Unlighted ranges

Although any two objects may be used as a range, the term is properly applied only to those pairs of structures built specifically for that purpose. Special shapes and markings will be used for the front and rear markers of a range for easier identification and more accurate alignment. Many different designs have been used in the past, but to make ranges more easily identifiable, and easier to use, the Coast Guard now has standardized on the use of rectangular daymarks, longer dimension vertical, painted in vertical stripes of contrasting colors, see color page I. The design of specific range daymarks will normally be found in the Light Lists.

Lighted ranges

Because of their importance and high accuracy in piloting, most range markers are equipped with lights to extend their usefulness through the hours of darkness. Entrance channels are frequently marked with range lights; the Delaware River on the Atlantic Coast and the Columbia River on the Pacific Coast are examples of this.

Range lights may be of any color used with aids to navigation—white, red, or green—and may show any of several characteristics. The principal requirement is that they be easily distinguished from shore backgrounds and from other lights. Front and rear lights will, however, often be of the same color (white is frequently used because of its greater visibility range), with different phase characteristics. Since both lights must be observed together for the proper steering of the craft, range lights will generally have

a greater "on" interval than will other lights. Range rear lights will normally be on more than their front counterparts. Many ranges now show an equal interval rear light and a quick-flashing front light.

Many range lights will be fitted with special lenses that result in a much greater intensity being shown on the range center line than off of it; the lights rapidly decrease in brilliance when observed from only a few degrees to either side. In some cases, the light will be visible only from on or very near to the range line; in other cases, a light of lesser intensity may be seen all around the horizon—this can be either from the main light source or from a small auxiliary "passing" light. Light is shown around the horizon when the front aid also serves to mark the side of a channel at a turn of direction.

Often range lights will be of such high intensity that they can be seen and used for piloting in the daytime, being of more value than the painted daymarks.

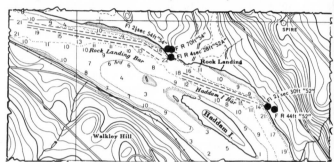

FIG. 1611. Lighted range markers are extensively used on the Connecticut River. When aligned by an observer in mid-channel, Rock Landing Range Front Light (flashing white, height 54 feet) shows below Rock Landing Range Rear Light (fixed red, height 70 feet). A similar range leads through Haddam Island Bar. Their daymarks are white diamonds with black centers. Details are given in the Light List.

DIRECTION LIGHTS

The establishment of a range requires suitable locations for two aids, separated adequately both horizontally and vertically. In some areas, this may not be possible and a single light of special characteristics will be employed.

A *direction light* is a single light source fitted with a special lens so as to show a white light in a narrow beam along a desired direction, with red and green showing to either side. The width of the sectors will depend upon the local situation, but red will be seen if the pilot is to the right of the center line as he approaches the aid from seaward, and green if he is to the left of the desired track. A typical direction light, at Deer Island, Massachusetts, shows white for a sector of 2.4° with red and green showing for 8.5° to either side. Another directional light in Delaware Bay has a white beam width of 1° 40' with red and green sectors of 6½° to either side.

Direction lights will normally have an occulting or equal interval characteristic, so they are easily followed.

Caution regarding direction lights

A pilot should not place too great reliance on the various colors of a direction light for safe positional information. As noted for light sectors, the boundaries between colors are not sharp and clear; the light shades imperceptibly from one color to the other along the stated direction lines.

CHAPTER 17

GOVERNMENT PUBLICATIONS

The typical boatman undoubtedly thinks first of charts when considering the publications that are issued by governmental agencies to aid his safe boating. This is certainly a valid thought—so much so that another chapter is devoted entirely to charts—but he should not overlook the many other publications that are available to make his boating safer and more enjoyable. Generally, these are issued by the same governmental agencies as are charts. Such publications will be considered in this chapter.

PUBLISHING AGENCIES

Agencies of the Federal Government that issue publications valuable to the boatman include:

National Ocean Survey (formerly the Coast & Geodetic Survey, and now including the Lake Survey Center), National Oceanic and Atmospheric Administration, Department of Commerce.

United States Coast Guard (transferred in 1967 from the Treasury Department to the Department of Transportation).

The U.S. Naval Observatory.

The Defense Mapping Agency Hydrographic Center.

U.S. Army Corps of Engineers (through its District Offices).

National Weather Service (formerly the U.S. Weather Bureau), also a part of NOAA.

Government Printing Office

The Government Printing Office, an independent agency, does much of the actual printing of the publications prepared by the agencies listed above. The Superintendent of Documents is responsible for the sale of most of these publications, but not all of them. Unfortunately, there seems to be no rule for the determination of whether a publication is sold by the GPO, or by the preparing agency —for example: H.O. 9 can be purchased from the GPO, but H.O. 103 cannot be bought there, only from the DMA Hydrographic Center and its sales agents.

Publications that are sold by the GPO can be purchased by mail. The address is Superintendent of Documents, Government Printing Office, Washington, D.C. 20402. There is also a retail bookstore in the GPO building at North Capital and H Streets in Washington where over-the-counter purchases can be made. Personal checks for the purchase of publications are acceptable; they should be made payable to the "Superintendent of Documents."

State agencies

Publications of interest to boatmen are also prepared by many State agencies, so many that it is not possible to list them all in this book. Boatmen should check with local

327

authorities in their own state and write ahead to other states when they expect to cruise into new waters. Information may be obtained that will add to safety and convenience, possibly avoiding legal embarrassment as well. "Ignorance is no excuse" applies both afloat and ashore!

The name of the state agency to be addressed will vary widely from state to state. Consult page 621 for the name and address of an office to which inquiries may be sent. Requests for information and literature should be as specific as possible.

SALES AGENTS

Various boating supply stores, marinas, and similar activities have been designated by governmental agencies as official *sales agents* for their publications. These agents accept responsibility for maintenance of adequate stocks of the various charts and documents of interest to mariners and boatmen in their respective areas.

Authorized sales agents may carry stocks of National Ocean Survey publications, some DMA Hydrographic Center publications, Coast Guard publications, or combinations of two or three of these. It does *not* hold true that because an activity is an agent for one type of publication it will have those of other governmental agencies.

Other information

Additional information on where to obtain certain specific government publications will be found on pages 571 and 608-610.

National Ocean Survey Publications _____

The National Ocean Survey (N.O.S.) is charged with the survey of the coast, harbors and tidal estuaries of the United States and its insular possessions. It issues the following publications relating to these waters as guides to navigation: Charts, Coast Pilots, Tide Tables, Tidal Current Tables, Tidal Current Charts, and chart catalogs.

In 1970, the National Ocean Survey was created from the former Coast & Geodetic Survey and the Army Engineers' Lake Survey District. This agency is part of the National Oceanic and Atmospheric Administration (which replaced the Environmental Science Services Administration) in the Department of Commerce.

TIDE TABLES

Tide Tables, fig. 1701, are of great value in determining the predicted height of the water at almost any place at any given time. These tables are calculated in advance and are published annually in four volumes, one of which covers the East Coast of North and South America and another the West Coast of these continents.

The Tide Tables give the predicted times and heights of high and low waters for each day of the year at a number of important points known as *reference stations*. The East Coast Tide Tables include 48 sets of detailed listings for such points as Portland, Boston, Sandy Hook, Baltimore, Miami, Pensacola, and Galveston. Additional

data are tabulated showing the differences in times and heights between these reference stations and thousands of other points, termed *subordinate stations*. From these tables, the tide at virtually any point along the coast can be easily computed.

The N.O.S. Tide Tables also include other useful data including tables of sunrise and sunset, reduction of local mean time to standard zone time, and moonrise and moonset.

The Tide Tables and their use in piloting are discussed at length in Chapter 20, pages 397-402.

TIDAL CURRENT TABLES

The Tidal Current Tables are in much the same format as the Tide Tables, see fig. 1702. However, instead of times of high and low waters, these tables give the times of maximum flood and ebb currents and times of the two slacks when current direction reverses. The times of slack water do *not* correspond to times of high and low tides, and the Tide Tables *cannot* be used to predict current situations. Velocity of the current at maximum strength is given in terms of knots (nautical miles per hour).

Tidal Current Tables are published in two volumes—Atlantic Coast of North America and Pacific Coast of North America and Asia. Included in each volume are tables from

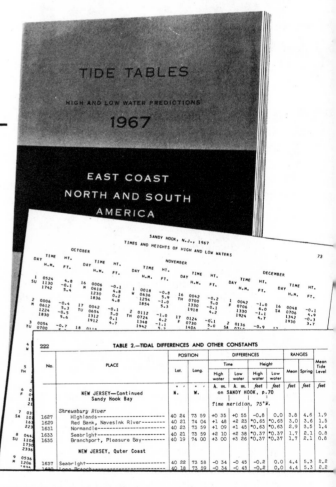

FIG. 1701 Tide Tables published by the National Ocean Survey provide necessary data for predicting height of tide at thousands of coastal points for any desired day and hour. Separate volumes are issued for the Atlantic-Gulf and Pacific Coasts.

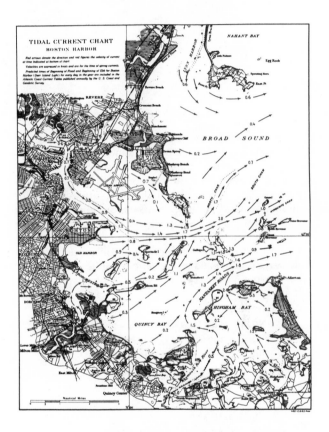

TIDAL CURRENT TABLES

PACIFIC COAST OF NORTH AMERICA AND ASIA

1967

FIG. 1702 Tidal Current Tables are prepared in much the same format as the Tide Tables. A system of a limited number of reference points together with thousands of subordinate stations permits calculation of current strengths and slacks at virtually any location of navigational interest.

cially where tidal currents are complex, often flowing in opposite directions at the same stage of tide, a real advantage can be gained in consulting one of these charts. A few minutes' study may well be the means of carrying a favorable current through the entire passage, instead of needlessly bucking an opposing flow for much or all of the time. As is the case for all current predictions, it must be remembered that these charts indicate normal conditions; a strong wind from certain directions may have a decided influence on both the strength of currents and the times that maximums are reached.

The New York Harbor Tidal Current Charts are used in conjunction with the annual tide tables. All other Tidal Current Charts are used with the annual tidal current tables for their respective areas. See also pages 409 and 410.

FIG. 1703 Tidal Current Charts are available for a number of major bodies of water where such flows are of significance in piloting. A series of twelve charts, for hourly intervals in the cycle of ebb and flood, comprise each Tidal Current Chart.

which may be calculated current velocity at any intermediate time and the duration of slack water or weak currents.

Tidal Current Tables and their use in piloting are covered in detail in Chapter 20, pages 406-409.

TIDAL CURRENT CHARTS

Tidal Current Charts are available for twelve bodies of water—Boston Harbor, Narragansett Bay to Nantucket Sound (two sets), Long Island Sound, Block Island Sound, New York Harbor, Delaware Bay and River, Upper Chesapeake Bay, Charleston (S.C.) Harbor, San Francisco Bay, and Puget Sound (two sets). Each set consists of a series of 12 reproductions of the chart of the locality, each of which indicates graphically the direction and velocity of tidal currents for a specific hour with respect to the state of the tide or current prediction for a major reference station. Currents in the various passages are indicated with red arrows and velocities are noted at numerous points; see fig. 1703. By following through the sequence of charts, hourly changes in velocity and direction are easily seen. These charts make it possible to visualize just how tidal currents act in various passages and channels throughout every part of the entire twelve-hour-plus cycle.

Where currents run at considerable velocity, and espe-

COAST PILOTS

The amount of information that can be printed on nautical charts is limited by available space and the system of symbols that is used. Additional information is often needed for safe and convenient navigation. The National Ocean Survey publishes such information in the *Coast Pilots*. These are printed in book form, covering the coastline in eight separate volumes.

Each Coast Pilot, see fig. 1704, contains sailing directions

329

FIG. 1704 The Coast Pilot is issued in eight volumes for various sections of the coastline. Each includes sailing directions, courses and distances between ports; information on hazards and aids to navigation; data on facilities for supplies and repairs; and much other useful information that cannot be conveniently shown on nautical charts.

United States Coast Pilot
EIGHTH EDITION · 1970

ATLANTIC COAST
Cape Henry to Key West

---

154   9. WESTERN LONG ISLAND SOUND

There are several marinas and boatyards in the harbor. Craft up to 12 tons can be hauled out for engine and hull repairs. Gasoline, diesel fuel, water, ice, storage facilities, lifts, and marine supplies are available. The town of Huntington maintains several launching ramps.

Lloyd Harbor extends westward from Huntington Bay nearly to Oyster Bay, from which it is separated by a narrow strip of beach at high water. Vessels drawing less than 7 feet can anchor just inside the entrance, where the depths are 7 to 11 feet. An abandoned light tower is about in the middle of the entrance.

Oyster Bay, on the south side of the sound about 5 miles westward of Eatons Neck Light, lies between Lloyd Neck and Rocky Point. The entrance and harbor are characterized by extensive shoals, boulder reefs, and broken ground making off from the shores. Vessels should proceed with caution if obliged to approach or cross shoal areas. The bay south of Cold Spring Harbor Light is a secure harbor, available for vessels of less than 18-foot draft. A fog signal is sounded at the light.

Lloyd Neck, between Huntington and Oyster Bays, is high and wooded, and has a high, yellow bluff on its north side 0.8 miles eastward of Lloyd Point. Many patches of boulders having least depths of 2 to 8 feet extend 0.2 to 0.5 mile offshore from **East Fort Point** to Lloyd Point. Small craft skirting this shore should keep well

Currents.—About 0.2 mile north of Cold Spring Harbor Light, the velocity is about 0.5 knot; about 0.2 mile north of Cove Point, 1.2 miles southwestward, it is about 0.8 knot. For predictions, the Tidal Current Tables should be consulted.

Ice.—During severe winters ice has been known to extend the full length of the bay during part of January and February.

Plum Point, the easternmost point of Centre Island, is marked at its south end by a small stone tower; boat landings are on the southwest side of the point. A yacht club with a prominent flagstaff is about 0.3 mile west of Plum Point. The yacht club landing has depths of about 9 feet. See appendix for **storm warning display**.

Cooper Bluff, at the northeast end of Cove Neck is prominent. A boulder reef extends nearly 0.3 mile northward from **Cove Point** at the northwest end of **Cove Neck**, and is marked by a lighted buoy.

Cold Spring Harbor, the southeasterly end of Oyster Bay, extends about 2.3 miles southward of Cooper Bluff. The seminary on the hill of **West Neck**, on the east side of the harbor, is prominent. The harbor is free of dangers if the shores are given a berth of about 0.3 mile, the depths being 15 to 18 feet to near its head.

The village of **Cold Spring Harbor** is on the eastern shore near the head of the harbor. An oil company

---

between ports in its respective area, including recommended courses and distances. Channels, with their controlling depths, and all dangers and obstructions are fully described. Harbors and anchorages are listed, with information on those points at which facilities are available for boat supplies and marine repairs. Information regarding canals, bridges, docks, etc., which cannot be adequately expressed on charts due to limitations of space, is provided in full in the Coast Pilots. Information on the Intracoastal Waterways is contained in the various applicable volumes.

The various volumes of the Coast Pilot cover areas as follows:

Atlantic Coast

No. 1 Eastport to Cape Cod
No. 2 Cape Cod to Sandy Hook
No. 3 Sandy Hook to Cape Henry
No. 4 Cape Henry to Key West
No. 5 Gulf of Mexico, Puerto Rico, and Virgin Islands

Pacific Coast

No. 7 California, Oregon, Washington, and Hawaii

Alaska

No. 8 Dixon Entrance to Cape Spencer
No. 9 Cape Spencer to Beaufort Sea

Note: Currently there is no Volume No. 6.

Coast Pilots are being converted to an automated (magnetic tape) typesetting process so that an updated edition may be issued each year. For all volumes so reprinted annually, *only* the one for the current year should be used; prior editions may not contain full and correct information essential for safe navigation.

For volumes not yet automated, an updating Supplement is issued each year; these are cumulative and only the latest year's is required. Such a Coast Pilot should be used *only* in conjunction with the latest Supplement. Annual Supplements are available free from local N.O.S. sales agents or from the National Ocean Survey, Rockville, Md. 20852.

THE GREAT LAKES PILOT

For the Great Lakes and other waters covered by the Lake Survey charts, the publication corresponding to the Coast Pilots is called the *Great Lakes Pilot,* fig. 1712. This is an annual publication, kept up to date during the navigation season by seven monthly supplements issued from May to November.

CHART CATALOGS

The National Ocean Survey issues free *Chart Catalogs,* fig. 1705, in three volumes for the Atlantic and Pacific

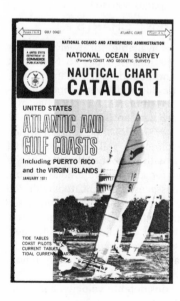

FIG. 1705 The National Ocean Survey issues catalogs of their nautical charts; these also include listings of other useful publications of the N.O.S. and other agencies. These catalogs show the area covered by each chart, the scale, price, etc. They are updated at intervals of 6 to 12 months.

Coasts, including offshore islands, and for Alaska. These are actually small-scale outline charts with diagrams delineating the area covered by each nautical chart published by the N.O.S. These catalogs are also sources of much additional information regarding charts and publications of other agencies, and the location of sales agents (shown both by a listing of the name and address of the agent and by a symbol on the chart-outline diagrams).

GREAT LAKES CHART CATALOGS

An excellent free catalog of Nautical Charts of the Great Lakes, fig. 1711, is available from the Lake Survey Center, N.O.S., 630 Federal Building, Detroit, Mich. 48226, where mail orders and counter sales of Lake Survey charts are handled. Lake Survey charts are also sold, over the counter only, at their sales offices in Sault Ste. Marie, Mich.; Buffalo, N.Y.; Cleveland, Ohio; Chicago, Ill., and Massena, N.Y.

Included in the waterways listed in the Lake Survey catalog, in addition to the Great Lakes and its outflow rivers, are Lake Champlain, the New York State Barge Canal System, and the Minnesota-Ontario Border Lakes. The catalog also supplies information on the Lake Survey's recreational chart series, designed especially for the operators of small pleasure boats, and other Lake Survey publications, such as the Great Lakes Pilot.

N.O.S. OFFICES

Nautical charts, Tide and Tidal Current Tables, Coast Pilots, and other publications of the National Ocean Survey

Distribution Division (C44)
National Ocean Survey
6501 Lafayette Avenue
Riverdales, MD 20840

FIG. 1706 If not available at local sales agents, publications and charts of the National Ocean Survey can be purchased by mail from the office listed above. A check or money order for the total price should accompany the order; the material will be sent postpaid.

can be purchased over-the-counter at the Distribution Office in Washington, D.C. at Connecticut Avenue and Van Ness Street, N.W., or by mail (prepaid) to the address shown in fig. 1706.

Other offices

Information regarding N.O.S. charts, publications, and activities can be obtained by addressing the National Ocean Survey, Rockville, Md. 20852. Field offices in various major port cities, formerly sources of information, were closed in mid-1969.

Coast Guard Publications

The United States Coast Guard prepares a major navigational publication and a number of minor ones. All of these are worthy of a boatman's serious consideration.

LIGHT LISTS

The USCG publication *List of Lights and Other Marine Aids* is commonly referred to as simply the "Light List." These Lists provide more complete information concerning aids to navigation than can be conveniently shown on charts, see fig. 1707. They are *not* intended to be used in navigation in place of charts and Coast Pilots, and should not be so used. Charts should be consulted for the location of all aids to navigation. It may be dangerous to use aids to navigation without reference to charts.

The Light Lists describe, for the use of mariners, the lightships, lighthouses, lesser lights, buoys, and daybeacons maintained in all navigable waters of the United States by the Coast Guard and various private agencies. (In this

(1)	(2) Name	(3) Location	(4) Nominal	(5) Ht.	(6) Structure		(7)
No.	Characteristic	Lat. N. Long. W.	Range	above water	Ht. above ground	Daymark	Remarks Year
			CALIFORNIA				TWELFTH DISTRICT
	SAN FRANCISCO BAY						
	South End						
	SAN FRANCISCO AIRPORT						
763	—*Channel Lighted Buoy 1* .... Fl. W., 4ˢ	In 13 feet	5	....	Black		
764.11	—CHANNEL LIGHT 3 .... Fl. W., 4ˢ	North end of the runway lighting catwalk. 37 37.5 122 22.5	5	10	SB		1966
765	—CHANNEL LIGHT 5 .... Fl. W., 4ˢ	Off end of south jetty 37 37.9 122 22.7	5	15	SB on pile		1941–1966
766	—AERO LIGHT .... Alt. Fl. W. and G., 10ˢ	At San Francisco International Airport. 37 37.0 122 23.0	....	....			Maintained by Federal Aviation Agency. 1929–1955
	COYOTE POINT						
767	—YACHT HARBOR 1						1960

FIG. 1707 Light Lists, published by the U.S. Coast Guard, provide more detailed information on aids to navigation than can be shown on charts. Five volumes cover all coasts, the Great Lakes, and the Mississippi River system. Light Lists are to be used with, not as a substitute for, nautical charts. Information in column 6 regarding daymarks is now being converted to abbreviations, such as "SB" for a black square daymark, "TR" for a red triangular daymark, etc.; see introductory pages of new volumes of the Light Lists.

usage, the Navy and all other non-USCG governmental organizations are considered to be "private agencies.") The data shown in the Lists includes the official name of the aid, the characteristics of its light, sound, and radio signals, its structural appearance, position, and other significant factors.

Light Lists are published in five volumes as follows:

Volume I—Atlantic Coast from St. Croix River,
Maine to Little River, S.C.

Volume II—Atlantic and Gulf Coasts from Little
River, S.C. to Rio Grande, Texas

Volume III—Pacific Coast and Pacific Islands

Volume IV—Great Lakes

Volume V—Mississippi River System

Within each volume, aids to navigation are listed by Coast Guard Districts in the following order: seacoast, major channels, Intracoastal Waterway, minor channel, and miscellaneous. Lighted and unlighted aids appear together in their geographic order, with amplifying data on the same page.

Seacoast aids are listed in sequence from north to south along the Atlantic Coast, from south to north and east to west along the Gulf Coast, and from south to north along the Pacific Coast. On the Atlantic and Gulf Coasts, aids along the Intracoastal Waterway are listed in the same sequence. For rivers and estuaries, the aids to navigation are shown from seaward to the head of navigation. Where an aid serves both a channel leading in from sea and the ICW, it will be listed separately in both sequences.

All volumes of the USCG Light Lists are for sale by the Superintendent of Documents, Government Printing Office; the volume for the local area concerned is sold by many of the authorized chart and publication sales agents.

RULES OF THE ROAD

The Coast Guard issues a series of free pamphlets setting forth the Rules of the Road for various bodies of water. These include the general "Inland Rules" (Publication CG-169), fig. 1708, the "Great Lakes Rules" (CG-172), and the "Western Rivers Rules" (CG-184). The International Rules of the Road, used on the open seas and outside of specified boundaries at major ports, are included with the Inland Rules in CG-169 in a convenient parallel column format.

FIG. 1708 Separate pamphlets are issued by the U.S. Coast Guard covering Rules of the Road for Inland Waters, the Great Lakes, and the Western Rivers. The International Rules, used on the high seas, are included in the pamphlet covering Inland Rules.

Copies of the Rules of the Road pamphlets may be obtained from Coast Guard Marine Inspection Offices in the major ports, or by writing to the Commandant (CHS), U.S. Coast Guard Headquarters, Washington, D.C. 20226.

RECREATIONAL BOATING GUIDE

An excellent collection of information on boat numbering, legal minimum equipment requirements, other equipment that should be carried, responsibilities when operat-

FIG. 1709 The official U.S. Coast Guard Recreational Boating Guide contains excellent summaries of information relating to legally required equipment, other items that should be aboard a boat, registration and numbering, responsibilities of a skipper, and services rendered boatmen by the Coast Guard Auxiliary.

ing a boat, emergency procedures, and U.S. Coast Guard Auxiliary services is published as the *Official U.S. Coast Guard Recreational Boating Guide* (CG-340), fig. 1709.

This publication also contains an example of a boating accident report, a Distress Information Sheet, and guides to the safe loading capacity of small boats.

The USCG Recreational Boating Guide is revised periodically when required by changes in the applicable laws and regulations. Copies may be purchased by mail from the Superintendent of Documents, or frequently may be found for sale at marinas or boating supply stores; the price is 60¢.

OTHER USCG PUBLICATIONS

The Coast Guard issues a number of publications relating to the safety of navigation and covering such topics as aids to navigation, applicable rules and regulations, general safety matters, etc. See page 609 for a more complete listing and information on where they may be obtained. Some of these are free, others are available for a nominal charge.

CG-290 is a small pamphlet covering federal requirements for recreational boats. Topics include laws and regulations, numbering and documentation, reporting accidents, approved equipment, etc. It, and CG-151 below, can be obtained from USCG Headquarters (G-BBE), Washington, D.C. 20590.

Another free USCG pamphlet is "Emergency Repairs Afloat" (CG-151). The Coast Guard reasons that if you can help yourself, they will have fewer emergency calls!

DMA Hydrographic Center Publications

The Defense Mapping Agency Hydrographic Agency has taken over certain functions of the U.S. Naval Oceanographic Office. DMAHC has several publications of interest to boatmen. Charts, publications, and other products of DMAHC are identified with a prefix to the individual chart or publication number as follows:

The identification of nautical charts has been changed to a system using a number of one to five digits, without prefix, as determined by the scale and assigned on a basis of regions and subregions. Publications and some other items will continue to have an "H.O." prefix until reprinted with a DMAHC publication number.

Oceanographic products, primarily publications, related to the dynamic nature of the oceans or the scientific aspects of oceanography will be identified with the letters "N.O.O." as a prefix to the publication or chart number.

BOWDITCH (H.O. 9)

The *American Practical Navigator,* originally written by Nathaniel Bowditch in 1799, and generally referred to simply as "Bowditch," is an extensive treatise on piloting, celestial navigation and other nautical matters. It is Publication No. H.O. 9, last revised in 1958 and reprinted with minor corrections in 1962 and 1966, see fig. 1710.

"Bowditch" has long been accepted as an authority on questions of piloting and navigation; a copy will be found useful on all but the smallest of boats. In addition to the lengthy text, the basic volume contains many mathematical tables as appendices. These tables alone are also available as a separate publication.

OTHER H.O. PUBLICATIONS

Other Hydrographic Center publications that may be found useful to a boatman include H.O. 117A, *Radio Navigation Aids;* H.O. 118A, *Radio Weather Aids;* and H.O. 103, *International Code of Signals, Visual* (see Chapter 26).

The Hydrographic Center publishes a series of *Sailing Directions* which provide supplementary information for foreign coasts and ports in a manner generally similar to the Coast Pilot for U.S. waters.

The *Lists of Lights* published by this agency likewise cover foreign waters and so are not duplicatory of the Coast Guard Light Lists. These are H.O. 111A through H.O. 116.

The Hydrographic Center's catalog of its charts is Publication No. N.O. 1N. It has an introduction in three parts plus lists of charts subdivided into ten "regions." It may be purchased as a whole or separately by regions. Regions 0, 1, and 2 would be of the most interest to American boatmen. See fig. 1710a.

Other H.O. publications include a number of tables for the reduction of celestial observations, and tables and charts for plotting lines of position from Loran-A and Loran-C measurements. These are of interest only to those yachtsmen making extensive voyages on the high seas.

Additional Hydrographic Center publications are listed on page 610.

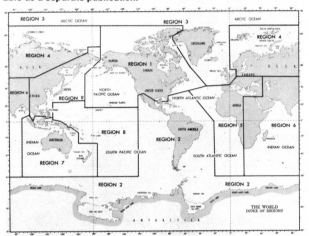

FIG. 1710 "Bowditch" is the name by which this popular and highly useful government publication is usually known. It contains a wealth of material on piloting, electronic and celestial navigation, and related topics. The mathematical tables contained in it are also available as a separate publication.

FIG. 1710a Charts formerly published by the Naval Oceanographic Office, and now by the Defense Mapping Agency Hydrographic Center, are numbered according to regions and subregions. The new system is a considerable improvement over the random numbering formerly employed.

Obtaining Oceanographic Office Publications

Branch offices of the DMA Hydrographic Center are located in Norfolk, Va.; Wilmington, Calif.; Honolulu, Hawaii; Rodman, C.Z.; and Yokosuka, Japan.

Charts and publications of the DMA Hydrographic Center are available for sale through authorized sales agents, and purchases should be made through these agents whenever possible. If not so available, charts may be purchased from the Branch Hydrographic Offices listed above, or by mail from the DMA Hydrographic Center, Washington, D.C. 20390, or from either of the DMA Hydrographic Depots listed below. Mail orders from purchasers located west of the Mississippi River (except Gulf of Mexico and the Canal Zone area) should be sent to:

DMA Hydrographic Center Depot, Clearfield, Utah 84016.

Mail orders from all other localities should be sent to:

DMA Hydrographic Center Depot, U.S. Naval Supply Depot, 5801 Tabor Ave., Philadelphia, Penna. 19120.

Orders submitted to the DMA Hydrographic Center, or to a DMA Hydrographic Center Depot must be accompanied by a check or money order made payable to the "DMA Hydrographic Center" for the amount of the purchase. Materials will be mailed at Government expense in regular printed-matter postal service. The added cost of requests for any special handling, such as air mail, special delivery, etc., must be borne by the purchaser.

Naval Observatory Publications

The U.S. Naval Observatory, Washington, D.C. publishes the *American Nautical Almanac.* This publication contains astronomical data necessary to boatmen who are concerned with celestial navigation, but is not needed for piloting. It can be purchased, in annual editions, from the Superintendent of Documents.

The Naval Observatory also participates in and assists the publication of other navigational documents such as the Tide Tables and celestial sight reduction tables, but it is not the agency directly responsible for them.

Army Engineers Publications

The Corps of Engineers of the U.S. Army has the responsibility for navigational and informational publications on major inland (non-tidal) rivers such as the Tennessee, Ohio, and Mississippi, and many lakes and reservoirs behind the large dams.

INTRACOASTAL WATERWAY BOOKLETS

The Army Engineers has prepared two paperbound booklets on the Intracoastal Waterway, which comes under its jurisdiction. These booklets contain descriptive material, photographs, small-scale charts, and tabulated data. Caution must be exercised, however, when using the distance tables as considerable differences exist between these publications and the N.O.S. charts of the Atlantic ICW. The Army Engineers use statute (not nautical) miles, and their zero point is at Trenton, N.J. rather than Norfolk, Va. Mileage differences will also be noted along the Gulf Intracoastal Waterway.

Unfortunately, these publications are *not* periodically updated, and they are of far less value than the corresponding volumes of the N.O.S. Coast Pilots with their annual supplements.

Bulletins on the Intracoastal Waterways are issued periodically by the Engineers District Offices. Addresses of these offices are given on page 608.

RIVERS AND LAKES INFORMATION

Regulations relating to the use of many rivers and lakes (reservoirs), *Navigational Bulletins,* and *Notices to Navigation Interests* are issued by various offices of the Corps of Engineers, U.S. Army, as listed on page 608. Other government publications relating to inland river and lake boating are also listed on that page, together with information as to where they may be obtained.

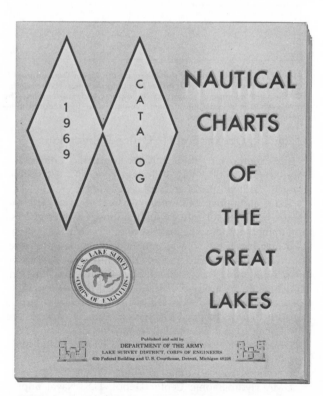

FIG. 1711 The Lake Survey chart catalog covers not only the Great Lakes, but also its outflow rivers, Lake Champlain, N.Y. State Barge Canal system, and Minnesota-Ontario border lakes.

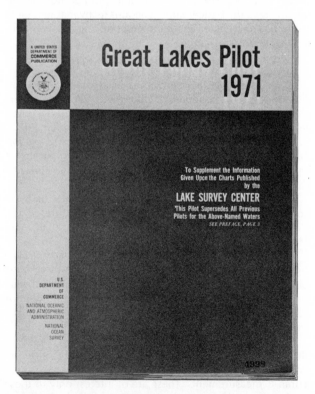

FIG. 1712 The Great Lakes Pilot is a comprehensive volume prepared to supplement information given on charts published by the Lake Survey. It is revised annually and kept up-to-date by supplements issued monthly during the navigation season (May-November).

National Weather Service Publications

The National Weather Service, a part of NOAA, Department of Commerce, prepares weather maps that appear in many newspapers, but boatmen generally make use greater of radio and television broadcasts of current weather and sea conditions and predictions.

To assist mariners and boatmen in knowing when and where to listen for radio and TV weather broadcasts, the Weather Service publishes a series of *Marine Weather Services Charts* in annual editions. These are discussed in more detail in pages 264-265 and 498.

Keeping Publications Up to Date

It is essential that certain navigational publications, as well as charts, be kept corrected and fully up to date with respect to the information contained in them. Incorrect, outdated information can be considerably more harmful than no information at all; a false sense of knowledge and confidence can easily lead to a dangerous situation.

Coast Pilots and Light Lists are the primary publications that need continual correction. Fortunately, the government has provided a convenient means for executing this most necessary function. The time and effort required are not great, provided a skipper keeps at it regularly and does not permit the work to build up a backlog.

NOTICE TO MARINERS

The Defense Mapping Agency Hydrographic Center publishes a weekly *Notice to Mariners* which is prepared jointly with the National Ocean Survey and the Coast Guard; see fig. 1713. These pamphlets advise mariners of important matters affecting navigational safety, including new hydrographic discoveries, changes in channels and navigation aids, etc. Besides keeping mariners informed generally, the Notice to Mariners also provides information specifically useful for updating the latest editions of nautical charts and publications. A revised format was introduced with Notice No. 1 of 1975.

Each issue contains instructions on how it is to be used to correct charts and other publications. Certain supplementary information is published at the beginning of each year, and portions are repeated at mid-year or at quarterly intervals.

LOCAL NOTICES TO MARINERS

The Commander of each Coast Guard District issues *Local Notices to Mariners,* fig. 1714. These are reproduced and mailed from the respective District offices, bringing information to users several weeks in advance of the weekly Notices that are printed in Washington, D.C. and mailed from there.

Local Notices are of particular interest to small-craft skippers, as the weekly Notices no longer carry information regarding inland and other waters not used by large ocean-going vessels.

Report all useful information

All boatmen are urged to cooperate with governmental agencies in keeping the buoyage system up to its highest

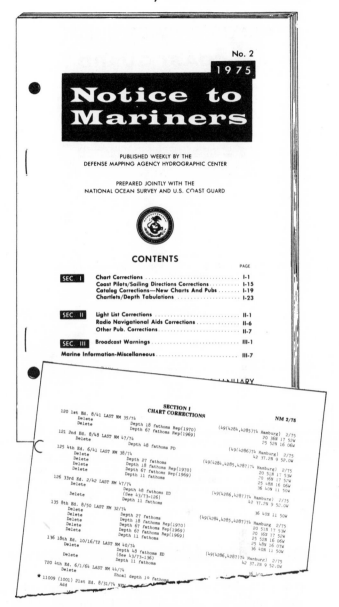

FIG. 1713. Notice to Mariners is a free weekly publication used to correct charts and other navigational publications. A single volume covers the major navigable waters of the world. Information appears in the form of descriptive paragraphs, inserts for pasting on charts, and cut-outs for insertion in volumes such as Light Lists. Information is limited to waters used by ocean-going vessels; for inland waters, Local Notices to Mariners must be used.

efficiency and helpfulness by reporting any facts that may come to their attention concerning damage to aids, malfunctioning of lights, shifting of shoals and channels, new hazards, etc. Defects in navigational aids and new hazards should be reported to the nearest Coast Guard activity by the fastest means available, including radio if the situation is of sufficient urgency. Suggestions for the improvement of aids to navigation should be sent to the Commandant, U.S. Coast Guard, Washington, D.C. 20590.

Data concerning dangers to navigation, changes in shoals and channels, and similar information affecting charts or publications of the N.O.S. should be sent to the Director, National Ocean Survey, NOAA, Rockville, Maryland 20852.

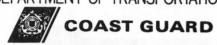

DEPARTMENT OF TRANSPORTATION

COAST GUARD

LOCAL NOTICE TO MARINERS

ISSUED BY: Commander, Seventh Coast Guard District
51 S. W. First Avenue, Miami, Florida 33130
Telephone: (305) 350-5621

BROADCAST NOTICE TO MARINERS

Information concerning aids to navigation promulgated by the following
broadcasts has been incorporated into this notice if still significant:

CG Miami BNM   1615-74 to 1663-74
CG Miami Selected BNM 222-74 to 230-74
CG San Juan BNM 278-74 to 284-74

LIGHT LIST REFERENCE: CG-160 Light List, Vol. II, 1974 Edition.

SPECIAL NOTE: UNLESS OTHERWISE INDICATED, MISSING AND DESTROYED STRUCTURES
ARE PRESUMED TO BE IN THE IMMEDIATE VICINITY. MARINERS SHOULD PROCEED WITH
CAUTION.

SPECIAL NOTICE

LORAN-C Off Air Time.

LORAN-C Rate SS7-W will be off the air for maintenance from 1400Z to 1900Z on
9 and 12 September 1974, with alternate dates of 10 and 13 September, same
times, in case of inclement weather.

Ref: LNM 35-74

SPECIAL NOTICE
Emergency Radiobeacon Evaluation

The U.S. Coast Guard will conduct field tests on emergency radiobeacons in the
Mobile, Alabama area from 1110Z to 2300Z alternately every ten minutes as follows:

a. 121.5, 157.15 and 243.0 MHZ 10-13 September 1974, 16-20 September, 23-27 September
1974. Characteristic A9 (swept tone) transmissions will be preceeded by voice
message "This is a Test" -and concluded by voice message "Test Complete".

REPORT DEFECTS IN AIDS TO NAVIGATION TO NEAREST COAST GUARD UNIT

DATE: 4 September 1974   NOTICE NO. 36-74

DEPARTMENT OF TRANSPORTATION U.S. COAST GUARD
CG-2938 HQ (REV. 10-73)
PREVIOUS EDITIONS ARE OBSOLETE

FIG. 1714 Local Notices to Mariners are published by each Coast Guard District on a "when required" basis, often several times per week. Information in Local Notices often reaches boatmen several weeks before it appears in weekly Notices from Washington. Check your local yacht club or marina for its file of Local Notices.

Quasi-Governmental Publications ———————

In addition to the governmental agencies and their publications noted above, there are several activities that can be best described as "quasi-governmental." Publications issued by them are of considerable interest to boatmen.

RADIO TECHNICAL COMMISSION FOR MARINE SERVICES

This organization with the long name is for obvious reasons better known by its initials, RTCM. It includes representatives of governmental agencies such as the FCC, the Coast Guard, NOAA, Maritime Administration, and others; user organizations, such as ocean steamship operating groups, Great Lakes shipping interests, and the United States Power Squadrons; equipment manufacturers; labor organizations; and communications companies such as the Bell System. The RTCM does not have authority to make binding decisions, but it wields considerable influence through its function as a meeting place for the presentation and resolution of conflicting views and interests.

The RTCM publishes *Marine Radio Telephony,* a booklet presenting a simplified interpretation of the FCC Rules and Regulations relating to the use of radios on ships and boats. The Fifth Edition (January 1974) has been extensively revised to cover recent regulatory changes with the shift to VHF-FM and single sideband. See fig. 2517.

This useful booklet can be ordered from the Radio Technical Commission for Marine Services, c/o Federal Communications Commission, Washington, D.C. 20554. The single copy price is $1.25, with discounts for quantity purchases.

NAVAL INSTITUTE PUBLICATIONS

The United States Naval Institute is not a governmental agency; rather it is a private association "for the advancement of professional, literary, and scientific knowledge in the Navy." One of its principal activities is the publication of books on naval and maritime matters.

The Naval Institute publishes a large number of books, but none will be more familiar to boatmen than *Dutton's Navigation and Piloting.* Like Bowditch, this volume has come to be an accepted authority on matters of piloting and navigation. Again like Bowditch, the current volume is an outgrowth of many years of development from an early work; the book was initially known as "Navigation and Nautical Astronomy" by Benjamin Dutton. This useful book can be purchased in boating supply and book stores, or directly by mail from the U.S. Naval Institute, Annapolis, Maryland, 21402. ⚓

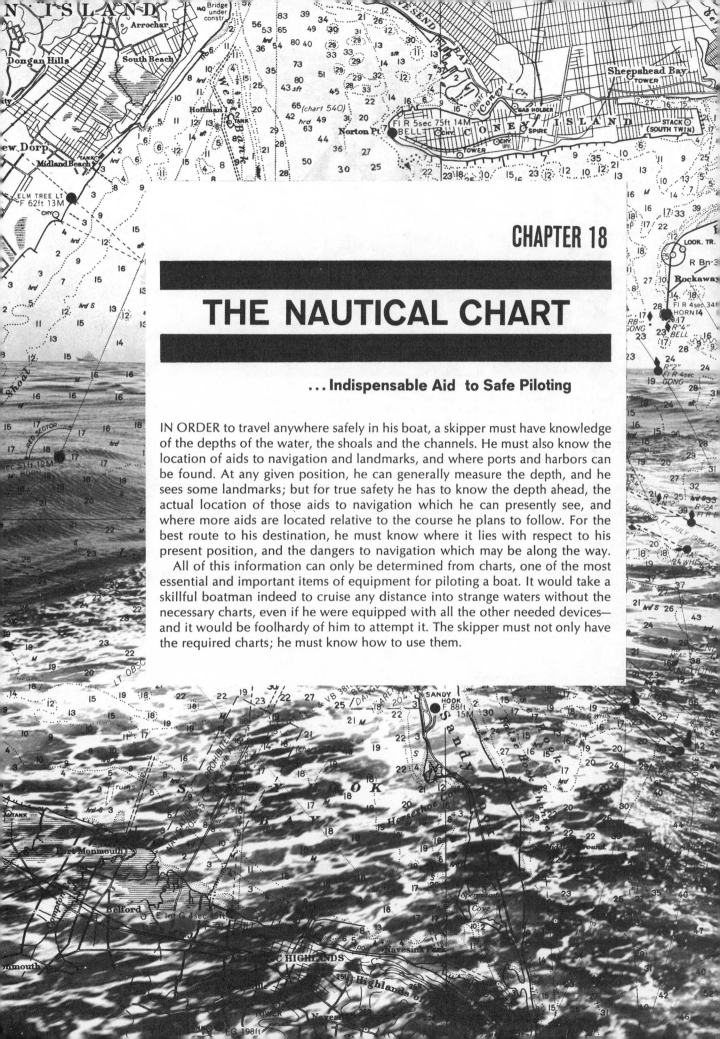

CHAPTER 18

THE NAUTICAL CHART

...Indispensable Aid to Safe Piloting

IN ORDER to travel anywhere safely in his boat, a skipper must have knowledge of the depths of the water, the shoals and the channels. He must also know the location of aids to navigation and landmarks, and where ports and harbors can be found. At any given position, he can generally measure the depth, and he sees some landmarks; but for true safety he has to know the depth ahead, the actual location of those aids to navigation which he can presently see, and where more aids are located relative to the course he plans to follow. For the best route to his destination, he must know where it lies with respect to his present position, and the dangers to navigation which may be along the way.

All of this information can only be determined from charts, one of the most essential and important items of equipment for piloting a boat. It would take a skillful boatman indeed to cruise any distance into strange waters without the necessary charts, even if he were equipped with all the other needed devices—and it would be foolhardy of him to attempt it. The skipper must not only have the required charts; he must know how to use them.

FIG. 1801   You are at Buoy "4" and the water is measured to be 18 feet deep, but what is the course to your destination, and how deep is the water along the way? Only a chart can give you this information —be sure that you have the right charts on board, and that you know how to use them.

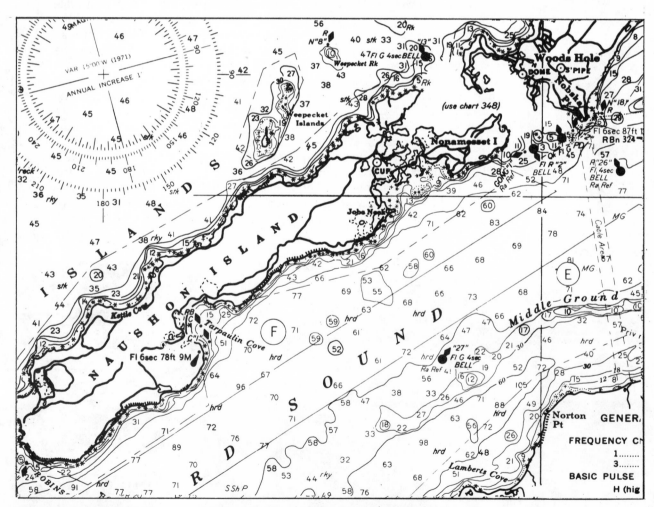

FIG. 1802   A nautical chart is a representation in miniature of a portion of the earth's surface with emphasis on natural and man-made features of particular interest to the navigator of a ship or boat.

CHARTS VS. MAPS

A *nautical chart,* fig. 1802, is a representation in miniature, on a plane surface, of a portion of the earth's surface emphasizing natural and man-made features of particular interest to a navigator. A map, fig. 1803, is a similar miniature representation for use on land in which the emphasis is on roads, cities, political boundaries, etc. For a boatman to refer to a chart as a "map" is to reveal his lack of nautical knowledge and experience.

A chart covers an area which is primarily water and includes such information as the depth of water, obstructions and other dangers to navigation, and the location and type of aids to navigation. Adjacent land areas are portrayed only in such detail as will aid a navigator—the shoreline, harbor facilities, prominent natural or man-made features, etc. Charts are printed on heavy-weight, durable paper so that they may be used as worksheets on which courses may be plotted and positions determined.

A basic requirement of a nautical chart is to provide the navigator with the proper information to enable him to make the *right* decision *in time to avoid danger.* Charts are prepared by various agencies of the Government to furnish the pilot or navigator with absolutely accurate representations of navigable bodies of water showing the depths, aids to navigation, shorelines, and other essential features. They differ from road maps both in the great amount of detailed information that they contain and in the precision with which they are constructed. The need for this accuracy can be appreciated when it is realized that an error of only a small amount in charting the position of a submerged obstruction could constitute a serious menace to navigation.

Several major oil companies produce a series of "cruising guides" which cover important boating areas, fig. 1804. These are useful in planning a nautical trip, but lack the detail, accuracy, and provision for revisions between printings (by means of Notices to Mariners) required for actual navigational use. Do *not* try to substitute them for official government charts.

GEOGRAPHIC COORDINATES

Charts will also show a grid of intersecting lines to aid in the description of a position on the water. These lines are the charted representations of a system of *geographic coordinates* which exist on the earth's surface, although in an unseen, imaginary sense like state boundaries.

The earth is nearly spherical in shape—it is slightly flattened along the polar axis, but the distortion is slight and

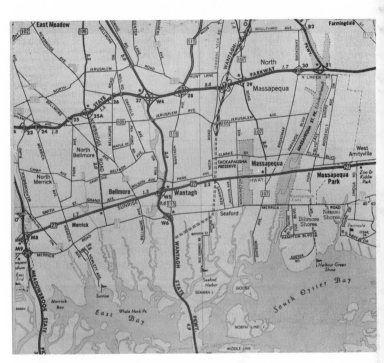

© General Drafting Co., Inc.

FIG. 1803 A map differs from a nautical chart in that the emphasis is on towns, roads, political boundaries, etc. It is designed primarily for motorists and should never be used for navigation.

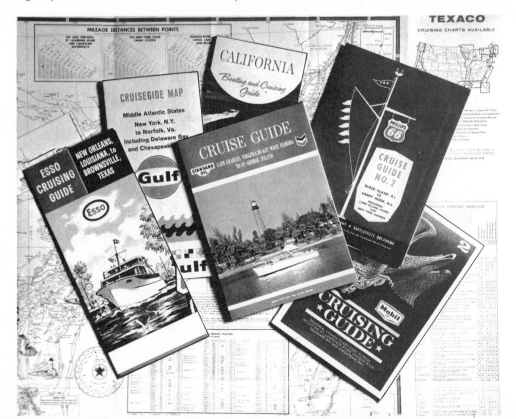

FIG. 1804 The major oil companies issue "cruising guides" which may be of great value in planning a cruise, but should never be depended upon for the actual navigation of a boat.

need be of concern only to scientists, not boatmen. A *great circle,* fig. 1805a, is the line traced out on the surface of a sphere by a plane cutting through the sphere at its center. This is the largest circle that can be drawn on the surface of a sphere. A *small circle,* fig. 1805b, is one marked on the surface of a sphere by a plane that does not pass through its center.

Meridians and parallels

Geographic coordinates are defined by two sets of great and small circles. One is a set of great circles each of which passes through the north and south geographic poles — these are the *meridians of longitude,* fig. 1806. The other set is a series of circles each established by a plane cutting through the earth perpendicular to the polar axis. The

For greater precision in position definition, degrees may be subdivided into *minutes* (60 minutes = 1 degree) and *seconds* (60 seconds = 1 minute).

From figures 1808b and 1809, it will be seen that the meridians of longitude get closer together as one moves away from the equator in either direction, and eventually converge at the poles. Thus the distance on the earth's surface between adjacent meridians is not a fixed quantity but varies with latitude. On the other hand, the parallels of latitude are essentially equally spaced and the distance between successive parallels is nearly the same. One degree of latitude is, for all practical purposes, 60 nautical miles: and *one minute of latitude may be taken as one nautical mile,* a relationship which we will later see is quite useful.

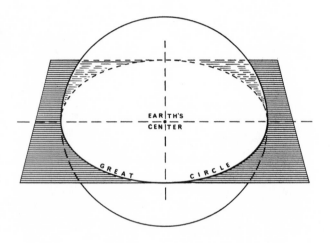

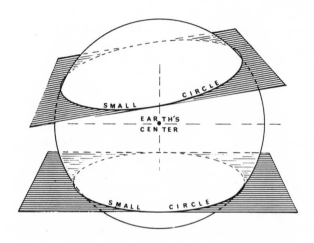

FIG. 1805 a   A GREAT CIRCLE is the line traced out on the surface of a sphere by a plane cutting through the center point of the sphere.   (From Dutton)

FIG. 1805 b   A SMALL CIRCLE is the line traced on the surface of a sphere by a plane which cuts through the sphere but does NOT pass through the center point of the sphere.

largest of these is midway between the poles and thus passes through the center of the earth, becoming a great circle; this is the *equator,* fig. 1807a. Other parallel planes form small circles which are known as the *parallels of latitude,* fig. 1807b.

Geographic coordinates are measured in terms of degrees (one degree is 1/360th of a complete circle). The meridian that passes through Greenwich, England is the reference for all measurements of longitude and is designated as the *prime meridian,* or 0°. The longitude of any position on earth is described as —° East or West of Greenwich, to a maximum in either direction of 180°. The measurement can be thought of as either the angle at the north and south poles between the meridian of the place being described and the prime meridian, or as the arc along the equator between these meridians, fig. 1808a. The designation of "E" or "W" is an essential part of any statement of longitude, abbreviated as "long." or "λ" (the Greek letter lambda).

Parallels of latitude are measured in degrees North or South from the equator, from 0° at the equator to 90° at each pole. The designation of latitude (abbreviated "L") as "N" or "S" is necessary for a complete description of position, fig. 1808b.

FIG. 1806   MERIDIANS of LONGITUDE are formed on the earth's surface by great circles which pass through the North and South Poles.
(From Bowditch)

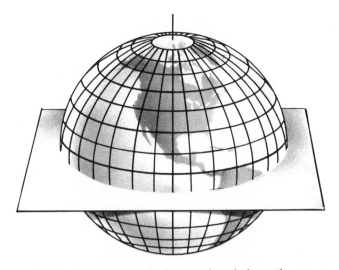

FIG. 1807 a The great circle that cuts through the earth perpendicular to the polar axis traces out the EQUATOR at the earth's surface.

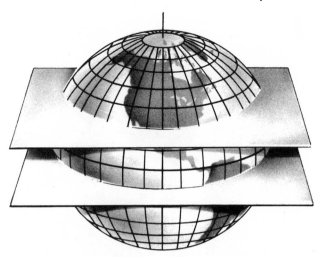

FIG. 1807 b PARALLELS of LATITUDE are the small circles formed at the earth's surface by planes perpendicular to the polar axis but not passing through the center of the earth. They are parallel to the plane of the Equator.

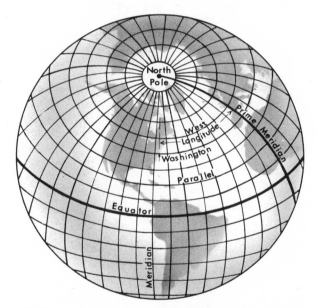

FIG. 1808 a Longitude is measured in degrees from the Prime Meridian (0°), which passes through Greenwich, England, East or West to a maximum of 180°. The designation of "E" or "W" is an essential part of any statement of longitude.

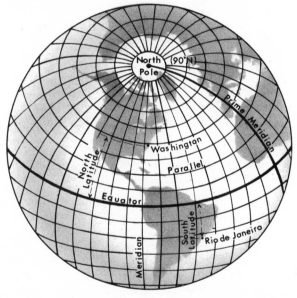

FIG. 1808 b Latitude is measured in either direction, North or South, from the Equator (0°) to the Poles (90°). Statements of latitude, abbreviated "L", must be labeled either "N" or "S" to be complete.
(From Bowditch)

CHART CONSTRUCTION

The construction of a chart for a portion of the earth's surface immediately produces the problem of representation of a spherical, three-dimensional surface on a plane, two-dimensional sheet of paper. Actually, it is impossible to accomplish this exactly. A certain amount of distortion is inevitable, but various methods, called *projections*, have been developed which provide practical and sufficiently accurate results.

The transfer of information from the sphere to the flat surface of the chart should be accomplished with as little distortion as possible in the shape and size of land and water areas, the angular relation of positions, the distance between points, and other more technical properties. Each of the different projections is superior to others in one or more of these qualities; none is superior in all characteristics. In all projections, as the area covered by the chart is decreased, the distortion diminishes, and the difference between various types of projections lessens.

Of the many techniques of projection that might be used, two are of primary interest to boatmen. The *Mercator projection* is an example of the most common; it is used for charts of ocean and coastal areas. The *polyconic projection* is employed for charts of the Great Lakes and inland rivers. The average skipper can quite safely navigate his boat using either type of chart without a deep knowledge of the techniques of projection. (For those who would know more of the various projection methods, see pages 359-363.

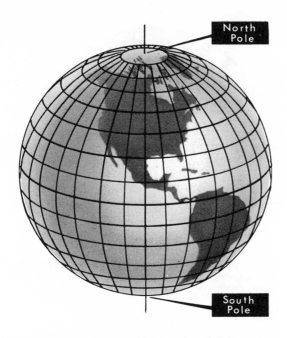

FIG. 1809 Meridians of longitude converge toward each other as one moves away from the Equator in the direction of either pole. All meridians meet at the North and South Poles.

DIRECTION

Direction is defined as the angle between a line connecting one point with another point and a base, or reference, line extending from the origin point toward the true or magnetic north pole; the angle is measured in degrees clockwise from the reference line. Thus direction on charts may be described as so many degrees "True" (T) or so many degrees "Magnetic" (M). The difference between these directions is "variation" and must be allowed for as described in Chapter 13. The principal difference in the use of charts on the Mercator projection and those on the polyconic projection lies in the techniques for measuring direction; this will be covered in Chapter 19 when the use of piloting instruments is considered.

Measurement of direction

To facilitate the measurement of direction, as in plotting bearings and laying out courses, most charts will have compass roses printed on them. A *compass rose,* fig. 1810, consists of two or three concentric circles, several inches in diameter and accurately subdivided. The outer circle has its zero at *true* north; this is emphasized with a star. The inner circle or circles are oriented to magnetic north. The middle circle, if there are three, is *magnetic* direction expressed in degrees, with an arrow printed over the zero point to indicate magnetic north. The innermost circle is also magnetic direction, but in terms of "points," and halves and quarters thereof; its use by modern boatmen will be limited. (One point = 11¼ degrees.) This innermost circle using the point system of subdivision may be omitted on some charts of the "small-craft" series.

The difference between the orientation of the two sets of circles is, of course, the magnetic variation at the loca-

tion of the compass rose. The amount of the variation and its direction (Easterly or Westerly) is given in words and figures in the center of the rose, together with a statement of the year that such variation existed and the annual rate of change. When using a chart in a year later than the date shown on the compass rose, it *may* be necessary to modify the variation shown by applying the annual rate of change. Such cases are, however, relatively rare as rates are quite small and differences of a small fraction of a degree may be ignored from a practical standpoint.

Each chart will have several compass roses printed on it at convenient locations where they will not conflict with navigational information. Roses printed on land areas may cause the elimination of topographical features in these regions.

Until a skipper has thoroughly mastered the handling of compass "errors," he should use only true directions and the true (outer) compass rose. Later, the magnetic rose may be used directly, thus simplifying computations.

Several cautions are necessary when measuring directions on charts. When large areas are covered, it is possible for the magnetic variation to differ for various portions of the chart. Check each chart when you first start to use it, and, to be sure, always use the compass rose nearest the area for which you are plotting. Depending upon the type and scale of the chart, graduations on the compass rose circles may be for intervals of 1°, 2°, or 5°. On some charts, the outer circle (true) is subdivided into units of 1° while the inner (magnetic) circle, being smaller, is subdivided into steps of 2°. Always check carefully to determine the interval between adjacent marks on each compass rose scale.

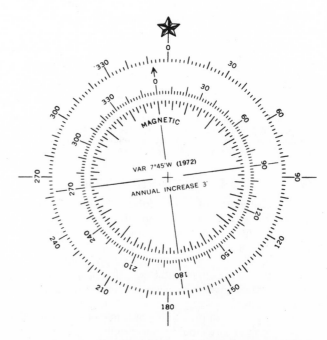

FIG. 1810 A compass rose graphically illustrates true and magnetic directions. The outer circle is in degrees with zero at true north. The inner circles are in degrees and "points" with their zero oriented to the magnetic north. Several will be found on each chart conveniently located for plotting courses and bearings.

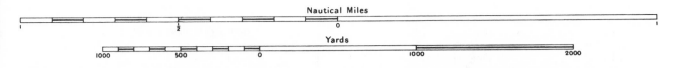

FIG. 1811 N.O.S. charts at scales of 1:80,000 or larger will have two sets of graphic scales. Each set consists of a scale of nautical miles and a scale of yards. On Intracoastal Waterway Charts, a scale of statute miles will also be shown. With the growing conversion to the metric system, some future chart editions will additionally carry a scale of kilometers.

DISTANCE

Distances on charts may be measured in statute or in nautical miles. The *statute (land) mile* of 5280 feet is the same as used on road maps; its use in boating is limited to the Great Lakes, inland lakes and rivers, and, since 1969, the Atlantic and Gulf Intracoastal Waterways. The *nautical mile* of 6076.1 feet is used on ocean and coastal waters.

It is sometimes necessary to convert from one unit to the other. This is not difficult—*1 nautical mile = 1.15 statute miles,* or roughly 7 nautical miles = 8 statute miles.

In navigation, distances of up to a mile or so usually are expressed in *yards,* a unit that is the same no matter which "mile" is used on the chart.

SCALE

As a chart is a representation in miniature of an area of navigable water, actual distances must be "scaled down" to much shorter dimensions on paper. This reduction is termed the *scale* of the chart. The basic way of describing the scale of a chart is its so-called *natural scale,* an expression of the relationship between a given distance on the chart to the actual distance that it represents on the earth. This may be expressed as a ratio, 1:80,000 meaning that 1 unit on the chart represents 80,000 units on the actual land or water surface, or as a fraction $\frac{1}{80,000}$ with the same meaning.

The ratio of chart to actual distance can also be expressed as a *numerical* or *equivalent scale.* This is such a statement as "1 inch = 1.1 miles," another way of expressing a 1:80,000 scale. Equivalent scales are not as commonly used on nautical charts as on maps, but they may be encountered from time to time on such publications as cruising guides.

It is important that at all times the pilot have clearly fixed in his mind the scale of the chart then being used—in order that he will not misjudge the distance to aids to navigation, dangers, etc. Quite often in a day's cruise, a skipper will use charts of different scales, changing back and forth between small-scale coastal charts and larger-scale harbor charts. Unless he is keenly aware of the scale

of the chart being used at the moment, a pilot may find himself unexpectedly in a dangerous position.

Large-scale and small-scale

When chart scales are expressed fractionally, confusion sometimes results from the use of the terms "large-scale" and "small-scale." Since the number that is varied to change the scale is in the *denominator* of the fraction, as it gets larger, the fraction, and hence the scale, gets smaller. For example, $\frac{1}{80,000}$ is a smaller fraction than $\frac{1}{40,000}$, and thus a chart to the former scale is termed a smaller-scale chart. The terms "large-scale" and "small-scale" are relative and have no limiting definitions. Scales may be as large as 1:5,000 for detailed harbor charts, or as small as 1 to several million for charts of large areas of the world.

Charts at a scale of 1:80,000 or larger will normally carry, in addition to a statement of scale, two sets of *graphic scales,* fig. 1811, each subdivided into conveniently and commonly used units. Note that one basic unit is placed to the *left* of the scale's zero point and is subdivided more finely than is the main part of the scale. The use of these graphic scales will be covered in Chapter 19.

When using Mercator charts, the navigator can take advantage of the fact that one minute of the *latitude* scale on each *side* of the chart is essentially equal to one nautical mile. On charts of a scale smaller than 1:80,000, the latitude scale will be the only means of measuring distance.

A *logarithmic speed scale,* fig. 1812, is printed on all charts of 1:40,000 or larger scale. Its use is explained in Chapter 19.

SOURCES OF CHARTS

Who issues charts

Charts are prepared and issued by several agencies of the Federal Government. This is not duplication, however, as different areas and types of charts are the responsibility of each office. The majority of boatmen will use charts prepared by the National Ocean Survey of the National

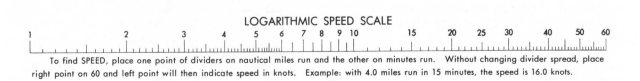

FIG. 1812 N.O.S. charts of 1:40,000 or larger scale will have a LOGARITHMIC SPEED SCALE from which a graphic calculation of speed may be made if the time of run is measured between two known points. See Chapter 19 for a detailed discussion of its use.

Oceanic & Atmospheric Administration, Department of Commerce. N.O.S. charts cover the coastal waters of the United States, including harbors and rivers extending inland to the head of tidal action.

On 1 July 1972, the Defense Mapping Agency was created by combining the mapping, charting, and geodetic activities of the Military Departments. The Naval Oceanographic Office became the Defense Mapping Agency Hydrographic Center. DMAHC publishes charts of the high seas and foreign waters based on its own and other nations' surveys. Boatmen will use DMAHC charts, for example, when cruising in the Bahamas. (The "N.O." prefix, which replaced the old "H.O." when charts were renumbered, has now been dropped and no prefix is used.) Canadian waters, however, are charted by that country's Hydrographic Service.

The Lake Survey Center of N.O.S. prepares and publishes charts of the Great Lakes, Lake Champlain, N.Y. State Barge Canal, and the Minnesota-Ontario Border Lakes.

Charts of major inland rivers such as the Mississippi and Ohio are issued by the U.S. Army Corps of Engineers. Also available are charts and "Navigational maps" of many inland lakes and canal systems.

Where to buy them

Charts may be purchased directly from the headquarters or field offices of the issuing agencies, or from retail sales agents. The government offices may be addressed as shown in fig. 1813. Sales agents are widely located in boating and shipping centers. The names of sales agents for N.O.S. and DMAHC charts are listed in Coast Pilots and periodically in Notices to Mariners as discussed in Chapter 17. Lake Survey charts are sold by designated offices as listed in their Chart Catalog and the Great Lakes Pilot. The Lake Survey is also establishing a system of local sales agents for their publications.

The cost of charts is amazingly little for the vast amount of information furnished to the navigator. The prices charged for charts include only a small part of the cost to the government for their production. Traditionally, it has been the duty of a country to aid safe navigation by publishing low-cost charts and nautical guides. Recent increases in chart prices have reflected only the general rise in costs, not a change in pricing policy.

N.O.S., Lake Survey, and DMAHC charts are sold by government offices and sales agents located in most boating

---

CHART ISSUING AGENCIES

⚓ National Ocean Survey, NOAA
Rockville, Maryland 20852

⚓ Defense Mapping Agency Hydrographic Center
Washington, D.C. 20390

FIG. 1813 Information on nautical charts can be obtained by writing to the appropriate headquarters at the address shown above. Regional and District Offices may also be able to provide answers to questions on charts.

---

areas; a discount is allowed to each dealer for his quantity purchases. Yacht clubs, boating organizations, etc., also may purchase charts in quantity for a discount; get details from the issuing agency.

The prudent skipper carries on his boat a full set of charts covering the waters that he cruises, and he regularly replaces worn-out or outdated charts with new ones. Charts are among his best boating bargains!

Chart catalogs

Catalogs are available from issuing agencies which indicate the area covered by each chart, the scale used, and the price. These will be found useful when planning a cruise into unfamiliar boating waters.

The N.O.S. catalog is issued in three volumes, each a large, accordion-folded sheet; they are free. Volume 1 covers the U.S. Atlantic and Gulf coastal waters. Volume 2 is for the West Coast and Pacific Islands. Volume 3 covers the Alaskan Coast.

DMAHC chart catalog, publication number 1-N, is issued in "Regions" at a price of 25¢ each. Region "0" covers U.S. coastal waters; Region "2" includes the Bahamian and West Indian cruising areas as well as the waters bordering Central and South America.

The Lake Survey annually publishes its chart catalog covering the Great Lakes, Lake Champlain, the New York Barge Canal System, and other waters. It is available without charge upon request.

What Charts Show

Charts include a great amount of information and a boatman should carefully study each chart soon after he purchases it, certainly well before he must use it to safely navigate his craft.

BASIC INFORMATION

Located at some convenient place on the chart, where space is available, will be found the *general information block,* fig. 1814. Here is the chart title which is descriptive of the waters covered (the chart number will not appear

here, but rather in several places around the margins), a statement of the type of projection used and the scale, the unit of measurement of depth (feet or fathoms—one fathom equals six feet—or meters), and the datum plane for such soundings.

Elsewhere on the chart where there is space available (normally in land areas), other information will be found, such as the meaning of abbreviations used on this chart, special notes of caution regarding dangers, the units of measurement of heights and the reference plane from

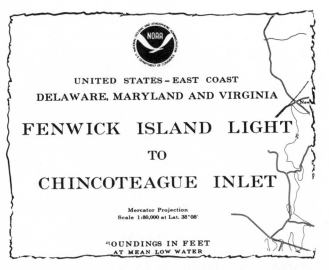

FIG. 1814 The title block shows the official name of the chart, the type of projection, scale, and datum and unit of measurement for depths. Printed nearby will be much valuable information—be sure to read all notes and data before using any chart.

which measured, tidal information, references to anchorage areas, and many other useful bits of data. *All* notes on charts should be read carefully and fully, as they may cover important information that cannot be graphically presented, such information applying to an extended length of a river or channel; see fig. 1815.

Editions and revisions

The edition number and date appear in the margin at the lower left-hand corner; immediately following these figures will be the date of the latest revised printing, if any. Figures 1816a and b illustrate these two cases. The typical nautical chart is printed to supply the normal demand for one or two years; quantities are so limited to provide for bringing it up to date as frequently as practicable. Charts may be reprinted as-is when the stock runs low, but a revised printing is more likely. Revisions include all changes that have been printed in Notices to Mariners since the preceding issue of the chart. When major changes in hydrography occur, such as new surveys revealing significant differences between charted depths and actual conditions, a new edition is published; it, too, will include all other changes which have been made in aids to navigation, etc.

Special charts, for which there is an urgent need, are printed directly from smooth drafting without engraving; these are designated as "Provisional Charts" and are so labeled in the title block. A chart constructed from unverified information will be marked as a "Preliminary Chart."

It is of the utmost importance that only the latest edition of a chart be used. All new editions supersede older issues, which should be discarded. New editions contain information published in Notices to Mariners, *plus* all other corrections that were too extensive for hand-application and so were not published in the Notices. Skippers are cautioned against using superceded charts that may not contain all information essential to safe navigation.

Between editions, charts should be corrected from information published in Notices to Mariners (see page 335). Charts are no longer kept corrected by the National Ocean Survey while in stock awaiting sale. The pur-

chaser of a chart should make every effort to check all Notices subsequent to the printed edition date and enter all applicable corrections. The safest chart is the one that is fully corrected up to date.

LATITUDE AND LONGITUDE SCALES

Nautical charts of the conventional type with the geographical north direction toward the top of the sheet will have latitude scales in each side border and longitude scales in the top and bottom borders. The meridians and parallels will be drawn across the chart as fine black lines at intervals of 2', 5', or 10' as determined by the scale of the particular chart.

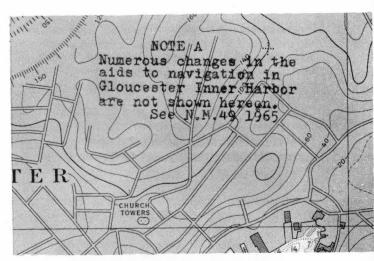

FIG. 1815 Charts will often have printed notes with information of considerable importance. These may concern navigation regulations, hazardous conditions at inlets, information on controlling depths that cannot be conveniently printed alongside the channel (as above), or other matters. Check each chart that you buy for such notes and read them carefully.

FIG. 1816 a The edition number and date are printed in the margin of each N.O.S. chart in the lower-left corner. Also shown here are the chart number

FIG. 1816 b Between editions, revised printings are made of charts to include all changes that have been published in Notices to Mariners. Be safe—do not use obsolete charts!

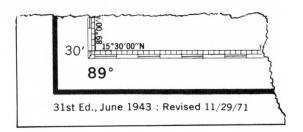

31st Ed., June 1943 : Revised 11/29/71

On N.O.S. charts having a scale larger than 1:49,000, such as on harbor charts, the subdivisions in the border scales are in terms of minutes and seconds of latitude and longitude, fig. 1818a.

On smaller-scale charts, the subdivisions are in minutes and fractions of minutes—charts at a scale of 1:80,000, such as 1210Tr, use minutes and tenths of minutes, fig. 1818b. Still smaller scale charts will use fifths or halves of minutes.

Where skewed projections are used, and north is not toward the top of the sheet, as on Intracoastal Waterway charts, the subdivisions of latitude and longitude are indicated along parallels and meridians at several convenient places, or near the graphic scales.

USE OF COLOR

Nearly all charts use color, pages M and N, to emphasize various features, and thus facilitate chart reading and interpretation. The number of different colors will vary with the agency publishing the chart and with its intended use. The National Ocean Survey makes use of five colors (and several shades of some of these) on their regular charts.

Land areas are shown in buff or yellowish color; water areas are white, the color of the paper, except for the shallower regions which are in blue. Areas that may be submerged at some tidal stages, but which uncover at others, are represented in green. Sand bars, mud flats, coral reefs, and marshes are typical of such green areas on charts. On some charts, water areas that have been swept with wire drags to ensure the absence of isolated rocks or coral heads may be shown in a greenish half-tone with the depth of the sweep indicated. This shade of green is lighter than the solid color used for uncovering areas and no confusion should result.

Nautical purple ink is used for many purposes on charts; it was selected for its good visibility under red light which is used on many vessels for reading charts during darkness because it does not destroy night vision as white light would. Red buoys are printed in this color, as are red daybeacon symbols. Lighted buoys of any color have a purple disc superimposed over the dot portion of the symbol to assist in its identification as a lighted aid to navigation. This same scheme is used with lighthouses, lights, lighted ranges, etc. Caution and danger symbols and notes are printed in nautical purple; also compass roses and recommended courses where shown. Black, of course, is used for most symbols and the bulk of printed information.

LETTERING STYLES

In order to convey to the chart reader as much information as possible in the clearest form, a system has been adopted whereby certain classes of information are printed in one style of lettering and other classes in another style.

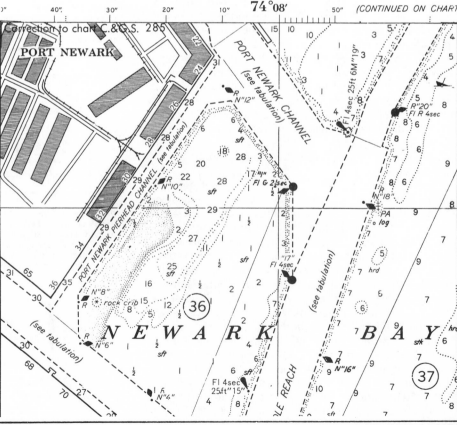

FIG. 1817 N.O.S. and Defense Mapping Agency Hydrographic Center (DMAHC) charts, and Light Lists and Coast Pilots, are corrected by Notices to Mariners. Illustrated is a typical extract showing some changes in Newark Bay, N.J. Not all corrections require a reproduction from the chart affected (in this case No. 285). The ammended section of chart shown is provided in the Notice as a loose insertion. The notes indicate which chart and Coast Pilot are affected.

★ 7(586)74. (12) NEW YORK AND NEW JERSEY—New York Harbor—Newark Bay—Chart amendment.—The accompanying reproduction of a portion of C. & G.S. Chart 285 shows changes in channel alignment, hydrography and aids to navigation.

Position: 40°40'30'' N., 74°08'00'' W.

NM 7 Feb. 16, 1974

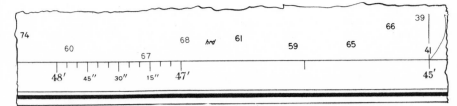

FIG. 1818 a On charts with scales of 1:49,000 or larger, the longitude and latitude scales in the borders are subdivided into minutes and seconds. On this extract from a 1:40,000 harbor chart, meridians are drawn at 5-minute intervals, tick marks are placed every minute, and one 1-minute interval is subdivided into units of 5 seconds each.

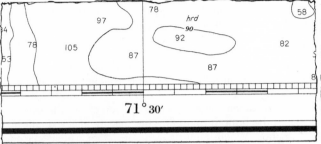

FIG. 1818(b) On charts with relatively small scales, the latitude and longitude border markings will be in minutes and fractions of minutes. On this 1:80,000 chart, meridians are drawn in every 10 minutes and the subdivisions are in minutes and tenths of minutes. On yet smaller scale charts, the smallest subdivision might be fifths, halves, or whole minutes of latitude and longitude.

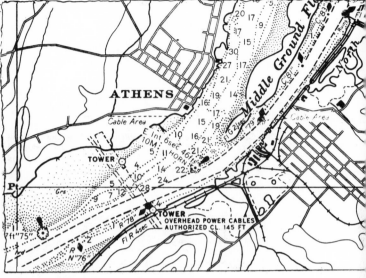

FIG. 1819 This chart excerpt illustrates the use of vertical lettering for features above water—"TOWER"—and leaning letters for underwater features—"hrd" and "Grs" for hard and grassy bottom at two places. Note also the designation of a CABLE AREA.

By knowing what type of lettering is used for which class of information, one can more easily and quickly grasp the data being presented.

VERTICAL lettering is used for features which are dry at high water and are not affected by movement of the water, except for the height of the feature above the water, which may be changed by tidal action. See the use of vertical lettering for the power line towers and the bell fog signal in fig. 1819.

LEANING, or slanting, lettering *(such as this)* is used for water, underwater, and floating features, except depth figures. Note the use in fig. 1819 of leaning lettering for *"hrd S"* meaning a hard sand bottom at that point.

On smaller-scale charts, a small reef (covering and uncovering with tidal action) often cannot be distinguished by symbol from a small islet (always above water); the proper name for either might be "— Rock." Following the standard of lettering, the feature in doubt is an islet if the name is in vertical letters, but is a reef if lettered in leaning characters.

Similarly, a piling visible above water at all tidal stages will be charted as "Pile," but one beneath the surface will be noted as *"subm pile."*

Periods after abbreviations are omitted in water and in land areas, but the lower-case *i* and *j* are dotted. Periods are used only where needed for clarity, as, for example, in certain notes.

WATER FEATURES

The information shown on charts is a combination of the natural features of the water and land areas and various selected man-made objects and features. Each item shown will have been carefully chosen for its value to those navigating vessels of all sizes.

Depths

The principal feature of concern to boatmen and mariners regarding water areas is the *depth*. For any system of depth information, there must be a reference plane, or *datum*. This is obvious in coastal areas where depths may change hourly as a result of tidal action; it is likewise true in inland areas where lake or river levels may also change, though more slowly on a seasonal basis. Each chart will have printed on it a statement of the datum from which all depths, also called *soundings,* are measured. The choice of the reference plane is based on many factors, most of them technical, but the primary consideration is that of selecting a datum near to normal low-water levels.

Planes of reference

Different planes of reference are used on charts of various boating areas. For charts along the Atlantic seaboard, the National Ocean Survey uses *mean low water* as the datum for soundings. On the Pacific Coast it is the *mean lower low water* that is used as a reference plane. (In some areas, one of the two daily low tides is markedly lower than the other—see Chapter 20 for a detailed discussion of tides.) Lake and river charts will generally use a datum which is based on past records of variations in level over many years. When entering strange waters, always be sure to check the chart for the statement of the datum used for depths.

Since by definition, "mean low water" is an average of low tide stages over a period of time, it can be seen that on approximately half the days individual low-water levels may be lower than the datum. This will result in actual

347

depths being shallower than the charted figures. However, these variations are not often great enough to affect navigation. Many charts will have a small box with a tabulation of the extreme variations from charted depths that may be expected, fig. 1820. Prolonged winds from certain directions, or persistent extremes of barometric pressure, may cause temporary local differences from charted depths. *It must always be remembered that exceptional conditions may occur at which time the water may be much shallower than indicated on the chart.*

	TIDAL INFORMATION			
Place	Height referred to datum of soundings (MLW)			
	Mean High Water	Mean Tide Level	Mean Low Water	Extreme Low Water
	feet	feet	feet	feet
Wilmington, Del.	5.3	2.9	0.0	−4.0
Chester, Pa.	5.4	2.9	0.0	−4.0
Billingsport, N.J.	5.5	3.0	0.0	−4.5
Phila. Pier 9N., Pa.	5.8	3.1	0.0	−5.0

FIG. 1820 Coast and Harbor Charts will usually have information on the normal range of tides and the extreme variations from charted depths that may be expected. Check all newly-purchased charts for this important information.

How depths are shown

Depth information is shown on the chart by many small printed figures. These indicate the depth at that point measured in feet or fathoms. A few charts may mix these units, using feet in shallower areas and fathoms offshore in deeper waters; such charts are relatively rare. Some newer charts have depths measured in meters and decimeters (tenths of a meter). The depth figures are only a small part of the many soundings taken by survey teams. Only the more significant and representative depths are selected for printing on the final chart.

The boatman can form some opinion of the characteristics of the bottom by noting the density of the depth information. Where depth figures are rather widely spaced, he can be assured of a reasonably flat or uniformly sloping bottom. Wherever the depths vary irregularly or abruptly, the figures will be more frequent and more closely spaced.

Fathom curves

Most charts will have *contour lines,* sometimes called *fathom curves,* connecting points of equal depth. Such lines will appear at certain depths as determined by the scale of the chart and the relative range of the depths. Typically, fathom curves are shown for 1, 2, 3 5, 10, and multiples of ten fathoms. Continuous solid lines or various combinations of dots and dashes are used to code the depth along each line, but it is often easier to learn a line's significance by inspection of the depth figures on either side of it.

On many charts, a blue tint is shown in water areas out to the curve that is considered to be the danger curve for that particular chart. In general, the 6-foot curve is considered the danger curve for small-craft and Intracoastal Waterway charts, the 12- or 18-foot curve for harbor charts, and the 30-foot curve for coast and general charts. (These types of charts are discussed in more detail on pages 356-358.) In some instances, the area between the 3-fathom and the 5- or 6-fathom curves may be tinted in a lighter shade of blue than the shallower areas. Thus it can be seen that while blue tint means shallow water, this symbolism does not have the same exact meaning on all charts. Check each chart that you use to determine at just what depth the coloring changes.

Charts on which no fathom curves are marked for water areas must be regarded with some suspicion and used with caution as this may indicate that soundings are too scarce to allow the lines to be drawn with accuracy.

Isolated soundings, shoaler than surrounding depths, should always be avoided, particularly if ringed around, as it is doubtful how closely the spot may have been examined and whether the least depth has been found.

Dredged channels

Dredged channels are shown on a chart by two dashed lines to represent the side limits of the improvement. The depth of the channel and the date on which such data were obtained will be shown within the lines or close alongside, see fig. 1821. A dredged basin will be similarly outlined with printed information on depths and date.

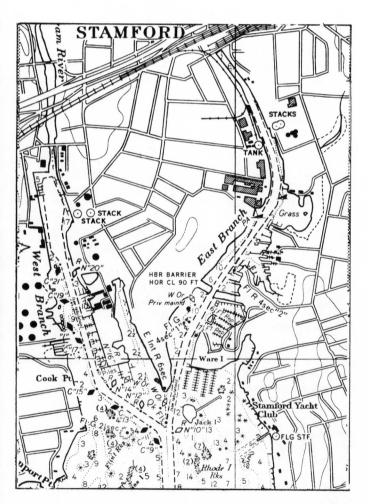

FIG. 1821 The side limits of "improved" (dredged) channels are marked by dashed lines. Information on the depth (and date of measurement) will often be printed between or alongside the dashed lines. In some cases, information on the width of the channel will also be shown.

The depth shown, such as "6 feet 1965," is the controlling depth through the channel on the date shown but does not mean that this depth exists over the full width of the channel.

Channels are sometimes described on charts in terms of specific width as well as depth; for example, "8 feet for width of 100 feet." The printing of such depth information does not insure that it may not have subsequently changed due to either shoaling or further dredging. Such changes do occur, and therefore if your craft's draft is close to the depth shown for the channel, local information on existing conditions should be obtained if possible before entering.

Detailed information for many dredged channels is shown in tabular form on the applicable charts, with revisions of the data published in Notices to Mariners as changes occur.

Nature of the bottom

The nature of the bottom, such as sand, rocky, mud, grass, etc., or a more general description such as "hard" or "soft," will be indicated for many areas by means of abbreviations. This information is of value when anchoring, and advantage should be taken of it wherever it appears. The meanings of these and other abbreviations are usually given on the face of the chart near the basic identification block; many are self-evident, the more frequently encountered ones should be memorized.

The shoreline

The shoreline shown on charts is the mean high-water line except in marsh or mangrove areas where the outer edge of vegetation (berm line) is used. It is represented by a solid line which gradually decreases in width up streams and rivers. Unsurveyed shoreline, or shoreline connecting two surveys that do not join satisfactorily, is represented by a dashed line. The outer limits of marsh are indicated by a fine solid line. On some large-scale charts, a low-water line will be indicated by a single row of dots.

The region between the high- and low-water lines will be tinted green, and may be labeled "Grass," "Mud," "Sand," etc.

FEATURES OF LAND AREAS

Features and characteristics of land areas are shown on nautical charts in only such detail as will be of assistance to a navigator. Details are usually confined to those near the shoreline or of such a prominent nature as to be clearly seen for some distance offshore.

How topography is shown

The general topography of land areas will be indicated by contours, form lines, or hachures. *Contours* are lines connecting points of equal elevation. The specific height, usually measured in feet, of such contour lines may be shown by figures placed at suitable points along the lines. The interval of height between adjacent contours is uniform over any one chart.

Form lines, or *sketch contours,* are shown by broken lines and are approximations of contours intended to give an indication of terrain formations without exact information on height. They are used in areas where accurate data are not available in sufficient quantity to permit the exact location of contours. The interval between form lines is not necessarily uniform and no height figures are given.

Hachures are short lines, or groups of lines, indicating approximately the location of steep slopes. The lines follow generally the direction of the slope, the length of the lines indicating the height of the slope.

Cliffs, vegetation and the shore

Cliffs are represented by bands of irregular hachures. The symbol is not an exact "plan view," but rather somewhat of a "side elevation"; its extent is roughly proportional to the height of the cliff. For example, a perpendicular cliff of 100 feet height will be shown by a hachured band wider than one representing a cliff of 15 feet with

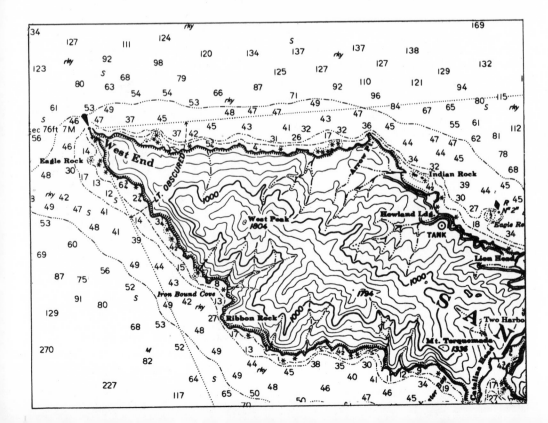

FIG. 1822 Information on the elevation of hills or mountain summits, or the tops of conspicuous landmarks, is often printed on a nautical chart. Heights are usually measured from Mean High Water in feet, but meters and decimeters (tenths of a meter) are now being used on some charts.

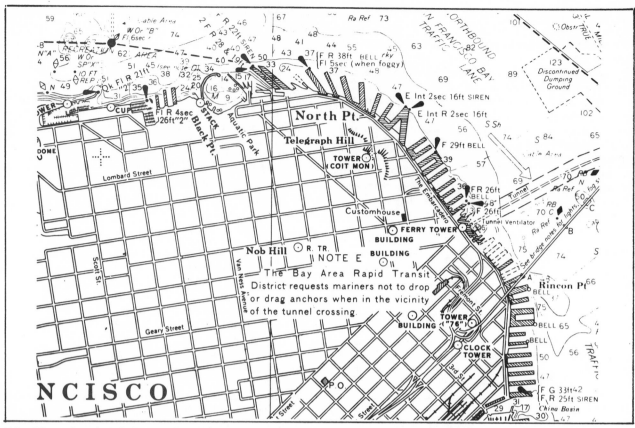

FIG. 1823 a On relatively large-scale charts, detailed information may be shown of the streets and buildings of a city or town, particularly near the waterfront. Some street names may be given, also the location of public buildings such as a customhouse and post office.

slope. According to the principles of "plan" drawing (viewing from directly above), a perpendicular cliff would be shown by one line only and could not be distinguished from an ordinary shoreline.

Spot elevations are normally given on nautical charts only for summits or the tops of conspicuous landmarks, fig. 1822. Heights are measured from mean high water.

The type of vegetation on land will sometimes be indicated by symbols or wording where such information may be of use to the mariner.

The nature of the shore is indicated by various symbols—rows of fine dots denote a sandy beach, small circles indicate gravel, irregular shapes mean boulders, etc.

MAN-MADE FEATURES

Man-made features on land will be shown in detail where they relate directly to water-borne traffic. Examples of these are piers, bridges, overhead power cables, and breakwaters. Other man-made features on land, such as built-up areas, roads, streets, etc., will be shown in some detail or will be generalized as determined by their usefulness to navigation and the scale of the chart. On large-scale charts the actual network of streets will at times be depicted, with public buildings such as the post office and customs house individually identified, fig. 1823a. On less detailed charts, the town or city may be represented by a halftone shaded area for the approximate limits of the built-up area with major streets and roads shown by single heavy lines, see fig. 1823b. Prominent isolated objects, tanks, stacks, spires, etc., will be shown accurately

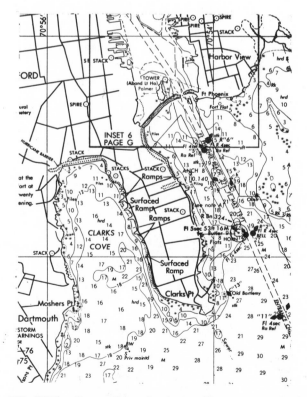

FIG. 1823 b On smaller-scale charts, cities, towns, and other built-up areas are generalized by "screening," a shading process that shows up as a darker, but not black, area. Only principal roads and streets are shown, these by a single, heavy solid line.

located in order that they may be used for taking bearings.

Specific descriptive names have been given to certain types of landmark objects for the purpose of standardizing terminology. Among the more often used are the following:

Building or **House**—the appropriate one of these terms is used when the entire structure is the landmark, rather than any individual feature of it.

Spire—a slender, pointed structure extending above a building. It is seldom less than two-thirds of the entire height of the structure, and its lines are rarely broken by intermediate structures. Spires are typically found on churches.

Dome—a large, rounded, hemispherical structure rising above a building; for example, the dome of the United States Capitol in Washington.

Cupola—a dome-shaped tower or turret rising from a building, generally small in comparison with the size of the building.

Chimney—a relatively small projection for conveying smoke from a building to the atmosphere. This term is used when the building is more prominent than the chimney, but a better bearing can be taken on the smaller feature.

Stack—a tall smokestack or chimney. This term is used when the stack is more prominent as a landmark than the accompanying buildings.

Flagpole—a single staff from which flags are displayed This term is used when the pole is not attached to a building.

Flagstaff—a flagpole arising from a building.

Radio Tower—a tall pole or structure for elevating radio antennas.

Radio Mast—a relatively short pole or slender structure for elevating radio antennas; usually found in groups.

Tower—any structure with its base on the ground and high in proportion to its base, or that part of a structure higher than the rest, but having essentially vertical sides for the greater part of its height.

Lookout Station or **Watch Tower**—a tower surmounted by a small house from which a watch is regularly kept.

Tank—a water tank elevated high above ground by a tall skeleton framework. *Gas Tank* and *Oil Tank* are terms used for distinctive structures of specialized design.

Standpipe—a tall cylindrical structure whose height is several times its diameter.

Tree—an isolated, conspicuous tree useful as a navigational landmark.

When two similar objects are so located that separate landmark symbols cannot be used, the word "TWIN" is added to the identifying name or abbreviation. When only one of a group of similar objects is charted, a descriptive legend is added in parentheses; for example, ("TALLEST OF FOUR)" or "(NORTHEAST OF THREE)".

Radio broadcasting station (AM) antennas are shown on charts where they may be used for taking visual or radio bearings. The call letters and frequency are often shown adjacent to the symbol marking the location of the towers.

Symbols and Abbreviations

The vast amount of information to be shown on a chart, and the closeness with which many items appear, necessitate the extensive use of symbols and abbreviations. It is essential that a boatman have a high degree of familiarity with the symbols and abbreviations encountered on the charts that he uses. A skipper must be able to read and interpret his charts quickly and accurately; the safety of his boat may depend on this ability. Knowledge will come with use, but dependence upon a build-up from experience alone may be costly—specific study is recommended.

INTERNATIONAL STANDARDS

Symbols are conventional shapes and designs which indicate the presence of a certain feature or object at the location shown on the chart. No attempt is made at an accurate or detailed representation of the object, but the correct location is shown. Symbols and abbreviations used on charts of the Defense Mapping Agency Hydrographic Center and National Ocean Survey, including the Lake Survey Center, have been standardized. These are published in a small pamphlet designated as Chart No. 1, available at 50¢ per copy. The same information is also printed on the

reverse side of Training Chart No. 1210Tr. These standardized symbols and abbreviations are in general conformance with world-wide usage as adopted by the International Hydrographic Bureau.

The standardized symbols and abbreviations are shown in figures 1844 a-o; they are grouped into *classifications* and are *numbered* in accordance with Chart No. 1. In these designations, vertical figures indicate that the symbol or abbreviation is in conformity with the standards of the International Hydrographic Bureau. Slanting figures mean that the symbol or abbreviation shown either differs from that of the IHB or else that it does not appear in its standards; those items which differ from the IHB standard are underlined. Where letter designations are enclosed in parentheses, the symbol or abbreviation is in addition to those on the international list.

These standardized abbreviations will be used on all new charts or new editions of existing charts by the National Ocean Survey and the Defense Mapping Agency Hydrographic Center. Older charts may continue to show other symbols and abbreviations until they are next revised and brought into conformity with the latest standards.

Charts / CHAPTER 18

Classification

In Chart No. 1, the standardized symbols and abbreviations are grouped into classifications as follows:

A—The Coast Line
B—Coast Features
C—The Land
D—Control Points
E—Units
F—Adjectives
G—Harbors
H—Topography
I—Buildings
J—Miscellaneous
    Stations
K—Lights
L—Buoys and Beacons
M—Radio Stations
N—Fog Signals
O—Dangers
P—Various Limits
Q—Soundings
R—Depth Contours
S—Quality of the Bottom
T—Tides and Currents
U—The Compass

Chart No. 1 also includes a table for the conversion of meters, fathoms, and feet.

BASIC SYMBOLS & ABBREVIATIONS

Simple inspection of many symbols will reveal a pattern or system to the way that they are formed. Knowledge of the general principles of chart symbols will facilitate learning of the details.

Buoys

Buoys, except mooring buoys, are shown by a diamond-shaped symbol and a small dot; the dot indicates the position of the buoy. To avoid interference with other features on the chart, it is often necessary to show the diamond shape at various angles to the dot; in some instances, the symbol might even appear "upside down." The symbol for a mooring buoy is number L22 in fig. 1844i; the small circle on the base line of the symbol indicates the position of the buoy.

A *black buoy* is shown as a solid black symbol without further identification of color. On charts using the normal number of colors, *red buoys* are shown in magenta; the

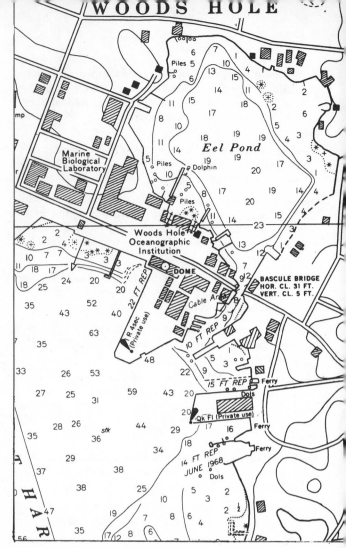

FIG. 1824 Ranges are excellent aids to navigation. They are charted by showing the front and rear markers with a line denoting the center of the range. This line is solid over the portion that is to be navigated, and dashed elsewhere.

FIG. 1825 This is a section from a "sailing chart." These charts, at scales of 1:600,000 or less, are the smallest scale series and cover long stretches of coastline. They are used by vessels approaching the coast from the high seas or when voyaging between distant coast ports.

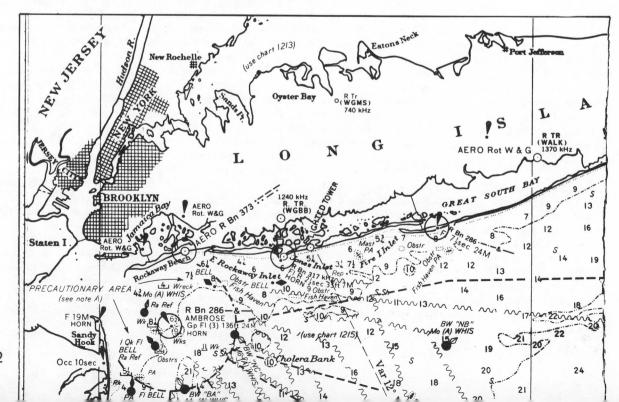

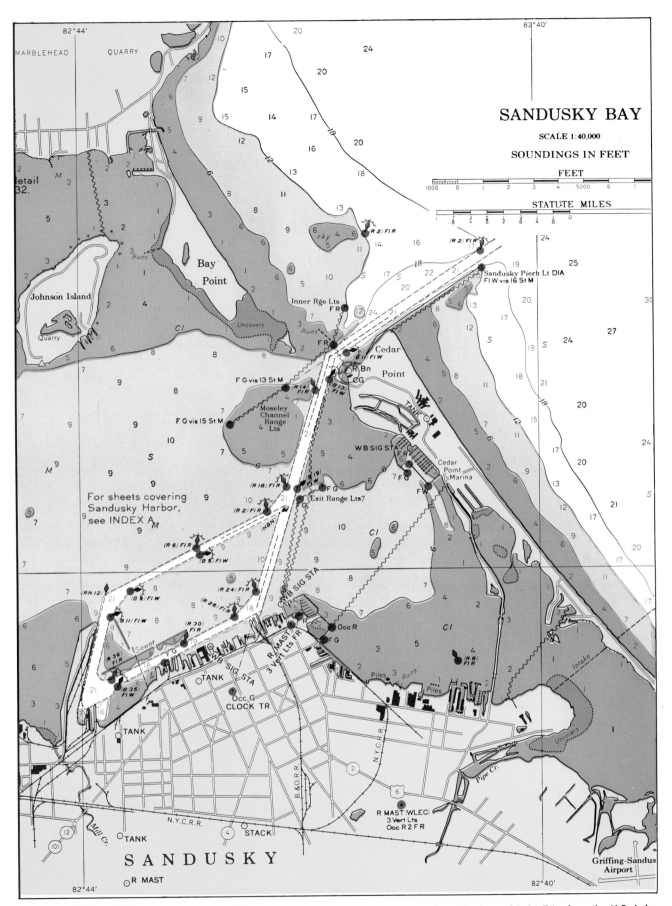

A portion (slightly less than half) of the chart for Sandusky Bay (eastern Bay (eastern end), south shore of Lake Erie, from the U.S. Lake Survey Recreational Craft Series Chart 14842—Port Clinton to Sandusky, Ohio. The spiral-bound volume includes 35 charts—lakes, rivers, harbors, and islands—and much data of value to the boatman. As reproduced above, the scale differs slightly from that (1:40,000) on which the original chart is drawn. Only charts as published by official sources should be used for navigation.

M

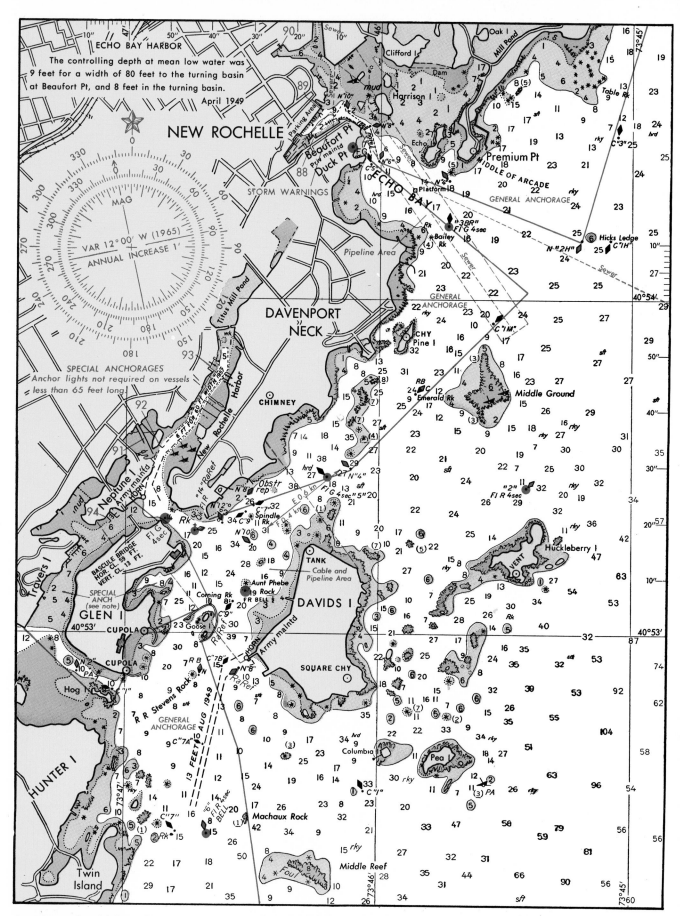

Inset 9 reproduced full-size from the National Ocean Survey's Small Craft series chart number 12364—New Haven Harbor Entrance and Port Jefferson to Throgs Neck—Long Island Sound, Connecticut, New York. Scale of this inset is 1:20,000, in which one mile (see distance on latitude scale from 40°53′ to 40°54′) measures about 3⅝ inches. The Small-Craft series of charts is produced in a format of maximum convenience to the operator of small boats. For more detailed information, see page 357.

N

letter "R" may also be shown adjacent to the symbol. Other buoys are shown by open outline symbols with the color indicated by an appropriate abbreviation, such as "Y" for yellow, "W Or" for white and orange, etc. On charts without colors, red buoys are printed as open symbols with the identifying abbreviation "R."

A buoy symbol with a line across its shorter axis indicates a *horizontally banded buoy*. For a junction buoy, if colors are used, the upper half (away from the dot) will be red and the lower half black. This is true whether in actuality the uppermost band is red (as on a nun buoy) or black (as on a can buoy). The letters "RB" will appear near the symbol. Other kinds of horizontally banded buoys, such as white-and-orange *special purpose buoys,* will be shown by an open symbol with appropriate letters for the colors.

A buoy symbol with a line across its longer axis represents a *vertically striped buoy*. No colors will be used on this symbol; the colors of such a buoy will be indicated by abbreviations, usually "BW" for black and white.

The type and shape of *unlighted buoys* is often indicated by an abbreviation such as "C" for can, "N" for nun, or "S" for spar.

Lighted buoys are indicated by the placing of a small magenta disc over the dot which marks the buoy's position. The color and characteristics of the light are indicated by abbreviations near the symbol. Buoys equipped with a *reflector* to increase their detection by radar are often indicated by the abbreviation "Ra Ref" in addition to other identification.

Daybeacons

The symbol for *daybeacons,* unlighted aids to navigation, is a small triangle. In general, the same scheme for indicating color is used as for buoys except that two colors are not combined in a single symbol. A red-and-black horizontally-banded daybeacon is printed as an open symbol with the description of colors abbreviated "RB."

Lights and Lighthouses

On older charts, lights and lighthouses are shown as black dots with a small magenta disc as for lighted buoys. On newer charts, the symbol will be a black dot with a magenta "flare" giving much the appearance of a large exclamation mark (!). In addition to color and characteristics of the light, there may be information, in abbreviated form, on the height of the light and its range of visibility for a standard height of eye of 15 feet.

Fog Signals

The type of *fog signal* on buoys, lights, and lighthouses so equipped will be indicated by a descriptive word or abbreviation adjacent to the chart symbol.

Identification by number

Buoys and lights are usually *numbered* (or less-frequently, designated with letters or combinations of letters and numbers). This identification is placed on the chart near the symbol and is enclosed in quotation marks to distinguish the figures from depth data or other numbers. Lighthouses and some major lights are named; the words

FIG. 1826   A small portion of Chart 12300. This is at a larger scale than Fig. 1825, but it still lacks many details. "General charts" should be used only for offshore navigation. Only major aids to navigation are shown. For comparison purposes, Figs. 1826 and 1828 show portions of the same area at progressively larger scales.

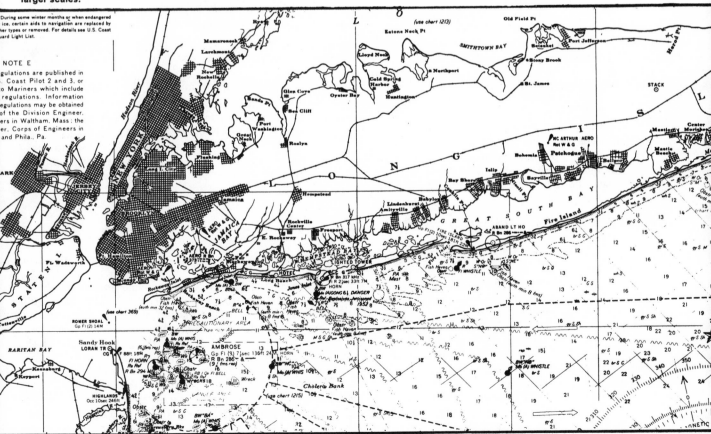

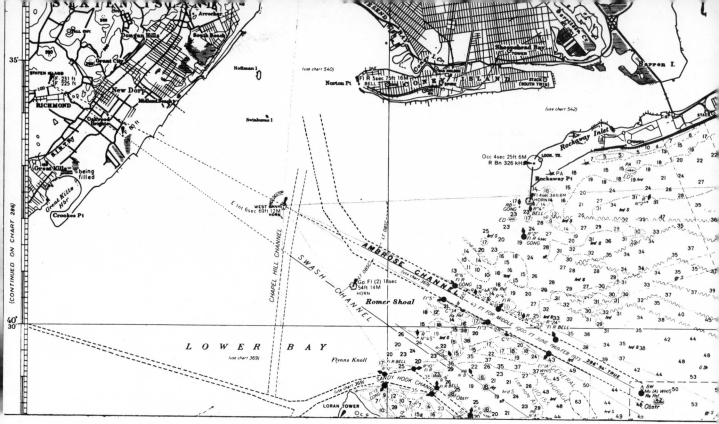

FIG. 1827 A portion of Chart 12326. "Coast charts," usually at a scale of 1:80,000, are used for closein coastwise navigation, entering and leaving harbors, and for cruising on some large inland bodies of water. The scale of this series is such that many more buoys and other aids to navigation can be shown. The depth of water is given in greater detail, the soundings being given in feet.

or abbreviations will be printed near the symbol where space permits.

Ranges

Ranges are indicated by the two symbols of the front and rear markers (lights or daybeacons), plus a line joining them and extending beyond. This line is solid over the distance for which the range is to be used for navigation; it continues on as a dashed line to the front marker and on to the rear marker, see fig. 1824.

Radiobeacons

Radiobeacons are indicated by a magenta circle around the basic symbol for the aid to navigation at which the beacon is located plus the abbreviation "R Bn." Aeronautical radiobeacons are shown only if they are useful for marine navigation; the same symbol is used and the iden-

tification "AERO" is added. The frequency, in KiloHertz, is given, as is the identifying signal in dots and dashes of the Morse code. Aeronautical radio ranges use the same symbol as beacons plus "AERO R Rge."

Dangers to navigation

Symbols are also used for many types of *dangers to navigation*. Differentiation is made between rocks that are awash at times and those which remain below the surface at all tides, between visible wrecks and submerged ones, and between hazards which have been definitely located and those whose position is doubtful. There are a number of symbols and abbreviations for objects and areas dangerous to navigation. The prudent skipper will spend adequate time studying them, with the greatest emphasis being placed on those types commonly found in his home waters.

Chart Numbering System _____

On 1 July 1974, all N.O.S. and Lake Survey charts were renumbered into a new system; a smaller number of DMAHC charts were renumbered at that time. The new system uses a logical sequence of numbers and eliminates the duplication of numbers for different charts prepared by different agencies, such as C&GS 234 and L.S. 234. Each U.S. chart will now have its own unique number.

The new system is based on the region/subregion concept adopted in 171 for all former H.O. charts. Boatmen will generally be concerned only with charts having *five-digit* numbers. Such charts have a scale of 1:2,000,000 or larger. The first digit refers to the region of the world, the second to a subregion, and the final three. assigned

systematically within the subregion, denote the specific chart area.

Region 1 includes the waters in and around the United States and Canada. Region 2 covers Central and South America, including both coasts of Mexico, the Bahamas, and the West Indies. There are a total of nine regions.

Region 1 has nine subregions designated counter-clockwise around North America from Subregion 11 for the Gulf of Mexico and the Atlantic Coast up to Cape Hatteras. Subregion 12 extends from there to the eastern tip of Long Island, and 13 goes on to the Canadian border. Subregion 14 covers the Great Lakes; 18 is the U.S. Pacific Coast.

The final three digits of a five-digit number are as-

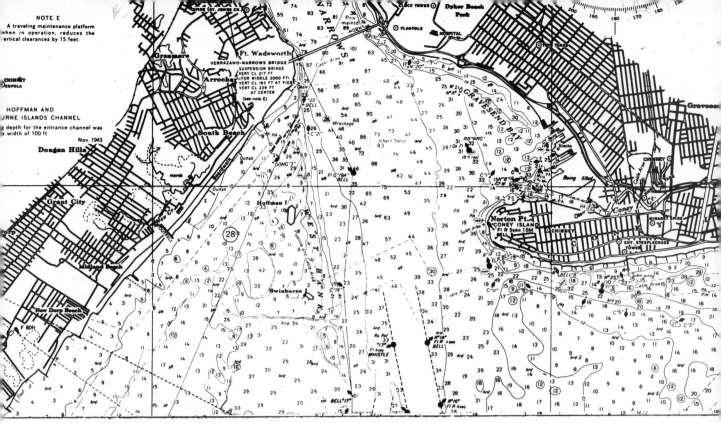

FIG. 1828   Portion of Chart 12327. This extract shows some of the same areas as the preceding three figures but at a greater scale and with more detail. "Harbor charts" at a scale of 1:40,000 or larger include all hazards and aids to navigation, some of which may have been omitted from smaller scale charts. More details of features on land are also shown.

signed counter-clockwise around the subregion or along the coast. Many numbers are left unassigned so that future charts can be fitted into the system.

A few examples of the new system may make it clearer. Old chart 141-SC, Miami to Marathon, Florida, is now numbered 11451—Region 1, Subregion 11, plus three new digits. Chart 848, Miami to Elliott Key, covering part of the same area at a larger scale, becomes 11465. Miami's harbor chart, 547, becomes 11468. All numbers are closely related. It is thus possible to use a new chart number to roughly identify the area covered by that chart.

Of lesser interest to boatmen is the balance of the new system. Charts with one-digit numbers have no scale and are not for navigation; an example is Chart No. 1, the booklet of chart symbols and abbreviations. Two digits indicate a chart on a 1:9,000,000 or smaller scale. Three-digit numbers indicate a scale of 1:2,000,000 to 1:9,000,000; there are only a few of these. Charts with two and three digits are numbered on an "ocean basin" concept rather than by regions. Four-digit numbers are used for special purpose and miscellaneous charts only. Training edition charts will continue to carry their old numbers.

Chart "Series"

FOUR N.O.S. SERIES

As previously mentioned, charts are published in a wide range of scales. For general convenience of reference, the issuing agencies have classified charts into "series" as follows:

1. Sailing Charts—the smallest scale charts covering long stretches of coastline; for example, Cape Sable, Newfoundland to Cape Hatteras, N. C.; or the Gulf of Mexico; or San Francisco to Cape Flattery, Washington; see fig. 1825. The charts of this series are published at scales of 1:600,000 and smaller. Sailing charts are prepared for the use of the navigator in fixing his position as he approaches the coast from the open ocean, or when sailing between distant coast ports. They show the offshore soundings, the principal lights and outer buoys, and landmarks visible at

great distances. Other than for ocean cruising races, the average boatman will have little use for charts in this series, except perhaps to plot the path of hurricanes and other tropical disturbances.

2. General Charts—the second series comprises charts with scales in the range of 1:100,000 to 1:600,000. These cover more limited areas, such as Cape May, N. J. to Cape Hatteras; or Mississippi River to Galveston Bay; or San Francisco to Point Arena, Calif. General charts are intended for coastwise navigation outside of offshore reefs and shoals when the vessel's course is mostly within sight of land and her position can be fixed by landmarks, lights, buoys, and soundings. Fig. 1826 is a portion of a general chart.

3. Coast Charts—this next larger scale series consists of charts for close-in coastwise navigation, for entering and

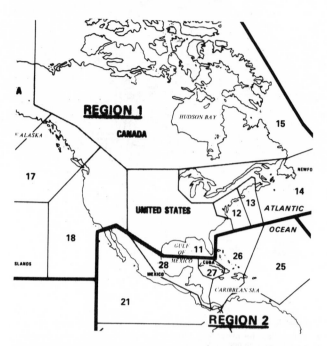

FIG. 1829 The above diagram shows the various subregions of Regions 1 and 2 of the new chart numbering system. The number of the subregion forms the first two digits of a five-digit chart number. The world-wide system of nine regions is shown in Fig. 1710a.

leaving harbors, and for navigating large inland bodies of water. The scales used range from 1:50,000 to 1:100,000 with most at 1:80,000. See fig. 1827. Typical examples of coast charts are the widely-used training chart No. 1210Tr, and such navigational charts as the series of five which cover Chesapeake Bay or 18746 which takes the California boatman from Long Beach or Newport to Santa Catalina Island and back. The average boatman will use several charts from this series.

4. Harbor Charts — this is the largest-scale and most-detailed series, see fig. 1828. Scales will range from 1:40,000 to 1:5,000, with an occasional insert of even larger scale. The scale used for any specific chart is determined by the need for showing detail and by the desired area to be covered by a single sheet. Skippers of small craft will find this the most generally useful type of chart.

Stowage and use

N.O.S. charts in the four series above are printed by accurate techniques on highly durable paper. Individual charts will range in size from approximately 19 x 26 to 36x54 inches. As they are among the most important tools of the navigator, they should be given careful handling and proper stowage. If circumstances permit, they should be stowed flat or rolled, and in a dry place. Charts should never be folded if this can be avoided.

It is advisable that permanent corrections be made in ink so that they will not be inadvertently erased; all other lines and notations should be made lightly in pencil so that they may be erased when no longer applicable without removing permanent information or otherwise damaging the chart.

Lake Chart series

Charts of the Great Lakes are also grouped into series. *General charts* include one of all the Lakes plus one for each lake. *Coast charts* are at a scale of 1:80,000 or 1:120,-000. *Harbor charts* have larger scales.

SELECTING THE PROPER CHART

From a consideration of the four categories of charts discussed above, it will be noted that most boating areas will appear on two charts of different series, and that some will be covered by three or four charts of different scales. Such charts will vary widely in the extent of the area covered and the amount of detail shown. The selection of the proper chart to use is important.

The chart catalogs (fig. 1830 is an example of one published by the National Ocean Survey) indicate graphically the area covered by each chart. Also included is a listing giving the name, scale, and price of each chart. These catalogs provide a starting point for the selection of the proper charts for your cruise. In general, the closer you will be to shoal water and dangers to navigation, the larger you will want the scale of the chart that you are using.

What coast charts show

Coast charts show only the *major* hazards and aids to navigation, and give generalized information on depths. Some charts in this series will omit entirely any details on portions thereof which are covered by larger scale charts. For example, Narragansett Bay appears on Chart 13218, but no details at all are given, merely a small note "(Chart 13221)." Other 1200 series coast charts include in their area coverage portions of the Atlantic Intracoastal Waterway, but the navigator is referred to the ICW route charts for all information on the inland route. Many coast charts include a small diagram outlining the areas covered by each larger scale chart—on No. 13218, this amounts to all or portions of 13 more-detailed charts.

What harbor charts show

Harbor charts will show more numerous soundings and *all* aids to navigation, and will permit the most accurate fixing of position from plotted bearings. The question may arise as to why ever select any but the largest-scale chart. The answer lies in the fact that as the scale is increased, the area that can be covered on a given size sheet of paper is proportionately reduced. Thus, for a cruise, many more charts of the harbor series would be required than from the coast series. Further, in some areas, continuous coverage from port to port is not possible from harbor charts alone. Another problem is that the increased number of larger-scale charts complicates the task of laying out a long run between ports.

The selection of the proper charts will usually result in a mixture of coast charts for the longer runs and harbor charts for entering ports and exploring up rivers and creeks. For some areas, one or more general charts, in addition to the coast and harbor charts, may be found useful. For example, the best route down Chesapeake Bay is more easily plotted on 12260 and 12220 than on the series of coast charts 12273 to 12221. When you have a variety of charts on board, duplication of area coverage may result but the right chart is available for the various specific requirements.

In the margin of many charts, you will find helpful information regarding the next chart to use when you are going in a particular direction. This note will take the form of a statement such as "(Joins Chart 13233)" or "(Continued on Chart 13236)."

"SMALL-CRAFT" CHARTS

The charts in the four series just discussed are referred to as "conventional" charts and are intended for flat or rolled stowage. There is another category, a fifth series, which is of special interest to boatmen—these are the *Small-craft Charts* of the National Ocean Survey, designed for more convenient use in the limited space available on boats, and for folded stowage, fig. 1831. (see also color plate, page N.) Originally, the letters "SC" following the number identified charts in the small-craft series, but this practice ceased with the new five-digit numbering system, and "SC" charts are now assigned an appropriate new-style number.

The first chart in this series was 101-SC of the Potomac River. It was introduced in 1957 and immediately was popular beyond all expectations. Requests were soon received from hundreds of boatmen throughout the United States for similar coverage of their waters. The years since 1959 have seen a steadily increasing number of "SC" charts published, as well as revised editions for those already out. As of October 1974, there were 85 small-craft editions printed, with more in the planning stage.

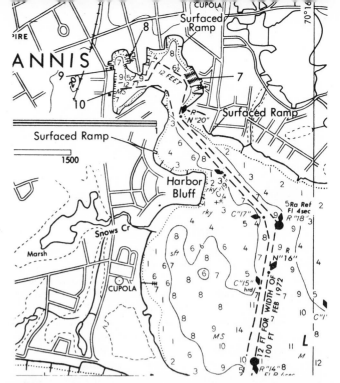

FIG. 1831 "Small-craft" Charts are a special series designed for the boatman. They are easier to use and stow, and contain added information of particular interest to the operators of power and sail boats. Included are data on boating facilities, tides and currents, weather broadcasts, etc.

printed front and back, accordion folded, and slipped into a suitable jacket.

Small-craft area charts, usually consisting of a conventional chart printed on lighter-weight paper with additional data for the small boat skipper. Half of the chart is printed on each side of the paper with a slight area of overlap in printed detail. The chart is accordion folded and issued in a protective jacket.

Facilities data

A unique feature of these most-modern charts is the variety of data printed on the chart and its protective jacket, fig. 1832. No longer is it necessary to use other sources to locate repair yards and marinas; their locations are clearly marked on the chart, and the available services and supplies are tabulated on the jacket. A tide table for the year, current and marine weather information, rules of the road, signals, and warning notes are included for ready reference.

Small-craft charts make frequent use of "insets" to show such features as small creeks and harbors in greater detail. Fig. 1833 shows an inset from Chart 12285 of the Potomac River.

Courses indicated

Many of the folio and route types of Small-craft charts will indicate a recommended track to be followed. The longer stretches of these tracks will be marked as to true course (some older charts showed magnetic courses; check each chart used) and the distance in miles and tenths. Route charts of the Atlantic Intracoastal Waterway also have tick marks every five miles indicating the accumulated distance southward from Norfolk, Virginia to Florida, fig. 1834. Facilities along the Atlantic ICW are designated in accordance with a numbering system that starts fresh with "1" on each chart of the series.

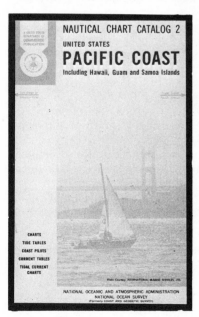

FIG. 1830 Chart Catalogs published by the various issuing agencies show the area coverage of each chart and greatly aid the skipper in the selection of the proper charts to be used in cruising unfamiliar waters. The title, scale, and prices are listed in tabular form. Shown here is one of the three volumes issued by the National Ocean Survey; all are available free upon request.

Types of small-craft charts

Small-craft charts are printed in three general formats termed folio, route, and area as follows:

Small-craft folio charts, consisting of three or four sheets printed front and back, accordion folded, and bound in a suitable cover.

Small-craft route charts, consisting of a single sheet

Revised annually

Small-craft charts are revised and reissued annually, usually to coincide with the start of the boating season in each locality. SC charts are *not* hand corrected by the N.O.S. after they are printed and placed in stock. The skipper should keep his chart up-to-date between yearly editions by applying all critical changes as published in the local and weekly editions of Notices to Mariners—this is not a great chore, *if* you keep up with the changes and don't get behind!

DMAHC CHARTS

Charts from the Defense Mapping Agency Hydrographic Center will be used by boatmen making long ocean voyages or visiting foreign waters (except Canada). The depicting of information will not differ much from the more familiar N.O.S. charts, and few difficulties will be encountered. Symbols and abbreviations will be familiar to the coastal boatman, but land areas will be found to be tinted gray rather than buff. Symbols will be different for lighted buoys and those with radar reflectors. Some charts will show depths and heights in meters and fractions, rather than in feet or fathoms.

The DMAHC often issues special editions for some of the major ocean sailing races. These are regular editions of the applicable charts overprinted with additional information for the yachtsman, including the direct rhumb line, typical sailing tracks for seasonal winds, additional current data, and other useful items. The publication of these special charts is well-publicized in Notices to Mariners and boating periodicals.

It must be remembered that many such charts are based on foreign surveys, fig. 1835. The authority for the charted information will always be given at will the date of the surveys. Check for this information, and apply appropriate judgment and caution when using charts of foreign waters; their accuracy and completeness will almost invariably be poor in comparison with N.O.S. charts of U.S. waters.

LAKE SURVEY CHARTS

As mentioned before, the polyconic projection method is used for most Lake Survey and Engineer charts; other small variations between these and coastal charts may be noted. LS charts may use as many as four different shades of blue in denoting various depths of water nearest the shore — the deeper the shade, the shallower the water. Often courses and distances (in statute miles) will be shown for runs between important points.

FIG. 1832 Small-craft Charts are printed on lighter weight paper than those in the conventional series. These "SC" charts are then folded and placed in protective jackets. Some are bound-in (114-SC on the left) and others are merely slipped into their jackets (831-SC on the right).

The Lake Survey prepares special editions of charts for the small-craft operator. These are called "Recreational Craft Charts" and are issued in a bound volume of large-scale individual charts of special interest to boatmen.

INLAND RIVER CHARTS

Boatmen on inland rivers will use charts that are different in many respects from those used in coastal waters. Often these will be called "navigational maps" and be issued in book form with several pages covering successive stretches of a river.

Probably the most obvious difference is the usual lack of depth figures. In lieu of these, there will generally be a broken line designating the route to be followed. In order to make the best use of the paper sheet, each page may be oriented differently; north will seldom be toward the top, its actual direction being shown by an arrow. Some symbols may vary slightly in appearance from those on "salt water" charts, and additional ones may be used as required by local conditions. Distances are often designated in terms of statute miles upriver from a specified origin point.

More detailed information on river charts will be found in Chapter 27; see pages 532-534, 544, and 547. A complete listing of where river charts and related publications can be obtained is presented on page 608.

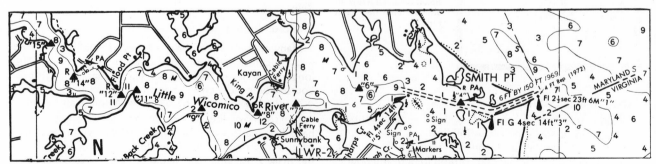

FIG. 1833 Insets are used liberally on Small-craft Charts to show local cruising areas in greater detail. This inset, No. 1 from Chart 12285, for the Little Wicomico River, is typical. Depths under six feet are tinted blue. Channel marks (black triangles in this reproduction) are in red and black on the original.

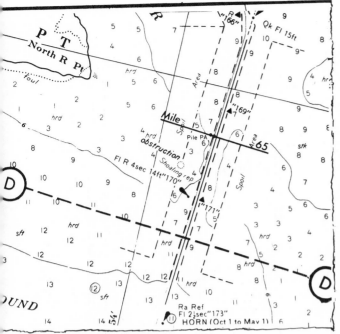

FIG. 1834 Charts of the Atlantic Intracoastal Waterway show a fine magenta line indicating the route to be followed. Tick marks are placed at five-mile intervals along this course line and are labeled with the accumulated mileage southward from Norfolk, Virginia. Since 1969, distances have been measured in statute miles. Passages over large bodies of water may show information on true course and distance. The "D-D" line on the chart extract above is a matching indicator to facilitate shifting from one chart to another.

CAUTIONS REGARDING USE

The production of charts is a major undertaking for the vast coastline and contiguous waterways of the United States. Our Atlantic coastline exceeds 24,500 nautical miles, the Gulf Coast 15,000 miles, the Pacific Coast 7,000 miles, and the Alaskan and Hawaiian shorelines total more than 30,000 nautical miles. The National Ocean Survey publishes more than 800 charts covering over two million square miles, and both of these figures continue to increase each year. In meeting its global responsibilities, the DMA Hydrographic Center puts out charts numbered in

the thousands, and there are, in addition, the many Army Engineer charts, or "Navigational maps."

It can easily be seen that the task of keeping so many charts up-to-date is literally staggering. Surveys are constantly being made in new areas and must be rechecked in old areas. An extensive program of cooperative reporting by boatmen is used by the National Ocean Survey and the Lake Survey to supplement the information-gathering capability of the Government.

Every effort is made by the charting agencies to keep their products accurate and up-to-date with changing editions. Major disturbances of nature such as hurricanes along the Atlantic coast and earthquakes in the Pacific Northwest cause sudden and extensive changes in hydrography, and destroy aids to navigation. The everyday forces of wind and wave cause slower and less obvious changes in channels and shoals.

All boatmen must be alert to the possibility of changes in conditions and inaccuracies in charted information. Most charts will cite the authorities for the information presented and frequently the date of the information will be given. Use additional caution when the surveys date back many years.

FIG. 1835 Many charts by the DMA Hydrographic Center are based on foreign surveys. This fact will be noted in the title block. Such charts should be used with caution, particularly if the surveys date back many years, as is often the case.

Chart Projections

The small craft skipper can safely navigate his boat without extensive knowledge of the various types of projection used in the preparation of charts. It is adequate to know that the projection of a spherical surface onto a plane surface inevitably results in some distortions; for small areas, these can be safely neglected.

As in almost any field, however, greater knowledge of the "how" and "why" will assist in understanding and using nautical charts. Hence the following paragraphs will provide additional detailed information on chart projections for those who would extend their knowledge in that direction.

The Mercator projection used in ocean and coastal waters and the polyconic projection used in inland lakes

and rivers have been mentioned earlier in this chapter. These, plus the gnomonic projection used in polar regions, will now be presented in more detail. There are many other systems of projection, but each has limited application and need not be considered here.

MERCATOR PROJECTION

The Mercator projection is often illustrated as a projection onto a cylinder. Actually, the chart is developed mathematically to allow for the known shape of the earth, which is not quite a true sphere. The meridians appear as straight, vertical lines, fig. 1836a. Here we have our first example of distortion, and it is quite obvious—the meridians no longer converge, but are now shown as being

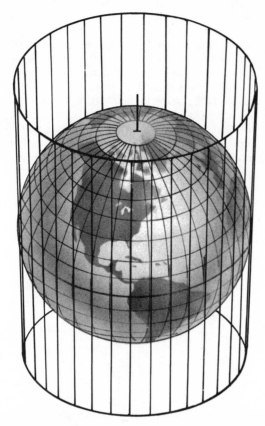

FIG. 1836 a   A Mercator projection starts with the placement of a cylinder around the earth parallel to the polar axis and touching the earth at the Equator. The meridians are projected out onto the cylinder and appear as a series of parallel straight lines when the cylinder is unrolled into a flat plane.

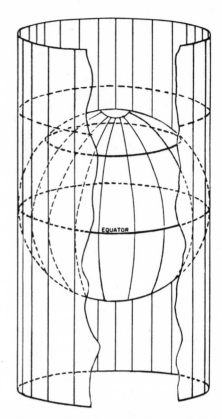

FIG. 1836 b   Parallels of latitude are projected onto the enveloping cylinder. They appear as parallel straight lines intersecting the meridians at right angles. The actual spacing of the meridians and parallels is adjusted to account for the true shape of the earth which is not an exact sphere. See text.

parallel to each other. This changes the representation of the shape of objects by stretching out their dimensions in an East-West direction.

To minimize the distortion of shape, one of the qualities that must be preserved as much as possible, there must be a stretching-out of dimensions in a North-South direction. The parallels of latitude appear as straight lines intersecting the meridians at right angles. Their spacing increases northward from the Equator, fig. 1836b, in accordance with a mathematical formula that recognizes the slightly oblate shape of the earth. This increase in spacing is not obvious in the case of charts of relatively small areas, such as in the harbor and coastal series, but it is quite apparent in Mercator projections of the world, fig. 1837, or of a large area such as covered by a sailing chart.

The Mercator projection is said to be "conformal," which means that angles are correctly represented and the scale is the same in all directions from any point.

By the Mercator technique of distortion, then counter-distortion, the shape of areas in high latitudes is correctly shown, but their size appears greater than that of similar areas in lower latitudes. An island, for example, in 60° latitude (Alaska) would appear considerably larger than an island of the same size located 25° above the equator (Florida). Its shape, however, would still be true to the actual proportions.

Advantages and disadvantages

The great value of the Mercator chart is that the meridians of longitude appear as straight lines all intersecting the parallels of latitude, also straight lines, at right angles to form an easily-used rectangular grid. Directions can be measured with reference to any meridian or any compass rose. The geographic coordinates of a position can easily be measured from the scales along the four borders of the chart. *We can draw upon a Mercator chart a straight line between two points and actually sail that course* by determining the compass direction between them; the heading is the same all along the line. Such a line is called a *rhumb* line. However, a great circle, the shortest distance between two points on the earth's surface, is a curved line on a Mercator chart; this is more difficult to calculate and plot. For moderate runs, the added distance of a rhumb line is insignificant, and this is the track that is used. Radio waves follow great circle paths and radio bearings on stations more than about 200 miles distant will require correction before being plotted on a Mercator chart.

The scale of a Mercator chart will vary with the distance away from the equator as a result of the N-S expansion. The change is unimportant on charts of small areas such as harbor and coastal charts, and the graphic scale may be used. The change in scale with latitude does become signi-

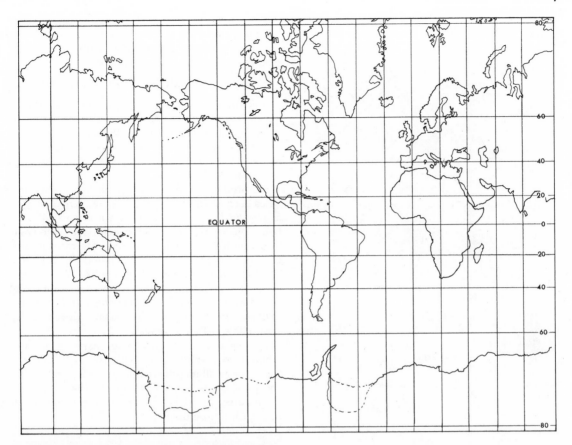

FIG. 1837 This Mercator projection of the world shows the considerable distortion in near-polar latitudes. Note that the spacing between parallels is not uniform, but increases as the distance from the Equator increases.

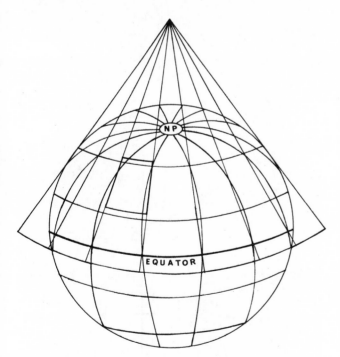

FIG. 1838 Polyconic projections are developed onto a series of cones tangent to the earth. Separate cones are used for each parallel of latitude. For clarity, the drawing above shows only one of these cones.

ficant, however, in charts covering greater areas, as on general and sailing charts. On such charts, it is necessary to measure distances using the latitude scale on either side margin, remembering that 1' of latitude is essentially 1 nautical mile. *Take care that distance is measured at a point on the latitude scale directly opposite the region of the chart being used. Never use the longitude scale at the top and bottom of the chart for measuring distance.*

POLYCONIC PROJECTION

Another form of chart construction is the *polyconic* projection. This method is based on the development of the earth's surface upon a series of cones, a different one being used for each parallel of latitude, fig. 1838. The vertex of the cone is at the point where a tangent to the earth at the specified latitude intersects the earth's axis extended. At the edges of the chart, the area between parallels is expanded to eliminate gaps.

The polyconic projection yields little distortion in shape, and relative sizes are more correctly preserved than in the Mercator projection. The scale is correct along any parallel and along the central meridian of the projection. Along other meridians, the scale increases with increased difference in longitude from the central meridian.

Parallels appear as nonconcentric arcs of circles and meridians as curved lines converging toward the pole, concave toward the central meridian, see fig. 1839. These characteristics contrast with the straight-line parallels and meridians of Mercator charts, and are the reasons why this

361

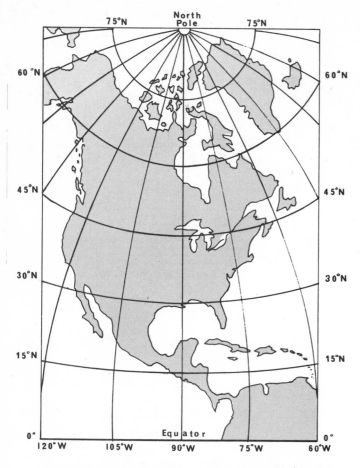

FIG. 1839 This polyconic projection of a large area emphasizes the curved characteristics of the parallels and meridians on this type of chart. Such curvatures exist on smaller area charts but are not so noticeable.

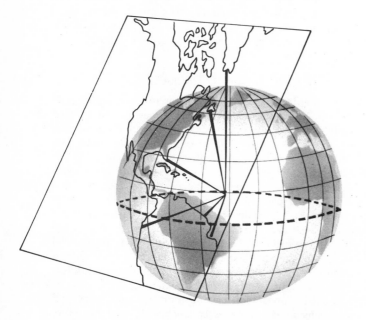

FIG. 1840 A Gnomonic projection is made by placing a plane surface tangent to the earth. Points on the earth's surface are then projected onto this plane. The point of tangency may be at any location.

projection is not so widely used in marine navigation. Directions from any point should be measured relative to the meridian passing through that point; in actual practice, the nearest compass rose is used.

GNOMONIC PROJECTION

A *gnomonic* chart results when the meridians and parallels of latitude are projected onto a plane surface tangent to the earth at one point, fig. 1840. For the oblique case, meridians appear as straight lines converging toward the nearer pole; the parallels, except for the equator, appear as curves, fig. 1841.

Distortion is great, but this projection is used in special cases because of its unique advantage—*great circles appear as straight lines,* which of course is not so with the other two projections discussed above. Probably the easiest way to obtain a great circle track on a Mercator or polyconic chart is to draw it as a straight line on a gnomonic chart and then transfer points along the line to the other chart using the geographic coordinates for each point. The points so transferred are then connected with short rhumb lines and the result will approximate, closely enough, the great circle path, fig. 1842a and b.

A special case of gnomonic chart projection occurs when a geographic pole is selected as the point of tangency. Now all meridians will appear as straight lines, and the parallels as concentric circles. The result is a chart easily used for polar regions where ordinary Mercator charts cannot be used.

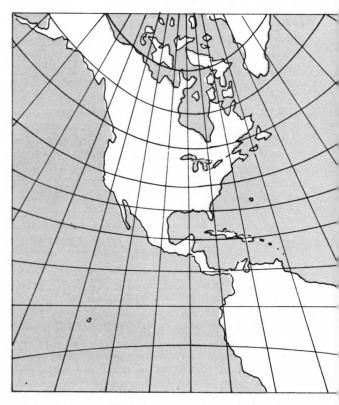

FIG. 1841 A chart made on the Gnomonic projection shows meridians as straight lines converging toward the nearer pole. The parallels, other than the Equator, appear as curves.

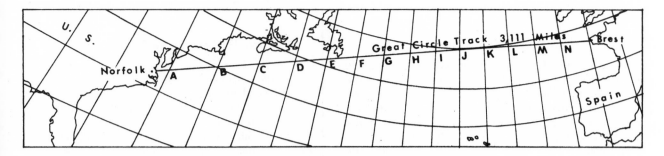

FIG. 1842 a A great circle provides the shortest distance between two points on the earth's surface, but is difficult to plot directly on a Mercator chart. An easier procedure is to draw it as a straight line on a Gnomonic chart, noting the latitude of each intersection of the track with a meridian.

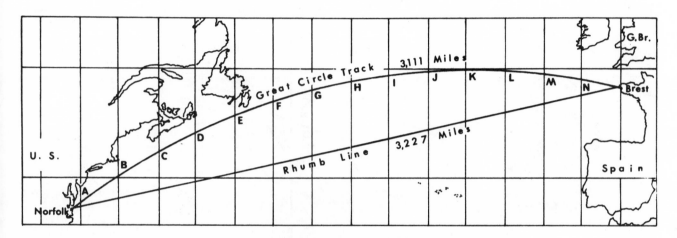

FIG. 1842 b Using the geographic coordinates of each point previously marked on the track, it is reconstructed on the Mercator chart by joining the points with short straight (rhumb) lines. This approximation can then be steered without great difficulty.

THE LAMBERT CONFORMAL PROJECTION

A projection can be made onto a single cone tangent to the earth at a single specified parallel of latitude; this is termed a *simple conic projection*. It is generally a poor projection as the scale is not correct except along the standard parallel. Areas not projected equally and correct angular relationships are not preserved.

The polyconic projection, previously considered, avoids some of these distortions, but only at the cost of the complexity of using a series of cones. Another technique to minimize the distortions of the simple conic projection is to have the cone *intersect* the earth's surface at two parallels. This general type is called a *conic projection with two standard parallels*.

If the spacing of the parallels is altered so that the distortion is the same along them as along the meridians, the projection becomes conformal, that is, the angular relationships are correctly represented, a highly desirable chart quality. This is known as the *Lambert conformal projection*. It is the most widely used conic projection,

although its use is more common among aviators than navigators. Its appearance is very much the same as the simple conic or polyconic projections. If the chart is not carried far beyond the standard parallels, and these are not a great distance apart, the distortion over the entire chart is small.

A straight line on this projection so nearly approximates a great circle that the two can be considered identical for most purposes of navigation. Radio bearings, from signals which are considered to travel great circle paths, can be plotted on a Lambert conformal chart without the correction needed when using a Mercator chart. This feature, gained without sacrificing conformality, has made this projection popular for aeronautical charts, since aircraft make much use of radio aids to navigation. It has made little headway in replacing the Mercator projection for marine navigation, except in high latitudes. In a slightly modified form, the Lambert conformal projection is sometimes used for polar charts.

PILOT CHARTS

No discussion of nautical charts would be complete without at least brief mention of a unique but valuable chart issued each month by the DMA Hydrographic Center. These *Pilot Charts* present in graphic form information on ocean currents and weather probabilities for that month, plus other data of interest to a navigator. Timely articles are printed on the reverse side of each chart. They are issued in two editions—

      (1) the North Atlantic Ocean,
      (2) the North Pacific Ocean.

Fig. 1843 below, is a portion of the front side of a North Atlantic Pilot Chart.

NAUTICAL CHART MANUAL

Those desiring to know more about the basic essentials of nautical chart construction and details of the current charting practices of the National Ocean Survey might wish to purchase the "Nautical Chart Manual," 6th Edition. This 213-page manual is available from the Superintendent of Documents, U.S. Government Printing Office, Washington, D.C. 20402. The price is $6.75.

⚓

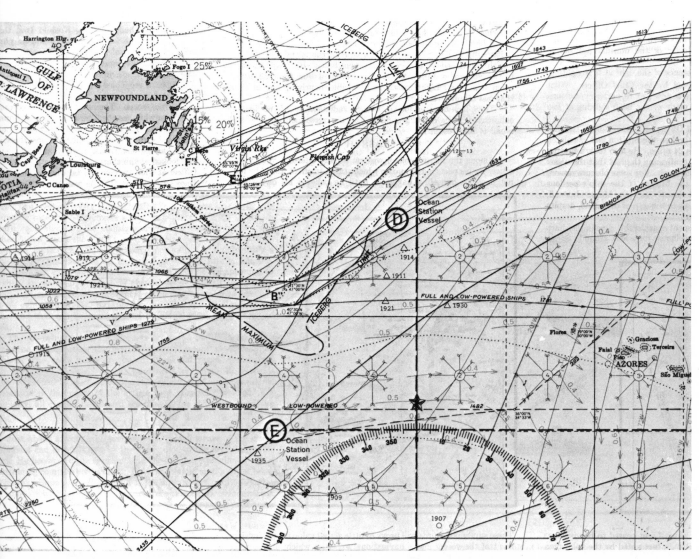

FIG. 1843 This is a small portion of the pilot chart of the North Atlantic for the month of May 1966. Dotted lines in blue on the original indicate the percentage of days in which fog can be expected for the month. The full lines represent the accepted tracks for full-powered and low-powered steamers. The wind rose (in blue on the original) in each 5-degree square shows the character of prevailing winds. Arrows fly with the wind. Length of the arrow gives percentage of the total number of observations in which the wind has blown from that point. The number of feathers shows the average force (Beaufort scale). Figures inside the circle give percentage of calms, light airs, and variable winds. Ocean station vessels (lettered red circles) supply meteorological information. The (red) long-short dashed line indicates extreme limit of ice. Outside this limit, triangles show where and when bergs have been sighted. Growlers are shown as small circles. Small (green) arrows indicate currents; velocity given in miles per day.

STANDARDIZED CHART SYMBOLS AND ABBREVIATIONS

The nautical chart can convey much or little to its user, depending upon the extent of his understanding of all those many small, odd shapes, marks, and lines. A great amount of information must be shown on a chart for safe navigation and, in many areas, there is little room for it. Thus, extensive use is made of *symbols* and *abbreviations*. To make chart reading easier, quicker, and surer, the various U.S. agencies that produce nautical charts have adopted a standardized system of abbreviations and symbols.

It is essential that a boatman have the ability to read and understand his charts rapidly and accurately. Knowledge of symbols and abbreviations is a "must" for this ability.

The standardized symbols and abbreviations are broadly grouped into classifications as follows:

A—The Coast Line
B—Coast Features
C—The Land
D—Control Points
E—Units
F—Adjectives
G—Harbors
H—Topography
I—Buildings
J—Miscellaneous Stations
K—Lights
L—Buoys and Beacons
M—Radio Stations
N—Fog Signals
O—Dangers
P—Various Limits
Q—Soundings
R—Depth Countours
S—Quality of the Bottom
T—Tides and Currents
U—The Compass

Most of the symbols used on nautical charts published by the National Ocean Survey and the DMAHC Hydrographic Center conform to the standards of the International Hydrographic Bureau (IHB), but a few do not. In the numbering of the symbols and abbreviations in fig. 1844 a to 1844(o) on this and the following pages, vertical figures indicate that the designated symbol or abbreviation is in conformity with the IHB standards. Slanting figures mean that it either

differs from the standard or does not appear in the international list. Where the figures are enclosed in *parentheses*, the symbol or abbreviations in addition to those included in the IHB standards. The symbols shown are from the 1972 edition of Chart No. 1; changes from the 1968 edition are indicated by a dagger (†) symbol before the number.

The symbols and abbreviations shown in fig. 1844 will be used on N.O.S. and DMAHC charts issued in the future. Cases may occur where older symbols still appear on charts that have not yet been reissued in the new editions.

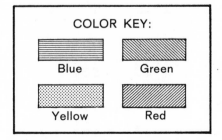

COLOR KEY:

Blue   Green

Yellow   Red

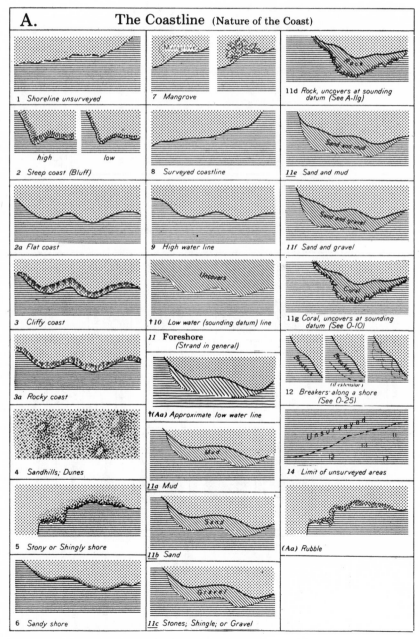

FIG. 1844 a   SYMBOLS—The coastline

F. Adjectives, Adverbs and other abbreviations

1	gt	Great
2	lit	Little
3	lrg	Large
4	sml	Small
5		Outer
6		Inner
7	mid	Middle
8		Old
9	anc	Ancient
10		New
11	St	Saint
12	conspic	Conspicuous
13		Remarkable
14	D Destr	Destroyed
15		Projected
16	dist	Distant
17	abt	About
18		See chart
18a		See plan
19		Lighted; Luminous
20	sub	Submarine
21		Eventual
22	AERO	Aeronautical
23		Higher
23a		Lower
24	exper	Experimental
25	discontd	Discontinued
26	prohib	Prohibited
27	explos	Explosive
28	estab	Established
29	elec	Electric
30	priv	Private, Privately
31	prom	Prominent
32	std	Standard
33	subm	Submerged
34	approx	Approximate
35		Maritime
36	maintd	Maintained
37	aband	Abandoned
38	temp	Temporary
39	occas	Occasional
40	extr	Extreme
41		Navigable
42	N M	Notice to Mariners
(Fa)	L N M	Local Notice to Mariners
43		Sailing Directions
44		List of Lights
(Fb)	unverd	Unverified
(Fc)	AUTH	Authorized
(Fd)	cl	Clearance
(Fe)	cor	Corner
(Ff)	concr	Concrete
(Fg)	fl	Flood
(Fh)	mod	Moderate
(Fi)	bet	Between
(Fj)		Fir
(Fk)	2nd	Second
(Fl)	3rd	Third
(Fm)	4th	Fourth
†(Fn)	DD	Deep Draft
†(Fo)	min	Minimum
†(Fp)	max	Maximum

D. Control Points

1	△	Triangulation point (station)
1a	○	Astronomic Station
†2	⊙	Fixed point (landmark, position accurate)
(Da)	○	Fixed point (landmark, position approx.)
3	· 256	Summit of height (Peak) (when not a landmark)
(Db)	⊛256	Peak, accentuated by contours
(Dc)	☼256	Peak, accentuated by hachures
(Dd)	⊙256	Peak, elevation not determined
(De)	⊕	Peak, when a landmark
4	Obs Spot	Observation spot
*5	BM.	Bench mark
6	View X	View point
7		Datum point for grid of a plan
8		Graphical triangulation point
9	Astro	Astronomical
10	Tri	Triangulation
(Df)	C of E	Corps of Engineers
12		Great trigonometrical survey station
13		Traverse station
14	Bdy Mon	Boundary monument
(Dg)	◇	International boundary monument

E. Units

No.	Abbr.	Term
1	hr	Hour
2	m; min	Minute (of time)
3	sec	Second (of time)
4	m	Meter
4a	dm	Decimeter
4b	cm	Centimeter
4c	mm	Millimeter
4d	m²	Square meter
4e	m³	Cubic meter
5	km	Kilometer
6	in	Inch
7	ft	Foot
8	yd	Yard
9	fm	Fathom
10	cbl	Cable length
11	M	Nautical mile
12	kn	Knot
12a	t	Ton
12b	cd	Candela (new candle)
13	lat	Latitude
14	long	Longitude
†14a		Greenwich
15	pub	Publication
16	Ed	Edition
17	corr	Correction
18	alt	Altitude
19	ht; elev	Height; Elevation
20	°	Degree
21	'	Minute (of arc)
22	"	Second (of arc)
23	No	Number
(Ea)	St M	Statute mile
(Eb)	msec	Microsecond
(Ec)	Hz	Hertz (cps)
(Ed)	kHz	Kilohertz (kc)
(Ee)	MHz	Megahertz (Mc)
(Ef)	cps	Cycles/second (Hz)
(Eg)	kc	Kilocycle (kHz)
(Eh)	Mc	Megacycle (MHz)

FIG. 1844 c   Control points, units, adjectives, adverbs

FIG. 1844 b   Features of the coast and natural features of the land

C. The Land (Natural Features)

1	Contour lines (Contours)
1a	Contour lines, approximate (Contours)
2	Hachures
2a	Form lines, no definite interval
2b	Shading
3	Glacier
4	Saltpans
5	○TREE Isolated trees
5a	Deciduous or of unknown type / Deciduous or of unspecified type
5b	Coniferous
5c	Palm tree
5d	Nipa palm
5e	Filao
5f	Casuarina
5g	Evergreen tree (other than coniferous)
6	Cultivated fields
6a	Grass fields / Grass
7	Paddy (rice) fields / Rice
7a	Park; Garden
8	Bushes
8a	Tree plantation in general
9	Deciduous woodland / Wooded
10	Coniferous woodland / Wooded
10a	Woods in general / Wooded
11	Tree top height (above shoreline datum) 2560
12	Lava flow
13	River; Stream
14	Intermittent stream
15	Lake; Pond
16	Lagoon (Lag) (Symbol used in small areas)
17	Marsh; Swamp
18	Slough (Slu.)
19	Rapids
20	Waterfalls
21	Spring

B. Coast Features

No.	Abbr.	Term
1	G	Gulf
2	B	Bay
(Ba)	B	Bayou
3	Fd	Fjord
4	L	Loch; Lough; Lake
5	Cr	Creek
5a	C	Cove
6	In	Inlet
7	Str	Strait
8	Sd	Sound
9	Pass	Passage; Pass
10	Thoro	Thorofare
10a	Chan	Channel
11		Narrows
12	Entr	Entrance
12a	Est	Estuary
13		Delta
14	Mth	Mouth
15	Rd	Road; Roadstead
16	Anch	Anchorage
16a	Hbr	Harbor
17	Hn	Haven
(Bb)	P	Port
18	P	Pond
19	I	Island
20	It	Islet
21	Arch	Archipelago
22	Pen	Peninsula
23	C	Cape
24	Prom	Promontory
25	Hd	Head; Headland
26	Pt	Point
27	Mt	Mountain; Mount
27a	Rge	Range
28		Valley
29	Pk	Summit
30		Peak
31	Vol	Volcano
32		Hill
33	Bld	Boulder
34	Ldg	Landing
35		Table-land (Plateau)
36	Rk	Rock
(Bc)		Isolated rock
(Bd)	Str	Stream
(Be)	R	River
(Bf)	Slu	Slough
(Bg)	Lag	Lagoon
(Bh)	Apprs	Approaches
	Rky	Rocky

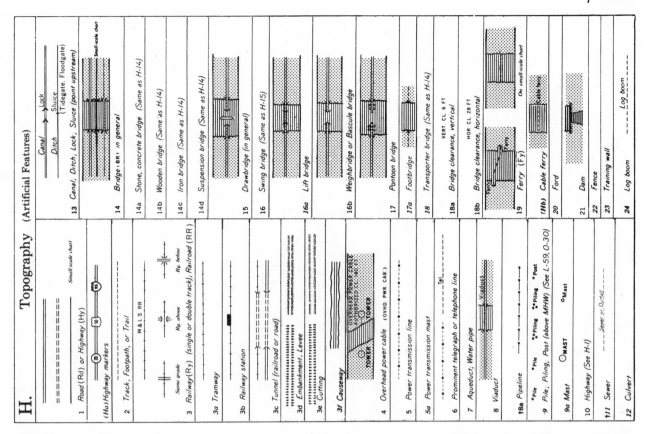

H. Topography (Artificial Features)

1	Road (Rd) or Highway (Hy)	13	Canal, Ditch, Lock, Sluice
	(Hu)Highway markers	14	Bridge (BR) in general
2	Track, Footpath, or Trail	14a	Stone, concrete bridge (Same as H-14)
3	Railway (Ry) (single or double track), Railroad (RR)	14b	Wooden bridge (Same as H-14)
		14c	Iron bridge (Same as H-14)
3a	Tramway	14d	Suspension bridge (Same as H-14)
3b	Railway station	15	Drawbridge (in general)
3c	Tunnel (railroad or road)	16	Swing bridge (Same as H-15)
3d	Embankment, Levee	16a	Lift bridge
3e	Cutting	16b	Weighbridge or Bascule bridge
3f	Causeway	17	Pontoon bridge
4	Overhead power cable (OVHD. PWR. CAB.)	17a	Footbridge
5	Power transmission line	18	Transporter bridge (Same as H-14)
5a	Power transmission mast	18a	Bridge clearance, vertical
6	Prominent telegraph or telephone line	18b	Bridge clearance, horizontal
7	Aqueduct, Water pipe	19	Ferry (Fy)
8	Viaduct	(Hb)	Cable ferry
†8a	Pipeline	20	Ford
†9	Pile, Piling, Post (above MHW) (See L-59, O-30)	21	Dam
9a	Mast	22	Fence
10	Highway (See H-1)	23	Training wall
†11	Sewer	24	Log boom
12	Culvert		

1844 e   **Artificial features of topography**

FIG. 1844 d   **Ports and harbors**

G. Ports and Harbors

1	Anch	Anchorage (large vessels)	20	Berth
2	Anch	Anchorage (small vessels)	20a	Anchoring berth
3	Hbr	Harbor	20b	Berth number
4	Hn	Haven	21	Dol	Dolphin
5	P	Port	22	Bollard
6	Bkw	Breakwater	23	Mooring ring
6a		Dike	24	Crane
7		Mole	25	Landing stage
8		Jetty (partly below MHW)	25a	Landing stairs
8a		Submerged jetty	26	Quar	Quarantine
(Ga)		Jetty (small scale)	27	Lazaret
9	Pier	Pier	*28	Harbor Master	Harbor master's office
10		Spit	29	Cus Ho	Customhouse
11		Groin (partly below MHW)	30	Fishing harbor
12	ANCH PROHIB	Anchorage prohibited (See P-25) (Screen Opt)	31	Winter harbor
12a		Anchorage reserved	32	Refuge harbor
12b		Quarantine anchorage	33	B Hbr	Boat harbor
13		Spoil ground	34	Dock	Stranding harbor (uncovers at LW)
(Gb)		Dumping ground	35		Dry dock (actual shape on large-scale charts)
(Gc)		Disposal area	36		Floating dock (actual shape on large-scale charts)
†(Gd)		Pump-out facilities	37		Gridiron; Careening grid
14	Fsh stks	Fisheries; Fishing stakes	38		Patent slip; Slipway; Marine railway
14a		Fish trap; Fish weirs (actual shape charted)	39		Ramp
14b		Duck blind	39a	Ramp	
15		Tunny nets (See G-14a)	40	Lock	Lock (point upstream) (See H-13)
15a	Oys	Oyster bed	41		Wet dock
16	Ldg	Landing place	42		Shipyard
17		Watering place	43		Lumber yard
18	Whf	Wharf	44	Health Office	Health officer's office
19		Quay	45	Hk	Hulk (actual shape on lrg scale charts)(See O-11)
			46	PROHIB AREA	Prohibited area
			46a		Calling-in point for vessel traffic control
			47		Anchorage for seaplanes
			48		Seaplane landing area
			49		Work in progress
			50		Under construction
			51		Work projected
			(Gd)		Submerged ruins

I. Buildings and Structures (continued)

61	Inst	Institute
62		Establishment
63		Bathing establishment
64	Ct Ho	Courthouse
65	Sch	School
(Ig)	H.S	High school
(Ih)	Univ	University
66	Bldg	Building
67	Pav	Pavilion
68		Hut
69		Stadium
70	T	Telephone
71		Gas tank; Gasometer
72	°Gab / GAB	Gable
73		Wall
74		Pyramid
75		Pillar
76		Oil derrick
(Ii)	Ltd	Limited
(Ij)	Apt	Apartment
(Ik)	Cap	Capitol
(Il)	Co	Company
(Im)	Corp	Corporation
(In)		Landmark (conspicuous object)
(Io)		Landmark (position approx.)

J. Miscellaneous Stations

1	Sta	Any kind of station
2	Sta	Station
3		Coast Guard station (Similar to LS. S.)
(Ja)		Coast Guard station (when landmark)
4	LOOK.TR	Lookout station; Watch tower
5		Lifeboat station
6		Lifesaving station (See J-3)
7	Rkt. Sta	Rocket station
8	PIL. STA	Pilot station
9	Sig Sta	Signal station
10	Sem	Semaphore
11	S. Sig Sta	Storm signal station
12		Weather signal station
†(Jb)	NWS SIG STA	Nat. Weather Service signal sta
13		Tide signal station
14		Stream signal station
15		Ice signal station
16		Time signal station
16a		Manned oceanographic station
16b		Unmanned oceanographic station
17		Time ball
18		Signal mast
19	°FS / °FP	Flagstaff; Flagpole
19a	°F. TR	Flag tower
20		Signal
21	Obsy	Observatory
22	Off	Office
(Jc)	BELL	Bell (on land)
(Jd)	HECP	Harbor entrance control post

FIG. 1844 g   Other buildings and structures, and miscellaneous stations

FIG. 1844 f   Buildings and structures

I. Buildings and Structures (see General Remarks)

1		City or Town (large scale)
(Ia)		City or Town (small scale)
2		Suburb
3	Vil	Village
3a		Buildings in general
4	Cas	Castle
5		House
6		Villa
7		Farm
8	Ch	Church
8a	Cath	Cathedral
8b	SPIRE / Spire	Spire; Steeple
9		Roman Catholic-Church
10		Temple
11		Chapel
12		Mosque
12a		Minaret
(Ib)		Moslem Shrine
13		Marabout
14	Pag	Pagoda
15		Buddhist Temple; Joss-House
15a		Shinto Shrine
16		Monastery; Convent
17		Calvary; Cross
17a		Cemetery, Non-Christian
18	Cem	Cemetery, Christian
18a		Tomb
19		Fort (actual shape charted)
20		Battery
21		Barracks
22		Powder magazine
23		Airplane landing field
24	Airport	Airport, large scale (See P-13)
(Ic)		Airport, military (small scale)
(Id)		Airport, civil (small scale)
25		Mooring mast
26	St (King St)	Street
26a	Ave (Locust Ave)	Avenue
26b	Blvd (Grand Blvd)	Boulevard
27	Tel	Telegraph
28	Tel.Off	Telegraph office
29	P.O	Post office
30	Govt. Ho	Government house
31		Town hall
32	Hosp	Hospital
33		Slaughterhouse
34	Magz	Magazine
34a		Warehouse; Storehouse
35	°MON	Monument
36	°CUP	Cupola
37	°ELEV	Elevator; Lift
(Ie)	Elev	Elevation; Elevated
38		Shed
39		Zinc roof
40	Ruins / °Ru	Ruins
41	°TR	Tower
(If)	ABAND LT HO	Abandoned lighthouse
42	WINDMILL	Windmill
43		Watermill
43a	WINDMOTOR	Windmotor
44	°CHY	Chimney; Stack
45	°S·PIPE	Water tower; Standpipe
†46		Oil tank
47	Facty	Factory
48		Saw mill
49		Brick kiln
50		Mine; Quarry
51	°Well	Well
52		Cistern
†53	TANK / °Tk	Tank
54		Noria
55		Fountain

K. Lights (continued)

69		Unwatched light
70	Occas	Occasional light
71	Irreg	Irregular light
72	Prov	Provisional light
73	Temp	Temporary light
(Ke)	D;Destr	Destroyed
74	Exting	Extinguished light
75		Faint light
76		Upper light
77		Lower light
78		Rear light
79		Front light
80	Vert	Vertical lights
81	Hor	Horizontal lights
(Kf)	VB	Vertical beam
(Kg)	RGE	Range
(Kh)	Exper	Experimental light
(Ki)	TRLB	Temporarily replaced by lighted buoy showing the same characteristics
(Kj)	TRUB	Temporarily replaced by unlighted buoy
(Kk)	TLB	Temporary lighted buoy
(Kl)	TUB	Temporary unlighted buoy

L. Buoys and Beacons (see General Remarks)

†1		Position of buoy
†2		Light buoy
†3	BELL	Bell buoy
†3a	GONG	Gong buoy
†4	WHIS	Whistle buoy
†5	C	Can or Cylindrical buoy
†6	N	Nun or Conical buoy
†7	SP	Spherical buoy
†8	S	Spar buoy
†8a	P	Pillar or Spindle buoy
†9		Buoy with topmark (ball) (See L-70)
†10		Barrel or Ton buoy
(La)		Color unknown
(Lb)	FLOAT	Float
†12	FLOAT	Lightfloat
13		Outer or Landfall buoy
14	BW	Fairway buoy (BWVS)
14a	BW	Mid-channel buoy (BWVS)
15	R	Starboard-hand buoy (entering from seaward)
16		Port-hand buoy (entering from seaward)
17	RB	Bifurcation buoy (RBHB)
18	RB	Junction buoy (RBHB)
19	RB	Isolated danger buoy (RBHB)
†20		Wreck buoy (RBHB or G)
20a		Obstruction buoy (RBHB or G)
21	Tel	Telegraph-cable buoy
†22		Mooring buoy (colors of mooring buoys never carried)
22a		Mooring
†22b	Tel	Mooring buoy with telegraphic communications
†22c	T	Mooring buoy with telephonic communications
23		Warping buoy
24	Y	Quarantine buoy
24a		Practice area buoy
25	Explos Anch	Explosive anchorage buoy
25a	AERO	Aeronautical anchorage buoy
26	Deviation	Compass adjustment buoy
27	BW	Fish trap (area) buoy (BWHB)
27a	W	Spoil ground buoy
28		Anchorage buoy (marks limits)
29	Priv maintd	Private aid to navigation (buoy) (maintained by private interests, use with caution)

FIG. 1844 i   Other lights, buoys and beacons

FIG. 1844 h   Lights

K. Lights

†1		Position of light
2	Lt	Light
(Ka)		Riprap surrounding light
3	Lt Ho	Lighthouse
†4	AERO AERO	Aeronautical light (See F-22)
4u		Marine and air navigation light
†5	Bn	Light beacon
†6		Light vessel; Lightship
8		Lantern
9		Street lamp
10	REF	Reflector
†11	Ldg Lt	Leading light
†12		Sector light
†13		Directional light
14		Harbor light
15		Fishing light
16		Tidal light
†17	Priv maintd	Private light (maintained by private interests; to be used with caution)
21	F	Fixed light
22	Occ	Occulting light
23	Fl	Flashing light
23a	E Int	Isophase light (equal interval)
24	Qk Fl	Quick flashing (scintillating) light
24a	I Qk Fl / Int Qk Fl	Interrupted quick flashing light
(Kb)	E Int	Equal interval (isophase) light
25a	S Fl	Short-flashing light
26	Alt	Alternating light
27	Gp Occ	Group occulting light
28	Gp Fl	Group flashing light
28a	S-L Fl	Short-long flashing light
28b		Group short flashing light
29	F Fl	Fixed and flashing light
30	F Gp Fl	Fixed and group flashing light
30a	Mo	Morse code light
31	Rot	Revolving or Rotating light
41		Period
42		Every
43		With
44		Visible (range)
(Kb)	M	Nautical mile (See E-11)
(Kc)	m; min	Minutes (See E-2)
(Kd)	sec	Seconds (See E-3)
45	Fl	Flash
46	Occ	Occultation
46a		Eclipse
47	Gp	Group
48	Occ	Intermittent light
49	SEC	Sector
50		Color of sector
51	Aux	Auxiliary light
52		Varied
61	Vi	Violet
62	Pu	Purple
63	Bu	Blue
64	G	Green
65	Or	Orange
66	R	Red
67	W	White
67a	Am	Amber
68	OBSC	Obscured light
68a	Fog Det Lt	Fog detector light (See Nb)

*National Ocean Survey has adopted a policy of using the small magenta disc for all floating lighted aids to navigation, and the magenta "flare" shape on all non-floating aids. This will be implemented as new chart editions are issued.

M. Radio and Radar Stations

1	°R. Sta	Radio telegraph station
2	°R. T	Radio telephone station
3	R. Bn	Radiobeacon
4	R. Bn	Circular radiobeacon
5	R.D	Directional radiobeacon; Radio range
6		Rotating loop radiobeacon
7	R.D.F	Radio direction finding station
(Ma)	TELEM ANT	Telemetry antenna
(Mb)	R RELAY MAST	Radio relay mast
(Mc)	MICRO TR	Microwave tower
9	R MAST / R TR	Radio mast / Radio tower
9a	TV TR	Television mast; Television tower
†10	R TR L (WBAL) 1090 kHz	Radio broadcasting station (commercial)
10a	°R. Sta	Q.T.G. Radio station
11	Ra	Radar station
12	Racon	Radar responder beacon
13	Ra Ref	Radar reflector (See L-Lf)
14	Ra (conspic)	Radar conspicuous object
14a		Ramark
15	D.F.S	Distance finding station (synchronized signals)
16	AERO R. Bn 302	Aeronautical radiobeacon
17	Decca Sta	Decca station
18	Loran Sta Venice	Loran station (name)
19	CONSOL Bn 190 Kc MMF	Consol (Consolan) station
(Md)	AERO R. Rge 342	Aeronautical radio range
(Me)	Ra Ref Calibration Bn	Radar calibration beacon
(Mf)	LORAN TR SPRING ISLAND	Loran tower (name)
(Mg)	R TR F R Lt	Obstruction light

N. Fog Signals

1	Fog Sig	Fog-signal station
2	HORN	Radio fog-signal station
3	GUN	Explosive fog signal
4		Submarine fog signal
5	SUB-BELL	Submarine fog bell (action of waves)
6	SUB-BELL	Submarine fog bell (mechanical)
7	SUB-OSC	Submarine oscillator
8	NAUTO	Nautophone
9	DIA	Diaphone
10	GUN	Fog gun
11	SIREN	Fog siren
12	HORN	Fog trumpet
13	HORN	Fog horn
†13a	HORN	Electric fog horn
14	BELL	Fog bell
15	WHIS	Fog whistle
16	HORN	Reed horn
17	GONG	Fog gong
18		Submarine sound signal not connected to the shore (See N-5,6,7)
18a		Submarine sound signal connected to the shore (See N-5,6,7)
(Na)	HORN	Typhon
(Nb)	Fog Det Lt	Fog detector light (See K 68a)

FIG. 1844 k   Radio and radar stations, fog signals

FIG. 1844 j   Buoys and beacons (continued)

L. Buoys and Beacons (continued)

†29 (cont.)	R	Starboard-hand buoy (entering from seaward)
	B	Port-hand buoy
30		Temporary buoy (See K i,j,k,l)
30a		Winter buoy
†31	HB	Horizontal stripes or bands
†32	VS	Vertical stripes
†33	Chec	Checkered
33a	Diag	Diagonal bands
41	W	White
42	B	Black
43	R	Red
44	Y	Yellow
45	G	Green
46	Br	Brown
47	Gy	Gray
48	Bu	Blue
48a	Am	Amber
48b	Or	Orange
†51		Floating beacon
†52	RW Bn / W Bn / R Bn / ▲Bn / △Bn	Fixed beacon (unlighted or daybeacon); Black beacon; Color unknown
(Lc)	MARKER / Marker	Private aid to navigation
53	Bn	Beacon, in general (See L-52)
54		Tower beacon
55		Cardinal marking system
56	Deviation Bn	Compass adjustment beacon
57		Topmarks (See L-9, 70)
58		Telegraph-cable (landing) beacon
59	Piles / Stumps	Piles (See O-30, H-9); Stakes; Stumps (See O-30); Perches
61	CAIRN / Cairn	Cairn
62		Painted patches
†63	TR	Landmark (position accurate) (See D-2)
†(Ld)	Tr	Landmark (position approximate)
64	REF	Reflector
65	MARKER	Range targets, markers
(Le)	W Or / W Or	Special-purpose buoys
66		Oil installation buoy
67		Drilling platform (See O-0b, O-0c)
70	Note:	TOPMARKS on buoys and beacons may be shown on charts of foreign waters. The abbreviation for black is not shown adjacent to buoys or beacons.
(Lf)	Ra Ref	Radar reflector (See M-13)

P. Various Limits, etc.

1	Leading line, Range line
2	Transit
3	In line with
4	Limit of sector
5	Channel, Course, Track recommended (marked by buoys or beacons) (See P-21)
(Pa)	Alternate course
6	Radar guided track
7	Submarine cable (power, telegraph, telephone, etc.)
7a	Submarine cable area
7b	Abandoned submarine cable (includes disused cable)
†8	Submarine pipeline
8a	Submarine pipeline area
9	Maritime limit in general
(Pb)	Limit of restricted area
10	Limit of fishing zone (fish trap areas)
11	U.S. Harbor Line
12	Limit of dumping ground, spoil ground (See P-9, G-13)
13	Anchorage limit
	Limit of airport (See I-23, 24)
13a	Limit of military practice areas
14	Limit of sovereignty (Territorial waters)
15	Customs boundary
16	International boundary (also State boundary)
17	Stream limit
18	Ice limit
19	Limit of tide
20	Limit of navigation
21	Course recommended (not marked by buoys or beacons) (See P-5)
22	District or province line
23	Reservation line (Options)
24	Measured distance
25	Prohibited area (See G-12, 46) (Screen Optional)
(Pd)	Shipping safety fairway
(Pe)	Directed traffic lanes

Q. Soundings

1	Doubtful sounding
2	No bottom found
3	Out of position
4	Least depth in narrow channels
5	Dredged channel (with controlling depth indicated)
6	Dredged area
7	Swept channel (See Q-9)
8	Drying (or uncovering) heights; in feet above chart (sounding) datum
†9	Swept area, not adequately sounded (shown by green tint)
†9a	Swept area adequately sounded (swept by wire drag to depth indicated)
10	Hair-line depth figures
10a	Figures for ordinary soundings
11	Soundings taken from foreign charts
12	Soundings taken from older surveys (or smaller scale chts)
13	Echo soundings
14	Sloping figures (See Q-12)
15	Upright figures (See Q-10a)
16	Bracketed figures (See Q-1, 2)
17	Underlined sounding figures (See Q-8)
18	Soundings expressed in fathoms and feet
22	Unsounded area
(Qa)	Stream

FIG. 1844 m ▼Various limits, and soundings

FIG. 1844 l Dangers

O. Dangers

1	Rock which does not cover (height above MHW) (See General Remarks)
2	Rock which covers and uncovers, with height in feet above chart (sounding) datum
†3	Rock awash at (near) level of chart (sounding) datum — Dotted line emphasizes danger to navigation
†(Oa)	Rock awash (height unknown)
4	Sunken rock (depth unknown) — Dotted line emphasizes danger to navigation
5	Shoal sounding on isolated rock
†6	Sunken rock not dangerous to surface navigation
6a	Sunken danger with depth cleared by wire drag (in feet or fathoms)
7	Reef of unknown extent
8	Submarine volcano
9	Discolored water
10	Coral reef, detached (uncovers at sounding datum)
	Coral or Rocky reef, covered at sounding datum (See A-11d, 11g)
11	Wreck showing any portion of hull or superstructure (above sounding datum)
	Obstruction (Fish haven)
	(Oc) Fish haven (fishing reef)
28	Wreck (See O-11 to 16)
12	Wreck with only masts visible (above sounding datum)
	Masts
	Wreckage (Wks)
29	Wreckage
13	Old symbols for wrecks
13a	Wreck always partially submerged
29a	Wreck remains (dangerous only for anchoring)
30	Submerged piling (See H-9, L-59) — Subm piles
†14	Sunken wreck dangerous to surface navigation (less than 11 fathoms over wreck) (See O-6a)
	Snags; Submerged stumps (See L-59) — Snags; Stumps
30a	Snags; Submerged stumps
31	Lesser depth possible
15	Wreck over which depth is known
32	Uncov Dries (See A-10; O-2, 10)
33	Cov Covers (See O-2, 10)
34	Uncov Uncovers (See A-10; O-2, 10)
15a	Wreck with depth cleared by wire drag
	Rep (1958) — Reported (with date)
35	Reported (with name and date)
16	Sunken wreck, not dangerous to surface navigation
	Eagle Rk (rep 1958)
36	Discol Discolored (See O-9)
37	Isolated danger
17	Foul ground — Foul
18	Overfalls or Tide Rips — Tide Rips (Symbol used only in small areas)
38	Limiting danger line
19	Eddies (Symbol used only in small areas)
20	Kelp, Seaweed — Kelp (Symbol used only in small areas)
39	Limit of rocky area
21	Bk Bank
22	Shl Shoal
23	Rf Reef (See A-11d, 11g; O-10)
23a	Ridge
24	Le Ledge
41	P A Position approximate
42	P D Position doubtful
43	E D Existence doubtful
44	P Pos Position
45	D Doubtful
46	Unexamined
†(Od)	L D Least Depth
25	Breakers (See A-12)
†26	Sunken rock (See O-4)
	(Oe) Crib — Subm Crib (above water)
	Platform (lighted) HORN
27	Obstr Obstruction
†(Of)	Offshore platform (unnamed)
†(Oh)	Submerged Well — Submerged Well (buoyed) — Hazel (lighted) HORN
†(Og)	Offshore platform (named)

U. Compass

Compass Rose

The outer circle is in degrees with zero at true north. The inner circles are in points and degrees with the arrow indicating magnetic north.

1	N	North
2	E	East
3	S	South
4	W	West
5	NE	Northeast
6	SE	Southeast
7	SW	Southwest
8	NW	Northwest
9	N	Northern
10	E	Eastern
11	S	Southern
12	W	Western
21	brg	Bearing
22	T	True
23	mag	Magnetic
24	var	Variation
25		Annual change
25a		Annual change nil
26		Abnormal variation; Magnetic attraction
27	deg	Degrees (See E-20)
28	dev	Deviation

T. Tides and Currents

1	HW	High water
1a	HHW	Higher high water
2	LW	Low water
(Ta)	LWD	Low water datum
2a	LLW	Lower low water
3	MTL	Mean tide level
4	MSL	Mean sea level
4a		Elevation of mean sea level above chart (sounding) datum
5		Chart datum (datum for sounding reduction)
6	Sp	Spring tide
7	Np	Neap tide
7a	MHW	Mean high water
8	MHWS	Mean high water springs
8a	MHWN	Mean high water neaps
8b	MHHW	Mean higher high water
8c	MLW	Mean low water
9	MLWS	Mean low water springs
9a	MLWN	Mean low water neaps
9b	MLLW	Mean lower low water
10	ISLW	Indian spring low water
11		High water full and change (vulgar establishment of the port)
12		Low water full and change
13		Mean establishment of the port
13a		Establishment of the port
14		Unit of height
15		Equinochal
16		Quarter; Quadrature
17	Str.	Stream
18		Current, general, with rate
19		Flood stream (current) with rate
20		Ebb stream (current) with rate
21		Tide gauge; Tidepole; Automatic tide gauge
23	vel.	Velocity; Rate
24	kn.	Knots
25	ht.	Height
26		Tide
27		New moon
28		Full moon
29		Ordinary
30		Syzygy
31	Fl.	Flood
32		Ebb
33		Tidal stream diagram
34		Place for which tabulated tidal stream data are given
35		Range (of tide)
36		Phase lag
(Tb)		Current diagram, with explanatory note

FIG. 1844 o   Tides and currents, the compass

FIG. 1844 n   Depth contours and tints, quality of the bottom

R. †Depth Contours and Tints (see General Remarks)

Feet	Fms/Meters
0	0
6	1
12	2
18	3
24	4
30	5
36	6
60	10
120	20
180	30
240	40

Feet	Fms/Meters
300	50
600	100
1,200	200
1,800	300
2,400	400
3,000	500
6,000	1,000
12,000	2,000
18,000	3,000

Or continuous lines, with values

5 (black)   100 (blue or black)

S. Quality of the Bottom

1	Grd	Ground
2	S	Sand
3	M	Mud; Muddy
4	Oz	Ooze
5	Ml	Marl
6	Cl	Clay
7	G	Gravel
8	Sn	Shingle
9	P	Pebbles
10	St	Stones
11	Rk, rky	Rock; Rocky
11a	Blds	Boulders
12	Ck	Chalk
12a	Ca	Calcareous
13	Qz	Quartz
13a	Sch	Schist
14	Co	Coral
(Sa)	Co Hd	Coral head
15	Mds	Madrepores
16	Vol	Volcanic
(Sb)	Vol Ash	Volcanic ash
17	La	Lava
18	Pm	Pumice
19	T	Tufa
20	Sc	Scoriae
21	Cn	Cinders
21a		Ash
22	Mn	Manganese
23	Sh	Shells
24	Oys	Oysters
25	Ms	Mussels
26	Spg	Sponge
27	K	Kelp
28	Wd	Sea-weed
	Grs	Grass
29	Stg	Sea-tangle
31	Spi	Spicules
32	Fr	Foraminifera
33	Gl	Globigerina
34	Di	Diatoms
35	Rd	Radiolaria
36	Pt	Pteropods
37	Po	Polyzoa
38	Cir	Cirripeda
38a	Fu	Fucus
38b	Ma	Mattes
39	fne	Fine
40	crs	Coarse
41	sft	Soft
42	hrd	Hard
43	stf	Stiff
44	sml	Small
45	lrg	Large
46	stk	Sticky
47	brk	Broken
47a	grd	Ground (Shells)
48	rt	Rotten
49	str	Streaky
50	spk	Speckled
51	gty	Gritty
52	dec	Decayed
53	fly	Flinty
54	glac	Glacial
55	ten	Tenacious
56	wh	White
57	bk	Black
58	vi	Violet
59	bu	Blue
60	gn	Green
61	yl	Yellow
62	or	Orange
63	rd	Red
64	br	Brown
65	ch	Chocolate
66	gy	Gray
67	lt	Light
68	dk	Dark
70	vard	Varied
71	unev	Uneven
(Sc)	S/M	Surface layer and Under layer
76		Fresh water springs in sea-bed

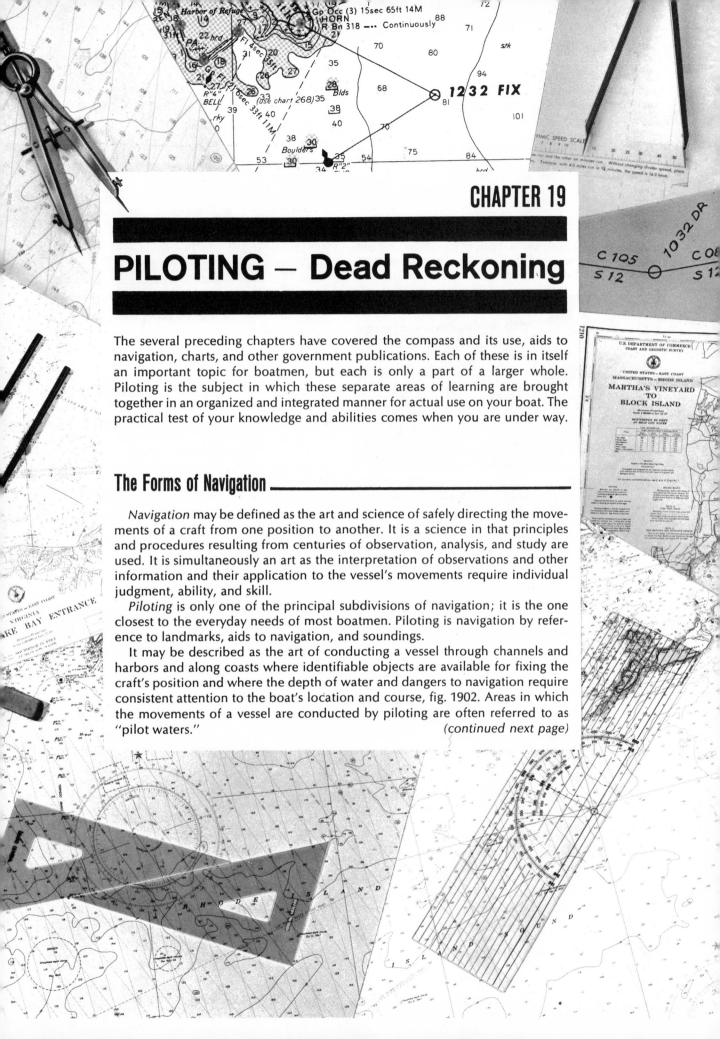

CHAPTER 19

PILOTING – Dead Reckoning

The several preceding chapters have covered the compass and its use, aids to navigation, charts, and other government publications. Each of these is in itself an important topic for boatmen, but each is only a part of a larger whole. Piloting is the subject in which these separate areas of learning are brought together in an organized and integrated manner for actual use on your boat. The practical test of your knowledge and abilities comes when you are under way.

The Forms of Navigation

Navigation may be defined as the art and science of safely directing the movements of a craft from one position to another. It is a science in that principles and procedures resulting from centuries of observation, analysis, and study are used. It is simultaneously an art as the interpretation of observations and other information and their application to the vessel's movements require individual judgment, ability, and skill.

Piloting is only one of the principal subdivisions of navigation; it is the one closest to the everyday needs of most boatmen. Piloting is navigation by reference to landmarks, aids to navigation, and soundings.

It may be described as the art of conducting a vessel through channels and harbors and along coasts where identifiable objects are available for fixing the craft's position and where the depth of water and dangers to navigation require consistent attention to the boat's location and course, fig. 1902. Areas in which the movements of a vessel are conducted by piloting are often referred to as "pilot waters." (continued next page)

Dead Reckoning / CHAPTER 19

Along with piloting, the boatman will often use another form of navigation, *dead reckoning,* a procedure by which the craft's approximate location at any time is deduced from its movements since the last accurate determination of position.

Other subdivisions of navigation are *electronic,* which will be touched on briefly in the following chapters insofar as specific systems are applicable to small craft, and *celestial,* which will be left to more advanced students and texts.

The importance of piloting

Piloting is a most important part of navigation, and perhaps the form requiring the least study but the most experience and best judgment. It is used by boatmen in

FIG. 1902 Piloting, by reference to landmarks and aids to navigation, is most often done in waters restricted by shoals and other dangers and which are relatively heavily traveled by other boats.

FIG. 1901 Piloting is the principal form of navigation used by boatmen. It requires study and practice, but it often becomes one of the major sources of enjoyment in boating. M. Rosenfeld.

rivers, bays, lakes, and close alongshore when on the open oceans. In such waters, the hazards to safe navigation may be quite frequent and the density of traffic quite high. The navigator of a craft of any size in pilot waters must have adequate training and knowledge; he must give his task close attention and constant alertness. Frequent determinations of position are usually essential, and changes in course or speed may be necessary at relatively short intervals.

The high seas vs. pilot waters

On the high seas, or well offshore in such large bodies of water as the Great Lakes, navigation can be more leisurely and relaxed. An error or uncertainty of position of a few miles will present no immediate hazard to the safety of the boat and its crew. But when one approaches the shore line, or the water shoals, a greater degree of accuracy is required. An error of only a few yards can result in running aground with certain embarrassment, and possibly much more serious consequences. The proximity of other craft requires constant knowledge of where the dangers lie and where one's own boat can be safely steered.

The enjoyment of piloting

Piloting can be "fun" for a boatman, but it will be most enjoyable when done without tension or anxiety; this happy state can be achieved only with a sound background of study and practice. The wise skipper "overnavigates" in times of fair weather so as to acquire the skill that will let him navigate his boat safely through fog or rain or night without fear or nervous strain.

The Dimensions of Piloting

The basic "dimensions" of piloting are direction, distance, and time. Other quantities which must be measured, calculated, or used, include speed, position, and depths and heights. A qualified pilot must have a ready understanding of how each of these dimensions is measured, expressed in units, used in calculations, and plotted on charts.

DIRECTION

Direction is the position of one point relative to another point without reference to the distance between them. As discussed earlier in the chapters on compasses and charts, modern navigation uses the system of angular measurement in which a complete circle is divided into 360 units called "degrees." Although each degree can in turn be subdivided into 60 minutes, the more common practice

in angular measurement in piloting is to use ordinary fractions such as ¹/₂ and ¹/₄, or decimal fractions in tenths.

True, magnetic, or compass

Directions are normally referred to a base line running from the origin point toward the geographic North Pole. Such directions can be measured on a chart with reference to the meridians of longitude and are called "true" directions. Measurements made with respect to the direction of the earth's magnetic field at that point are termed "magnetic" directions, and those referred to local magnetic conditions as measured by the craft's compass are designated "compass" directions, see fig. 1903. *It is of the utmost importance to always designate the reference used for directional measurement, true (T), magnetic (M), or compass (C).*

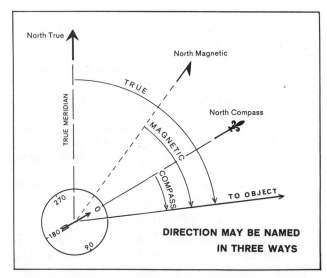

FIG. 1903 Direction is one of the basic "dimensions" of piloting. It can be measured with respect to True, Magnetic, or Compass North. Always be sure to designate the reference used.

Directions and angles

The basic system of measurement uses the reference direction as 0° (North) and measures clockwise through 90° (East), 180° (South), and 270° (West) around to 360° which is North again. Directions are expressed in three-digit form such as 005°, 030°, 150°, etc. Note that zeros are added before the figures denoting direction if necessary to make a three-digit number, for example, 005° or 030°, fig. 1904a. *Angles* which are *not* directions are expressed in one, two, or three digits as appropriate, 5°, 30°, 150°, etc., fig. 1904b.

Occasionally, directions will be expressed as so many degrees east or west of North or South, such as N30°E (030°), S20°E (160°), S40°W (220°), or N15°W (345°), fig. 1905. This form of expression, "direction in quadrant," is useful for some types of computations, but it is not employed for general navigational purposes.

Directions in the "point" system

The "point" system of angular measurement, so widely used in the days of sailing ships, has now fallen almost completely from practical use in navigation. It divided a complete circle into 32 points of 11¼ degrees each which could then be further subdivided fractionally. It is cumbersome to use and complicates calculations; with respect to the piloting of modern small craft, it is now of historical interest only.

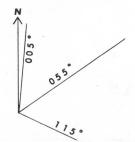

FIG. 1904a Directions are always designated by a *three-digit* number. Add zeros before a single or double-digit number as shown here.

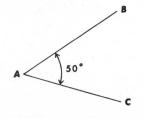

FIG. 1904b An angle between two directions, as distinguished from the directions themselves, is *not* expressed as a three-digit number. An angle such as BAC above is shown as simply 50°, not as 050°.

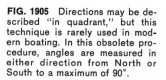

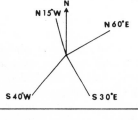

FIG. 1905 Directions may be described "in quadrant," but this technique is rarely used in modern boating. In this obsolete procedure, angles are measured in either direction from North or South to a maximum of 90°.

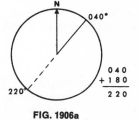

FIG. 1906a

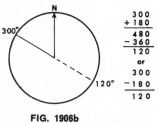

FIG. 1906b

The *reciprocal* of a direction is simply the opposite direction, shown here as a broken line. To find a reciprocal, add 180° to the given direction. If the total exceeds 360°, subtract that amount. Alternatively, subtract 180° from the given direction if it is greater than that amount.

Reciprocals

For any given direction, there is its *reciprocal*. This latter direction is the direct opposite, differing by 180°. Thus the reciprocal of 030° is 210°, and the reciprocal of 300° is 120°. To find the reciprocal of any direction, simply add 180° if the given direction is less than the amount; or subtract 180°, if it exceeds that figure, as shown in fig. 1906.

DISTANCE

This is the second of the basic dimensions of piloting. *Distance* is defined as the spacial separation between two points without regard to the direction of one from the other. It is commonly thought of as the length of the shortest line that can be drawn between the two points.

Nautical and statute miles

The basic unit of distance in piloting is the *mile,* but, as noted in Chapter 18, there are two types of miles that a boatman may encounter. The *statute mile* is used on inland bodies of water such as the Mississippi River and its tributaries, the Great Lakes, etc. (also the Atlantic and Gulf Intracoastal Waterways since 1969). It is 5280 feet in length, the same mile commonly used on land.

On the high seas and connecting tidal waters, the unit of measurement is the *nautical mile* of 6076.1 feet. This "salt-water" mile is essentially equal to one minute of latitude, and this relationship is often used in navigation. Nautical miles are slightly longer than statute miles, and the comparison is usually taken as 7 nautical miles equals 8 statute miles. More accurately, the conversion of nautical miles into statute miles is done by using the factor of 1.15.

It is quite possible to cruise from an area using one kind of mile into waters where the other kind is used. Care must be exercised at such times to determine which type of mile is being used and so specify in calculations.

For shorter distances, a few miles or less, the unit of measurement may be the *yard;* feet are seldom used as a unit of horizontal distance in boating. With the coming of the metric system, boatmen must expect greater use of *meters* and *kilometers;* we must become familiar with these units and conversion to and from English units.

TIME

The third basic dimension of piloting is *time*. Although the pilot does not need so accurate a knowledge of the exact time of day as does a celestial navigator, ability to determine the passage of time and to perform calculations with such *elapsed time* is essential. A boat should have aboard a clock or watch of reasonable time-keeping accuracy; a second one in reserve is desirable. For many practical problems in piloting, a stop watch will be found useful.

Units of time

The units of time used in boating are the everyday ones of *hours* of 60 *minutes* each. In piloting, measurements will not often be carried to the preciseness of *seconds* of time although decimal fractions of minutes may occasionally occur in calculations. Seconds and fractions of minutes may be used in competitive events such as races and predicted log contests, but seldom otherwise.

The 24-hour clock system

In navigation, including piloting, the time of day is expressed in a 24-hour system that eliminates the necessity for using the designations of "am" and "pm." Time is written in four-digit figures; the first two are the hour and the second pair represent the minutes. The day starts at 0001, one minute after midnight, 12:01 am in the old system. 0100 would be 1 am, 1000 is 10 am, and 1200 is noon. The second half of the day continues in the same pattern with 1300 being 1 pm, 1832 being 6:32 pm, etc., to 2400 for midnight. Time is spoken as "zero seven hundred" or "fifteen forty." The phrase "hours" should *not* be used. The times of 1000 and 2000 are correctly spoken as "ten hundred" and "twenty hundred," *not* as "one thousand" or "two thousand."

When performing arithmetic computations with time caution must always be exercised to remember that when "borrowing" or "carrying" there are *60* minutes in an hour, and not 100. As obvious and simple a matter as this may be, the mistake occurs all too often.

Time zones

A navigator in pilot waters must also be alert to *time zones*. Even in coastal or inland waters, it is possible to cruise from one zone to another resulting in the necessity for changing clocks, the plot on the chart, and the log; plus one's arrival time at the next port.

A further complication in time is the prevalence of "daylight time" in many boating areas during the summer months. Government publications are in standard time; local sources of information such as newspapers and radio broadcasts will undoubtedly use daylight time if it is in effect. Daylight time is one hour *later* than standard time. When going from standard time to daylight, *add* one hour; from daylight to standard, *subtract* one hour.

SPEED

No matter how fast or slow one's craft may be, speed is an essential dimension of piloting. *Speed* is defined as the number of units of distance that would be traveled in a specified unit of time.

The basic unit of speed is *miles per hour*, whether these be nautical or statute miles, as determined by location. A special name, *knot*, has been given to the nautical mile per hour. Note well that the word "knot" includes the element of time—to say "knots per hour" is not only incorrect, it is a mark of ignorance.

Conversion of knots and MPH

The conversion factors between statute miles per hour (MPH) and knots are the same as for the corresponding units of distance—1 knot = 1.15 MPH, or 7 knots roughly equals 8 MPH.

The unit "knot" may be abbreviated either as "kn." or "kt."; the former has a somewhat greater usage.

POSITION

The ability to describe accurately the position of his craft is an essential requirement for a pilot, and one that marks him as well qualified. To realize the importance and the difficulties of this seemingly simple task, one has only to listen to his radio on 2182 kHz on a weekend afternoon during the boating season. The hesitant, inadequate, and inaccurate attempts by skippers to simply say where they are must surely irritate the Coast Guard and embarrass all competent boatmen!

Relative and geographic coordinates

Position may be described in relative terms or by geographic coordinates. When defined as a *relative position*, the location of the craft is described as being a certain distance and direction from a specified identifiable point such as a landmark or aid to navigation. A boat's position may be described with varying degrees of preciseness as determined by the accuracy of the data on which it is based. A skipper might say that he was "about two miles southwest of Brenton Reef Light"; or if he had the capability of being more precise, he could say, "I'm 2.2 miles, 230°. True from Brenton Reef Light." In relative positioning, the distance may, of course, be essentially zero, as would be the case with a position report such as "I am at Lighted Whistle Buoy 2." See fig. 1907.

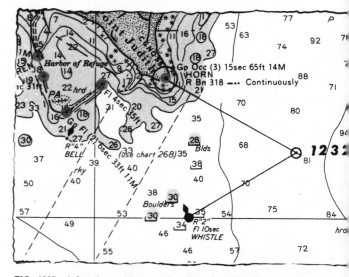

FIG. 1907 A boat's position may be described in "relative" terms. It is stated to be at a certain distance and direction from an identifiable object such as an aid to navigation. In this example, it would be "1.8 miles, 120 degrees True from Point Judith Light."

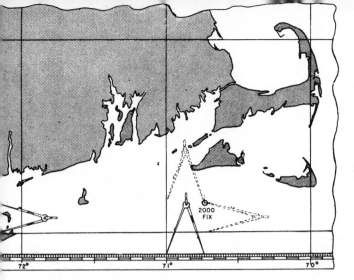

FIG. 1908 The position of a boat can be described in terms of "geographic coordinates." Using the subdivisions of the chart's borders, the latitude and longitude of the plotted position are measured and recorded. (from DUTTON'S NAVIGATION AND PILOTING)

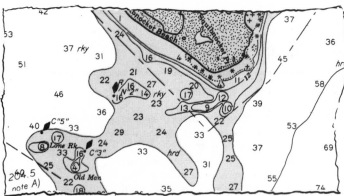

FIG. 1909 Depth is a "dimension" of piloting that is often of the greatest importance to the safety of a boat and its crew. Be sure that you know whether the charted depths on the chart you are using are shown in feet or fathoms.

The preceding examples of position description have all used visible identifiable objects. It is also possible to state one's *geographic position* in terms of *latitude* and *longitude* using those nice straight, uniformly-spaced lines on charts which so unfortunately do not appear on the surface of the water. Using this procedure, the position is measured from the markings on either side and the top or bottom of the chart.

The units of measurement for geographic coordinates are *degrees* and *minutes,* but this degree is not quite the same unit as used in the measurement of direction, nor is this minute the same as the unit of time. Care must be used to avoid confusion between these units of position and other units with similar names. For precise position definition, one may use either *seconds* or *tenths of minutes* as determined by the chart being used. Typically, the smallest unit on the marginal scales of N.O.S. coast charts will be tenths of minutes, but for harbor charts it will be seconds; see page 355.

In a statement of geographic position, latitude is given first, before longitude, and the figures must be followed by "North" or "South" as appropriate. In U.S. waters, the latitude is, of course, always "North," even for the most unreconstructed "rebel." Similarly, longitude must be designated "East" or "West" to be complete; all U.S. waters are in West longitude, fig. 1908.

DEPTHS

The *depth* of the water is important both for the safety of a boat in preventing grounding and for navigational purposes. Thus, this vertical measurement from the surface of the water to the bottom is an essential dimension of piloting. Measurements may be made continuously or only occasionally as determined by the circumstances, but you can be sure that at some time or another on almost any cruise, knowledge of the depth will become critically important.

In pilot waters, depths will normally be measured in *feet*. In open ocean waters, the small craft operator may find himself on charts indicating depths in *fathoms* of six feet each. It is important to check each chart when purchased and again when used to note the unit of measurement of depth, fig. 1909.

In many areas, depths will fluctuate somewhat from the printed figures on charts due to tidal changes. Charts will indicate the *datum* used, the reference plane from which measurements were made. They will also indicate the normal range of tidal variations and the extreme low-water condition that must be considered.

HEIGHTS

The height, or elevation, of certain objects will be of concern to the pilot. The height of some landmarks and lighted aids to navigation may determine their range of visibility. Of more critical importance, however, are such vertical measurements as the clearance under a bridge, fig. 1910. *Heights,* or vertical dimensions upward from the surface of the water, are measured in *feet*. It should be noted that in tidal areas, the datum, or plane of reference, for heights is *not* the same as for depths. Examine each chart closely and note the datum from which heights are measured.

The usual datum for the measurement of heights is *mean high water*. This will be an imaginary plane surface above the mean low-water datum for depths by an amount equal to the *mean tide range*; the height of mean high water will usually be shown on a chart.

FIG. 1910 Charts will show the heights of bridges or other structures that will affect navigation. Heights are measured vertically in feet, usually from mean high water (MHW).

The Instruments of Piloting

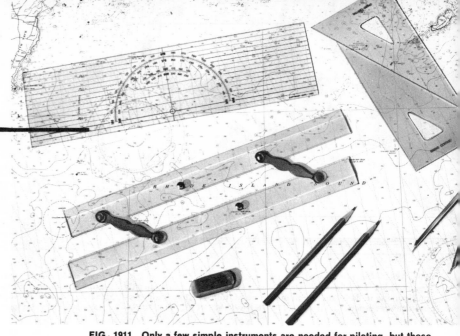

The practice of piloting in coastal and inland waters requires the use of a few simple tools or instruments, fig. 1911. These are not particularly expensive items, but they should be of good quality, well cared for, and used with the proper respect. A skilled man in any profession or trade is known by his tools, when that term is used in its broadest sense. A navigator may well be judged by his instruments and how he uses them.

FIG. 1911 Only a few simple instruments are needed for piloting, but these should be of good quality, used with respect, and properly maintained.

DIRECTION

Many instruments are used in the measurement of direction. Some are concerned with such measurement directly, and others with its measurement on a chart. Still other instruments are used to both measure direction from a chart and to plot directions from observations.

Determining Direction

The basic instrument on a boat for the determination of direction is a *compass*. With rare exceptions, this will be a *magnetic* compass as shown in fig. 1912 and described in Chapter 13. Directions obtained from this instrument will be "compass" directions and will require correction for deviation and variation as covered in that chapter.

A *gyro* compass is a complex device capable of indicating the true north direction without regard to magnetic conditions. However, its size, weight, electrical power requirements, and particularly its high cost, limit its use to the largest and most luxurious yachts. The average boatman must make do with a magnetic compass, but, properly used, this traditional piloting instrument will serve him well.

The compass is used primarily to determine the direction in which the craft is headed. Depending upon its location, and how it is mounted, the steering compass may also be used for determining the direction of other objects from the boat. Rough readings may be taken by sighting across the compass itself and estimating the reading of the compass card. More exact readings can be taken if a pair of *sight vanes* can be mounted on the compass as illustrated in fig. 1913. Sights taken with a steering compass are satisfactory as to accuracy, but are generally limited by physical considerations to objects forward of the beam.

Pelorus. A more flexible instrument for measuring the direction of objects from the boat is the *pelorus,* fig. 1914. This simple device consists of a set of sighting vanes mounted over a circular scale calibrated in degrees like a compass card. A means must be provided for mounting or temporarily locating the pelorus so that it may be properly oriented to the fore-and-aft center line of the boat. Peloruses may be purchased or made in the home workshop; see fig. 1915.

The circular scale of a pelorus is usually made so that it may be rotated to a desired position and there clamped in place. With the scale so set that 000° is dead ahead, over or parallel to the center line of the boat, the directions that are then measured are termed *relative bearings*.

FIG. 1912 A magnetic compass is the basic instrument for measuring direction on a boat. See Chapters 13 and 14 for detailed coverage of the compass.

FIG. 1913 The compass can be used to determine the direction from the boat to an object such as an aid to navigation. Greater accuracy will be obtained if *sight vanes* are used as shown here.

FIG. 1914 A *pelorus* is used to take bearings on objects from a boat. It consists of a set of sights mounted over an angular scale calibrated like a compass card.

The sight vanes placed on a compass, or those of a pelorus, may be replaced with a small telescope having cross-hairs. Greater accuracy will be achieved, but the telescope must be of low power in order to have a wide enough field of view to pick up and hold objects at a distance despite the movements of the boat.

Even greater flexibility of use can be obtained with one of several patented instruments now on the market. Each of these consists of a small magnetic compass conveniently mounted for holding in front of one's eyes, plus a set of sights and a prismatic optical system for simultaneously observing a distant object through the sights and reading the compass card. Internal lighting for night use is usually provided. Typical of these instruments is the Hand Bearing Compass (fig. 1916) with open sights. Fig. 1917 illustrates how some small compasses may be unshipped from their mounting and held at eye level to take a bearing.

Plotting directions

Once direction has been determined by compass, pelorus, or other device, it must be plotted on the chart. For this action, there are a number of instruments available. These same tools will be used when the problem is the determination of direction from the chart itself.

Course plotters. These are pieces of clear plastic, usually rectangular in shape, with one or more semi-circular angular scales marked thereon, see fig. 1918. The center of these scales is at or near the center of one of the longer sides of the plotter and is usually emphasized with a small circle or "bull's-eye." There are normally two main scales, one from 000° to 180° and the other from 180° to 360°; each is calibrated in degrees. There may also be smaller auxiliary scales offset 90° from the main scales. Lines are marked on the plotter parallel to the longer sides. Some instruments have distance marks along the edges corresponding to the more commonly-used chart scales.

Course plotters are used in the following manner:

1. *To determine the direction of a course or bearing from a given point,* place the plotter on the chart so that one of its longer sides is along the course or bearing line and slide the plotter until the bull's-eye is over a *meridian.* The true direction is then read on the scale where it is intersected by the meridian. Easterly courses are read on the scale that reads from 000° to 180°, and westerly courses are read on the other main scale, see fig. 1919.

These may be converted to compass directions or compass bearings, by numerically adding the heading of the boat as read from the steering compass at the instant of observation (subtract 360° from this sum if it exceeds that amount). A steady hand at the wheel is required, and the observer should call "Mark" at the time that he reads the pelorus so that the helmsman may simultaneously read the boat's compass. Alternatively, the helmsman may call a series of "marks" as he is on the prescribed heading, remaining silent if the boat falls off to either side. When using this technique, the observer takes his reading only when the helmsman is indicating that he is directly on the correct heading.

A second method of using a pelorus is to set the scale so that it matches the compass for the heading being steered. Readings then taken with the pelorus are directly compass bearings without further conversion. Two cautions must be observed — the craft must be directly on course at the time of observation; and, when correcting for *deviation,* the value used is that for the *heading* of the boat, *not* that for the observed direction. Because of these possible errors, particularly the latter one, this technique should be avoided, or used only with much practice and great care.

FIG. 1915 A pelorus may be purchased or it is easily made in a home workshop. A compass rose or card diagram such as Fig. 1310 or 1335 is cut out and mounted on a wooden or metallic base. A set of rotatable sighting vanes completes the pelorus.

FIG. 1916 A hand bearing compass has the advantage that it may easily be used from almost any place on a boat. Be careful, however, of using it near large masses of magnetic material that will introduce deviation errors.

FIG. 1917 Some compasses, like this Corsair, are so mounted (particularly on small boats) that they can be easily unshipped and held at eye-level for taking bearings. The same precautions regarding deviation must be observed as for a hand bearing compass.

If it is more convenient, the course or bearing may be lined up with one of the marked parallel lines rather than the edge of the course plotter. In measuring courses and bearings, it is not absolutely necessary to actually draw in the line connecting the two points, the plotter can be aligned using only the two points concerned. Usually, however, it will be found easier and safer to draw in the connecting line.

When the direction to be measured is within 20° or so of due North or South, it may be difficult to reach a meridian by sliding the course plotter across the chart. The small inner auxiliary scales have been included on the plotter for just such cases. Slide the plotter until the bull's-eye intersects a *parallel of latitude* line. The intersection of this line with the appropriate *auxiliary* scale indicates the direction of the course or bearing, see fig. 1920.

2. *To plot a specified direction (course or bearing) from a given point,* put a pencil on the origin point, keep one of the longer edges of the course plotter snug against the pencil, and slide the plotter around until the center bull's-

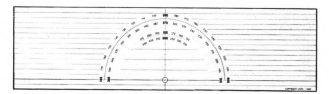

FIG. 1918 A *course plotter* is a single rectangular piece of transparent plastic ruled with circular scales and a set of lines parallel to its longer sides. Shown here is the model used by the U.S. Power Squadrons.

FIG. 1919 The course plotter is lined up with the course line along one of the longer sides, and then is moved until a meridian cuts through the "bull's eye." Direction can then be read from the appropriate main scale.

eye and the desired mark on the appropriate main scale both lie along the same meridian. With the plotter thus positioned, draw in the specified direction from the given point.

Alternatively, the plotter may first be positioned using the bull's-eye and scale markings without regard to the specified origin point. The plotter is then carefully slid up or down the meridian until one of the longer edges is over the origin point and then the direction line is drawn in.

For directions nearly North or South, one of the small auxiliary scales can be used in conjunction with a parallel of latitude.

3. *To extend a line* which must be longer than the length of the course plotter, place a pair of dividers, opened to three or four inches, tightly against the edge of the plotter and then slide the plotter along using the divider points as guides. Draw in the extension of the course or bearing line after the plotter has been advanced.

4. In piloting, it is sometimes necessary *to draw a new line parallel to an existing course or bearing line.* For such situations, the parallel lines marked on the course plotter may be used as guides.

Course protractors. Many pilots use a *course protractor*, fig. 1921, as their primary plotting tool. This instrument, with its moving parts, is not as easily used as the course plotter described above; but, when it is employed with care, it gives as satisfactory results.

In using the course protractor *to measure the direction of a course or bearing,* its center should be placed on the chart exactly over the specified origin point, such as the boat's position or an aid to navigation. The arm of the protractor is then swung around to the nearest compass rose on the chart, making the upper edge of the arm (which is in line with the center of the compass part of the course protractor) pass directly over the center of the compass rose.

Holding the course protractor arm firmly in this position, the compass part of the protractor is then turned around until the upper edge of the arm cuts across the same degree marking of the protractor compass as it does at the compass rose. The compass and the rose are now parallel. Holding the protractor compass firmly against the chart, the protractor arm is then moved around until its edge cuts across the second point involved in the course

FIG. 1920 If a meridian cannot be easily reached, as may be the case with courses within a few degrees of North or South, use the *auxiliary* inner scales and a *parallel* of latitude as shown here.

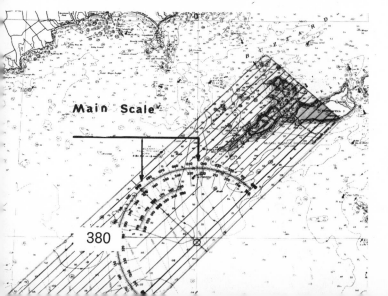

Main Scale

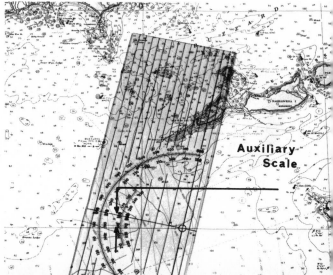

Auxiliary Scale

or bearing. The direction in degrees can then be read directly from the protractor compass scale.

To lay off a line in a specified direction from the given point, the protractor rose is first lined up with the compass rose on the chart as in the preceding instructions. Then the arm is rotated until the desired direction is indicated on the compass scale, and the line is drawn in; this line will have to be extended back to the origin point after the course protractor has been lifted off the chart.

Parallel rulers. A traditional instrument for measuring and plotting directions on charts is a set of *parallel rulers*. Their use on boats has declined somewhat in recent years, but they are still capable of giving good results if the navigator is careful to avoid slippage. Parallel rulers may be

FIG. 1922 *Parallel rulers* are a traditional charting instrument. The two straightedges are kept in parallel alignment by the connecting links. Directions are transferred from one place to another by "walking" the rulers across the chart.

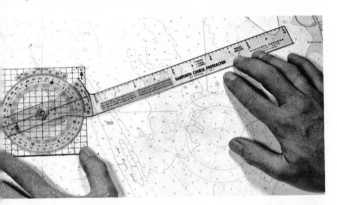

FIG. 1921 Some skippers prefer to use a *course protractor* as their primary plotting tool. It consists of two pieces of plastic movable with respect to each other.

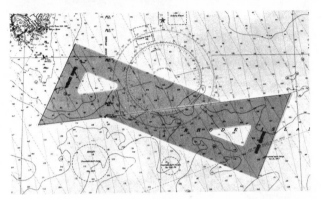

FIG. 1923 A pair of ordinary drawing triangles can be used for transferring a direction from one part of a chart to another, but not for great distances. See text for method of their use.

made of black (as shown in fig. 1922) or clear transparent plastic material. The two rulers are connected by metal linkages so that the edges always remain parallel. To measure the direction of a line, one ruler is lined up with the desired objects on the chart and then the pair is "walked" across the chart to the nearest compass rose by alternately holding one ruler and moving the other. To plot a line of stated direction, the process is essentially reversed; the procedure is started at the compass rose and worked to the desired origin point.

Drawing triangles. A pair of ordinary plastic *drawing triangles* can also be used for transferring a direction from one part of a chart to another, although not for very great distances. The two triangles need not be similar in size or shape. The two hypotenuses (longest sides) are placed together and one of the other sides of one triangle is lined up with the course or bearing line, or with the desired direction at the compass rose, fig. 1923. The other triangle is held firmly in place as a base, and the first one is slid along in contact with it, carrying the specified line to a new position while maintaining its direction. If necessary, the triangles may be alternately held and slid for moving somewhat greater distances.

Courser. One rather unique direction instrument, particularly useful in outboards or other situations of limited space, is a "Courser," a patented device consisting of a sheet of flexible plastic upon which are ruled a series of parallel lines, fig. 1924. One line is placed over the course or bearing to be measured and another will fall across or near the center of a compass rose on the chart. By slight adjustments to the Courser, directions can be read off the

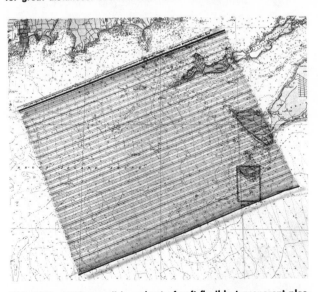

FIG. 1924 A "Courser" is a sheet of soft flexible transparent plastic on which parallel lines have been ruled. It is simple and convenient to use in smaller boats, and the accuracy obtained with it is adequate for such applications.

rose with sufficient accuracy for practical use in a small boat.

An ordinary *drawing protractor* may find some use aboard a boat for measuring angles, but it is not a highly useful instrument and can be omitted. A chart compass rose can always be used for angle measurement if this becomes necessary.

FIG. 1925 A *radar set* on a boat can measure the direction and distance to other boats, aids to navigation, prominent structures and terrain features, etc. The use of radar is covered more fully in Chapter 25.

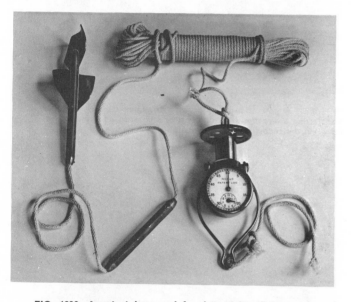

FIG. 1926 A *patent log*, used for determining distance run and speed. A log line connects the rotator to a registering device near the stern of the boat. The log line must be long enough to clear the wake as it is towed astern. In use, the rotator revolves as it is towed through the water, and the line transmits this rotary motion to the registering device which is calibrated so that the distance can be read directly from the dial.

FIG. 1927 A more modern patent log consists of a much smaller impeller mounted on the bottom of the boat connected to a dialed instrument for measuring speed and distance run through the water.

DISTANCE

Distance to an object can be measured directly by *radar*, fig. 1925; and distance traveled can be measured directly by a *summing log,* figs. 1926 and 1927. However, few boats are equipped with either of these items of equipment. Distance is usually measured in piloting by taking it from a chart.

Chart measurements for distance

Dividers. Distance is measured on a chart with a pair of *dividers*, fig. 1928a. The two arms of this small drafting instrument can be opened as desired, and the friction at the pivot is sufficient to hold them in place with the same separation between the points. Most dividers have some means for adjusting this friction; it should be enough to hold the arms in place, but not so much as to make opening or closing difficult. A special type of dividers has a center cross-piece (like the horizontal part of the capital letter "A") which can be rotated by a knurled knob to set and maintain the opening between the arms, fig. 1928b; thus the distance between the points cannot accidentally change. This type of dividers is particularly useful if kept set to some standard distance, such as one mile to the scale of the chart being used.

The dividers are first opened to the distance between two points on the chart, then they are transferred without change to the chart's graphic scale (see fig. 1929). Note that the zero point on this scale is not at the left-hand end, but rather is one basic unit up the scale. This unit to the left of zero is more finely divided than are the remaining basic units. For the measurement of any distance, the right-hand point of the dividers is set on the basic unit mark that will result in the left-hand point falling somewhere on the more-finely-divided unit to the left of the zero. The distance measured is the sum of the basic units counted off to the right from the scale's zero point plus the fractional unit to the left from zero. In fig. 1929, the distance is 1.4 nautical miles.

If the distance on the chart cannot be spanned with the dividers opened widely (about 60° is the maximum practical opening), set them at a convenient opening for a whole number of units on the graphic scale or latitude subdivisions, step this off the necessary number of times, then measure the odd remainder. The total distance is then the simple sum of the parts stepped off and measured separately, fig. 1930.

To mark off on the chart a desired distance, set the right point of the dividers on the nearest lower whole number of units, and the left point on the remaining fractional part of a unit measured leftward from zero on the scale. The dividers are now properly set for the specified distance at the scale of the chart being used and can be applied to the chart. If the distance is too great for one setting of the dividers, it may be stepped off in several increments.

Charts at a scale smaller than 1:80,000 will not have a graphic scale. In lieu thereof, distances are measured on the latitude scales at either side of the chart. Care should be taken to measure on these scales near the same latitude as the portion of the chart being used; in other words, move directly horizontally across the chart to either of its sides to use the scales.

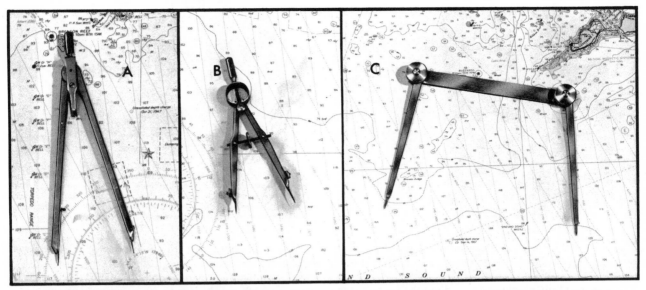

FIG. 1928 Dividers are used to measure distances on a chart. A—Friction at the pivot holds the arms to the desired opening. B—In this type of dividers, an adjustable center cross-arm maintains the separation between points and avoids accidental changes. C—Long-legged dividers enable the pilot to step off long runs on a chart, without "walking" them.

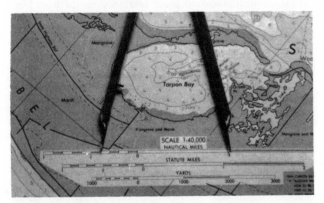

FIG. 1929 After the dividers have been set for the distance on the chart between the points concerned, they are moved to the graphic scale or latitude subdivisions at the edge of the chart. Distance is measured on these scales as described in the text.

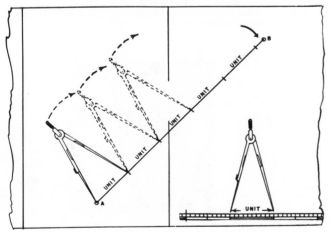

FIG. 1930 When a chart distance is too great to be measured with a single setting of the dividers, open the points to a convenient whole number of units. Step these along the chart for the required number of times and then measure any small left-over distance (arrow) in the usual manner. (Figs. 1908 and 1930 are based on DUTTON'S NAVIGATION AND PILOTING, copyright © 1957 and 1958 by U. S. Naval Institute, Annapolis, Maryland.)

With a little experience, dividers can be set and used with one hand. Making sure that the friction at the pivot is properly adjusted, practice this technique until it can be used with ease; such ability will add convenience and speed to your piloting work.

An instrument that looks much like a pair of dividers, except that a pencil lead or pen is substituted for one point, is called a *compass* (or *drawing compass* to distinguish it from a magnetic compass). This is used primarily for drawing arcs or circles.

Distance can also be measured across a chart with reduced, but generally acceptable, accuracy by using a *chart measurer*, fig. 1931. This device has a small wheel that is rolled along the chart; the wheel is internally geared to an indicating dial. Chart measurers will read distances directly in miles at various typical chart scales; separate models are available for charts using statute and nautical miles. They are particularly useful in measuring distances up rivers with many bends and changes of direction.

TIME

Every pilot, no matter how small his craft, should have a dependable and reasonably accurate timepiece. This can be a clock, wrist watch, or pocket watch. Long-term accuracy is of secondary importance in piloting, but short-term errors, those accumulated over the length of a day or half-day, should be small. A knowledge of the time of day within a few minutes will usually be sufficient. A clock, if used, should be mounted where it is clearly visible from the helm-seat or plotting table. If two clocks are used, be sure that they show the same time.

Elapsed time is usually of greater interest than *absolute* time. A stop watch will often be handy although it cannot be classed as a necessary instrument of piloting. Most stop watches have a second hand that makes one revolution for each minute, but there are some that sweep completely around in 30 seconds, and even a few that have a 10-second period. Know for sure the type of stop watch that you are using.

FIG. 1931 If a *chart measurer* is rolled across a chart, between two points, an indicating dial will show the distance directly for typical chart scales. It is especially useful in measuring distances on waterways with many bends and curves.

FIG. 1933 Many small boats are fitted with a simple device that measures speed by the pressure built up in a probe as a result of the movement of the boat through the water. Accuracy is quite good, but it must be remembered that it is speed through the water that is measured, and not speed made good over the bottom.

SPEED

Speed is a dimension that can be measured directly or calculated from knowledge of distance and time. Direct reading instruments are convenient, but they give only the relative speed through the water, and not the speed made good between two geographic points.

In years gone by, speed through the water was measured by use of a *chip log,* fig. 1932. More modern marine speedometers use the static pressure built up in a small tube by motion of the boat, fig. 1933, an impeller turned by the passing water, or a finger-like strut projecting below the bottom of the boat, fig. 1934. Many different models are available in a wide variety of speed ranges from those for sailboats to models reading high enough for fast speedboats.

Speed can be calculated from a knowledge of the distance covered and the elapsed time, to be discussed later in this chapter, or by the use of special calculating devices. These calculators are specialized adaptations of slide rules used for general mathematical calculations; they may be either linear or circular in form, figs. 1935a and b.

DEPTH

This most important dimension of piloting can be measured manually or electronically. A hand *lead line,* fig. 1936, is simple, accurate, and not subject to breakdowns. It does have the disadvantages, however, of being awkward to use, inconvenient in bad weather, and capable of giving only one or two readings per minute; a lead line can be used only at quite slow speeds.

Many small craft today are equipped with an *electronic depth sounder.* These devices can clearly, accurately, and most conveniently provide measurements of the depth of water beneath the boat. Moreover, soundings are indicated many times each second, so frequently that they appear to be a smooth, continuous measurement of depth. For more information on these relatively inexpensive but most useful piloting aids, see Chapter 25, pages 499 to 501.

FIG. 1934 This speedometer, designed primarily for sailboats, is actuated by a strut or finger which projects below the bottom of the boat. A modern solid-state electronic instrument, it measures speed variations to 1/100 knot. An optional feature measures distance up to 999.9 nautical miles.

FIG. 1932 The old chip log, consisting of the log-chip, log-line, and log-glass. The log-chip is a thin piece of wood, weighted so that it will float vertically. The chip is thrown from the stern and the log-line is allowed to flow freely over the rail. The line is marked at intervals of 47 feet 3 inches, called "knots," and the number of knots that pass over the rail in the time that it takes the glass to empty is a direct measure of the speed.

FIG. 1934 a Unipas-300, a versatile 12-volt solid-state navigational instrument, measures depth on 25- or 100-foot scales; speed, on various scales from 0-2.5 or 0-25 knots, with sensitivity as fine as .01 knot; and distance logged, in steps of .001 mile. Plug-in modules provide for twin-engine synchronization, wind-speed measurement, detection of gasoline vapors, and a battery check. At anchor, it will even measure current velocity.

MISCELLANEOUS PILOTING TOOLS

Among the most important of all piloting tools are the ordinary *pencils* and *erasers*. Pencils should be neither too hard nor too soft. If too hard, there will be a tendency to score into the chart paper; if too soft, smudging may result. A medium, or No. 2, pencil will often be found to be satisfactory, but personal preferences may cause some variation. Pencils should be kept well sharpened, and several should be handy to the piloting table.

FIG. 1935a Speed need not be measured directly; it may be calculated from a knowledge of distance and time. A circular calculator as shown here will make all speed-time-distance computations quickly and accurately.

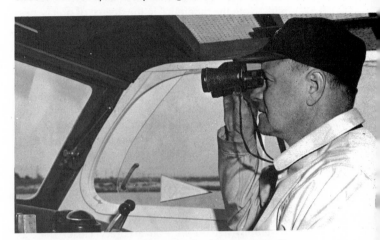

FIG. 1937 A good pair of binoculars is almost a necessity on a boat. The size most often recommended is designated "7 x 50." The eyepieces may be individually or centrally focused.

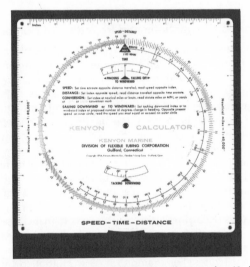

FIG. 1935b This calculator enables the pilot to solve 18 different types of navigational problems—speed-time-distance, conversions and measurement, and includes special aids for the sailboatman, even a plotting board on the reverse side.

A soft eraser of the "Pink Pearl" type will be satisfactory for most erasures; an art gum eraser can be used for general chart cleaning.

Binoculars. A good pair of *binoculars* will be found essential for most piloting situations, fig. 1937. In selecting a pair of binoculars, it should be remembered that higher powers will result in greater magnification, bringing distant objects closer, but only at the cost of a more limited field of view. An adequate field of view is essential on small boats with their rapid and sometimes violent motion. Binoculars are designated by two figures, such as "6x30" or "10x50." The first figure indicates the power of magnification, the second is the diameter of the front lens in millimeters. This latter characteristic is important in night use. Most authorities recommend a 7x50 set of binoculars as best suited for marine use.

The binoculars may be individually focused (IF) for each eye, or centrally focused (CF) for both eyes, with a minor adjustment on one eyepiece to balance any difference between a person's two eyes. The choice between IF and CF glasses is a matter of personal preference.

Binoculars should be kept in their case when use is not imminent. When taken out, they should be carefully placed where they cannot be thrown from a table or ledge to the deck and damaged; protect your binoculars from any rough usage.

A boat should be equipped with several *flashlights* for emergency use. One of these should have a red lens or filter in order that it may be used to read charts and other printed matter at night without undue loss of night vision by a person who must both check the chart and act as helmsman or lookout.

FIG. 1936 Depth can be measured manually with a marked weighted line—a lead line. Markings can be of the traditional type with strips of leather and rags, or with modern direct-reading plastic tags.

MEASUREMENTS

In considering the measurement of various quantities in piloting, and the calculations in which they are used, some attention must first be given to standards of accuracy and precision. Statements of distance as 32 miles or 32.0 miles are not quite the same thing. The former merely says that to the best of observation and measurement the distance is not 31 nor 33 miles; the latter says that it is not 31.9 nor 32.1 miles. Note the difference in the degree of preciseness of these two statements of the same distance. Never write 32.0 for 32 unless your measurements are sufficiently precise to warrant such action.

STANDARD LIMITS OF ACCURACY

The navigation of various sizes of vessels naturally involves different standards of precision or accuracy as befitting the different conditions encountered. The piloting of small craft does not permit so high a degree of accuracy as on large ships that offer a more stable platform.

Direction

Direction is measured in small-craft navigation to the nearest whole degree. It is not reasonable to measure or calculate directions to a finer degree of precision when a boat is seldom steered with an accuracy closer than 2° or 3°.

Distance

Distances are normally expressed to the nearest tenth of a mile. This degree of precision, roughly 200 yards, is reasonable in consideration of the size of the craft and other measurement standards.

Time

Time is measured and calculated to the nearest minute. Fractions of a minute are rarely of any significance in routine piloting. In contests, however, time will be calculated to decimal fractions and used in terms of seconds.

Speed

Speed is calculated to the nearest tenth of a knot or mile-per-hour. It is seldom measurable to such fine units, but a calculation to the nearest tenth is not inconsistent with the expressed standards of accuracy of distance and time. This same degree of precision is used in calculations of current velocity.

Position

Geographic coordinates will be expressed to the nearest tenth of a minute of latitude and longitude, or to the nearest second, as determined by the scale of the chart. As explained in Chapter 18, latitude and longitude markings will be subdivided into minutes and seconds on the larger-scale charts (1:49,000 and larger) and in fractions of minutes on smaller-scale charts (1:50,000 and smaller).

Depths and heights of tide

Tidal variations in the depth of water are normally tabulated to the nearest tenth of a foot, fig. 1938; calculations are carried out to the same degree of precision. It must be recognized, however, that modifications to tidal action resulting from winds and atmospheric pressure variations make such a degree of precision hardly warranted.

PORTLAND, MAINE, 1966

TIMES AND HEIGHTS OF HIGH AND LOW WATERS

	OCTOBER						NOVEMBER				
DAY	TIME H.M.	HT. FT.	DAY	TIME H.M.	HT. FT.	DAY	TIME H.M.	HT. FT.	DAY	TIME H.M.	
1 SA	0542	0.3	16 SU	0600	-1.0	1 TU	0024	8.3	16 W	0118	
	1148	9.1		1212	10.9		0618	0.8		0712	
	1806	0.1		1836	-1.8		1230	9.4		1330	
							1854	-0.2		2000	
2 SU	0012	8.7	17 M	0048	9.8	2 W	0100	8.1	17 TH	0212	
	0612	0.5		0648	-0.5		0654	0.9		0806	
	1224	9.1		1300	10.6		1306	9.3		1418	
	1836	0.1		1924	-1.3		1936	-0.1		2048	
3 M	0048	8.5	18 TU	0142	9.2	3 TH	0148	7.9	18 F	0306	
	0648	0.7		0742	0.1		0736	1.1		0900	
	1254	9.1		1354	10.0		1354	9.2		1512	
	1918	0.1		2024	-0.8		2024	0.0			
4 TU	0124	8.2	19	0236	8.6	4					
	0724	0.9									
	1336										

FIG. 1938 Heights of tides are tabulated in the tables of daily predictions to the nearest tenth of a foot. However, local conditions of wind and barometric pressure will often cause variations of greater magnitude.

Arithmetic Calculations and Rounding of Numbers

Any mathematical expression of a quantity will have a certain number of "significant figures." These can perhaps be better explained through the use of examples rather than by a complicated definition. The quantity "4" has one significant figure; 4.0 or 14 has two significant figures; 5.12, 43.8, or 609 each has three significant figures, etc.

A quantity ending in one or more zeros may have a varying number of significant figures as determined by the degree of precision with which it was measured. The number 150 may have either two or three significant figures; 2000 may have one, two, three, or four significant figures.

Consideration must be given to the number of significant figures occurring in the result of mathematical calculations, especially multiplication and division. Results should not have an excessive and unwarranted number of significant figures. For example, if 83 is multiplied by 64, the result is 5312. But note that this quantity has four significant figures whereas each of the input quantities had only two significant figures. A more meaningful statement of the result would be 5310 or even 5300.

The process of reducing the number of significant figures is called "rounding." In order to have uniform results, rules have been established for the rounding of numbers.

1. If the digit to be rounded off is "4" or less, it is dropped or changed to a zero.

8.23 can be rounded to 8.2

432 can be rounded to 430

2. If the digit to be rounded off is "6" or larger, the preceding digit is raised to the next higher value and the rounded digit is dropped or changed to a zero.

8.27 can be rounded to 8.3

439 can be rounded to 440

3. If the digit to be rounded off is a "5," the rounding is to the nearest *even* value.

8.25 is rounded to 8.2

435 is rounded to 440

This rule may seem somewhat arbitrary, but it is followed

for consistency in results; it has the advantage that when two such rounded figures are added together and divided by two for an average, the result will not present a new need for rounding.

4. Rounding can be applied to more than one final digit; but all such rounding must be done in *one* step. For example: 6148 is rounded to 6100 in a single action; do not round 6148 to 6150, and then round 6150 to 6200.

In many of the statements of accuracy requirements in the preceding section, the phrase "to the nearest ———" has been used. Rounding is used to reduce various quantities to such limitations. For example: if you calculated the distance traveled in 5 minutes at 13 knots, you would get 1.08 miles. However, distance is normally stated to the nearest tenth of a mile, and so the proper expression for distance run would be 1.1 mile.

FIG. 1939 A Dead Reckoning plot should always be maintained when a boat is off-shore or cruising in large, open bodies of water.

M. Rosenfeld.

Dead Reckoning

When operating his boat offshore in large bodies of water, a pilot should have at all times at least a rough knowledge of his position on the chart. Basic to such knowledge is a technique of navigation known as *dead reckoning,* usually abbreviated to *DR.* This is the advancement of the boat's position on the chart from its last accurately determined location, using the course (or courses) steered and the speed (or speeds) through the water. No allowance is made for the effects of wind, waves, current, or steering errors.

Terms used in dead reckoning

At this point, we will deal with only those terms related to *dead reckoning.* Later, when the influence of current is being considered, additional terms will be introduced and defined.

The *DR track* (or *DR track line)* is the path that the boat is expected to follow (no current) represented on the chart by a line drawn from the last known position using courses and speeds through the water. The path the boat actually travels may be different due to one or more offsetting influences, to be considered later.

Course is the direction of the DR track line. Courses are normally plotted as true direction*s,* three-digit figures with zeros added—8° becomes 008. Some skippers may label courses as magnetic or compass directions.

Heading is the direction in which the boat is pointed at any given time. The term is usually used in connection with the direction in which a boat must be steered in order to make good a desired path, allowing for various offsetting influences. Headings are often stated in terms of magnetic or compass directions.

Speed, abbreviated as "S," is the rate of travel through the water. This is the DR track speed; it is used, together with elapsed time, to determine *DR positions* along the track line.

The Basic Principles of Dead Reckoning

It is important that the pilot adhere to certain basic principles of dead reckoning.

1. A DR track is always started from a known position.

2. Only true courses steered are used for determining a DR track.

3. Only the speed through the water is used for determining distance traveled and a DR position along the track.

Although it may appear unusual to ignore the effects of a current that is known to exist, this is always done for reasons that will be established later.

The importance of dead reckoning

A DR track should always be plotted when navigating in large, open bodies of water. It is the primary representation of the path of the boat, the base to which other factors, such as the effect of current, are applied. Dead reckoning can be considered to be the basic method of navigation to which corrections and adjustments from other sources of information are applied.

At the same time, it must be remembered that this DR track is rarely a representation of the boat's actual progress. If there were no steering errors, speed errors, or external influences, the DR track could be used as a means of determining the craft's position at any time desired, as well as the ETA (Estimated Time of Arrival) at a stated destination. Despite the fact that this will rarely, if ever, be the case, a DR plot is highly desirable at all times as a safety measure in the event of unexpected variations in current, and it is most useful in the event of a sudden fog or other loss of visibility.

PLOTTING

Fundamental to the use of dead reckoning is the use of charts and plots of the craft's intended and actual positions.

FIG. 1940a The course is labeled above the line as shown here. The direction is indicated as a three-digit number (zeroes added as necessary) followed by "T," "M," or "C" for True, Magnetic, or Compass as appropriate, spaced about the width of one character. Omit the degree symbol "°"

FIG. 1940b Speed is labeled below the course line. Write in the letter "S", a space, and the speed in knots or MPH as appropriate. Distance may be shown along a course segment using "D" and the number of statute or nautical miles below the course line.

Basic requirements

The basic requirements of plotting are *accuracy, neatness,* and *completeness.* All measurements taken from the chart must be made carefully, all direct observations must be made as accurately as conditions on a small craft will permit, and all calculations should be made in full and in writing. If time permits, each of these actions should be repeated as a check; errors can be costly!

Neatness in plotting is essential to avoid confusion of information on the chart. The drawing in on charts of excess or overly-long lines, or the scribbling of extraneous notes, may obscure small bits of vital information.

In addition to being neat, information on a chart must be complete. Often a pilot will have need to refer back to information that he placed on the chart hours, or even days, ago. It could be dangerous if he should have to rely on memory to supply part of the details. In some cases, the piloting duties may be shared among several persons; here it is obvious that all plotted information must be fully identified.

The use of standardized procedures for identifying information on charts will ensure neatness, completeness, and understandability to any person who uses it.

Labeling

Lines on charts should be drawn lightly and no longer than necessary. Be alert to the fact that a straightedge must be placed a slight distance off the desired position of the line to be drawn to allow for the thickness of the pencil point, no matter how finely it is sharpened.

The requirements of neatness and completeness combine to establish a need for *labeling.* To meet these requirements, certain rules and procedures have been established. The proper labeling of any plot is essential.

Immediately after any line is drawn on a chart, or any point is plotted, it should be labeled. The basic rules for labeling are:

1. The label for any *line* is placed *along* that line.

2. The label for any *point* should *not* be along any line; it should make such an angle with any line that its nature as the label of a point will be unmistakably clear.

The above basic rules are applied in the labeling of DR plots in the following manner:

1. The label indicating the direction of a DR track is placed *above* the track line as a three-digit number; "T," "M" or "C" may follow to indicate True, Magnetic, or Compass. Note that the degree symbol "°" is omitted.

2. The speed along the track is indicated by numerals

placed *under* the track line, usually directly beneath the direction, fig. 1940b. Units, knots or MPH, are omitted.

3. A known position at the start of a DR track, a *Fix,* to be discussed later, is shown as a circle across the track line. It is labeled with the time, in four-digit notation (24-hour clock system) followed by "FIX," fig. 1941.

4. A DR position, calculated as a distance along the track at the set speed through the water, is shown as a half-circle along the track line; it is labeled with the time in four-digit style; see fig. 1942.

5. When planning and pre-plotting a run, speed, which is often affected by sea conditions, may not be known in advance. In this case, distance, D, may be labeled below the course line; as before, units are not shown.

Further applications of the basic rules of labeling will be given as additional piloting procedures and situations are introduced in subsequent chapters.

All lines on a chart should be erased when no longer needed to keep the chart clear. Erasures should be made as lightly as possible to avoid damage to the surface of the chart and its printed information.

FIG. 1941 A known position of the boat is plotted as a dot with a small circle around it. If it is along a line, the dot will not show separately. Label the position with the time as a four-digit number in the 24-hour system plus the word "FIX".

FIG. 1942 A dead reckoning position along a track is plotted as a half-circle along the track line plus the time. The letters "DR" are not needed as this symbol is not used for any other purpose.

D, T, AND S CALCULATIONS

As mentioned earlier, calculations involving distance (D), time (T), and speed (S) are often done by means of a small calculator. The use of such a device is perfectly acceptable, but the good pilot can accurately and quickly make his calculations without one, using only a simple set of equations and ordinary arithmetic. An ability to make arithmetical computations is necessary as a calculating device may not always be available.

The three basic equations are:

$$D = ST \qquad S = \frac{D}{T} \qquad T = \frac{D}{S}$$

Where D is distance in miles, T is time in *hours,* and S is speed in knots or miles per hour as determined by the type of mile being used. Note carefully that T is in hours in these basic equations. To use time in *minutes,* as is more normally the case, the equations are modified to read:

$$D = \frac{ST}{60} \qquad S = \frac{60D}{T} \qquad T = \frac{60D}{S}$$

Examples of the use of these practical equations may serve to make them clearer:

1. You are cruising at 14 knots; how far will you travel in 40 minutes?

$$D = \frac{ST}{60} \qquad D = \frac{14 \times 40}{60} = 9.3 \text{ miles}$$

Note that the calculated answer of 9.33 is rounded to

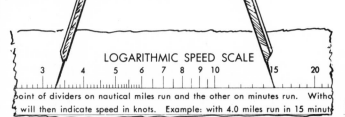

LOGARITHMIC SPEED SCALE

3   4   5   6   7 8 9 10   15   20

point of dividers on nautical miles run and the other on minutes run. Witho
will then indicate speed in knots. Example: with 4.0 miles run in 15 minute

FIG. 1943a On some charts, a logarithmic speed scale may be used to graphically determine speed. First, set one point of your dividers on the scale division indicating the miles traveled, and the other on the number corresponding to the time in minutes.

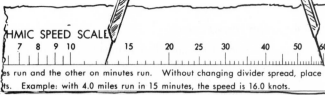

HMIC SPEED SCALE

7 8 9 10   15   20   25   30   40   50 60

es run and the other on minutes run. Without changing divider spread, place
ts. Example: with 4.0 miles run in 15 minutes, the speed is 16.0 knots.

FIG. 1943b With the dividers maintaining the same spread, transfer them so that the right point is on the "60" of the scale (right end). The left point will indicate the speed in knots or MPH, as determined by the type of mile used.

the nearest tenth according to the rule for the degree of accuracy to be used in stating distance.

2. On one of the Great Lakes, it took you 40 minutes to travel 11 miles; what is your speed?

$$S = \frac{60D}{T} \qquad S = \frac{60 \times 11}{40} \qquad = 16.5 \text{ MPH}$$

3. You have 9½ miles to go to reach your destination, your cruising speed is 11 knots; how long will it take you to get there?

$$T = \frac{60D}{S} \qquad T = \frac{60 \times 9.5}{11} \qquad = 52 \text{ minutes}$$

Note again the rounding of results; the calculated answer of 51.8 minutes would be used as 52 minutes, except in contests where it would probably be used as 51 minutes 48 seconds.

The three practical equations of distance, time, and speed should be carefully memorized. Practice using them until you become thoroughly familiar with them and can obtain your answers to typical problems quickly and accurately.

Use of logarithmic scale on charts

Charts of the National Ocean Survey at scales of 1:40,000 and larger will have printed on them a logarithmic speed scale. To find speed, place one point of your dividers on the mark on the scale indicating the distance in nautical miles, and the other point on the number corresponding to the time in minutes, fig. 1943a. Without changing the spread between the divider arms, place the right point on the "60" at the right end of the scale; the left point will then indicate on the scale the speed in knots, see fig. 1943b.

This same logarithmic scale can also be used *to determine the time* required to cover a given distance at a specified speed (for situations not exceeding one hour). Set the two divider points on the scale marks representing speed in knots and distance in miles. Move the dividers, without changing the spread, until the right point is at "60" on the scale; the other point will indicate the time in minutes.

Likewise, *distance can be determined* from this logarithmic scale using knowledge of time and speed. Set the right point of the dividers on "60" and the left point at the mark on the scale corresponding to the speed in knots. Then, without changing the spread, move the right point to the mark on the scale representing the time in minutes; the left point will now indicate the distance in nautical miles.

N.O.S. charts will have instructions for determining speed printed beneath the logarithmic scale, but not the procedures for determining distance or time. In all cases, you must know two of the three quantities in order to determine the other.

Use of S-D-T calculators

It is not possible here to give detailed instructions for the operation of all models of speed-distance-time calculators. In general, such devices will have two or more scales, each logarithmically subdivided. The calculator will be set using two of the factors and the answer, the third factor, will be read off at an index mark.

If you have a calculator for S-D-T problems, read the instructions carefully and practice with it sufficiently, using simple, self-evident problems, to be sure of obtaining reliable results, even under the stress of difficult situations or emergencies.

SPEED CURVES

Although some boats may be equipped with marine speedometers, the more-often used method of determination of speed is through the use of engine speed as measured by the *tachometer* in revolutions per minute (RPM). A *speed curve* is prepared as a plot on cross-section (graph) paper of the boat's speed in knots or MPH for various engine speeds in RPM.

Factors affecting speed curves

The speed that a boat will achieve for a specified engine setting may be affected by several factors. The extent of each effect will vary with the size of the boat, type of hull, and other characteristics.

Load is a primary factor influencing a boat's speed. The number of persons aboard, the amount of fuel and water in the tanks, and the amount and location of other weights on board will affect the depth to which the hull sinks in the water and the angular trim. Both displacement and trim may be expected to have an effect on speed.

Another major factor affecting speed is the *underwater hull condition*. Fouling growth, such as barnacles or moss, increases the drag, the resistance to movement through the water, and slows the speed of the boat at any given engine RPM.

Whenever preparing speed data on a boat, the loading and underwater hull conditions at the time of the trials should be noted with the figures for RPM and speed. If a speed curve is made at the start of a boating season when the bottom is clean, it should be checked later on in the season if the boat is used in waters where fouling is a problem. A new speed curve may be required, or it may be possible to determine what small corrections can be applied to get a more accurate measure of speed. A good skipper also knows what speed differences he may expect from full tanks to half to nearly empty; the differences can be surprising in many boats.

Obtaining speed curves

Speed curves are obtained by making repeated runs over a known distance using different throttle settings and timing each run very accurately. Any reasonable distance can be used. Ordinarily, it should not be less than a half-mile in order that small timing errors will not excessively influence the results; it need not be more than a mile, to avoid excessive time and fuel requirements for the trials.

The run need not be an even half-mile or mile if the distance is accurately known. Do not depend upon floating aids to navigation — they may be slightly off-station, and, in any event, they have some scope on their anchor chains and will swing about under the effects of wind and current. Many areas will have *measured miles* (or half-miles), fig. 1944. These are accurately surveyed distances with each end marked by ranges. Use these courses whenever possible; they can be depended upon for accuracy and calculations are made easier by the even-mile distance. But do not let the absence of such a measured mile in your local waters keep you from having a speed curve for your boat. Use accurately charted wharves, fixed aids to navigation, points of land, etc.

In most speed trials, it will be necessary to run the known distance twice, once in each direction, in order to allow for the effects of current. Even in waters not affected by currents, it is advisable to make round-trip runs for each throttle setting to allow for wind effects.

For each *one-way* run, measure the time required; steer the boat carefully so that the most direct, the shortest run is made. Compute the speed for each run by the equations previously used. If a measured mile is used for the speed trials, speeds can be found easily by use of the table on page 603. If the measured distance is an exact half-mile, the tabulated speeds must be divided by two. Then average the *speeds* of each run of a pair at a given RPM to determine the true speed of the boat through the water. The strength of the current is one-half the difference between the speed in the two directions of any pair of runs. *Caution:* do *not* average together the *times* of a pair of runs to get a single time for use in the calculations; this will *not* give the correct value for speed through the water.

If time is measured with a regular clock or watch, be

RPM	N-S		S-N		Average Speed	Current
	Time	Speed	Time	Speed		
900	7m 54s	7.60	11m 25s	5.26	6.43	1.17
1100	6 53	8.72	9 14.2	6.50	7.61	1.11
1300	6 08.8	9.76	7 36.8	7.88	8.82	.94
1500	5 35.8	10.72	6 40.4	9.00	9.86	.86
1700	5 10.8	11.59	5 54.2	10.17	10.88	.71
1900	4 38.0	12.96	5 06.4	11.76	12.36	.60
2150	3 48.6	15.75	4 05.6	14.73	15.24	.51

FIG. 1945 Tabulated results of speed trials made for "Trident." Note that runs were made in each direction to account for the effect of current. Entries were made in the log as to fuel and water loads aboard and condition of the bottom of the hull.

careful in making the subtractions to get elapsed time. Remember that there are 60 seconds in each minute, not 100, and likewise 60 minutes in one hour. Most people are so used to decimal calculations that foolish errors are sometimes made when "borrowing" in the subtraction of clock times.

If one is willing to use a slightly more complex equation, the boat's speed through the water (or the strength of the current) can be found from a single calculation using the times of the two runs of each pair.

$$S = \frac{60D(Tu + Td)}{2TuTd} \qquad\qquad C = \frac{60D(Tu - Td)}{2TuTd}$$

Where S is speed through the water in knots or MPH
  C is current in knots or MPH
  Tu is time upstream, in minutes
  Td is time downstream, in minutes
  D is distance, in nautical or statute miles

In the preparation of a speed curve for a boat, sufficient pairs of runs should be made to provide points for a plot of speed versus RPM; some six or eight points will usually be enough for a satisfactory curve. With some types of hulls, there will be a break in the curve at a critical speed when the hull changes from displacement action to semi-planing action. At this portion of the curve, additional, more closely-spaced measurements may be required. For this reason, it is often a good idea to calculate speeds during runs and make a rough plot as you go along.

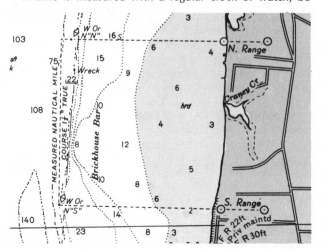

FIG. 1944 Many boating areas have *measured mile* courses established for making accurate speed trials. These will be shown on the chart of the area.

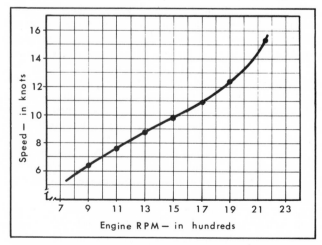

FIG. 1946 The speed curve for "Trident" plotted from the data of fig. 1945. This curve is truly accurate only for load and underwater hull conditions similar to those on the day of the trials.

It may also be found desirable to calculate the strength of the current for each pair of runs. It will probably be noted that the current values will vary during the speed trials, but such variations should be small and in a consistent direction, either steadily increasing or decreasing, or going through a slack period. The best results will normally be obtained if the trials are run at a time of minimum current.

Example of a Speed Curve

A set of speed trials was run for the motor yacht "Trident" over the measured mile off Kent Island in Chesapeake Bay, fig. 1944. This is an excellent course as it is marked both by buoys offshore and by ranges on land. The presence of the buoys aids in steering a straight run from one end of the course to the other; the ranges are used for greater accuracy in timing.

On this particular day, it was not convenient to wait for slack water, but a time was selected that would result in something less than maximum ebbing current. A table was set up in the log, and runs were made in each direction at speeds of normal interest from 900 RPM to 2150 RPM which was maximum for the 6-71 diesels.

The results of the runs are shown in fig. 1945. An entry was also made in the log that these trials were made with fuel tanks 0.35 full, the water tanks approximately ⅓ full, and a clean bottom. The column of the table marked "Current" is not necessary, but it serves as a "flag" to quickly expose any inconsistent data. Note that on these trials the current is decreasing at a reasonably consistent rate.

After the runs had been completed, a plot was made on cross-section paper of the boat's speed as a function of engine RPM. This resulted in the speed curve shown as fig. 1946.

DEAD RECKONING PLOTS

With knowledge of dead reckoning terms and principles, the rules for labeling points and lines, and the procedures for making calculations involving distance, time, and speed, it is possible to consider now the use of DR plots.

There are several specific rules for making and using DR plots.

1. A DR plot should be made when leaving a known position, fig. 1947.

2. A DR position should be shown whenever a change is made in course, fig. 1948a, or in speed, fig. 1948b.

3. A DR position should be plotted each hour on the hour, fig. 1949.

4. A new DR track should be started each time the boat's position is fixed. The old DR position for the same time as the fix should also be shown at the end of the old DR track, see fig. 1950.

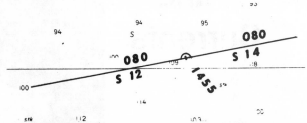

FIG. 1948b If a variation in speed is made without a change in direction, a DR position is plotted on the track and new labels of course and speed are entered following it.

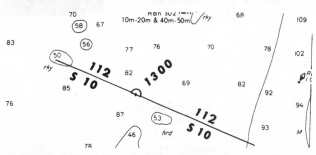

FIG. 1949 A DR position should be plotted each hour on the hour along the track even though there is no change in course or speed. These plots will keep the pilot informed of his progress and are useful in sudden emergencies.

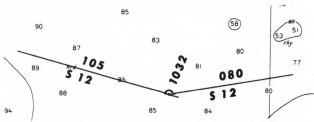

FIG. 1947 A dead reckoning plot is started when leaving a known position. The time of that position is plotted as a Fix (full circle symbol); course and speed are labeled along the DR track.

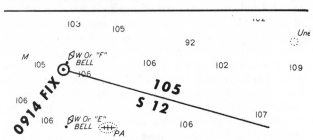

FIG. 1948a Whenever a change in course is made a DR position (half-circle symbol) is plotted for that time; the new course and speed are labeled along the new track.

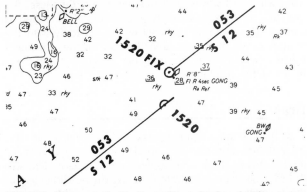

FIG. 1950 Whenever the boat's position is fixed, such as by passage close by a buoy as shown here, a DR position is plotted for that time, calculated from speed and distance information. The fix is also plotted and a new DR track is started. The difference between the DR position and the Fix for the same time indicates the effect of offsetting influences such as current.

Tides and currents are of much interest and concern to the skipper who does his boating on coastal waters. Time invested in mastering their theory and practice will pay dividends in the form of increased safety, convenience, and economy. And too, there is the satisfaction of developing an ability to deal with natural phenomena that you can't change, but which can often be used to your advantage.

CHAPTER 20

PILOTING —Tides and Currents

FIG. 2001 Boatmen in coastal regions must learn to cope with tidal conditions. The range from high water to low may be only inches, or it may be many feet.

Dead Reckoning and Currents

In the preceding chapter, it was noted that a dead reckoning plot is based upon the course steered and the boat's speed through the water. Even though offsetting factors were known to exist, they were *not* included in a DR plot. Thus, it can readily be seen that while a DR plot is a basic representation of a boat's motion, it fails to account for all existing circumstances.

Offsetting influences that will make the boat's actual path diverge from the DR track include current, leeway from wind and waves, and steering errors. Of these, the one that can be most easily and accurately handled is current. The extent of its effect will vary widely with the relative values of current strength and boat speed through the water, but often the influence of current can be a major factor in piloting.

Tides vs. Current

Perhaps at this point we should pause to make clear the proper meaning and use of several terms that are often loosely and incorrectly used. *Tide* is the rise and fall of the ocean level as a result of changes in the gravitational attraction between the earth, moon, and sun. It is a *vertical* motion only. *Current* is a *horizontal* motion of water from any cause. *Tidal current* is the flow of water from one point to another that results from a difference in tidal heights at those points. How often have you heard others say (or perhaps even said it yourself) that "The tide is certainly running strongly today!" This is not correct, for tides may be high or low, but they do not "run." Obviously, the correct expression would have been "The (tidal) current is certainly strong today." Remember — tide is vertical change; current is horizontal flow.

Tides

As tidal action is a primary cause of currents, let us consider it first, and save our consideration of currents for later. Actually, tides in themselves are important factors in the safe navigation of watercraft as will be discussed in the following pages.

Tides originate in the open oceans and seas, but are only noticeable and significant close to shore. The effect of tides will be observed along coastal beaches, in bays and sounds, and up rivers generally as far as the first rapids, waterfall, or dam. Curiously, the effect of tides may be more noticeable a hundred miles up a river than it is at the river's mouth. Coastal regions in which the water levels are subject to tidal action are often referred to as "tidewater" areas.

Definition of Terms

In addition to the basic definition of tide as given above, certain other terms used in connection with tidal action must be defined. The *height of tide* at any specified time is the vertical measurement between the surface of the water and the *tidal datum* or reference plane. Do not confuse "height of tide" with "depth of water." The latter is the total distance from the surface to the bottom. The tidal datum for an area is selected so that the heights of tide are normally positive values, but the height can at times be a small negative number when the water level falls below the datum.

High water, or *high tide,* is the highest level reached by an ascending tide. Correspondingly, *low water,* or *low tide,* is the lowest level reached by a descending tide, fig. 2003. The difference between high and low waters is termed the *range* of the tide.

The change in tidal level does not occur at a uniform rate; starting from, say, low water, the level builds up slowly, then at an increasing rate which in turn tapers off as high water is reached. The decrease in tidal stage from high water to low follows a corresponding pattern of a slow buildup to a maximum rate roughly midway between stages followed by a decreasing rate. At both high and low tides, there will be periods of relatively no change in level; these are termed *stand.* *Mean sea level* is the average level of the open ocean and corresponds closely to mid-tide levels offshore.

TIDAL THEORY

Tidal action can be studied both from a theoretical view and in terms of actual conditions. It is perhaps best approached from an initial consideration of basic principles, with practical departures from theory being noted afterwards. As briefly mentioned earlier, tidal theory is based on the gravitational attraction between the earth on one hand, and the moon and sun on the other. In order to simplify the presentation of these effects, they will be described separately, although, of course, in actual practice, they both act simultaneously. Although the sun has a lesser effect on tides than the moon, its gravitational

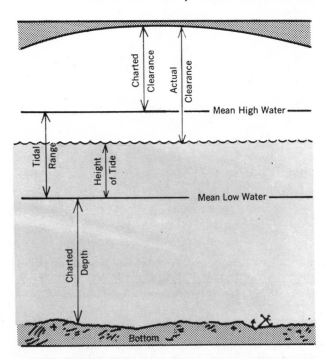

FIG. 2003 This diagram illustrates the relationship between some of the terms used to describe tidal conditions. Terms are defined in the text. Mean lower low water may be substituted for mean low water in some areas.

action is easier to visualize, and so it will be considered first.

Earth-Sun Effects

Each year the earth and the sun revolve around a common point located close to the center of the sun; for all practical considerations, the earth can be thought of as revolving around the sun. Just as a stone tied to the end of a string tends to sail off when a young boy whirls it about

FIG. 2002 The rise and fall of ocean tidal levels will cause a flow first into and then out of inland bodies of water such as bays, sounds, and the lower reaches of rivers. These tidal currents may have important effects on the piloting of boats in such waters. *(from Kodachrome by Wm. H. Koelbel)*

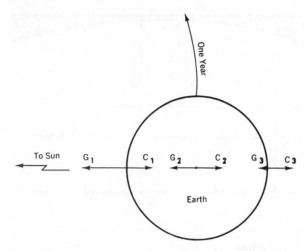

FIG. 2004 Tides result from the differences between centrifugal forces—C_1, C_2, and C_3—and gravitational forces—G_1, G_2, and G_3. The forces shown here are those of the interaction of earth and sun; corresponding forces result from the earth-moon relationship.

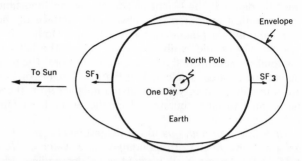

FIG. 2005 Inequalities of gravitational and centrifugal forces result in high tides on opposite sides of the earth at the same time, on the side away from the sun as well as the side toward it. Low tides will occur midway between these areas.

his head, so the earth tends to fly off into space. This is known as centrifugal force; it is designated as C in fig. 2004. (Remember that we are talking about the centrifugal force related to the sun-earth system, and not that of the day-night spinning of the earth on its axis.)

The earth is kept from flying off into space by the gravitational attraction of the sun, designated G in fig. 2004. Now, since the earth does not fly off into space, nor does it fall into the sun, C_2 and G_2 (at the center of the earth) must be equal.

Keeping mathematics at a minimum, we need only note that gravitational attraction varies inversely with the square of the distance between the objects, and centrifugal force varies directly with the radius of rotation—the distance from the sun in this case. Thus G_1 is greater than G_2 and G_3 is less. Likewise, C_1 is less than C_2 or C_3. With G_2 equal to C_2, there will be unbalanced forces at both sides—G_1 being greater than C_1 and C_3 being greater than G_3. These differences called SF_1 and SF_3 in fig. 2005, are the vertical tidal forces. Note that SF_1 points toward the sun and SF_3 away, and that SF_1 is essentially equal to SF_3.

Continuing our theoretical analysis, we can think of the earth as being a smooth sphere uniformly covered with water (no land areas). The two forces SF_1 and SF_3 will cause a flow of water toward their locations building up a bulge on either side of the earth in line with the earth-sun line; this is marked as "envelope" in fig. 2005. These points would accordingly experience a rising of the water level, a high tide. Between those two points, around the earth, the water would be drawn away, and such places would have a low tide.

As the earth turns on its axis, once in twenty-four hours, inside this envelope of water, each point on the earth's surface would then have two high and two low tides each day, following each other in alternate and regular succession.

Earth-Moon Effects

The moon is commonly thought of as revolving about the earth; actually, the two bodies revolve around a common point on a monthly cycle. This point is located about

2900 miles from the center of the earth toward the moon (about 1100 miles deep inside the earth). By just the same logic as applied to the earth-sun system, a second set of tidal forces is developed. In explaining tidal forces in the earth-moon system, however, one must always remember to think of both the earth and the moon as revolving around a common point, rather than the moon merely going around the earth. It is only by the former concept that we can get the necessary centrifugal forces for tides on the earth.

Spring and Neap Tides

Let us now combine the earth-sun and earth-moon systems. Due to the fact that the moon is much closer to the earth (about 238,860 miles away), its tidal forces are approximately 2½ times greater than those of the sun (roughly 92,900,000 miles distant). The result is that the observed tide usually "follows the moon," but the action is somewhat modified by the sun's relative position. The two high and two low waters each day occur about 50 minutes later

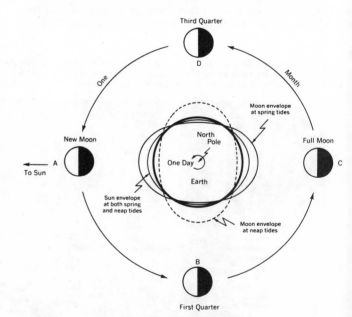

FIG. 2006 At new and full moon, combined gravitational "pull" of sun and moon acts to produce maximum effect; at these times, tidal ranges are greatest. At first and third quarters of the moon, the two gravitational forces partially offset each other and the net effect is at a minimum; tidal ranges are then least.

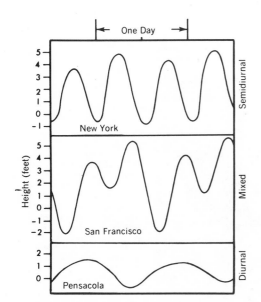

FIG. 2007 Characteristics of the daily cycle of tides vary widely at different places. Shown here are three basic types—from the top, semi-diurnal, mixed, and diurnal.

than the corresponding tides of the previous day.

In the course of any one month, the three bodies line up sun-moon-earth (position A in fig. 2006) and sun-earth-moon (position C). These are the times of the new and full moon, respectively. In both cases, the sun's effect (or "envelope") lines up with and reinforces the moon's effect, tending to result in greater-than-average tidal ranges (about 20%), called *spring tides;* note carefully that this name has nothing to do with the season of the year.

At positions B and D in fig. 2006, when the moon is at its first and third quarters, the tidal "bulge" due to the sun is at right angles to that caused by the moon (they are said to be "in *quadrature*"). The two tidal effects are in conflict and partially cancel each other, resulting in smaller-than-average ranges (again about 20%); these are *neap tides.*

It should also be noted that the tidal range of any given point varies from month to month, and from year to year. The monthly variation is due to the fact that the earth is not at the center of the moon's orbit. When the moon is closest to the earth, the lunar influence is at its maximum; tides at these times will have the greatest ranges. Conversely, when the moon is farthest from the earth, its effect, and tidal ranges, are the least.

In a similar manner, the yearly variations in the daily ranges of the tides are caused by the changing gravitational effects of the sun as that body's distance from the earth becomes greater or less.

ACTUAL TIDES

We have been considering the tidal forces and their envelope rather than the actual tide as we observe it in the sea. Why do they differ? The following are the main reasons:

1. Great masses of land, the continents, irregularly shaped and irregularly placed, act to interrupt, restrict, and reflect tidal movements.

2. Water, although generally appearing to flow freely, is actually a somewhat viscous substance and therefore

lags in its response to tidal forces.

3. Friction is present as the ocean waters "rub" against the ocean bottom.

4. The depth to the bottom of the sea, varying widely, influences the speed of the tidal motion horizontally.

5. The depths of the ocean areas and the restrictions of the continents often result in "basins" which have their own way of responding to tidal forces.

Although these reasons account for great differences between theoretical tidal forces and actual observed tides, there nevertheless remain definite, constant relationships between the two at any particular location. By observing the tide, and relating these observations with the movements of the sun, moon, and earth, these constant relationships can be determined. With this information, tides can be predicted for any future date at a given place.

Types of Tides

A tide which each day has two high waters approximately equal in height, and two low waters also about equal, is known as a *semidiurnal* type. This is the most common tide, and, in the United States, occurs along the east coast (fig. 2007, New York).

In a monthly cycle, the moon moves north and south of the Equator. Fig. 2008 illustrates the importance of this action to tides. Point A is under a bulge in the envelope. One half-day later, at point B, it is again under the bulge but the height is not as large as at A. This situation, combined with coastal characteristics, tends to give rise to a "twice daily" tide with unequal high and/or low waters in some areas. This is known as the *mixed* type of tide; see fig. 2007, San Francisco. The term "low water" may be modified to indicate the more pronounced of the two lows. This tidal stage is termed *lower low water* and is averaged to determine the *mean lower low water* (MLLW); this is used as the tidal datum in many areas subject to mixed tides. Likewise, the more significant of the higher tides is termed *higher high water.*

Now consider point C in fig. 2008. At this place, it is still under the bulge of the envelope. One half-day later, at point D, however, it is above the low part. Hence, the tidal forces tend to cause only one high and one low water each day (actually each 24 hours and 50 minutes approximately). This is the *diurnal* type, typified by Pensacola in fig. 2007.

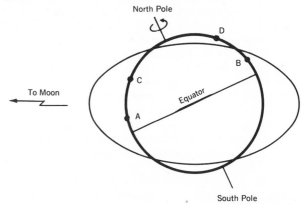

FIG. 2008 The moon travels north and south of the earth's equatorial plane. This change results in variations in the daily tidal cycle at any given location. Similar, but lesser, effects result from changes in the sun's position with respect to the earth.

FIG. 2009 Watch out for falling tides! A prudent skipper knows not only the depth of water when he anchors, but also how it is going to change over the next 12 hours or so. In this river in Nova Scotia, the river bed will be exposed for about five hours; in the sixth hour the flood will rush in as a "bore" and rise 20 feet.
(from Kodachrome by Wm. H. Koelbel)

Whenever the moon is farthest north (as in fig. 2008) or south, there will be a tendency to have the diurnal or mixed type. When the moon lies over the Equator, we tend to have the semidiurnal type. These are *Equatorial tides* and the tendency toward producing inequality is then at a minimum.

The above theoretical considerations are, however, modified by many practical factors such as the general configuration of the coastline.

Special Tidal Situations

Peculiarities in the tide can be found almost everywhere, but none compare with those in the Bay of Fundy. Twice each day, the waters surge in and out of the Bay, producing, at Burntcoat Head, the highest tidal range in the world —a typical rise and fall of nearly 44 feet. At springs, according to Sailing Directions for Nova Scotia, it rises 51½ feet —on perigee springs, 53 feet.

This great range is often attributed to the funnel-like shape of the Bay, but this is not the main cause. Just as the water in a wash basin will slosh when you move your hand back and forth in just the right period of time, depending upon the depth of water and the shape of the basin, so the tide will attempt to oscillate water in bays in cycles of 12 hours and 25 minutes. It would be a coincidence indeed if a bay were of such a shape and depth as to have a complete oscillation with a period of exactly 12 hours and 25 minutes. A bay, however, can easily have a part of such an oscillation; such is the case in the Bay of Fundy.

A further factor in creating the large tidal ranges in the Bay of Fundy is the circumstance that they are controlled by the Gulf of Maine tides which, in turn, are controlled by the open ocean tides. The relationships between these tides are such as to exaggerate their ranges.

THE IMPORTANCE OF TIDES

A good knowledge of tidal action is essential for safe navigation. The skipper of a boat of any size will be faced many times with the need for knowledge of the time of high water and low water, and their probable heights. He may be faced with the desirability or necessity of crossing some shoal area, passable at certain tidal stages but not at others. He may be about to anchor, and the scope to pay out will be affected by the tide's range. He may be going to make fast to a pier or wharf in a strange harbor and will have need of tidal information if he is to adjust his lines properly for overnight.

Tidal effects on vertical clearances

The rise and fall of the tide will change the vertical clearance under fixed structures such as bridges or overhead power cables. These clearances are stated on charts and in Coast Pilots as heights measured from a datum which is *not* the same plane as used for depths and tidal predictions. The datum for heights is normally mean high water (MHW).

It will thus be necessary to determine the height of MHW above the tidal datum. On the East Coast, where the tidal datum is mean low water (MLW), the plane of mean high water is above MLW by the "mean range" which is listed in Table 2 of the Tide Tables, fig. 2010, for each reference and subordinate station.

On the West Coast, or in any area where the tidal datum is mean lower low water (MLLW), slightly more complicated calculations are required. Here, MHW is above the tidal datum by an amount equal to the sum of the "mean tide level" plus one-half of the "mean range"; both of these values appear in Table 2 for the West Coast.

If the tide level at any given moment is below MHW, the vertical clearance under a bridge or other fixed structure is then greater than the figures shown on the chart; but if the tide height is *above* the level of MHW, then the clearance is *less*. Calculate the vertical clearance in advance if you anticipate a tight situation, but *also* observe the clearance gauges usually found at bridges. Clearances will normally be greater than the charted MHW values, but will occasionally be less.

SOURCES OF TIDAL INFORMATION

The basic source of information on the time of high and low water, and their heights above (or below) the datum, is the *Tide Tables* published by the National

Ocean Survey, fig. 2010. Any predictions appearing in newspapers, or broadcast over radio and TV stations, will have been extracted from these tables. The cover jackets of charts in the small-craft series will also include excerpts from the Tide Tables as applicable to the area covered by the chart, fig. 2011.

Not to be overlooked is the possibility of "local knowledge." Never be hesitant to ask experienced local watermen when you are in unfamiliar waters and need information of any kind. The best of tables prepared by electronic computers sometimes cannot compare with a knowledge of what to expect that is based on years of local experience.

TIDE TABLES

The National Ocean Survey Tide Tables are of great value in determining the height of water at any place at a given time. These are calculated in advance and published annually. There are four volumes, one of which covers the East Coast of North and South America, and another the West Coast of these continents.

These Tables can usually be bought at any authorized sales agent for N.O.S. charts. The price for each volume is $2.00.

The Tide Tables give the predicted times and heights of high and low water for each day of the year at a number of important points known as *reference stations*. Portland, Boston, Newport, and Sandy Hook are examples of points for which detailed information is given in the East Coast Tables. Reference stations in the West Coast Tables include

FIG. 2010 The National Ocean Survey uses modern electronic computing equipment to prepare advanced predictions of tidal levels at many points. These are published in the annual Tide Tables.

San Diego, the Golden Gate at San Francisco, and Aberdeen, Washington.

Additional data are tabulated showing the difference in times and heights between these reference stations and thousands of other points termed *subordinate stations*. From these tables, the tide at virtually any point of significance along the coasts can easily be computed. The West Coast Tide Tables contain predictions for reference sta-

tions and differences for about 1100 subordinate stations in North and South America.

The heights given in Tide Tables must, of course, be reckoned from some plane of reference, or tidal datum. From the discussion earlier in this chapter, it is evident that there are a number of different planes to which the heights might be referred. In actual practice, the predictions in the Tables are based on the same datum as that used in making the charts for any given locality. The datum used for the Atlantic Coast is *mean low water* (MLW), which is the average of *all* low-water levels. On the Pacific Coast, where the mixed type of tide is more prevalent, it is the average of the lower of the two low waters occurring each day (MLLW).

All of the factors that can be determined in advance are taken into account in tide predictions, but in the use of the tables, it must be remembered that certain other factors which have a pronounced influence on the height of tides, cannot be forecast months or years in advance. Such influences include barometric pressure and wind. In many areas, the effect of a prolonged gale of wind from a certain quarter is sometimes sufficient to offset all other factors. Tidal rivers may be affected by changes in the volume of water flowing down from the watershed. Normal seasonal variations of flow are allowed for in the predictions, but unexpected prolonged wet or dry spells may result in significant changes to the predictions of tidal heights. Intense rainfall upriver may result in changes to both the heights and times of tides; these effects may not appear downstream for several days.

Caution should therefore be exercised whenever using the Tide Tables, especially since low waters may at times go considerably lower than the level predicted.

Explanation of the Tables

Table 1 of the Tide Tables, fig. 2012, gives the predicted times and heights of high and low water at the main reference stations and is practically self-explanatory. Where no sign is given before the predicted height, the quantity is positive and is to be added to the depths as given on the chart. When the value is preceded by a minus (−) sign, the "heights" are to be *subtracted* from charted depths.

Time is given in the four-digit system from 0001 to 2400 (see page 376). In many areas, caution must be exercised regarding *daylight time.* The Tide Tables are published in terms of local *standard* time, and a correction must be applied if you are in a DT locality.

While there are normally two high and two low tides each date, they are, on an average, nearly an hour later each succeeding day. Consequently, there will be instances when a high or low tide may skip a calendar day, as indicated by a blank space in the Tide Tables, fig. 2013. If it is a high tide, for example, that has been skipped, it will be noted that the previous corresponding high occurred late in the foregoing day, and the next one early in the following day; see the sequence for the late evening high tides of 1, 2, and 3 February in fig. 2013.

It may also be noted from a review of the Tide Tables that at some places there will be only one high and one low tide on some days, with the usual four tides on other days. This is not a diurnal tide situation, where a single high and low would occur every day. The condition considered here arises when the configuration of the land and the periods between successive tides are such that one tide is reflected back from the shore and alters the effect of the succeeding tide.

Sometimes the diurnal inequality (the difference in the height of the two high or two low waters of a day) is so increased as to cause only one low water each day. These tides are not unusual in the tropics and consequently are called *tropic tides.*

Table 2, Tidal Differences and Constants, fig. 2014, gives the information necessary to find the time and height of tide for thousands of subordinate stations by the application of simple corrections to the data given for the main reference stations. The name of the applicable reference station in each case is given in bold-face type at the head of the particular section in which the subordinate station

is listed. The following information is given in separate columns of Table 2:

a. Latitude and longitude of the subordinate station.
b. Differences in time and height of high (and low) waters at the subordinate station and its designated reference station.
c. Mean and spring (or diurnal) tidal ranges.
d. Mean tide level.

Note carefully that the existence of a "minus tide" means that the actual depths of water will be *less* than the figures on the chart.

To determine the time of high or low water at any station in Table 2, use the column marked Differences, Time. This gives the hours and minutes to be added to (+) or subtracted from (−) the time of the respective high or low water at the reference station shown in bold-face type next *above* the listing of the subordinate station. Be careful in making calculations near midnight. The application of the time difference may result in crossing the line from one day to another. Simply add or subtract 24 hours as necessary.

The height of the tide at a station in Table 2 is determined by applying the height difference or ratio. A plus sign (+) indicates that the difference, in feet and tenths, is to be added to the height at the designated reference station for the same time; a minus sign (−) indicates that it should be subtracted.

Where height differences would give unsatisfactory predictions, *ratios* may be substituted for heights. Ratios are identified by an asterisk. These are given as a decimal fraction by which the height at the reference station is to be multiplied to determine the height at the subordinate station.

In the columns headed Ranges, the *mean range* is the difference in height between mean high water and mean low water. This figure is useful in many areas where it may

FIG. 2011 Small-craft charts give annual tidal predictions for reference stations covered by that chart. Information tabulated for marinas and other boating facilities includes tidal ranges at such locations and time differences from a reference station.

FIG. 2012 Table 1 of the Tide Tables lists daily predictions of the time and height of high and low tides at selected reference stations.

FIG. 2013 An extract from Table 1 showing how a high tide may occasionally be omitted near midnght; see text for explanation. Similarly, a low tide near midnight may be skipped about once each two weeks.

TABLE 2.—TIDAL DIFFERENCES AND OTHER CONSTANTS

No.	PLACE	POSITION		DIFFERENCES				RANGES		Mean Tide Level
		Lat.	Long.	Time		Height		Mean	Diurnal	
				High water	Low water	High water	Low water			
		° ′	° ′	h. m.	h. m.	feet	feet	feet	feet	feet
	WASHINGTON—Continued	N.	W.	on PORT TOWNSEND, p.94						
	Admiralty Inlet—Continued			*Time meridian, 120°W.*						
897	Port Townsend (Point Hudson)--------	48 07	122 45	-0 04	-0 04	+0.3	+0.1	5.3	8.6	5.2
899	Marrowstone Point------------------	48 06	122 41	+0 09	+0 07	+0.5	0.0	5.6	8.8	5.3
901	Oak Bay----------------------------	48 01	122 43	+0 15	+0 29	+1.0	+0.1	6.0	9.4	5.6
	Hood Canal			on SEATTLE, p.98						
903	Port Ludlow------------------------	47 55	122 41	-0 27	-0 18	*0.88	*0.88	6.4	9.9	5.9
905	Port Gamble------------------------	47 51	122 35	-0 17	-0 17	*0.91	*0.91	6.7	10.3	6.2
907	Bangor Wharf-----------------------	47 45	122 44	-0 20	+0 04	-0.3	0.0	7.3	10.9	6.4
908	Zelatched Point, Dabob Bay---------	47 43	122 49	-0 10	-0 05	0.0	+0.1	7.5	11.3	6.6
909	Seabeck----------------------------	47 38	122 50	-0 03	+0 03	+0.3	+0.1	7.8	11.6	6.8
911	Union------------------------------	47 21	123 06	-0 09	+0 04	+0.4	0.0	8.0	11.7	6.8
	Puget Sound									
913	Point No Point---------------------	47 55	122 32	-0 16	-0 16	*0.92	*0.92	6.7	10.4	6.1
915	Port Madison-----------------------	47 42	122 32	-0 08	-0 08	+0.1	0.0	7.7	11.4	6.6
917	Poulsbo, Liberty Bay---------------	47 44	122 39	+0 02	+0 08	+0.6	+0.1	8.1	11.9	6.9
919	Brownsville, Port Orchard----------	47 39	122 37	+0 02	+0 08	+0.4	0.0	8.0	11.7	6.8
921	SEATTLE (Madison St.), Elliott Bay--	47 36	122 20	Daily predictions				7.6	11.3	6.6
923	Eighth Ave. South, Duwamish River---	47 32	122 19	+0 05	+0 07	-0.1	0.0	7.5	11.1	6.5
925	Port Blakely-----------------------	47 36	122 30	+0 02	+0 03	+0.2	0.0	7.8	11.5	6.7
927	Pleasant Beach, Rich Passage--------	47 36	122 32	+0 01	+0 07	+0.2	0.0	7.8	11.5	6.7
929	Bremerton, Port Orchard------------	47 33	122 38	+0 07	+0 12	+0.4	0.0	8.0	11.7	6.8
931	Tracyton, Dyes Inlet---------------	47 37	122 40	+0 30	+0 56	+1.0	0.0	8.6	12.3	7.1
933	South Colby, Yukon Harbor----------	47 31	122 32	+0 01	+0 07	+0.3	0.0	7.9	11.6	6.7
935	Des Moines-------------------------	47 24	122 20	+0 03	+0 09	+0.4	0.0	8.0	11.7	6.8
937	Burton, Quartermaster Harbor--------	47 23	122 28	+0 07	+0 13	+0.6	0.0	8.2	11.9	6.9
939	Gig Harbor-------------------------	47 20	122 35	+0 06	+0 14	+0.6	0.0	8.2	11.8	6.9
941	Tacoma, Commencement Bay------------	47 17	122 25	+0 07	+0 06	+0.5	0.0	8.1	11.8	6.8
943	Arietta, Hale Passage--------------	47 17	122 39	+0 23	+0 36	+1.7	0.0	9.3	13.0	7.4
945	Home, Von Geldern Cove, Carr Inlet--	47 16	122 45	+0 27	+0 39	+2.3	+0.2	9.7	13.6	7.8
947	Wauna, Carr Inlet------------------	47 23	122 38	+0 20	+0 36	+1.8	0.0	9.4	13.1	7.5
949	Steilacoom-------------------------	47 10	122 36	+0 22	+0 35	+1.8	0.0	9.4	13.1	7.5
951	Hyde Point, McNeil Island----------	47 12	122 39	+0 23	+0 41	+2.1	+0.2	9.5	13.4	7.7
953	Sequalitchew Creek, Nisqually Reach-	47 07	122 40	+0 24	+0 42	+2.1	+0.1	9.6	13.4	7.7
955	Longbranch, Filucy Bay-------------	47 13	122 45	+0 26	+0 39	+2.2	+0.1	9.7	13.5	7.7
957	Henderson Inlet--------------------	47 09	122 50	+0 27	+0 45	+2.6	+0.2	10.0	14.0	8.0
959	Vaughn, Case Inlet-----------------	47 20	122 46	+0 35	+0 47	+2.8	+0.2	10.2	14.1	8.1
961	Allyn, Case Inlet------------------	47 23	122 49	+0 27	+0 46	+2.8	+0.2	10.2	14.1	8.1
963	Walkers Landing, Pickering Passage--	47 17	122 56	+0 35	+0 47	+2.9	+0.2	10.3	14.3	8.1
965	Arcadia, Pickering Passage----------	47 12	122 56	+0 35	+0 54	+3.0	+0.2	10.4	14.4	8.2
967	Shelton, Oakland Bay---------------	47 13	123 05	+1 12	+1 54	+2.8	-0.2	10.6	14.2	7.9
969	Burns Point, Totten Inlet----------	47 07	123 03	+0 36	+0 54	+3.6	+0.2	11.0	15.0	8.5
971	Rocky Point, Eld Inlet-------------	47 04	123 01	+0 34	+0 52	+3.3	+0.3	10.6	14.7	8.4
973	Dofflemyer Point, Budd Inlet--------	47 08	122 54	+0 29	+0 47	+3.1	+0.2	10.5	14.4	8.2
975	Olympia, Budd Inlet----------------	47 03	122 54	+0 31	+0 46	+3.1	+0.2	10.5	14.4	8.2
	Possession Sound and Port Susan									
977	Mukilteo---------------------------	47 57	122 18	-0 08	-0 12	-0.3	-0.1	7.4	11.0	6.4
979	Everett----------------------------	47 59	122 13	-0 09	-0 11	-0.2	0.0	7.4	11.1	6.5
981	Tulalip----------------------------	48 04	122 17	+0 02	-0 02	0.0	0.0	7.6	11.2	6.6
982	Kayak Point------------------------	48 08	122 22	-0 04	-0 01	-0.4	-0.1	7.3	10.9	6.3
983	Stanwood,[1] Stillaguamish River------	48 14	122 22	+0 18	+2 10	*0.63	*0.29	5.7	7.4	3.6

*Ratio.
[1]The low water seldom falls below the chart datum.

FIG. 2014 Table 2–Tidal Differences and Other Constants. Data are given for hundreds of subordinate stations so that predictions can be made for almost any point of significance to navigation.

Duration of rise or fall, see footnote.	TIME FROM THE NEAREST HIGH WATER OR LOW WATER														
h. m.	h. m.	h. m.	h. m.	h. m.	h. m.	h. m.	h. m.	h. m.	h. m.	h. m.	h. m.	h. m.	h. m.	h. m.	h. m.
4 00	0 08	0 16	0 24	0 32	0 40	0 48	0 56	1 04	1 12	1 20	1 28	1 36	1 44	1 52	2 00
4 20	0 09	0 17	0 26	0 35	0 43	0 52	1 01	1 09	1 18	1 27	1 35	1 44	1 53	2 01	2 10
4 40	0 09	0 19	0 28	0 37	0 47	0 56	1 05	1 15	1 24	1 33	1 43	1 52	2 01	2 11	2 20
5 00	0 10	0 20	0 30	0 40	0 50	1 00	1 10	1 20	1 30	1 40	1 50	2 00	2 10	2 20	2 30
5 20	0 11	0 21	0 32	0 43	0 53	1 04	1 15	1 25	1 36	1 47	1 57	2 08	2 19	2 29	2 40
5 40	0 11	0 23	0 34	0 45	0 57	1 08	1 19	1 31	1 42	1 53	2 05	2 16	2 27	2 39	2 50
6 00	0 12	0 24	0 36	0 48	1 00	1 12	1 24	1 36	1 48	2 00	2 12	2 24	2 36	2 48	3 00
6 20	0 13	0 25	0 38	0 51	1 03	1 16	1 29	1 41	1 54	2 07	2 19	2 32	2 45	2 57	3 10
6 40	0 13	0 27	0 40	0 53	1 07	1 20	1 33	1 47	2 00	2 13	2 27	2 40	2 53	3 07	3 20
7 00	0 14	0 28	0 42	0 56	1 10	1 24	1 38	1 52	2 06	2 20	2 34	2 48	3 02	3 16	3 30
7 20	0 15	0 29	0 44	0 59	1 13	1 28	1 43	1 57	2 12	2 27	2 41	2 56	3 11	3 25	3 40
7 40	0 15	0 31	0 46	1 01	1 17	1 32	1 47	2 03	2 18	2 33	2 49	3 04	3 19	3 35	3 50
8 00	0 16	0 32	0 48	1 04	1 20	1 36	1 52	2 08	2 24	2 40	2 56	3 12	3 28	3 44	4 00
8 20	0 17	0 33	0 50	1 07	1 23	1 40	1 57	2 13	2 30	2 47	3 03	3 20	3 37	3 53	4 10
8 40	0 17	0 35	0 52	1 09	1 27	1 44	2 01	2 19	2 36	2 53	3 11	3 28	3 45	4 03	4 20
9 00	0 18	0 36	0 54	1 12	1 30	1 48	2 06	2 24	2 42	3 00	3 18	3 36	3 54	4 12	4 30
9 20	0 19	0 37	0 56	1 15	1 33	1 52	2 11	2 29	2 48	3 07	3 25	3 44	4 03	4 21	4 40
9 40	0 19	0 39	0 58	1 17	1 37	1 56	2 15	2 35	2 54	3 13	3 33	3 52	4 11	4 31	4 50
10 00	0 20	0 40	1 00	1 20	1 40	2 00	2 20	2 40	3 00	3 20	3 40	4 00	4 20	4 40	5 00
10 20	0 21	0 41	1 02	1 23	1 43	2 04	2 25	2 45	3 06	3 27	3 47	4 08	4 29	4 49	5 10
10 40	0 21	0 43	1 04	1 25	1 47	2 08	2 29	2 51	3 12	3 33	3 55	4 16	4 37	4 59	5 20

Range of tide, see footnote.	CORRECTION TO HEIGHT														
Ft.	Ft.	Ft.	Ft.	Ft.	Ft.	Ft.	Ft.	Ft.	Ft.	Ft.	Ft.	Ft.	Ft.	Ft.	Ft.
0.5	0.0	0.0	0.0	0.0	0.0	0.0	0.1	0.1	0.1	0.1	0.1	0.2	0.2	0.2	0.2
1.0	0.0	0.0	0.0	0.0	0.1	0.1	0.1	0.2	0.2	0.2	0.3	0.3	0.4	0.4	0.5
1.5	0.0	0.0	0.0	0.1	0.1	0.1	0.2	0.2	0.3	0.4	0.4	0.5	0.6	0.7	0.8
2.0	0.0	0.0	0.0	0.1	0.1	0.2	0.3	0.3	0.4	0.5	0.6	0.7	0.8	0.9	1.0
2.5	0.0	0.0	0.1	0.1	0.2	0.2	0.3	0.4	0.5	0.6	0.7	0.9	1.0	1.1	1.2
3.0	0.0	0.0	0.1	0.1	0.2	0.3	0.4	0.5	0.6	0.8	0.9	1.0	1.2	1.3	1.5
3.5	0.0	0.0	0.1	0.2	0.2	0.3	0.4	0.6	0.7	0.9	1.0	1.2	1.4	1.6	1.8
4.0	0.0	0.0	0.1	0.2	0.3	0.4	0.5	0.7	0.8	1.0	1.2	1.4	1.6	1.8	2.0
4.5	0.0	0.0	0.1	0.2	0.3	0.4	0.6	0.7	0.9	1.1	1.3	1.6	1.8	2.0	2.2
5.0	0.0	0.1	0.1	0.2	0.3	0.5	0.6	0.8	1.0	1.2	1.5	1.7	2.0	2.2	2.5
5.5	0.0	0.1	0.1	0.2	0.4	0.5	0.7	0.9	1.1	1.4	1.6	1.9	2.2	2.5	2.8
6.0	0.0	0.1	0.1	0.3	0.4	0.6	0.8	1.0	1.2	1.5	1.8	2.1	2.4	2.7	3.0
6.5	0.0	0.1	0.2	0.3	0.4	0.6	0.8	1.1	1.3	1.6	1.9	2.2	2.6	2.9	3.2
7.0	0.0	0.1	0.2	0.3	0.5	0.7	0.9	1.2	1.4	1.8	2.1	2.4	2.8	3.1	3.5
7.5	0.0	0.1	0.2	0.3	0.5	0.7	1.0	1.2	1.5	1.9	2.2	2.6	3.0	3.4	3.8
8.0	0.0	0.1	0.2	0.3	0.5	0.8	1.0	1.3	1.6	2.0	2.4	2.8	3.2	3.6	4.0
8.5	0.0	0.1	0.2	0.4	0.6	0.8	1.1	1.4	1.8	2.1	2.5	2.9	3.4	3.8	4.2
9.0	0.0	0.1	0.2	0.4	0.6	0.9	1.2	1.5	1.9	2.2	2.7	3.1	3.6	4.0	4.5
9.5	0.0	0.1	0.2	0.4	0.6	0.9	1.2	1.6	2.0	2.4	2.8	3.3	3.8	4.3	4.8
10.0	0.0	0.1	0.2	0.4	0.7	1.0	1.3	1.7	2.1	2.5	3.0	3.5	4.0	4.5	5.0
10.5	0.0	0.1	0.3	0.5	0.7	1.0	1.3	1.7	2.2	2.6	3.1	3.6	4.2	4.7	5.2
11.0	0.0	0.1	0.3	0.5	0.7	1.1	1.4	1.8	2.3	2.8	3.3	3.8	4.4	4.9	5.5
11.5	0.0	0.1	0.3	0.5	0.8	1.1	1.5	1.9	2.4	2.9	3.4	4.0	4.6	5.1	5.8
12.0	0.0	0.1	0.3	0.5	0.8	1.1	1.5	2.0	2.5	3.0	3.6	4.1	4.8	5.4	6.0
12.5	0.0	0.1	0.3	0.5	0.8	1.2	1.6	2.1	2.6	3.1	3.7	4.3	5.0	5.6	6.2
13.0	0.0	0.1	0.3	0.6	0.9	1.2	1.7	2.2	2.7	3.2	3.9	4.5	5.1	5.8	6.5
13.5	0.0	0.1	0.3	0.6	0.9	1.3	1.7	2.2	2.8	3.4	4.0	4.7	5.3	6.0	6.8
14.0	0.0	0.2	0.3	0.6	0.9	1.3	1.8	2.3	2.9	3.5	4.2	4.8	5.5	6.3	7.0
14.5	0.0	0.2	0.4	0.6	1.0	1.4	1.9	2.4	3.0	3.6	4.3	5.0	5.7	6.5	7.2
15.0	0.0	0.2	0.4	0.6	1.0	1.4	1.9	2.5	3.1	3.8	4.4	5.2	5.9	6.7	7.5
15.5	0.0	0.2	0.4	0.7	1.0	1.5	2.0	2.6	3.2	3.9	4.6	5.4	6.1	6.9	7.8
16.0	0.0	0.2	0.4	0.7	1.1	1.5	2.1	2.6	3.3	4.0	4.7	5.5	6.3	7.2	8.0
16.5	0.0	0.2	0.4	0.7	1.1	1.6	2.1	2.7	3.4	4.1	4.9	5.7	6.5	7.4	8.2
17.0	0.0	0.2	0.4	0.7	1.1	1.6	2.2	2.8	3.5	4.2	5.0	5.9	6.7	7.6	8.5
17.5	0.0	0.2	0.4	0.8	1.2	1.7	2.2	2.9	3.6	4.4	5.2	6.0	6.9	7.8	8.8
18.0	0.0	0.2	0.4	0.8	1.2	1.7	2.3	3.0	3.7	4.5	5.3	6.2	7.1	8.1	9.0
18.5	0.1	0.2	0.5	0.8	1.2	1.8	2.4	3.1	3.8	4.6	5.5	6.4	7.3	8.3	9.2
19.0	0.1	0.2	0.5	0.8	1.3	1.8	2.4	3.1	3.9	4.8	5.6	6.6	7.5	8.5	9.5
19.5	0.1	0.2	0.5	0.8	1.3	1.9	2.5	3.2	4.0	4.9	5.8	6.7	7.7	8.7	9.8
20.0	0.1	0.2	0.5	0.9	1.3	1.9	2.6	3.3	4.1	5.0	5.9	6.9	7.9	9.0	10.0

FIG. 2015 Table 3–Height of Tide at Any Time. This table is used in determining tide level at intermediate times between low and high waters.

be added to mean low water to get mean high water (MHW), the datum commonly used for the measurement of vertical heights above water, bridge and other vertical clearances, etc. The *spring range* is the average semidiurnal range occurring twice monthly when the moon is new or full. It is larger than the mean range where the type of tide is either semidiurnal or mixed, and is of no practical significance where the tide is of the diurnal type. Where this is the situation, the table gives the *diurnal range,* which is the difference in height between mean higher high water and mean lower low water.

Table 3, fig. 2015, is provided in order that detailed calculations can be made for the height of the tide at any desired moment between the times of high and low waters. It is equally usable for either reference stations in Table 1 or the subordinate stations of Table 2. Note that Table 3 is not a complete set of variations from one low to one high. Since the rise and fall are assumed to be symmetrical, only a half-table need be printed. Calculations are made from a high or low water, whichever is nearer to the specified time. In using Table 3, the nearest tabular values are used; interpolation is not necessary.

If the degree of precision of Table 3 is not required (it seldom is in practical piloting situations), a much simpler and quicker estimation can be made by using the following one-two-three rule of thumb. The tide may be assumed to rise or fall 1/12 of the full range during the first and sixth hours after high and low water stands, 2/12 during the second and fifth hours, and 3/12 during the third and fourth hours. The results obtained by this rule will suffice for essentially all situations and locations, but should be compared with Table 3 calculations as a check when entering new areas.

The table shown at the bottom of page 440 has been prepared from the above rule of thumb to supply multiplying factors for half-hour intervals of a rising or falling tide.

The Tide Tables also include four other minor tables which, although not directly related to tidal calculations, are often useful. Table 4 provides sunrise and sunset data at five-day intervals for various latitudes. Table 5 lists corrections to convert the local mean times of Table 4 to standard zone time. Table 6 tabulates times of moonrise and moonset for certain selected locations. Table 7 lists other useful astronomical data such as the phases of the moon, solar equinoxes and solstices, etc.

Each Table is preceded by informative material which should be read carefully prior to its use.

EXAMPLES OF TIDAL CALCULATIONS

The instructions in the Tide Tables should be fully adequate for the solution of any problem. However, examples will be worked out here for various situations as guides to the use of the various individual tables. Comments and cautions relating to the solution of practical problems involving the Tide Tables will also be given.

Example 1. Determination of the time and height of a high or low tide at a reference station.

Problem: What is the time and height of the evening low tide at Seattle on Sunday, 1 October 1967?

Solution: Using Table 1, fig. 2012, it will be seen directly that the evening low water occurs at 2124 Pacific Standard Time on this date and that the height is 4.2 feet above the tidal datum of mean lower low water.

Notes: a. Observe that if the date had been 3 November, the tide level at low water stand would have been a *minus* figure, −3.0 feet. At this time, the water level is predicted to be *below* the datum and actual depths will be *less* than those printed on the charts of this area.

b. Observe that if the date had been 4 November, there would have been no solution as the normal progression of the tides on a cycle of roughly 24 hours and 50 minutes has moved the normal evening low tide past midnight and into the next day. Thus, Saturday, 4 November has only three tides rather than the usual four.

c. It should be further noted that the reference stations are also listed in Table 2 and additional information is shown there. This table, fig. 2014, indicates, for reference stations as well as subordinate stations, the specific location for which predictions are given, the mean and spring (or diurnal) tidal ranges, and the mean tide level.

d. Remember to add one hour if you are in an area using daylight saving time.

Example 2. Determination of the time and height of a high or low tide at a subordinate station.

Problem: What is the time and height of the morning low water at Shelton on Oakland Bay, Puget Sound on Tuesday, 5 December 1967?

Solution: From the Index to Table 2 in the back of the Tide Tables, Shelton is found to be Subordinate Station No. 967. It is then located in Table 2 (fig. 2014). First, note that the Reference Station shown next *above* this place is "Seattle." Then note the time and height differences for Shelton for *low* waters; be sure to use the correct columns.

Th differences are then applied as follows:

Time		Height
00 48	At Seattle	−2.5 feet
1:54	Differences	−0.2
02 42	At Shelton	−2.7 feet

Thus, at Shelton on 5 December 1967, the predicted morning low water will occur at 0242 PST with a height of −2.7 feet (2.7 feet *below* the tidal datum).

Notes: a. If the date had been 5 October, the morning low water at Seattle for that date is at 1130. Adding the time difference of 1ʰ 54ᵐ would have resulted in a time prediction for Shelton of 1324, which is *not* a *morning* tide at the subordinate station. In this case, it would be necessary to use the low water at the reference station that occurs before midnight on the *preceding* day. At Seattle on 4 October, there is a low water at 2318; adding the time difference gives a morning low tide at Shelton of 0112 on 5 October.

b. Observe that if the subordinate station had been Port Gamble on Hood Canal, the height would be determined by multiplying the height at the reference station by the *ratio* of 0.91 rather than adding or subtracting a difference in feet. (Ratios may be either greater or less than 1.) Note also that here the time differences are *negative;* the high and low waters at the subordinate station occur *earlier* than at the reference station of Table 1.

c. The use of minus time differences with predictions of

FIG. 2016 Table 4—Local Mean Time of Sunrise and Sunset. Times are tabulated for various dates and latitudes, usually at intervals of 5 days and 2°; interpolation is used for exact dates and locations.

Date	30° N.		32° N.		34° N.		36° N.		38° N.		40° N.	
	Rise	Set	Rise	Set	Rise	Set	Rise	Set	Rise	Set	Rise	Set
	h. m.	h. m.	h. m.	h. m.	h. m.	h. m.	h. m.	h. m.	h. m.	h. m.	h. m.	h. m.
Jan. 1	6 56	17 11	7 01	17 07	7 06	17 02	7 11	16 57	7 16	16 51	7 22	16 44
6	6 57	17 15	7 02	17 11	7 06	17 06	7 11	17 01	7 17	16 56	7 22	16 49
11	6 57	17 19	7 02	17 15	7 06	17 10	7 11	17 05	7 16	17 00	7 22	16 54
16	6 57	17 23	7 01	17 19	7 05	17 15	7 10	17 10	7 15	17 05	7 20	17 00
21	6 56	17 27	6 59	17 24	7 '04	17 20	7 08	17 15	7 12	17 11	7 18	17 05
26	6 54	17 32	6 57	17 28	7 01	17 25	7 05	17 21	7 09	17 16	7 14	17 11
31	6 51	17 36	6 55	17 33	6 58	17 29	7 02	17 26	7 06	17 22	7 10	17 17
Feb. 5	6 48	17 40	6 51	17 37	6 54	17 34	6 58	17 31	7 01	17 27	7 05	17 23
10	6 45	17 44	6 47	17 42	6 50	17 39	6 53	17 36	6 56	17 33	7 00	17 29
15	6 41	17 48	6 43	17 46	6 45	17 44	6 48	17 41	6 50	17 39	6 54	17
20	6 36	17 52	6 38	17 50	6 40	17 48	6 42	17 46	6 44	17 44		16 47
25	6 31	17 56	6 32	17 55	6 34	17 53	6 36	17 51	6 39			16 47
											6 47	16 43
Mar. 2	6 26	18	6 27	17 58	6 28	17 57	6 29				6 52	16 39
7	6 20	18 03	6 21	18 02	6 22	18 0		6 48	16 44		6 58	16 37
12	6 14	18 06	6 14			16 47	6 53	16 42				
17	6 09	18 09			6 48	16 51	6 58	16 46	7 03	16 35		
22	6 02			16 56	6 52	16 51	6 57	16 46	7 02	16 40	7 08	16 35
27		00	6 51	16 56	6 56	16 52	7 01	16 46	7 07	16 41	7 12	16 35
		17 01	6 54	16 58	6 59	16 53	7 04	16 48	7 10	16 42	7 16	16 36
	17 03	6 52	17 05	6 56	17 00	7 01	16 55	7 07	16 49	7 12	16 44	7 18 16 38
27	6 54	17 08	6 59	17 03	7 04	16 58	7 09	16 53	7 15	16 47	7 20	16 41
Jan. 1	6 56	17 11	7 01	17 07	7 06	17 01	7 11	16 56	7 16	16 50	7 22	16 44

Local mean time. To obtain standard time of rise or set, see Table 5.

FIG. 2017 Table 5—Reduction of Local Mean Time to Standard Time. A correction, obtained from this table, is applied to the time of sunrise or sunset computed from Table 4 to get the time of the event in standard zone time. A further correction of one hour is needed for Daylight Saving Time.

Difference of longitude between local and standard meridian	Correction to local mean time to obtain standard time	Difference of longitude between local and standard meridian	Correction to local mean time to obtain standard time	Difference between local and standard meridian
° ′	Minutes	° ′	Minutes	°
0 00 to 0 07	0	7 23 to 7 37	30	15
0 08 to 0 22	1	7 38 to 7 52	31	30
0 23 to 0 37	2	7 53 to 8 07	32	45
0 38 to 0 52	3	8 08 to 8 22	33	60
0 53 to 1 07	4	8 23 to 8 37	34	75
1 08 to 1 22	5	8 38 to 8 52	35	90
1 23 to 1 37	6	8 53 to 9 07	36	105
1 38 to 1 52	7	9 08 to 9 22	37	120
1 53 to 2 07	8	9 23 to 9 37	38	135
2 08 to 2 22	9	9 38 to 9 52	39	150
2 23 to 2 37	.10	9 53 to 10 07	40	165
2 38 to 2 52	11	10 08 to 10 22	41	180
2 53 to 3 07	12	10 23 to 10 37	42	
3 08 to 3 22	13	10 38 to 10 52	43	
3 23 to 3 37	14	10 53 to 11 07	44	
3 38 to 3 52	15	11 08 to 11 32	55	
3 53 to 4 07	16	13 53 to 14 07	56	
4 08 to 4				
6 38 to 6 52	27	14 08 to 14 22	57	
6 53 to 7 07	28	14 23 to 14 37	58	
7 08 to 7 22	29	14 38 to 14 52	59	

If local meridian is east of standard meridian, subtract tion from local time.
If local meridian is west of standard meridian, add the to local time.

tides to occur shortly after midnight at the reference station may result in a change of date backward into the preceding day. Always be careful in making calculations close to 2400.

Example 3. Determination of the level of the tide at a reference station at a given time between high and low waters.

Problem: What is the height of the tide at Seattle at 1820 on Saturday, 2 December 1967?

Solution: From Table 1, we first note that the given time of 1820 falls between a high tide at 1554 and a low tide at 2318. We compute the time difference and range as follows:

Time	Height
23 18	11.8 feet
15 54	−3.6
7:24 time difference	15.4 feet range

Thus our desired tide level is on a falling tide whose range is 15.4 feet (since the low water height is a negative value, we are subtracting a minus number which is arithmetically equivalent to adding the numerical values).

The desired time is nearer to the time of the high water, so calculations will be made in Table 3, fig. 2015, using this starting point.

18 20	Desired time
15 54	Time of nearest high or low water
2:26	Difference

The given time is $2^h 26^m$ after the nearest high water. Table 3 is used to the nearest tabulated value; do not interpolate. Entering the *upper* part of the Table on the line for Duration of rise or fall of $7^h 20^m$, (nearest value to $7^h 24^m$), read across to the entry nearest $2^h 26^m$; this is $2^h 27^m$ in the tenth column from the left. Follow *down* this column into the *lower* part of Table 3 to the line for Range of Tide of 15.5 feet (nearest value to actual range of 15.4 feet). At the intersection of this line and column is found the correction to the height of the tide; in this case, 3.9 feet.

Since we have noted that in this example the tide is falling, and we are calculating from high water, the correction is subtracted from the height of high water: $11.8 - 3.9 = 7.9$.

The predicted height of the tide at Seattle at 1820 PST on 2 December 1967 is 7.9 feet above the tidal datum.

Notes: a. Be sure that calculations are made for the right pair of high and low tides; be sure that the calculations are made for the *nearest* high or low water.

b. Be careful to apply the final correction to the nearest high or low water as used in its computation; do not apply it to the range; apply it in the right direction, down from a high, or up from a low.

Example 4. Determination of the height of tide at a subordinate station at a given time.

Problem: What is the height of the tide at Port Ludlow at 0930 on Saturday, 2 December 1967?

Solution: First, the times of the high and low waters on either side of the stated time must be calculated for the subordinate station using Tables 1 and 2. This is done as follows:

High water	06 06	At Seattle	12.8 feet
	−:27	difference/ratio	0.88
	05 39	At Point Ludlow	11.3 feet
Low water	11 06	At Seattle	7.7 feet
	−:18	difference/ratio	0.88
	10 48	At Point Ludlow	6.8 feet

Next, we calculate the time difference and range:

10 48	11.3
05 39	6.8
5:09 time difference	4.5 feet range

The time from the nearest high or low is calculated:

10 48
09 30
1:18 time from nearest low

With the data from the above calculations, enter Table 3 for a Duration of rise or fall of $5^h 09^m$ (use $5^h 00^m$), a time from nearest high or low of $1^h 18^m$ (use $1^h 20^m$), and a range of 4.5 feet. From these data, we find a correction to height of tide of 0.7 feet. We know that the tide is falling and that the nearest time of stand was the low water at 1048. From these facts, we can see that the correction is to be *added* to the low water height; $6.8 + 0.7 = 7.5$.

The height of the tide at Port Ludlow at 0930 PST on 2 December 1967 is predicted to be 7.5 feet above the datum.

Note: Be sure to use the high and low tides occurring *at the subordinate station* on either side of the given time. It may be that in some instances with large time differences, a correction of times from the reference station to the subordinate station will show that you have selected the incorrect pair of tides; in this case select another high or low tide so that the pair used at the subordinate station will bracket the given time.

Example 5. Determination of the time of the tide reaching a given height at a reference station.

Problem: At what time on the afternoon of 4 October 1967 will the height of the rising tide reach 10 feet at Seattle?

Solution: This is essentially Example 3 in reverse. First, determine the range and duration of rise (or fall).

16 48	High water	11.9 feet
10 48	Low water	2.3
6:00	Duration	9.6 feet range

It is noted that the desired difference in height of tide is $11.9 - 10.0 = 1.9$ feet. Enter the *lower* part of Table 3 on the line for a range of 9.5 feet (nearest value to 9.6) and find the column in which the correction nearest 1.9 feet is tabulated; in this case, the nearest value (2.0) is found in the ninth column from the left. Proceed *up* this column to the line in the upper part of the Table for a Duration of $6^h 00^m$ (here the exact value can be used). The time from nearest high or low found on this line is $1^h 48^m$. Since our desired level is nearer to high water than low, this time difference is subtracted from the time of high water; $1648 - 1:48 = 1500$.

Thus the desired tidal height of 10 feet above datum is predicted to occur at 1500 PST on 4 October.

Note: A similar calculation can be made for a subordinate station by first determining the applicable high and low water times and heights at that station.

Example 6. Determination of vertical clearance.

Problem: What will be the vertical clearance under the fixed west span of the bridge across the Hood Canal near Port Gamble, Washington, at the time of morning high tide on 2 December 1967?

Solution: Chart 185-SC states the clearance to be 35 feet. The datum for heights is mean high water; the tidal datum is mean lower low water.

From Tables 1 and 2, we determine the predicted height of the tide at the specified time:

At Seattle	12.8 feet
ratio	0.91
At Port Gamble	11.6 feet

From Table 2, we calculate the height of mean high water for Port Gamble:

Mean tide level	6.2 feet
½ mean range	3.4
Mean high water	9.6 feet above tidal datum

The difference between predicted high water at the specified time and MHW is 11.6 − 9.6 = 2.0 feet. The tide is above MHW and the bridge clearance is reduced, 35 − 2.0 = 33 feet.

On the morning of 2 December 1967, the clearance at high tide under the fixed west span of the bridge across Hood Canal near Port Gamble is predicted to be 33 feet; this is *less* than the clearance printed on the chart.

ASTRONOMICAL DATA FROM THE TIDE TABLES

Table 4 gives sunrise and sunset information for various latitudes at five-day intervals. If more precise times are needed, interpolation can be used. Times are *local* meridian and must be corrected to standard zone time.

Example 7. Determination of the time of sunrise at a specified location.

Problem: What is the time of sunrise at Catalina Harbor, Santa Catalina Island on 12 February 1967?

Solution: From Table 2, we note that the latitude and longitude of the given point are 33° 26′N, 118° 30′W.

Fig. 2016 is an extract from Table 4; the applicable entries are set up as follows:

	32°N	34°N
Feb 10	0647	0650
Feb 15	0643	0645

Then we interpolate to the nearest minute vertically for the desired date:

	32°N	34°N
Feb 10	0647	0650
Feb 12	**0645**	**0648**
Feb 15	0643	0645

Next, interpolation is done horizontally for the latitude of the given point:

	32°N	**33° 26′N**	34°N
Feb 12	0645	**0647**	0648

This time of 0647 is local meridian time and must be corrected to zone time by Table 5, fig. 2017. The meridian of Pacific Standard Time is 120° W (from Table 1, bottom of any page).

120° 00′	
118° 30′	
1° 30′	Longitude difference

From Table 5, the time correction for 1°30′ is 6 minutes. Since Catalina Harbor is *east* of the zone meridian, the correction is *subtracted*; 0647 − 6ᵐ = 0641.

On the morning of 12 February 1967, the time of sunrise at Catalina Harbor is 0641 PST.

Notes: a. Interpolation can be done first horizontally for the latitude difference and then vertically for the desired date. The results may vary slightly due to rounding to the nearest minute, but the difference should not exceed one minute.

b. Calculations for the time of sunset are made in exactly the same manner.

c. Latitude and longitude data may be taken from a chart or any other source.

d. Times must be corrected for daylight time, if in effect.

Times of moonrise and moonset

Table 6 gives daily times for moonrise and moonset for selected points. Correction or interpolation for other points is *not* possible.

Currents

Current is the horizontal motion of water. This motion may be the result of any one of several factors, or of a combination of two or three. Although certain of these causes are of greater importance to a boatman than are others, he should have a general understanding of all.

TIDAL CURRENTS

Boatmen in coastal areas will be most affected by *tidal currents*. The rise and fall of tidal levels is a result of the flow of water to and from a given locality. This flow results in tidal current effects.

The normal type of tidal current, in bays and rivers, is the *reversing* current that flows alternately in one direction and then the opposite. Off-shore, tidal currents may be of the *rotary* type, flowing with little change in strength, but slowly and steadily changing direction.

A special form of tidal current is the *hydraulic* type such as flows in a waterway connecting two bodies of water. Differences in the time and height of the high and low waters of the two bays, sounds, etc., cause a flow from one to the other and back again. A typical example of hydraulic current is the flow through the Cape Cod Canal with Massachusetts Bay at one end and Buzzards Bay at the other.

Remember to use the terms correctly—tide is the *vertical* rise and fall of water levels; current is the *horizontal* flow of water.

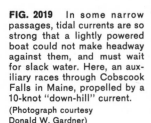

FIG. 2018 The major ocean currents of interest to boatmen are the Gulf Stream off the East Coast and the California Current along the Pacific Coast.

OTHER TYPES OF CURRENT

Although most piloting situations involving current are concerned with tidal currents, there will be times when river, ocean, and wind-driven currents must be considered.

River currents

Boatmen on rivers above the head of tidal action must take into account *river currents*. (Where tidal influences are felt, river currents are merged into tidal currents and are not considered separately.) River currents will vary widely with the width and depth of the stream, the season of the year, recent rainfall in the river basin, etc.

Ocean currents

Off-shore piloting will frequently require knowledge and consideration of *ocean currents*. These result from regions of relatively constant winds such as the often-mentioned "trade winds" and "prevailing westerlies." The rotation of the earth and variations in water density are also factors in the patterns of ocean currents.

The ocean currents of greatest interest to boatmen are the Gulf Stream and the California Current, fig. 2018. The *Gulf Stream* is a northerly and easterly flow of warm water along the Atlantic Coast of the United States. It is quite close to shore along the southern part of Florida, but moves progressively further to sea as it flows northward, where it both broadens and slows.

The *California Current* flows generally southward and a bit eastward along the Pacific Coast of Canada and the United States, turning sharply westward off Baja California (Mexico). It is a flow of colder water and, in general, is slower and less sharply defined than the Gulf Stream.

Wind-driven currents

In addition to the consistent ocean currents caused by sustained wind patterns, local *wind-driven currents* may be established by temporary conditions. The effect of wind blowing across the sea is to cause the surface water to move. The extent of the effect varies with many factors, but generally a steady wind for 12 hours or longer will result in a discernible current.

For a rough rule-of-thumb, the strength of a wind-driven current can be taken as 2% of the wind's velocity. The direction of the current will *not* be the same as that of the wind, a result of the earth's rotation. In the Northern Hemisphere, the current will be deflected to the right to a degree determined by the latitude and the depth of the water. The deflection may be as small as 15° in shallow coastal areas, or as great as 45° on the high seas; it is greater in the higher latitudes.

DEFINITIONS OF CURRENT TERMS

Currents have both strength and direction. The proper terms should be used in describing each of these characteristics.

The *set* of a current is the direction *toward* which it is flowing. A current that flows from North to South is termed a southerly current and has a set of 180°. (Note carefully the difference here from the manner in which wind direction is described—it is exactly the opposite: a wind from North to South is called a northerly wind with a direction of 000°.)

FIG. 2019 In some narrow passages, tidal currents are so strong that a lightly powered boat could not make headway against them, and must wait for slack water. Here, an auxiliary races through Cobscook Falls in Maine, propelled by a 10-knot "down-hill" current.
(Photograph courtesy Donald W. Gardner)

FIG. 2020 Table 1 of the Tidal Current Tables. Daily predictions are listed for the times and strengths of maximum flood and ebb currents, and the time of slack water, at major reference stations.

CHESAPEAKE BAY ENTRANCE, VA., 1967

F—FLOOD, DIR. 305 TRUE   E—EBB, DIR. 125 TRUE

SEPTEMBER

DAY	SLACK WATER TIME H.M.	MAXIMUM CURRENT TIME H.M.	VEL. KNOTS	DAY	SLACK WATER TIME H.M.	MAXIMUM CURRENT TIME H.M.	VEL. KNOTS
1 F	0400	0030	1.1E	16 SA	0448	0130	1.3E
	0800	0554	0.4F		0942	0718	0.7F
	1542	1224	1.4E		1700	1336	1.6E
	2154	1836	1.1F		2254	1954	1.0F
2 SA	0436	0118	1.3E	17 SU	0524	0206	1.3E
	0906	0648	0.6F		1030	0754	0.8F
	1630	1312	1.6E		1742	1418	1.6E
	2236	1924	1.3F		2324	2024	1.0F
3 SU	0512	0200	1.4E	18 M	0554	0242	1.4E
	1006	0736	0.8F		1112	0830	0.9F
	1718	1400	1.8E		1824	1454	1.6E
	2318	2012	1.4F		2348	2100	0.9F
4 M	0554	0236	1.6E	19 TU	0630	0318	1.4E
	1100	0824	1.1F		1148	0906	0.9F
	1806	1442	1.9E		1854	1530	1.5E
	2354	2054	1.4F			2124	0.9F
5 TU	0630	0318	1.7E	20 W	0012	0342	1.4E
	1148	0906	1.2F		0700	0936	1.0F
	1854	1530	2.0E		1224	1606	1.5E
		2136	1.4F		1930	2154	0.8F
6 W	0036	0400	1.8E	21 TH	0030	0412	1.3E
	0712	0954	1.4F		0730	1006	1.0F
	1242	1618	1.9E		1300	1642	1.4E
	1942	2218	1.4F		2006	2224	0.7F
7 TH	0112	0442	1.8E	22 F	0054	0442	1.3E
	0800	1042	1.4F		0806	1042	1.0F
	1336	1712	1.8E		1336	1718	1.2E
	2030	2306	1.2F		2048	2254	0.6F

OCTOBER

DAY	SLACK WATER TIME H.M.	MAXIMUM CURRENT TIME H.M.	VEL. KNOTS	DAY	SLACK WATER TIME H.M.	MAXIMUM CURRENT TIME H.M.	VEL. KNOTS
1 SU	0400	0042	1.4E	16 M	0454	0136	1.3E
	0854	0624	0.8F		1018	0730	0.9F
	1612	1248	1.6E		1718	1354	1.5E
	2200	1854	1.2F		2236	1954	0.8F
2 M	0436	0124	1.6E	17 TU	0524	0206	1.4E
	0954	0712	1.1F		1054	0806	0.9F
	1700	1336	1.8E		1800	1430	1.5E
	2236	1942	1.3F		2300	2024	0.8F
3 TU	0518	0206	1.7E	18 W	0554	0242	1.4E
	1048	0800	1.3F		1136	0836	1.0F
	1748	1424	1.9E		1830	1506	1.4E
	2318	2030	1.4F		2324	2054	0.7F
4 W	0600	0248	1.9E	19 TH	0624	0306	1.4E
	1142	0848	1.5F		1206	0906	1.1F
	1836	1512	2.0E		1906	1542	1.4E
		2112	1.3F		2342	2118	0.7F
5 TH	0000	0330	1.9E	20 F	0654	0336	1.4E
	0648	0936	1.6F		1242	0942	1.1F
	1236	1606	1.9E		1942	1618	1.3E
	1924	2154	1.2F			2148	0.6F
6 F	0036	0418	1.9E	21 SA	0006	0406	1.3E
	0736	1024	1.6F		0730	1012	1.1F
	1330	1654	1.8E		1318	1654	1.2E
	2018	2242	1.1F		2024	2224	0.5F
7 SA	0118	0506	1.8E	22 SU	0030	0436	1.3E
	0824	1118	1.5F		0806	1054	1.0F
	1424	1748	1.6E		1400	1730	1.1E
	2112	2330	0.9F		2106	2300	0.4F

The *drift* of a current is its velocity, normally in knots (except for river currents which will be in MPH). As noted in the preceding chapter, current drift is stated to the nearest tenth of a knot.

A tidal current is said to *flood* when it flows in from the sea and results in higher tidal stages. Conversely, a tidal current *ebbs* when the flow is seaward and water levels fall.

Slack vs. Stand

As these currents reverse, there are brief periods of no discernible flow, called *slack,* or *slack water.* The time of occurrence of slack is *not* the same as the time of *stand,* when the vertical rise or fall of tide has stopped. Tidal currents do *not* automatically slack and reverse direction when tide levels stand at high or low water.

High water at a given point simply means that the level there will not get any higher. Further up the bay or river, the tide will not have reached its maximum height and water must therefore continue to flow in so that it can continue to rise. The current can still be flooding after stand has been passed at our given point and the level has started to fall.

For example, let us consider the tides and currents on Chesapeake Bay. High tide occurs at Baltimore some 7 hours after it does at Smith Point, roughly half way up the 140 miles from Cape Henry at the entrance to Baltimore. On a certain day, high water occurs at 1126 at Smith Point, but slack water does not occur until 1304. The flooding current has thus continued for $1^h 38^m$ after high water was reached.

Corresponding time intervals occur in the case of low water stand and the slack between ebb and flood currents.

In many places, the time lag between a low or high water stand and slack water is not a matter of minutes but hours. At The Narrows in New York Harbor, flood current continues for about 2 hours after high water is reached and the tide begins to fall, ebb for 2½ hours after low water stand. After slack, the current increases until mid-flood or mid-ebb, then gradually decreases. Where ebb and flood last for about six hours—as along the Atlantic seaboard—current will be strongest about three hours after

slack. Thus, the skipper who figures his passage out through The Narrows from the time of high water, rather than slack, will start about two and a half hours too soon and will run into a current at nearly its maximum strength.

NEED FOR KNOWLEDGE

Currents, primarily of the tidal type, will affect many boating situations. Currents will be a definite factor in piloting in tidal rivers, bays, and sounds. Coastal currents, resulting from waves striking the beaches at an angle, will often influence coastal piloting problems.

Effect on course and speed made good

A current directly in line with a boat's motion through the water will have a maximum effect on the speed made good, but with no off-course influence. The effect can be of real significance in figuring your ETA at your destination. It can even affect the safety of your craft and its crew if you have figured your fuel too closely and run into a bow-on current.

A current that is nearly at a right angle to your course through the water will have a maximum effect on the course made good and a minor effect on the distance you must travel to reach your destination. The off-course effect can be of great importance if there are shoals or other hazards near your desired track.

Knowledge of current set and drift can be applied to assist your cruising. Departure times can be selected to take advantage of favorable currents, or at least to minimize adverse effects. A 12-knot boat speed and a 2-knot current, reasonably typical situations, can combine to result in either a 10-knot or a 14-knot speed made good—the 40%

gain of a favorable current over an opposing one is significant both in terms of time en route and fuel consumed.

Even lesser currents have some significance. A half-knot current would hinder a swimmer and make rowing a boat noticeably more difficult. A one-knot current can seriously affect a sailboat in light breezes.

Difficult locations

In many boating areas, there will be locations where current conditions can be critical.

Numerous ocean inlets are difficult, or even dangerous, in certain combinations of current and onshore surf. In general, difficult surf conditions will be made more hazardous by an outward-flowing (ebbing) current. The topic of inlet seamanship is covered in more detail on pages 528-547.

There are a number of narrow bodies of water where the maximum current velocity is such as to make passage impossible at times for boats of limited power, and to seriously slow boats of greater engine power, fig. 2019. Such narrow passages are particularly characteristic of Pacific Northwest boating areas, but do occur elsewhere. Currents in New York City's East River reach a maximum of 4.6 knots, and at the Golden Gate of San Francisco velocities greater than 5 knots occur. Velocities of $3\frac{1}{2}$ to 4 knots are common in much-traveled passages like Woods Hole, Mass., and Plum Gut, at the eastern end of Long Island, N. Y.

FIG. 2021 Table 2—Current Differences and Other Constants. Data are given for hundreds of subordinate stations so that predictions for current may be made for many points of navigational significance.

No.	PLACE	POSITION		TIME DIFFERENCES		VELOCITY RATIOS		MAXIMUM CURRENTS			
								Flood		Ebb	
		Lat.	Long.	Slack water	Maximum current	Maximum flood	Maximum ebb	Direction (true)	Average velocity	Direction (true)	Average velocity
		° ′	° ′	h. m.	h. m.			deg.	knots	deg.	knots
	DELAWARE BAY and RIVER—Continued	N.	W.	on DELAWARE BAY ENTRANCE, p.58							
				Time meridian, 75°W.							
1091	Fisher Point	39 59	75 04	+5 45	+5 25	0.8	0.9	40	1.4	225	1.7
1093	Torresdale, west of channel	40 02	74 59	(¹)	+5 50	0.5	0.8	45	0.9	225	1.6
1095	Rancocas Creek, off Delanco	40 03	74 58	+6 15	+6 15	0.6	0.5	90	1.0	270	0.9
1097	Bristol, south of	40 05	74 52	(²)	(²)	0.7	0.8	25	1.3	200	1.6
1099	Burlington Island, channel east of	40 06	74 50	(³)	(³)	0.5	0.9	20	0.9	205	1.8
1101	Whitehill	40 08	74 44	-----	⁴+7 00	----	0.7	----	----	235	1.4
	DEL., MD. and VA. COAST										
1103	Indian River Inlet (bridge)	38 37	75 04	+0 10	+0 10	1.0	1.1	265	1.8	85	2.1
1105	Fenwick Shoal Lighted Whistle Buoy 2	38 25	74 46	See table 5.							
1107	Winter Quarter Shoal Lightship⁵	37 55	74 56	See table 5.							
	on CHESAPEAKE BAY ENTRANCE, p.64										
1109	Cape Charles, 70 miles east of	37 05	74 51	See table 5.							
1111	Smith Island Shoal, southeast of	37 05	75 43	-2 10	-2 10	0.3	0.3	300	0.3	70	0.4
1113	Chesapeake Lightship	36 59	75 42	(⁶)	(⁶)	----	----	----	----	----	----
1115	Cape Henry Light, 2.2 miles SE. of	36 54	75 59	-1 15	-1 30	1.0	0.6	345	1.0	165	0.9
	CHESAPEAKE BAY										
1117	Cape Henry Light, 1 mile north of	36 56	76 00	0 00	-0 25	1.1	1.3	280	1.1	90	2.0
1119	Cape Henry Light, 1.8 miles north of	36 57	76 00	-0 05	-0 15	1.2	1.0	290	1.2	100	1.5
1121	CHESAPEAKE BAY ENTRANCE	36 59	76 00	Daily predictions				305	1.0	125	1.5
1123	Cape Henry Light, 4.6 miles north of	37 00	75 59	-0 35	-0 50	1.3	0.9	295	1.3	105	1.3
1124	Cape Charles Light, 9.5 mi. WSW. of	37 04	76 05	+0 10	0 00	1.5	0.9	320	1.5	125	1.4
1125	Cape Henry Light, 8.3 mi. NW. of	37 02	76 07	-0 05	-0 10	1.0	0.7	330	1.0	135	1.1
1126	Lynnhaven Roads	36 55	76 05	-0 35	-0 40	0.8	0.6	280	0.8	70	0.9
1127	Lynnhaven Inlet bridge	36 54	76 06	-2 05	-2 35	0.6	0.9	180	0.6	0	1.4
	Chesapeake Bay Bridge Tunnel										
1128	Chesapeake Beach, 1.5 miles N. of	36 57	76 07	-0 15	-0 20	0.8	0.6	305	0.8	100	0.9
1129	Thimble Shoal Channel	36 58	76 07	-0 40	-0 40	1.4	0.9	310	1.4	95	1.3
1130	Tail of the Horseshoe	37 00	76 06	-0 25	-0 40	0.9	0.7	300	0.9	110	1.0
1131	Middle Ground, channel west of	37 03	76 05	-0 25	-0 10	1.6	0.9	335	1.6	150	1.3
1132	Chesapeake Channel	37 02	76 04	-0 15	-0 15	1.8	1.0	335	1.8	145	1.5
1133	Fisherman I., 3.2 miles WSW. of	37 04	76 02	-0 55	-1 05	1.2	1.1	330	1.2	135	1.6
1134	Fisherman I., 1.4 miles WSW. of	37 05	76 00	(⁷)	-1 05	1.8	0.7	330	1.8	140	1.1
1135	Fisherman I., 1.8 miles south of	37 04	75 59	-0 45	-1 10	1.6	0.9	320	1.6	120	1.4
1136	Fisherman I., 0.4 mile west of	37 06	75 59	-0 45	-1 10	2.0	1.3	5	2.0	175	2.0
1137	Fisherman I., 1.1 miles NW. of	37 06	76 00	(⁸)	-0 40	1.8	1.1	355	1.8	165	1.6
1139	Cape Charles, off Wise Point	37 07	75 58	(⁹)	(⁹)	0.7	0.1	305	0.7	75	0.2
	Little Creek										
1141	North of east jetty	36 56	76 11	-1 50	-2 00	0.9	0.7	280	0.9	75	1.0
1143	0.5 mile north of west jetty	36 56	76 11	-1 10	-1 15	0.9	0.6	275	0.9	110	0.9
1145	Old Plantation Flats Light, west of	37 14	76 04	+1 10	+0 50	1.2	0.9	5	1.2	175	1.3
1146	York Spit Channel	37 13	76 09	+0 55	+0 55	0.8	0.7	10	0.8	195	1.1
1147	Wolf Trap Light, 0.5 mile west of	37 23	76 12	+1 05	+1 05	1.0	0.8	15	1.0	190	1.2
1148	Wolf Trap Light, 5.8 miles east of	37 23	76 04	+1 45	+1 45	0.9	0.9	15	0.9	175	1.3
1149	Stingray Point, 5.5 miles east of	37 35	76 10	+1 50	+2 20	1.0	0.6	345	1.0	180	0.9
1150	Stingray Point, 12.5 miles east of	37 34	76 02	+1 40	+2 05	1.0	0.5	30	1.0	175	0.8

¹ Flood begins, $+6^h 55^m$; ebb begins, $+5^h 00^m$.
² Flood begins, $+6^h 55^m$; maximum flood, $+5^h 30^m$; ebb begins, $+4^h 55^m$; maximum ebb, $+6^h 10^m$.
³ Flood begins, $+7^h 30^m$; maximum flood, $+5^h 45^m$; ebb begins, $+4^h 15^m$; maximum ebb, $+6^h 45^m$.

TIDAL CURRENT PREDICTIONS

Without experience or official information, local current prediction is always risky. East of Badgers Island in Portsmouth, Maine, for example, the average ebb current flows at a maximum velocity of less than a half-knot. Yet, southwest of the same island, it averages 3.7 knots.

One rule is fairly safe for most locations—the ebb is stronger and lasts longer than the flood. Eighty percent of all reference stations on the Atlantic, Gulf, and Pacific coasts of the U.S. report currents stronger at the ebb. This is normal because river flow adds to the ebb, but hinders the flood.

On the Atlantic coast, expect to find two approximately equal flood currents and two similar ebb currents in a cycle of roughly 25 hours. On the Pacific coast, however, two floods and ebbs will differ markedly. On the Gulf coast, there may be just one flood and one ebb in 25 hours. In each case, these patterns are, of course, generally similar to tidal action in the respective areas.

Don't try to predict current velocity from the time that it takes a high tide to reach a given point from the sea's entrance. Dividing the distance from Cape Henry to Baltimore by the time that it takes high water to work its way up Chesapeake Bay gives a speed of 13 knots. True maximum flood current strength is only about one knot.

Another useful truism about tidal currents is that tidal currents at different places *cannot* be forecast from their tidal ranges. You would expect strong currents at Eastport, Maine, where the difference between successive high and low waters reaches as much as 20 feet. And you would be right; there are three-knot currents there. But Galveston, Texas, with only a two-foot range of tides has currents up to more than two knots. So has Miami with a three-foot range, and Charleston, S. C. with a six-foot range—these are stronger currents than Boston where the range is often more than 10 feet and as strong as at Anchorage, Alaska where it's as much as 35 feet from some highs to the next low.

A good forecasting rule for all oceans: expect strong tidal currents where two bays meet. The reason: tidal ranges and high water times in the two bodies of water are likely to be different.

For the coasting skipper, here is another tidal current fact that may be useful: near the beach, flood and ebb don't usually set to and from the land, but rather parallel with the coast. This is as true off New Jersey and Florida as it is off California and Oregon. A few miles offshore, however, and in some very large bays, the current behaves quite differently—the rotary current mentioned previously in this chapter.

TIDAL CURRENT TABLES

At any given place, current strength varies with the phases of the moon and its distance from the earth. It will be strongest when tidal ranges are greatest—near new and

TABLE A

Interval between slack and maximum current

Interval between slack and desired time	1 20	1 40	2 00	2 20	2 40	3 00	3 20	3 40	4 00	4 20	4 40	5 00	5 20	5 40
0 20	0.4	0.3	0.3	0.2	0.2	0.2	0.2	0.1	0.1	0.1	0.1	0.1	0.1	0.1
0 40	0.7	0.6	0.5	0.4	0.4	0.3	0.3	0.3	0.3	0.2	0.2	0.2	0.2	0.2
1 00	0.9	0.8	0.7	0.6	0.6	0.5	0.5	0.4	0.4	0.4	0.3	0.3	0.3	0.3
1 20	1.0	1.0	0.9	0.8	0.7	0.6	0.6	0.5	0.5	0.5	0.4	0.4	0.4	0.4
1 40		1.0	1.0	0.9	0.8	0.8	0.7	0.7	0.6	0.6	0.6	0.5	0.5	0.4
2 00			1.0	1.0	0.9	0.9	0.8	0.8	0.7	0.7	0.6	0.6	0.6	0.5
2 20				1.0	1.0	0.9	0.9	0.9	0.8	0.8	0.7	0.7	0.6	0.6
2 40					1.0	1.0	1.0	0.9	0.9	0.8	0.8	0.7	0.7	0.7
3 00						1.0	1.0	1.0	0.9	0.9	0.8	0.8	0.8	0.7
3 20							1.0	1.0	0.9	0.9	0.9	0.8	0.8	0.8
3 40								1.0	1.0	1.0	0.9	0.9	0.9	0.9
4 00									1.0	1.0	1.0	1.0	0.9	0.9
4 20										1.0	1.0	1.0	1.0	1.0
4 40											1.0	1.0	1.0	1.0
5 00												1.0	1.0	1.0
5 20													1.0	1.0
5 40														1.0

TABLE B

Interval between slack and maximum current

Interval between slack and desired time	1 20	1 40	2 00	2 20	2 40	3 00	3 20	3 40	4 00	4 20	4 40	5 00	5 20	5 40
0 20	0.5	0.4	0.4	0.3	0.3	0.3	0.3	0.3	0.2	0.2	0.2	0.2	0.2	0.2
0 40	0.8	0.7	0.6	0.5	0.5	0.5	0.4	0.4	0.4	0.4	0.3	0.3	0.3	0.3
1 00	0.9	0.8	0.8	0.7	0.7	0.6	0.6	0.5	0.5	0.5	0.5	0.4	0.4	0.4
1 20	1.0	1.0	0.9	0.8	0.8	0.7	0.7	0.6	0.6	0.6	0.5	0.5	0.5	0.5
1 40		1.0	1.0	0.9	0.9	0.8	0.8	0.7	0.7	0.7	0.6	0.6	0.6	0.6
2 00			1.0	1.0	0.9	0.9	0.9	0.8	0.8	0.7	0.7	0.7	0.7	0.6
2 20				1.0	1.0	1.0	0.9	0.9	0.8	0.8	0.8	0.7	0.7	0.7
2 40					1.0	1.0	1.0	0.9	0.9	0.9	0.8	0.8	0.8	0.7
3 00						1.0	1.0	1.0	0.9	0.9	0.9	0.9	0.8	0.8
3 20							1.0	1.0	1.0	0.9	0.9	0.9	0.9	0.8
3 40								1.0	1.0	1.0	1.0	0.9	0.9	0.9
4 00									1.0	1.0	1.0	1.0	0.9	0.9
4 20										1.0	1.0	1.0	1.0	1.0
4 40											1.0	1.0	1.0	1.0
5 00												1.0	1.0	1.0
5 20													1.0	1.0
5 40														1.0

FIG. 2022 Table 3—Velocity of Current at Any Time. Using the appropriate part, A or B, of this table, the velocity of current at intermediate times between maximum strength and slack may be calculated for either a reference or a subordinate station. Table B is for use at Cape Cod Canal, Hell Gate, or Chesapeake and Delaware Canal <u>only</u>; use Table A for all other locations.

DURATION OF WEAK CURRENT NEAR TIME OF SLACK WATER

Table A

Maximum current	Period with a velocity not more than—				
	0.1 knot	0.2 knot	0.3 knot	0.4 knot	0.5 knot
Knots	*Minutes*	*Minutes*	*Minutes*	*Minutes*	*Minutes*
1.0	23	46	70	94	120
1.5	15	31	46	62	78
2.0	11	23	35	46	58
3.0	8	15	23	31	38
4.0	6	11	17	23	29
5.0	5	9	14	18	23
6.0	4	8	11	15	19
7.0	3	7	10	13	16
8.0	3	6	9	11	14
9.0	3	5	8	10	13
10.0	2	5	7	9	11

Table B

Maximum current	Period with a velocity not more than—				
	0.1 knot	0.2 knot	0.3 knot	0.4 knot	0.5 knot
Knots	*Minutes*	*Minutes*	*Minutes*	*Minutes*	*Minutes*
1.0	13	28	46	66	89
1.5	8	18	28	39	52
2.0	6	13	20	28	36
3.0	4	8	13	18	22
4.0	3	6	9	13	17
5.0	3	5	8	10	13

FIG. 2023 Table 4—Duration of Slack. Although actual slack water is only a momentary event, current velocity is quite small for a significant period while the direction is reversing. Part A or B of this table is used in the same situations as for Table 3.

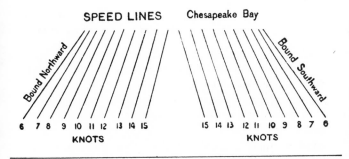

SPEED LINES   Chesapeake Bay

Bound Northward

Bound Southward

6 7 8 9 10 11 12 13 14 15   15 14 13 12 11 10 9 8 7 6
KNOTS   KNOTS

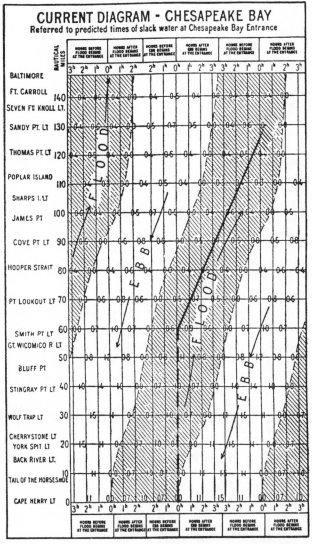

FIG. 2024 Current Diagrams from the Tidal Current Tables (East Coast volume only) provide a quick and simple way of determining the best speed and time of departure for a run up or down several of the major waterways subject to tidal currents.

full moon—and weakest when tidal ranges are least—near first and last quarters. Current velocity may vary as much as 40 percent above and below its average value.

The relationship between currents and tides makes possible the prediction of tidal currents. The National Ocean Survey publishes two volumes of predictions annually; one covers the Atlantic Coast of North America and the other the Pacific Coast of North America and Asia.

Each volume includes for its area, predictions of tidal currents in bays, sounds, and rivers, plus ocean currents such as the Gulf Stream. General information on wind-driven currents is also included although these, of course, result from temporary, local conditions and so cannot be predicted a year or more ahead. Your own past experience and "local knowledge," the advice of experienced watermen of the area, will be the best source of information regarding the effect of storm winds on local waters and their currents.

Tidal Current Tables are available at authorized sales agents for N.O.S. charts. The cost of each volume is $2.

Description of the Tables

The format and layout of the *Tidal Current Tables* is much the same as for the *Tide Tables* discussed earlier in this chapter. A system of reference stations, plus constants and differences for subordinate stations, is used to calculate the predictions for many points.

Table 1. There are 20 *reference stations* in the Atlantic Coast volume and 10 for the Pacific Coast. The Gulf of Mexico is included in the Atlantic Coast volume. For each station, there are tabulated the predicted times and strengths of maximum flood and ebb currents, plus the times of slack water. The direction of the flood and ebb currents is also listed, see fig. 2020.

Table 2. Time differences and velocity ratios are listed for hundreds of *subordinate stations*, fig. 2021. The location of these stations is described in terms of place names or position relative to identifiable points; the latitude and longitude are also given as an aid to their precise location. The direction and strength of typical maximum currents for each station are also tabulated. A number of subordinate stations will have only the footnoted entry "Current too weak and variable to be predicted." This information, even though negative in nature, is useful in planning a cruise.

Table 3. This table, fig. 2022, provides a convenient means for determination of the strength of the current at times intermediate between slack and maximum velocity. Use nearest tabulated values without interpolation.

Table 4. Although slack water is only a momentary event, there is a period of time on either side of slack during which the current is so weak as to be negligible for practical piloting purposes. This period, naturally, varies with the maximum strength of the current, being longer for weak currents. Two sub-tables, fig. 2023, predict the duration of currents from 0.1 to 0.5 knot by tenths for normal reversing currents and for the hydraulic currents found at certain specified locations.

Table 5. For the Atlantic Coast only, information is given on rotary tidal currents at various offshore points of navigational interest. These points are described in terms of general location and specific geographic coordinates. Predictions of velocity and direction are referred to times after maximum flood at designated reference stations.

Current Diagrams

For a number of major tidal waterways of the United States, a *current diagram,* such as fig. 2024, is provided in the Tidal Current Tables. These give a graphic means of quickly and easily selecting a favorable time for traveling in either direction along these routes.

Tides and Currents / CHAPTER 20

Time

The Tidal Current Tables list all predictions in *local standard time*. Be sure to make a conversion to daylight time if you are piloting in an area using such "fast" time; this is done by adding one hour to the tabulated times.

Cautions

As with tidal predictions, the data in the Tidal Current Tables may often be upset by sustained abnormal local conditions such as winds or rainfall. Use the current predictions with caution during and immediately after such weather abnormalities.

It should also be noted carefully that tidal current predictions are generally for a *spot location only;* the set and drift may be quite different only a mile or less away. This is at variance from predictions of high and low tides which can usually be used over fairly wide areas in the vicinity of the reference or secondary station.

EXAMPLES OF TIDAL CURRENT CALCULATIONS

The Tidal Current Tables contain all the information needed for the determination of such conditions as the time of maximum current and its strength, the time of slack water, the duration of slack (actually, the duration of the very weak current conditions), etc. Examples will be given of typical problems and their solution, plus comments and cautions to be used in connection with such situations.

Example 1. Determination of the time and strength of maximum current, and the time of slack, at a reference station.

Problem: What is the time and strength of the maximum ebb current at Chesapeake Bay Entrance during the afternoon of 17 October 1967?

Solution: As with the Tide Tables, the answer is available for a reference station by direct inspection. Fig. 2020 is a typical page from the Tidal Current Tables; we can see that the maximum ebb current on the specified afternoon is 1.5 knots setting 125° True; it is predicted to occur at 1430 EST.

Problem: What is the time of the first slack before ebb at this station on 17 October 1967?

Solution: Table 1 does not directly identify the slacks as being "slack before ebb" or "slack before flood"; this must be determined by comparison of the slack time with the nature of the next occurring maximum current.

From fig. 2020, we can see that the earliest slack that will be followed by an ebbing current at Chesapeake Bay Entrance on 17 October is predicted for 1054 EST.

Notes: a. Times obtained from the Tidal Current Tables are *standard;* add one hour for daylight time if in effect.

b. The set of the current for a reference station is found at the *top* of the page in Table 1; it is also given in Table 2 where further information, such as the geographic coordinates of the station, and the average velocity of maximum flood and ebb currents, is listed.

c. The normal day at Chesapeake Bay Entrance, where the tide is of the semi-diurnal type, will have four slacks

and four maximums. The tidal cycle of 24^h and 50^m will result in the occasional omission of a slack or maximum.

Example 2. Determination of the time and strength of maximum current, and the time of slack, at a subordinate station.

Problem: What is the time and strength of the morning flood current in Lynnhaven Inlet at the bridge on 21 September 1967?

Solution: Table 2, fig. 2021, gives time differences and velocity ratios to be applied to the predictions at the appropriate reference station. There is an Index to Table 2 in the rear of the Tidal Current Tables if it is needed to locate the given subordinate station.

In this problem, the time difference and velocity ratio are applied as follows:

10 06	at Chesapeake Bay Entrance	1.0 knot
−2:35	difference/ratio	0.6
07 31	at Lynnhaven Inlet	0.6 knot

The set (direction) of the current is also noted from the appropriate column of Table 2; in this case, it is 180° True.

Thus the predictions are for a maximum current of 0.6 knot setting 180° True at Lynnhaven Inlet bridge at 0731 EST on 21 September 1967.

Problem: What is the time of the first afternoon slack water at Lynnhaven Inlet bridge on 6 September 1967?

Solution: From Table 2, the time difference is found to be −2:05. This is applied to the time of slack at the reference station:

19 42	at Chesapeake Bay Entrance
−2:05	difference
17 37	at Lynnhaven Inlet bridge

The time of the first afternoon slack water at Lynnhaven Inlet bridge on 6 September 1967 is 1737 EST.

Notes: a. Observe that often there may be two separate time differences, one for slack and the other for maximum current, either flood or ebb. More complex situations with varied time differences will be shown by special footnotes to Table 2 where required. Note also that the velocity ratios may differ between ebb and flood.

b. Note that the direction of the current at a subordinate station must be taken from Table 2. It will nearly always differ from that at the reference station. No statement of current is complete without giving direction as well as strength.

c. The locations in Table 2 are usually a point some distance and direction from a landmark or aid to navigation. There may be several subordinate stations referred to the same base point (see subordinate stations 1117 to 1124, and 1149-1150 in fig. 2021); be sure to use the correct subordinate station.

Example 3. Determination of the current at an intermediate time at a reference station.

Problem: What is the velocity and set of the current at Chesapeake Bay Entrance at 1300 EST on 3 October 1967?

Solution: The time of slack and maximum current (ebb or flood) which bracket the desired time are found from Table 1. The interval between these times is determined, as is the interval between the desired time and the slack.

```
14 24
10 48
 3:36  interval, slack—maximum current
13 00
10 48
 2:12  interval, slack—desired time
```

With these time intervals, Table 3A is used to determine the ratio of the velocity of the current at the desired time to its maximum velocity. The nearest tabulated values are used, no interpolation. In this example, the ratio at the intersection of the line for 2ʰ 20ᵐ and the column for 3ʰ 40ᵐ is found to be 0.8. Multiply the maximum current by this decimal factor, $1.9 \times 0.8 = 1.5$.

From the times used, we note that the current is ebbing. From the top of Table 1, we determine that the direction is 125° True.

Thus, at 1300 EST on 3 October 1967, the current at Chesapeake Bay Entrance is predicted to have a velocity of 1.5 knots and be setting 125° True.

Notes: a. Except as specially indicated, use Table 3A, the upper portion of Table 3. The lower, B, portion is for use in designated waterways only.

b. Be sure that the interval is calculated between the desired time and the time of *slack,* whether or not this time is nearer to the given time than the time of maximum current.

c. Note that calculations of current velocity are rounded to the nearest tenth of a knot.

Example 4. Determination of the current at an intermediate time at a subordinate station.

Problem: What is the velocity and set of the current at a point 5½ miles east of Stingray Point at 1700 EDT on 5 October 1967?

Solution: First, the predictions for slack and maximum current must be found for the subordinate station after converting 1700 EDT to 1600 EST for entering the Tables.

Slack		Maximum	
12 36 at Chesapeake Bay			
Entrance		16 06	1.9 knots, Ebb
+1:50 difference/ratio		+2:20	0.6
14 26 at subordinate station		18 26	1.1

With the information developed above, and the desired time, further calculations are made as follows:

```
18 26
14 26
 4:00  interval, slack—maximum current
16 00  (EST)
14 26
 1:34  interval, slack—desired time
```

Using Table 3A, fig. 2022, the velocity ratio is found to be 0.6; then $1.1 \times 0.6 = 0.7$. From Table 2, the direction is seen to be 180° True.

The current at 1700 EDT at a point 5½ miles east of Stingray Point on 5 October 1967 is predicted to be 0.7 knot setting 180° True.

Note: Calculations for the strength at an intermediate time of a hydraulic current, such as in the Cape Cod Canal or at Hell Gate in East River, New York City, are handled

exactly as above, except that the lower, B, part of Table 3 is used.

Example 5. Determination of the duration of slack (weak current) at a designated point.

Problem: For how long will the current be less than 0.4 knots around the time of slack before ebb on the morning of 4 October 1967 at Chesapeake Bay Entrance?

Solution: From Table 1 (fig. 2020), for this date, the maximum currents on either side of this slack (at 1142) are 1.5 knots flood at 0848 and 2.0 knots ebb at 1512.

Using Table 4A (fig. 2023), the duration of current less than 0.4 knot is determined for each maximum. One-half of each such duration is used for the period from 0.4 to 0 knots and then 0 to 0.4 knots.

The value for the ending flood current is one-half of 62, or 31 minutes; for the beginning ebb current, it is one-half of 46, or 23 minutes.

On 4 October 1967 at Chesapeake Bay Entrance, the predicted duration of a current less than 0.4 knot is $31 + 23 = 54$ minutes; from $1142 - 31 = 1111$ until $1142 + 23 = 1205$. **Notes:** a. If the maximum strengths of the ebb and flood currents are essentially the same, only one figure need be taken from Table 4. Interpolate as necessary.

b. Use the A or B portion of Table 4 in the same manner as for Table 3.

Example 6. Use of a Current Diagram

Problem: For an afternoon run up Chesapeake Bay from Smith Point to Sandy Point Light at 10 knots on 20 October 1967, what time should you depart from Smith Point for the most favorable current conditions?

Solution: We use the current diagram for Chesapeake Bay and a graphic solution, fig. 2024. Draw a line on the diagram parallel to the 10-knot northbound speed line so that it fits generally in the center of the shaded area marked "Flood." Project downward from the intersection of this line with the horizontal line marked Smith Point Light to the scale at the bottom of the diagram. The mark here will be seen to be "0ʰ after ebb begins at the entrance."

Referring to Table 1, it will be seen that on the given date, the afternoon slack before ebb occurs at 1242.

For a run up Chesapeake Bay to Sandy Point Light at 10 knots on the afternoon of 20 October 1967, it is predicted that the most favorable current conditions will be obtained if you leave Smith Point Light at about 1242 EST or 1342 EDT.

Notes: a. Similar solutions can be worked out for southbound trips, but it is likely that on longer runs you will be faced with both favorable and unfavorable current conditions. Selection of starting time may be made, however, to minimize adverse conditions.

b. Conditions shown on Tidal Current Diagrams are averages and for typical conditions; small variations should be expected in specific situations.

TIDAL CURRENT CHARTS

The National Ocean Survey also publishes a series of *Tidal Current Charts.* These are available for 12 bodies of water, from Boston Harbor around to Puget Sound (see complete listing on page 329).

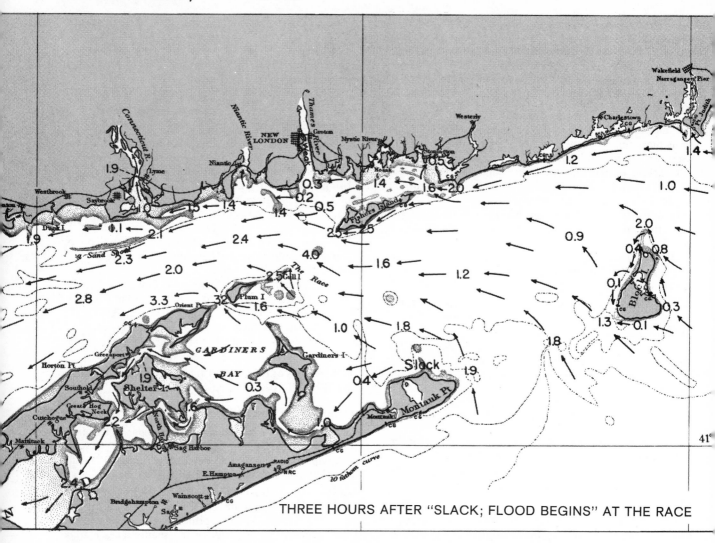

THREE HOURS AFTER "SLACK; FLOOD BEGINS" AT THE RACE

FIG. 2025 Tidal Current Charts are published for certain major bodies of water. Each is a set of 12 small-scale chartlets showing currents existing at hourly intervals throughout a complete cycle of flood and ebb.

Tidal Current Charts are made up in the form of a series of 12 reproductions of a small-scale chart of the area. Each of the charts depicts the direction and velocity of the current for a specific time in terms of hours after the predicted time of the beginning of flood or the beginning of ebb at the appropriate reference station. See fig. 2025. The currents in various passages and portions of the body of water are indicated by arrows and numbers. By following through the sequence of the charts, the hourly changes in strength and direction are easily seen.

These charts must be used with caution as tidal current strengths may vary widely between points separated by only a short distance.

Tidal Current Charts are periodically updated from new surveys and only the latest edition should be used.

TIDAL CURRENT DIAGRAMS

A development of the "computer age," *Tidal Current Diagrams* are a series of 12 monthly graphs to be used with Tidal Current Charts instead of the Tidal Current Tables. The diagram method is more convenient as the graphs indicate directly, from the date and time, the chart to be used

and the speed correction factor to be applied.

Tidal Current Diagrams are presently available only for use with the Tidal Current Charts of the Block Island Sound and Long Island Sound areas. A new set of diagrams is required for each year; the price is $2.

RIVER CURRENTS

River currents, above tidal action, will consistently flow in one direction, but the velocity may vary widely. For further information on river currents and river piloting, see Chapter 27.

SUPPLEMENTARY SOURCES OF INFORMATION

The ultimate source of current information is your own eyesight and past experience, fig. 2026. These are most helpful even where there are predictions from the N.O.S. tables. As noted before, the tabular data are to be expected under "normal" conditions, and may be easily upset by unusual circumstances. Strong winds will, for example, drive water into or out of bays and modify tidal levels and currents.

0.3 KNOT

1.0 KNOT

These photographs by Larry Riordan show clearly how buoys can be a helpful aid in estimating the direction and strength of current. Even though some data are available in Current Tables, predictions may be in error because of wind. Turbulence and eddies around a buoy increase with current velocity. In very strong currents, buoys may tow completely under.

Note (top left) how at 0.3 knot a wake is evident and the buoy inclines slightly. Doubling the velocity (0.6 knot, at left) increases the disturbance on both sides of the buoy. At 1.0 knot (top right) it leans over and a whirlpool-like eddy has developed. Finally, at 2.2 knots (bottom right), the wake has whitened. Buoy shapes affect the pattern and inclination.

0.6 KNOT

2.2 KNOTS

FIG. 2026 Tidal current predictions are often upset by temporary local conditions of wind or rainfall. There is no substitute for an ability to interpret currents from visual observations. This excellent set of photographs shows visible indications on a buoy of currents of various strengths. Be careful; do not overestimate current velocity.

Currents and Piloting

One of the most interesting problems in small-craft piloting is the matter of currents, their effect upon boat speed, the determination of courses which must be steered to make good a desired path, and the time required to reach a destination. This is often know as *current sailing*.

Contrary to popular belief, the solution of current problems is really comparatively simple and does not require the use of higher mathematics to obtain results of practical accuracy. Indeed, when the fundamental principles have been mastered, the working out of current problems can be fun.

As a boat is propelled through the water, by oars, sails, or motor, and as it is steered, it moves with respect to the water. At the same time, the water may be moving with respect to the bottom and the shore as a result of current. The resultant motion of the boat is the net effect of these two motions combined, with regard to both velocity and direction. The actual track made good over the bottom will not be the same as the DR track, neither in terms of course nor speed.

The importance of tidal currents should not be underestimated. Unexpected current is always a threat to the skipper because it can carry his craft off course, possibly into dangerous waters. The risk is greater with slower boat speeds and under conditions of reduced visibility. A prediction of current effect can be added to a plot of a DR track to obtain an *estimated position (EP)* plotted as a small square with a dot in the center, fig. 2027.

Leeway

Before proceeding further with current effects, let us here introduce, and then dispense with, the term *leeway*. By definition, leeway is the leeward (away from the wind)

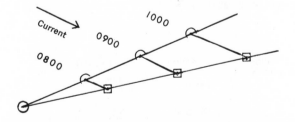

FIG. 2027 If the current is known, or can be estimated, a DR plot (half-circles) can be modified to show a series of Estimated Positions (squares) showing the effect of current.

motion of a vessel due to the wind. The term is most applicable to sailing craft, but it can be appreciable on larger motorboats and yachts. Its effect, however, need not be considered separately from current; the two may be lumped together, plus such factors as wave action on the boat, and the total offsetting influence termed "current."

411

Sailing Directions emphasize the necessity of taking such influences into account. A typical caution might read: "The directions 'steer' or 'make good' a course mean, without exception, to proceed from a point of origin along a track having the identical meridional angle as the designated course. Vessels following the directives must allow for every influence tending to cause deviation (not to be confused with compass deviation—Ed) from such track, and navigate so that the designated course is continuously being made good."

DEFINITION OF CURRENT SAILING TERMS

The terms "Course" and "Speed" were used in DR plots for the motion of the boat through the water without regard to current. Now this most important influence will be studied and additional terms must be introduced.

The *intended track* is the expected path of the boat, as plotted on a chart, after consideration has been given to the effect of current.

Track, abbreviated as TR, is the direction (true) of the intended track line.

Speed of advance, SOA, is the intended rate of travel along the intended track line.

It must be recognized that the intended track will not always be the actual track, and so two more terms are needed.

Course over the ground, COG, is the direction of the *actual* path of the boat, the track made good.

Speed over the ground, SOG, is the actual rate of travel along this track; sometimes termed "Speed made good."

CURRENT SITUATIONS

A study of the effects of current resolves itself into two basic situations, as follows:

1. When the direction of the current, its *set,* is in the same direction as the boat's motion, or is in exactly the opposite direction.

2. When the direction of the current is at an angle to the boat's course, either a right or an oblique angle.

The first situation is, of course, the simplest and most easily solved. The velocity of the current, the *drift,* is added to, or subtracted from, the speed through the water to obtain the speed over the ground. The course over the ground (or intended track) is the same as the DR course—COG equals C, as does TR.

CURRENT DIAGRAMS

When the boat's motion and the set of the current form an angle with each other, the solution for the resultant course and speed is more complex, but still not difficult. Several methods may be used, but a graphic solution using a *current diagram* will usually be found to be the easiest to understand.

Basically, a current diagram represents the two component motions separately, as if they occurred independently and sequentially, which, of course, they do not. These diagrams can be drawn in terms of velocities or distances. The former is easier and is usually used; current diagrams in this book will be drawn in terms of velocities and labeled as shown in fig. 2028. If distances are plotted, be sure to use the same period of time for each component motion—one hour is commonly used since the units of distance will then be the same numerically as the units of speed.

Accuracy of current diagrams

The accuracy with which the resultant course and speed can be determined depends largely on the accuracy with which the current has been determined. Values of the current usually must be taken from tidal current tables or charts, or estimated by the skipper from visual observations; see fig. 2026.

Current diagrams may also be called "vector triangles of velocity," a profound title for a simple graphic procedure. The term "vector" in mathematics means a quantity that has both magnitude and direction. Directed quantities are important things. In current sailing, the directed quantities are the motions of the boat and the water (the current).

Vectors

A vector may be represented graphically by an arrow, a segment of a straight line with an arrowhead indicating the direction, and the length of the line scaled to the velocity, fig. 2029. If we specify that a certain unit of length is equal to a certain unit of speed—e.g., that 1 inch equals 1 knot—then two such vectors can represent graphically two different velocities. Any speed scale may be used, the larger the better for accuracy. The size of the available paper and working space will normally control the scale.

Current diagrams may be drawn on a chart either as part of the plot or separately. They may also be drawn on plain paper; in this case, it is wise to draw in a north line as the

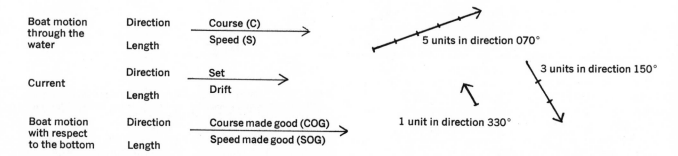

FIG. 2028 The component lines of a current diagram must always be correctly and completely labeled. Direction is shown above the line; velocity is noted below the line. Typical labels are shown above.

FIG. 2029 A vector is a line representing a *directed quantity.* It has direction (shown by the arrowhead) and magnitude (length). Any convenient scale may be selected to indicate magnitude.

reference for measuring directions.

Since boats are subject to two distinct motions—the boat through the water, and the water with respect to the bottom—we will now consider how the resultant motion, or vector sum, is obtained by current diagrams.

Vector triangles

When the two motions are not in line with each other, they form two sides of a triangle, fig. 2030. Completing the triangle gives the third side which will be a vector representing the resultant motion or velocity. Thus, when any two velocity vectors are drawn to the same scale and form the sides of a velocity triangle, the third side will be the resultant velocity vector (the vector sum of the other two), and its direction and magnitude may be measured from the diagram.

It may be an aid to the visualization of the component motions if a time period of one hour is used and the points that are the corners of the triangle are considered as positions of the boat before and after certain motions, as follows:

O—the origin.

DR—the DR position of the boat as a result solely of its motion through the water.

W—the position of the boat solely as a result of the motion of the water.

P—the position (intended or actual) of the boat as a result of the combined action of the component motions.

(It should be noted that, in some cases, two of the above letters are applicable to a position; it is customary to use only one.)

"Tail-to-head" relationship. Note very carefully how the vectors for boat motion through the water and the current are drawn. These vectors are always drawn "tail-to-head," *not* so that both are directed out from the same source. (This rule applies only when one of the vectors is current; not when they both represent boat's motion.)

If both boat motion through the water and current are known, either may be drawn first from the origin; fig. 2031b will give the same resultant motion as fig. 2031a.

The four "Cases" of current problems

There are four typical current problems, different combinations of known and unknown factors. For convenience, we will call them Case 1, 2, etc.

CASE 1—Known: Boat's course (C) and speed (S) through the water; current set and drift.

To be determined: The intended (expected) track (TR) and speed of advance (SOA).

This is the determination of the effect of a known current if no allowance is made for its effect.

CASE 2—Known: Boat's course (C) and speed (S) through the water; the course (COG) and speed made good (SOG).

To be determined: The set and drift of the current.

This is the determination of the nature of an unknown current from observation of its effect.

CASE 3—Known: Boat's speed through the water (S), the set and drift of the current, and the intended track (TR).

To be determined: The course to be steered (C) and the speed of advance (SOA) along the intended track.

This is the determination of corrected course to be steered, but without regard for the effect on speed or ETA.

CASE 4—Known: The set and drift of the current, the intended track (TR), and the speed of advance desired (SOA).

To be determined: The course to be steered (C) and speed to be run through the water (S). This is the "rendezvous" or "contest" case where the destination and the time of arrival are specified.

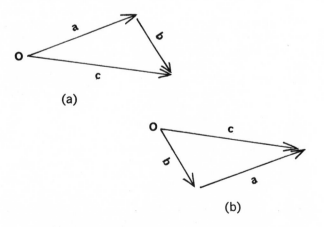

(a)

(b)

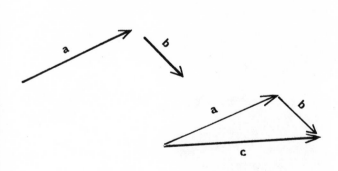

FIG. 2030 **Vectors may be combined graphically to determine the vector sum. Typically, vectors *a* and *b* above, representing component motions, are combined as vector *c*, the resultant motion of the two components.**

FIG. 2031 **The two vector triangles shown above appear to be different because in one vector *a* was drawn before vector *b*, and in the other, *b* was drawn before *a*. The resultant vector, *c*, however, is exactly the same for either procedure.**

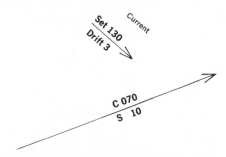

FIG. 2032 If a boat is traveling through the water on a course of 070°, and the current is setting in the direction 130°, it is obvious that the craft will be set off course to starboard. The question of how much, and the effect on speed over the bottom, is what must be determined. A current diagram will provide the answers.

Illustrative examples

Let us first consider **Case 1**—the effect of current on a boat's course and speed. If the set of the current is as shown in fig. 2032, then the boat will be set off to the right of the direction in which it is being steered. We will use a current diagram to determine the exact extent of this effect, the path the boat can be expected to follow and its speed (the intended track and speed of advance).

We first draw in a north line as a reference for measuring directions, fig. 2033a, and then the vector for the boat's speed through the water, O-DR, a line drawn from the origin in the direction 070° for a length of 10 units, fig. 2033b. Next we add the vector for current, DR-W, three units in the direction 130°, fig. 2033c. Note that we have remembered to observe the "tail-to-head" relationship rule. (Either of these two vectors could have been drawn first; the triangle would appear differently, but the result will be the same.) Because these vectors form two sides of a triangle of velocities, the third side O-W, fig. 2033d, is the resultant velocity at which the boat moves with respect to the bottom under the combined influences of its propulsion and the current. The point W can now be relabeled "P." The intended (or expected) track (TR) and the speed of advance (SOA) can be measured from the O-P line. In this example, it turns out that the boat can be expected to sail a course over the ground of 083° and to have a speed of advance of 11.8 knots. Note that the directions of these vectors are always plotted as *true* directions.

Summarizing briefly, we have drawn vectors to indicate independently the motion of the boat from two different influences, its own propulsion and the current. Actually, of course, the boat will *not* go first from O to DR and then on to P. All the time, it will travel directly along the intended track O-P. The boat is steered on course C, the direction of O-DR, but, due to the effect of current, it is expected to travel along the intended track O-P. This is the route that must be considered for shoals and other hazards to navigation.

Cruising men can never afford to ignore the effect of current. Down East, for example, in Maine waters big tidal ranges often cause baffling current conditions, compounded by unusual influences of headlands and river currents. Fog in such areas places a special premium on piloting skill.

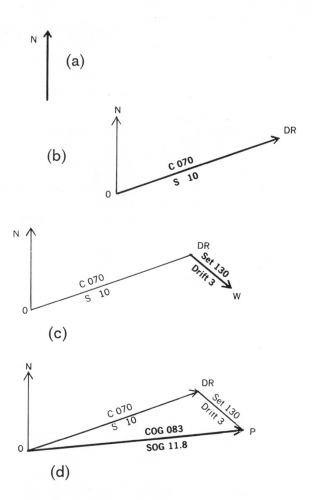

FIG. 2033 Current Diagram—CASE 1. These diagrams illustrate the step-by-step graphical solution: (a) the reference North line; (b) the vector for boat's motion through the water; (c) the vector for current, the motion of the water with respect to the bottom; and finally (d) the vector for the resultant motion of the boat with respect to the bottom.

FIG. 2034 Current Diagram — CASE 2. The prevailing current (actually the net effect of all offsetting influences) can be found graphically from a vector triangle of velocities.

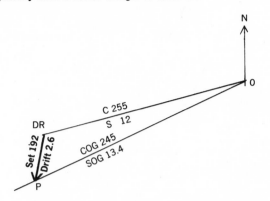

Now for a **Case 2** situation in which you know the course you have steered and the speed through the water from either the speed curve of your boat or a marine speedometer. It is also obvious to you that you did not arrive at your DR position. From your chart plot, you have been able to determine the course and speed over the ground. Current has acted to set you off your course—you desire to know its set and drift.

After again drawing a north reference line, plot vectors for your motion through the water—C 255°, S 12 knots; and your motion with respect to the bottom—COG 245°, SOG 13.4 knots. See fig. 2034. These vectors are both drawn outward from the origin, O, to points DR and P respectively. The "tail-to-head" rule is not applicable as neither of these vectors represents current. The action of the current has been to offset your boat from DR to P (which is also point W in this case), thus the set is the direction *from* DR *toward* P, and the drift is the length of this line in scale units.

In fig. 2034, the current is found to be setting 192° with a drift of 2.6 knots. This is the *average* current for the time period and location of the run from O to P for which the calculations were made; it is not the current at P. For the next leg of your cruise, these current values can be used as is, or modified as required by the passage of time and/or the continuing change in position of the boat.

Case 3 is a typical cruising situation—here, you know the track you desire to make good (TR 080°), you have decided to run at your normal cruising speed through the water (S 10 knots), and you have calculated (or estimated) the current's set (140°) and drift (4 knots). What you desire to know is the course to be steered (C) and the speed of advance (SOA) which can be used to figure your estimated time of arrival (ETA).

Draw in a north line and measure directions from it, fig. 2035a. Plot the current vector, O-W, at the specified direction and length, and a line (not a vector yet) in the direction of the intended track—this line should be of indefinite length at this time. From point W, swing an arc, with dividers or drawing compass, equal in length to the speed through the water in scale units. The point at which this arc intersects the intended track line is point P and the vector triangle has been completed. The direction of W-P is the course to be steered (C 060°); the length of the vector O-P is the speed over the ground (SOG 11.4) and from this the ETA can be calculated.

Let us look at the reasoning behind this graphic solution of Case 3. Again considering the component motions separately for the sake of simplicity, the boat is moved by current from O to W. It is to move from W at the specified speed through the water, but must get back on the intended track line; the problem is to find the point P on the track which is "S" units from point W. The solution is found by swinging an arc as described above.

Remember that all vectors are plotted as *true* directions, including C, the course to be steered in the preceding solution. This must be changed to a compass direction (course) for actual use at the helm.

In accordance with the principles of dead reckoning, it is desirable to plot the DR track even though a current is known to exist. This line, drawn from point O in the direction C and with a length of S scale units, forms a basis for consideration of possible hazards if the current is not as calculated or estimated, fig. 2035b.

FIG. 2035 Current Diagram — CASE 3. If you know your desired track, and have decided upon your speed through the water, a graphical solution (a) can be used to determine the course to be steered and the speed of advance. For safety's sake, a DR plot from the origin should be added as in (b).

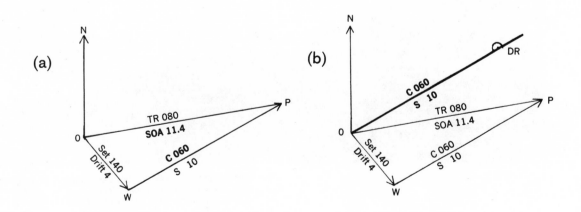

(a)

(b)

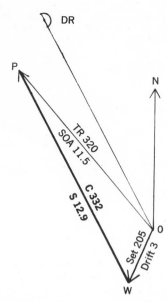

FIG. 2036 Current Diagram—CASE 4. This problem concerns the course to be steered and the speed at which to run in order to arrive at a specified destination at a predetermined time. This could be useful in a predicted log contest or in rendezvousing with another boat.

A **Case 4** situation is an interesting variation of Case 3—you desire to arrive at a specified point at a given time. It may be that you are competing in a predicted log contest, or merely that you have agreed to meet friends at that time and place. In addition to the data on current that you have, you have decided upon your track and your speed of advance. For fig. 2036, let us assume that the current sets 205° at 3 knots. You need to make good a track of 320°, and a quick distance-time-speed calculation sets your required speed of advance at 11.5 knots.

From the north reference line, draw the current vector O-W and the intended track vector O-P. Complete the triangle with the vector W-P which will give you the course to be steered (C 332 True) and the speed to run through the water (S 12.9) to arrive at the destination at the desired time. Line O-DR should be drawn in from the origin as a dead reckoning track for the sake of safety.

Solutions of Cases 1, 2, 3, and 4 using tabular data, rather than graphic plots, are given in pages 441-447.

These tables should not be used without a clear understanding of the fundamentals of current sailing, the component motions and their relationships to each other. These fundamentals, and the terms and symbols used, should be learned from simple graphic solutions as presented above.

FIG. 2037 Ability to estimate the set and drift of currents on a proposed course is of paramount importance to contestants in a predicted log race, where accuracy of the highest order is required to win.

CHAPTER 21
PILOTING—Position Determination

The art of piloting reaches its climax in *position determination*. Underway on a body of water of any size, where the safety of your boat and its crew is at stake, it's not "where you ought to be," or "where you think you are," but your knowledge of "where you are for sure" that counts. The development of an ability to determine your position quickly and accurately under a wide range of conditions should be one of your primary goals as a skipper.

The need for position determination

In three of the current sailing situations covered in the preceding chapter, the set and drift of the current were taken as known values. In everyday cruising, it is more than likely that the strength and direction of the actual current will be somewhat different from that calculated or estimated. Local wind conditions or abnormal rainfall will frequently upset tabular predictions; estimates based on visual observations of current will often be inaccurate unless the boatman has had considerable experience. Because of these uncertainties, current sailing solutions can be considered only as *estimates* of present positions and of future motions and positions.

Buoy positions are usually reliable; the Coast Guard expends much effort in keeping them on station and operating properly. They are, however, not infallible, and the position of a boat should be determined by other means as often as practicable.

Accurate position determination whenever the opportunity presents itself is essential in order that the safety of the craft can be verified, or corrective action taken promptly. By so doing, the true effects of the current may also become known. Further, such fixing of position makes possible the start of a new DR plot, fresher and more accurate than the old one.

Frequent position determination is an essential safety precaution. No matter how safe your boat is, no matter how experienced you are in boating, no matter how good the weather nor how calm the seas, emergencies can arise, and suddenly, too. Knowledge of where you are, extended from a *recent* position determination, can be of the greatest value when you must call for help. Or, if it is another boat that has trouble, you can set the most direct course to render assistance if you are sure of where you are.

THE SKIPPER'S RESPONSIBILITIES

It is the duty of a skipper to fix the position of his craft with such degree of precision and at such frequent intervals as is required by the proximity to hazards to safe navigation. This is an absolute requirement of the person in charge of the vessel, whether he is personally doing the piloting or this is being done by another person. He can assign the function, but he cannot delegate his responsibility.

The actual procedures in position determination will vary widely in practice. Proceeding down a narrow channel, positioning will be informal and a chart plot will not be maintained. But this does not mean that position de-

St. Petersburg Times Photo by Dan Hightower

FIG. 2101 The skipper of any boat is responsible for the safety of it and of all persons on board. He must be able to determine his position accurately, and do so as often as required by prevailing conditions.

termination is being omitted; indeed, it is being done essentially continuously by visual reference to the aids to navigation. On the other hand, during an open ocean passage, a plot will be maintained, but positions will be determined, other than by DR calculations, perhaps only three or four times each day.

Between the extremes cited above, there will be found the normal cruising situations in pilot waters. Cruising just offshore, or in the larger inland bodies of water, a skipper will usually maintain a plot of his track with periodic checks on its accuracy, perhaps every 15 or 20 minutes, perhaps at hourly intervals.

The ability to determine the position of his craft to an acceptable degree of accuracy under any condition of visibility is essential to safe boating. The absence of this ability, or any limitation on it, should restrict the extent of a person's boating activities, setting the boundaries of the water areas and weather conditions into which he will enter.

DEFINITION OF TERMS

A *line of position (LOP)* is a line, in actuality or drawn on a chart, at some point along which an observer is presumed to be located, fig. 2102. A LOP may result from observation or measurement; from visual, electronic, or celestial sources. It may be straight or curved; a circular LOP is sometimes referred to as a *circle of position,* fig. 2103. A line of position may be *advanced* (moved forward) or *retired* (moved backward) in time according to the movement of the vessel during the time interval involved. In piloting, the more usual situation will be the advancement of a previously taken LOP to the time of another LOP just taken.

A *bearing* is the direction of an object from the observer, expressed in degrees as a three-digit number—005°

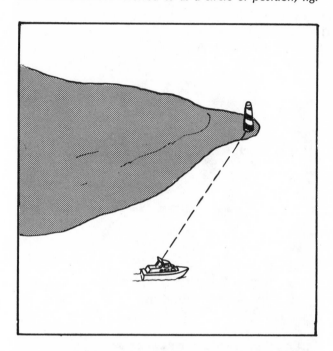

FIG. 2102 Position determination is based on "lines of position." These are lines, in actuality or on a chart, along which the observer is presumed to be located. A single line will not determine position, but it does tell the observer where he is *not* located, and such information is often useful.

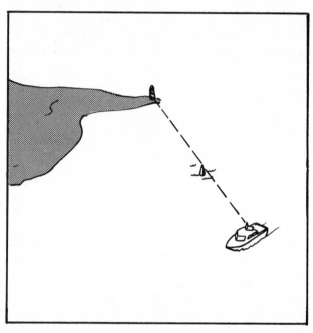

FIG. 2104 When *two* objects can be observed in line, an excellent line of position is established. Such "ranges" may have been set up with specific aids to navigation, or they may be any two identifiable objects such as ordinary navigational aids, landmarks, or natural or man-made features.

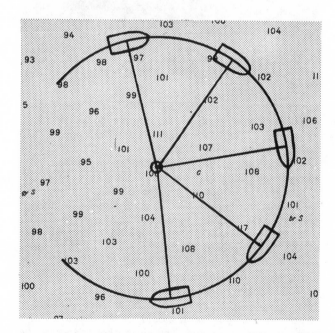

FIG. 2103 Lines of position may be curved as well as straight. A measurement of distance from an identified object yields a circular LOP. It may be plotted as a complete circle or as only a partial arc.

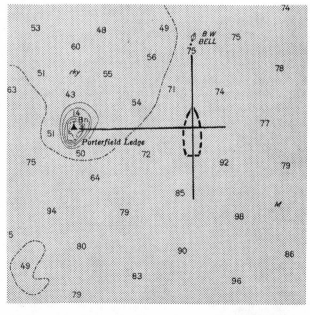

FIG. 2105 A "fix" is an accurately determined position for the observer and his craft. It is not based on any prior position, but is determined from currently observed lines of position or other data.

062°, 157°, etc. A *true bearing* is a bearing measured with reference to the true north direction as 000°. *Magnetic* and *compass bearings* are, respectively, observations with reference to the local magnetic north direction or to the craft's steering compass as it is affected by deviation at that moment. A *relative bearing* is a bearing measured with reference to the ship's heading—it is measured clockwise from the fore-and-aft line with 000° being dead ahead,

090° broad on the starboard beam, 180° dead astern, etc. (An older method of measuring relative bearings 180° to port or starboard is seldom used any more; it made calculations more complicated than necessary.)

A *range* consists of two objects that can be observed in line with each other and the observer, fig. 2104.

A *fix* is an accurately located position determined without reference to any prior position, fig. 2105. A *running fix* is a position that has been determined from LOPs at least one of which has been taken at a different time and advanced or retarded to the time of the other observation.

An *estimated position (EP)* is the best position obtainable short of a fix or good-quality running fix. It is the most probable position, determined from incomplete data, or from data of questionable accuracy.

Lines of Position

Lines of position are the basic elements of position determination. By definition, the observer, and his craft, are located somewhere along a LOP. If two LOPs intersect, the only position at which the vessel can be, and be on both lines, is their intersection. Thus, the usual fix is determined by the crossing of two lines of position.

Labeling

Since LOPs are also lines that are drawn on a chart, it is essential that they be labeled immediately, and that such labels conform to a standardized system. A label should contain all information necessary for identification, but nothing further that might cause confusion or clutter up the chart. The information to be recorded for each line of position is the time that it was observed or measured and its basic dimension, such as direction toward, or distance from, the object used.

A bearing is a LOP that has time and direction. Fig. 2106 shows several examples of correctly labeled bearings. Time is always shown *above* the line of the bearing, and direction *below* the line. Time is given as a four-digit figure in the 24-hour clock system. Directions are *true* and are written as a three-digit group with zeros prefixed as necessary.

A circle of position has dimensions of time and distance; it may be plotted as a complete circle, fig. 2107a, or merely as a partial circle, an arc, as in fig. 2107b. Time is labeled above the curved line and distance, with units, is shown below the line.

A range is a line of position whose direction is self-evident from the two points which define it. In this case, only time need be shown; it is placed above the line as for other LOPs; see fig. 2108.

Do not draw the line completely through the chart symbols for the two objects used as the range; this will avoid the necessity for subsequent erasure across the symbols. Draw the line neatly and no longer than necessary; it need not extend all the way to the front range marker or other object if the two features used to form the range are clearly evident.

A line of position that has been advanced (or retired) in time is labeled with *both* times above the line, the time of original observation or measurement and the time to which it has been advanced (or retired). The time of the original LOP is written first, followed by a dash and then

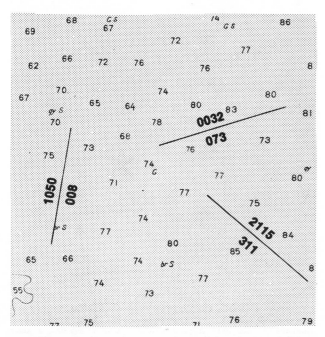

FIG. 2106 The correct labeling of lines of position is most important; unlabeled lines on a chart can only be a source of confusion. The time is always shown above the line (in 24-hour clock system) and direction below the line as a three-digit number without the "o" symbol.

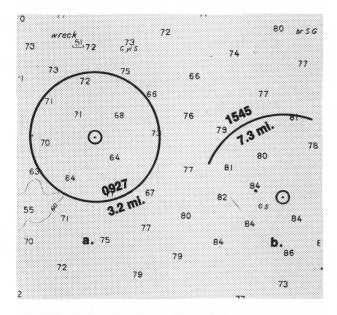

FIG. 2107 Circles of position are labeled in the same general manner as straight lines of position. The time is placed above the line and the distance below, as it would normally be viewed and read. Thus, the time may be "inside" or "outside" the circle as determined by the curvature of the arc.

419

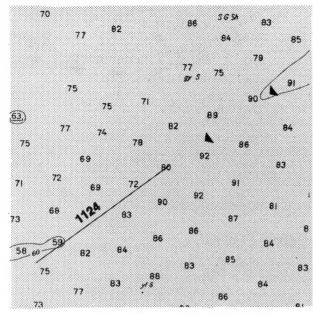

FIG. 2108 Since a range is based on the relationship between the two sighted objects, it is often used without a measurement of its actual direction. Ranges need be labeled only with the time of the observation.

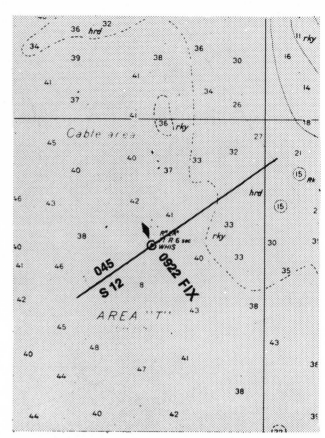

FIG. 2110 A simple, but excellent, determination of position occurs when a boat passes close alongside an aid to navigation or other identifiable point. A good pilot always notes the time of such an event on his chart.

the second time, fig. 2109.

Always label lines of position as soon as they are drawn. Unmarked lines on a chart can easily be a source of confusion. If labeling is put off until a later time, mistakes may be made.

FIXES

As previously defined, a fix is an accurately located position for a vessel. On many occasions in small-craft piloting, position will be established by passing close by an

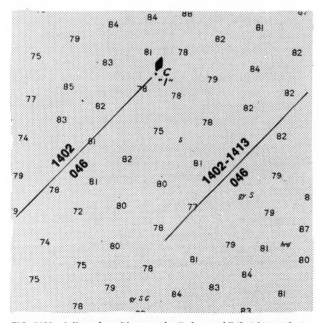

FIG. 2109 A line of position may be "advanced," that is, used at a later time than when it was observed if it is replotted to account for the movement of the boat since the time of observation. An advanced LOP is labeled with the original time and the time for which it is replotted. The direction, of course, remains the same.

identifiable object, usually an aid to navigation. This is, of course, a fix of the highest possible accuracy, and a skipper should always note the time of such an event on his chart plot, fig. 2110.

Fix from two LOPs

The typical fix obtained from lines of position will be the intersection of two such lines. It is important to consider the effect of the angle of intersection between the two LOPs on the accuracy of the position determination. Let us look first at the situation where the two lines cross at right angles, 90°, fig. 2111a. If there should be an error of, say, 2° in one LOP, the resulting fix from this mistake would be off only a short distance.

Consider now fig. 2111b in which the intersection angle is only 30°. An error of 2° in one LOP would result in a considerably greater change in the location of the intersection.

Two lines of position should intersect as nearly as possible at right angles; the angle of intersection should never be less than 60° nor more than 120° if this can be avoided.

Where there is no alternative, a fix from two lines of position intersecting at angles of 30° to 60° (120° to 150°) can be used, but only with caution. A position from two LOPs intersecting at less than 30° (more than 150°) is of too dubious accuracy for safe navigation. **Areas of uncertainty.** Lines of position will normally be stated as having a specific direction, such as 072°, 147°, etc. In actuality, there may be an uncertainty in each line of two or three, or even more, degrees. This condition can be shown graphically on the chart by additional lines drawn lightly on either side of the basic LOP; this should always be done if such uncertainty could mean the difference between a safe position and a hazardous one.

Lines of position from various sources and techniques will have different degrees of uncertainty. Only experience will give the pilot the ability to judge various methods and assign relative values of probable accuracy.

If two LOPs, each with its graphic representation of uncertainty, are drawn, the result is an *area of uncertainty* about the intersection of the lines of position; there is an element of doubt about the location of the fix. Figs. 2112a and b show how the angle of intersection alters this area of uncertainty and why it is desirable to have the LOPs cross as nearly as possible at 90°. Based on the mathematics of statistics and probability, the area of uncertainty is elliptical (circular if the LOPs cross at 90°) rather than the quadrilateral formed by the outside limiting lines for each bearing. In actual piloting, this distinction is more theoretical than practical. A detailed discussion of this topic, including the additional complexities that arise if one line of position can be considered to be more accu-

rate than the other, is beyond the scope of this book, but may be found in Bowditch, Chapter 29.

More than two LOPs

Since most lines of position obtained in small-craft piloting (except possibly ranges) are reasonably, but certainly not exactly, accurate, it is highly desirable to use more than two LOPs to reduce the uncertainty of position. There is no theoretical upper limit to the number of lines of position that can be used, but practical considerations with a boat underway will normally limit the pilot to three LOPs.

Ideally, since the observer is presumed to be on all three lines of position, they will intersect in a common point, fig. 2113a. The much more likely result is that when the observations are plotted, the lines will form a triangle, fig. 2113b.

The use of three LOPs results in a modification of the previously stated rule about the desirable intersection angle of the lines. For optimum results, the three lines should each differ in direction as closely as possible to 60° (or 120°), fig. 2114. In this configuration, an inaccuracy in any of the LOPs will result in the minimum net error of position.

An alternative technique to the above is to obtain two

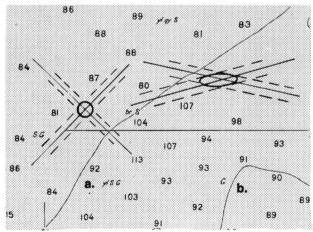

FIG. 2111 Lines of position taken from a small craft are seldom precisely accurate. Selection of an optimum angle of intersection between LOPs reduces the uncertainty of position. Shown here is the difference that a change of 2° in one LOP makes in the intersection point when the lines cross at 90° or at 30°.

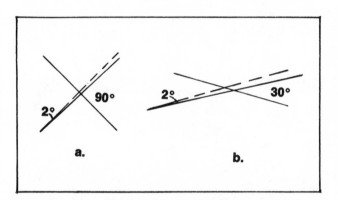

FIG. 2112 When each of two LOPs may have an inaccuracy of several degrees, there is an *area of uncertainty* around the intersection point. This is least, a circle, when the angle of intersection is 90°. Angles of 60° to 90° are satisfactory; those of 30° to 60° may be used with caution.

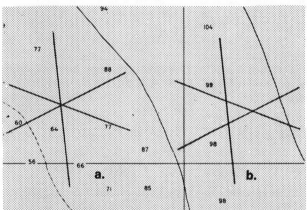

FIG. 2113 The use of more than two LOPs will enhance confidence in the resulting fix. Ideally, three lines of position will intersect at a common point, as in *a* above. More often in actual piloting, a triangle will be formed as shown in *b*. If the triangle is unreasonably large for the prevailing conditions, the observations should be checked or discarded.

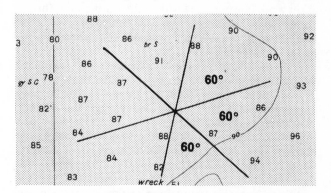

FIG. 2114 For an optimum set of three observations, the lines of position should cross at 60° to each other. This will seldom be exactly possible in actual piloting situations, but should be kept in mind as fundamentally desirable.

lines of position at nearly 90° to each other, and then a third LOP making an angle of approximately 45° with those of the original pair, figs. 2115a and b. This procedure has the advantage of providing an optimum two-LOP plot in the event that a change of visibility or other circumstance should suddenly prevent the third observation.

Triangles of position

As noted above, three lines of position will usually form a *triangle of position*. If this triangle is quite large, it is probable that there is a significant error in one or more of the LOPs, and a check should be made of the observations, calculations, and plotting.

If, however, the triangle is relatively small (and "relatively" will have to be defined in each situation as determined by the techniques used, the experience of the observer, the size of the boat, sea state, and other conditions), it can be assumed that no more than normal inaccuracies and uncertainties exist. In the everyday practice of piloting on boats, it is customary to use the center of the triangle of position, as estimated by eye, for the fix.

Labeling fixes

A fix is shown on a chart plot as a small circle with a dot in its center; it is labeled with the time followed by the letters "FIX"; see fig. 2116a. A running fix is labeled with the time and "R FIX"; fig. 2116b.

The track line or bearing lines do not extend through the circle so that the position dot will be more distinct. If the fix is obtained by passing close to a buoy or other aid to navigation, the dot or center of the symbol may be used for the plot. The usual distance off, 50 to 100 yards or so, is not significant at typical chart scales; greater distances are estimated and the fix is plotted in the correct direction from the aid at a scaled distance.

THE VALUE OF A SINGLE LOP

The preceding discussion has centered on the use of two or more lines of position for obtaining a fix. While admittedly this is the most desirable situation, the value of a single LOP should not be overlooked.

Basically, a single line of position cannot tell a pilot where he is at the moment, but it can, within the limitations of its accuracy, tell him where he is *not*. If he is presumed to be somewhere along the LOP, then he cannot be at a position appreciably distant from the line. This information, although lacking in detail and negative in sense, may often be of value to a navigator concerned with the safety of his vessel.

A single line of position can frequently be combined with a DR position to obtain an "estimated position." This EP is the point along the LOP that is closest to the DR position for the same time. A line is drawn from the DR position perpendicular to the LOP until it intersects that line. An estimated position is marked by a dot within a square; the line does not go through the square. As a square is used only for estimated positions, it is not necessary to add "EP"; time may be omitted as it appears on the LOP.

It is also possible to obtain an "estimated position with current" from a single LOP if the set and drift of the current have been determined from predictions or from its effect on the boat's course and speed made good. From

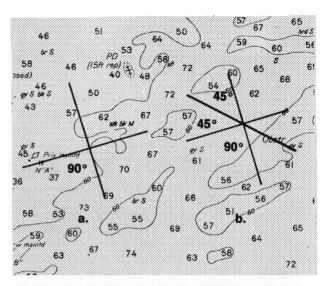

FIG. 2115 An alternative procedure for taking three observations is to select the first two objects so that their LOPs will cross at as near 90° as possible, *a* above. Then the third sight is taken so that its plotted LOP will cross the other two at approximately 45°, as in *b* above. If circumstances prevent the pilot from getting the third sight, he will still have a near-optimum two-LOP fix.

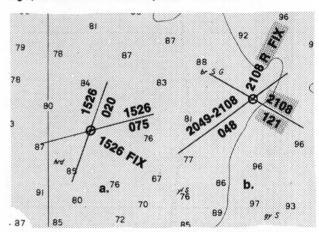

FIG. 2116 A *fix* is labeled with the time followed by "FIX" not written parallel to any line. A *running fix* is labeled with the time and "R FIX".

the DR position for the specified time, a line is drawn to scale to represent the effect of the current since the DR track was started from the last fix. This line is drawn in the direction of the set of the current and for a length equal to the "total drift," the distance found by multiplying the drift by the elapsed time since the last fix. This total drift line is labeled and from its end another line is drawn perpendicular to the LOP until it intersects that line; see fig. 2117c. The intersection is the *EP with current*; it is labeled in the same manner as before (the fact that current has been included is obvious from the plot).

In using an EP, make generous allowances for the uncertainty of the position; always err on the side of safety.

In some piloting situations, a single bearing on an object can be advanced and crossed with a later LOP on the same object. This will result in a running fix, not as desirable as a fix from two independent lines of position, but far better than a DR position or the pilot's "best guess."

Running fixes, and the use of a single LOP with depth measurements, will be discussed later in this chapter.

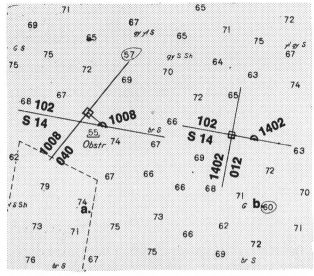

FIG. 2117 An *estimated position* can be obtained from a single line of position. It is the point on the LOP closest to the DR position for that time, see *a* above. If a beam bearing is used, the EP will fall along the DR track, as in *b* above.

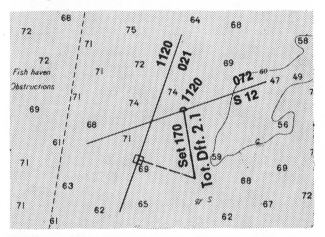

FIG. 2117c If information about the current is available, an improved "estimated position with current" can be plotted. The off-setting effect of the current since the start of the DR track is calculated and plotted; the nearest point on the LOP from this current-influenced point is the EP.

FIG. 2118 A very simple, yet fully accurate method of taking bearings is to "aim" the boat directly at the sighted object and read the compass. Brief off-course swings for this purpose will not materially affect the DR plot but be sure that there are no hazards close alongside your course. Correct such compass bearings to true directions before plotting them.

Visual Observations

For the pilot of a typical motorboat or sailboat, the primary source of lines of position will be visual observations. These will include direct and relative bearings, ranges, and horizontal and vertical angle measurements. Correct identification of the sighted object is essential. Other methods and equipment may lead to LOPs such as those from radio direction finding, radar, and depth measurements, but these will normally be secondary to visual observations.

SIMPLE VISUAL BEARINGS

It will amaze the novice pilot (and perhaps some of the more experienced ones, too) how much navigational information can be obtained from the most simple of visual bearings, those directly ahead or broad on the beam.

Bearings dead ahead

Bearings taken directly ahead require no auxiliary equipment; the boat's steering compass will suffice. Only insignificant effects will be made on the DR track of a boat if the bow is momentarily swung off course and pointed toward an object on which it is desired to take a bearing. The craft should be held on this new heading long enough for the helmsman to properly line up on the object and for the compass to settle down and be read. This is normally a matter of less than a minute, perhaps only 20 or 30 seconds.

To use this technique, the pilot must be sure enough of his general location that the off-course swing can be made safely. But if such is the situation, he should not hesitate to use this quick and simple way of getting a line of position. The accuracy of bearings obtained by this method will normally be considerably greater than those of the more complex techniques to be discussed later.

The procedure of taking bearings dead ahead by "aiming" the boat at the object sighted upon has an additional advantage in that it can be accomplished by the helmsman alone, without the assistance of another person. Other methods will generally require the services of a second individual as the bearing-taker while the helmsman continues his normal duties, plus reading the steering compass at the time of the observation.

Beam bearings

If the observed aid to navigation or landmark is well around on either beam, it may not be feasible to make so great a deviation from the normal heading being steered in order to take a dead-ahead bearing. Or perhaps the limited width of the available deep water does not permit so large an excursion from the DR track. In this case, the other simple bearing technique may be used.

Determine some portion of the boat that is at a right angle to the fore-and-aft axis of the craft. Among the possibilities are bulkheads, seat backs, deck seams, etc. Sights taken along these features will determine when the observed object is directly abeam—a relative bearing of 090° or 270°.

The boat may be held on course and the passage of time awaited until sighting along the pre-selected portion of the boat indicates that the aid to navigation or other object is exactly broad on the beam. Its direction then is, of course, 90° greater or less than the direction read from the boat's compass at that moment.

If waiting until the object comes abeam in the normal course of events is not feasible or desirable, then the heading of the craft can sometimes be temporarily altered slightly as needed to bring the sighted object directly on the beam more quickly. Should such a temporary change of heading be made, the pilot must be sure that the 90° is added to, or subtracted from, the compass reading at the exact moment that the sighted object is abeam; do not use the normal base course.

Correction of compass bearings

The pilot should always remember that in either of these types of observations the bearings that are taken are *compass bearings*. It will be necessary to correct them for deviation and variation (see Chapter 13) and then plot them as *true* bearings. Any of the plotting instruments and techniques described in Chapter 19 may be used.

Beam bearings are obtained by adding 90° to or subtracting 90° from the boat's *true* heading. Be sure to correct the boat's compass heading for deviation and variation *first*, and *then* add the 90° if the observation was to starboard or subtract the 90° if the sighting was on the port beam. Do not use the direction of the bearing for entering the craft's deviation table; use the heading.

Plotting bearings

The direction measured by the visual observation is *from the boat toward the object.* When plotting is being done, the position of the boat is not known, but it is still possible to draw the line so that it will have the correct direction and lead toward, to, or through the chart symbol for the sighted object. The particular plotting instrument used will determine the exact procedures used.

It is also possible to plot a line of position outward from the sighted object by using the *reciprocal* of the corrected observed bearing. (In fact, this is the formally correct procedure, but it is usually by-passed in favor of the more direct technique mentioned in the paragraph above.) Here, caution must be taken to *first* correct the observed compass (or relative) bearing to a true direction, and then add or subtract 180° to obtain the reciprocal; do not reverse this sequence.

MORE SOPHISTICATED BEARINGS

The procedures just described above for bearings dead ahead and broad on the beam will suffice in many situations, but not in all. It may be neither safe nor convenient to alter the boat's heading for the purpose of taking a bearing.

Greater flexibility of navigation is obtained if bearings can be taken in any direction without a change in the normal heading of the craft. Such bearings will involve the use of the boat's compass, a pelorus or hand bearing compass, or some combination of these instruments.

Using the boat's compass

On many boats, it will be possible to take bearings directly over the steering compass, at least through a limited angle on either side of the bow. As determined by the construction of the compass, it may be feasible to sight directly over the card and get bearings of acceptable accu-

racy. On other models, a set of sighting vanes may be placed on the compass for greater precision in direction measurement. The directions in which bearings may be taken using the boat's steering compass will normally be limited by the nearby superstructure of the boat. Bearings taken using the boat's compass must be corrected for the deviation on the heading of the boat, *not* that for the bearing direction, and for the variation of the locality.

Using a hand-held compass

Direct visual bearings can also be taken using a hand-bearing compass, or even with the boat's compass if it is a model that has been designed for quick and easy dismounting with accurate remounting. It is normally not feasible to prepare a deviation table for such hand compass use because of the many different positions and circumstances connected with this procedure. Careful tests should be made to determine the locations about the boat, if any, at which a hand-held device can be used without deviation errors. These tests are best made from known positions by taking bearings on objects whose actual direction can be established from the chart. If deviation-free locations can be found on board, then correction will be required for magnetic variation only, to obtain true bearings for plotting.

Using a pelorus

Alternatively, a pelorus may be used to measure directions, usually as relative bearings. This instrument is, of course, not affected by magnetic disturbances on the boat and may be used at any location from which the desired object can be seen. The caution to be observed in this case is that the pelorus must be accurately aligned with the fore-and-aft axis, the keel-line, of the vessel. The correct positioning of the pelorus should be worked out for several locations on the boat so that sights may be taken on an object regardless of its relative position with respect to the boat.

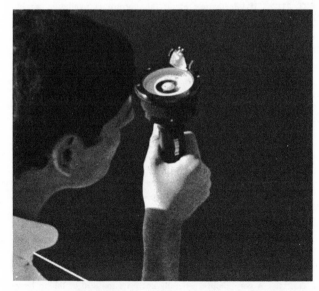

FIG. 2119 A hand bearing compass can be used to take direct readings on objects that cannot be sighted over the boat's steering compass. Before using such an instrument on your boat, however, make checks to find locations at which it will not be affected by local magnetic influences.

The scale of the pelorus can be aligned to the boat's heading and observations made directly in terms of compass bearings, but this procedure is generally less desirable than the technique of relative bearings to be described below. In all cases, the compass bearings must be converted to true bearings before plotting.

An exception to the above statement can be made in the case of an *experienced* pilot. It is possible to omit the step of correction from magnetic to true direction and plot in terms of magnetic bearings. This procedure, while appearing to be a handy short cut, has two pitfalls. First, it requires the use of the magnetic directions circle of the compass roses printed on the chart plus the use of a plotting instrument that determines direction from these compass roses rather than from the meridians and parallels; this rules out use of the convenient and accurate course plotter. Secondly, this technique requires the use of magnetic directions for all purposes, such as courses, ranges, set of current, etc., or else a confusing mixture of directions. Because of these two serious disadvantages, the possibility of plotting bearings as magnetic directions will be noted here, but will be discarded immediately in favor of the "old reliable" procedure of using only true directions on the chart.

RELATIVE BEARINGS

Relative bearings are those taken with respect to the vessel alone, without reference to geographic directions. Relative bearings offer some advantages, but also have some built-in problems.

The instrument for taking relative bearings is the pelorus. As noted before, it has the advantage of being usable anywhere on the boat if properly oriented. Its disadvantage is that close coordination is required between two persons, the bearing-taker and the helmsman. The heading of the boat at the instant of observation must be known, and direct communication between these two individuals is required.

To take a relative bearing, the scale of the pelorus is set with 000° dead ahead. The helmsman is alerted to the fact that a bearing is about to be taken; he concentrates on steady steering and continuously reads the compass. When the observation is made, the bearing-taker calls out "Mark," and reads the scale of the pelorus. (It is very helpful if the bearing-taker calls out "Stand by" a few seconds before his "Mark.") At the word "Mark," the helmsman notes the reading of the steering compass and calls it off to the observer or other person who will compute the bearing. If the compass should be swinging at the moment, so that an accurate reading cannot be taken, the helmsman calls out that information and the pelorus reading is discarded; another attempt is then made to take the bearing.

As noted in Chapter 19, an alternative technique is to have the helmsman call a series of "Marks" when, but only when, he has the boat directly on course. The bearing-taker makes his observation only when it is so indicated that the boat is on the specified heading.

When the relative bearing has been taken by either of the above techniques, it must be converted to a true bearing for plotting. This is done by adding the numerical values of the relative bearing and the *true* heading of the boat at the instant of observation. If the sum so obtained is more than 360°, that amount is subtracted. The true bearing can then be plotted and labeled.

If the true heading is not known for any reason, such as the boat's being momentarily off-course when the bearing was taken, it is, of course, necessary that it be determined before the addition of the preceding paragraph can be accomplished. *Always be sure to use the deviation value for the heading of the boat, and not for the bearing angle.* This is an often-made error, and one that must be continually guarded against.

In fig. 2121a, an observer on a boat heading 047° takes a relative bearing on a buoy of 062°. To determine the true bearing of this aid to navigation, these two numbers are added, 047° + 062° = 109°.

FIG. 2120 A pelorus eliminates the magnetic difficulties that may be experienced with a hand-held compass. It can be used at any point from which the target object can be seen. A pelorus must, however, be properly oriented to the fore-and-aft axis of the boat.

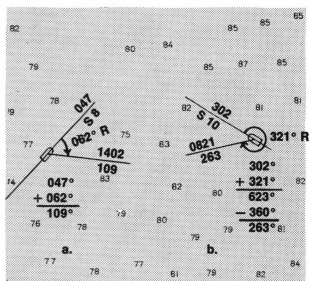

FIG. 2121 Relative bearings must be converted to true bearings before they are plotted. To do this, the relative bearing is added to the true heading of the craft at the moment of observation. If the sum exceeds 360°, that amount is subtracted.

In fig. 2121b, the boat is heading 306° by its compass when a relative bearing of 321° is measured. The variation is 6°W and the deviation (for the compass heading of 306°) is 2°E. The true heading of the boat is thus 306° − 6° + 2° = 302°. The sum of the relative bearing, 321° and the true heading 302° is 623°; therefore 360° is subtracted and a value of 263° is found to be the true bearing of the object.

If the pilot is so fortunate as to have multiple objects on which to take bearings, he should select the nearer ones (provided, of course, that desirable angles of intersection between the LOPs will result). An angular error of 1° will result in a lateral error of about 100 feet at a distance of one mile—at two miles, the *same* angular error will cause a lateral displacement of 200 feet; at three miles, 300 feet, etc.

RANGES

Lines of position from ranges are of exceptional value in position determination. They are free from all of the magnetic effects that might cause errors in bearings taken with a compass or a pelorus. Such LOPs are also easily obtained, much more so than those from bearings. Ranges can be absolutely accurate, as accurate as the charted positions of the two objects lined up in the observation. No matter how small the boat, how rough the water, or how poor the visibility, if you can see the objects come into line, you can plot a good line of position on your chart and so have half of an accurate fix.

Ranges can be classified into two groups. First, there are those that consist of two aids to navigation constructed specifically to serve as a range and are charted with a special symbol, see fig. 1824, page 352. The true direction of such ranges can be determined from the information in the Light List for the rear marker. Ranges are particularly useful in determining compass deviation because of their high accuracy.

It is not necessary, however, to have an especially constructed pair of aids to navigation in order to have a range. Any two objects that can be identified by sight and on the chart form a natural range and can be used in the same manner as one consisting of two formally established navigational aids. Among such objects are ordinary aids to navigation of all types; spires, radio towers, flagpoles, stacks, etc.; identifiable portions of bridges, such as center spans; and other prominent, isolated features; see fig. 2122. Caution should be exercised in using points of land as either a front or rear range mark; errors may be made in attempting to sight on the exact end of the point, particularly if it is of low elevation.

The taking of a LOP from a range requires no more than the observation of the time that the two objects came into line. The LOP is plotted on the chart by lining up the symbols for the two objects with a straightedge and drawing a light solid line over such portion of the chart where the LOP has significance. The line will normally not be drawn all the way back to the two objects that established the range. Its actual direction will not ordinarily need to be determined. The line should be labeled as soon as it is drawn on the chart.

This line of position can be crossed for a fix with another range, or with any other form of LOP. If such is not available at the time, the LOP from the range may often be advanced later and used as part of a running fix.

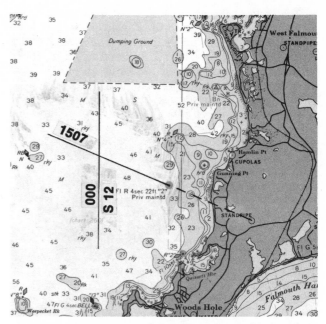

FIG. 2122 Pilots are not limited to those ranges that have been established as such by the Coast Guard or other authorities. Any two identifiable objects can be used. Here, a skipper northbound in Buzzards Bay can get an excellent line of position when light "2" lines up with the standpipe ashore.

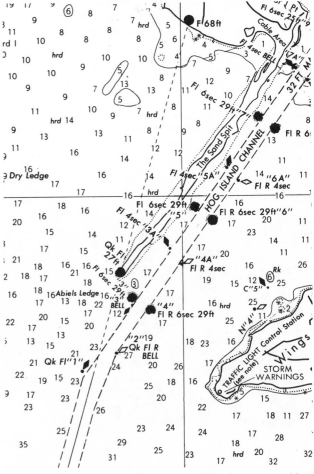

FIG. 2123 Ranges are excellent means of keeping your position centered in a channel, but caution must be exercised not to follow them beyond their proper limits. One or two buoys may be used to mark the beginning or end of a range-marked channel, the point at which to make a change of course.

Never pass up an opportunity to obtain a line of position from a range; there are none better. And there is no better fix than one obtained from the intersection of two ranges.

Ranges are often established by the Coast Guard or other authority to mark the center of important waterways, usually dredged channels or natural channels with hazards close on either side. When so established, the range center line will be printed on the chart, see fig. 1827, page 354. Such ranges will normally be used for direct steering rather than as a line of position, but there is no reason that they should not be used for the latter purpose if desired.

Two cautions should be observed in steering up or down a channel marked by a range. A vessel traveling in the opposite direction on the range will be on a collision course, or will pass too close aboard for comfort. Secondly, the beginning and end of the range, the ends of the solid portion of the line on the chart, must be noted carefully—a range can be followed for too great a distance on either end. Buoys will often be used to mark the spot at which to turn onto or off of the range line, fig. 2123. Always study your chart carefully when using a range.

HORIZONTAL ANGLES

A fix may also be obtained by measuring the two horizontal angles between the lines of sight to three identifiable objects, without a measurement of the relative or geographic direction to any of them. This procedure avoids the inaccuracies involved in relative or compass bearings. Such horizontal angles can be measured to a high degree of accuracy (as close as $1/2°$) with a sextant.

For plotting these horizontal angles, a *three-arm protractor*, fig. 2124, is the preferred instrument. Each side arm is set for the angle measured to its side of the line of sight to the center object. Then the instrument is moved about on the chart until the arms line up with the symbols for the objects sighted upon in measuring the angles. There is a small hole in the center of the protractor through which a pencil point can be placed to mark the fix on the chart.

The same general technique can be used without a special instrument by drawing lines with the proper angles between them on a piece of transparent paper, fig. 2125. This is then moved about as before until the lines and points are properly related.

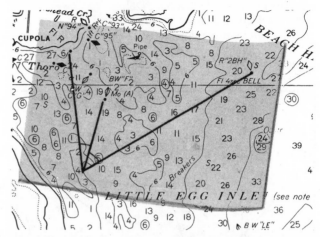

FIG. 2125 If a three-arm protractor is not available, the angles can be drawn on a sheet of transparent paper. This is then moved about on the chart until correctly positioned.

Some caution must be exercised in selecting the objects between which the angles are to be measured. Three points, not in a straight line, will all lie on the circumference of a specific circle, such as points X, Y, and Z in fig. 2126a. An angle measured between X and Y, or Y and Z, will be the same measured at A or B, or at any point on the circular arc from X around through A and B to Z. Thus,

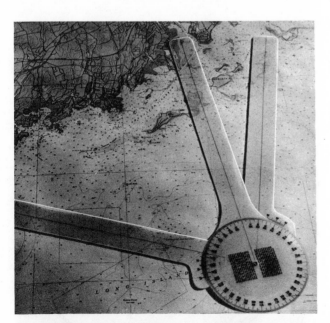

FIG. 2124 A three-arm protractor is a specialized plotting instrument used with the two-horizontal-angles technique of position determination. When the angles have been set, the arms are lined up with the appropriate chart symbols; then the position is marked with a pencil point through a hole in the center of the device.

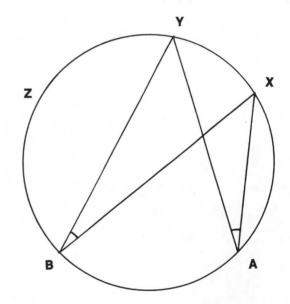

FIG. 2126a In using the two-horizontal-angles method of positioning, the center of the three objects, Y in this illustration, should *not* be farther away from the observer than the other two. If this caution is neglected, the result may be an indeterminate solution called a "revolver," as shown above, where the boat may be at any point on a circle containing the three objects.

if the observer should be on the circle, his position will be indeterminate. This situation, known as a "revolver," can occur if the center object sighted upon is farther away from the observer than the other two. By selecting three objects so that they are essentially in line, or that the center one is closer to the observer, an indeterminate situation is avoided. (If the center object is closer, a circle still exists, but it curves away from the observer, and he could not possibly be on it.) See fig. 2126b.

A "revolver" should be avoided; but if one does develop, it can be made determinate by the addition of another LOP, such as a single bearing on one of the three objects, or on any other point.

This technique of using the two horizontal angles is not often used in practical piloting, but it does offer excellent results when high accuracy is needed. Fig. 2127 illustrates an instrument developed especially for the measurement of horizontal angles and bearings.

VERTICAL ANGLES

A circular line of position represents points at a constant distance from a specific object. Such distances are often found by the measurement of vertical angles with a marine sextant, or with a specialized device for such purposes alone.

The height of many natural and man-made features is

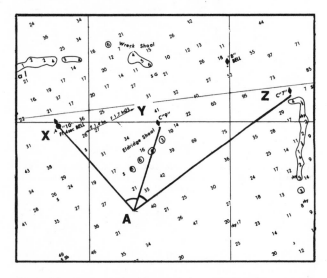

FIG. 2126b If the center object is on line with the other two, or is nearer to the observer, as Y is above, an indeterminate solution is avoided and a fix is found.

FIG. 2127 The Ilon position finder is a specialized instrument that determines a fix from a combination of the compass bearing to an object and the horizontal angle between that line of sight and the line to a second object.

FIG. 2128 A marine sextant, most commonly used for celestial navigation sights, may also be used in piloting for the measurement of vertical or horizontal angles.

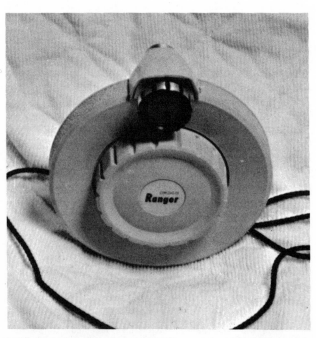

FIG. 2129 If a vertical or horizontal dimension of a distant object is known, this simple optical rangefinder can make an accurate measurement of the distance to it.

shown on charts. Such objects include lighthouses, bridges, radio towers, and generally similar features. Caution must be exercised to determine if the height shown is that above the structure's base on land or the vertical distance above the chart's datum for heights, usually mean high water. Frequently, a correction may be required for the tidal level at the time of observation, its difference from MHW, see Chapter 20. On such features as lighthouses, the height usually given is that of the *light,* not that of the top of the structure.

Using a sextant, the vertical angle is measured between the base and the top or other part of the structure, fig. 2128. This angle and the known height can be used to de-

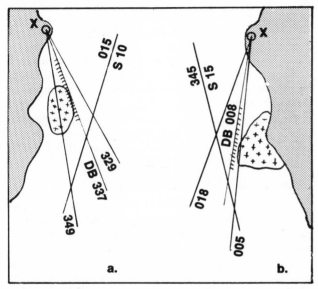

FIG. 2130 A *danger bearing* **can be established so as to avoid an unmarked hazardous area. In** *a* **above, any bearing on object** *X* **that is more than 337° indicates a potentially hazardous position for the boat. In** *b,* **the reverse is true, bearing less than 008° are indications of possible danger if the craft continues on the same course.**

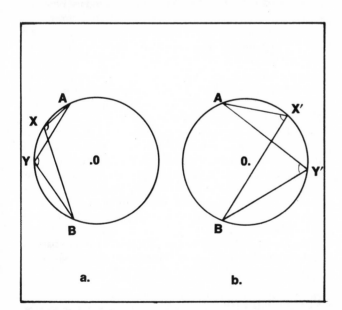

FIG. 2131a and b The various points at which there is a constant angle between the lines of sight to two objects form a circle. The angle between the lines to *A* **and** *B* **is the same at** *X* **or** *Y.* **At points** *X'* **and** *Y',* **the angle is likewise the same.**

termine the distance from the observer to the object. Solution can be had from plane geometry formulas, or from specially prepared tables such as Table 9 in Bowditch.

Special range finder instruments are now being marketed which use the principle of matching images much like the focusing mechanism of many cameras. It is still necessary, however, to know the height (or a horizontal dimension) of the object on which the observation is made. Fig. 2129 shows one such instrument.

DANGER BEARINGS AND ANGLES

The safety of navigation can often be insured without the establishment of a complete fix. As noted earlier, a single line of position has value—if it is of reasonable accuracy, it can assure you that you are somewhere along it and not elsewhere. A line of position can be chosen, in many piloting situations, that will keep a boat in safe water without precisely defining its position.

Danger bearings

A bearing line can be established so that positions on one side will assure the craft's being in safe waters, while a position on the other side may signify a hazardous situation; such a *danger bearing* is shown in fig. 2130. Here, a shoal, unmarked by any aid to navigation, lies offshore; the problem is to pass it safely. A lighthouse is observed on shore just beyond the shoal, and is identified on the chart. The danger bearing is a line from the lighthouse just tangent to the shoal on the safe side. This line is drawn on the chart and its direction is measured. The line is labeled with the direction preceded by the letters "DB." (No time is shown as it is not an actual observation.) For greater emphasis, short hachures may be added on the side toward the danger; and, if available, the use of a red pencil for this line is desirable to make it stand out from other lines on the chart.

As the boat approaches the hazardous area, a series of observations are made on the selected object. In the example shown in fig. 2130a, any bearing on the lighthouse *less* numerically than the danger bearing indicates a *safe* position; any bearing *greater* than the danger bearing indicates that the boat is in or approaching the shoal area if it continues on the same course. Should the danger area lie to starboard, rather than to port as in fig. 2130b, the "greater" and "less" factors above would be reversed.

Danger bearings cannot always be established for the safe passage of hazardous areas, but their use should be considered whenever conditions permit. It is necessary to have a prominent object, although it need not be an aid to navigation, that can be seen from the boat and positively identified on the chart. This object should lie beyond the danger area in the same general direction as the course of the boat as it approaches and passes the area to be avoided.

HORIZONTAL DANGER ANGLES

A horizontal angle measured between two identifiable fixed objects defines a circle of position. In fig. 2131, an observer at *X* or *Y* would measure the same angle between *A* and *B;* he would also measure the same angle at any point along that semi-circular arc. If the observer were on the other side of the center of the circle, at *X'* or *Y',* or other point on that arc, a constant angle also would be observed. This angle, however, is not the same as that measured across the circle at X and Y. Note that the angle will be greater than 90° if the sighted objects are on the same side of the circle as the observer, as in fig. 2131a, and less than 90° if they are on the opposite side as in fig. 2131b.

Such a circle may be established to indicate the boundary between positions of safety and those of possible danger. When such a LOP is set up, the angle defined by the circle is termed the *horizontal danger angle*.

Fig. 2132 illustrates the use of a single horizontal danger angle to avoid an unmarked shoal area. The problem is to

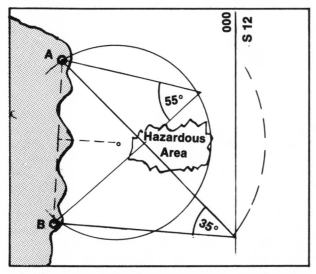

FIG. 2132 Horizontal angles between *A* and *B* are measured as the boat approaches the hazardous area. Any angle *less* than the *horizontal danger angle* of 55° indicates that the boat is in safe waters.

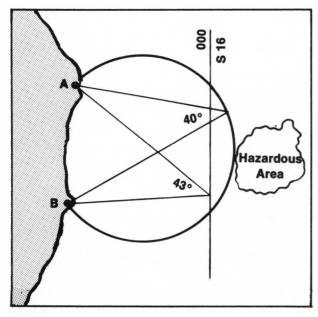

FIG. 2133 In this situation, it is desired to pass inshore of an unmarked hazardous area. The horizontal danger angle is established as before, but now the safe angular measurements are those greater than the horizontal danger angle.

stay sufficiently offshore to miss the hazard. The horizontal danger angle is found by drawing a circle that includes two prominent identifiable objects ashore, *A* and *B* in fig. 2132, and the shoal area. The circle is established by drawing a line between the sighted objects, and then drawing a second line at right angles to the first line at its midpoint. The center of the circle is found by trial-and-error along this second line so that the arc includes the desired points.

Lines are then drawn to *A* and *B* from any point on the circle near the shoal area and the angle between them is measured; in this example, it is 55°.

If the angle between the objects, measured from the boat as it approaches the area, is *less* than the horizontal danger angle, then the radius of the circle on which the boat is located is larger, and the boat is farther offshore in *safe* waters. On the other hand, if the measured horizontal angle is greater than the danger angle, the boat is closer in and may be in or approaching a hazardous area. The angle is preferably measured with a sextant, but it can be calculated from the difference between two compass or relative bearings.

Should the piloting situation require passage inshore of a shoal area, fig. 2133, a single horizontal danger angle can again be used. In this case, *safe* waters are indicated by angles *greater* than the danger angle.

Double horizontal danger angles

The two situations described above can be combined into *double horizontal danger angles* where the requirement is for a safe passage between two offshore hazardous areas. Fig. 2134 is essentially a combination of the two preceding illustrations. The principles are the same; here the safe horizontal angles are those *between* upper and lower danger limits.

Vertical danger angles

A circle of position, obtained from a vertical angle measurement, can also be used to mark the boundary between safe and hazardous waters. With a selected prominent object identified visually and on the chart, a circle is drawn using that object as the center and having a radius that will just include all of the hazardous area. The radius is measured from the chart and converted to a vertical angle by geometric formula or Table 9 in Bowditch. The danger circle is then labeled with the *vertical danger angle*. Fig. 2135 shows such a circular LOP outlining a shoal area.

As the boat approaches the dangerous area, a series of vertical angle measurements are taken on the selected object. Measurement of a vertical angle *less* than that specified as the vertical danger angle indicates that the observer is farther offshore, and consequently he is in *safe* waters.

Measurements of distance directly from an optical range finder can be substituted for vertical angles if such a device is on board.

Corresponding situations would prevail for safe passage inshore of a hazardous area, or between two danger areas, as was shown for horizontal danger angles.

Positioning Procedures

As mentioned earlier, the "basic" fix is obtained by crossing two lines of position. A third LOP is desirable, but this can be obtained in only a limited number of situations. It is assumed for the fix that the observations or measurements for these LOPs are made simultaneously, and this may often be the procedure on a naval ship or other large vessel. On small craft, however, the normal situation will be that of a single bearing-taker and one piece of equipment. Of necessity, therefore, observations will be taken sequentially rather than concurrently. If the observations are taken quickly, the distance traveled between them will be negligible, and adherence to the procedures to be described here will minimize the error from sequential observations.

As a result of the movement of the boat along its course, the observed bearing angles will be changing. Consider the relative *rate of change* of the bearing to each object to be sighted upon; those on the beam will be changing at a more rapid rate than those nearly dead ahead or astern; those on nearer objects will be changing more rapidly than those at greater distances.

For the most accurate determination of a fix from two lines of position, first take a sight on the object with the *least* rate of change, then on the other object, and finally a repeat on the first object. Use the second observation and the average of the first and third bearings (which are, of course, on the same object). If circumstances permit only one observation on each object, it is usually preferable to take the more rapidly changing bearing last and then make an immediate chart plot of both bearings.

If you are able to take observations on three objects, take them in descending order of rate of change of bearing and consider taking a repeat of the first bearing, if possible, for averaging as before.

The time of the fix should be that of the approximate middle of the series of observations. At typical boat cruising speeds and chart scales, a difference of a minute or two will not be significant. At 12 knots, a boat will travel 1/5 mile in one minute; on a 1:80,000 scale chart, this distance of approximately 400 yards is less than 3/16 inch.

Positioning standards of precision

As set forth in Chapter 19, there are generally accepted standards of precision in describing position of a vessel. If geographic coordinates are used, latitude and longitude, in that sequence, are stated to the nearest tenth of a minute on charts with scales of 1:50,000 or smaller, and to the nearest second on charts of larger scale.

If the position is stated with respect to some aid to navigation or landmark, direction from that point is given to the nearest degree (true) and distance is given to the nearest tenth of a mile.

THE RUNNING FIX

The lack of a second object on which to make an observation may at times prevent the immediate determination of the boat's position by a normal fix, even though one good line of position has been established. In such situations, a somewhat less accurate determination of position may be made by a *running fix (R Fix)*. In this technique there is one line of position at the time of the running fix and another from a different time, usually earlier. This latter LOP must be replotted from its position at the time of its measurement to account for the movement of the boat during the intervening time. The act of advancing the first LOP brings it to a common time with the second obser-

vation so that their intersection may be considered as a determination of position. It should be noted that this line so advanced (or retired) may have resulted from an observation on the *same* object as that used for the second sighting at the time of the running fix, or on a different object.

Advancing a line of position

A line of position is advanced as follows:
(1) A point is selected on the original LOP. This can be

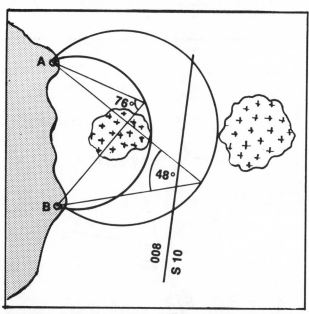

FIG. 2134 For passage between two unmarked hazardous areas, *double horizontal danger angles* may be used. This technique is essentially the combination of the two preceding situations; a safe passage is indicated by measurement of horizontal angles between specified upper and lower limits.

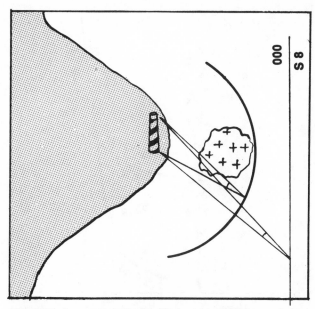

FIG. 2135 A measurement of vertical angle establishes a circle of position at a specific distance from a point. Such an angle can be calculated for an object of known height so as to insure that a boat does not get too close. Safe vertical angles are those *less* than the *vertical danger angle*.

the intersection of the line with the DR track, *X* in fig. 2136, or any point on the LOP, such as *X'*.

(2) The selected point is moved in an amount equal in distance and direction to the boat's motion during the time interval involved. This is most easily measured from the DR position at the time of observation to the DR position for the advanced time.

(3) The new LOP is drawn in through the advanced point parallel to the original LOP.

(4) The advanced LOP is labeled as soon as it is drawn: both times are shown above the line and the direction beneath it.

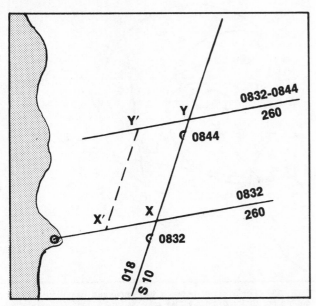

FIG. 2136 A line of position is *advanced* by moving forward any point on it an amount equal to the boat's motion during the time interval and re-drawing the line through this advanced point.

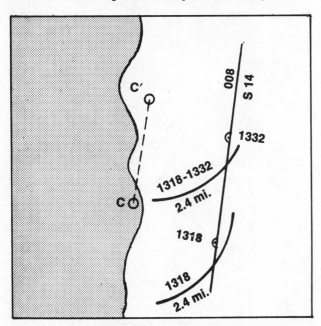

FIG. 2137 A circle of position, or circular LOP, is advanced by merely moving the center point an amount equal in direction and distance to the motion of the boat during the time interval, and redrawing the circle on the new center. In the illustration above, C = C' is equal to the spacing between the two DR positions.

Advancing a circular LOP

If the LOP to be advanced is circular, as would be the case with a distance measurement by vertical angle or range finder, the center of the circle is the point advanced by the procedure described above, fig. 2137. The circle or arc is redrawn using the new center, and is then labeled as for any other advanced LOP.

Advancing a LOP with course and/or speed changes

The advancement of the selected point on the initial LOP must take into account all changes in course and/or speed of the boat during the time interval. It is frequently a convenient procedure to calculate and plot the DR positions for the time of the initial observation and for the advanced time. The movement of the selected point on the initial LOP should parallel and equal a line drawn between these two DR positions. This technique is particularly useful if there has been more than one change in course and/or speed, fig. 2138.

Advancing a LOP with current

The advancement of a line of position may take into account current effects if they are adequately known or can be estimated. The selected point on the initial LOP is first advanced for DR speeds and courses, and then for the set and drift of the current, both calculations using the elapsed time interval between the two observations; see fig. 2139.

The accuracy of advanced LOPs

The accuracy of an advanced line of position can be only as good as the accuracy of the initial observation *decreased* by any errors or uncertainties in the navigator's data for the boat's course and speed (and current data, if used). Obviously, the longer the time interval over which

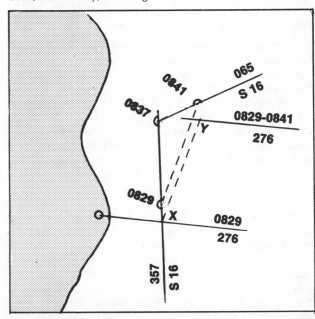

FIG. 2138 The advancement of a LOP must take into consideration all changes of course and/or speed during the time interval. The net effect can be determined by drawing a light line between the DR positions for the two times concerned. The selected point on the original LOP is advanced in the same direction and distance as this net effect line.

the sight is advanced, the greater the uncertainties become. The interval should, therefore, be the minimum possible, and, in piloting, should rarely exceed 30 minutes. (In navigation on the high seas, celestial lines of position are often advanced several hours, but the accuracy of positioning is less critical in these circumstances.)

The same criteria for the angle of intersection of lines of position apply to running fixes as were discussed previously for normal fixes. Running fixes involving three lines of positions (two of them advanced) are possible but are unusual in actual piloting practice.

Lines of position may be retired, moved back to an earlier time, in a similar manner. Such retrograde movement is, however, quite rare in piloting situations.

Running fixes and DR plots

The DR plot may be interrupted and restarted from a running fix if it is considered of reasonable accuracy. In all cases, however, a fix obtained from two or more essentially simultaneous observations or measurements is to be preferred over a running fix.

OBSERVATIONS ON A SINGLE OBJECT

In addition to the technique of the running fix using advanced lines of position, position information can be obtained from successive observations on a single object by means of several other more specialized procedures. These include: bow-and-beam bearings, doubling the angle on the bow, two bearings and run between, and two relative bearings.

Bow-and-beam bearings

Position determination is easily accomplished by the technique of taking two particular successive bearings on an object to one side or the other of the craft's course. The first bearing is taken when the object sighted upon

bears either 45° to starboard (RB 045°) or to port (RB 315°). The second bearing is taken when the same object is broad on the respective beam (RB 090° or 270°), fig. 2140. The time of each bearing having been noted, the time interval is found, and then the distance traveled between the two sightings is calculated using the boat's speed. Because of the nature of the triangle established by the two bearings and the course line, the boat is away from the sighted object at the time of the second (beam) bearing at the same distance as that traveled during the time interval. This distance is that traveled *over the bottom;* correction to the DR track should be made for any current or other offsetting influence if such information is known or can be estimated. Since there is a LOP (the beam bearing) and a distance, the position of the craft has been determined. It should be noted that this position is *not* necessarily the intersection of the second bearing and the course line; the craft may be off its intended track.

The principal advantage of this procedure is the ease with which it can be accomplished. Beam bearings are easily taken, and 45° relative bearings can be quickly set up using crude sights oriented with an ordinary plastic drafting triangle. On some boats, it may be possible to make the 45° sight over the steering compass. The bow-and-beam technique often can be done by the helmsman without assistance.

Doubling the angle on the bow

This is a more generalized application of the same principles as those involved in bow-and-beam bearings, in which a 45° angle was doubled to 90°. Geometric principles establish that whenever an angle on the bow is doubled, the distance from the position at which the second bearing is taken to the object sighted upon is equal to the distance traveled (over the bottom) during the time

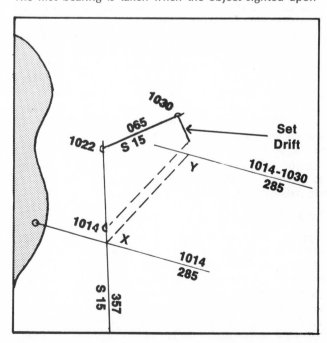

FIG. 2139 If the LOP is to be advanced with allowance for current, the same procedure as before is followed, except that a further movement is made from the second DR position to account for the current during the time interval and obtain an estimated position.

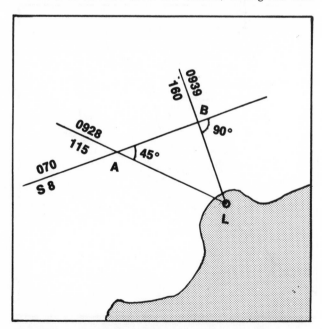

FIG. 2140 If a bearing is taken when an object bears 45° on either bow (RB = 045° or 315°), and again when the same object is broad on the beam (RB = 090° or 270°), the distance to the object at the time of the second bearing will be equal to the distance run (over the bottom) between the bearings; B-L = A-B.

433

interval between the two observations, fig. 2141. The angle referred to above is the relative bearing to starboard or to port. A relative bearing of, say 340° measured in the conventional manner, must be converted to an angle of 20° to port for the purpose of "doubling"; in this case, the doubled angle would be RB 320° (40° to port).

The doubling-of-the-bow-angle technique has the advantage of determining the boat's position *before* the sighted object is abeam. With information as to the boat's position at such an earlier moment, the course can be projected ahead on the chart. Should the craft be traveling too close to shore for passing a headland, a more adequate warning of the dangerous course will thus be in hand, and corrective action can be taken sooner.

This technique does, however, have a disadvantage in that it requires the possession and use of a pelorus or other instrument for measuring relative bearings with reasonable accuracy. Another disadvantage is that a second person is needed as a bearing-taker.

Two-bearings-and-run-between

With only a single object upon which sights can be taken, another method, known as "two-bearings-and-run-between" for lack of a better name, may be used. In this procedure, a bearing is taken on the object, the boat proceeds along her course, and a second bearing is taken after the angle has changed by at least 30°. This second bearing may be taken before or after the sighted object is passed abeam. From the times of each bearing, the time interval is calculated, and from this, the distance run is determined.

Both bearings are plotted, as is the course of the boat, fig. 2142. A pair of dividers is opened to the distance run between the two bearings and is then moved parallel to the course line until the points fall on the bearing lines.

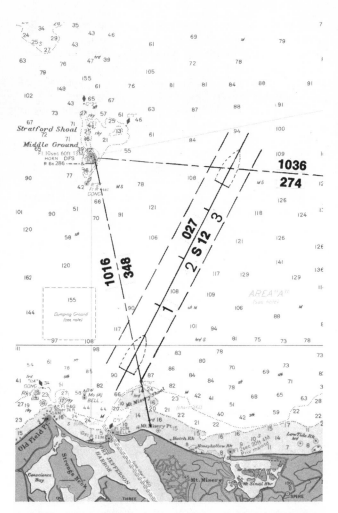

FIG. 2142 If two bearings are taken on a single object as the boat passes it, and are plotted on the chart, then only one point can be found on each LOP so that the course and distance made good will fit between these LOPs.

The divider points now indicate the positions of the boat at the times of the first and second bearings.

As before, the distance run must be that *over the bottom;* suitable corrections must be made for any current. The accuracy of this technique depends upon many factors: the accuracy of each of the two bearings, the accuracy of the calculation of the distance run over the bottom, and the accuracy with which the boat was steered during the interval between the two sightings. The net effect of this compounding of accuracies is to make the positions so determined somewhat less certain than the other techniques described above.

Two relative bearings

A more generalized solution from two relative bearings can be used if a copy of "Bowditch" is on board. Table 7 of that book uses two items of information—the angle between the course and the first bearing (the first relative bearing) and the difference between the course and the second bearing (the second relative bearing). Columns of the Table are in terms of the first item and lines are in terms of the second item above; the interval between tabular entries is two degrees in both cases.

For any combination of the two relative bearings within the limits of Table 7, two factors will be found. The first

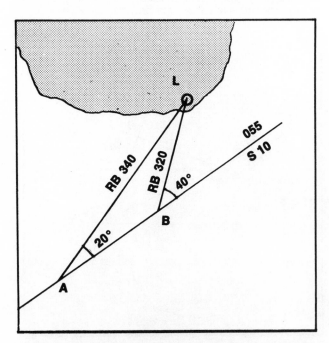

FIG. 2141 If two observations are made so that the second relative bearing is twice that of the first (as measured from the bow to either starboard or port), then the distance to the sighted object at the time of the second bearing is the same as the distance made good between the sightings; again, *L-B = A-B.*

number is a factor by which the distance run between the bearings is multiplied to obtain the distance away from the sighted object at the time of the second bearing. The second factor of the same entry in Table 7 is the multiplier to be used to determine the distance off when the object is abeam, assuming, of course, that the same course and speed are maintained. See fig. 2143.

Electronic Piloting

Although electronic navigation is essentially a topic in itself, and outside of the scope of piloting, brief mention will be made here of two techniques which have direct comparability and applicability to visual piloting.

RADIO BEARINGS AND FIXES

With relatively simple equipment, observations can be made of the direction to radio stations, even though such "objects" lie far beyond visual range, either as a result of night, fog, or simply great distance. See fig. 2144. Bearings can be taken on radiobeacons operated by the Coast Guard as aids to navigation; some aeronautical ranges and beacons operated by the FAA; on standard AM radio broadcast stations; and on stations in the 2-3 MHz marine band, including both shore and ship stations. In general, the desirability for use in radio direction finding is in descending order as listed above. Radio bearings can be taken under any condition of visibility, and on stations at ranges as great as hundreds of miles; accuracies will, of course, be more favorable with nearer stations.

Radio bearings are taken with a *radio direction finder*, usually referred to as an RDF if it is manually operated, or as an ADF if the bearings are taken and displayed automatically. These items of electronic equipment are discussed more fully in Chapter 25, pages 502 to 506.

Using radio bearings

Radio bearings are plotted in essentially the same manner as visual bearings. They are not as sharp as visual observations, however; an accuracy of 2° to 3° is the best that can be expected, and this precision will be achieved only with experience. Accordingly, it is advisable to obtain three radio LOPs, and even so, the position so determined should not be considered as precise as one from visual bearings.

Accurate identification of the station being received is essential, and the exact location of the transmitting antenna must be plotted on the nautical chart if it is not already shown there. Radiobeacons, both marine and aeronautical, are normally plotted on nautical charts, although sometimes additional aeronautical beacons can be found on aviation charts and transcribed to nautical charts. The antenna location of a few standard AM broadcasting radio stations will be found on charts identified by call letters and frequency, but often others can be added. Antenna locations in latitude and longitude for many stations are tabulated on the reverse side of Marine Weather Services Charts, see page 265.

Radio bearings taken on a station more than approximately 200 miles distant must be corrected if they are to be plotted on a Mercator chart. (The exact distance will vary with latitude and the relative position of the vessel and the radio station.) This correction is required because

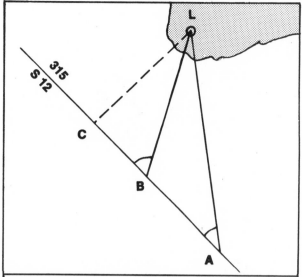

TABLE 7
Distance of an Object by Two Bearings

Difference between the course and second bearing	34°		36°		38°		40°		42°		44°		46°	
44	3.22	2.24												
46	2.69	1.93	3.39	2.43										
48	2.31	1.72	2.83	2.10	3.55	2.63								
50	2.03	1.55	2.43	1.86	2.96	2.27	3.70	2.84						
52	1.81	1.43	2.13	1.68	2.54	2.01	3.09	2.44	3.85	3.04				
54	1.63	1.32	1.90	1.54	2.23	1.81	2.66	2.15	3.22	2.60	4.00	3.24		
56	1.49	1.24	1.72	1.42	1.99	1.65	2.33	1.93	2.77	2.29	3.34	2.77	4.14	3.43
58	1.37	1.17	1.57	1.33	1.80	1.53	2.08	1.76	2.43	2.06	2.87	2.44	3.46	2.93
60	1.28	1.10	1.45	1.25	1.64	1.42	1.88	1.63	2.17	1.88	2.52	2.18	2.97	2.57
62	1.19	1.05	1.34	1.18	1.51	1.34	1.72	1.52	1.96	1.73	2.25	1.98	2.61	2.30
64	1.12	1.01	1.25	1.13	1.40	1.26	1.58	1.42	1.79	1.61	2.03	1.83	2.33	2.09
66	1.06	0.96	1.18	1.07	1.31	1.20	1.47	1.34	1.65	1.51	1.85	1.69	2.10	1.92
68	1.00	0.93	1.11	1.03	1.23	1.14	1.37	1.27	1.53	1.42	1.71	1.58	1.92	1.78
70	0.95	0.89	1.05	0.99	1.16	1.09	1.29	1.21	1.43	1.34	1.58	1.49	1.77	1.66
72	0.91	0.86	1.00	0.95	1.10	1.05	1.21	1.15	1.34	1.27	1.48	1.41	1.64	1.56
74	0.87	0.84	0.95	0.92	1.05	1.01	1.15	1.10	1.26	1.21	1.39	1.34	1.53	1.47
76	0.84	0.81	0.91	0.89	1.00	0.97	1.09	1.06	1.20	1.16	1.31	1.27	1.44	1.40
78	0.80	0.79	0.88	0.86	0.96	0.94	1.04	1.02	1.14	1.11	1.24	1.22	1.36	1.33
80	0.78	0.77	0.85	0.83	0.92	0.91	1.00	0.98	1.09	1.07	1.18	1.16	1.28	1.27

FIG. 2143   Distance off at time of second bearing, L-B, and distance off when abeam, **L-C,** can be found by applying multiplying factors to the distance run, **A-B.** These factors for various pairs of angles will be found in Table 7 of Bowditch.

FIG. 2144   Radio direction finders (RDFs) can be used to take bearings on transmitters located a fraction of a mile, or several hundreds of miles, distant. Lines of position can be found at night, in fog, or when visibility is good but the station is too far away to be seen.

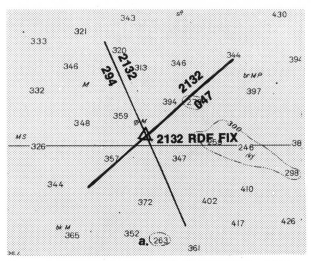

FIG. 2145a Because the accuracy of a fix derived from radio bearings is usually less than that of one obtained from visual observations, it should be labeled "RDF FIX".

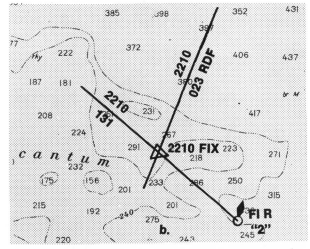

FIG.2145b If a combination of LOPs includes one from an RDF measurement, it may be well to add the letters "RDF" above the line where applicable.

radio waves travel via the most direct route, a great circle path, and this does not plot as a straight line on a Mercator chart; see page 363. Table 1 in Bowditch provides the correction factor and instructions on how it should be applied. No correction is needed for nearer stations, or on stations at any distance if the plotting is done on a gnomonic chart.

A sequence, or "round," of several radio bearings on different radiobeacons or other stations can normally be taken quickly enough so that any movement of the boat during this time can be ignored and the lines of position can be plotted as of the mid-time of the sequence. If any appreciable time delays are encountered, however, an RDF line of position can be advanced or retarded in the same manner as a visual LOP.

To assist in plotting RDF bearings, special charts are available for some areas. These are commercial adaptations of government charts with compass roses entered on each radiobeacon or other usable station. Alternatively, a skipper may apply adhesive, transparent plastic compass roses to regular nautical charts at the location of sources of signals upon which radio bearings can be taken.

In considering the accuracy of radio bearings, it must be kept in mind that these are referenced to the boat's heading as determined by its magnetic compass. Any compass deviation must be known and taken into consideration before bearings can be plotted. Any sloppy steering or yawing off-course as a result of rough water will directly affect the RDF bearings.

Labeling RDF bearings and fixes

In view of the lesser accuracy of RDF bearings as compared to visual sighting, and particularly those radio bearings taken on distant stations, it is desirable that the fix obtained from such lines of position be so identified. A

FIG. 2146 Marine radiobeacons are included in Coast Guard Light Lists with the related visual or audible aid to navigation. If the transmitting antenna is not at the principal aid, its distance and direction from it will be given. Frequencies, characteristic signal, ranges, and schedules of operation are tabulated in the front pages of each Light List volume.

(1)	(2)	(3)	(4)	(5)	(6)		(7)
No	Name Characteristic	Location Lat. N. Long. W.	Nominal Range	Ht. above water	Structure Ht. above ground	Daymark	Remarks Year
		TEXAS					EIGHTH DISTRICT
	GULF COAST (Chart 1288) (NO 11041) Port Mansfield Fish Haven South Buoy. **BRAZOS SANTIAGO LIGHT** . . . . . . Fl. W., 5ˢ	In 63 feet . . . . 26 45.0 97 15.1 On shore on dwelling of lifeboat station. 26 04.4 97 09.8	 23	. . . 52	Orange and white horizontal bands; nun. White lifeboat station dwelling.		Private aid. RADIOBEACON: Antenna 135 yards 199½° from center of Coast Guard Station Building. See p. XVIII for method of operation. Emergency light of reduced intensity showing Fl. W. 5ˢ obscured from 075 to 150° if main light is extinguished. 1853–1953

223
3411
J4226

different symbol is employed to make the probable lesser accuracy more apparent—a dot enclosed within a *triangle* (rather than in a circle) and this is labeled as an "RDF FIX;" see fig. 2145a.

If RDF bearings must be used to establish a position in possibly hazardous waters, it is advisable to plot additional lines two or three degrees (or more if conditions make for a reduction of normal accuracy) on either side of the basic LOP. These will clearly show the possible *area,* rather than specific position, in which the RDF-equipped boat is located; see fig. 2112.

Although it is of much lesser accuracy, an RDF Running Fix is better than no position information beyond dead reckoning if only one radiobeacon or other station can be used. Just as with visual techniques, an initial radio bearing is taken and plotted. Then after sufficient movement of the boat to ensure an adequate change in direction, a second radio bearing is taken on the same signal source and is plotted. One or the other of these LOPs can be advanced or retarded to a common time and thus an RDF Running Fix is established.

Combined lines of position

It is often possible, or necessary, to combine an RDF line of position with a visual bearing or range; this might occur when only one visual LOP could be obtained and is was necessary to cross it with another LOP from any source to get a fix. If radio lines of position are mixed with visual bearings or ranges, the former should be identified by adding the letters "RDF" below the line following the direction figures; see fig. 2145b.

Radio direction finding may also help the skipper whose craft is *not* equipped with an RDF. By establishing communications on the 2-3 MHz marine band, an RDF-equipped boat or Coast Guard unit can take bearings on his signals as he gives a "long count" and then advise him of his position or home in on him to render assistance. There are, however, some limitations on this procedure. The newer single-sideband signals are not as good for direction finding purposes as the older double-sideband signals, and as yet RDFs for the VHF-FM band are not widely available.

RADAR BEARINGS AND DISTANCES

Radar is another item of electronic equipment that is covered in greater detail in Chapter 25, but which will be considered here in connection with piloting situations. Radar has unique advantages in that a single instrument can measure both direction and distance (range), and that these measurements can be accomplished under visibility conditions that would preclude visual observations.

Radar observations

Measurements of direction by radar are *not* as accurate as those by visual sightings, but radar will penetrate darkness; light and moderate rain without difficulty, and heavy rain with some reduction in effectiveness; fog; and other restrictions that would prohibit visual bearings or range measurements.

On the other hand, measurements of distance by radar can be quite accurate, much more so than such observations taken by vertical sextant angles or with simple optical range finders.

Use of radar information

Radar data are used in the same manner as information from visual observations. Lines of position are combined to obtain fixes—typical combinations include two bearings, a bearing with a distance measurement to the same or another object, or two distance measurements. A fix obtained by radar bearings and/or distance measurements is labeled with the time and "RAD FIX"; see fig. 2147.

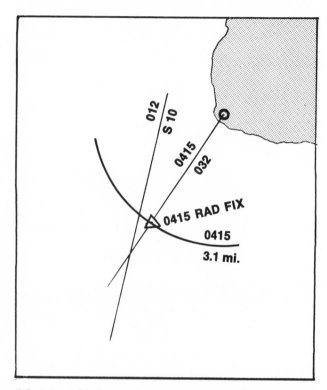

FIG. 2147 A fix obtained from radar lines of position is labeled on the chart as "RAD FIX". In the example above, a fix has been obtained on a single object by measurement of both bearing and distance.

When visibility conditions permit, a frequent combination, and an excellent one, is that of a visual bearing on an object and a radar measurement of distance to that same point.

Radar distance measurements also may be used in the same manner as distance determinations by vertical sextant angle to avoid a shoal area delineated by a circular LOP from a prominent object identifiable on the radarscope.

Radar observations on isolated objects such as buoys, offshore lighthouses, etc., usually are made without difficulty in identification of the object on the radarscope. When the radar target is on shore, however, some problems may be encountered in picking out the exact object on which the bearing and range information is to be obtained. Navigate with caution when using radar information from such objects. Even more so than other types of piloting, radar requires practice and the building up of experience. If you have a radar, use it often in non-critical times so that you can employ it and have the advantage of its unique capabilities when its use is essential. You must be capable of using it with competence and confidence when it is needed.

Depth Information in Piloting

Information on the depth of water under a vessel is usually considered to be merely a safety matter for the prevention of running aground. In actuality, such data can be of considerable value in piloting. The essential characteristic of depth information is the fact that although it cannot tell the pilot where he is, it can tell him *positively* where he is *not*. If an accurate measurement of depth gives a reading of 26 feet, you may be at any number of places where such is the depth, but you certainly are not at a position where the depth is significantly greater or less.

HOW DEPTH INFORMATION IS OBTAINED

Data on the depth of the water beneath a craft can be obtained manually or electronically. A hand lead line, see page 385, is a time-honored instrument of piloting, and every boat should have one of a length suitable for the waters usually sailed. It is accurate and dependable in use, although far from efficient or convenient. The modern-day trend is toward electronic depth sounders that can provide information at a much faster rate and with the convenience of reading a simple dial. They can also measure great depths that would be impracticable with a lead line. Electronic sounders are discussed in detail in Chapter 25, page 499 to 501.

USE OF DEPTH INFORMATION

In using depth information, regardless of how obtained, a correction for the height of tide may be required. The use of Tide Tables and the necessary calculations with their data are covered in Chapter 20.

Depth data can be combined with a line or lines of position obtained from other means to yield positional information. Under some circumstances, depth information alone may be of value in position determination.

Depth information and a single LOP

If the bottom of the body of water being navigated has some slope, and this slope is reasonably uniform, it may be possible to get positional information from a single LOP, typically a beam bearing, and a depth reading. The bearing line is plotted and then examined for a spot where the depth figure on the chart agrees with the measured depth as corrected for the tidal stage; be sure that there aren't several such depths along the LOP, fig. 2148. Such a location should be considered as an Estimated Position (EP) rather than a Fix.

Matching measured depths to the chart

In some instances, a rough estimate of the position of a boat can be obtained by matching a series of depth readings, appropriately corrected for the prevailing height of the tide, with depths printed on the chart. Depth readings are taken and recorded at regular time intervals, such as those corresponding to intervals of distance of one-tenth to one-half mile, as determined by the scale of the chart concerned, the density of printed depth figures, etc. (Electronic depth sounders can provide far more depth measurements than can be used.) These depths are marked on a piece of transparent paper at intervals determined by the scale of the chart, fig. 2149a. This piece of paper is then moved about on the chart, keeping the line of sound-

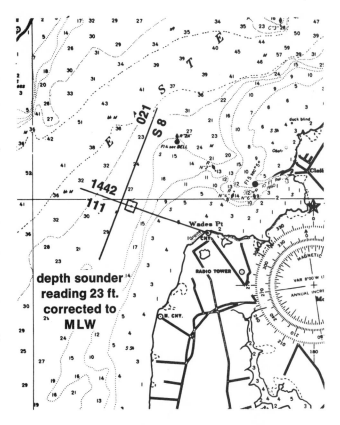

depth sounder reading 23 ft. corrected to MLW

FIG. 2148 Depth information can often be used with a single LOP, such as a simple beam bearing, to determine an estimated position.

ings parallel to a line representing the course steered while they were being taken. A maximum degree of match is sought between the observed depths and the charted depths; exact concurrence should not be expected.

In the example shown here, the 60-foot depth as measured is aligned with the 10-fathom curve on the chart, and a search for a match is started. If the line of soundings is moved north of the position shown in fig. 2149b, the depths at the outer end would still be in general agreement, but the mismatch at the inshore end would generally show that the line was incorrectly placed. If the line were moved down the chart, keeping it parallel to the course sailed, then the 37-foot measurement near the inshore end would mismatch with the actual 48-foot depth. The matching found by the location shown in fig. 2149b is as close as may be expected, and this position of the line can be considered to fairly well indicate the track of the craft as the soundings were made.

Position determination by the use of depth data is not well suited to shorelines that are foul with offshore rocks, or areas that have varying, irregular depths. Nor can this technique be used where the depth is quite uniform with few or no variations. There are, however, many situations where it can, and should, be used.

Position checking by depth data

If an EP has been determined by some other method or combination of methods, consideration should be given to checking it by a depth measurement. Remember that confirmation cannot be positive, but that denial can be quite

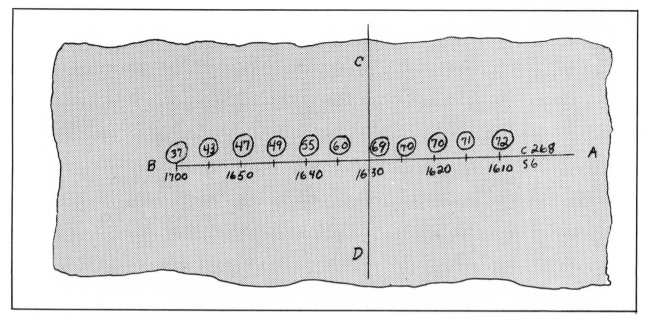

FIG. 2149a   Position by a line (or chain) of soundings. The sound-ings are taken at regular intervals and plotted on transparent paper as shown.

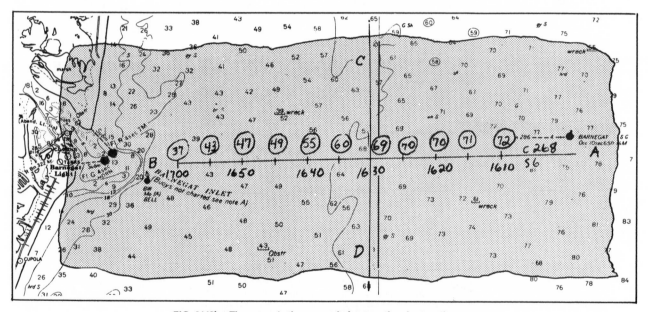

FIG. 2149b   The paper is then moved about on the chart until meas-ured depths correspond with the charted depths.

certain if there is a significant difference between the depth at the boat's actual location and that charted for the estimated position. If such should be the case, a further verification of the estimated position is a necessity, per-haps even an urgent necessity!

Fathom curve sailing

When cruising along a coast that has a fairly uniformly sloping bottom offshore, piloting can often be simplified by an examination of the chart for a fathom curve that will keep the craft in safe waters generally and will avoid any specific hazards. The boat is then steered so as to keep the

reading of the electronic depth sounder within a few feet of the selected depth. If readings increase, the boat is gently steered toward shore; if they decrease, the wheel is put over a bit to edge farther offshore.

For the sake of safety, the chart should be checked for the *full* distance that this technique is to be used to be sure that there are no sudden changes in depth, or bends in the depth curve, that might result in an unexpectedly hazardous situation. For added safety, this examination of the chart should be carried beyond the intended end of fathom-curve sailing to prevent unexpected hazards from arising should your speed over the bottom be greater than anticipated.

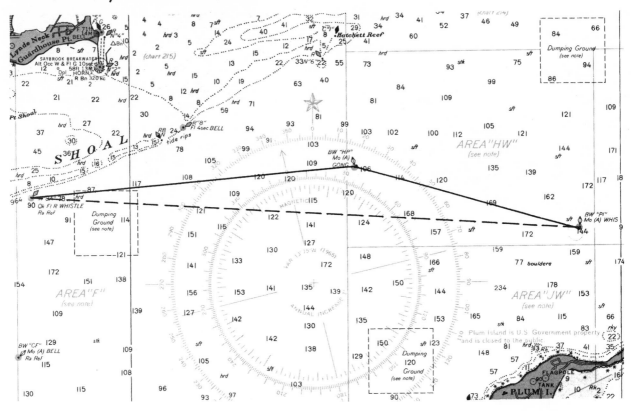

FIG. 2150 As a general rule, it is better practice to lay two short courses between buoys than one long one. This is especially true in thick weather.

Practice — and More Practice

Position determination is the part of piloting that truly cannot be learned "from the book." Study is important, it is essential, but the skipper must put into actual practice the various procedures and techniques. He must know the rules and principles involved, but he must also be able to *apply* them. Make a habit of "over-navigating" during daylight and good weather conditions so that you will be experienced and capable at night or in foul weather.

TABLE FOR FINDING HEIGHT OF TIDE ABOVE LOW WATER AT ANY HOUR OF THE EBB OR FLOOD		
FALLING TIDE Hours after high water	RISING TIDE Hours after low water	CONSTANT Rising or Falling
0	6	1.0
½	5½	0.98
1	5	0.92
1½	4½	0.84
2	4	0.75
2½	3½	0.63
3	3	0.50
3½	2½	0.38
4	2	0.26
4½	1½	0.16
5	1	0.08
5½	½	0.025

1. Find rise of tide for given day in Tide Tables (difference between heights of nearest high and low tides)
2. Enter column 1 or 2 on line corresponding to time for which height of tide is to be calculated
3. In column 3, find constant given for that time
4. Multiply constant obtained in (3) by total rise of tide (1)

Preceding pages in this chapter have provided all of the basic information required for the safe navigation of a boat in pilot waters —the dimensions and instruments of piloting, the procedures of dead reckoning, calculations involving tides and currents, and position determination. The material to be presented in this supplementary section extends beyond these fundamentals. These are techniques that will be useful in specialized situations, or which may provide a quicker or easier solution to a piloting problem. The material of this section might be considered as "graduate study" in small-craft piloting. These techniques should not be approached without a thorough understanding of Chapters 19 and 20, and the basic methods already discussed in Chapter 21. FIG. 2152 (left): Current problems, for example, may be solved with the aid of precomputed speed factors and course corrections—but first understand the principles.

PILOTING—Specialized Techniques

Current Problem Solutions from Tabulated Factors

When a boat moves in water that is in itself in motion with respect to the bottom as a result of current, two effects must be considered. One of these is the difference in speed over the bottom as compared with speed through the water. The other effect is the variation between the course steered and the path actually traveled.

THE VARIOUS CURRENT SAILING PROBLEMS

The effects mentioned above can be approached from several viewpoints:
  (a) with a selected course and speed, together with a known or estimated current, *determining the track and speed of advance* that may be expected;
  (b) with a desired track and speed to be run through the water, plus knowledge of the current, *determining the course to steer and the speed of advance* that may be expected; and
  (c) with a desired track and speed of advance to be made good, and knowledge of the current, *determining the course to steer and the speed to run through the water.*

In all current situations, there are three pairs of direction and speed values—*boat with respect to the water, water with respect to the bottom,* and *boat with respect to the bottom.* For the solution of current sailing problems, in general, four of the above six quantities will be known (or estimated) and the other two are to be determined.

In Chapter 20, graphic solutions using vectors were used, see pages 392 to 416.

Such current problems can also be solved using data derived from an electronic digital computer. Solutions from these tables of data should not be attempted, however, without a thorough understanding of the relationships between the various quantities involved, as are shown in the graphic plots of Chapter 20. An understanding of the graphical procedure will reduce the chances of

misinterpreting the tables, or of using the factors incorrectly. For easier understanding, the same terms, abbreviations, and designations of problems (Case 1, Case 3, etc.) will be used here as in Chapter 20.

DISTANCE, TIME, AND SPEED CALCULATIONS

Where no current is present, the pilot's problem is a simple matter of *determining the time required to run a given distance in slack water.* Even where there is current, slack water speed (or speed through the water without reference to current) is a basic factor. The formulas for D, T, and S, see page 388, can be used, but the table of fig. 2151 is a handy means of achieving the same results. It was developed primarily for the cruising boatman who is interested in relatively long runs involving hours and minutes of time.

Slack water speed solutions

The use of fig. 2151 is simple, as the following examples will illustrate:
  Example A. At 13 knots, how long does it take to go 36 miles?
  Answer: Reading directly from the table, $2^h 46^m$.
  Example B. At 11 knots, how long does it take to go 43.6 miles?
  Answer: Reading from the table—

to go 43. miles,	$3^h 55^m$
to go .6 miles,	3^m
to go 43.6 miles	$3^h 58^m$

  Example C. At 14.3 knots, how long does it take to go 26.4 miles?
  Answer: From the table, in the same manner as for Example B:

to go 26.4 miles at 14 knots,	$1^h 53^m$
to go 26.4 miles at 15 knots,	$1^h 46^m$
Difference in time for 1 knot,	7^m

  Hence, to go 26.4 miles at 14.3 knots requires $1^h 53^m - (0.3 \times 7^m) = 1^h 51^m$.

SPEED—6 TO 27—IN MILES PER HOUR

DISTANCE—.1 TO 90—IN MILES

Dist. miles	6.0	7.0	8.0	9.0	10.0	11.0	12.0	13.0	14.0	15.0	16.0	17.0	18.0	19.0	20.0	21.0	22.0	23.0	24.0	25.0	26.0	27.0
.1	01	01	01	01	01	01	01	00	00	00	00	00	00	00	00	00	00	00	00	00	00	00
.2	02	02	02	01	01	01	01	01	01	01	01	01	01	01	01	01	01	01	01	00	00	00
.3	03	03	02	02	02	02	02	01	01	01	01	01	01	01	01	01	01	01	01	01	01	01
.4	04	03	03	03	02	02	02	02	02	02	02	01	01	01	01	01	01	01	01	01	01	01
.5	05	04	04	03	03	03	03	02	02	02	02	02	02	02	02	01	01	01	01	01	01	01
.6	06	05	05	04	04	03	03	03	03	02	02	02	02	02	02	02	02	02	02	01	01	01
.7	07	06	05	05	04	04	04	03	03	03	03	02	02	02	02	02	02	02	02	02	02	02
.8	08	07	06	05	05	04	04	04	03	03	03	03	03	03	02	02	02	02	02	02	02	02
.9	09	08	07	06	05	05	05	04	04	04	03	03	03	03	03	03	02	02	02	02	02	02
1.0	10	09	08	07	06	05	05	05	04	04	04	04	03	03	03	03	03	03	03	02	02	02
2.0	20	17	15	13	12	11	10	09	09	08	08	07	07	06	06	06	05	05	05	05	05	04
3.0	30	26	23	20	18	16	15	14	13	12	11	11	10	09	09	09	08	08	08	07	07	07
4.0	40	34	30	27	24	22	20	18	17	16	15	14	13	13	12	11	11	10	10	10	09	09
5.0	50	43	38	33	30	27	25	23	21	20	19	18	17	16	15	14	14	13	13	12	12	11
6.0	1 00	51	45	40	36	33	30	28	26	24	23	21	20	19	18	17	16	16	15	14	14	13
7.0	1 10	1 00	53	47	42	38	35	32	30	28	26	25	23	22	21	20	19	18	18	17	16	16
8.0	1 20	1 09	1 00	53	48	44	40	37	34	32	30	28	27	25	24	23	22	21	20	19	18	18
9.0	1 30	1 17	1 08	1 00	54	49	45	42	39	36	34	32	30	28	27	26	25	23	23	22	21	20
10.0	1 40	1 26	1 15	1 07	1 00	55	50	46	43	40	38	35	33	32	30	29	27	26	25	24	23	22
11.0	1 50	1 34	1 23	1 13	1 06	1 00	55	51	47	44	41	39	37	35	33	31	30	29	28	26	25	24
12.0	2 00	1 43	1 30	1 20	1 12	1 05	1 00	55	51	48	45	42	40	38	36	34	33	31	30	29	28	27
13.0	2 10	1 51	1 38	1 27	1 18	1 11	1 05	1 00	56	52	49	46	43	41	39	37	35	34	33	31	30	29
14.0	2 20	2 00	1 45	1 33	1 24	1 16	1 10	1 05	1 00	56	53	49	47	44	42	40	38	37	35	34	32	31
15.0	2 30	2 09	1 53	1 40	1 30	1 22	1 15	1 09	1 04	1 00	56	53	50	47	45	43	41	39	38	36	35	33
16.0	2 40	2 17	2 00	1 47	1 36	1 27	1 20	1 14	1 09	1 04	1 00	56	53	51	48	46	44	42	40	38	37	36
17.0	2 50	2 26	2 08	1 53	1 42	1 33	1 25	1 18	1 13	1 08	1 04	1 00	57	54	51	49	46	44	43	41	39	38
18.0	3 00	2 34	2 15	2 00	1 48	1 38	1 30	1 23	1 17	1 12	1 08	1 04	1 00	57	54	51	49	47	45	43	42	40
19.0	3 10	2 43	2 23	2 07	1 54	1 44	1 35	1 28	1 21	1 16	1 11	1 07	1 03	1 00	57	54	52	50	48	46	44	42
20.0	3 20	2 51	2 30	2 13	2 00	1 49	1 40	1 32	1 26	1 20	1 15	1 11	1 07	1 03	1 00	57	55	52	50	48	46	44
21.0	3 30	3 00	2 38	2 20	2 06	1 55	1 45	1 37	1 30	1 24	1 19	1 14	1 10	1 06	1 03	1 00	57	55	53	50	48	47
22.0	3 40	3 09	2 45	2 27	2 12	2 00	1 50	1 42	1 34	1 28	1 23	1 18	1 13	1 09	1 06	1 03	1 00	57	55	53	51	49
23.0	3 50	3 17	2 53	2 33	2 18	2 05	1 55	1 46	1 39	1 32	1 26	1 21	1 17	1 13	1 09	1 06	1 03	1 00	58	55	53	51
24.0	4 00	3 26	3 00	2 40	2 24	2 11	2 00	1 51	1 43	1 36	1 30	1 25	1 20	1 16	1 12	1 09	1 05	1 03	1 00	58	55	53
25.0	4 10	3 34	3 08	2 47	2 30	2 16	2 05	1 55	1 47	1 40	1 34	1 28	1 23	1 19	1 15	1 11	1 08	1 05	1 03	1 00	58	56
26.0	4 20	3 43	3 15	2 53	2 36	2 22	2 10	2 00	1 51	1 44	1 38	1 32	1 27	1 22	1 18	1 14	1 11	1 08	1 05	1 02	1 00	58
27.0	4 30	3 51	3 23	3 00	2 42	2 27	2 15	2 05	1 56	1 48	1 41	1 35	1 30	1 25	1 21	1 17	1 14	1 10	1 08	1 05	1 02	1 00
28.0	4 40	4 00	3 30	3 07	2 48	2 33	2 20	2 09	2 00	1 52	1 45	1 39	1 33	1 28	1 24	1 20	1 16	1 13	1 10	1 07	1 05	1 02
29.0	4 50	4 09	3 38	3 13	2 54	2 38	2 25	2 14	2 04	1 56	1 49	1 42	1 37	1 32	1 27	1 23	1 19	1 16	1 13	1 10	1 07	1 04
30.0	5 00	4 17	3 45	3 20	3 00	2 44	2 30	2 18	2 09	2 00	1 53	1 46	1 40	1 35	1 30	1 26	1 22	1 18	1 15	1 12	1 09	1 07
31.0	5 10	4 26	3 53	3 27	3 06	2 49	2 35	2 23	2 13	2 04	1 56	1 49	1 43	1 38	1 33	1 29	1 25	1 21	1 18	1 14	1 12	1 09
32.0	5 20	4 34	4 00	3 33	3 12	2 55	2 40	2 28	2 17	2 08	2 00	1 53	1 47	1 41	1 36	1 31	1 27	1 23	1 20	1 17	1 14	1 11
33.0	5 30	4 43	4 08	3 40	3 18	3 00	2 45	2 32	2 21	2 12	2 04	1 56	1 50	1 44	1 39	1 34	1 30	1 26	1 23	1 19	1 16	1 13
34.0	5 40	4 51	4 15	3 47	3 24	3 05	2 50	2 37	2 26	2 16	2 08	2 00	1 53	1 47	1 42	1 37	1 33	1 29	1 25	1 22	1 18	1 16
35.0	5 50	5 00	4 23	3 53	3 30	3 11	2 55	2 42	2 30	2 20	2 11	2 04	1 57	1 51	1 45	1 40	1 35	1 31	1 28	1 24	1 21	1 18
36.0	6 00	5 09	4 30	4 00	3 36	3 16	3 00	2 46	2 34	2 24	2 15	2 07	2 00	1 54	1 48	1 43	1 38	1 34	1 30	1 26	1 23	1 20
37.0	6 10	5 17	4 38	4 07	3 42	3 22	3 05	2 51	2 39	2 28	2 19	2 11	2 03	1 57	1 51	1 46	1 41	1 37	1 33	1 29	1 25	1 22
38.0	6 20	5 26	4 45	4 13	3 48	3 27	3 10	2 55	2 43	2 32	2 23	2 14	2 07	2 00	1 54	1 49	1 44	1 39	1 35	1 31	1 28	1 24
39.0	6 30	5 34	4 53	4 20	3 54	3 33	3 15	3 00	2 47	2 36	2 26	2 18	2 10	2 03	1 57	1 51	1 46	1 42	1 38	1 34	1 30	1 27
40.0	6 40	5 43	5 00	4 27	4 00	3 38	3 20	3 05	2 51	2 40	2 30	2 21	2 13	2 06	2 00	1 54	1 49	1 44	1 40	1 36	1 32	1 29
41.0	6 50	5 51	5 08	4 33	4 06	3 44	3 25	3 09	2 56	2 44	2 34	2 25	2 17	2 09	2 03	1 57	1 52	1 47	1 43	1 38	1 35	1 31
42.0	7 00	6 00	5 15	4 40	4 12	3 49	3 30	3 14	3 00	2 48	2 38	2 28	2 20	2 13	2 06	2 00	1 55	1 50	1 45	1 41	1 37	1 33
43.0	7 10	6 09	5 23	4 47	4 18	3 55	3 35	3 18	3 04	2 52	2 41	2 32	2 23	2 16	2 09	2 03	1 57	1 52	1 48	1 43	1 39	1 36
44.0	7 20	6 17	5 30	4 53	4 24	4 00	3 40	3 23	3 09	2 56	2 45	2 35	2 27	2 19	2 12	2 06	2 00	1 55	1 50	1 46	1 42	1 38
45.0	7 30	6 26	5 38	5 00	4 30	4 05	3 45	3 28	3 13	3 00	2 49	2 39	2 30	2 22	2 15	2 09	2 03	1 57	1 53	1 48	1 44	1 40
46.0	7 40	6 34	5 45	5 07	4 36	4 11	3 50	3 32	3 17	3 04	2 53	2 42	2 33	2 25	2 18	2 11	2 05	2 00	1 55	1 50	1 46	1 42
47.0	7 50	6 43	5 53	5 13	4 42	4 16	3 55	3 37	3 21	3 08	2 56	2 46	2 37	2 28	2 21	2 14	2 08	2 03	1 58	1 53	1 48	1 44
48.0	8 00	6 51	6 00	5 20	4 48	4 22	4 00	3 42	3 26	3 12	3 00	2 49	2 40	2 32	2 24	2 17	2 11	2 05	2 00	1 55	1 51	1 47
49.0	8 10	7 00	6 08	5 27	4 54	4 27	4 05	3 46	3 30	3 16	3 04	2 53	2 43	2 35	2 27	2 20	2 14	2 08	2 03	1 58	1 53	1 49
50.0	8 20	7 09	6 15	5 33	5 00	4 33	4 10	3 51	3 34	3 20	3 08	2 56	2 47	2 38	2 30	2 23	2 16	2 10	2 05	2 00	1 55	1 51
51.0	8 30	7 17	6 23	5 40	5 06	4 38	4 15	3 55	3 39	3 24	3 11	3 00	2 50	2 41	2 33	2 26	2 19	2 13	2 08	2 02	1 58	1 53
52.0	8 40	7 26	6 30	5 47	5 12	4 44	4 20	4 00	3 43	3 28	3 15	3 04	2 53	2 44	2 36	2 29	2 22	2 16	2 10	2 05	2 00	1 56
53.0	8 50	7 34	6 38	5 53	5 18	4 49	4 25	4 05	3 47	3 32	3 19	3 07	2 57	2 47	2 39	2 31	2 25	2 18	2 13	2 07	2 02	1 58
54.0	9 00	7 43	6 45	6 00	5 24	4 55	4 30	4 09	3 51	3 36	3 23	3 11	3 00	2 51	2 42	2 34	2 27	2 21	2 15	2 10	2 05	2 00
55.0	9 10	7 51	6 53	6 07	5 30	5 00	4 35	4 14	3 56	3 40	3 26	3 14	3 03	2 54	2 45	2 37	2 30	2 23	2 18	2 12	2 07	2 02
56.0	9 20	8 00	7 00	6 13	5 36	5 05	4 40	4 18	4 00	3 44	3 30	3 18	3 07	2 57	2 48	2 40	2 33	2 26	2 20	2 14	2 09	2 04
57.0	9 30	8 09	7 08	6 20	5 42	5 11	4 45	4 23	4 04	3 48	3 34	3 21	3 10	3 00	2 51	2 43	2 35	2 29	2 23	2 17	2 12	2 07
58.0	9 40	8 17	7 15	6 27	5 48	5 16	4 50	4 28	4 09	3 52	3 38	3 25	3 13	3 03	2 54	2 46	2 38	2 31	2 25	2 19	2 14	2 09
59.0	9 50	8 26	7 23	6 33	5 54	5 22	4 55	4 32	4 13	3 56	3 41	3 28	3 17	3 06	2 57	2 49	2 41	2 34	2 28	2 22	2 16	2 11
60.0	10 00	8 34	7 30	6 40	6 00	5 27	5 00	4 37	4 17	4 00	3 45	3 32	3 20	3 09	3 00	2 51	2 44	2 37	2 30	2 24	2 18	2 13
61.0	10 10	8 43	7 38	6 47	6 06	5 33	5 05	4 42	4 21	4 04	3 49	3 35	3 23	3 13	3 03	2 54	2 46	2 39	2 33	2 26	2 21	2 16
62.0	10 20	8 51	7 45	6 53	6 12	5 38	5 10	4 46	4 26	4 08	3 53	3 39	3 27	3 16	3 06	2 57	2 49	2 42	2 35	2 29	2 23	2 18
63.0	10 30	9 00	7 53	7 00	6 18	5 44	5 15	4 51	4 30	4 12	3 56	3 42	3 30	3 19	3 09	3 00	2 52	2 44	2 38	2 31	2 25	2 20
64.0	10 40	9 09	8 00	7 07	6 24	5 49	5 20	4 55	4 34	4 16	4 00	3 46	3 33	3 22	3 12	3 03	2 55	2 47	2 40	2 34	2 28	2 22
65.0	10 50	9 17	8 08	7 13	6 30	5 55	5 25	5 00	4 39	4 20	4 04	3 49	3 37	3 25	3 15	3 06	2 57	2 50	2 43	2 36	2 30	2 24
66.0	11 00	9 26	8 15	7 20	6 36	6 00	5 30	5 05	4 43	4 24	4 08	3 53	3 40	3 28	3 18	3 09	3 00	2 52	2 45	2 38	2 32	2 27
67.0	11 10	9 34	8 23	7 27	6 42	6 05	5 35	5 09	4 47	4 28	4 11	3 56	3 43	3 32	3 21	3 11	3 03	2 55	2 48	2 41	2 35	2 29
68.0	11 20	9 43	8 30	7 33	6 48	6 11	5 40	5 14	4 51	4 32	4 15	4 00	3 47	3 35	3 24	3 14	3 05	2 57	2 50	2 43	2 37	2 31
69.0	11 30	9 51	8 38	7 40	6 54	6 16	5 45	5 18	4 56	4 36	4 19	4 04	3 50	3 38	3 27	3 17	3 08	3 00	2 53	2 46	2 39	2 33
70.0	11 40	10 00	8 45	7 47	7 00	6 22	5 50	5 23	5 00	4 40	4 23	4 07	3 53	3 41	3 30	3 20	3 11	3 03	2 55	2 48	2 42	2 36
71.0	11 50	10 09	8 53	7 53	7 06	6 27	5 55	5 28	5 04	4 44	4 26	4 11	3 57	3 44	3 33	3 23	3 14	3 05	2 58	2 50	2 44	2 38
72.0	12 00	10 17	9 00	8 00	7 12	6 33	6 00	5 32	5 09	4 48	4 30	4 14	4 00	3 47	3 36	3 26	3 16	3 08	3 00	2 53	2 46	2 40
73.0	12 10	10 26	9 08	8 07	7 18	6 38	6 05	5 37	5 13	4 52	4 34	4 18	4 03	3 51	3 39	3 29	3 19	3 10	3 03	2 55	2 48	2 42
74.0	12 20	10 34	9 15	8 13	7 24	6 44	6 10	5 42	5 17	4 56	4 38	4 21	4 07	3 54	3 42	3 31	3 22	3 13	3 05	2 58	2 51	2 44
75.0	12 30	10 43	9 23	8 20	7 30	6 49	6 15	5 46	5 21	5 00	4 41	4 25	4 10	3 57	3 45	3 34	3 25	3 16	3 08	3 00	2 53	2 47
76.0	12 40	10 51	9 30	8 27	7 36	6 55	6 20	5 51	5 26	5 04	4 45	4 28	4 13	4 00	3 48	3 37	3 27	3 18	3 10	3 02	2 55	2 49
77.0	12 50	11 00	9 38	8 33	7 42	7 00	6 25	5 55	5 30	5 08	4 49	4 32	4 17	4 03	3 51	3 40	3 30	3 21	3 13	3 05	2 58	2 51
78.0	13 00	11 09	9 45	8 40	7 48	7 05	6 30	6 00	5 34	5 12	4 53	4 35	4 20	4 06	3 54	3 43	3 33	3 23	3 15	3 07	3 00	2 53
79.0	13 10	11 17	9 53	8 47	7 54	7 11	6 35	6 05	5 39	5 16	4 56	4 39	4 23	4 09	3 57	3 46	3 35	3 26	3 18	3 10	3 02	2 56
80.0	13 20	11 26	10 00	8 53	8 00	7 16	6 40	6 09	5 43	5 20	5 00	4 42	4 27	4 13	4 00	3 49	3 38	3 29	3 20	3 12	3 05	2 58
81.0	13 30	11 34	10 08	9 00	8 06	7 22	6 45	6 14	5 47	5 24	5 04	4 46	4 30	4 16	4 03	3 51	3 41	3 31	3 23	3 14	3 07	3 00
82.0	13 40	11 43	10 15	9 07	8 12	7 27	6 50	6 18	5 51	5 28	5 08	4 49	4 33	4 19	4 06	3 54	3 44	3 34	3 25	3 17	3 09	3 02
83.0	13 50	11 51	10 23	9 13	8 18	7 33	6 55	6 23	5 56	5 32	5 11	4 53	4 37	4 22	4 09	3 57	3 46	3 37	3 28	3 19	3 12	3 04
84.0	14 00	12 00	10 30	9 20	8 24	7 38	7 00	6 28	6 00	5 36	5 15	4 56	4 40	4 25	4 12	4 00	3 49	3 39	3 30	3 22	3 14	3 07
85.0	14 10	12 09	10 38	9 27	8 30	7 44	7 05	6 32	6 04	5 40	5 19	5 00	4 43	4 28	4 15	4 03	3 52	3 42	3 33	3 24	3 16	3 09
86.0	14 20	12 17	10 45	9 33	8 36	7 49	7 10	6 37	6 09	5 44	5 23	5 04	4 47	4 32	4 18	4 06	3 55	3 44	3 35	3 26	3 18	3 11
87.0	14 30	12 26	10 53	9 40	8 42	7 55	7 15	6 42	6 13	5 48	5 26	5 07	4 50	4 35	4 21	4 09	3 57	3 47	3 38	3 29	3 21	3 13
88.0	14 40	12 34	11 00	9 47	8 48	8 00	7 20	6 46	6 17	5 52	5 30	5 11	4 53	4 38	4 24	4 11	4 00	3 50	3 40	3 31	3 23	3 16
89.0	14 50	12 43	11 08	9 53	8 54	8 05	7 25	6 51	6 21	5 56	5 34	5 14	4 57	4 41	4 27	4 14	4 03	3 52	3 43	3 34	3 25	3 18
90.0	15 00	12 51	11 15	10 00	9 00	8 11	7 30	6 55	6 26	6 00	5 38	5 18	5 00	4 44	4 30	4 17	4 05	3 55	3 45	3 36	3 28	3 20

FIG. 2151 Time required to run a known distance at a specified speed. Time is shown in hours and minutes. Distances and speeds may be in nautical miles and knots, or in statute miles and MPH. Times for whole miles and fractions may be combined. See text.

The technique of interpolating between speeds in Example C is not precisely correct from a pure mathematics viewpoint. The error, if any, however, will be negligible in practical piloting situations, and the procedure is quite acceptable.

CURRENT PROBLEM SOLUTIONS

In solving current sailing problems with tabulated data, the pilot will still use the terminology developed in earlier chapters. For review, these terms are as follows:

Course (C)—the direction of the DR track, the direction the boat is steered through the water.

Speed (S)—the speed of the boat through the water, the DR track speed.

Set—the direction *toward* which the current is flowing.

Drift—the velocity of the current.

Track (TR)—the direction of the desired (expected) track line.

Speed of Advance (SOA)—the desired (expected) speed along the intended track line.

The terms *Course over the Ground (COG)* and *Speed over the Ground (SOG)* are used only with Case 2 problems which will not be considered in these tabular solutions.

Whenever distance and speed appear in the above definitions, and in the examples to follow, the units may be either statute miles and MPH, or nautical miles and knots.

Special terms

In the solution of current problems by tabulated factors, it is necessary to introduce certain additional terms not previously employed in the graphic solution of such problems.

$$\textit{Drift}, \text{ in percent} = \frac{\text{Drift} \times 100}{\text{Speed, or SOA, as specified}}$$

Relative set is the angle measured from the course steered (C), or from the desired (expected) track (TR), to the set of the current, measured either clockwise or counter-clockwise so that the angle is less than 180°. When measured in a *clockwise* direction, relative set is *positive;* when measured in a *counter-clockwise* direction, relative set is *negative*. In some cases, relative set will be figured with respect to course (C); in other cases, with respect to track (TR).

Fig. 2153 shows graphically the relationship of relative set and course change (CC) to the previously used terms of course, track, set, etc. for Case 1 problems.

Relative set is calculated as shown in the examples shown below:

Relative set = Set − Course, 180° or less to starboard or port.

Set	060	300
Course	−025	−340
Relative set	+035	−040

If (Set − C) is numerically greater than 180°, and positive, subtract 360° obtaining a *negative* relative set less than 180°

Set	240
Course	−030
	+210
	−360
Relative set	−150

If (Set − C) is numerically greater than 180°, and negative, add 360°, obtaining a *positive* relative set less than 180°.

Set	060
Course	−300
	−240
	+360
Relative set	+120

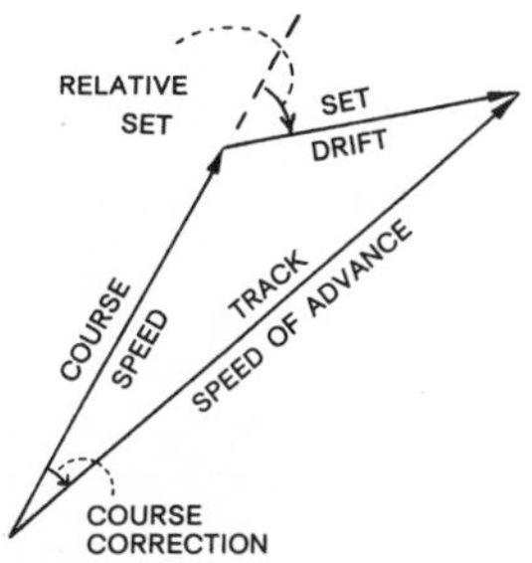

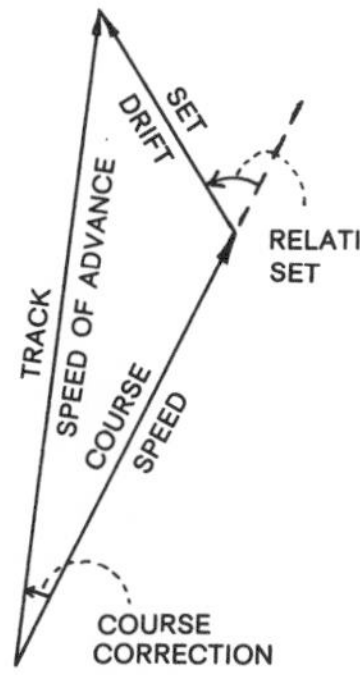

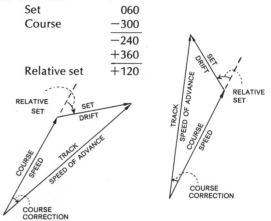

FIG. 2153 The tabular solution of current problems introduces two new terms—*relative set* and *course correction* (CC). The relationship of these terms to the more familiar directions and velocities are shown above for Case 1 problems.

Fig. 2154 and subsequent tables will yield a multiplying quantity, termed Speed Factor (SF), and an angle, called Course Change or Course Correction (CC). The use of these factors will be explained in connection with each of the three types of current problems to be solved by the tables.

Case 1 solutions by tabular factors

In Case 1, the pilot has selected the course that he will steer and the speed at which he will operate his boat with respect to the water (the engine rpm setting that he will use). He also has information on the set and drift of the current from predictions or visual observations. He desires to know *the direction of the path that the boat may be expected to follow with respect to the bottom (TR) and*

FIG. 2154 Case 1—To find Track and Speed of Advance from knowledge of Course and Speed through the water, plus relative set and percent drift. This table yields Speed Factors (SF) and Course Corrections (CC).

DRIFT—in percent of speed over water

2		4		6		8		10		12		14		16		18		20	
SF	CC	SF	CC	SF	CC	SF	CC	SF	CC	SF	CC	SF	CC	SF	CC	SF	CC	SF	CC
1.020	00	1.040	00	1.060	00	1.080	00	1.100	00	1.120	00	1.140	00	1.160	00	1.180	00	1.200	00
1.020	00	1.040	00	1.060	00	1.080	00	1.100	00	1.120	01	1.140	01	1.159	01	1.179	01	1.199	01
1.020	00	1.039	00	1.059	01	1.079	01	1.099	01	1.118	01	1.138	01	1.158	01	1.178	02	1.197	02
1.019	00	1.039	01	1.058	01	1.077	01	1.097	01	1.116	02	1.136	02	1.155	02	1.175	02	1.194	02
1.019	00	1.038	01	1.057	01	1.076	01	1.095	02	1.114	02	1.133	02	1.152	03	1.171	03	1.190	03
1.018	00	1.036	01	1.055	01	1.073	02	1.091	02	1.110	03	1.128	03	1.147	03	1.166	04	1.184	04
1.017	01	1.035	01	1.052	02	1.070	02	1.088	03	1.106	03	1.123	04	1.141	04	1.159	04	1.177	05
1.016	01	1.033	01	1.050	02	1.067	02	1.083	03	1.100	04	1.118	04	1.135	05	1.152	05	1.169	06
1.015	01	1.031	01	1.047	02	1.063	03	1.079	03	1.095	04	1.111	05	1.127	05	1.144	06	1.160	06
1.014	01	1.029	02	1.043	02	1.058	03	1.073	04	1.088	04	1.103	05	1.119	06	1.134	06	1.150	07
1.013	01	1.026	02	1.040	03	1.053	03	1.067	04	1.081	05	1.095	06	1.110	06	1.124	07	1.139	08
1.012	01	1.023	02	1.036	03	1.048	04	1.061	04	1.073	05	1.086	06	1.100	07	1.113	08	1.127	08
1.010	01	1.021	02	1.031	03	1.042	04	1.054	05	1.065	06	1.077	06	1.089	07	1.101	08	1.114	09
1.009	01	1.018	02	1.027	03	1.036	04	1.046	05	1.056	06	1.067	07	1.077	08	1.088	09	1.100	09
1.007	01	1.014	02	1.022	03	1.030	04	1.038	05	1.047	06	1.056	07	1.065	08	1.075	09	1.085	10
1.005	01	1.011	02	1.017	03	1.024	04	1.030	05	1.038	06	1.045	07	1.053	08	1.061	09	1.069	10
1.004	01	1.008	02	1.012	03	1.017	04	1.022	06	1.028	07	1.034	08	1.040	09	1.046	10	1.053	11
1.002	01	1.004	02	1.007	03	1.010	05	1.014	06	1.018	07	1.022	08	1.026	09	1.031	10	1.037	11
1.000	01	1.001	02	1.002	03	1.003	05	1.005	06	1.007	07	1.010	08	1.013	09	1.016	10	1.020	11
.998	01	.997	02	.997	03	.996	05	.996	06	.997	07	.998	08	.999	09	1.001	10	1.003	11
.997	01	.994	02	.991	03	.989	05	.988	06	.986	07	.985	08	.985	09	.985	10	.985	12
.995	01	.990	02	.986	03	.982	05	.979	06	.976	07	.973	08	.971	09	.969	10	.968	12
.993	01	.987	02	.981	03	.976	04	.970	06	.966	07	.961	08	.957	09	.954	10	.950	11
.992	01	.984	02	.976	03	.969	04	.962	05	.955	07	.949	08	.944	09	.938	10	.933	11
.990	01	.981	02	.971	03	.962	04	.954	05	.946	06	.938	07	.930	09	.923	10	.917	11
.989	01	.978	02	.967	03	.956	04	.946	05	.936	06	.927	07	.918	08	.909	09	.900	10
.987	01	.975	02	.963	03	.951	04	.939	05	.927	06	.916	07	.905	08	.895	09	.885	10
.986	01	.972	02	.959	03	.945	03	.932	04	.919	05	.906	06	.894	07	.882	08	.870	09
.985	01	.970	02	.955	02	.940	03	.926	04	.911	05	.897	06	.883	07	.870	08	.856	09
.984	01	.968	01	.951	02	.936	03	.920	04	.904	04	.889	05	.874	06	.859	07	.844	08
.983	01	.966	01	.949	02	.932	02	.915	03	.898	04	.882	05	.865	05	.849	06	.833	07
.982	00	.964	01	.946	02	.928	02	.910	03	.893	03	.875	04	.858	05	.840	05	.823	06
.981	00	.963	01	.944	01	.925	02	.907	02	.888	03	.870	03	.851	04	.833	04	.815	05
.981	00	.961	01	.942	01	.923	01	.904	02	.885	02	.866	02	.846	03	.827	03	.808	04
.980	00	.961	00	.941	01	.921	01	.902	01	.882	01	.862	02	.843	02	.823	02	.804	02
.980	00	.960	00	.940	00	.920	00	.900	01	.881	01	.861	01	.841	01	.821	01	.801	01
.980	00	.960	00	.940	00	.920	00	.900	00	.880	00	.860	00	.840	00	.820	00	.800	00

22		24		26		28		30		32		34		36		38		40	
SF	CC	SF	CC	SF	CC	SF	CC	SF	CC	SF	CC	SF	CC	SF	CC	SF	CC	SF	CC
1.220	00	1.240	00	1.260	00	1.280	00	1.300	00	1.320	00	1.340	00	1.360	00	1.380	00	1.400	00
1.219	01	1.239	01	1.259	01	1.279	01	1.299	01	1.319	01	1.339	01	1.359	01	1.379	01	1.399	01
1.217	02	1.237	02	1.257	02	1.277	02	1.296	02	1.316	02	1.336	03	1.356	03	1.376	03	1.396	03
1.214	03	1.233	03	1.253	03	1.273	03	1.292	03	1.312	04	1.331	04	1.351	04	1.371	04	1.390	04
1.209	04	1.228	04	1.247	04	1.267	04	1.286	05	1.305	05	1.325	05	1.344	05	1.363	05	1.383	06
1.203	04	1.222	05	1.241	05	1.259	05	1.278	06	1.297	06	1.316	06	1.335	07	1.354	07	1.373	07
1.196	05	1.214	06	1.232	06	1.250	06	1.269	07	1.287	07	1.306	07	1.324	08	1.343	08	1.361	08
1.187	06	1.204	07	1.222	07	1.240	07	1.258	08	1.275	08	1.293	09	1.311	09	1.329	09	1.347	10
1.177	07	1.194	07	1.211	08	1.228	08	1.245	09	1.262	09	1.279	10	1.297	10	1.314	11	1.331	11
1.166	08	1.182	08	1.198	09	1.214	09	1.231	10	1.247	10	1.263	11	1.280	11	1.297	12	1.314	12
1.154	08	1.169	09	1.184	10	1.199	10	1.215	11	1.230	11	1.246	12	1.262	13	1.278	13	1.294	14
1.141	09	1.155	10	1.169	11	1.183	11	1.198	12	1.212	12	1.227	13	1.242	14	1.257	14	1.272	15
1.126	10	1.139	11	1.152	11	1.166	12	1.179	13	1.193	13	1.206	14	1.220	15	1.235	15	1.249	16
1.111	10	1.123	11	1.135	12	1.147	13	1.159	14	1.172	14	1.184	15	1.197	16	1.211	17	1.224	17
1.095	11	1.105	12	1.116	13	1.127	14	1.138	14	1.149	15	1.161	16	1.173	17	1.185	18	1.197	18
1.078	11	1.087	12	1.096	13	1.106	14	1.116	15	1.126	16	1.136	17	1.147	18	1.158	18	1.169	19
1.061	12	1.068	13	1.076	14	1.084	15	1.093	16	1.102	17	1.111	18	1.120	18	1.130	19	1.140	20
1.042	12	1.049	13	1.055	14	1.062	15	1.069	16	1.076	17	1.084	18	1.092	19	1.100	20	1.109	21
1.024	12	1.028	13	1.033	15	1.038	16	1.044	17	1.050	18	1.056	19	1.063	20	1.070	21	1.077	22
1.005	13	1.008	14	1.011	15	1.015	16	1.019	17	1.023	18	1.028	19	1.033	20	1.038	21	1.044	22
.986	13	.987	14	.989	15	.991	16	.993	17	.996	18	.999	20	1.002	21	1.006	22	1.010	23
.967	13	.966	14	.966	15	.966	16	.967	17	.968	19	.969	20	.971	21	.973	22	.976	23
.948	13	.945	14	.943	15	.942	16	.941	17	.940	19	.940	20	.940	21	.940	22	.941	24
.929	12	.925	14	.921	15	.917	16	.915	17	.912	19	.910	20	.908	21	.907	22	.907	24
.910	12	.904	13	.899	15	.894	16	.889	17	.885	18	.881	20	.877	21	.874	22	.872	23
.892	12	.884	13	.877	14	.870	15	.864	17	.858	18	.852	19	.847	20	.842	22	.837	23
.875	11	.865	12	.856	13	.848	15	.839	16	.831	17	.824	18	.817	20	.810	21	.804	22
.859	10	.847	12	.837	13	.826	14	.816	15	.806	16	.797	18	.788	19	.779	20	.771	22
.843	10	.831	11	.818	12	.806	13	.794	14	.782	15	.771	16	.760	18	.750	19	.740	20
.829	09	.815	10	.801	11	.787	12	.774	13	.760	14	.747	15	.735	16	.722	18	.710	19
.817	08	.801	09	.786	10	.770	10	.755	11	.740	12	.726	14	.711	15	.697	16	.684	17
.806	07	.789	07	.772	08	.756	09	.739	10	.723	11	.707	12	.691	13	.675	14	.660	15
.797	05	.779	06	.761	07	.743	07	.725	08	.708	09	.690	10	.673	11	.656	11	.639	12
.790	04	.771	05	.752	05	.733	06	.714	06	.696	07	.677	07	.659	08	.641	09	.622	10
.784	03	.765	03	.745	03	.726	04	.706	04	.687	05	.668	05	.648	06	.629	06	.610	07
.781	01	.761	02	.741	02	.721	02	.702	02	.682	02	.662	03	.642	03	.622	03	.603	03
.780	00	.760	00	.740	00	.720	00	.700	00	.680	00	.660	00	.640	00	.620	00	.600	00

the speed of advance over the bottom (SOA) that will result from the current's effect.

Fig. 2154 can be used to solve the above problem. The tables of this figure are entered with the drift, in percent of speed through the water, at the top (columns labeled 2 to 40), and the relative set of the current (lines labeled 000° to 180° at the left side). The intersection of the appropriate column and line yields a Speed Factor (SF) and Course Change (CC).

In Case 1 problems, speed (S) is a known value; it is multiplied by SF to get the value for the speed of advance (SOA). In this type of current problem, the Course steered (C) is also a known value. Thus, "CC" is "Course Change," the angle by which the boat is set off course by the current. It is applied as follows:

Track (TR) = C + CC, when relative set is positive.

= C − CC, when relative set is negative.

Three examples will be used to illustrate the application of these tabular factors. Graphic plots of each example are shown as aids to understanding, but they are not required, and are not normally drawn.

Example D. (Fig. 2155)

Known: Course = 076° True
Speed = 8 knots
Set = 324°
Drift = 3 knots

To be determined: Track and Speed of Advance
Solution: Relative set = 324° − 076° = +248°
248° − 360° = −112°

Percent drift = $\frac{3 \times 100}{8}$ = 38

From the table: for 110°, CC = 22°, SF = 0.940
for 115°, CC = 22°, SF = 0.907
by interpolation, for 112°, CC = 22°, SF = 0.927
Thus: Track = 076° − 22° = 054° True
Speed of Advance = 8 x 0.927
= 7.4 knots

Example E. (Fig. 2156)

Known: Course = 331° True
Speed = 9 knots
Set = 021°
Drift = 2.5 knots

To be determined: Track and Speed of Advance
Solution: Relative set = 021° − 331° = −310°
+360°
+050°

Percent drift = $\frac{2.5 \times 100}{9}$ = 28

From the table: CC = 10°
SF = 1.199
Thus: Track 331° + 10° = 341°
Speed of Advance = 9 x 1.199
= 10.8 knots

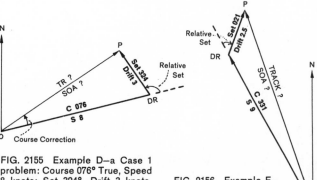

FIG. 2155 Example D—a Case 1 problem: Course 076° True, Speed 8 knots; Set 324°, Drift 3 knots. Find Track and Speed of Advance. See text for solution by tabular factors of fig. 2154.

FIG. 2156 Example E—a Case 1 problem with positive relative set. See text for solution.

Example F. (Fig. 2157)

Known: Course = 015° True
Speed = 10 knots
Set = 156°
Drift = 2 knots

To be determined:
Track and Speed of Advance
Solution:
Relative set = 156° − 015° = +141°

Percent drift = $\frac{2 \times 100}{10}$ = 20

From the table: CC = 9
SF = 0.854
Thus: Track 015° + 9° = 024°
Speed of Advance = 10 x 0.854
= 8.5 knots

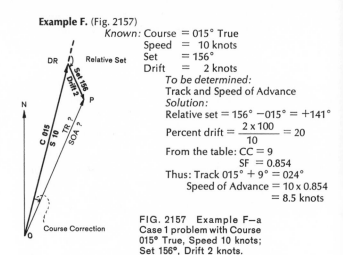

FIG. 2157 Example F—a Case 1 problem with Course 015° True, Speed 10 knots; Set 156°, Drift 2 knots.

Case 3 solutions by tabular factors

In Case 3 current sailing problems, the pilot has determined the direction of the track line that he desires to make good (TR) and has selected his rpm speed (S). He also has information on the set and drift of the current. He desires to determine what course he should steer through the water (C) and to know what speed of advance (SOA) will be achieved at this throttle setting.

In this Case (and in Case 4 problems to be examined later), relative set is the angle between the current and the desired track; see fig. 2158.

Relative set = Set − Track, 180° or less
to starboard or port.

As before, relative set is positive when measured clockwise and negative when measured counter-clockwise. Follow the same rules as for Case 1 if the subtraction gives you an angle greater than 180°.

Fig. 2159 may be used for the solution of this particular current sailing problem. As speed (S) is again a known quantity, it is multiplied by SF as before to obtain speed of advance (SOA).

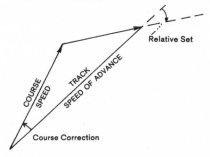

FIG. 2158 In Case 3 and 4 current sailing problems, the relative set is measured between the current and the intended track. The course correction remains as the angle between track and course as in Case 1.

In Case 3, the course to be steered (C) is a desired rather than a known value, and it must be determined by the application of a correction to the desired track (TR). Thus the tabulated angle "CC" is termed "Course Correction" and is used as follows:

Course to be steered (C)
= TR − CC, when the relative set is positive.
= TR + CC, when the relative set is negative.

DRIFT—in percent of speed over water

2	4	6	8	10	12	14	16	18	20	22	24	26	28	30	32	34	36	38	40
SF CC	SF CC	SF CC	SF CC	SF CC	SF CC	SF CC	SF CC	SF CC	SF CC	SF CC	SF CC	SF CC	SF CC	SF CC	SF CC	SF CC	SF CC	SF CC	SF CC
1.020 00	1.040 00	1.060 00	1.080 00	1.100 00	1.120 00	1.140 00	1.160 00	1.180 00	1.200 00	1.220 00	1.240 00	1.260 00	1.280 00	1.300 00	1.320 00	1.340 00	1.360 00	1.380 00	1.400 00
1.020 00	1.040 00	1.060 00	1.080 00	1.100 00	1.119 00	1.139 01	1.159 01	1.179 01	1.199 01	1.219 01	1.239 01	1.259 01	1.279 01	1.299 01	1.318 02	1.338 02	1.358 02	1.378 02	1.398 02
1.020 00	1.039 00	1.059 01	1.079 01	1.098 01	1.118 01	1.138 01	1.157 02	1.177 02	1.196 02	1.216 02	1.235 02	1.255 03	1.275 03	1.294 03	1.314 03	1.333 03	1.353 04	1.372 04	1.392 04
1.019 00	1.039 01	1.058 01	1.077 01	1.096 01	1.115 01	1.135 02	1.154 02	1.173 03	1.192 03	1.211 03	1.230 04	1.249 04	1.268 04	1.287 04	1.306 05	1.325 05	1.343 05	1.362 06	1.381 06
1.019 01	1.037 01	1.056 01	1.075 02	1.093 02	1.112 02	1.130 03	1.149 03	1.167 04	1.186 04	1.204 04	1.222 05	1.240 05	1.259 05	1.277 06	1.295 06	1.313 07	1.331 07	1.349 07	1.366 08
1.018 00	1.036 01	1.054 01	1.072 02	1.090 02	1.107 03	1.125 03	1.143 04	1.160 04	1.178 05	1.195 05	1.212 06	1.230 06	1.247 07	1.264 07	1.281 08	1.298 08	1.315 09	1.331 09	1.348 10
1.017 01	1.034 01	1.052 02	1.068 02	1.085 03	1.102 03	1.119 04	1.135 05	1.152 05	1.168 06	1.184 06	1.201 07	1.217 07	1.233 08	1.248 09	1.264 09	1.280 10	1.295 10	1.311 11	1.326 12
1.016 01	1.033 01	1.049 02	1.064 03	1.080 03	1.096 04	1.111 05	1.127 05	1.142 06	1.157 07	1.172 07	1.187 08	1.202 09	1.216 09	1.231 10	1.245 11	1.259 11	1.273 12	1.287 13	1.301 13
1.015 01	1.030 01	1.045 02	1.060 03	1.075 04	1.089 04	1.103 05	1.117 06	1.131 07	1.145 07	1.158 08	1.172 09	1.185 10	1.198 10	1.211 11	1.224 12	1.236 13	1.249 13	1.261 14	1.273 15
1.014 01	1.028 02	1.042 02	1.055 03	1.068 04	1.081 05	1.094 05	1.107 06	1.119 07	1.131 08	1.143 09	1.155 10	1.167 11	1.178 11	1.189 12	1.200 13	1.211 14	1.222 15	1.232 16	1.242 16
1.013 01	1.025 02	1.038 03	1.050 04	1.061 04	1.073 05	1.084 06	1.095 07	1.106 08	1.117 09	1.127 10	1.137 11	1.147 11	1.157 12	1.166 13	1.175 14	1.184 15	1.193 16	1.201 17	1.209 18
1.011 01	1.022 02	1.033 03	1.044 04	1.054 05	1.064 06	1.074 07	1.083 08	1.092 08	1.101 09	1.110 10	1.118 11	1.126 12	1.134 13	1.141 13	1.149 15	1.155 16	1.162 17	1.168 18	1.174 19
1.010 01	1.019 02	1.029 03	1.038 04	1.046 05	1.055 06	1.063 07	1.070 08	1.078 09	1.085 10	1.092 11	1.098 12	1.104 13	1.110 14	1.116 15	1.121 16	1.126 17	1.130 18	1.134 19	1.138 20
1.008 01	1.016 02	1.024 03	1.031 04	1.038 04	1.045 06	1.051 07	1.057 08	1.063 09	1.068 10	1.073 12	1.077 13	1.082 14	1.086 15	1.089 16	1.092 17	1.095 18	1.097 19	1.099 20	1.101 21
1.007 01	1.013 02	1.019 03	1.025 04	1.030 05	1.035 06	1.039 08	1.043 09	1.047 10	1.051 11	1.054 12	1.056 13	1.059 14	1.061 15	1.062 16	1.063 17	1.064 19	1.064 20	1.064 21	1.063 22
1.005 01	1.010 02	1.014 03	1.018 04	1.021 06	1.024 07	1.027 08	1.029 09	1.031 10	1.033 11	1.034 12	1.035 13	1.035 15	1.035 16	1.035 17	1.034 18	1.033 19	1.031 20	1.029 22	1.026 23
1.003 01	1.006 02	1.009 03	1.011 05	1.013 06	1.014 07	1.015 08	1.015 09	1.015 10	1.015 11	1.014 13	1.012 14	1.010 16	1.007 17	1.005 18	1.001 20	.998 21	.993 22	.989 23	.982 23
1.002 01	1.003 02	1.003 03	1.004 05	1.004 06	1.003 07	1.002 08	1.001 09	.999 10	.997 11	.995 13	.992 14	.989 15	.985 16	.980 17	.976 19	.971 20	.965 21	.959 22	.952 23
1.000 01	.999 02	.998 03	.997 05	.995 06	.993 07	.990 08	.987 09	.984 10	.980 12	.976 13	.971 14	.966 15	.960 16	.954 17	.947 19	.940 20	.933 21	.925 22	.917 24
.998 01	.996 02	.993 03	.990 05	.986 06	.982 07	.978 08	.973 09	.968 10	.963 11	.957 13	.950 14	.943 15	.936 16	.928 17	.920 19	.911 20	.902 21	.892 22	.882 23
.996 01	.992 02	.988 03	.983 05	.978 06	.972 07	.966 08	.960 09	.953 10	.946 11	.938 13	.930 14	.922 15	.913 16	.903 17	.893 18	.883 20	.873 21	.861 22	.850 23
.995 01	.989 02	.983 03	.976 04	.969 06	.962 07	.955 08	.947 09	.938 10	.929 11	.920 12	.911 13	.901 15	.890 16	.879 17	.868 18	.857 19	.844 20	.832 22	.819 23
.993 01	.986 02	.978 03	.970 04	.961 05	.953 06	.943 08	.934 09	.924 10	.914 11	.903 12	.892 13	.881 14	.869 15	.857 16	.844 17	.831 19	.818 20	.804 21	.790 22
.991 01	.982 02	.973 03	.964 04	.954 05	.943 06	.933 07	.922 08	.911 09	.899 10	.887 12	.875 13	.862 14	.849 15	.836 16	.822 17	.808 18	.793 19	.778 20	.763 21
.990 01	.979 02	.969 03	.958 04	.946 05	.935 06	.923 07	.910 08	.898 09	.885 10	.872 11	.858 12	.844 13	.830 14	.816 15	.801 16	.786 17	.770 18	.754 19	.738 20
.988 01	.977 02	.964 03	.952 04	.939 05	.926 06	.913 07	.900 08	.886 08	.872 09	.857 10	.843 11	.828 12	.813 13	.797 14	.781 15	.765 16	.749 17	.732 18	.715 19
.987 01	.974 02	.960 03	.947 04	.933 04	.919 05	.904 06	.890 07	.875 08	.860 09	.844 10	.829 11	.813 11	.797 12	.780 13	.765 14	.747 15	.730 16	.712 17	.695 18
.986 01	.971 02	.957 02	.942 03	.927 04	.912 05	.896 06	.880 07	.865 07	.849 08	.832 09	.816 10	.799 11	.782 11	.765 12	.748 13	.730 14	.712 15	.695 16	.676 16
.985 01	.969 01	.953 02	.937 03	.921 04	.905 04	.889 05	.872 06	.855 07	.838 07	.821 08	.804 09	.787 10	.769 10	.751 11	.733 12	.715 13	.697 13	.679 14	.660 15
.984 01	.967 01	.950 02	.933 03	.916 03	.899 04	.882 05	.865 05	.847 06	.830 07	.812 07	.794 08	.776 09	.758 09	.739 10	.721 11	.702 11	.684 12	.665 13	.646 13
.983 01	.965 01	.948 02	.930 02	.912 03	.894 03	.876 04	.858 05	.840 05	.822 06	.803 06	.785 07	.766 07	.748 08	.729 09	.710 09	.691 10	.672 10	.653 11	.633 12
.982 01	.964 01	.945 01	.927 02	.908 02	.890 03	.871 03	.853 04	.834 04	.815 05	.796 05	.777 06	.758 06	.739 07	.720 07	.701 08	.681 08	.662 09	.643 09	.623 10
.981 01	.962 01	.943 01	.924 02	.905 02	.886 02	.867 03	.848 03	.829 04	.810 04	.790 04	.771 05	.752 05	.732 05	.713 06	.693 06	.674 07	.654 07	.634 07	.615 08
.981 01	.961 01	.942 01	.923 01	.903 01	.884 02	.864 02	.845 02	.825 03	.805 03	.786 02	.766 03	.747 03	.727 04	.707 04	.687 05	.668 05	.648 05	.628 06	.608 06
.980 01	.961 01	.941 01	.921 01	.901 01	.882 01	.862 01	.842 02	.822 02	.802 02	.783 02	.763 02	.743 03	.723 03	.703 03	.683 03	.663 03	.644 04	.624 04	.604 04
.980 00	.960 00	.940 00	.920 00	.900 00	.880 01	.860 01	.841 01	.821 01	.801 01	.781 01	.761 01	.741 01	.721 01	.701 01	.681 02	.661 02	.641 02	.621 02	.601 02
.980 00	.960 00	.940 00	.920 00	.900 00	.880 00	.860 00	.840 00	.820 00	.800 00	.780 00	.760 00	.740 00	.720 00	.700 00	.680 00	.660 00	.640 00	.620 00	.600 00

FIG. 2159 Case 3—To find Course to be steered and Speed of Advance from knowledge of desired Track and Speed through the water, plus relative set and percent drift. This table yields Speed Factors (SF) and Course Corrections (CC) to be applied as shown in text.

In other words, the course correction is toward the current.

Again, three examples will be used to illustrate the application of the tabular factors; these will actually be the same situations as the previous examples, but with different known and unknown elements.

Example G. (Fig. 2160)

Known: Track = 054° True
Speed = 8 knots
Set = 324°
Drift = 3 knots

To be determined: Course and Speed of Advance

Solution: Relative set = 324° − 054° = 270°
$$-360°$$
$$-090°$$

Percent drift = $\dfrac{3 \times 100}{8} = 38$

From the table: CC = 22°
SF = 0.925

Thus: Course = 054° + 22° = 076°
Speed of Advance = 8 × 0.925
= 7.4 knots

FIG. 2160 Example G—a Case 3 problem: Track 054° True; Speed 8 knots; Set 324°, Drift 3 knots. Desired: Course and Speed of Advance. See text for solution by tabular factors of fig. 2159.

Example H. (Fig. 2161)

Known: Track = 341° True
Speed = 9 knots
Set = 021°
Drift = 2.5 knots

To be determined:
Course and Speed of Advance

Solution:
Relative set = 021° − 341° = −320°
$$+360°$$
$$+040°$$

Percent drift = $\dfrac{2.5 \times 100}{9} = 28$

From the table: CC = 10°
SF = 1.198

Thus: Course 341° − 10° = 331°
Speed of Advance = 9 × 1.198
= 10.8 knots

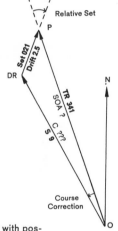

FIG. 2161 Example H—a Case 3 problem with positive relative set. Note that relative set is measured with respect to the desired Track.

Example I. (Fig. 2162)

Known: Track = 024° True
Speed = 10 knots
Set = 156°
Drift = 2 knots

To be determined:
Course and Speed of Advance

Solution:
Relative set = 156° − 024° = +132°

Percent drift = $\dfrac{2 \times 100}{10} = 20$

From the table: for 130°, CC = 9°, SF = .860
for 135°, CC = 8°, SF = .849
by interpolation, for 132°, CC = 9°, SF = .856

Thus: Course = 024° − 9° = 015°
Speed of Advance = 10 × 0.856
= 8.6 knots

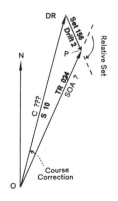

FIG. 2162 Example I—a Case 3 problem with desired Track 024° True; Speed 10 knots; Set 156°, Drift 2 knots. To be determined: Course to be steered and Speed of Advance.

445

DRIFT—in percent of speed of advance

Rel. Set	2 SF	2 CC	4 SF	4 CC	6 SF	6 CC	8 SF	8 CC	10 SF	10 CC	12 SF	12 CC	14 SF	14 CC	16 SF	16 CC	18 SF	18 CC
000	.980	00	.960	00	.940	00	.920	00	.900	00	.880	00	.860	00	.840	00	.820	00
005	.980	00	.960	00	.940	00	.920	00	.900	01	.881	01	.861	01	.841	01	.821	01
010	.980	00	.961	00	.941	01	.921	01	.902	01	.882	01	.862	02	.843	02	.823	02
015	.981	00	.961	01	.942	01	.923	01	.904	02	.885	02	.866	02	.846	03	.827	03
020	.981	00	.963	01	.944	01	.925	02	.907	02	.888	03	.870	03	.851	04	.833	04
025	.982	00	.964	01	.946	02	.928	02	.910	03	.893	03	.875	04	.858	05	.840	05
030	.983	01	.966	01	.949	02	.932	02	.915	03	.898	04	.882	05	.865	05	.849	06
035	.984	01	.968	01	.951	02	.936	03	.920	04	.904	04	.889	05	.874	06	.859	07
040	.985	01	.970	02	.955	02	.940	03	.926	04	.911	05	.897	06	.883	07	.870	08
045	.986	01	.972	02	.959	03	.945	03	.932	04	.919	05	.906	06	.894	07	.882	08
050	.987	01	.975	02	.963	03	.951	04	.939	05	.927	06	.916	07	.905	08	.895	09
055	.989	01	.978	02	.967	03	.956	04	.946	05	.936	06	.927	07	.918	08	.909	09
060	.990	01	.981	02	.971	03	.962	04	.954	05	.946	06	.938	07	.930	09	.923	10
065	.992	01	.984	02	.976	03	.969	04	.962	05	.955	07	.949	08	.944	09	.938	10
070	.993	01	.987	02	.981	03	.976	04	.970	06	.966	07	.961	08	.957	09	.954	10
075	.995	01	.990	02	.986	03	.982	05	.979	06	.976	07	.973	08	.971	09	.969	10
080	.997	01	.994	02	.991	03	.989	05	.988	06	.986	07	.985	08	.985	09	.985	10
085	.998	01	.997	02	.997	03	.996	05	.996	06	.997	07	.998	08	.999	09	1.001	10
090	1.000	01	1.001	02	1.002	03	1.003	05	1.005	06	1.007	07	1.010	08	1.013	09	1.016	10
095	1.002	01	1.004	02	1.007	03	1.010	05	1.014	06	1.018	07	1.022	08	1.026	09	1.031	10
100	1.004	01	1.008	02	1.012	03	1.017	04	1.022	06	1.028	07	1.034	08	1.040	09	1.046	10
105	1.005	01	1.011	02	1.017	03	1.024	04	1.030	05	1.038	06	1.045	07	1.053	08	1.061	09
110	1.007	01	1.014	02	1.022	03	1.030	04	1.038	05	1.047	06	1.056	07	1.065	08	1.075	09
115	1.009	01	1.018	02	1.027	03	1.036	04	1.046	05	1.056	06	1.067	07	1.077	08	1.088	09
120	1.010	01	1.021	02	1.031	03	1.042	04	1.054	05	1.065	06	1.077	06	1.089	07	1.101	08
125	1.012	01	1.023	02	1.036	03	1.048	04	1.061	04	1.073	05	1.086	06	1.100	07	1.113	08
130	1.013	01	1.026	02	1.040	03	1.053	03	1.067	04	1.081	05	1.095	06	1.110	06	1.124	07
135	1.014	01	1.029	02	1.043	02	1.058	03	1.073	04	1.088	04	1.103	05	1.119	06	1.134	06
140	1.015	01	1.031	01	1.047	02	1.063	03	1.079	03	1.095	04	1.111	05	1.127	05	1.144	06
145	1.016	01	1.033	01	1.050	02	1.067	02	1.083	03	1.100	04	1.118	04	1.135	05	1.152	05
150	1.017	01	1.035	01	1.052	02	1.070	02	1.088	03	1.106	03	1.123	04	1.141	04	1.159	04
155	1.018	00	1.036	01	1.055	01	1.073	02	1.091	02	1.110	03	1.128	03	1.147	03	1.166	04
160	1.019	00	1.038	01	1.057	01	1.076	01	1.095	02	1.114	02	1.133	02	1.152	03	1.171	03
165	1.019	00	1.039	01	1.058	01	1.077	01	1.097	01	1.116	02	1.136	02	1.155	02	1.175	02
170	1.020	00	1.039	00	1.059	01	1.079	01	1.099	01	1.118	01	1.138	01	1.158	01	1.178	02
175	1.020	00	1.040	00	1.060	00	1.080	00	1.100	00	1.120	01	1.140	01	1.159	01	1.179	01
180	1.020	00	1.040	00	1.060	00	1.080	00	1.100	00	1.120	00	1.140	00	1.160	00	1.180	00

Rel. Set	20 SF	20 CC	22 SF	22 CC	24 SF	24 CC	26 SF	26 CC	28 SF	28 CC	30 SF	30 CC	32 SF	32 CC	34 SF	34 CC	36 SF	36 CC	38 SF	38 CC
000	.800	00	.780	00	.760	00	.740	00	.720	00	.700	00	.680	00	.660	00	.640	00	.620	00
005	.801	01	.781	01	.761	02	.741	02	.721	02	.702	02	.682	02	.662	03	.642	03	.622	03
010	.804	02	.784	03	.765	03	.745	03	.726	04	.706	04	.687	05	.668	05	.648	06	.629	06
015	.808	04	.790	04	.771	05	.752	05	.733	06	.714	06	.696	07	.677	07	.659	08	.641	09
020	.815	05	.797	05	.779	06	.761	07	.743	07	.725	08	.708	09	.690	10	.673	11	.656	11
025	.823	06	.806	07	.789	07	.772	08	.756	09	.739	10	.723	11	.707	12	.691	13	.675	14
030	.833	07	.817	08	.801	09	.786	10	.770	10	.755	11	.740	12	.726	14	.711	15	.697	16
035	.844	08	.829	09	.815	10	.801	11	.787	12	.774	13	.760	14	.747	15	.735	16	.722	18
040	.856	09	.843	10	.831	11	.818	12	.806	13	.794	14	.782	15	.771	16	.760	18	.750	19
045	.870	09	.859	10	.847	12	.837	13	.826	14	.816	15	.806	16	.797	18	.788	19	.779	20
050	.885	10	.875	11	.865	12	.856	13	.848	15	.839	16	.831	17	.824	18	.817	20	.810	21
055	.900	10	.892	12	.884	13	.877	14	.870	15	.864	17	.858	18	.852	19	.847	20	.842	22
060	.917	11	.910	12	.904	13	.899	15	.894	16	.889	17	.885	18	.881	20	.877	21	.874	22
065	.933	11	.929	12	.925	14	.921	15	.917	16	.915	17	.912	19	.910	20	.908	21	.907	22
070	.950	11	.948	13	.945	14	.943	15	.942	16	.941	17	.940	19	.940	20	.940	21	.940	22
075	.968	12	.967	13	.966	14	.966	15	.966	16	.967	17	.968	19	.969	20	.971	21	.973	22
080	.985	12	.986	13	.987	14	.989	15	.991	16	.993	17	.996	18	.999	20	1.002	21	1.006	22
085	1.003	11	1.005	13	1.008	14	1.011	15	1.015	16	1.019	17	1.023	18	1.028	19	1.033	20	1.038	21
090	1.020	11	1.024	12	1.028	13	1.033	15	1.038	16	1.044	17	1.050	18	1.056	19	1.063	20	1.070	21
095	1.037	11	1.042	12	1.049	13	1.055	14	1.062	15	1.069	16	1.076	17	1.084	18	1.092	19	1.100	20
100	1.053	11	1.061	12	1.068	13	1.076	14	1.084	15	1.093	16	1.102	17	1.111	18	1.120	18	1.130	19
105	1.069	10	1.078	11	1.087	12	1.096	13	1.106	14	1.116	15	1.126	16	1.136	17	1.147	18	1.158	18
110	1.085	10	1.095	11	1.105	12	1.116	13	1.127	14	1.138	14	1.149	15	1.161	16	1.173	17	1.185	18
115	1.100	09	1.111	10	1.123	11	1.135	12	1.147	13	1.159	14	1.172	14	1.184	15	1.197	16	1.211	17
120	1.114	09	1.126	10	1.139	11	1.152	11	1.166	12	1.179	13	1.193	13	1.206	14	1.220	15	1.235	15
125	1.127	08	1.141	09	1.155	10	1.169	11	1.183	11	1.198	12	1.212	12	1.227	13	1.242	14	1.257	14
130	1.139	08	1.154	08	1.169	09	1.184	10	1.199	10	1.215	11	1.230	11	1.246	12	1.262	13	1.278	13
135	1.150	07	1.166	08	1.182	08	1.198	09	1.214	09	1.231	10	1.247	10	1.263	11	1.280	11	1.297	12
140	1.160	06	1.177	07	1.194	07	1.211	08	1.228	08	1.245	09	1.262	09	1.279	10	1.297	10	1.314	11
145	1.169	06	1.187	06	1.204	07	1.222	07	1.240	07	1.258	08	1.275	08	1.293	09	1.311	09	1.329	09
150	1.177	05	1.196	05	1.214	06	1.232	06	1.250	06	1.269	07	1.287	07	1.306	07	1.324	08	1.343	08
155	1.184	04	1.203	04	1.222	05	1.241	05	1.259	05	1.278	06	1.297	06	1.316	06	1.335	07	1.354	07
160	1.190	03	1.209	04	1.228	04	1.247	04	1.267	04	1.286	05	1.305	05	1.325	05	1.344	05	1.363	05
165	1.194	02	1.214	03	1.233	03	1.253	03	1.273	03	1.292	03	1.312	04	1.331	04	1.351	04	1.371	04
170	1.197	02	1.217	02	1.237	02	1.257	02	1.277	02	1.296	02	1.316	02	1.336	03	1.356	03	1.376	03
175	1.199	01	1.219	01	1.239	01	1.259	01	1.279	01	1.299	01	1.319	01	1.339	01	1.359	01	1.379	01
180	1.200	00	1.220	00	1.240	00	1.260	00	1.280	00	1.300	00	1.320	00	1.340	00	1.360	00	1.380	00

RELATIVE SET—000 TO 180

FIG. 2163 Tabulation of Speed Factors (SF) and Course Corrections (CC) for the solution of Case 4 current sailing problems. Be careful to use the proper set of tabular factors for a Case 1, 3, or 4 problem; there is a separate table for each Case.

It might be supposed that the course corrections and speed factors above would be the same as those found in the preceding table and used in the examples for Case 1, but a careful comparison of the tables will reveal that this is not so. To illustrate, let us suppose that the drift is 20 percent and the relative set is 90°. Using the table of fig. 2154 for Case 1, we find that the current sets us off course by 11°. From the table of fig. 2159, however, we find that we must alter course 12° to compensate for the same current situation.

Also, when the course is not corrected, the speed factor is 1.020, which means that our speed of advance is two percent greater than our speed through the water (but, of course, it isn't getting us where we want to be). If, as in Case 3, we do "crab" into the current by the required 12°, the speed factor is 0.980, meaning that our actual speed of advance is two percent less than our speed through the water. Obviously, the two cases, and their respective tabulated factors, are different.

Case 4 solutions by tabular factors

This is a variation of Case 3 in which the pilot knows both where he wants to go and when he desires to arrive. Thus he has a desired track (TR) and speed of advance (SOA) in addition to the known or estimated set and drift of the current. He needs to determine *the course to be steered (C) and the necessary speed through the water (S).*

Fig. 2163 enables the pilot to determine these desired quantities without the construction of a vector diagram. Instead, he uses another set of course corrections (CC) and speed factors (SF). These factors are not the same as in either of the preceding tables and must be used for Case 4 problems only.

The speed to be run through the water (S) is determined by multiplying the desired speed of advance (SOA) by the tabular factor SF. The course to be steered is found by adding the correction angle CC to, or subtracting it from, the track (TR) in the same manner as for Case 3.

Course to be steered (C)

= TR − CC, when the relative set is positive.

= TR + CC, when the relative set is negative.

The same basic examples as before will be used, but again with different combinations of known and unknown elements.

Example J. (Fig. 2164)

Known: Track = 054° True
SOA = 7.4 knots
Set = 324°
Drift = 3 knots

To be determined: Course and Speed

Solution: Relative set = 324° − 054° = 270°
−360°
−090°

Percent drift = $\frac{3 \times 100}{7.4} = 40$

From the table: CC = 22°
SF = 1.077

Thus: Course = 054° + 22° = 076°
Speed = 7.4 x 1.077 = 8 knots

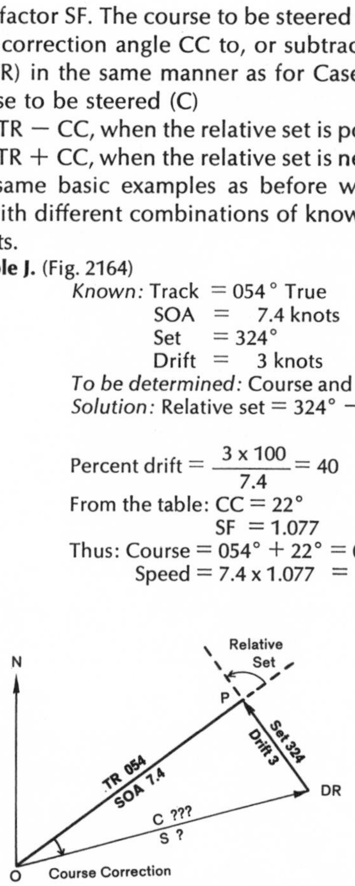

FIG. 2164 Example J—a Case 4 problem: Track 054° True, Speed of Advance 7.4 knots; Set 324°, Drift 3 knots. To be found: Course to be steered and Speed to be run through the water. See text for solution by tabular factors of fig. 2163.

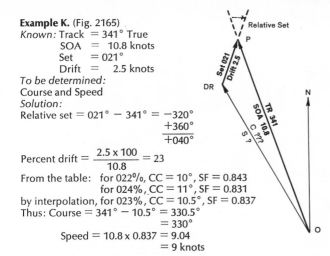

Example K. (Fig. 2165)
Known: Track = 341° True
SOA = 10.8 knots
Set = 021°
Drift = 2.5 knots
To be determined:
Course and Speed
Solution:
Relative set = 021° − 341° = −320°
$$+360°$$
$$+040°$$

Percent drift = $\dfrac{2.5 \times 100}{10.8} = 23$

From the table: for 022%, CC = 10°, SF = 0.843
for 024%, CC = 11°, SF = 0.831
by interpolation, for 023%, CC = 10.5°, SF = 0.837
Thus: Course = 341° − 10.5° = 330.5°
= 330°

Speed = 10.8 × 0.837 = 9.04
= 9 knots

FIG. 2165 Example K—a Case 4 problem in which both the Track and Speed of Advance are specified. The Course to be steered and the Speed to be run through the water are the values to be found by the application of tabulated course correction and speed factor.

FIG. 2166 Example L—a Case 4 problem to be solved by use of the factors from fig. 2163. Given: Track 024° True, Speed of Advance 8.6 knots; Set 156°, Drift 2 knots. To be found: Course and Speed.

Example L. (Fig. 2166)
Known: Track = 024° True
SOA = 8.6 knots
Set = 156°
Drift = 2 knots
To be determined:
Course and Speed
Solution:
Relative set = 156° − 024° = +132°

Percent drift = $\dfrac{2 \times 100}{8.6} = 23$

From the table, by double interpolation,
for 132°/23% : CC = 8.3°
SF = 1.167
Thus: Course = 024° − 8.3° = 015.3°
= 015°

Speed = 8.6 × 1.167 = 10 knots

PILOTING IN CURRENTS: GENERAL RESUME OF THE THREE CASES

		CASE 1	CASE 3	CASE 4
KNOWN: Set and Drift, plus		Course	Track	Track
		Speed Through Water	Speed Through Water	Speed of Advance
DESIRED:		Speed of Advance	Speed of Advance	Speed Through Water
		Track	Course	Course
Calculate Before Using Table	% Drift	$\dfrac{\text{Drift} \times 100}{\text{Speed Through Water}}$	$\dfrac{\text{Drift} \times 100}{\text{Speed Through Water}}$	$\dfrac{\text{Drift} \times 100}{\text{Speed of Advance}}$
	Relative Set	SET−COURSE (180° or less to port or starboard)	SET−TRACK (180° or less to port or starboard)	SET−TRACK (180° or less to port or starboard)
Read from table, interpolating, if necessary	SF	Speed factor	Speed factor	Speed factor
	CC	Course Change	Course Correction	Course Correction
ANSWERS		Speed of Advance = (Speed through water) X SF	Speed of Advance = (Speed through water) X SF	Speed Through Water = (Speed of Advance) X SF
	If Rel. Set is positive (to St'bd.)	TRACK = COURSE + CC	COURSE = TRACK − CC	COURSE = TRACK − CC
	If Rel. Set is negative (to Port)	TRACK = COURSE − CC	COURSE = TRACK + CC	COURSE = TRACK + CC

Summary of tabular factor solutions

Fig. 2167 is a consolidated presentation of the procedures used in the solution of current sailing problems using tabulated factors of course and speed corrections. The numbering of the cases corresponds to the basic presentation of current problems in Chapter 20 and the examples above.

In all of the cases presented here, the set and drift of the current were considered to be known values, as determined from the Tidal Current Tables or Charts, or from visual observations. Thus, Case 2 of the current sailing problems—the determination of the characteristics of an unknown current from the measurement of its effects—is omitted from this tabular technique.

FIG. 2167 Summary of the procedures for the solution of certain current sailing problems by the use of pre-computed factors and corrections.

Specialized Positioning Procedures

In addition to the generally used procedures for position determination previously described in this chapter, there are other, more specialized, techniques. These should not be scorned as "short cuts"; they will provide valid position information and fixes under the particular circumstances that permit their use.

COMBINATIONS OF RELATIVE BEARINGS

The bow-and-beam-bearings technique has already been described, fig. 2140. This was a particular set of two relative bearings, 045° and 090° (or 315° and 270°). It was included there because of its basic simplicity and the ease with which such a pair of bearings could be obtained. There are other combinations of relative bearings, not so easily obtained, but quite easily used.

Special pairs of bearings

The following sets of bearings have such a relationship to each other that the run between the first bearing and the second will nearly equal the distance away from the sighted object when it is passed abeam:

20°-30°, 21°-32°, 22°-34°, 23°-36°, 24°-39°, 25°-41°, 27°-46°, 29°-51°, 30°-54°, 31°-56°, 32°-59°, 34°-64°, 35°-67°, 36°-69°, 37°-71°, 38°-74°, 39°-77°, 40°-79°, 41°-81°, 43°-86°, 44°-88°.

There are also additional pairs of angles that could theoretically be used, but these involve half-degrees and have been omitted here as such precision is not usually obtainable on small craft.

It should be noted that these are pairs of relative bearings to port as well as to starboard. In the table above, "20°-30°" can be either relative bearings 020° and 030°, or 340° and 330°; "31°-56°" can be either RB 031° and 056°, or RB 329° and 304°; etc.

The 7/8th rule

If observations are made when the relative bearings are 30° and 60° on either bow, simple calculations will give *two* useful items of information. The distance run between the two bearings is equal to the distance to the object at the time of the second bearing (doubling the angle on the bow). Also, this same distance, fig. 2168, multiplied by $^7/_8$ is the distance that the craft will be off from the sighted object when it is broad on the beam, provided that course and speed are not changed.

The 7/10th rule

A situation comparable to the preceding rule is that which exists when the two relative bearings are $22^1/_2°$ and 45° to port or starboard (assuming that bearings can be taken to a half-degree). In this case, as before, the distance away from the sighted object at the time of the second bearing is equal to the distance run between bearings, but the multiplier is 7/10 to determine the distance off the sighted object when it is abeam.

THREE BEARINGS AND RUN BETWEEN

The technique of using *two* bearings and the run between them was illustrated in fig. 2142. The positional information derived from this procedure was dependent upon the assumption that the course and speed made good with respect to the bottom during the run between bearings was accurately known. Along strange coasts, without current predictions or means of estimating current effects, this assumption is often of doubtful validity.

By taking a *third* bearing and timing a second run (between the second and third bearings), enough additional known factors are entered into the problem so that no assumption need be made about the course made good nor the actual speed over the bottom. All that is required for this technique is a prominent object or mark on shore, plus the means for taking bearings and measuring time intervals.

As soon as you spot the object, "X" in fig. 2169, take a bearing on it and note the exact time; record both items of information. Plot the bearing line on your chart, line XA in fig. 2169(a). Next, when the object is exactly broad on the beam, note the time. Plot this line of position on the chart. Later, when the bearing to X has changed enough to give a good angle of intersection, take a third bearing and again note the time carefully. Plot this line, XC. Be sure that throughout this procedure you are maintaining a steady course and speed through the water.

Since you have recorded the time of each bearing, you can determine the two elapsed times, and compute the *ratio* between these intervals.

For example, if you ran for $32^1/_2$ minutes between the first and second (beam) bearings, and then for $22^1/_2$ minutes more to the third bearing, the ratio would be $32^1/_2/22^1/_2$, which can be reduced to 6.5/4.5.

Through a convenient point, B, on the beam bearing line, draw a light "construction" line in the direction of your course (C) as steered. Using point "B" as the reference or zero point, measure off to each side, along the construction line, distances proportional to the ratio of the time intervals using any convenient scale, fig. 2169(b).

Erect perpendiculars to the construction line at the spots determined by these proportionate distances. These lines, drawn at 90° angles to the construction line, intersect the bearing lines XA and XC at points A' and C' respectively, fig. 2169(c).

Connect points A' and C' with a line and you have your answer. Line A'-C' is the course you are making good and

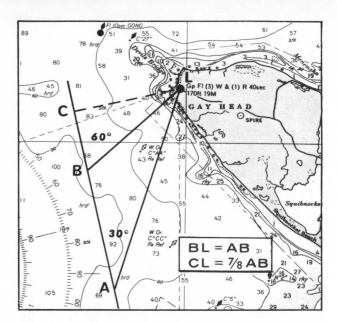

FIG. 2168 If observations are made when the relative bearings of a fixed object are 30° and 60°, and the distance made good between these observations is calculated, the pilot can determine his distance from the object both at the time of the second bearing and when it is abeam by the "$^7/_8$th Rule."

includes the effects of currents, wind, and errors in steering. Its direction may be taken from the chart and compared with the intended course. It should be noted that this is *not the actual track*—the selection of the scale to represent the two time intervals would determine the location of points A' and C', and hence the line's location, although not its direction.

It is because *ratios* are used, and not actual speeds, that an accurate speed over the bottom is not needed here as it was in the case of the technique of *two* bearings and run between. Although it does not allow the navigator to determine his position nor his speed over the bottom, this technique does show plainly whether he is making good his intended course, or is being set onto or off the shore; it helps determine whether the actual track parallels the beach or not.

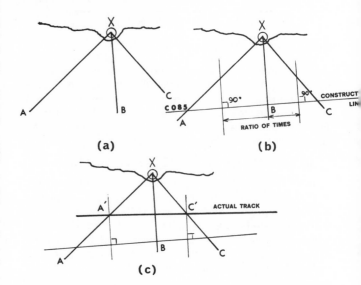

FIG. 2169 The actual track of a boat under unknown conditions of current can be determined by taking three bearings on a single object. See text for details of this technique.

Relative Motion

The easiest way to acquire what is often called a "sailor's eye" is to learn the simple, but basic, principles of *relative motion*. The term "relative motion" scares some people, but it is really quite a simple subject to master. It is also one of the most useful skills that a boatman can acquire as it gives quick and accurate answers to problems involving moving vessels.

For example, you find that your motorboat is converging on another boat that has the right of way. If you hold your present course and speed, will you clear her? Or your sailboat is beating to windward on a port tack, and you find a boat coming in on the starboard tack. Will you cross safely ahead, or must you pass astern? Or you have laid a course for a buoy, making allowance for the current. Have you made the right allowance? Relative motion will give you the answers to all such questions.

When a boat is under way, its movement across the water is termed *actual motion*. If it is anchored, the movements of another craft appear in their actual relationship to the earth's surface; you are observing that boat's actual motion. But if you get under way, the movement of the other boat appears to be different because you are now observing *relative motion*. Some objects, especially moving ones, seem to be doing things that are not actually happening; elements of what may be almost an optical illusion can exist.

Let us suppose that you are under way and proceeding north at 5 knots up a marked channel. You sight another boat coming directly toward you; this other craft is also making 5 knots. The two boats are converging at a *relative speed* of 10 knots which is simply the sum of your speed and his. Both craft are passing the stationary channel markers at the same actual speed, but the distance between them is lessening at a rate which is the sum of the individual speeds.

As the other boat approaches, you recognize the skipper as a friend and turn around to join him on his southerly course. As soon as the boats are alongside each other on the same course and at the same speed, *relative motion* ceases to exist because the other boat stays in the same place relative to your boat. Only *actual motion* remains—that of your boat past the buoys and over the bottom. If the other craft develops engine trouble and slows down, there is again relative motion between the two vessels. He will appear to be moving aft because of his reduced speed. Thus, the rule may be stated as follows: *relative motion is present only when the actual movements of two or more objects are not the same.*

Relative bearings

The bearing of an object is usually taken as a relative bearing; these were discussed in pages 352a, b. See fig. 2170. With practice, the relative bearing of an object can be estimated within five or ten degrees. It must be remembered that a change in course of your own boat will change the relative bearings of all objects around it. Thus, if you are on a course of 050° True and sight an object bearing 090° relative, the true bearing of that object will be 140°, fig. 2171a. Come left to a course of 020°, and although the true bearing will remain unchanged at 140°, the rela-

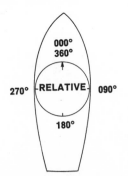

FIG. 2170 In determining relative motion in small-craft piloting, much use is made of relative bearings measured clockwise from 000° dead ahead.

tive bearing will now become 120°, fig. 2171b.

In small craft piloting, approximations will usually suffice in relative motion problems and special instruments are not needed. A steady hand at the wheel or tiller, a clear eye, and a rough mental diagram are all that are needed. A pelorus can be used, but seldom is, in actual practice.

TO CROSS OR NOT TO CROSS

When determining the relative motion of another boat, it is necessary either to convert relative bearings to compass (or true) bearings, or to maintain a steady course. In practice, it is easier to maintain a steady course, with the result that any change in relative bearing will be the result of a change in the positions of the boats relative to each other, rather than the result of the changing course of your craft. Since the desired information is the changing positions of the boats relative to each other, the actual value of the relative bearing is of far less importance than the direction and rate of change, if any.

Collision bearings

What we want to know in any crossing or converging situation is: will we cross ahead of, or astern of, the other boat, or will we hit her? Because the two boats are considered relative to each other, it is convenient to think of one's own boat as stationary—relative to the other boat. Thus, we have three basic situations:

1. The relative bearing of the other boat moves ahead (toward the bow), or
2. The relative bearing of the other boat moves aft, or
3. The relative bearing of the other boat remains constant.

Fig. 2172a illustrates the first situation, that of a boat passing ahead. This illustration indicates the actual successive positions of the two boats. Fig. 2172b represents

FIG. 2171 If a boat's heading changes, the relative bearing of an object is changed by the same amount. From the situation in *a* below to that in *b*, the true heading of the boat has changed from 050° to 020°; the relative bearing has changed by the same amount, from 090° to 120°. (Note that the sum of the heading and the relative bearing remains constant.)

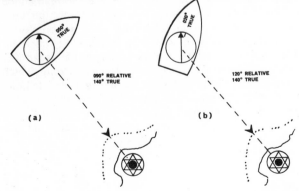

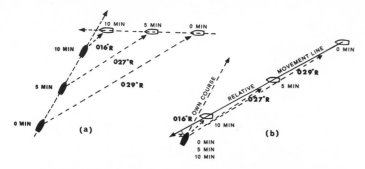

FIG. 2172 The positions of two boats are shown for three intervals of time separated by five minutes each. In *a*, the actual positions of each craft are shown. In *b*, the motion of the other boat is shown *relative* to our craft. In both cases, the relative bearings move forward on our boat and the other craft will cross ahead of us. The distance *x* is the separation at the *point of closest approach*.

the same situation shown in terms of motion relative to our own boat as stationary. The bearing change is then more clearly seen.

The line connecting the positions of the other boat in fig. 2172b is the *line of relative movement,* the relative course and relative distance traveled by the other boat in relationship to our boat. Provided both boats maintain course and speed, it is a straight line. In this situation, when the line of relative motion is extended, it passes the bow of our "stationary" boat; therefore, the other boat following that line relative to us will cross ahead. The distance "*x*" fig. 2172b is the distance apart that the two boats will be at the *closest point of approach* (CPA).

The second case, in which the relative bearing moves aft, is the opposite of the first situation. The relative mo-

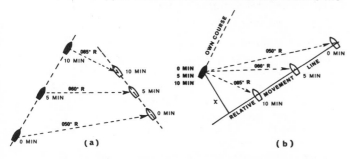

FIG. 2173 In this crossing situation, the relative bearings move aft, and the other boat will pass astern of us (we will pass ahead of her). The actual successive positions of each craft are shown in *a*, and relative motion is shown in *b*.

tion line passes astern, and so will the other boat. Figs. 2173a and b illustrate this situation.

If the relative bearing does not change, the line of relative motion will pass through our boat's position, the distance "*x*" is zero, and the two boats will collide unless one or both changes course or speed. See figs. 2174a and b.

It is important to note that figs. 2172-2174 are intended to illustrate situations rather than actual chart plots on a boat. The position of the other craft could not be plotted unless distance as well as bearing information was available, and this is unlikely unless your boat has radar. The significance here is that *bearing information only*, which is available to any pilot, will by its change, if any, tell him whether he will pass ahead, astern, or "through" the other craft. The closest point of approach can be determined only if an actual plot based on distances is made, but lack of this information is not significant.

Rules for crossing situations

The foregoing discussion, formulated into rules, results in the following procedures for a crossing situation:

1. Maintain a reasonably steady course and speed.
2. Observe the relative bearing of the other boat only when you are on your specified compass course. You must be on the *same* course each time you take a relative bearing.
3. Watch the other boat for changes in course or speed which would obviously upset the relative motion conditions.
4. (a) If the relative bearing moves ahead, the other boat will pass ahead.
   (b) If the relative bearing moves aft, the other craft will pass astern.
   (c) If the relative bearing is steady, there is a dangerous possibility of collision.

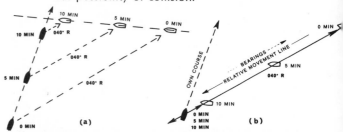

FIG. 2174 Here is a crossing situation in which the relative bearing does *not* change! A collision will result if both craft maintain course and speed. Note that in *b* the line of relative movement passes *through* our boat and the value of *x* is reduced to zero.

Offsetting effects of current or wind

There is another useful application of relative motion in the case of allowances for offsetting the effects of current and/or wind.

In fig. 2175, the boat has been put on a course that her skipper believes will put her close aboard the buoy marking the shoal. At the time of the first bearing, "0" minutes, the buoy bears 340° relative. Five minutes later, the relative bearing has changed to 350°. It is clear from this change that the boat is being set down more than expected and that the relative movement line of the buoy will pass ahead of the boat, i.e., the boat will pass on the shoal side of the buoy. If the bearings on the buoy remained steady, the boat would pass close to it; and if the bearings shifted gradually away from the bow, the skipper would know that he would clear the shoal safely.

In fig. 2175a, the problem is shown in terms of the boat moving relative to the buoy. In fig. 2175b, the boat is considered to be stationary and the relative movement line is that of the buoy. Note that the relative movement lines in the two representations are parallel, equal, and opposite.

FIG. 2175 Relative motion considerations are also applicable when the other "craft" is stationary, such as a buoy. The change, if any, of the relative bearings on the object can be used to determine on which side of it you will pass. In *a* and *b* below, the motion is considered relative to the buoy and to your boat, respectively.

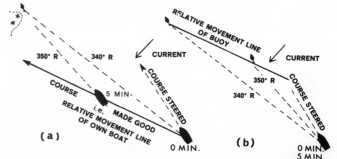

The Maneuvering Board

Since 1920, the U.S. Naval Oceanographic Office (formerly the Hydrographic Office) has published a plotting sheet known as the *Maneuvering Board* (now N.O. 5090, or 5091 with larger sheets). maritime services for the solution of relative motion problems. Complicated movements of large task forces, as well as the tracking of a single ship, are plotted on maneuvering boards to facilitate the solution of problems of interception and the determination of the course and speed of radar contacts.

Use on boats

Here we will consider a few of the simpler, though useful, applications of the maneuvering board, using only the plotting sheet, parallel rulers or equivalent, and a pair of dividers. For the fortunate yachtsman who has radar aboard, however, the applications are increased ten-fold.

Description of the sheet

To observe the physical appearance of a maneuvering board, examine fig. 2176 which shows one reduced about 40% from its original size of approximately 12 inches square. On it is printed, in green, a large circle with bearing lines radiating outward from the center every 10 degrees, and 10 concentric circles ½ inch apart to indicate speed or distance. At the right and left sides are lines of scale with numbered marks spaced equal to the distance between the concentric circles. Thus, a speed line drawn out to the fifth circle could indicate 5, 10, 15, 20, or 25 knots as determined by your choice of scale.

At the bottom of the sheet are three lines divided into logarithmic scales for use in solving time, distance, and speed problems. If two of these quantities are known, the third may be found by drawing a line between the known values on the appropriate scales, and finding the answer at the intersection of this line with the third scale.

In fig. 2177, observe the solution to three problems: (1) if you run 6 miles in 30 minutes, your speed is 12 knots; (2) to run 6 miles at 12 knots will require 30 minutes; or (3) running at 12 knots for 30 minutes, you will cover 6 miles. Distance, time, speed—knowing two, you can quickly, easily, and accurately solve for the third. This alone makes the maneuvering board a handy device, but it is only a small sample of its usefulness.

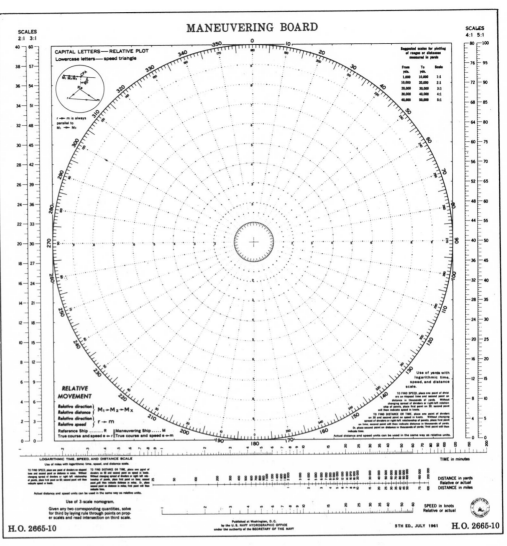

FIG. 2176 The U.S. Navy-Oceanographic Office (formerly the Hydrographic Office) publishes pads of a useful plotting sheet known as a *maneuvering board*. These sheets are particularly handy when plotting situations or relative motion.

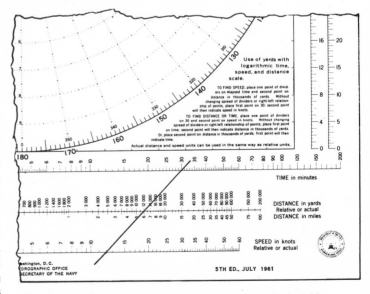

FIG. 2177 Extract from a maneuvering board showing the logarithmic distance-time-speed scales. The problem illustrated by the line drawn across the scales is discussed in the text.

451

The bearing lines and circles of distance facilitate the plotting of positions of other craft or objects relative to the boat on which the maneuvering board is being used. These radial lines and concentric circles can also be used for vector diagrams with lines drawn to represent actual and relative motion. Each vector, according to its length and direction, depicts a statement of fact in the problem. For example: a vector line to indicate a course of 040° and a speed of 5 knots would be drawn outward along the 40° bearing line to a length of 5 units, i.e., to the fifth circle. If the speed is greater than 10 units (knots or MPH), use is made of the 2:1, 3:1, 4:1, or 5:1 scales at the sides of the chart.

A vector line indicates graphically the direction and velocity of an element of the problem, such as the course and speed of your boat, another boat, the wind, or the current. In some instances, the vector will not be drawn from the center of the sheet, but its direction is always measured with reference to the center point and the outer circular scale.

Points on diagrams of positions are labeled with upper-case (capital) letters; points on vector diagrams are labeled with lower-case letters.

Maneuvering boards come in pads of 50 sheets. Each sheet is printed on both sides, and the paper is sufficiently heavy that both sides may be used. Both N.O. 5090 and N.O. 5091 include condensed instructions in each of the four corners, outside the circular scale. The pad comes with a cover sheet on which is printed a "sample problem" but this, unfortunately, is a problem of interest to naval task force commanders, not boatmen.

USE OF THE MANEUVERING BOARD

N.O. 5090 or 5091 sheets may be used for plots of the relative motion of two vessels in a crossing situation as shown in figs. 2172-2174. These sheets are particularly useful on board radar-equipped craft where distance as well as bearing can be measured. Fig. 2178, for example, is a re-plot of fig. 2173b on a maneuvering board sheet.

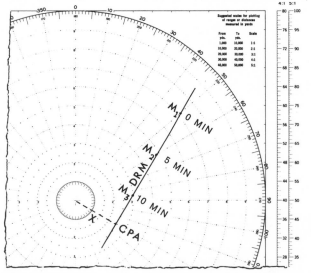

FIG. 2178 This is a re-plot of the situation of fig. 2173b on a Maneuvering Board sheet. Note that the plot has been rotated so that the direction of one's own boat is toward the top of the sheet (RB 000° dead ahead). The direction of relative motion (DRM) can be readily taken from the sheet, and the point of closest approach (CPA) and "miss distance" easily determined.

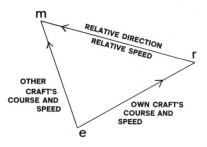

FIG. 2179 A vector triangle of relative motion. The course and speed of your own craft is plotted as e-r and the apparent (relative) motion of the other craft as r-m. The triangle can be closed with the line e-m which is the *actual* course and speed of the other craft.

From a plot such as fig. 2178, with successive relative positions of the other craft plotted at recorded times, the direction of relative movement (DRM) and speed of relative movement (SRM) can be found. SRM is determined from the logarithmic scales at the bottom of the sheet using distance and time as the known factors. Knowing these relative motion quantities, and the course and speed of your own boat, a *vector triangle* can be used to determine the *actual* course and speed of the other craft. The relationships between these quantities are shown in fig. 2179. Point e, always at the center of the maneuvering board, represents earth, the reference for actual motion. Point r is the outer end of the speed vector, e-r, for the reference craft (your boat). The vector r-m represents the relative motion of the maneuvering (other) craft. By completing the triangle with the vector e-m, always outward from the point e at the center, the actual course and speed of the other boat are found. When such a vector triangle is drawn on a maneuvering board sheet, as in fig. 2180, the actual course can be read directly from the outer circular scale, and the actual speed can be read from the convenient concentric circles of the sheet, remembering to apply the same scale factor as used in plotting the speed of your own boat.

True wind problem

Fig. 2181 illustrates what is called a *true wind problem*.

Situation: Your sailboat is close-hauled on true course 080°, speed 5 knots. The apparent (relative) wind is coming over the starboard side from 125° true with a velocity of 15 knots.

Problem: You want to sail your boat as close to the wind as possible, say at an angle of 45° off the true wind. You wish to know the direction and velocity of the *actual* wind so as to be able to determine whether you can lay the mark on the next tack, and the best course that you will be able to make to windward.

Solution: Draw your course and speed vector, e-r, along the bearing line for 080° outward from the center for 2½ circles (5 knots at a scale of 2:1). From point r, draw a line for the relative wind in the direction *toward* which the wind is traveling; use parallel rulers or another plotting instrument to transfer this direction from the bearing line out to the point r. With dividers, measure off the length for 15 knots along the 2:1 scale at the left side of the chart; lay off this distance along the relative wind line and so obtain the vector for that element of the problem. Where this vector ends is point w.

Next, draw a line from point e at the center to point w;

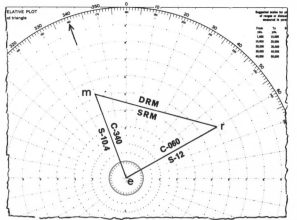

FIG. 2180 This is a re-plot of the preceding illustration on a Maneuvering Board sheet. The actual course of the other craft can be read directly from the outer scale of figures and the speed from the concentric rings; note that in this example the speed ratio is 2:1, each circle represents 2 knots or MPH.

this vector, e-w, represents the direction and velocity of the *true wind*. Since wind direction is never expressed in terms of where it is going (blowing toward), we look directly across the board and see that it is blowing *from* 142°. The velocity of 12 knots is read directly from the circles, the sixth circle at a scale of 2:1. Now it can be seen that the motion of your boat through the water has caused the apparent wind to come from a direction 17° counterclockwise from its true direction. (The actual wind velocity is seen to be less than the apparent velocity, but this information is not pertinent to this particular problem.)

To determine our course for sailing at an angle of 45° to the actual wind on the next, port, tack, it is merely a matter of adding 45° to the true wind direction of 142° to get 187°.

Current sailing problems

One problem common to both sail boats and motor boats is that of choosing the correct course in traversing an area where the current will set the craft off her intended track if allowances are not made. In fig. 2182 we have the graphic solution of two questions. What is the current doing? What course do we take to correct for it?

Assume that your boat is on course 320° at a speed of 6 knots to pass close aboard a light vessel that now, at 0800, is dead ahead, 9 miles distant. As you progress through the water on your specified course, you notice that the light vessel appears to be moving to your left. This indicates that a current is at work on your port side.

To learn the set and drift of the current, and the course needed to correct for it: Plot the 0800 position of the light vessel from you—320°, 9 miles. Fix your present position and determine from the chart the new relative position of the light vessel. In fig. 2182 this is 310° and 7 miles; label this position with the time, 0829.

Now, draw in your boat's course and speed vector, e-r, of 320° and 6 knots, using a 2:1 scale ratio and the third circle. Note that the same scale ratio does not have to be used for both distance and speeds; it must, however, be constant within either category.

With parallel rulers or other plotting instrument, transfer the direction of the line of relative movement between the two plots of the light vessel's position to point r and draw in a line to some convenient length. After measuring the distance "traveled" by the light vessel, solve for its relative speed using the distance-time-speed logarithmic

scales. In this case, 2.4 miles in 29 minutes gives 5.2 knots.

Using the speed scale factor of 2:1, the speed of 5.2 knots is laid off along the line drawn from r. The point so found is labeled m and a line drawn *from m to e* at the center represents the set and drift of the current. This is found to be 080° and 3 knots.

With this information, we can now determine a new course to correct for the effect of the current. Remembering that our vessel *never* leaves the center of the maneuvering board, we must make the light vessel "come to us." A line drawn from the 0829 position of the light vessel, the broken line in fig. 2182, is the line that we wish the light vessel to follow on its way to us.

Parallel a line to this, starting at a convenient distance out, beyond the third circle (6 knots at our 2:1 speed scale), and draw toward point m in the same direction as the intended track of the light vessel; this is line a-m in the illustration. Where this relative movement line crosses the third circle is the course to steer for a speed of 6 knots —287°. It should be noted that there are many possible

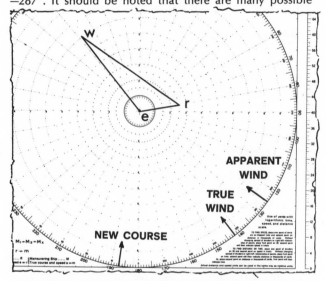

FIG. 2181 The maneuvering board can be used to determine the velocity and direction of the true wind to aid in setting a new course on the next tack. See the text for details of this technique.

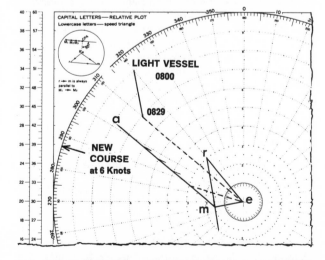

FIG. 2182 In this problem, a maneuvering board sheet enables the pilot to determine the current setting the boat off the desired track. It is also possible to graphically determine the necessary new course to be steered for any given speed.

combinations of courses and speeds available along this line, and that any increase in speed would bring a lesser course change, and vice versa. For example: looking out along the line *a-m*, we would find that for 8 knots, the course would be 293°; for 10 knots, 297°; for 12 knots, 299°.

Other uses for the maneuvering board

The examples above have barely touched on the many uses of the maneuvering board sheets. There are many more applications—all interesting, but of lesser direct use in small-craft boating. Those interested in this topic in more detail can satisfy their curiosity in the many pages of *Bowditch* and *Dutton* devoted to the maneuvering board and its uses.

A pad of N.O. 5090 or 5091 maneuvering boards may be obtained almost anywhere that Oceanographic Office publications are sold. The cost is only a few cents for each sheet, a small price to pay for safety and interesting, easy piloting!

Longshore Piloting

There are a number of specialized techniques that might well be a part of every skipper's piloting skills. Their practicability has been thoroughly tested.

DELIBERATE OFFSET OF COURSE

One of these specialized piloting techniques is used in making a landfall. The essence of it is this—lay your course, *not* for your objective, but decidedly to one side to allow for possible inaccuracies in the offsetting effect of the current, or to account for possible uncertainties of position. The advantage of this procedure lies in the fact that should you not arrive at your destination at the scheduled time, you have a near-certainty, rather than considerable doubt, as to which way you should turn to reach your objective.

The technique is best explained by use of an example.

Situation

Let us assume that you have been fishing somewhere in the area between Block Island and Martha's Vineyard. After several hours of trolling, drifting, and just circling around, your position is quite problematical. Just as you decide that your fishing luck has run out for the day and it is time to head for Block Island Harbor, fog sets in to make the situation more interesting.

Your best "guesstimate," in the absence of any positional information, is that you are somewhere to the east of bell buoy "1", marked as point *B* in fig. 2183; you believe that you are somewhere in the vicinity of point *A* on the chart.

Solution with deliberate offset of course

It's a good plan to lay your course for the off-lying bell buoy—as a matter of fact, that's what they are there for—but even if there were no such buoy, there can be merit in laying the course decidedly off to one side of the ultimate objective, Block Island Harbor.

Suppose you lay your course AB to the bell buoy and miss it by 1/8 mile to the north. When you pick up the 3-fathom (18-foot) curve, at *C*, you know you are north of

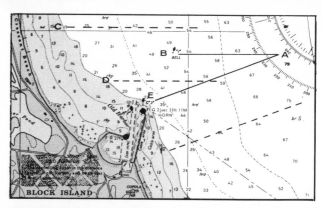

FIG. 2183 If you are caught in a fog somewhere offshore in the vicinity of point A, the inclination might be to head directly for the harbor entrance at E. It is much safer, however, to deliberately head for a point more to the north on a course that will take you past the bell buoy at B. The text explains why.

the harbor—a fact confirmed by the realization that you would have picked it up much sooner if you were south of the harbor entrance.

Had you missed it by 1/8 mile to the south, and picked up the 3-fathom curve at *D*, you could still follow the curve southeastward to buoy *C* "3". Even if your position were 1/4 mile south of *A* when you laid your course westward, you would still pick up the 3-fathom curve at the harbor entrance.

You find added assurance of your general position above the harbor entrance when you find depths holding generally at 3 fathoms on your course southeastward. If your calculations were completely wrong and you ran southeastward from any point below the harbor entrance, depths would increase.

Solution without deliberate offset of course

Consider, however, what could happen if you missed your objective E by 1/4 mile to the south if the course had been laid direct to buoy *C* "3". Picking up the 3-fathom curve at F, you could not be sure whether you were north or south of the entrance.

Your first conclusion might be that, since you have run a few minutes overtime before reaching the 3-fathom curve, you are north of the harbor. But don't forget that you didn't accurately know your starting point. Suppose you had been several minutes eastward of where you thought you were when the fog set in. In this event, the additional few minutes running time before reaching 18-foot depths is reasonable.

On the assumption that you are indeed somewhat to the north of the harbor, you turn south, proceeding slowly and carefully. A few minutes pass, but still no buoy or harbor entrance. How far to continue? That buoy may be just ahead, obscured by the fog. On the other hand, doubt creeps in. You couldn't have been that far off in your reckoning—or could you? So there you are, in a fog—literally and figuratively.

General procedures

In the first example above (where we laid a course for the bell) the intended track was laid about 3/8 mile to the north of the objective (the harbor entrance). How much deliberate offset of course is made in any given case varies within limits determined by what you feel would be a maximum error under the circumstances. On a long run in from offshore, making a landfall on a beach that trends in a straight line for miles in either direction with few marks of identification even if visibility is good, you may prefer to make an allowance of a mile or more. It adds little to the total run, but eliminates much uncertainty. But don't use this technique blindly, without regard to possible dangers that may line the beach. Study the chart carefully and adapt the procedure to the situation at hand.

Crossing the Gulf Stream

This same procedure may be used in crossing the Gulf Stream. Rather than attempting to make an exact allowance for the distance you will be set northward, a somewhat overly-generous allowance is made, with the knowledge that if you don't pick up your target landmark after the allotted passage time, you have only to turn northward. It can be comforting to know the proper direction in which to turn, rather than to have to make a choice with perhaps a 50-50 chance of being wrong.

The same technique can be used in recrossing the Gulf Stream on your westward passage back to Florida. Again, over-allow for the northward offsetting influence of the Stream and plan to turn northward as you approach the coast if you see no identifiable landmarks.

NIGHT PILOTING BY TIMETABLE

Another specialized piloting technique that will go far toward increasing the pleasure of nighttime piloting is the establishment of a "timetable" for your particular cruise.

Preparing the timetable

When you anticipate a night run, don't wait until you are on your way before studying out courses, distances, running times, etc. Go over the entire trip in advance and acquaint yourself thoroughly with the separate legs of the cruise, the aids to navigation that you will pass, the characteristics of the lights, and other items of piloting interest.

Then set up a timetable, assuming that you will leave your point of departure at exactly 0000, and note in orderly fashion the predicted time of arrival abeam of every light and buoy on both sides of your intended track. Alongside each entry, show the characteristics of the navigational aid and the compass course at the time. You can also enter into your timetable the approximate times that major lights can be expected to become visible.

Using the timetable

Invest in an alarm clock or watch with a luminous dial and set it for 12 o'clock when you start your run from the point of departure on which your predetermined timetable is based. Then as the flashing, occulting, or other lights successively wink over the horizon, you won't have to dash below to puzzle out characteristics and identify each in turn. The elapsed time from your start will clue you as to the identity of the aid to navigation.

The timetable will aid you in knowing where you are at any time, what light you just passed, what the characteristics will be of the next light to appear, and when that should happen. The use of elapsed time, rather than actual clock time, allows flexibility in the starting time; it is not necessary to revise your entire timetable if you take your departure earlier or later than originally planned. If any discrepancy creeps in consistently between when events should happen and when they actually do, the hands of the clock or watch can be shifted as needed.

NIGHT COASTWISE PILOTING BY SHORE LIGHTS

For night piloting alongshore, the lights of towns and settlements along the beach can be used to estimate distances offshore. An experienced boatman reports that he has been able to maintain a course approximately 5½ miles offshore going down the Jersey coast simply by keeping in sight of the reflected glow in the sky above lights in towns along the shore.

The appearance of direct rays of light would be a signal indicating that the distance offshore was decreasing to 5 miles or less, whereupon it would be advisable to haul off until only the reflected glow was visible once more. The objective of keeping so far offshore was to avoid the extensive areas of fish net stakes, and yet not lose contact with land.

The distance that the direct rays will be seen will be determined by the height of the observer's eye, and should be determined by the individual skipper for his own boat. The principles involved, however, remain the same for all craft.

FOLLOWING THE BEACH

Elsewhere, we have considered how a boat may be piloted along a coast by following a constant depth, or fathom curve. It is possible, however, that the sounder might be inoperative or not available for some other reason. It is well to have another means of following the shoreline approximately when visibility conditions permit the observation of objects on the beach.

Let's say that you wish to parallel the Jersey or Long Island beach (or any average coast where there are no hills or mountains ashore to stand out prominently at long range). Fig. 2184 shows such a coastline. From the deck of a typical small boat at sea, you will be unable to see the beach if you are more than about 4½ miles offshore, due to the earth's curvature. If you can just make out the beach, you are approximately 4 miles out. This, naturally, will not hold true if there is haze or fog.

FIG. 2184 With just a little effort, you can determine for your height of eye on your boat the distances off shore at which you can see the beach and certain features of the buildings. Your distances shouldn't vary much from those shown here for a typical boat.

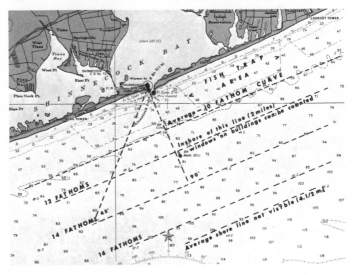

Specialized Piloting Techniques / CHAPTER 21

Distance off by visibility of details

Now as you follow the coast, you will probably trend in closer without realizing that you are off your intended track. Buildings appear, and you find that you can distinguish detail enough to make out individual windows of houses. This means that you are roughly within 2 miles of the beach.

Thus, you have established two limits, by keeping within sight of the beach, but far enough off that you cannot count windows, you are averaging 2 to 4 miles offshore. Meticulous pilots may object that this is too loose, but there are many cruises that do not require any higher degree of precision.

Check for your height-of-eye

The 2-mile distance at which windows can be counted will not vary with the observer's height of eye. This is a matter of distance and detail. The 4- to 4½-mile limits of visibility for the beach itself, however, are subject to variation from one boat to another. These are average figures; establish more exact distances for your own craft by using the bow-and-beam bearings technique or any other positioning procedure.

A NEW POSITION FINDER

Earlier in this chapter, we considered a positioning technique using two horizontal angles between the lines of sight to three identifiable objects. See figs. 2124-2126. Although this is a standard method, it has not been widely used on small boats because a sextant is normally required to measure the angles and a three-arm protractor to plot them accurately. As a sextant would be a relatively large investment for this use only, those who do not venture onto the high seas and use celestial navigation do not normally have one aboard.

The Weems Position-Finder is a combination instrument that can be used both to measure the angles and do the chart plotting. It eliminates the need for a sextant for making observations, and the attendant steps of reading angles from the sextant scale and setting these values on the protractor. This results in a saving of time, effort, and risk of error. As the observations are taken, the arms of this instrument are locked in position, and the device becomes, in effect, a three-arm protractor with the angles already set. The actual values of the angles need never be known. The solution is entirely independent of the compass or other instruments. The optical principle employed is shown in fig. 2185.

FIG. 2187 The position-finder in place on a chart. The arms are set directly as the observations are made, and no angles need be read in order to determine the fix. The three arms are aligned with the chart symbols for the objects sighted upon; the observer's position is at the center of the instrument.

The observing portion of the device, fig. 2186, consists of a fixed horizon mirror, A, in which the reflected image of one object is seen immediately below the true image of the center object viewed over the top of the mirror. This is called a horizon mirror because it has the same function as the horizon mirror of a marine sextant.

The rotatable index mirror, B, is moved by the index arm, C, to reflect the image of the right or left object into the fixed mirror. By viewing through the slot in the center of this mirror, it is possible to use this one mirror for both the right and left angles. This is not possible with a sextant, where the index mirror is offset and can be used for only one horizontal angle at a time.

The plotting portion of the position-finder consists of three arms, pivoted at one center point, at which a pencil mark can be made through a hole onto the chart. The center arm is permanently located with an etched centerline at 90° to the plane of the horizontal mirror. The two movable arms can be locked in position during the observations, avoiding the need for any reading of scales and subsequent setting of the arms before plotting. The inside edges of the movable arms are used for plotting.

Using the position-finder

Three objects are selected that can be identified visually and on the chart. The procedure is to measure the angle between the line of sight to the center object and those to the right-hand and left-hand objects. The two angles cannot be measured simultaneously. If it is apparent that one angle is changing at a more rapid rate than the other, the angle changing more slowly should be measured first and the angle changing more rapidly last; otherwise, it is not important which angle is measured first.

Each angle is measured in accordance with the detailed instructions furnished with the instrument. As the angles are measured, the movable arms are locked into place. The instrument is then transferred to the chart and used as a conventional three-arm protractor, lining up each arm with the respective chart symbol and marking the position with a pencil through the hole in the center of the device. Fig. 2187 shows the Position-Finder in place on a chart.

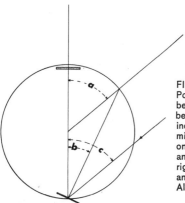

FIG. 2185 Optical principle of Position Finder. Angle *a* is angle between two objects on shore being observed. Angle *b* is amount index arm, and therefore index mirror, is turned. This is always one-half of angle *a*. Angle *c* is angle of light rays coming from right hand object to index mirror and reflected to horizon mirror. Always the same as angle *a*.

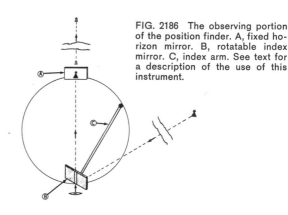

FIG. 2186 The observing portion of the position finder. A, fixed horizon mirror. B, rotatable index mirror. C, index arm. See text for a description of the use of this instrument.

ECHO PILOTING

An approximate method of determining distance, in passages or other bodies of water where there are sheer cliffs that will produce echoes, is to sound a short blast of the whistle or horn, and time, preferably with a stop watch, the interval before the echo is received.

Divide this interval in seconds by two (because the sound has to travel to the shore and return as the echo), and multiply that figure by 1100, a rough value for the speed of sound in air in feet per second. (Actually, at 32°F, the speed is 1088 feet per second and at 72°F it is 1132 fps, but the figure of 1100 is close enough for the accuracy of the timing method used.)

For example, you sound a short blast on your horn and time the interval until the return of the echo as five seconds. Half of this time is 2½ seconds; multiply by 1100, and you have 2650 feet or a distance off of slightly less than one-half nautical mile.

This is sometimes called "dog-bark navigation" and is used to a limited extent in the inside passage to Alaska on the British Columbia coast. If an echo can be received from both shores, a vessel can be kept in the approximate middle of the passage by holding such a course that an echo will be received simultaneously from both sides.

THE RULE-OF-SIXTY

Another useful specialized piloting technique is the *Rule-of-Sixty*. It provides a simple, practical way of changing course to clear an off-lying danger area without a lot of chart work. Again, the technique is best explained with an example.

Let's assume in this case that you have come out of Portsmouth Harbor and are running a southerly course down the coast to Cape Ann. See fig. 2188. Somewhere out off Newburyport you pick up dead ahead the light on Straitsmouth Island, marked C in the figure. Your course made good along the line AC has been 164° True. A bell buoy has been placed a mile and a half eastward of the light to mark a number of rocks and ledges that must be cleared. It is obvious that you must make a change of course for safety. The problem is how much?

Instead of getting out the chart and plotting a position and a new course to clear the bell buoy, you can apply the Rule-of-Sixty and get a new course with a simple mental calculation. You know from the chart or Light List that the light on Straitsmouth Island is visible for 8 miles, assuming good visibility. (With less than perfect visibility, you will have to establish your distance from the light by other means. But on this night, the visibility is good and you can accept the distance as 8 miles when the light appears on the horizon.)

The procedure is to divide 60 (the rule) by 8 (the distance); the result is 7.5. Since you want to clear the light by a mile and a half, you multiply 7.5 by 1.5 and get 11.25. This is rounded to 11, and is the number of degrees that you must change your course. Thus, your new course is 164° − 11° = 153° True. Long before you need to be concerned about the rocks and ledges, you will pick up the bell buoy north of Flat Ground and then the light on the bell buoy at D.

Although this technique is quite valid and acceptable as a specialized procedure, it should not be considered a full

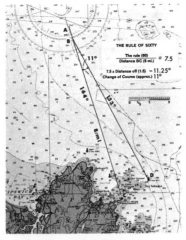

FIG. 2188 The Rule of Sixty can guide you in determining how much to change course to clear an obstacle seen ahead at a known distance. The rule can be applied without making a chart plot of the situation.

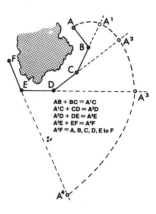

FIG. 2189 The length of the several straight courses required to pass around a point of land can be added graphically and measured all at one time, rather than measuring them separately and adding the distances numerically.

substitute for the basic and conventional procedure of accurately determining your position and plotting a revised course. There may be circumstances where the Rule-of-Sixty will be useful, such as on a single-handed passage or under conditions too rough for accurate plotting, but consider it a "secondary" method rather than a first-choice method.

DETERMINING THE DISTANCE AROUND A HEADLAND

A pilot may be confronted with the problem of determining the total distance to be covered when rounding a headland or point of land in a series of short, straight courses. There is a graphic method that will give a quick and accurate solution.

In fig. 2189, the boat is at A. You want to know the total run to F on the other side of the point if you proceed to B, then C, D, and E in turn.

In the figure, lines are drawn from point to point, but after you become familiar with the technique, you can merely swing the legs of your dividers from point to point so as to ensure that the invisible line determined by the points will be far enough offshore to be safe.

Step-by-step procedures

The starting point is A; use a pair of dividers and measure the distance to B. Keep the dividers' leg point that is at B on that point, and swing the other leg around from A to the right until it touches the broken line extended backwards from C to B at A¹. Hold this dividers' point on A¹, and extend the other leg from B to C.

Now hold the point at C fast and swing the other point around from A¹ until it touches the broken line extended backward from D to C at A². Hold this point fast at A² and open the dividers further, as before, until the point at C reaches to D.

This same step-by-step procedure is repeated to find A³ and A⁴. When the dividers have been finally extended from A⁴ to F, they are set to measure the total distance around the headland using the chart's graphic scale or latitude markings.

This technique saves much time and is more accurate than the usual procedure of measuring each leg separately and adding the distance together to get the total run.

457

Fig. 2201

Mastless motorboat. At the stern, US, Yacht, or USPS Ensign. At the bow, club burgee, Squadron pennant, private signal, officer's flag, or USCG Aux. Ensign (but only one of these at a time).

Note: The Ensigns of the U.S. Power Squadrons and the U.S. Coast Guard Auxiliary may be flown *only* by members of those organizations in good standing.

Fig. 2202 *(above)*

Typical outboard cruiser or open boat with radio antenna. A USPS officer's flag or past officer's signal may be flown from the antenna at the same height as if on a signal mast. A USCG Auxiliary Ensign may be flown from the same location, but only one flag at a time.

Fig. 2203 *(left)*

Small cruiser having signal mast without spreader. Same flags as Fig. 2202.

Chapter 22

FLAG ETIQUETTE

How to fly your flags afloat—

Where and when to fly them—

Flag, pennant or burgee, which?—

Origin of the national and yacht ensigns—

Flags for masts ashore—

Etiquette in foreign waters

Fig. 2204
Cruiser with bow and stern staffs, with signal mast and spreader. At bow, Squadron pennant or club burgee. Aft, US, Yacht, or USPS Ensign. At masthead, officer's flag, private signal, or USCG Aux. Ensign. At starboard spreader, USPS Ensign (if not flown aft), absent flag, or guest flag.

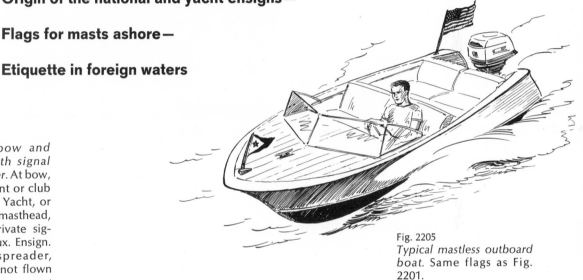

Fig. 2205
Typical mastless outboard boat. Same flags as Fig. 2201.

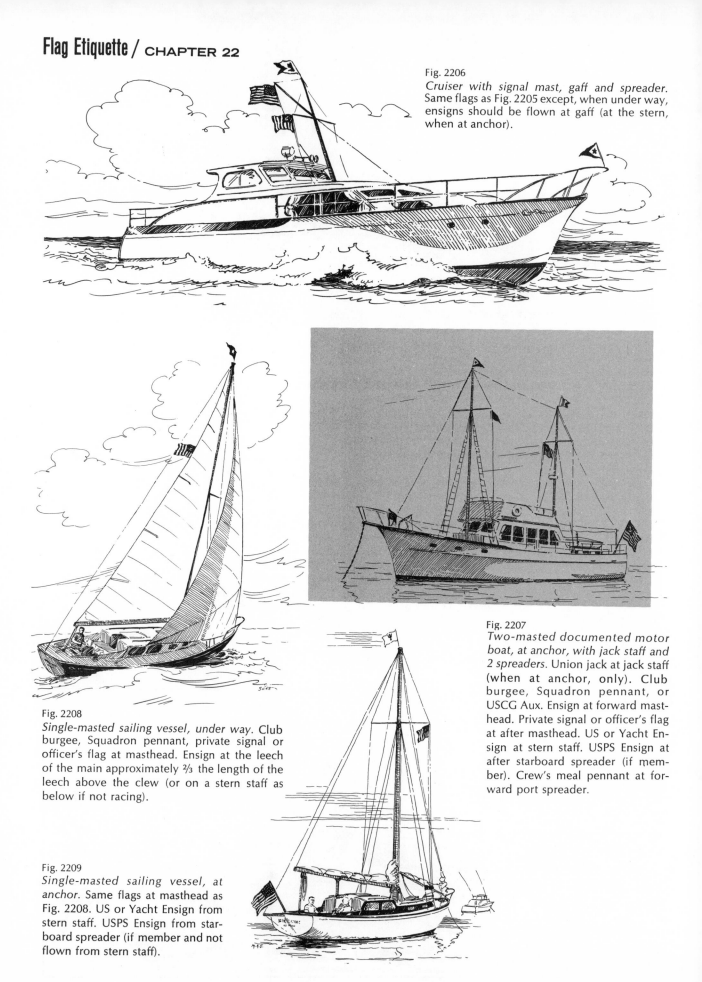

Fig. 2206
Cruiser with signal mast, gaff and spreader. Same flags as Fig. 2205 except, when under way, ensigns should be flown at gaff (at the stern, when at anchor).

Fig. 2208
Single-masted sailing vessel, under way. Club burgee, Squadron pennant, private signal or officer's flag at masthead. Ensign at the leech of the main approximately ⅔ the length of the leech above the clew (or on a stern staff as below if not racing).

Fig. 2207
Two-masted documented motor boat, at anchor, with jack staff and 2 spreaders. Union jack at jack staff (when at anchor, only). Club burgee, Squadron pennant, or USCG Aux. Ensign at forward masthead. Private signal or officer's flag at after masthead. US or Yacht Ensign at stern staff. USPS Ensign at after starboard spreader (if member). Crew's meal pennant at forward port spreader.

Fig. 2209
Single-masted sailing vessel, at anchor. Same flags at masthead as Fig. 2208. US or Yacht Ensign from stern staff. USPS Ensign from starboard spreader (if member and not flown from stern staff).

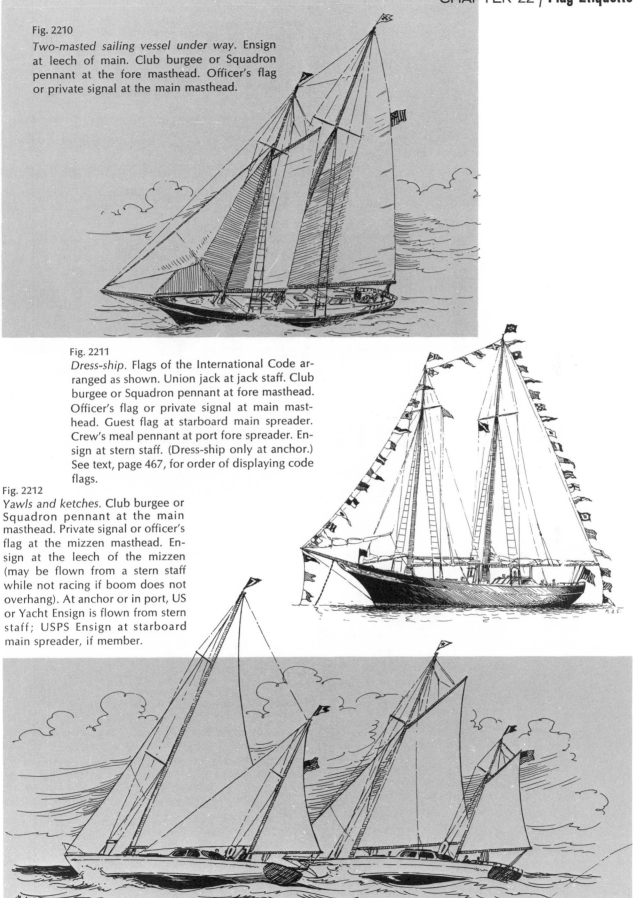

Fig. 2210
Two-masted sailing vessel under way. Ensign at leech of main. Club burgee or Squadron pennant at the fore masthead. Officer's flag or private signal at the main masthead.

Fig. 2211
Dress-ship. Flags of the International Code arranged as shown. Union jack at jack staff. Club burgee or Squadron pennant at fore masthead. Officer's flag or private signal at main masthead. Guest flag at starboard main spreader. Crew's meal pennant at port fore spreader. Ensign at stern staff. (Dress-ship only at anchor.) See text, page 467, for order of displaying code flags.

Fig. 2212
Yawls and ketches. Club burgee or Squadron pennant at the main masthead. Private signal or officer's flag at the mizzen masthead. Ensign at the leech of the mizzen (may be flown from a stern staff while not racing if boom does not overhang). At anchor or in port, US or Yacht Ensign is flown from stern staff; USPS Ensign at starboard main spreader, if member.

461

U.S. ENSIGN

U.S. ENSIGN, the one and only U.S. National flag, proper for all yachts, without reservation. Old Glory, the flag with 50 stars and 13 stripes. Flown, when at anchor, at the stern staff. When under way in inland waters, and when meeting or passing other vessels on the high seas, weather and rig permitting, by: motor yachts at the stern staff; by motor yachts with mast and gaff at the gaff.

U.S. POWER SQUADRON ENSIGN

U.S. YACHT ENSIGN

U.S. COAST GUARD AUXILIARY ENSIGN

Marconi-rigged sloops and cutters, when under sail, fly the ensign at the leech of the mainsail approximately ⅔ the length of the leech above the clew. When Marconi-rigs have more than one mast, the ensign is flown from the leech of the aftermost sail.

Gaff-rigged sloops and cutters, when under sail, fly the ensign at the peak of the mainsail gaff. When gaff-rigs have more than one mast, the ensign is flown from the peak of the aftermost gaff.

A sailboat of any rig, when under sail but not racing, may, in lieu of the above, fly its ensign from a stern staff if desired and the aftermost boom does not so overhang as to prevent the mounting of a stern staff.

Under power alone, or when at anchor or made fast, the ensign should be flown from the stern staff of all sailboats. If an overhanging boom requires that the staff be off-center, it should be on the starboard side.

U.S. POWER SQUADRONS ENSIGN is flown as an outward and visible signal to other craft that the boat is commanded by a member of the USPS in good standing, one who is an able seaman, with a knowledge of things nautical, and competent to handle his craft.

The preferred location for flying the USPS Ensign is the starboard yardarm or spreader, underway and at anchor, and made fast to the shore, on motor and sailing craft. It may be flown from a stern staff in lieu of the US or Yacht Ensign, but this is usually done only on smaller boats lacking a mast. On sailboats underway, it may be flown from the aftermost peak or leech in place of other ensigns, but this is rarely seen.

U.S. YACHT ENSIGN, by custom and by rulings of governing authorities, may be flown on recreational boats of all sizes in lieu of the U.S. Ensign. Originally, the flying of the Yacht Ensign was restricted to documented vessels of a special classification, but all such restrictions have now been removed. Many yacht clubs now provide in their by-laws that the Yacht Ensign be flown regardless of size or documentation status.

Strictly speaking, the Yacht Ensign is *not* the American flag. Thus, it is proper that a 50-star U.S. Ensign be substituted for the Yacht Ensign whenever the craft is taken into international or foreign waters.

U.S. COAST GUARD AUXILIARY ENSIGN, known as the "Blue Ensign," is flown *day and night* on a boat that has been approved as a facility for the current year. Here's how:

☐ On a vessel without a mast—at the bow staff.
☐ On a vessel with one mast—at the truck.
☐ On a vessel with two or more masts—at the main truck.
☐ NEVER in place of the national ensign.

The USPS Ensign may be flown at its proper location on boats displaying the USCG Aux. Ensign to indicate that the owner is a member of both organizations.

YACHT CLUB BURGEE, generally triangular in shape, sometimes swallow-tail; may be flown by day only or day and night as set by the rules of the Yacht Club concerned.

Flown from the bow staff of mastless and single-masted vessels (foremost truck of vessels with two or more masts); at the main truck of yawls and ketches.

Burgee may be flown under way and at anchor. It is, however, permissible to substitute the private signal for the burgee on single-masted yachts without bow staff when under way.

SQUADRON PENNANT. A distinguishing Squadron pennant which has been authorized by the Governing Board of USPS may be flown in lieu of a club burgee and from the same positions. This pennant may be flown by day only or both day and night.

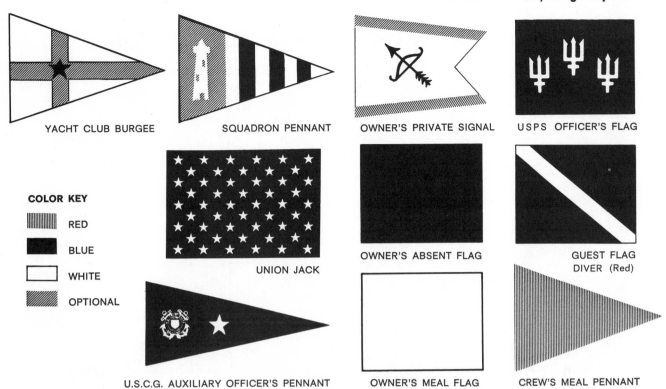

YACHT CLUB BURGEE

SQUADRON PENNANT

OWNER'S PRIVATE SIGNAL

U.S.P.S. OFFICER'S FLAG

COLOR KEY

|||||||| RED

BLUE

WHITE

OPTIONAL

UNION JACK

OWNER'S ABSENT FLAG

OWNER'S MEAL FLAG

GUEST FLAG
DIVER (Red)

CREW'S MEAL PENNANT

U.S.C.G. AUXILIARY OFFICER'S PENNANT

OWNER'S PRIVATE SIGNAL, generally swallow tail in shape, sometimes rectangular or pennant, flown from masthead of single-masted motor and sailing craft, or from the aftermost masthead of motor or sailing craft with two or more masts; may be flown by day only or day and night.

Mastless motorboats may fly this signal from the bow staff in lieu of a club burgee; see fig. 2201 and 2204.

OFFICER'S FLAG, rectangular in shape, blue (with white design) for senior officer(s); red for next lower in rank; white (with blue design) for lower rank. Other officer's flag (except fleet captain) may be swallow tail or triangular in shape, as provided in the regulations of those organizations making provisions for such flags. Flown in place of private signal on all rigs of motor and sailing vessels except on single-masted sailing vessels, when it is flown in place of burgee at masthead.

UNION JACK, a rectangular blue flag with 50 white stars. The Union Jack may be displayed *only* at the jackstaff on sailing yachts and at the jackstaff on motor yachts with more than one mast, between morning and evening colors, and only while at anchor on Sundays or holidays, or when dressing ship. The Union Jack shall never be substituted for or replace the club burgee.

ABSENT FLAG, rectangular blue flag, flown during owner's absence in daylight hours. Flown from starboard yardarm, starboard main spreader or equivalent, provided USPS Ensign is not flown at this hoist. (Replaced at night, at anchor, by blue light.)

GUEST FLAG, a rectangular blue flag, crossed diagonally by a white stripe, flown during daylight, when owner is absent but guests are on board. Flown from the starboard yardarm, starboard main spreader or equivalent, provided USPS Ensign is not being flown from this hoist.

U.S.C.G. AUXILIARY OFFICER'S PENNANT, or a past officer's burgee (same design except swallow-tail shape), flies day and night when officer is on board. On a vessel without a mast, flown at the bow staff in lieu of the Auxiliary flag. On a vessel with a mast, at starboard spreader.

Only *one* officer's pennant or burgee may be flown at one time. An incumbent officer's pennant takes precedence. When the Aux. Ensign is displayed, it is improper to hoist a guest, owner absent, meal, cocktail, or novelty flag.

OWNER'S MEAL FLAG, a white rectangular flag, flown at anchor, during daylong meal hours of owners, from the main starboard spreader or yardarm, if the USPS Ensign is not at this hoist. (Replaced by white light at night.)

CREW'S MEAL PENNANT, red, flown during daylight, at anchor, during meal hours of the crew at the fore port yardarm or spreader. Seldom seen now.

RAISING AND LOWERING FLAGS. On a typical cruiser, fig. 2204, "colors are made" each morning at 0800. The ensign at the stern is hoisted (or its staff set in place). This is followed by the USPS Ensign at the starboard yardarm if the skipper is a member of USPS. Then, if not already flying on a day-and-night basis, comes the club burgee or Squadron pennant at the bow and private signal at the masthead. (An officer's flag, if flown in lieu of a private signal, would be flown continuously.)

If the craft bears a valid USCG Aux. Facility decal, it would be flying, day and night, the Auxiliary Ensign at the masthead. A USCG Aux. officer's pennant or burgee may be flown, day and night, at the starboard yardarm.

At sunset, colors not properly flown on a day-and-night basis should be lowered in reverse sequence, the ensign at the stern always being the last to be secured. If you are leaving your boat before sunset and will not be aboard at that time, colors should be secured before departing.

FLYING FLAGS AT YACHT CLUB HOISTS ASHORE

These diagrams illustrate how flags can be displayed for a variety of situations and on different types of yacht club masts and poles.

NOTES: The flag of the Senior Club Officer present on the club grounds or aboard his boat in the club anchorage, or Storm Signal flags can be substituted for the International Code Flags shown in the diagrams, except in the case illustrated at bottom left. The diagrams show hoists as if you were standing ashore facing seaward.

If only a Yacht Club single pole with no yard or gaff, only the U.S. Flag should be flown, at the truck.

If a pole with yardarm only, the U.S. Flag should be flown at truck, Club burgee at starboard yardarm, USPS Ensign or other organizational flag may be flown at port yardarm during activities ashore of such organization.

On national holidays and on days of special yachting significance, it is permissible to fly the flags of the International Code.

The code for "flying flags ashore at Yacht Clubs" may be followed for flags flown ashore at the homes of yachtsmen.

Signal flags, such as storm and weather flags, etc. should be flown from a conspicuous hoist.

Flags of yachting organizations should not be flown from commercial establishments, except by special permission.

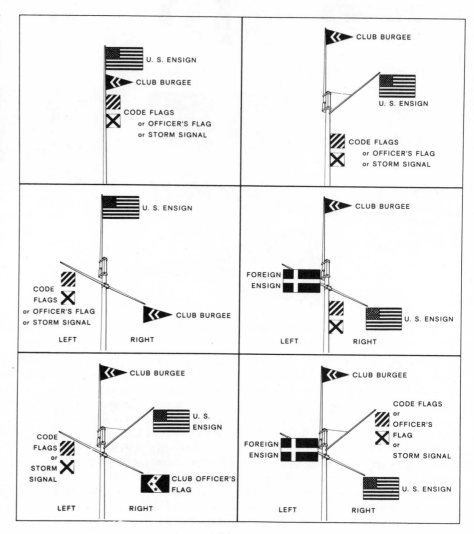

About Pennants

Pennant or Burgee. Adrift in a foggy sea of semantics, a sea lawyer could easily founder, groping for the right terms to describe those bits of bunting he flies from the truck and bow staff. Basically, there are four shapes his signals may take—rectangular, triangular, rectangular swallow-tailed, and triangular swallow-tailed. What to call them? Pennants or burgees?

We can't go far wrong if we think of a *pennant* as a flag smaller at the fly than at the hoist which is (1) commonly pointed, triangular (2) often truncated, as in some Navy signals (3) sometimes swallow-tailed (4) occasionally a long thin streamer.

The *burgee* we might regard as a swallow-tailed flag which is (1) often rectangular (2) may be pennant-shaped (3) by popular usage, the identifying signal of a yacht club, regardless of shape.

Naval Reserve Pennants. There are two types of Naval Reserve pennant. (See illustrations, pages P and Q.) The *Naval Reserve Yacht Pennant* is displayed at the fore truck by yachts and vessels commanded or owned by Naval Reserve Officers, designated by the Secretary of the Navy as suitable for service as naval auxiliaries in time of war. The *Naval Reserve Yacht Owners Distinguishing Pennant* is a personal flag flown, preferably at the fore truck, on yachts owned by, or under the command of, individuals who donated yachts or other craft for use by the Navy during World War II. Those awarded this pennant are not necessarily members of the U.S. Naval Reserve.

Racing Pennant. A distinctive pennant has been designed by the Sea Cliff (N.Y.) Yacht

Club as an identifying signal for racing boats. The field is blue, with white fluorescent strip in the middle, and red anchor superimposed. Cruising yachts carry it at the starboard spreader; smaller boats fly it from the leech of the mainsail. It aids race committees in distinguishing contesting boats; other boats, hopefully, will give them a wide berth. It is suggested that other clubs follow Sea Cliff's lead, standardizing on the design illustrated below.

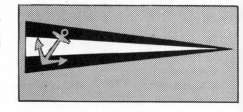

FLAGS

When and How
to Fly Them

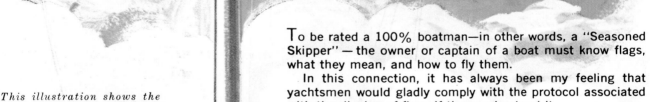

This illustration shows the Union Jack flying at the port yardarm. Correct practice dictates that this flag can be flown only on Sundays or Holidays.

Diagrams illustrating how to fly various flags on a yacht club mast ashore will be found on page 464.

NOTE:—*While it is true that no naval or other authority can be quoted for the display of the Union Jack on a yacht club mast ashore, a long-standing precedent has been established in its widespread use by the better yacht clubs.*

To be rated a 100% boatman—in other words, a "Seasoned Skipper" — the owner or captain of a boat must know flags, what they mean, and how to fly them.

In this connection, it has always been my feeling that yachtsmen would gladly comply with the protocol associated with the display of flags if they understood it.

With these thoughts in mind, the editors of Motor Boating have prepared this special section containing illustrations of flags in full color and authoritative information concerning their use.

There is a right way to fly every flag. Following this guide, you can be sure you are displaying your flags correctly.

As a long-time proponent of propriety in the flying of flags aboard ship, it gives me considerable pleasure to recommend this feature to our readers.

Charles F. Chapman

U.S. GOVERNMENT and ARMED SERVICES FLAGS

Except for those of the Army, Navy, and Coast Guard, the flags illustrated on this page won't often be seen flying from small craft. Nevertheless, they are presented here with the thought that every American will want to be able to identify whatever flag he may see afloat—or ashore. For a complete discussion of flag etiquette, see pages 458-472.

PRESIDENT OF THE UNITED STATES

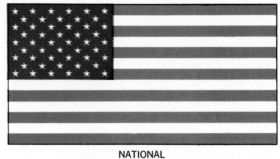

NATIONAL
ENSIGN AND MERCHANT FLAG

VICE PRESIDENT

SECRETARY OF STATE

SECRETARY OF TREASURY

SECRETARY OF DEFENSE

ATTORNEY GENERAL

COAST GUARD ENSIGN

JOINT CHIEF OF STAFF

POSTMASTER GENERAL

SECRETARY OF LABOR

COAST GUARD COMMANDANT

SECRETARY OF THE NAVY

SECRETARY OF THE ARMY

SEC. OF AGRICULTURE

SEC. HEALTH, ED. & WELF.

COAST GUARD REAR ADMIRAL

ADMIRAL, U. S. NAVY

CORPS OF ENGINEERS
(U. S. Army)

SEC. OF INTERIOR

FISH AND
WILD LIFE SERVICE

BOW
PENNANT

U. S. CUSTOMS

NAVAL RESERVE
YACHT PENNANT

ARMY TRANSPORTATION
CORPS

SEC. OF COMMERCE

NATIONAL OCEAN SURVEY

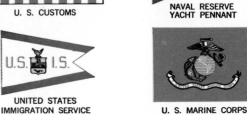

U.S. I.S.

UNITED STATES
IMMIGRATION SERVICE

U. S. MARINE CORPS

SECRETARY, AIR FORCE

P

YACHTING FLAGS

NATIONAL
ENSIGN AND MERCHANT FLAG

UNION JACK

YACHT ENSIGN

U. S. POWER SQUADRONS' ENSIGN

YACHT CLUB BURGEE

YACHT PRIVATE SIGNAL

NAVAL RESERVE
YACHT OWNERS'
DISTINGUISHING PENNANT

YACHT OWNER ABSENT

YACHT OWNER'S MEAL

YACHT GUEST FLAG

YACHT CREW'S MEAL

QUARANTINE INTERNATIONAL Q

TRANSPORTATION

YACHT PROTEST

DIVER

NOTE: Navy Department regulations provide that the Union Jack should be the same size as the union of the ensign flown from the stern. See page 464 on two types of Naval Reserve pennant.

GENERAL COMMENTS

COLORS: Though the term "colors" is frequently used to include all flags on a boat, a strict interpretation would restrict its use to the national flag which identifies the nation to which the boat belongs. The term "colors" or "making colors" is also used to refer to the ceremony of hoisting the boat's flags at 0800 and lowering at sunset.

WHEN TO FLY FLAGS: A boat's flags should be flown from 0800 to sundown except as otherwise noted in the chart on Page X. At sundown flags should be lowered, whether the boat is underway, at anchor, or made fast. However, if you *enter* or *leave* port *before* 0800, it is permissible to hoist your flags while there is sufficient light for them to be seen. Likewise, if you are *entering* or *leaving* port after sundown, the same holds true. During bad weather at sea, flags may or may not be flown, at the captain's discretion.

At 0800 the national ensign should be hoisted first, followed by the USPS Ensign (if you are a member of the U. S. Power Squadrons in good standing, and in command of the boat), the yacht club burgee, officer's flag, and/or private signal. USCG Auxiliary Ensign, and Auxiliary officer pennants and burgees, may be flown night and day on currently inspected facilities; these are in lieu of yacht club burgees, officer's flags, and private signals. Flags are hoisted smartly, but lowered ceremoniously. Flag officers' flags, though displayed day and night, may be temporarily lowered and hoisted at colors.

At U.S.P.S., C.G. Auxiliary, or Club rendezvous, marine parades, etc., on order of the Commanding Officer, flags may be flown after sundown but must be lowered at or before midnight, as ordered.

SIZE OF FLAGS: The national ensign, yacht ensign, USPS engine, whichever is flown, should be a minimum of 1″ on the fly per foot of overall length of boat. The hoist should be two-thirds the fly. The burgee, private signal, and flag officer's flag should be a minimum of ½″ on the fly for each foot of the highest masthead above the water on sailing yachts, and ⅝″ on the fly for each foot of overall length for motorboats.

When the USPS Ensign is flown from the starboard yardarms on motorboats, the fly should be ⅝″ per foot of overall length of boat.

SALUTING: Never salute, or answer a salute, by dipping the U.S. national ensign. Salute by dipping the yacht ensign, or the USPS ensign, when flown at the stern or gaff of motor craft, stern staff of sailing vessels, under power or at anchor. Never salute by dipping a flag flown from the yardarm or spreader.

MISCELLANEOUS

CHARTER: When a boat is chartered, use flags of the charterer.

DISTRESS: Though not official, flying the U.S. Ensign upside down is universally recognized as a distress signal.

OPTIONAL: Flags authorized by naval, military, government, or yachting organizations, may be displayed at option, providing the procedure for flying such flags specified by these organizations is followed. No other flag should be displayed, except when making signals with international code flags or when dressing ship.

QUARANTINE: The plain yellow flag is a signal meaning "I request pratique"—formal admittance upon arrival at a foreign port, or return to U.S. Fly where most easily seen, usually starboard spreader or radio antenna.

TRANSPORTATION: Code flag "T" is used to call club tender.

PROTEST: For sailors who race. See illustration.

DIVERS: Display when diving is in progress. See illustration. Do not fly underway.

STRIKING: "Striking colors" is a naval term meaning surrender. *Never* use in yachting.

UNITED STATES POWER SQUADRONS FLAGS and INSIGNIA

USPS ENSIGN

The Ensign of United States Power Squadrons may be displayed only by enrolled members of USPS. It is an outward and visible sign that the vessel displaying it is under the charge of a person who has made a study of piloting and small boat handling, and will recognize the rights of others and the traditions of the sea. The Squadrons' Ensign also marks a craft as being under the command of a man who has met certain minimum requirements and is so honored for meeting them. This honor may not be bought, sold, rented, loaned or given away. The USPS Ensign is displayed, during the hours from 0800 to sundown, from the stern staff or from the starboard yardarm of a power vessel. On craft under sail, it is flown from the leach or peak of the mainsail or aftermost sail.

USPS OBJECTIVES

Shall be to establish a high standard of skill in handling and navigation of yachts, to encourage the study of the science of navigation, and small boat handling, to cooperate with the agencies of the United States Government charged with the enforcement of the laws and regulations relating to navigation and to stimulate interest in activities which will tend to the upbuilding of our Army, Navy, Coast Guard and Merchant Marine.

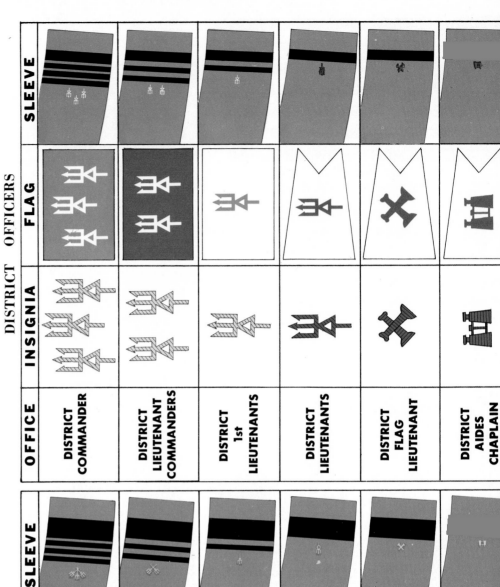

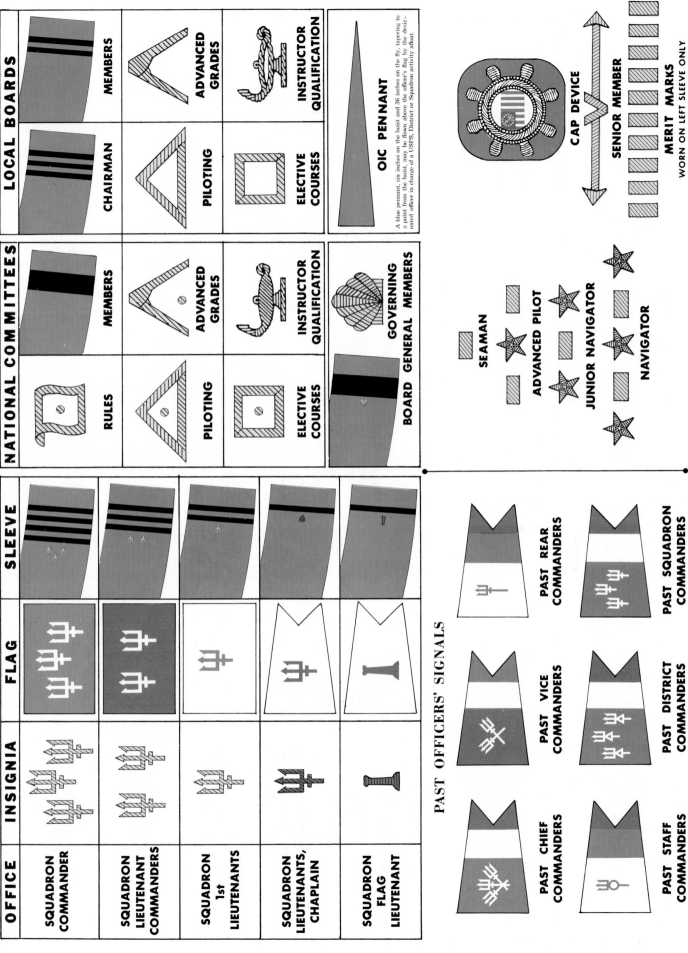

LOCAL BOARDS

MEMBERS	CHAIRMAN
ADVANCED GRADES	PILOTING
INSTRUCTOR QUALIFICATION	ELECTIVE COURSES

OIC PENNANT

A blue pennant, six inches on the hoist and 36 inches on the fly, tapering to a point from the hoist, may be flown above the officer's flag by the designated officer in charge of a USPS, District or Squadron activity afloat.

NATIONAL COMMITTEES

RULES	MEMBERS
PILOTING	ADVANCED GRADES
ELECTIVE COURSES	INSTRUCTOR QUALIFICATION
BOARD GENERAL MEMBERS	GOVERNING BOARD GENERAL MEMBERS

CAP DEVICE

SENIOR MEMBER

MERIT MARKS
WORN ON LEFT SLEEVE ONLY

SEAMAN

ADVANCED PILOT

JUNIOR NAVIGATOR

NAVIGATOR

OFFICE	INSIGNIA	FLAG	SLEEVE
SQUADRON COMMANDER			
SQUADRON LIEUTENANT COMMANDERS			
SQUADRON 1st LIEUTENANTS			
SQUADRON LIEUTENANTS, CHAPLAIN			
SQUADRON FLAG LIEUTENANT			

PAST OFFICERS' SIGNALS

PAST CHIEF COMMANDERS

PAST VICE COMMANDERS

PAST REAR COMMANDERS

PAST STAFF COMMANDERS

PAST DISTRICT COMMANDERS

PAST SQUADRON COMMANDERS

S

U.S. COAST GUARD AUXILIARY FLAGS

COAST GUARD ENSIGN

COAST GUARD AUXILIARY

THE AUXILIARY FLAG, known as the "Blue Ensign" (at left), may be flown day and night on a currently inspected facility. **Never** in place of the national ensign.

When the Blue Ensign is displayed, it is improper to hoist a guest, owner absent, meal, cocktail, or novelty flag.

AN OFFICER'S PENNANT, or a past officer's burgee, flies day and night when the officer is on board.

NATIONAL COMMODORE

NATIONAL VICE COMMODORE
(With small star, Nat. Rear Commodore)

CHIEF OF DEPARTMENT
3 Bars—Division Chief
2 Bars—Branch Chief
1 Bar—Aide to National Commodore

DISTRICT COMMODORE

DISTRICT VICE COMMODORE
(White field, blue markings: Dist. Rear Commodore)

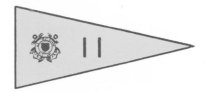

DISTRICT STAFF OFFICER

DIVISION CAPTAIN

DIVISION VICE CAPTAIN

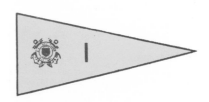

DIVISION STAFF OFFICER

FLOTILLA COMMANDER

FLOTILLA VICE COMMANDER

FLOTILLA STAFF OFFICER

U.S. COAST GUARD AUXILIARY PAST OFFICERS' BURGEES

Past elected officers who are not currently holding office, but are active or permanent members of the U. S. Coast Guard Auxiliary, may display the burgee of the highest office held in the same manner as prescribed for officers' pennants. Past officers' burgees are of the same design as present officers' pennants, except for their shape.

PAST DIVISION CAPTAIN

Past staff officers of the U. S. Coast Guard Auxiliary who are not currently holding appointive office, but who are active members, may display the burgee of the highest appointed office held, in the same manner as prescribed for staff officers' pennants. Burgees have the same hoist dimensions as pennants, with the fly 1½ times the hoist.

T

U.S. COAST GUARD AUXILIARY INSIGNIA

OFFICER	METAL COLLAR and SHOULDER INSIGNIA [1.]	SHOULDER BOARDS [2.]	SLEEVE [3.]
National Commodore			
National Vice Commodore District Commodore National Rear Commodore			
District Vice Commodore With Red "A": Department Chief			
District Rear Commodore With Red "A": Division Chief			
Division Captain With Red "A": Branch Chief District Staff Officer			
Division Vice Captain Flotilla Commander With Red "A": Aide Asst. Dist. Staff Officer			
Flotilla Vice Commander With Red "A" Division Staff Officer			
Flotilla Staff Officer (Red "A")			

Notes: 1. Large metal shoulder insignia is worn on blue raincoats; the same insignia in smaller size is worn on khaki, blue flannel, and khaki tropical shirts.

2. Shoulder Marks are worn on khaki coats, blue overcoats, and white tropical shirts.

3. Sleeve Grade stripes are worn on blue coats; braid goes only halfway around the sleeve.

CAP DEVICE

SHIELD
Current Officer

SHIELD
Staff Officer

SHIELD
Past Officer

Silver Collar
Insignia-Member

AUXILIARY AVIATOR

U

WHEN AND WHERE TO FLY FLAGS ON BOATS

FLAG	WHEN FLOWN	Power Boat with Bow and Stern Staffs Only	Power Boat with Bow and Stern Staffs and Single Mast	Single-Masted Sailing Yacht	Power Boat or Sailing Yacht With Two Masts	FOOTNOTES
U.S. ENSIGN OR U.S. YACHT ENSIGN[1]	0800 to Sundown[5]	Stern Staff[3]	Stern Staff[3]	At anchor or underway: from stern staff (except when racing). (Optional: from peak if gaff-rigged, or from leach of mainsail if Marconi-rigged[4]).	At anchor or underway: from stern staff (except when racing). (Optional: from after peak if gaff-rigged, or from leach of aftermost sail if Marconi-rigged[4]).	[1] A USPS member has the option of flying the U.S. Ensign, the U.S. Yacht Ensign or the USPS Ensign.
USPS ENSIGN[1]	0800 to Sundown[5]	Stern Staff[3]	Stern Staff or Starboard Spreader[2 and 3]	As Above	As Above	[2] If the USPS Ensign is flown from the Spreader, the U.S. Ensign or the U.S. Yacht Ensign should be flown from the stern staff.
SQUADRON PENNANT OR YACHT CLUB BURGEE	0800 to Sundown or Day and Night While Boat Is In Commission	Bow Staff	Bow Staff	At Bow Staff If Yacht So Equipped; Otherwise At Masthead	Foremost Masthead	[3] On boats with outboard motors and on sailing yachts with overhanging booms, the stern staff to be located to starboard of motor or boom.
FLAG OFFICER'S (RECTANGULAR)	Day and Night While Boat is in Commission	Not Flown[6]	At Masthead Instead of Private Signal	At Masthead Instead of Squadron Pennant or Yacht Club Burgee	Aftermost Masthead Instead of Private Signal	[4] Approximately two-thirds of the length of the leach above the clew.
APPOINTED OFFICER'S (SWALLOWTAIL)	0800 to Sundown or Day and Night While Boat Is In Commission	Not Flown	At Masthead Instead of Private Signal	At Masthead Instead of Squadron Pennant or Yacht Club Burgee	Aftermost Masthead Instead of Private Signal	[5] Yachts that will be unmanned at color time shall make evening colors beforehand.
USPS PAST OFFICER'S SIGNAL	0800 to Sundown or Day and Night	Not Flown	At Masthead	At Masthead	Aftermost Masthead	[6] On mastless boats with a radio antenna, it may be flown from the antenna at a height equivalent to where it would be if there were a mast. (Note: the USPS Ensign shall **never** be flown from antenna.)
PRIVATE SIGNAL	0800 to Sundown or Day and Night	Not Flown	At Masthead	At Masthead	Aftermost Masthead	[7] To be flown above officer's flag.
UNION JACK	0800 to Sundown, At Anchor Only, On Sundays and Holidays or When Dressing Ship[5]	Not Flown	Not Flown	Not Flown	Jack Staff	**NOTICE:** Where the same hoist is indicated for more than one flag or signal, the choice is optional. The flying of two flags or signals from the same hoist is **Not Authorized**, except in the case of the OIC pennant or International Code Flags.
GUEST FLAG	0800 to Sundown When Owner is Absent, But Guests are on Board[5]	Not Flown	Starboard Spreader	Starboard Spreader	Starboard Main Spreader	
OFFICER-IN-CHARGE (OIC) PENNANT	Day and Night During Activity for which Authorized[6]	Not Flown	At Masthead[7]	At Masthead[7]	Aftermost Masthead[7]	

NOTE — When a motor yacht with mast and gaff is under way, the ensign (U.S., USPS or U.S. Yacht) should be flown at the gaff instead of the stern staff. A mastless boat may display, on a staff erected on the superstructure, the flag designated by this code to be flown from masthead of single-masted boats.

"And yet, though silent, it speaks to us—speaks to us of the past, of the men and women who went before us, and of the records they wrote upon it." —PRESIDENT WILSON

The Flag of Your Country

THE FLYING of flags and colors on motor craft, sailing and other yachts is governed largely by custom. Few, if any, laws or government regulations have ever been enacted on this subject. Mention has seldom if ever been made by Congress in all of its years, of any requirements for the flying of any flag on numbered, undocumented or unlicensed vessels or yachts. Documented yachts are expected to fly the yacht ensign but the enforcement of even this regulation is questionable.

A review or a brief history of the United States National Flag should permit one to better understand some of the fundamentals on which many of the customs of flags and colors are based, especially their evolution for use on the water.

The origin and early history of the use of national flags is very indefinite. This is especially true of the national ensign of the United States. Early Colonial and American history makes very little mention of our flag or flags. Our Navy seems to have begun the use of the Stars and Stripes immediately after the Continental Congress had passed an Act in June, 1777, establishing the Stars and Stripes as the flag of this country. However, it was not until 1895 or some 30 years after the close of the Civil War, that the United States cavalry was given the right to carry the Stars and Stripes as the national standard. It was in 1841 that the infantry first used the national colors. Not until 1876 did the Marines carry the Stars and Stripes.

As the Navy made use of the national flag from the beginning and the other branches of the U.S. government were slow in adopting it, it emphasizes that the Stars and Stripes as the national ensign is a flag of the sea and its right to be flown from yachts is clearly established.

On the subject of the origin and development of the flag from which the Stars and Stripes has been evolved, accounts are too conflicting to warrant placing much credence in them. Prince Edward, afterwards Edward I of England, about the middle of the last half of the 13th century, adopted the Red Cross of St. George, on a white field, as the national flag of England. After James VI of Scotland ascended the throne of England in 1603, as James I, he was much annoyed by the wrangling between the masters of English and Scotch ships when they met at sea as to which one should dip its colors to the other. Therefore, in 1606, he stopped this annoyance and to help unite the two kingdoms into one country, combined the two crosses into a new flag, which subsequently became known as the Union

Jack. This he required all vessels of both countries to carry at their mainmast. A century later when the two countries agreed upon their union, a national agreement required the union of the crosses to be used on flags, banners, standards, and ensigns both at sea and on land.

Near the beginning of the revolution, General Washington assigned to the various officers as a distinction of rank, ribbons varying in color and these were worn by them until something more formal was designed. There were practically no flags or colors although some of the individual companies of the Colonial Army are supposed to have brought with them those which they had previously used. Later General Washington urged the various Colonels to provide for their regiments colors of such design as might appeal to them. This was frequently done and in many instances, some designs of 13 units were used to represent the 13 colonies.

Some of the colonies adopted flags of their own. Massachusetts adopted the Pine Tree, with the motto An Appeal to Heaven. Rhode Island selected one having an anchor and the word Hope and within the canton a union of 13 white stars on a blue field, said to be the first flag on which the 13 colonies were represented by 13 stars.

South Carolina's flag has an interesting history. In September 1775, the Committee of Safety of Charleston instructed Colonel William Moultrie to take possession of Fort Johnson on James Island, which he did. The uniforms of their troops were blue with a silver increscent in the cap. Soon realizing that a flag was needed, he improvised one having a blue field with a white increscent in the canton. This was the flag which sergeant Jasper so gallantly rescued on June 28, 1776, when the fort of palmetto logs on Sullivans Island was attacked by the British Fleet under Admiral Sir Peter Parker. It was under this flag that the Declaration of Independence was read to the people of Charleston on August 8, 1776. When the state came to officially adopt a flag, it took the one which Colonel Moultrie had designed and in recognition of the good services of the palmetto logs, placed upon it a palmetto tree.

While our first flag act was adopted June 14, 1777, by resolution of the Continental Congress and reading as follows: "Resolved, That the flag of the United States be thirteen stripes, alternate red and white; that the union be thirteen stars, white in a blue field, representing a new constellation" yet there is nothing to show that the Revolutionary Army ever carried any flags furnished by the Amer-

465

ican Congress. Those which were carried were purely personal, each made by or for some officer, company or regiment, and represented the sentiments of the makers. However, the United States Navy began to use the flag immediately after it was authorized by the Continental Congress.

History records only one Stars and Stripes that was carried by the American Army during the Revolutionary War. It was carried by the North Carolina Militia at the Battle of Guilford Courthouse, March 15, 1781, but the stripes were blue and red and the union had a white field with 13 eight-pointed stars. There is also another flag hanging in the State House at Annapolis, which it is claimed was carried by the Third Maryland Regiment in 1781. It has 13 five-pointed stars, one in the center, and 12 arranged in the form of a circle around it. In both of these cases, the flags were purely personal, not official.

The Stars and Stripes preserved in the State House of Boston is claimed to have flown over Fort Independence during the American Revolution but was not carried by the Army. In 1863 each battery of artillery and each company of cavalry was allowed to carry a small flag consisting of Stars and Stripes but that privilege was revoked at the end of the Civil War. The U.S. Marines did not carry the Stars and Stripes as national colors until 1876, yet those which they carried as such in the Mexican and Civil Wars had an eagle in the union.

In none of the three acts adopting the United States national flag is there any mention as to how the stars should be arranged or how many points they should have. In one of the first flags, the stars were sometimes arranged in a circle or with one star in the center and the remaining 12 either in the form of a circle or hollow square, or three horizontal rows of 4, 5 and 4 stars respectively. In a later flag, they were also arranged in several different orders, three horizontal rows of five each or three vertical rows of five each; sometimes in the quincunx order as was the flag that floated over Fort McHenry when Key wrote the Star Spangled Banner.

Apparently about 1841, when the United States Infantry was first given the right to carry the Stars and Stripes, there was a desire on the part of some to preserve their old national colors in the union of the new flag. One of these had an eagle with a bunch of arrows in one claw and the Indian pipe of peace in the other with 13 stars above and a like number below. During the Mexican War, the Fourth Indiana Volunteers carried a flag having in the union an eagle standing on a segment of the globe with a bunch of arrows in one claw, as though intending to conquer the earth.

Near the beginning of the 20th Century, the different departments of our National Government appointed representatives to confer and see if they could not bring order out of chaos. The proportions of Naval flags and Army colors were quite different, the former being much longer in proportion to its height, the latter being much shorter to avoid interfering with the color or standard bearer. It was decided to leave the Army colors alone but to fly the Naval flag from flagstaffs and from Government buildings.

Accordingly, following the recommendations of this committee, President Taft, in 1912, issued an executive order defining minutely the proportions and other details of the Stars and Stripes, at the same time approving a cus-

tom which had existed in the Navy of placing on their small boats flags having only 13 stars instead of the full complement. The use of only 13 stars on our small or boat flags was discontinued by an executive order of President Wilson, dated May 29, 1916, and now all flags, colors, etc., used by the United States Government are required to have their full complement of 50 stars. In all of the discussion by the conference it does not appear that there was any mention whatsoever of the yacht ensign or the rights or duties of yachts or any other vessels to fly any particular flag.

From the foregoing it will be seen that the United States has only one flag. The use of the yacht ensign is misleading. England has, by law, created a flag for its navy, another for its merchant service, another for yachts and another for its land forces; each is a national flag and entitled to the position and courtesy due the colors of a nation. But, in the United States, wherever, whenever and for whatever purpose the national colors are flown, there is but one flag to fly.

The place of honor for the national colors on land and sea is as follows: on land on a straight mast, at the head; on a mast with a gaff, at the gaff. At sea and at anchor on a steam or motor vessel, at the flag staff aft; on vessels under sail, at the peak; and on vessels with a gaff, at this gaff when under way.

There has never been passed a law compelling boats to fly the national flag or none at all from the place of honor. It has probably never been contemplated that a loyal citizen would ever do otherwise. Yet, we are free to do as we

The American flag is flying here, properly, from the gaff at a yacht club station. The club burgee is at the masthead.

M. Rosenfe

like and in the use of this freedom there has grown the custom of flying the yacht ensign at the point of honor at shore stations and aboard yachts. There are today ardent yachtsmen in high places who believe this custom aboard yachts should be continued.

The yacht ensign had its beginning on August 7, 1848, when the Congress passed "an act to authorize the Secretary of the Treasury to license yachts and for other purposes" providing for the enrollment and licensing of yachts and exempting them from entering and clearing at Customhouses. The third paragraph of the act provided "that all such licensed yachts shall *use a signal* of the form, size and colors prescribed by the Secretary of the Navy." (This paragraph has been subsequently reenacted as Sec. 4215 Revised Statutes of the United States.) The Secretary of the Navy acted promptly, and on August 26, 1848, he requested the New York Yacht Club to submit a design for this signal. The design they submitted on January 9, 1849, was the then adopted American ensign, which carried thirteen stars in a circle in the blue field and the thirteen red and white stripes (the Betsy Ross flag), in which they placed a fouled anchor in the center of the circle of stars. The Secretary of the Navy accepted the suggestion of the New York Yacht Club and authorized the adoption of the design.

It is the design of the yacht "signal" that has resulted in the present confusion because its similarity in appearance to the national ensign promptly led yachtsmen to fly the "signal" now known as the yacht ensign in place of the national ensign and the custom has grown until at present nearly all pleasure craft, from outboard speedsters up, are flying the "signal" as an ensign. The yacht ensign was created only as a signal for yachts enrolled and licensed (documented) and exempted them from entering and clearing at Custom-houses. Presumably it was to be flown in addition to the national ensign on documented yachts. To fly it from a club mast ashore signifies nothing.

Under present law it is the general rule that "the ownership of a vessel determines its national character." Several cases bear upon this and explain also how else a vessel's nationality may be proved.

In one called the Merritt (17 Wall 582, 21 L.Ed. 682) Mr. Justice Hunt, writing for the U.S. Supreme Court in October 1873, observed that "The documents a vessel carries furnish the only evidence of her nationality."

In the 1880's, U.S. v. Seagrist (27 F. Cas. No. 16,245) held that the register of a vessel, while proper evidence of nationality, is not indispensable, and the flag and ownership of the vessel may be proved by *any* competent evidence.

In 1894 in St. Clair v. United States (154 U.S. 134) the Supreme Court ruled not only that the "certificate of the vessel's registry, and its carrying the American flag, was admissible in evidence," but that "such evidence made, at least, a *prima facie* case . . . of the nationality of the vessel. . . ." This means that such evidence is sufficient to prove the points for which it is introduced unless it is contradicted by other evidence.

Conclusion: Generally the nationality of a vessel is determined by the nationality of her owner. Her papers or her flag may indicate otherwise, however, but neither is conclusive on the issue. Both elements are entitled to prima facie weight—that is, they will stand unless overcome by other evidence. Obviously there are no exclusive ways

Never fly the American flag from the masthead of a mast equipped with a gaff, as illustrated here. Just as on a ship, the gaff, even though lower in height, is the place of honor.

to prove this matter in a court of law; all material and relevant evidence on the issue will be allowed.

DRESSING SHIP

On national holidays, at regattas, and on other special occasions, yachts often dress ship with International Code signal flags. Flag officers' flags, club burgees, and national flags are not used. The ship is dressed at 8:00 A.M. and remains so dressed from morning to evening colors. (While at anchor only.) See fig. 2211, page 461.

In dressing ship, the yacht ensign is hoisted at the peak or staff aft, and the jack at the jackstaff. Then a rainbow of flags of the International Code is arranged, reaching from the waterline forward to the waterline aft, by way of the bowsprit end to the foretop masthead, then across to the main topmast, and down to the main boom end, allowing several flags to touch the water line from both the bowsprit end and the main boom end. To keep the flags in position, a weight should be attached to the end of each line. Where there is no bowsprit, flags will start at the stemhead. Flags and pennants should be bent on alternately, rather than in any indiscriminate manner. Since there are twice as many letter flags as numeral pennants, it is good practice, as in the Navy, to follow a sequence of two flags, one pennant, etc., etc., throughout. In order to effect a degree of uniformity in yacht procedure, the following arrangement has been proposed:

Starting from forward, AB2, UJ1, KE3, GH6, IV5, FL4, DM7, PO Third Repeater, RN First Repeater, STo (zero), CX9, WQ8, ZY Second Repeater.

The arrangement here proposed is designed to effect a harmonious color pattern throughout.

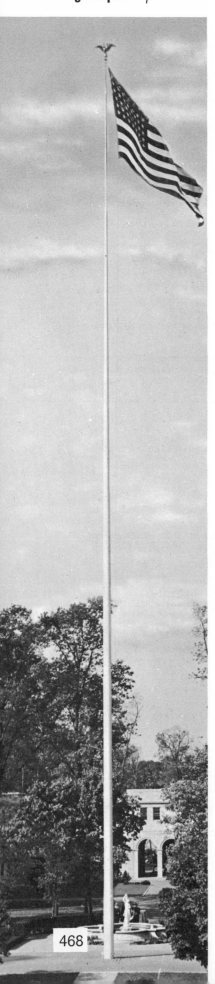

The Evolution of the United States Flag

GRAND UNION:
Before the American Revolution, the Colonies used a flag with a British ensign as the canton, plus 13 alternate red and white stripes signifying the original Colonies.

GADSDEN FLAG:
Even before 1776, there were those who resented anything in our flag resembling the British ensign. The Gadsden flag was developed about this time with a coiled rattlesnake on a yellow field with the words "Don't Tread On Me." Other flags used by some of the Colonies carried such slogans as "Liberty or Death."

BUNKER HILL FLAG:
In the New England area, the pine tree of Maine was the popular flag emblem. This appeared on the banner hoisted by the Colonies at Bunker Hill. It showed a red background with the pine tree in the canton. Another was the British blue ensign with a pine tree in the canton.

FIRST "STARS AND STRIPES":
Congress passed the first flag resolution on June 14 (now flag day), 1777. The battle of Bennington in August of the same year is believed to mark the first display of Old Glory with 13 stars and 13 stripes, with 11 stars arranged in a semi-circle and one in each corner. The 76 denotes the year of Independence.

COWPENS FLAG:
This flag, consisting of 12 white stars in a circle with one in the center, with 13 alternate red and white stripes, was first carried in the battle of Cowpens, January 1781.

BETSY ROSS FLAG:
The legend has it that Betsy Ross of Philadelphia was asked in 1776 to design a national flag suggested by General Washington. She is credited with making the stars 5-pointed and arranging them in a circle on the national flag.

FLAG OF 1795:
This flag had 15 stripes and 15 stars indicating the 15 States at that time. Five new stars were added during the five years this flag flew, but no additional stripes. This flag is credited with being the first official flag to fly over the Capitol in Washington.

FLAG OF THE CONFEDERACY:
Of the four Confederate flags, the one shown was most popular and best known; it consisted of a blue cross arranged diagonally across a red field. On the cross were 13 stars.

FLAG OF 1912:
Two stars were added to the flag when this design became offical, representing the new States of Arizona and New Mexico. The stars were arranged in six rows of 8 stars each and remained unchanged for 47 years.

OLD GLORY OF TODAY:
With the admission of the 49th and 50th States, Alaska and Hawaii, 2 more stars were added to the flag, making a total of 50, arranged in 5 rows of 6 stars each and 4 rows of 5 stars each. The flag became official on July 4, 1960.

The United States ensign proudly flies from the tallest single-masted, unguyed flagpole in the world (172 ft.) at the United States Merchant Marine Academy, Kings Point, N. Y.

Suggested Flag Ceremonies and Etiquette at Yacht Club and Squadron Meetings

FLAG CEREMONIES AT SQUADRON MEETINGS

It is better to place the flags with ceremony than to consider them merely a part of the decorations and equipment.

The route of march in advancing the colors will depend upon the size and layout of the meeting place, width of aisles, etc. In the following it is assumed that the flag of the United States and the USPS flag are to used, mounted on staffs, and with stands properly located in advance.

In small or congested rooms the following is recommended.

The bearer of the flag of the United States stands at the right side of the room, as viewed by the audience, with the bearer of the USPS flag on the opposite side of the room, in the open space between the first rows of chairs and the speaker's platform. If there is no raised platform for the head table or speaker, the bearers of the U.S. and USPS flags take positions opposite from the positions indicated (see paragraph 4 Display of Flags at Squadron Meetings).

The Commander raps his gavel for order, and as soon as obtained announces "We will now have the presentation of the colors. All please rise and stand at attention."

As soon as this is accomplished the Commander orders, "Color Guard—Present the colors." The Color Guard, on the order, marches in opposite directions across the room in front of the speaker's platform. At the center point and just before passing, each comes to a distinct stop facing each other. The bearer of the USPS flag dips his flag slightly and as soon as his flag is back up in carrying position both bearers continue their march and place the flags in their respective stands.

As soon as each flag is placed both bearers step back and come to the position of breast salute, facing the flag of the United States.

Referring back in the above, as soon as the bearers start their march across the room, the Commander orders all present "Breast Salute."

As soon as the bearers have come to the position of breast salute as above, the Commander orders "Two." (Second count of the salute routine.) On this order all present return to the position of attention and the color bearers retire.

The Commander then raps his gavel and orders all present "Be seated" or calls for the Invocation, after which he seats the audience.

If a larger hall is used or more formal ceremonies are desired, the flags may be marched up the center aisle or right aisle. If in single file, with the United States flag in the lead, if abreast with the U.S. flag on the right of marchers.

If marching up the center aisle, at the point where the cleared space between the front seats and the table is reached, the bearer of the USPS flag stops momentarily and allows the bearer of the U.S. flag to cross in front of him. The flag dip is used only when the flags meet from opposite directions as in the first method above.

The Commander follows the same sequence of orders as for the first method above.

COLOR RETIRING CEREMONIES

Color retiring ceremonies may properly and easily be followed at all formal business meetings, where there is a definite moment of official closing. It is not recommended at social gatherings.

Color retiring ceremonies are as follows:

Just before declaring the meeting adjourned the Commander gives the order "Color Guard, stand by to retire the colors." On receiving this order, the Color Guard advances and stands directly in front of their respective colors. When both are in position the Commander orders "Attention" and all present rise and stand at attention. When this is accomplished the Commander orders "Color Guard, secure the colors."

Each color bearer at this command removes his flag from the stand and together do an about-face to face the audience, and then hoist the flags to carry position.

As soon as this is accomplished the Commander orders "Breast salute" and all present except the color bearers comply. As soon as the position of breast salute is accomplished, the color bearers step off together to retrace their presentation march. If the first method described for presenting colors is used, the dipping ceremony is repeated just before they cross in the center of the room. In this method, as soon as the colors reach the side of the room, or if the aisle method is used, as soon as the colors pass from sight or reach the back of the room, the Commander orders "Two" and all present return to the position of attention.

The Commander may now order the meeting adjourned, or may seat the audience first if there are to be informal activities following.

On a shore mast equipped with gaff, at yacht clubs and similar marine installations such as marinas, USPS and USCG Auxiliary shore headquarters, etc., the U.S. Ensign should be flown from the gaff, the position of honor. The illustration above, made from a poster issued by the U.S. Government, shows Old Glory flying from the gaff. Even though there may be positions at a greater height above the ground, yet the flying of the ensign from the gaff is not a violation of the statutes that "no flag should be displayed 'above' the U.S. Ensign."

DISPLAY OF FLAGS AT YACHT CLUB AND SQUADRON MEETINGS

1. The flag of the United States should be displayed either from a staff, or flat against the wall above and behind the speaker's table.

2. The flag of the United States should never be draped or laid over anything except a casket, at which time special rules apply.

3. When displayed flat against a wall it should be fastened along the upper edge only, with the union to the flag's right, to the left as viewed by the audience. This applies whether the flag is hung with stripes vertical or horizontal. The horizontal position of the stripes is preferable.

4.* When displayed on a staff indoors, in an enclosure where there is no platform at the head of the room, the U.S. ensign is stood at the right of the audience; but if there is a platform, the U.S. ensign is displayed on a staff at the left of the audience, namely, at the right of the speaker. The USPS ensign, if also displayed, is stood at

* See USPS Officers Manual.

the left of the audience where there is no platform, and at the right of the audience (left of the speaker) if there is a platform. If the Canadian ensign is also to be so displayed, it should be at the right of the audience where there is no platform, and at the right of the speaker where there is a platform but just inboard of the U.S. ensign.

5. If the flag of the United States, and another, are displayed with crossed staffs, as at the head of a room, the flag of the United States should be at the flag's right, to left as viewed by the audience, and with its staff in front of the other.

6. If the flag of the United States is displayed with other flags in a group, from staffs, it should be in the center and slightly higher or in front of the other flags.

7. If the USPS flag is to be displayed flat against a wall, it is hung as prescribed for the Flag of the United States, as in paragraph 3 above, but on the opposite wall.

DISPLAY OF STATE FLAGS

Any citizen of any state, according to P/C William B. Matthews, Jr., Boating Administrator for the State of Maryland, may fly the flag of that state unless it is specifically prohibited by law.

On a *vessel with one or more masts,* the State flag is flown at the main masthead in place of the private signal, officer's flag, or Coast Guard Auxiliary Ensign.

On a *mastless boat,* the State flag would be flown at the bow staff in place of a club burgee.

It should be understood that, when a State flag displaces a Coast Guard Auxiliary Ensign at the masthead, an Auxiliary officer cannot fly his officer's pennant from the starboard yardarm. When the State flag at the masthead displaces the flag of an officer of a yacht club or the USPS, he cannot fly his officer's flag at any hoist.

The flying of a State flag at the stern of a boat is *not* proper; nor is it proper to fly from this place of honor any Confederate, "pirate," or other "gag" flag.

Honoring Other National Flags

Just as a certain code of etiquette has been adopted to govern the display of flags by American yachts on the waterways of our own nation, so too there is a certain accepted procedure to which pleasure boats should properly adhere when they cross international boundaries into the waters of another nation.

There are only a limited number of positions from which flags may be properly displayed on motor boats and consequently when a foreign flag is to be flown, it must displace one of the flags commonly flown in home waters.

Unfortunately, the customs observed in various foreign waters differ from each other; in case of doubt, inquire locally or observe other U.S. craft.

It is preferable for U.S. vessels while in international or foreign waters to fly the U.S. Ensign (50-star flag) at the stern rather than the Yacht or USPS Ensign.

It would be normal while in foreign waters *not* to fly at all the flags of purely U.S. organizations such as the USPS and USCG Auxiliary. An exception might be made for cruising groups from these organizations.

MOTOR BOATS

For the purposes of this flag code, motor boats may be divided into three general groups: (1) mastless vessels, having bow and stern staffs only; (2) single-masted motor vessels, with spreader; and (3) vessels with two masts.

Mastless vessels. A motor boat having only bow and stern staffs, if in home waters, would fly the yacht club burgee forward and her own ensign aft. In foreign waters, she must obviously keep her own ensign at the place of

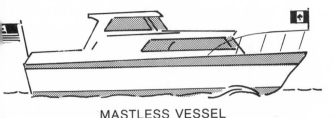

MASTLESS VESSEL

On the Great Lakes and along the eastern Canadian border, the foreign national flag (often called a "courtesy ensign") is flown from the bow staff. This displaces the club burgee which then may be flown from the starboard spreader. See illustrations on this page and page 472.

On other waters such as the Pacific Northwest, the Bahamas, and the Mexican Pacific Coast, a different procedure is followed. Here, it is expected that the U.S. boats will fly the local national flag from the starboard spreader, retaining the club burgee at the bow. See illustrations this page and page 472.

Motor vessels with two masts. Some of the larger motor craft have two masts. Assuming that the mainmast has no gaff, then the practice is as follows. Her own ensign is at

honor aft. Therefore she has no alternative but to display the national flag of the foreign country which she is visiting at the bow staff in place of her own club burgee. Under no circumstances should she try to fly both flags from one staff at the same time. That principle holds consistently true throughout all flag etiquette.

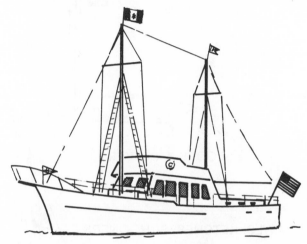

MOTOR VESSEL WITH TWO MASTS

NOTE:—

Ashore, it is common practice among U. S. yacht clubs on the border to fly the Canadian flag at the masthead, with the U.S. flag at the gaff, when they have Canadian entries in races or Canadian flag officers officially in the club house.

Motor vessels with one mast. Consider next the motor vessel with one mast and spreader—possibly the most common of all arrangements aboard cruising motor boats—her own ensign remains at the stern staff and her private signal or officer's flag at the masthead.

the stern staff as usual, and her private signal or officer's flag stays at the main masthead. The club pennant goes to the bow staff, making way for the foreign national flag at the fore masthead. This is correct practice whether the vessel is under way or laying at anchor, or at a dock.

The only variation of this procedure for two-masted vessels is found when the mainmast is equipped with a gaff. In such cases, the craft's own national ensign is flown at the gaff when underway, just as in home waters.

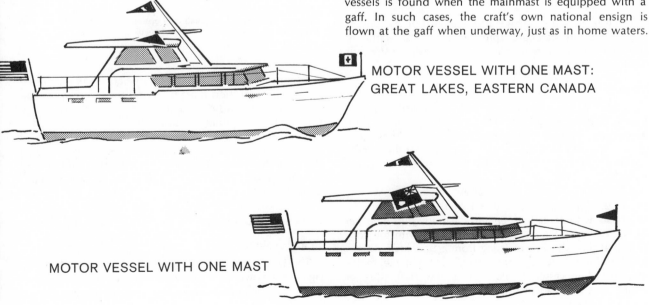

MOTOR VESSEL WITH ONE MAST:
GREAT LAKES, EASTERN CANADA

MOTOR VESSEL WITH ONE MAST

471

SAILING VESSELS

Where foreign flag flies to starboard

In the majority of foreign waters, where the courtesy ensign is flown from the starboard spreader on masted motorboats, a similar procedure is followed for sailing vessels.

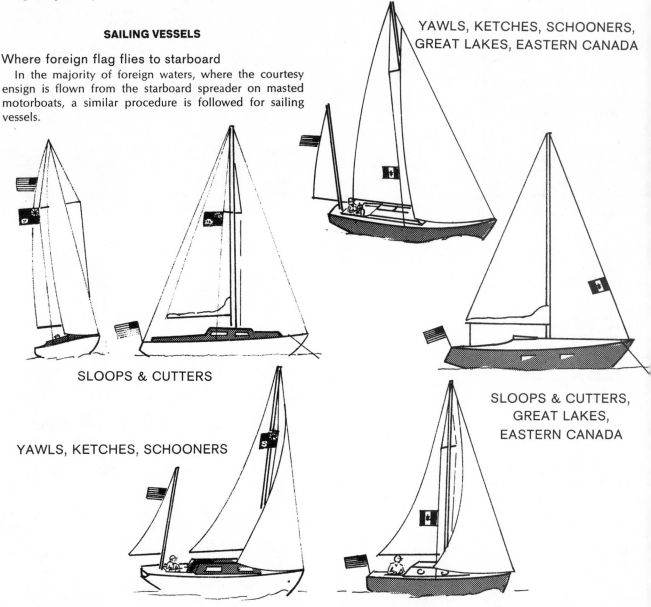

SLOOPS & CUTTERS

YAWLS, KETCHES, SCHOONERS, GREAT LAKES, EASTERN CANADA

YAWLS, KETCHES, SCHOONERS

SLOOPS & CUTTERS, GREAT LAKES, EASTERN CANADA

Sailboats underway under sail may optionally fly their own national ensign from a stern staff as shown above.

The foreign national flag is flown, at anchor and underway, from the starboard spreader (foremost starboard spreader if there is more than one mast). See illustrations on this page.

Where foreign flag flies forward

In those waters where it is the custom for motorboats to fly the courtesy ensign from the bow staff, problems arise when applying this procedure to sailing vessels. These craft do not normally have bow staffs and a place for the foreign national flag must be found that best approximates that location.

On sailing vessels of all rigs *at anchor* in these waters, the foreign national flag is flown from the forestay at a height so as to be easily seen and clear any personnel on deck, yet not so high as to be inconsistent with the concept that this is in lieu of flying from a bow staff. This is usually about ⅓ of the mast height. (If a large multi-masted sailing vessel should have a bow staff, it is, of course, used, instead of the more general procedure described above.)

As this location is not practical when *underway under sail*, another location must be found for the courtesy ensign. On sloops and cutters, it is flown from the starboard shroud, again at a height above deck of about ⅓ of the mast height. On ketches and yawls, this is the starboard shroud of the mainmast. Schooners fly the foreign national flag from the foremost starboard shroud, or from the foremost masthead (where it would displace the flags normally flown there).

Sailing vessels *underway under power* may fly the courtesy ensign from either the forestay or starboard shroud.

In all foreign waters

The US Ensign, club burgee, officer's flag, and private signal are flown in a similar manner as in home waters (except for schooners underway in certain areas as noted above).

Many boatmen spend their time afloat with little or no thought to the customs and etiquette of yachting. This is regrettable, for their activities can be more enjoyable both to themselves and to others with some knowledge and practice of doing things "the proper way."

A *custom* is defined in one dictionary as "the habitual practice; the usual way of doing a thing in given circumstances." Such long-standing practices and procedures have usually developed out of trial and error over many years into the "best," or "safest," or "most appropriate" method. By adhering to yachting customs, a boatman is benefiting from long years of others' experience — to defy custom is really to miss a fine opportunity. A love of boats and the water should be accompanied by respect for the traditions and long-established customs of the sea.

Etiquette has been described as "a prescribed or accepted code of usage as established for any occasion." Since recreational boating is a purely voluntary activity, let us drop the "prescribed" aspect of that description and emphasize the "accepted" qualities of the usages. If etiquette were regarded as no more than blind adherence to certain set conventionalities and amenities of social life, there might be sound reasons why one could question the need for, or desirability of, conforming to relatively rigid rules of conduct.

Just as soon, however, as one realizes that these principles of etiquette are not mere arbitrary laws demanding conformity on the part of all individuals— that they are basically the natural expressions of those who instinctively conduct themselves in a sincerely considerate manner toward all others, regardless of rank or race—it becomes quite obvious why anyone should seek to follow the practices that distinguish the true gentleman and yachtsman.

YACHTING CUSTOMS and ETIQUETTE

CHAPTER 23

Customs in general

In the varied relationships of people in many walks of life, a natural body of customs and accepted procedures inevitably develops to govern such relationships. Nowhere is this better exemplified than in the various branches of government service. In the departments that are concerned with diplomacy and statesmanship, observance of the correct form is inextricably woven into the act itself. In the military services, it is safe to say that efficient functioning could not be achieved without the many established customs and procedures.

Customs in Boating

The direct application of all naval customs and forms of etiquette to boating activities would be quite inappropriate and quickly rejected by most boatmen. There are, however, many customs and items of service etiquette that can be used as-is or modified for the circumstances of non-military small craft. Other boating customs derive directly from the ways of the sea and seafaring men.

The Skipper

By custom and by law, the skipper of a craft has the sole ultimate responsibility and authority aboard, especially in emergencies. These are spelled out in some detail in Chapter 7; here it is enough to note that these duties and powers have developed over the years, first as desirable and necessary practices, then as customs, and finally, in many cases, into legal requirements.

Leadership

Even on non-military and non-commercial small craft leadership is an important requirement. Getting things done by a willing and happy crew is a large step forward in putting the "pleasure" into pleasure boating. Proper attention to customs and etiquette provides a basis for effective leadership.

Leadership is said to be largely a matter of intelligent and just administration of authority. Knowledge along technical lines and of practical matters does not automatically provide the capability for leadership. This involves a study and cultivation of such qualities as self-control, judgment, courage, earnestness, sympathy, and loyalty, to name just a few of the many necessary attributes. One of the best methods of acquiring these qualities is to consciously take stock of one's own shortcomings with a view toward eliminating deficiencies and developing the desired characteristics—do this rather than demand in one's crew a degree of perfection that one has not himself attained.

Discipline

Leadership and discipline, including self-discipline, are logically considered in conjunction with each other—they are inseparable. Given a group of individuals in which all have the qualities of leadership developed to a greater or lesser degree, discipline will give each person an appreciation of the authority and responsibilities of their appointed or elected leader. Consequently, they will each work at assigned tasks in mutual cooperation, and will not waste time or mental effort in envy of their superior's position. The leader, in turn, will have the ability to inspire his subordinates to self-development and the voluntary

FIG. 2301 By law as well as long-established custom, the skipper of a boat has the sole ultimate responsibility and authority for the actions of the craft and the safety of all those aboard.

acceptance of higher responsibilities. It is an error for any leader to believe that he can grow no more; the effective leader grows as well as the men he leads.

It should be quickly apparent that the principles above have great applicability to the world of boating. The yacht club, Power Squadron, or unit of the Coast Guard Auxiliary that reflects an understanding of these ideas will flourish. Of all places, there is none where the demand for capable leadership and discipline is more vital than aboard a vessel, whether it be a large yacht, an ocean-racing sailboat, or a motorboat of any size. The skipper has, and must have, the final authority; he must be equal to that responsibility. If he is worthy of his trust as a "leader," he will get the cooperation of his crew by "leading" and not by driving.

PERSONAL SALUTES

Hand salutes are not often given by civilian boatmen, although they may be used in some formal ceremonies. In a way, this lack of personal saluting is unfortunate, for what better way is there to say "thank you" to a cooperative bridge tender or to the skipper of a boat that slowed down in passing you than to give him a snappy—but not exaggerated—hand salute. Its meaning will never be misunderstood and it will often be much appreciated. It is more of a show of appreciation than merely a wave of the hand in greeting.

Origins

The practice of hand salutes is believed to have had its origins at least as far back as the days of the Romans, when the raising of one's hand, palm forward, was a gesture to show that no dagger was concealed in it. The native American Indians used much the same gesture to indicate a lack of harmful intent. Today, happily, we have other motives when showing respect for superiors.

Uncovering the head also dates back to ancient days. Certain types of headgear, however, were not easily removed, and so the present day salute evolved as a gesture in which the hand is raised to the visor of the cap in much the same manner as if the visor of a helmet were going to be lifted.

Exchanging salutes

Etiquette prescribes that in ceremonies a person junior in rank or seniority should salute first. It is emphasized that this deference to superiors does not imply an admission of inferiority, no more than one could logically be accused of cowardice when displaying a wholesome respect for laws. Those who might take the attitude that a salute is undemocratic should recognize that such an act is merely an extension of the courtesies of everyday life. The salute, thus understood, becomes an opportunity to respect the authority an official represents with no thought of personal inferiority.

BOARDING AND LEAVING
GOVERNMENT SHIPS

It is not inappropriate for a civilian boatman in an organizational uniform, or even in informal clothing but wearing a uniform or visored cap, to observe the proper naval etiquette when boarding and leaving a ship of the Navy, Coast Guard, Coast & Geodetic Survey, or other gov-

FIG. 2302 Of all places, there is none where the demand for capable leadership and discipline is more vital than aboard an ocean-racing sailboat. The skipper must have final authority.

ernmental agency. He can be assured that his actions will be promptly and properly responded to by the personnel of the watch.

Procedures

When reaching the upper platform of the gangway or accommodation ladder, the person about to board, and before stepping aboard, should stop, then turn toward the stern of the vessel and salute the national ensign. He then turns back to the Officer of the Deck (O.O.D.), salutes, and says: "Request permission to come aboard, sir." The O.O.D. returns both salutes as they are given and with the second one says "Permission granted."

When leaving the vessel, the individual first salutes the Officer of the Deck and says: Request permission to leave ship, sir." The O.O.D. returns the salute and grants permission. At the top of the gangway or other platform, the departing person stops, faces aft, and salutes the U.S. Flag; the O.O.D. returns this salute also, but says nothing.

If the individual is *not* wearing a cap, the *salutes* are *omitted*, but the request for permission to board or depart is made as noted above.

DAILY COLOR CEREMONIES

If a boatman is at a yacht club, or a military or naval base, where formal morning and evening color ceremonies are held, he should follow the actions of local personnel who are not in formation. If he is outdoors when the flag is raised or lowered, and he is wearing a uniform or visored cap, he should face the flag and give a hand salute, holding it until the ceremony is completed. If he is wearing a civilian hat, this should be removed and held over the left breast. If no headgear is worn, the right hand should be placed over the left breast. This is the "breast salute." Women not in uniform stand at attention and give the

breast salute. Automobiles are stopped and personnel remain inside.

The above rules do not, of course, apply if the boatman is engaged in hoisting or lowering his own colors. He should complete his actions and then, if the official ceremonies have not ended, he should stand at attention, and salute if appropriate.

On official occasions, the same salutes as above are given for the playing of the Star Spangled Banner or national anthem of another country.

Yachting Etiquette

Etiquette in yachting takes many forms, but all are essentially the act of showing consideration and courtesy to others. The range of correct etiquette extends from simple everyday actions to formal daily routines and official ceremonies.

Boarding another boat

The etiquette to be observed when coming on board another person's boat is derived from that explained above for boarding a naval vessel. Salutes are seldom exchanged, but a simple request for permission to come aboard is always in good taste. An occasion for saluting might be if the individual boarding were wearing a uniform cap and the craft were that of the commodore of the yacht club or the commander of a Power Squadron.

When leaving another's boat, the naval form of requesting permission is not used. A simple statement of thanks for the hospitality or best wishes for a pleasant cruise is sufficient.

SALUTES BETWEEN VESSELS

In formal ceremonies such as a rendezvous of a yacht club or Power Squadron, the fleet of boats present may pass in review before the flagship of the commodore or USPS commander. In such cases, each craft will salute as it passes. In other isolated instances, joining a club cruise or passing a ship with a high public official embarked, salutes may be exchanged between vessels.

Dipping the ensign in salute

Federal law prohibits dipping the Flag of the United States (the 50-star flag) to any person or thing, and only government vessels are permitted to dip the national ensign in reply to a dip.

The law does, however, permit organizational or institutional flags to be dipped. Thus the U.S. Power Squadrons Ensign, when flown from stern or gaff, may be dipped to salute another craft, or dipped in reply to a dip.

The status of the Yacht Ensign (13 stars in a circle around an anchor on a blue field) is not spelled out clearly, but since the law specifically covers only the Flag of the United States, the assumption has been made that the Yacht Ensign may be dipped.

In a fleet review of a unit of the Power Squadrons, the USPS Ensign should be flown from the stern staff or gaff if a suitable size flag is available. In this way, the flag dipped would be that of the organization holding the review.

All vessels in any review, flying either the USPS or Yacht Ensign at the stern or gaff, should dip that flag when their

FIG. 2303 "Dressing ship" is an old custom applicable to yachts as well as to naval and merchant vessels. This is done only on special occasions and the proper procedures must be followed to be correct.

YACHT ROUTINES

The following regulations, particularly applicable to a consideration of yachting etiquette, are taken from that portion of the New York Yacht Club code entitled *Yacht Routine*. These deal with salutes, boats (meaning tenders and dinghies), and general courtesies. Other sections, not given here, relate primarily to the display of flags, signaling, and lights.

The routines of other yacht clubs may be considerably less formal and detailed than that which follows, but whatever routines are used they are likely to have been derived from the procedures of the New York Yacht Club.

Salutes

All salutes shall be made by dipping the ensign once, lowering the ensign to the dip and hoisting it when the salute is returned. All salutes shall be returned.

Whistles shall never be used in saluting.

Guns may be used to call attention to signals, but their use otherwise shall be avoided as much as possible.

Vessels of the United States and foreign navies shall be saluted.

When a flag officer of the Club comes to anchor, he shall be saluted by all yachts present, except where there is a senior flag officer present.

When a yacht comes to anchor where a flag officer is present, such officer shall be saluted. A junior flag officer anchoring in the presence of a senior shall salute.

Yachts passing shall salute, the junior saluting first.

All salutes shall be answered in kind.

A yacht acting as Race Committee boat should neither salute nor be saluted while displaying the Committee flag.

Boats

Upon entering and leaving boats, deference is shown seniors by juniors entering first and leaving last.

When in boats, flag officers display their flags, captains (owners) their private signals, and members (non-owners) the club burgee. When on duty, the fleet captain and race committee display their distinctive flags. The flag of the senior officer embarked takes precedence. A flag officer embarked in a boat not displaying his distinctive flag should be considered as present in an unofficial capacity.

When two boats are approaching the same gangway or landing stage, flag officers shall have the right of way in order of seniority.

Whenever possible, boat booms shall be rigged in at night. Otherwise, a white light shall be shown at the end. All boats made fast to the stern of a yacht at anchor shall show a white light at night.

Courtesies

When a flag officer makes an official visit, his flag, if senior to that of the yacht visited, shall be displayed in place of the burgee while he is on board.

A yacht may display the personal flag of a national, state, or local official when such individual is on board, or the national ensign of a distinguished foreign visitor. This flag should be displayed in place of the private signal or officer's flag for the President of the United States, and in place of the burgee for all other officials and visitors.

On Independence Day, and when ordered on other occasions, a yacht shall, when at anchor and the weather

bow comes abreast of the stern of the flagship and return it to full height when their stern clears the bow of the flagship.

On this occasion, the Flag of the United States should *not* be flown, but if it is, *do not dip it* and use only the hand salute described below. Do not dip any flag other than the flag being flown at the stern staff or the gaff (including the equivalent position on a Marconi sail).

Hand saluting

When a vessel is officially reviewing a parade of other vessels, the senior officer present stands on the deck of the reviewing ship with his staff in formation behind him. Only he gives the hand salute in return to salutes rendered him.

On a boat passing in review, if the skipper has his crew and guests in formation behind him, only he gives the hand salute. If the crew and guests are in uniform and standing at attention at the rail facing the reviewing boat as they pass, they all give the hand salute. The criterion is whether or not the other persons aboard are in formation. If in formation, only the skipper salutes; but if not in formation, all salute.

For both situations, the hand salute is given as the flag is dipped and is held until it is raised again.

Gun salutes

Guns should not be used in salutes between yachts unless ordered by a national authority or by the senior officer present.

FIG. 2304 Cruising will usually take a boatman well away from familiar home waters. He should be alert to the peculiarities of local customs and should conform to the way in which things are done at the club or harbor he is visiting.

permits, *dress ship* from morning to evening colors. See pages 461 and 467.

After joining the Squadron during the Annual Cruise, a yacht shall request permission before leaving.

Cruising

When cruising away from home waters, the wise skipper keeps a sharp eye out for local customs. It is a mark of courtesy to conform to local procedures and practices.

While visiting at a yacht club of which you are not a member, observe the actions and routines of the local owner-members, and particularly the club officers. This is especially important with respect to evening colors. Not all clubs strictly calculate the daily time of sunset, and some may be earlier than you would normally expect.

If you will be off your boat at the time of evening colors —in the clubhouse for dinner, for example—be sure to take down your flags before you leave your craft.

Be a good neighbor

Consideration of the other skipper is an important element of yachting etiquette. Don't anchor too close to another boat so as to give cause for concern for the safety of both craft; consider the state of the tide and the effect of its range on the radius about which you will swing. Use a guest mooring only with permission; tie up to a fuel pier only briefly.

In the evening hours at an anchorage, don't disturb your neighbors on other boats. Sound travels exceptionally well across water and many cruising boatmen turn in early for dawn departures. Keep voices down and play radios only at low levels. If you should be one of the early departees, leave with an absolute minimum of noise.

Be a good neighbor in other ways, too. Don't throw

trash and garbage overboard. Secure flapping halyards; they can be a most annoying source of noise for some distance. When coming into or leaving an anchorage area, do so at a dead slow speed to keep your wake and wash at an absolute minimum.

Passing other boats

A faster boat overtaking and passing a slower one in a narrow channel should slow down *sufficiently* to cause no damage or discomfort. Often overlooked is the fact that it may be necessary for the *slower* boat itself to reduce speed. If that boat is making, say, 8 knots, the faster boat can only slow down to about 10 knots in order to have enough speed differential left to get past. At this speed, the passing boat may unavoidably make a wake that is uncomfortable to the other craft. In such cases, the overtaken boat should slow to 4 or 5 knots to allow herself to be passed at 6 or 7 knots with little wake.

If adequate depths of water extend outward on one or both sides of the course, it is the courteous thing for the passing boat to swing well out to a safe side to minimize the discomfort of the overtaken boat.

Proper etiquette calls for power boats to pass sailing craft astern or well to leeward.

GUESTS ABOARD

If you are invited to go cruising for a day, a weekend, or a more extended period, there are many things to be considered—clothes, promptness, gifts, aids, noise, smoking, privacy, and time.

FIG. 2305 Whenever circumstances such as the depth of water permit, power boats should observe the proper etiquette of passing sailboats on their lee side or crossing under their stern. Consideration of the other skipper is a mark of a good yachtsman. The wake must always be kept down to a reasonable level.

Take a minimum of *clothes*, packed in collapsible containers, or at least in suitcases that will nest inside each other when empty—storage space is severely limited aboard boats. Bring one outfit of "city clothes" for use at those places ashore requiring such dress. Bring two bathing suits if you plan to do much swimming—at times, things dry slowly around a boat. For additional comments on boating clothing and shoes, see Chapter 24.

For the *stowage of clothing* you bring aboard, the skipper may assign a special locker which he has cleared for your convenience. Don't scatter gear and clothing all over the boat. Use the locker provided, keep it orderly, and thus help the skipper keep things shipshape.

When a *sailing time* is given, be there ahead of time. The skipper generally chooses a time with a purpose in mind—the tides and currents, normal weather patterns, the length of the planned run, etc.

Meal times are set for the convenience of the galley hand. It is inconsiderate for a tardy guest to delay meals. In any event, it is bad manners to be late for a meal.

Rising and *bedtimes* are a matter of convenience to everyone aboard because of the generally limited washing and toilet facilities. Get up promptly when the skipper or paid hands are heard moving about. Use the head as expeditiously as possible, make up your bunk, stow any loose gear about the cabin, and appear on deck. When the skipper suggests that it is time to retire for the evening, take the hint and bed down.

Noise on a boat seems to amplify, so walk and speak softly and your shipmates will be glad you're aboard.

Smoking is stopped, of course, when gasoline is to be taken aboard, but care is the order of the day even when smoking is permissible. A carelessly flicked cigarette ash or butt has started many a fire in a chair, awning, or compartment. Cigars leave a particularly unpleasant after-odor and should be enjoyed only in the open air.

Many small particles—pipe tobacco and ashes, peanut shells, bits of potato chips, crumbs, etc.—have a way of getting into cracks, crevices and corners, and there defying the ordinary cleaning facilities found on a boat. Use care with all of these things.

Privacy becomes valuable on a protracted cruise. Part of every day should be set aside for getting away from everyone else aboard. Your cruisemates will be more glad of your company if it is not constant.

Should occasions arise where you board the boat from a *dinghy*, or have an opportunity to use the skipper's dinghy (with his permission, of course) use care in coming alongside. Unship oarlocks which could scar the boat's planking, and stow oars in the boat; never leave them in the oarlocks.

Gifts are certainly not expected, but are always acceptable. Be sure, however, that they are appropriate for boating—if in doubt, make it liquid and consumable. When invited on board for a day or a week, ask what you can bring. If the owner wants to provide all of the food and drink, the guest might take the cruising party ashore for a good dinner at the first port of call. Buying part of the fuel is looked upon as a partial charter by some government agencies, but bringing food or liquid refreshment is not so regarded.

Assistance on board a boat can be useful, or it can do more harm than good. If you don't know what to do, sit down out of the way and be quiet. Always keep out of the line of vision of the helmsman and be particularly quiet and unobtrusive when the craft is being docked or undocked.

If being on board is not a new experience, or you wish to learn to be more useful, you may ask what you can do to help. Ask, however, when things are calm and uneventful; don't ask in the midst of getting under way or coming alongside a pier.

Above all, if you are assigned to do something, do exactly that. If you think that the instructions were wrong, say so, but don't go off on your own when the skipper thinks that you are doing what he asked.

FIG. 2306 Having guests aboard for a day's cruise or longer period can add to a boat owner's enjoyment of his recreation by sharing his enjoyment with others. Guests can do their part by "fitting in" with the routine of the craft.

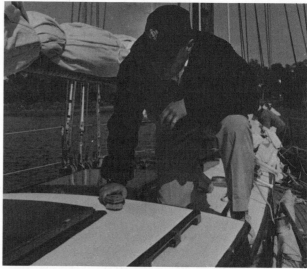

FIG. 2307 Guests aboard for a cruise may offer their assistance in the operation of the craft or in the daily chores. They should not, however, tackle work without the skipper's knowledge and should work under proper supervision.

CHAPTER 24

BOATING CLOTHING and UNIFORMS

FIG. 2401 Many boatmen find an informal visored cloth cap the most practical form of headgear afloat. It is comfortable, provides good shade for the eyes, and stays on well in a breeze. Club emblems, but no insignia of rank, may be worn on such caps.

(Photograph by Frank Rohr)

The subject of "clothing and uniforms" encompasses both the matter of wearing or not wearing a uniform and that of safe, sensible apparel for today's boating. In each of these areas rather strong differences of opinion will be found to exist.

When it comes to clothing, most boatmen have rather strong convictions as to whether or not they should, or must, abide by any arbitrary set of regulations. The spokesmen of one faction argue that they go afloat for pleasure and relaxation, and propose to dress as they please—for comfort and practicability. The other group advocates strict adherence to all the proprieties, frowning on those who do not conform to the dictates of etiquette, whether it be in dress, the display of flags, or other areas.

Who is right? Actually neither, in the sense that the other would be wrong. There is room for differences of opinion, and no logical reason why each group and individual should not be entitled to his own position and actions.

Good taste

Few boatmen would deliberately violate the principles of good taste in regard to dress aboard their craft. In some cases, it is merely a matter of not realizing that such principles exist. Errors are often made in the use of various devices and insignia worn on uniforms, and in the choice of articles of uniforms themselves. Generally these practices would be corrected if the wearer knew that he was in error.

One thing is certain. The clothing that might be appropriate and acceptable in one situation may be decidedly in bad taste in another. It would be hard to say who would be more uncomfortable—the outboarder in shorts at a yacht club dinner party or the commodore in spotless whites tinkering with a balky engine under a blazing sun.

Origins of present-day clothing

The clothing that is worn while boating today has developed over the years from the quite stiff and formal uniforms of the late 1800's and early years of this century. The steady trend toward smaller, owner-operated craft has taken its toll on the rigid customs of yachting circles—the "dressing for dinner" routine. The establishment of many small, much less formal yacht clubs and boating clubs has likewise supported the gradual change to a more informal mode of attire. A third factor is the general trend of modern life to an easier, more casual mood.

These developments all combine to make a full yachting uniform something of a rarity aboard present-day craft or at typical yacht clubs.

479

Yacht Club Uniforms

Essentially all yacht clubs provide in their by-laws for uniforms and insignia of rank. In actual practice, however, there will be found a wide variance in the degree to which such apparel is worn. In a very few clubs, the officers, many members who are boat owners, and even some non-owner members have uniforms and will wear them on formal occasions. Hardly ever will full uniforms be worn while cruising or at every-day activities around the clubhouse. It should be noted, though, that members are not required to have uniforms; their purchase and use are purely optional.

Uniforms in typical clubs

In most yacht and boating clubs, the officers will own uniforms, but few members will have them. Rare indeed in these clubs would be a uniform on a member who did not own a boat.

In the smaller and even less formal clubs, the uniforms of officers and members may be limited by general agreement and custom to the wearing of a uniform cap only, worn with any boating clothes of good taste. This is not "wrong" although it may be viewed with disfavor by older, more tradition-minded yachtsmen. It is well in tune with the informality of modern life and family-style boating, particularly outboarding.

When uniforms are worn

Yacht and boating club uniforms are typically worn only on special occasions, although it is quite reasonable to wear a uniform cap with regular clothing while engaged in ordinary activities while afloat or at the club piers. Formal occasions for uniform wearing might include the ceremonies at the beginning of a new season, the installation of officers, holiday regattas, and the like. The best guidance at any club regarding the wearing or non-wearing of the full uniform or cap only is the policy adhered to by the majority of the officers and members.

On board and under way, the cap will probably be the only item of uniform worn on owner-operated boats. On larger craft where there are paid hands to take care of the operation of the yacht, a uniform for the owner would seem to be in far better taste, as well as more sensible, than on a small boat where the owner-captain must break out his own anchor, swab his own deck, and attend to numerous other chores both clean and dirty.

Derivation of the uniform

On one point, at least, there can be little argument. For the occasions where a uniform is appropriate, it should certainly follow the style prescribed by yacht clubs as correct. For authority, no better source can be found than the code to which the New York Yacht Club has adhered for many years. While there may be minor deviations in the practices of other clubs, the N.Y.Y.C. rules are the basic form on which the others are patterned.

Basic uniforms

The service dress uniform prescribed for yacht club officers and members is normally a double-breasted sack coat of navy blue or white cloth, serge or flannel, with trousers of the same material or of white drill. The cap is of navy blue cloth and has a patent leather visor, black chin strap, and black buttons. The white cap is of the same style with a fixed or removable cover. White shirts with black or dark ties are appropriate; some clubs have ties of their own design. White or black shoes are worn to match the trousers; boating shoes are not worn with a uniform except under limited circumstances afloat when advisable for safety.

Cap emblems

There are a number of styles of yachting caps offered by the manufacturers of uniforms. In every case, an emblem or device will be found on the front of the band over the visor. This identifies the club to which the individual belongs and indicates his status in the club. See figures 2402(a), (b), (c), (d). The central part of the device will be an enameled metal or silk embroidered disc showing the distinctive emblem of the club, basically its burgee. This is placed at the intersection of two crossed fouled anchors in gold embroidery.

Insignia of rank

If the yachtsman holds the office of commodore, there will be three gold stars around the anchors, one at the top and one at each side. See fig. 2402(a).

COMMODORE ★ ★ ★
Trefoil with 4 additional black stripes; 3 gold stars within loops.

VICE COMMODORE ★ ★
Trefoil with 3 additional black stripes; 2 gold stars within side loops.

REAR COMMODORE ★
Trefoil with 2 additional black stripes; 1 gold star in center loop.

FIG. 2402(a) Yacht club officers are distinguished by insignia on sleeve and cap. Stars of current officers are gold, those of past officers, when used, are silver.
(All insignia illustrations courtesy Commodore Uniform Company, Inc.)

The vice-commodore of the club, next lower in rank, has the same device except that he is entitled to two stars, one on each side of the anchors.

The third-ranking officer, the rear commodore, rates one star, placed above the device the same as the top star of the commodore.

Members and staff officers

The N.Y.Y.C. code prescribes that captains (owners of boats) and ex-flag officers rate only the two gold fouled anchors without the gold stars of incumbent officers. In some clubs, however, this practice is modified to authorize past officers to wear silver stars of the same number and in the same locations.

In most yacht clubs, a member who is not a boat owner uses a cap device with a *single* fouled anchor placed vertically, fig. 2402(c). Some clubs, however, omit this separate insignia and allow the wearing of two crossed fouled anchors for all members not holding office.

Other officers of a club (often referred to as "staff officers") are distinguished by certain symbols in gold placed above the regular cap emblem, fig. 2402(b). A fleet captain, for example, is identified by a horizontally placed anchor. The secretary is entitled to a maple leaf; the treasurer, an acorn; the measurer, a short bar; and a member of the race committee, a half-inch anchor placed vertically. A fleet surgeon is identified by a red cross.

Variations exist in some clubs—the letter M for the measurer; the letters RC for race committeemen.

Sleeve insignia

Rank and status are also indicated by stripes on each sleeve of the uniform coat, fig. 2402(a). On blue uniforms, the stripes are black; on white coats, they are white.

A commodore wears five stripes of mohair braid, the upper one taking the shape of what is known as a trefoil—this might be described as a triple loop, one part vertical and the others horizontal. In each loop of the trefoil, the commodore wears a gilt star. Regulations, of course, prescribe the width of the braid, how far from the cuff the

lower stripe is and how far apart the others are, the size of the stars, etc.

The vice-commodore wears four stripes, the upper one being a trefoil, and there are two stars, one in each horizontal loop.

The rear-commodore has three stripes with one star in the upper loop of the trefoil formed by the top stripe.

Boat owners and staff officers are entitled to two stripes, the upper one having the trefoil; they, of course, have no stars. Members not owning boats wear a single stripe which has the trefoil.

Ex-flag officers continue to wear the stripes designating their former rank, but omit the stars that they were entitled to while holding office.

No gold braid

Note particularly that in all of the uniform descriptions above there is *no* mention of *gold braid* for the yachtsman, whether member, owner, or officer. The only gold permissible is the gold fouled anchors of the cap device, the stars on cap and sleeve, and the insignia of the staff officers.

The yachtsman does *not* wear a gold chin strap on his cap, nor is there any sanction for the wearing of gold embroidery on the cap visor as is worn by senior Navy and Coast Guard officers—the so-called "scrambled eggs." This has been seen in some boating circles in recent years, but is entirely incorrect and improper for a boatman.

Formal dress

In some of the older clubs, the uniform regulations prescribe a mess jacket for the most formal occasions. This might be compared with a tuxedo or dinner jacket of civilian dress. The yacht club mess jacket is single-breasted, of blue undress worsted, with rolling collar made with a long roll, and pointed lapels. It is trimmed with black silk braid and appropriate collar and sleeve ornaments.

In most clubs, however, the more formal uniform will consist of the regular service dress coat with a bow tie substituted for the usual four-in-hand tie.

STAFF OFFICERS' INSIGNIA

FIG. 2402(b) Cap insignia worn by staff officers are illustrated at the right. Sleeve insignia is shown above—trefoil with one additional black stripe, and insignia of officer in the center loop (in this case the gold anchor of the Race Committee).

RACE COMMITTEE

FLEET CAPTAIN

FLEET SURGEON

SECRETARY

TREASURER

MEASURER

481

Blazers

A relatively recent development in boating clothing is the wearing of a blazer jacket with matching or contrasting slacks. This is a comfortable and attractive alternative to the full club uniform except on formal occasions. It has been widely adopted and its use continues to spread.

Blazers are dark blue, two- or three-button style, single-breasted with a left upper and two lower patch pockets. Either black or gilt buttons may be prescribed by the club's rules for the front and sleeves of the jacket.

A patch of the club burgee on crossed fouled anchors, or other design derived from the club insignia, is worn on the upper left pocket. The blazer is not, however, an item of uniform and thus no insignia of rank is worn on the sleeve or elsewhere on the blazer. The club uniform cap should be worn with the blazer only if authorized by the club's rules.

UNIFORMS OF PAID CREW

The uniform regulations of the New York Yacht Club, from whence most other clubs' procedures are derived, include a complete set of descriptions of uniforms for various *paid* crew members. Crews, in general, are much smaller today than they were in the days of very large sail and steam yachts when the regulations were originally drafted, but logical adaptations to current conditions can easily be made.

Rare indeed will be the yacht paid captain—"sailing master" in NYYC terminology—in blue uniform with four gold sleeve stripes, or chief engineer with three red stripes, overseeing a crew of mates, assistant engineers, boatswains, oilers, coxswains, and launchmen. If blue crew uniforms are seen, it will be noted that the trefoil device of club members is not worn by professionals.

The typical work and cruising uniform of paid crew is khaki. Blue coats and trousers may be worn in port or for more formal occasions. White uniforms may be worn in warm or hot climates.

Caps for paid crew

The cap is the distinguishing device of the professional. See fig. 2402(d). The use of gold for the chin strap is as proper for the paid crewmen as it is improper for the owner. Further, the insignia above the gold strap is always quite different. There is no single accepted design for the cap ornament for the professional. Many owners have adopted an embroidered design consisting of their club burgee and their personal flag crossed and partially surrounded by a gold wreath. Others use a more simple design of crossed clear anchors (*not* the fouled anchors of the owner's emblem) within a plain gold circle. Engineering personnel would wear a three-bladed propeller in lieu of the anchors.

Skippers and mates of charter fishing boats may be seen using the last design described above with or without the word "captain" or "mate" embroidered in gold above the circle.

CLUB UNIFORMS IN GENERAL

Having read all of the above, one might reach the conclusion that most boatmen own a wardrobe full of uniforms and never relax in anything less formal. That, how-

ever, is not at all true. While the formal occasions mentioned contribute in large measure to the general good fellowship and enjoyment found in yachting circles, if the sport were ever to lose its basic character as a freedom from shore-based conventions, it would very rapidly lose some of its virtues, and most likely many of its followers.

OWNER - CLUB MEMBER

MEMBER (non-owner)

OWNER (non-member)

FIG. 2402(c) While practice varies among yacht clubs, the cap and sleeve insignia illustrated here satisfy the dictates of etiquette. Above— the boat-owning yacht club member has a trefoil with one additional black stripe on the sleeve; the member who owns no boat has the trefoil without additional stripes.

CAP INSIGNIA FOR YACHTING PROFESSIONALS

FIG. 2402(d) Traditionally correct devices for paid hands aboard yachts. Crossed flags in gold wreath may be used, at the yacht owner's discretion, by professional officers and crewmen. Crossed anchors in gold wreath often designate the paid captain. Crossed anchors (in circle) are worn by deck officers, propeller in circle by engineer officers. Lettering in gold wreath (below) is self-explanatory.

FIG. 2403 Officers and members of the U.S. Power Squadrons may wear a variety of uniforms for different climates and occasions. Uniform "C" shown here with long-sleeve white shirt, black tie, and long white trousers is typical of those worn at outdoor summer ceremonies such as flag-raisings. The Sea Explorer Scouts forming the color guard are not a part of the USPS, but many Squadrons do sponsor such units.
(Photograph by Frank P. Beauchamp)

USPS Uniforms

Although the United States Power Squadrons is not a military organization, it has a rather full set of uniforms, winter and summer, formal and informal. These are not required to be worn by all members, and many do not, but they are authorized and specified if desired. Most officers will wear uniforms for meetings, rendezvous ceremonies, and other special occasions. Uniforms are not generally worn to various USPS educational classes.

Uniform combinations

The USPS uniforms range from informal white Bermuda shorts worn with open-neck, short-sleeve shirt to regular dark blue coat and trousers that can be worn with four-in-hand tie during the day or with bow tie for evening events. In between are uniforms consisting of the short-sleeve shirt and long white trousers, or a long-sleeve white shirt and black tie worn with the same trousers. See fig. 2403. The blue uniform coat may also be combined with white trousers for more formal affairs in warm climates. Although not a part of the uniform series, there is a USPS blazer that may be worn for many occasions.

Insignia of rank

Officer's rank in the United States Power Squadrons is indicated on the uniform coat by sleeve braid and embroidered insignia. A varying number of black stripes, up to four, is used as on yacht club uniforms, but in addition there are three different widths of braid used in combination. The long-sleeved white shirt also carries the sleeve insignia but not the braid.

Uniform cap

As with yacht clubs, there is a uniform cap that is worn both with the various uniforms and by itself with informal boating clothes. The rank of various local, District, and National officers is also indicated on the cap. A USPS cap ornament may be worn on non-uniform boating caps, but in such cases no insignia of rank is shown.

Further information

Details of the USPS uniforms and insignia of rank are spelled out in the by-laws of that organization and are illustrated in the officers' manual. A table of information on officers' sleeve braid and insignia, cap insignia, and flags will be found on pages R and S.

Coast Guard Auxiliary Uniforms

The uniforms worn by officers and members of the Coast Guard Auxiliary have evolved through several distinct phases over recent years. The uniforms are now more "military" than "yachting" although the organization remains basically civilian in nature. Its supervision and administration by the regular Coast Guard does not change the Auxiliary's non-military status. The title of "Commodore" in various combinations remains in use also as a carry-over from earlier days.

Uniform combinations

The uniforms of the USCGAux—and that is the correct abbreviation, not USCGA—include a "service dress" in blue, khaki, and combination (blue coat with white trousers); working uniforms in blue and khaki (with boating shoes optional); and tropical whites. Members of the Auxiliary would not, of course, need all of these uniforms, only those appropriate to their area and normal duties. A black bow tie may be worn with the combination service dress uniform for formal evening events. There are also uniform jackets, raincoats, and overcoats.

Insignia of rank

The rank of various officers is now indicated by sleeve braid, shoulder boards, and pin-on insignia, all patterned after those worn by regular Coast Guard officers, but with differences designed to distinguish the Auxiliarist.

Braid on sleeves and shoulder boards is of silver rather than gold and is worn in stripes, half-stripes, and broad stripes in a series comparable to those worn by Ensigns to Rear Admirals of the Coast Guard and Navy. The Auxiliary, however, does not use rank titles like those of the regular and reserve services. Braid is prescribed for the office held rather than for rank titles. Sleeve braid rings go only half-way around each sleeve.

Shoulder boards worn with khaki uniforms carry the same number of stripes as the sleeves of blue coats; these are also used with the overcoat. Shoulder boards of the most senior officers are solid silver braid with one or two stars as appropriate.

The Auxiliary shield is worn above the stripes of both shoulder boards and sleeve rings.

Collar insignia, worn on the khaki and blue shirts, consist of the same series of designs used for officers of the Armed Forces, but with a letter "A" in blue or red super-

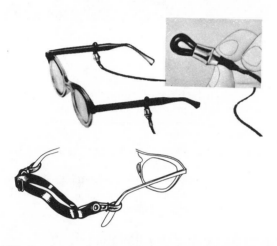

FIG. 2404 Eyeglasses, if accidentally dropped overboard, are likely to be lost. To prevent this, "keeper" cords or holders are available. Light flotation devices may also be attached to the frames.
(Courtesy Commodore Uniform Company, Inc.)

imposed. Similar insignia in slightly larger size are worn on the uniform raincoat.

Rank insignia of the Coast Guard Auxiliary are illustrated on page V.

Uniform caps

Officers and members of the Auxiliary wear frame caps similar to those used by regular officers; white and khaki covers are used—the blue cover is no longer used by the Coast Guard and Navy.

The chin straps of members' frame caps are black, those of officers are silver. Visor ornamentation in silver is worn on the caps of senior officers.

A "working cap" of boating style is authorized in blue and khaki. The fore-and-aft "garrison" cap has been reduced to an optional item only.

INFORMAL CLOTHING

Informal boating clothing varies widely with the individual, the area, and the activities engaged in. Essentially the only degree of uniformity exists at the two extremes—

top and bottom, cap and shoes. In between, the individual is "on his own," guided only by good sense and good taste. "Gag" or extreme uniforms and clothing do not meet the latter criterion and should be avoided.

Caps

The yachtsman who is particular to wear the correct style of yachting cap on formal occasions may often go hatless in the summer time. The sun is strong around the water, however, and protection of some kind for head and eyes is usually necessary, which probably gives rise to the custom of wearing the yachting cap even when other parts of the uniform are omitted. See fig. 2401.

When informal boating caps of the visored style, often referred to as "flat-top" or "flight deck" type, are worn, the careful skipper adds no organizational or rank insignia except as prescribed by the organization concerned.

Especially among the sailing enthusiasts a white cloth hat with wide brim all around, frequently with green underneath or with a green transparent visor, is popular.

Sun glasses

Sun glasses are widely used afloat to prevent eye strain from sun glare. Glasses with Polaroid lenses are among the best as they are particularly efficient in glare reduction.

Those individuals who must wear glasses with prescription lenses for distant vision will find it highly desirable to have a pair made with the prescription in tinted glass. The tint must be dark enough to cope adequately with the extreme degrees of brightness found on and near the water. Persons using bifocals for both near and distant vision correction will also find the use of tinted glass most desirable while afloat.

Regular eyeglasses or sun glasses must be protected from accidental loss overboard. See fig. 2404. A keeper chain or cord can be worn around the back of the person's neck, or a light flotation device can be attached to the frames to keep them from sinking if dropped into the water.

Foot-gear

Shoes that cannot be relied upon to give you a sure, slip-proof footing on a wet or slippery deck are highly dangerous on a boat. Coupled with this is the necessity of using a type of sole and heel that will not scratch fine decks.

For all-around use afloat, the best informal footwear available is a sneaker type of shoe with cloth uppers and soles of special material and designs that can be depended upon to give a grip on a wet, heeling deck. Slits in the soles of Sperry Topsiders, Randy Boatshus, and others provide an effective "squeegee" action. For more dressy occasions, shoes with leather uppers, but the same non-slip soles, are available.

Cork soles and special designs are available that will not pick up grit and sand when worn ashore, to be tracked back on deck when returning to the boat. Ordinary sneakers or tennis shoes may be worn provided they do not have a smooth sole that would permit slipping on a wet deck. Crepe-soled shoes, though comfortable, are doubtful items on a boat.

Women may wear much the same footgear as men. High heels, obviously, have no place on a boat.

BAGGAGE

Closely related to clothing for boatmen is the luggage that they and their guests use to bring aboard such apparel and related personal items. Storage space always seems to be at a premium on boats, and baggage should be soft and collapsible if possible. Canvas duffel bags are probably the most practical luggage, but other types that will fold and stow flat can be used.

IN SUMMARY

Summing up on the question of what to wear while boating, it would seem reasonable to say that if the occasion requires the use of a uniform, then the uniform should be correct in detail according to the regulations and customs of the organization concerned. If, on the other hand, the clothing is being chosen for informal wear, comfort and utility would seem to be the major considerations.

FIG. 2406 A flotation jacket is comfortable, light weight and functional, serving not only as a practical garment but providing buoyancy like a life preserver if the wearer should fall overboard.
(Courtesy Commodore Uniform Company, Inc.)

FIG. 2405 Foul weather gear is essential for most boatmen, especially those on sailing craft. It should provide full protection from wind-driven rain and spray. The type shown above is of international orange color to provide the greatest visibility should the wearer fall overboard. Matching boots with non-slip soles complete the outfit.

Foul-weather gear

Wet weather clothing is essential afloat. You may have a closed-in deckhouse for protection while under way, but there will be occasions when you must go on deck regardless of rain to make fast to a pier, handle an anchor, or pick up a mooring.

Oilskin slickers and sou'westers were the traditional heavy-weather garments, but now foul-weather gear is made of more modern materials and in a variety of styles. See fig. 2405. Articles are available that are light-weight and comfortable to wear. Check your boating store or mail order catalog for the protective clothing best suited to your boating activities.

The secret of greater comfort is to put on foul-weather gear *before* you get wet. It is equally effective in keeping moisture *in* as well as out if you delay in donning it until after you are partially or thoroughly wet.

Clothing for warmth

Boating activities are often extended into months of chilly weather. Special parka-style coats with hood attached are made for yachtsmen, where warmth and light weight, together with wind- and water-resistant qualities, are prime requisites. These are made of soft waterproof canvas or synthetic material, backed up with a lining for warmth.

A recent development is the flotation jacket which will not only provide warmth on deck but also a considerable measure of buoyancy should the wearer fall overboard. See fig. 2406.

Don't mix uniforms

Since the insignia and devices used by yacht clubs differ from those prescribed for the USPS, it is evident that breaches of etiquette would result from wearing, at the same time, articles associated with two different organizations. This might be compared with wearing two socks that were not mates, or a brown shoe and a black one. For example, fouled anchors belong on the cap of an amateur yachtsman, the member of a yacht club. In the center of these anchors belong the yacht club insignia, not the USPS emblem. Again, the sleeve braid with trefoil identifies the member of a yacht club; USPS insignia of rank or merit marks would definitely be improper in combination with such braid.

Similarly, items of the USCGAux uniform, or rank insignia of that organization, should never be mixed with USPS or yacht club apparel or insignia.

The key to correct practice, of course, is to wear the insignia of only one organization at any one time. And, naturally, to avoid the use of any uniform item or insignia to which you are not entitled.

CHAPTER 25

FIG. 2501 Electronic equipment now makes boating safer and more pleasurable — radiotelephones, direction finders, depth sounders, radar sets, loran receivers, fuel vapor detectors, and many others.

ELECTRONIC EQUIPMENT AND ITS USE

THE EVER-INCREASING variety of electronic equipment that is available for small craft places on all boatmen the burden of knowing more about this subject. "Electricity" and "electronics" are generally mysterious topics to the average person on the water; you can't see or feel them, but you know that they exist from their effects. The typical boatman shrinks from technical details on electricity and electronics, yet if he fails to put them to work for him on his boat, he is seriously neglecting valuable assistance easily available to him.

The owner of a boat of any size should know four things about electronic equipment—(1) what items are available for his craft, see fig. 2501, (2) how, in very general terms, such equipment operates, (3) how it should be used for greatest effectiveness, and (4) what he should and should not do regarding its maintenance. Such knowledge and understanding will mean not only greater safety on the water, but also increased convenience and pleasure. There is no intention or expectation of making an electronics technician out of Mr. Average Boatman, but he will be surprised how much can be understood and how much better his equipment will serve his requirements when used with greater knowledge of its capabilities and limitations. Technical language will be kept at a minimum in this chapter; only enough details will be included as are needed to make the necessary explanations.

"Electrical" and "electronic" are terms often used in an overlapping manner. In this chapter, *electronic* will be the term applied to equipment primarily employing tubes and transistors. *Electrical* equipment will be considered to include such things as motors, generators, lights, etc. The items of electronic equipment to be covered here are radiotelephones, direction finders, depth sounders, radar, loran, consolan, automatic steering devices, and several minor items.

Electrical Systems

Electrical power must be considered briefly before electronic equipment for this is the life-blood of such devices as radios, direction finders, and the like. Although a few transistorized items may operate from self-contained batteries, the bulk of electronic equipment is powered from the boat's electrical system. With many of today's outboard motors having generators or alternators, there is almost no lower limit to the size of boat which can have one or more electronic devices, but the total load must not exceed the electrical system's capacity.

Voltages

Electronic equipment is available for input voltages of 6, 12, 32, or 115, the first three being for direct current (DC) systems, and the last for alternating current (AC) operation. By far the most popular voltage is 12; its primary advantages are the widest selection of items and generally the lowest cost.

Six-volt systems are regarded today as obsolete; the lower voltage requires higher currents for the same power, and this results in heavier wiring or excessive voltage drops

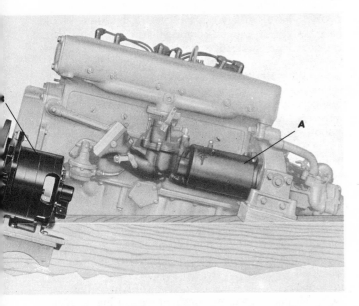

FIG. 2502   Basic source of electrical power for operation of electronic equipment is a generator (A) or alternator (B) driven by main engine. Most electrical systems are 12-volts DC; some older boats have 6-volt. Larger craft may use 32 volts.

between the battery and the load. The use of 32-volt equipment has the advantage of requiring even smaller currents for a given load than do 12-volt systems, but many items such as low and medium power radios, depth sounders, etc., are largely unavailable in this voltage rating. A 32-volt electrical system also has the disadvantage of requiring a larger and more expensive battery.

The current popularity of 12-volt systems in automobiles makes economical the use of such generators, batteries, and regulators on boats. Equipment powered by 115 volts AC can be used, but the primary power must be continuously generated as AC cannot be stored in batteries as can DC. Thus, except where specifically mentioned as being different, it will be assumed throughout this chapter that

items of electronic equipment being discussed are powered from a 12-volt DC electrical system.

Generators and Alternators

On essentially all boats, the basic source of electrical power will be a generator or an alternator driven by a main engine. See fig. 2502. The difference between these electrical devices is technical and the boat owner need not concern himself with them, except to know that the alternator is the more modern of the two and has the advantage of a greater output at low engine rpm. The external result is the same with both devices: a DC voltage somewhat greater than that of the battery (about 14 volts for a 12-volt system) so that energy can be put into the battery against its natural tendency to discharge into a completed circuit.

The flow of electricity from the generator or alternator into the battery will be through a *voltage regulator*. This device prevents the generator from charging at a rate in excess of its capacity, prevents the battery from being overcharged, and cuts out the generator from the circuit when the engine is not running in order to prevent the generator from acting as a load on the battery and running it down. For more on the operation of such generators and alternators, see books and pamphlets on engine electrical systems.

For boats that are in port with people aboard for a considerable portion of the time, it may be necessary to install a *charger*. This electrical device takes 115-volt AC shore power, *transforms* it to a lower voltage, and then *rectifies* it to DC. Thus as energy is taken from the boat's battery, it is replaced from shore power and the battery is completely or partially protected from becoming discharged.

Storage Batteries

Fortunately, DC electrical energy can be stored in batteries, and electronic equipment can be used without the operation of the main engine. See fig. 2503. There are several types of storage batteries that might be used in a boat but cost, that most practical of considerations, eliminates all but the lead-acid type used in automobiles.

In connection with electronic equipment, the basic question may be stated as "Is there enough storage capac-

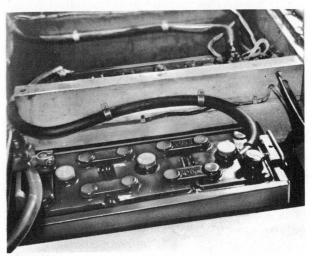

FIG. 2503   Direct current (DC) electrical energy can be stored in a battery. Boats commonly use automobile-type lead-acid batteries.

ity in the boat's electrical system for me to add this new equipment?" Capacity is measured in *ampere-hours*—the product of current drain in amperes multiplied by time in hours. This must be computed for all electrical loads, lights, motors, pumps, etc., as well as for electronic equipment. And there must be enough left over to start the main engine if only one set of batteries is installed! If the estimate of demand exceeds capacity (or if this has been found out the hard way!), a larger battery is needed. The installation of a larger battery may or may not require a larger generator and new regulator. The ratio of running time to idle time will determine this.

Wiring

If the generator and battery are the heart of a boat's electrical system, then the wires supplying the power to the electronic equipment are the veins and arteries. The wires must be heavy enough, of sufficient cross-sectional area, to carry the current of the loads connected to that

Fig. 2504
RECOMMENDED WIRE GAUGE SIZES
12-Volt Systems
Length of wire in feet — Source to Load

Current in Amps	10 or less	15	20	30	40	50
5	14	12	12	10	8	8
10	12	10	8	6	6	5
15	10	8	6	5	4	3
20	8	6	6	4	2	2
30	8	6	5	3	2	1

FIG. 2504   The table above, extracted from AB&YC Safety Standard E-9, 1970, specifies the wire gauge to be used versus conductor length for a voltage drop of not more than 3% in a 12-volt system. If a larger drop can be tolerated by a less critical item of equipment, smaller wire can be used. See Fig. 1015 for wire gauges allowing a drop of not more than 10%. Length is measured, one way, along path followed by wiring.

circuit. Adequate size is determined by two factors: heating effect and voltage drop. The passage of current through a wire increases its temperature; obviously it must not become so hot that it is a fire hazard. As a general rule of thumb, a wire should not become appreciably warm to the touch when carrying its full load.

The voltage drop problem is the more common one. The heating losses just mentioned result in a lower voltage being delivered to the load than is put into the wire at the generator/battery end. The voltage drop increases with a greater load, being directly proportional to the current in the wire. If the conductors are not of adequate size, the voltage delivered may be too low to operate the electronic device or other load efficiently.

Most, but not all, boats are delivered with wiring adequate for the installed equipment. The problem normally arises as additional accessories are installed. The solution requires either the replacement of existing wires with larger conductors, or the installation of additional main circuits back to the battery (assuming, always, that the various load combinations have been calculated and the

battery capacity is adequate).

The gauge number of wire runs opposite to its size; the larger the wire, the smaller the gauge number. Wires of smaller diameter than 16 gauge should not be used for any purpose in a boat's electrical system; most circuits should have heavier wire. The voltage drop is proportional to the length of the circuit between source and load. The longer the circuit, the larger the wire must be to prevent an excessive drop. Figures 2504 and 1015 provide information as to the minimum size of wire to be used for various loads and lengths in a 12-volt system. For a 6-volt system, subtract 2 from the gauge numbers in either table. For a 32-volt system, 4 may be added, but never use wire smaller than #16.

The insulation of wiring used on boats should be suitable for the damp conditions which will be found below decks; thermoplastic insulation is best. Stranded wire should be used rather than solid; all wiring should be well secured and protected from abrasion and chafing.

Switches, Fuses, Circuit Breakers

Of the utmost importance in the electrical system providing power to the boat's electronic equipment are the various protective devices, including *switches, fuses,* and *circuit breakers.* Every marine electrical system should have a *main distribution center* where there are switches and overload protective devices. In addition to the switches on the individual pieces of electronic gear which are used to turn them on and off in regular operation, the various loads should be connected together into several *branch circuits,* each with a protective element and a means of shutting off power. This is necessary in order that a short-circuit or other failure on one branch circuit will not require turning off all electrical power.

The combining of loads into branch circuits should be carefully considered, as should the selection of the existing circuit to which a new accessory is to be connected. Loads which are likely to be used at the same time should be connected to different branch circuits; likewise, the loads that are most vital to the boat's safety should be connected to different branch circuits.

Further, there should be a *master switch* by means of which all electrical power can be cut off in case of fire, for working on the electrical system, or when the boat is to be left unattended. An excellent type of master switch is an enclosed, explosion-proof, heavy-duty switch which can be mounted directly at the battery and operated remotely from the instrument panel by means of a cable such as is used on engine chokes and throttles.

Overload protection may be by means of either fuses or circuit breakers. Fuses are less expensive initially, but are a one-time-use device. The cartridge type which fits into clips is preferred over the screw-in plug type often found on shore. The cartridge type is less subject to loosening under vibration, with resulting poor contact. On circuits with motors, be sure to use a "slow-blow" type of fuse in order to withstand the initial starting current surge without going to an overly large capacity fuse for the wiring to be protected. Circuit breakers are a greater initial expense, but there are no spares to be bought and carried aboard as there are with fuses. Many types of circuit breakers can be tripped manually and thus can additionally serve as switches.

Radiotelephones

When the subject of electronic equipment for boats arises, the first thought probably will be "radio." See fig. 2505. The principal purpose of a radio on any recreational boat is *safety*. Certain other uses are authorized, but by law these are secondary to safety communications.

Safety Communications

A boat's radio may be used to summon assistance in a wide variety of situations. A leak may have started, involving risk of sinking; the motor may have failed in the face of worsening weather; or there may have been illness or injury to some person aboard. The possibilities of radio's adding to the safety of a boat and its crew are virtually unlimited.

There are many stations listening on the distress frequency—Coast Guard shore facilities, lighthouses, and craft of all sizes, plus many commercial stations on shore. In addition, the regulations of the Federal Communications Commission (FCC) require that a listening watch be maintained when the radio equipment of a boat is turned on but is not actively being used to communicate with another station. Thus there is a high degree of likelihood— a near certainty—that someone (probably many) will hear your distress call and either come to your assistance or get help for you.

Operational Communications

In addition to its safety value, a radio on a boat may be used for contacts with other boats for "operational" communications. The large number of marine band stations, and the few radio channels available, have made it necessary for the government to impose severe restrictions on the use of radios. As defined by the FCC, operational communications are limited to matters relating to "navigation, movement, and management." *Navigation* includes the actual piloting of a vessel, while *movement* relates to future moves of the boat such as might occur during a club cruise. Radio messages of the *management* category pertain to the obtaining of fuel, dockage, repairs, etc., and are limited to matters too urgent to permit handling by slower means of communication.

Business Communications

A third type of operational radio traffic is called "business communications," but this is limited to commercial and government craft, and so need not be considered here. Note that for talking between recreational boats, the *only* permitted kinds of radio transmission are *safety* and *operational* communications as narrowly defined by the FCC. Social and personal conversations between boats— any "superfluous" communications—are strictly prohibited.

Ship-to-shore Communications

In most areas of the United States, a radio on a boat also makes possible contact with various commercial shore stations on channels designated for that purpose. Through these stations, the boat becomes part of the nationwide telephone system; calls may be placed to, or received from, any home or business telephone. The restrictions placed on boat-to-boat contacts do not apply on these channels; calls placed through a "Marine Operator" may

FIG. 2505 A radiotelephone, properly selected, installed, and used, can provide safety and operational communications to other boats, the Coast Guard, and to shore stations.

be of a personal or social nature. The charges for ship-to-shore calls are quite reasonable.

EQUIPMENT

The selection of a radiotelephone is much like that of a new automobile—there are many manufacturers and many models. A number of factors must be considered in determining which is the "right" set for your boat. The legal requirements of the FCC must be met; beyond that, intended usage and price will be the primary considerations.

Frequency bands

Radiotelephones for ships and boats operate on two frequency bands. Generally speaking, these are called medium frequency (MF) and very high frequency (VHF). [We say "generally speaking" because many MF sets will also cover some high frequency (HF) channels used for longer range communications on inland waters and the high seas; these are quite different from VHF.]

Equipment operating in the Citizens Band may also be used on boats. These sets, however, are not in the "maritime service" as established by the FCC; see pages 512-514.

Radio frequencies are measured in kilohertz (kHz) and megaHertz (MHz); one MHz = 1,000 kHz. The older terms of "kilocycle" and "megacycle" are now being phased out.

Characteristics of MF and VHF

MF radio signals (2-3 MHz band) have a range that is determined by transmitter power, the presence or absence of interfering signals, static and noise on the air, and whether it is day or night. Exact ranges are impossible to set, only approximations can be given. Daytime ranges under "normal" conditions of interference *might* range from 40 miles for a 35-watt set to 65 miles for one of 150 watts power. At night, signals will be heard at greater distances, but the interference level also rises as more can be heard. Interference is considerable on MF due to the large number of stations within reception range. Signals are heard strongly at close distances, and fade away gradually as the stations are separated.

VHF signals have much less range, but much more "solid" communications over these shorter distances. Transmission range is only slightly greater than "line of sight;" it is much more affected by antenna height than by transmitter power. The normal boat-to-boat range is only about 8 to 12 miles. Ship-to-shore ranges are usually greater as the shore station antenna can be much higher. Beyond these distances, VHF signals drop off abruptly with little warning. The possibility of interferring signals is much as such stations must be relatively nearby. There is also a desirable freedom from static caused by lightning and local electrical noises since VHF sets use frequency modulation (FM). There are many more available channels on VHF; some are reserved exclusively for non-commercial boats, and yacht clubs and marinas.

Equipment selection

The date 1 January 1972 marked the beginning of a whole new era in marine radio communications; the "air" will never be quite the same again. Essentially all recreational boats will have to gradually shift from their present radio equipment to one or two sets of newer design and very different operating characteristics.

The situation in 1971

Probably 98% of the recreational boats on the air in 1971 were equiped with MF transmitters operating in the 2-3 MHz band using amplitude modulation (AM) with double sidebands (DSB). The few available frequencies were very badly congested; the transmissions of commercial and recreational craft competed on the two intership channels; the same frequencies were used for communications over distances of 1 mile, 10 miles, 100 miles, or more. Even with the maximum allowable power, attempts at boat-to-boat communications were often frustrating. Safety communications. too, were adversely affected by the large number of boats using 2182 kHz for initial calls, frequently between craft within sight of each other.

The solution—general policies

The FCC, after extended consideration, adopted policies that would restrict *all* short-range communications to VHF, keeping the MF (and HF) frequencies much clearer for longer-range contacts. VHF sets would be limited to 25 watts output and in addition would have to have a switch which would cut power to 1 watt where that was sufficient for talking across short distances.

To further reduce interference on the MF and HF channels, the FCC is phasing out DSB operation in favor of single sideband (SSB) transmissions which occupy less than half as much of the limited and crowded radio spectrum.

A five-year transition period is allowed for the conversion of equipment. By 1 January 1977, the change-over must be fully implemented.

The solution—implementation

The above policies will be implemented as follows:

1. Since 1 January 1972, no more medium frequency, double sideband (MF/DSB) radios have been licensed as

FIG. 2506 Select antenna of good quality, as large as can be safely mounted. Install clear of other metallic objects, as high as possible.

new installations on boats.

2. If you had a MF/DSB set on your boat with a valid license on 31 December 1971, you can continue to use it until 1 January 1977 *if you keep your license renewed.* You cannot reinstate your license if it lapses!

3. If you change your boat for a new one between now and 1 January 1977, you can move your MF/DSB set from your present boat to the new one. A license modification is required; send in your old license with your application.

4. If you sell your boat to a new owner, and leave your radio on it, he *cannot* get a license for it. He must remove and discard the set.

5. Since 1 January 1972, *all new radio installations on boats must be VHF.* You cannot install only a MF/SSB set. You must first install VHF, then you must be able to show a *need* for a MF/SSB set, that you have necessary communications beyond VHF range.

6. On 1 January 1977, all DSB operation must cease; only SSB can then be used in the MF and HF bands.

VHF Equipment

The new regulations have given a considerable boost to the manufacture of VHF sets. Many more models are now on the market giving a wider selection, and prices have come down with increased production.

Power. The maximum power for VHF is 25 watts *output,* which equates roughly to 50 watts input for comparison with older MF/DSB sets. Power, however, is not a significant factor in VHF range or ability to override interference. Sets are available with output power in the order of 3, 5, 15, and 25 watts. Because of the technical characteristics of FM, an external amplifier can be added later to a 3 or 5 watt set if the need arises for the full 25 watts power.

Antenna. A good antenna, mounted as high as possible, is essential for an effective VHF installation. (Sailboats with a masthead antenna will have a significant advantage over powerboats.) No ground plate is needed.

Channel capacity. A fully adequate number of channels is necessary to obtain the best use of a VHF set. Although the FCC requires only three channels, the wise skipper will equip his craft with a set having at least 6, and preferably 12, channels. (Some sets will be advertised with 6½, 12½, etc., channels; the fraction refers to "receive only" frequencies such as the NOAA weather broadcasts.) See fig. 2509 for recommended "channelization" of sets with various capacities.

SSB equipment

The first thing that will be noticed about single sideband equipment is the price tag! These modern sets are quite complicated as compared with the MF/DSB radios that have been used for many years. Modulation circuitry is more complex and the frequency stability requirement is ten times more rigid. SSB sets can easily cost three to five times the price of a DSB radio.

SSB sets will have the same 150 watts power limit as with DSB equipment, but the more modern modulation technique provides greater "talk" power, and this should result in greater range—not to mention the better communications resulting from lessened interference.

The decreased bandwidth of SSB signals allows for more channels in the MF band. Five new frequencies have been made available, four of which may be used by recreational boats; these are for SSB *only* and not all frequencies are available in all areas. The full list of available intership frequencies is given on page 493.

The operation of SSB equipment is more complex than for DSB sets. Skippers must carefully study their instruction manuals and follow their guidance carefully.

Installation and Maintenance

Radio equipment may be physically installed and electrically connected by the boat owner or any person. Before it is put on the air, however, the set must be checked out by a person holding a first or second class license who will make certain tests required by the FCC rules. Radio installations on gasoline-powered boats will generally require some form of ignition noise suppression or shielding; this is a job for a technician. With regard to maintenance, an unlicensed person is limited to matters which will not affect the quality of the signal on the air. For example, he can replace bad fuses, tubes, etc., but cannot change crystals, or adjust antenna loading.

RADIO LICENSES

With over 200,000 marine radio stations on the air, the need for licensing and regulations can easily be seen. The FCC issues its Rules and Regulations in various "Parts," of which "Part 83—Stations on Shipboard in the Maritime Service" is applicable to recreational boats.

To control the use of radio stations, holding down interference and making possible emergency and essential communications, a system of licenses is used. Recognizing that harmful interference could result from either mal-

functioning equipment or from misuse of a properly operating set, licenses are required for both the station (see fig. 2510) and the person operating it. Although it is termed a station license, the FCC authorization is essentially concerned with the transmitting component only. The set owner need not concern himself with the many technical requirements for equipment provided that he has a set that is "type accepted."

The Station License

A station license may be issued to a U.S. Citizen or an alien individual, but not a foreign government or its representative (if a corporation, see section 82.23 of the FCC Rules.) Application is made on Form 502 which is either mailed to the FCC, Gettysburg, Penna. 17325, or taken to one of the more than 30 FCC field offices. The fee for a station license is $4 for the five-year term. The actual issuance of the license will take perhaps as long as 30 days, but if the applications is personally taken to an FCC office, you will be given an interim license which will permit immediate use of your set; the fee for station license plus interim permit is $10.

Radio station licenses are issued in the name of the *owner* and the *vessel*. A station license is not automatically transferred to another person upon sale of the boat, nor may a license be moved with the radio set to a new craft owned by the same person. A simple change in the name of the boat or licensee (but not a change in ownership),

PRIORITY LIST OF VHF-FM CHANNELS
FOR RECREATIONAL BOATS

Channel Number	Frequency (MHz) Transmit	Receive	Communications Purpose
16	156.800	156.800	DISTRESS, SAFETY and CALLING (mandatory)
06	156.300	156.300	Intership safety communications (mandatory)
22	157.100	157.100	Primary liaison with USCG vessels and USCG shore stations, and for Coast Guard marine information broadcasts
68	156.425	156.425	Non-commercial intership and ship to coast (marinas, yacht clubs, etc.)
09	156.450	156.450	Commercial and non-commercial intership and ship to coast (commercial docks, marinas, & some clubs)
26	157.300	161.900	Public telephone, first priority
28	157.400	162.000	Public telephone, first priority
25	157.250	161.850	Public telephone
27	157.350	161.950	Public telephone
13	156.650	156.650	Navigational—Bridge to Bridge (1 watt only) Mandatory for ocean vessels, dredges in channels, and large tugs while towing. Army installing for communications with boats in their locks. Will be found, also, on Army operated bridges
14	156.700	156.700	Port Operations channel for communications with bridge and lock tenders. Some Coast Guard shore stations have this channel for working
70	156.525	156.525	Non-commercial only, intership
WX-1		162.550	
WX-2		162.400	
12	156.600	156.600	Port Operations—traffic advisory—still being used as channel to work USCG shore stations.
72	156.625	156.625	Non-commercial intership (2nd priority)

FIG. 2509 This table lists the required and recommended VHF channels for recreational boats. Not all radios can be set up for all these channels, nor will all skippers wish to buy a full set of crystals, hence the priority sequence. Four public telephone channels are listed; there are also other, less-used channels. Select the one or ones needed for your cruising area. Consider use of a separate receiver for the second weather frequency; some areas use a third weather frequency. Coast Guard Auxiliary boats may use Channel 83 (157.175 MHz) for drills, patrols, and similar official activities.

FIG. 2510 Transmitter on boat must have radio station license issued by Federal Communications Commission (FCC). No license required for receiver, radio direction finder, or depth-sounder.

FIG. 2511 In addition to station license, person in charge of set must have operator's permit. Either Restricted Radiotelephone Operator Permit or Third Class Radiotelephone Operator Permit is generally satisfactory for voluntarily-equipped boats.

or his address does *not* require license modification. Just send a letter to the FCC advising them of the change; a copy of this letter must be posted with the license.

The regulations require that a station license be conspicuously posted aboard the vessel. At the end of its five-year term, it must be renewed if continued operation of the station is desired. Form 405-B is used for renewal; it should be sent to Gettysburg with a $4 renewal fee before the expiration of the license. If, but only if, timely application for renewal has been made, operation may continue even should the renewed license not be received before the expiration date. If the use of the radio station is permanently discontinued at any time, the license must be returned to the FCC in Washington for cancellation.

The Operator's Permit

A personal license is required for the operation of any marine band radio station. The average boatman will obtain either a *Restricted Radiotelephone Operator Permit* or a *Third Class Radiotelephone Operator Permit*. See fig. 2511. Higher class licenses are available for persons with technical training and experience, but they are needed only for making tuning adjustments and repairs. An unlicensed person may talk into the microphone of a radio, but a licensed operator must be present and responsible for the use of the station.

An applicant for any grade of license may be either a U.S. citizen or an alien. A Restricted Permit is obtained by submitting an application on FCC Form 753. This form contains all necessary instructions, including where to mail it; there is no need to appear in person at any FCC office. The permit is issued, without test or examination, by "declaration." The applicant must be at

least 14 years old and "certify" that he (1) can receive and transmit spoken messages in the English language; (2) can keep a rough log in English, or in a foreign language translatable into English; (3) is familiar with the applicable laws, treaty provisions, rules, and regulations; and (4) understands his responsibility to keep currently informed of the regulations, etc. The Restricted Permit fee, $4, is valid for the lifetime of the person to whom issued, unless, of course, it is suspended or revoked.

For the Third Class Operator Permit, there is no age limit, but an examination is required. This test is non-technical, covering only operating rules and procedures; questions are all of the multiple-choice type. You will find the examination not at all difficult if you prepare yourself for it properly. A free Study Guide is available from FCC offices. For skippers of recreational boats the privileges of this higher class license are no greater than those of a Restricted Permit, but it is a matter of pride for many to qualify and post it on their craft. Boats that carry more than six passengers for hire, however, are "compulsorily equipped" and must have a crewman with at least a Third Class Permit. The fee for a Third Class Permit is $4, and it is issued for a five-year term; the fee for renewal for another five years is $2.

If your radio operator permit is lost, or becomes so mutilated that it is illegible, you should immediately apply for a duplicate. The fee is $2 and the same form as for an original is used. State the circumstances fully, and, if the license has been lost, you must certify that a reasonable search has been made. Continued operation is authorized if a signed copy of the application for a duplicate is posted. Should a lost license be found later, either it or the duplicate must be sent at once to the FCC for cancellation.

FIG. 2512 The FCC Rules require that a radio transmitter be secure against use by unauthorized persons. A set in an exposed location, as above, can be fitted with a key-operated switch for its electrical power. Physical security may also be used, such as a lock for the panel door in fig. 2513.

RADIO OPERATING RULES

Hand in hand with licensing, radio operating rules have been established to bring order out of chaos on the air and reduce the interference that would inevitably result from the overcrowded conditions on the few frequencies available. Actually, the legally required procedures are only a bare minimum and must be supplemented with voluntary procedures for the most efficient communications.

As stated before, radio communications (other than ship-shore telephone calls) must be necessary and of a "safety" or "operational" nature. Even within these limitations, a system of priorities has been established to make sure that the more important messages get through. First, of course, are *distress* calls and related follow-up messages; these are identified by the signal "Mayday" and receive "absolute priority" over other communications. Second are *urgent* messages; these are defined as relating to the safety of a ship, aircraft, or other vessel, or of some person on board or in sight. Urgent communications are identified by the signal "Pan." In third place on the priority list are *safety* messages, those concerning the safety of navigation or giving important weather warnings; these transmissions are identified by the safety signal, "Security."

The system of priorities has been established to ensure that the message that *has* to get through does so without delay. No station or operator has any exclusive rights to any frequency; the nature of his traffic determines whether he should transmit or keep silent. One of the most important FCC regulations requires that an operator *listen before transmitting* to ensure that he will not interfere with the communications of others, and particularly not with distress or other priority traffic. See fig. 2518.

Frequencies for Calling and Distress

The most important channel in the MF band is 2182 kHz —the International Radiotelephone Distress Frequency. In order to keep one channel relatively clear of traffic so that even a weak distress call can be heard, the use of this frequency is limited to distress traffic and the initial contact between vessels. This latter use as a "Calling Frequency" is permitted to ensure that when a station is not working on another channel, it is listening on 2182 kHz for calls. Thus many stations are constantly monitoring the distress frequency and a call for help is much more likely to be heard.

Listening on 2182 kHz is not only a logical procedure, it is legally required. A "voluntarily equipped" boat need not have its radio turned on, but if it is, it must be tuned to the distress and calling frequency when not being actively used on another channel.

On the VHF band, 156.8 MHz—Channel 16—is used in a similar manner for distress, safety, and calling.

FIG. 2513 Radio station license must be posted near equipment. On voluntarily-equipped boats, an Operator Permit may be posted. Alternatively, a Restricted Permit or a Verification Card for a Third Class Permit may be carried in one's personal possession.

Ship-to-ship and Ship-to-shore Channels

After making their initial contact on 2182 kHz, boats using the MF band *must* shift from the calling channel to a "working" frequency to communicate with each other.

2638 kHz	All areas
2003 kHz	Great Lakes only
2830 kHz	Gulf of Mexico only
2738 kHz	All areas other than Great Lakes and Gulf of Mexico
2142 kHz	Pacific Coast south of 42° North latitude, daytime only
*2082.5 kHz	All areas
*2093.0 kHz	Commercial fishing vessels only
*2203.0 kHz	Gulf of Mexico (other than commercial fishing vessels)

*May be used *only* on single sideband

Frequencies shown for a single area only may be used inter-area for vessels within 200 miles of each other, one within that area and the other outside.

A similar system of a calling frequency (also used for distress) and multiple working channels is used on the VHF band. If VHF equipment is on board, it *must* be tried first, if no contact is made, then MF may be used.

For communications with the Coast Guard, see page 516.

For ship-to-shore calls, a third set of channels is used. These will vary for the different Marine Operators along the coasts, Great Lakes, and elsewhere. The frequencies for your area can be found in Part 83 of the FCC Rules.

Legal Requirements

Legal operation of a radio station aboard a boat requires four things. First, a license for the station, properly posted.

FIG. 2514 Every radio station licensed in Marine Service must have current copy of Part 83, FCC Rules and Regulations. See text for details.

FIG. 2515 Every radio station on a boat must have radio log. Requirements are simple, but don't neglect them!

Second, an operator's license. This may be posted, or a Restricted Permit or a Verification Card for a Third Class Permit may be carried on one's person. Third, a station log. Fourth, an up-to-date copy of Part 83 of the FCC Rules on board or in a secure place on shore.

Part 83 will be found with two other parts in Volume IV of the FCC Rules and Regulations. See fig. 2514. This volume may be purchased by mail from the Superintendent of Documents, Government Printing Office, Washington, D.C. 20402. The price is $9.50, including a subscription to changes to this volume as issued. Changes are mailed in the form of reprinted pages; it is a simple task to remove old pages and insert new ones.

The Radio Log

Log keeping for a radio station on a voluntarily equipped boat has been made much easier than it used to be, but don't let this simplification stop you from meeting the present minimum requirements of the FCC. See fig. 2515. Each page of the log must show the name of the vessel and the radio call sign; each entry must be signed by the person making it. Entries are required for all distress calls heard or transmitted, for all urgent and safety communications transmitted, and any information related to maritime safety. The log must also show the time of starting and ending of a listening watch on 2182 kHz or 156.8 MHz (Channel 16), but remember that the keeping of such a watch is not mandatory on recreational boats.

All installation, service, and maintenance work performed on the radio equipment must be logged. It is *not* necessary to make entries for ordinary communications to other boats, the Coast Guard, or shore stations. Logs must be retained for one year following the last entry, except for unusual circumstances described in the Rules. Logs must be made available' for inspection upon request from any authorized FCC representative. Inspection of the station by such an official must be permitted at any reasonable hour, and at such frequent intervals as may be determined necessary in the discretion of the FCC.

Rules Governing Transmissions

Transmissions on the calling channel must be limited to the securing of an agreement as to the working frequency to be used, and this may not take longer than two minutes. Any one calling transmission must not take longer than 30 seconds and, if no reply is heard, you must wait two minutes before calling again. Another two minutes must separate a second and a third attempt to make contact and, if these fail, a delay of 15 minutes is required before a new calling cycle can be started (the 15 minutes may be reduced to 3 if other stations will not receive interference from the calls).

Once contact is made on a working frequency, the exchange of transmissions (between boats) must (1) be of a legally proper nature, (2) be of the minimum length possible, and (3) not exceed three minutes in length. After concluding the contact, neither boat shall re-contact the other until 10 minutes have elapsed. The stations may, however, communicate with others during this time. These time limitations do not apply in emergency situations, nor do they apply to ship-shore telephone calls.

The Communications Act of 1934, together with the FCC Rules, strictly prohibit the use on the air of any language which is "obscene, indecent, or profane." This is watched as closely as possible by various government monitoring stations and violators have been taken into court a number of times. Special, more severe, penalties are specifically provided for this offense.

Procedure for Station Identification

The FCC has established certain procedures to be followed in identifying your station on the air. Such identification must be given in the English language by stating the official call sign. Phonetic words for the letters may be used but are not legally required; any understandable word may be employed, but use of the international aviation and military alphabet is recommended. See fig. 2516. if the station is operating under an interim authorization, it may not have received its call sign. In this case, identification must be made by announcing the name of the craft *and the name of the licensee.* The licensee's name is required because of the great number of boats with identical or similarly sounding names. It is often erroneously omitted, but this is a violation subject to penalties.

Radio stations must be identified, as a minimum, at the beginning and end of an exchange of transmissions with another station, but identification of *each* transmission is *not* required. If both 2182 kHz (or 156.8 MHz) and a working frequency are used, the beginning and ending identification is required on *both* frequencies. Identification must be made of each transmission for any other purpose, such as a test. If transmissions continue for more than 15 minutes, the station must be identified at intervals of 15 minutes or less, except that on a ship-shore telephone call this may be deferred until the end of such call.

Secrecy Requirements

The Communications Act of 1934 and the Rules of the FCC protect the *secrecy* of communications. No person may divulge to another person, except the addressee or his authorized agent, any knowledge gained from receiving or intercepting radio transmissions not addressed to himself, *nor shall he use such knowledge for his own benefit.* This basic point of law should be carefully noted by all who operate radios on boats. It does not apply to distress communications nor to broadcasts for the general use of the public, but it does apply to *all* other conversations heard on the air. It could even be construed to apply to the fellow who listened to find out where the fish were biting and then moving in on the good spots.

OPERATING PROCEDURES

The FCC Rules contain only a few instances of specific operating procedures, chiefly in connection with emergency communications. The various examples of operating procedures given below are in conformance with the regulations, but go further than the legal requirements; they are offered as examples of good practices on the air. See fig. 2517.

How to Make a Call

Listen carefully to make sure that the channel you want to use is not busy. If it is busy, you will hear voices, or from most public shore stations, an intermittent busy tone. Except in a safety emergency, don't interrupt.

Standard Phonetic Spelling Alphabet

A	ALFA	N	NOVEMBER
B	BRAVO	O	OSCAR
C	CHARLIE	P	PAPA
D	DELTA	Q	QUEBEC
E	ECHO	R	ROMEO
F	FOXTROT	S	SIERRA
G	GOLF	T	TANGO
H	HOTEL	U	UNIFORM
I	INDIA	V	VICTOR
J	JULIETT	W	WHISKEY
K	KILO	X	X-RAY
L	LIMA	Y	YANKEE
M	MIKE	Z	ZULU

FIG. 2516 **When receiving conditions are poor, use phonetic equivalents for individual letters in spelling out difficult words such as name of boat or person.**

When the conversation is to take place on a ship-to-ship frequency—unless you have reached an agreement in advance as to the time and frequency, establish contact on 2182 kHz (or 156.8 MHz) and the shift to the agreed-upon intership channel.

When the conversation is to take place through a commercial shore station—make your initial contact on a working frequency of that station; this will speed your call.

Both of these practices are designed to relieve the load on 2182 kHz and 156.8 MHz so that their utility for safety purposes will not be jeopardized.

Steps to Follow in Making a Call (other than a Distress, Urgency, or Safety Call)

Boat-to-boat calls—Listen to make sure 2182 kHz (or 156.8 MHz) is not busy. If it is free, put your transmission on the air and say—

"(Name of boat called) This is (Name of your boat and call sign), Over." To avoid confusion, always observe the proper sequence of call signs—state the name or call sign of the *other station first,* then give your own identification after saying 'This is'—don't reverse the sequence.

(If necessary, the identification of the station called, and your boat's name and call sign may each be given two or three times, but not more; the entire calling transmission must not take longer than 30 seconds.)

Listen for a reply. If no contact is made, repeat the above after an interval of at least two minutes. After establishing contact switch to the agreed upon intership working channel. One exchange of communications shall not exceed three minutes after establishing contact on the working frequency. After conversation is completed, say—

"This is (name of your boat and call sign), Out."

You shall not establish contact thereafter with the same boat until 10 minutes has elapsed.

Ship-to-shore Service

Listen to make sure that the working channel you wish to use is not busy. See fig. 2518. If it is clear, put your transmitter on the air and say—

"(Location) Marine Operator This is (Name of your boat and call sign), Over."

Listen for a reply. If no contact is made, repeat after an interval of at least two minutes.

When the Marine Operator answers, say—

"This is (Name of your boat and call sign) calling (telephone number desired), Over."

After the telephone conversation is completed, say—

"This is (Name and call sign of your boat), Out."

How to Receive a Call

Your boat can be reached only when your receiver is turned on and tuned to the frequency over which you expect to receive calls.

The receiver you use to maintain watch on 2182 kHz (or

FIG. 2518 To minimize interference, FCC has established strict rules. Listen before transmitting and do not interfere with communications in progress. Keep contacts short and observe time limitations.

FIG. 2517 Booklet "Marine Radio Telephony" contains extracts from FCC Rules plus explanations to make them easily understood. Available from Radio Technical Commission for Marine Services, c/o FCC, Washington, D.C.

156.8 MHz) will assure that you get calls addressed to you by other boats. For calls from public shore stations, you will generally need to keep a receiver tuned to a working frequency of the station for that area. It is urged that you have one receiver for watch-keeping and a second one to ensure that you can be reached by a public shore station over a working channel. This will help to keep 2182 kHz and 156.8 MHz free for their primary purpose of securing help.

Steps in Receiving a Call

Boat-to-boat calls—When you hear your boat called, put your transmitter on the air and say—

"(Name of boat that called) This is (Name of your boat and call sign), Over."

Switch to the agreed upon intership channel. After the conversation is completed, say—

"This is (Name of your boat and call sign), Out."

Shore-to-ship calls—When you hear the name of your boat called, put your transmitter on the air and say—

"(Name of station that called) This is (Name of your boat and call sign), Over."

After the conversation is completed, say—

"This is (Name of your boat and call sign), Out."

FIG. 2519 RADIOTELEPHONE ALARM SIGNAL (two alternate audio tones of different pitch) attracts attention to boats in trouble. Some larger radios now have built-in generator for this signal; separate units available for other sets.

Distress, Urgency, Safety

In an emergency as part of the marine safety and communications system, you have help on 2182 kHz or 156.8 MHz at your fingertips wherever you may be.

Only when grave and imminent danger threatens your boat and immediate help is required, use the distress procedure—radiotelephone alarm signal (if available) and MAYDAY. Transmitted on 2182 kHz or 156.8 MHz, it should be heard by many boats, as well as by the Coast Guard and public shore stations within range.

FIG. 2520 Prudent skipper tunes in latest weather bulletins before plotting day's course, especially when considering long run offshore.

The *Radiotelephone Alarm Signal* consists of two audio tones, of different pitch, transmitted alternately. The purpose of this signal is to attract the attention of persons on watch, and, at some stations, to actuate automatic devices giving an alarm. It shall be used *only* to announce that a distress call or message is about to follow. (Exception: it may be used with the Urgency Signal in two specified instances. See FCC Rules.) Coast Guard shore radio stations are now equipped with devices to generate this signal, and such devices are now being built into some larger models of boat radios. See fig. 2519.

The Distress Procedure—"Mayday"

Distress communications include the following actions:

1. The RADIOTELEPHONE ALARM SIGNAL (whenever possible) followed by—
2. The DISTRESS SIGNAL "MAYDAY."
3. The DISTRESS MESSAGE.
4. Acknowledgment of Receipt of Distress Message.
5. Further Distress Messages and other communications.
6. Transmission of the Distress Procedure by a boat or shore station not itself in distress.
7. Termination of Distress Situation.

The DISTRESS CALL consists of:

—the Distress Signal MAYDAY, spoken three times;
—the words THIS IS;
—the identification (name and call sign) of the craft in distress, spoken three times.

The DISTRESS MESSAGE follows immediately and consists of:

—the Distress Signal MAYDAY, spoken three times;
—the identification of the craft;
—particulars of its position (latitude and longitude, or true bearing and distance in miles from a known geographical position);
—the nature of the distress and the kind of assistance desired;

—any other information that might facilitate the rescue; especially a description of the boat: length, color, type, etc.; and the number of persons aboard; OVER.

Example of Distress Procedure

"(Alarm Signal, if available, for one minute). Mayday, Mayday, Mayday This is Yacht Blue Duck, WZ 1234, Yacht Blue Duck, WZ 1234, Yacht Blue Duck, WZ 1234:

Mayday, Yacht Blue Duck, WZ 1234, 133 degrees true, 12 miles from Montauk Point. Struck submerged object, taking on water fast, engine disabled, estimate cannot stay afloat more than one hour. Four persons on board. Blue Duck is a 26-foot cabin cruiser, white hull. Maintaining watch on 2182 kHz (or 156.8 MHz or Channel 16). This is yacht Blue Duck, WZ 1234, Over."

General Rules for Distress

With your life at stake, you have a far better chance by following the correct procedure, but the provisions of the International Radio Regulations authorize a vessel in distress to use *any means* at its disposal to attract attention, make known its position, and obtain help.

Stay on 2182 kHz (or 156.8 MHz), but if no answer to a distress call is received, repeat it on any other available frequency on which attention might be attracted.

Speak slowly and distinctly. Use phonetic words for letters when necessary, especially when giving the letters of your call sign.

You may be requested to transmit a "long count" or other suitable signals to permit direction finding stations to determine your position; always end your transmission with the name and call sign of your boat.

If you have to abandon ship, the radio transmitter should be locked on the air, if considered necessary and conditions permit. The purpose of this is to locate you by radio direction finding bearings. If you have already been visually located, do not lock your transmitter on the air as the signal would interfere with rescue operations.

All vessels having knowledge of distress traffic, and which cannot themselves assist, are *forbidden* to transmit on the frequency of the distress traffic; but they should listen and follow the situation until it is evident that assistance is being provided. Always listen before transmitting. It is *unlawful* for any radio operator to *willfully* or *maliciously interfere with* or cause interference to *any radio communication* or *signal*. No person shall knowingly transmit, or cause to be transmitted, any *false* or *fraudulent signal of distress* or *communication* relating thereto.

Radio Silence

The signal "Seelonce Mayday" has been adopted internationally to control transmissions on the distress frequency, telling all other stations to leave the air and maintain radio silence. This signal is to be used *only* by the unit in distress and the station controlling the distress traffic. Any other station which considers it necessary to advise one or more other stations of the need to keep off the air should use the signal "Seelonce Distress" followed by its identification.

The signal to indicate the end of radio silence and permission to resume normal operation is "Seelonce Feenee."

The oddly spelled words above are phonetic equivalents from the French as adopted for international use.

If You Hear a MAYDAY Call

If you are not in distress, but hear a "Mayday" call, this is what you should do:

1. *Listen—Do Not Transmit.*
2. Try to determine if you are the craft in the best position to take action, or if some other vessel is better located or better equipped.
3. *If* yours is the logical boat to render assistance, reply to the distress message as follows:

"(Name of craft in distress) This is (Name of your boat and call sign), Received Mayday (your position, your course and speed toward the scene of the distress, and your estimated time of arrival), Over."

4. If yours is not the logical boat to take action, maintain radio silence, but continue to monitor the frequency closely for any further developments—make an entry in your radio log of the Mayday call and your actions.

When another station retransmits a distress message, the words "Mayday Relay" must be spoken three times before station identification.

Use "Mayday" sparingly

The distress signal "Mayday" should be used *only* when the vessel is "threatened with *grave* and *immediate danger* and requests *immediate assistance.*" It should *not* be used for situations such as being out of fuel, running aground, or engine failure under conditions of no immediate danger. Reserve "Mayday" for true emergencies of real hazard to life and property; don't "cry wolf" when it is not a desperate situation. Make an ordinary call for assistance, or if there is some degree of urgency short of distress, use the urgency signal "Pan" spoken three times before the call.

The safety signal "Security"—pronounced "Saycuritay"—is spoken three times before transmissions such as those relating to defects in aids to navigation and weather warnings; it is used mainly by shore stations.

Test Transmissions

Always remember, when making tests, to take every precaution not to cause interference to others. Listen before testing, to make sure that the frequency is not busy. You must obtain the consent of any station affected before proceeding. If the air appears clear, put your transmitter on the air and say—

"This is (name of your boat and call sign) Test."

If you hear no station tell you to "Wait," you may proceed, saying "Testing" followed by a number count or other phraseology that will not confuse listeners.

At the end of the test, announce the name and call sign of your boat, and your general location.

Calls may not be made to Coast Guard stations on 2182 kHz for "radio checks." If a two-way communication is *necessary,* a call may be made to another ship station, preferably on a working frequency. General calls—those not addressed to a partiffcular station—may be made *only* for test purposes.

Weather Reports

When aboard your boat, you can keep up to date on weather and other marine information by listening to the working frequencies of public or U.S. government shore stations. See fig. 2520. Coast Guard stations transmit weather and other information on 2670 kHz after a preliminary announcement on 2182 kHz.

The National Weather Service publishes a series of *Marine Weather Services Charts* at only 15c each. In addition to showing where weather warnings are displayed day and night, these charts give the frequency and schedules of radio (AM and FM) and TV stations broadcasting weather reports and forecasts. See page 264.

Don't take chances—the information on weather conditions is there—get it.

VIOLATIONS AND PENALTIES

Hopefully, you will never be in violation of the FCC Rules and will have no need for knowledge of the procedures and penalties involved. Yet things do not always work out that way, so it is just as well to be informed.

If you receive a citation of violation from the FCC, you must reply in duplicate within 10 days, to the office that issued the citation. See fig. 2522. If a complete reply cannot be given in that time, an interim reply must be sent and supplemented as soon as possible. If for reasons beyond your control, you cannot reply at all within 10 days, do so at the earliest date practicable, and fully support your reasons for the delay. Each letter to the FCC must be complete and contain all the facts without cross-reference to other correspondence. The answer must contain a full explanation of the incident and describe the actions taken to prevent a recurrence of it. If personnel errors are involved, your reply must state the name and license number of the operator concerned.

You may be lucky, however, and receive a "warning notice" rather than a citation. In this instance, no reply is required. The FCC form that you receive will indicate whether or not an answer is necessary. If one is required, don't get yourself into further trouble by failing to answer *within 10 days.*

Revocation and Suspension of License

A station license may be revoked for any one of a number of specified violations of the Communications Act or the FCC Rules. Operator licenses and permits normally are not revoked but are suspended for varying periods of time.

FIG. 2522 If you receive citation for violation of FCC Rules and Regulations, submit written reply within ten days. No reply required if you receive "warning," rather than citation.

Notice of suspension must be given in writing and is not effective until 15 days after receipt. Within this period, you can apply for a hearing, and this automatically defers the suspension until after the hearing has been held and the FCC has ruled.

Fines Imposed

In addition to the revocation or suspension of licenses, the FCC can prosecute violators in the Federal District

Courts. Any violation of the Communications Act may be punished by a fine of not more than $10,000, or imprisonment for not more than one year, or both. A second offense, not necessarily a repeat of the first, increases the maximum limit on the prison term to two years. For a violation of any FCC rule, regulation restriction, or condition, or of any treaty provision, a court may additionally impose a fine of not more than $500 for *each and every day* during which the violation occurred.

Administrative Forfeitures

To avoid the delays, costs, and general cumbersomeness of formal court prosecutions, the FCC has the authority to levy its own "administrative forfeitures," actually small fines, for 12 specified violations. These fines are in addition to any other penalties that may be imposed by law.

Among these twelve, the violations of principal concern to the operators of radio stations of boats are:

—Transmission of any unauthorized communications on a distress or calling frequency.

—Failure to identify the station at the times and in the manner prescribed by the Rules.

—Interference with a distress call or distress communications.

—Operation of a station without a valid permit or license of the proper grade.

—Transmission of any false call contrary to the Rules.

—Failure to respond to official communications from the FCC.

The maximum forfeiture for a single violation, or a series of violations all falling within a single category as listed above, is $100. If, however, more than one category is involved, the maximum liability is raised to $500 for a station licensee, or $400 for an individual operator. It should be noted that the term "operator" may be applied to any person using the equipment, whether or not licensed by the FCC. In some cases, if two different persons are involved, forfeitures may be assessed against both the station licensee and the person who was operating the station.

The procedures for the imposition of these administrative fines have been kept simple, yet ample protection is afforded to the rights of individuals. Upon receipt of a "notice of apparent liability for forfeiture," the addressed person has open to him three courses of action. He can pay the fine and so close the incident; or he may, within 30 days, submit a written statement to the FCC giving reasons why he should be allowed to pay a lesser fine, or none at all; or he may request an interview with an FCC official. These last two courses of action can be combined, submitting both an explanation and a request for an interview. If either or both of these actions are taken, the FCC will review all of the information relative to the case, and make a final determination.

There is no judicial appeal from the FCC's ruling, and you had best pay up as there are established procedures for turning over cases of non-payment to a District Attorney for prosecution.

Depth Sounders

Depth sounders (fig. 2523) closely rival radiotelephones as the most popular item of electronic equipment for boats; they have a wide range of use—lakes, rivers, bays, and off-shore. Your sounder can be one of the most interesting and useful devices on your boat.

Depth sounders are a modern replacement for the hand-held lead line used for uncounted centuries to determine the depth of water beneath a ship. This electronic device furnishes a vastly greater amount of information, and does it with much greater ease, especially in nasty weather. It provides safety as well as convenience in boating, and so is doubly advantageous to have on board.

How Depth is Measured

Depth is determined by measuring the round-trip time for a pulse of ultrasonic energy to travel from the boat to the bottom of the water and be reflected back to the point of origin. See fig. 2524. The frequency of the audio pulses generally lies between 50,000 and 200,000 cycles per second, too high to be heard by human ears. Their average velocity through the water is approximately 4800 feet per second; slight variations in speed will occur between salt and fresh water and with different temperatures. The resulting small errors, however, can be safely ignored for the relatively shallow depths of interest to the operators of recreational boats.

Probably the greatest advantage of the electronic device over the hand-held lead line is the essentially continuous nature of the information furnished. Depth sounders vary

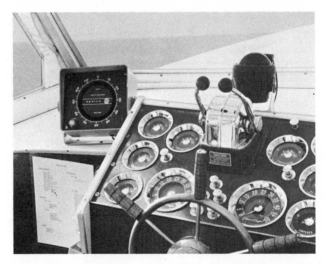

FIG. 2523 Depth sounders are popular on all waters. This compact, inexpensive device gives many indications of depth each second.

widely in the rate at which readings are taken, but in all cases many more soundings are taken than could be accomplished by hand. Current equipment takes readings at rates between 1 and 30 *each second.*

Components of a Depth Sounder

The major components of a depth sounder are a source of energy (transmitter), a means of sending out the pulses and picking up the echoes (transducer), a receiver to amplify the weak echoes, and a visual presentation of the information. See fig. 2525. The transducer usually takes the form of a round block of hard ceramic material several inches in diameter and an inch or so thick. In many cases, it is given an oblong, streamline shape to reduce drag.

The visual presentation of information on the depth of the water is accomplished by either an "indicator" or a "recorder." The indicator provides a non-permanent indication of the depth, in most cases by the use of a flashing light, although in a few units an ordinary electric meter is used with a suitably calibrated dial. The flashing light is mounted on the end of an arm which rotates around a scale much like the second hand of a clock, only much faster. The zero of the scale is usually at the top of the dial and a flash of light occurs there when the outgoing pulse leaves the transducer on the boat's bottom. A second flash

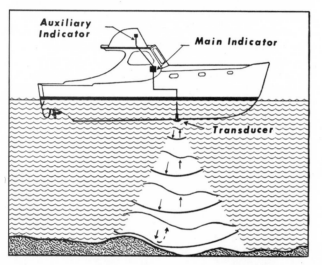

FIG. 2524 An electronic depth sounder measures depth by sending pulses of high frequency sound waves, reflected back from bottom. Distance measured by time taken by pulses for round-trip.

occurs when the pulse is received back at the transducer, having been reflected back from the bottom of the water. The deeper the water, the longer it will take for the echo to return to the boat; the longer this takes, the farther the arm will have rotated around the dial. (Fig. 2526.) Thus the scale of depths increases clockwise around the face of the indicator.

Principle of the Depth Sounder Illustrated

An example may make this clearer. If the sounder has a depth range of 240 feet, at full scale the sound pulses will have traveled a round-trip distance of 480 feet. Taking the speed of sound in water at 4800 feet per second, the round-trip will have taken 1/10 second. Therefore the arm carrying the flashing light must make one full rotation in 1/10 second; this is 10 rps or 600 rpm.

If the depth is only, say, 80 feet, the echo will cause the light to flash when the arm has made only 1/3 of a full revolution, and the flash will occur at a position corresponding to four o'clock on a clock dial. In many models, it is possible to detect greater than full-scale depths by turning up the sensitivity control until a flash is seen on the "second trip around" of the rotating arm. Using the same sounder as in the preceding example, if the water was known to be quite deep, and a weak reading of 60 feet was seen with the sensitivity control well advanced, it could mean an actual depth of 300 feet (full scale plus 60 feet). Some models are now calibrated with two sets of numbers around the dial for first and second revolutions of the flashing light. Caution is essential to avoid reading the depth as much greater than is actually the case.

With the recording type of sounder, a permanent record is made of the depths, and notations as to the boat's position can be made directly on the paper tape. See fig. 2527. The paper moves horizontally from a supply roll to a take-up spool at the rate of one inch in several minutes. A dry method of chemically marking the paper is normally used to avoid the messiness of ink. A recording type of depth sounder has some advantages, but this type is more expensive. Some models are now available with both flashing light indicator and a permanent paper tape record of the depths.

Correction to "Zero" Depth

If you have a sounder on your boat, you must know its "zero" depth. In most instances, the transducer is mounted on the hull several feet below the water surface and, as

FIG. 2526 On this sounder, indicator shows flash of light at "0" on scale and another opposite depth.

FIG. 2525 Typical depth sounder consists of two units, transducer on bottom of boat and electronics package with indicator near helmsman. Model shown has calibrated meter with two ranges.

FIG. 2527 With recording type of sounder, depth is measured many times each second and presented as series of dots on scaled tape.

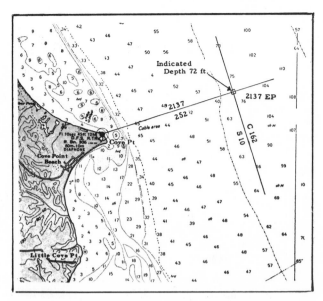

FIG. 2528 Navigator notes that Cove Point Light is abeam at 2137 but can get no other line of position. Depth sounder showing depth of 72 feet gives Estimated Position (EP).

depths are measured from the transducer, the indications will be neither the depth of water from the surface nor the depth beneath the keel of the boat. On some models, the zero flash can be offset on the dial to its depth below the surface, then the indicated depths are correspondingly increased to show directly the full distance between the water surface and the bottom without need for adding a correction. This is advantageous when the sounder is used for navigation.

The nature of the bottom of the body of water will have an effect on the appearance of the flash which indicates the depth. Learn how to determine roughly the nature of the bottom by the characteristics of the flashing light; a surprising amount of information can be obtained. Sharp, clear indications mean a hard bottom. Conversely, broad and fuzzy flashes indicate a soft, muddy bottom. Multiple flashes, each fairly sharp, can result from rocky bottoms; the ultrasonic pulses are reflected more or less horizontally to adjacent rocks before being returned upward. The added time delays for these sideward bounces make them show up as if they were at greater depths. Additional flashes at multiples of the least depth indicated may result, in shallow water with a hard bottom, from pulses being reflected downward again by the craft's hull following the first round-trip. Two or even three round-trips may occur; the cure for this is to turn back the sensitivity control until only the first indication is seen. In *all* cases of multiple flashes, play it safe and assume that the minimum reading is the true depth! As the depth indication flash will always have some width, be sure to read the "trailing" edge, or least indicated depth. This is the correct value.

Application in Piloting

The primary application of an electronic depth sounder is to assist in the safe navigation of the boat in unfamiliar waters. It can provide much useful information, but must be used with care as *it makes no predictions ahead.*

Information on the depth of water is reassuring in itself; furthermore, it can be used to assist in determining the boat's position. It can be used to make rough position data somewhat more exact. For example, if only a single line of position (LOP) is available, an estimated position (EP) can often be obtained from the additional knowledge of the depth of the water. See fig. 2528. This requires a fairly uniform sloping bottom and some knowledge of the state of the tide. Many times, a rough EP can be obtained from indications of an abrupt change in depth.

A line of soundings can sometimes be matched with chart figures to locate the boat's track. See pages 439 and 543. This is most easily done on depth recorders, but is also possible on indicating types by logging depths at regular time intervals. Depths are plotted on a strip of paper with their distance apart matched to the scale of the chart and the speed of the boat. The paper strip is moved about on the chart parallel to the boat's course until the depths match. This technique is not possible in all locations and should be used with caution lest an erroneous conclusion as to the boat's position lead to danger. Often in conditions of low visibility, a boat can be navigated to a desired destination by using the depth sounder to follow along a path of roughly constant depths. This is the technique of "following a fathom curve."

A depth sounder may also be used navigationally in a negative sense. If your depth indication agrees with the charted depth for your estimated position, you may, *or may not,* be there; the same depth figures occur in many places on any chart. If, however, your sounder shows a considerably different value than that charted for your DR (dead reckoning) position, it is an almost sure indication that your DR is *not* correct. Thus, while a depth sounder cannot positively confirm a DR plot, it can surely call it wrong.

The location of fish with a depth sounder is possible, but you may be disappointed with your results at first. Experience is required and you will improve with practice. Detection will generally be limited to schools of fish or quite large single fish. The echoes are quite weak and the sensitivity control will have to be advanced.

Radio Direction Finders

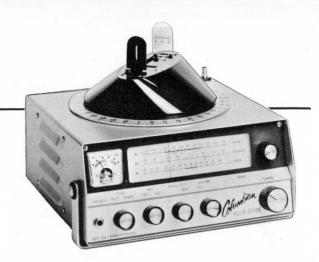

On the seacoasts of the United States, and on the Great Lakes and other large inland bodies of water, a *radio direction finder* (RDF) is an important piece of electronic equipment. See fig. 2529. Primarily installed as a safety item, it can also be a great convenience to the boat operator. It is the primary radio aid to navigation for small craft.

A complete radio direction finding system consists of four components:

1. One or more radio transmitters at known locations.
2. An RDF set on the boat.
3. Charts covering both the location of the transmitters and the area of operation of the boat.
4. A person who knows the operation of the system.

To be fully effective, the RDF system must be used with competence and confidence — an incorrect radio bearing can lead to disaster; a correct bearing that is ignored because of mistrust can be equally disastrous.

Special RDF Features

Basically, an RDF is a radio receiver with two additional features. First and vitally important is the directional antenna. Usually, this antenna is rotatable so that the set may be secured firmly in a convenient location. The directional antenna employed with an RDF set is an improved version of the simple loop used on portable receivers, the directional characteristics of which are familiar to most boatmen. This antenna may take the form of a loop a foot or so in diameter or it may appear as a plastic bar measuring about an inch square by some six inches in length. Both types will be mounted on top of the set; either will do the job.

FIG. 2529 When visibility is poor, RDF can help fix position, or navigator may "home in" on transmitter near his destination.

As the antenna is rotated through 360°, these directional antennas show two positions of maximum signal strength and two positions of minimum sensitivity called "nulls." With properly balanced construction and no local interfering objects, the two maximum signal positions will be separated by 180°, as will be the nulls which are found 90° in either direction from the maximums. It is characteristic of these antennas that the maximum signal points are broad and poorly defined, while the nulls are marked and precise. For this reason, the nulls are used for direction finding.

The second special feature of RDFs is a visual null indicator. While the operator can judge by ear the position of the antenna at minimum signal with fair accuracy, a more precise bearing can be obtained by observing a visual indicator. This is normally a small electric meter, read for either a maximum or minimum deflection of its needle in accordance with the instructions for the particular set being used.

FIG. 2530 Radiobeacon charts are published in Light Lists. As reproduced here, not to be used for navigation. The frequency, identification signal, and schedule of operation are shown on this chart.

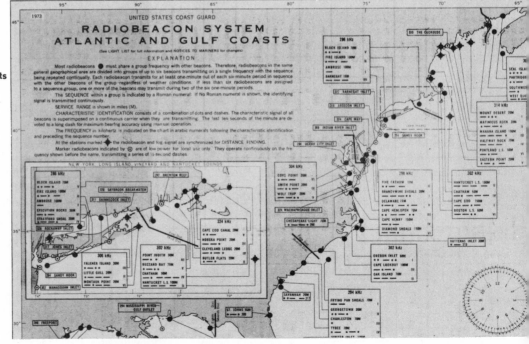

(1)	(2)	(3)	(4)	(5)	(6)	(7)
	Name	Location	Nominal	Ht.	Structure	
			Range	above	Ht. above	
No.	Characteristic	Lat. N. Long. W.		water	ground Daymark	Remarks Year
			FLORIDA			**EIGHTH DISTRICT**
	GULF COAST					
137	**CAPE SAN BLAS LIGHT**	On cape.	25	101	White, square skeleton tower, inclosing stair cylinder; with black lantern house.	Obscured from 211° to 251°.
J3366	**Fl. W.,** 20ˢ	29 40.3 85 21.4				RADIOBEACON: Antenna 702 feet 208° from lighthouse. See p. XVIII for method of operation.
					96	1849–1919
138	*Cape San Blas Outer Shoal Lighted Bell Buoy 30.*	In 60 feet, off shoals.	7	. . . .	Red	Ra ref.

FIG. 2531 The location of the antenna of a radiobeacon is shown in the Light List under the listing of the basic aid to navigation with which it is associated.

RDF Frequency Bands

Radio direction finders normally cover three frequency bands: a low frequency (LF) beacon band, the standard AM radio broadcast band, and the 2-3 MHz MF communications band. The LF beacon band is of primary interest for the marine radiobeacons operated by the Coast Guard on frequencies between 285 and 325 kHz at locations along or just off our coastlines and the Great Lakes. See fig. 2530. Aeronautical beacons, somewhat lower and higher in frequency, are also within the tuning range of these sets and can be used for direction finding. (These aero beacons, or "ranges" as they are called, are an excellent source of weather information at 15 and 45 minutes past each hour.)

Coverage of the standard AM radio broadcast band is desirable because of the large number of stations on which bearings can be taken. It should be noted, however, that the accuracy of bearings on this band will not be quite as good as it will on the LF beacon band. The 2-3 MHz marine band is generally used only for special purposes such as "homing" since the accuracy of bearings is still less on these higher frequencies. RDFs are being developed for the VHF-FM band but are not yet generally available.

A direction finder can readily double as an entertainment receiver, particularly if it is of the low-drain transistor type. Coverage of the marine band permits the RDF to be used to monitor a second communications channel when the radiotelephone's receiver is tuned to 2182 kHz. Usually, a direction finder is tunable to any frequency in the band rather than being crystal-controlled on spot channels. This characteristic permits the monitoring of frequencies to which the boat's radio is not tuned. The pretuned spot-frequency feature may also be present on the more expensive models to permit more accurate tuning and quicker frequency changes.

Precise knowledge is required of the antenna location of the radiobeacon or other type of station. For the low frequency band, the locations of Coast Guard operated beacons are shown on standard navigation charts and are listed in Light Lists published by the U.S. Coast Guard. (Fig. 2531.) The *Marine Weather Services Charts* previously described list many broadcast band radio station antenna locations by latitude and longitude. If not already shown

FIG. 2532 For accurate RDF bearings, you must have table of radio deviation corrections. RDF shown here has built-in sighting vanes for visual bearings, or separate pelorus may be used.

on your area's nautical charts, these locations may be plotted from this information. Aeronautical radio ranges and beacons are similarly listed and may be plotted if not already shown on your charts.

Marine Radiobeacons

Marine radiobeacons are divided into four classes according to their power and normal reliable range:

Class A . . . . .200 miles
Class B . . . . .100 miles
Class C . . . . 20 miles
Class D . . . . 10 miles
    (marker beacons)

A few of the primary beacons, and the short-range markers, operate continuously. The others are "sequenced"; up to six beacons operating in turn on the same frequency, each being on the air for one minute and then off while the others take their turn. The sequence of operation can be determined from the charts or by reference to the Light List. It is indicated by a Roman numeral immediately following the frequency; if no Roman numeral is shown, the beacon operates continuously.

Radio Deviation

All RDFs are subject to local deviation errors caused by the reflection of the radio signals by nearby wires and other metallic objects. This is generally similar to the effect of masses of iron on a magnetic compass. One important difference, however, is that the radio bearing errors vary with respect to the *relative* bearing angle; the heading of the boat is not the deciding factor as it is with compass deviation. A table, or curve, must be prepared to show the corrections for RDF error on various relative bearings. Separate tables will generally be required for each of the frequency bands.

Determining RDF Deviation Error

RDF deviation errors are determined by comparison of observed radio bearings with known correct bearings. Either of two methods may be used. The simplest is to take radio bearings on a radiobeacon or other type of transmitting antenna within sight, at the same time having another person take direct visual bearings. See fig. 2532. The difference between these readings is the radio deviation error. If no radio station is within sight, take radio bearings from a known location and compare them with correct bearings as taken from a chart. Avoid doing this while made fast to the club pier; erroneous readings may result from reflections caused by adjacent boats. In both cases, the deviation corrections have the same numerical value as the errors, but with the opposite sign.

Calibration readings should be taken of a strong local station which is received clearly without interference. A complete deviation correction table, preferably in steps of not more than 15°, should be prepared for the low frequency band. Then spot checks can be made to determine if the same corrections will apply on higher frequency bands or if separate tables must be made for each band. Correction tables should be checked at least annually, and additionally if the direction finder is relocated on the boat or major changes are made in the electrical wiring, rigging, etc.

Direct and Reciprocal Bearings

Due to the technical characteristics of a loop antenna, two nulls can be found 180° apart. In most situations, the navigator's general knowledge of his approximate position will suffice to eliminate the reverse reading. If this is not

FIG. 2534 Taking radio bearing, antenna is rotated to locate null, angle read from scale. Reading, normally, is a relative bearing.

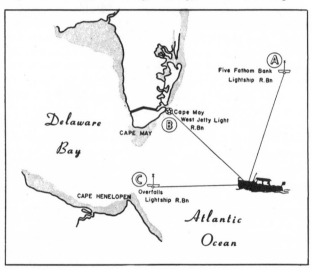

FIG. 2535 Boat shown here could determine position by bearings on any two radiobeacons at "A," "B" and "C." Better fix would be obtained by using all three beacons.

possible, or to be absolutely sure, special measures can be taken. Nearly all direction finders have either an integral auxiliary "sense" antenna or a connection terminal for an external antenna. By operating a switch, this antenna is connected into the circuit to change the directional characteristics to a single null and single maximum pattern. Simple procedures will then indicate which of the previous nulls is the direct bearing and which is the reciprocal reading. (The sense antenna is not left in the circuit all the time as more precise readings are obtained from the loop alone.)

Always use a portable RDF set from the same position on the boat; a change in location may require a completely new deviation table. See fig. 2533. As an RDF contains strong magnets in the speaker and meter, be sure to keep it at least several feet away from the boat's compass, both while in and out of use.

FIG. 2533 To ensure accuracy always use portable RDF from same position. Do NOT, however, place it too close to compass. Speaker magnet may affect it; three feet is safe minimum separation.

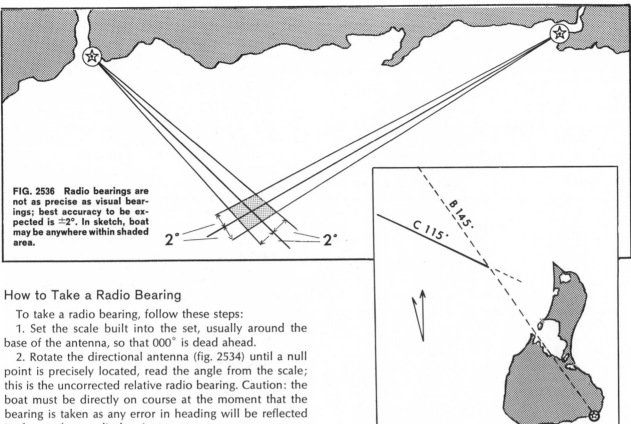

FIG. 2536 **Radio bearings are not as precise as visual bearings; best accuracy to be expected is ±2°. In sketch, boat may be anywhere within shaded area.**

FIG. 2537 **Using single radio bearing, skipper notes bearing of 145° on Southeast Pt., Block Island, will bring him safely to Great Salt Pond. He holds his 115° heading, taking frequent radio bearings. When they increase to 145°, he changes course and homes on signal to entrance buoy.**

How to Take a Radio Bearing

To take a radio bearing, follow these steps:

1. Set the scale built into the set, usually around the base of the antenna, so that 000° is dead ahead.

2. Rotate the directional antenna (fig. 2534) until a null point is precisely located, read the angle from the scale; this is the uncorrected relative radio bearing. Caution: the boat must be directly on course at the moment that the bearing is taken as any error in heading will be reflected in the resultant radio bearing.

3. If there is any doubt as to whether the reading just taken is the direct or reciprocal bearing, use the sense antenna to identify it. If the reading is the reciprocal, do *not* add or subtract 180°, take a new bearing.

4. Having determined the direct bearing angle, apply the proper deviation correction; the sum is the corrected relative radio bearing.

5. Add the boat's *true* heading, subtracting 360° if the sum exceeds that amount; this is now the true radio bearing from the boat, plot in the same manner as a visual bearing.

The above steps outline in basic terms the correct procedures to be followed in taking a radio bearing. In the use of any particular RDF set, however, the manufacturer's manual should be studied and the instructions followed closely.

Plotting the Radio Bearing

If the transmitting station is more than 200 miles away, and the plotting is to be done on a Mercator chart, a further correction is necessary before plotting. This small correction is required because the great circle path along which radio waves travel does not plot as a straight line on this type of chart. The amount of correction, and the procedure for applying it, can be found in Table 1 of Bowditch.

Radio bearings are plotted in the same manner as visual bearings, and the use of an RDF requires the same degree of piloting knowledge and plotting skill. Radio bearings do not have as high a degree of precision as visual bearings, and for this reason a three-bearing fix is desirable. See fig. 2535. The best probable accuracy for radio bearings is on the order of plus or minus 2°, and some experience and

practice are required to reach this precision. In situations involving close proximity to dangerous waters, a careful navigator will draw additional lines 2° to either side of the corrected bearing; these will indicate graphically the probable limits of his position; see fig. 2536.

Position-finding by Radio Bearings

Radio bearings can also be used in any of the other forms of position plotting—bow and beam bearings, doubling the angle, danger angles, etc. If only a single radio bearing can be obtained, it is possible to combine this with a visual bearing, an astronomical line of position, or a depth reading to determine an estimated position. (Fig. 2537.) Remember that this EP will be no better than the accuracy of the poorest method used, and navigate accordingly.

In order to ensure the most accurate position from radio bearings:

1. Take bearings from as strong signals as possible.

2. Use the low frequency band in preference to higher frequencies.

3. Avoid taking bearings on radio stations located inland, particularly those behind coastal hills or mountains.

4. Take three or more bearings on different stations if possible; make sure that you identify the station correctly

and know the location of the transmitting antenna.

5. Take bearings so that the intersection angle is at least 30⁰, preferably 90⁰ for two-station fixes or 60⁰ for three-station fixes.

More on position finding with RDF bearings will be found in Chapter 21.

Factors Affecting Accuracy

There are two circumstances which tend to degrade the accuracy of radio bearings. "Night effect" is the term applied to the fact that all radio bearings taken at night, but particularly those made near sunset and sunrise, show a broader and sometimes shifting null. This makes less precise any bearing taken at these times, and efforts should be made to take bearings under these conditions only on stations less than 30 to 40 miles distant. If this is not possible, the next best procedure is to take a series of readings on each station and average them for a mean reading; but still consider the accuracy to be less than that of a reading taken in the daytime.

The second special circumstance of lessened accuracy comes into effect when the radio waves travel approximately parallel to a coastline for any appreciable portion of the distance from the transmitting station to the RDF. There is a bending effect on the signals which can be as much as 10°, pulling the waves in toward the land. Fortunately, the effect is to make the boat appear closer to land than it actually is.

Homing with an RDF

In addition to determination of the position of a boat, an RDF can be used in several other interesting ways. When the directional antenna is set on 000° relative, the craft may be directed toward a radio station by steering so as to keep the signal strength at the deepest point of the null. One RDF model has a direct-reading meter which shows the helmsman whether he is to the right or left of his course. This homing procedure provides a simple navigational technique for getting into port when visibility conditions are bad or other navigational aids are not available; but be sure that the direct course doesn't lead into shoal waters or other dangerous areas. Many harbor entrances have low-power "marker" radiobeacons, usually at the outer end of a jetty if one exists.

Homing also makes possible the steering of a boat on the most direct course to the scene of a distress situation. Such an application normally makes use of signals in the 2-3 MHz marine communications band. Here the accuracy

of radio bearings is less than on lower frequency bands, but the homing process works satisfactorily because the signal strength gets stronger as the source is approached. Caution must be exercised not to run directly into the source of the signals (this may seem like rather obvious advice, but it has happened!).

Use and Care of an RDF

Throughout any consideration of the purchase, installation, and use of a radio direction finder, it must be remembered that such an item of electronic equipment is first of all a safety device. Any other planned use, such as an auxiliary receiver, is a bonus feature only, and must not be allowed to detract from readiness for its primary use when needed. Most portable RDFs are powered by small drycell ("flashlight") batteries; many models have a swtich position for the null meter so that battery strength may be checked at any time. It is advisable to carry a set of spare batteries on cruises to guard against the possibility of loss of RDF capability should the unit be accidentally left on for an extended period of time. Batteries should be replaced annually, whether indicated or not, to ensure freshness and adequate life when needed.

An RDF should be used often in periods of good visibility so as to gain familiarity with its operation under circumstances permitting visual checks on the radio bearings which are obtained. Frequent practice reduces the personal error component of the total error in radio bearings, thus improving the overall accuracy. If these procedures are followed, there is every reason for a boat owner to trust his RDF to bring him safely into port under any conditions of visibility.

Automatic Radio Direction Finders

An automatic radio direction finder (ADF) indicates on a dial the direction to a transmitter once it has been tuned in—no swinging of a loop, no 180° ambiguity.

ADFs cover the same frequency bands as manual RDFs and use the same types of transmitting stations. They are, of course, more complex in circuitry and thus more expensive. The antenna is continuously rotated, either mechanically or electronically, whenever the set is turned on. Often such equipment is a fixed installation with a remote antenna, but portable models are available.

The advantages of ADFs lie in their ease and speed of operation. They are, however, subject to the same radio deviation as manual RDFs and a correction table must be prepared.

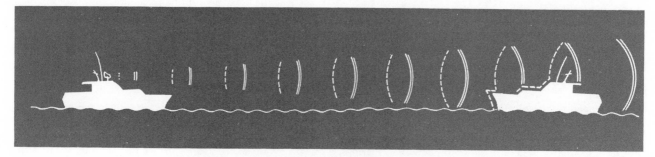

FIG. 2539 A marine radar set operates by sending brief pulses of super high frequency radio waves, reflected back by other ships, navigational aids and land masses. Sketch shows pulse traveling outward and echo returning. Speed is so great echoes are received before next pulse is transmitted.

FIG. 2540 Most radars have two major sections. Shown is antenna and upper electronics unit containing transmitter and portion of receiver. Antenna must be mounted high to have clear "look" in all directions.

Radar

Radar is an excellent means of marine navigation and is used on vessels of all sizes down to boats about 30 feet in length. Although size, power requirements, and cost limit its use on recreational boats, its capabilities and limitations should be known to all boatmen for their own safety when cruising on waters navigated by radar-equipped vessels.

Radar Principles

A radar set sends out brief pulses of super-high frequency radio waves that are reflected by objects at a distance. The time that it takes for the pulse to go out and the echo to return is a measure of the distance to the reflecting object. See fig. 2539. In broad principles, this is the same technique as previously described for depth sounders, except that transmission is through air rather than water, and radio waves have been substituted for ultrasonic pulses. A refinement has been made in that the radar pulses are sent out in a very narrow beam which can be pointed in any direction around the horizon and used to determine direction as well as distance.

Components of a Radar Set

The major components of a radar set are:

1. The *transmitter* which generates the radio waves; it includes the *modulator* which causes the energy to be sent out in brief pulses.

2. The *antenna* which radiates the pulses and collects the returning echoes. See fig. 2540. The antenna is highly directional in its horizontal characteristics, but 8 to 10 times wider vertically. The beam pattern can be thought of as being like a fan turned up on edge. The beam's narrow horizontal directivity gives it a fairly good angle-measuring capability, while its broadness in the vertical plane helps keep the beam on an object despite any rolling or pitching of the vessel.

3. The *receiver* which detects the returned reflections and amplifies them to a usable strength. See fig. 2541.

4. The *indicator* which provides a visual display of objects sending back reflections.

Radars operate at frequencies far above the usual radio communications bands. At such super-high frequencies, radar pulses act much like light waves in that they travel in essentially straight lines. They travel at the speed of light, 186,000 miles per second. For each nautical mile of distance to the target, only a fraction more than 12 microseconds are required for the round-trip of the outgoing pulse and the returned echo. Pulses, each of which lasts for only a fraction of a microsecond (one millionth of a second), are sent out at a rate of from 600 to 4000 each second depending upon the design of the equipment. The directional antenna rotates at a rate of one revolution in about 4 seconds. The round-trip time for a pulse is so short that the antenna has not appreciably moved before the reflection is returned.

The Plan Position Indicator (PPI)

Marine navigational radars use a Plan Position Indicator (PPI) type of display. A circular cathode ray tube of a special type from 5 to 20 inches in diameter is used. See fig. 2542. The center of the face represents the position of the radar-equipped vessel and the presentation is roughly like that of a navigational chart.

A bright radial line on the face of the tube represents the radar beam; it rotates in synchronism with the antenna. Reflections show up as points or patches of light depending upon the size of the echo-producing object. The persistence of the screen is such that the points and patches of light do not completely fade out before the antenna has made another rotation and they are restored to brilliance. Thus the picture on the radarscope is repainted every few seconds.

Radar Range Scales

The relative bearing of an object is indicated directly on the screen; a position corresponding to the "12" on a clock face is directly ahead. The distance to the object is proportional to the distance from the center of the screen to the point of light which is the echo. On most radars, concentric circles of light are used as range markers to make the estimation of distances both easier and more accurate. All radar sets have multiple range scales which may be selected to suit the purpose for which the radar is being used. Longer range scales provide coverage of greater areas, but at a cost of less detail and poorer definition.

Radar sets have both a maximum and a minimum range, each of which is of importance in the operation of the equipment. The maximum range is determined by the transmitter power and the receiver sensitivity, provided, of course, that the antenna is at a sufficient height above water that the range is not limited by the distance to the horizon. See fig. 2543. (The radar pulses normally travel with just a slight amount of bending; thus the radar horizon is about 15% farther away than the visual horizon.)

Because a radar pulse has a definite duration, and therefore occupies a definite length in space as it moves outward from the antenna, there is a minimum range within which objects cannot be detected. This minimum range, usually between 20 and 50 yards, is important when maneuvering in close quarters, as when passing buoys at the side of a narrow channel.

Units for Small Craft

Radar sets for small craft usually consist of two units. Modern design of the components makes it possible to combine the antenna, transmitter, and a portion of the receiver into a single unit installed on a mast or on the pilothouse. This unit, usually weighing between 60 and 120 pounds, should be located as high as possible in order to avoid limiting the range of the set. The antenna should have an unobstructed "look" in all directions. The remainder of the receiver and the indicator are located near the helmsman's position. Improved design techniques have resulted in indicator units so small that they may be fitted into a pilothouse in any number of positions.

Because radar sets radiate radio frequency energy, they must be licensed by the FCC, but this is not difficult to do for commercially produced equipment. No license is required to operate a radar, but for its installation and maintenance, the technician must have a second- or first-class radio operator's license with a special "ship radar" en-dorsement. The owner and station licensee of a marine radar installation is responsible that only a properly licensed individual does all of the technical work on the equipment.

Principal Applications

Radars have two principal applications aboard ships and small craft. They are often thought of primarily as anti-collision devices, but are even more often used to assist in the piloting of the vessel.

Radar was originally conceived for the detection and tracking of ships and aircraft. It offers an excellent means of extending the coverage of a visual lookout, especially at night and under conditions of reduced visibility. This greater range of detection affords more time for a ship to maneuver to avoid another craft or an obstacle.

Radar serves another valuable function in the piloting of a vessel approaching a coastline or traveling in confined waters. It has real advantages even in the daytime, and, of course, becomes particularly helpful at night or in fog.

Fixes by Radar

The daytime advantages of radar stem from its ability to measure distance. Often a landmark or navigation aid can be seen and a visual bearing easily obtained. If, however, only one such object can be seen, only a single line of position is obtained and a fix is not possible. With a measurement of distance by radar, a fix becomes possible. See fig. 2544. The bearing could have been made by radar simultaneously with the range measurement, but a visual bearing is more precise and should be used if possible. The capability of getting a fix from a single object is often of great importance to the navigator.

Fixes may also be obtained in low visibility situations—from a single radar bearing and range measurement, from crossed bearings (fig. 2545—but this is not too accurate due to the finite width of the radar beam), and preferably from distance measurements to two or more points that can be identified on both the radar screen and the chart. More than two ranges or bearings should be taken and plotted to prevent the possibility of a false fix which might occur if one of the echoes on the scope were incorrectly

FIG. 2541 (Left) Lower section of radar set contains remainder of receiver, indicator, and all operating controls, located within easy view of helmsman, but not too close to compass.

FIG. 2542 (Right) Marine radars present information on ships, buoys, shorelines, etc. as patches of light on face of PPI scope. Radar-equipped boat is at center of scope.

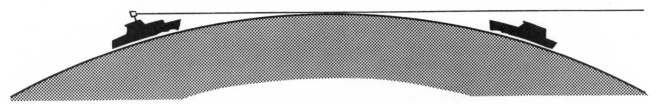

FIG. 2543   Maximum range of radar set on small craft is more likely to be limited by antenna height than by transmitter power. Radar waves bend slightly but distance to radar horizon is only 15% greater than to optical horizon.

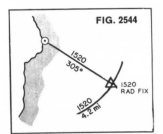

FIG. 2544

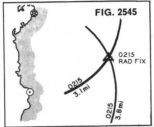

FIG. 2545

FIG. 2544   Radar fix may be obtained from single object, using both distance and bearing measurements. Navigator must be sure he has correctly identified object on both radar scope and chart.

FIG. 2545   Getting navigational fix by plotting distance to two identifiable objects as measured by radar. Radar measurements of distance provide more accurate fix than do radar bearings. Ranges to more than two objects are desirable.

identified. In all cases, the use of radar lines of position and fixes is the same as for visual plotting, giving due consideration to the lesser accuracy of bearing information. See figs. 2546 and 2547 for additional illustrations of radar plotting.

Coastline Pictures on the PPI

The use of radar to determine a vessel's approximate position from observation of the presentation of a coastline on a radarscope is not a safe procedure. The image seen on the PPI will often vary appreciably from the appearance of a chart. This is true despite some widely publicized photographs of radar screens showing such distinctive patterns as New York harbor appearing nearly identical with the actual scene. Because the radar beam, as narrow (1° to 4°) as it is, does have a finite width, and because the pulse, as brief (0.1 to 0.5 microsecond) as it is, does have a definite length in space, the picture on a radar PPI scope is not an exact replica of the land area or other object returning the echoes. Normally, radar echoes will be returned from buildings, hills, etc., some distance inland from the shorelines shown on charts.

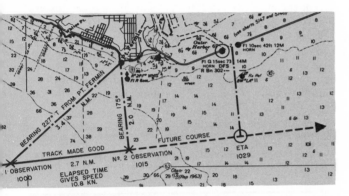

FIG. 2546   For greatest benefit, radar information must be plotted. Here two successive measurements of bearing and range of a fixed point on shore provide data to plot track and speed made good by radar-equipped boat. Track can be projected ahead to give estimated time of arrival (ETA) at any point. Effect of currents may be determined by comparison of heading and slack-water speed with track and speed made good.

Passive Radar Reflectors

The motorboat owner who does not have a radar can still do something to increase his safety in relation to this item of electronic equipment. He can equip his craft with a *passive radar reflector*. See fig. 2548. This simple and inexpensive item consists of thin lightweight metal sheets, or areas of fine-mesh metal screening, arranged in mutually perpendicular planes. These may fold for storage, but must remain rigid with respect to each other when opened for use. A relatively small reflector with each metal surface only about two feet square will provide a radar reflection as strong as that from a medium-sized steel ship. The echo from the wooden hull of a small craft is so weak as to be easily overlooked in the echoes from the waves if a reflector is not used. With a passive reflector hoisted as high as possible, the operator of a small craft can be sure that his boat will be detected on the radar screens of passing ships. Often Coast Guard or other rescue craft searching for a boat in distress are radar-equipped; the use of a passive radar reflector greatly increases the chances of being quickly spotted.

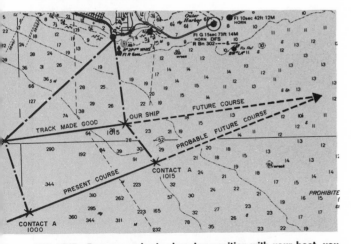

FIG. 2547   Because radar is changing position with your boat, you cannot depend upon appearance of radar-scope to give indication of course and speed of another vessel. It is necessary to make radar plot. Shown are track and speed of your vessel as established in fig. 2546, plus actual track and speed of another craft based on two successive radar measurements of relative bearing and distance. Both tracks may be projected ahead to evaluate possibility of collision should neither craft change course or speed.

Electronics / CHAPTER 25

Electronic Navigation Systems

There are a number of electronic navigation systems that are available to skippers of offshore cruising and fishing boats as well as to navigators of larger ships. These vary in degree of complexity and cost of receiving equipment. Many boatmen will probably never use any of them personally, but it is desirable to have a general familiarity with their method of operation, and their advantages and disadvantages.

The most widely used electronic navigation system is *Loran* which is currently operational in two versions, Loran-A and Loran-C. (A third form, Loran-D, is for military applications only.) Another system is *Omega* which is now operational with wide-area coverage, and complete global coverage scheduled for 1976.

Decca is a short-range, high-accuracy electronic navigation system that is available only in limited areas; it is more widely used in Europe than North America. Decca is unique in that in the United States it is commercially operated rather than by a governmental agency.

The aeronautical VHF navigations system called *VOR*, or *Omnirange,* is sometimes used by boats, but its short range is a severe limitation. (Aircraft can use this system out to hundreds of miles by reason of their high altitudes; Omni-equipped boats are limited to about 10-20 miles by the line-of-sight characteristics of the signals.

There is also an electronic navigation system based on the use of satellites, but the complexity and cost of equipment eliminates it from consideration by boatmen.

LORAN

Loran (LOng RAnge Navigation) now exists in two forms: Loran-A, also called Standard Loran, and Loran-C. These are both basic navigation systems for ocean-going ships and offshore fishing vessels; they can also be used to advantage by boats on open-water passages. Loran has the disadvantage of being dependent upon the reliable operation of electronic equipment both on shore and on the vessel.

Loran is a passive system; there is no transmitter on board the vessel, but a relatively complex and expensive receiver is required. Loran is a valuable supplement to celestial navigation, particularly when weather conditions prevent the taking of sights.

Loran-A

Frequencies between 1750 and 1950 kHz are employed by Loran-A. A pair of transmitters send out pulses of radio waves which are received on board the vessel. The difference in time of arrival of the pulses from each station is measured electronically, and this information is used to determine a line of position. The pulses are not sent out simultaneously, but are synchronized in a predetermined

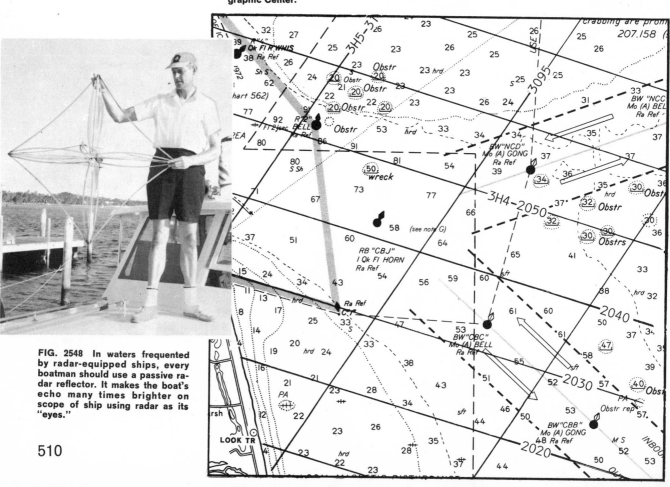

FIG. 2549 Portion of Chart 12221 published by the National Ocean Survey showing sets of Loran lines of position—in a different color for each set. Although position may be determined from Loran tables, direct plotting on a chart is the simplest and quickest way of getting a fix. Generally similar charts showing Omega lines of position are published by the Defense Mapping Agency Hydrographic Center.

FIG. 2548 In waters frequented by radar-equipped ships, every boatman should use a passive radar reflector. It makes the boat's echo many times brighter on scope of ship using radar as its "eyes."

manner. A second pair of pulses is used to determine another LOP and the result is a Loran fix. Normally, one station is common to each of the two pairs; it is called the "master" and the others are "slaves."

A line of position can usually be determined in about two minutes; training in the use of a Loran receiver is required, but skill is soon acquired with practice. Loran stations must be accurately identified and the controls of the receiver manipulated properly to measure the time difference in arrival of the pulses. Thereafter, the position may be obtained from tables or plotted directly on readily available charts. As with other navigational techniques, three LOPs will give a better fix than two; coverage is such as to make this possible in many areas.

Loran-A has different day and night ranges because of the radio frequencies involved. Daytime reception using "ground waves" is the most accurate and average ranges are about 500 miles. This can be extended by the use of "sky waves" to as much as 1200 miles as determined by the power of the transmitter. Reception at night, also using sky waves, may extend out to 1400 miles, but with lessened accuracy. Range is reduced when the pulses must cross land areas, but accuracy is not degraded.

Accuracy of a Loran-A line of position varies over the coverage area of the stations used; it is greatest near the base line (line *between* the two stations). Ground wave LOPs should give a fix within 1½ miles accuracy over 80% of the normal coverage area. The accuracy when using sky waves will be degraded to a position uncertainty of 5 to 7 miles.

Loran-C

The transmitters of Loran-C operate on 100 kHz in groups of one master and several slave stations. This system uses pulse matching (as in Loran-A) and cycle matching techniques for rough and fine positioning respectively.

As a result of the lower frequency, Loran-C has a ground wave (most reliable) range of up to 1200 miles, with sky wave reception extending out to more than 3000 miles. Accuracy of position depends upon the method of reception. Automatic equipment gives more precise locations than manually operated receivers. Automatic tracking and cycle matching will provide positions within ¼-mile or less to a nominal distance of 1000 miles from the master station. Manual reception, with cycle matching will give locations accurate to 1 to 3 miles out to 700 miles. Without cycle matching, this reduces to 3 to 10 miles at the same distances from the master station.

Loran-C is scheduled to eventually replace Loran-A but the changeover will be gradual and dependent upon expansion of the Loran-C network. Overlap of the two systems will be provided and Loran-A will not be finally phased out until 1979 in some areas and 1980 in other areas.

Loran receivers

Receivers for Loran are widely available in many models. The simpler, less expensive units require manual tuning and human-operator matching of the signals. More sophisticated models feature automatic tracking, and some even provide for automatic signal acquisition.

Basic models of receivers are for Loran-A only, but units are also made that will receive both "A" and "C" signals. Dual receivers are available which will track and display two Loran readings simultaneously, enabling the navigator to plot a fix more quickly and easily than by having to take sequential readings. Loran receivers are not inexpensive, the price is several times that of a radiotelephone, but they do provide full-time, all-weather navigational assistance.

FIG. 2551 Here navigator uses special radio receiver to pick up loran signals. Loran, simple to operate, provides quick fixes of good accuracy. One reading gives line of position from special chart or tables. Another on second pair of signals gives information for loran fix.

OMEGA

The *Omega* electronic navigation system uses very low frequency (VLF) radio waves; three different frequencies from 10.2 to 13.6 kHz are used. Such VLF signals have considerable range and stability over day and night paths. An advantage of the system is that complete global coverage can be obtained by the use of only six transmitters properly situated. Ideally, stations would be located at the North and South Poles and 90° apart on the Equator; such a requirement must, of course, be modified to meet practical considerations. In actual practice, the Omega network will have eight transmitting sites to allow for possible equipment failures and off-air time for routine maintenance. The transmitters are located approximately 6,000 miles apart and at any point signals from at least four stations wil be usable. As the global network of stations is established, transmitters will be operated by the U.S. (by USCG personnel) and by foreign nations.

The Omega system

The Omega system was originally developed by the U.S. Navy for its submarines, surfaced or submerged (VLF signals can be received while under water), as well as for surface vessels and aircraft. Receiving equipment is now available, however, for civilian ships and aircraft, including fishing and recreational boats. Omega equipment is now quite expensive, but advancing technology and increased production can be expected to bring price reductions.

Omega fixes

Omega stations transmit continuous-wave signals, rather than pulses, for approximately one second out of every ten seconds on each frequency used. Signals from a single pair of stations on a single frequency can furnish a hyperbolic line of position, but rough position knowledge is required to within about eight miles to identify the set of lines, called a "lane," within which the receiver is located. Use of a second frequency reduces the need for position knowledge to 24 miles, and use of a third frequency extends this to 72 miles.

Two or more lines of position are combined in the normal manner to obtain an Omega fix. Station pairs should be selected so as to get lines crossing at large angles, as near 90° as possible for two lines, or 60° for three lines. As with Loran, special charts are used with over-printed Omega lines of position. Receivers have "lane counters" to keep a record of the number of lanes crossed since the counter was re-set after a fix was established, and so lessen the problem of lane identification.

Omega signals are affected by sky-wave propagation conditions and it is necessary to refer to published correction tables in the use of this system. The nominal all-weather accuracy is one mile in the daytime and two miles at night. Special techniques are available within local areas for increased degree of precision in position fixing, this is known as *differential omega,* and is useful for high-accuracy work such as surveys.

The signals from Omega transmitters are controlled by atomic frequency standards and can be used for adjusting or calibrating less accurate frequency standards; these signals can also be used for highly accurate time data.

By mid-1974, the Omega system is expected to have five fully operational stations providing complete coverage of the Northern Hemisphere, except for the SE portion of the North Atlantic Ocean, SW portion of the North Pacific, and the Indian Ocean. The target date for full global coverage from eight stations is 1976; status reports are published at intervals in Notices to Mariners.

Automatic Steering Devices

Automatic steering devices are electrical or electro-hydraulic equipment used to hold a boat on a predetermined heading. They are often, but erroneously, referred to as "automatic pilots"; they do no part of the piloting of a boat.

In lieu of the direct application of human muscle power to the steering mechanism of a boat, electric or hydraulic motors may be used to move the rudder to the desired angle and to hold it there. See fig. 2552. The control of these motors may be made automatic by the addition of a direction-sensing element and suitable electronic amplifiers. Either magnetic or gyroscopic compasses can be used to sense heading changes, but the former is nearly always used because of its lower cost.

Most automatic steering devices have controls which allow temporary manual over-riding of the automatic controls with the boat returning to the preset heading when the over-ride switch is released. This permits brief course changes to avoid obstructions or other boats without having to reset the desired heading. Local control boxes on long cords make possible the maneuvering of the boat while away from the normal helm position. This control of the craft, however, does not include throttle changes or forward-reverse shifting.

The use of automatic steering devices is simple. They do much to relieve boredom and fatigue on long, straight stretches. The device can, under most circumstances, steer

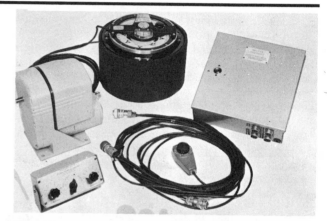

FIG. 2552 Automatic steering mechanism can do better job than human helmsman! Components are shown—magnetic compass with sensing attachments, electronic amplifier, steering motor, and control boxes.

a straighter course than a human helmsman. The disadvantage in this equipment lies in its misuse, excessive reliance on the device and failure to keep a person at the helm as a lookout ready to take over immediately if a dangerous situation should develop. It must also be remembered that the sensing element is usually no more "intelligent" than a magnetic compass; it is subject to all of the same outside corrupting influences such as tools, portable radios, beer cans, etc., if they are placed too close.

Citizens Band Radio

Citizens Band (CB) radio operations must be considered separately from those of the 2-3 MHz and VHF bands as they come under an entirely different set of FCC Rules. The CB sets are relatively inexpensive, easy to install, and simple to operate. See fig. 2553.

The Citizens Radio Service (CRS) is unique; it is not intended to duplicate any other radio service. It is *not* a substitute for the safety features of the regular marine radio service in the 2-3 MHz band, nor for the ship-to-shore connections into the public telephone system. Likewise, it is *not* a new type of hobby or amateur service for casual contacts at great distances. The CRS has its own particular functions and these do not overlap or conflict with other established services. As the result of widespread misuse of CB sets, the FCC, in April 1965, tightened its rules to control CRS operations more strictly.

Citizens Band communications can relate to either the business or social activities of the licensee, but they must be "necessary"—messages which could be sent by other means, or which need not be sent at all, are not permitted by FCC regulations. CB stations may not, of course, be used to further any illegal activity.

CB LICENSES

Licenses for stations in the Citizens Band have been made as easy as possible to obtain, and operator permits are not required at all. There are only a minimum of legal restrictions on the applicant and the equipment. To get a station license, a person may be either a U.S. citizen or an alien individual, but must be at least 18 years of age. A license also can be issued to a corporation, but not to any foreign government or a representative thereof. Licenses may not be transferred to another person; prompt report by letter is required for a change in address (but not for a change in approved equipment). Licenses are good for 5 years; renewal requires the same form and fee.

Application for a CB station license is made on Form 505 available from any FCC office, but mailed to Gettysburg, PA when completed. *A license and call sign must have been received before a station can be used.* A check or money order for $4 must accompany an application for a station license, which may, at no additional cost, include any number of sets owned by the same individual or organization.

In licensing equipment to be used on the Citizens Band, the FCC primarily envisions separate complete communications systems to meet the needs of individual licensees. This system would normally communicate within itself, and contacts with other stations heard on the air would be the exception rather than the normal mode of operation. In this connection, a "station" is all of the equipment used by a licensee in his system, and a "unit" is the term applied to a particular transmitter-receiver combination. Thus a *station* normally consists of at least two *units,* although it may consist of many more. Only in well-justified instances will the FCC license a single-unit station in the Citizens Band. The planned use of a Class D set by a boat owner belonging to a group operating a CB system would be an example of justification for licensing a single unit.

AUTHORIZED CHANNELS

The FCC has authorized 23 channels for the Citizens Band; they are generally referred to by channel number rather than frequency in megacycles. Any of them may be used by any licensee *for communications between units of one station.* For contacts between different stations, *only* channels 10 through 15, plus 23 may be used. Channel 9 is reserved for "emergency communications involving the

FIG. 2553 Citizens Band radios find many applications in boating, car, home or summer cottage. Model shown is specially designed for marine use.

immediate safety of life or the immediate protection of property." It is also available for "communications necessary to render assistance to a motorist" (but *not* for aid to boatmen!). Two points *must* be noted: (1) Although Channel 9 may be used for marine emergencies, it is *not* a substitute for the regular maritime distress frequencies of 2181 kHz and 156.8 MHz; and (2) Channel 9 is *not* to be used for "calling" to make initial contact with another station or unit in a manner similar to 2182 kHz in the marine band.

Citizens Band Class D stations are limited to 4 watts output power on AM and 12 watts peak power on single sideband. Normally, an antenna must not extend more than 20 feet higher than the building on which it is mounted. The usual reliable range is on the order of five miles, but may extend to 15 miles or more. These are groundwave ranges; skywave transmission of CB signals will often occur and cause signals to be heard at distances of several thousand miles despite their low power. The FCC Rules prohibit exchanges between stations more than 150 miles apart.

Communication between an unlicensed unit and a licensed station is prohibited. All low-powered (100 milliwatts) "handi-talkies" used with a CB station must have been included in the CB license application. If so licensed, they must be properly identified on the air.

OPERATING PROCEDURES

Operation of a Citizens Band station is quite simple. No specific operating procedures need be learned and used; no log is required. However, there are regulations which must be known and obeyed.

The FCC Rules require that *all* communications be restricted to the *minimum practicable transmission time,* but no time limits are placed on intercommunications between units of the same station. Between different stations, however, an exchange must be limited to a maximum of 5 minutes; after its completion, both stations must remain off the air for an additional 5 minutes, monitoring the frequency just used. A station called during this waiting period may break silence to advise the other station to stand-by. Avoidance of this waiting period by changing to another channel is prohibited.

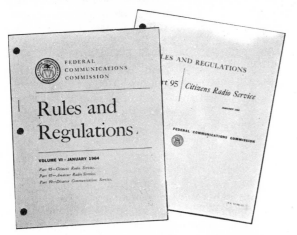

FIG. 2554 Each CB licensee must have on hand CURRENT copy of Part 95 of FCC Rules and Regulations. See text for details.

Station identification must be given at the beginning and end of each exchange of transmissions on each frequency used. If the contact continues for more than 15 minutes (legal only between units of the same station), identification must be made at least each 15 minutes. The Rules specifically require that *each letter and digit* of the call sign must be transmitted separately and distinctly. For example, 2951 must be said as "two nine five one," not as "twenty-nine fifty-one"; and 4500 as "four five zero zero," not as "forty-five hundred." Only standard phonetic alphabets may be used for the letters of the call sign.

The CB Rules now provide priority for transmissions involving the immediate safety of life of persons or protection of property. Under such conditions, the regulations restricting inter-station contacts to certain channels, limiting the durations of exchanges, etc., are waived, provided that a report is made to the FCC after the emergency is over. There are no other priorities.

The usual prohibitions against profane, obscene, and indecent language apply to the Citizens Band. Plain language must be used, except that abbreviations and normal operating signals (such as the "10" Code) are permitted, provided that a list of such signals and their meaning is kept in the station records. Although no operator permit is required, CB stations may be operated only by the licensee, members of his immediate family, his employees, and certain other individuals specifically authorized in the regulations. CB stations may *not* be operated by a person who has had his own license revoked or has surrendered it for cancellation as the result of rule violations. The licensee must remember that he retains full responsibility for all use of all units of his station. The same system of administrative forfeitures (small fines) that applies to marine band radio operations is also applicable to CB.

The FCC now requires that a CB licensee have a *current* copy of the applicable Rules, now Part 95. See fig. 2554. The only practicable way of complying is to purchase a copy of the FCC Rules and Regulations, Volume VI, from the Superintendent of Documents, Government Printing Office, Washington, D. C. 20402. The price of $5.35 includes a subscription to the mailing service for changes as they are issued.

Miscellaneous Electronic Equipment

There are many small items of electronic equipment that can be installed on a boat for the greater safety and convenience of the owner and his guests. The boatman should consider each for possible installation on his craft, not forgetting that each item will usually add a bit to the load on the battery and electrical wiring.

FUEL VAPOR DETECTORS

A *fuel vapor detector* is considered by many boatmen to be an essential piece of safety equipment aboard any craft using gasoline as fuel. See fig. 2555. These devices provide a visual warning of the build-up of any dangerous concentration of fuel vapors in the bilges. Frequently, such a device also provides an audible alarm in addition to the visual warning.

The installation of a fuel vapor detector is not difficult electrically or mechanically, but it is essential that it be done correctly. The location of the detector unit is important if the maximum safety benefit is to be obtained. Have your installation checked by a surveyor or safety inspector from your insurance company. Even the best fuel vapor detector is no substitute for electric bilge blowers, forced ventilation fans that pull air and fumes out of the lower parts of your boat's interior.

AUXILIARY RECEIVERS

If your boat does not have a direction finder that can be used as an *auxiliary receiver,* the boat owner should consider the purchase of one of several compact and lightweight receivers that are available at a reasonable price. See fig. 2556. This additional receiver can serve the functions previously mentioned of monitoring a second communications channel or of backing up the regular receiver in case of its failure. If the auxiliary receiver is of the transistorized type, the added battery drain is negligible, or it may be operated from its self-contained dry batteries. Models are available with either continuous tuning or several crystal-controlled fixed frequencies. This latter type lacks the flexibility of the former, but has the advantage of quick and sure tuning. These small receivers, if they have self-contained batteries, may be taken ashore on a beach or in the dinghy if you leave your boat for any reason.

MARINE CONVERTERS

The growing use of electrical equipment on boats has resulted in a steadily increasing demand for power from the craft's batteries. The generator or alternator on the boat's engine will suffice to keep the batteries charged if the engine is operated a large enough percentage of the time that the electrical equipment is in use. There is no way to state a general figure as to what proportion of the

FIG. 2555 Fuel vapor detector, properly installed and used, will warn of explosive vapors in bilge. Models available with audible alarm and visual indicator.

FIG. 2556 With auxiliary receiver, second marine band channel may be monitored, or you can listen to frequency for which your radio-telephone does not have a crystal. Model shown operates from self-contained batteries. Keep it at least two feet from compass.

FIG. 2557 Boat batteries are normally charged by generator or alternator driven by main engine. At dockside, marine converter keeps batteries up by converting shoreside AC power to DC at proper voltage for boat's electrical system.

time is required as individual conditions will vary too widely.

If you are one of the boat owners who finds that all too often his battery is down so far that it won't start the engine, then you are a candidate for a *marine converter.* See fig. 2557. This relatively simple electrical device converts the 115-volt AC dockside electricity into the 6, 12, or 32 volts DC required for the boat's electrical system. It is essentially a continuous-duty battery-charger with control circuits to permit it to operate safely left unattended.

INVERTERS

It may seem a bit contradictory to immediately discuss a means of getting 115-volt AC electrical power from the boat's low voltage DC system just after having considered the reverse process, but there is a reason. There is no way to store AC in a battery, and if AC is needed when away from the shore, the only means of getting it (without installing an auxiliary generating plant) is to "invert" the DC power from the batteries into AC.

Alternating current aboard a boat of any size is useful for the powering of television or hi-fi sets, tape recorders, electric razors, electric mixers or other small household appliances. Small inverters are available using vibrators or transistors and these will quietly and efficiently supply you with small amounts of "shore-type" electricity. These DC to AC converters are *not* suitable for use with electrical devices whose function is to produce heat, such as toasters and irons; the power required for such items is beyond the capacity of inverters.

AUXILIARY GENERATING PLANTS

Inverters using vibrators or transistors are usually limited to a power rating of not more than 250 watts. If greater amounts of 115-volt AC power are required for cooking, air conditioning, or heating, the installation of a small

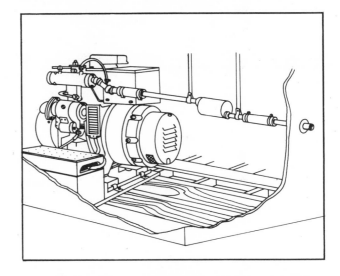

FIG. 2558 Inverters can change DC electrical power of boat's batteries to 115-volts AC for operation of shore-type electrical equipment, up to a few hundred watts. For heavier loads, install auxiliary electric plant driven by its own gasoline or diesel engine. (Diagram from Technical Bulletin T-021, Installation of Onan Marine Generating Plants.)

auxiliary generating plant should be considered. See fig. 2558. These units are available in sizes from 500 watts to 10 kilowatts or more, with either gasoline or diesel engines to match the type of fuel used in the main engines.

Calculation of the size of generator you will need is not difficult as nearly all items of electrical equipment are plainly rated in watts of power consumed. Be careful, however, about loads that are not constant. For example, an electric refrigerator unit may consume only about 100 watts *average* power since it does not run continuously, but while it is running it may require 400 watts, and the momentary starting load will be even greater. Be generous and be safer; install an electric plant with an adequate excess or reserve capacity. You will soon think of more electrical and electronic gear to add to your boat.

INTERCOM SYSTEMS

While most people think of a boat as being too small and compact to have internal communications problems, there are numerous possible applications for simple intercom systems. See fig. 2559. The interior of many larger cruisers, particularly those of the double-cabin type, are so divided that voices do not carry well from one compartment to another. A simple three-station intercom system connecting the bridge, forward cabin, and after cabin will

FIG. 2559 Small intercom system permits easy communication between all areas aboard cruisers and yachts. Master unit shown controls five substations, including one on foredeck, useful when anchoring or docking.

make possible easy conversation between these locations and save many steps. On a boat with a small crew, such as a couple living aboard by themselves, a quick and easy means of internal communications is truly a safety item as the helmsman need not leave the controls or divert his attention to carry on a conversation or summon assistance.

On a larger boat, the intercom system can be extended to include a unit in a weather-proof box on the foredeck.

Then you can have constant contact between the person at the boat's controls and the person raising or lowering the anchor, or handling the docking lines. Just try to get up a badly fouled anchor without communicating with the helmsman, and you will quickly appreciate this small electronic device.

RUDDER POSITION INDICATORS

A simple and inexpensive, but very useful, item is a *rudder position indicator*. See fig. 2560. These are standard equipment of large vessels and tugboats, but are seldom found on recreational boats. This small degree of use probably results from a lack of knowledge of the availability of the device and how it works. A small unit is in-

FIG. 2560 Rudder position indicators are always found on large ships and tugs, infrequently on small craft. They deserve wider use. Knowledge of rudder angle helps when docking, undocking, entering canal locks, etc.

stalled at the rudder post and wires are run forward to a meter located within easy view of the helmsman. This meter is calibrated in degrees of right or left rudder. A quick glance will instantly tell the exact position of the rudder at that moment; such information is of considerable value when getting under way or docking with little steerageway. Once you have and use one of these electronic items, you will never be without it.

Communications with the Coast Guard

Radio communications with Coast Guard shore stations and vessels follow slightly different procedures than those with other recreational boats or commercial ships. Every skipper should know these procedures and have his radio set up to operate on the proper frequencies.

Initial calls should be made on 2182 kHz or Channel 16 (156.8 MHz); these frequencies are "guarded" by all Coast Guard units. Expect to be asked to shift to a special working frequency if it is not a Mayday situation. On the MF band, this is 2670 kHz in all areas. (This is a "government" frequency and must **not** be used except to the USCG and USCG Auxiliary.)

On VHF-FM,, the working frequency to the Coast Guard for all non-distress communications is now 157.100 MHz, send and receive—this is variously called Channel 22, 22A, or 22CG, and has replaced Channel 12 which was initially used.

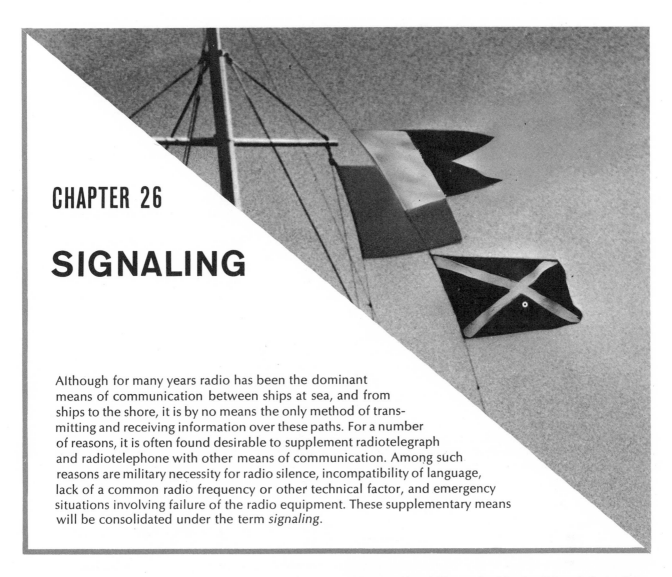

CHAPTER 26

SIGNALING

Although for many years radio has been the dominant means of communication between ships at sea, and from ships to the shore, it is by no means the only method of transmitting and receiving information over these paths. For a number of reasons, it is often found desirable to supplement radiotelegraph and radiotelephone with other means of communication. Among such reasons are military necessity for radio silence, incompatibility of language, lack of a common radio frequency or other technical factor, and emergency situations involving failure of the radio equipment. These supplementary means will be consolidated under the term *signaling*.

FIG. 2601 Aboard this vessel arriving in a U.S. port, the two-letter International Code flag signal AM (Alfa Mike) at the masthead signifies "Have you a doctor?" and the single-letter Q (Quebec) at the starboard yardarm is flown to "request pratique."   (Rosenfeld photo)

The forms of signaling

The principal forms of signaling are: (1) flag-hoist, (2) flashing light, and (3) semaphore. These are all visual means; signaling by audible methods, such as by Morse code on the boat's horn, is of little practical use. Sound signals as used in the Rules of the Road are covered elsewhere and will not be repeated here.

VISUAL SIGNALING

Visual signaling should not be a new or strange concept to the average boatman, although he probably lacks the detailed knowledge to read such signals. The yachtsman crossing a busy harbor will certainly see many ships flying signal flags; and should it be a naval harbor, such as Hampton Roads or San Diego, he will undoubtedly also see flashing signal lights, and perhaps sailors sending semaphore.

The value of visual signaling

The time taken to acquire a rudimentary knowledge of visual signaling can be of value to a boatman in at least two ways. Not the least of these is the pleasure and satisfaction of knowing what is going on and being able to explain it to the other crew members and guests aboard his boat. Merchant ships, fig. 2602, will be flying signal flags indicating the presence of a pilot aboard, the handling of dangerous cargoes, an imminent sailing, and other interesting facts. Naval and Coast Guard vessels, fig. 2603, probably will be flying many more flags, some signifying simple facts like those noted above, and others signaling more complex naval messages and maneuvers. Being able to read and know the meaning of at least a portion of these signal flags, or other types of signals, will give the boatman a greater sense of "belonging" to the maritime world around him.

The greater value, however, in a knowledge of signaling lies in the added margin of safety that it can provide. So much dependence is placed today on the boat's radio-telephone that one often overlooks the possibility of its not being available when needed. It need not be an electronic failure that precludes your communicating with another craft; it could be merely a lack of a common frequency or type of modulation. Radio will undoubtedly remain your primary means of boat-to-boat and boat-to-shore communications, but don't overlook the added possibilities of signaling.

Signal Codes

For more than two thousand years, information and orders have been communicated between ships by means of flags. In the days of the ancient Greeks and Romans, battles were begun by the hoisting of streamers of various colors. These were first raised on the vessel carrying the commander of the naval force—hence the term "flagship."

The development of modern flag-hoist signaling may be said to date from 1340 when the British Navy officially listed two signals—one for all captains to come to the flagship and the other that the enemy had been sighted. By 1530, the French Navy was using a signal code with five meanings.

Signal books first appeared in 1673 when an English system was established using flags of different colors hoisted at various places to give a series of meanings. The 1738 French signal code used ten numerical flags in groups of three for transmitting prearranged messages. By 1780, this technique had been expanded by the addition of two "repeaters" so that only 12 flags, rather than 30, would be needed for all combinations, 000 to 999. The code book was prepared in both alphabetical and numerical sections for encoding and decoding. This is essentially the same format as is used for signal books today. The French system also provided for the relaying of signals to the more distant ships in a formation, again just as is currently done in naval forces at sea.

The first American flag code was proposed in 1797 em-

ploying numeral pennants and repeaters for 290 signals, and in 1802 a modified version was adopted for use by the Continental Navy. Flag-hoist signaling has been used by the American Navy continuously since then.

In 1817, the British adopted a code of signals for merchant ships different from that used by the Royal Navy. In other countries, non-naval vessels used various signal systems that usually were published by private individuals or groups. These prevailed until 1857 when a new English "commercial code" was established that was gradually adopted by other countries. Because more combinations were needed than could be obtained with ten pennants in combinations of three, a new set of 18 flags was adopted and named after letters of the alphabet—the consonants, less X, Y, and Z. These flags could not be used for spelling out words as the vowels were missing; coded meanings were still employed for geographical locations, common words and phrases, combinations of letters or single letters, and numbers. More than a dozen of these flags are still used in the original design as adopted in 1857; others have been changed to increase their readability under difficult conditions of visibility.

In 1897, the alphabet was filled out with flags for the missing letters and was officially designated as the International Code of Signals. Experience with this code during World War I revealed many deficiencies, and it was subsequently revised in a series of conferences and meetings. Numeral pennants were added to eliminate the need for using code groups of letters for sending numbers, and three substitutes (repeaters) were added to expand the possible combinations of four-flag hoists. The 1930 Code was made truly international by being standardized in official versions in seven languages. Since 1955, the flags have been associated with the phonetic alphabet now so widely used in radio-telephone communications.

THE REVISED INTERNATIONAL CODE

Between 1961 and 1964 an international committee met periodically and drew up a new Code of Signals. The revised Code is intended primarily for situations related to the safety of navigation and persons, especially where language difficulties arise. Official versions of the new Code are now published in nine languages. It is suitable for transmission by *all* means of communications, including radiotelephony.

H.O. 102

The revised International Code of Signals became effective on 1 April 1969. For American use, it has been published by the Naval Oceanographic Office as H.O. 102. This new volume replaces both the old H.O. 103 used for visual signaling and H.O. 104 used for radio. The book can be purchased from local sales agents, or it can be ordered by mail from the U.S. Naval Oceanographic Office, Washington, D.C. 20390.

H.O. 102 includes both general procedures applicable to all forms of communication and specific rules for flag signaling, flashing light signaling, sound signaling, radio-telegraphy, radiotelephony, and signaling by hand flags, using either semaphore or the Morse code.

Principles of coding

The revised Code is based on the principle that each

FIG. 2602 Merchant ships are often seen flying a single flag from the International Code of Signals. This vessel has the "H" flag hoisted to signify that there is a pilot aboard. The "G" flag woud have indicated a request for a pilot. All of the alphabet flags have a special meaning when flown singly as well as when used in groups of two or more.

U. S. COAST GUARD PHOTO

FIG. 2603 Naval and Coast Guard ships make much use of signal flags for communicating with other vessels. Each flag represents a letter, number or special meaning. Government ships always hoist the flags of their call letters when entering or leaving port.

signal will have a complete meaning. It thus omits the vocabulary method that was a part of the old Code. The Geographical Section, not being considered essential, was dropped. By these means, it was possible to reduce considerably the volume of the Code and achieve greater simplicity.

The signals used consist of: (1) single-letter signals allocated to meanings which are very urgent, important, of very common use; (2) two-letter signals for general messages; and (3) three-letter signals (all beginning with "M") for medical messages.

In certain cases, *complements* are used—an added nu-meral following the basic two-letter signal. Complements express: (1) variations in the meaning of a basic signal; (2) questions and answers related to the meaning of the basic signal; and (3) supplementary, specific, or more detailed meanings.

Spelling

When names must be sent, or other words for which there are no signal groups in the International Code, they must be spelled out. The signal group YZ *may* be used to indicate that the groups which follow are plain language words rather than code signals; it can, however, be omitted if the spelling is obvious. The "alphabetical signals" formerly used have been discontinued.

Special procedures

The International Code of Signals provides special procedures for many purposes such as signaling time, courses and bearings, geographical coordinates, etc. The details of these procedures are too lengthy for inclusion in this book; the boatman needing such knowledge will find it in full in H.O. 102. This volume is a "must" for a boatman who may need to communicate with foreign ships or shore stations; it is a necessity for any skipper who carries a full set of signal flags and uses them to communicate with other yachts or with Naval and Coast Guard vessels. It is an interesting book to have aboard even if such signaling is not contemplated.

The problem of compiling a code from which expressions in any one of nine languages might be taken was a difficult one, and certain principles must be followed in its use. These are outlined in the instructions in H.O. 102 and should be read carefully before attempting to use the code itself. Otherwise, because of the form used, erroneous interpretations might be placed on a message sent in code.

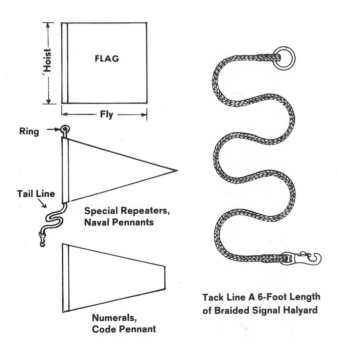

FIG. 2604 Flags and pennants of the International Code of Signals are joined together with snaps and rings. The "tail line" extending below each flag provides the spacing beween them in each group; the "tack line" provides a greater spacing between two groups hoisted on the same halyard.

Typical code signals from H.O. 102

The simple single-letter signal codes are shown beneath the flags on page W. Typical two-letter groups are listed in fig. 2615.

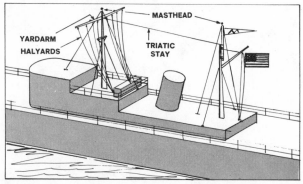

FIG. 2605 Signal flags are normally hoisted on halyards rising to the yardarms. In some situations, particularly on naval vessels, hoists may be made at more than one location simultaneously. See text for sequence in which such multiple hoists are read.

Flag-hoist Signaling

The set of international code flags prescribed for flag-hoist signaling consists of 26 alphabetical flags, 10 numeral pennants, three substitutes, and the answering pennant. The names "substitute" and "repeater" are used interchangeably in publications on flag-hoist signaling. In either case, they are pennants that are employed as replacements for flags (or pennants) already used once in a hoist, since there is only one of each letter or number in a set.

Five standardized colors are used for signal flags—red, white, blue, yellow, and black. Most of the flags are of two colors, selected and arranged for maximum contrast. Two flags are of a single solid color, several use three colors, and one uses four colors. Each flag and pennant has a piece of line sewn into its hoist edge, extending slightly above the cloth to a metal ring, and for several inches below the cloth ending in a snap hook. This "tail line"

provides the spacing between the flags of a hoist; the combination of snaps and rings permits the rapid joining together of the individual flags and their connection onto a signal halyard. See fig. 2604.

The flags and pennants of the International Code are shown in full color on page W. Also indicated here are the meanings of the flags when flown singly. Of these, probably the most often seen will be the "B" flag, displayed while a ship is carrying or handling an explosive cargo, and the "H" flag flown when a pilot is on board.

Special naval flags and pennants

The boatman may sometimes see vessels of the U. S. Navy and Coast Guard flying signals that include flags and pennants not found in the International Code. The Navy uses a set of *numeral flags* as well as the regular pennants for numbers. In addition, special flags and pennants have been adopted for naval formations and maneuvers.

The U. S. Navy uses the three substitutes of the International Code and has added its own fourth substitute.

The special naval flags and pennants are shown in color at the bottom of page X.

FLAG SIGNALING PROCEDURES

Signal flags are flown singly and in combinations of two or more; see page X. Flags and pennants may be mixed as required.

When signaling by means of the flags and pennants of the International Code, it is advisable to show only a single *hoist* at a time. A hoist means one or more *groups* displayed from a single halyard. The signal is read from the top down. Each group of letters and/or numerals constitute a separate signal; when several groups are used on a single hoist, they must, of course, be separated to convey the correct meaning. A *tackline,* a six-foot length of line with a snap hook in one end and a ring in the other, is used as a spacer to separate the groups.

FIG. 2606 Flag hoists are read from the top flag down. If there should be more than one halyard in use from the same yardarm at the same time, the hoists are read from outboard inward as shown above.

TYPICAL SIGNALS FROM A YACHT CLUB SIGNAL CODE

A — The course will be _____.
H — Communicate with me via radiotelephone.
L — Come within hail.
Q — Race will finish off _____.
T — Send club launch.
BF — Anchor for night at _____.
CQ — Captains and guests are invited on board this yacht at _____.
CZ — Congratulations, well done.
DC — Mail for you ashore at _____.
IR — Monday
JQ — 0730
NG — Bangor, Maine
SG — Newport, R. I.
AQP — N.N.E.
ARU — S.W.

FIG. 2607 In a typical yacht club signal code, single letters will consist of special, racing, and emergency signals; two-letter groups will represent general and designating signals, and days of the week and hours of the day; three-letter groups are compass signals.

Signals should be kept flying until acknowledged. There are occasions when more than one hoist need be displayed simultaneously; in such cases, an order of sequence must be followed in order to interpret the message correctly. The hoists are read in the following order: (1) masthead, (2) triatic stay, (3) starboard yardarm, and (4) port yardarm, fig. 2605.

In cases where more than one hoist is flown from a yardarm, they are read from outboard inward, fig. 2606. When a vessel displays more than one hoist from a triatic stay, they are read from the foremost one aft.

The terms *superior* and *inferior* are often used in relation to signals. A signal is superior to another if hoisted

FIG. 2608 On boats equipped with a full set of signal flags and pennants, a flag chest or locker may be built in, with letter or name plates to identify code flags in their individual pigeonholes.

before the latter, either in point of time or hoist. If hoisted after, it is inferior.

Obviously, a visual signal is going to fail in its purpose if it is not clearly visible. For that reason, signals should always be flown where they can be seen best by the receiving vessel or shore station. This means that each flag must stand out clearly, not fouled by the halyard, sails, etc.

Signal groups

If every message transmitted by flag signals had to be spelled out letter by letter, it is obvious that the procedure would become impossibly lengthy, wasting much time and effort. Many typical messages have been given two-letter signals in the revised Code. One of the first steps in gaining proficiency in visual signaling is to become thoroughly familiar with the code book. With such knowledge, one will naturally frame his messages so as to use phrasing for which code groups have been provided, lessening the number of words that must be spelled out.

Calling and answering

When calling a particular vessel, her signal letters are hoisted superior to the message that is to follow. Otherwise, in the absence of such signal letters, the message would be understood to be addressed to all vessels in sight of the signal. If the vessel's signal letters are not

known, she can be requested to hoist them by displaying the code letter group CS and hoisting your own signal letters at the same time. As another alternative, display of the code group YQ would convey the message: "I wish to signal to the vessel on bearing indicated from me." This signal would, of course, be accompanied with another hoist indicating the bearing concerned so as to distinguish between several vessels that might be within sight.

In order to understand the procedure followed in answering a signal, there are several terms that should be explained. A signal is said to be *at the dip* when it is hoisted only about half as high as the halyard will permit. It is said to be *close up* when it has been hoisted as high as possible. See page X center left.

In receiving signals, the vessel or vessels addressed should hoist the answering pennant at the dip when each hoist is seen, closing up to indicate that the signal is understood. Then when the hoist on the transmitting ship is hauled down, the answering pennant on the receiving vessel is lowered to the dip again so as to be ready to acknowledge the next hoist in a similar manner when that one is understood. This continues until the message is completed, at which time the answering pennant alone is hoisted aboard the transmitting ship; this signal is acknowledged by the receiving ship as before, after which the answering pennants are hauled down.

When a hoist can not be clearly distinguished, the answering pennant is kept at the dip on the receiving ship and a signal is hoisted to convey the reason for the difficulty. If, on the other hand, the signal can be distinguished but not understood, the letters ZL are hoisted.

Substitutes or Repeaters

With every set of code flags there are included three *substitutes*. These permit the repetition of a signal flag in a group without carrying extra sets of flags. In the procedures of the International Code, substitutes repeat the same *class* of flag that precedes them; that is, following alphabetical flags they repeat them, but if used with numeral pennants they repeat such pennants.

Considering then only the class of flag directly preceding the substitute, the first substitute repeats the top such flag; the second substitute, the second flag from the top; and the third substitute, the third flag from the top. An answering pennant used as a decimal point is disregarded. For example: if the signal were T1330, the hoist would be: T, 1, 3, second substitute, 0. See the illustration on page X, upper right. A particular substitute is never used more than once in the same group. If the signal were BBCB, the hoist would read: B, first substitute, C, second substitute. Note that the first substitute has been used once in place of the second letter and cannot be used again. However, as used it represented the letter B, and so it can be repeated by use of the second substitute; see page X.

Naval procedures

Flag-hoist signaling procedures between Naval and Coast Guard vessels will vary from that used by merchant ships and yachts. These differences stem from the different and special requirements of naval formations and maneuvers. They need not cause any concern to boatmen, however, for in communications with non-naval craft, these vessels will use International Code procedures.

YACHT CLUB SIGNAL CODES

Many yacht clubs have adopted signal codes of their own that are not in conformity with the International Code. The purpose of the signals prescribed in such codes is principally to provide a means of communication between craft of the club's fleet. These local codes permit quicker and easier signaling for matters of particular interest to that group. See fig. 2607.

While the codes do vary between different clubs, there is a tendency toward standardization of both the signals and the procedures. The interpretation of club signals will generally require the availability of that club's signal code as published in its year book.

Most clubs provide that when using the club code the burgee is hoisted over the code flags; the absence of the burgee indicating that the hoist should be read from the International Code of Signals. In other cases, the procedures provide that the three signal flags YV 1 can be hoisted to indicate specifically that the International Code is being used, its absence indicating the use of the club code. It is necessary to know the procedures of the particular club concerned.

General yachting uses of signal flags

Most boats will not carry a full set of signal flags and pennants, fig. 2608, but may carry one or more for special use under certain conditions.

The flying of the single flag "Q" when returning from a foreign port is correct and desirable in accordance with its International Code meaning "My vessel is healthy and I request free pratique." See fig. 2601. *Pratique* is the formal term for permission to use a port.

The code flag "T" is often seen flying on boats at yacht club moorings. Its meaning at such times is a request for "transportation"—a call for the club launch to come alongside and pick up passengers for shore. This is not in accordance with the International Code of Signals, but has general acceptance and understanding through wide usage.

Another single code-flag signal is the flying of the letter "M" to signify "Doctor on board"; this differs from the revised International Code meaning. Not yet in general use, its value is gradually being recognized and the practice is spreading. While most, if not all, doctors look to their boating hours as a time "to get away from it all," knowledge that a boat has a doctor on board is of great importance should an accident happen within sight; it is to be hoped that the practice of flying the "M" flag will be adopted by more and more physicians and surgeons.

SPECIAL FLAGS

Many flags will be seen on boats that undoubtedly "signal" a meaning, but nonetheless will not be found in any signal code, International or yacht club.

The more official of these flags include the owner absent, guest aboard, and meal flags described on page 463. Next in line would come the cocktail flag, the meaning of which is never in doubt, closely followed by a newer flag bearing a foaming mug of beer. For the non-alcoholically inclined, there is now a flag decorated with a pot of coffee, obviously inviting the beholder to "come on over and have one."

Boats operating out of sport-fishing ports will often be seen flying flags bearing the likeness of various game fish, indicating their catch for that day. Unhappily, you may also see boats flying the "skunk" flag signifying "no luck today."

A special flag that must be strictly honored is the "diver down" flag—rectangular red with a single white diagonal stripe. Keep well away from any boat or float displaying this signal.

There seems to be an ever-expanding list of what might be called "comic" flags. These are not particularly in good taste in yachting circles, but as they can be considered as signaling information, their existence will be noted here. Among such flags are the ball-and-chain (wife aboard), witch-on-a-broom (wife not on board), battle-axe (mother-in-law aboard), and two sleeping rabbits (do not disturb). See fig. 2609.

There is also the skull-and-crossed-bones "pirate" flag that is often seen, but which apparently has no standardized meaning, if indeed it has any meaning beyond its decorative (?) value.

BATTLE-AXE
MOTHER-IN-LAW ABOARD

SKUNK
(NO FISH CAUGHT)

COCKTAIL

COFFEE

BALL & CHAIN
WIFE ABOARD

WITCH—
WIFE ASHORE

BEER

BUNNIES—SLUMBER
DO NOT DISTURB

FIG. 2609 Many boats will be seen flying the so-called "novelty" or "gag" flags. While in somewhat questionable taste in strict yachting circles, it must be admitted that, properly used, they do "signal" information to other craft.

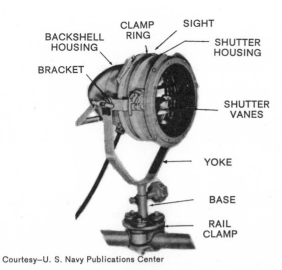

Courtesy—U. S. Navy Publications Center

FIG. 2610 For short-range signaling, naval vessels will use small searchlights not much larger than those found on motorboats. The flashes of light are formed by opening and closing shutter vanes in front of the light source. The Navy also uses several larger sizes of signal searchlights up to 36-inch carbon-arc lights.

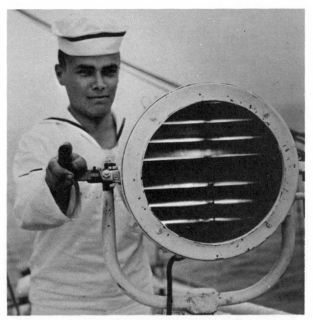

Courtesy—United States Coast Guard

Flashing Light Signaling

Signaling by short and long flashes of light is widely used by naval forces. It is much faster than hoists of code flags and has a much greater range than semaphore signaling. It maintains the radio silence sometimes needed for security.

Navy vessels may use small or large signal searchlights, yardarm or masthead lights, or special security devices. For normal ranges from one ship to another, a small search-light about the size of those mounted on medium-sized boats will be used, fig. 2610. These lights will be bright enough for signaling during the day or night. To communicate over greater distances, which may be several miles or more, large and powerful arc-light searchlights will be found on major naval vessels.

Searchlights of all sizes are normally used to communicate with another specific vessel or with a shore station. For signaling to all ships around a harbor or in a formation at sea, use will be made of the yardarm or masthead blinker lights, less powerful but capable of being read

from any direction, fig. 2611. Security can be achieved by using cones over the signal searchlight to restrict the light pattern, or by using infrared devices that require special receiving equipment to read the signals being sent.

Small-craft use

Flashing light signaling is useful also to boatmen. It has the advantage of needing little or no special equipment; an ordinary flashlight is usually used as the signaling light. There is, however, the disadvantage that a knowledge of the Morse code is required.

Generally, flashing light signals from a boat are limited to nighttime use by the low power of the light source. The boat's searchlight cannot be turned on and off fast enough for the practical transmission of Morse code dots and dashes—the Navy's signal searchlights are left on continuously during use, with shutters being rapidly opened and closed to make the short and long flashes of light. The short but definite time for the filament of a boat's search-light to come up to brilliance and die out is too great for message sending, but would be satisfactory for such special use as the three shorts, three longs, and three shorts of an SOS signal. (••• — — — •••)

THE INTERNATIONAL MORSE CODE

As noted above, the International Morse Code of *dots* and *dashes* is used for flashing light signaling. The flashes and the spaces between them are defined in terms of *units* —a *dot* is *one* unit long; a *dash* is *three* units; the space between the dots and dashes of a single character (letter or number) is one unit long, between characters it is three units, and between words or groups it is five units in length. The length of a "unit" is roughly set by the skill of the operator and the speed at which he can transmit accurately; it is always well to transmit somewhat more slowly than one's maximum capability to minimize errors—and, in

FIG. 2611 For non-directional flashing light signaling, a vessel may be equipped with yardarm blinker lights. They may also be located as a pair at a masthead. With these lights the range over which signals can be sent is much less than that of a searchlight.

A • —	J • — — —	R • — •	Period • — • — • —
B — • • •	K — • —	S • • •	Comma — — • • — —
C — • — •	L • — • •	T —	Interrogative • — • — — • — (RQ)
D — • •	M — —	U • • —	Distress Call • • • — — — • • • (S̄O̅S̅)
E •	N — •	V • • • —	From — • • • (DE)
F • • — •	O — — —	W • — —	Invitation to transmit (go ahead) — • — (K)
G — — •	P • — — •	X — • • —	Wait • — • • • (A̅S̅)
H • • • •	Q — — • —	Y — • — —	Error • • • • • • • • (EEEE etc.)
I • •		Z — — • •	Received • — • (R)
			End of each message • — • — • (A̅R̅)

1 • — — — —	2 • • — — —	3 • • • — —
4 • • • • —	5 • • • • •	6 — • • • •
7 — — • • •	8 — — — • •	9 — — — — •
		0 — — — — —

NOTE:
A dash is equal to three dots.
The space between parts of the same letter is equal to one dot.
The space between two letters is equal to three dots.
The space between two words is equal to five dots.

FIG. 2612   The International Morse Code, with certain simple procedure signals.

case of doubt, it is better to exaggerate slightly the lengths of dashes and spaces than it is to shorten them.

The letters of the alphabet, numbers, and punctuation marks are signaled in Morse code by combinations of dots and dashes. Letters have from one to four components, numbers have five, and punctuation symbols have six. The basic Morse code is shown in fig. 2612.

Time is required to memorize the Morse code characters for the letters, numbers, and simple punctuation marks; but it *can* be done by anyone, and it is well worth the effort required. Once learned, and occasionally used, it will not be forgotten and may prove extremely valuable some day in an emergency.

FLASHING LIGHT PROCEDURES

Formal procedures have been prescribed for the establishment and carrying out of communications by flashing light. The boatman need know only the barest fundamentals, enough for emergencies, leaving the full details, as described in H.O. 102, to the professional signalman.

Establishing contact

A vessel desiring to establish flashing light communications with another trains its light on the other and sends the other's call letters, if known, or the signal A̅A̅, A̅A̅, etc. (• — • —, • — • —, etc.). This is discontinued when the vessel called answers.

T̅T̅T̅T̅T̅, etc. (— — — — —, etc.) is the signal used to answer the above call; it is discontinued when the first ship stops calling.

Procedure signals

Certain letters and combination of letters have been given special procedural meanings. They are, in effect, brief messages in themselves. Some of the more basic signals are given below with their meanings; the bar over the letters means that they are run together and transmitted as a single character.

T (—) is the single dash flash signifying the receipt of each word or code group in a message.

R (• — •) means "Message received."

EEEEE, etc. (• • • • • •, etc.) is the erase sign, signifying that a mistake has been made. It is answered by the receiving ship with the same signal. When answered, the sending ship repeats the *last word or group sent correctly* and then goes ahead with the rest of the message.

RQ   Interrogative, or "The significance of the previous group should be read as a question."

C   Affirmative, or "The significance of the previous group should be read in the affirmative."

N   Negative, or "The significance of the previous group should be read in the negative. When used with voice transmissions, the procedure signal is 'NO'."

"C" and "N" (or "NO") can be used singly to indicate an affirmative or negative statement or reply. When "N" (or "NO") or "RQ" are used to change an affirmative signal into a negative statement or a question, they are sent after the main signal.

OK   Acknowledging a correct repetition, or "It is correct."

CS   "What is the name or identity signal of your vessel (or station)?"

DE   "From" (used to precede the name or identity signal of the calling station.

RPT   Repeat signal: "I repeat" or "Repeat what you have sent" or "Repeat what you have received."

Many of the above procedure signals may be used with means of communication other than flashing light. When used by voice, the letters are spoken from the phonetic alphabet, except for "NO" which is spoken as the word.

Using the repeat sign

When the repeat sign is sent singly, it means "Repeat all of the last message." It can be used in conjunction with the signs AA, AB, WA, or WB and an identifying word or the signals AA, AB, BN, WA, and WB plus an identifying group or groups (or word or words) to request the repetition of a portion of a message.

AA   All after . . .
AB   All before . . .
BN   All between . . . and . . .

WA   The word or group after . . .
WB   The word or group before . . .
For example:
RPT alone means to repeat the entire message.
RPT AA RED means "Repeat all after the word Red."
RPT AB MJ means "Repeat all before the group MJ."
RPT WA EY means "Repeat the group after the group EY."
RPT WB BOY means "Repeat the word before the word Boy."
RPT BN FR TX means "Repeat the groups between the groups FR and TX."

Repeat signs are not to be used when a message is not understood or when a message as decoded is unintelligible. In such cases, suitable signals taken from the Code are to be used.

Use of International Code groups

YV is the international code group indicator, used in messages transmitted by Morse code as the first group of the coded text and signifies that the message that follows consists of code groups, not plain language.

FLASHING LIGHT SIGNALING BY BOATS

Although the average boatman may have little regular use for flashing light signaling, this means of communications may prove of great value in emergencies. Take, for example, the situation in which a boat is aground at night. It may be unsafe for another boat to approach close enough for shouting back and forth across the gap between them—there may be uncertainty as to where the shoal water lies, or the other craft may draw considerably more water and thus have to stand off at a distance. Knowledge of the Morse code, being able to receive as well as send, will permit the exchange of vital information using nothing more than an ordinary flashlight. Knowledge of plain language is used and numbers are spelled out.

Use of the signal YV (or "INTERCO" by voice) and groups from the International Code of Signals will provide a means of getting around a language barrier.

Semaphore Signaling —————

Semaphore signaling may make a boatman think of his Boy Scout days, but actually this means of communication is used more at sea than on land. A pair of skilled naval signalmen "talking" rapidly back and forth with semaphore flags is an interesting sight and a thoroughly practical one.

Semaphore signaling is normally done with a pair of hand flags for greater visibility. Such flags can be omitted for signaling over short distances, although the use of handkerchiefs, rags, etc. will aid in the reading of the signals.

The semaphore alphabet

Information is transmitted in semaphore signaling by the position of the sender's two hands. For each character, each hand will be in one of eight possible positions, vertically up or down, straight out to either side, or at positions midway between, fig. 2613.

The semaphore alphabet is shown in fig. 2614. The *break sign* (or *front*, as shown in the illustration) is most important; it is used between words and, without a pause, between double letters appearing in a word. In semaphore plain language is used and numbers are spelled out.

SEMAPHORE PROCEDURES

The desire to communicate by semaphore is indicated by sending the signal K 1 by any means. The other ship hoists the answering pennant at the dip to acknowledge the signal, and closes it up when she is ready to receive. If unable to communicate by semaphore, the reply is the signal YS 1. For simple boating situations, it is sufficient to use the attention sign, waving both arms from straight out to vertically upward.

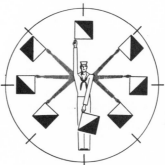

Courtesy—United States Coast Guard

FIG. 2613   The semaphore signaling code is based on the position of the sender's two hands (flags). There are eight basic positions as shown; for any character, one hand is at a position and the other hand is at one of the seven remaining positions.

Each letter is sent distinctly with the sender's flags (or hands) moving directly from the positions of one letter to those of the next, and then dropping to the break (front) position at the end of the word. The sender then waits for the receiver to send "C" indicating that the word has been received and the message should be continued. At the end of the message, the signal AR is sent; if at any time a mistake is made, a series of Es is made, then the *full last word sent correctly* is retransmitted followed by the word in which the error was made and the rest of the message.

SEMAPHORE SIGNALING BY BOATMEN

Semaphore signaling has its advantages and its disadvantages for use from recreational boats. It permits communications over greater distances than a voice will carry, even when amplified through a loud-hailer; it is effective where wind or breakers would drown out sound. A typical use of semaphore might be from a stranded boat to a Coast Guard rescue craft that could not approach close enough for shouting back and forth.

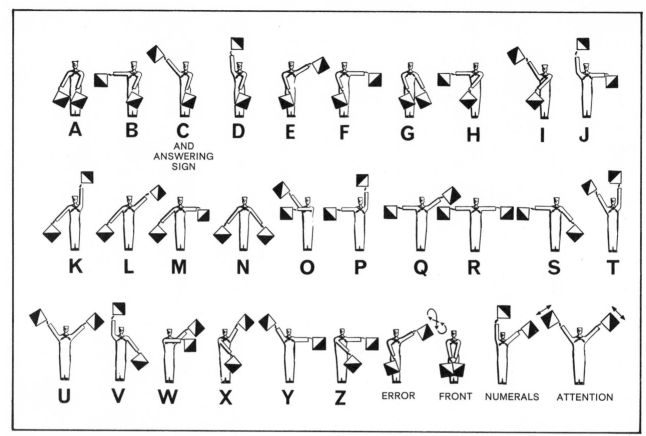

FIG. 2614 The Semaphore Signaling Code.

Courtesy: U. S. Navy Training Publications Center

Semaphore requires no special equipment, as does flag-hoist signaling. It is probably more satisfactory for day use than flashing light. On the other hand, it requires learning a new code and regular practice to develop *any* degree of competence. Another disadvantage is that it is not usable for communications at night.

Even though a boatman does not develop a full qualification in semaphore signaling, a knowledge of the letter "R" is often useful. "R" has wide recognition (as "Roger" on radiotelephone circuits) as meaning "received and understood." The semaphore "R"—both arms stretched straight out to the sides—is a simple, but highly effective, way of signaling to another person that you "got the message." Clearly and distinctly given, it is a much more satisfactory means of acknowledging information or instructions than a careless wave of one hand.

Sound Signaling

Signaling by sound using the boat's horn or whistle is possible, but has severe limitations.

Sound signaling should be used only with the greatest of caution, due to the confusion that it might create with passing or fog signals. A good rule for boatmen would be to become familiar with its principles and procedures, but never to use it except in emergencies or situations in which one was certain that no misunderstandings could possibly arise from its use.

A sound signal should be as brief as possible, and, except in an emergency, communications should be limited to the single-letter signals. In fog or on inland waters, where traffic is heavy, sound signals must be kept to an absolute minimum.

SOUND SIGNALING PROCEDURES

The Morse code is used for signaling by sound, with calling and answering procedures generally similar to those used for flashing light. The receiving craft makes no signal as the message is sent unless a character is missed in which case the repeat signal RPT is immediately signaled. When the message is completed, the sending ship signals $\overline{AR}$; if the message has been fully received, the other ship acknowledges by sending R.

Further details on signaling by sound will be found in H.O. 102.

**Two-letter groups
from the International Code of Signals.**

AE	I must abandon my vessel.
CJ	Do you require assistance?
CN	I am unable to give assistance.
JI	Are you aground?
JL	You are running the risk of going aground.
JW	I have sprung a leak.
KN	I cannot take you in tow.
LN	Light (name follows) has been extinguished.
LO	I am not in my correct position. (To be used by a lightship.)
LR	Bar is not dangerous.
LS	Bar is dangerous.
MF	Course to reach me is . . .
MG	You should steer course . . .
NF	You are running into danger.
NG	You are in a dangerous position.

PD	Your navigation light(s) is (are) not visible.
PT	What is the state of the tide?
QX	I request permission to anchor.
RY	You should proceed at slow speed while passing me (or vessels making this signal).
UF	You should follow pilot boat (or vessel indicated).
UO	You must not enter harbor.
UT	Where are you bound for?
YK	I am unable to answer your signal.
YX	I wish to communicate by radiotelephony on frequency indicated.
ZM	You should send (or speak) more slowly.
ZP	My last signal was incorrect. I will repeat it correctly.
ZQ	Your signal appears incorrectly coded. You should check and repeat the whole.

FIG. 2615

The Medical Signal Code

An interesting part of the International Code of Signals is its "Medical Signal Code." This section permits the exchange of information on the condition of a sick or injured person, and a diagnosis and recommended treatment for him, regardless of language barriers. Any means of communication may be used. Details may be given between ships or ship and shore by the use of letter and number groups which can be coded from any of the nine official languages—English, French, German, Greek, Italian, Japanese, Norwegian, Russian, and Spanish.

Medical advice should be sought and given in plain language whenever possible, but if language difficulties are encountered, the International Code groups should be used. Even when plain language is used, the wording of Medical Code should be used and its instructions followed as far as possible.

The Medical Signal Code is easily recognized in communications a: each basic code group consists of three letters (as contrasted with the main body of code groups which are limited to basic signals of two letters); it is made even more distinctive by the use of "M" as the first letter of each three-letter group. As with other portions of the International Code of Signals, other letters or numbers may be added to the basic signal to modify its meaning; such as "C" for an affirmative modification, "N" or "NO"

for negative, and "RQ" to give it an interrogative sense. For example: "MFE" means "Bleeding is severe"; "MFE N" means "Bleeding is not severe"; and "MFE RQ" means "Is bleeding severe?"

Locations of pain or injury are communicated by use of a basic signal followed by a number taken from a chart of the human body. For example: "MDF 10" indicates "Patient is in pain in the middle of chest." "MGC 14" signals "Patient has a compound fracture of the forearm." (The side of body or limb affected may be indicated if important to the diagnosis or treatment.)

Other code groups can be used to describe the patient's age, sex, previous illnesses, temperature, pulse, breathing, duration of symptoms, and many other items of information that would be required for diagnosis and treatment recommendations.

Diagnosis is communicated with a basic signal plus a number from a listing of common diseases. For example: "MQE 52" carries the message "Probable diagnosis is influenza." Another situation might result in "MQP" (I cannot make a diagnosis) and "MQC" (Please answer the following questions).

Treatments are likewise coded into groups of three letters plus numbers as required. A table of 37 standard medicines normally available on ships is included with the Medical Signal Code. "MTD 32" means "You should give aspirin tablets" and "MTI 2" means "You should give two

tablets by mouth" and "MTQ 4" means "You should repeat every four hours." Thus with a combination of signals a complete set of treatment instructions has been given.

The Medical Signal Code is quite complete, and it can literally be a "life saver" when in foreign waters with a language problem. Use of the code may be preferable to the chance of misunderstanding when each person only poorly comprehends what the other is saying.

Signaling and the Boatman

Knowledge and ability in signaling can bring both added pleasure and safety to a boatman. Pleasure can be had from being able to recognize and understand simple flag hoists or other visual signals. Safety will surely result from being able to use such methods of communications in an emergency, his or someone else's. Visual signals can often mean the difference between the communication of vitally necessary information, even though slowly and tediously, and no communication at all. Such signals are particularly valuable when one's boat has no radio, or the set on board fails to work when needed.

The more knowledge and ability in signaling the better, but expertness is neither expected nor needed. Simple knowledge of the code flags, the Morse alphabet, or the semaphore code, plus the rudiments of procedure, are all that are required. The boatman should make the effort to learn the fundamentals of signaling, and he should keep in practice. Some day when least expected, it could mean a great difference to all on board his boat.

INTERNATIONAL FLAGS AND PENNANTS

ALPHABET FLAGS			NUMERAL PENNANTS
Alfa — Diver Down; Keep Clear	**K**ilo — Desire to Communicate	**U**niform — Standing into Danger	1
Bravo — Dangerous Cargo	**L**ima — Stop Instantly	**V**ictor — Require Assistance	2
Charlie — Yes	**M**ike — I Am Stopped	**W**his-key — Require Medical Assistance	3
Delta — Keep Clear	**N**ovem-ber — No	**X**ray — Stop Your Intention	4
Echo — Altering Course to Starboard	**O**scar — Man Overboard	**Y**ankee — Am Dragging Anchor	5
Foxtrot — Disabled	**P**apa — About to Sail	**Z**ulu — Require a Tug	6
Golf — Want a Pilot	**Q**uebec — Request Pratique	**REPEATERS** — 1st Repeat	7
Hotel — Pilot on Board	**R**omeo	2nd Repeat	8
India — Altering Course to Port	**S**ierra — Engines Going Astern	3rd Repeat	9
Juliett — On Fire; Keep Clear	**T**ango — Keep Clear of Me	CODE — Code and Answering Pennant (Decimal Point)	0

W

How International Code Flags are Used in Signaling

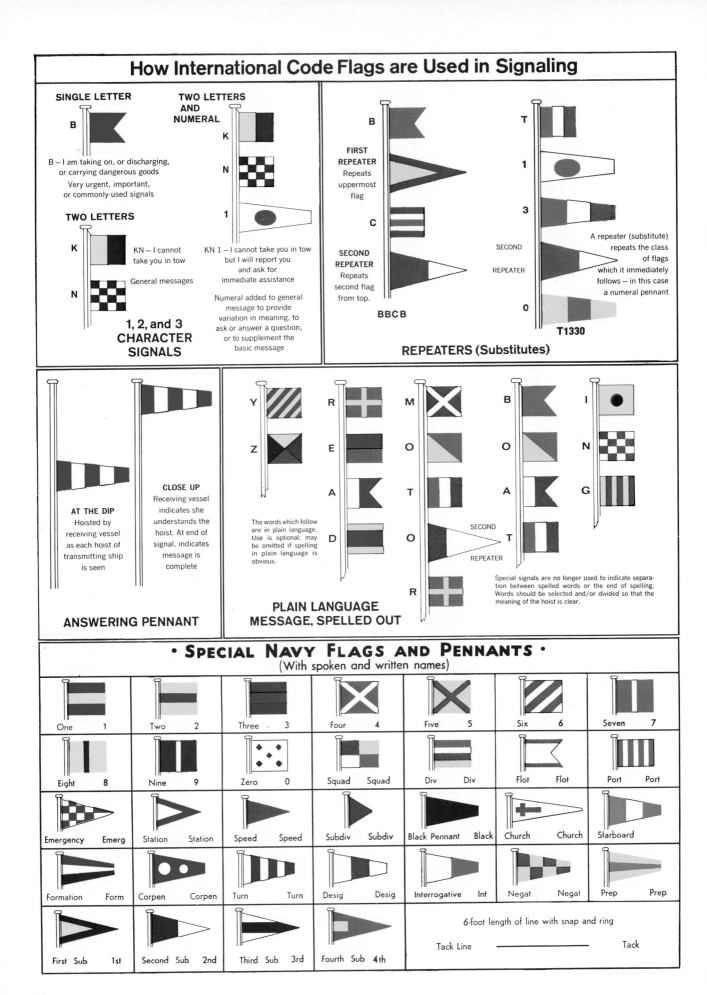

SINGLE LETTER

B

B — I am taking on, or discharging, or carrying dangerous goods

Very urgent, important, or commonly-used signals

TWO LETTERS

K

N

KN — I cannot take you in tow

General messages

1, 2, and 3 CHARACTER SIGNALS

TWO LETTERS AND NUMERAL

K

N

1

KN 1 — I cannot take you in tow but I will report you and ask for immediate assistance

Numeral added to general message to provide variation in meaning, to ask or answer a question, or to supplement the basic message

REPEATERS (Substitutes)

B

FIRST REPEATER Repeats uppermost flag

C

SECOND REPEATER Repeats second flag from top.

BBCB

T

1

3

SECOND

REPEATER

0

A repeater (substitute) repeats the class of flags which it immediately follows — in this case a numeral pennant

T1330

ANSWERING PENNANT

AT THE DIP Hoisted by receiving vessel as each hoist of transmitting ship is seen

CLOSE UP Receiving vessel indicates she understands the hoist. At end of signal, indicates message is complete

PLAIN LANGUAGE MESSAGE, SPELLED OUT

Y
Z
A
D

R
E
A
D
O
R

M
O
T
O

SECOND
REPEATER

B
O
A
T

I
N
G

The words which follow are in plain language. Use is optional; may be omitted if spelling in plain language is obvious.

Special signals are no longer used to indicate separation between spelled words or the end of spelling. Words should be selected and/or divided so that the meaning of the hoist is clear.

• SPECIAL NAVY FLAGS AND PENNANTS •
(With spoken and written names)

One 1	Two 2	Three 3	Four 4	Five 5	Six 6	Seven 7
Eight 8	Nine 9	Zero 0	Squad Squad	Div Div	Flot Flot	Port Port
Emergency Emerg	Station Station	Speed Speed	Subdiv Subdiv	Black Pennant Black	Church Church	Starboard
Formation Form	Corpen Corpen	Turn Turn	Desig Desig	Interrogative Int	Negat Negat	Prep Prep
First Sub 1st	Second Sub 2nd	Third Sub 3rd	Fourth Sub 4th			

6-foot length of line with snap and ring

Tack Line ———————— Tack

X

INLAND BOATING

Tom Bottomley photo

*Boating on inland lakes, rivers, and canals is different in some respects from that on
coastal rivers, bays and sounds, and along our salt-water shores.
Or perhaps to keep peace among all hands, we might say that coastal boating
is different from that on inland waters! The differences are not total; many aspects
of safe and enjoyable recreational boating are the same on all waters,
but differences do exist and must be carefully considered for full safety.*

The pleasures of inland boating

For the cruising boatman who has never laid his course inland, there are many surprises in store. He is likely to have regarded the interior waterways as little better than glorified "canals" to be used only as links between large bodies of salt water. Cruising them for their own sake might never occur to him, and canalling, in his mind, would be synonymous with "ditch-crawling."

As a matter of fact, some of the finest cruising this country affords can be found on the vast network of interconnected rivers and lakes which give access to areas far removed from tidal waters. Throughout the United States there are more than 30,000 miles of improved inland waterways. The Mississippi River system alone embraces more than 12,000 miles of waterways navigable by small craft—the largest such network in the world. Using the Mississippi, the Great Lakes, the New York State Barge Canal, and other waterways linking these with the Atlantic and Gulf Intracoastal Waterways, a boatman can circumnavigate the entire eastern portion of the United States, a cruise of more than 5,000 miles. Only a small portion of this would be in the open sea, although the Great Lakes are, of course, sizeable bodies of water, comparable to the ocean insofar as small craft cruising is concerned.

To these vast networks of interconnected waterways must be added the many isolated rivers and the hundreds, if not thousands, of lakes large enough for recreational boating. Many of these lakes have been formed behind dams in regions far removed from what is normally thought of as "boating areas." Today, there is virtually no place in our nation where one should be surprised to see a sign reading "marina" or "boating supplies"; truly, "inland boating" has no geographical boundaries.

Limitations

All cruising areas have their disadvantages and limitations. On rivers and lakes, shoals and rocks may be a factor. On other rivers, you may have problems of overhead clearance; there may be streams where a fixed bridge will arbitrarily determine your "head of navigation."

On some of our principal inland waterways, the overhead clearance is severely limited—on the New York State Canal System, for example, it is only 15½ feet. Masts on sailboats and auxiliaries must be unstepped and secured on deck for transit; on motorboats, all signal masts, radio antennas, and outriggers must be folded down or otherwise kept low and out of the way.

Fixed overhead power cables are usually high enough to cause no problems to masted vessels, and this clearance is noted on charts. High water stages on rivers naturally reduce overhead clearances under bridges and similar structures by the amount of the rise above normal levels. Chart books for the Ohio River give examples of how to calculate existing clearances at open river stages from the vertical clearances charted for normal pool stages and at 1936 high water stage, shown on charts.

529

FIG. 2701 Many inland waterways have been constructed to link major bodies of water to make possible through navigation. Seen above is the Illinois Waterway which interconnects the Great Lakes with the Mississippi River System for both commercial and recreational vessels.

River Piloting

While rivers seldom offer great open expanses similar to coastal waters where the usual techniques of navigation are needed, they do demand unique piloting skills. Here, local lore often outweighs some of the fundamental piloting principles which are the coastal skipper's law. Ever-changing conditions on rivers put a premium on local knowledge and elevate river navigation to the status of more an art than a science.

The fundamental difference is, of course, the closeness of the shore, usually with easily identifiable landmarks or aids to navigation. Knowledge of one's position, therefore, is *not* a problem. The skill of piloting here lies in the careful direction of the craft so as to avoid hazards, and on many rivers, this is not a simple or easy matter.

FIG. 2702 The eastern part of the United States has an extensive network of inland waterways, natural and man-made or man-improved. Additions have been made in recent years, and further extensions are either authorized or are in the planning stage.

LEGEND

━━━ IMPROVED INTRACOASTAL WATERWAY
●●● OPEN BAY WATER
■ ■ ■ AUTHORIZED FOR IMPROVEMENT
──── PRINCIPAL IMPROVED CONNECTING WATERWAYS

Water Level Changes

Because inland waters may be termed "non-tidal," it does *not* follow that there are no fluctuations in level. On the coast, there are daily changes in height, normally two highs and two lows each day. Inland, the variations are more apt to be of a seasonal nature as spring freshets, loaded with debris, flood down from the headwaters, overflow banks, and course on down to the sea at considerable velocities. The annual changes in level can be astounding; at St. Louis, the seasonal fluctuation in river level from flood conditions in late winter and early spring to normal levels in late summer and fall may range to as much as 40 to 50 feet. In some smaller navigable streams, sudden hard rains may raise the water level several feet in a matter of hours.

FIG. 2705 The upper Mississippi River is no longer a free-flowing stream, but a series of permanent pools regulated by navigation dams. Many craft of all types spend pleasant hours and days on these waters; the houseboat shown here is anchored out of the channel below Dam No. 4.

AIDS TO NAVIGATION

The larger inland rivers, those that are navigable from the sea, have aids to navigation maintained by the U.S. Coast Guard. Many of the lights, buoys, and daybeacons are similar in appearance and significance to those discussed in Chapters 15 and 16, but a few are of special design for their particular "inland" purpose. Many rivers under state jurisdiction will have aids to navigation conforming to the Uniform State Waterway Marking System; see pages 314-316 and color page L.

The "right" and "left" banks of a river

Designation of the banks of a river may at first be confusing. Left and right banks are named relative to a craft's course *downstream*. The left bank, in river terminology, is the one on your left hand as you face in the direction that the river flows; the right bank is that one on your right when you face downstream.

On the New York State Canal System, however, when regulations refer to the "starboard" side of the canal, they mean the right side when entering from Waterford. Thus the starboard side of the Champlain Canal is the east side; but on the Barge (Erie) Canal westward, the north side becomes the starboard side.

Mileage markers

Aids to navigation along the banks of many major rivers are conspicuously marked with mileages which correspond

FIG. 2703 River piloting differs from that in coastal waters in that the skipper usually can tell at all times where he is quite precisely. Here, the navigational problems consist mainly of avoiding underwater hazards such as shoals, sand bars, and snags.

FIG. 2704 The U.S. Coast Guard is responsible for the maintenance of aids to navigation on inland rivers under Federal jurisdiction.

FIG. 2706 The banks of a river are designated as "right" and "left" as one stands looking downstream.　　Corps of Engineers, U.S. Army

FIG. 2707 The daymark for this lighted aid to navigation consists of two white boards in the form of an "X"; there is also a mileage sign.

to the distance from a designated zero reference point. It is always an easy matter, therefore, to get a "fix." All you need to do is read the mileage as posted on one of the daybeacons or light structures and compare with the mileage figures given on the chart. The mileage figures take the place of the arbitrary odd and even numbers that are used on coastal waters. They are a great convenience in computing distance travelled and speeds being made good.

Lights

Most lights on major rivers, such as the Mississippi, show through 360°—visible, that is, all around the horizon. In some cases, however, light is projected in one direction only. Some of these directional aids supplement the power of an all-around light by a lens which increases its intensity in one direction only. The width of the arc through which the directional beam is visible varies with navigational need of the locality. A concentrated beam may be used in a long narrow reach, but a wider spread in a more open area where conditions are less critical.

Generally speaking, lights on the Western Rivers are placed strategically at the upper and lower ends of "crossing" (see page 536) as marks to steer by, with additional lights between as required by conditions. Where there are no crossings, lights are used along the banks as passing lights. Reference to the chart of the locality will reveal how a specific light is to be used.

Daymarks

On the Mississippi River, daymarks are usually white diamond shapes with number boards at the top to give the mileage. In the center a red triangle is used for left bank aids (when descending the river) and a vertical black rectangle for right bank aids. Daymarks will have a reflector at each of the four corners, red on the left bank and white or green on the right bank.

Daymarks on some rivers may consist of two white boards placed on trees on shore in the form of a large "X"; see fig. 2707.

Buoys

The skipper who is familiar with the basic U.S. system of buoyage will have no difficulty whatever with buoyage on rivers. They will generally follow the same basic principles whereby black can-type buoys will be on the left and red nun-type buoys will be on the right when proceeding from seaward, which, of course, is upstream.

Sometimes, as on the Mississippi, buoys will be topped with white for improved visibility against shore backgrounds.

Buoys on the Mississippi River carry reflectors similar to those used on shore aids—red on the left (when descending) side of the channel and white or green on those on the right (descending) side. Lighted buoys show a white or red light if on the left side of a channel, a white or green light if on the right side. Buoys marking wrecks show a quick flashing light of an appropriate color. Buoys marking channel junctions or obstructions are red and black horizontally banded and if lighted show an interrupted quick-flashing characteristic.

Color illustrations

Buoys and daymarks used on the "Western Rivers" (see definition on page 38) are illustrated in color on page K. For those used on other waters, see pages I and J.

Caution required

In all cases, buoys should be followed with reference to whatever charts or navigational maps may be available, as deviations from conventional systems may be found on some rivers. On the New York State Canals, for example, buoys are alike *in shape* on both sides of the channel, although the color of the buoy and light will differ; red buoys and red lights on the "starboard" side (as defined above) and white buoys and white lights on the port side.

The chart will invariably prevent confusion and misunderstanding in following any system of buoyage. The symbols for buoys on charts of the Ohio River, for exam-

FIG. 2708 Portion of Lake Survey Chart 14852 for the Saint Clair River, scale 1:40,000 on polyconic projection, in which distortion is small and relative sizes are correctly preserved. Depths are referred to the sloping surface of the river at specified lake levels above mean tide at New York. Note the International Boundary in midstream, and the separate channels for traffic up- and down-stream.

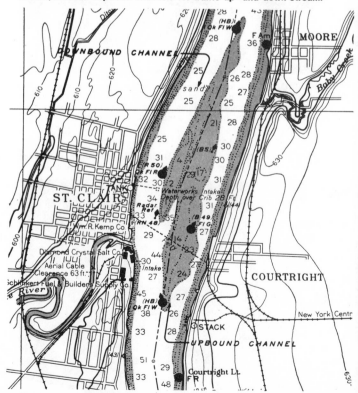

ple, are unique to that waterway and may cause initial confusion to strangers until carefully studied.

Ranges

On some rivers, such as the Hudson and the Connecticut, where channels through flats in the river are stabilized and maintained through dredging, ranges with conspicuous markers on shore are of great aid to the skipper in staying within the limits of a narrow channel. Aligning the front and rear markers, he can hold his course safely in mid-channel despite any off-setting forces of current or wind.

CHARTS

River charts are commonly in the form of books of "navigational maps," each page covering successive short stretches of the river in strip form. A typical example is the bound volume published annually by the Mississippi River Commission, Vicksburg, Miss., to cover that river from Cairo, Illinois to the Gulf of Mexico. This is on a scale of 1:62,500, or approximately one inch to the mile. All of the depth information (with a few exceptions) and detailed positions of rocks, reefs, shoals, and ledges so familiar on coastal charts are omitted. In their place, the course of the river is traced in blue tint between heavy black lines delineating the banks. A broken red line is used to indicate the channel line. Navigation lights are shown by a star with a white dot in the center together with a number which indicated its distance upstream from a fixed reference point—in this case, A.H.P., "Above the Head of Passes." The Head of Passes is the point not far above the mouth of the river where the river splits into separate channels leading through the delta into the Gulf. Mileages are given every five miles (statute), with red circles at one mile intervals. Mileages above and below the Head of Passes are printed in red. A detailed table is given in the book listing in alphabetical order all towns, cities, bridges, mouths of tributary rivers, and other important features adjacent to the main channel, with distances (AHP) in miles and the numbers of the map on which each feature appears.

River charts are usually on a polyconic projection (see

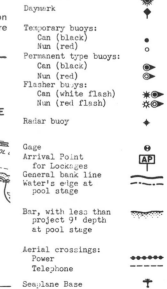

FIG. 2709 On charts of Pools 25 and 26 (Mississippi River and Illinois Waterway) hazards are shown in bright red. Distances are in statute miles above a specified reference point.

LEGEND

▬ HAZARD AREA (LESS THAN 6 f) BELOW EL 418.0 POOL 26)
/////// SNAG, STUMPS, AND UNDERWATER HAZARDS
- - - - SUBMERGED GOVERNMENT DIKE
⊗ GOVERNMENT GAGE
210 RIVER MILEAGE
⚓ HARBOR OR TIE UP POINT

pages 361-362), and elevations normally refer to a specified mean water level.

Variations in river charts

Not all river charts use the same symbol and coloring scheme. Before using any such chart, a skipper should make a careful study of its *legend*. This will give the symbols used for aids to navigation together with the associated abbreviations, information on topographic and hydrographic features that are shown, and probably illustrations of any characteristics that are peculiar to that chart. A few minutes study of an unfamiliar chart will prove very valuable before venturing out on strange waters.

Some charts of the Middle and Upper Mississippi Rivers are done only in black and white with no color to help distinguish significant features.

In the book of charts for the Illinois Waterway, the main channel is shown in white with shoal areas tinted blue.

FIG. 2710 Ohio River chart. Arrow (top) indicates true north, seldom at top of chart. Arrow at left indicates direction of river flow. Note symbols for cans and nuns (see legend, right). Location of bulletin board showing river gages is shown on chart.

Right, legend of symbols used on navigation charts of the Ohio River. Some of these are illustrated on the chart extract shown.

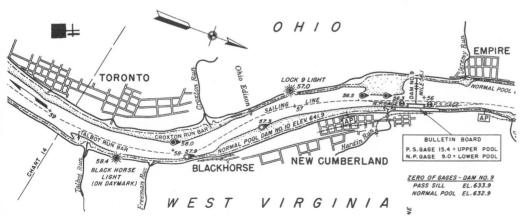

A small booklet of charts for Navigation Pools 25 and 26 of the Mississippi River is distinguished primarily by the fact that it shows hazard areas (under 6-foot depths) in bright red shading, harbors or anchorage areas with an anchor symbol, and the availability of fuel, water, marine railways, launching ramps, and repair and docking facilities at specified locations.

The charts in the book for the New York State Canals, published by the Lake Survey Center, Detroit, are much like the coastal area charts described in Chapter 18. Land areas are tinted buff, channels of 12 feet or more are white, lesser depths are tinted light blue with depth contour lines for 6 and 12 feet, and distinct black lines delineate the banks. Buoy symbols, diamonds with dots, have magenta discs if they are lighted. Aids to navigation are numbered and scattered depth figures give the skipper a good idea as to whether he dare venture out of the channel to seek an anchorage or for any other reason. Rocks and wrecks are indicated with standard symbols from Chart No. 1 (see page 371). Arrows indicating current flow direction, used on many other inland charts, do not appear on those of New York inland waterways.

Missing from the river chart or navigational map is the compass rose of coastal and off-shore charts which enables the navigator to lay a compass course and determine true and magnetic course and bearings. River charts generally show instead a simple arrow to indicate true north; on strip charts, north may not necessarily be at the top of the sheet. On charts of the Lower Mississippi, parallels of latitude and meridians of longitude are printed, but most river charts omit such information.

PUBLICATIONS

Charts can convey to the river skipper a great amount of information, and he should always use the most detailed and latest editions obtainable, but they cannot show all that he needs to know. The limitations of space and the necessary use of symbols and abbreviations require that additional data be published in the form of books and pamphlets.

Engineer publications

The Army Engineers at Vicksburg, Miss., publish an informational pamphlet, "Mississippi River Navigation" which contains not only a great deal of interesting background information on navigation of that river, but also a few pages with explicit instructions "For Part-Time Pilots," the recreational boatmen who use the great river in such large numbers.

Since conditions on the Mississippi, Ohio, and other major rivers are in a constant state of change, with channels shifting and water levels fluctuating, the river boatman must keep posted on the latest information at all times. The various Army Engineer District and Division offices issue a number of publications to provide data on current conditions. These are variously termed *Divisional Bulletins, Navigational Bulletins, Navigation Notices, Notices to Navigational Interests* (weekly), and *Special Notices to Navigation Interests* (as required). These show river conditions such as channel depths, and widths, estimated current velocities, controlling bridge clearances for specified stretches of rivers, construction projects and other hazards, and facilities such as marine railways and lifts.

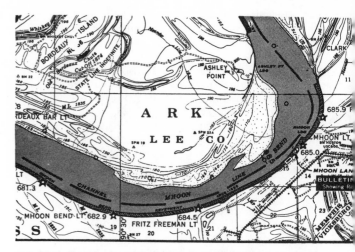

FIG. 2711 Section of a typical Mississippi River chart. On the original, the shaded areas appear in blue tint. Channel lines, lights and mileages are printed in red. River stages, or heights, are given on the bulletin boards, locations of which are indicated on the chart in red. Small circles are 1 statute mile apart. Parallels of latitude and meridians of longitude appear, but no compass rose, as used on coastal charts.

Coast Guard Notices

The 2nd Coast Guard District, with Headquarters at St. Louis, issues *Local Notices to Mariners* with information on changes in aids to navigation, hazards to navigation, and other matters within Coast Guard cognizance. The USCG also publishes "Channel Reports" periodically with the least depth found by Coast Guard Cutters and Buoy Tenders on their patrols of various sections of the major rivers.

Light List

One of the most helpful documents to the river skipper is the Light List, Volume V, published by the Coast Guard and covering all of the Mississippi River System. In it all lights, buoys, and other aids to navigation are tabulated, together with the river mileage (in statute miles) from the specified reference point. Aids are described in much more detail than can be shown by symbols and abbreviations on charts.

NAVIGATION "TOOLS"

The compass is but little use on river boats and binoculars become the primary piloting tool to aid the skipper in sighting from one navigational aid to the next. In fog, this means that recreational boat traffic comes pretty much to a standstill, although large commercial craft normally carry on using their radar for "eyes." This should not be taken to mean that a compass can be dispensed with on all inland rivers; some are wide enough that navigation can be continued on in fog using a compass, speed curve, watch or clock, *and due caution*.

LOCAL KNOWLEDGE

Not even the best of charts and publications can "tell all" about a particular body of water. Many rivers are particularly prone to seasonal or irregular changes of condition, and a skipper new to a specific stretch of river should take advantage of every opportunity to ask experienced and responsible local people about special hazards or recent changes in conditions.

Name of aid Character and period of light	Number of miles from Grafton	Bank or side of channel	Remarks
Island Bend Daymark_____	258. 9	Left___	
Island Light_____	258. 8	Right__	Visible 360° with 3° directional
W., 2 sec.			
Island Light_____	256. 0	Right__	Visible 360° with 3° directiona
W., 2 sec.			
Light_____	255. 1	Right__	3° directional light oriented dowr
W., 2 sec.			
I. & P. Ry Bridge, vertical lift. Clear-	254. 1	_____	
es: Horizontal, 141 feet; vertical, closed			
feet, open 47.5 feet, above pool stage.			
Island Bridge Daymark_____	254. 1	Left___	Painted on bridge pier.

ILLINOIS WATERWAY—Illinois River

FIG. 2712 Charts show much of the information needed for safe navigation of the rivers, but they cannot "tell all." The USCG Light List, Volume V, furnishes many details on aids to navigation that are not shown on charts by symbols and abbreviations.

RIVER CURRENTS

Broadly speaking, river currents, although they may fluctuate in velocity, will trend always in one direction—from the headwaters to the mouth. Despite this, tidal rivers connecting with the sea may feel the effect of tidal conditions occurring at the mouth, backing the water up so that a skipper can take advantage of a favorable current going *upstream* when tidal conditions are right. On the Hudson, for example, an economy-minded skipper electing to run at 9 to 10 knots, and properly selecting his starting time, can carry a favorable current all the way from New York City to Albany, 150 miles inland. Tides at this latter city, even so far from the sea, may range in excess of six feet, although at the other points far *downstream* the range will be only *half* that amount.

Current velocities

The strength of river currents varies widely from river to river, and from season to season for any particular river. Velocities on the Mississippi will range between 1 and 6 mph under average conditions, depending upon the particular section of that river concerned. At extreme high water stages, current strengths may be much greater, 9 mph or more in narrow and constricted areas.

River currents sometimes attain such speeds that navigation upstream is not feasible, although capably handled craft can safely be taken down. Such is the case in the Galop Rapids of the St. Lawrence where the velocity may run as much as 12 to 13 mph. Some river boats have power enough to ascent certain rapids, but, as a general rule, it is best to avoid them by using the canals and locks that by-pass them, unless the skipper has local knowledge or engages the service of a local pilot.

"Selecting" your current

River currents have been the subject of extensive studies and their characteristics are of the utmost importance to the masters of deep-draft commercial vessels. The surface current acting on a small craft may, in fact, be actually contrary to that which grips the keel of a large ship near the river bottom. Even with respect to surface currents alone, there is a variation from bank to mid-stream. Fric-

tion of the bank and bottom retards velocity. The skipper of the commercial vessel—where fuel costs and time of run are of considerable importance—knows this difference. He uses the strength of the mid-stream current to aid his run downstream. Returning upstream, he runs as close to the bank as he safely can, even turning into small coves behind points of land to take advantage of any counter-current that flows opposite to the main stream.

Perhaps the economic factors that the professional pilot weighs so carefully are of less significance to the recreational boatman. Even so, the small craft skipper can profitably heed the same principles and cut his running time and fuel costs by running courses that make the river's current work for him, or at least minimize its adverse effect. It is only simple arithmetic to note that a 12-mph boat in a 4 mph current is making good either 8 or 16 mph, a significant effect! Even for a faster 20-mph craft, the difference between 16 and 24 mph speeds is 50%. Steer your course so that you can "select" your current; take advantage of your relatively shallow draft, but don't run aground!

CHANNELS AT RIVER BENDS

River channels have a basic tendency for the flow of water to carry across the stream on the outside of the bend, scouring out a natural channel at the outside while depositing a bar extending out from the point around which it is turning. Exceptions to the above may occur where there are unusual bottom contours or man-made structures exist.

Study a river chart which gives the depths (those prepared by the Nation Ocean Survey do) and note this characteristic. Then when you are on a river where the "navigational maps" give no data as to the depths (such as those for the Mississippi and Ohio), you will have a better feeling for where the deeper water will be found. Try to visualize the picture as if you were in an aircraft above and looking down on the river and your boat. This understanding of the natural channels at bends will make you less likely to run straight courses from marker to marker, cutting corners and running the risk of hanging up on a bar.

The proper course at each bend is, of course, a curved line conforming roughly to the trend of the river as a whole. If there are no aids to navigation to guide you, a general rule is to keep about one-quarter of the river's width off the outside bank.

On some river charts even the markings showing the

FIG. 2713 Typical crossing channel, as illustrated in chart book, Cairo to Gulf of Mexico. Note how channel sweeps toward outside of bend. Channel line, lights and mileages in red on original.

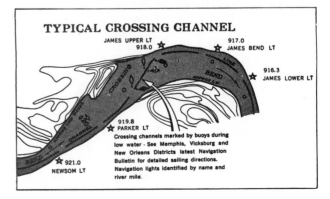

TYPICAL CROSSING CHANNEL

JAMES UPPER LT
918.0

917.0
JAMES BEND LT

916.3
JAMES LOWER LT

919.8
PARKER LT

921.0
NEWSOM LT

Crossing channels marked by buoys during low water - See Memphis, Vicksburg and New Orleans Districts latest Navigation Bulletin for detailed sailing directions. Navigation lights identified by name and river mile.

FIG. 2714 The most often encountered hazards in river cruising are shoals and sandbars. In some waters, caution must be exercised for underwater rocks.

topography ashore supply clues as to what may be expected in the river itself. Contour lines crowded close together on land at the water's edge indicate a cliff rising steeply from the bank, with good chances of deep water close under the bluff. The cliff or hill may at the same time provide a prominent landmark to steer by.

Channel "crossing"

Where there is an "S" curve—a curve in one direction followed by a curve in the opposite direction—the straight section between the curves is termed a "crossing." On major rivers, these are usually marked by ranges or directional lights. In some instances, such as at low later stages, buoys may be added to mark the route of best water; these buoys may be found in pairs or singly; see fig. 2713.

"EYEBALL" PILOTING

Much of a good river pilot's success depends on his acquired skill in interpreting what he sees. Experience is the true teacher, but some fundamentals can be discussed in a book.

No flat statement can be made as to the relative depth of water indicated by certain sets of surface conditions. On one hand, where there is a chop in the channel, there may be areas of relatively smooth slicks over the bars, especially if there is any weed growth present. As against this, there will be combinations of wind-current conditions where the channel will be comparatively smooth with ripples revealing the bars.

In some narrow river channels, with wind against the current, a small sea builds up in which the larger waves disclose the deeper water, growing progressively smaller until there are no seas at the channel's edge. But under any given set of conditions, the boatman with an eye peeled for natural signs will, with the aid of his chart and the buoys, quickly learn to read the signs that the river has for those eager to understand its secrets.

Watch your wake

If you will glance astern while in unfamiliar waters, your wake can provide a clue to the safety of your course. When the natural sequence of waves in your wake is broken, there must be something to have disturbed it. As it rolls off into shallow water, the smooth undulations will give way to a sharper formation, even cresting on the flats in miniature "breakers." When they encounter a shoal or a flooded area where submerged stumps lie close to the surface, the wake will show the difference. When any short, peaked unnatural wake closes up toward your stern, sheer

off, and fast, away from the side on which this telltale signal appears.

Shoals

Shoaling is a serious problem in most rivers. Spring floods build up current velocities, stir up silt in river bottoms, wash away portions of river banks, and carry this total load of dirt in suspension to be deposited in the form of mud flats and sand bars where the strength of the current lessens; these become hazards to safe navigation. The Connecticut River is a good example of this, where considerable expenditures are required annually to keep channels dredged to authorized depths. In the Mississippi River, a jellied mass of muck, called flocculation, is deposited as a sediment on the river bottom to a depth of 10 to 15 feet. Deep-draft vessels plow through it, and high water stages of the river flush it out into the Gulf, so the Army Engineers do not bother to dredge it at low water stages. Over the centuries, this is how the river's delta has been built up.

On a smaller scale, a bar or shoal is often formed at the mouth of a river where the current slows to a degree where the silt is no longer held in suspension. On bars of this kind, bad seas may build up in strong outflowing currents opposed by an on-shore wind. This may even occur inland at the confluence of some rivers, with disturbed surface conditions where smooth water would normally be expected.

Practice makes perfect

Gradually developing a sense of river piloting, you'll become more acutely conscious of the actual track you should make good over the bottom relative to nearby shoals and the side limits of channels. Where currents do occasionally flow diagonally across your course, you will allow for them instinctively and look astern frequently to help maintain that sense of position.

River Seamanship

Boatmen on inland rivers are subject to many of the requirements for safety and good seamanship covered in earlier chapters. A skipper must also be prepared for certain conditions specifically related to those waters on which he is boating.

Boat handling at piers and on entering or leaving slips may be made more complicated by swift river currents. Grounding hard on river shoals may be more troublesome than it is on tidewater, where the next rising tide will often free a craft without any other assistance.

RIVER CRUISING

One of the greatest of all the many pleasures in boating is "cruising," or in other words, going somewhere in your craft. This can be most enjoyable on inland rivers, but requires adequate planning and careful execution.

Problems of where to make fast (tie up) or anchor for the night are a part of cruising in any waters. On coastal waters, the problem may be essentially a matter of finding a sheltered cove or basin to avoid the risk of a rough night in an exposed anchorage. As a rule on the rivers, shelter from blows is closer at hand, yet there are areas great enough in expanse to work up a sizeable chop or even

seas, especially when the wind opposes the current. Then, too, there is the matter of having protection in narrow waterways from passing river traffic and the wake and wash resulting therefrom. Finally, there is always the question of personal preference as to whether one seeks the seclusion of quiet anchorages off the beaten track, or prefers the activity usually associated with towns and cities.

The development in recent years of many new marinas on some of the inland waterways—the Tennessee River network, for example—has been a great boon to river cruising. Not only do these provide a place to make fast for the night, but fuel, supplies, and other necessities are generally available at the marina or close at hand.

Safety harbors and landings

On the Tennessee River, and others, safety harbors and landings have been provided for use in case of bad weather, mechanical difficulties, or other emergencies. Their locations are shown on charts. Safety harbors are usually coves off the navigable channel. Direction boards on shore indicate the entrance and cross boards mark the upper limits.

Safety landings are areas where the banks have been cleared of stumps, boulders, snags, or other underwater hazards so that craft may safely come to shore. Upper and lower limits are marked by direction boards. These signs

are color-coded on the Tennessee, white if a 9-foot depth is available at all water level stages, orange if this depth is not available at lower levels.

The New York State Barge Canal provides terminals at intervals along the route; these are used intermittently by commercial craft, but are available to recreational boats at other times. Of concrete with rather rough faces, these require adequate fendering when used by small craft.

In order to allow for the seasonal range in water levels, or stages, on Western Rivers, most marinas and yacht clubs are afloat on strings of barges, necessitating a long climb up the river bank at low-water stages to get to town.

Anchoring

Frequently study of the chart or navigational map will reveal a likely place to anchor for the night. A widening of the river may offer an opportunity to get out of the reach of traffic, or a small tributary or slough may invite exploration (entering with caution, checking depths as you go), or the natural configuration of river banks and bars may provide a natural "harbor" with complete protection. Islands occurring in mid-river often leave a secondary channel for small-craft on the opposite side from that used by large, deep-draft commercial vessels. When a river cuts a channel behind a section of bank, a "towhead" is formed. Sometimes these are filled in or dammed across at the upper end by river deposits, forming a nautral protected harbor which can be entered from the lower end.

At times, a skipper can get his craft behind a pile dike, a type of structure used on rivers to protect banks from washing away. The dike juts out into the river and, by making fast to one of the piles just inside the outer end, on the downstream side, the boat will have protection not only from passing traffic but from floating debris as well.

Use caution outside channels

When entering sloughs between islands or an island and the bank in search of an anchorage, beware of submerged wing dams at the upstream end. To be safe, always enter and leave from the downstream end.

When anchoring on the larger rivers near a sandbar or island—or when beaching a small boat to go ashore at such a place—a good rule to follow is to pick the downstream rather than the upper end. If an anchor drags, or if for any other reason you get aground on the upstream end, the current will be pushing you harder ashore, complicating the task of getting free. Water at the downstream end is likely to be quieter and the eddies which normally exist

FIG. 2717 At Mile 715.0 on the Lower Mississippi River, just a few miles below Memphis, pleasure craft anchor on the back side of a bar in slack water with complete protection from the wake of passing towboats. There are many such bars along the Mississippi from Baton Rouge on north. The river boatman will find them a snug haven for anchorage at night or during severe weather.   J. D. Tennison, Jr.   Photo

there may help to free a grounded craft.

Sandy bars that are exposed during periods of low water may be quite unstable. Caution, therefore, should be exercised in using them for camping or swimming.

Check characteristics of the bottom

The character of the bottom varies widely on inland waterways. Particularly in their lower reaches, river bottoms are often soft mud, pointing to the desirability of carrying at least one anchor with broad flukes of a design that will dig down until it reaches good holding strength. In such spots, an anchor with spidery arms and flukes will cut through and provide no holding power at all; yet on a hard bottom, such an anchor might be highly efficient and needed rather than the other type described above.

When anchoring over rocky bottoms or in areas infested with snags and roots, it is highly desirable to rig a "trip line," a light line from the anchor's crown long enough to reach the surface where that end is buoyed. If the anchor snags and will not come free in a normal fashion, pick up the buoy and raise the anchor by the trip line, crown first. Some anchors are provided with slip rings, shear pins, or other devices to make them snag proof; see Chapter 6 for additional information.

An anchor light should be left burning all night if there is danger of being run down by other vessels; in case of doubt as to the necessity for an anchor light, be on the safe side and have one showing.

FIG. 2718 A typical Mississippi river bank riprapped with cement to protect banks against erosion. Boatmen must use care near such banks due to risk of damage to the boat's bottom. J. D. Tennison, Jr.

Making fast to the bank

In many areas, cruising boatmen make fast (tie up) to the river's bank for a lunchtime break in the day's journey, or even overnight. In so doing, caution is essential. The first necessity is that there be adequate depths and the area is free of underwater obstacles; approach slowly. It is advisable to avoid vertical banks that may be in a stage of active caving; exposed tree roots in the bank should be viewed with suspicion as possible evidence of recent erosion. Rock riprap along the banks can be rough on a boat's bottom; see fig. 2718.

One trick used on Western Rivers is the so-called "river hitch." To make fast to the bank for the night, the boat's bow is held up to the bank with power while a line is run to a nearby tree. Then a sapling is cut, some 15 to 20 feet long, and lashed from bank to stern to hold the stern *off*, while another line to shore is used to hold the stern *in*.

Allowance for water level changes

As a general rule, when making fast for the night on inland rivers, lines need not be put out with allowance for the tidal changes common on the coasts, except, of course, on tidal rivers (a six-foot range at Albany on the Hudson, for example). On non-tidal waterways, however, there is always the chance of a change in level with hard thunderstorms or otherwise heavy rainfalls. It is advisable to observe the practices of local craft, and be guided accordingly.

Making fast to a barge or float which will itself rise or fall with a change in levels is advantageous. Here, it is only necessary to leave enough slack in lines as may be required for comfort and safety if a passing vessel throws a disturbing wake.

River cruising problems

Boatmen cruising the rivers bring back widely conflicting reports of hazards encountered, or the absence of them. Perhaps this may be attributed to the fact that one made his cruise in the early spring, encountering high water, flood conditions, racing currents, and much floating debris. Another, no doubt, has made his trip under ideal conditions in September or October with water levels at a low stage and currents at reasonable velocities so that few, if any, obstacles were encountered. There is that much difference in seasonal conditions. River navigation at extreme flood conditions, is not as a rule to be recommended without the services of an experienced pilot.

FIG. 2719 The moderate current flow in many smaller inland rivers cán increase considerably—rapidly and without warning—as a result of heavy rainfall upstream. Caution must be exercised during times of summer thunderstorms.

Gary Miller photo

Eddies and "whirlpools"

A typical example of this conflict in reports of conditions encountered or observed is the story of "sand boils" in the Mississippi caused by sand piling up on the river bed. One skipper reports that these whirlpool-like disturbances were so violent that they almost threw his boat out of control. Another might say, in more favorable months, they were no worse than surface eddies, felt, but certainly of no danger to the boat.

Problems from silt

Some river boatmen have reported underwater bearings ruined, engine jackets filled with silt, and water pump impellers worn out at the end of one river run. Others have observed no difficulties of these types. As a general rule, as in all places where the water is heavily laden with silt, the logical course is to provide, in advance, whatever protection is possible in the form of effective raw water strainers, fresh water cooling systems, cutless-type underwater bearings, and pump impellers of a type that will handle mud and sand better than bronze gears.

Debris

Floating and partially submerged debris, such as tree trunks and branches, constitute a navigational hazard for small craft and a sharp lookout should be maintained in waters where such have been seen or reported. Floating debris is usually at its worst in the spring months when flood or near-flood water levels have swept away downed trees and other items that litter the banks of waterways just above the normal water line.

Towed-under buoys

River currents sometimes flow so fast that buoys are towed under, leaving only a V-shaped eddy on the surface to reveal their location. Sometimes the top of the buoy will

FIG. 2720 River flow increases markedly during times of spring thaws and run-off. In some locations the current strength becomes so great as to pull buoys beneath the surface of the water, where they become hazards rather than aids to navigation.

be visible to a boat bound upstream, or the wake of a passing vessel will expose it momentarily.

The V-shaped surface eddy of a towed-under buoy always points upstream as its "wake" divides downstream around it. Any surface disturbance such as this is to be avoided, as a submerged obstacle is likely lurking beneath. This, however, is not to be confused with the condition where two currents meet at the downstream end of a middle bar with converging eddies that may also show as a V-shape, but in this case pointing downstream.

Misplaced buoys

Another hazard of river piloting at spring-time high water levels is the shifting of buoys from their charted positions when they are dragged by large floating trees or logs.

Hazards generally

Some rivers present special hazards. The Army Engineers caution against regarding the Mississippi with insufficient respect. The lower river is very large, with low-water widths of ½-mile and bank-full widths up to 9,000 feet. Those bank-full stages generally occur between December and July, most frequently in March or April. Low-water stages occur in the fall months, October and November.

Lake Pepin typifies the kind of exposed area that may be encountered, even on the upper river. This "lake," actually a broadening of the river proper, is 21 miles long and up to 2½ miles in width; sizeable seas can build up in such a body of water.

Many kinds of equipment are found at work along rivers, especially the larger ones. Hydraulic pipeline dredges may have long lengths of floating pipeline which must be avoided. Bank protection equipment carried on barges may extend several hundred feet from shore into the stream, frequently in the swiftest part of the current. Small craft should keep *well* clear of such equipment because of the hazard of being swept under it. In general, boats should exercise both caution and consideration when passing any form of construction or maintenance work, slowing down to avoid doing any damage with their wake. Regulations exist governing lights and day shapes for dredges and other "floating plant" working on river projects, and for the passing of such equipment by other vessels; see "Army Engineer Navigation Regulations" on page 83.

Signals

Whistle signals for passing other vessels, fog or otherwise restricted visibility, and other situations are prescribed by the Rules of the Road and Pilot Rules for the waters concerned, either Inland or Western Rivers. Details will be found in Chapter 5.

Signals for the opening of drawbridges are not uniform in all waters; it will be necessary to consult local regulations, or ask local watermen. For the major rivers, information will be available from Army Engineer District and Division Offices; see page 610

PASSING COMMERCIAL TRAFFIC

Most of our inland waterways handle considerable commercial traffic. Whether cruising on a river, or just out for a day on the water, the recreational skipper must know how to handle a situation involving his craft and a large commercial vessel. In a channel of narrow width, a big tug

FIG. 2721 Among the longest "vessels" in the world, along with the big ocean liners and the supertankers, are the tows on Western Rivers made up of barges pushed by a towboat at the stern. Length often exceeds 1000 feet. They should always be passed with great care, especially at bends. U.S. Army Corps of Engineers photo

or tanker requires the better part of the available water. As she approaches, you'll see a sizeable bow wave built up ahead of her, and the water drawn away by suction to lower the level at her sides amidships. Give such vessels as wide a berth as you possibly can, and be alert for violent motions of your boat as she passes.

Tugs with tows astern in narrow waterways present a real problem to approaching small craft. Fortunately, most of the "towing" today is done by pushing scows and barges ahead of the tug. This keeps the whole tow under better control as a single unit. Passing at a bend is more dangerous than on a straightaway, and in many instances should be avoided entirely. The tug and its barges cannot help but make a wide swing; where there is ample room to pass at the beginning of the turn, there may be none at all later. If small craft *must* pass at a bend, it is usually wiser for them to take the *inside* of the curve regardless of how this affects the normal side for passing.

Jumbo tows on the Mississippi

Big rafts of barges bunched together on the Mississippi River in one vast tow may cover many acres in extent. The prudent recreational craft skipper will appreciate the problems of handling such colossal floats and will never jeopardize their activities, regardless of any considerations of right-of-way. Integrated tows are often made up of a bow-piece, a group of square-ended barges, and a towboat (at the stern) all lashed together in one streamlined unit 1000 feet or more in length. At night, to an observer in a small boat, the towboat's light may be more conspicuous than those on the tow far out ahead. On certain rivers, tests have been made with a bright flashing amber light on the center of the leading barges to make them more readily seen, but this has not been regularly adopted.

Thus it can be seen that special caution is needed when running rivers at night, even though the river itself be so well lighted as to make this feasible. When commercial traffic is using powerful searchlights, their blinding beams may make it impossible for the boatman to see anything at all. Shore lights may add to the difficulty because of their reflections in the water. Then, too, in some rivers, especially in flood, there's the hazard of floating trees and other partially submerged debris that could not be seen in time, if at all, in the darkness.

Give all tows a wide berth

On all rivers, recreational craft should give tows a wide berth. In particular, they should *stay away from in front of tows* when underway. If the small craft should happen to lose power in such a spot, it might be impossible for the tow to stop or steer clear. With the way she carries, a commercial tow may at times travel a half-mile or more before she can come to a full stop.

Boats equipped with VHF/FM radiotelephones should call the tug and coordinate the passing before it is started.

WATCH YOUR WAKE

Much inland boating is done on rivers that are relatively narrow. Skippers should so regulate the speed of their craft that no *destructive* wake is caused. The banks of the river may be close to the boat's course, and excessive wake can cause damage to shoreside installations. Some wake is almost inevitable from motorboats, but it must not be "destructive"; keep your speed, and your wake, at a minimum when passing boats, and piers and other shoreline facilities.

Canal Boating

Before the days of dams and locks, many of our rivers were unnavigable. Water coursing down valleys at the land's natural gradient, dropping perhaps hundreds of feet in tens of miles, runs too fast and encounters too many natural obstacles for safe navigation. To overcome them, engineers dam natural waterways at strategic spots, creating a series of "pools" or levels that may be likened to a stairway. Good examples of how closely these can resemble an actual flight of stairs will be found at places like Waterford, N.Y., and the Rideau Waterway at Ottawa where vessels descend or ascent a series of locks in immediate succession. This section will cover boating on both completely man-made waterways, which might be termed "pure canals," and on "canalized" natural rivers.

Water levels

To a river pilot, the term "pool stage" indicates the height of water in a pool at any given time with reference to the datum for that pool. On many rivers, pool stages are posted on conspicuous bulletin boards along river banks so as to be easily read from passing vessels. Locations of these bulletin boards are given on charts.

On the Ohio, gauge readings are displayed at the power-houses of the dams. These indicate depths of the pool impounded by the dam *next below*. A depth of 9 feet is uniformly taken to indicate the pool at normal elevation. A reading of 8.7 feet would indicate that the lower pool at this dam is 0.3 foot below normal elevation. These readings are preceded by the letters NP (normal pool) in white on a green background.

LOCKS AND DAMS

Dams on our inland waterways, without locks, would restrict river cruising to the individual pools and would prevent through navigation except for small craft which were light enough to be portaged around the dams. Locks, in conjunction with the dams, provide the means for watercraft to move from level to level. Locks vary in size,

FIG. 2722 Locks and dams make rivers navigable by changing levels in successive stages. On some waterways, locking through on a Sunday is somewhat reminiscent of highway motoring. Note the need for many fenders on each craft.

but since they almost invariably handle commercial traffic, their limiting dimensions offer no restriction to the movement of recreational boats. On the New York State Barge Canal, a tanker will almost fill a lock, with very little room to spare; in fact, the tanker or barge was designed to fit the canal lock, and not vice versa!

Principles of locks and locking

Locks are watertight (or almost so) chambers with gates at each end. Valves are provided to admit water as required. When a vessel needs to be locked upstream to a higher level, the upstream gates are first closed, valves are opened to let the water run out to the lower level, and then the downstream gates are opened. The vessel enters the lock through the opened lower gates; these are then closed and water is allowed to flow in from above through another set of valves until the chamber is full to the upper pool level. Next the upstream gates are opened and the vessel is free to resume her course upstream. Locking a vessel down is the reverse of this process.

Water is not pumped at locks; the natural flow is utilized and this is why some canals must impose restrictions limiting the number of lockings each day during droughts or annual dry seasons.

Variations in lock design

There are various kinds of locks, all of which accomplish the same end result of effecting a change of level. Gates may swing to the side or roll back; sometimes they lift vertically permitting water traffic to pass under them.

At some smaller locks where the water level change is not great, valves are omitted and water flows into or out of the chamber by opening the gates just a crack at first, then gradually widening the opening as the levels begin to equalize inside and outside the gates.

On the Trent Waterway in Canada, a hydraulic elevator lifts the boat in a water-filled chamber, and at another location a marine railway actually hauls the boat out to get her up and over a hill. Through passage on a waterway like the Trent is obviously limited to craft within the capacity of the railway to haul it, both as to length and weight.

Whistle signals

Signals are prescribed for vessels approaching a lock and these are answered by the lockmaster. These vary in different areas; the river boatman should familiarize himself with the special signals applicable to the particular waterway he is using. At many locks, VHF/FM radios are used for direct communications between vessels and the lockmaster.

The Army Engineers at Pittsburgh publish an informative illustrative leaflet entitled "Locking Through," which sets forth, very concisely, the main essentials as they apply to the Ohio River. Several other Army Engineer offices publish generally similar pamphlets for the waters under their control.

FIG. 2723 Locks at dams provide the means for boats to go "uphill" and "downhill" to and from lakes and "pools" of different elevations. Without locks, such navigation would be impossible. Here the lift is 80 feet at Fort Loudon Dam on the Tennessee.

FIG. 2724 Locks are massive chambers of concrete and steel which may be flooded and emptied through valves and gates. On many waterways, commercial craft are designed to fit the lock chambers with only inches to spare.

FIG. 2725 On some heavily traveled waterways, locks have been built in pairs. This is a view of the upstream side of Alton Lock and Dam No. 24 on the Mississippi above St. Louis. The landward lock is considerably larger than the riverward lock; signals indicate which to use.

FIG. 2726 The locks shown here at Lockport on the New York State Barge Canal have a double set of gates. Variations from the basic design of a chamber with one set of gates at each end may be found on many waterways.

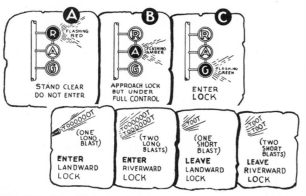

FIG. 2727 Signal lights and air horn signals used on the Western Rivers to control traffic at locks. (From "Locking Through," prepared by Army Engineers.)

FIG. 2728 Skippers of recreational boats must be prepared for rough and dirty walls in lock chambers. Fenders that are adequate in design and number are essential—and they must be in position before entering the lock.

Sound signals

On the Ohio River, vessels sound a long and short blast on the whistle from a distance of not more than one mile from the lock. When approaching a lock, boats must wait for the lockmaster's signal before entering. When bound downstream, they must stay in the clear at least 400 feet upstream from the end of the guidewall leading along the bank into the lock. Approach must be made through the buoyed channel directly to the lock, keeping clear of the spillway sections of the dam. Boats must take care not to obstruct the movement of any large commercial vessel that may be leaving the lock. When bound upstream, small craft must keep clear of the turbulent water that is invariably found beneath a dam.

Where locks are in pairs (designated as landward and riverward), the lockmaster on the Ohio may also use an air horn to give directions as follows: one long, enter landward lock; two longs, enter riverward lock; one short, leave landward lock; two shorts, leave riverward lock.

On the New York State Canal System, a skipper signals his request for lockage by sounding three distinct blasts.

Manual signals

On the Mississippi, signs are placed on the river face of the guidewall warning small craft not to pass a certain point until signalled by the lock tender. Near this sign, a signal cord is placed. Small craft with horns not loud enough to attract the attention of the lock attendant may use this to alert him that passage is desired. Generally similar arrangements are found on the Okeechobee Waterway crossing Florida and elsewhere.

Signal lights

Traffic signal lights at the Ohio locks resemble those you find on city streets—red, amber or yellow, and green, vertically arranged. Flashing red warns: do not enter, stand clear. Flashing amber cautions: approach, but under full control. Flashing green is the go-ahead: all clear to enter.

On New York State Canals, a fixed green is the signal to enter; a fixed red required the vessel to wait.

Precedence at locks

The Secretary of the Army has established an order of priority for the users of locks controlled by the Engineer Corps. The precedence in the handling of traffic is as follows: (1) U.S. Military craft; (2) mail boats; (3) commercial passenger craft; (4) commercial tows; (5) commercial fishermen; (6) non-commercial craft. In the descending order ot precedence, the lockmaster also takes into account whether vessels of the same priority are arriving at landward or riverward locks (if locks are paired), and whether they are bound upstream or downstream.

Recreational boats *may,* at the discretion of the lockmaster, be locked through with commercial vessels if a safe distance can be maintained between them and the commercial vessels are *not* carrying petroleum products or other hazardous substances.

LOCKING PROCEDURES

The concrete walls of locks are usually rough and dirty. Some of the older locks have been metal-sheathed on the inside surfaces, but most are hard on small craft. Consequently, a boat will need adequate fender protection. Ordinary cylindrical fenders will pick up dirt and roll on the wall to smear the topsides. Fender boards consisting of a plank (generally 2 by 6 inches, several feet long) suspended horizontally outside the usual fenders hung vertically, will normally work well amidships or where sides are reasonably straight.

Bags of hay have the same objection as cylindrical fenders, except on heavily flared bows at the edge of the deck where they flatten down and work fairly well. Auto tires wrapped in burlap would be ideal except that their use is illegal in most canals (if they came adrift they would sink and probably foul the lock's valves).

As you can't be sure which side of the next lock you will be using, it's wise to have duplicate fender systems, one for each side.

Have enough line

Another essential in locking is adequate line. How heavy it must be depends on the size of the boat; how long it must be, on the depth of the locks. Lines can be slightly smaller in diameter than one's normal mooring lines; ½-inch manila is often used for boats in the 35 to 50 foot size range, ⅜-inch for smaller craft. (Manila is suggested in preference to synthetic material because of its lower cost; locking lines will soon get too dirty for further use and must be discarded.)

In general, each line (bow and stern) will have to be at least twice the depth of the deepest lock that is expected to be encountered. The reason for this is to permit running the bight of the line around a bollard on the top of the lock wall, using it doubled. Then at the lower level when you are ready to cast off after locking down, you can turn loose one end and haul in on the other without assistance

FIG. 2729 The easiest locking through is accomplished where the mooring posts are recessed into the chamber walls and float up and down with changes in water level. Here, lines do not have to be adjusted during the locking process.

from above (which you are not likely to get anyway); see fig. 2728.

Use of ladders and other methods

Ladders are often recessed into lock walls for safety reasons should someone be unlucky enough to fall in. On some canals, small craft may follow a ladder up or down, rung by rung, holding on with boathooks or short lengths of line. On other canals, this is not permitted by the rules and the ladders must be kept clear for emergency use.

In addition to large bollards at the top, some locks have other posts recessed in the walls at intervals in a vertical line. Locking up, lines can be cleared successively from lower posts and transferred to higher ones within reach. Locking down would use the reverse procedure.

In some of the newer locks, floating mooring posts are built into the side walls, moving up or down with changes in the water level in the lock. This makes for the simplest and easiest of all locking through as relatively short lines

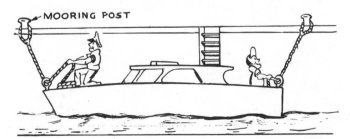

FIG. 2730 Larger boats should use two separate mooring lines leading from bow and stern to separate mooring posts on the lock wall. This will require a person at each end of the boat to pay out or take in mooring lines as the water level changes.

From "Locking Through" U.S. Army Engineers

FIG. 2731 Small boats, and larger craft with only one person aboard, may use one long line securely fastened at one end of the boat with the bight of the line around the mooring post on the lock wall and the free end of the line around a cleat at the other end of the boat. This will allow the person at the free end of the line to pay out or take in mooring as the water level changes.

FIG. 2732 Recreational craft may sometimes be locked through with commercial vessels. Skippers must beware of considerable turbulence behind these from their large propellors and powerful engines; be especially wary of tugs.

can be used to make fast, and they need not be adjusted as the boat moves up or down.

Tend your lines carefully

Rising or falling, stand by your lock lines at all times and tend them carefully. This requires a crewman forward and another aft; with only two persons aboard, it is usually possible for the helmsman to move to and tend the aft line. One of the most dangerous practices is to make fast to a bollard above and then secure the line to a bitt or cleat on the boat. If the level drops unexpectedly, the boat can be "hung," with risk of serious damage.

In some locks, coming up, special caution is required at the top of the lift. The boat may have been adequately fendered to keep her off the lock wall, but if the water rises to nearly completely fill the lock chamber, the boat's gunwale will be above the top of the wall and the top-sides below would then be unprotected from the lip of the chamber, particularly at a bow with flare.

Entering and leaving

It is always imperative to enter locks, and leave them, at a slow speed with the craft under full control. This is especially true when locking through with other boats. Sometimes, especially on fleet cruises, it will be necessary to make fast two abreast at each lock wall. This is entirely practicable if all boats are intelligently handled.

Occasionally one hears cautions concerning the possibility of a boat being tossed about as water boils into the lock from open valves. This is a possibility, and one for which a skipper must be on the alert, but in almost all instances the lock tenders on our inland waterways are careful to control the rate of inflow to minimize any turbulence in the lock chamber, and there is no real need to fear the locking process for this reason. With a light craft, however, some thought should be given to extra caution when locking through in company with large commercial vessels. A boat directly astern of a tug ("tow boat"), for example, can be subjected to quite a bit of being tossed around when the big propellor of the tug starts to kick out its wash astern on leaving the lock.

Approaching a lock from upstream

Caution is especially necessary when approaching a lock from the upstream side; the marked channel must be followed closely. Some years ago, a cruiser bound down the Hudson River missed the lock at Troy, which lies far toward the east bank, and went *over* the dam. By rare good fortune, she was able to continue her journey to New York under her own power. Looking down the river from above many dams, it is virtually impossible to see any break in the water's surface, yet there is no excuse for

FIG. 2733 Extract from one of the Illinois Waterway charts. With wicket-type dams which can be lowered at high-water stages, traffic uses the navigable pass through the dam, indicated by "high water sailing line." System of lights, explained on chart, shows whether lock or navigable pass is to be used. Lights and nun buoys in red on original.

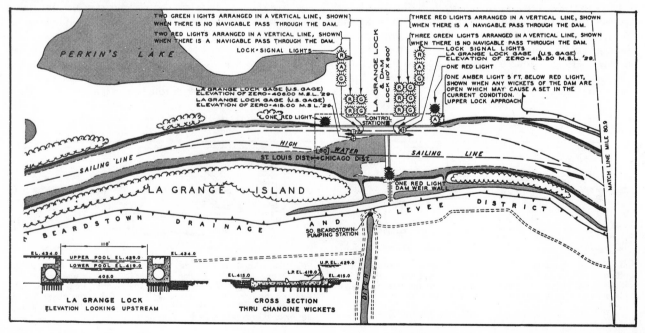

FIG. 2734 A view of the wickets at one of the Ohio River movable dams. Wickets are held in an upright position during low water stages of the river. At high water, they can be lowered, creating a navigable pass which river boats use without locking. J. M. Wallace photo

FIG. 2735 Often canals consist of entirely artificial "land cuts." West of Rochester, the New York State Barge Canal passes through such a section. Speed limit is 6 statute miles per hour.

such an occurrence if the skipper pays attention to the buoys as indicated on the chart, or to the general configuration of the dam and locks if there are no buoys.

Actually, there are times and places where it is proper to go *over* a dam, strange as that may sound. On the Ohio River, a moveable type of dam is used which has a lock chamber on one side and "bear traps" on the other. In the middle, between them, there are moveable wickets that can be held in an upright position during low water stages and lowered at times of high water. When the wickets are up, water traffic necessarily uses the lock. With the wickets down, at high water, boats run through the navigable pass, over the dam without locking. By day, it is important to watch the bulletin boards at the locks to know whether the lock or the navigable pass is to be used. At night, distinguishing lights are shown at the guide walls. When the navigable pass is being used, the gauge reading on the power house bulletin board shows the depth of water over the pass sill at the dam. The reading is in white on a red background, and is preceded by the word "Pass."

SAFETY FIRST

Recreational boatmen *must* keep clear of the spillway area below dams. The fishing in such areas may be particularly good, but the hazards are great—a good catch is

not worth your life! These water areas are subject to sudden changes as gates and valves in the dam are opened and closed; placid waters may become very turbulent with no warning at all, a heavy stream of water may unexpectedly boil up from beneath the surface. Spillway areas can be extremely dangerous for small craft; heed the warning signs and stay out.

ARTIFICIAL LAND CUTS

Not all waterways are merely improved versions of natural rivers and lakes. Artificial land cuts are often needed to interconnect navigable waterways and provide continuous passage between major bodies of water. Lake Champlain is accessible from the upper reaches of the Hudson River only because of a 24-mile completely artificial waterway cut into the land. A dredged land cut is also found at the western end of the New York State Barge Canal to connect Lake Erie with rivers in the middle of the state.

Narrow land cuts pose problems of their own. A typical cross section of a dredged canal might have a surface width of, for example, 125 feet, but a bottom width of only 75 feet, with a depth of 12 feet. If normal cruising speeds were maintained through such portions of a canal, the bank would be quickly washed down into the channel with a consequent aggravation of maintenance problems. Thus, in such artificial waterways, speed limits are rigidly enforced. In New York State Canals, the limit is 6 mph in the land cuts and 10 mph in the canalized river and lake

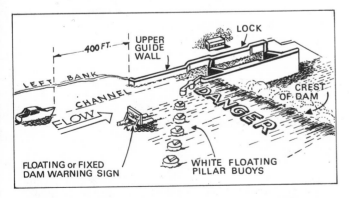

FIG. 2736 Extreme caution is required when approaching a dam and lock from upstream. Check your chart carefully; watch for aids to navigation and direction signs. Keep at least 400 feet upstream from the guide wall until signaled to enter the lock.

FIG. 2737 The many dams constructed for power and flood control purposes have created lakes ideal for inland boating. This is a typical scene showing many varied types of recreational activity on Lake Carlyle.

sections. A telephone network between the various locks enables lock tenders to know when a boat is due; speeders are quite easily caught! Some sets of locks also operate on time schedules and it serves no purpose to go too fast as one only has to wait when he reaches the next lock.

Some of the land sections of canals are cut through solid rock, perhaps only 100 feet or less in width. This makes a virtual trough with ragged walls of blasted rock. In a confined channel such as this, the wakes of a group of boats may combine and reinforce each other in a synchronized pattern, building up out of all proportion to the wakes of each craft individually. Unless speed is held down as required by the circumstances, regardless of the legal limit, small craft can get out of control, with the ultimate possibility of being thrown into the rock walls and suffering serious damage.

REGULATIONS

Lock permits, once required for non-commercial craft on the New York State Barge Canal, are no longer needed. On the Western Rivers, no special permission or clearance is necessary for passage through the locks. There are, however, regulations to be observed, and copies of these should be obtained from the Engineer District Offices at Chicago or St. Louis.

When craft are anchored at night along the side of the New York State Canals, authorities require the use of a red, rather than a white, anchor light.

Lake Boating

The term "lake boating" has extreme limits. The water area involved can range from the smallest of natural or man-made lakes and reservoirs to the Great Lakes, really inland seas. Some lakes are "protected waters" at all times; others can produce waves to hazard the largest of recreational craft and even ships of considerable size.

While it is true that an inland boatman can cruise hundreds of miles continuously on rivers and canals and never be more than a very short distance from shelter in case of bad weather, the larger lakes must be treated with considerable respect. Lake Superior, for example, is the largest body of fresh water in the world. Deep, with rock-lined coasts and subject to storms and fog as well, it can present a challenge to even the saltiest skipper. Lake Erie, although smaller than Lake Superior, is comparatively shallow. In a gale of wind, seas cannot shape up in the normal pattern of open ocean waves. Consequently, they are short and steep, frequently breaking in heavy squalls. Even Lake Oneida in mid-state New York on the Barge Canal route can build up seas that will test the abilities of an offshore boat.

Water levels

Lake levels vary from year to year and show a seasonal rise and fall as well, low in the winter and high in the summer. The Lake Survey Center, Detroit, publishes monthly bulletins during the navigation season showing current and projected levels of the Great Lakes, plus average and

FIG. 2738 Boatmen on some inland lakes encounter spectacular scenery. This is a view on Lake Powell in Utah, near the Arizona boundary.

Tom Bottomley photo

keeps track of where he is at all times. The very largest lakes will require the plotting of courses; the use of a compass; time, speed, and distance caluculations; and even bearings and fixes.

Great Lakes charts

Charts of the Great Lakes, published by the Lake Survey Center of the National Ocean Survey, are excellent, covering features of the navigable water in great detail. They show depths of water (the lesser depths in blue tint), safe channels, submerged reefs and shoals, aids to navigation, adjacent shorelines with topographic features and landmarks, types of bottom, and much related information. Scales of the charts vary from as large as 1:2,500 to 1:20,000 for harbor charts to 1:400,000 or 1:500,000 for general charts of individual lakes. The smallest scale used is for the general chart of all the Great Lakes at 1:1,200,000. The projection used for Lake Survey charts is basically polyconic, but a few are additionally published with a Mercator projection; see Chapter 18.

On Great Lakes charts, a compass rose will be found, showing both true and magnetic directions with the variation stated. In parts of the Great Lakes, the variation reduces to zero. In some locations, great deposits of iron ore in the earth produce strong local effects; this is most pronounced along the north shore of Lake Superior where variation has been observed to change from 27° to 7° within a distance of 650 feet!

Many lake charts show some of the principal routes between major ports, giving the course in degrees (true)

record levels. More current information is contained in weekly reports released each Thursday to newspapers and radio and television stations.

In larger lakes, a steady, strong wind will lower levels to windward and pile up water on the leeward side. Barometric pressure can also exert an influence on lake levels, sometimes causing a sudden and temporary, but drastic, oscillation of considerable magnitude; this phenomenon is called a "seiche."

LAKE PILOTING

Many smaller lakes are not of a size to require "navigation" by the skipper; charts often do not exist for such bodies of water. On the larger lakes, however, shore lines may run to many miles of length and the prudent boatman

FIG. 2739 Reproduction (reduced more thana half) of typical page from the Lake Survey Recreational Chart Series 14853 covering the Detroit River, Lake St. Clair, and the St. Clair River. Charts of this kind are prepared for the express purpose of providing the boatman with a maximum of navigational information in convenient form. In these volumes, data are included which is not available on other chart series. In the original, Lake St. Clair (below) is shown on a scale of 1:60,000; Belle Isle and a portion of the Detroit River 1:15,000. On the original, two tints of blue are used to define limits of the shoaler areas (up to one and two fathoms), thus emphasizing navigable deep-water channels which appear in white, with soundings in feet in black figures. Land areas are tinted light yellow.

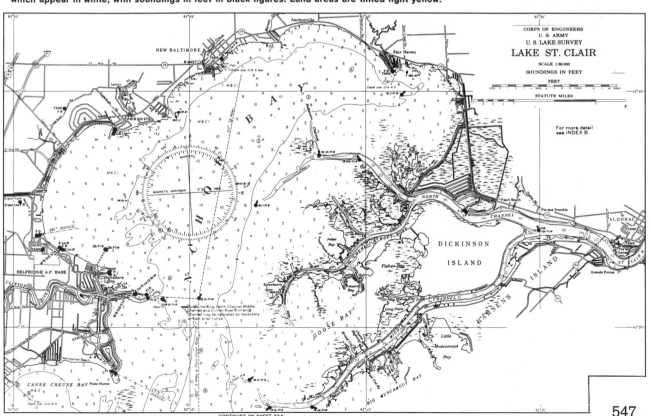

and distance in statute miles. Comparative elevations are referred to mean tide as calculated at New York City. Local heights and depths are measured from an established datum for each lake.

The Great Lakes are partly Canadian waters and there are excellent charts available for these areas from the Canadian Hydrographic Survey, Ottawa.

Great Lakes Pilot

To supplement the information available on Great Lakes charts, boatmen should have a copy of the current edition of the *Great Lakes Pilot,* published annually by the Lake Survey Center, Detroit. This most useful volume provides detailed information that cannot be shown on charts. Included are full descriptions of the waters charted, laws and regulations governing navigation, bridge clearances, signals for locks and bridges, dimensions and capacities of marine railways, and weather information. Purchasers of the Pilot get, free, seven monthly supplements (May through November) to keep the Pilot up-to-date.

Great Lakes Light List

The U.S. Coast Guard publishes the Light List, Volume IV, covering the Great Lakes; see page 331.

In this Light List, Canadian buoys and lights are identified by the letter "C"; except for minor differences in design, the system of buoyage used in Canadian waters is the same as used by the United States.

Caution along some shores

When cruising in some lakes, such as Lake Champlain, the depth becomes a factor. Along some shores, which may be particularly inviting because of their scenic attractions, the skipper may find depths of several hundred feet running right up to sheer cliff shores. If power fails, the anchor will be of little use in such deep water, and if the breeze is toward those cliffs, he is in danger of a lee shore.

RULES AND REGULATIONS

Many smaller inland lakes do not fall under federal jurisdiction and are regulated by the states or agencies thereof; see page 30. Others are, however, "navigable waters of the United States" where federal rules and reg-

ulations apply. Boatmen should check on the status of unfamiliar waters if there are any doubts.

Rules of the Road

The U.S. Inland Rules of the Road will apply to vessels on some of the waters covered in this chapter. Others will be governed by the Great Lakes Rules or the Western Rivers Rules; see page 38 for the boundaries of these sets of rules of the road, and remember that the "Western Rivers Rules" do not apply to rivers on the West (Pacific) Coast of the United States.

Pollution control regulations

Many inland lakes are used as sources of municipal water supplies or have their water quality maintained for other reasons. Boatmen visiting new bodies of water should check carefully for any special regulations regarding overboard discharges.

USCG BOATING SAFETY DETACHMENTS

The U.S. Coast Guard has jurisdiction on all "Navigable Waters of the United States" as defined on page 30. Coast Guard stations will be found on the Great Lakes, the larger rivers, and some other major bodies of water, but many of the smaller inland rivers and lakes do not have regular USCG facilities. On these waters, the Coast Guard meets its responsibilities and asserts its authority through mobile teams called *Boating Safety Detachments,* abbreviated *BOSDET.* During each boating season, these detachments travel thousands of miles and visit nearly every state; they will be seen in areas where one would hardly expect to note the presence of a *Coast* Guardsman.

Personnel and equipment

Each BOSDET normally consists of a Chief Petty Officer and two other enlisted men. These men have been carefully selected for such independent duty and have been given special schooling. Their equipment includes a 16 to 18 foot outboard or I-O boat together with a trailer for it pulled by a light pickup or carryall type of truck. The boats are clearly marked with the Coast Guard name and distinguishing stripe; many craft are equipped with the revolving blue light prescribed for law enforcement vessels.

Activities

The BOSDETs' function is educational and advisory as much as it is law enforcement. They would much rather counsel and assist boatmen, but in the event of flagrant violations they can, and do, issue citations. Team personnel are often seen at boat shows, boating or fishing club meetings, U.S. Power Squadrons and USCG Auxiliary classes, and similar functions—all on the basis that "an ounce of prevention is worth a pound of cure." Safety patrols on the water are a major activity of BOSDETs, with emphasis on the peak days of each weekend—their personal "days off" must come in the middle of the week!

The new authority to turn back boats in unsafe conditions, granted by the Federal Boat Safety Act of 1971, will undoubtedly be used more by BOSDETs than any other type of Coast Guard unit. Boats may be directed to return to port or may be escorted back if unsafe either in their condition, equipment, or loading, or if weather and sea conditions are hazardous for that size or type of craft.

FIG. 2740 Coast Guard Boating Safety Detachments bring their twin functions of advice and enforcement to inland boating areas under Federal jurisdiction. U. S. Coast Guard photo

OUTBOARD BOATING

The pleasures of recreational boating are not related in any way to the size of one's craft. Some skippers have never had a truly small craft; they desired, and could afford, boats of 40 or more feet in length. Others have never owned boats larger than 18 to 22 feet or so, either for economic reasons or their preferred style of boating. Both these groups have equally enjoyed their time on the water. So, too, have other boatmen who have changed the size of their boat—upward, downward, or both—as dictated by their boating areas, available time, or other reasons. Boating is fun—fun for the skipper, his family, and guests—in any size of boat. It is more fun when it is done with the added safety that comes with knowledge.

This chapter is focused on the smaller craft up to 26 feet in length, covering the special considerations of selection, equipment, and use of such boats on the water. This is a convenient dividing point as it separates the Coast Guard categories of Classes A and 1 from Classes 2 and 3. In actuality, the boats most relevant to this chapter will fall in the 15 to 22 or 24 foot range. Based on recent Coast Guard statistics, 96.4% of all registered boats were in the first two size classes, and of these 90.5% were outboard propelled.

CHAPTER 28

Much that has preceded this chapter is applicable to outboard boating. The basics of aids to navigation, the compass, chart reading, weather, safety, seamanship, and many other topics are applicable as a whole or in large part to the outboard boatman. And here it might be pointed out that except for details of the motor, we include the skipper of the boat with inboard-outboard (out-drive, stern drive) propulsion.

The laws and regulations relating to outboard boats will be found with those relating to larger motorboats in Chapters 2 through 5 and they will not be repeated here. Outboard skippers should carefully study those applicable to the length of his craft.

For a great many outboard skippers this chapter might have been entitled "Trailer Boating," for their craft spend more time on land on trailers than they do in the water. Yet such would not be correct as a trailered boat is no different in its safe operation than any others once it is in the water—it is then just a "boat." The only differences are its land transportation and storage, both of which topics are covered in Chapter 29, "Boat Trailering."

The Boat

Outboard boats, those craft suitable for equipping with a detachable motor, come in an extremely wide range of design, size, construction material, and cost. They range from 8-foot or smaller prams that can be "car-topped" or even used as a dinghy for a boat small enough that *it* fits into the outboard category, to large hulls capable of carrying two motors of more than a hundred horsepower each. The craft that we will consider in this chapter may be of entirely open construction or have a small but comfortable cabin with bunks, galley, and a head.

THE USE OF THE BOAT

The key to the selection of the "right" boat for a particular skipper is the use or uses to which it will be put. No craft can do everything best—quite obviously the craft for water skiing is not the boat for fishing by trolling, the boat for an afternoon outing is not the craft for a weekend or week's cruise, the competitive racer is not a family boat. Probably no boating family will agree on just one or even

FIG. 2801 Outboard boating is not entirely "a world unto itself"—many of the basic aspects of boating covered in earlier chapters are applicable to smaller craft powered with an outboard motor, or an out-drive unit.

FIG. 2803 Many outboards are used for fishing in protected waters or, with due caution, offshore. These range from simple, displacement-type utility craft to complex and expensive "fishing machines."

FIG. 2802 Except for details of the motor, inboard-outboard craft are much like outboards. They are generally of the same size, handle alike, and are used for the same types of waterborne recreation.

FIG. 2804 Displacement hulls ride down in the water, while planing hulls derive lift from their forward motion and tend to ride "on" the water. Each type has its use and careful selection is advisable when choosing your boat.

Many boat designs for outboard motors have a single, rather conventional hull, but there is an increasing tendency toward wider craft which have greater horizontal stability and more interior space for passengers. Underwater, these have, in effect, two or three hull shapes although they are not catamarans or trimarans; a number of trade names are applied to patented hull designs of this type, often called "cathedral" hulls.

Flat bottom (displacement type) hulls. Usually rowboats or skiffs 14' to 18'; used for fishing or utility purposes on shallow streams and small protected lakes. They are not fast, are generally heavy and roomy. (Some light, flat bottom boats plane and are fast.)

Round bottom (displacement) hulls. Dinghies, tenders, car-top craft, occasionally runabouts 12' to 18'. These hulls at slow speeds are often more easily driven and maneuvered than the flat-bottom craft. (Many fast, light, round bottom boats will also plane.)

Vee-bottom hulls. Commonly used for runabouts, utilities, and cruisers when speed is a factor. Forward undersection is usually deep "V" in shape. Bottom flattens toward amidships, until at the stern it becomes broad and flat.

Hydroplane (planing) hulls. Generally used for racing. Bottom, which is flat, may be "stepped," i.e., divided into two levels, about amidships. The resultant notch reduces wetted surface, increasing speed.

Other terms that may be used are "utility" and "runabout." A utility and a runabout, in effect, are practically interchangeable terms. Both craft function about the same, are about the same size, take about the same horsepower, etc. The runabout, however, is generally considered to be a bit faster and more luxuriously equipped than a utility of comparable size.

two uses, and few families can afford a separate craft for each type of activity enjoyed by its members, so compromise is inevitable. If, however, all possible factors are considered in advance of selecting "the boat," the likelihood of disappointment will be lessened. Not to be overlooked, also, is the type of waters upon which it will be used, protected lakes and rivers, or coastal bays and off shore.

Hull designs

There are two basic hull types, displacement and planing—and many variations of the latter. Displacement boats cruise *through* the water; planing hulls lift and skim *over* the surface.

Often it is difficult to make a sharp distinction between "displacement" and "planing" types of hulls. Planing hulls receive a large part of their support at normal speeds from the dynamic reaction of the water against the bottom, and a lesser part from buoyancy which diminishes with increased speed, but never quite disappears at any speed. Generally, planing begins when the water breaks cleanly away at the chines and transom. In these days of high horsepower, many cruisers are actually planing hulls, and, of course, practically all runabouts are planing type.

FIG. 2805 Although this runabout demonstrates great carrying capacity, she should never carry so many passengers. Overloading is dangerous practice in small craft. No one should be permitted on forward deck while under way.

Size and loading

Economic considerations are, of course, a primary aspect in the choice of the size of an outboard boat, but its use and the typical number of persons to be aboard at any one time must also be considered. Coast Guard regulations require that boats under 20 feet (except sailboats and some special types) manufactured after 31 October 1972 *must* carry a "capacity plate" showing maximum allowable loads computed from complex formulas developed by the American Boat & Yacht Council. Plates on outboard boats show both maximum weight, in pounds, for persons, and maximum weight for motor, gear, *and persons*. Plates for inboard, inboard-outboard, and unpowered craft show only the maximum weight for gear and persons.

Boats manufactured before this regulation *may* carry a capacity plate prepared from earlier formulas. If there is no such plate, there is a double check which, if properly used, will help prevent overloading.

First, a check of the *number* of persons:

$$\frac{L \times B}{15} = \underline{\hspace{1cm}} \text{ number of persons}$$

L = Overall Length

B = Maximum Width (Both dimensions in feet and tenths of feet)

The results, taken to the nearest whole number, gives the *number of persons* that can be put aboard without crowding in good weather conditions.

Second, one must *also* check the weight-carrying capacity to be certain the boat is adequate for that number of persons, taking into account their actual weight as well as the weight of engine, fuel, and equipment.

The *weight carrying capacity* of a small boat having a conventional hull can be checked by determining the allowable weight in pounds from the expression:

$$7.5 \times L \times B \times De = \underline{\hspace{1cm}} \text{ pounds for persons, engine, fuel and equipment}$$

L is Overall Length

B is Maximum Width

De is *Minimum* Effective Depth of the Boat

Measure De at the *lowest point* that water can enter. This takes account of low transom cut-out or credits an acceptable engine well. All dimensions are in feet and tenths.

Having figured the total weight-carrying capacity of your boat by the above method, now use Table 28-1 to find the capacity that is available for *people.*

In any particular loading situation, the skipper should *obey whichever value,* from the number-of-persons formula or the weight capacity available for people, *sets the lower limit.*

Construction material

Small light boats are made of three basic materials: wood, metal, and fiber-reinforced plastics. Although "fiberglass" is now the leader in new boat construction for a number of reasons including lessened maintenance and adaptability to mass production, recent registration figures gave a remarkably balanced picture for all Class A and 1 registered boats. In round figures, there were 1.3 million craft of wood; 1.6 million of metal (almost entirely aluminum), and 1.7 million of fiberglass.

WEIGHT AND PERSON CAPACITY TABLE

(1)	Weight Carrying Capacity of Boat	_____	lbs.
	Add weight of:		
	—outboard motor . . .	_____ lbs.	
	—battery	_____ lbs.	
	—fuel tank and fuel (gas = 6 lbs. per gal.) .	_____ lbs.	
	—equipment: anchor, oars, radio, etc. . .	_____ lbs.	
(2)	Total	_____	lbs.
(3)	Remaining Weight Available for Persons . .	_____	lbs.
	[Subtract (2) from (1)]		

Table 28-1 This table, used as described in the text, guides the skipper in determining the number of persons that can be safely carried, based on weight-capacity considerations.

Personal preferences and cost will undoubtedly be the controlling factor in the selection of a new or used craft, but the boatman will not go wrong with any of these materials if he purchases a well-designed and honestly-built craft.

Special design features

Many craft will have special design features for particular applications such as sport fishing. These invariably add to the cost of a boat and should be avoided unless that use will be made of the boat.

A design feature that can well be looked for on any outboard for the aspect of safety is the "motor well." Most craft have a transom that is "cut down" or lowered where

FIG. 2806 When the transom of a boat is cut down for the motor—and no full-height bulkhead is forward of the cut-down area—this reduced freeboard at the stern must be taken into consideration when figuring the craft's safe capacity.

FIG. 2807 A "motor well" is formed when there is a full-height transverse partition forward of the outboard motor. This is an important safety feature as it keeps the stern from being a low point for the entry of water into the hull.

FIG. 2808 Every small boat should have added buoyancy material to keep it, its motor, and its crew afloat if it swamps. It is extremely desirable that it float in an upright position; this is accomplished by placing the buoyant material high in the hull around the gunwales.

the motor or motors are to be attached; this is necessary so that the motor will be low enough that the lower unit and propeller will be well below the bottom of the hull. Such a mounting provides efficiency for the motor, but may seriously jeopardize the safety of the craft by providing an easier point of access for water into the hull. Safety can be maintained by an inner bulkhead forward of the motor that is not cut down, that is fully as high as the sides of the boat. The space aft of this bulkhead to the cut down transom is the motor well, and self-bailing drains should be provided at each corner; see fig. 2807.

Added buoyancy

Still another step can be taken to ensure the safety of your passengers and boating rig—built-in flotation. This can take the form of sealed air chambers or masses of plastic foam. In either case, there must be enough added buoyancy to support the weight of the boat and motor even though completely flooded.

It is very desirable that the added buoyance be located *high* in the hull so that the craft, if swamped, will float in any upright position and not capsize. Such a way of floating provides much greater safety for the skipper and his passengers. Persons in the water will be able to hold on more easily and it may be possible to recover some form of emergency signalling, bailing, or other needed equipment.

For boats less than 20 feet in length (except sailboats and some special types), Coast Guard regulations specify flotation performance and materials. These are effective for craft manufactured after 31 July 1973.

The Motor and Accessories

An outboard motor is a *detachable* power plant of from one to six cylinders which is complete with drive shaft and propeller. The fuel tank and operating controls are usually separate, but may be integral on the smallest motors. It is a gasoline-fueled motor, nearly always of two-cycle design. It is normally raw-water cooled, and may be either manually or electrically started in the medium and larger size models.

Inboard-Outboards

A newer type of mechanical propulsion for small craft combines a conventional marine inboard engine with a drive unit that closely resembles the lower unit of an outboard motor. This is variously termed "inboard-outboard (I-O)," "outdrive," "stern drive," or other generally similar descriptive words or phrases. It seeks to combine the greater power and efficiency of an inboard engine (four-cycle) with the directed-thrust steering, tilt-up action, and other advantageous features of outboard propulsion.

Boats of I-O design can generally be included with outboards, except for matters directly relating to the engine. They are usually in the size category of medium and larger outboard craft, handle similarly, are used for the same general purposes, and can be trailered.

OUTBOARD MOTOR SELECTION

The first question *always* seems to be, "How much horsepower?" Such other factors as weight, electric starting, even price, seem to routinely come second to "horse-

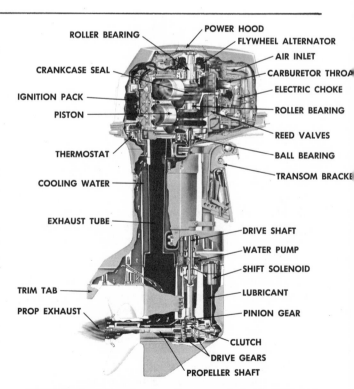

FIG. 2809 An outboard motor offers many desirable features for smaller craft. It is detachable for storage and servicing; it gives great maneuverability with "power steering"; and it can tilt up if the lower unit strikes a submerged obstruction.

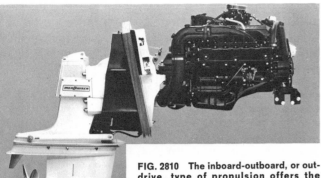

FIG. 2810 The inboard-outboard, or out-drive, type of propulsion offers the economy and power of an inboard engine without giving up outboard features such as directed-thrust steering and tiltability.

FIG. 2811 Use of an inboard-outboard drive unit will permit installation of diesel power in quite small craft. Cost may be greater than for a gasoline engine, but there are operating economy and safety features.

FIG. 2812 For use on protected inland waters with a utility type of craft, a motor of 10 horsepower is adequate. More power would be wasted on this displacement type of hull, and might be unsafe.

FIG. 2813 Water-skiing takes speed, and this requires horsepower. Typically, motors of 40 horsepower or more are used on planing types of hulls for this fast, exciting sport.

power." Outboard motors have been available for essentially all this century, with a slow rate of increase in horsepower until World War II, and a startlingly rapid rise in power ratings in recent years. The larger outboard motors have long ceased to be a *readily* detachable piece of machinery that one could walk up a pier with, carrying it by one hand. Power ratings of stock motors are now well past 100 hp, with weights in excess of 250 pounds.

Enough, but not too much!

The horsepower required for a boat will depend upon the size and weight of the craft (loaded), and the speed that it is desired to make. A displacement hull of 14 feet or so will serve adequately for lake and river fishing with a 10 hp motor, and any greater power will be largely wasted in attempting to drive the craft faster than "hull speed."

For water skiing behind a planing hull, typically a 16 to 18 footer, a skipper should consider 40 to 75 horsepower. A larger engine will make the boat go faster (provided that the hull has the capacity for the greater power), but *not* at all in proportion to the increase in engine power. Very roughly, horsepower must be tripled or even quadrupled to double the speed.

For cruising about, either day trips or longer ventures, the typical outboard craft is a planing-type hull. It may not be operated at its maximum attainable speed, but "running on a plane" is both more enjoyable and economical

than pushing one's way through the water in the displacement mode. The size of motor must be considered from a consideration of the boat *and* its normal load of persons and equipment. No specific recommendation can be made — each situation is a case unto itself — but the boatman would be well-advised to make a trial run of any boat and motor combination prior to closing a purchase deal. These trials should be made *with load,* either actual or simulated with weights, and figuring a bit of excess for later additions. If at all possible, try the "rig" (outboarders' language for a boat and motor combination, sometimes also including a trailer) in various conditions of wind and water that are typical of how it is expected to be used.

FIG. 2814 Outboard motors have steadily grown in size until now the largest models produce 125 hp or more, and weigh over 250 pounds—a long way in both categories from the early models of only a few horsepower!

Rating plates

USCG regulations require that all outboard boats over 20 feet in length (except sailboats and certain special types) manufactured after 31 October 1972 must show the maximum horsepower on the required "capacity plate."

Lacking a rating plate, the maximum safe horsepower may be calculated from two dimensions of the boat, length and width *at the stern*. The product of these dimensions, in feet and tenths, taken to the nearest whole number, gives a "factor" which can be applied to Tables 28-2 and 28-3. These tables are illustrated graphically as fig. 2816 and 2817, respectively. For flat bottom, hard chine boats, the capacities of Tables 28-2 and fig. 2816 must be reduced by one increment. The horsepower ratings from Table 28-3 and fig. 2817 may be increased to the next greater multiple of 5 hp.

Both the tables and the figures referred to above are for outboard craft only. They give the maximum horsepower whether from one engine or two. Length is measured from the stem to the transom along a straight line parallel to the keel; do not include extensions such as outboard motor brackets in this measurement.

A couple of examples may make these calculations a bit more clear. First, consider a round-bottom dinghy measuring 10 feet in length and 3 feet, 8 inches across its stern. The product of 10 x 3.7 gives a factor 37. From either Table 28-2 or fig. 2816, we can see that this craft should be limited to a 5 hp motor.

For a larger outboard boat with a length of 17 feet and a stern width of 5 feet, 2 inches, the factor would be 17 x 5.2 or 88.4, used as 88. *If* the craft had *both* remote steering and a 20-inch high transom, the horsepower capacity calculation would be $(2 \times 88) - 90 = 86$, which can be rounded up to 90. This might be either a single 90 hp motor or twins of 45 hp each. If this craft lacked *either* remote steering or a transom height of 20 inches (or both), the horsepower capacity would be calculated as $(\frac{3}{4} \times 88) - 20 = 46$, used as 50 hp, a significant reduction.

Recent research has shown that a series of carefully planned and instrumented tests can sometimes result in safe higher horsepower ratings than those produced by using the USCG calculations. The average skipper, however, should continue to use the above method unless he is satisfied that the manufacturer has responsibly established a higher rating.

Electric starting?

Early outboard motors were started by winding a short length of rope around the top of the flywheel for about two turns and then giving a strong pull—or perhaps several! This method, with refinements such as built-in pull cords that automatically retract and rewind themselves, remain in use for smaller and some medium horsepower motors. As the power ratings increased, it became necessary to go to electric starting motors to provide the required cranking power. This feature proved popular with boatmen, and their crews, and soon was extended downward to medium-power models, often as an optional accessory.

FIG. 2815 Before buying a combination of boat and motor, try it out under varying conditions of wind and water, and be sure to have a full normal load, live or simulated aboard.

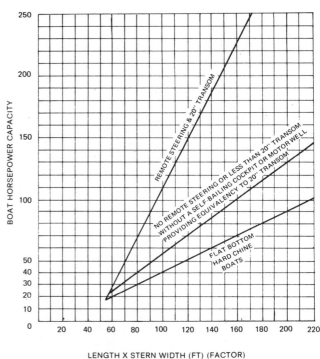

BOAT HORSEPOWER CAPACITY CURVES

FIG. 2817 For "factors" (product of length and width at the stern) greater than 57, the proper line on the above diagram is chosen as determined by such design characteristics as location of steering controls, presence of motor well, etc.

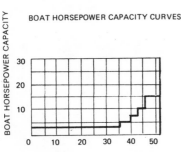

BOAT HORSEPOWER CAPACITY CURVES

FIG. 2816 If the product of length and width at the stern is less than 57, the diagram (left) will graphically indicate the maximum safe horsepower.

Multiply overall length ____ x stern width ____ = factor ____ (nearest whole number)					
If this factor is	thru 35	36–39	40–42	43–45	46–52
H.P. capacity is	3	5	7–1/2	10	15

Table 28-2 The product of boat length times width at the stern gives a "factor" which can be used with this table to determine the maximum safe horsepower for the hull.

	Remote steering and 20" Transom or equivalent	No remote steering or Transom less than 20" or equivalent	
		Flat Bottom Hard Chine Boats	Other Boats
If this factor is	over 52.5	over 52.5	over 52.5
H.P. capacity is	(2 x factor) - 90	(1/2 factor) - 15	(0.8 factor) - 25
H.P. capacity = ____ (raise to next higher multiple of 5)			

Table 28-3 When the "factor" is greater than 52.5, multiplication and subtraction are used to determine the maximum safe horsepower for hulls in each of three general categories.

FIG. 2818 Twin outboard motors give a greater degree of security from complete loss of power, but only at the cost of greater investment, weight, and fuel consumption. Their use over a single, larger motor must be carefully considered.

Electric starting requires additional equipment — and weight and cost — the starting motor, a battery, control wiring, etc., but the considerable added convenience is usually greatly appreciated by all concerned. In general, motors under 10 hp will be manually started, and those over 40 hp will be electrically started; motors between these sizes may have either method of starting.

Nearly all electrically started outboard motors are also equipped with an *alternator* to supply electricity for battery charging and the operation of other accessories. This feature may not be automatically included on motors that have electric starting as an additional-cost option.

Single or twins?

Many outboard hulls are designed at the transom to allow the fitting of either one or two motors. There are definite advantages and disadvantages of each method for the same total horsepower. Some years ago, the largest available motors did not have enough power for larger craft or higher speeds; the use of multiple motors was the only solution. Now, a single large motor may well supply all the power that the hull can safely handle, and a choice must be made, one large single or smaller twins?

The reason most often advanced for twin motors rather than a single one of the total horsepower is added safety. Outboard motors are very reliable if given adequate care, but failures do occur, and many a boatman has made it home "on one" when the other was incapacitated.

The disadvantages, however, are many and must be considered. Greater initial cost (not twice as much but about 1⅓ times the price of a single large motor), a second battery or larger single one, more complex control systems, greater weight in the boat (about 50% more), greater underwater drag, and greater fuel consumption (again not doubled, but greater by ⅓ to ½); all these are negative factors that must not be overlooked. Twin motors, and their batteries and fuel tanks, will also take up greater space within the boat than that used for a single-motor installation.

A special case in the larger outboard cruiser where the use of two motors is required to meet horsepower needs, and where the weight and space penalties are less important. Twin motors here will also allow the use of more efficient propellers with larger blade area.

The consideration above has been of the same total horsepower in a single or twin motors. Let us now look at a comparison of one motor with two of the same size (always assuming that the doubled horsepower is within the capacity of the hull). If a boat has performed to certain standards with one motor, what may be expected if a second, identical motor is added? First of all, the speed will *not* be doubled. The added weight and drag, combined with hydrodynamic factors, will hold the speed increase to roughly 25%, although this will vary widely with specific installations. Even if both motors are operated at the same rpms, fuel consumption will not be doubled as the second motor seems to "help" the first one; very roughly, the total fuel consumption will be about 1½ times that of the single motor rig.

A big one and a little one

A combination seen more and more often is that of a single large motor adequate for all normal operation, plus a smaller motor of 4 to 10 horsepower. The smaller motor is used for trolling while fishing—large motors do not like to run at idle speeds for extended periods of time—and for emergency back-up. A 6 hp motor will move a medium size outboard hull at 3 or 4 mph and get you home or to assistance if the main unit fails.

PROPELLORS

An outboard motor is sold complete with a propellor; this is a "stock" propellor, a suitable propellor for an average boat under average conditions. (Some outboard motors, especially the larger models—are offered with a choice of several propellors.) The stock propellor will undoubtedly be usable on your craft, but it probably will *not* be the optimum in pitch or diameter, or both Consideration should be given to changing to a more suitable

Outboard Boating / CHAPTER 28

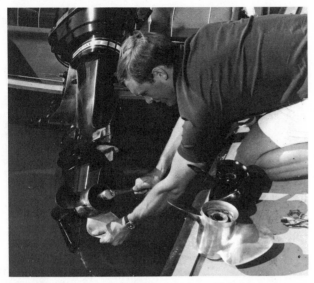

FIG. 2819 One of the advantages of outboard boating is ease with which a propeller can be changed in the case of damage or to have a more optimum diameter and pitch for a particular use of the boat.

FIG. 2820 Light but very strong propellors are being made of stainless steel coated with Teflon. Much stronger than aluminum or bronze, these blades can be made thinner for higher efficiency and performance.

propellor for *your* boat.

Manufacturers do publish tables of recommended propellor sizes for various applications, but these can serve as little more than initial guides. The answer lies in experimentation—unless you should be so lucky as to know another skipper who has an identical boat and motor combination, and whose style of boating matches yours.

The "right" propellor for any craft in a specific application is the one which allows the motor to turn up to its full rated rpm, but no more. It is necessary for the motor to turn up full rated rpm to develop full rated power; but if it will turn faster than that, the propellor is too small and full power is not being developed at the rated maximum rpm (which must not be exceeded except for brief tests).

If the craft is used for more than one type of activity, such as cruising, fishing, water skiing, etc., it may be that the same motor will require different propellors for the most efficient operation in each usage. As a spare propellor is an excellent safety item, the purchase of a more efficient propellor is not all "added expense"—the stock propellor becomes the spare.

Materials

Most stock propellors are aluminum, as are those normally purchased for more optimum performance. Propellors of bronze are also available; these are stronger and more easily repaired, but are more expensive.

Propellors of stainless steel and other high-strength alloys are advantageous for special applications, but are even more costly than bronze. Plastic is used for the propellors of some of the smaller motors, and a recent development is a teflon-coated steel propellor, said to be very strong and efficient yet light in weight.

Number of blades

For a stock propellor, most outboard motors are equipped with a three-blade type. For lighter loads, and faster speeds, a two-blade propellor may do a better job.

For lower rpm use on heavier craft, it may be desirable to install a four-blade propellor. The number of blades, is, of course, a factor closely inter-related to diameter and pitch.

Pitch

The pitch of a propellor determines its "bite" on the water, and thus the rpm which the motor can turn up, (this is also affected by propellor diameter). This in turn is related to the speed of the craft through the water—a lighter, faster boat will use a propellor of greater pitch, and a heavier, slower craft will use one of lesser pitch. Again, experimentation is really the only way of selecting the best match of propellor to the boat.

There are available on the market propellors for medium-size motors that allow an adjustment of pitch over a wide range. These are quite useful if load and speed conditions vary greatly, but this should not interfere with the carrying of a second, spare propellor.

If a single motor is "doubled up" with another similar to it, this will call for a change of propellor on the original motor. The faster speed obtained with the added horsepower will call for a greater pitch, probably one, but possibly two, inches more; again, only actual trials will tell for sure.

Shear pins and slip clutches

Somehow, outboard motors seem to run aground more than inboards, or at least the lower parts of the motor strike the bottom more often. To prevent damage to the

FIG. 2821 Having the correct propellor pitch is essential to optimum performance. Here the skipper is adjusting the dial which changes the pitch on this special propellor. If pitch is not adjustable, it may be a wise move to carry several propellors of different pitch for use under varying conditions.

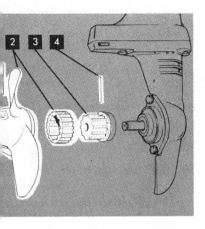

FIG. 2822 Smaller outboard motors commonly use a "shear pin" to protect the drive shaft and other parts of the motor should the propellor strike a submerged obstruction. Driving power is transmitted through a pin of soft metal which will break if the propellor hits something. This pin must be replaced if sheared; several spares must be carried on board.

A shear pin is made of a relatively soft metal. It is installed so as to transmit the drive from the propellor shaft to the propellor, and is strong enough for this. Upon impact with a rock or other hard object by a propellor blade, this pin is broken, sheared off near each end, and the propellor is effectively disconnected from the motor. The outboard motor is then inoperative insofar as thrust is concerned until the propellor hub, and perhaps the propellor itself, is removed and a new pin installed.

To overcome the nuisance of having to replace sheared pins, manufacturers developed slip clutches in which a rubber inner hub is used to transmit the drive power. Under normal loads, there is no slippage, but upon impact with a hard object by a propellor blade (or even with the sudden load of a too-quick shift of gears), the rubber hub slips somewhat to absorb the strain. Obviously, there is here no internal component that need be replaced after impact, and yet it provides adequate protection for the motor, clearly an improvement over shear pins.

drive shaft and gears, and possibly other internal parts of the motor, these are equipped with either a *shear pin* (smaller motors) or a *slip clutch* (larger motors).

Equipment

The outboard boat must first of all meet legal requirements for equipment according to its size classification. The federal requirements have been spelled out in Chapter 3 and will not be repeated here. The craft must also carry any additional equipment required by state and/or local regulations. (The Federal Boat Safety Act of 1971 provides that no state or local jurisdiction can enforce regulations that are not identical with Federal regulations except as specifically authorized. This provision, however, has been suspended for all state and local regulations in effect as of 10 August 1971 pending the issuance of new and more detailed Federal regulations under the authority of the 1971 Act.) Boatmen venturing into new waters subject to other regulations than "at home" should check with a marina operator, park ranger, or other local authority to avoid inadvertant violations.

Navigation lights

Even if you plan absolutely never to use your boat at night, it should be equipped with navigation lights in accordance with the waters on which it *may* be found some evening after sunset. Engine trouble, fuel problems, unexpectedly good fishing, or other situations may keep you out longer than you intended. See Chapter 4 for details on the navigation lights for each class of boat or various waters.

Several items regarding legal requirements for navigation lights should be especially noted by the outboard skipper. Nearly all OB craft are delivered with a red-green combination light forward and an all-around white light aft. Such lights are legal, on U.S. waters *only,* if they are properly used *and meet the requirements of the regulations.* All too often the aft light is not high enough to meet the requirements for *all-around* visibility, especially when the craft is underway and the bow rises or when the canvas top is raised. Some lights are on a telescoping stem so that they may be lowered when not in use during daylight for convenience and to protect the mounting from accidental damage. Even when raised, these are usually too low to

FIG. 2823 This stern light is too low to meet the legal requirements for all-around visibility—its beams will be blocked in some directions by the motor. For safety's sake, be sure that your white light can be seen from all directions when running or at anchor.

be seen from ahead. The prudent skipper will check his craft and make sure that he can be seen at night from *any* direction; the white light is even more important than the colored lights as it will be seen at a greater distance. These checks should be made both with the boat underway when the white light is a "running" light, and with the craft dead in the water simulating use of the white light as an anchor light.

Under the regulations of the old Motorboat Act of 1940 (which are continued in effect under the new Act until specifically superceded), boats up to 26 feet in length *may* carry the white all-around light off the centerline of the craft as is sometimes made necessary by the positioning of the outboard motor.

It should also be noted that the white all-around aft light described above does *not* meet the requirements of International Rules of the Road. These Rules require two separate white lights as described on pages 64(s) to 64(u).

Outboard Boating / CHAPTER 28

No exception is made for outboards, although it is permissible for the after 12-point light to be located off the centerline for craft less than 26 feet in length. If your fishing or cruising takes you beyond the boundary lines between Inland and International Rules, see page 31, then you must equip your boat with navigation lights to meet the requirements of those waters.

EQUIPMENT FOR SAFETY

Equipment for safety and convenience was also covered in Chapter 3 for boats in general. Here we will consider some of these, plus other, more specialized items specifically related to outboards.

Life saving devices

Outboards are more likely to capsize than are larger inboard craft, and consequently there is a greater possibility of the skipper and crew finding themselves in the water. The wise outboard skipper does not skimp on personal flotation devices. Although buoyant cushions are less expensive and are legally acceptable, life preservers or buoyant vests, see pages 52-56, offer substantially greater personal protection; they are worn rather than grasped and so provide greater safety for the injured or exhausted person. It should be an absolute "rule of the boat" that adult non-swimmers and all children *wear* a life preserver or buoyant vest *at all times* when the craft is underway. At the higher speeds of most outboards, there may not be time to locate and put on a life jacket when a sudden emergency occurs.

"Special purpose life saving devices" *approved by the Coast Guard,* such as some hunter's jackets and some water skiing *vests,* are legally acceptable items for smaller boats not carrying passengers for hire; ski *belts,* however, are not so approved and are not acceptable in meeting the legal requirements although their use is recommended while water skiing.

Paddle or oar

Required in some state and local jurisdictions, and by the Coast Guard Auxiliary for their courtesy examination decal, a paddle or pair of oars should be on all outboard boats. They could be the only way of reaching safety in the event of motor failure. Most outboard craft row or paddle quite clumsily and with considerable effort, but it can be done, and the means to do so should be on board.

Anchor and line

Every outboard should be equipped with a suitable anchor and line adequate in length for anchoring in es-

FIG. 2824 Regardless of the normal dependability of the outboard motor, small boats should be equipped with a paddle or two, or a pair of oars for emergency use. Some craft can be propelled manually more easily than others, but all can be so worked to safety, even tho slowly.

FIG. 2825 Every boat should carry at least one anchor and line of sufficient length for the waters cruised. The anchor may be used in a variety of situations, see text, and is essential in case of engine failure.

FIG. 2826 A scoop or hand bailer of some sort is a very desirable back-up to the pump or other means of removing rain and spray from the boat. These may be purchased inexpensively or home made easily. A large sponge is frequently useful for getting that last little bit of water out of the boat.

FIG. 2827 Every boat, even the smallest, should be equipped with distress signalling equipment. This should include an orange flag and orange smoke signals for day use, plus red flares for nighttime emergencies. All these should be kept dry in a waterproof container.

sentially all areas in which the boat is used. Obviously, this requirement must be applied with reason when the craft is used off very deep coasts, but do err on the side of having too much rather than too little when you decide on the length of your anchor line.

Anchors may be used in their normal manner, or specially in the case of outboards, when the craft is beached or nearly so. If the boat is fully beached, the anchor may be carried up on shore to keep the craft from drifting away on a rising tide or from the wake of passing vessels. If it is not desired to quite fully beach, the anchor may be used to hold the boat away from the shore, pulling against a line made fast to some object on the land.

Bailer

All small boats should be equipped with a manual bailer. This can be a scoop purchased or home-made from a household plastic jug; see fig. 28-26. Transom drains are effective underway for many fast craft, but must have a means of closure when not in use. Manual or even electric pumps may be found on larger outboards. A large sponge is frequently convenient for getting that last little bit of water out of a small boat.

Distress signals

An outboard boat should be equipped with a distress signalling package consisting of several daytime orange

FIG. 2828 An electric lantern is an excellent item for any small boat whether or not operation after darkness is planned. If it will float, like the one shown that's an extra advantage for they do sometimes get dropped overboard.

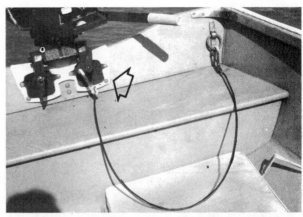

FIG. 2829 A safety chain or cable is an excellent item for smaller boats on which the outboard motor is installed and removed at various times. It will prevent loss if the clamps work loose; it should be fastened just as soon as it will reach, and remain fastened as long as possible as the motor is being detached.

smoke signals, several nighttime red flares, and an orange flag (sea dye marker is also advisable for boats that will operate off-shore). Even though nighttime use of the craft is not contemplated, you may find yourself stranded out on the water after dark, so carry red flares. Do *not*, however, consider such flares a substitute for the orange smoke signals, which are much more effective for use in daylight.

Flashlight or lantern

Every outboard craft should be equipped with a flashlight or electric lantern whether or not it is ever intended to use the boat after dark. This item should be waterproof and it is desirable that it float if accidentally dropped into the water. Extra batteries, stored in a waterproof container, will often prove valuable in an emergency. Batteries in the flashlight or lantern, and the spares, should be renewed at the start of each boating season regardless of their apparent condition.

OPERATIONAL EQUIPMENT

A magnetic compass is an item of equipment that cannot be placed solely in either the safety or operational category; it fits both! Almost all outboards in their various applications can make good use of a compass. Select one of adequate size and quality, and install it properly. See Chapters 13 and 14 for additional information.

As most outboards are relatively open craft, it is particularly important that the compass be kept shielded from the sun's direct rays. When not in use, place a cover over its top; this should be completely light-tight, colored plastic or cloth will not do an adequate job.

Charts

One or more charts should be carried covering the waters being used. Learn to use a chart with your compass, and do use it under favorable conditions even where such use is not strictly necessary. This practice is excellent training and will prepare you for use with confidence and efficiency should an emergeny arise. Make a point of keeping track at all times of where you are on a body of water.

Tools

Every boat, no matter how small, should carry at least a few simple hand tools. The minimum should be a screwdriver, pair of pliers, and an adjustable open-end wrench. Consideration might be given to having two or more screwdrivers and wrenches in different sizes.

Safety chain

Most outboard motors are clamped to the craft's transom (a few of the larger ones may be through bolted). To protect against accidental loss overboard should the clamps loosen with vibration, a short *safety chain* (or cable) is often used between a connecting point on the motor and a ring securely fastened to the hull of the boat. Chains or lengths of steel cable, frequently plastic-coated to reduce rusting, may be inexpensively purchased for this purpose already equipped with snap fittings at each end; this is "cheap insurance" against an accidental dunking of an expensive motor, or its possible total loss in deep water.

Extra fuel tanks

The very smallest outboard motors have an integral fuel tank, but those of three or more horsepower now normally operate from external tanks which are more convenient with their larger capacity. Larger rigs, boats of 18 feet or so in length with high horsepower motors, usually have built-in tanks.

It is often necessary to carry additional fuel in order to make long runs without stops. A skipper should carefully select any container or spare fuel tank; it must be made for that specific use. The material of the tank and its design must be satisfactory for containing gasoline in a marine (often salt water) environment. Homemade or converted tanks are very often hazardous.

Steering and other controls

The simplest outboard motors are directly controlled at the motor itself. A steering handle, or tiller, is used to turn the motor from side to side for steering the craft. A throttle to control motor speed may be incorporated into the tiller or may be a separate lever on the motor. A gear shift lever —for forward, neutral, and reverse—is located on the side of the motor. Controls for choking and carburetor jet adjustment are usually on the front of the motor.

In order to locate the skipper further forward than at the immediate stern next to the motor, *remote controls* are necessary. These are of two different kinds, a wheel for steering and a lever or levers for the throttle and gear shifting.

Steering controls may consist of a continuous loop of metallic cable (usually plastic covered) running from one side of the engine forward, around a drum on the shaft of the steering wheel, and back aft to the other side of the

FIG. 2830 The use of a steering wheel and remote motor controls will permit the operator of a small outboard boat to sit further forward. This improves the longitudinal trim and makes for safer operation.

motor. Pulleys are used to guide the cable, which may run forward on one side of the boat and aft on the other, or may run fore and aft on the same side. Another form of steering that gives excellent results is rod steering in which a stiff linkage is pushed back and forth in a protective sheath. Rack and pinion type of gearing at the steering wheel shaft imparts the push or pull which moves the motor from side to side around its central pivot. Rod steering gives smooth control and is free of the hazards of the exposed cables of the other type.

Hydraulic steering is feasible and quite good, but is rarely found on outboards. Likewise, automatic steering mechanisms, erroneously called "automatic pilots," are available for quite small boats, but are seldom found on outboards.

Throttle and gear shift controls also consist of a stiff cable within a sheath to transmit the back and forth motion required. With some equipment, the two controls are combined at the helm into a single lever which is pushed forward to go ahead faster and pulled backward, through a neutral center position, to go faster sternward. This mechanism is somewhat more complex than separate throttle and gear shift controls, and may give some troubles, but it does offer considerable operating convenience.

Tachometers

The need for an efficient propeller, and the importance of trials, have been mentioned above. The skipper must be able to measure engine rpm and boat speed; the former requires a *tachometer* and the latter is more easily done with a speedometer, both relatively inexpensive instruments.

An electronic tachometer can be fitted to essentially any outboard motor; it is a simple job requiring little technical know-how and only an hour or two of the skipper's time. This instrument, when properly calibrated, will indicate *motor* revolutions per minute and guide you in the selection of a propellor which will allow the motor to develop its full rated rpm and power.

Speedometers

Speed can be checked by timed runs over measured distances, but a *speedometer* for an outboard boat is such a simple device that one should be considered. Direct-reading speed indicating devices for smaller craft normally operate from the pressure of the water on a pickup head as the craft moves forward. This, too, can be easily installed by the average outboard owner. Accuracy may be only moderate, but it can be calibrated by timed runs over known distances; see page 390. Even if not accurate in absolute terms, it can be adequately used to determine the relative speeds obtained with various motor and propeller combinations. Calibration is, however, necessary if it is to be used in navigation.

Electronic depth sounders

Many outboard craft can carry an electronic depth sounder and put it to good use. Special transom mounts are available for smaller boats where through-hull mounting may not be practical. More on this very useful item of electronic equipment will be found in Chapter 25.

Radiotelephones

Radios—either VHF, marine-band, or CB—are often installed on outboards that have a battery for electric-starting motors and an alternator to keep the battery charged. VHF equipment, with its smaller antennas, is especially suitable for smaller boats. Care should be taken to intall equipment that is suitable for the craft and its intended operation; consult an expert (not just a salesman!) if you don't have the knowledge to make the choice yourself. In many applications, radios may fit into the "safety" rather than "operational" category; buy wisely. See also Chapter 25.

Boat covers

Many outboard boats have a cover of canvas or similar material. Some styles will cover the boat from the stem to and including the upper part of the motor; other designs will only cover the open parts of the craft. These are excellent for keeping rain and dirt out of the boat and will provide protection to any varnished or painted wood surfaces. Covers should, however, be used with caution as adequate ventilation of the interior of the boat is a *must* if mildew, "dry rot," and other forms of fungus growth are to be avoided; vents of proper design should be a part of the cover.

FIG. 2831 Outboard and inboard-outboard boats are especially suited for use on snorkeling or scuba-diving expeditions. Their shoal draft and the tiltability of the lower unit make them desirable for in-shore or over-reef work.

The cover must fit the boat it is used with, and must be capable of being adequately secured by means of snaps or a drawstring. (Snaps or other mechanical fasteners should be protected from corrosion by a non-staining lubricant; a silicone grease stick is excellent for this purpose.) Covers are of perhaps their greatest value when a boat is being trailered, but they must be fastened down adequately to prevent wind damage. In outdoor storage, a cover must also be adequately supported internally to prevent the formation of pools of rain water that will stretch and eventually tear the cover, dumping the water into the boat.

REGISTRATION AND NUMBERING

Boats are subject to the registration requirements of their "state of principal use" or the Coast Guard; see Chapter 2. Effective in 1974, the previous exemption from registration and numbering for boats with motors of less than 10 hp (or lesser specified horsepower in some states) was removed by the Federal Boat Safety Act of 1971. Now all "mechanically propelled" boats must be numbered if they are not documented. Additionally, some states have extended registration to cover "all watercraft," or "sailboats over 16 feet in length," or other categories of boats.

Operation

As noted earlier in connection with considerations of selecting the boat, an outboard rig can be used for many, widely varied purposes—fishing, water skiing, cruising, skin diving, and others. In each of these applications, greater safety and enjoyment will result from knowing and using the proper boating practices.

Boarding

Before a boat can be used, one must get on board it. There is a right and a wrong way—perhaps several wrong ways—and the difference becomes increasingly important as the size of the boat decreases.

If you are boarding from a beach, climb in over the bow when practicable. When boarding from a float or low pier, step aboard as nearly amidships, both from side to side and stem to stern, as possible. Bend your body so that your weight is kept low, thus helping to keep the boat stable. Grasp the gunwale (the top of the boat's sides) for balance. In a small outboard, do not step on the gunwale or you will most likely flip the craft.

Do not carry bulky or heavy items of gear or supplies while boarding. If you are alone, place these items on the pier where you can reach them once you are safely aboard; or have someone ashore hand them to you.

MOTOR ADJUSTMENT

Begin your outboarding by installing the motor properly —the manufacturer's diagrams will help in doing this. Basically, the task is to seat the motor squarely on the center of the transom and securely tighten the bracket screws. Some motors come with special mounting plates; with others you may desire to use a rubber pad to reduce vibrations and prevent the transom from being marred. The safety chain mentioned above as desirable equipment should be connected between the motor and the hull.

If twin motors are to be used, they should be mounted with the proper spacing between them. The AB&YC rec-

FIG. 2832 Although the wide beam of a cathedral-hull craft gives it considerable lateral stability, a safer way to get aboard is with both hands free. Large or heavy objects should be left on the pier until you are safely aboard; then reach back for them, or have someone hand them to you.

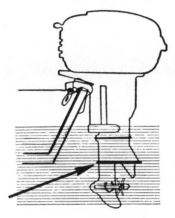

FIG. 2833 The proper relationship between the motor and the boat's hull is very important. The anti-cavigation plate should be in line with the bottom of the hull at the stern for a proper flow of water to the propellor.

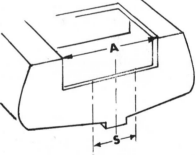

FIG. 2834 The AB&YC recommended dimensions for the sketch above are: "A" 33 inches for single motors, 54 inches for twins of less than 61hp each, and 60 inches for twins of 61 or more horsepower. The centerline spacing —"S"—should be 22 inches for under 61hp and 26 inches for larger motors.

ommended center-to-center separation is 22 inches for motors under 61 hp and 26 inches for larger motors. Standardized motor well dimensions are recommended to manufacturers which will allow this spacing.

If a combination of a large and small motor is used, the large unit is mounted on the craft's centerline, with the small "kicker" off to one side, usually on a bracket designed for such use. (Such brackets allow the small motor to be raised entirely clear of the water to reduce drag when it is not in use, yet keep it out of the boat.) The low horsepower of the small motor will prevent any significant steering problems from its off-center placement.

Motor height

Although there has been a high degree of standardization in the design of transom cut-outs for motor mounting, it is wise to check that the lower unit is correctly located with respect to the bottom of the hull. Motors are made in different shaft lengths, 15 and 20 inches are common, and modifications can be made if necessary at the transom to ensure proper motor positioning. The *anti-cavitation plate* on the lower unit should line up with the transom chine; see fig. 2833. If the motor is too high, a smooth flow of water will not reach the propellor and it will not be able to get a proper "grip" on the water. This may cause *cavitation* with definitely less efficient boat operation and possible damage to the propeller or motor through excessive rpm. If the motor is too low, drag will be increased due both to the greater area of the lower unit in the water and a distorted flow over and under the anti-cavitation plate. Attention to this detail of installation will provide both increased speed and decreased fuel consumption.

Thrust line adjustment

Most outboard motors have a tilt adjustment to vary the angle of thrust of the unit. For best performance, the drive of the propeller should be in a line parallel to the flat surface of the water at the boat's most efficient operating angle whether as a planing hull or in the displacement mode.

If the motor is too close in to the transom, the thrust line is upward from horizontal, pushing the stern up and the bow down making the boat "plow" through the water unnecessarily. On the other hand, if the motor is tilted too far out from the transom, the thrust line is below the horizontal and the bow is forced up to ride high while the stern "squats"; see fig. 28-35.

Boats differ in design, and loading conditions vary widely with any specific craft, so manufacturers make the adjustment of the tilt angle as easy as possible. On inboard-outboards and some larger outboard motors, there is an electric or electro-hydraulic drive for powered adjustment of the tilt angle; just push the button for "up" or "down."

The wise skipper is aware of the inefficiency of an improper thrust angle and does not neglect to change the tilt adjustment to meet his current operating conditions.

The "best" tilt angle may vary with water conditions. On some craft, an adjustment with the motor a bit more out (bow up) for smooth water may give more speed, but this should be checked for your individual craft. A bit more in (bow down) may give a more "solid" ride in choppy waters, but again only actual trials will tell for sure.

FIG. 2836 Many hulls can be had in nearly identical form as either outboards or inboard-outboards. The prospective skipper should consider carefully the advantages and disadvantages of both these types of propulsion.

Special applications of tilt

While underway, the tilt feature of outboard motors and I-O lower units can be used to advantage for several special situations.

If the propellor becomes fouled with weeds, it is often easy to stop the motor, tilt it up, clear off the vegetation, lower the motor, restart it, and continue on your course. If a smaller motor shears its pin, this can frequently be replaced by tilting the motor and working on it in this position, rather than having to remove the whole unit and bring it into the boat.

It may be possible to partially tilt the motor or I-O lower unit so as to reduce the draft of the craft and get over shoal areas. Do this with caution, however; take care not to tilt so much that the cooling water intake comes above the surface, and watch out that the propellor does not strike rocks or other hard objects that might damage it; proceed slowly when using this technique.

Mixture controls

Many outboard motors will have controls for adjusting the fuel-air mixture ratios to obtain optimum performance at low and/high motor speeds. These are external to the motor cover so that they may be easily adjusted underway; see fig. 28-37. Follow the manufacturer's instructions con-

MOTOR ANGLE ADJUSTMENT

FIG. 2835   It is most important for efficient operation of an outboard motor that its thrust be horizontal when the boat is in running trim. Motors are easily adjusted to secure the proper thrust line. Adjustment on smaller motors is made by moving pin (1) to different notches.

INCORRECT
CAUSES BOAT TO "PLOW"

INCORRECT
CAUSES BOAT TO "SQUAT"

CORRECT
GIVES MAXIMUM PERFORMANCE

tained in the manual for the model being used in order to obtain the best results and to minimize the possibility of any damage to the motor from incorrect settings. Smaller motors will have adjustments for both low and high speed operation; medium size and larger motors will normally have only one adjustment, that for low rpm use, the high-speed carburetor jet being fixed.

Changes in fuel, air temperature, and altitude (such as going to mountain lakes from lower elevations or sea level, and vice versa) may require changes in mixture controls. Any adjustment should be made with the motor thoroughly warmed up and the boat loaded to its normal trim.

Essentially all motors will have a manual choke for use when starting.

FUELS AND OILS

Two-cycle outboard motors use a mixture of gasoline and lubricating oil. It is essential that both of these be of the correct type and that the mixture ratio be as specified by the manufacturer of the motor.

Fuels

The drive for a cleaner environment has resulted in the introduction of many gasolines in the "no-lead" and "low-lead" categories. In many of these, other chemicals have been added to maintain the octane rating and other desirable characteristics. These newer fuels have in numerous cases proven to be unsatisfactory, or even unsafe, in marine engines, especially in two-cycle outboard motors.

Automobile engines operate in circumstances of frequently changing speeds and loads. City driving is stop and go; highway driving has its up and down grades, or acceleration to pass another vehicle. On the other hand, marine use frequently involves sustained periods of heavy load at unvarying rpm. The differences in these two sets of operating conditions are significant to engines and their fuels.

Outboard motors are generally of relatively low compression ratios and can use fuels of quite modest octane rating. "Old fashioned" marine white gasoline (which is lead-free, but without the newer replacement additives) is satisfactory; regular leaded automotive fuel is also satisfactory. Do *not* use the modern *no-lead* car gasolines unless you have been advised by a responsible representative of the motor manufacturer that a specific fuel of this type is satisfactory for an outboard motor of your model and year; some low-lead gasolines may be used with adjustment of the ignition timing, but again seek *reliable* advice rather than risk extensive internal damage to your motor.

Oils

The typical outboard motor uses its lubricating oil mixed into the gasoline fuel supply; there is no separate crankcase for oil as there is in automotive and marine four-cycle engines. Thus special properties (low "ash" for example) are required of outboard oil, and many "normal" features such as detergents must be limited or avoided.

The best oil to use in a two-cycle motor is oil that is specifically made and sold for that purpose by oil companies or engine manufacturers. This is SAE-30 or 40 weight oil that burns cleanly and has no harmful compounds. It is not necessary to use oil bearing the label of the motor manufacturer—they don't make it, although presumably they do set the specifications for it—but such

FIG. 2837 Outboard motors will have one or more carburetor controls brought out to the front of the motor case for easy adjustment during use. Follow the manufacturer's instructions in the manual.

Pints of Oil per Gal. of Gas	GASOLINE TO OIL RATIO TABLE					
		Pints when applied to				
	ACTUAL RATIO	2 Gal	3 Gal	4 Gal	5 Gal	6 Gal
1/12	96:1	1/6	1/4	1/3	5/12	1/2
1/6	48:1	1/3	1/2	2/3	5/6	1
1/5	40:1	2/5	3/5	4/5	1	1-1/5
1/3	24:1	2/3	1	1-1/3	1-2/3	2
3/8	21:1	3/4	1-1/8	1-1/2	1-7/8	2-1/4
1/2	16:1	1	1-1/2	2	2-1/2	3
3/4	11:1	1-1/2	2-1/4	3	3-3/4	4-1/2

TABLE 28-4 This table shows the correct amount of oil to be used for different fuel-oil ratios and for various amounts of gasoline. Pints can be translated to ounces by multiplying by 16. Oil containers are frequently marked in fractions of a pint and in ounces.

usage is an easy and sure way of ensuring compatibility between oil and motor.

If in an emergency, "two-cycle oil" cannot be obtained, use the least expensive grade of automotive oil (it is less likely to have additives!) in #30 weight, *not lighter.*

Oil-fuel mixture ratios

The outboard motor manufacturers specify the correct ratio of gasoline to oil for each of their motors. In past years the ratio was often 24 to 1, but technological advances have now moved this to 50 to 1 for most motors of U.S. manufacture. The amount of oil is frequently translated somewhat roughly to ounces or fractions of a pint per gallon of gasoline for partial tank fillings or for tanks of non-standard size.

"Pre-mix"

Many marinas now have special pumps dispensing a mixture of gasoline and oil. In some instances, the mixture is fixed, usually 50 to 1; at other pumps, controls can be set to deliver a mixture at any one of several standard ratios.

Fueling Procedures

There are two aspects of fueling an outboard that must be given careful consideration—safety and the proper mixing of the oil and gasoline. First of all, extinguish all flames and tell everyone nearby that there will be no smoking. Get all persons off the boat who are not participating in the fueling.

Fueling portable tanks

It is wise to remove portable fuel tanks from the boat whenever possible and take them ashore to be filled. Make

FIG. 2838 As a safety measure, portable tanks should be removed from a boat and filled on the pier. After filling, they should be wiped clean and dry before being put back on board.

sure that the gas pump hose nozzle is in contact with the rim of the tank fill opening to prevent the generation of a spark of static electricity which might cause an explosion.

Oil properly mixed with gasoline will *not* separate later, but the initial mixing procedure requires careful attention; follow these steps for a three or six gallon tank:

(1) Put in approximately one gallon of gasoline.

(2) Pour in *all* the oil that is to be added.

(3) Replace the cap on the tank and shake *vigorously* —you can't shake it up too much!

(4)   Remove the filler cap, add the balance of the gasoline without delay, and replace the cap. It wouldn't hurt to shake the tank some more, but a full tank is much heavier and cannot be shaken as vigorously as one with only a gallon in it.

(5) Wipe off the outside of the tank, and return it to the boat (if it has been removed for filling) *after* any odor of fumes has disappeared.

For the sake of safety, portable fuel tanks should be secured in the craft. A simple way is to provide wooden blocks on the hull or floor-boards to prevent sideways or endways movement of the tank, with a strap or straps over the top of the tank to hold it down in rough going.

Fueling larger tanks

If your outboard carries fuel tanks which would be impractical to remove for fueling—anything larger than a six-gallon tank would probably be so considered—or permanently installed fuel tanks, your fueling procedures will closely resemble those for inboards; see pages 205-206. Before taking on fuel, close all doors, hatches, windows, etc., to keep any gasoline vapors from getting below. After fueling, open them all and allow time for ventilation to clear these areas before starting the engine.

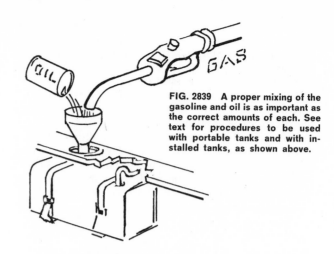

FIG. 2839   A proper mixing of the gasoline and oil is as important as the correct amounts of each. See text for procedures to be used with portable tanks and with installed tanks, as shown above.

The mixing of gasoline and oil for larger tanks that cannot be shaken up can be done in several ways—all of which are time-consuming but *very* important, even more so than getting the exact fuel-oil mixture ratio.

One method is to use a metal funnel that has a screen filter (metal so that a grounding connection can be made from hose nozzle to tank). This funnel is inserted in the tank or fill pipe and as gasoline flows thru it, oil is added at the same time, apportioning the oil flow rate and allowing the stream of gasoline to blend thoroughly with the oil.

A second method is to mix the fuel and oil in batches in a separate five- or six-gallon tank using the same procedures as for portable tanks described above. The mixed fuel is then poured into the larger tank. On tanks *not* larger than about 15 gallons, it is permissible to mix the total amount of oil in one five- or six-gallon tank of gasoline, pouring the mixture into the larger tank, and then adding the remainder of the gasoline directly. Do *not*, as should now be clear, pour oil directly into the tank—it will not mix properly!

Check the fuel system now for leakage. Carefully wipe up any spillage (discard the rag, don't stow it in the boat), and hose down with fresh water if possible. Remember to thoroughly ventilate the boat before starting the motor; there is a hazard of an explosion even though the outboard with its motor external to the hull is safer in this respect than an inboard. It is essential that you be alert for gasoline vapors which are heavier than air and can sink into the lower parts of the hull just waiting for a spark or flame. A power bilge blower may be a wise investment, especially on an outboard cruiser.

BOAT HANDLING

The general principles of boat handling are covered in Chapter 8. The important difference with respect to outboards (and inboard-outboards) is that they steer with a directed thrust of the propellor rather than by the flow of water past a rudder. This makes for easier and more positive steering in many situations, but it has a distinctly different "feel" and one must become accustomed to it if one is experienced in handling inboards. The reaction of the boat to a turning of the motor thrust line will be different at slow speeds and at planing speeds; it will vary with hulls of different design and with motors of widely different horsepower ratings. A wise skipper will handle an unfamiliar craft with considerable respect until he understands its reactions to his actions at the wheel and throttle.

FIG. 2840 Proper trim is important. In illustration above, boat lists heavily to port. Weight should be distributed to keep on even keel, as shown below.

Trim

The number of seats in a boat is *no* indication of the number of persons she can carry safely. Overloading is a major cause of boating accidents—stay within the limits of your craft. The factors affecting trim become ever more critical as the load approaches the capacity, and as the boat's size decreases.

Have all weight evenly distributed so that the boat will trim properly—level from side to side and slightly down at the stern, never down at the bow. Passengers should be seated toward the centerline of the craft and not hanging over the sides; not too many forward or aft. It the load is concentrated near the bow or stern, the boat will plow or drag needlessly, reducing your safety margin and increasing your fuel consumption. Proper trim is essential to proper performance.

Trim your boat as well as possible *before* getting underway. In smaller craft, it is dangerous for passengers to attempt to change places or move about while she is scooting along briskly. If such movement becomes essential, slow or stop the boat first, remembering in rough weather to keep enough momentum to retain steerage control and to keep the craft headed into wind and waves. Have the person who must move keep low and near the boat's centerline.

FIG. 2842 An outboard boat—and an inboard-outboard, too—steer by changing the direction of thrust of the lower unit of the motor.
This gives positive, effective control, but one must practice to get the "feel" of it.

Stability

Outboard craft are often operated at relatively high speeds and their stability becomes a matter of safety. Some hulls will run straight ahead quite steadily, but have a tendency to heel excessively, or even "flip over," when turned sharply.

The presence of an external keel, and its relative size has a major effect on the directional stability of a small boat. Smaller, faster craft have little need for much keel; larger, cruiser-type hulls which are slower will have a more pronounced keel. Greater directional stability naturally resists turning; attempting to make a sharp turn at too high a speed for the amount of keel carried may result in its broaching, flipping over sidewards. Conversely, a boat with little or no keel or skeg has little directional stability and may skid out sideways when a turn is attempted at excessive speed—initially the boat will point off in the new direction but actually continue to travel along essentially its old course.

FIG. 2843 An anti-tilt latch is found on most outboard motors. It prevents the lower unit from flipping up when the motor is put in reverse gear, but should be released while running forward normally so that the motor can tilt up if a submerged obstruction or shoal water is encountered.

INCORRECT

*OVERLOAD FORWARD
CAUSES BOAT TO "PLOW"*

INCORRECT

*OVERLOAD AFT
CAUSES BOAT TO "SQUAT"*

CORRECT

*BALANCED LOAD
GIVES MAXIMUM PERFORMANCE*

FIG. 2841 Fore-and-aft trim is also important for a comfortable ride and the most efficient operation.

FIG. 2844 The bow of a fast-moving outboard is not the safest place to ride! Never let an adult or small child ride with his or her feet dangling over the side—one slip and it's into the propellor!

The faster a boat goes, the less keel it requires, and the more important it is to reduce speed to a safe value before starting a turn; never turn more sharply than necessary; normal operation seldom requires a sudden, sharp, high-speed turn.

Reversing

Most outboard motors have a reverse gear that enables the boat to be backed. (Very small motors usually do not have such gears, but can be pivoted around 180° to give thrust in the opposite direction.) Unless restrained, an outboard motor has the tendency to tilt itself up and out of the water when the thrust is reversed. On many models, there is a manually-operated *reverse lock* that must be latched into place to keep the motor down while engaged in backing maneuvers. For normal running, however, it is important that this latch be released so that the lower unit will be free to tilt up if it strikes an underwater obstruction.

On some larger motors, especially those with electric shifting, anti-tilt latch operation is automatically interlocked with reverse operation.

SAFE OPERATION

Exercise your knowledge of the Rules of the Road, but also exercise good judgment, whether you have the right-of-way or not. Small craft should stand clear as far as possible from large yachts and commercial vessels. Watch their wakes carefully. Dont count on ships to look out for you; they need more, much more, room to stop, are more difficult to turn, and sometimes have "blind spots"—areas which are blocked to the helmsman's vision. Never assume that the pilot of a vessel sees you; keep well clear.

Stand clear of hazards

Should you come upon a tow in the bend of a river, or one maneuvering near shore, note whether the tow is swinging to starboard or port, and give it the room it needs.

You should not bring your boat near a moored vessel. If circumstances make this necessary, be exceedingly wary. Strong river currents moving under a moored barge can pull a small craft beneath the surface. A cross current—a current that is running at or about a right angle to your course—requires great caution. If you get into such a situation, give any object, floating free or made fast, an extra wide berth.

No one on the bow

It is extremely dangerous for anyone, especially children, to ride on the bow of a small boat with their legs dangling over the side. If one slipped off, it is very likely that he would be run over by the boat before the skipper could take any action—and a propellor easily makes hamburger of a human body, often with fatal or crippling results.

Watch the weather

Keep your mind on your course and boat handling, but keep an eye on the weather even of the morning forecast was for fair skies and gentle breezes. Weather is important to all boatmen, but especially so for the outboarder with his smaller craft. Learn to recognize threatening cloud formations. Train yourself to be sensitive to shifts in wind directions; a shift in the wind often is advance notice of a coming change in the weather. Know and observe official warnings.

Leave word behind

If you are going offshore or for a relatively long run on inland waters, or even just fishing some distance away from home, make someone ashore familiar with your plans in as much detail as possible. Should trouble develop, the Coast Guard will render all assistance possible on water where they operate; the more that they can be told of your plans, the more help they can be.

To help the Coast Guard assist you, the following steps are recommended:

(1) Let someone know your plans for the day, including destination or time of return, planned stops enroute, and similar details; provide a *good* description of the craft.

(2) Never use "Mayday" on the radiotelephone unless there is a great danger and immediate assistance is required; don't use it for such a situation as running out of fuel.

Distress-signals

Every outboard skipper should know the standard distress signals, see pages 87-88, and carry one or more types of emergency signalling equipment. These must be in good condition and ready for immediate use. If no distress

FIG. 2845 When you go out fishing, leave word behind where you intend to go and when you plan to return. Be sure, also, that someone on shore has a complete and accurate description of your craft, including motor.

equipment is on board, an outboard boatman in need of help can always signal this fact by slowly and repeatedly raising and lowering his arms outstretched to each side while he stands in his craft (or from a kneeling position if rough water conditions would make standing hazardous).

Local knowledge

Whenever boating in unfamiliar waters, take advantage of "local knowledge"; watch the operation of boats piloted by skippers who are at home in these waters, and don't hesitate to ask questions about possible hazards.

A boat has no brakes!

Many persons who have not handled a small boat have the misconception that one can be maneuvered and stopped as easily as an automobile—'tain't so! But much can be done with a boat if one takes it slowly and easily. The new boat owner should practice the leaving from and returning to piers, and other maneuvers, until he has developed both skill and confidence; take it very cautiously and gently at first, and gradually build up to the procedures of experienced skippers.

Always slow down gradually rather than pulling the throttle back quickly. All boats have a stern wave that will catch up with and pass the craft if it comes to an abrupt stop. This can bring water into the boat, especially if it has a low-cut transom with no motor well.

Fuel consumption

An important aspect of outboarding safety is *not* running out of fuel! Each skipper should make tests and keep records to establish the rate of fuel consumption at various typically-used throttle settings (rpm as read on the tachometer). He should follow this up with a rough check on the number of hours run since last filling his tank. He should also know his fuel consumption on a per-mile basis to aid in planning cruises.

COURTEOUS OPERATION

Keep your boat's speed under control at all times—don't be a "show-off!" Respect the rights, and comforts, of others afloat; slow down not only when your craft is in danger, but also when it's a matter of courtesy to others. When passing other craft going in the same or opposite direction, give them a wide berth if possible, or drop

FIG. 2846 This 19-foot craft, with either outboard or I-O power, can provide overnight accommodations for two adults and a child; more could use sleeping bags in the cockpit. Cruising is quite feasible for weekends or other short trips.

FIG. 2847 Keep an eye on the weather! Don't let good fishing take all your attention; watch out for thunderstorms building up or line squalls approaching. Head for home or a safe harbor in ample time—come back another day to catch that "bigger" one.

down to a slow speed. When passing through or by an anchorage, throttle down to your slowest speed and keep an alert lookout for mooring, swimmers, debris, etc.

It is courteous to keep down your wake and wash so as to not cause damage to other boats. It's a wise action, too, for you are legally responsible for any damage to other boats or persons from the waves you leave behind you.

EMERGENCIES

Various studies have shown the following to be the major causes of boating accidents:

    (1) Overloading, overpowering, and improper trim.

    (2) High speed turns, especially in rough water.

    (3) Failure to keep a sharp lookout for obstructions.

    (4) Going out in bad weather (or not starting for home soon enough when good weather turns bad).

    (5) Standing in a moving boat.

    (6) Having too much weight too high in the boat, as when someone sits on the deck of a small outboard.

    (7) Leaks in the fuel system.

    (8) Going too far offshore.

Each of these factors, and others not listed here, can and should be avoided. A carefully matched boat, motor, and propellor, operated in accordance with the law and with courtesy will go a long way toward eliminating accidents and even distressing moments. But some possibility of troubles always remains; be prepared to act in emergency.

Squalls and storms

If your boat gets caught in a squall or heavy seas, slow down immediately, maintaining only enough power to head her into or at a slight angle to the wind and waves. Have everyone put on life preservers, including yourself. Don't try to smash your boat through the waves at high speed in an attempt to get home sooner—that's inviting disaster. Instead, take the seas as gently as possible on the bow. The hull may pound, and the waves may toss up a lot of spray, but you will have your best control over the craft. If you don't run this way, you might get caught broadside in a trough and possibly capsize.

Keep enough weight at the stern in stormy weather to hold the propellor in the water. Since an outboard has no rudder, if the propellor comes out, control is lost. Should the motor quit, rig some sort of sea anchor, see pages 165-166, to hold the bow up to the seas.

Don't let water accumulate in the boat. If rain, spray, or waves bring water into the bilges, pump or bail it out immediately. Water inside a boat must not be allowed to build up to an amount that could affect the trim and stability of the craft.

Whenever safely possible, of course, get to a protected harbor rather than attempt to ride out a storm. But don't let your desire for a harbor upset your judgment. Avoid a course that will put large waves on your stern; they can swamp the boat, although self-bailing motor wells reduce this hazard. There is risk, too, of "pitchpolling" (turning end over end) in a heavy following sea by being driven too fast before it.

If you must turn in a heavy sea, watch for a lull in the wave formation in which to do it so that you won't get caught broadside in a trough by an approaching wave. Always cross a large wave, or wake, at about a right angle; this lets you maintain the best control over your boat.

Capsizes

Stay with the boat if it capsizes! Almost invariably the temptation is to try to swim to shore if land is in sight, and almost always the shore is farther than it appears. Most outboard boats will remain afloat, even if filled with water; more and more are being designed so that they will not only float but will do so in an upright position. A boat is a much larger and more easily seen object than a person in the water; stay with the boat and you will receive help much more quickly than if you swim off on your own.

Rescuing a person in the water

One of the leading causes of death in boating accidents is drowning. Many of these fatalities result from people falling overboard. As the skipper of your craft, it is your responsibility to know how to rescue such a person. You

FIG. 2849 When anyone is in the water near an outboard or I-O craft, especially near its stern, the motor should be stopped, not just shifted into neutral. A boat's propeller can cause serious injuries—even fatal ones—to the human body. Be sure—stop that motor!

should practice the maneuvers necessary to accomplish this; a ring buoy or buoyant cushion can be used as the simulated victim. Practice enough so that you will be able to react instinctively and correctly; minutes saved may mean a life saved.

As soon as someone falls overboard, maneuver the boat's stern away from him. Shift into neutral immediately (kill the motor if you do not have a gearshift) and throw a buoyant cushion or life jacket near the victim—try to get it close, but don't try to hit him with it. Make sure that you are well clear of the person in the water before shifting into gear again.

Circle around quickly, selecting a course that will allow you to approach the person with the boat headed into the wind or waves. Approach him slowly, now, taking care to come alongside and not over him. Stop the motor before attempting to get the victim aboard.

When alongside, extend a paddle or boathook to him, or toss him one end of a line. *With the motor stopped,* lead him around to the stern, where the freeboard is the lowest, if there is enough space at the transom for him to get aboard without hurting himself on the motor. If it is not feasible, help the victim aboard over the side as far aft as possible. In either case, the use of a boarding ladder will be of help. To avoid a capsize while he is coming aboard, other passengers should shift their weight to the opposite side to maintain trim as much as possible. When helping a person aboard, hold him under the armpits and lift gently.

In case of an accident

If you are involved in a boating accident, you are required to stop and give whatever help you can without seriously endangering your boat or passengers. You must also identify yourself and your boat to any person injured or to the owner of any property damaged. See pages 36-37 for additional details.

If you see an accident without being a part of it, you may now render assistance without fear of liability. The Federal Boat Safety Act of 1971 contains a "good samaritan" section which provides that any person who renders assistance at the scene of a vessel accident will not be liable for civil damages from such action if he acts as a reasonably prudent man would have acted under the same circumstances.

FIG. 2848 Courteous boat operation is a mark of a knowledgable and safe skipper. Slow down when near other craft and yield to those that have the right of way.

FIG. 2850 A skipper who will take the time and trouble to learn can do much of his own motor maintenance work. He should have a copy of the manufacturer's service manual for the year and model of his unit.

Maintenance

Proper maintenance of an outboard rig pays off in many ways—increased safety, greater enjoyment through fewer breakdowns or other mechanical troubles, and increased pride in one's property as well as decreased depreciation. Careful attention to all aspects of maintenance, large and small, should be given to hull, motor, and equipment, and the trailer, too, if one is used.

HULL MAINTENANCE

The details of hull maintenance will, of course, depend upon the material of which it is made. Wood and metal are painted (a few aluminum craft are left bare), and fiberglass hulls are waxed. Whatever is required, do not neglect it, for the cost of materials and effort will be repaid well in beauty and resale value. On a wooden hull particularly, attention to the maintenance of paint and varnish will prevent deterioration of the structure itself. Pages 182-183 provide additional information on hull maintenance.

In any waters, but particularly salt, a boat should have a complete hosing down with fresh water after each use. Periodically, it should be washed down with soap or detergent rather than merely being hosed off.

Anti-fouling paints

In all but the cleanest of fresh waters, and in all salt water areas, a hull that is left afloat between periods of use will collect growth of marine grass, slime, and/or barnacles unless it is protected with *anti-fouling paint*, see pages 183-184.

Ventilation

Adequate ventilation of the interior of a boat is essential to a wooden hull, and is very advantageous for craft of other materials. Open drawers, side panels, etc., and let fresh air in when the boat is not in use. This will aid in the prevention of mildew and dry rot, and generally result in a "sweeter smelling" boat free of damp, musty odors.

MOTOR MAINTENANCE

The most important guide to outboard motor maintenance is the owner's manual furnished by the manufacturer. If you have lost yours, or bought a used motor without one, get a manual without delay; read it and carry out faithfully all its instructions. You will have greater reliability and lower repair bills.

The recommendations given above for hosing off and washing down the boat include the motor's exterior surfaces as well. Deposits of salt or pollution-laden water can quickly attack the unit's exterior finish. Although modern outboard motors are made of aluminum alloys that are designed to resist internal corrosion from salt water, an occasional flush-out with fresh water is desirable. Special fittings can be inexpensively purchased which clamp over the cooling water intake and allow the motor to be run "high and dry" with water being supplied through a hose from a nearby faucet.

On a boat that stays in the water between uses, the outboard motor (or I-O lower unit) should be tilted so that as much as possible of the lower unit—all of it if possible—is completely out of the water. This will lessen the possibility of any electrolytic action between the aluminum motor and dissimilar metals nearby, and will prevent the build-up of marine growth on the lower unit and propellor. Do not put a tight, airproof cover (a plastic bag is particularly bad) around the upper part of the motor; this will result in condensation and fast corrosion of metal parts. A loosely fitted cover to protect from dirt and rain is desirable, but ventilation should be provided.

Spark plugs

Much of the ignition system of an outboard motor should give no trouble if given normal care. Spark plugs, however, are "replaceable" items, ones that can be expected to "wear out" with use and require periodic replacement. A spare set should always be on board as that wear-out point just might come when least expected or convenient. The spare plugs should be in a sealed container to protect them from corrosion or breakage; plugs for marine use are normally sold in such packages.

Spark plugs for outboard motors are of a specific design for their application and the proper type should always be used. They come in various "heat" ranges and it is essential that the proper degree of heat be used for best results. Most motors are sold with a "normal heat" range set of plugs that will be satisfactory for average uses and loads. If the motor is to be lightly loaded (running cooler), a higher heat range ("hotter") plug may be desirable to prevent the build-up of deposits in the cylinders. If, on the other hand, the motor is to be heavily loaded (run hotter), a "colder" plug may be required. A plug type should be used that operates cleanly, without fouling at all engine speeds.

Spark plugs should be removed and replaced carefully lest the porcelain insulator be damaged; use a special spark plug wrench if possible. When installing or reinstalling a plug, the proper tightening is essential, too much can be as bad as too little. Unless specific instructions otherwise are furnished, install a plug finger tight and then give it one-half turn with a wrench, not more.

Used spark plugs can often provide a clue to any misoperation of the motor or incorrect selection of the plugs themselves. Specifics of diagnosis are beyond the scope of this book but will be found in specialized volumes.

FIG. 2851 Spark plugs are a vital part of an outboard motor. Two-cycle operation makes them susceptible to troubles. Take care to select the right type and heat range for your use; keep them cleaned and properly adjusted.

Fuel system

The most likely source of trouble with an outboard motor is the fuel system; here, too, the proper maintenance will forestall difficulties. The first precaution is to keep dirt and other foreign particles out of the fuel tank and lines; if in doubt as to the cleanliness of fuel, strain it through a funnel with a fine-screen filter. Secondly, fuel has a definite storage life and it is frequently more economical to discard old, unused fuel than to run the risk of gumming in the carburetor floats and jets.

In the event of apparent fuel starvation of an outboard motor when you know that your tank is not empty, first check the fuel filter on the motor. On most units, this is easily removed for inspection and cleaning.

Propellor

For smooth, vibration-free operation, the blades of a propellor must be free of distorting bends and major nicks and gouges on the edges; the propellor as a whole must have proper dynamic balance.

Minor nicks in blades can be filed smooth, at some risk of disturbing the balance of the propellor. More major damage will require the services of a properly outfitted shop. Often it is less expensive to replace an aluminum propellor than it is to repair it; bronze propellors are more "repairable."

FIG. 2852 Propellors should run without vibration. To do this, they must not have bent or warped blades, and each blade should be free of any major nicks or broken off pieces.

Motor overboard!

No, not "man overboard," but "motor overboard!" Despite the best of intentions and the availability of a safety chain, a motor sometimes does get dropped into the water, or perhaps the whole boat swamps and the motor gets dunked. Whatever the situation, prompt and correct "first aid" is essential.

Actually, less deterioration will occur underwater than when the motor is brought up and exposed to the air—so keep it down until you are fully prepared to take restorative actions. Ideally, once the motor is brought to the surface it should be again submerged in an oil bath; if this is not practicable, fresh water may be used to keep air from it until it can be rushed to a shop for disassembly, cleaning, and inspection. Don't attempt this work yourself unless you have done it before and have a maintenance manual.

EQUIPMENT MAINTENANCE

It is essential that all items of equipment aboard an outboard boat be given proper maintenance if they are going to have an economic life and be operable when needed. This is true of such simple items as buoyant cushions and such complex items as electronic depth sounders.

Basically, equipment needs to be kept clean and dry. If it is of the type that gets wet in use, it should periodically be washed off with fresh water to remove salt or other contaminants. Beyond these simple basics, details will be found in the manufacturer's instruction book on most pieces of equipment.

As an open outboard boat is more exposed to rain and spray than other craft, special attention should be given to electrical wiring and fittings such as the sockets for navigation and other lights. Movable mechanical parts, such as steering mechanisms and other control cables, should be kept lightly greased or protected by a spray-on coating. Batteries should be kept charged and the water level in the cells checked at least monthly.

FIG. 2853 Houseboats are frequently powered by inboard-outboard units, and sometimes by outboard motors. The same advantages and disadvantages of such types of propulsion apply to these craft as they do for runabouts and small cruisers.

Boat Trailering

CHAPTER 29

FIG. 2900   The addition of a trailer can greatly widen a boatman's scope of operation. His craft can be taken to nearby or far-distant bodies of water. With this added capability comes a need for further knowledge—the proper selection, use, and care of the trailer itself.

When an outboard boatman adds a trailer to his "rig" of hull and motor, or for his inboard-outboard craft, he adds a whole new dimension to his world of recreational boating. No longer is he confined to his local body of water—he can venture literally countless miles from his home port in search of new cruising areas or fishing grounds. Singly or in organized groups, the "trailer boatman" takes to the highway for day, week-end, or longer trips. Land journeys of hundreds of miles are not uncommon, and some skippers even travel thousands of miles for special boating adventures. Yet for others, trailering is merely a short haul from the local ramp to one's own backyard for storage and maintenance between uses on nearby waters. Trailering is whatever the skipper wants to make of it; the possibilities are limitless.

With this new dimension of boating comes a need for additional knowledge. When his craft is on the water, the trailer boatman is no different from any other skipper of a similar boat; but there is, however, a need for knowledge regarding the selection, use, and maintenance of his added major item of "equipment," the trailer itself. These matters are the concern of this chapter.

FIG. 2901   One advantage of trailer boating is that after use the craft can be taken home with the skipper for storage and minor maintenance. Frequently, it can be worked on in evening hours during the week, thus saving weekends for on-the-water use.

What a trailer provides

A boat trailer performs multiple functions and offers many advantages—probably more than you would think of on a quick review. Although a trailer is basically a means of transporting a boat across land distances, it also serves as the boat's "storage slip" when it is not in use, and its servicing "dry dock" when work is needed.

The "storage" aspects of boat trailering can be important. There is no need to pay rent for a slip at a marina (if you can find one, as space is steadily becoming more difficult to obtain in many boating areas). Many localities have free public ramps for launching, but even if a ramp or hoist fee must be paid for each use, these rarely approach the costs of regular slip rental. Dry storage on a trailer has a further advantage in that it eliminates the problems of fouling on the bottom of the hull—annual or semi-annual repainting is not required, nor is boat performance degraded as fouling accumulates between paintings. In coastal areas, there is the further advantage that often the boat will spend its non-working days in an environment much freer of salt air and spray, thus reducing inevitable corrosion and deterioration.

The secondary function of a trailer as a "dry dock" or "marine railway" can be very useful and money-saving. The craft and motor can be taken to the service facility, which always results in a smaller bill than if the repairmen has to come to the craft. Work gets done faster and better if the boat is at the shop, even though that may be only a short distance from the marina slip. Then, too, much work on small craft is often done by the skipper, with perhaps the aid of his family "crew." Consider the time saved if the boat is home in the driveway or backyard, as compared with being miles away at a marina; work can often be done on week days after work or dinner, rather than having to be put off until the weekend. Home workshop, tools, and other facilities can be used, and a boat in a stable position on shore is a more "workable" object than one that may bounce around in the water at its marina slip. Many items of work on the hull and external drive parts can only be

571

FIG. 2902 A trailer is of little use without a vehicle to pull it. The car-trailer combination must be considered as a whole, and each unit must match the other for safe and trouble-free operation.

done by an owner if he has his boat high and dry on his own property; financial savings can be significant.

The Car-Trailer Combination

An item essential for trailer boating that is often overlooked is the automobile that will pull the rig. As boats, and their trailers, get larger and heavier, just any car won't do. If you are considering pulling a new boat trailer with your present car, or if you have a rig now and are planning the purchase of a new car, it would be advisable to discuss the project with a knowledgable and responsible representative of the car dealer, or perhaps with several such persons.

It is quite possible that your present car, or a new one, will require modifications in order to be a trouble-free "tractor" for your boat trailer. These are discussed later in this chapter.

Trailer Selection and Equipping

As noted above, a trailer serves several functions, transportation and storage being the principal ones. The use to which it will be put will influence the selection of the trailer to be bought. If the trailer is to be used for short local hauls and home storage only, money can be saved by purchasing a light-duty unit. If, on the other hand, long, cross-country, high-speed trips are in the offing, the greater cost of a heavy-duty trailer is necessary to avoid time-consuming troubles and added expenses later.

Trailers, like boats and motors, come in many varieties. They are variously equipped with electric winches, adjustable keel rollers, finger-tip controls for loading and launching, etc. Your problem is to get the right combination, the right trailer for your boat and motor, and your type of trailering. There are many makes and models to choose from—take time to select wisely.

ADEQUACY

The trailer for your boat must be adequate in both weight-carrying capacity and length. Under-buy in either of these aspects and your craft will ultimately suffer.

You must have a trailer able to carry the weight of your boat, motor(s), *and the gear stowed in the boat.* This last factor is all-too-often overlooked in making calculations of

required trailer capacity. Having figured the total weight, check the prospective trailer's capacity, usually found on a plate affixed to the frame. If the load to be carried is within 100 pounds of the trailer's stated capacity, buy the *next larger* model. Don't underestimate; if possible, actually check the weight of the hull as some boat manufacturers seem to list the weight of their craft a bit on the light side. Make a detailed list of each item you plan to carry in the boat and its weight, and be sure to include a generous allowance for "miscellaneous"! It is wise to over-allow somewhat as experience always results in items being added to the equipment list, with few deletions. When all is done, it is advisable to get actual weight measurements on a truck scale; first the empty trailer and then the boat and trailer, preferably once without any gear, and finally with full load of items normally carried. You may be surprised at the final gross weight!

Length

The length of a trailer is critical as it is absolutely essential that the stern area, and especially the transom, be adequately supported. It must be possible to so position the boat on the trailer bed that the transom is *directly* over the aftermost supports; see fig. 2905. If there is *any* overhang, the hull will be distorted; this is true for outdrive craft, but it is particularly important for hulls with outboard motors which put their full weight on the transom.

There must not be a "sag" in the hull, or a "hook" (in the stern, from too short a trailer). Such things may change the shape of your boat permanently, affecting your speed in the water and the general handling characteristics of the craft.

Supports

A boat's natural environment is the water. Here the hull is uniformly supported and there are no concentrations of pressure on the hull. A trailer, like any dry-land cradle, is an unnatural place for a boat, so you must baby the craft all you can. Make the trailer bed as "comfortable" as possible. See that it fits the contours of the hull (special trailers are made for the modified catamaran or "cathedral" hull). Plenty of padding and bracing may be needed. Treat the boat right on the trailer and you'll get the sought-for results in the water.

Supports may take the form of rollers or of padded bars or stringers, or a combination of some of each. Each type has its advantages and disadvantages; the way that the boat will normally be launched and loaded must be considered.

Rollers of hard rubber are widely used on trailers that tilt and allow the craft to move backward into the water by gravity. Their disadvantage is in the very nearly point con-

FIG. 2903 Houseboats, too, can be trailered if their beam is not so great as to violate state highway restrictions. Their greater weight will require a multiple-axle trailer.

tact with the keel and the consequent high pressure on the hull there. The more rollers there are, the better the load is shared, *provided* that the height of each is adjusted properly; the depth of the indentation into the roller by the keel is a rough guide as to the weight being carried at that point.

Padded bar rests provide the maximum area in contact with the hull, and thus the minimum of point contact pressure. These are excellent for boats that normally are lifted from the trailer, as by slings from a crane. They have considerable surface friction, however, and are generally unsuitable for use where the boat must slide back from the trailer into the water unless special features are provided.

Some trailers of excellent design use a combination of these two forms of support. Rollers provide the basic support for the keel, and padded rests are levered into position to provide additional support for the transom after the craft has moved fully up the rollers and onto the trailer. The levering action allows the padded rests to be lowered out of contact with the hull just before launching so that their friction does not impede the movement of the hull under the force of gravity.

There should also be side supports to hold the boat firmly in position on the trailer and a bow chock into which the stem fits so as to prevent further forward movement of the craft on the trailer bed. All of these supports must be adjustable and so positioned that they carry out their intended function. The fore and aft location of the bow chock is especially critical as this is what ensures that the transom will be directly above its supports as it must be. This positioning of the boat on the trailer also directly affects the downward weight on the trailer tongue and coupling. Any unbalanced condition, once the hull is properly mated to the trailer bed, is properly corrected by shifting the location of the axle and wheels, *not* the bow chock.

SAFETY ASPECTS

Safety must be a primary consideration in the selection of a trailer—safety on one's investment in boat and motor, safety of personnel in its use, and the safety of other vehicles on the road. A few dollars more spent initially on the trailer may prevent much greater losses later.

Hitches and couplings

The American Boat & Yacht Council Safety Standard A-15 for boat trailers includes specifications for couplings (on the trailer) and hitches (on the car). These require a larger coupling ball for larger and heavier trailers. This may seem natural, but a Federal Highway Safety Standard proposed in 1970 to be effective in 1972 would *reverse* the size requirement sequence; smaller (but still adequately strong) balls would be used on heavy-duty hitches, with larger balls on light-duty hitches, in a series of five gross-weight classes. The reasoning behind this inverse size sequence is that if a heavy-duty trailer had a *small* coupling, it could not be mated with a light-duty hitch which would have too large a ball to fit. Thus a hitch could not be overloaded, either inadvertently or by deliberate intent of risk.

A hitch on the rear end of a car should be secured to the

FIG. 2904 Care must be exercised when trailering that an excess weight of gear is not placed in the boat. Items that are heavy or which have sharp edges and corners must be securely fastened down so that they will not shift about while on the road.

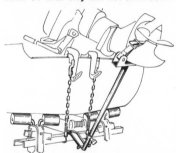

FIG. 2905 As the full weight of an outboard motor is carried on the transom of a boat, it is essential that there be adequate support directly under this portion of the hull. The supports must be there and the boat must be properly positioned with respect to them.

FIG. 2906 Hull supports in the form of rollers provide for the greatest ease in launching and reloading, but do not distribute the contact pressure over a wide area as do padded bar rests. Each type thus has its own advantages, and many trailers use a combination of the two.

vehicle's frame either with bolts (using lock washers) or by welding. A light-duty hitch attached to the rear bumper should *not* be used. For heavier loads, there are available "weight distributing" or "equalizing" hitches which mechanically apply leverage to both the trailer and the towing vehicle. When properly adjusted, such a hitch lessens the load on the rear of the car and permits it to operate in a

FIG. 2907 The winch line alone should not be depended upon for keeping the bow of the boat in place. A separate chock should be on the front of the trailer into which the bow fits snugly. A separate hold-down lashing—in addition to the winch line—is desirable for maximum security of the boat on the trailer.

more level attitude. These are more expensive, but are necessary for trailers of more than 3,500 pounds gross weight and are desirable for those in the 2,000 or 3,500 pound category.

Safety chains

A safety chain between the trailer and the towing car is a must, and the use of two is desirable. The size of the chain must be adequate for the trailer with which it is used; its minimum breaking strength should be 1½ times the maximum gross trailer weight and any connecting hooks and attaching hardware should be of equivalent strength.

Brakes

The type and design of brakes on a boat trailer are often a matter of state or local regulations, the requirements of which must be met. In general, brakes are necessary for rigs of 1,500 pounds or more gross weight. It may be well to have even better brakes than the minimum legal requirements as they could be a key factor in the safety of the rig, car, and persons.

Many trailers have hydraulic "surge" brakes which act automatically as the towing vehicle slows. Although such brakes act *after* the car's brakes, the time lag is so brief there is no tendency for the rig to "jackknife."

There are electric trailer brakes which act automatically

as the car's brakes are activated, and also electric brakes that are manually controlled by the driver.

Automatic brakes are desirable as the driver does not have to remember each time to apply them, but manually-controlled brakes provide more flexible operation.

An excellent feature, required in some jurisdictions for larger trailers, is a "breakaway" device which will automatically apply the trailer's brakes if that unit becomes detached from the towing car, as in the case of a hitch failure.

Tie-downs

As determined by its design, every trailered boat should be held firmly in place with tie-downs. Starting at the bow —the winch cable should not be solely depended upon to hold the boat onto the trailer and the bow down into its chock. There should be an additional tie-down of a lashing and turnbuckle. Moving aft—straps may be fitted across the hull to hold the craft firmly against the supports of the trailer and prevent any bouncing up and down on rough road surfaces. To further prevent such up and down movement, there should be separate lashings with turnbuckles at each side of the transom. If a trailer as purchased does not have adequate hold-down straps and fittings, these should be added before any extensive trip is made.

FIG. 2909 Winches are used to gain added pull to get the boat back onto its trailer. Both manual and electrical models are available with gear ratios as required by the weight of the boat and motor.

Wheels and tires

Tire failures on the road are one of the most prevalent and annoying troubles of boat trailering, and one of the least necessary. An understanding of the differences between car and trailer tires, and proper selection and maintenance, will virtually eliminate tire troubles.

Usually trailer wheels are smaller in diameter than those of the car with which it is used, and with smaller tires to match. The smaller diameter means both heavier loading and faster turning. For higher-speed, long-distance highway trailering, favor a larger wheel diameter over a smaller one, and select a tire capable of meeting the service you will expect of it.

Electrical system

A boat trailer's electrical system powers its lights—tail, stop, license plate, marker, and turn signal—and in many cases, a braking system also. Good quality components and careful installation are essential for safety and long trouble-free operation. Wires should be protected from mechanical abrasion, road splash, and other physical damage. It is important that there be a ground wire as a part of the electrical system between the trailer and the car; do not depend upon the trailer coupling and hitch to provide a "return

FIG. 2908 When being transported, a boat must be firmly held down into its trailer bed so that it cannot shift about or rise and fall independently. When in storage at rest, the tie-downs may be slacked off a bit to reduce any distorting strains on the hull.

path" for electrical currents. Connectors should be heavy-duty and waterproof.

Check carefully all state and local regulations regarding the number and placement of lights on a boat trailer of your size. Frequently, it is recommended that tail, stop, license plate, and turn signal lights be mounted high, either on the boat or on a bar placed across the boat's transom, but in some jurisdictions such a high and/or temporary location may not be legally acceptable.

Trailers will normally be sold equipped with several light reflectors. The Safety Standard for Boat Trailers issued by the American Boat & Yacht Council, see pages 192-193, calls for four amber and two red reflectors. Additional reflectors and/or reflector tape may be added as deemed necessary by the owner.

GENERAL FEATURES

There are a number of optional features for boat trailers, the selection of which will depend upon the craft and its owner.

Winch

A winch is used with all but the very smallest of trailered boats. Designs and capacity vary considerably; both manual and electrical models are available.

Two-speed manual winches have a low-speed, high mechanical advantage mode of operation for heavy pulls, with a faster operating mode for use once the pull becomes easier. Electrical winches are powered from the car's battery and the motor makes the work of loading a heavy boat onto a trailer more of a "push button" task than hard labor.

All winches should have a hand brake and an anti-reverse latch or lock for safety. The winch cable may be of synthetic line, but steel cable is frequently used. If you use

the latter, also buy a pair of heavy gloves as a steel winch cable must never be touched with bare hands.

The winch should be mounted on a stand that can be adjusted fore and aft to match the positioning of the boat on the trailer bed. Vertically, the winch cable should come off the top of the drum level with (or slightly above, but never below) the eye in the stem of the boat into which the hook connects; the winch should be capable of adjustment on its stand to meet this requirement.

Tilting bed trailers

Many trailer designs feature a bed or frame that is hinged so that it can tilt up for easier launching and reloading. With such a model, it will not be necessary to back the trailer into the water, an action to be avoided if at all possible.

Walkway

Many trailers have a narrow walkway down one side of the frame inside the wheels. This permits a person to get out *over* the water to attach the hook of the winch cable rather than to wade out and get wet feet. It is a simple feature and can often be added by the purchaser if one is not a part of the basic trailer.

Accessories

In addition to the basic features and options of boat trailers, there are accessories which will make trailering both safer and more enjoyable.

Parking wheel

Some trailers include a front parking wheel, and one can be added in most cases where it is not standard equipment. A parking wheel should be on an adjustable shaft so that the height of the tongue of the trailer from ground level can be varied. The wheel will aid in maneuvering the trailer when it is detached from the car and will make hitching up an easier and safer job. The height can also be adjusted to give the proper angle to the boat when it is parked for storage.

Jack and lug wrench

Every over-the-road boat trailer rig should include a jack for the trailer; most automobile jacks are useless if the trailer should have a flat tire. The jack need not be elaborate, many simple designs are available, but it must fit the situation.

FIG. 2910 Many trailers employ a hinged bed that may be tilted up to facilitate launching and reloading. This normally makes it unnecessary to run the trailer into the water more than a few inches.

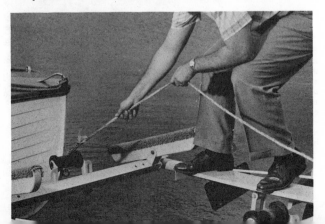

FIG. 2911 (Left) A walkway on a trailer is useful for attaching or releasing the winch line without getting one's feet wet. Such a walkway may go down either side of the trailer bed and should have a non-skid surface.

FIG. 2912 (Right) Every trailer should be equipped with a spare wheel and tire. Their availability will often prevent delays of hours or days if trouble is encountered on the road far from a source of repairs or replacement.

FIG. 2913 (Left) A small stand at the front end of the trailer will allow it to be parked in a level position. This is often equipped with a small wheel for greater maneuverability. The stand may or may not be adjustable, but must swing up to clear the road.

FIG. 2914 (Right) Many boats are of such beam that their width obstructs the driver's rearward vision unless special extended arms are used on the mirrors. These should be installed on both sides of the car for maximum rearward vision and safety.

As trailer wheels are generally smaller than those on automobiles, the size of the wheel lugs may be different. If the lug wrench for your car is not usable with your trailer wheels, be sure to purchase and carry one that will fit.

Spare wheel and tire

One of the best investments that a trailer boatman can make is a spare wheel and tire. Service for the smaller tire sizes usually used on trailers, or a replacement if one is ruined, is seldom available on a highway. The availability of your own spare might mean the saving of many hours, or even days, should trouble occur on a trip.

A related item for possible emergency replacement is a set of wheel bearings. These can cause trouble unexpectedly, and they, too, can be difficult to locate in out-of-the-way places.

Emergency signals

Every trailering rig should have highway flares, flags, reflectors, and similar equipment to set out if a flat tire, overheated bearing, or other trouble should cause an emergency stop along the shoulder of a road.

Wheel chocks

A pair of wheel chocks should be a part of every trailer rig; these are usually triangular in shape and made of wood. The chocks should be of a suitable size and shape for use with either the car's wheels (when launching or reloading) or the trailer's wheels (when parking on sloping ground).

Cover

Although a cover for the boat is not strictly an accessory for a trailer, it is a very desirable item in connection with road travel. One of these, properly fitted and secured for high-speed travel will keep dust and dirt, trash, rain, and other "undesirables" out of the boat when it is on the road. See Chapter 28 for further considerations regarding boat covers.

Insurance

Every trailer boatman should know *fully* the status of his insurance coverage when he is engaged in pulling a trailer with his car. It is quite possible that your policy allows for trailer operation, but it might not, or there might be limitations. Check your policy carefully and, if necessary, consult your insurance agent. If an endorsement is needed, don't delay or neglect to get it, even at the cost of a small additional premium—be protected, especially in your liability coverage.

CAR MODIFICATIONS

A car used with a trailer may require some modifications in the way of "beefing up" to give fully satisfactory performance. Rear springs and/or shock absorbers may have to be replaced with heavier duty units because of the added weight transferred from the tongue of the trailer. The turn signal flasher unit on many passenger cars is not satisfactory for the additional load of flashing the trailer's lights; a heavy duty unit can be quickly and easily substituted for the standard flasher.

Wide side mirrors

Driving with a boat trailer behind the car is not as easy as ordinary driving, especially when the craft is high and wide. A second external rear-view mirror on the right side of the car will make passing both safer and less nerve-straining. Where the boat is quite wide, consideration should be given to the installation of external mirrors specially designed to project out far enough to be effective, the type often seen on cars pulling house trailers.

Front bumper hitch

A hitch on the front end of a car is frequently useful in special launching situations. Where a ramp is slippery—such as at low water stages in tidal areas—or where the ramp is unsurfaced and soft, the use of a front hitch permits the car to be turned around so that the rear driving wheels will have better traction.

Other advantages of using a front hitch for launching or retrieving the boat include better maneuverability of the car-trailer combination in tight quarters, and the availability of the car's headlights for night illumination.

As the front hitch is used only for short distances and

FIG. 2915 A hitch on the front of the car can be very useful in some launching situations. As this hitch is used in only limited cases, a bumper mounting is acceptable rather than being secured to the frame as is necessary for rear, towing hitches.

FIG. 2916 When the load—boat, motor, gear, and trailer itself—gets too heavy to be shared between a single pair of tires, it is necessary to add a second axle and its pair of tires. For some of the heaviest loads, three axles are used.

special situations, a bumper-mounted hitch is acceptable, but heavy pulling strains should be avoided so as not to damage the car.

MULTIPLE-AXLE TRAILERS

As the length of a boat increases, so does its weight, and at an even greater rate. There is a definite upper limit to the weight-carrying capacity of trailer tires, and when the boat-plus-trailer gross weight exceeds the safe capacity of two tires, the only solution is the addition of another axle and pair of tires. Even with large tires such as 6.00-12 in a 6-ply rating, the gross weight limit for two is about 2500 pounds; more weight means more tires.

Characteristics

The general discussion of boat trailer features and characteristics mentioned above are applicable to trailers with two, or more, axles. These, because of their greater size and weight, more often will have electrical brakes, a front parking wheel, and weight-distributing hitches.

Trailering

Safety and freedom from troubles in boat trailering depends as much on proper preparations as on correct procedures while "underway" on the road. Preparations are not complicated or difficult, but even a single item overlooked can make for problems. It is an excellent idea to have a check list, *and to use it.* Such a list can be typed and then sealed in plastic; thus waterproofed, it can be attached to the trailer tongue where it cannot be overlooked in the hitching-up process. No standard check list can be given here; it is a matter of your own personalized list for your boat, trailer, and type of use.

GENERAL PREPARATIONS

Let's start properly with the "horse before the cart"—the car which pulls the trailer is, of course, a vital element in the trailering process. The vehicle should be in good mechanical condition and fully serviced prior to the trip; don't depend on stopping soon for fuel or water or other service once you're on your way.

Loading the Boat

The trailer, too, should have been lubricated and given any other service well ahead of the time for departure. All gear that is to be carried in the boat must be properly stowed. Soft and light items such as sleeping bags or cushions may be left loose, but heavy items or hard ones with sharp corners and projections, such as an anchor, must be secured firmly in place. If the motor is of the electric-starting type, the battery, although relatively small, is a particularly heavy item and must be firmly held in position, preferably in a fiberglass box.

Don't try to carry too much in a boat on a trailer, but don't overlook any essential items; use a checklist. Remember those items that you had aboard when you last checked your gross weight on those truck scales—don't let your gross weight creep up. Consider traveling with empty tanks and filling up with fuel and water at your destination—often 100 to 300 pounds, or even more, can be saved by this action as fuel weighs 6.6 pounds per gallon, and water is even heavier at 8.3 pounds per gallon.

Weight distribution

Consideration also must be given to the distribution of gear in the trailer, switching around light and heavy items to bring the trailer into proper balance. In extreme cases, such as with craft of unusual design, it may be necessary to relocate the axle and wheels with respect to the trailer frame to get a proper balance for the loaded trailer.

The optimum weight on the trailer coupling at the end of the tongue is approximately 7% of the gross weight, with any value between 5% and 10% being acceptable. For a larger boat-trailer combination of, say 3,000 pounds, this means 150 to 300 pounds at the coupling—here a parking wheel with screw-action adjustment is an obvious necessity.

For smaller, lighter rigs, the weight on the tongue can be estimated when it is picked up from the ground. A more accurate measurement, however, is desirable and can usually be easily made with the use of household bathroom scales. This method is really a necessity as tongue weights approach and exceed 100 pounds.

Effects of improper tongue weight

The most readily apparent condition of maldistribution of weight on the trailer is a too-heavy tongue. Here the rear of the car sags excessively, the hitch is in danger of striking the road surface on bumps, and the trailer follows poorly because of faulty balance.

Too-light a tongue weight also can cause highway problems as there may even be an *upward* thrust on the hitch as the car moves along. This, too, makes driving difficult as the trailer will tend to sway and whip from side to side.

Check your tongue weight carefully before starting out, but also observe how your trailer follows. It may be that your particular rig or hitch will ride better with a tongue load toward either the high or low side of the allowable range.

Preparing the boat

The outboard motor should be tilted up and secured firmly in that position. If no travel latch is provided, a block of wood can be inserted between the motor and the transom and the motor lashed down against it to keep it in place. The lower unit of an outdrive may be in either the down or tilted position as recommended by the manufacturer of the craft, but if tilted, it must be secured in that position.

Tops and covers

A folding canvas top should be in the down position; these are not made to take the wind speeds of highway travel—50 mph down a road will have the same effect as a gale wind of that velocity, or even more if moving into a natural head wind! Take down all flags; these, too, are not made to stand the whipping of such strong "winds."

The boat cover should be on and securely fastened so that the wind, and dust and dirt, will not get in under the edge. If the trip is to be made on dirt roads, a simple cover of canvas or plastic should be placed over the winch on the front of the trailer to keep out dirt and grit that might interfere with its smooth mechanical operation.

Securing the boat

All tie-downs must be correctly tightened—not too much, not too little. They should not be so tight as to compress or otherwise distort the hull, but they must be tight enough so that there is no relative movement between the boat and the trailer supports; all vertical motion should be as a single unit and absorbed by the springs of the trailer. Additional tie-downs, not needed for storage, may be added, especially at the bow and transom; the anti-reverse latch of the winch should be checked.

Tire Pressure

More trailering problems on the road develop from incorrect tire pressure than any other single cause. Trailer tires use higher pressures than regular passenger car tires, and the pressure used must be right for both the size of the tire and the load carried by it (gross weight less tongue weight, divided by the number of tires).

Trailer tires must not be overloaded; the "ply rating" of

FIG. 2917 When on the road trailering, a full boat cover will keep dirt, dust, and other undesirables out of the boat. The cover shown here protects from stem to stern, including the motor; other designs cover only the open areas of the hull.

the tire is an important factor to be considered in determining the maximum load capacity. Table 29-1 gives the tire load capacity for various size tires and inflations at highway speeds; the highest figure on each line is the maximum inflation pressure and load and *must not be exceeded*. Remember that these are "cold" pressures, readings taken before the trip is started. Tire pressures will increase during the trip due to heating, but do *not* bleed out air to reduce pressure as this is a normal change anticipated in the setting of the cold pressure.

Effects of incorrect inflation

Tires that are under-inflated tend to bulge at the area in contact with the ground. As the tire turns, this area changes with a resulting constant flexing of the sidewalls. This is an abnormal strain on the tire and will shorten its life, if actual failure doesn't occur on the road.

Excess tire pressure is equally bad. In the worst case, the pressure will rise during driving to such a point that the sidewalls burst and you have a "blow-out." At best, there will be excessive wear in the center of the tread and shortened tire life.

Know your loads; know your correct tire pressure—check tires *before* each trip.

Check wheel lugs

The lug nuts or bolts on each trailer wheel should be checked periodically for tightness; this is not necessary for every trip, but it should not be neglected. Looseness can cause uneven tread wear, and if a wheel should come off while driving, a serious accident is likely.

Tools and Spares

Before starting out on a trailering trip, make sure that you have in your boat (or car) all necessary spares and tools—especially the spare wheel and tire (properly inflated) for the trailer, and the lug wrench to use if making a change becomes necessary.

Be sure that you carry a spare bulb or two for the trailer lights (at least one of each type if not all are the same)—these may burn out and should be replaced immediately for safety (and, too, to prevent being stopped by the police!).

TABLE 29-1 This table gives load capacities per tire for various tire sizes and inflation pressures (measured cold before starting). The underlined value on each line is the maximum inflation-load value for that tire at highway speeds.

TIRE LOAD CAPACITY AT VARIOUS INFLATIONS													
Tire Size	Ply Rating	30	35	40	45	50	55	60	65	70	75	80	85
4.80/4.00 x 8	2	380											
4.80/4.00 x 8	4	380	420	450	485	515	545	575	600				
5.70/5.00 x 8	4		575	625	665	710							
6.90/6.00 x 9*	6		785	850	915	970	1030	1080					
6.90/6.00 x 9*	8		785	850	915	970	1030	1080	1125	1175	1225	1270	
20 x 8.00-10	4	825	900										
20 x 8.00-10	6	825	900	965	1030	1100							
20 x 8.00-10	8	825	900	965	1030	1100	1155	1210	1270	1325			
20 x 8.00-10	10	825	900	965	1030	1100	1155	1210	1270	1325	1370	1420	1475
4.80/4.00 x 12	4	545	550	595	635	680	715	755	790				
5.30/4.50 x 12	4	640	700	760	810	865	915						
5.30/4.50 x 12	6	640	700	760	810	865	915	960	1005	1045	1090	1135	
6.00 x 12	4	855	935	1010									
6.00 x 12	6	855	935	1010	1090	1160	1230	1290					
6.50 x 13	6	895	980	1060	1130	1200	1275						

Laws and Regulations

It is presumed that the prudent trailer-boating skipper is familiar with the laws and regulations of his state and local community regarding the use of his rig. If, however, you are venturing farther than normal from home base, don't assume that the requirements are the same everywhere. Check carefully into all requirements and restrictions before starting out. Information can usually be obtained from police departments, automobile clubs, or boating clubs, either locally or these in the new area.

HOOKING-UP

Before mating the trailer's coupling to the car's hitch, the ball may be lightly coated with grease to reduce friction. After joining the two units, make sure that the coupling is tightened properly and locked in accordance with its design. Now connect the safety chains *immediately* so that they won't be forgotten. Most trailers use "S" hooks, fig. 2918; a safer connection can be made with a "scissor" hook or a shackle or clevis. If a single chain is used, it should be long enough to go around the drawbar of the

WRONG   RIGHT

FIG. 2918 There is a right and a wrong way to hook up trailer safety chains. The open end of the hook should go up through the hole, never down into it. Two chains are better than one!

hitch and back to the trailer to fasten onto the frame or the chain itself near its beginning. *The chains must have no more slack than is necessary for making sharp turns; they should not be long enough to permit the coupling to fall to the road if the trailer should suddenly become unhitched.* Next, the parking wheel should be raised to its proper position for on-the-road travel, and the electrical connections made between the car and trailer. (A neat trick is to have the electrical cord on the trailer long enough so that the connector can be placed *inside* the car trunk to protect it from rain and road splash; the trunk lid will close easily over the wires without damage.)

A final check

Now you *should* be ready to move out—but are you? Make a final run-down of the check list. Check all lights with someone in the car depressing the brake pedal and operating the switches; check all functions, tail, license plate, stop, turn, and marker (if used). And don't forget to ask each member of the crew, "Have you forgotten anything?"

ON THE ROAD

Driving a car pulling a trailer can be quite different from driving the car only, especially if it is one of the lighter and less powerful models. There will be less acceleration ability, and more time and distance will be required to stop.

If this is your first experience in trailering, or if you are "moving up" in terms of size and weight of your rig, take time to learn the driving characteristics of your new combination—practice in light traffic before taking to crowded freeways and major roads on weekends.

FIG. 2919 In many areas, there may be a lower speed limit for cars pulling trailers than for those not so encumbered. This is in recognition of the greater weight and longer stopping distance of car-trailer combinations. Read and heed such signs.

Driving

The first principle to note in driving with a trailer behind is "No passengers in the trailer!" This is very unsafe and is illegal in nearly all jurisdictions. The rule should be applied liberally, and not even pets allowed to ride in the trailer.

Drive as smoothly as possible—no sudden jerks in starting, and well-anticipated, easy stops. Jerks and sudden stops put added loads on the trailer connection, the boat itself, and the gear stowed in it. Avoid quick turns and sudden swerves; these can make a car-trailer combination harder to handle.

Check your brakes

Just as soon as you start out towing a trailer—before you leave your own property if possible—test your brakes and those of the trailer if it is so equipped.

Look and listen

Watch the trailer in the rear-view mirrors as much as possible and keep an ear open for the development of unusual noises from that direction. If a car passes you making hand signals to you, pull off and make a check to see what might be wrong.

Drive carefully

Observe all speed limits; these are often slower for cars with trailers, and for good reasons. Don't "tail-gate"; re-

FIG. 2920 Even a small car can pull a boat and trailer combination of limited size. Whatever the weight of the rig, the car's driving characteristics will be changed while towing, and the driver must be constantly alert to the differences.

FIG. 2921 A thorough check should be made upon arrival at the ramp to detect any unsatisfactory conditions resulting from the trip. These may need correction before starting on the return journey.

member that your stopping distance is extended because of the trailer; leave more-than-normal space between your car and the vehicle ahead of you. Use added caution in passing; remember that your overall length is twice as much as normal, or more, and your car will have to be well ahead of the passed vehicle before there will be room for you to pull back into lane—and remember, too, that your acceleration to pass is going to be less than you normally have. Keep in the proper lane; on multi-lane highways, this will normally be the right-hand, or "truck," lane. If there is only one lane in each direction, and a pile-up of traffic begins to form behind you, it is courteous and a contribution to safety to pull off to the side (where you can safely do so) and let the faster cars get past you.

On city streets, and in other restricted areas, the driver of a car-trailer combination must swing a bit wider than usual in turns to allow for the trailer which will tend to "cut across the corner" slightly rather than following in the tracks of the towing car—it can be embarrassing to bump the trailer tires up over the curb when turning at a street intersection!

Stop and Check

On long highway hauls at relatively high speeds, it is important to stop occasionally and see how the rig is riding. This need not be overdone, but to neglect it is to invite troubles, if not a real disaster. A suggested plan for long trips is to pull off and make a thorough inspection after 5 to 10 miles of open road speeds, then again at about 50 miles, and thereafter at intervals of about 100 miles. The initial check should not be delayed too long after starting out lest an initial defect or human error build up to a problem before it is detected. Stopping intervals must of course, be adjusted to the availability of suitable locations, especially on heavily traveled roads.

Use a regular procedure

At each roadside check, the wise skipper has a regular procedure to follow to ensure that nothing is overlooked. The hitch should be checked for tightness and the safety chains for the right amount of slack. Check the tires visually; remember that a build-up of pressure is normal and don't bleed off air in the belief that it is excess. Feel all wheel bearings; warmth is ok, but if they are too hot to touch, you have a problem. Let them cool off and then drive as slowly as practicable to a service station for dis-

assembly and inspection. Be sure also to check all tie-downs and take a look inside the trailer at the stowed gear. Check all lights even though it is daytime, especially the stop and turn signals.

Check the car, too

At each stop, take the time, too, to check the car's tires and lights. Don't check radiator water unless there have been signs of overheating, and then do so with great caution if a pressure-type is used as on most cars.

When Conditions Are Bad

Driving in rain, fog, or other condition of reduced visibility is always somewhat more hazardous, but it is especially so when the added length of the car and trailer combination must be considered, and its less favorable acceleration and stopping characteristics. High winds, particularly cross winds, present added hazards to trailers and may exclude such vehicles from some roads and bridges at these times; be alert for caution or prohibition signs at toll booths and bridge aproaches.

Pulling Tandem-axle Trailers

It has been noted that the "following" characteristics of trailers with two axles can sometimes be improved by *not*

FIG. 2922 With a little ingenuity, a trailered small cruiser can be made to serve as your overnight accommodations on long overland trips by camping in authorized trailer parks.

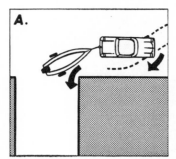
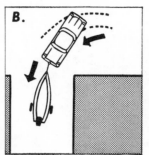
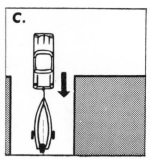

FIG. 2923 Remember, trailer always backs in direction opposite to that of car. (a) Driver swings close to launching ramp, then cuts car away from ramp, placing trailer at angle to ramp and driveway. (b) He cuts wheels of car to left, backs slowly into ramp, as trailer moves to right. (c) Driver straightens wheel after "jackknifing" car-and-trailer until both are in line, then backs slowly down ramp.

inflating all four tires equally. If you are experiencing any weaving back and forth of your boat trailer at highway speeds, try varying tire pressures by 5 or 10 pounds with the front wheels softer and the rear wheels harder than nominal pressure, or vice versa. No specific guidance can be given, except to try various combination of pressures and check for either improved or worsened handling characteristics.

ON ARRIVAL

When you reach your destination, make a final check just as you would have done at an intermediate stop. Even if the tie-downs are to be removed soon, for example, it is well to know whether or not they have tended to work loose, and similarly with the hitch and safety chains. Hot wheel bearings or even warm ones, must be allowed to cool down before launching; if they are too hot, it may be an indication that they will have to be serviced before starting out on the return trip.

Maneuvering the Trailer

Although the proper procedures for driving a car so as to maneuver a trailer in a desired manner will be described here, there is no substitute for experience and deliberate practice. A large shopping center parking lot on a Sunday or other day of light use makes an excellent practice ground; place some empty boxes or similar objects to mark limits for parking, backing, and other "precision" maneuvers.

Backing up

Learn how to back in a straight line and how to turn while backing so as to put your trailer just where you want

it. A trailer *always backs* in a direction *opposite* to that of the car! This causes much confusion to beginners, and can even embarrass experienced drivers if they forget this basic fact when hurrying or in the stress of an emergency. When backing, turn your car's steering wheel in the direction to which you wish the trailer to go—it's true that your car's front end will go in the opposite direction, but the trailer will head off just as you desired.

The key to success in backing a trailer is *slowness;* make all moves slowly and watch the results carefully. If things are not going well, if the trailer is tending to jack-knife on you, don't panic, just stop, pull *ahead* a few feet to straighten out the car-trailer combination, and then try again, *slowly* and with *less* turning of the car's wheels.

Practice, and practice again

Success will not normally come quickly or without some embarrassing moments, but backing a trailer is a skill that can be acquired. If ever the saying, "Practice makes perfect" were applicable, it is to the art of trailer maneuvering.

SPECIAL TIPS

When trailering a boat for any distance, it is a good idea to remove the fire extinguisher from the craft and carry it readily accessible in the car. All too often, a passing boat on a trailer is the target of a carelessly or deliberately discarded cigar or cigarette from a passing vehicle. The fire extinguisher may be unreachable if it is in the boat when a fire starts, so have it in the car, but don't forget to return it to the boat before the craft is used on the water.

The American Automobile Association has prepared a booklet, "Trailer Pointers and Driving Hints" check your local automobile club office for a copy.

Launching and Retrieving

The act of transferring a boat from its trailer to the water is *launching*; the reverse process is *retrieval,* or *loading.* Both of these actions must be planned and done with care to avoid troubles, either damage to the craft and its outboard motor or outdrive unit, or injuries to personnel.

USING A RAMP

A sloping surface extending both above and below the water surface, used for launching and retrieving trailered boats is called a *ramp.* Using a ramp is not the best way to get a craft into the water, but it is by far the most often

used method, and all trailer boatmen should be qualified in this technique.

Ramps vary widely in their characteristics, including their "quality." Many are surfaced with concrete or asphaltic paving; others are unsurfaced, hard packed dirt or sand, sometimes reinforced with wood or steel planking. Some ramps are only wide enough for one launching operation at a time; others are much wider and several trailers can be backed down side-by-side for simultaneous launching or retrieval.

The quality aspects of a ramp relate to its slope, extent

FIG. 2924 Ramps vary widely in size and nature of surface. This wide, paved launching ramp can handle six boats at a time. On busy days, one boat is launched every three minutes.

into the water, and condition of the surface. The angle of slope is not critical, but it must be steep enough that a trailer need not be backed down so far into the water that its wheel bearings get wet. On the other hand, it must not be so steep that an excessive pull is required to get a loaded trailer up and off the ramp. The ramp must extend far enough into the water that trailers can be backed down at any water level without running off the lower end. (Many surfaced ramps develop a sharp drop-off at the lower end where dirt washes away; serious problems can be encountered in getting trailer wheels back up over this "lip" if they are rolled too far down and off the hard surface.) A dirt or sand ramp must be firm enough to support the trailer and car wheels; a surfaced ramp must not have a coating of slippery slime that could make footing dangerous and provide inadequate traction for the car's driving wheels.

Preparations for Launching

First of all, remember to allow time for the wheel bearings to cool down if there is any chance of their getting wet. If a hot bearing is put into colder water, the sudden temperature change has the effect of creating a partial vacuum inside and sucking in water, a most undesirable circumstance.

While the bearings are cooling down, the boat cover can be removed, folded, and stowed in the car or boat. Tie-

downs can be removed and stored in a safe place, but leave the winch line taut. If the outboard motor or out-drive unit has been in the down position during trailering —unlikely, but possible—it should now be tilted up.

At this time, it may be desired to remove or relocate some of the equipment that has been transported in the boat, remembering that it will take an up angle as it is launched. If the craft has been trailered with empty or only partially filled fuel and water containers, these may be filled at this time unless there is a pier to move the boat to after it is in the water.

Use two lines

Attach a both a bow and a stern line; a boat cannot adequately be controlled with only one line (you can't "push" on a line!), but it can be safely and accurately moved about with two. Put over the side any fenders that might be needed, such as if the boat will be moved to a pier or seawall once it is in the water.

"Preview" the launching

Study the launching ramp and surrounding water area; check for any hazardous conditions such as a slippery or too short ramp, estimate the wind and current effects.

In case of doubt, don't hesitate to ask another skipper who has just launched his boat or taken it out of the water. If you have the time, perhaps while waiting for your trailer's

FIG. 2925 A trailer should not be backed farther into the water than is shown above. Wheel bearings, especially, should not be submerged. A tilt-bed trailer will usually make this possible.

FIG. 2926 Especially on weekends and holidays, a popular ramp can be a very busy place with many boatmen waiting to launch or haul-out. The courteous skipper uses the ramp quickly and moves off promptly with both his boat and his car-trailer combination.

wheel bearings to cool off a bit, watch the launching operations of others, noting any peculiarities of this ramp which may be new to you.

Check and double-check

Now check the drain plug, if one is used; and as a final item, *re-check the drain plug*. It is quite embarrassing to launch your craft and have it start filling up with water, perhaps damaging gear placed on the floor boards. It can, and does, happen to experienced skippers who get careless about their preparations—don't let it happen to you. Look about, too, and see that *no* item of preparation has been forgotten.

The Actual Launching

Line up the car and trailer so that the backing process will be as straight and short as possible. On a wide ramp with multiple launching positions, give due regard to others and don't take up more than your share of the available space.

Back the car to the launching spot, preferably where the trailer's tires are just at the water's edge. (If ramp conditions are unfavorable, and you have a front bumper hitch, consider whether it is worthwhile to unhitch the trailer, turn the car around, and hook up again before spotting the trailer on the ramp.) Set the parking brake on the car and block a wheel on each side for added safety. Have one person man the winch controls and one, preferably two, others take the lines running from the bow and stern of the boat.

Release the tilt latch on the trailer if it is of this type. Tighten the winch brake and release the anti-reverse lock; do *not* disconnect the winch cable from the boat. The craft should then slide down and off the trailer easily, its speed controlled by the winch brake; a push or two might be needed to get it started. Be sure that the motor is tilted up so that the propeller and skeg will not dig into the bottom as the boat slides down.

When the boat is in the water, floating free of the trailer, unhook the winch line; move the boat aside and make it fast to a pier, beach it, or otherwise secure it temporarily. Return the tilted trailer bed to a horizontal position and

latch it in place. The winch line may be rewound on the drum if desired, but it can often be adequately secured by catching the hook on an after member of the trailer frame and taking up the slack.

Remove the car's wheel blocks and drive it to an authorized parking area—give consideration to others by clearing the ramp area promptly and selecting a parking spot that will not take up unnecessary space or block others. If at all possible, hose down with fresh water any parts of the trailer that got wet during the launching operation. Have a padlock on the coupling or safety chain to prevent theft of the trailer while you are enjoying your boating. Place chocks at its wheels if the trailer is detached from the car and the parking area has any slope.

At the boat, lower the motor or outdrive unit to its operating position and connect the fuel line if necessary. Make all other preparations for getting underway, such as transfer of gear from the car, load up your crew, and clear away from the launching area as rapidly as can be done with safety.

Reloading on the Trailer

Beach the boat or make it fast to a pier while someone goes to get the car and trailer from the parking area. If the outboard motor is not to be used further in the next day or so, it is an excellent idea to disconnect the fuel line with the motor still running at a fast idle. Let it run until all the fuel in the motor is used up; this will help prevent the formation of gum and deposits in the carburetor and fuel lines.

Back the trailer to the water's edge, again stopping, if possible, before the wheels and axles are submerged. Set the car brakes and block the wheels. (A front bumper hitch is even more useful in retrieval where the pull is harder than it is in launching). Release the trailer tilt latch and push the frame into the up position. Tilt the boat's motor and work the craft into position to move onto the first rollers with the keel of the boat straight with the centerline of the trailer; again, both a bow and stern line will make for easier handling unless conditions are favorable for someone to wade into the water and man-handle the craft into position. Run out enough winch cable and engage the hook

FIG. 2927 With the line attached to the eyebolt in the boat's stem, the winch is cranked so as to pull the craft up onto the trailer bed. If it is a two-speed winch, "low gear" may be used to start the boat up as this is the heaviest pull.

FIG. 2928 Cranes are often used to unload sailboats from their trailers and put them into the water, especially keel-boats that are not adaptable to the usual "slide-off" procedures.

in the eye in the stem of the boat; watch out for kinks in the cable and never handle a steel line except with gloves.

Crank in on the winch line and the boat should come easily onto the trailer bed; a tilted frame will come down to the horizontal position by itself as the boat moves up it. Often a winch has a lower-geared speed (higher mechanical advantage) which is useful for the initial pull to get the boat started up the trailer bed and a higher-speed mode to complete the loading when the pull gets easier.

Do not allow anyone to be in line with the winch cable, especially if a synthetic material is being used. A broken cable snaps like a broken rubber band and can throw a hook or fitting great distances. Serious injuries, even death, can result from being struck by a broken winch cable or fitting. *Keep clear!*

When the boat is fully onto the trailer, latch down the tilt mechanism (if it is of this type), remove the blocks from the car's wheels, and move the rig clear of the ramp so that others can use it. Don't overlook the other preparations that must be made for road travel, but do get away from the launching area to do them.

USING A CRANE

The use of a crane with padded slings is probably the launching method that is easiest on the craft. Done with care, this method puts a minimum of abnormal strains on the hull. Slings are normally provided by the crane operator, but should be checked for adequacy by the skipper before he entrusts his craft to them. The owner should know the proper placement of the slings for a safe balance of his boat.

Two lines, bow and stern, should always be used to control any swinging motion of the boat while it is hanging from the crane hoist between the trailer and the water.

Some cranes are fitted with hooks to engage in lifting eyes on the boat. This is generally not a good method as it concentrates the strains on the hull at two or three points. With proper planning and adequately installed eye bolts through the keel, however, it is possible to use this technique. Keep the boat light, removing loose gear, portable fuel tanks, and possibly the motor. Always use lines to control any swinging motion while the craft is up in the air.

Land Storage

A trailered boat is normally stored on land between uses, spending more time just sitting on its trailer bed than in the water or being hauled down a road. Thus for the sake of both the boat and trailer, land storage must be done properly.

Protection against theft of the boat and trailer can be at least partially achieved by installing one of the specially designed fittings that goes on the coupling of the trailer and is secured with a keyed lock—if they can't "hitch up," they can't haul it away!

As for the car when it is not pulling the trailer, the ball of the hitch can be covered with a small plastic bag secured

by a short length of cord or elastic. This will prevent any grease on the ball from rubbing off on clothing and will provide some protection from rusting.

Keep water out

Rainwater is undesirable in the boat for many reasons and a collection of it can rapidly increase the weight on the trailer, often beyond the trailer's capacity. A cover is desirable, but with or without one, the tongue of the trailer should be raised enough to cause rainwater to flow aft and run out through a drain hole. The tongue can be raised by the parking wheel, or lacking this, it can be kept elevated by securely blocking it up; the plug must, of course, be out.

If a cover is used, it must be adequately supported so that pockets of rainwater will not form, stretch the material, and possibly break through. Cross-supports under the cover and frequent fastening points around the edge will keep the cover sag-free; small sand bags in lieu of snap fasteners will ensure tautness but allow some "give" for shrinkage which occurs when the cover gets wet (such cover hold-downs, however, are not suitable for road travel).

Ease strains on the hull

A boat must be quite firmly held down to the trailer bed when it is being moved, particularly on rough roads or at high speeds. It need *not* be so tightly tied down when just sitting in storage, and the hull will be subjected to less strains and distortions if the tie-downs are slacked off a bit or some of them are removed.

Blocking up a trailer

If a rig is not going to be used for weeks or months, the trailer frame should be jacked up and placed on blocks to take the weight off the springs and tires. Blocking up must be adequate—at enough points to avoid distorting the frame which is undesirable in itself and which could transmit distortions to the boat's hull. The blocks need not be high, just enough to take the greater part of the load. If, however, the trailer wheels are clear of the ground, the air pressure in the tires should be reduced to 10 to 15 pounds. Remember that you must have means at hand to restore pressure when the blocks are taken out for the next trip; don't deflate tires unless you can pump them up again right there.

For long periods of land storage, consideration should

FIG. 2929 Folding canvas tops are subject to damage if the boat is towed at highway speeds. Be sure top is in the down position before starting on a trip, and take down all flags and pennants too.

also be given to removal of the battery, motor, and accessories, especially electrical ones, from the boat to more protected storage indoors. This may both prevent theft and provide for less deterioration.

Frequent checks

Don't forget the boat just because it is in land storage and out of regular use. Set up a schedule of weekly visits by yourself or someone else acting for you. Doing this at the same time each week will prevent forgetfulness or neglect.

On each visit to the craft, check for any signs of deterioration such as rust or peeling paint and don't let little problems grow into big ones before you take corrective action.

Maintenance

There is a need for regular maintenance on all items of boating equipment, and the trailer is no exception, especially if it is used around salt water. A bit of regular care and periodic major maintenance will protect your investment and ensure carefree use with a maximum of enjoyment and a minimum of "cussing."

Wheel bearings

The trailer's wheel bearings will need careful maintenance more than any other item. Basically, it is a problem of keeping water out and grease in. Use a proper grade of grease of high quality—if you didn't receive instructions with the trailer when you bought it, get guidance from the dealer or from an automotive mechanic familiar with trailer wheel bearings.

Bearings should be repacked at least annually, more often if adverse conditions are met. They should be inspected and repacked after *each* time that the trailer is submerged to such a depth that water reaches the bearings.

Tire maintenance

Whenever the trailer's wheels are removed for bearing lubrication, take advantage of this opportunity to carefully inspect each tire for imbedded objects in the tread, side-wall cracks or damage, or other signs of impending trou-

bles. Replace tires which have any serious damage or defects. When reinstalling the wheels on the trailer, switch the right side for the left so as to "rotate" the tires and even up tread wear.

Frame and mechanical parts

Rust and corrosion can quickly get a start and spread on a boat trailer. Hose it off with fresh water at every opportunity and keep painted surfaces intact. Touch up promptly wherever painted surfaces get scratched or scraped.

All bare metal surfaces, such as mating parts, latches, etc., should be protected by a light coat of grease. The winch should be lubricated regularly in accordance with its instruction book or with general good mechanical practices if no specific guidance is available.

Rollers on the trailer must be kept free of rust and well oiled so that they turn freely and added strains do not occur when the boat is moved on or off the trailer.

Electrical system

Water is a great enemy of electrical systems. Keep moisture out of light housings and connectors; drain holes help keep dampness from building up in such fixtures.

A light coat of grease or vaseline will fight off corrosion and lengthen the life of all electrical connectors.

FIG. 2930 Sailboats on trailers with their masts up and in the vicinity of overhead electric power lines present a very serious safety hazard—use extreme caution in these circumstances.

Sailboats, Too!

The attention of this chapter has been primarily focused on the trailering of outboard and I-O runabouts and fishing craft, as these predominate in numbers. But many small sailboats, too, are trailered from home parking areas to various bodies of water for racing or day-sailing. The same advantages of mobility, dry storage, "at home" maintenance, etc., apply here as well as for motorboats.

Much of what has been said earlier about trailers and their selection, use, and maintenance will be applicable to sailboat trailering. The selection of a sailboat trailer is just as critical and the supports must be just as carefully designed, perhaps even more so. Sailboats will usually be launched and reloaded using slings from a crane. For this reason, the supports will normally be of the padded-bar type, placed and adjusted to fit the contours of the hull; excellent support can be obtained if these are properly positioned.

The problem of the mast

Sailboats are trailered with their masts unstepped and carried in a horizontal position. Special holders for this must be mounted on the boat or the trailer. The mast will usually far overhang the hull and must be marked with warning flags and/or lights to meet local police regulations; extra care is required in driving a car pulling a trailer with such an extended length.

Maintenance

Sailboat trailers will rarely be immersed in the water and so wheel bearings will be less of a troublesome item, but all other maintenance will be required as for trailers in general. Padding on supports should be replaced when, due to its exposure to the weather, it begins to harden and lose its cushioning ability.

FIG. 2931 Sailboats can be "trailer boats"—and many are! Quite a few centerboard designs can be launched directly from trailers as shown above. Special provisions must be made for raising and lowering the mast, and for transporting it.

CHAPTER 30

As with almost any form of modern-day human endeavor, there is a certain amount of "paperwork" involved with the ownership and operation of a boat. Although never really enjoyable, these necessary tasks and processes can be made less burdensome and more effective by an orderly and efficient approach.

A boat of almost any size larger than a dinghy or a sailboard is a relatively complex item that must be properly used and maintained for safety, efficient operation, maximum enjoyment, and the protection of one's investment in her. The use and maintenance of a craft might well be lumped together and termed "boat management"; the proper documents and records are a vital part of this function.

This chapter will offer broad guidance in connection with the paperwork of "boat management." It will remain the responsibility of each owner-skipper to work out the specific actions and records for his boat as every craft and its use are highly individualized matters. What is best for a cabin cruiser just won't be right for an outboard runabout or a sailboat—what is adequate for the weekend user of a Class 1 boat will fall short of meeting the needs of a cruising yachtsman. But in *all* cases, there is a requirement for a certain amount of

"BOAT MANAGEMENT"

Certificates and Documents

The term "ship's papers" has a long and honored history. Nearly all vessels, including the smallest of boats, have some official or legal papers relating to them. Even a rowing dinghy or a sailboat of any size completely without mechanical propulsion (and thus exempt from any requirement for registration and numbering) will have a bill of sale or purchase receipt.

Many items can be included in any listing of "ship's papers" for a recreational craft. Among these are the Certificate of Number or yacht document; radio licenses, both station and operator's; survey reports; insurance policies; personal certificates; etc.

REQUIRED PAPERS

The owner of a boat registered by the Coast Guard, or by a state under a numbering plan approved in accordance with the Federal Boat Safety Act of 1971, is issued a "Certificate of Number." This must be on board the craft whenever it is in use (with a few specified exceptions), and to facilitate this, the law prescribes that it shall be of "pocket size." If lost or destroyed, immediate action must be taken to obtain a duplicate, but use of the boat can continue while waiting for this to arrive.

In a number of states, a sticker or decal must be attached to the boat in a specified location. Broadly speaking, this small item can be considered a part of the ship's papers. It is visual evidence from a distance that the craft's registration is currently valid.

Documents

Boats over a specified minimum size *may* be "documented" by the Coast Guard in lieu of registration and numbering. Information on this procedure is given in Chapter 2.

Craft that are documented must carry this paper on board, and it must be renewed annually. These documents are valid for one year from date of issue or renewal; there is no calendar or other fixed year.

A Certificate of Number or document must be produced for inspection by a law-enforcement official upon his request.

Radio Licenses

A radio station aboard a boat must be licensed by the Federal Communications Commission. This includes "marine band" (2-3MHz) sets, VHF radiotelephones, and Citizen Band equipment, plus radar sets. No license is required for small "handitalkies" on CB frequencies provided that their power is not over 0.1 watt. No license is required for radio direction finders, loran receivers, electronic depth sounders, and other types of equipment that do not *transmit* radio signals.

For the operation of marine band and certain other radio transmitters, the individual must have an operator's license or permit. None is required for CB sets or radar equipment.

Posting of Licenses

The radio station license must be on board the boat, posted in a prominent location as near as practicable to the position from which the equipment is operated. A Restricted Radiotelephone Operator Permit may be carried on an individual's person; any higher class of license must be posted.

Copy of FCC Rules

Each radio station on a boat must have a copy of the current edition of Part 83 of the FCC Rules and Regulations. This *should* be on board and available for ready reference, but the regulations allow that it be kept in a "suitable place on shore."

A radio log, required by the Rules, must be maintained;

this will be covered later in this chapter.

Additional information on the "paperwork" related to marine radio stations will be found in Chapter 25.

OPTIONAL BOAT PAPERS

Although not required by any law or regulation, an annual Courtesy Motorboat Examination by the Coast Guard Auxiliary is an excellent check on a craft's safety and "readiness for sea." If this examination is passed, a sticker will be awarded and the inspection form will be signed by the Auxiliarist and given to the Skipper. This signed form should be stowed safely away with the others of the ship's papers.

Personal certificates

If a motorboat is not carrying "passengers for hire," there is no requirement for the operator to have a Coast Guard license—state requirements may differ and should be checked. (The term "non-commercial operation" is often used in this connection, but it is not strictly correct as a person commercially fishing, crabbing, lobstering, etc., does not need a USCG operator's license provided he has no passengers for hire on board.)

The circumstances of when a guest aboard is, or is not, a "passenger for hire" have been examined in some detail in Chapter 2. It has also been held that a salesman, broker, or owner demonstrating a boat to a prospective buyer must have an operator's license or else place the craft under the command of a licensed individual.

Many skippers, however, do get a USCG license in one or more of the categories in which they are issued, just for the sake of having one rather than from any regular need for it. If so, it should be posted where it can readily be seen. If nothing more, it may serve to reassure any nervous "landlubber" guests aboard for a cruise!

Likewise, the Skipper's membership certificate in the United States Power Squadrons, with its endorsements for qualifications in Advanced Grades and Elective Courses is often posted on his boat rather than at home ashore. The same, too, is frequently done with one's certificate of membership in the United States Coast Guard Auxiliary. As with a USCG operator license, these documents all attest to the owner's established qualifications and abilities —they should be proudly displayed.

Insurance Papers

Most boats are, or should be, covered by insurance policies; see page 64. The owner may either keep his policy on board, or ashore in a secure place such as a safe deposit box.

If the policy is not carried on board, there should at least be a memorandum of information in the ship's papers regarding it. It should list the insurance company, policy number, coverages, expiration date, and other pertinent information such as the agent's name, address, and telephone numbers, both office and residence.

Logs and Log Keeping

An important part of the paperwork of "boat management" is the maintenance of the legally required or otherwise desirable logs. The plural form of "log" is used as it is often convenient to keep separate records of navigational, engine, and radio operations. These, however, can be within the same covers or binder if such is desired.

Developing your log format

The first step in log-keeping is to have logs that fit your needs. It is useless to follow a format that provides space for recording many items of information that are not applicable to your style of boating—for example, the nature of the bottom as brought up by an "armed" lead, or true headings if you regularly use magnetic readings from the chart. Trying to use an unsuitable log format is a bad practice as it may lead to the neglect of making any entries at all. Many printed logs simply do not meet an individual's requirements—if they do, fine; but if they do not, then develop your own style for the data that you find necessary and useful at a later date. It is wasted effort to record information for which you have no future use.

A log should be kept in columnar form insofar as practicable, rather than in paragraph style, but columns should not be set up for data that are only occasionally entered as this would result in much wasted space.

Printed log books are available from *Motor Boating Books* and at most marine supply stores. These may be used as they are, or column headings may be modified. In general, the use of a loose-leaf notebook form of a log should be avoided as pages can get lost. Much more desirable is a bound, hard-cover book—often a "record" book, available from office supply stores, will do nicely for the boatman who rules his own columns. It is quite possible that *your* needs will be met by such a book ruled in just three columns—"Date," "Time," and "Remarks"—other entries may be many, but probably will not be so grouped as to make additional columns useful.

Determining needs

It may take some time to determine just what is needed and what is not. Your requirements for log data may not even "jell" until after you have made a second cruise over some of the same areas months or more later; then you will learn just what information you should have recorded on your first visit there.

In considering which form to use, or in designing one of your own, be systematic. List the items that you wish to enter; consider their relative value. Sort possible entries

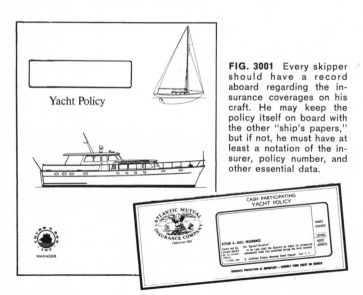

FIG. 3001 Every skipper should have a record aboard regarding the insurance coverages on his craft. He may keep the policy itself on board with the other "ship's papers," but if not, he must have at least a notation of the insurer, policy number, and other essential data.

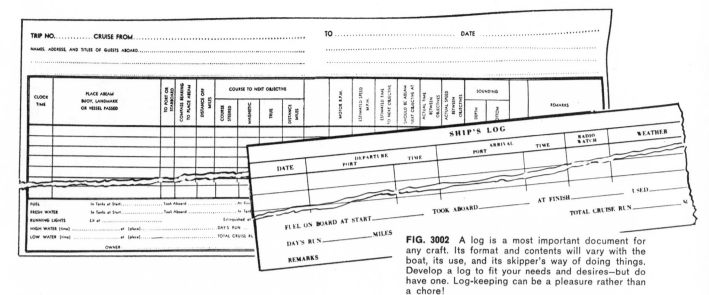

CLOCK TIME	PLACE ABEAM BUOY, LANDMARK OR VESSEL PASSED	TO PORT OR STARBOARD	COMPASS BEARING TO PLACE ABEAM	DISTANCE OFF MILES	COURSE TO NEXT OBJECTIVE				MOTOR R.P.M.	ESTIMATED SPEED M.P.H.	ESTIMATED TIME TO NEXT OBJECTIVE	SHOULD BE ABEAM NEXT OBJECTIVE AT	ACTUAL TIME BETWEEN OBJECTIVES	ACTUAL SPEED BETWEEN OBJECTIVES	SOUNDING		REMARKS
					COURSE STEERED	MAGNETIC	TRUE	DISTANCE MILES							DEPTH	BOTTOM	

TRIP NO.......... CRUISE FROM .... TO .... DATE ....

NAMES, ADDRESS, AND TITLES OF GUESTS ABOARD ....

FUEL   In Tanks at Start.................... Took Aboard .... At Fue...
FRESH WATER   In Tanks at Start.................... Took Aboard .... In Tank...
RUNNING LIGHTS Lit at ....   Extinguished a...
HIGH WATER (time) .... at (place)........................ DAYS RUN ...
LOW WATER (time) .... at (place)........................ TOTAL CRUISE RL...
OWNER:

SHIP'S LOG

DATE	DEPARTURE PORT	TIME	ARRIVAL PORT	TIME	RADIO WATCH	WEATHER

FUEL ON BOARD AT START........ TOOK ABOARD .... AT FINISH .... USED ....
DAY'S RUN .... MILES
REMARKS   TOTAL CRUISE RUN ....

FIG. 3002 A log is a most important document for any craft. Its format and contents will vary with the boat, its use, and its skipper's way of doing things. Develop a log to fit your needs and desires—but do have one. Log-keeping can be a pleasure rather than a chore!

into two categories—frequent and occasional. The first group will guide you in establishing columns; the second category can be put in a general column headed "Remarks." Once you have worked out your needs, reduce your log-keeping to those items only, and buy or prepare a form most convenient to record them. Be careful, however, that you don't overlook data for which you may have only infrequent use, but which would be invaluable in case of accident, breakdown, tax or insurance inquiry, etc. —don't be too brief!

DECK LOGS

A "deck log" is a record of navigational data—the time that you started a day's run and the time of reaching your destination, plus times of passing important navigational aids or landmarks and towns or cities. These latter items are particularly useful when cruising in inland waters where a constant speed cannot be maintained and you might later want to know the running time between such points. If your cruising takes you offshore, you will probably include your various headings and speeds, with the time of any change in either.

Other information that should be entered in the log are the names of any persons aboard other than the usual family "crew." Entries might be made of the weather—wind, visibility, sea conditions, etc.—at the start of the day's run and any significant changes. Entries should, of course, be made of any unusual events on board or seen; for example, engine trouble on your boat, or assistance rendered to another craft. These entries should be made in full detail so that reliance need not be placed on one's memory at a later date.

It is frequently useful to record in your log your operating expenses, such as fuel and dockage charges. Such records must, of course, be kept if you are able to take advantage of any business-related tax deductions. It is often of interest to record fuel prices at stops where no fuel is taken on, or dockage fees at brief daytime stops; this information may be of use in planning future cruises.

A log for every boat

A deck, or navigational, log should be kept by every boatowner and used for all activities—local outings, fishing trips, water skiing runs, etc., as well as "cruises." It is ad-

visable that a boat's log account for *every* day, in port or underway. The former may easily be done by such a simple entry as "8-12 June. In regular slip; no one aboard." This may later prove to be a useful and valuable record.

Validating the log

Regardless of format, certain essential elements should be entered. Each page should be numbered and the craft's name should appear somewhere on the page, usually at the top. Each day's entries, or a combined entry for several days in port, should be signed by the skipper as he completes them at the end of the day concerned. This authenticated record may be needed in connection with an insurance claim, a law suit, or other investigation. If a boat owner can state under oath that it is his practice to keep a daily log and then present a signed entry for the day involved, he has gone a long way toward legally establishing the situation as seen by him. Be sure that you *never* make erasures in a log—if you need to correct an item, rule out the old material without making it illegible, and then write in the correct entry if there is space, or make reference to where it will be found elsewhere in the log.

FIG. 3003 It is important that the log entries for each day's use, or period of time in port, be validated by the skipper with his signature. This may have important legal aspects if the log is ever needed to establish facts in a court of law.

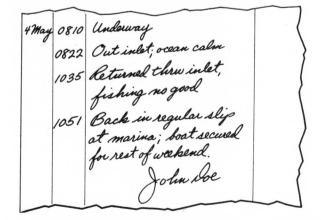

4 May | 0810 | Underway
| 0822 | Out inlet; ocean calm
| 1035 | Returned thru inlet, fishing no good
| 1051 | Back in regular slip at marina; boat secured for rest of weekend.
| | *John Doe*

Initial the correction and add the date if it is made on a later day.

Why not an illustrated log?

With a bit of proper planning, log-keeping can be interesting and fun—and the log itself will be of interest and use long after a cruise is over. Why not consider an illustrated log? Use marginal sketches if you or your mate has the artistic ability; or put in photographs of scenes, events, and people.

ENGINE LOGS

An engine log is kept in terms of hours of operation and is valuable in timing oil changes and other items of preventive maintenance. Record all routine maintenance and other significant events such as any troubles, repairs, etc. If a record is kept in the engine log of the addition of crankcase oil to maintain the proper level, any increase will soon become apparent and consumption can be accurately computed. Any increase in the use of oil may be a valuable warning of internal engine troubles. Likewise, fuel consumption can be periodically figured in terms of engine hours and any unusual change noted.

Hours can be estimated, or roughly figured from the deck log, but the easiest and by far the best way is by use of an electric engine-hour meter. Such an instrument is not expensive, and a typical installation can be made in an hour or two by the average skipper. An engine log for the dinghy's outboard motor is not beyond reason, but here we confine ourselves to estimates of the running time if we remember to make an entry promptly after each use.

RADIO LOG

If your craft is equipped with a radio transmitter, a certain amount of log-keeping is required by the FCC Rules and Regulations. In recent years, the number of entries that are required has been greatly reduced, but there is no excuse accepted for a lack of these if your station is inspected. Refer to your copy of Part 83 of the FCC Rules and keep at least the minimum log. You may want to add more to your radio log relating to contacts with the Coast Guard, other boats, or the marine operator.

LOG-KEEPING TECHNIQUES

A most important feature of good log-keeping is the making of entries while the facts are fresh in your mind—the very best time is immediately after the occurrence of the event. On a small craft this may present problems—you may not be able to write neatly, or even legibly, due to the boat's motion; the cockpit of a sailboat may be far too wet for "paperwork." One solution to this is the use of a small portable tape recorder; some are now so small that they can easily be held in one hand, complete with built-in microphone. Thus the skipper can keep a running record of events and transcribe them later into the permanent log when he has reached a sheltered marina slip or a quiet anchorage. The use of a tape recorder will ensure that no event is overlooked, nor will the log be messy or unreadable at a later date. One caution however, watch your tape supply—don't get caught at the end of a day with no data because you ran to the end of a reel or cassette and didn't notice!

FIG. 3004 An excellent way to keep notes for logs —deck, engine, or radio, while underway is the use of a small hand-held tape recorder. Using this procedure, the actual log can be written up after the day's run and will be much more legible than one written at the helm while underway.

Retention of logs

Since the maintenance of a deck or engine log is voluntary on a recreational boat, its retention is at the owner's discretion. In any case, it should be kept in a safe place until any possibility of litigation has passed. Many skippers keep their logs permanently and read them with fond memories years later. A radio log *must be retained* for the period specified by the current regulations.

How about a "Fog"?

One further thought on log-keeping—the skipper's logs may well be supplemented by a "female's log," or "fog" for short. In this record, the skipper's wife records the names of boats seen, new friends made (and don't forget addresses), new recipes discovered, points of interest ashore, and any other bits of information that will aid her in planning for other cruises or will just bring back memories. If you are a "shutter-bug," here is the place to record enough information about your picture-taking so that months later you will not be wondering what in the world that particular photograph was intended to show.

Instruction Books

It is most important that a boat owner have instruction manuals or data sheets for all equipment installed on his craft. Such papers are of great value in the performance of routine maintenance to keep the equipment working properly, or whenever repairs are necessary. These instruction books will normally include a "parts list" which will help greatly in obtaining the correct replacement components when needed.

The prudent skipper ensures that he has a *complete* set of instruction books. He starts with the main engines and goes straight through the inventory to the smallest motor, pump, horn, etc. There should be no item categorized as "too small," "too insignificant," or "too dependable" for inclusion in this check-up.

Rare, indeed, is the craft that has a complete set of manuals when it is purchased, either new or used. Those that are not on board must be obtained—sometimes from a local dealer, but more often directly from the manufacturer of that particular item of equipment. The boat owner can usually determine the manufacturer's address from the name plate on the equipment or from advertising in *Motor Boating* or other publications.

Model and serial numbers

When making this check of equipment, it is wise to make a note of *both* model and serial numbers for all items. These can be recorded in a notebook set up for this purpose or in the back of a log book. The latter location is usually quite convenient, but it requires the transcribing of information when one volume of a log is filled and another is started.

When writing for an instruction book or a replacement part for any piece of equipment, be sure to include *both* model and serial numbers as often there are variations in design after a certain serial number without a change in model designation.

Parts lists

Parts lists must include as a minimum the identification of those units which normally wear out with the passage of time and whose replacement is a matter of routine maintenance, especially those whose replacement is within the capability of the skipper or crew.

Much more desirable is to have the instruction manual or parts book so complete that it shows the identification of *all* parts and sub-assemblies. This will facilitate the ordering of proper replacements in the event of any sort of breakdown, and much time may be saved thereby.

Names and addresses

Instruction manuals, parts lists, and the like should be annotated with the name, address, and telephone number of the nearest source of supply—the local dealer or his source, the area distributor. If service technicians must be obtained from a different firm, this, too, should be recorded with all necessary details.

Sailboats

Sailboats should have complete information on each sail carried—manufacturer, date made, cloth type and weight, and all dimensions, including those relating to battens, if these are used. It is so much easier to take measurements under ideal conditions at one's convenience, and then look up the information in a notebook or log when needed, than it is to have to measure under adverse conditions, perhaps in an emergency.

INFORMATION ON THE BOAT

Very few, if any, boats are delivered with what might be termed an instruction book on the craft itself. Such a document would typically include electrical wiring diagrams for each system of different voltage; a drawing of the fresh water system's pumps, lines, and valves; a diagram of the fuel lines and valves; information on the location of all seacocks and other through-hull fittings; and similar information regarding the boat and systems that are not a part of accessory equipment.

Unfortunately, some manufacturers consider that they have provided such a manual when they place on board each new boat a simple, generalized booklet of "safe boating tips," and nothing else.

If not found on board the boat when it is purchased, some or all of the above documents may possibly be obtained by writing to the manufacturer of the craft, being sure to include all available identification data including hull number. On a used boat, all such information, either coming with the boat or later obtained from the builder, should be verified as previous owners may have modified or added to one or more of the systems. In all probability, the owner will have to search out and record much of the information discussed above.

Docking plan

For medium-size and larger craft, those over, say, 30 feet in length, there should be a "docking plan." This drawing shows where slings should be placed if the boat is to be lifted, or where shoring blocks must be placed if she is to be hauled on a marine railway. Close attention to this plan will prevent excessive stresses being placed on the hull when the craft is taken out of the water.

Safe stowage of books

It is important that all instruction books, parts lists, and similar publications be on board, but kept safe from damage or loss. Usually, it will be most convenient to place them in a waterproof plastic envelope and then put that in a secure place. On larger craft, where water damage is less likely, a large heavy-paper case with lettered or numbered subdividers makes an excellent means of filing these documents for the easiest retrieval when needed.

Check Lists

As the size of one's boat increases, its operation becomes more complex and there are more details to be remembered and executed at such times as getting underway or docking. While it should not be carried to extreme degrees that would complicate boat operation to the extent of decreasing enjoyment, the use of "check lists" can be valuable from a viewpoint of both safety and the avoidance of embarrassing situations. Their use can have real value in the prevention of expensive accidents and equipment damage.

Applications

The situations for which check lists can be prepared, and their level of detail, will, of course, vary with the size, type, and use of the craft. They may well vary, too, with the personality of the skipper. Typically, for a cruising Class 2 or 3 boat there will be check lists for:
1. Getting underway
2. Approaching a pier or mooring
3. Securing after a day's operations
4. Departure from the boat for a day or more
5. Periodic routine preventive maintenance

Importance for single-handed operation

Check lists are of particular importance and value for the person who is aboard by himself. Single-handed operation of a boat requires the maximum of thought and preplanning. Once underway, many tasks become much more difficult, if not impossible of accomplishment with safety, than if they had been performed before lines were cast off. A check list will minimize the reliance that must be placed on one's memory during the final minutes before casting off, and reduce the penalties for any forgetfulness.

Boat Management / CHAPTER 30

DEVELOPMENT OF CHECK LISTS

The contents of any check list will vary so much with the individual craft and her skipper that it will not be possible here to give more than sample items which may or may not be applicable to another person's situation.

Probably the most significant single characteristic of any check list is that it is a "living" document—it is never "completed" and final; it must always be considered as being under review each time that it is used.

Getting underway

Before getting underway from a marina berth, many "disconnections" must be made—electric cords, water hose, possibly a telephone connection, and most certainly the lines which have held the craft fast to the pier or pilings. Forget just one of any of these and you're in trouble, but fast!

Even the most elementary "housekeeping" chores are candidates for a pre-departure check list. Trash and garbage should be put in proper containers ashore rather than being taken along for a day's cruise. Water tanks should be topped off, if appropriate, and certainly fuel tanks should be checked. Use of a check list helps prevent the omission of an item because each of two persons thought the other had done it.

Not too silly an item for family groups is a final headcount of all children and pets. Even if the individual is missed before the craft gets far away, it can mean another docking and undocking, an unnecessary waste of time.

For the single-hander, there are such matters as the proper setting of switches and valves, the raising or lowering of a radio antenna, or even the setting of the craft's colors. All of these are minor tasks, but they cannot be done underway without leaving the helm unattended.

Coming into port

When approaching a pier or wharf, a much better landing will be achieved, and embarrassment often avoided, if the proper lines are laid out where needed and fenders are placed ready for use if required. Once made fast to the shore, there will be switches to be turned and valves to be opened or closed. Notations must be made for log entries while the information is still fresh in one's mind. Supplies of fuel and water should be checked so that refills can be arranged as needed.

FIG. 3005 Larger craft should have on board diagrams of the electrical system—systems, if there is more than one voltage involved—and the network of tanks, valves, and lines of the fuel system. These will be of great value when troubles must be found and fixed.

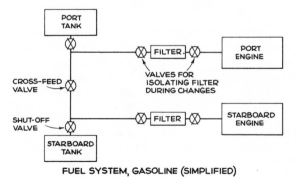

FUEL SYSTEM, GASOLINE (SIMPLIFIED)

FIG. 3006 A "docking plan" is a sketch indicating where a craft's keel ends and where shoring blocks must be placed if she is to be hauled on a railway or elevator platform. It shows where slings must be located if the boat is to be lifted out.

Departure from the boat

This is a very important check list as items which are overlooked when leaving will often not be remembered until their execution is impracticable or even impossible. Primary choices for this list are items relating to the safety and security of the unattended craft—turning off fuel valves, the proper setting of electrical switches, pumping out the bilge and leaving the switch on automatic (if one trusts the switch) or making arrangements for such periodic pumping out as may be needed, and the physical security of ports, windows, hatches, and doors.

Routine maintenance check lists

Routine maintenance check lists will include both items based on use of the craft (usually in terms of engine hours) and on calendar dates (weekly, monthly, etc., checks). Typical of the former are crankcase oil level checks and oil changes, and oil and fuel filter changes.

On a calendar basis are such matters as checking the water in storage battery cells, pressure gauges on dry-chemical fire extinguishers, and all navigation lights. The proper operation on and off of automatic bilge alarms or pump switches should be checked by deliberately running water into the boat. Seacocks should be periodically operated closed and open several times to ensure their free and easy operation if needed quickly in an emergency. Equipment and supplies carried on board for emergency use should be inspected for any signs of deterioration.

CHECK LISTS MUST BE USED

The most important aspect of check lists is that they must be used *regularly*. They must be used if they are to be of any value to the skipper, and they must be used if they are to be kept up to date and increase in usefulness.

A pre-departure check list must be gone through *each* time the craft is gotten underway. A list prepared and filed away is of little value, and it may build up a false sense of security. For safety and to avoid any embarrassment, the boatman should train himself to automatically reach for the list when he is ready to start an operation for which a check list has been established. He should be like the aircraft pilot who goes through such a check list *every* time, no matter how many years experience he has or how many times he has taken off and landed that day.

The value of a check list lies in its use, not in its existence!

CHAPTER 31

"What's that odd-looking flag on that boat over there?"

"What flag? Oh, you mean the one with blue and white vertical stripes?"

"Yes, that one—it has a red union for the anchor and stars, rather than the usual blue field."

"That's the Ensign of the United States Power Squadrons."

"The United States . . . what? What's that?"

"The United States Power Squadrons—a volunteer organization dedicated to making boating safer through education rather than legislation. I took their free Boating Course—you should take it too."

- "Perhaps I will; tell me more."

The United States Power Squadrons

FIG. 3101 The USPS Ensign is usually flown from the starboard spreader on a sailboat or a motorboat with a mast. On any craft, however, it can be displayed on a staff at the stern as shown above, and this is the normal procedure for smaller boats.

The United States Power Squadrons is a non-governmental, private membership organization, self-supporting in its efforts to enhance boating safety through education. Somewhat contrary to its name, which has more historical significance than current-day literal meaning, it is *not* limited to the owners of motorboats; many sailboat skippers belong, as well as quite a few individuals who do not own a boat at all.

Purposes

The purposes of the USPS are best described by a direct quotation from its Constitution—

"The objects of the United States Power Squadrons shall be to establish a high standard of skill in the handling and navigation of yachts; to encourage the study of the science of navigation, piloting, seamanship, and small boat handling; to cooperate with agencies of the United States Government charged with the enforcement of the laws and regulations relating to navigation; and to stimulate interest in activities which will tend to the upbuilding of our Army, Navy, Coast Guard, and Merchant Marine."

The USPS Ensign

The Ensign of the United States Power Squadrons may be flown on boats only when they are skippered by members of the organization. Rules for where and when it can be flown are given on page 462 and V.

The USPS Ensign consists of seven *blue* and six white vertical stripes with a union of *red* on which is the same white fouled anchor and circle of stars as on the yacht ensign; see color illustration on pages Q, R.

In the form of decals and stickers, automobile emblems, boating cap insignia, etc., the USPS design can be worn or displayed only by members in good standing.

THE ENSIGN is the name of the USPS monthly publication.

HISTORICAL DEVELOPMENT

In 1912, the motorboat was beginning to challenge the sailboat for a place in the field of recreational boating. A group in the Boston Yacht Club felt that there was a serious lack of knowledge on the part of some who were taking up this new form of boating, and decided to inprove the situation by conducting classes. This program led to formation of the "Power Squadron of the Boston Yacht Club," and set the educational basis for the USPS which remains its primary function.

Formation of a national organization

On 2 February 1914, a meeting was held at the New York Yacht Club that resulted in the formation of the "United States Power Squadrons." Following World War I, the programs of the USPS were reorganized into a new format that emphasized instruction as a service to boatmen and boating in general. The old distinctions between "power" and "sail" faded, and the Squadrons began to have an appeal to all who used boats of any type. The word spread, and Squadrons were formed on the Great Lakes, in Florida, on the Pacific and Gulf Coasts, and on inland rivers and lakes.

Growth after World War II

During World War II, the USPS again provided training to thousands of men before their entry into military service or the Merchant Marine. With the end of this war, boating boomed, and with it, the USPS. Squadrons were formed in many new areas, including Japan and Okinawa, as well as Hawaii, Alaska, Puerto Rico, and the Canal Zone.

MEMBERSHIP

The USPS is a private organization and membership is by invitation. Members must be male U.S. citizens over 18 years of age who have met entrance qualifications set by the national organization and who have been elected by the local unit. As it is a volunteer organization depending upon its membership for support, an important aspect of a prospective member's qualifications is his willingness to "give" of his time and talents as well as "take" from the USPS of knowledge and improved skills.

There are also provisions for Apprentice status for male youths between 12 and 21 years of age, and for a "Certificate Holder" status for women who have passed the qualifying examination. Individuals in both of these groups must be U.S. citizens.

In 1971, provisions were made for the affiliation, for educational purposes only, of men and women who are not citizens of the United States.

ORGANIZATION

The basic unit of the USPS is the local *Squadron*. These have names of geographic significance and may have as few as 20 to 30 members or as many as 1200 or more.

Squadrons are grouped into *Districts* which are numbered; this is the intermediate level between the local unit and the *National* organization.

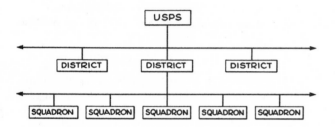

FIG. 3102 The above organizational diagram is greatly simplified; there are 30 Districts and more than 380 squadrons. The number of Squadrons in a District varies from 5 to more than 30. Each echelon is led by elected officers.

Officers

All levels of organization are led by elected officers. Squadrons and Districts have a *Commander,* plus several *Lieutenant Commanders* and *Lieutenants*. The USPS as a whole is directed by a *Chief Commander* and five department heads with the rank of *Vice Commander.* National Committee Chairmen and other staff officers hold the rank of *Rear Commander* or *Staff Commander.* All officers are unpaid volunteers; there is a small paid office staff at the National Headquarters at Montvale, N.J.

Uniforms, insignia, and flags

The USPS has a series of blue and white uniforms suitable for a wide variety of occasions and climates. The purchase of a uniform is optional for members, but is expected of officers. The various uniforms, plus insignia and flags of officers, are shown on pages 483, R, and S.

The USPS today

In 1975 the United States Power Squadrons were comprised of more than 83,000 members. There were 436 Squadrons assigned to 32 Districts.

FIG. 3103 USPS members may wear any one of a series of blue and white uniforms as determined by the nature of the Squadron activity and the climate. A blazer is available for informal occasions. The purchase of a uniform is not required of all members.

Educational Programs

The educational programs of the USPS are a major activity. There are four major areas of educational effort. One of these is for the general public. The other programs are for members only, and include two for further personal study and one for the internal training of the membership to improve their teaching abilities.

THE USPS BOATING COURSE

Each local Squadron is required to give each year at least one series of classes of the *USPS Boating Course* for the general public. Many Squadrons give the classes two or more times each year, varying the place and/or night of the week so as to reach the greatest number of boatmen and their families.

The USPS Boating Course is focused on the vast, and steadily growing, number of men and their families who go out on the water each year in small craft. The course covers the basic areas of piloting, seamanship, and small boat handling. The major topics are—

Handling Under Normal Conditions
Handling Under Adverse Conditions
Seamanship and Common Emergencies
Rules of the Road
Compass and Chart Familiarization
Aids to Navigation
Running Lights and Equipment
Inland Boating
Mariner's Compass and Piloting
Boat Trailering

The course material is prepared and distributed on a national basis, as is the end-of-course examination. Instruction is by local USPS members, supplemented in some instances by outside experts and specialists. The course is given free of charge by the local Squadron, although students will usually find it desirable to purchase a textbook, notebook binder, plotting instruments, etc., if they do not already have them. In some areas, the course is presented as a part of the adult education program of a local school system and a small registration fee is charged by that organization; no part of this money goes to the USPS or any member.

Family groups are encouraged to take the USPS Boating

FIG. 3104 As a public service function, each Squadron annually presents the USPS Boating Course for the general public. This course covers all aspects of basic boating safety and is in furtherance of the aim of "safety through education, not legislation."

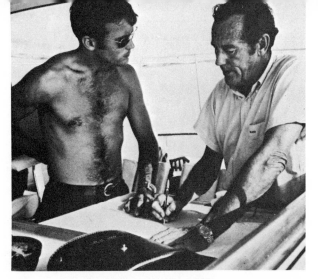

FIG. 3105 The USPS also has a progressive series of courses for its members. The initial courses are Seamanship and Advanced Piloting in which the basic material of the public course is studied in more detail and advanced aspects.

Course together; the minimum age is 12 years. Boating is widely enjoyed as family recreation, and both safety and pleasure are enhanced if all are knowledgeable.

THE ADVANCED GRADES PROGRAM

In keeping with its stated purpose of encouraging the study of the science of navigation, the USPS offers its members a progressive series of four courses.

The primary purpose of the *Seamanship Course* is to provide basic information about boating to people who have had little or no experience on the water. Knowledgeable boatmen, however, will find it quite valuable as a refresher course. The material covered in "S" applies to both motorboats and sailboats. The course includes instruction in "marlinespike seamanship" to develop a working knowledge of useful knots, bends, hitches, and splices.

The *Advanced Piloting Course* covers the basic principles and more important practices of pilotage, including modern electronic methods. The lessons will prove to be of great interest and practical value to the small boat skipper as much of the knowledge can be applied at once to the use of his own craft. This course includes a thorough study of the mariner's compass and its errors. The student is instructed in the use of government publications concerned with piloting. He learns how to determine the height of the tide or the strength of a tidal current at any specified time. Further instruction is given in the use of charts, in the laying of courses, and in the determination of position by bearings, angles, and soundings.

The *Junior Navigator Course* teaches the "sailings"—the mathematical counterpart of plotting. The practical use of the marine sextant is covered, including the taking and reduction of sights on the sun, moon, planets, and stars. A main objective of this course is to provide instruction sufficiently complete in itself that the graduate could navigate out of sight of land and bring his craft safely back to port.

The *Navigator Course* deals with alternative methods, special situations, and more advanced techniques. It aims to develop greater skill in the taking if sights and higher precision in position finding. Throughout the course, orderly methods for carrying out the day's work of a navigator at sea are emphasized. The grade of "N" is the

FIG. 3106 The Advanced Grades program of USPS education culminates in the Junior Navigator and Navigator Courses covering celestial navigation. The final grade of "N" is highly esteemed by members.

highest awarded by the USPS—its "PhD" in the field of boating study.

THE ELECTIVE COURSES PROGRAM

The USPS also offers to its members, apprentices, and woman's certificate holders four "elective" courses in speciality subjects; these do not constitute a series and may be taken in any sequence.

Engine Maintenance familiarizes students with the general construction, operating principles, and simple maintenance of marine gasoline and diesel engines, including outboard motors. As one of the major objectives of the course is to make the skipper a self-reliant and effective trouble-shooter, the diagnosis of all types of engine troubles is emphasized. EM is *not* intended to produce trained *mechanics,* only well-informed and resourceful *users* of marine engines.

Marine Electronics focuses on the legally proper and most effective *use* of marine radios and other electronic equipment that can be installed on boats for greater safety and convenience. This is *not* a technical course, and is well within the capabilities of the average USPS member. Students are prepared to take the FCC exam for a Third Class Radiotelephone Operator Permit.

The *Sail Course* is proof that the USPS is not just for the motorboat skipper! It covers sail terminology, types of rigs

595

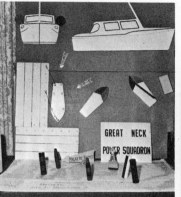

FIG. 3107 At the Annual Meeting of the USPS there is a large exhibition of teaching aids developed by the local Squadrons. These are shown both for the recognition of achievement and for the mutual benefit gained from an exchange of ideas.

and hulls, the theory of sailing with emphasis on the balance of hull and sails, stability, and other related topics.

The *Weather Course* is concerned with what the weather is all about and how its many variations can be predicted. We may not be able to do anything about it, but we can boat more safely, and more comfortably, too, if we understand something about it. Throughout the course, the student is encouraged to make observations and predictions on his own, so that he may apply the principles learned in class to his activities on the water.

INSTRUCTOR QUALIFICATION

The USPS depends almost entirely upon its own membership as a source of instructors for all courses. For members who would like to teach, yet hesitate to do so for lack of experience, and for those now teaching who would like to increase their classroom effectiveness, the *Instructor Qualification* program can be of great value.

The *Instruction Techniques Course* covers such topic areas as the principles of teaching and the preparation of effective lesson plans. The new *Instructional Aids Course* guides the novice teacher in the availability and use of a

wide range of teaching aids including films, slides, overhead projector transparencies, chalkboards, flip charts, and many others.

Topics to be covered will include such diverse subjects as the use and care of hand tools, predicted log racing, water skiing, the magnetic compass, and others.

SUPPLEMENTAL PROGRAMS

To provide further educational "packages" for members who have completed their basic boating education, the USPS is developing a series of *Supplemental Programs*. These generally are shorter and below the level of USPS courses.

FIG. 3109 The USPS also engages in other programs oriented toward increased boating safety. Squadrons and individual members assist in the Cooperative Charting Program for the correction and improvement of nautical charts issued by the Coast & Geodetic Survey and the Lake Survey.

Other Activities

The USPS participates in a *Cooperative Charting Program* with the Coast & Geodetic Survey and the Lake Survey. In this effort, the boating activities of thousands of USPS members are coordinated toward the reporting of errors, omissions, and changes for nautical charts and related publications. The limited field facilities of these federal agencies are thus much strengthened and expanded, and all boatmen are assured of more correct and accurate charts of the waters they use.

Many Squadrons also participate in events of a local nature such as boat shows and the annual observance of National Safe Boating Week.

Social Activities

It's not "all work and no play" in the USPS. Squadrons hold a wide variety of social activities both afloat and ashore. Each District has a Fall and a Spring Conference. These are working sessions, but they are usually preceded or followed by evening social gatherings. The national-level Annual Meeting each January combines both intense official events with those of a much lighter nature.

The Canadian Power Squadrons

In Canada, the Canadian Power Squadrons (CPS) is organized along lines generally similar to the USPS and conducts roughly equivalent education programs. There are close lines of communication and a well-developed sense of brotherhood between these two organizations.

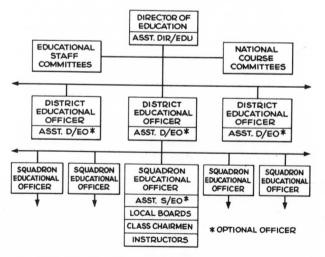

FIG. 3108 The Educational Department is the largest sub-unit of the USPS. Many members holding other offices or engaging in other tasks also teach on the local level or serve on national and district committees of the Department. At any time, approximately 80% of the membership is active in educational work.

The U.S. Coast Guard and Coast Guard Auxiliary

FIG. 3201 The United States Coast Guard is a military service although it is not normally under the Department of Defense. It is unique in its dual roles of public service in time of peace and naval operations in time of war.   U.S. Coast Guard Photo

The never-ending work of the United States Coast Guard (USCG) touches upon the activities of the vast majority of U.S. boatmen. Even far from salt-water "coasts," far up the major rivers of this nation, the work of Coast Guardsmen assists and protects the boating public. In many of its functions, the Coast Guard is ably assisted by its civilian supporting organization, the Coast Guard Auxiliary (USCG Aux). (Note the correct abbreviation; it is *not* "USCGA," this stands for Coast Guard Academy.)

The principal activities of the Coast Guard relating to boating are in the areas of law enforcement and safety. These take many forms as will be discussed in this chapter. Auxiliarists do not have law-enforcement powers, but do engage in a wide variety of activities, afloat and ashore, that further the cause of safety on the water.

The United States Coast Guard

The **U.S. Coast Guard** is a military service and a branch of the Armed Forces. It is *not,* however, normally a part of the Department of Defense. In peacetime, the USCG functions as an agency of the Department of Transportation. In time of war or national emergency, though, the Coast Guard, or units thereof, may be transferred to the Navy.

The Coast Guard Ensign

The flag of the Coast Guard, its distinctive Ensign, is closely connected with its history. The red and white *vertical* stripes number *16,* the number of states in the Union when the flag was first authorized in 1799.

The Coast Guard Ensign is illustrated in color on plate T. It has the unusual feature that it is flown *day and night* on active USCG units afloat and ashore—a constant reminder that the Coast Guard is always on duty to render assistance.

Coast Guard cutters, ships, boats, aircraft, vehicles, etc., are easily identified by the distinctive red band with USCG emblem and blue stripe.

FUNCTIONS RELATING TO BOATING

Boatmen come into contact with the Coast Guard in both of its major areas of law enforcement and safety. Many of the federal laws relating to boating are implemented by regulations issued by the Commandant of the USCG.

Boating regulations

The Federal Boat Safety Act of 1971 is the basis for the registration and numbering of motorboats. Although the Coast Guard performs this task itself in only three states and two other jurisdictions, the boat registration systems of those states that carry out this function for themselves must be approved by the Commandant. Coast Guard patrol vessels may check the registration papers of boats on all U.S. waters.

Boats of more than a specified minimum size may be "documented" rather than registered and numbered. In

FIG. 3202 Coast Guard mobile boarding teams extend law enforcement and general boating safety activities to inland areas of navigable waters subject to federal jurisdiction. Such teams can also conduct limited rescue operations if an emergency arises.

FIG. 3203 Amphibious vehicles along the shore and helicopters in the air support the search and rescue operations of Coast Guard small craft and cutters. Every available means is used to save lives and property in times of emergency.

all states and territories, this function is performed by officials of the Coast Guard.

Coast Guard regulations also spell out the details of the safety equipment required by the Act of 1971. USCG personnel are authorized to make inspections of boats to determine the adequacy of such equipment.

Safety activities

Coast Guard craft make frequent patrols to keep a watchful eye for any reckless operation of boats and all hazards to navigation. They may make spot checks of boat registrations and required equipment. Races, regattas, and other marine events are patroled to ensure the safety of both participants and spectators.

Safe Boating Centers have been established in a number of major locations of small craft activity. At these, boatmen can get information, advice, and assistance on problems relating to safety on the water—the Coast Guard would much rather prevent an accident than to rescue one's victims!

Aids to navigation

The Coast Guard is responsible for the operation of many thousands of aids to navigation, from unlighted buoys and daybeacons to very large lighthouses. The USCG also operates hundreds of radiobeacons and many of the stations of the world-wide Loran-A and Loran-C systems.

This is a quiet and unspectacular, but most necessary, service to all who travel on the water. The installation and maintenance of lighted and unlighted aids to navigation is a major function of the Coast Guard and one that affects most boatmen every time that they leave their moorings.

Search and rescue

The rescue of mariners in distress is probably the most dramatic activity of the Coast Guard, the one that makes the headlines when a ship goes down at sea in a storm. Less publicized, but equally important, are the many instances when the USCG comes to the aid of the boatman who has lost his way at sea, gone aground, suffered dismasting or engine failure, or who has merely run out of fuel. Many boatmen, and especially their wives, venture out on the waters, offshore or inland, with a greater sense of security knowing that the Coast Guard is standing by to help, living up to its motto, "Semper Paratus"—"Always Ready."

Search and rescue units include amphibious vehicles, motorboats, and ships known as "cutters," a term with which historical reference for the Coast Guard. Fixed-

wing aircraft and helicopters both extend the search capabilities of surface vessels and in many cases perform rescue mission themselves when wind and sea conditions permit.

ORGANIZATION

The Commandant of the Coast Guard, an Admiral, and his staff are located at *USCG Headquarters* in Washington, D.C. Operational activities are geographically grouped into *Districts* each under its Commander, a Rear Admiral. Fig. 1502 shows the boundaries of the Districts of the contiguous 48 states; the 14th District is in Hawaii and the 17th District covers Alaskan waters. For better coordination of operational matters, primarily search and rescue, the Districts of the Atlantic/Gulf of Mexico and Pacific coasts have been placed under Atlantic and Pacific Area commands, respectively.

The operating units of the Coast Guard, the individual bases, stations, cutters, boats, aircraft units, etc., may be under the direct control of a District, or these may be under an intermediate level, the *Group*.

Officers and enlisted personnel

Personnel of the Coast Guard include commissioned officers, warrant officers, and enlisted men. Ranks are the same as in the U.S. Navy. To replace uniforms that were generally similar to those of the Navy, the Coast Guard has recently developed a new uniform of a distinctive new "Coast Guard Blue" color cloth. The distinguishing USCG device is a small shield worn above an officer's stripes and on the lower right sleeve of an enlisted man's uniform shirt or jacket.

There is a Coast Guard Reserve to support the regular establishment. Women now serve in both commissioned and enlisted ranks in the regular Coast Guard as well as the Reserves.

OTHER COAST GUARD FUNCTIONS

Functions of the Coast Guard not directly related to boating include the Merchant Marine Inspection Program that establishes and enforces safety standards for both vessels and crews, and oceanographic research activities. Coast Guard icebreakers and cutters of reinforced construction often are busy keeping northern harbors open for commercial navigation in winter, and they also operate in the Arctic and Antarctic. In spring, cutters and aircraft with the International Ice Patrol keep track of the movement of icebergs into Atlantic shipping lanes.

The final major function of the Coast Guard is to maintain at all times a high state of readiness to function as a specialized service in the Navy in time of war.

FIG. 3204 The Coast Guard Auxiliary includes both women and men as members. Many ladies have qualified in specialty subjects and participate actively in all aspects of Auxiliary work—education, examination, and operations.

FIG. 3205 Boats that are owned by members of the USCG Aux and have met the higher inspection standards of a "Facility" may fly the blue and white flag of the Auxiliary. If the owner is an officer, elected or appointed, he may also fly the pennant of his office.

FIG. 3206 Members of the Coast Guard Auxiliary make thousands of free voluntary courtesy checks each year on boats of all sizes and types. Deficiencies are brought to the attention of the owner, but are not reported to any law-enforcement officials.

The Coast Guard Auxiliary

The **Coast Guard Auxiliary** is a *civilian* organization functioning under the direction of the Commandant of the Coast Guard. It is composed of persons interested in the Coast Guard and its principles, dedicated to the interests of their country, and concerned about the safety and welfare of their fellow men. Despite its uniforms and insignia, the Auxiliary is a non-military body.

The Auxiliary has a wide range of members. Eligibility extends to persons, male or female, who are over 17 years of age, U.S. citizens, and who own not less than a 25% interest in a boat, aircraft, or amateur radio station (or who have some other special qualification useful to the Auxiliary). An Auxiliarist is normally enrolled initially as a "conditional member" subject to further training and qualification to become "Basically Qualified," and then an "Operational (AUXOP) Member." The boat, aircraft, or radio station on which membership is based is termed a "Facility."

The Auxiliary flag

A boat that has qualified as a facility may fly the Coast Guard Auxiliary flag—popularly known as the "Blue Ensign." This is a rectangular blue flag with a white diagonal slash on which is the USCG Aux emblem; see color illustration on page T.

The Auxiliary flag shares with the regular USCG Ensign the distinction of being authorized to fly from boats *day and night.*

PURPOSES

The U.S. Coast Guard Auxiliary has several fundamental purposes which are stated as follows in the Act of Congress that established the organization—

To promote safety and effect rescues on and over the high seas and on the navigable waters.

To promote efficiency in the operation of motorboats and yachts.

To foster a wider knowledge of, and better compliance with, the laws, rules, and regulations, governing the operation of motorboats and yachts.

To facilitate other operations of the Coast Guard.

ACTIVITIES

In carrying out its stated purposes, the Auxiliary has three basic program areas—Education, Examinations, and Operations. All of these are focused on the objective of greater safety for those who go on the water in boats.

Education

The Auxiliary offers several courses to the boating public, tailored to meet the needs of various types of boatmen and their families. Courses consist of from one to twelve lessons; classes are held in the evenings or on weekends. Constant attention is given to the improvement of these courses and the development of new lessons or courses as required.

Members of the Auxiliary are actively encouraged to take "specialty" courses to improve their knowledge and increase their value to the organization. Typical subjects include vessel examination, communications, search and rescue, patrol procedures, administration, and others.

Examinations

Many members of the Coast Guard Auxiliary are active in the "Vessel Examination" program. Boat owners are urged each year to request a "Courtesy Motorboat Examination." This purely voluntary action ensures that a thorough check is made of the craft and its equipment. Boats that pass are awarded the CME sticker for the current calendar year. Craft that do not pass are *not* reported to any authority—the owner is advised of the deficiencies and is encouraged to resubmit his boat for another check when they have been corrected.

Auxiliarists are also busy each year checking the craft of other members to determine their fitness for continued designation as "Facilities." Higher standards and equipment requirements are placed on such boats as they will be allowed to fly the Auxiliary flag. The highest standards are required for a craft that is designated an "Operational Facility" and will be used in operational programs under Coast Guard orders.

Operational programs

Personnel and craft of the Auxiliary are used to perform various missions in such fields as search and rescue and regatta patrols, where the resources of the regular Coast Guard are not sufficient to meet the demands placed upon them. This often occurs on weekends and during holiday periods. For such duties, orders are issued by a designated Coast Guard officer.

Auxiliary members have *no law enforcement powers*. In those cases where such is needed, a Coast Guard officer or petty officer will be embarked in the Auxiliary vessel and the craft will fly the regular Coast Guard Ensign.

FIG. 3207 **Coast Guard Auxiliarists give up many hours of their own family boating time to conduct search and rescue missions and safety patrols for the assistance and protection of their fellow boatmen. Such activities support and extend the efforts of regular Coast Guard units.**

Auxiliary craft also conduct informal "Safety Patrols" without official orders. Other types of patrols include those to check on aids to navigation, or as a part of the Cooperative Charting Programs of the National Ocean Survey, including its Lake Survey Center, for the reporting of any errors and needed changes on charts.

Auxiliary operational facilities are often used to supplement regular Coast Guard units in search and rescue operations. Auxiliary aircraft aid in this work and are used

to make "twilight patrols" at the end of days of heavy boating activity to spot any craft that may need aid in reaching port safely.

Auxiliarists donate their time and abilities to the cause of safety on the water; there is no compensation for services rendered, except personal satisfaction, and only minor reimbursement of expenses, limited to activities under official orders.

Fellowship Activities

Units of the Auxiliary work hard at their basic responsibilities, but not to the complete exclusion of social activities. Rendezvous, parties, dances, and other events which tend to promote goodwill and fellowship are held on appropriate occasions.

ORGANIZATION

The basic unit of the Coast Guard Auxiliary is the *Flotilla*. This is a group of members and their facilities who work together in the various programs. Membership varies from the tens to the hundreds of individuals.

Flotillas are grouped geographically into *Divisions;* this is the normal intermediate level between the local flotilla and the District. In some cases, a District is divided into two or more Regions for better control.

Officers

All units of the Auxiliary are headed by their own elected officers—Flotilla Commander, Division Captain, or District Commodore. These are assisted by other elected and appointed officers. The USCG Aux as a whole is headed by a National Commodore, with a Vice Commodore, two Rear Commodores, and staff officers.

UNIFORMS, INSIGNIA, AND FLAGS

Although the Auxiliary is *not* a military or naval organization, its members, other than those in a conditional status, are authorized a series of uniforms—blue, white, and khaki—quite similar to those worn by regular Coast Guard personnel. Uniforms are available for dress, ordinary service, and working situations. The purchase and maintenance of uniforms is optional for the individual, but are required for activities such as patrols and other duty under official orders. See also pages 483-484.

Officers' insignia

A series of "rank" insignia from single gold bars to two silver stars, each with the distinctive Auxiliary "A" superimposed, has been established for officers of the USCG Aux. These are shown on page U.

The boats of officers of the Auxiliary are identified by pennants of special design for each office or level of office. These are illustrated on page T. Past officers may fly a burgee of generally similar design, but of different shape from the pennants of active officers.

WHY NOT JOIN?

If you're an eligible boatman, or fit into one of the other categories, why not join the Auxiliary? You are sure to learn much for your boating safety and enjoyment, and there is nothing finer than the sense of satisfaction that comes from helping others. Ask any Coast Guard unit or Auxiliarist where *you* can "sign up."

UNITED STATES COAST GUARD AUXILIARY
FLAG CODE CONFIGURATIONS

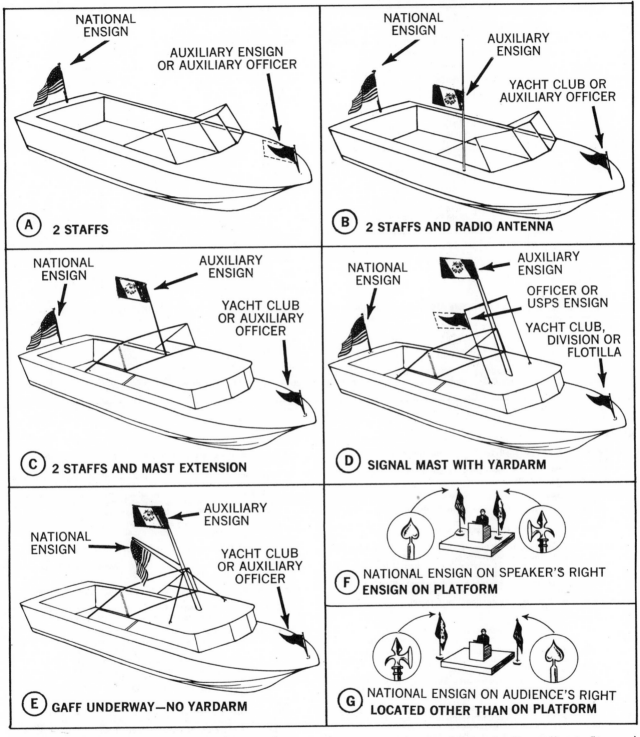

A 2 STAFFS

NATIONAL ENSIGN

AUXILIARY ENSIGN OR AUXILIARY OFFICER

B 2 STAFFS AND RADIO ANTENNA

NATIONAL ENSIGN

AUXILIARY ENSIGN

YACHT CLUB OR AUXILIARY OFFICER

C 2 STAFFS AND MAST EXTENSION

NATIONAL ENSIGN

AUXILIARY ENSIGN

YACHT CLUB OR AUXILIARY OFFICER

D SIGNAL MAST WITH YARDARM

NATIONAL ENSIGN

AUXILIARY ENSIGN

OFFICER OR USPS ENSIGN

YACHT CLUB, DIVISION OR FLOTILLA

E GAFF UNDERWAY—NO YARDARM

AUXILIARY ENSIGN

NATIONAL ENSIGN

YACHT CLUB OR AUXILIARY OFFICER

F NATIONAL ENSIGN ON SPEAKER'S RIGHT ENSIGN ON PLATFORM

G NATIONAL ENSIGN ON AUDIENCE'S RIGHT LOCATED OTHER THAN ON PLATFORM

The information on page 496 has been drafted to show in tabular form what the United States Coast Guard Auxiliary has approved as a flag code for power vessels. The problem would be simplified if there were no diversification of sizes and types of boats, thus providing a uniform number and arrangement of positions at which the flags might be displayed. To illustrate typical configurations on small craft for the display of the national ensign, Auxiliary ensign, USPS ensign, yacht club or Auxiliary officer's flag, and division or flotilla pennant, the chart above provides a key for the respective types, depending on what staffs, yard-arms and halyards may be available. In addition to config-urations shown for boats, figures F and G illustrate correct procedure when the national and Auxiliary ensigns are displayed at meetings ashore, the practice depending on whether or not the ensign is located on the platform.

UNITED STATES COAST GUARD AUXILIARY FLAG CODE FOR POWER VESSELS

FLAG	NATIONAL ENSIGN	COAST GUARD ENSIGN	AUX. ENSIGN	AUX. OFFICER PENNANT OR BURGEE	YACHT ENSIGN	USPS ENSIGN	USPS OFFICER FLAG	YACHT CLUB PENNANT OR UNIT	YACHT CLUB OFFICER FLAG	HOUSE FLAG	GAG FLAGS — MEAL, ETC.
FACILITY NORMAL CONDITION — FLOWN (STATUS 1)	STERN STAFF OR GAFF (Note #1)	NO	TRUCK — BOW STAFF (Note #2) (Note #14)	STB'D. YARD — BOW STAFF (Note #3) (Note #6)	(Note #4)	STB'D. YARD ONLY (Note #5)	(Note #6)	BOW STAFF (Note #10)	STB'D. YARD (Note #6)	NO (Note #7)	NO (Note #8)
UNDER ORDERS — FLOWN (STATUS 2)	STERN STAFF OR GAFF (Note #1)	NO	TRUCK — BOW STAFF (Note #2) (Note #14)	STBD. YARD — BOW STAFF (Note #3) (Note #15)	NO (Note #15)	NO (Note #15)	NO (Note #15)	NO (Note #15)	NO (Note #15)	NO (Note #7)	NO (Note #8)
UNDER ORDERS USCG OFFICER ABOARD — FLOWN (STATUS 3)	STERN STAFF OR GAFF (Note #1)	TRUCK (Note #16)	NO (Note #16)	NO (Note #16)	NO (Note #16)	NO (Note #16)	NO (Note #16)	NO (Note #16)	NO (Note #16)	NO (Note #7)	NO (Note #8)
HOURS FLOWN	0800 TO SUNSET	DAY AND NIGHT UNDER ORDERS (Note #13)	DAY AND NIGHT (Note #9)	OFFICER ABOARD DAY AND NIGHT	0800 TO SUNSET (Note #4)	0800 TO SUNSET Note #5	DAY AND NIGHT (Note #6)	0800 TO SUNSET (Note #11)	DAY AND NIGHT (Note #12)	(Note #7)	NO

NOTES

#1 **The National Ensign** shall be flown from the stern staff on a power boat except when the vessel is equipped with a gaff, in which case the ensign is flown from the stern staff at anchor, and the gaff when underway.

#2 **Auxiliary Ensign**
(a) Shall be flown from the main truck when the vessel is equipped with a mast(s).
(b) Without a mast, from the bow staff.

#3 **Auxiliary Officer**—Pennant or burgee shall be flown from the starboard yardarm when the vessel is equipped with a signal mast. If the vessel has no mast, it may be flown in lieu of the Auxiliary ensign from the bow staff. The pennant of a current officer shall take precedence over his own higher ranking past officer's burgee. However, as a matter of courtesy to a visiting officer, display the highest ranking officer flag (pennant or burgee).

#4 **The Yacht Ensign**
(a) The flying of the yacht ensign on any yacht, numbered or documented, is neither mandatory nor forbidden.
(b) A documented yacht operating under official orders, becomes a Government vessel, and Government vessels *may not* fly the "Yacht ensign."
(c) All facilities *not documented* shall fly the U.S. ensign, whenever the Auxiliary ensign is flown.

#5 **USPS Ensign**—This is the only "service" organization recognized by this code. The USPS ensign may be flown only from the starboard yardarm of a signal mast, *never* from the stern staff or gaff. On facilities flying the Auxiliary ensign, this position of honor is *reserved* for the national ensign.

#6 **Officer Flags**—Auxiliary, USPS, yacht or boat club, either pennants or burgees, are flown from the starboard yardarm, except as noted in #3. Only *one* of these flags may be flown at a time.

#7 **House Flag**—The owner's private signal known as a house flag is correctly flown at the truck between morning and evening colors;

therefore, it *cannot* be flown at the same time as the Auxiliary ensign.

#8 **Gag Flags**—Because of the quasi-official status of an Auxiliary facility, cocktail flags, ball-and-chain, or other humorous flags *shall not* be flown when the Auxiliary ensign is flown. Other flags, such as crew's pennant, owner's meal flag, guest flag, absent flag, also shall not be flown with the Auxiliary ensign.

#9 **The Auxiliary Ensign**—may be flown *day* and *night* on currently inspected facilities displaying decal, while in commission.

#10 **The Yacht Club Pennant**—can be flown from the bow staff.

#11 **The Yacht Club Pennant, Flotilla, or Division, Unit Flags**—shall be flown from 0800 to sunset.

#12 **Yacht Club Officer Flags**—shall be displayed day and night.

#13 **The Coast Guard Ensign**—shall be flown day and night while the facility is under orders with a Coast Guard officer aboard.

#14 **No Signal Mast**—When a boat is equipped with a bow and stern staff, and does not have a signal mast, but has a radio antenna, the Auxiliary ensign may be properly displayed by substituting the antenna for a signal mast. The height of the uppermost portion of the hoist of the Auxiliary ensign should be affixed at a point approximately ⅔ the height of the antenna. *No additional* antennas or outriggers may be utilized.

#15 **A Facility Under Official Orders** (STATUS 2) shall be permitted to fly the Auxiliary officer's pennant or burgee, in addition to the U.S. and Auxiliary ensigns. All other flags—yacht ensign, USPS ensign, yacht club pennants, officer flags, flotilla, division, etc. *shall not* be flown.

#16 **Coast Guard Officer Aboard Facilities Under Orders** (STATUS 3) the Coast Guard Ensign substitutes for the Auxiliary ensign; *all* other flags except the national ensign shall be taken down. This includes Auxiliary officer pennants or burgees, yacht ensign, unit flags, USPS ensign, yacht or boat club flags, etc.—only two flags shall be permitted—the national ensign and the Coast Guard ensign.

SEE UNITED STATES COAST GUARD AUXILIARY FLAGS IN FULL COLOR, PAGE T

USEFUL TABLES

TABLE I—SPEED OVER A MEASURED MILE

Sec.	1 min.	2 min.	3 min.	4 min.	5 min.	6 min.	7 min.	8 min.	9 mid.	10 min.	11 min.	12 min.
0	60.000	30.000	20.000	15.000	12.000	10.000	8.571	7.500	6.667	6.000	5.455	5.000
1	59.016	29.752	19.890	14.938	11.960	9.972	8.551	7.484	6.654	5.990	5.446	4.993
2	58.064	29.508	19.780	14.876	11.921	9.945	8.531	7.469	6.642	5.980	5.438	4.986
3	57.143	29.268	19.672	14.815	11.881	9.917	8.511	7.453	6.630	5.970	5.430	4.979
4	56.250	29.032	19.565	14.754	11.842	9.890	8.491	7.438	6.618	5.960	5.422	4.972
5	55.384	28.800	19.459	14.694	11.803	9.863	8.471	7.423	6.606	5.950	5.414	4.965
6	54.545	28.571	19.355	14.634	11.765	9.836	8.451	7.407	6.593	5.941	5.405	4.959
7	53.731	28.346	19.251	14.575	11.726	9.809	8.431	7.392	6.581	5.931	5.397	4.952
8	52.941	28.125	19.149	14.516	11.688	9.783	8.411	7.377	6.569	5.921	5.389	4.945
9	52.174	27.907	19.048	14.458	11.650	9.756	8.392	7.362	6.557	5.911	5.381	4.938
10	51.428	27.692	18.947	14.400	11.613	9.730	8.372	7.347	6.545	5.902	5.373	4.931
11	50.704	27.481	18.848	14.343	11.576	9.704	8.363	7.332	6.534	5.892	5.365	4.925
12	50.000	27.273	18.750	14.286	11.538	9.677	8.333	7.317	6.522	5.882	5.357	4.918
13	49.315	27.068	18.653	14.229	11.502	9.651	8.314	7.302	6.510	5.873	5.349	4.911
14	48.648	26.866	18.557	14.173	11.465	9.626	8.295	7.287	6.498	5.863	5.341	4.905
15	48.000	26.667	18.461	14.118	11.429	9.600	8.276	7.273	6.486	5.854	5.333	4.898
16	47.368	26.471	18.367	14.062	11.392	9.574	8.257	7.258	6.475	5.844	5.325	4.891
17	46.753	26.277	18.274	14.008	11.356	9.549	8.238	7.243	6.463	5.835	5.318	4.885
18	46.154	26.087	18.182	13.953	11.321	9.524	8.219	7.229	6.452	5.825	5.310	4.878
19	45.570	25.899	18.090	13.900	11.285	9.499	8.200	7.214	6.440	5.816	5.302	4.871
20	45.000	25.714	18.000	13.846	11.250	9.474	8.182	7.200	6.429	5.806	5.294	4.865
21	44.444	25.532	17.910	13.793	11.215	9.449	8.163	7.186	6.417	5.797	5.286	4.858
22	43.902	25.352	17.822	13.740	11.180	9.424	8.145	7.171	6.406	5.788	5.278	4.852
23	43.373	25.175	17.734	13.688	11.146	9.399	8.126	7.157	6.394	5.778	5.270	4.845
24	42.857	25.000	17.647	13.636	11.111	9.375	8.108	7.143	6.383	5.769	5.263	4.839
25	42.353	24.828	17.561	13.585	11.077	9.351	8.090	7.129	6.372	5.760	5.255	4.832
26	41.860	24.658	17.476	13.534	11.043	9.326	8.072	7.115	6.360	5.751	5.248	4.826
27	41.379	24.490	17.391	13.483	11.009	9.302	8.054	7.101	6.349	5.742	5.240	4.819
28	40.909	24.324	17.308	13.433	10.976	9.278	8.036	7.087	6.338	5.732	5.233	4.813
29	40.450	24.161	17.225	13.383	10.942	9.254	8.018	7.073	6.327	5.723	5.225	4.806
30	40.000	24.000	17.143	13.333	10.909	9.231	8.000	7.059	6.316	5.714	5.217	4.800
31	39.561	23.841	17.062	13.284	10.876	9.207	7.982	7.045	6.305	5.705	5.210	4.794
32	39.130	23.684	16.981	13.235	10.843	9.184	7.965	7.031	6.294	5.696	5.202	4.787
33	38.710	23.529	16.901	13.187	10.811	9.160	7.947	7.018	6.283	5.687	5.195	4.781
34	38.298	23.377	16.822	13.139	10.778	9.137	7.930	7.004	6.272	5.678	5.187	4.774
35	37.895	23.226	16.744	13.091	10.746	9.114	7.912	6.990	6.261	5.669	5.180	4.768
36	37.500	23.077	16.667	13.043	10.714	9.091	7.895	6.977	6.250	5.660	5.172	4.762
37	37.113	22.930	16.590	12.996	10.682	9.068	7.877	6.963	6.239	5.651	5.165	4.756
38	36.735	22.785	16.514	12.950	10.651	9.045	7.860	6.950	6.228	5.643	5.158	4.749
39	36.364	22.642	16.438	12.903	10.619	9.023	7.843	6.936	6.218	5.634	5.150	4.743
40	36.000	22.500	16.364	12.857	10.588	9.000	7.826	6.923	6.207	5.625	5.143	4.737
41	35.644	22.360	16.290	12.811	10.557	8.978	7.809	6.910	6.196	5.616	5.136	4.731
42	35.294	22.222	16.216	12.766	10.526	8.955	7.792	6.897	6.186	5.607	5.128	4.724
43	34.951	22.086	16.143	12.721	10.496	8.933	7.775	6.883	6.175	5.599	5.121	4.718
44	34.615	21.951	16.071	12.676	10.465	8.911	7.759	6.870	6.164	5.590	5.114	4.712
45	34.286	21.818	16.000	12.632	10.435	8.889	7.742	6.857	6.154	5.581	5.106	4.706
46	33.962	21.687	15.929	12.587	10.405	8.867	7.725	6.844	6.143	5.573	5.099	4.700
47	33.644	21.557	15.859	12.544	10.375	8.845	7.709	6.831	6.133	5.564	5.092	4.693
48	33.333	21.429	15.789	12.500	10.345	8.824	7.692	6.818	6.122	5.556	5.085	4.687
49	33.028	21.302	15.721	12.457	10.315	8.802	7.676	6.805	6.112	5.547	5.078	4.681
50	32.727	21.176	15.652	12.414	10.286	8.780	7.660	6.792	6.102	5.538	5.070	4.675
51	32.432	21.053	15.584	12.371	10.256	8.759	7.643	6.780	6.091	5.530	5.063	4.669
52	32.143	20.930	15.517	12.329	10.227	8.738	7.627	6.767	6.081	5.521	5.056	4.663
53	31.858	20.809	15.451	12.287	10.198	8.717	7.611	6.754	6.071	5.513	5.049	4.657
54	31.579	20.690	15.385	12.245	10.169	8.696	7.595	6.742	6.061	5.505	5.042	4.651
55	31.304	20.571	15.319	12.203	10.141	8.675	7.579	6.729	6.050	5.496	5.035	4.645
56	31.034	20.455	15.254	12.162	10.112	8.654	7.563	6.716	6.040	5.488	5.028	4.639
57	30.769	20.339	15.190	12.121	10.084	8.633	7.547	6.704	6.030	5.479	5.021	4.633
58	30.508	20.225	15.126	12.081	10.056	8.612	7.531	6.691	6.020	5.471	5.014	4.627
59	30.202	20.112	15.063	12.040	10.028	8.592	7.516	6.679	6.010	5.463	5.007	4.621

Table I (right), boat speed over a measured 1-mile course can be picked out by inspection. For example, if it takes 4 minutes and 19 seconds to run a statute mile (5280-foot) course, the boat's speed is 13.9 statute miles per hour. If the course were a nautical mile (6076.1 feet), the speed is 13.9 knots (nautical miles per hour).

TABLE II

Height (feet)	Distance (nautical miles)	(statute miles)	Height (feet)	Distance (nautical miles)	(statute miles)	Height (feet)	Distance (nautical miles)	(statute miles)
5	2.6	2.9	70	9.6	11.0	250	18.1	20.8
10	3.6	4.2	75	9.9	11.4	300	19.8	22.8
15	4.4	5.1	80	10.2	11.8	350	21.4	24.6
20	5.1	5.9	85	10.5	12.1	400	22.9	26.3
25	5.7	6.6	90	10.9	12.5	450	24.3	27.9
30	6.3	7.2	95	11.2	12.8	500	25.6	29.4
35	6.8	7.8	100	11.4	13.2	550	26.8	30.9
40	7.2	8.3	110	12.0	13.8	600	28.0	32.3
45	7.7	8.8	120	12.5	14.4	650	29.1	33.5
50	8.1	9.3	130	13.0	15.0	700	30.3	34.8
55	8.5	9.8	140	13.5	15.6	800	32.4	37.3
60	8.9	10.2	150	14.0	16.1	900	34.3	39.5
65	9.2	10.6	200	16.2	18.6	1,000	36.2	41.6

TABLE II Distance to the horizon, or geographic range, for various heights of eye. To find the range to a distant object or light above the horizon, determine the distance separately for the height at each end and then add the two distances; do not add heights and make a single determination of range. Ranges given here are optical and may vary slightly with different conditions of refraction. Ranges for VHF radio and radar are about 15% greater, but also may vary with atmospheric conditions.

Bilge Ventilation

Gasoline in its liquid and vapor states is potentially dangerous, but this fact need *not* make recreational boating hazardous. All that is required is a respect for its potential, combined with safe boat construction and sensible operating procedures. To enjoy safe boating, one need only follow Coast Guard regulations and good common sense.

WHEN REQUIRED

The "proper and efficient" ventilation of boat bilges was established as a requirement by the Motorboat Act of 1940 for all boats employing volatile fuels (gasoline) with certain limited exceptions, boats built before 25 April 1940 and those of "open" construction.

Open construction defined

The Coast Guard has prepared a set of specifications to guide the boat owner as to whether his craft meets the definition of "open construction." To qualify for exemption from the bilge ventilation regulations, the boat must meet *all* of the following conditions.

(1) As a minimum, engine and fuel tank compartments must have 15 square inches of open area directly exposed to the atmosphere for each cubic foot of *net* compartment volume. (Net volume is found by determining total volume and then subtracting the volume occupied by the engine, tanks, other accessories, etc.)

(2) There must be no long or narrow unventilated spaces accessible from the engine or fuel tank compartments into which a fire could spread, unless the space meets requirements of item 3 below.

(3) Long, narrow compartments, such as side panels, if joining engine or fuel tank compartments and not serving as ducts, must have at least 15 square inches of open area per cubic foot through frequent openings along the compartment's full length.

Note: It was formerly required that all fuel and engine compartments have at least one square inch of open area per cubic foot within one inch of the bilge level or floor so that fuel vapors could drain out into open areas; this requirement has now been deleted.

Be safe—be sure

If your craft does not meet one or more of the specifications above, or if there is *any* doubt, *play it safe and provide an adequate ventilation system.* To err on the safe side will not be costly; it may save a great deal, perhaps even a life.

Diesel-powered boats

Diesel fuel does not come within the Coast Guard's definition of a "volatile" fuel, and thus bilge ventilation legal requirements are not applicable. It is, however, a sensible step to provide essentially the same ventilation system for your boat even if it is diesel-powered.

VENTILATION FUNDAMENTALS

If a boat will entrap fumes, i.e., it is not an "open" boat, it is required to have at least two ventilator ducts fitted with cowls at their openings to the atmosphere.

The ventilators, ducts, and cowls must be installed so that they provide for efficient removal of explosive or flammable gases from bilges of *each* engine and fuel tank compartment. Intake ducting must be installed to extend from the cowls to at least midway to the bilge or at least below the level of the carburetor air intake. Exhaust ducting must be installed to extend from the lower portion of the bilge to the cowls in the open atmosphere. Ducts should not be installed so low in the bilge that they could become obstructed by a normal accumulation of bilge water.

Cowls attached to intake and exhaust ducts should be located and trimmed for maximum effectiveness, and so as to prevent recirculation of fumes through the bilges.

ACTIONS OF 1966-67 AND 1971-72

The Coast Guard in 1966 and 1967 took action to implement much more stringently existing laws and regulations regarding "proper and efficient" bilge ventilation. The law did not change, only the interpretation and enforcement thereof.

These tightened regulations were continued by the 1971 Federal Boat Safety Act and its implementing regulations. Lack of adequate bilge ventilation can result in an order from a Coast Guard Boarding Officer for "termination of unsafe use" of the craft; see page 36.

ACCEPTABLE VENTILATION SYSTEMS

No foolproof ventilation system has been developed. The efficiency of various shaped cowls and ducts, the size and location of components, the capacity of mechanical blowers, and the choice of materials are all related to safety. There is no such thing as a ventilation system "approved by the Coast Guard." There has been, however, a great deal of study and thought, some testing, and years of experience upon which to base requirements. These have led to the conclusion that, *as a minimum,* fresh air must be ducted into *each* engine and fuel tank compartment, and dangerous fumes ducted out of the craft.

To create a flow through the ducting system, at least when underway or when there is a wind, cowls (scoops) or other fittings of equal effectiveness are needed on all ducts. A wind-actuated rotary exhauster or mechanical blower is considered equivalent to a cowl on an exhaust duct.

Ducts required

If it wasn't clear before, there's no mistaking it now: *ducts* are a necessary part of the ventilation system. A mere hole in the hull won't do; that's a vent, not a ventilator. "Vents," the Coast Guard explains, "are openings that permit venting, or escape of gasses due to pressure differential. Ventilators are openings that must be fitted with *cowls* to direct the flow of air and vapors in or out of *ducts* that channel movement of air for the actual displacement of fumes from the space being ventilated."

Ducting materials

For safety and long life, ducts should be made of non-ferrous, galvanized ferrous, or sturdy high-temperature-resistant non-metallic materials. Ducts should be routed clear of, and protected from, contact with hot engine surfaces.

Text continued on page 607

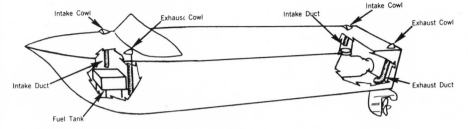

STERN-DRIVE RUNABOUT—Note that all engine and fuel tank compartments need to be efficiently ventilated. Hence, not only the engine area aft should be ducted, but the fuel compartment forward also. As on all installations, an electric exhaust blower is recommended, to be installed externally if it is not of the sealed or arcless type.

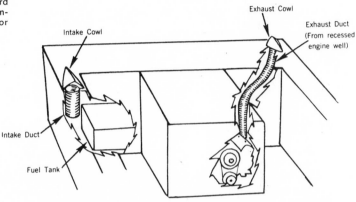

STERN-DRIVE INSTALLATION—Be sure the cowls are arranged to prevent the exhaust being picked up by the intake. If you can't spread them sufficiently apart horizontally (4 feet), to achieve this you probably can work it out by arranging one higher than the other. Where a power-driven exhaust blower is used in a *separate* duct, its duct may terminate in a flush fitting without a cowl. If the blower is in a natural ventilation duct, a cowl must be used and located so as to be in a normal suction situation.

INSTALLATION WHERE TRANSOM FUEL TANK IS USED—The requirements remain the same: at least two cowl-fitted ventilators properly ducted and of sufficient capacity.

INSTALLATION WHERE AFT SEAT IS USED—Where the fuel tank is under a stern seat, ventilate as illustrated in the diagram. It's a good idea to be sure you can get to the tank quickly, if for nothing else, to inspect it. Hinge the seat if it is not already so constructed.

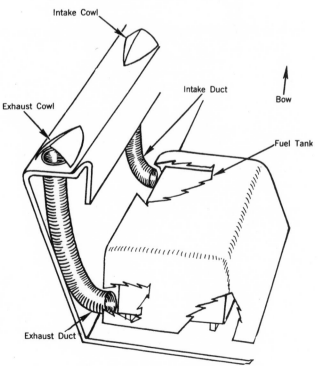

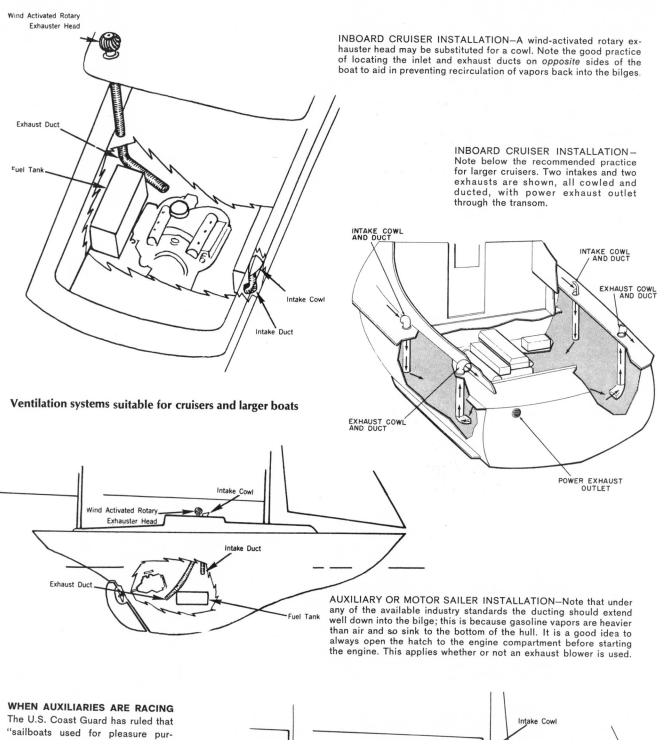

Wind Activated Rotary
Exhauster Head

Exhaust Duct

Fuel Tank

Intake Cowl

Intake Duct

INBOARD CRUISER INSTALLATION—A wind-activated rotary exhauster head may be substituted for a cowl. Note the good practice of locating the inlet and exhaust ducts on *opposite* sides of the boat to aid in preventing recirculation of vapors back into the bilges.

INBOARD CRUISER INSTALLATION— Note below the recommended practice for larger cruisers. Two intakes and two exhausts are shown, all cowled and ducted, with power exhaust outlet through the transom.

INTAKE COWL
AND DUCT

INTAKE COWL
AND DUCT

EXHAUST COWL
AND DUCT

EXHAUST COWL
AND DUCT

POWER EXHAUST
OUTLET

Ventilation systems suitable for cruisers and larger boats

Intake Cowl

Wind Activated Rotary
Exhauster Head

Intake Duct

Exhaust Duct

Fuel Tank

AUXILIARY OR MOTOR SAILER INSTALLATION—Note that under any of the available industry standards the ducting should extend well down into the bilge; this is because gasoline vapors are heavier than air and so sink to the bottom of the hull. It is a good idea to always open the hatch to the engine compartment before starting the engine. This applies whether or not an exhaust blower is used.

WHEN AUXILIARIES ARE RACING
The U.S. Coast Guard has ruled that "sailboats used for pleasure purposes need not be ventilated when under sail alone and may block off cowls and ducts leading to engine and fuel compartments when under sail alone."

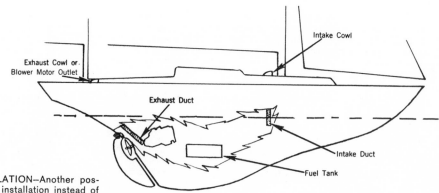

Intake Cowl

Exhaust Cowl or
Blower Motor Outlet

Exhaust Duct

Intake Duct

Fuel Tank

AUXILIARY OR MOTOR SAILER INSTALLATION—Another possible ventilation arrangement is the midship installation instead of the fore and aft one as above.

NATURAL VS. MECHANICAL VENTILATION

The systems described above provide for ventilation without mechanical assistance. The efficiency of a "natural" ventilation system is greatest when there is a breeze from forward of the beam. This will normally occur when underway or at anchor, and some of the time when in a slip. Although less efficient when the wind is abaft the beam, some scouring effect in bilges may be expected even then.

Mechanical blowers

To provide a positive means of exhausting vapors when there is little or no movement of air, and especially before starting engines when risk of explosion is greatest, mechanical blowers are *recommended* for engine spaces. This is not, however, a legal requirement.

It is suggested that ducting separate from the natural ventilation system be installed for mechanical blowers. Exhaust blowers should be of the sealed or arcless type, and, if located within the compartment being ventilated, be positioned as high as possible. Blower fan blades or impellers should be non-sparking; if installed in the exhaust duct of the natural ventilation system, they should not interfere with functioning of the duct as a natural ventilator.

Exterior terminations of separate power exhaust ducts may be fitted with flush louvered fittings instead of cowls.

Positioning of cowls

Normally, the intake cowl will face forward in an area of free airflow underway, and the exhaust cowl will face aft where a suction effect can be expected.

The two cowls, or sets of cowls, should be located with respect to each other, horizontally and/or vertically, so as to prevent return of fumes removed from any space to the same or any other space. Intake cowls should be positioned to avoid pick-up of vapors from fueling operations.

Air for carburetors

Openings into the engine compartment for entry of air to the carburetor are in addition to requirements of the ventilation system.

Size of ducts

Ventilation must be adequate for the size and design of the craft. There should be no constriction in the ducting system that is smaller than the minimum cross-sectional area required for reasonable efficiency. Where a stated size of duct is not available, the next *larger* size should be used.

Small motorboats. To determine the minimum crosssectional area of the cowls and ducts for motorboats having small engine and/or fuel tank compartments, see Table 10-1, which is based on *net* compartment volume (as previously defined).

Cruisers and larger boats. For most cruisers and other large motorboats, Table 10-2, which is based on the craft's beam, is a practical guide for determination of the minimum size of ducts and cowls.

GENERAL SAFETY PRECAUTIONS

Ventilation systems are *not* designed to remove vapors in large quantities such as might be caused by breaks in fuel lines, leaking tanks, or dripping carburetors. If gas odors are detected, repairs are generally needed.

Before starting the engine, especially on calm days and on boats without a power ventilation system, the engine compartment should be opened to dissipate any vapors that may be present. The smaller the compartment, the quicker an explosive mixture of gasoline vapors can develop.

Regardless of the ventilation system installed, always open hatches and use your nose to detect any gasoline odors. Even the slightest trace should warn you to search for the cause and to ventilate the compartment thoroughly before pressing the starter switch.

PASSENGER-CARRYING VESSELS

Vessels that carry more than six passengers *for hire* are subject to special regulations. Consult the nearest Coast Guard Marine Inspection Office for details.

TABLE 10-1			
	One *intake* and One Exhaust System		Two *Intake* and Two Exhaust Systems
Net volume (cu. ft.)	Minimum inside diameter for each duct (inches)	Area sq. in. for cowl	Minimum inside diameter for each duct (inches)
Up to 8	2	3	
10	2¼	4	
12	2½	5	
14	3¾	6	
17	3	7	
20	3¼	8	2½
23	3½	10	2½
27	3¾	11	3
30	4	13	3
35	4¼	14	3
39	4½	16	3
43	4¾	19	3
48	5	20	3

TABLE 10-2—*Two* Intake and *Two* Exhaust Systems		
Vessel beam (feet)	Minimum inside diameter for each duct (inches)	(Area square inches)
7	3	7
8	3¼	8
9	3½	9
10	3½	10
11	3¾	11
12	4	12
13	4¼	13
14	4¼	14
15	4½	15
16	4½	16
17	4½	17
18	5	18
19	5	19

Where To Obtain Charts, Cruising Information, And Other Publications

CHARTS OF VARIOUS WATERWAYS

Charts, U. S. Coastal Waters—Charts of coastal waters such as the Atlantic, Pacific and Gulf Coasts, the Hudson River as far north as Troy, and the Atlantic and Gulf Intracoastal Waterways, are published by the National Ocean Survey, Rockville, Md., 20852, and are available from them, their distribution offices, or any of their sales agents, listed semi-annually in the Oceanographic Office Notice to Mariners.

Charts, Great Lakes—Charts of the Great Lakes and connecting rivers, Lake Champlain, New York State Canals, Lake of the Woods, and Rainy Lake are available from the Lake Survey Center, 630 Federal Bldg., Detroit, Mich. 48226. They also publish a catalog of charts issued by that office.

Charts, New York State Canals—A bound booklet of charts of the New York State canals (Champlain, Erie, Oswego, and Cayuga-Seneca), east of Lyons, is available from the Lake Survey Center, 630 Federal Bldg., Detroit, Mich. 48226.

Charts, Mississippi River and Tributaries—(*Middle & Upper Mississippi River; Cairo, Ill. to Minneapolis, Minn.*)
(*Middle Mississippi River; Cairo, Ill. to Grafton, Ill.*)
(*Mississippi River from Cairo, Ill. to Gulf of Mexico*)
(*Small Boat Navigation Chart; Alton, Ill. to Clarksville on the Mississippi River and Grafton, Ill., to LaGrange, Ill. on the Illinois River*)
(*Illinois Waterways; from Grafton, Ill. to Lake Michigan at Chicago and Calumet Harbors*)
U. S. Army Engineer District, 210 N. 12th Street, St. Louis, Missouri, 63101.

The offices listed below will supply exhaustive lists of available charts, detailing sources, prices, scales, and exact sections covered.

Mississippi River and connecting waterways, north of Ohio River—U. S. Army Engineer Division, North Central, 536 South Clark St., Chicago, Ill. 60605.

Mississippi River and tributaries, below Ohio River—Mississippi River Commission, P.O. Box 80, Vicksburg, Miss. 39181. This office also has a free booklet, "Mississippi River Navigation," discussing history, development and navigation of the river.

Ohio River and tributaries; Pittsburgh, Pa., to the Mississippi River—U. S. Army Engineer Division, P.O. Box 1159, Cincinnati, Ohio 45201.

Tennessee and Cumberland Rivers—U. S. Army Engineer District, P. O. Box 1070, Nashville, Tenn. 37202. Another general information source for the Tennessee is the Tennessee Valley Authority, Maps and Engineering Records Section, 102A Union Bldg., Knoxville, Tenn.

Missouri River and tributaries—U. S. Army Engineer District, 6012 U. S. Post Office and Court House, Omaha, Neb. 68102.

Charts, Canadian Waters—Charts of Canadian waters are available from Hydrographic Chart Distribution, Canadian Hydrographic Service, Department of Mines and Technical Surveys, 615 Booth St., Ottawa, Canada. These include charts of Canadian coastal waters; Canadian sections of the Great Lakes including Georgian Bay; the St. Lawrence River; Richelieu River; Ottawa River; The Rideau Waterway; and other Canadian lakes, canals, etc.

Prices and details are given in a Coastal and Inland Waters Catalog; indexes of charts for any area in Canada are available free from the address above.

Charts, Foreign Waters—These are published by the Defense Mapping Agency Hydrographic Center, Washington, D. C. 20390, and are available through any of the sales agents listed twice a year in Notice to Mariners, published by the Defense Mapping Agency Hydrographic Center. A general catalog and ten regional catalogs are available.

NOTICE TO MARINERS

Notice to Mariners—This is a weekly pamphlet published by the Defense Mapping Agency Hydrographic Center, Washington, D. C. 20390. It is issued so mariners may keep nautical charts and Coast Pilots up to date. Twice a year the Notices contain lists of Branch Hydrographic offices; U. S. Coast Guard District offices; National Ocean Survey District offices; U. S. Engineer offices; agents for the sale of Oceanographic Office charts and publications; data on all publications of the Hydrographic Center; data on the various Coast Pilots, Tide Tables, Current Tables and Tidal Current Charts sold by the National Ocean Survey; data on U. S. Coast Guard Light Lists; and a list of agents for the sale of National Ocean Survey and Coast Guard publications.

Local Notices, of interest primarily within the limits of each of the Coast Guard Districts, are issued by Commanders of the respective districts, and are available from their district offices.

COAST PILOTS

Coast Pilots—For coastal waters, and the Atlantic and Gulf Intracoastal Waterways, these are published by the National Ocean Survey, Rockville, Md. 20852, and are available from them, their distribution offices, or sales agents as listed semi-annually in Notice to Mariners. These volumes supplement the information given on charts, with detailed descriptions of routes, courses, distances, depths, harbors, sources of supplies, tides, currents, weather, list of yacht clubs, facilities for repairs, etc.

For the Great Lakes and other waters covered by Lake Survey charts, the publication corresponding to the Coast Pilot is called the Great Lakes Pilot. This is an annual publication, kept up-to-date during the navigation season by seven monthly supplements issued from May to November. It is obtained from the Lakes Survey Center, 630 Federal Bldg., Detroit, Mich. 48226.

For Canadian waters—available from Hydrographic Chart Distribution, Canadian Hydrographic Office, Dept. of Mines and Technical Surveys, 615 Booth St., Ottawa, Canada. Details are given in the Coastal and Inland Waters Catalog available from Hydrographic Chart Distribution at the address given above. A descriptive list of Pilots and Sailing Directions is also available.

LIGHT LISTS

Light Lists—These are published by the U. S. Coast Guard and are for sale by the Superintendent of Documents, Washington, D. C. 20402, or any of the Coast Guard sales agents listed semi-annually in the Oceanographic Office Notice to Mariners. They describe lighted aids, radio beacons, fog signals, unlighted buoys, and daymarks. Vol. I covers Atlantic Coast from St. Croix River, Me., to Little River, S. C. Vol. II, Atlantic and Gulf Coasts from Little River, S. C., to Rio Grande River, Tex., and the Antilles. Vol. III, Pacific Coast and Islands. Vol. IV, Great Lakes. Vol. V, Mississippi River.

TIDE AND CURRENT TABLES

Tide Tables, Current Tables and Tidal Current Charts—These are also publications of the National Ocean Survey, Rockville, Md. 20852, and may be obtained from them, their distribution offices, or from any of their sales agents listed semi-annually in Notice to Mariners.

RULES OF THE ROAD

Rules of the Road—Rules of the Road are published for three areas, namely: C.G. No. 169—Certain inland waters of the Atlantic and Pacific coasts and of the coast of the Gulf of Mexico; C.G. No. 172—The Great Lakes and their connecting and tributary waters and the St. Mary's River; and C.G. No. 184—The Western Rivers and the Red River of the North. They are published by the U. S. Coast Guard and copies may be obtained from Coast Guard Marine Inspection Offices in principal ports, or the Commandant (CHS), U. S. Coast Guard, Washington, D. C. 20226.

Handbook of Boating Laws—in four editions for Southern, Northeastern, North Central and Western states. Lists state requirements for registering, numbering, equipment and small boat operation; fuel tax laws; boat trailer laws; and applicable federal regulations. Available from Outboard Boating Club, 333 N. Michigan Ave., Chicago, Ill. 60601.

NEW YORK STATE CANALS

Rules and Regulations Covering Navigation and Use of the New York State Canal System—A booklet by this title is published by and is available from New York State Dept. of Public Works, Division of Operation and Maintenance, Albany, N. Y. It contains a description of the New York Canal System, and regulations pertaining to use of the canal. Applications for free season permits to use the canals should be made to the same office.

Canal Guide Book for the New York State Barge Canal System and Connecting Navigable Waterways—A booklet of great value in cruising the Hudson River, Lake Champlain, New York State canals, and connecting Canadian waterways, including the St. Lawrence River and parts of Lake Erie and Lake Ontario. Lists sources of supplies such as fuel, oil, engine repairs, fresh water, provisions, anchorage and dockage. Available from Cruising Guide Book, 146 Sheridan Avenue, Albany, N. Y. 12210.

The Northwest Passage—Cruise kit and guide book, with charts, for Hudson River, Champlain Canal and Lake Champlain. Division of Motor Boats, New York Conservation Dept., Albany, N. Y. 12226.

The Grand Canal—Cruise kit and guide book, with charts, for Erie Canal, Oswego Canal, and the Cayuga Seneca Canals. Division of Motor Boats (address above).

INTRACOASTAL WATERWAYS

Waterway Guide—A publication detailing for the yachtsman a vast amount of information concerning the inland waterways. The Northern Edition covers the coast from Maine to New York; the Middle Atlantic Edition from New York to Sea Island, Ga.; the Southern Edition from Sea Island, Ga., to Florida and Gulf Coast to New Orleans; the Great Lakes Edition from New York to the Great Lakes with connecting Canadian canals and rivers. Available from Waterway Guide, Inc., 238 West St., Annapolis, Md. 21401.

Intracoastal Waterway Booklets—Comprehensive descriptions of the Intracoastal Waterway, with data on navigation, charts, distances, etc. Prepared by Corps of Engineers, U. S. Army, and sold by Superintendent of Documents, Washington, D. C. 20402. In two sections: (1) Atlantic Section, Boston to Key West, (2) Gulf Section, Key West to Brownsville, Tex.

Intracoastal Waterway Bulletins—Frequent bulletins giving latest information on the condition of the Intracoastal Waterway are published by the Corps of Engineers. These are available from the following District Offices of the Army Engineers: 803 Front St., Norfolk, Va. 23510; P. O. Box 1890, Wilmington, N. C. 28401; P. O. Box 919, Charleston, S. C. 29402; P. O. Box 889, Savannah, Ga. 31402; P. O. Box 4970, Jacksonville, Fla. 32201; P. O. Box 2288, Mobile, Ala. 36601; P. O. Box 1229, Galveston, Tex. 77551.

OTHER CRUISING PUBLICATIONS

Cruising Charts, Guides and Booklets—Some of the large oil companies provide free cruising services for yachtsmen. These companies will go to considerable length to provide such items as cruising charts from which the itinerary can be planned, harbor booklets showing the facilities available in all the principal ports, mimeographed outlines of various cruises containing a digest of up-to-date information on the waterways involved, etc. Sources for this kind of material include: Texaco Waterways Service, 135 E. 42nd St., New York 17, N. Y.; Gulf Tourgide Bureau, Box 8056, Philadelphia 1, Pa. (east of Mississippi); Mobil Touring Service, Mobil Oil Co., 150 E. 42nd St., New York 17, N. Y.; Esso Touring Service, 15 W. 51st St., New York 19, N. Y.

Cruising Guide to the New England Coast—Descriptions of harbors, anchorages, and waterways by Fessenden Blanchard. Includes Hudson River, Long Island Sound and the New Brunswick coast. Available from Sailing Book Service, 34 Oak Ave., Tuckahoe, N. Y. 10707.

Cruising Guide to the Southern Coast—Blanchard's guide to the Intracoastal Waterway—Norfolk to New Orleans, including other Florida waterways. Sailing Book Service (address above).

Cruising Guide to the Chesapeake—Another Blanchard guide, with a wealth of information on Chesapeake Bay. Sailing Book Service (address above).

Yachtsman's Guide to Northern Harbors—Harbors, boat basins and services around Long Island, and seacoast of New England. Seaport Publishing Co., 843 Delray Ave., S.E., Grand Rapids 6, Mich.

Guide for Cruising Maryland Waters—Prepared by Maryland Dept. of Tidewater Fisheries. Twenty full-color charts, with more than 200 courses and distances plotted. Maryland Board of Natural Resources, State Office Bldg., Annapolis, Md. Available from the same address is the booklet Maryland Marine Facilities.

Boating Atlas of Tidewater Virginia—An atlas of 53 charts in full color covering the ocean front, lower Chesapeake Bay, the James, York, Rappahannock and Potomac Rivers. Includes buoyage system, rules of the road, location of marine facilities, state and Coast Guard regulations, notes from the Coast Pilot, Tide Tables, safety suggestions, and a course protractor. Distributed by Paxton Co., 1019 Main St., Norfolk, Va.

Florida Boating—Pamphlet giving data on waterways, charts, Florida boat registration, and water safety regulations, fishing licenses, area maps and information, plus a directory of marine facilities throughout the state. Available from Florida Development Commission, Carlton Bldg., Tallahassee, Fla.

Yachtsman's Guide to the Great Lakes—Harbors, services, supplies on the Great Lakes, St. Lawrence, Richelieu and Hudson Rivers, Lake Champlain, and New York State Barge Canal. Seaport Publishing Co., 843 Delray Ave., S. E., Grand Rapids, Mich. 49506.

Cruising the Georgian Bay—Cruising information, with 23 pages of Ontario Government Aerial Survey Maps and tabulations of services and facilities at ports. Bellhaven House, 12 Dyas Road, Don Mills, Ontario.

Cruising the North Channel—Covers the waterway between Manitoulin Island and the north shore of Lake Huron. Bellhaven House, see address above.

Cruising the Trent-Severn Waterway—A cruising guide, including rules and regulations, supply points and services, mileages and general data. British Book Service, see address above.

Trailer Boating Where the North Begins—Written especially for the small boatman, and includes the Muskoka, Parry Sound, and Lake-of-Bays areas of Ontario. Bellhaven House, see address above.

Harbor Guide to the Upper Mississippi River—From Minneapolis to St. Louis, including St. Croix River. Covers harbors (services and location), cities and towns (population, transportation, shopping centers, tourist interest), locks and dams, mileage charts, source of navigation charts, history of river. Available from Mildred Quimby, 801 South Michigan, Prairie du Chien, Wisconsin.

Yachtsman's Guide to the Bahamas—A complete guide book for a cruise in the Bahamas. The data it contains is much like the information found in Coast Pilots. The Customs and Immigration information will be found especially valuable to those who have never cruised to foreign waters. Available from Tropic Isle Publishers, Inc., P. O. Box 613, Coral Gables, Fla. 33134.

Yachtsman's Guide to the Caribbean—Island, port and anchorage charts on courses from Florida through the Bahamas to the Greater Antilles and the Leeward and Windward Islands; lists of facilities, refueling places, customs and port formalities on all islands in the Caribbean. Seaport Publishing Co., 843 Delray Ave. S. E., Grand Rapids, Mich. 49506.

The Alluring Antilles—This cruising guide provides accurate, precise and ample information about every island in the West Indies. D. Van Nostrand Co., Inc., 120 Alexander St., Princeton, N. J. 08540.

Virgin Islands—Eggleston's descriptions of islands, harbors, people, history, passages, and facilities. Illustrated. Sailing Book Service, 34 Oak Avenue, Tuckahoe, N. Y. 10707.

U. S. COAST GUARD PUBLICATIONS

Recreational Boating Guide—CG-340. 77 pp. Information on boat numbering; legal minimum equipment requirements; other equipment you should carry; responsibilities when operating; aids to navigation; hints on safety afloat; emergency procedures; and U. S. Coast Guard Auxiliary services. Contains copies of Federal Boating Act of 1958, and the Motorboat Act of April 25, 1940; sample of Application for Number form; Boating Accident Report; and Radio Distress Information Sheet. Superintendent of Documents, Government Printing Office, Washington, D. C. 20402.

Pleasure Craft—CG-290. Digest of boating laws and regulations. Numbering. Boating accidents. Sales to aliens. Law enforcement. Documentation. C. G. approved equipment. Equipment requirements. Suggestions for safety. U. S. Coast Guard offices.

Marine Aids to Navigation of the United States—U. S. Coast Guard Publication CG-193. Illustrated. 32 pages. U. S. Coast Guard, Washington, D. C. 20590. Basic principles underlying the marking of coasts and waterways with lighthouses, lightships, fog signals, radiobeacons, loran, and buoys. Treats primarily of the manner in which the physical characteristics of various aids to navigation serve the mariner.

Emergency Repairs Afloat—U. S. Coast Guard publication CG-151. The Boatman's pocket guide to engine trouble shooting, emergency repairs, how to stay afloat, and recommended basic hand tools and spare parts. Available from Boating Safety Offices at Coast Guard District Headquarters, or by mail from U.S.C.G. Headquarters, Washington, D. C. 20590.

Rules and Regulations for Uninspected Vessels—U. S. Coast Guard publication CG-258. Currently under revision to add the requirements of the Federal Boat Safety Act of 1971 to the remaining provisions of the Motorboat Act of 1940. When available, every boat owner should have a copy. To be obtainable from District Offices or USCG Headquarters (G-CAS), Washington, D. C. 20590.

Rules and Regulations for Numbering Undocumented Vessels—U. S. Coast Guard publication CG-267. Being revised; expected to later become available from District Offices or USCG Headquarters (G-CAS), Washington, D. C. 20590.

The Skipper's Course—CG-433. 85 pages, illustrated. A concise self-teaching text covering legal requirements, safety afloat, rules of the road, general good operating practices, handling emergencies, and other information essential for the beginning boatman. Includes many quizzes and an end-of-course test, all with answers. Price $1.50 from Superintendent of Documents, Government Printing Office, Washington, DC 20402.

A Pocket Guide for Visual Distress Signals—CG-152. 16 pages, illustrated. Description and guidance for the use of many distress signals suitable for boats. Free from Coast Guard District offices, or Headquarters, U.S. Coast Guard, Washington, DC 20590.

GASOLINE TAX REFUNDS

Gasoline Tax Refunds—Some states allow a refund, in whole or in part, of the gasoline tax when the fuel is used for boat purposes. However, the regulations differ greatly and it would be well for the yachtsman to become familiar with these regulations in advance.

MISCELLANEOUS PUBLICATIONS OF THE
DEFENSE MAPPING AGENCY HYDROGRAPHIC CENTER

The DMA Hydrographic Center produces charts and Sailing Directions (Pilots) and lists of lights of all oceans and seas, and of foreign coasts and islands and harbors, but only general charts of the coasts of the United States.

Information on DMA Hydrographic Center Charts and Publications. H. O. Pub. 1-N. Catalog listing some of the more popular index charts, world charts, general nautical charts, magnetic charts, pilot charts, bathymetric charts, special charts, plotting charts, oceanographic and bottom sediment charts, aeronautical charts, loran charts, published by the DMA Hydrographic Center, with information on H. O. nautical, aeronautical and oceanographic publications. Free Introduction, Part I, is a general listing.

Sailing Directions are books supplementing the nautical charts issued by the DMA Hydrographic Center. They contain descriptions of coast lines, harbors, dangers, aids, port facilities, and other data which cannot be conveniently shown on charts.

Daily Memorandum carries a synopsis of the latest information relating to dangers and aids to navigation, including reports of drifting buoys, wreckage, and other hazards together with advance items that will appear in the Notice to Mariners. The Daily Memorandum is issued locally by the Branch Hydrographic Offices and the most urgent of the reports are also broadcast by radio under the title, Government Hydro All Ships and Stations, and rebroadcast locally.

Pilot Charts of the North Atlantic Ocean, North Pacific Ocean are issued monthly. These present information on average winds and currents, percentages of gales and calms, and other hydrographic data of a varied nature.

H.O. Pilot Charts

#576 Atlas of Pilot Charts—South Atlantic Ocean and Central American Waters.
#577 Atlas of Pilot Charts—South Pacific, Indian Oceans.
#1400 Pilot Chart of the North Atlantic Ocean (Monthly).
#1401 Pilot Chart of the North Pacific Ocean (Monthly).

H.O. Lists of Lights and Fog Signals

Light Lists published by the DMA Hydrographic Center give detailed descriptions of navigational lights and fog signals, and mention signals of various kinds operated at lighthouses.

H.O. 111A and 111B cover the Coast of North and South America (only the seacoast lights of the United States), the West Indies, and the Hawaiian Islands.

H.O. 112 covers islands of the Pacific and Indian Oceans, Australia, Asia, and the East Coast of Africa.

H.O. 113 covers the West Coasts of Europe and Africa, the Mediterranean Sea, Black Sea, and the Sea of Azov.

H.O. 114 covers the British Islands, English Channel, and North Sea.

H.O. 115 covers Norway, Iceland, and Arctic Ocean.

H.O. 116 covers the Baltic Sea with Kattegat, Belts and Sound, and Gulf of Bothnia.

H.O. 111A, 111B, 112, 113 are revised and reissued annually and H.O. 114, 115, 116 at less frequent intervals. H.O. 114, 115, 116 are corrected by annual supplements containing changes that have taken place during the year or years since the books were published. These supplements are mailed free of charge to purchasers of the books. Weekly corrections to the Light Lists are published in the section, Corrections to H.O. Light Lists, at the end of the Notice to Mariners. This section includes minor corrections not appearing in the main body of the Notice.

Other H.O. Publications of the DMA Hydrographic Center

Chart #1—Nautical Chart Symbols and Abbreviations.
#9 American Practical Navigator. Originally by Nathaniel Bowditch, LL.D. etc. Revised (Including the Useful Tables.)
#234 Breakers and Surf; Principles in Forecasting.
#601 Wind, Sea, and Swell: Theory of Relations in Forecasting.

#602 Wind Waves at Sea, Breakers and Surf.
#102 International Code of Signals.
#117 Radio Navigational Aids. Marine Direction-Finding Stations, Radiobeacons, Time Signals, Navigational Warnings, Distress Signals, Medical Advice and Quarantine Stations, Loran, Consol, and Regulations Governing the Use of Radio in Territorial Waters.
#118 Radio Weather Aids. General weather information, broadcast schedules, international index numbers with locations of stations, key groups, and call signs.
#151 Tables of Distances Between Ports.
#2100 World Star Chart.
#226 Handbook of Magnetic Compass Adjustment and Compensation.

WEATHER

Weather Forecasting—National Oceanic & Atmospheric Administration. Illustrated. 40 pages. Generally accepted facts and theories of meteorology and some of the principles of weather forecasting, in popular style. Atmospheric Pressure, Circulation of the Atmosphere, Weather Forecasting, and An Atmospheric Survey, concerning the gathering of information by the Weather Service stations for weather maps. Superintendent of Documents, Washington, D. C. 20402.

The Hurricane—National Oceanic & Atmospheric Administration. Illustrated. 22 pages. An interesting paper dealing solely with the hurricane. The general information contained in this publication should be known by all who go to sea. Superintendent of Documents, Washington, D. C. 20402.

Circular R. W. B. 1151 Preparation and Use of Weather Maps at Sea—National Weather Service. Illustrated. 100 pages. The Ship's weather observation, Radio weather message and its uses, Radio weather bulletins, Preparation of weather maps, Weather types, Tropical storms. Drawing inferences from weather map.

The Daily Weather Map, Weekly Series—National Weather Service. A complete explanation of the maps, including all symbols and tables used in plotting the data appears on the reverse side of the Sunday map only. Annual subscription, $7.50; airmail, add $5.20. Superintendent of Documents, Washington, D. C. 20402.

MISCELLANEOUS PUBLICATIONS

Rules of the Nautical Road—U. S. Naval Institute, Annapolis, Md. Revised edition by Lt. Alfred Prunski, U.S.C.G., of the textbook by Captain Raymond F. Farwell, U.S.N.R., designed to show new changes in International Rules which took effect January 1, 1954. Gives comparison with up-to-date Inland Rules and Pilot Rules. Includes interpretations of rules by courts.

The American Nautical Almanac—United States Naval Observatory. Copies purchased from the Superintendent of Documents. A compact publication containing all the ephemeris material essential to the solution of problems of navigational position. Contains a Star Chart which shows the position of the stars used in navigation. Instructions for its use are included. The Star Chart may be purchased separately. (Star Chart in larger form may be purchased from Oceanographic Office sales agents.)

Tide and Current Investigations of the Coast and Geodetic Survey—National Ocean Survey, Washington, D. C. 20230. Illustrated. 50 pages. Types and forms of tides, earthquake waves, tidal currents, and wind currents.

First Aid—Supt. of Documents, Washington, D. C. 20402. Illustrated. 160 pages. This is one of the best first aid manuals obtainable. Only first aid instruction is given.

Miscellaneous Publication No. 9. The Ship's Medicine Chest and First Aid at Sea—United States Public Health Service. Illustrated. 498 pages. Prepared especially for seafaring people. An excellent treatise. Sections included give special instruction for emergency treatment, and First Aid by Radio. (Superintendent of Documents, Washington, D. C. 20402.)

Magnetic Poles and the Compass—National Ocean Survey. Superintendent of Documents, Washington, D. C. 20402.

EXTRACTS FROM THE FEDERAL BOAT SAFETY ACT OF 1971

(Public Law 92-75, Approved 10 August 1971)

Be it enacted by the Senate and House of Representatives of the United States of America in Congress assembled, That this Act may be cited as the "Federal Boat Safety Act of 1971."

Declaration of policy and purpose

SEC. 2. It is hereby declared to be the policy of Congress and the purpose of this Act to improve boating safety and to foster greater development, use, and enjoyment of all the waters of the United States by encouraging and assisting participation by the several States, the boating industry, and the boating public in development of more comprehensive boating safety programs; by authorizing the establishment of national construction and performance standards for boats and associated equipment; and by creating more flexible regulatory authority concerning the use of boats and equipment. It is further declared to be the policy of Congress to encourage greater and continuing uniformity of boating laws and regulations as among the several States and the Federal Government, a higher degree of reciprocity and comity among the several jurisdictions, and closer cooperation and assistance between the Federal Government and the several States in developing, administering, and enforcing Federal and State laws and regulations pertaining to boating safety.

Definitions

SEC. 3. As used in this Act, and unless the context otherwise requires—

(1) "Boat" means any vessel—

(A) manufactured or used primarily for noncommercial use; or

(B) leased, rented, or chartered to another for the latter's noncommercial use; or

(C) engaged in the carrying of six or fewer passengers.

(2) "Vessel" includes every description of watercraft, other than a seaplane on the water, used or capable of being used as a means of transportation on the water.

(3) "Undocumented vessel" means a vessel which does not have and is not required to have a valid marine document as a vessel of the United States.

(4) "Use" means operate, navigate, or employ.

(5) "Passenger" means every person carried on board a vessel other than—

(A) the owner or his representative;

(B) the operator;

(C) bona fide members of the crew engaged in the business of the vessel who have contributed no consideration for their carriage and who are paid for their services; or

(D) any guest on board a vessel which is being used exclusively for pleasure purposes who has not contributed any consideration, directly, or indirectly, for his carriage.

(6) "Owner" means a person who claims lawful possession of a vessel by virtue of legal title or equitable interest therein which entitles him to such possession.

(7) "Manufacturer" means any person engaged in—

(A) the manufacture, construction, or assembly of boats or associated equipment; or

(B) the manufacture or construction of components for boats and associated equipment to be sold for subsequent assembly; or

(C) the importation into the United States for sale of boats, associated equipment, or components thereof.

(8) "Associated equipment" means—

(A) any system, part, or component of a boat as originally manufactured or any similar part or component manufactured or sold for replacement, repair, or improvement of such system, part, or component;

(B) any accessory or equipment for, or appurtenance to, a boat; and

(C) any marine safety article, accessory, or equipment intended for use by a person on board a boat; but

(D) excluding radio equipment.

(9) "Secretary" means the Secretary of the Department in which the Coast Guard is operating.

(10) "State" means a State of the United States, the Commonwealth of Puerto Rico, the Virgin Islands, Guam, American Samoa, and the District of Columbia.

(11) "Eligible State" means one that has a State boating safety program which has been accepted by the Secretary.

Applicability

SEC. 4. (a) This Act applies to vessels and associated equipment used, to be used, or carried in vessels used, on waters subject to the jurisdiction of the United States and on the high seas beyond the territorial seas for vessels owned in the United States.

(b) Sections 5 through 11 and subsections 12(a) and 12(b) of this Act are applicable also to boats moving or intended to be moved in interstate commerce.

(c) This Act, except those sections where the content expressly indicates otherwise, does not apply to—

(1) foreign vessels temporarily using waters subject to United States jurisdiction;

(2) military or public vessels of the United States, except recreational-type public vessels;

(3) a vessel whose owner is a State or subdivision thereof, which is used principally for governmental purposes, and which is clearly identifiable as such;

(4) ships' lifeboats.

Boat and Associated Equipment Standards and Use

Safety regulations and standards

SEC. 5. (a) The Secretary may issue regulations—

(1) establishing minimum safety standards for boats and associated equipment, and establishing procedures and tests required to measure conformance with such standards. Each standard shall be reasonable, shall meet the need for boating safety, and shall be stated, insofar as practicable, in terms of performance;

(2) requiring the installation, carrying, or using of associated equipment on boats and classes of boats subject to this Act; and prohibiting the installation, carrying, or using of associated equipment which does not conform with safety standards established under this section. Equipment contemplated by this clause includes, but is not limited to, fuel systems, ventilation systems, electrical systems, navigational lights, sound producing devices, fire fighting equipment, lifesaving devices, signaling devices, ground tackle, life and grab rails, and navigational equipment.

(b) A regulation or standard issued under this section—

(1) shall specify an effective date which is not earlier than one hundred and eighty days from the date of issuance, except that this period shall be increased in the discretion of the Secretary to not more than eighteen months in any case involving major product design, retooling, or major changes in the manufacturing process, unless the Secretary finds that there exists a boating safety hazard so critical as to require an earlier effective date; what constitutes major product redesign, retooling, or major changes shall be determined by the Secretary;

(2) may not compel substantial alteration of a boat or item of associated equipment which is in existence, or the construction or manufacture of which is commenced before the effective date of the regulation; but subject to that limitation may require compliance or performance to avoid a substantial risk of personal injury to the public that the Secretary considers appropriate in relation to the degree of hazard that the compliance will correct; and

(3) shall be consistent with laws and regulations governing the installation and maintenance of sanitation equipment.

Prescribing regulations and standards

SEC. 6. In establishing a need for formulating and prescribing regulations and standards under section 5 of this Act, the Secretary shall, among other things—

(1) consider the need for and the extent to which the regulations or standards will contribute to boating safety;

(2) consider relevant available boat safety standards, statistics and data, including public and private research, development, testing, and evaluation;

(3) consider whether any proposed regulation or standard is reasonable and appropriate for the particular type of boat or associated equipment for which it is prescribed;

(4) consult with the Boating Safety Advisory Council established pursuant to section 33 of this Act regarding all of the foregoing considerations.

Display of labels evidencing compliance

SEC. 7. The Secretary may require or permit the display of seals, labels, plates, insignia, or other devices for the purpose of certifying or evidencing compliance with Federal safety regulations and standards for boats and associated equipment.

Exemptions

SEC. 9. The Secretary may, if he considers that boating safety will not be adversely affected, issue exemptions from any provision of this Act or regulations and standards established thereunder, on terms and conditions as he considers appropriate.

Federal preemption

SEC. 10. Unless permitted by the Secretary under section 9 of this Act, no State or political subdivision thereof may establish, continue in effect, or enforce any provision of law or regulation which establishes any boat or associated equipment performance or other safety standard, or which imposes any requirement for associated equipment, except, unless disapproved by the Secretary, the carrying or using of marine safety articles to meet uniquely hazardous conditions or circumstances within the State, which is not identical to a Federal regulation issued under section 5 of this Act.

Prohibited acts

SEC. 12. (a) No person shall—

(1) manufacture, construct, assemble, introduce, or deliver for introduction in interstate commerce, or import into the United States, or if engaged in the business of selling or distributing boats or associated equipment, sell or offer for sale, any boat, associated equipment, or component thereof to be sold for subsequent assembly, unless—

(A) it conforms with regulations and standards prescribed under this Act, or

(B) it is intended solely for export, and so labeled, tagged, or marked on the boat or equipment and on the outside of the container, if any, which is exported.

(2) affix, attach, or display a seal, label, plate, insignia, or other device indicating or suggesting compliance with Federal safety standards, on, in, or with a boat or item of associated equipment, which is false or misleading;

(3) fail to furnish a notification as required by section 15 (a) or exercise reasonable diligence in fulfilling the undertaking given pursuant to section 15 (c) of this Act.

(b) No person shall be subject to any penalty contained in this section if he establishes that he did not have reason to know in the exercise of due care that a boat or associated equipment does not conform with applicable Federal boat safety standards, or who holds a certificate issued by the manufacturer of the boat or associated equipment to the effect that such boat or associated equipment conforms to all applicable Federal boat safety standards, unless such person knows or reasonably should have known that such boat or associated equipment does not so conform.

(c) No person may use a vessel in violation of this Act or regulations issued thereunder.

(d) No person may use a vessel, including one otherwise exempted by section 4(c) of this Act, in a negligent manner so as to endanger the life, limb, or property of any person. Violations of this subsection involving use which is grossly negligent, subject the violator, in addition to any other penalties prescribed in this Act, to the criminal penalties prescribed in section 34.

(e) No vessel equipped with propulsion machinery of any type and not subject to the manning requirements of the vessel inspection laws administered by the Coast Guard, may while carrying passengers for hire, be used except in the charge of a person licensed for such service under regulations, prescribed by the Secretary, which pertain to qualifications, issuance, revocation, or suspension, and related matters.

(f) Section 12(e) of this Act shall not apply to any vessel being used for bona fide dealer demonstrations furnished without fee to business invitees. However, if on the basis of substantial evidence the Secretary determines, pursuant to section 6 hereof, that requiring vessels so used to be under the control of licensed persons is necessary to meet the need for boating safety, then the Secretary may promulgate regulations requiring the licensing of persons controlling such vessels in the same manner as provided in section 12(e) of this Act for persons in control of vessels carrying passengers for hire.

Termination of unsafe use

SEC. 13. If a Coast Guard boarding officer observes a boat being used without sufficient lifesaving or firefighting devices or in an overloaded or other unsafe condition as defined in regulations of the Secretary, and in his judgment such use creates an especially hazardous condition, he may direct the operator to take whatever immediate and reasonable steps would be necessary for the safety of those aboard the vessel, including directing the operator to return to mooring and to remain there until the situation creating the hazard is corrected or ended.

Notification of defects; repair or replacement

SEC. 15. (a) Every manufacturer who discovers or acquires information which he determines, in the exercise of reasonable and prudent judgment, indicates that a boat or associated equipment subject to an applicable standard or regulation prescribed pursuant to section 5 of this Act either fails to comply with such standard or regulation, or contains a defect which creates a substantial risk of personal injury to the public, shall, if such boat or associated equipment has left the place of manufacture, furnish notification of such defect or failure of compliance as provided in subsections (b) and (c) of this section, within a reasonable time after the manufacturer has discovered the defect.

(b) The notification required by subsection (a) of this section shall be given to the following persons in the following manner—

(1) by certified mail to the first purchaser for purposes other than resale: *Provided,* That the requirement for notification of such first purchaser shall be satisfied if the manufacturer exercises reasonable diligence in creating and maintaining a list of such purchasers and their current addresses and sends the required notice to each person on said list at the address appearing thereon;

(2) by certified mail to subsequent purchasers, if known to the manufacturer;

(3) by certified mail or other more expeditious means to the dealers or distributors of such manufacturer to whom such boat or associated equipment was delivered.

(c) The notification required by subsection (a) of this section shall contain a clear description of such defect or failure to comply, an evaluation of the hazard reasonably related thereto, a statement of the measures to be taken to correct such defect or failure to comply, and an undertaking by the manufacturer to take such measures at his sole cost and expense.

Rendering of assistance in casualties

SEC. 16. (a) The operator of a vessel, including one otherwise exempted by subsection 4(c) of this Act, involved in a collision, accident, or other casualty, to the extent he can do so without serious danger to his own vessel, or persons aboard, shall render all practical and necessary assistance to persons affected by the collision, accident, or casualty to save them from danger caused by the collision, accident, or casualty. He shall also give his name, address, and the identification of his vessel to any person injured and to the owner of any property damaged. The duties imposed by this subsection are in addition to any duties otherwise imposed by law.

(b) Any person who complies with subsection (a) of this section or who gratuitously and in good faith renders assistance at the scene of a vessel collision, accident, or other casualty without objection of any person assisted, shall not be held liable for any civil damages as a result of the rendering of assistance or for any act or omission in providing or arranging salvage, towage, medical treatment, or other assistance where the assisting person acts as an ordinary, reasonably prudent man would have acted under the same or similar circumstances.

Numbering of Certain Vessels

Vessels requiring numbering

SEC. 17. An undocumented vessel equipped with propulsion machinery of any type shall have a number issued by the proper issuing authority in the State in which the vessel is principally used.

Standard numbering

SEC. 18. (a) The Secretary shall establish by regulation a standard numbering system for vessels. Upon application by a State the Secretary shall approve a State numbering system which is in accord with the standard numbering system and the provisions of this Act relating to numbering and casualty reporting. A State with an approved system is the issuing authority under the Act. The Secretary is the issuing authority in States where a State numbering system has not been approved.

(b) If a State has a numbering system approved by the Secretary under the Act of September 2, 1958 (72 Stat. 1754), as amended, prior to enactment hereof, the system need not be immediately revised to conform with this Act and may continue in effect without change for a period not to exceed three years from the date of enactment of this Act.

(c) When a vessel is actually numbered in the State of principal use, it shall be considered as in compliance with the numbering system requirements of any State in which it is temporarily used.

(d) When a vessel is removed to a new State of principal use, the issuing authority of that State shall recognize the validity of a number awarded by any other issuing authority for a period of at least sixty days before requiring numbering in the new State.

(e) If a State has a numbering system approved after the effective date of this Act, that State must accept and recognize any certificate of number issued by the Secretary, as the previous issuing authority in that State, for one year from the date that State's system is approved, or until its expiration date, at the option of the State.

(f) Whenever the Secretary determines that a State is not administering its approved numbering system in accordance with the standard numbering system, or has altered its system without his approval, he may withdraw his approval after giving notice to the State, in writing, setting forth specifically wherein the State has failed to meet the standards required, and the State has not corrected such failures within a reasonable time after being notified by the Secretary.

Exemptions

SEC. 19. (a) The Secretary, when he is the issuing authority, may exempt a vessel or class of vessels from the numbering provisions of this Act under such conditions as he may prescribe.

(b) When a State is the issuing authority, it may exempt from the numbering provisions of this Act any vessel or class of vessels that has been exempted under subsection (a) of this section or otherwise as permitted by the Secretary.

Description of certificate of number

SEC. 20. (a) A certificate of number granted under this Act shall be pocket size, shall be at all times available for inspection on the vessel for which issued when the vessel is in use, and may not be valid for more than three years. The certificate of number for vessels less than twenty-six feet in length and leased or rented to another for the latter's noncommercial use of less than twenty-four hours may be retained on shore by the vessel's owner or his representative at the place from which the vessel departs or returns to the possession of the owner or his representative. A vessel which does not have the certificate of number on board shall be identified while in use, and comply with such other requirements, as the issuing authority prescribes.

(b) The owner of a vessel numbered under this Act shall furnish to the issuing authority notice of the transfer of all or part of his interest in the vessel, or of the destruction or abandonment of the vessel, within a reasonable time thereof, and shall furnish notice of any change of address within a reasonable time of the change, in accordance with prescribed regulations.

Display of number

SEC. 21. A number required by this Act shall be painted on, or attached to, each side of the forward half of the vessel for which it was issued, and shall be of the size, color, and type as may be prescribed by the Secretary. No other number may be carried on the forward half of the vessel.

Safety certificates

SEC. 22. When a State is the issuing authority it may require that the operator of a numbered vessel hold a valid safety certificate issued under terms and conditions set by the issuing authority.

Regulations

SEC. 23. The issuing authority may prescribe regulations and establish fees to carry out the intent of sections 17 through 24 and section 37 of this Act. A State issuing authority may impose only terms and conditions for vessel numbering (1) which are prescribed by this Act or the regulations of the Secretary concerning the standard numbering system, or (2) which relate to proof of payment of State or local taxes.

State Boating Safety Programs

Establishment and acceptance

SEC. 25. In order to encourage greater State participation and consistency in boating safety efforts, and particularly greater safety patrol and enforcement activities, the Secretary may accept State boating safety programs directed at implementing and supplementing this Act. Acceptance is necessary for a State to receive full rather than partial Federal financial assistance under this Act. The Secretary may also make Federal funds available to an extent permitted by subsection 27(d) of this Act to national nonprofit public service organizations for national boating safety programs and activities which he considers to be in the public interest.

Boating safety program content

SEC. 26. (a) The Secretary shall accept a State boating safety program which—

(1) incorporates a State vessel numbering system previously approved under this Act or includes such a numbering system as part of the proposed boating safety program;

(2) includes generally the other substantive content of the Model State Boat Act as approved by the National Association of State Boating Law Administrators in conjunction with the Council of State Governments, or is in substantial conformity therewith, or conforms sufficiently to insure uniformity and promote comity among the several jurisdictions;

(3) provides for patrol and other activity to assure enforcement of the State boating safety laws and regulations;

(4) provides for boating safety education programs;

(5) designates the State authority or agency which will administer the boating safety program and the allocated Federal funds; and

(6) provides that the designated State authority or agency will submit reports in the form prescribed by the Secretary.

(b) The requirements of subparagraph (a) (2) of this section shall be liberally construed to permit acceptance where the general intent and purpose of such requirements are met and nothing contained therein is in any way intended to discourage a State program which is more extensive or comprehensive than suggested herein, particularly with the regard to safety patrol and enforcement activity commensurate with the amount and type of boating activity within the State, and with regard to public boat safety education, and experimental programs which could enhance boating safety.

Consultation and cooperation

SEC. 32. (a) In carrying out his responsibilities under this Act the Secretary may consult with State and local governments, public and private agencies, organizations and committees, private industry, and other persons having an interest in boating and boating safety.

(b) The Secretary may advise, assist, and cooperate with the States and other interested public and private agencies, in the planning, development, and execution of boating safety programs. Acting under the authority of section 141 of title 14, United States Code, and consonant with the policy defined in section 2 of this Act, the Secretary shall insure the fullest cooperation between the State and Federal authorities in promoting boating safety by entering into agreements and other arrangements with the State whenever possible. Subject to the provisions of chapter 23, title 14, he may make available, upon request from a State, the services of members of the Coast Guard Auxiliary to assist the State in the promotion of boating safety on State waters.

Boating Safety Advisory Council

SEC. 33. (a) The Secretary shall establish a National Boating Safety Advisory Council (hereinafter referred to as "the Council"), which shall not exceed twenty-one members, whom the Secretary considers to have a particular expertise, knowledge, and experience in boating safety. Insofar as practical, to assure balanced representation, members shall be drawn equally from (1) State officials responsible for State boating safety programs, (2) boat and associated equipment manufacturers, and (3) boating organizations and members of the general public. Additional persons from those sources may be appointed to panels to the Council which will assist the Council in the performance of its functions.

(b) In addition to the consultation required by section 6 of this Act the Secretary shall consult with the Council on any other major boat safety matters related to this Act.

Criminal penalties

SEC. 34. Any person who willfully violates section 12(c) of this Act or the regulations issued thereunder shall be fined not more than $1,000 for each violation or imprisoned not more than one year, or both.

Civil penalties

SEC. 35. (a) In addition to any other penalty prescribed by law any person who violates subsection 12(a) of this Act shall be liable to a civil penalty of not more than $2,000 for each violation, except that the maximum civil penalty shall not exceed $100,000 for any related series of violations. Whenever any corporation violates section 12(a) of this Act, any director, officer, or executive employee of such corporation who knowingly and willfully ordered or knowingly and willfully authorized such violation shall be individually liable to the civil penalties contained herein, in addition to the corporation: *Provided, however,* That no such director, officer, or executive employee shall be individually liable under this subsection if he can demonstrate, by a preponderance of the evidence, (1) that said order or authorization was issued on the basis of a determination, in the exercise of reasonable and prudent judgment, that the nonconformity with standards and regulations constituting such violation would not cause or constitute a substantial risk of personal injury to the public, and (2) that at the time of said order or authorization he advised the Secretary in writing of his action under this proviso.

(b) In addition to any other penalty prescribed by law any person who violates any other provision of this Act or the regulations issued thereunder shall be liable to a civil penalty of not more than $500 for each violation. If the violation involves the use of a vessel, the vessel, except as exempted by subsection 4(c) of this Act, shall be liable and may be proceeded against in the district court of any district in which the vessel may be found.

(c) The Secretary may assess and collect any civil penalty incurred under this Act and, in his discretion, remit, mitigate, or compromise any penalty prior to referral to the Attorney General. Subject to approval by the Attorney General, the Secretary may engage in any proceeding in court for that purpose, including a proceeding under subsection (d) of this section. In determining the amount of any penalty to be assessed hereunder, or the amount agreed upon in any compromise, consideration shall be given to the appropriateness of such penalty in light of the size of the business of the person charged, the gravity of the violation and the extent to which the person charged has complied with the provisions of section 15 of this Act or has otherwise attempted to remedy the consequences of the said violation.

(d) When a civil penalty of not more than $200 has been assessed under this Act, the Secretary may refer the matter for collection of the penalty directly to the Federal magistrate of the jurisdiction wherein the person liable may be found for collection procedures under supervision of the district court and pursuant to order issued by the court delegating such authority under section 636(b) of title 28, United States Code.

Casualty reporting systems

SEC. 37. (a) The Secretary shall prescribe a uniform vessel casualty reporting system for vessels subject to this Act, including those otherwise exempted by paragraphs (1), (3), and (4) of section 4(c).

(b) A State vessel numbering system and boating safety program approved under this Act shall provide for the reporting of casualties and accidents involving vessels. A State shall compile and transmit to the Secretary reports, information, and statistics on casualties and accidents reported to it.

(c) A vessel casualty reporting system shall provide for the reporting of all marine casualties involving vessels indicated in subsection (a) of this section and resulting in the death of any person. Marine casualties which do not result in loss of life shall be classified according to the gravity thereof, giving consideration to the extent of the injuries to persons, the extent of property damage, the dangers which casualties create, and the size, occupation or use, and the means of propulsion of the boat involved. Regulations shall prescribe the casualties to be reported and the manner of reporting.

(d) The owner or operator of a boat or vessel indicated in subsection (a) of this section and involved in a casualty or accident shall report the casualty to the Secretary in accordance with regulations prescribed under this section unless he is required to report to a State under a State system approved under this Act.

(e) The Secretary shall collect, analyze, and publish reports, information, or statistics together with such findings and recommendations as he considers appropriate. If a State accident reporting system provides that information derived from accident reports, other than statistical, shall be unavailable for public disclosure, or otherwise prohibits use by the State or any person in any action or proceeding against an individual, the Secretary may utilize the information or material furnished by a State only in like manner.

General regulations

SEC. 39. The Secretary may issue regulations necessary or appropriate to carry out the purposes of this Act.

Savings provision

SEC. 40. Compliance with this Act or standards, regulations, or orders promulgated hereunder shall not relieve any person from liability at common law or under State law.

Miscellaneous provisions

SEC. 41. (a) The following are repealed:

(1) Section 7, as amended, and sections 13 and 14 of the Motorboat Act of 1940, Public Law 76–484, April 25, 1940 (54 Stat. 165);

(2) The Federal Boating Act of 1958, Public Law 85-911, September 2, 1958 (72 Stat. 1754), except subsections 6(b) and 6(c) thereof;

(3) The Act of March 28, 1960, Public Law 86-396 (74 Stat. 10); and

(4) The Act of August 30, 1961, Public Law 87-171 (75 Stat. 408).

(c) Any vessel, to the extent that it is subject to the Small Passenger Carrying Vessel Act, May 10, 1956 (70 Stat. 151), or to any other vessel inspection statute of the United States, is exempt from the provisions of this Act.

(e) Regulations previously issued under statutory provisions repealed, modified, or amended by this Act continue in effect as though promulgated under the authority of this Act until expressly abrogated, modified, or amended by the Secretary under the regulatory authority of this Act.

EXTRACTS FROM COAST GUARD REGULATIONS
RELATING TO THE MOTORBOAT ACT OF 1940

**(These Regulations are retained in effect by the Federal Boat Safety Act of 1971
until specifically replaced by new regulations issued under the authority of that Act.)**

24.01 Authority and Purpose

24.01–1 Purpose of regulations.

24.01–1(a) The purpose of the regulations in this subchapter is to set forth uniform minimum requirements for motorboats, certain motor vessels, and barges carrying passengers when towed by motorboats or motor vessels in accordance with the intent of the Motorboat Act of April 25, 1940, as amended· (54 Stat. 163–167; 46 U.S.C. 526–526t). The regulations are necessary to carry out the provisions of the Motorboat Act of April 25, 1940, and such regulations have the force of law.

24.05 Application

24.05–1 Vessels subject to the requirements of this subchapter.

24.05–1(a) This subchapter shall be applicable to all vessels indicated in column 6 of Table 24.05–1(a), and shall apply to all such United States flag vessels, and to all such foreign vessels, except as follows:

24.05–1(a)(1) Any vessel operating exclusively on inland waters which are not navigable waters of the United States.

24.05–1(a)(2) Any vessel while laid up and dismantled and out of commission.

24.05–1(a)(3) With the exception of vessels of the U.S. Maritime Administration, any vessel with title vested in the United States and which is used for public purposes.

24.10 Definition of Terms Used in this Subchapter

24.10–1 Approved. This term means approved by the Commandant unless otherwise stated.

24.10–3 Carrying passengers for hire. The carriage of any person or persons by a vessel for a valuable consideration, whether directly or indirectly flowing to the owner, charterer, operator, agent or any other person interested in the vessel.

24.10–17 Motorboat.

24.10–17(a) This term means any vessel indicated in column 6 of Table 24.-05–1(a), 65 feet in length or less which is equipped with propulsion machinery (including steam). The length shall be measured from end to end over the deck excluding sheer. This term includes a boat temporarily or permanently equipped with a detachable motor, since such a boat is also subject to the Act of April 25, 1940, as amended (46 U.S.C. 526–526u), and the regulations promulgated thereunder. For the purpose of this subchapter, motorboats are included under the term "vessel" unless specifically noted otherwise. The various classes of motorboats are as follows:

Class A—Any motorboat less than 16 feet in length.

Class 1—Any motorboat 16 feet or over and less than 26 feet in length.

Class 2—Any motorboat 26 feet or over and less than 40 feet in length.

Class 3—Any motorboat 40 feet or over and not more than 65 feet in length.

24.10–17(b) The expression "length shall be measured from end to end over the deck excluding sheer" means a straight line measurement of the overall length from the foremost part of the vessel to the aftermost part of the vessel, measured parallel to the centerline. Bow sprits, bumpkins, rudders, outboard motor brackets, and similar fittings or attachments, are not to be included in the measurement. Length shall be stated in feet and inches.

24.10–19 Motor vessel. This term means any vessel more than 65 feet in length, which is propelled by machinery other than steam.

24.10–23 Passenger. A passenger is every person, other than the master and the members of the crew or other persons employed or engaged in any capacity on board a vessel in the business of that vessel. In the case of a vessel on an international voyage a child under one year of age is not counted as a passenger.

24.10–27 Vessel. Where the word "vessel" is used in this subchapter, it shall be considered to include all vessels indicated in column 6 of Table 24.05–1(a), except as otherwise noted in this subpart.

24.15 Equivalents

24.15–5 Canadian pleasure craft temporarily using navigable waters of the United States.

24.15–5(a) Uninspected Canadian pleasure craft (uninspected vessels) temporarily using navigable waters of the United States may carry in lieu of the equipment required by the Motorboat Act of 1940 (46 U.S.C. 526–526u) and the regulations in this subchapter, the equipment as required by the laws of the Dominion of Canada and the regulations of the Department of Transport, Ottawa, Canada.

25.01 Application

25.01– Applicable to all vessels.

25.01–1(a) The provisions of this part shall apply to all vessels except as specifically noted.

25.05 Navigation Lights and Shapes, Whistles, Foghorns, Fog Bells, and Gongs

25.05–1 Vessels operating on waters governed by the International Rules of the Road.

25.05–1(a) All vessels (including motorboats) operating on waters governed by the International Rules of the Road (33 U.S.C. 1051–1094) shall be equipped with the navigation lights and shapes, whistles, foghorns, fog bells, and gongs as required by those rules.

25.05–10 Vessels operating on waters governed by the Inland, Great Lakes, or Western Rivers Rules of the Road.

25.05–10(a) All vessels, other than motorboats, operating on waters governed by the Inland, Great Lakes, or Western Rivers Rules of the Road (33 U.S.C. 154–232, 241–295, 301–355) shall be equipped with the navigation lights and shapes, whistles, foghorns, fog bells, and gongs as required by the Rules of the Road applicable to the waters on which the vessel is navigated.

25.05–10(b) All motorboats operating on waters governed by the Inland, Great Lakes, or Western Rivers Rules of the Road shall be equipped with the following:

25.05–10(b)(1) Navigation lights as set forth in the Motorboat Act of April 25, 1940, as amended (46 U.S.C. 526–526u) or, in lieu thereof, the lights required by the International Rules of the Road.

25.05–10(b)(2) An efficient whistle or other sound producing mechanical device as set forth in Table 25.05–10(b)(2), except:

25.05–10(b)(2)(i) Motorboats engaged in a race which has been previously arranged or announced, or while engaged in such navigation as is incidental to the tuning up of the motorboat and engines for the race, need not carry the devices required by Table 25.05–10(b)(2).

25.05–10(b)(3) An efficient fog bell, except that the following motorboats need not carry such a bell:

25.05–10(b)(3)(i) Motorboats of less than 26 feet in length (Classes A and 1).

25.05–10(b)(3)(ii) Motorboats engaged in a race previously arranged or announced, or while engaged in such navigation as is incidental to the tuning up of the motorboat and engines for the race.

25.05–15 Light intensity standards

25.05–15(a) Navigation lights shall be of sufficient intensity so that the candlepower outside lens is not less than that amount corresponding to the required distance of visibility as specified in Table 25.05–15(a).

25.05–15(b) Reserved.

25.05–15(c) Reserved.

25.05–15(d) The light intensity standards of this section shall apply to new navigation lights installed and replacements of existing lights made on or after January 1, 1973. Such lights shall be of an approved type.

25.30 Fire Extinguishing Equipment

25.30—1 Application.

25.30—1(a) The provisions of this subpart, with the exception of section 25.-30—90, shall apply to all vessels contracted for on or after November 19, 1952. Vessels contracted for prior to that date shall meet the requirements of section 25.30—90.

25.30—5 General provisions.

25.30—5(a) Where equipment in this subpart is required to be of an approved type, such equipment requires the specific approval of the Commandant. Such approvals are published in the Federal Register, and in addition, are contained in Coast Guard publication CG—190,"Equipment Lists."

25.30—5(b) All hand protable fire extinguishers, semiportable fire extinguishing systems, and fixed fire extinguishing systems shall be of an approved type.

25.30—10 Hand portable fire extinguishers and semiportable fire extinguishing systems.

25.30—10(a) Hand portable fire extinguishers and semiportable fire extinguishing systems are classified by a combination letter and number symbol. The letter indicating the type of fire which the unit could be expected to extinguish, and the number indicating the relative size of the unit.

25.30—10(b) For the purpose of this subchapter, all required hand portable fire extinguishers and semiportable fire extinguishing systems are of the "B" type; i.e., suitable for extinguishing fires involving flammable liquids, greases, etc.

25.30—10(c) The number designations for size will start with "I" for the smallest to "V" for the largest. For the purpose of this subchapter, only sizes I through III will be considered. Sizes I and II are considered hand portable fire extinguishers and sizes III, IV, and V are considered semiportable fire extinguishing systems which shall be fitted with suitable hose and nozzle or other practicable means so that all portions of the space concerned may be covered. Examples of size graduations for some of the typical hand portable fire extinguishers and semiportable fire extinguishing systems are set forth in Table 25.30—10(c).

25.30—10(d) All hand portable fire-extinguishers and semiportable fire extinguishing systems shall have permanently attached thereto a metallic nameplate giving the name of the item, the rated capacity in gallons, quarts, or pounds, the name and address of the person or firm for whom approved, and the identifying mark of the actual manufacturer.

25.30—10(e) Vaporizing-liquid type fire extinguishers containing carbon tetrachloride or chlorobromomethane or other toxic vaporizing liquids are not acceptable as equipment required by this subchapter.

25.30—10(f) Hand portable or semiportable extinguishers which are required on their nameplates to be protected from freezing shall not be located where freezing temperatures may be expected.

25.30—10(g) The use of dry chemical, stored pressure, fire extinguishers not fitted with pressure gauges or indicating devices, manufactured prior to January 1, 1965, may be permitted on motorboats and other vessels so long as such extinguishers are maintained in good and serviceable condition. The following maintenance and inspections are required for such extinguishers:

25.30—10(g)(1) When the date on the inspection record tag on the extinguisher shows that 6 months have elapsed since last weight check ashore, then such extinguisher is no longer accepted as meeting required maintenance conditions until reweighed ashore and found to be in a serviceable condition and within required weight conditions.

25.30—10(g)(2) If weight of the container is ¼ ounce less than stamped on container, it shall be serviced.

25.30—10(g)(3) If the outer seal or seals (which indicate tampering or use when broken) are not intact, the boarding officer or marine inspector will inspect such extinguisher to see that the frangible disc in neck of the container is intact; and if such disc is not intact, the container shall be serviced.

25.30—10(g)(4) If there is evidence of damage, use, or leakage, such as dry chemical powder observed in the nozzle or elsewhere on the extinguisher, the container shall be replaced with a new one and the extinguisher properly serviced or the extinguisher replaced with another approved extinguisher.

25.30—10(h) The dry chemical, stored pressure, fire extinguishers without pressure gauges or indicating devices manufactured after January 1, 1965, shall not be labeled with the marine type label described in Section 162.028—4 of this title nor shall such extinguishers manufactured after January 1, 1965, be carried on board motorboats or other vessels as required equipment.

25.30—15. Fixed fire extinguishing systems.

25.30—15(a) When a fixed fire extinguishing system is installed, it shall be of an approved carbon dioxide type, designed and installed in agreement with the applicable provisions of Subpart 76.15 of Subchapter H (Passenger Vessels) of this chapter.

25.30—20 Fire extinguishing equipment required.

25.30—20(a) Motorboats.

25.30—20(a)(1) All motorboats shall carry at least the minimum number of hand portable fire extinguishers set forth in Table 25.30—20(a)(1), except that motorboats less than 26 feet in length, propelled by outboard motors and not carrying passengers for hire, need not carry such portable fire extinguishers if the construction of such motorboats will not permit the entrapment of explosive or flammable gases or vapors.

25.30—20(a)(2) The intent of this regulation is illustrated in Figure 25.30—20 (a1) where fire extinguishers are required if any one or more of the specified conditions exist, and in Figure 25.30—20 (a2) where specified conditions do not, in themselves, require that fire extinguishers be carried.

25.35 Backfire Flame Control

25.35—1 Requirements

25.35—1(a) Every gasoline engine installed in a motorboat or motor vessel after April 25, 1940, except outboard motors, shall be equipped with an acceptable means of backfire flame control.

25.35—1(b) Installations made before November 19, 1952, need not meet the detailed requirements of this subpart and may be continued in use as long as they are serviceable and in good condition. Replacements shall meet the applicable conditions in this section.

25.35—1(c) Installations consisting of backfire flame arresters bearing basic Approval No. 162.015 may be continued in use as long as they are serviceable and in good condition. Replacements shall meet the applicable conditions in this section.

25.35—1(d) Installations consisting of engine air and fuel induction system and given a basic Approval No. 162.015 may be continued in use as long as they are serviceable and in good condition. Replacements shall meet the applicable conditions in this section.

25.35—1(e) The following are acceptable means of backfire flame control for gasoline engines:

25.35—1(e)(1) A backfire flame arrester constructed in accordance with the specification regulations contained in Subpart 162.041 of Subchapter Q (Specifications) of this chapter and it shall be specifically approved by the Commandant. The flame arrester shall be suitably secured to the air intake with flametight connection.

25.35—1(e)(2) An engine air and fuel induction system which provides adequate protection from propagation of backfire flame to the atmosphere equivalent to that provided by an approved backfire flame arrester. A gasoline engine utilizing an air and fuel induction system, and operated without an approved backfire flame arrester shall have such installation tested and labeled in accordance with the specifications contained in Subpart 162.042 of Subchapter Q (Specifications) of this chapter and such system shall be specifically approved by the Commandant.

25.35—1(e)(3) Any attachment to the carburetor or location of the engine air induction system by means of which flames caused by engine backfire will be dispersed to the atmosphere outside the vessel in such a manner that the flames will not endanger the vessel, persons on board, or nearby vessels and structures. All attachments shall be of metallic construction with flametight connections and firmly secured to withstand vibration, shock, and engine backfire. Such installations do not require formal approval and labeling, but will be accepted by Coast Guard law enforcement officers on the basis of compliance with this subpart.

25.40 Ventilation

25.40–1 Tanks and engine spaces.

25.40–1(a) All motorboats or motor vessels, except open boats, the construction or decking over of which is commenced after April 25, 1940, and which use fuel having a flashpoint of 110°F. or less, shall have at least 2 ventilator ducts, fitted with cowls or their equivalent, for the efficient removal of explosive or fla.nmable gases from the bilges of every engine and fuel tank compartment. There shall be at least one exhaust duct installed so as to extend from the open atmosphere to the lower portion of the bilge and at least one intake duct installed so as to extend to a point at least midway to the bilge or at least below the level of the carburetor air intake. The cowls shall be located and trimmed for maximum effectiveness and in such a manner so as to prevent displaced fumes from being recirculated.

25.40–1(b) As used in this section, the term "open boats" means those motorboats or motor vessels with all engine and fuel tank compartments, and other spaces to which explosive or flammable gases and vapors from these compartments may flow, open to the atmosphere and so arranged as to prevent the entrapment of such gases and vapors within the vessel.

25.40–1(c) Where alterations are needed for existing motorboats or motor vessels to comply with the requirements in this section, such alterations shall be accomplished as soon as practicable but in any case shall be completed by June 1, 1966.

25.45 Liquified Petroleum Gas

25.45–1 Prohibited on vessels carrying passengers for hire.

25.45–1(a) On vessels carrying passengers for hire, the use of liquefied petroleum gases and certain flammable liquids for cooking, heating, or lighting is prohibited by Parts 146 and 147 of Subchapter N (Dangerous Cargoes) of this chapter.

26.15 Boarding

26.15–1 May board at any time.

26.15–1(a) In addition to any other authority provided by law, the boarding of vessels is authorized by subsection 8(c) of the Federal Boating Act of 1958 (46 U.S.C. 527e(c)), which reads as follows:

Commissioned, warrant, and petty officers of the Coast Guard may board any vessel required to be numbered under this Act at any time such vessel is found upon the navigable waters of the United States, the Commonwealth of Puerto Rico, the Virgin Islands, Guam, and the District of Columbia, or on the high seas, address inquiries to those on board, require appropriate proof of identification therefrom, examine the certificate of number issued under this Act, or in the absence of such certificate require appropriate proof of identification of the owner of the vessel, and, in addition, examine such vessel for compliance with this Act, the Act of April 25, 1940, as amended, and the applicable rules of the road.

26.15–1(b) To facilitate the boarding of vessels by the commissioned, warrant, and petty officers of the Coast Guard in the exercise of their authority, every vessel subject to the Federal Boating Act of 1958, or the Act of April 25, 1940, as amended (46 U.S.C. 526–526u), if under way and upon being hailed by a Coast Guard vessel or patrol boat, shall stop immediately and lay to, or shall maneuver in such a way as to permit the boarding officer to come aboard. Failure to stop to permit a boarding officer to board a vessel or refusal to comply will subject the operator or owner to penalties provided in these laws.

26.15–1(c) Coast Guard boarding vessels will be identified by the display of the Coast Guard ensign as a symbol of authority and the Coast Guard personnel will be dressed in Coast Guard uniform. The Coast Guard boarding officer upon boarding a vessel will identify himself to the master, owner, or operator and explain his mission.

26.20 Exhibition of Motorboat Operator's License

26.20–1 Must Be Available.

26.20–1(a) Any person to whom a license as a motorboat operator has been issued shall have such license in his possession and available for immediate production to any Coast Guard boarding officer at all times during which any vessel which he is operating is carrying passengers for hire.

26.25 Crew Requirements

26.25–1 Licensed Personnel.

26.25–1(a) Every motorboat, as defined by the Act of April 25, 1940, as amended (46 U.S.C. 526), and any other vessel of fifteen gross tons or less propelled by machinery other than steam, while carrying passengers for hire, shall be operated or navigated by a person duly licensed for such service by the Coast Guard. This licensed operator shall be in charge of such motorboat or vessel, regardless of whether or not the passengers carried for hire are on such motorboat or vessel or are carried on a non-self-propelled vessel being towed or pushed by such motorboat or vessel. See Section 157.30–30 of Subchapter P (Manning of Vessels) for special provisions with regard to use of superior licenses for motorboat operator's license.

26.25–1(b) Certain uninspected vessels of 200 gross tons and upward are required to carry licensed officers. For details of these provisions see Subchapter P (Manning of Vessels) of this chapter, and the applicable law.

EXTRACTS FROM COAST GUARD REGULATIONS RELATING TO THE FEDERAL BOAT SAFETY ACT OF 1971

PART 173—VESSEL NUMBERING AND CASUALTY AND ACCIDENT REPORTING

Subpart A—General

173.1 Purpose. This part prescribes requirements for numbering vessels and for reporting casualties and accidents to implement sections 17, 18, and 37 of the Federal Boat Safety Act of 1971.

173.3 Definitions. As used in this part:

(a) "Act" means the Federal Boat Safety Act of 1971 (85 Stat. 213; 46 U.S.C. 1451, et seq.).

(b) "Issuing authority" means a State that has a numbering system approved by the Coast Guard or the Coast Guard where a number system has not been approved. Issuing authorities are listed in Appendix A of this part.

(c) "Operator" means the person who is in control or in charge of a vessel while it is in use.

(d) "Owner" means a person who claims lawful possession of a vessel by virtue of legal title or equitable interest therein which entitles him to such possession.

(e) "Person" means an individual, firm, partnership, corporation, company, association, joint-stock association, or governmental entity and includes a trustee, receiver, assignee, or similar representative of any of them.

(f) "Reporting authority" means a State that has a numbering system approved by the Coast Guard or the Coast Guard where a numbering system has not been approved. Reporting authorities are listed in Appendix A of this part.

(g) "State" means a State of the United States, the Commonwealth of Puerto Rico, the Virgin Islands, Guam, American Samoa, and the District of Columbia.

(h) "State of principal use" means the State on whose waters a vessel is used or to be used most during a calendar year.

(i) "Use" means operate, navigate, or employ.

Subpart B—Numbering

173.11 Applicability. This subpart applies to each vessel equipped with propulsion machinery of any type used on waters subject to the jurisdiction of the United States and on the high seas beyond the territorial seas for vessels owned in the United States except—

(a) Foreign vessels temporarily using waters subject to U.S. jurisdiction;

(b) Military or public vessels of the United States, except recreational-type public vessels;

(c) A vessel whose owner is a State or subdivision thereof, which is used principally for governmental purposes, and which is clearly identifiable as such;

(d) Ships' lifeboats;

(e) A vessel which has or is required to have a valid marine document as a vessel of the United States.

173.13 Exemptions. Where the Coast Guard issues numbers, the following classes of vessels are exempt, under section 19(a) of the Act, from the numbering provisions of the Act and this part:

(a) A vessel that is used exclusively for racing.

(b) A vessel equipped with propulsion machinery of less than 10 horsepower that—

(1) Is owned by the owner of a vessel for which a valid certificate of number has been issued;

(2) Displays the number of that numbered vessel followed by the suffix "1" in the manner prescribed in 173.27; and

(3) Is used as a tender for direct transportation between that vessel and the shore and for no other purpose.

173.15 Vessel number required.

(a) Except as provided in 173.17, no person may use a vessel to which this part applies unless—

(1) It has a number issued on a certificate of number by the issuing authority in the State in which the vessel is principally used; and

(2) The number is displayed as described in 173.27.

(b) This section does not apply to a vessel for which a valid temporary certificate has been issued to its owner by the issuing authority in the State in which the vessel is principally used.

173.17 Reciprocity.

(a) Subsection 18(c) of the Act states:

When a vessel is actually numbered in the State of principal use, it shall be considered as in compliance with the numbering system requirements of any State in which it is temporarily used.

(b) Subsection 18(d) of the Act states:

When a vessel is removed to a new State of principal use, the issuing authority of that State shall recognize the validity of a number awarded by any other issuing authority for a period of at least 60 days before requiring numbering in the new State.

173.19 Other numbers prohibited. No person may use a vessel to which this part applies that has any number that is not issued by an issuing authority for that vessel on its forward half.

173.21 Certificate of number required.

(a) Except as provided in 173.13 and 173.17, no person may use a vessel to which this part applies unless it has on board—

(1) A valid certificate of number or

temporary certificate for that vessel issued by the issuing authority in the State in which the vessel is principally used; or

(2) For the vessel described in paragraph (b) of this section, a copy of the lease or rental agreement, signed by the owner or his authorized representative and by the person leasing or renting the vessel, that contains at least—

(i) The vessel number that appears on the certificate of number; and

(ii) The period of time for which the vessel is leased or rented.

(b) Section 20(a) of the Act states in part:

The certificate of number for vessels less than 26 feet in length and leased or rented to another for the latter's noncommercial use of less than 24 hours may be retained on shore by the vessel's owner or his representative at the place from which the vessel departs or returns to the possession of the owner or his representative.

173.23 Inspection of certificate. Each person using a vessel to which this part applies shall present the certificate or lease or rental agreement required by 173.21 to any Federal, State, or local law enforcement officer for inspection at his request.

173.25 Location of certificate of number. No person may use a vessel to which this part applies unless the certificate or lease or rental agreement required by 173.21 is carried on board in such a manner that it can be handed to a person authorized under 173.23 to inspect it.

173.27 Numbers: Display; size; color.

(a) Each number required by 173.15 must—

(1) Be painted on or permanently attached to each side of the forward half of the vessel except as allowed by paragraph (b) or required by paragraph (c) of this section;

(2) Be in plain vertical block characters of not less than 3 inches in height;

(3) Contrast with the color of the background and be distinctly visible and legible;

(4) Have spaces or hyphens that are equal to the width of a letter other than "I" or a number other than "1" between the letter and number groupings (Example: DC 5678 EF or DC–5678–EF); and

(5) Read from left to right.

(b) When a vessel is used by a manufacturer or by a dealer for testing or demonstrating, the number may be painted on or attached to removable plates that are temporarily but firmly attached to each side of the forward half of the vessel.

(c) On vessels so configured that a number on the hull or superstructure would not be easily visible, the number must be painted on or attached to a backing plate that is attached to the forward half of the vessel so that the number is visible from each side of the vessel.

(d) Each number displayed on a tender exempted under 173.13 must meet the requirements of paragraph (a)

of this section and have a space or hyphen that is equal to the width of a letter other than "I" or a number other than "1" between the suffix and the number. (Example: DC 5678 EF 1 or DC–5678–EF–1.)

173.29 Notification to issuing authority. A person whose name appears as the owner of a vessel on a certificate of number shall, within 15 days, notify the issuing authority in a manner prescribed by the issuing authority of—

(a) Any change in his address;

(b) The theft or recovery of the vessel;

(c) The loss or destruction of a valid certificate of number;

(d) The transfer of all or part of his interest in the vessel; and

(e) The destruction or abandonment of the vessel.

173.31 Surrender of certificate of number. A person whose name appears as the owner of a vessel on a certificate of number shall surrender the certificate in a manner prescribed by the issuing authority within 15 days after it becomes invalid under paragraph (b), (c), (d), or (e) of 173.77.

173.33 Removal of number. The person whose name appears on a certificate of number as the owner of a vessel shall remove the number and validation sticker from the vessel when—

(a) The vessel is documented by the Coast Guard;

(b) The certificate of number is invalid under paragraph (c) of 173.77; or

(c) The vessel is no longer principally used in the State where the certificate was issued.

173.35 Coast Guard validation sticker. No person may use a vessel except a vessel exempted in 173.13 that has a number issued by the Coast Guard unless it has the validation sticker issued with the certificate of number displayed within 6 inches of the number.

Subpart C—Casualty and Accident Reporting

173.51 Applicability.

(a) This subpart applies to each vessel used on waters subject to the jurisdiction of the United States and on the high seas beyond the territorial seas for vessels owned in the United States that—

(1) Is used by its operator for recreational purposes; or

(2) Is required to be numbered under this part.

(b) This subpart does not apply to a vessel required to have a certificate of inspection under Chapter I of Title 46, Code of Federal Regulations.

173.53 Immediate notification of death or disappearance.

(a) When, as a result of an occurrence that involves a vessel or its equipment, a person dies or disappears from a vessel, the operator shall, without delay, by the quickest means available, notify the nearest reporting authority listed in Appendix A of this part of—

(1) The date, time, and exact location

of the occurrence;

(2) The name of each person who died or disappeared;

(3) The number and name of the vessel; and

(4) The names and addresses of the owner and operator.

(b) When the operator of a vessel cannot give the notice required by paragraph (a) of this section, each person on board the vessel shall notify the casualty reporting authority or determine that the notice has been given.

173.55 Report of casualty or accident.

(a) The operator of a vessel shall submit the casualty or accident report prescribed in 173.57 to the reporting authority prescribed in 173.59 when, as a result of an occurrence that involves the vessel or its equipment—

(1) A person dies;

(2) A person loses consciousness or receives medical treatment or is disabled for more than 24 hours;

(3) Damage to the vessel and other property damage totals more than $100; or

(4) A person disappears from the vessel under circumstances that indicate death or injury.

(b) A report required by this section must be made—

(1) Within 48 hours of the occurrence if a person dies within 24 hours of the occurrence;

(2) Within 48 hours of the occurrence if a person loses consciousness or receives medical treatment or is disabled for more than 24 hours or disappears from a vessel; and

(3) Within 5 days of the occurrence or death if an earlier report is not required by this paragraph.

(c) When the operator of a vessel cannot submit the casualty or accident report required by paragraph (a) of this section, the owner shall submit the casualty or accident report.

173.57 Casualty or accident report. Each report required by 173.55 must be in writing, dated upon completion, and signed by the person who prepared it and must contain, if available, at least the following information about the casualty or accident:

(a) The numbers and names of each vessel involved.

(b) The name and address of each owner of each vessel involved.

(c) The name of the nearest city or town, the county, the State, and the body of water.

(d) The time and date the casualty or accident occurred.

(e) The location on the water.

(f) The visibility, weather, and water conditions.

(g) The estimated air and water temperatures.

(h) The name, address, age, or date of birth, telephone number, vessel operating experience, and boating safety training of the operator making the report.

(i) The name and address of each

operator of each vessel involved.

(j) The number of persons on board or towed on skiis by each vessel.

(k) The name, address, and date of birth of each person injured or killed.

(l) The cause of each death.

(m) Weather forecasts available to, and weather reports used by, the operator before and during the use of the vessel.

(n) The name and address of each owner of property involved.

(o) The availability and use of personal flotation devices.

(p) The type and amount of each fire extinguisher used.

(q) The nature and extent of each injury.

(r) A description of all property damage and vessel damage with an estimate of the cost of all repairs.

(s) A description of each equipment failure that caused or contributed to the cause of the casualty.

(t) A description of the vessel casualty or accident.

(u) The type of vessel operation (cruising, drifting, fishing, hunting, skiing, racing, or other), and the type of accident (capsizing, sinking, fire, or explosion or other).

(v) The opinion of the person making the report as to the cause of the casualty.

(w) The make, model, type (open, cabin, house, or other), beam width at widest point, length, depth from transom to keel, horsepower, propulsion (outboard, inboard, inboard outdrive, sail, or other), fuel (gas, diesel, or other), construction (wood, steel, aluminum, plastic, fiberglass, or other), and year built (model year), of the reporting operator's vessel.

(x) The name, address, and telephone number of each witness.

(y) The manufacturer's hull identification number, if any, of the reporting operator's vessel.

(z) The name, address, and telephone number of the person submitting the report.

173.59 Where to report. A report required by 173.55 must be submitted to—

(a) The reporting authority listed in Appendix A of this part where the vessel number was issued, or, if the vessel has no number, where the vessel is principally used; or

(b) The reporting authority where the casualty or accident occurred, if it occurred outside the State where the vessel is numbered or principally used.

Subpart D—Issue of Certificate of Number

173.71 Application for certificate of number. Any person who is the owner of a vessel to which 173.11 applies may apply for a certificate of number for that vessel by submitting to the issuing authority, listed in Appendix A of this part, where the vessel will principally be used—

(a) An application on a form and in a manner prescribed by the issuing au-

thority; and

(b) The fee required by the issuing authority.

173.73 Duplicate certificate of number. If a certificate of number is lost or destroyed, the person whose name appears on the certificate as the owner may apply for a duplicate certificate by submitting to the issuing authority that issued the certificate—

(a) An application on a form or in a manner prescribed by the issuing authority; and

(b) The fee required by the issuing authority, if any.

173.75 Temporary certificate. A temporary certificate valid for not more than 60 days after it is issued may be issued by an issuing authority pending the issue of a certificate of number. A temporary certificate is not valid after the date that the owner receives the certificate of number from the issuing authority.

173.77 Validity of certificate of number.

(a) Except as provided in paragraphs (b), (c), (d), and (e) of this section, a certificate of number is valid until the date of expiration prescribed by the issuing authority.

(b) A certificate of number issued by an issuing authority is invalid after the date upon which—

(1) The vessel is documented or required to be documented under Part 67 of Title 46, Code of Federal Regulations;

(2) The person whose name appears on the certificate of number as owner of the vessel transfers all of his ownership in the vessel; or

(3) The vessel is destroyed or abandoned.

(c) A certificate of number issued by an issuing authority is invalid if—

(1) The application for the certificate of number contains a false or fraudulent statement; or

(2) The fees for the issuance of the certificate of number are not paid.

(d) A certificate of number is invalid 60 days after the day on which the vessel is no longer principally used in the State where the certficate was issued.

(e) The certificate of number is invalid when the person whose name appears on the certificate involuntarily loses his interest in the numbered vessel by legal process.

173.79 Expiration of Coast Guard certificate of number. A certificate of number issued by the Coast Guard expires 3 years from the date it is issued.

173.85 Coast Guard fees.

(a) In a State where the Coast Guard is the issuing authority the fees for numbering are—

(1) Original number and two validation stickers—$6;

(2) Renewal of number and two validation stickers—$6;

(3) Duplicate certificate of number—$1; and

(4) Replacement of lost or destroyed validation sticker—$0.25 each.

(b) Fees must be paid by check or money order made payable to the "U.S. Coast Guard," except when the application is made in person by the owner, the fee may be paid in cash.

Appendix A—Issuing Authorities and Reporting Authorities

(a) The State is the issuing authority and reporting authority in:

STATE

Alabama—AL.	Nebraska—NB.
Arizona—AZ.	Nevada—NV.
Arkansas—AR.	New Jersey—NJ.
California—CF.	New Mexico—NM.
Colorado—CL.	New York—NY.
Connecticut—CT.	North Carolina—NC.
Delaware—DL.	North Dakota—ND.
Florida—FL.	Ohio—OH.
Georgia—GA.	Oklahoma—OK.
Hawaii—HA.	Oregon—OR.
Idaho—ID.	Pennsylvania—PA.
Illinois—IL.	Puerto Rico—PR.
Indiana—IN.	Rhode Island—RI.
Iowa—IA.	South Carolina—SC.
Kansas—KA.	South Dakota—SD.
Kentucky—KY.	Tennessee—TN.
Louisiana—LA.	Texas—TX.
Maine—ME.	Utah—UT.
Maryland—MD.	Vermont—VT.
Massachusetts—MS.	Virginia—VA.
Michigan—MC.	Virgin Islands—VI.
Minnesota—MN.	West Virginia—WV.
Mississippi—MI.	Wisconsin—WS.
Missouri—MO.	Wyoming—WY.
Montana—MT.	

(b) The Coast Guard is the issuing authority and reporting authority in:

STATE

Alaska—AK.	Guam—GM.
American Samoa—AS.	New Hampshire—
District of Columbia—	NH.
DC.	Washington—WN.

(c) The abbreviations following the names of the State listed in paragraphs (a) and (b) are the two capital letters that must be used in the number format to denote the State of principal use as prescribed in 174.23 of this chapter.

PART 174—STATE NUMBERING AND CASUALTY REPORTING SYSTEMS

Subpart A—General

174.1 Applicability. This part establishes a standard numbering system for vessels and a uniform vessel casualty reporting system for vessels by prescribing requirements applicable to the States for the approval of State numbering systems.

Subpart B—Numbering System Requirements

174.11 Applicability of State numbering system.

(a) Except as allowed in paragraph (c) of this section, a State numbering system must require the numbering of vessels to which 173.11 of this chapter applies.

(b) A State numbering system may require the numbering of any vessel subject to the jurisdiction of the State unless prohibited by the regulations in Part 173 of this chapter.

(c) A State numbering system may exempt from its numbering requirements any vessel or class of vessels to which 173.13 of this chapter applies.

174.13 Owner or operator requirements. A State numbering system must contain the requirements applicable to an owner or a person operating a vessel that are prescribed in the following sections of Part 173 of this chapter:

(a) Paragraph (a) of 173.15 *Vessel number required of this chapter.*

(b) Section 173.19 *Other numbers prohibited of this chapter.*

(c) Paragraph (a) of 173.21 *Certificate of number required of this chapter.*

(d) Section 173.23 *Inspection of certificate of this chapter.*

(e) Section 173.25 *Location of certificate of number of this chapter.*

(f) Section 173.29 *Notification to issuing authority of this chapter.*

(g) Section 173.31 *Surrender of certificate of number of this chapter.*

(h) Section 173.33 *Removal of number of this chapter.*

(i) Section 173.71 *Application for certificate of number of this chapter.*

(j) Section 173.73 *Duplicate certificate of number of this chapter.*

(k) Section 173.77 *Validity of certificate of number of this chapter.*

174.15 Validation stickers.

(a) If a State issues validation stickers, its numbering system must contain the requirements that stickers must be displayed within 6 inches of the number and the stickers must meet the requirements in paragraphs (b) and (c) of this section.

(b) Validation stickers must be approximately 3 inches square.

(c) The year in which each validation sticker expires must be indicated by the colors, blue, international orange, green, and red, in rotation beginning with blue for stickers that expire in 1973.

174.17 Contents of application for certificate of number.

(a) Each form for application for a certificate of number must contain the following information:

(1) Name of the owner.

(2) Address of the owner, including ZIP code.

(3) Date of birth of the owner.

(4) Citizenship of the owner.

(5) State in which vessel is or will be principally used.

(6) The number previously issued by an issuing authority for the vessel, if any.

(7) Whether the application is for a new number, renewal of a number, or transfer of ownership.

(8) Whether the vessel is used for pleasure, rent or lease, dealer or manufacturer demonstration, commercial passenger carrying, commercial fishing, or other commercial use.

(9) Make of vessel.

(10) Year vessel was manufactured or model year.

(11) Manufacturer's hull identification number, if any.

(12) Overall length of vessel.

(13) Type of vessel (open, cabin, house, or other).

(14) Whether the hull is wood, steel, aluminum, fiberglass, plastic, or other.

(15) Whether the propulsion is inboard, outboard, inboard-outdrive, or sail and name of engine manufacturer if available.

(16) Whether the fuel is gasoline, diesel, or other.

(17) The signature of the owner.

(b) An application made by a manufacturer or dealer for a number that is to be temporarily affixed to a vessel for demonstration or test purposes may omit items 9 through 16 of paragraph (a) of this section.

(c) An application made by a person who intends to lease or rent the vessel without propulsion machinery may omit items 15 and 16 of paragraph (a) of this section.

174.19 Contents of a certificate of number.

(a) Except as allowed in paragraphs (b), (c), and (d) of this section, each certificate of number must contain the following information:

(1) Number issued to the vessel.

(2) Expiration date of the certificate.

(3) State of principal use.

(4) Name of the owner.

(5) Address of owner, including ZIP code.

(6) Whether the vessel is used for pleasure, rent or lease, dealer or manufacturer demonstration, commercial passenger carrying commercial fishing or other commercial use.

(7) Manufacturer's hull identification number (if any).

(8) Make of vessel.

(9) Year vessel was manufactured.

(10) Overall length of vessel.

(11) Whether the vessel is an open boat, cabin cruiser, houseboat, or other type.

(12) Hull material.

(13) Whether the propulsion is inboard, outboard, inboard-outdrive, or sail.

(14) Whether the fuel is gasoline, diesel, or other.

(15) A quotation of the State regulations pertaining to change of ownership or address; documentation, loss, destruction, abandonment, theft, or recovery of vessel; carriage of the certificate of number on board when the vessel is in use; rendering aid in a boat accident; and reporting of vessel casualties and accidents.

(b) A certificate of number issued to a vessel that has a manufacturer's hull identification number assigned, may omit items 8 through 14 of paragraph (a) of this section if the manufacturer's hull identification number is plainly marked on the certificate.

(c) A certificate of number issued to a manufacturer or dealer to be used on a vessel for test or demonstration purposes may omit items 7 through 14 of paragraph (a) of this section if the word "manufacturer" or "dealer" is plainly marked on the certificate.

(d) A certificate of number issued to a vessel that is to be rented or leased without propulsion machinery may omit items 13 and 14 of paragraph (a) of this section if the words "livery vessel" are plainly marked on the certificate.

174.21 Contents of temporary certificate. A temporary certificate issued pending the issuance of a certificate of number must contain the following information:

(a) Make of vessel.

(b) Length of vessel.

(c) Type of propulsion.

(d) State in which vessel is principally used.

(e) Name of owner.

(f) Address of owner, including ZIP code.

(g) Signature of owner.

(h) Date of issuance.

(i) Notice to the owner that the temporary certificate is invalid after 60 days from the date of issuance.

174.23 Form of number.

(a) Each number must consist of two capital letters denoting the State of the issuing authority, as specified in Appendix A of Part 173 of this chapter, followed by—

(1) Not more than four numerals followed by not more than two capital letters (example: NH 1234 BD); or

(2) Not more than three numerals followed by not more than three capital letters (example: WN 567 EFG).

(b) A number suffix must not include the letters "I," "O," or "Q," which may be mistaken for numerals.

174.25 Size of certificate of number. Each certificate of number must be approximately 2½ by 3½ inches.

174.27 Duration of certificate of number. A certificate of number must not be valid for more than 3 years.

174.29 Temporary certificate of number. A State may issue a temporary certificate of number that is effective for not more than 60 days.

174.31 Terms and conditions for vessel numbering. A State numbering system may condition the issuance of a certificate of number on—

(a) Title to, or other proof of ownership of a vessel except a recreational-type public vessel of the United States; or

(b) The payment of State or local taxes, except for a recreational-type public vessel of the United States.

Subpart C—Casualty Reporting System Requirements

174.101 Applicability of State casualty reporting system.

(a) A State casualty reporting system must require the reporting of vessel casualties and accidents involving vessels to which 173.51 of this chapter applies.

(b) The State casualty reporting system may require vessel casualty or accident reports resulting in property damage of less than $100.

174.105 Owner or operator casualty reporting requirements. A State vessel casualty reporting system must contain the following requirements of Part 173 of this chapter applicable to an owner or a person operating a vessel:

(a) Section 173.55 *Reporting of casualty or accident of this chapter.*

(b) Section 173.59 *Where to report of this chapter.*

(c) Section 173.53 *Immediate notification of death or disappearance of this chapter.*

(d) Section 173.57 *Casualty or accident report of this chapter.*

(e) Section 173.61 *Rendering of assistance in casualties of this chapter.*

174.107 Contents of casualty or accident report form. Each form for reporting a vessel casualty or accident must contain the information required in 173.57 of this chapter.

Part 175—Equipment Requirements

Subpart A—General

175.1 Applicability.

This part prescribes rules governing the use of boats on waters subject to the jurisdiction of the United States and on the high seas beyond the territorial seas for boats owned in the United States except—

(a) Foreign boats temporarily using waters subject to U.S. jurisdiction;

(b) Military or public boats of the United States, except recreational-type public vessels;

(c) A boat whose owner is a State or subdivision thereof, which is used principally for governmental purposes, and which is clearly identifiable as such;

(d) Ship's lifeboats.

175.3 Definitions.

As used in this part:

(a) "Boat" means any vessel manufactured or used primarily for noncommercial use; leased, rented, or chartered to another for the latter's noncommercial use; or engaged in the carrying of six or fewer passengers.

(b) "Recreational boat" means any vessel manufactured or used primarily for non-comercial use; or leased, rented, or chartered to another for the latter's non-commercial use. It does not include a vessel engaged in the carrying of six or fewer passengers.

(c) "Vessel" includes every description of watercraft, other than a seaplane on the water, used or capable of being used as a means of transportation on the water.

(d) "Use" means operate, navigate, or employ.

(e) "Passenger" means every person carried on board a vessel other than—

(1) The owner or his representative;

(2) The operator;

(3) Bona fide members of the crew engaged in the business of the vessel who have contributed no consideration for their carriage and who are paid for their services; or

(4) Any guest on board a vessel which is being used exclusively for pleasure purposes who has not contributed any consideration, directly or indirectly, for his carriage.

(f) "Racing shell, rowing scull, and racing kyak," means a manually propelled boat that is recognized by national or international racing associations for use in competitive racing and one in which all occupants row, scull, or paddle, with the exception of a coxswain, if one is provided, and is not designed to carry and does not carry any equipment not solely for competitive racing.

Subpart B—Personal Flotation Devices

175.11 Applicability.

This subpart applies to all recreational boats that are propelled or controlled by machinery, sails, oars, paddles, poles, or another vessel except racing shells, rowing sculls, and racing kayaks.

175.13 Definitions.

As used in this subpart:

(a) "Personal flotation device" means a device that is approved by the Commandant under 46 CFR Part 160.

(b) "PFD" means "personal flotation device."

175.15 Personal flotation devices required.

(a) Except as provided in § 175.17, no person may use a recreational boat less than 16 feet in length or a canoe or kayak unless at least one PFD of the following types or their equivalents listed in Table 175.23 is on board for each person:

(1) Type I PFD.

(2) Type II PFD.

(3) Type III PFD.

(4) Type IV PFD.

(b) No person may use a recreational boat 16 feet or more in length, except a canoe or kayak, unless at least one PFD of the following types or their equivalents listed in Table 175.23 is on board for each person:

(1) Type I PFD.

(2) Type II PFD.

(3) Type III PFD.

(c) No person may use a recreational boat 16 feet or more in length, except a canoe or kayak, unless at least one Type IV PFD or its equivalent listed in Table 175.23 is on board in addition to the PFD's required in paragraph (b) of this section.

175.17 Exceptions.

(a) A person using a canoe or kayak that is enclosed by a deck and spray skirt need not comply with § 175.15 if he wears a vest-type lifesaving device that—

(1) Has no less than 150 separate permanently inflated air sacs made of not less than 12 mil polyvinylchloride film and has not less than 13 pounds of positive buoyancy in fresh water, if worn by a person who weighs more than 90 pounds; or

(2) Has no less than 120 separate permanently inflated air sacs made of not less than 12 mil polyvinylchloride film and has not less than 8½ pounds of positive buoyancy in fresh water, if worn by a person who weighs 90 pounds or less.

(b) A Type V PFD may be carried in lieu of any PFD required in § 175.15 if that Type V PFD is approved for the activity in which the recreational boat is being used.

175.19 Stowage.

(a) No person may use a recreational boat unless each Type I, Type II, Type III, or Type V PFD required by § 175.15 or § 175.17 is readily accessible.

(b) No person may use a recreational

boat unless each Type IV PFD required by § 175.15 is immediately available.

175.21 Conditions; approval; marking.

No person may use a recreational boat unless each device required by § 175.15, or each device allowed by § 175.17, is—

(a) In serviceable condition;

(b) Legibly marked with the approval number as specified in 46 CFR Part 160 for items subject to approval; and

(c) Of an appropriate size for the person for whom it is intended.

175.23. Personal flotation device equivalents.

Table 175.23 lists devices that are equivalent to personal flotation devices.

TABLE 175.23

Devices marked	Are equivalent to
160.002 Life preserver	Performance Type I personal flotation device
160.003 Life preserver	Performance Type I personal flotation device
160.004 Life preserver	Performance Type I personal flotation device
160.005 Life preserver	Performance Type I personal flotation device
160.009 Ring life buoy	Performance Type IV personal flotation device
160.047 Buoyant vest	Performance Type II personal flotation device
160.048 Buoyant cushion	Performance Type IV personal flotation device
160.049 Buoyant cushion	Performance Type IV personal flotation device
160.050 Ring life buoy	Performance Type IV personal flotation device
160.052 Buoyant vest	Performance Type II personal flotation device
160.053 Work vest	Performance Type V personal flotation device
160.055 Life preserver	Performance Type I personal flotation device
160.060 Buoyant vest	Performance Type II personal flotation device
160.064 Special purpose water safety buoyant devices.	A device intended to be worn may be equivalent to Type II or Type III. A device that is equivalent to Type III is marked "Type III Device—may not turn unconscious wearer." A device intended to be grasped is equivalent to Type IV.

Part 177—Correction of Especially Hazardous Conditions

Action to Correct Especially Hazardous Conditions

177.01 Purpose and applicability.

This part prescribes rules to implement section 13 of the Federal Boat Safety Act of 1971 which govern the correction of especially hazardous conditions on boats using waters subject to the jurisdiction of the United States and on the high seas beyond the territorial seas for boats owned in the United States, except operators of—

(a) Foreign boats temporarily using waters subject to United States jurisdiction;

(b) Military or public boats of the United States, except recreational-type public boats;

(c) A boat whose owner is a State or subdivision thereof, which is used principally for governmental purposes and which is clearly indentifiable as such;

(d) Ship's lifeboats.

177.03 Definitions.

As used in this part:

(a) "Act" means the Federal Boat Safety Act of 1971 (85 Stat. 213; 46 U.S.C. 1451, et seq.)

(b) "Boat" means any vessel—

(1) Manufactured or used primarily for noncommercial use; or

(2) Leased, rented, or chartered to another for the latter's noncommercial use; or

(3) Engaged in the carrying of six or fewer passengers.

(c) Coast Guard Boarding Officer" means a commissioned, warrant, or petty officer of the Coast Guard having authority to board any vessel under the Act of August 4, 1949, 63 Stat. 502, as amended (14 U.S.C. 89).

(d) "Operator" means the person who is in control or in charge of a boat while it is in use.

(e) "Use" means operate, navigate, or employ.

(f) "Vessell" includes every description of watercraft, other than a seaplane on the water, used or capable of being used as a means of transportation on the water.

177.05 Action to correct an especially hazardous condition.

An operator of a boat who is directed by a Coast Guard Boarding Officer to take immediate and reasonable steps necessary for the safety of those aboard the vessel, under section 13 of the Act, shall follow the direction of the Boarding Officer, which may include direction to—

(a) Correct the especially hazardous condition immediately;

(b) Proceed to a mooring, dock, or anchorage; or

(c) Suspend further use of the boat until the especially hazardous condition is corrected.

177.07 Other unsafe conditions.

For the purpose of section 13 of the Act, "other unsafe condition" means a boat—

(a) Does not display the navigation lights prescribed by 46 CFR 25.05 between sunset and sunrise;

(b) Has fuel leakage from either the fuel system or engine;

(c) Has an accumulation of fuel in the bilges or a compartment other than a fuel tank;

(d) Does not meet the ventilation requirements for tanks and engine spaces prescribed by 46 CFR Subpart 25.40; or

(e) Does not meet the requirements for backfire flame control prescribed by 46 CFR Subpart 25.35.

177.09 Penalties.

An operator of a boat who does not follow the directions of a Coast Guard Boarding Officer prescribed in § 177.05 is, in addition to any other penalty prescribed by law, subject to—

(a) The criminal penalties of section 34 of the Federal Boat Safety Act of 1971 which provides that "Any person who willfully violates section 12(c) of this Act or the regulations issued thereunder shall be fined not more than $1,000 for each violation or imprisoned not more than 1 year, or both," and

(b) The civil penalties of subsection 35(b) of the Federal Boat Safety Act of 1971 which provides "In addition to any other penalty prescribed by law any person who violates any other provision of this Act or the regulations issued thereunder shall be liable to a civil penalty of not more than $500 for each violation. If the violation involves the use of a vessel, the vessel, except as exempted by subsection 4(c) of this Act, shall be liable and may be proceeded against in the district court of any district in which the vessel may be found.

Effective 1 July 1974, Federal Regulations provide that "No person may operate a vessel, except a foreign vessel or a vessel less than 26' in length, unless it has a placard at least 5" x 8", made of durable material, fixed in a conspicuous place in the machinery spaces, or at the bilge and ballast pump control station, stating the following:

Various marine insurance companies are making such placards in suitable sizes available without charge to boat skippers and others.

> ### DISCHARGE OF OIL PROHIBITED
> The Federal Water Pollution Control Act prohibits the discharge of oil or oily waste into or upon the navigable waters and contiguous zone of the United States if such discharge causes a film or sheen upon, or discoloration of, the surface of the water, or causes a sludge or emulsion beneath the surface of the water. Violators are subject to a penalty of $5,000."

GENERAL INDEX

In a textbook such as **Piloting, Seamanship and Small Boat Handling,** its value to the student, and to all readers for reference purposes, is immeasurably enhanced by a comprehensive general index.

Where multiple listings make it desirable, the reader may turn to a basic head, such as compass, flags, lights, etc., and conveniently find the particular phase of the subject in question. Concerned with variation of the compass, for example, he may find it as a sub-head under the broad listing of "compass," or may turn directly to "variation" where various aspects of variation are, in turn, sub-headed. Generous use of cross-references has been made throughout.

Note: All color plates are designated by the letters A through X, and placed in the following sequence:

A-D   (Navigation Lights), between text pages 64 (f)-64(g).
I-L   (Buoyage Systems), between text pages 304-305.
M-N   (Nautical Charts) between text pages 352-353.
O-V   (Flags and Insignia), between text pages 464-465.
W-X   (International Code Flags), between text pages 526-527.

See also the Nautical Terminology Index beginning on next page, and the Table of Contents, on page v.

A

PAGE

Abandoning Ship 181
Abbreviations Used on Charts 351-354, 365-372
Absent Flag, Owner's ....463, Q, V
Accidents Afloat 620
Accidents, Outboard 568
Accuracy In Piloting, Standard Limits of 386, 431
Actual Current 413, 415
Actual Track 412
Adjust Your Compass 274, 292-296
Advancing a Line of Position 419, 420, 431-433
Advection Fog 251-253
Adverse Conditions, Boat Handling under..........161-170
Agencies for Government Publications 327, 344 608-610
Agonic Line 273
Aground, Aiding a Vessel 170-173
Aid, First 211, 214
Aids to Course Conversion 276-278, 298
Aids to Navigation 300-326
   Buoys ....303-307, I, J, K, L
   Daybeacons 302, 307, 308, 312, 353
   Defined 300
   Directional Lights 326
   Fog Signals ....304, 305, 322-324, I, J
   Intracoastal Waterway 312, 313
   Lightships 324, 325
   Minor Lights 308, 309, 312
   Offshore Light Towers 325
   On Charts ....351-354, 369-371, M, N
   Operating Agencies 301
   Primary Seacoast Lights 317-322
   "Private" Aids 301
   Protection by Law 302
   Purpose 300, 301
   Ranges 325, 326
   River 326, 531
   Secondary Lights 317, 320-322
   State-maintained ....301, 302, 314-316, L
   Types 302, 303
Air Masses, Labeling 238
Aircraft Distress Signals 87
Alien or Random Magnetism 291
Alongshore Piloting 454-457
Alphabet, Phonetic ....495, W
American Boat & Yacht Council 192, 193
American Ensign, Display of ....458-468, O-R, V
American Lighthouses 318, 319

PAGE

American National Red Cross 192, 207, 213
American Nautical Almanac 333, 610
American Practical Navigator
   278, 292, 333, 421, 429, 434, 435, 454, 610
Anchor or Anchors
   Bend 98, 221
   Bowline 98, 99, 220
   Buoy 106, 107, 110, 111
   Care of 112
   Definitions 91
   Evolution of 90
   Holding Power of 99, 108, 109
   Load on 100
   Multiple 114
   Number and Weight 98
   Parts of 91, 92
   Rode 95-99
      Braided Synthetic 96
      Care and Inspection 112, 113
      Chain 96, 97
      Manila 96, 97
      Nylon 95
      Nylon-and-chain 97
   Selection of 91-95
   Stowage of 100, 101
   Types of
      Ancient 90
      Burying 91, 93, 94
      Folding 94
      Grapnels 94, 96
      Kedges 92, 94
      Lightweight 90-93
      Mushroom 95, 113, 115
      Navy 90, 91, 94
      Plow 91, 92, 94, 99, 100
      Sea 95, 165, 166
      Stockless 91, 94
Anchoring 89-115, 136, 138
   Approaching Anchorage 103
   Buoys, Use of 106, 107, 110, 111
   Chafe, Protection Against 112
   Cautions 112
   Chart, Use of 103
   Docking, When 110, 136, 138
   Dragging, What to Do 105, 106

PAGE

Equipment 91–102
Fouled Anchor, Clearing 108–111
Getting Under Way 107, 477
Hand Signals, Use of 106
Kedging 111
Letting Go 105
Lights Required 64j, 111
Making Fast 105
Night, at 111
Ranges, Use of 103
Rivers on the 537
Rocky Bottoms, on 108, 110, 111
Scowing 111
Selecting an Anchorage 103
Setting the Anchor 105
Stern Anchors, Use of 110
Swinging Circles 104
System 91, 92
Techniques 136, 138
Trip Lines, Use of 110, 111
Two Anchors, Use of 109, 110
Without Power 106
Yawing, How to Stop 109
Anemometer 255
Aneroid Barometer 257
Angle
Course as an 275, 387
Deviation as an 274, 275, 282, 298, 374, 375
Direction as an 270, 272, 375
Variation as an 272, 273, 275, 298
Angle, Danger .429, 430
Angular Equivalents, Points and Quarter Points 271
Angular Measurement 375
Annual Change in Variation 272, 274, 298, 342
Antenna, Radio 490, 491
Apparent Motion of Compass Card 287, 298
Application for Numbers 616, 618, 620
Applying Variation and Deviation
To Bearings 299, 424
To Courses in Degrees 276, 277, 298, 424
To Courses in Points 278, 298
Arctic Sea Smoke 253
Arrival, Estimated Time of 387
Art of Docking 154–157
Artificial Land Cuts 545
Artificial Respiration 212
Assignments, Reading
USCG Auxiliary Study Course 639
USPS Instruction Courses 639
Assistance, Coast Guard 177, 180, 181
Assisting Vessels, Towing Off, etc. 172–175
Attraction, Local 273
Automatic Radio Direction Finder 506
Automatic Steering Devices 512
Autopilots 512
Auxiliaries
Flags for . . . . .460–463, 470, 471, 472, V
Lights for . . . . .64b, d
Auxiliary (Coast Guard) Flags of . . . . . . 458, 460, 602, T
Auxiliary Electric Plant 515, 516
Auxiliary, USCG, Courtesy Motorboat Examinations . .191, 192,
599, 600
Average Bearing 282, 431
Average Speed of Boat 389–391
Azimuth Ring 282

B

Back Splice 231
Backing .129–132, 152, 153

PAGE

Backing, Rule for Boats 76
Bar, Approaching a 164–167
Bar, Flinders 295
Barges, Lights for . . . . .64f, g, A–D
Barometer, The 257, 258
Barometer and Wind Changes 258
Barometer Rules 258
Basic Piloting 373–391, 417–424
Batteries, Storage 199, 200, 487, 488
Beacons . . . . .302, 307, 308, 312, 353, I–L
Beam, Points on 9
Beam Seas, Handling a Boat in 163, 164, 170
Bearing or Bearings
Averaging a Round of 282, 431
Bow and Beam 433
Compass 282, 299, 378, 379, 419, 424
Converting to True 298, 424
Cross 420–422, 431–433
Danger 429
Defined 9, 16, 418, 419
Determining Deviation by 282
Magnetic 282, 379, 419
Of the Sun .278, 295
Plotting 379–381, 418–421, 447–454
Position by 419–426, 433–437, 447, 448
Radar 437, 508, 509
Radio 435–437, 503–506
Relative 378, 379, 425, 426, 434, 435, 449, 450
Simple Visual 423, 424
Taking 378–381, 423–426
Beaufort Scale 255
Becket Bend 220
Bell Buoys 304
Bell (Fog) 304, 322–323
Bends, Knots and Hitches 220–221
Bends, Rules for Meeting at 74, 76
Bilges, Air Ducts for 605–607
Bilges, Definition 6
Bilge Ventilation 605–607
Binnacle 269, 281, 287–289
Binoculars 385
Blackwall Hitch 221
Blade Thrust of Propeller, Unequal 124, 125
Block and Rope Sizes, Table 227
Blocks and Tackles 225–227
Board, Maneuvering 451–454
Boarding and Leaving Another Boat 475, 476
Boarding and Leaving Government Ships 474, 475
Boat Construction Terminology 3–6
Boat Handling
Adverse Conditions, under 161–170
Anchors in Docking, Use of 110, 136–138
Backing 129, 132, 152, 153
Beam Seas, in 163, 164, 170
Current, Effect of 121
Docking 134, 138, 152–157
Factors Affecting Control 149
Fenders, Use of 145, 146
Following Seas, in 164, 169, 170
Getting Under Way 131, 477
Headway, Checking 131
Heaving Lines 141, 172
Heaving to .165–167
In the Trough of Seas 163, 164, 170
Mooring Lines 138–142, 148
Moorings, Handling Boat at 133, 134
Orders to Crew 149
Outboard 564

NAUTICAL TERMINOLOGY INDEX

Words and phrases listed here cover boating objects and actions described and/or defined in Chapter 1.

Admiralty law   27
Aft   3
Aground   8
Aids to navigation   16
Aloft   3
Anchor chock   27
Auxiliary   2
Abaft   3
Abeam   9

Aboard   3
Abovedeck   3
Abreast   9

Backing blocks   18
Backs (wind)   20
Backstays   14
Baggy wrinkle   26
Balanced helm   23

Balanced rudder   20
Ballast   13
Bar   17
Barometer   11
Batten-down   26
Battens (sail)   20
Batten-seam   5
Beam   6
Beam seas   12

Bearings   9, 16
Bedding compound   10
Belay   8
Belaying pin, 8, 22
Belayed   10
Below   3
Bends   7
Berths   6
Bight   8

Piles, Maneuvering at 146, 147, 150
Principles 120
Propeller Action .123-130
Propeller Hand, Left and Right 123
Response of Boat to Propeller and Rudder 127-130
Reversing 128-132, 152, 153
Rudder Action 126, 152
Running on Inlet 164, 165, 167
Running before the Sea 164, 169, 170
Screw Current .123, 124
Shallow Waters, in 169, 170
Slips, Maneuvering at 132, 133, 146-148, 156, 157
Springs, Use of 138-147, 152
Terminology 122, 138
Turning at a Dock 141, 142
Turning Circles .126, 127
Turning in Close Quarters 132, 148
Twin-Screw Boats, Handling 150-155
Undocking 142-145, 155, 156
Wind and Current, Effect of 121
Winding Ship 141
Boat Maintenance 181-189, 209-211
Boating Clothing and Uniforms 479-485
Boating Safety, Basic Guides 214
Boats, Etiquette When Entering and Leaving 475, 476
Border Scales on Charts 345-347
Bosun's Locker 228
Bottoms for Anchoring, Nature of 103
Boundaries of High Seas—Where From 31
Bow and Beam Bearings, Fix from 433
Bow, Points on 9
Bowditch
      278, 292, 333, 421, 429, 434, 435, 454, 610
Bowline 220
Box Compass 269, 290
Boxing the Compass 270
Braided Synthetic Rope 96, 98
Breakers, Handling Boats in 164, 165, 167
Breaking Inlets, Seamanship in 164, 165, 167
Breast Line 138
Briefs, Compass 298, 299
Broaching 164, 169
Buoyage Systems . . . . .309, I, J, K, L, 316
Cardinal 309, 315
Foreign 316
Great Lakes .309, 310
Intracoastal Waterway (ICW) . . . . .312, 313, J
Lateral 309-316
Uniform State (USWMS) . . . . .314-316, L
Western Rivers . . . . .316, K
Buoyant Cushions, Required by Law 54
Buoys . . . . .303-316, I-L
Anchorage Areas . . . . .M, P, 313
Bell . . . . .304, I, K
Can . . . . .303-305, I-L
Cautions in Using 307
Characteristics . . . . .303-306, I-L
Chart Symbols for . . . . .M, N, 352, 353, 365-372
Color Charts . . . . .I-L
Combination 304
Daylight Controls 305
Disposable 294
Gong 304, 305
Light Characteristics 306, 307, 310-311
Lighted . . . . .305, 307, 310-312, I-K, 316
Mooring, ...107, 113
Numbering . . . . .309-312, I-K, 316

Nun . . . . .303, 304, 311, I-K
Quarantine Anchorage Areas . . . . .I-K
Radar Reflector 304-306
Sound Signals . . . . .304-305, I-K
Special Purpose 313-314
Special Type 314
Station 312
Unlighted . . . . .303, 304, I-K
Whistle .304, 305, I
Wreck 311
Burdened and Privileged Vessels 67
Burgees . . . . .462, 464, 602, Q-V

C

Cabin Heaters, Safe Installation of 205
Cable-laying Vessels 64j, 85
Fog Signals 85
Lights 64g
Calculating Slack Water Speeds in a Current 390
Can Buoys . . . . .303-305, I-L
Canadian Waters, Flags Flown in 471, 472
Canal Boating .540-546
Dams 540-546
Locks & Locking 541-545
Manual Signals 542
Precedence at Locks 542
Regulations 546
Safety 545
Signal Lights 542
Whistle Signals 541-542
Canal Boats, Lights . . . . .B, C
Canvas Repairs 231
Cap Devices .480-484, U
Caps, Informal 484
Caps, Uniform .480-484
Capsize, Outboard Boat 568
Car-Trailer Combination 572
Carburetor Safety Features 196, 197
Card, Compass, "a dial" 270, 288
Card, Deviation 286
Cardinal Headings, Compensation on 294, 295, 299
Care and Maintenance of Boat and Engine
      181-189, 209-211
Care of the Compass 291
Carrying Passengers for Hire 45
Cases, Current Sailing Problems 413-416, 441-447
Casualty, Report of 33-34
Catalogs, Chart 330, 333, 334, 356, 357
Cat's Paw Knot 221
Caution in Thick Weather 78, 79, 82, 86, 167
Caution in Use of Charts 359
Caution in Using Buoys 307, 417
Ceremonies (Flag) and Etiquette at Yacht Club and USPS
      Meetings 469, 470
Certificate of Number 36, 613, 622
Chafing Gear .112, 231
Chain for Anchor Rode 96, 97
Chain of Soundings, Fix from 438-439, 501
Changes in Deviation due to Ship's Heading 279-281
Changes in Variation 272, 273, 342
Channel Crossings, River 536
Channel, Rule for Winding 73, 76, 81
Characteristics of Lights 306-311, 320-322
Charted Depth .348, 393

Bilge 6
Bilge keels 17
Binoculars 11
Bitter end 8
Bitts 10
Blankets (in sailing) 24
Blocks 8
Boarding ladder 10
Boards (tacks) 23
Boat 2
Boathook 10
Boatmen 3
Bobstay 22
Bollard 26
Bolt rope 20

Boom 14
Boom crutch 23
Boom vang 22
Boot top 19
Boot topping 20
Bow 3
Bow lines 7
Bowsprit 15
Breakwaters 7
Breasthook 19
Bridge 6
Brightwork 20
Broad on the beam 9
Broad on the bow 9
Bulkheads 5

Bulwarks 5, 18
Bunks 6
Buoys 16
Burgee 11
Butt blocks 5
Button (of oars) 24

Cabin 3
Camber (deck) 19
Canoe 24
Canvas (sails) 14
Capsize 9
Capstan 27
Carburetor 13
Carlings (carlines) 19

Carries away 11
Carvel planking 5
Catamaran 4
Cathedral hull 4
Catwalks 7
Caught in stays (irons) 23
Caulked 5
Cavitation 26
Ceilings 5
Centerboard 13
Centerboard trunk 13
Chafing gear 26
Chainplates 22
Charlie Noble 26
Charter 26

	PAGE
Charted Height	350
Charted Visibility	321-322, 353
Charts	
Abbreviations Used on	351-354, 365-372
Accuracy of	359
Aids and Dangers to Navigation	352-354, 365-372
Catalogs	330, 333, 334, 356, 357
Cautions in Using	359
Coast	355
Compared with Maps	339
Consolan	510
Construction	341, 359-363
Correction of	345, 346, 359
Dates on	345
Depths on	347-349
Distortion of	359-363
Editions and Revisions	345
Fathom Curves	348, 501
General	355
Geographic Coordinates	339, 340
Gnomonic	362, 363
Great Lakes	355, 356, 358, 547
Harbor	355
How Buoys are Shown	352, 353, 369, 370
Hydrography on	347-349
Information Shown on	344-351
Inland Waterways	357, 358
Lambert Conformal	363
Land Features	349, 350
Large Scale vs. Small Scale	343
Lettering on	346, 347
Man-made Features	350, 351
Notes on	344, 345
Pilot	364
Planes of Reference	347-348, 350
Projection, Methods of	341, 359-363
Publishers of	343, 344, 608-610
Radiobeacon	502
Ranges	352, 354, 371
River	358, 533-534
Sailing	354
Scales	343, 354, 355
Series of	354-358
Small Craft	357, M, N
Sources	343, 344, 608-610
Stowage of	355
Symbols	351-354, 365-372
Tidal Current	329, 409-410, 608
Topography on	349, 350
Use of Color	346
Variation from	272, 274, 298, 342
Water Features	347, 349
Where to Buy	344, 608
Check Lists, Pre-departure	208
Chip Log	384
Chocks	112
Church Pennant	X
Circle, Great	340
Circle of Position	418
Circle, Small	340
Circuit Breakers, Electric	488
Citizens' Band Radio	512-514
Classes of Motor Boats	33, 615
Clearing Anchorage or Mooring	107-108, 133, 134, 477
Clearing Customs When Going Abroad	48
Cleat, How to Make Fast to	105, 221
Clothing, Boating	479-485
Clothing, Informal	484-485
Cloud Form Changes, Significance of	261, E, F, G, H
Cloud Formations, Log Symbols for	259, 260
Clouds	238, 239, 242-244, 246, 259, 260
Clouds, Classification of	259, 260
Clouds (color plates)	F, G

	PAGE
Clove Hitch	220
Coast Charts	355
Coast Guard	
Auxiliary Courtesy Examination	61, 191, 192, 599-600
Auxiliary Facilities, Equipment Carried	62
Districts	301
Documentation of Craft	41
Ensign	597, P
Flags, Auxiliary	458, 460, 462, 600, 602
How They Aid Stranded Vessels	180-181, T, V
Publications, U.S.	331, 332, 608-610
Radio Frequency	490
Registration Numbers	613
Coast Pilots	329, 330, 334, 608
Coastal Fog	252, 253
Coastal Warning Facility Charts	264, 265
Code	
Flag Etiquette	469, 470, 602, V
Flags, International	461, 467, 517-522, W, X
Morse	523-525
Signal	517-527, W, X
Signals, Typical	520, 527
USCG Auxiliary Flags	462, 602, T, U
USPS Flags	462, R, S
Yacht Club Signal	520, 522
Coiling Rope	230
Cold-surface Fog	253
Color Ceremonies, Daily	475
Color Retiring Ceremonies	469
Color, Use of on Charts	346, 352-354, 365-372
Coloring of Buoys	306, 310-316, I-L
Colors of Lights on Buoys	310-312, 316, I-L
Combination Buoys	304
Combination of Bearings in Getting a Fix	420-422, 433-435, 447-448
Compass Bearings	282, 299, 378-379, 447-450
Compass, Dry	278, 288
Compass, Dumb, See Pelorus	
Compass, Gyro	278, 378
Compass, The Mariner's	
Accuracy of	278
Azimuth Ring on	282, 378
Adjusting, See Compensation	
Box	269, 290
Boxing the	270-271
Briefs	298, 299
Card, Graduations of	270, 271, 288
Suspension of	268
Care of	291
Compensation, Compensating	274, 281, 292-295, 298
Construction of	268
Conversion Rules (Courses)	276-278
Conversion Table, Points-Degrees	271
Course Defined	275, 387
Deviation or Deviations	
By Bearing of the Sun	278
Card	286
Caused by Windshield Wipers	296, 297
Changes in, Random	291, 296
Curve of	283-285
Defined	274
Depends on Ship's Heading	279-281
Determining	282, 283
Observational	299
Quadrantal	299
Radio	503, 504
Random	296-297
Residual, After Compensation	274, 295, 297
Semicircular	299
Tables	274, 282, 285, 296, 297, 299
Dumb, See Pelorus	
Electric Wires near	269
Error (so-called) CE	275, 277, 278

NAUTICAL TERMINOLOGY INDEX

Chines 17

Chocks 10

Chop (waves) 12

Clawing off 20

Clear 11

Cleats 10

Clevis 26

Clew 20

Close aboard 9

Closed cooling system 13

Close-hauled 16

Coamings 5

Cockpits 5

Collision bulkhead 19

Colors 11

Companion ladders 5

Companionways 5

Compartments 6

Compass course 16

Compass error 16

Compasses 11

PAGE

'Errors' are not Errors 278
How to Apply Var. and Dev. 276-278
Installing the, See Mounting Aboard
Liquid, See The Mariner's
Location of, See Mounting Aboard
Lubber's Line 269, 270, 278, 288, 289
Lubber's Line, a "Hand" 298
Magnetic Environment of 281, 291, 299
Maintenance of 291
Mounting Aboard 269, 290, 291
Points, See Card, Graduations of
Principles Governing its Operation 267
Refilling 291, 298
Review of 298, 299
Rose, The 272-274, 342
Selecting a 287, 288, 298
Sight Vanes on 378, 424
Spherical 267, 268, 287, 289-291
Steering by 169, 275, 288
Swing in Gimbals 268
Testing Site for 290
Trust Your 278
Variation 272, 273, 275-278, 298, 299, 342
Why it Works 267
Zeroing-in 289, 293
Compass, Sun 278
Compensating Magnets 288, 289, 292-295, 299
Concealed Magnets Aboard 290, 291 295, 296, 299
Construction, Safety Features 194-202
Contours on Charts 348-350
Converging Courses 449-450
Conversion of Relative Bearings 419, 425-426
Conversion Table, Compass Points and Degrees 271
Conversion Table, Inches and Millibars 234
Converting Compass to Magnetic, Napier Diagram 285
Converting Courses, Rules for 275-278
Cordage 215
Cordage Table, Weight and Strength 216
Course or Courses
    An Angle 275, 387
    Conversion, Rules for 275-278, 298
    Crossing 449-450
    Defined 275, 298, 387
    Great Circle 362, 363
    Kinds of 275, 298
    Laying or Plotting 379-381, 387-388, 391, 443-447
    On Mercator Charts 359-361, 363
    Over the Ground 411
    Plotter 379, 380
    Protractor 380, 381
    Ranges as a 282, 426, 427
    Reciprocal Sailing 293, 375
    Sailing off, Effects of 297, 426
    Steering by Compass 169, 275, 288
    True 374, 375, 387
Courses (Educational)
    USCG Auxiliary 191, 599
    US Power Squadrons 191, 595-597
Courtesies, Official 476, 477
Courtesy Motorboat Examination, USCGAux 61, 191, 599
CQR Plow Anchor 92
Crew, The 116-119, 161, 175-177
Cross Bearings 420-422, 431-433, 447-448
Cross Signals 71, 81
Crossing Ahead 449-450
Crossing Channel 536
Crossing Courses, Rule for 71
Cruising Etiquette 477, 478
Current or Currents
    Allowing for 411-416, 441-447
    Charts, Tidal 329, 409-410, 608
    Defined 392, 402

PAGE

Determining Actual 413, 415
Determining Slack Water Speeds in 390
Drift 404
Diagrams 407, 409, 411-416, 441-447
Ebb and Flood 404
Estimating Strength Visually 411
Hydraulic 402
Kinds of 402, 403
Piloting in 411-416
River 403, 535
Set of 403, 412, 442-447
Slack 404
Tables 328, 329, 404-409
Tidal 402
Triangles 411-416, 443-447
Wind-driven 403
Current Problems, Using Tables 441-447
Current and Wind, Effect on Boat 121, 169
Currents, Effect on Breakers 165, 167
Custom, Defined 473
Customs and Etiquette, Yachting 473-478
Customs and Immigration Regulations 48
Customs and Usages 473-478
Cyclones, Extra-Tropical 241, 243

D

Danforth Anchor 91-94, 100, 101, 111, 115
Danger Angle, Horizontal 429-430
Danger Angle, Vertical 430
Danger Bearings 429
Danger Curves 348
Danger of Collision 69, 449-450
Danger Signal 69, 76, 85
Dangers to Navigation, How Shown on Chart 354, 371
Danger Zone 71
Datum, Chart, Heights 350
Datum, Tidal 334, 347, 348, 384
Daybeacons ....302, 307-309, 312, 353, I
    Characteristics ....308, I
    Use of ....308, 312, I
Day Marks for Vessels ....I-L
Daymarks, Western Rivers 569
Dead Reckoning
    Definitions 387
    Instruments 378-387
    Importance of 387
    Plots 391
    Track 387, 388, 391
    Weaknesses of 387, 417
Deadweight Tonnage 25
Decal, USCG Auxiliary 61, 191, 600
Deckhouses 3
Degrees and Points, Compass 271
Demagnetization 291, 295, 296, 299
Depth Sounders 384, 499-501, 560
Depths, Measurement of 384, 499-501
Deviation(s) See listings under Compass
Dewpoint 249-251
Diagram, Current 407, 409, 411-416, 441-447
Diagram, Napier 283-285
Dinghy, The 134, 166
Dip Needle 272
Dipping the Ensign 475, 476
Direction
    Defined 342, 374

Composite construction 19
Corinthian 3
Counter 18
Course 16
Covering board 19
Cradle 7
Crest (waves) 12
Cross sea 12

Cruiser 2
Cuddy 3
Current 12
Cutter 15
Cutwater 18

Daggerboard 13
Davits 27

Daybeacons 17
Dead ahead 9
Dead astern 9
Deadlight 6
Dead reckoning 16
Deadweight tonnage 25
Deadwood 12
Deck 3

Deck beams 19
Deck horse (boom horse) 23
Deckhouse 3
Deep-vee hull 4
Departure 16
Depth (of hull) 6
Depthsounder 11
Deviation 16

PAGE

Measurement of 342, 374, 375
Units 342, 374, 375
Direction as an Angle 270, 272
Direction Finders, Radio ...435-437, 502-506
Directional Lights 326
Disabled Vessel Day Mark ....64(I)
Disable Vessel Lights ....64(I)
Discharge Screw Current 123, 124
Discipline and Leadership 116, 474
Displacement Tonnage 25
Distance Around a Headland, Determining 457
Distance, Defined, Units of 375
Distance, Measurement of, on Charts 343, 382-384
Distance-time-speed Calculations 388, 389
Distance-time-speed Tables 442
Distortion on Charts 359-363
Distress Signaling Equipment 203
Distress Signals 87, 180, 203, 204, 496-498, 566-567
Ditty Bag 231
Diurnal Inequality of Tides 395
Dividers, Use of 382, 383
Docking 134-138, 152-157
Documenting of Vessels 41
Double Horizontal Danger Angles 430
Doubling the Angle 433
Doubt, When Giving Signals 69, 76, 85
DR (see Dead Reckoning)
Dragging Anchor, How to Test for 109
Drawbridges, Signals 77
Dredged Channels 348, 349
Dredges and Vessels Aground, Passing 83
Dredges, Day Marks 64n, 64r
Dredges, Lights ....64m, 64n, B
Dredging Buoy 313
Dressing Ship 461, 467
Drift of Current 404
Drift Lead, Use of 111
Drogues 95, 165, 166
Drowning, First Aid for the 212
Dry-bulb Thermometer 250
Dry Compass 278, 288
Dumb Compass, See Pelorus
Duties of Privileged and Burdened Vessels 67
Dutton's 336, 454
Duty of Man at Wheel 116-119, 121, 122

E

Earth's Magnetism 267, 268, 279
Easterly Var. and Dev., How to Apply ...276-278
Ebb Current 404
Echo Piloting 457
Echo Sounding 384, 438-439, 499-501
Eddies & Whirlpools, River 539
Editions of Charts 345
Effects of Sailing Off Course 297, 426
Electrical Systems 199-201, 487, 488
Electrical Wiring 200, 201, 488
Electric Wires near Compass 269
Electronic Equipment 486-516
Emergencies, Preparation for ..161-163, 175-181, 208, 567
Emergency Procedures 175-181
Engine, Care of 186, 187
Engine Exhaust Systems 198, 199
Engine Fuel Systems, Safety Aspects of ..196-198
Engines, Ventilation of 604-607
Ensign
   Coast Guard ....605, P
   Honoring a National 471, 472

PAGE

U. S. ....458-468, O-Q, V
USCGAux ....458, 460, 462, 599, 601-602 T
(USPS), Display of ....459-464, 593, R, S
Yacht ....462, 467, P, V
Entering a Country 48
Equator 340, 341
Equatorial Tides 396
Equipment
   Care of 181, 182
   Carried by USCGAux Facilities 62
   Classes of Motor Boats 64a
   Electronic 486-516
   Not required 202-205, 378-385, 427-428
   Outboard Boat 557-558
   Required by Law 51
   Safety 51-63, 202, 204
Error, Gyro 278
Errors in Running Fixes 432, 433
"Errors" of the Compass, How to Apply ..276-278
Estimated Current 411
Estimated Position
   Defined 411, 419
   Plotting and Labeling ..411, 419, 422-423, 433, 438-439
   With Current 422
Estimated Time of Arrival (ETA) 387
Etiquette
   Cruising 477-478
   Defined 473
   Flag ....458-472, 604-605, O-V
   Yachting 475-478
Examinations
   For License to Operate Motor Boats for Hire........45
   Radio License 492
Examinations, by USCGAux, Courtesy ..61, 191-192, 599-600
Exhaust Systems, Engine 198-199, 607-610
Eternal Compensators, Compass 292, 294-295, 299
External Conditions Affecting Boat Handling 121
Eye Splice, How to Make 222

F

Faking 229-230
Fathom Curves 348, 439, 501
FCC Rules and Regulations 489-499, 512-514
Fenders 145-146
Ferries, Lights for ....64f, A
Fuels & Oils, Outboard Motor 563
Fueling, Outboard 564
Fiber Rope, Care and Inspection 112-113
Fiber Rope, Kinds of 228
Figure Eight Knot 220
Filling Gasoline Tanks 205-206
Fire
   Classes of 178
   Emergencies 178-179
   Extinguishers 56-57, 178-179, 210
   Prevention 196-201, 209-210, 604-607
Fire Protection Standards for Motor Craft 193-194
First Aid 211-214
   Instruments 213
   Kits 211, 213
   Supplies 213
Fish Net Buoys 313
Fisherman's Bend 221
Fishing Vessels
   Day Marks 64n
   Fog Signals 86
   Lights ....64f, 64k, A

NAUTICAL TERMINOLOGY INDEX

Displacement hull   4
Displacement tonnage   25
Dock   6
Documentation   25
Dog watches   11
Dolphin   7
Dolphin striker   22
Double-ended (paddles)   25

Double-ender (boat)   4
Double-planked   5
Downwind   16
Dowsed (doused) sail   14
Draft   6
Drift (of current)   25
Drogue   9
Drydock   6

Dry rot   19

Engine beds   12
Engine compartment   13
Engine instruments   13
Ensign   11
Entrance   18
Even keel   9

Eye bolts   4

Fagged   8
Faked (flaked) down   27
False keel   4
Fastenings   18
Fathom   11
Fenders   10

PAGE

Rights of 75
Fitting-out Preparations 181-188
Fix
  By Bearing and Depth 438, 501
  By Crossed Bearings 420-422, 431-434, 447-448
  By Radar 437, 508-509
  By Sextant 427-431
  By Soundings 438-439, 501
  Defined 388, 419
  From Depth Information 438-439, 501
  Labeling 388, 391, 422
  Running 431-433
Flag Ceremonies, Yacht Club and USPS Meetings 469
Flag Etiquette ....458-472, 601-602, O, V
Flag of Your Country ....465-472, O, P, Q, V
Flag (US), Evolution of 468
Flag-hoist Signaling ....518-522, W, X
Flag Signaling Procedures ....520-522, X
Flags, How Flown
  Armed Services .... P
  Dressing Ship 461, 467
  Foreign Waters 470-471, 472
  Government .... P
  Homes of Yachtsmen 464
  International Code ......461, 467, 517-523, 527, W, X
  Masts Ashore 464, 466-469
  Motor Boats ....458-463, 470-472, Q, V
  Outboard Boats 458-459
  Past Officers' .... S, T
  Sailboats ....460-463, 470-472, Q, V
  State 470
  Tables, Where to Fly ....464, 601-602, V
  USCGAux ....458, 460, 462-463, 601-602, T, U
  U S Power Squadrons ....458-464, 469-472, Q, V
  USPS Officers ....594, R, S
  Yacht Club Masts ....464, 466-467, O
Flame Arrestors (for Carburetors) 196-197
Flashing Light, Signaling 523-525
Flemishing Down 101, 229-230
Flinders Bar 295
Float Plans 208
Flood Current 404
Fog
  Cautions in Using Fog Signals 307, 323-324
  Distribution of 254
  Horn 323
  How It Forms 249
  Judging Likelihood 250
  Seasonal Frequencies 254
  Signals 77, 81, 85-87
  Speed in 79, 87, 167
  Types of 251-253
Folding Anchors 94
Following Seas, Handling Boat in 164, 169-170
Foot-gear for Boating 484
Force, Magnetic Lines of 267-268
Forecasting Weather 238-240
Foreign Ports, Arrival at 48
Foreign Waters, What Flags to Fly 470-472
Fouled Anchor 110
Fronts, Cold and Warm 235, 237, 240, 242
Fuel Filler Pipes and Vents 197
Fuel Lines 197
Fuel Pumps 197-198
Fuel System Safety 196-198
Fuel Tanks 196-197
Fuel Vapor Detectors 514
Fueling Safety Precautions 205-206
Fuses 488

G

Gaff Rig 14
Galley, Safety in the 204-205
Gasoline Fumes 196-198, 604-607
General Charts 355
Generators 487, 515
Geographic Coordinates 339-341, 376-377
Geographic Position 339-341, 376-377
Gimbals 268
Gnomonic Projection 362-363
Gold Braid, Not for Yachtsmen 481
Gong Buoys 304-305
Good Seamanship, Rule of 79
Government Publications 327-336, 397, 406, 608-610
  Army Engineers 334, 608, 610
  Bowditch (H.O.9)
            278, 292, 333, 421, 429, 434-435, 454, 610
  Chart Catalogs 330, 333-334, 356-357, 608
  Coast and Geodetic Survey ...328-331, 344-372, 397-410
  Coast Guard 331-332, 608
  Coast Pilots 329-330, 334, 608
  Government Printing Office 327, 609-610
  Great Lakes Pilot 334, 608
  H.O. Publications 333, 610
  Light Lists 331-332, 608, 610
  Local Notices to Mariners 335-336, 608, 610
  Naval Institute 336
  Naval Oceanographic Office 332-333, 608, 610
  Notices to Mariners 335, 345, 571, 611, 613
  R.T.C.M. 336, 496
  Rules of the Road 332, 608, 610
  Sales Agents 328, 344, 608, 610
  Tidal Current Tables 328, 404-409, 608
  Tide Tables 328, 397-402, 608
  Weather Service 232-235, 264-265, 335, 610
Government Regulation of Motor Boats 29-50, 611-622
Government Vessels, Boarding and Leaving 474-475
Government Vessels, Flags for .... P
Grapnel Anchors 94, 96
Great Circle
  Comparison with Rhumb Line 362-363
  Defined 340
  On Gnomonic Charts 362-363
  On Mercator Charts 359-361, 363
Great Lakes Buoyage System ....309-310, I
Great Lakes Charts 358, 547
Great Lakes Light List 548
Great Lakes Pilot 334, 548, 608
Grommet Strap 231
Gross Tonnage 25
Ground Fog 251
Ground, Radio 490-491
Ground Tackle 91-102
Guest Flag ....459, 461, 463, Q, V
Guest Aboard, Suggestions for 116-119, 477-478
Gun Salute 476
Gunter Rig, Sliding 24
Gyro Compass 278, 378

H

Hachures on Charts 349-350
Half-hitches 221
Hand Lead 384-385
Hand Salutes 474
Handling Boats under Adverse Conditions 161-170
Handling, Practical Hints on 120-127, 528-547

Fetch (an objective) 23
Fid 26
Fife rails 22
Fin keel 23
Flam 18
Flame arrestor 13
Flare 4
Flat bottom 4
Flemish down 27
Flood tide 12
Floors 5

Flotsam 26
Flying bridge 6
Following sea 12
Fore-and-aft 3
Fore-and-aft rigged 15
Forecastle (fo'c's'l) 6
Forepeak 6
Forestays 14, 21
Forestaysail 15
Forward 3
Foul 11

Founder 9
Frames 3
Freeboard 6
Fuel pumps 13
Furled sail 14

Gaff 14
Gaff-rigged 14
Galley 6
Gangway 27

Garboard strake 4
Genoas 21
Gimbals 11
Gooseneck fitting 23
Grab rails 10
Gross tonnage 25
Grounds 8
Ground tackle 8
Gunter (sliding gunter) 24
Gunwale 4
Guys 22

	PAGE
Harbor Charts	355
Hawsepipes	101
Heading	387
Head-on, Rule for Meeting	70
Head Seas	163, 169
Headway, Checking	131
Heaters	205
Heaving Lines	141, 173
Heaving to	165-167
Heavy Weather, Handling in	161-170
Heeling Magnets	281-295
Height of Tide at Any Hour	397-400
Helm, the	6
Helmsmanship	121-122, 168-170, 288
Herreshoff Anchor	93, 95
High Seas, Fog Signals on	85-87
High Water (Tide), Determining Time of	397-399
Highs, Barometric	235-236, 239, 258
History of U S Flag	465-468
Hire, License to Operate Motor Boats for	45
Hitches, Knots and Bends	220-221
Hitches, Two Half	221
Hockle in Rope	100
Holding Power of an Anchor	108-109
Homing with RDF	506
Honoring Other National Flags	471-472
Horizontal Danger Angle	429-430
Horizontal Sextant Angles for Getting a Fix	429-431
Horns, Fog	58, 323
Horsepower, Safe, for Outboards	206
Hull, Care and Inspection of	182-183, 211
Hull, Construction of	121, 194-196
Hull Construction, Safety Aspects of	194-196, 604-607
Hull Design, Outboard	550
Hull Inspection	182, 183, 211
Hurricanes	243-245
Hydraulic Current	402
Hydrography	347-349

I

Identification of Radio Station	495-496, 513-514
Immigration and Customs Regulations	48
Impeller-type Log	382, 384
Inboard-outboard Drives	124, 126, 552
Informal Clothing	484-485
Inland Boating	529-548
Inland Boating Limitations	529
Inland and International Rules, Where they Apply	31
Inland Rules, Lights Required by	64c-64o, A-C
Inland Steamers, Lights for	64f, A
Inland Waters, Fog Signals for	77-79
Inland Waterways, Charts of	357-358
Inlets, Handling Boats at	164-165, 167
Insignia	
Cap	480-484, U
Rank	480-484, 600
Shoulder and Collar	484, R, S, U
Sleeve	480, 482, 600, R, S, U
USCGAux (Color Plate)	U
USPS (Color Plate)	R, S
Inspection of Rope	219
Inspections, Maintenance	186-189, 209-211
Installing the Compass	269, 290-291
Instruments, Piloting	267-299, 378-385, 427-428, 456
Intended Track	412
Intercom Systems	516

	PAGE
Intercardinal Courses, Deviation on	295
Internal Compensators	288-289, 293-295, 299
Internationl Code Flags	461, 467, 517-522, 527, W, X
International and Inland Rules, Where they Apply	31
International Morse Code	523-525
International Rules, Lights Required by	64g, 64s-64x, D
Intracoastal Waterway Aids to Navigation	312-313, J
Intracoastal Waterway Charts	357-358
Inverter, Electrical	515
Isobars	235
Isogonic Lines	273

J

Jack, Uuion	O, Q, V

K

Kedge Anchors	92, 94
Kedging Off a Bar	111, 171
Keeping Track of Your Position	417-440
Kellets	106-107
Ketch Rig	15
Knockabout Rig	15
Knots and Splices, Strength of	219
Knots, Bends and Hitches	220-221
Knot, Unit of Speed, Defined	11, 376

L

Labeling	
Bearings	419-420, 435-437
DR Plots	388, 391
Fixes	388, 391, 420, 422, 436-437, 509
Lines of Position	419-420
Lake Boating	546-548
Cautions	548
Charts, Great Lakes	547
Great Lakes Light List	548
Great Lakes Pilot	548
Piloting	546
Pollution Control	548
Rules & Regulations	548
Rules of the Road	548
USCG Safety Detachments	548
Lake Charts	358
Lambert Projection	363
Lateral System of Buoyage	309-316, I-L
Intracoastal Waterway	312-313
Numbering	309-312
Uniform State	314-316, L
U. S. and Canadian	316
Western Rivers	316, K
Latitude	340-341, 377
Launching Ramps	581-582
Launching & Retrieving from a Trailer	581-584
Laws for Motor Boats	29-50, 611-621
Laws (Numbering) by States	622
Laying a Course	391, 415-416, 444-447, 457
Lay-up, Winter	188-189
Leadership and Discipline	116, 474
Lead Line	384-385
Leaks and Damage Control	179-181
Leeway	9, 411
Left Rudder	122

NAUTICAL TERMINOLOGY INDEX

Hail (from a port)	25	Head (of sail)	20	Hitches	7	Inboard cruiser	2
Halyards	16, 22	Headroom	6	Hogged	25	Inboard engine	12
Harbor	7	Headsail	15	Hoist (of flag)	11	Inboard-outboard	12
Harden (sails)	16	Head sea	12	Holds	26	In irons	23
Hauled out	7	Headway	9	Hood ends	18	Internal ballast	13
Hauling parts	8	Heat exchanger	13	Horn timber	19		
Hawse pipe	27	Heave	8	Houseboats	2	Jaws (of gaff)	21
Hawsers	8	Heaving line	8	Hull	3	Jetties	7
Head	6	Heel (of mast)	21	Hydrofoil	2	Jettison	26
Heading	16	Helm	6	Inboard	3	Jetsam	26

	PAGE
Legal Equipment	51-60
License to Operate Motor Boats for Hire	45, 46
Licenses, Radio	491, 492
Lifelines (Liferails)	195
Life Preservers	53-55
Light Characteristics	306, 311, 320-321
Flashing	306, 311, 320-321
Occulting	311, 320-321
Sectors	321-322, 369
Light List	331, 332, 548, 608, 610
Light Phase Characteristics	306-307, 311, 320-321
Light Requirements	64b-66, A-D
Light Station	317-319
Light Station, Offshore	325
Lighted Buoys	305-307, 310-312, 316, I-K
Lighthouse Structures, Types of	317-321
Lighthouses, American	318-319
Lightning Protection	201-202
Lights (Aids to Navigation)	317-326
Cautions in Using	322
Directional	326
How Designated on Charts	353, 369
Identification	322
Minor	308-309, 312, I-K
Offshore Towers	325
Primary Seacoast	317-322
Range	325-326
Secondary	317, 320-322
Visibility	321-322
Lights, Diagram of Visibility in Points	64d
Lights for Boats	64b-66, A-D
Anchorage	64j
Auxiliaries	64h
Barges	B-C
Cable-laying Vessels	64f, 64n, A
Canal Boats	64f, A
Color Illustrations	A, C-D
Disabled Vessels	64q
Dredges	B, C, 64m
Ferry Boats	64f, A
Fishing Boats	64f, A
Fixed White Light, on Stern	64e
Great Lakes Rules	64p-64r
Illustrated Color Pictures	A, C-D
Inland Rules	64c-64l, A-C
International Rules	64g, 64s-64x, D
Moorings, Floating Plant	64m, B-C
Motor Boats	64d-64e
Naval Vessels	64 (I)
Owner Absent at Night	463
Pilot Vessels	64k, 64w
Sailing Vessels	64f, 64h, A
Scows	B-C
Screens for	64e
Seagoing Vessels	64g, 64s, D
Small Vessels Under Way	64e
Steamers, Inland	64f, A
Steam Vessels Under Way	64f, A
Steam Vessels, Towing	64f, 64j, 64p, A
Tow Boats	64f, A
Vessels Towed	B-C
Wrecking Steamers	64f, A
Lights, Range	325-326
Lightships	324-325
Lightweight Type Anchors	90-93, 101
Line, Care of	113, 217-219
Line of No Variation (Agonic)	273

	PAGE
Lines, Handling	138-142, 149
Lines, Mooring	138-141
Lines of Force	267-268
Lines of Position	418-420, 447, 456-457
Lines of Variation (Isogonic)	273
Local Attraction	273
Local Notices to Mariners	335-336, 608
Local Piloting Knowledge	397
Locks, Passing through	543-544
Log	
Chip	384
Keeping a	588
Modern	382, 384
Patent	382
Radio	494
Weather	261
Logarithmic Speed Scale	343, 389
Longitude	340-341, 377
'Longshore Piloting	454-457
Long Splice	224
Lookouts	167, 176
Loran	511, 512
Lows, Barometric	235-236, 239, 258
Low Tide (Low Water)	393
Lubber's Line	268-269, 278, 288-289, 298
Luff Tackle	226-227
Lug Rig	24
Luggage for Boating	478, 485
Luminous (Nominal) Range of Lights	321-322

M

Magnet(s)	
Compass	268
Concealed	290-291, 295, 299
Compensating	288-289, 292-295, 299
Heeling	281, 295
Magnetic	
Bearing	282, 379, 419
Course, Compared with Compass Course	274-276, 296-298
Course, Compared with True Course	272, 275-276, 298
Course, Defined	275, 298
Disturbances, Local	273
Environment of the Compass	279-281, 289, 290, 299
Field of the Earth	267-268, 279
Geographic North, and	268, 272, 279
Influences, Concealed in Hull	290-291, 295-296, 299
Meridian	268, 272, 274-275, 289
Polar Areas (Poles)	272-273
Variation, see under Compass, The Mariner's	
Magnetism	
Alien or Random	291
The Compass'	268
The Earth's	267-268, 279
Hidden	290-291, 295-296, 299
The Ship's	274, 279-281, 290, 292-294, 299
Maintenance of Boat and Engine	181-189, 209-211, 569
Maintenance for Safety	209-211
Maintenance of the Compass	291
Maintenance, Outboard Equipment	570
Maintenance, Outboard Motor	569-570
Maintenance, Trailer	585
Maneuvering Board	451-454
Maneuvering in Close Quarters	132, 148
Manila Anchor Line	96-97, 216-219

Jib 15	King plank 19	Leather (of oars) 24	Lines (hull) 17
Jib-boom 22	Knees (structural) 5, 19	Leeboards 23	List 9
Jib-headed 14	Knockabout 15	Leech (leach) 20	Lockers 6
Jibing 15	Knots 7	Lee shore 20	Log 11
Jibstay 21	Knot (nautical mile per hour) 11	Leeward 10	Loom (of oars) 24
Jumper stays 22		Leeway 10	Loose-footed sail 20
Jury mast 21	Landfall 11	Length on the waterline 6	Lower unit 12
Jury rig 21	Lateen rig 24	Lifelines 5	Lubberly 17
	Law, admiralty 27	Life preservers 10	Lubber's line 11
Kedge 8	Lay a course 25	Liferails 5	Luff 20, 23
Kedging 8	Lay down (hull lines) 25	Lift 2	Lug rig 24
Keel 3	Lazarettes 6	Lights 18	
Keelson 4	Lazy jacks 22	Limber chain 19	Magnetic course 16
Ketch 15	Lead 11	Limber holes 19	Mainsail 15

PAGE

Manila, Comparative Properties 216-217
Manila, Care of 113, 217-219
Man-overboard Procedures 176-177
Map, The Weather 236, 239
Marconi Rig 14
Marine Converters, Electric 514-515
Markers (Regulatory) State ....314, 316, L
Marks, Lead Line 385
Marlinespike Seamanship 215-231
Masts, Flags to Fly at ....458-461, 464, 466-469, V
MAYDAY Radio Calls 496-498
Meal Flags ....463, Q, V
Mean Low Water 347-348, 393-395
Mean Lower Low Water 347-348, 393-395
Measuring Distance on a Chart 343, 382, 383
Mean Sea Level 393
Meeting Head-On, Rules for 70
Meeting in Winding Channel 73-74, 81
Mercator Chart
    Direction on 359-361, 363
    Distance on 343, 360, 382-383
    Great Circle on 359-361, 363
    Rhumb line on 359, 363
Mercator Projection 359-361, 363
Meridian, True or Geographic 272, 340
Mile, Nautical and Statute 375
Mileage Markers, River 531
Millibars, Conversion Table 234
Minor Lights ....308-309, 312, I-K
Mississippi River Buoyage 316
Mixed Tides 395-396
Moon, Effect of, on Tides 393-396
Mooring or Moorings
    Anchors, use of 114-115, 136-138
    Bitts 112
    Buoys 107, 113, 115
    Diagrams 113-114
    Inspection of 115
    Leaving and Picking up 133-134, 477
    Lines 113-115, 138-142, 148
    Permanent 113-115
    Snubbers, Use of 115
    Swivels 98-99, 113
    Tables 114, 115
    Wind or Current, in 134-138
Morse Code, International 523-525
Motor Adjustment, Outboard 561-562
Motor Boat Act of 1940, Excerpts from 615-618
Motor Boat, Definition of 2, 615
Motorboat Examination, Courtesy, USCGAux
                    61, 191-192, 599-600
Motorboat Handling 120-157, 161-170, 172-175
Motor Boats, Classes of 33, 615
Motor Boats, Lights for ....64b-66, 615, B, C
Motor Sailers 2
Motor Sailers, Rules for 64h
Mounting the Compass 269, 290
Mouse a Hook 231
Mouth-to-mouth Artificial Respiration 212
Multiple-Axle Trailers 577
Mushroom Anchors 95, 113-115

N

Names of Code Flags .... W
Napier Diagram 283, 285
National Fire Protection Association 194

PAGE

Natural Scale of Charts 343
Nautical Chart Manual 364
Nautical Charts 337-372
Nautical Mile, length of 375
Nautical Terms 1-28
Naval Reserve Owner's Distinguishing Pennant .... 464, P
Naval Reserve Yacht Pennant .... 464, P
Naval Vessels, Procedures When Boarding or Leaving
                                        474-475
Naval Vessels, Rights of .... 64(I)
Navigating Instruments ...267-299, 378-385, 427-428, 456
Navigation, Aids to 300-326
Navigation, Aids to on Charts ....352-354, I-L
Navigation, Forms of 373-374
Navigation Lights (in Color) ....A, C-D
Navigation Lights, Outboard 557
Navigation Tools, River Piloting 534
Navigational Aids 300-326
Navy Anchor 90-91, 94
Naval Signal Flags ....521, X
Neap Tides 394-395
Needle, Dip 272
Negligent Operation, Penalty for 36, 38, 39, 614
Net Tonnage 25
Night Piloting 455
Non-magnetic Ship 272, 279, 281
Norman Pin 112
Northill Anchor 91, 93, 95
Notes on Charts 344-345
Notice to Mariners 335, 345, 608, 610
Notices to Mariners, Local 335-336, 608
Number Certificate on Motor Boats 34, 613
Numbering
    Fees Charged for 35
    Of Buoys ....309-312, 316, I-L
    Of Motor Boats 34, 613
    Records, Availability of 621
Numbers, How Displayed 35-36
Numbers, How to Obtain 622
Numerical Scale of Charts 343
Nun Buoys ....303-304, 311, I-L
Nylon Rope 95-97, 99, 112-115, 215-218

O

Observational Deviation 299
Observations, Weather 255
Ocean Currents 403
Ocean-going Vessels, Lights for ....64g, 64s-66, D
Oceanographic Office Publications 333-334, 608, 610
Officers and Crew, Licensed 45, 618
Officers' Flags ....599-602, 604-605, T-W
Officers, Yacht Club, Insignia 480-482
Official Courtesies 476-477
Offshore Light Stations 325
Oil, Use of 166-167
Omega 511-512
Operation of Compass, Principles 267
Operation of Motor Boats, Licensed 45, 618
Orders to Crew When Docking 149
Outboard Boating 549-570
    Capsizes 568
    Courtesy 567
    Accidents 568
    Added Buoyancy 552
    Basics 549
    Boat Handling 564
    Electronic Depth Sounders 560

NAUTICAL TERMINOLOGY INDEX

Marconi rigged 14
Marina 7
Marine ways (railways) 7
Marine surveyor 17
Marlinespike seamanship 7
Masts 13
Masthead 21
Masthead fitting 21

Mast partners 21
Mast step 21
Measurement
    (admeasurement) 25
Misses stays 23
Mizzen 15
Mizzenmast 15
Monkey's fist 8

Mooring 8
Motorboats 2
Motorsailer 2
Multi-hull 4
Multi-step hull 4
Mushroom anchor 8

Nautical miles 11

Naval architect 17
Navigation 16
Neap tides 12
Net (registered) tonnage 25
Net tons 25
Norman pin 10

Oarlock 24

PAGE

Emergencies 567
Equipment 557
Equipment Maintenance 570
Fuel & Oils 563
Fueling 564
Hull Design 550
Hull Maintenance 569
Inboard-Outboard Drives 552
Lower Unit 123
Maintenance 569-570
Motors 552
Motor Adjustment 561-562
Motor Maintenance 569-670
Motor Selection 552-557
Navigation Lights 557
Operation 561-568
Operational Equipment 559
Propellers 555
Radiotelephones 560
Registration & Numbering 561
Safe Operation 566-567
Safety Cabin, Motor 559
Safety Equipment 558
Shear Pins, Motor 556
Size & Loading 551
Special Design Features 565
Stability 565
Tachometers 560
Overhand Knot 220
Overtaking, Rule for 72, 81, 84
Owners' Private Signals ....463, Q, V

P

Painter (Dinghy), Definition 8
Painting 182-185
Parallel Course, Rule for 72, 81, 84
Parallel Rulers 381
Parallels of Latitude 340-341
Parcelling 230
Passenger-carrying Vessels, (Small), Rules for ...45-49, 607
Passengers for Hire, When Boat Is Carrying 45
Passengers, Liability for 45
Passenger Vessels, License for Operating 45-47
Passing 72, 81, 84
Passing a Line 141, 172-174
Past Officers' Flags .... S, T
Patent Log 382
Patrol Vessels (Government), Lights for 64n, 64o
Pelorus 278, 378-379
Penalties for Violation of Boat Safety Act 614
Penalties for Violation of Radio Rules 498-499
Pennant, Racing 464
Pennants and Burgees ....464, Q-T
Pennants, USCGAux .... T
Permits to Cruise, Canadian 48
Phases of Lights 306-307, 320-321
Phonetic Alphabet ....495, W
Pictorial Rule for Course Conversion ...277-278, 298
Piles, Maneuvering Around 146-147, 150
Pilot
  Chart 364
  Coast 329-330, 334, 608
  Rules ....64 (I), 64r
  Vessels, Lights for ....64g, 64k, D
  Waters 374
Piloting
  Basic 373-391, 417-424
  Defined 373
  In Current 411-416, 441-447

Instruments 267-299, 378-385, 427-428, 456
Lake 546
'Longshore 454-457
Methods 373-457
Need for Practice 440
Nighttime 455
River 530-536
Specialized Techniques 441-457
Unmarked Coasts 448
Use of Soundings 438-439, 455, 501
Pitchpoling 164
Pitch, Propeller 124
Planes of Reference, Charts 347-348, 350
Plotter, Course 379-380
Plotting
  Bearings 379-381, 418-421, 447-454
  Courses 379-381, 387-389, 391, 443-447
  Position, Three-arm Protractor 427, 456
  Radio Bearings 435-437, 505-506
Plow Anchor
  CQR 92, 100
  Plowright 92, 94, 99
Point Courses, Rules for Conversion 278, 298
Point Graduation, Compass Card 270, 271
Points and Degrees, Compass 270, 271
Points on Bow, Beam and Quarter 9
Poles, Magnetic 272-273
Pollution Control on Lakes 548
Pollution, Law Regarding 49-50, 119
Polyconic Projection 361-362
Port Tack 15
Position Determination 417-440
Position Estimated 411, 419
Position Finder, Weems 456
Position, Fining a Boat's 417-440
Position Finding
  Horizontal Angles 427-431, 456
  More Than Two Lines of Position 421-422, 448
  Radio 435-437, 505-506
  Ranges 426-427
  Sextant Angles 429-431
  Simple Visual Bearings 423-424
  Specialized Techniques 447-448
  Two Lines of Position 420-421
  Using Depth Information 438-439, 501
  Value of a Single Line of Position ...422, 433-435
  Vertical Angles 428-430
Position, Keep Track of Your 417, 440
Position, Line of 418-420
Position, Plotting a 391, 422
Positioning Procedures 417-440
Precipitation Fog 251, 253
Precipitation Symbols 233
Predicting Fog 250
Preparation for Rough Weather 162-163, 208
Pressure Indicators 237
Prime Meridian 340
Principles of Compass Compensation 292
Principles Governing Operation of Compass 267
Privileged and Burdened Vessels 67
Projections, Chart 341, 359-363
Propeller Hand, Left and Right 123
Propeller, Influence on Steering 123-130
Propellers, Outboard 555-556
Protection from Lightning 201-202
Protractor, Course 380-381
Psychrometer 250-251
Publications for River Pilots 534
Publications, Government 327-336, 397, 608-610

Oars 24
Offshore wind 20
Off soundings 27
On soundings 27
Outboard 3
Outboard cruiser 2
Outboard engine 12
Outfoots 24
Outpoints 24
Overall length 6
Overhang 4, 18

Overhead 6
Painter 8
Passage 11
Patent log 11
Peak (of sail) 20
Pennant 11
Pennant (pendant) 8
Pier 7
Piles 7
Piloting 16
Pinched (in sailing) 23

Pin rails 22
Pitch 9
Pitchpoling 9
Plain sail 21
Planing hull 4
Planks 3
Plates 3
Plots 16
Plumb 4
Points 9
Port 3, 6

Porthole 6
Portlight 6
Powerboats 2
Pram 2, 4
Propeller 12
Propeller post 12
Propeller shaft 12
Pulpit 5
Punt 4

Quarter 4

Q

PAGE

Quadrantal Deviation 299
Quarantine, Anchorage (Yellow) Buoys . . . . 313, I-K
Quarter, Points on 9
Quarter-Points 270-271

R

Racing Outboards, Special Exemptions 657
Racing Pennant 464
Radar 506-509
Radar Bearings 437, 508-509
Radar, Fixing Position by 437, 508-509
Radar Reflector Buoys 304, 306
Radar Reflectors (for Boats) 509
Radiation Fog 251
Radio
  Antenna and Ground 490-491
  Bearings 435-437, 503-506
  Citizens' Band 512-514
  Communications, Types of 489
  Deviation 503-504
  Direction Finder, Operation of 502-506
  Distress Call Procedures 496-498
  Distress Frequency 493
  Installation and Maintenance 491
  Licenses 491-492
  Log 494
  Navigational Aids 503
  Operator Permits 492
  Outboard Boats 560
  Procedures, Operating 492
  Violations and Penalties 498-499
  Weather Reports 498
Radio Direction Finder (RDF) Bearings . . . 435-437, 503-506
Radio Position Finding 435-437, 503-506
Radiobeacons 435-436, 503
Radiotelephones 489-499
  Alarm Signal 497
  Frequencies 489-494
  Operating Procedures 495-498
  Power-Range Relationship 490
  Rules for Use 493-498
Rafting 110-111, 145
Rain Fog 253
Raised Deck Cruiser 6
Random Deviations 296-297
Range, Determining Deviation by Sailing a 282
Range, Geographic, of a Light 321-322
Range Lights . . . . 64d, 64f, A-D, 64g, 325-326
Range, Luminous, of a Light 321-322
Range of Tide 395-397
Range of Visibility of Lights 321-322
Ranges (Aids to Navigation) 302, 325-326
Ranges, How Shown on Chart . . 352, 354, 369, 371, 426, M
Ranges in Piloting 326, 352, 354, 426-427
Rate of Change in Variation 272-274, 298
Reaching 16
Reading Assignments
  UCGAux Study Course 639
  USPS Courses of Instruction 639
Reciprocal Courses, in Compensation 293-295
Reciprocal Courses, Steering by Disposable Buoy 294
Reciprocal Directions 375
Reciprocal Headings, Zero-ing In a Compass 289
Reckless Operation, Penalty for 38, 39, 614

PAGE

Recreational Boating Guide 332
Red Cross, American National 192, 207, 213
Reef Knot 220
Reeving Line Bend 221
Reference List of Government Publications 608-610
References, USCGAux Study Course 639
References, USPS Instruction Courses 639
Refilling or Topping Off a Compass 291, 298
Reflectors 306, 308, 316, 509
Registration Laws, State 622
Registration Numbers, for Motor Boats . . 29, 34-35, 561, 613
Registration Numbers, Placement on Hull 36, 613
Regulations
  Canal 546
  Customs and Immigration 48
  FCC 489-495, 512-513
  Federal Boating Act of 1958 619-621
  Motor Boats, Government 29-50, 611-621
  Radio 489-495, 512-513
  Trailering 579
Regulatory Markers, State . . . . 314-316, L
Relative Bearings 378-379, 425-426, 434-435, 449-450
Relative Motion 449-450
Repeat Signs and Signaling . . . . . . 518-521, 524-526, W, X
Repeater Code Flags . . . . 518-521, W, X
Report of Accident or Casualty 36-37, 614
Report to Customs on Entering 48
Rescue 180-181
Residual Deviations 274, 295-297
Respiration, Artificial 212
Responsibilities and Duties of Skipper
                        116-119, 417, 474, 587-592
Resuscitation (First Aid) 212
Reverse, Handling in Boats 128, 132, 152-153
Revisions of Charts 345
Revolver, Danger of 427-428
Rhumb Line 360
Rhumb Line, Comparison with Great Circle 363
Right of Way 67-88
  Auxiliaries 70
  Ferry Boats 74
  Fishing Vessels 75
  Sailing Vessels 74
Rigs of Sailing Vessels 14
Ring, Azimuth 282, 378
Rivers
  Aids to Navigation 531
  Currents 535
  Mileage Markers 531
  Right & Left Banks 531
  Water Level Changes 531, 538
River Piloting 530-536
  Buoys 532
  Caution Required 532
  Channels at Bends 535
  Channel Crossings 536
  Charts 533-534
  Coast Guard Notices 534
  Daymarks 532
  Engineer Publications 534
  Light List 534
  Local Knowledge 534
  Navigation Tools 534
  Publications 534
  Ranges 533-540
River Seamanship 536-540
  Anchoring 537

NAUTICAL TERMINOLOGY INDEX

Rabbetting   18
Rafted   10
Rail   5
Raised deck cruiser   6
Raked   4
Raked masts   13
Raw water cooling   13

Reaching   16
Reaching jibs   21
Reduction gears   12
Reef bands   22
Reef cringle   22
Reef points   22
Reeved   8

Registration   25
Relative bearing   16
Render   8
Reverse gears   12
Reverse sheer   18
Ribs   3
Rig   14

Rigging   14
Ring bolts   4
Rips (waves)   12
Rode (anchor)   8
Roll   9
Roller reefing   23
Rope   7

	PAGE
Bottom Characteristics	538
Cruising	536-538
Cruising Problems	538
Eddies & Whirlpools	538
Making Fast to Beach	538
Passing Commercial Traffic	539-540
Problems with Buoys	539
Safety Harbors	537
Signals	539
Use Caution	537

Rodes
Care and Inspection	112-113
Kinds	95-97
Marking for Scope	102
Securing	97-98

Rolling Hitch	221
Rolling Period	170

Rope
Care of	112-113, 217
Handling	112-113, 217-219
Inspect, How to	112, 219
Manila	96, 113, 217-219
Measurement of	229
New Rope, How to Uncoil	113, 228
Nylon	95-97, 99, 112-115, 215-218
Synthetic	96, 215-218
Terminology	228
Uses, Table of	218

Rose, Compass	272-274
Rotary Tidal Currents	402
Rough Water, Use of Oil in	166-167
Rounding of Numbers	386-387
Routine, Yacht	476-477

Rudder
Action of	126, 152
Action of Propeller on	123-130
Balanced	122, 123
Position Indicators	516
Right and Left	122

Rule of Sixty	457
Rules of the Road, Lake	548
Rules of the Road, Proposed Changes	66, 88

Rules
FCC	489-495, 512-513
Bearing Conversion	297, 298, 379, 424
Course Conversion	275-278, 298
Lights, Inland	64c-64o, 64f, A-C
Lights, International	64g, 64s-64x, D

Rules of the Nautical Road (Publication)	608
Rules of the Road	64b-88, 332
Rulers, Parallel	381
Running an Inlet	164-165
Running Fix	431-433

S

Safe Loading of Boats	206
Safety, Canal	545
Safety Equipment	52-63, 202-204, 611, 615-618
Safety Equipment, Outboard	558
Safety Features in Boat Construction	194-202, 604-607
Safety in Operations	205-209
Safety in the Water	207-209
Safety on Deck	195
Safety Organizations	191-194
Safety Practices Afloat	161-163, 190-214

	PAGE
Cabin Heaters	205
Diesel-powered Boats	198
Electrical Installations	199-201, 210-211
Operational Aspects	205-209
Ventilation Methods	604-607, 618
Safety Precautions in Fueling	205-206
Safety Standards for Small Craft (ABYC)	192-193
Sailboat Trailering	586
Sailing Charts	352, 354

Sailing Vessels
Fog Signals	78, 81, 85
Lights for	64f, 64h, A
Rules for	74, 84
Types of	15

Sails, Care of	187-188, 231
Sales Agents for Government Publications	328, 344, 608-610
Salutes Between Vessels	475-476
Salutes, Hand	474
Salutes, Personal	474
Samson Post	105, 112
Sand Anchors	93, 95
Scale, (Logarithmic), Speed	343, 389
Scale, Chart, Natural Numerical, Graphic	343
Schooner Rig	15
Scope	101-102
Scowing an Anchor	111
Scows, Lights for	B, C
Screens for Lights	64e
Screw Current	123-124
Scuppers, Definition	5, 18
Sea Anchor	95, 165, 166
Sea-Claw Anchor	96
Sea Level, Mean	393
Sea Smoke	251-253
Sea Surface at Various Wind Velocities	265-266
Seamanship	158-189
In Fog	167-168
Marlinespike	215-231
Outboard	549-570
Preparation for Rough Weather	162-163
Seaman's Terminology	1-28, 122, 138
Sedan Cabins	6
Seizing	231
Selecting a Compass	287, 288, 298
Semaphore Signaling	525-526
Semidiurnal Tides	395-396
Semicircular Deviation	299
Sentinels	106-107
Series of Soundings, Fix from	438-439, 501
Serving	230
Set of Current	403, 412, 442-447
Seven-eighths Rule	447-448
Seven-tenths Rule	448
Sextant Angle, Position by	429-431
Shackles	97-99, 113
Shallow Water, Boat Handling in	169, 170
Shapes of Buoys	303-305, 311, 316, I-K
Shear Pins, Outboard	556
Sheepshank	221
Sheet Bend	220
Ship, Non-magnetic	279
Ships, Government, Boarding and Leaving	474-475
Ship's Magnetism	274, 279-281, 290, 292-294, 299
Ship's Magnetism, Testing for	290, 299
Shore, Flags to Fly on	464, 466-467
Short Splice	223
Side Splice	222
Sideboards	146

Round bottom	4	Sailboats	2	Sea cocks	19
Round up (into wind)	23	Sails	13	Sea kindly	27
Rowboats	2, 24	Samson post	10	Sedan cruiser	6
Rowlock	24	Scarph (scarf)	19	Seized	8
Rubrail	18	Schooners	15	Semi-displacement hull	4
Rudder	4	Screw (propeller)	12	Semi-planing hull	4
Runabouts	2	Scudding	16	Set (of current)	25
Running rigging	14	Sculling	24	Shackle	26
		Scuppers	5, 18	Shaft logs	12
Sagged	25	Sea anchor	9	Shear pin	13

Sheaves	8
Sheer	3
Sheer strake	4
Sheets	16
Sheet block	23
Ship	2
Ship-shape	26
Shrouds	14
Sights (sextant)	16
Signal mast	20

	PAGE
Sight Vanes	282, 378, 424
Signal Code, International	518-527, W, X
Signal Code, Yacht Club	520, 522
Signaling	
Flag-hoist	520-522, W, X
Flashing Light	523-525
International Code Flags	517-522, 527, W, X
Semaphore	525-526
Sound	526
Visual	517-522
Signals	
Canal Lights	542
Danger	69, 81, 85
Distress	87, 180, 496-498
Flag	518-522, W, X
Navy Flags	P
River	539
Storm	263-264
Whistle	69, 84
Single-bearing Fix	438
Single Whip	226-227
Sixty, Rule of	457
Size of Buoys	304
Skipper, Duties and Responsibilities	
	116-119, 417, 474, 587-592
Slack of Current	404
Slack Water Speed, Calculating in a Current	389-391
Sleeve Insignia	480, 482, 600, R, S, U
Sliding Gunter Rig	24
Slips, Maneuvering at	132-133, 146-148, 154-157
Sloop Rig	14, 15
Small Craft Charts	357, 358, M, N
Small Craft Warnings	263-264
Sound and Radio Signals, Synchronization of	437, 506
Sound in Air, Velocity of	265
Sound in Water, Velocity of	499
Sound Signaling	526
Sounding, Echo	384, 438-439, 499-501
Soundings, Position by	438-439, 501
Spar Buoys	304, I-K
Specialized Piloting Techniques	441-457
Speed	
Curves	389-391
Defined	376, 387
Distance-Time Calculations	442
In Fog	79, 82, 86, 167
Made Good	412, 444-447
Over the Ground	412
Scale, Logarithmic	343, 389
Units	376
Speedometers, Marine	382, 384
Spheres, Quadrantal	295, 299
Spherical Compass	267-268, 287, 289-291
Splice	
Back	231
Eye	222-223
Long	224
Short	223
Splices and Knots, Strength of	219
Splicing	222-224
Spring Lines	138-147, 152
Spring Tides	394-396
Sprit Rig	24
Squadron Pennants	463, V
Square Knot	220
Stability, Outboard	565
Stand of the Tide	393

	PAGE
Standards of Accuracy (Precision)	386, 431
Standing Lug Rig	24
Starboard Tack	15
Starting Motor, Safety Precautions	131, 206
Starboard-to-Starboard Passing	71
State Buoyage, Uniform	314-316, L
State Flags	470
State Laws, Numbering	622
Station Buoys	312
Station Model	233
Statute Mile, Length of	375
Staysail Rigs	21
Steam Fog	251, 253
Steamers, Lights for Inland	64f, A
Steering	
Automatic	512
By Compass	169, 275, 288
Effects of Wind and Sea	169
Hints	129, 152
Off Course, Effect of	297
Reciprocal Course	293
Stern Anchors	110
Stockless Anchors	94
Stop Watch	383
Stopper on a Rope	231
Storm Signals and Warnings	263-265
Storms, Various Types of	241-249
Stoves, Safety Practices	204-205
Stowage of Ground Tackle	100-101
Stranding and Kedging Off	171-172
Strap on a Rope	231
Strength of Cordage, Table	216
Strength of Knots and Splices, Table	219
Study Assignments, USCGAux Courses	639
Study Assignments, USPS Courses	639
Submarine Construction, Day Marks for Vessels Engaged In
	559
Submarine Distress Signals	87, W, X
Substitute Code Flags	518-521, W, X
Suction Screw Current	123-124
Sun, Bearings of	278, 295
Sun Glasses	484
Sunrise and Sunset, Determining Time of	399, 402
Sun Glasses	278
Sunrise and Sunset, Determining Time of	399-400, 402
Superstructure and Stability	195-196
Surveys, Boat	194
Swimming Tips	207-208
Switches, Electrical	488
Swivels	98, 99
Symbols	
Chart	351-354, 365-372
Cloud	259-260
Precipitation	233
Weather	232, 233
Synchronized Signals for Distance Finding	436-437, 506
Synthetic Rope	96

T

Table or Tables	
Compass Points and Degrees	271
Current	328, 329, 404-409, 608
Deviation	282, 285, 296-297, 299
Height of Tide at Any Hour	440
Holding Power of Anchors	108
Loads on Anchor, Horizontal	100

NAUTICAL TERMINOLOGY INDEX

Sister frames 19	Speed curve 11	Stand (of tidal level) 25	Stem bands 18
Skeg 4	Spinnakers 21	Standing lug rig 24	Stern 3
Skin 3	Splices 7	Standing parts (of line) 8	Stern drive 12
Slack (of current) 25	Sport fisherman 6	Standing rigging 14	Stern lines 7
Slides (sail) 20	Spreaders 22	Stand by 11	Sternway 9
Sloop 15	Spring lines 7	Starboard 3	Stiff (vessel) 23
Small craft 2	Spring tides 12	Statute miles 11	Stopwater 19
Sole 19	Sprit rig 24	Staysails 21	Storm anchor 8
Sounding pole 11	Square-rigged 14	Steadying sail 2	Stove 11
Spars 13	Stanchions 5	Stem 4	Strake 4, 18

	PAGE
Sizes of Mooring Equipment	114-115
Speed over Measured Mile	603
Speed Factors and Course Corrections	442-447
Tidal Current	328-329, 397-402, 608
Time-speed-distance	442
Weight and Strength, Fiber Cordage	216
Tacking	15
Tackle, Calculating Power	226
Tackle, Kinds of	226
Tackles, Blocks and	225-227
Taking on Fuel	205-206
Terms, Nautical	1-28
Testing Compass Site for Magnetism	290
Testing for Random Deviations	296-297
Texas-Tower Type Light Stations	325
Thimble, Synthetic Rope	97, 98
Three-Arm Protractor	427
Three Bearings and Runs Between	448
Three-point Problem	429-431, 456
Through-hull Fittings	196
Thunderstorms	245-247
Tidal Current Charts	329, 409-410, 608
Tidal Current Tables	328-329, 397, 404, 608
Tidal Currents	402
Tidal Data, Reference Points for	347-348, 393
Tidal Day, Length of	395
Tidal Range	395-397
Tide of Tides	
Cause of	392
Correction for Height	393, 397-402, 440
Equatorial	396
Height, at Any Time	393, 397-402, 440
Neap	394-395
Relation to Current	392
Spring	394-396
Tables	328-329, 397-404, 608
Tropic	398
Timber Hitch	221
Time, Calculation	376, 388-389
Time-speed-distance Tables	442
Times, Units	376
Tire Pressure, Trailer	578
Trailers & Trailering	549, 571-586
To Cross or Not to Cross	449-450
Tonnage	41
Topography on Charts	349-350
Tornadoes, Characteristics of	247-248
Tow Boats, Lights for	64f, A-C
Towing	174-175
Towing Lights	64f, A-C
Track, DR	387-388, 391
Trailers	
Car	572, 576
Driving with	579-581
Features	575-576
Hitches & Couplings	573-574, 576
Land Storage	584-585
Launching & Retrieving	581-584
Launching Ramps	581-582
Maintenance	585
Multpile Axle	577
Regulations	579
Sailboat	586
Selection & Equipment	572-577
Tire Pressures	578
Tongue Weight	577

	PAGE
Tops & Covers	578
Using a Crane	584
Wheels & Tires	574
Triangle of Position	422
Triangles, Vector	413, 442-447
Trip Line in Anchoring	110-111
Tropic Tides	398
True and Magnetic Directions Compared	272, 275-277, 298
True Course, Defined	275
True Wind Problem	452-453
Trunk Cabin Cruiser	6
Trust Your Compass	278
Turning at a Dock	141-142
Turning Circles	127
Turning in Close Quarters	132, 148
Twin Screw Boats, Handling	150-157
Two Bearings and Run Between	434
Two Half Hitches	221
Two-fold (Double) Tackle	226, 227
Types of Boats	2, 15, 24, 458-461
Types of Sailboats	15, 24

U

Ultraviolet Ray Damage to Synthetic Lines	112
Under Way, Preparing to Get	131
Undocking	142-145, 155-156
Uniform State Waterway Marking System	314-316, L
Uniforms	
Don't Mix	485
No Gold Braid for Yachtsmen	481
Paid Crew	482
USCGAux	483-484, 600
U S Power Squadrons	483, 594
Yacht Clubs	480-482
Union Jack	461, 463, O, V
Unlighted Beacons	302, 307, 308, 312, 353, I-L
USCG Auxiliary	
Curtesy Examinations	61, 191, 599
Flag Code	601, 602
Flags (Color Plate)	T
Organization and Functions	191, 192, 597-600
Officers' Flags	601, 602, T
Sleeve Insignia (Color Plate)	U
Study Course References	639
U S Coast Guard Publications	608-609
USCG Safety Detachments	548
USC&GS Small Craft Charts	357-358, M, N
U S Flag, History and Origin of	465-468
U S Lake Survey Small Craft Charts	358
U S Power Squadrons	
Ensign, Display of	458-464, Q, R, V
Flag	458-464, 469-470, Q, R, V
Flag Ceremonies	469-470
Insignia and Officers' Flags	594, R, S
Flags (Color Plate)	R, S
Instruction Courses, References	639
Organization and Functions	191, 593-597
Uniforms	483, 594
Use of Oil on Rough Waters	166-167

V

Vanes, Sight, on Compass	282, 378, 424
Variation, See also under Compass, The Mariner's	
An Angle	272-273, 275

Stringers 19		
Strip planking 5		
Struts 12		
Suit of sails 14		
Superstructure 3		
Swab 27		
Swamp 9		
Swells (ground swells) 12		
Swimming platform 10		
Tachometer 13		
Tack (of sail) 20		
Tacking 15		

Tackle 8
Taffrail 18
Taffrail log 19
Tangs 22
Tenders 2
Throat (of sail) 20
Thole pins 24
Through-hull fittings 19
Thwart stanchion 24
Tiller 23
Tidal current 12
Tide 12
Time allowance 20

Toe rails 5
Tonnage 25
Topping lift 22
Topsides 4
Trailboards 22
Transom 4
Traveller 23
Travelling lifts 7
Trim 9
Trimaran 4
Truck (of mast) 21
True course 16

Trunk cabin 6
Tumble home 4
Turnbuckle 14
Turn of the bilge 17
Underway (under weigh) 8
Union Jack 11
Unlaying 8
Utility boats 2
V-drive 12
Variation 16
Vee-bottom 4

	PAGE
Annual Change in	272-274, 298, 342
Applied	275-278, 298-299
Changes with Location	273
Defined	272
Find Amount and Direction on Charts	272-273, 298, 342
Lines (Isogonic)	273, 350
Vector Triangles	413
Vectors	412-413
Ventilation of Fuel and Engine Compartments	604-607
Verbal Aids for Course Conversion	276, 278, 298
Vertical Danger Angle	430
Vertical Sextant Angle	428-429
Vessel, Government, Boarding and Leaving	474-475
Vessel Inspecting Flies USCG Flag	192
VHF Radio	263, 491
Visibility of Lights (Aids to Navigation)	321-322
Visual Signaling	517-527
Vocabulary	1-28

W

Warm-surface Fog	253
Warnings, Storm	263-265
Watch Required, Radio	493
Watch, Tackle	227
Water-skiing Safety	209
Waterspouts	248-249
Weather	232-266, E-H
Changes, Estimating	238
Flags	263-264
Instruments	251, 255, 257
Log	261-262
Map	236, 239
Map, Analysis	235-240
Map, How to Read	232-235
Map, Newspaper	235
Map, Typical	236, 239
Observations, Local	261
Preparation of Local Forecasts	238
Publications on	610
Reports, Radio	263-265, 498
Signals	263-265, 497
Signs, Visual	259
Symbols	233
Weather Warnings	263-265, 498
Weight of Cordage, Table	216
Westerly Var. and Dev., How to Apply	276-278
Wet-bulb Thermometer	250
Wet-weather Clothing	485
Whip, Single	226-227
Whipping a Rope End	221
Whistle Buoys	304, 305

	PAGE
Whistle on Motor Boats	58
Whistle Signals	69, 84
Whistle Signals, Canal	541-542
Wildcats	96
Winches and Windglasses	96, 104, 112
Wind	
Force, Effect on Sea	265-266
Observations	255
Pattern Changes	240
Pressure Table	265
Scale, Beaufort	255-256
True and Apparent	255-256, 452-453
Wind and Current, Effect on Boat	121, 411-416, 441-447
Wind and Sea Conditions	257
Wind-driven Currents	403
Windshield Wipers	296-297
Winding Channels, Rule for	73, 76, 81
Winding Ship	141
Winter Lay-up	188-189
Wire Rope	
Anchor Line	107
Splicing	224
Use and Care	229-230
Wiring, Electrical	200, 488
Wiring, Electrical, Near Compass	269
Worming, Parcelling and Serving	230-321
Wreck Buoys	311

Y

Yacht Club	
Burgees	462, 464, O-Q, V
Flags to Fly at	464, 466-467, O
Moorings	113, 114
Signal Codes	520, 522
Yacht Club Uniforms	480-482
Yacht Ensigns	462, 467, Q, V
Yacht Routine	476-477
Yacht Safety Bureau	193-194
Yachting Customs and Etiquette	473-478
Yachts, Lights for Steam	64f, A-C
Yachtman's Anchor	64g, 93
Yawl Rig	15
Yellow (Quarantine Anchorage) Buoys	313

Z

Zero-ing-in Compensators	289, 298
Zero-ing-in, Analogous to Compensation	293

NAUTICAL TERMINOLOGY INDEX

Veers (wind) 20	Water pump 13	Whipped 8	Yacht 2
Vessel 2	Waterways 18	Whisker pole 24	Yacht basin 7
Voyage 11	Waves 12	Winch 11	Yachtsmen 3
	Wearing ship 15	Windless 27	Yards 14
Wake 9	Weather helm 23	Windward 10, 16	Yaw 9
Wash 9	Weather shore 20	Wing and wing 23	Yawls 15
Watches 11	Wedges 18	Working anchor 8	
Waterlight 26	Well-found 27	Worm shoe 4	
Waterline 6	Wharf 7		Z-drive 12

REFERENCES FOR INSTRUCTION COURSES

BOATING COURSE

Section 1
Handling Under Normal
Conditions .... pages 52-57, 87-108, 116-119,
155-157, 263, 551-555,
561-567

Section 2
Handling Under Adverse
Conditions ... pages 161-168, 174-181, 567-568

Section 3
Seamanship and Common
Emergencies ..... pages 201, 205-206, 215-224,
497-498, 563-564, 604-607

Section 4
Rules of the Road .... pages 67-88

Section 5
Compass and Chart
Familiarization .... pages 267-269, 287-291,
337-359, 365-372

Section 6
Aids to Navigation .... pages 300-326, I-L

Section 7
Running Lights and
Equipment ....pages 64(b)-66, 557-561, A-D

Section 8
Inland Boating ....pages 529-548

Section 9
Mariner's Compass and
Piloting ....pages 272-282, 292-299,
373-391, 417-424

Section 10
Boat Trailering ....pages 571-586

SEAMANSHIP COURSE

Section 1
Types of Boats & Propulsion
Systems ....pages 2, 6, 12-15, 24, 550,
552-557

Section 2
Hull Design and
Construction........... pages 2-3, 17-18, 121,
194-196

Section 3
Equipment and
Regulations ... pages 27-66, 557, 560, 604-607

Section 4
Marlinspike ....pages 215-231

Section 5
Stability and Trim .... pages 551-552, 565-566

Section 6
Factors Governing Normal Boat
Handling ....pages 120-131, 150, 155, 564-567

Section 7
Docking ....pages 131-149, 151-157

Section 8
River Piloting, Locking, & Boat
Trailering ....pages 529-548, 571-586

Section 9
Anchors, Anchoring, & Permanent
Moorings ....pages 89-115

Section 10
Boat Handling Under Adverse
Conditions ......pages 77-79, 161-170, 567-568

Section 11
Stranding, Towing, Damage Control,
and Rescue ....pages 170-181

Section 12
Fire Prevention and
Control ....pages 56-57, 178-179, 196-202,
204-206, 209-210, 564

Section 13
Lay-up, Fitting Out, and
Repairs ....pages 181-189, 217-220, 569-570,
585-586

Section 14
Flags and Pennants, Flag Etiquette,
Manners and Customs ....pages 458-485

Section 15
Rules of the Road ....pages 64(b)-88

ADVANCED PILOTING COURSE

Section 1
Charts ....pages 337-388, 533-534, 547-548

Section 2
Aids to Navigation .....pages 300-336, 502-503

Section 3
The Compass ....pages 267-299, 378-379

Section 4
Bearings ....pages 417-432

Section 6
Time-Speed-Distance ....pages 375-376,
382-391, 441-442

Section 7
Tides ....pages 392-402

Section 8
Current Tables ....pages 402-410

Section 9
Current Piloting .... pages 411-416

Section 10
Positioning ....pages 417-440

Section 11
The Log ....pages 588-590

USCG AUXILIARY REFERENCES FOR STUDY COURSE

BOATING SAFETY & SEAMANSHIP COURSE

The Safe Way To Boating Enjoyment
Chapters 10, 12, 28 ....pages 190-214,
263, 549-570

The Sailors' Language
Chapters 1, 29 ....pages 1-28, 571-586

Boat Handling
Chapters 6, 8, 28 ....pages 89-115, 120-157,
549-570

Legal Requirements
Chapters 2, 3 ....pages 29-64(a)

Rules Of The Road
Chapters 4, 5 ....pages 64(b)-88

Aids To Navigation
Chapters 15-17, 27 ....pages 300-336,
529-548

Charts And Compass
Chapters 13-14, 18-19, 21 ....pages 267-299,
337-391, 417-457

Marine Engines
Chapters 10, 28 ....pages 190-214, 549-57

Marlinspike Seamanship
Chapters 9, 11 ....pages 174-175, 215-231

Sailboats
Chapters 1. 9, 10 ....pages 13-16, 20-24,
187-188. 190-214

Weather
Chapter 10 ....pages 232-266

Radiotelephone
Chapter 25 ....pages 489-499

WHERE TO APPLY FOR NUMBERING CERTIFICATES

The Federal Boat Safety Act of 1971 continued the pattern previously established by the Federal Boating Act of 1958 whereby powered craft could be registered and numbered by State authorities if the State had set up a program for such actions in accordance with Federal standards. Approval of the State system by the U. S. Coast Guard is required in each case for the sake of state-to-state uniformity.

By July 1972, the Coast Guard had officially approved the numbering systems of all states except Alaska, New Hampshire, Washington, and Washington, D. C. In these jurisdictions application forms for Coast Guard registration numbers may be obtained through local post offices or any Coast Guard facility. In Guam, application should be made to the Officer in Charge, Marine Inspection, U. S. Coast Guard.

Boats principally used in states having an approved number-

ing law are numbered exclusively by the state; Coast Guard numbers are obsolete. In compliance with the Federal Act all of these state laws grant 60-day reciprocity to out-of-state boats awarded numbers pursuant to Federal law or a federally approved state numbering system.

The Outboard Boating Club of America (333 No. Michigan Ave., Chicago, Ill. 60601) has compiled all available information on state boating laws in handbooks for various regions of the country. These include not only the registration and numbering requirements, but also all related laws on equipment, operation, use of trailers, etc., which readers are urged to obtain.

Given below are extracts from OBC data, listing agencies responsible for boat numbering laws.

ALABAMA Department of Conservation, State Administrative Building, Montgomery, Alabama 36104.

ALASKA The State of Alaska does not have a boat registration and numbering law, but general information on boating can be obtained from Department of Natural Resources, Division of Lands, 344 6th Ave., Anchorage, Alaska 99501.

ARIZONA Game and Fish Department, 2211 W. Greenway Rd., Phoenix, Ariz. 85023.

ARKANSAS Revenue Department, State Revenue Building, Little Rock, Ark. 72201.

CALIFORNIA Department of Harbors and Watercraft, 1416-9th Street, Room 1336, Sacramento, California 95814.

COLORADO Game, Fish & Parks Department, 6060 Broadway, Denver, Colorado 80216.

CONNECTICUT Boating Commission, Department of Agriculture & Natural Resources, State Office Building, Hartford, Connecticut 06115.

DELAWARE Small Boat Safety Division, Commission of Shell Fisheries, P. O. Box 512, Lewes, Delaware 19958.

FLORIDA State Board of Conservation, 107 West Gaines Street, Tallahassee, Florida 32304.

GEORGIA State Game and Fish Commission, Room 715, Trinity-Washington Bldg., Atlanta, Ga. 30334.

HAWAII Harbors Division, Department of Transportation, Box 397, Honolulu, Hawaii 96809.

IDAHO Motor Vehicle Division, Department of Law Enforcement, P. O. Box 34, Boise, Idaho 83707.

ILLINOIS Conservation Department, 400 South Spring Street, Springfield, Illinois 62706.

INDIANA Department of Natural Resources, 605 State Office Building, Indianapolis, Indiana 46209.

IOWA State Conservation Commission, State Office Building, 300 4th Street, Des Moines, Iowa 50319.

KANSAS Forestry, Fish & Game Commission, P. O. Box 1028, Pratt, Kan. 67124.

KENTUCKY Division of Boating, Department of Public Safety, New State Office Bldg., Frankfort, Ky. 40601.

LOUISIANA Wild Life & Fisheries Commission, Wild Life & Fisheries Building, 400 Royal Street, New Orleans, Louisiana 70130.

MAINE Bureau of Watercraft Registration and Safety, State Office Building, Augusta, Maine 04330.

MARYLAND Department of Chesapeake Bay Affairs, State Office Building, Annapolis, Maryland 21404.

MASSACHUSETTS Division of Motorboats, 100 Nashua Street, Boston, Massachusetts 02114.

MICHIGAN Department of State, 2100 N. Larch Street, Lansing, Mich. 48906.

MINNESOTA Department of Conservation, 625 North Robert Street, St. Paul, Minnesota 55101.

MISSISSIPPI Boat and Water Safety Commission, Suite 240, 720 President St., Jackson, MS 39202.

MISSOURI Boat Commission, P. O. Box 603, Jefferson City, Missouri 65101.

MONTANA State Board of Equalization, Capitol Building, Helena, Montana 59601.

NEBRASKA State Game, Forestation & Parks Commission, Lincoln, Nebraska 68509.

NEVADA Fish and Game Commission, Box 10678, Reno, Nev. 89501.

NEW HAMPSHIRE Division of Motor Vehicles, Department of Safety, 85 Loudon Road, Concord, New Hampshire 03301. The State of New Hampshire registers powerboats operated on inland or nontidal waters. As this registration system does not com-

ply with the Federal Boating Act of 1958, the Coast Guard has retained the responsibility for registering and numbering undocumented vessels with more than 10 horsepower chiefly used on navigable waters of the United States within the territorial limits of New Hampshire.

NEW JERSEY Bureau of Navigation, Department of Conservation & Economic Development, Box 1889, Trenton, New Jersey 08625.

NEW MEXICO State Park and Recreation Commission, P. O. Box 1147, Santa Fe, New Mexico 87501.

NEW YORK Division of Motorboats, State Conservation Department, New York State Campus, 1220 Washington Avenue, Albany, New York 12226.

NORTH CAROLINA Wildlife Resources Commission, Box 2919, Raleigh, North Carolina 27602.

NORTH DAKOTA State Game & Fish Department, Bismarck, North Dakota 58501.

OHIO Watercraft Division, Department of Natural Resources, 1952 Belcher Dr., Columbus, Ohio 43224

OKLAHOMA State Tax Commission, 2101 N. Lincoln Blvd., Oklahoma City, Okla. 73105.

OREGON State Marine Board, State Agriculture Building, 635 Capitol Street, N.E., Salem, Oregon 97310.

PENNSYLVANIA Miscellaneous License Division, Pennsylvania Dept. of Revenue, Harrisburg, Pennsylvania 17127.

RHODE ISLAND Registry of Motor Vehicles, Executive Department, State Capitol Building, Providence, Rhode Island 02903.

SOUTH CAROLINA Wildlife Resources Department, P. O. Box 167, Columbia, South Carolina 29202.

SOUTH DAKOTA Department of Game, Fish & Parks, State Office Building, Pierre, South Dakota 57501.

TENNESSEE Game & Fish Commission, 706 Church Street, Doctors Building, Nashville, Tennessee 37203.

TEXAS Highway Department, Motor Vehicle Division, 40th & Jackson, Austin, Texas 78703.

UTAH Boating Division, Utah State Park & Recreation Commission, 132 South Second West, Salt Lake City, Utah 84101.

VERMONT Marine Division, Department of Public Safety, Montpelier, Vermont 05602.

VIRGINIA Game & Inland Fisheries Commission, P. O. Box 1642, Richmond, Virginia 23213.

WASHINGTON The State of Washington does not have a boat registration and numbering law, but the Washington State Parks and Recreation Commission, P. O. Box 1128, Olympia, Wash. 98501, can furnish general information on boating in the state.

WEST VIRGINIA Department of Natural Resources, State Office Building, Charleston, West Virginia 25305.

WISCONSIN Conservation Department, P. O. Box 450, Madison, Wisconsin 53701.

WYOMING Game & Fish Commission, P. O. Box 1589, Cheyenne, Wyoming 82001.

DIST. OF COLUMBIA The District of Columbia does not have a boat registration and numbering system; this is done by the Coast Guard. General information about boating regulations and restrictions can be obtained from the Harbor Precinct, Metropolitan Police Department, 550 Maine Avenue S.W., Washington, D.C. 20024.

PUERTO RICO Marine Operations Department, Ports Authority, San Juan, P.R.

VIRGIN ISLANDS Department of Commerce, Marine & Aviation Services, Charlotte Amalie, St. Thomas Island, Virgin Islands.

MARLINESPIKE SEAMANSHIP

Illustrated here are some common knots, bends, hitches, and splices. See Chapter 11, Pages 215-231 for details.

Overhand

The simple overhand knot is used to keep the end of a rope from unlaying.

Figure Eight

The figure eight knot. This does not jam.

Square or Reef Knot

The square or reef knot is a most useful and common knot. The rope manipulated by the right hand (this is the rope leading from the left side of the sketch and terminating in the arrow in A) is turned over the other rope in tying both the first and second half of the knot.

Sheet or Becket Bend

The sheet or becket bend is used for tying two lines together. It will not slip even if there is great difference in the sizes of the lines.

Clove Hitch

The clove hitch is used for making a line fast temporarily to a pile or a bollard.

Bowline

The bowline is considered a knot second in usefulness only to the square knot. The bowline will not slip, does not pinch or kink the rope as much as some other knots, and does not jam and become difficult to untie. By tying a bowline with a small loop and passing the line through the loop the running bowline is obtained. This is an excellent form of running noose.

Two Half Hitches

Two half hitches are used for making a line fast to a bollard, ring, timber, or stanchion. Note that the knot consists of a turn around the fixed object and a clove hitch around the standing part of the line.

Correct Method of Making Fast to a Cleat

Correct method for making fast to a cleat is shown. The half hitch which completes the fastening is taken with the free part of the line. The line can then be freed without taking up slack in the standing part.

Incorrect Method of Making Fast to a Cleat

Common incorrect method of making fast to a cleat is shown. The half hitch is taken with the standing part of the line and the line consequently can not be freed without taking up slack in the standing part. Accidents have been caused by the use of this type of fastening on lines which must be freed quickly.

Fisherman's Bend

The fisherman's bend, also called the anchor bend, is made by taking two round turns around the ring, then passing the end under both turns to form a half hitch around the standing part of the line. For further security, a second half hitch is taken around the standing part only.